D1001410

34

REGIONAL ATLAS OF THE WORLD

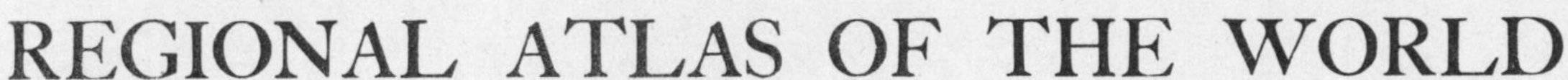

PRINTED IN SCOTLAND BY
JOHN BARTHOLOMEW AND SON LTD
12 DUNCAN STREET, EDINBURGH, 9

THE
REGIONAL ATLAS
OF THE WORLD

BY

JOHN BARTHOLOMEW
M.C., M.A., F.R.S.E.

INTRODUCTION BY

A. G. OGILVIE, O.B.E., F.R.S.E.
PROFESSOR OF GEOGRAPHY EDINBURGH UNIVERSITY

EDINBURGH
THE GEOGRAPHICAL INSTITUTE

1948

DEDICATED
TO THE ROYAL SCOTTISH GEOGRAPHICAL SOCIETY
MEMBERS OF WHICH, FROM ITS FOUNDATION
TO THE PRESENT DAY, HAVE TAKEN
A LEADING PART IN THE
ADVANCEMENT OF
GEOGRAPHY

CONTENTS

Introduction by Prof. A. G. Ogilvie, O.B.E.

CONTENTS

CONTENTS

GENERAL INDEX

INTRODUCTION

By Prof. A. G. OGILVIE, O.B.E.

THE word 'Regional' in the title of this atlas may be used as a text, in suggesting uses for the atlas which go far beyond cursory reference. The word 'region' denotes a tract of land of rather vague limits; but the addition of an adjective such as 'climatic,' 'linguistic' or 'agricultural' reminds us that tracts of country may be delimited more or less precisely by reference to the distribution of a single type of climate, of language or of agricultural practice. So various kinds of region exist in virtue of physical qualities and also of human groupings and activities. The main body of the maps in this atlas depict systematically and by uniform methods one physical type, the orographical region; and one human type, the political region—the state. But it should be realised that the introductory series of maps of smaller scale provides a wealth of information on the distribution of many phenomena over the earth. To make the fullest use of the atlas, then, the reader should compare the maps of larger scale with those of the introductory series. By doing so he will be able to add vastly to the information available on the 'regional' map itself.

There is only one completely satisfactory method of representing the earth in miniature: by the terrestrial globe. The flat map is the substitute, indispensable because of its convenience, but imperfect in one way or another just because it is flat. With a large globe direct comparison of region with region may be made easily. To achieve this with an atlas all the maps should be drawn on the same scale; and such an atlas would certainly fail to meet certain obvious purposes. For this reason the various maps in this atlas have been drawn on scales that are simple multiples of one another. Thus the regions for which the average (British) reader requires most detail are given on the scale 1:1,000,000, i.e., 1 mm. = 1 km. and 1 inch = nearly 16 miles; a larger number appear at half this scale, 1:2,000,000, others at 1/5 m., 1/10 m., and so on. Study of these in turn will reveal the degree of detail that is appropriate to each. In the representation of relief the same series of tints is used throughout, and on all but a few maps the tints indicate the same range of altitude. Similar uniformity characterizes the other conventional signs and the lettering throughout. Thus a great deal may be learned by simple comparison of any group of maps in the atlas.

Now to return to the series of maps showing the earth as a whole and different distributions

INTRODUCTION

thereon: the one which is obviously of first importance—the distribution of population (p. 1) —is given special prominence and a novel projection of the globe. Since this is an ' equal-area ' projection the extent of the various human habitats can be accurately compared. Moreover the map also shows one of the limiting factors of man's environment, the average (annual) temperature of the air. These lines, however, are drawn as if there were no mountains : to represent the irregularities due to cooler air on these would have made the map illegible. This drawing of population densities may well evoke the questions :—' what are the causes of the irregular pattern

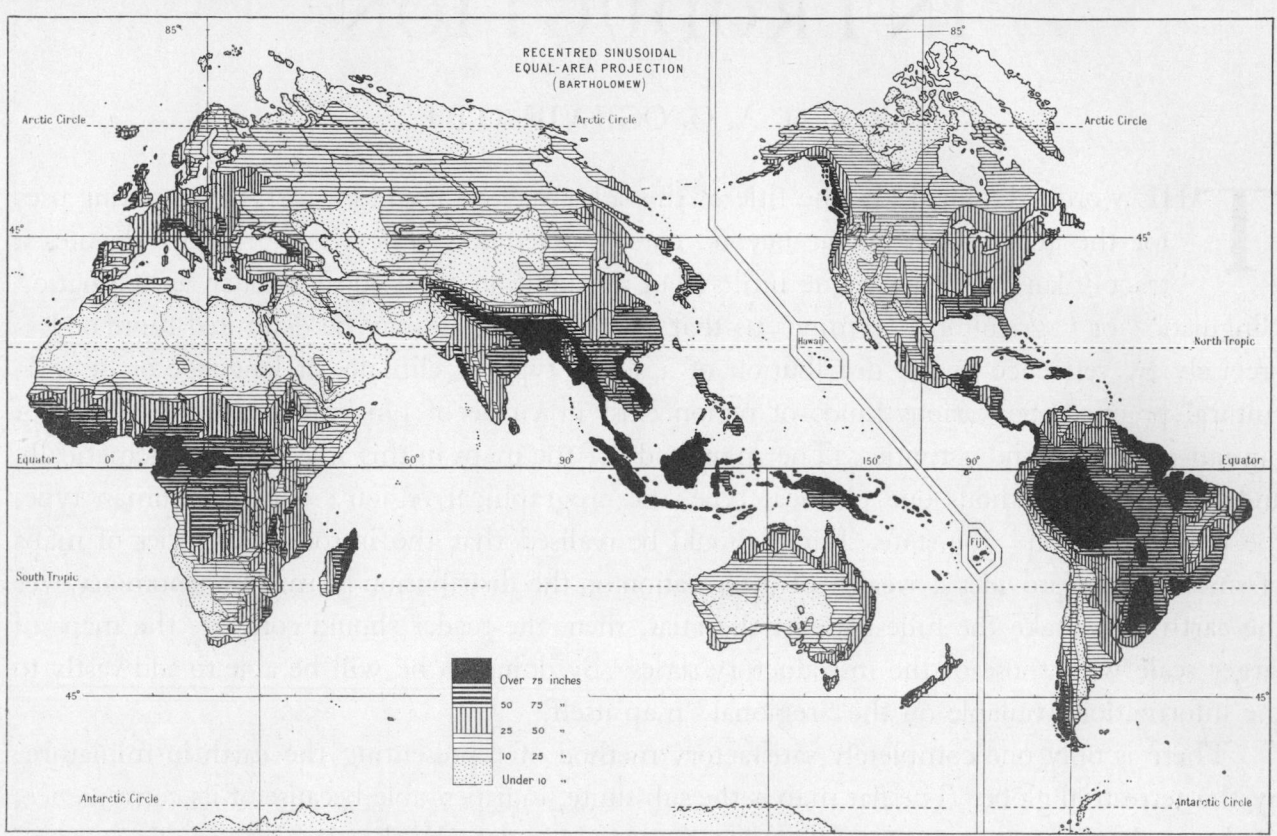

FIG. 1. ANNUAL RAINFALL OF THE WORLD

of mankind on the earth ? ', and ' will the pattern be the same after the lapse of another century ? '. To the first question the other distribution-maps together can be made to give a reasonably complete answer, since they depict the various physical elements of human environment ; but the historical factor must also be borne in mind. Moreover, the maps given require the addition of at least two others that possess special importance :—that of the distribution of average total rain for the year, and that of the minerals coal, oil and iron-ore (Figs. 1 and 2). The annual rainfall accounts in large measure for the relative success with which food may be produced ; but the seasonal rainfall and temperature (pp. 6-7) are also vital since, in general, crops will be heavier where rain is abundant during the warm season: one of the chief reasons for the great densities of population in India and China. Two of the great masses of the human race, then, are found in lower northern latitudes where the annual rainfall exceeds 50 inches. The third mass,

in Europe, and its offshoot in North America correspond to a rainfall between 50 and 25 inches.

Coal and iron are basic to the heavy industries ; and their distribution, particularly that of coal, since we are still largely in the 'coal-age,' is related to the concentration of manufacturing peoples. Petroleum, which is quickly extracted and easily transported, has been less effective in gathering manufactures and large population to a region. Some indication of this may be gleaned by comparing the railway net of Texas where there are great oilfields (p. 133) with the much

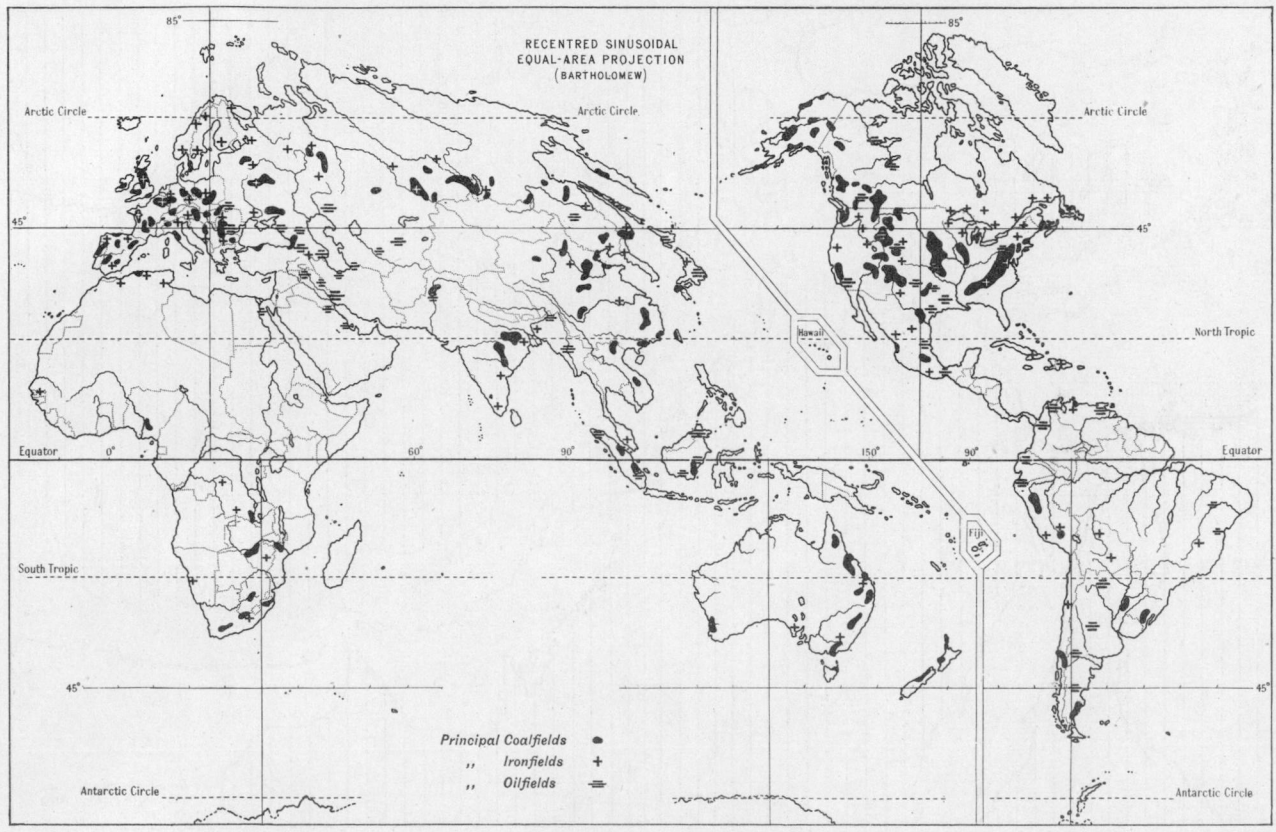

FIG. 2. DISTRIBUTION OF COAL, IRON AND OIL

closer mesh of the railways in Ohio (p. 129) a productive agricultural state with vast and varied industries based upon coal.

It is interesting to compare the maps of two regions with high densities of population. The same map, of the Eastern United States, reflects the vast traffic where highly organised manufactures depend upon resources of coal and iron. Page 87 covers much of North-Eastern India —on a slightly larger scale. Here the railways, though drawn more prominently, are seen to be much more widely spaced, despite the presence of the greatest coal and ironfields of India (squares F and Gd) and large textile industries. The great majority of the huge rural population promote little railway traffic.

The alluvial plain of the Ganges, again, with its dense population, may be usefully contrasted with the comparatively empty plain of Mesopotamia, shown, at less than half the scale, on pp.

INTRODUCTION

78-79. This is likewise an alluvial plain, but the difference of population is mainly a matter of the amounts of rainfall, over 40 inches and under 10 inches respectively. The area included on this map of 'The Middle East,' 1/10 m., contains the greatest known reserves of mineral oil in the world ; petroleum has long been extracted west of the Caspian Sea, for shorter periods along the borders of Persia and Iraq, and still more recently on the west coast of the Persian Gulf. Yet apart from oil pipelines there is little sign of all this on the map ; and one reason has been stated above. Moreover, in looking to the future, it is well to recall that the life of even great oilfields

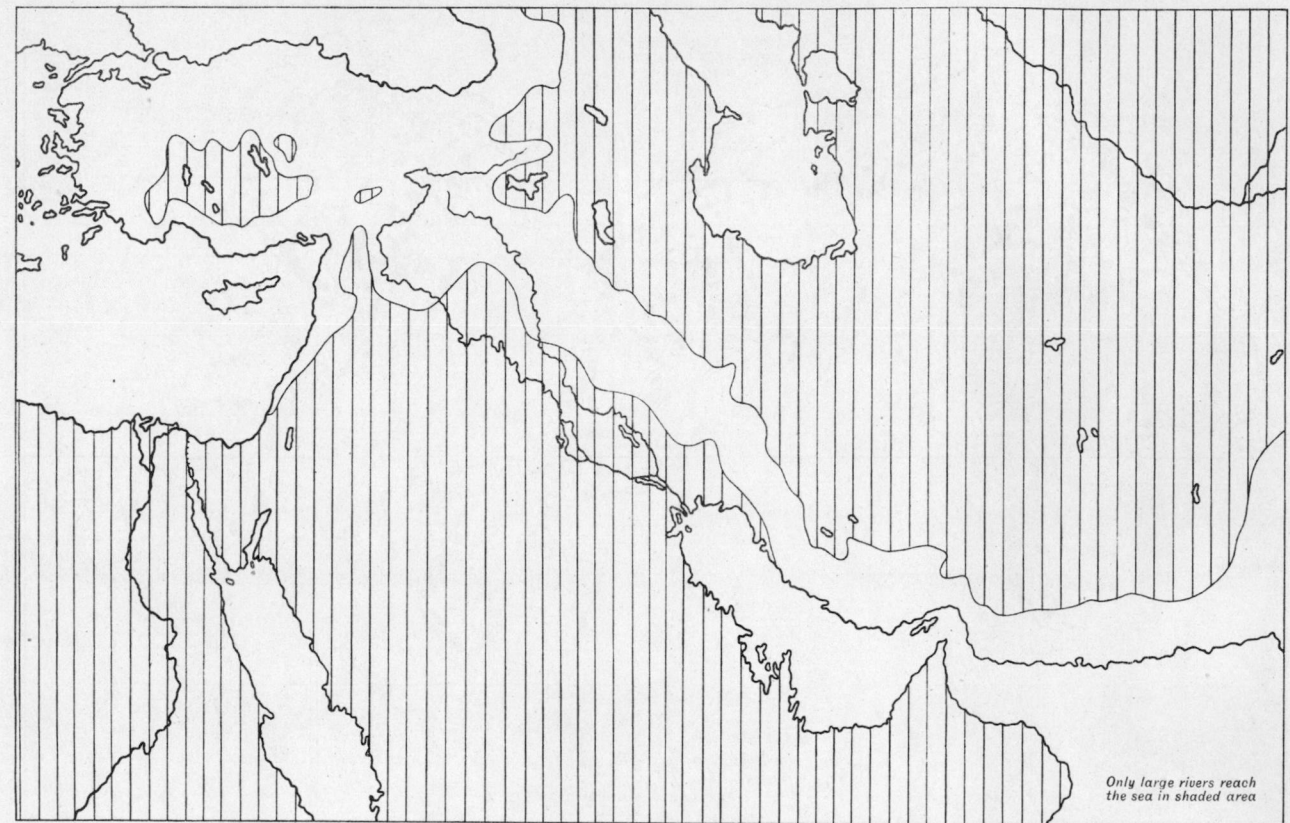

Only large rivers reach the sea in shaded area

FIG. 3. INTERIOR DRAINAGE, MIDDLE EAST

is short compared to that of similar deposits of coal and iron. Many of these latter on the other hand still await full development, as in Brazil and China, and this is true even of the Asian resources of the U.S.S.R. ; all these would seem likely to cause concentration of population in the future.

An atlas of this kind makes no attempt to 'tell the whole story' about any region. One may be allowed, however, to suggest to the reader, by brief consideration of a few sketch-maps, that he may seek further information from other sources and so amplify the maps of an atlas in the study of regions. So we may refer again to 'The Middle East' or South-Western Asia (pp. 78-79). The plate includes in whole or part the following OROGRAPHICAL REGIONS :— (1) the great zone of mountains extending from Anatolia to Afghanistan enclosing a number of basins that are themselves high plateaux; (2) to north of this, parts of the lowland of Thrace,

INTRODUCTION

the Caucasian furrow, parts of the Caucasus Mountains and the lowland of Turkistan ; (3) south of the mountain zone, the Mesopotamian lowland, the ranges and furrows of Syria, Palestine and Sinai, the tilted plateau of Arabia with the mountains of Oman in the south-east ; finally, a fragment of Africa. The climate of all of these is semi-arid or arid, except for the western seaboards (Fig. 1). Consequently most of the rivers carry water only periodically or even at irregular intervals. Furthermore, owing to the fact that geological forces have produced surfaces that slope away from the ocean, many streams which do flow every year send their water to be

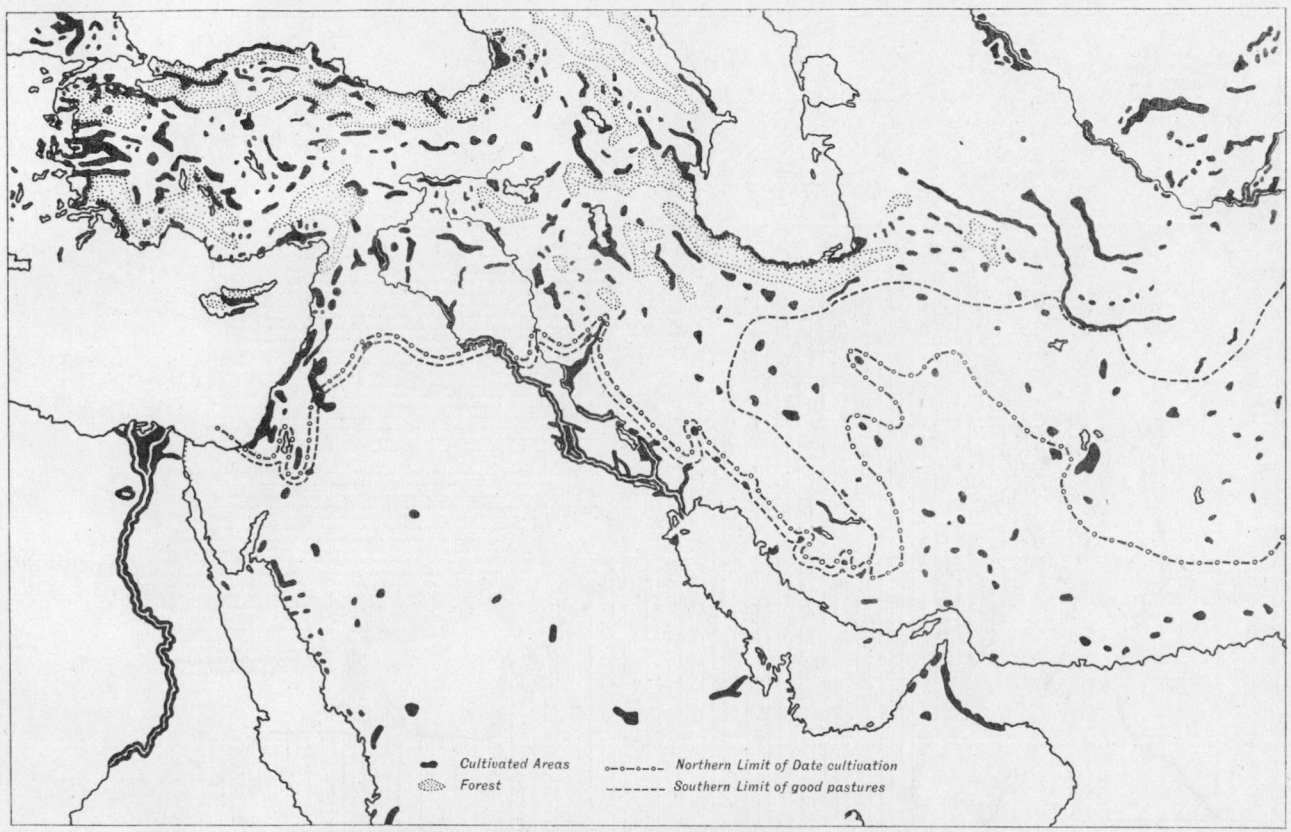

— Cultivated Areas	o—o—o—o—	Northern Limit of Date cultivation
Forest	---------	Southern Limit of good pastures

FIG. 4. CULTIVATION, MIDDLE EAST

evaporated in these interior basins, the largest of them containing the Caspian Sea. Fig. 3 then, shows the huge area that is not drained to the ocean ; but a few 'stronger' rivers, the Nile, Euphrates and Tigris succeed in passing through these tracts.

Restricted water has ever limited human activities and largely determined their character in The Middle East, except on the large deltas and near the east end of the Black Sea. Thus Fig. 4 shows all but the smallest patches that are under cultivation ; their total area is remarkably small, but it is greatest where rainfall exceeds 25 inches. Where this is under 10 inches agriculture is practised solely by irrigation, from wells or the 'stronger' rivers, and south of the limit of the date palm, determined by temperature, this tree is a principal object of cultivation. All the substantial tracts of remaining forests are on the mountains, and again with the heavier rainfall. The rest of the land is used only for grazing, which implies movement of flocks through-

out the year or from season to season, according to water and vegetation. It is this movement, perpetual or intermittent, above all which characterizes the life of The Middle East and renders it, in this connection at least, a single large region. But there are all gradations from settled life on the western coasts to pure nomadism in Arabia and inner Persia ; moreover there are many differences between life in the mountains and life in the plains. Fig. 5 emphasises this since the ethnic boundaries follow the mountain foot, with Arabs and Turkmens on the plains to south and north-east respectively, while in the highland zone Persians in the east and Turks in the

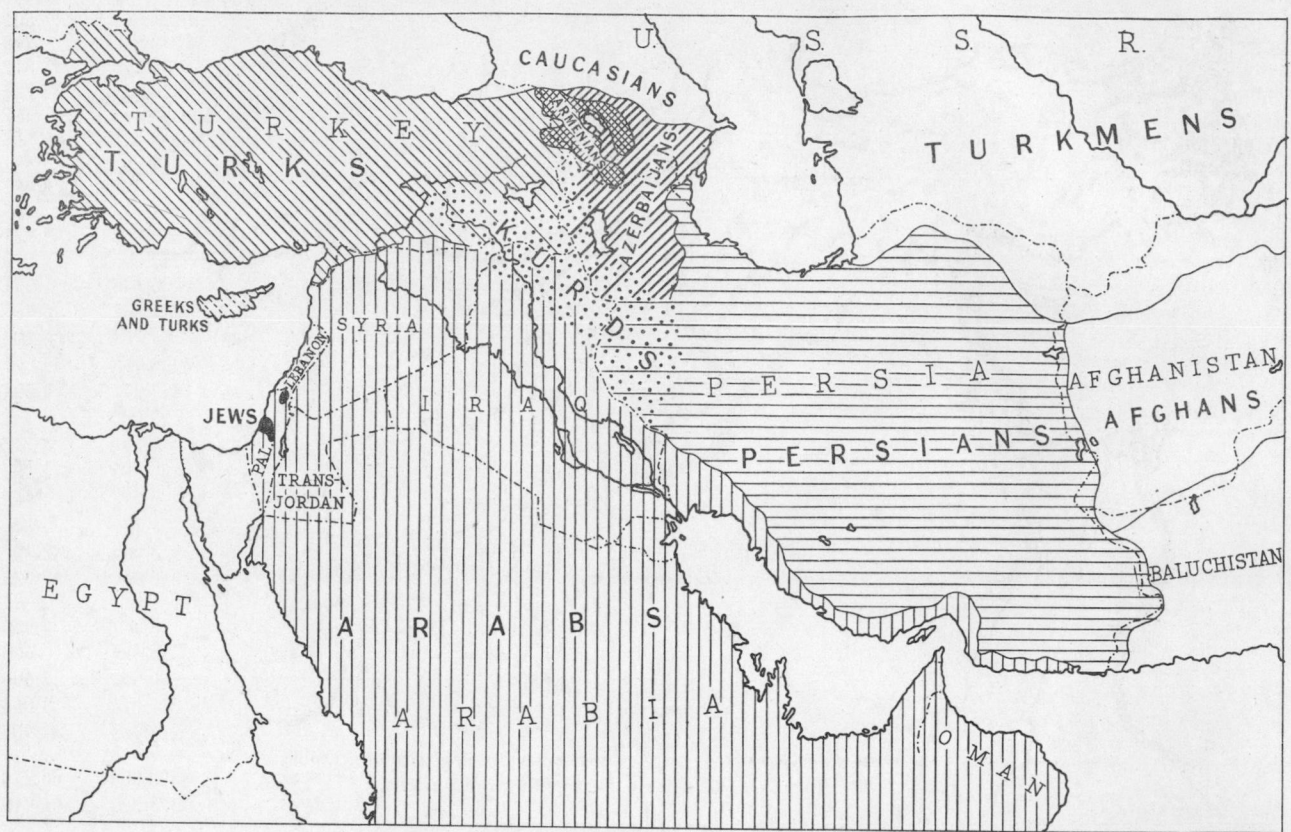

FIG. 5. ETHNOGRAPHIC GROUPS, MIDDLE EAST

west are imperfectly separated by the Kurds and the Armenian remnant in the centre. The boundaries of states coincide substantially with the ethnic limits. But there are exceptions, notable in regard to the Kurds, the Tartars of Azerbaijan and the Turkmens of northern Persia and Afghanistan ; less so in the case of the Arabs. But the political problem of Palestine and the Jews remains.

These, then, are some of the aspects of geography which must be considered in the comparative study of regions. There are evidently regions of different orders and of different kinds. In this case the mountain zone and the lowlands alike might be divided otherwise than by existing national boundaries. But the three States of the mountains, Turkey, Iran and Afghanistan have good geographical reasons for political affinity; and so have the five principal States of the south, the ‘Arab League’ which, together with Palestine occupy the lower bridge-lands between the seas.

STATES OF THE WORLD

	Area (sq. miles)	Population
ABYSSINIA, *see* Ethiopia.		
AFGHANISTAN, *Kingdom*	250,000	12,000,000
ALBANIA, *Republic*	10,629	1,003,124
ANDORRA, *Republic*	191	5,231
ARGENTINA, *Republic*	1,079,965	14,130,000
AUSTRALIA, *Dominion*	2,974,671	7,630,000
New Guinea, *Mandated Territory*	93,000	675,369
Papua, *Commonwealth Territory*	90,540	339,000
AUSTRIA, *Republic*	32,393	6,652,720
BAHREIN, *Sheikhdom*	213	120,000
BELGIUM, *Kingdom*	11,775	8,386,553
Belgian Congo, *Colony*	902,082	10,381,700
Ruanda-Urundi, *Mandated Territory*	20,152	3,775,335
BHUTAN, *Kingdom*	18,000	300,000
BOLIVIA, *Republic*	514,400	3,722,700
BRAZIL, *Republic*	3,275,510	41,356,605
BRITISH EMPIRE, *Commonwealth*	14,435,060	539,870,000
Aden, *Colony and Protectorate*	69,600	190,000
Anglo-Egyptian Sudan, *Condominium*	967,500	6,342,477
Bahamas, *Colony*	4,404	68,903
Basutoland, *Protectorate*	11,716	562,411
Bechuanaland, *Protectorate*	275,000	265,756
British Guiana, *Colony*	89,480	346,982
British Honduras, *Crown Colony*	8,598	59,965
British North Borneo, *Protectorate*	29,500	270,223
British Solomon Islands, *Protectorate*	11,000	94,105
Brunei, *Sultanate under British protection*	2,226	30,135
Cyprus, *Colony*	3,572	383,967
Falkland Is. and Dependencies, *Crown Colony*	5,618	2,785
Fiji Islands, *Crown Colony*	7,083	198,379
Gambia, *Colony and Protectorate*	4,068	199,520
Gibraltar, *Crown Colony*	2	21,372
Gold Coast, *Colony, Protectorate and Mandate*	91,843	3,962,520
Hong Kong, *Colony*	391	1,071,893
Jamaica, *Crown Colony*	4,628	1,223,241
Kenya, *Colony and Protectorate*	224,960	3,534,862
Leeward Islands, *Federal Colony*	423	92,010
Malayan Union, *Protectorate*	49,610	4,124,549
Malta, *Self-Governing Colony*	122	286,000
Newfoundland & Labrador, *Dominion (status deferred)*	152,700	305,000
New Hebrides, *Condominium*	5,108	43,000
Nigeria, *Colony, Protectorate & Mandate*	372,674	20,641,814
Nyasaland, *Protectorate*	37,374	1,686,045
Rhodesia, Northern, *Colony*	290,320	1,381,829
Rhodesia, Southern, *Self-Governing Colony*	150,333	1,448,393
Sarawak, *Protectorate*	50,000	490,585
Sierra Leone, *Colony & Protectorate*	27,940	1,793,100
Singapore, *Colony*	220	769,216
Somaliland, *Protectorate*	68,000	344,700
Swaziland, *Protectorate*	6,705	156,715
Tanganyika, *Mandated Territory*	340,000	5,283,893
Trinidad and Tobago, *Colony*	1,980	484,900
Uganda, *Protectorate*	93,981	3,829,705
Windward Islands (*Colony*)	826	283,658
Zanzibar (and Pemba), *Protectorate*	1,020	250,000

	Area (sq. miles)	Population
BULGARIA, *Republic* (Sept. 1946)	42,796	6,477,939
BURMA, *Republic* (Jan. 1948)	261,610	16,823,798
CANADA, *Dominion*	3,694,863	11,506,655
Alberta	248,800	796,169
British Columbia	359,279	817,861
Manitoba	219,723	729,744
New Brunswick	27,473	457,401
North-West Territories	1,253,438	12,028
Nova Scotia	20,743	577,962
Ontario	363,282	3,787,655
Prince Edward Island	2,184	95,047
Quebec	523,860	3,331,882
Saskatchewan	237,975	895,992
Yukon	205,346	4,914
CEYLON, *Dominion*	25,332	5,981,000
CHILE, *Republic*	296,717	5,200,000
CHINA, *Republic*	3,406,488	459,675,840
COLOMBIA, *Republic*	439,997	9,523,000
COSTA RICA, *Republic*	23,000	746,596
CUBA, *Republic*	44,164	4,777,284
CZECHOSLOVAKIA, *Republic*	50,500	13,452,980
DENMARK, *Kingdom*	16,575	4,045,232
DOMINICAN REPUBLIC	19,325	1,826,407
ECUADOR, *Republic*	226,000	3,200,000
EGYPT, *Kingdom*	386,000	17,625,000
EIRE, *Republic, affiliated member of British Commonwealth*	26,601	2,989,700
ERITREA, *Italian Colony*	15,574	600,573
ETHIOPIA (Abyssinia), *Empire*	350,000	7,600,000
FINLAND, *Republic*	117,975	3,863,753
FRANCE, *Republic*	212,735	41,907,056
French Colonial Empire, excluding Syria	4,598,000	66,215,400
GERMANY	373,000	65,910,999
GREAT BRITAIN, *Kingdom, see* United Kingdom.		
GREECE, *Kingdom*	50,184	7,534,975
GUATEMALA, *Republic*	45,452	3,450,732
HAITI, *Republic*	10,204	3,284,000
HONDURAS, *Republic*	44,275	1,205,504
HUNGARY, *Republic* (Feb. 1946)	35,875	9,106,252
ICELAND, *Republic* (May 1944)	39,709	125,618
INDIA	1,583,183	388,803,000
Hindustan, *Dominion*	1,200,000	240,000,000
Hyderabad, *Princely State*	82,500	16,194,000
Pakistan, *Dominion*	190,000	70,000,000
INDONESIA, *Republic*	214,832	49,060,000
IRAN, *see* Persia.		
IRAQ, *Kingdom*	116,600	4,560,456
ITALIAN SOMALILAND, *Italian Colony*	194,000	1,021,572
ITALY, *Republic* (June 1946)	116,764	43,578,000
JAPAN, *Empire*	147,702	73,114,308
JUGOSLAVIA, *Republic* (Nov. 1945)	95,576	15,703,000
LEBANON, *Republic*	19,000	1,047,745
LIBERIA, *Republic*	43,000	1,500,000

STATES OF THE WORLD

	Area (sq. miles)	Population
LIBYA, *Italian Colony*	679,385	888,401
LUXEMBOURG, *Grand Duchy*	999	296,913
MEXICO, *Republic*	768,944	22,226,561
MONGOLIA, *Republic*	1,500,000	850,000
MUSCAT AND OMAN, *Sultanate*	82,000	500,000
NEPAL, *Independent Kingdom*	54,000	7,600,000
NETHERLANDS, *Kingdom*	13,203	9,048,600
Curaçao, *Colony*	403	105,617
Surinam (Guiana), *Colony*	54,291	191,044
NEW ZEALAND, *Dominion*	104,935	1,769,964
Nauru, *Mandated Territory*	8	3,352
Western Samoa, *Mandated Territory*	1,133	62,287
NICARAGUA, *Republic*	57,143	1,095,481
NORWAY, *Kingdom*	124,556	3,123,883
PALESTINE, *former Mandate*	10,460	1,033,314
PANAMA, *Republic*	28,576	635,836
PARAGUAY, *Republic*	153,400	1,114,773
PERSIA, *Kingdom*	628,000	15,000,000
PERU, *Republic*	532,000	7,200,000
PHILIPPINE ISLANDS, *Republic*	115,600	16,971,100
POLAND, *Republic*	130,470	34,775,698
PORTUGAL, *Republic*	35,490	8,139,484
ROMANIA, *Republic* (Dec. 1947)	91,670	16,500,000
SALVADOR, *Republic*	13,176	1,987,930
SAUDI ARABIA, *Kingdom*	913,000	6,000,000
SIAM (Thailand), *Kingdom*	200,148	15,718,000
SOUTH AFRICA, UNION OF, *Dominion*	472,550	11,250,000
South-West Africa, *Mandated Territory*	317,725	350,000
SPAIN, *Republic*	196,607	27,285,487
Spanish West Africa, *Colony*	110,100	50,000
Spanish Guinea, *Colony*	10,300	167,002
Spanish Morocco, *Colony*	18,454	1,284,000
SWEDEN, *Kingdom*	173,839	6,522,827
SWITZERLAND, *Republic*	15,944	4,260,719
SYRIA, *Independent State*	39,487	2,860,411
TANGIER, *International Zone*	225	100,000
TIBET, *Monastic State*	469,294	2,500,000
TRANSJORDAN, *Kingdom*	34,740	400,000
TRIESTE, *International Zone*	300	262,514
TRUCIAL OMAN, *Sheikhdom*	6,000	80,000
TURKEY, *Republic*	296,492	19,000,000
UNITED KINGDOM	93,675	47,934,000
England and Wales	58,343	41,460,000
Scotland	29,798	5,045,000
Northern Ireland	5,238	1,288,000
UNITED STATES OF AMERICA, *Republic* (including overseas possessions)	3,735,223	150,621,231
Alabama	51,078	2,832,961
Arizona	113,580	499,261
Arkansas	52,725	1,949,387
California	156,803	6,907,387
Colorado	103,967	1,123,296
Columbia, District of	61	663,091
Connecticut	4,899	1,709,242
Delaware	1,978	266,505
Florida	54,262	1,897,414
Georgia	58,518	3,123,723
Idaho	82,808	524,873
Illinois	55,947	7,897,241
Indiana	36,205	3,427,796
Iowa	55,986	2,538,268

	Area (sq. miles)	Population
UNITED STATES OF AMERICA—*continued*		
Kansas	82,113	1,801,028
Kentucky	40,109	2,845,627
Louisiana	45,177	2,363,880
Maine	31,040	847,226
Maryland	9,887	1,821,244
Massachusetts	7,907	4,316,721
Michigan	57,022	5,256,106
Minnesota	80,009	2,792,300
Mississippi	47,420	2,183,796
Missouri	69,270	3,784,664
Montana	146,316	559,456
Nebraska	76,653	1,315,834
Nevada	109,802	110,247
New Hampshire	9,024	491,524
New Jersey	7,522	4,160,165
New Mexico	121,511	531,818
New York	47,929	13,479,142
North Carolina	49,142	3,571,623
North Dakota	70,054	641,935
Ohio	41,122	6,907,612
Oklahoma	69,283	2,336,434
Oregon	96,350	1,089,684
Pennsylvania	45,045	9,900,180
Rhode Island	1,058	713,346
South Carolina	30,594	1,899,804
South Dakota	76,536	642,961
Tennessee	41,961	2,915,841
Texas	263,644	6,414,824
Utah	82,346	550,310
Vermont	9,278	359,231
Virginia	39,899	2,677,773
Washington	66,977	1,736,191
West Virginia	24,090	1,901,974
Wisconsin	54,715	3,137,587
Wyoming	97,506	250,742
Total, Continental United States	2,977,128	131,669,275
Alaska	586,400	73,023
Guam	206	23,394
Hawaii	6,454	423,330
Panama Canal Zone	553	51,827
Puerto Rico	3,435	1,869,255
Samoa	76	16,493
Virgin Islands	133	24,889
URUGUAY, *Republic*	72,153	2,146,545
U.S.S.R. (Union of Soviet Socialist Reps.)	8,708,070	193,267,186
Armenia, S.S.R.	11,640	1,281,599
Azerbaijan, S.S.R.	33,460	3,209,727
Estonia, S.S.R.	17,610	1,120,000
Georgia, S.S.R.	37,570	3,542,289
Karelia, S.S.R.	69,720	900,000
Kazak, S.S.R.	1,072,000	6,145,937
Kirgiz, S.S.R.	76,900	1,459,301
Latvia, S.S.R.	24,840	1,950,000
Lithuania, S.S.R.	31,600	2,879,070
Moldavia, S.S.R.	13,200	2,200,000
Russia, S.F.S.R.	6,609,000	109,279,000
Tadzhik, S.S.R.	55,700	1,485,091
Turkmen, S.S.R.	189,370	1,253,985
Ukraine, S.S.R.	225,200	38,500,000
Uzbek, S.S.R.	159,170	6,282,446
White Russia, S.S.R.	81,090	10,400,000
VATICAN CITY, *Papal State*	109 ac.	1,025
VENEZUELA, *Republic*	352,143	3,491,159
YEMEN, *Kingdom*	23,900	900,000
YUGOSLAVIA, *see* Jugoslavia.		

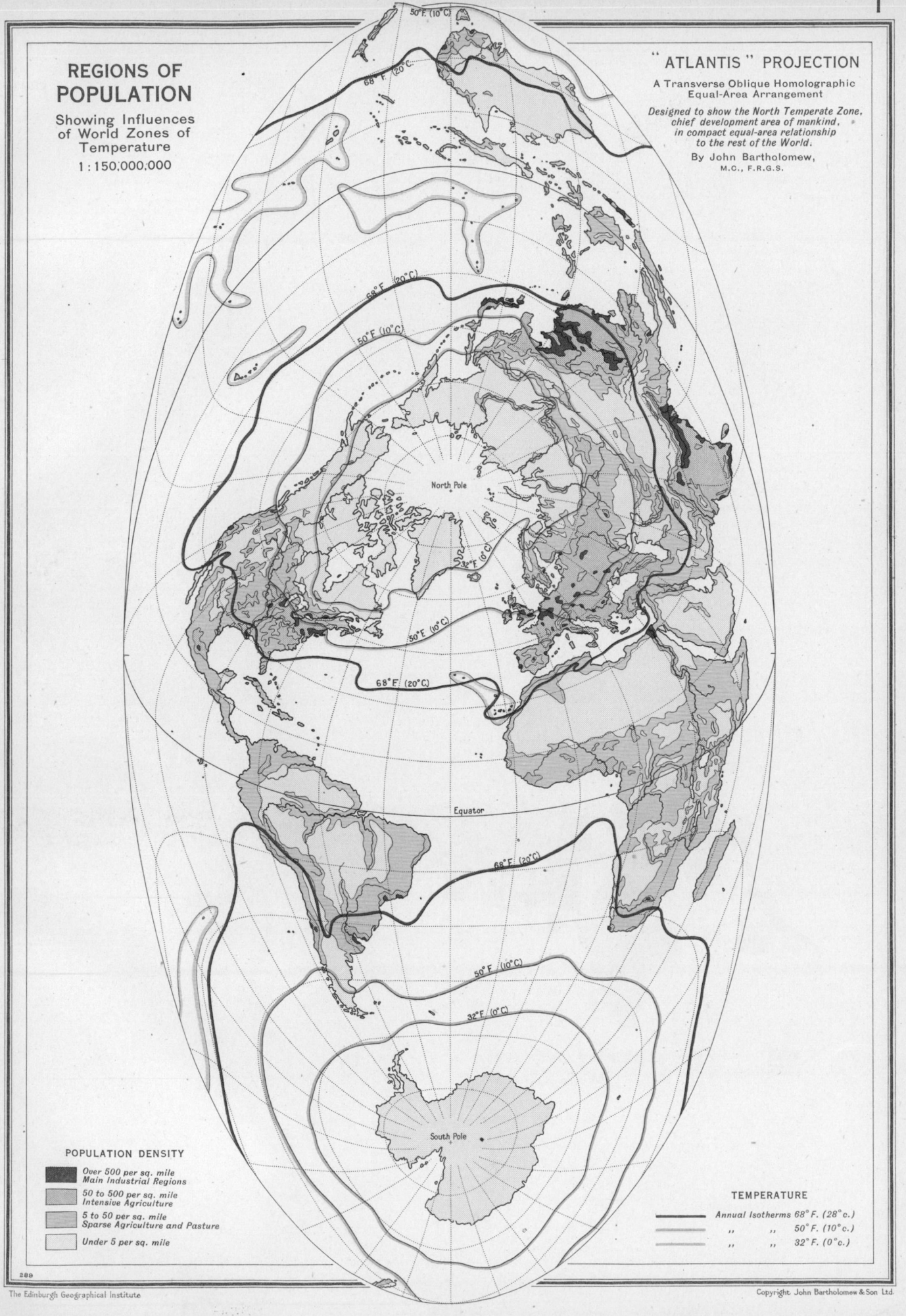

REGIONS OF POPULATION

Showing Influences
of World Zones of
Temperature
1 : 150,000,000

"ATLANTIS" PROJECTION

A Transverse Oblique Homolographic
Equal-Area Arrangement

*Designed to show the North Temperate Zone,
chief development area of mankind,
in compact equal-area relationship
to the rest of the World.*

By John Bartholomew,
M.C., F.R.G.S.

POPULATION DENSITY

- Over 500 per sq. mile
  Main Industrial Regions
- 50 to 500 per sq. mile
  Intensive Agriculture
- 5 to 50 per sq. mile
  Sparse Agriculture and Pasture
- Under 5 per sq. mile

TEMPERATURE

Annual Isotherms 68° F. (28° c.)
     ,,   ,,   50° F. (10° c.)
     ,,   ,,   32° F. (0° c.)

The Edinburgh Geographical Institute

Copyright. John Bartholomew & Son Ltd.

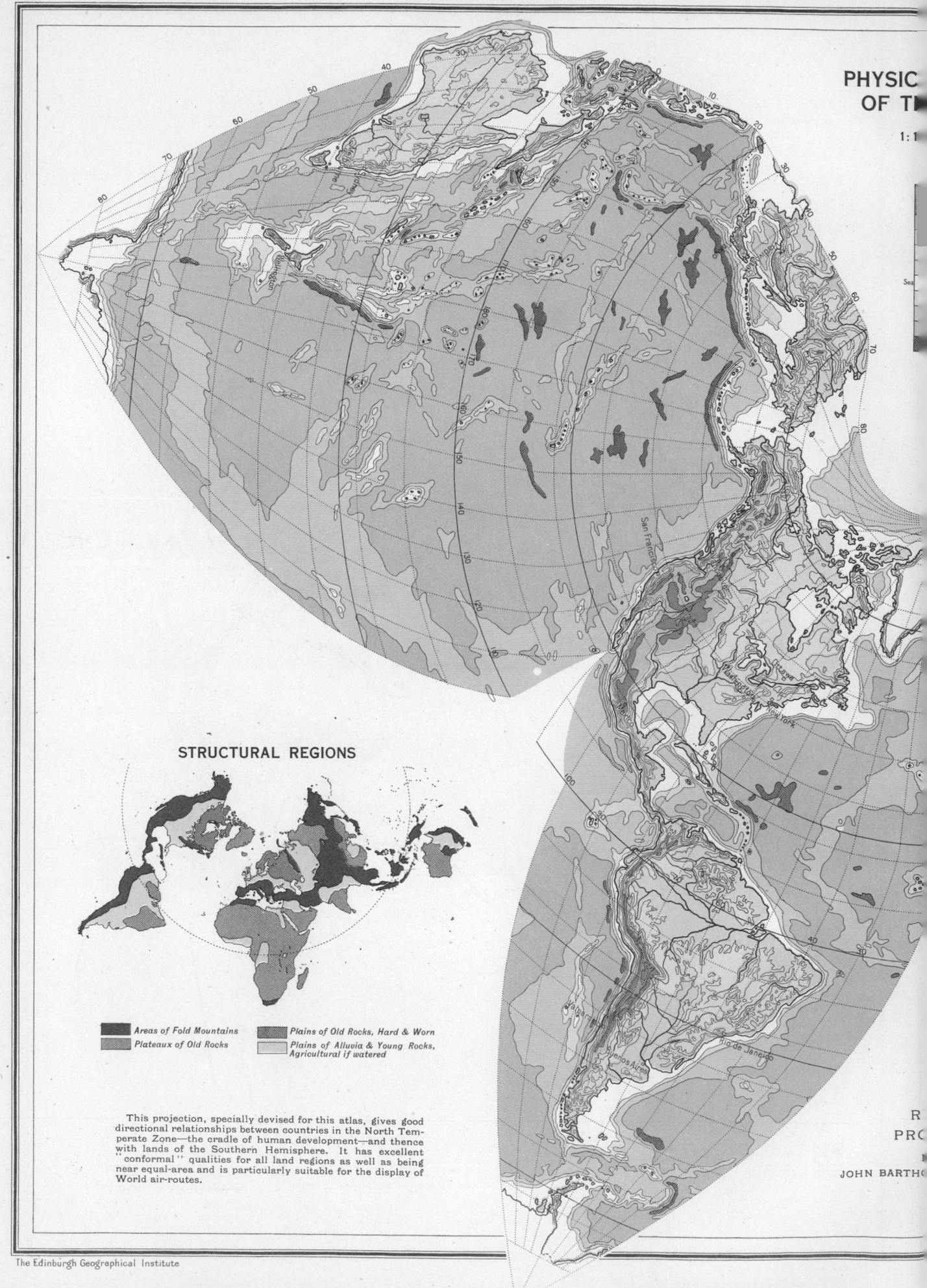

PHYSIC
OF T

1 : 1

STRUCTURAL REGIONS

Legend:
- ■ *Areas of Fold Mountains*
- ▨ *Plateaux of Old Rocks*
- ▧ *Plains of Old Rocks, Hard & Worn*
- ▢ *Plains of Alluvia & Young Rocks, Agricultural if watered*

This projection, specially devised for this atlas, gives good directional relationships between countries in the North Temperate Zone—the cradle of human development—and thence with lands of the Southern Hemisphere. It has excellent "conformal" qualities for all land regions as well as being near equal-area and is particularly suitable for the display of World air-routes.

R
PRO

JOHN BARTHO

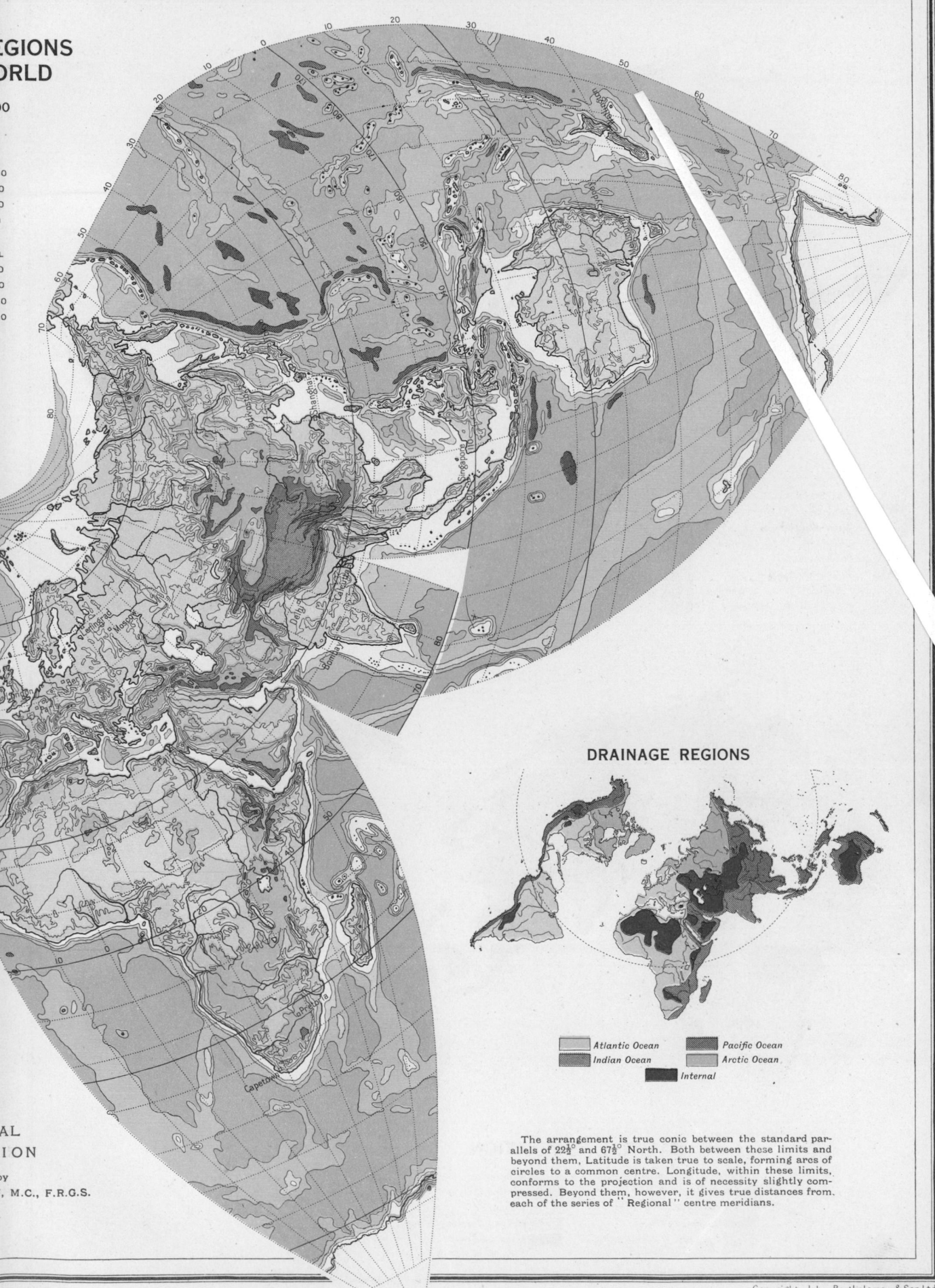

REGIONS
WORLD

DRAINAGE REGIONS

Atlantic Ocean
Indian Ocean
Pacific Ocean
Arctic Ocean
Internal

The arrangement is true conic between the standard par-
allels of $22\frac{1}{2}°$ and $67\frac{1}{2}°$ North. Both between these limits and
beyond them, Latitude is taken true to scale, forming arcs of
circles to a common centre. Longitude, within these limits,
conforms to the projection and is of necessity slightly com-
pressed. Beyond them, however, it gives true distances from
each of the series of " Regional " centre meridians.

AL
TION
by
, M.C., F.R.G.S.

Copyright-John Bartholomew & Son, Ltd.

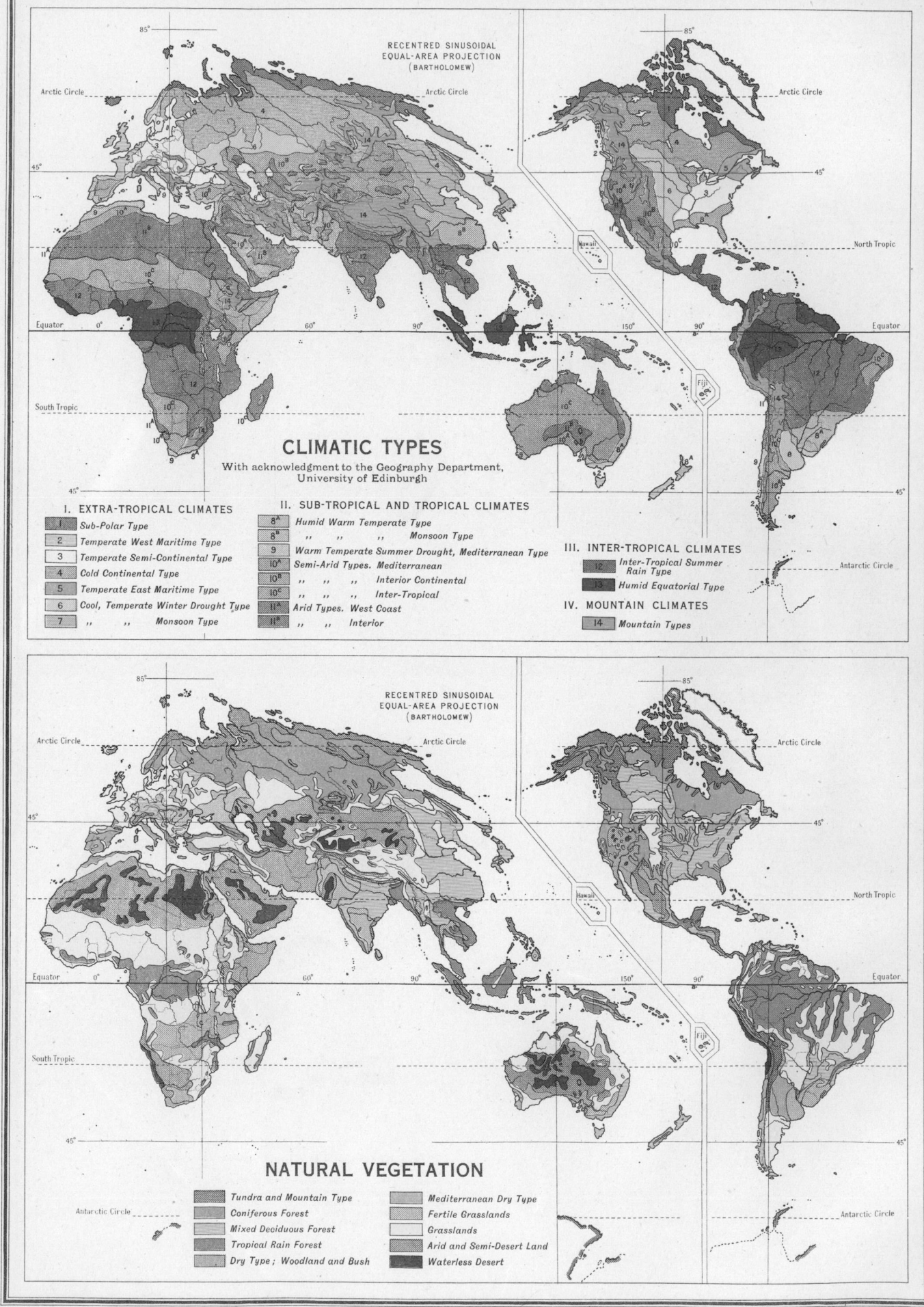

RECENTRED SINUSOIDAL
EQUAL-AREA PROJECTION
(BARTHOLOMEW)

CLIMATIC TYPES

With acknowledgment to the Geography Department,
University of Edinburgh

I. EXTRA-TROPICAL CLIMATES

1 Sub-Polar Type
2 Temperate West Maritime Type
3 Temperate Semi-Continental Type
4 Cold Continental Type
5 Temperate East Maritime Type
6 Cool, Temperate Winter Drought Type
7 ,, ,, Monsoon Type

II. SUB-TROPICAL AND TROPICAL CLIMATES

8A Humid Warm Temperate Type
8B ,, ,, ,, Monsoon Type
9 Warm Temperate Summer Drought, Mediterranean Type
10A Semi-Arid Types. Mediterranean
10B ,, ,, ,, Interior Continental
10C ,, ,, ,, Inter-Tropical
11A Arid Types. West Coast
11B ,, ,, Interior

III. INTER-TROPICAL CLIMATES

12 Inter-Tropical Summer Rain Type
13 Humid Equatorial Type

IV. MOUNTAIN CLIMATES

14 Mountain Types

RECENTRED SINUSOIDAL
EQUAL-AREA PROJECTION
(BARTHOLOMEW)

NATURAL VEGETATION

Tundra and Mountain Type
Coniferous Forest
Mixed Deciduous Forest
Tropical Rain Forest
Dry Type ; Woodland and Bush

Mediterranean Dry Type
Fertile Grasslands
Grasslands
Arid and Semi-Desert Land
Waterless Desert

The Edinburgh Geographical Institute

1 : 160,000,000

Copyright John Bartholomew & Son Ltd.

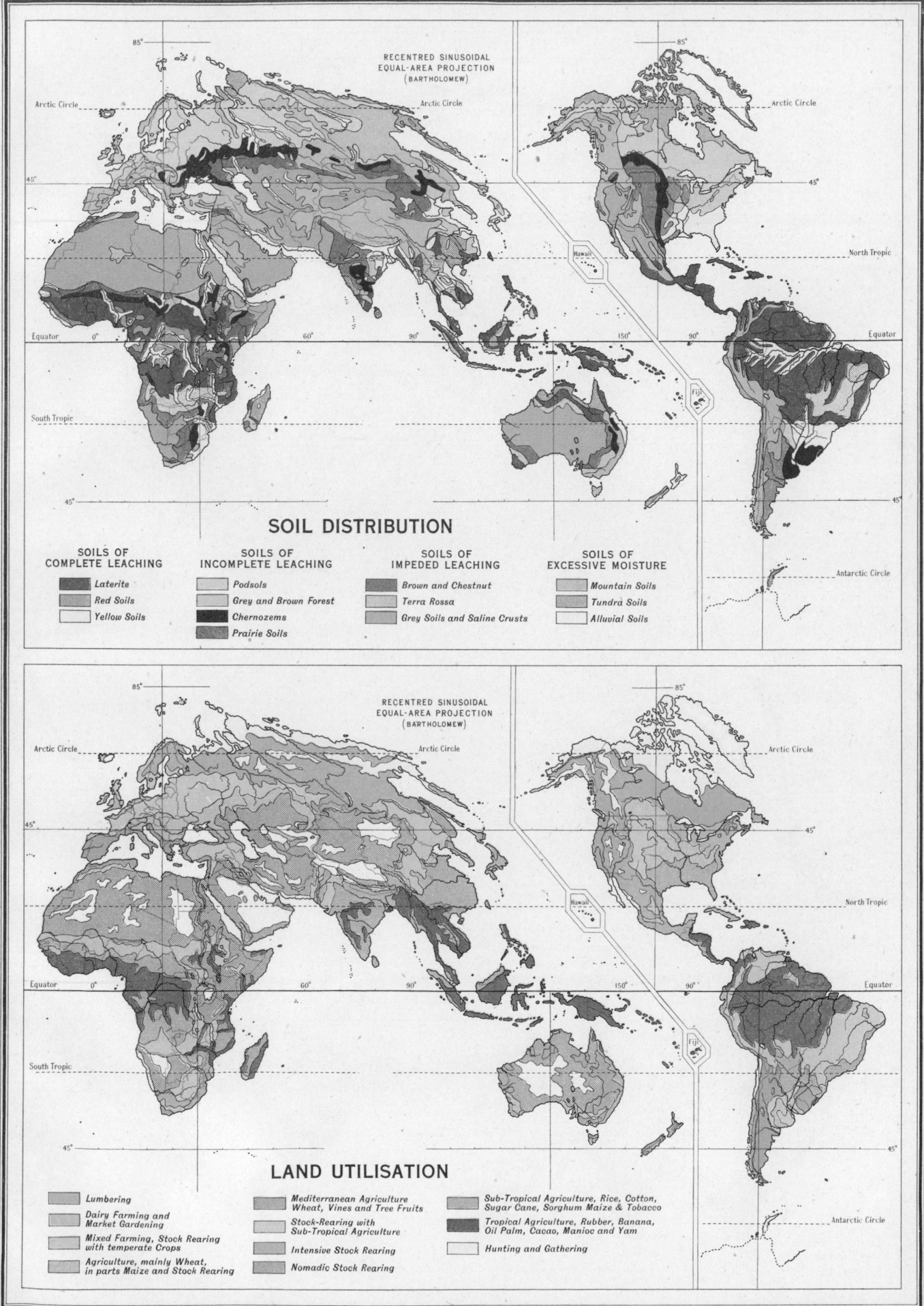

**RECENTRED SINUSOIDAL
EQUAL-AREA PROJECTION
(BARTHOLOMEW)**

SOIL DISTRIBUTION

SOILS OF COMPLETE LEACHING	SOILS OF INCOMPLETE LEACHING	SOILS OF IMPEDED LEACHING	SOILS OF EXCESSIVE MOISTURE
Laterite	Podsols	Brown and Chestnut	Mountain Soils
Red Soils	Grey and Brown Forest	Terra Rossa	Tundra Soils
Yellow Soils	Chernozems	Grey Soils and Saline Crusts	Alluvial Soils
	Prairie Soils		

**RECENTRED SINUSOIDAL
EQUAL-AREA PROJECTION
(BARTHOLOMEW)**

LAND UTILISATION

Lumbering

Dairy Farming and Market Gardening

Mixed Farming, Stock Rearing with temperate Crops

Agriculture, mainly Wheat, in parts Maize and Stock Rearing

Mediterranean Agriculture Wheat, Vines and Tree Fruits

Stock-Rearing with Sub-Tropical Agriculture

Intensive Stock Rearing

Nomadic Stock Rearing

Sub-Tropical Agriculture, Rice, Cotton, Sugar Cane, Sorghum Maize & Tobacco

Tropical Agriculture, Rubber, Banana, Oil Palm, Cacao, Manioc and Yam

Hunting and Gathering

The Edinburgh Geographical Institute

Copyright John Bartholomew & Son, Ltd.

1 : 160,000,000

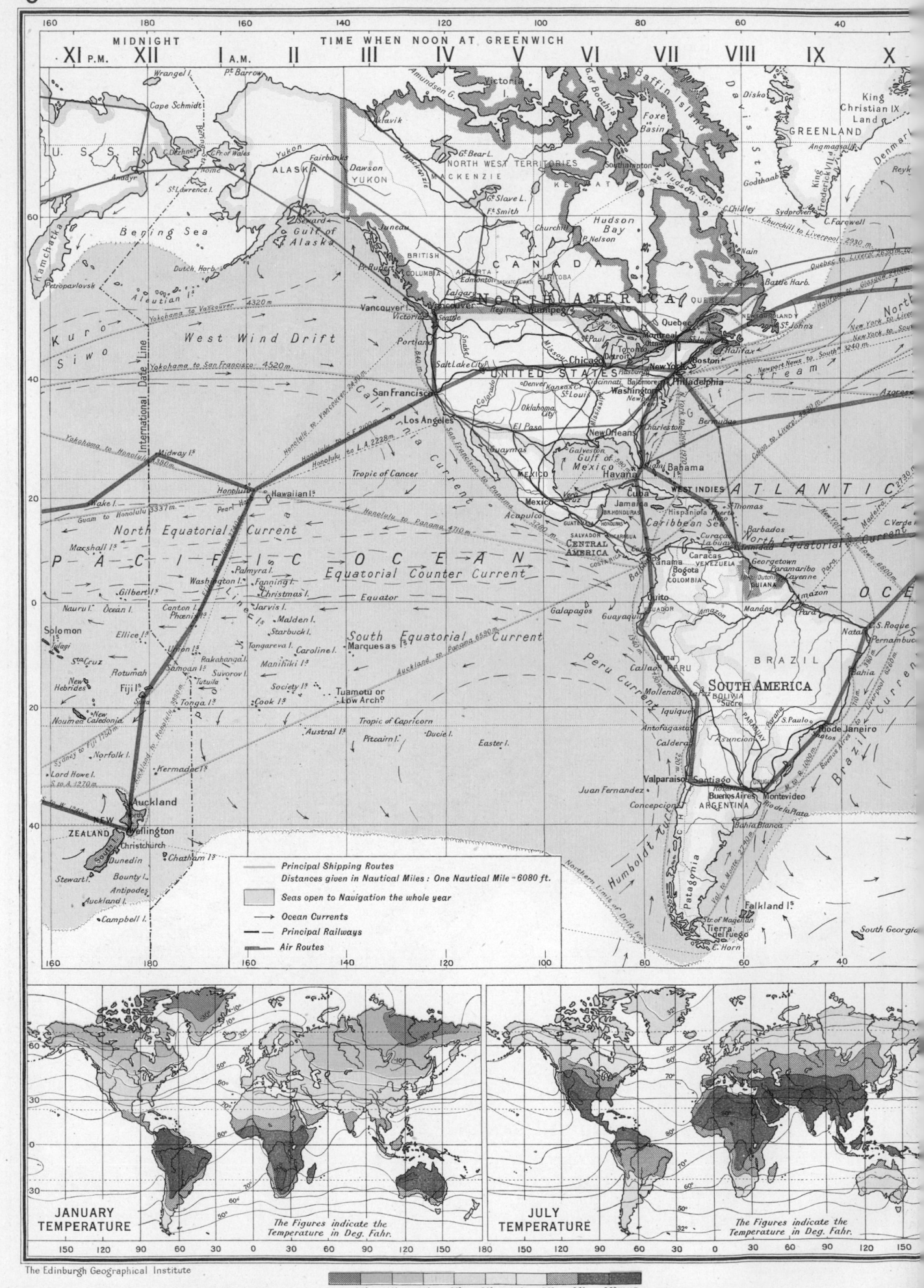

TIME WHEN NOON AT GREENWICH

XI P.M.   XII   I A.M.   II   III   IV   V   VI   VII   VIII   IX   X

MIDNIGHT

—— Principal Shipping Routes
Distances given in Nautical Miles : One Nautical Mile = 6080 ft.

Seas open to Navigation the whole year

→ Ocean Currents

– – – Principal Railways

Air Routes

JANUARY TEMPERATURE   *The Figures indicate the Temperature in Deg. Fahr.*

JULY TEMPERATURE   *The Figures indicate the Temperature in Deg. Fahr.*

The Edinburgh Geographical Institute

-30°   -10°   10°   32°   50°   60°   70°   80°   90° FAHR.

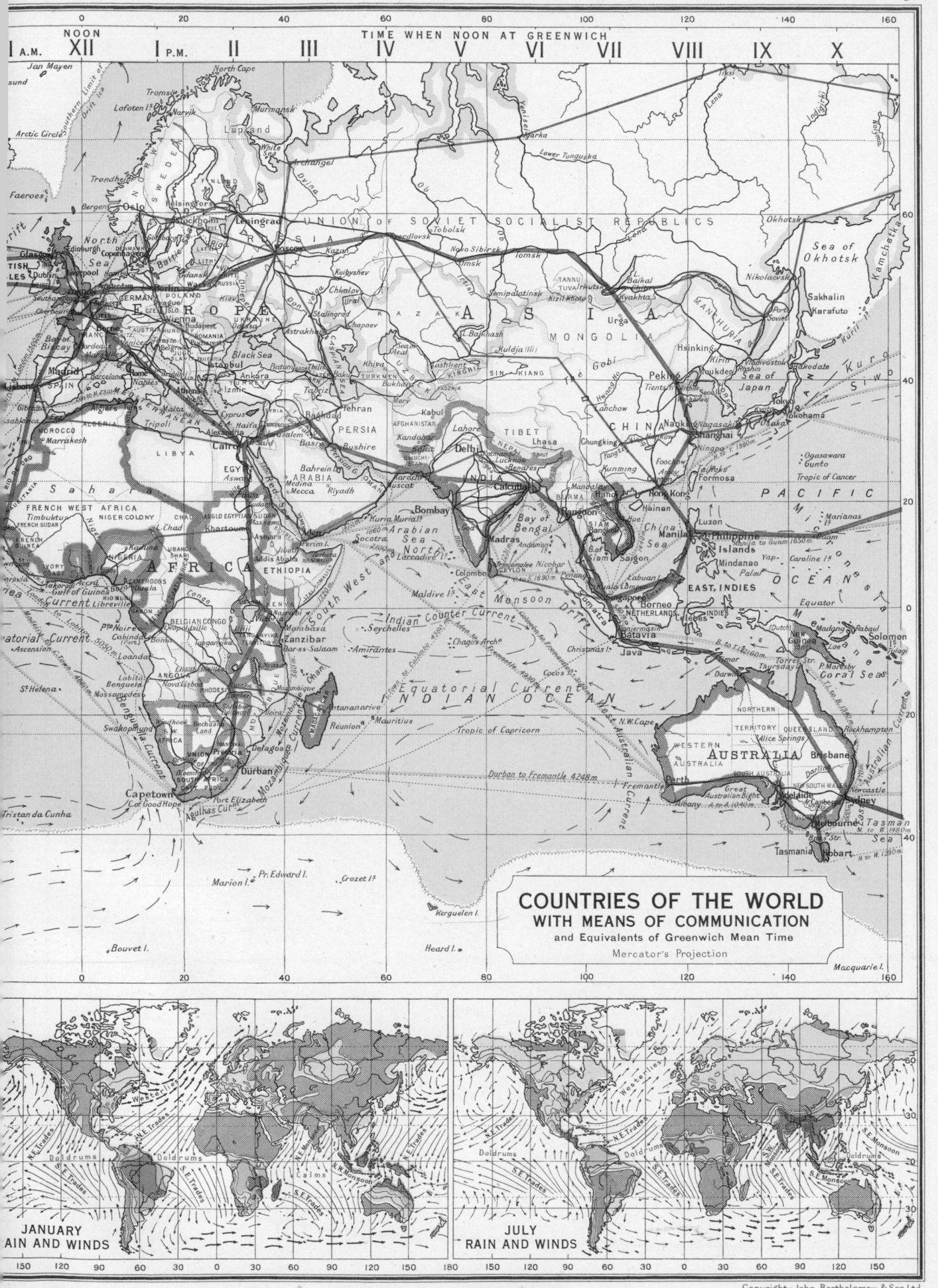

NOON
I A.M. XII I P.M. II III IV V VI VII VIII IX X

COUNTRIES OF THE WORLD
WITH MEANS OF COMMUNICATION
and Equivalents of Greenwich Mean Time
Mercator's Projection

JANUARY
RAIN AND WINDS

JULY
RAIN AND WINDS

Copyright-John Bartholomew & Son.Ltd.

1 2 4 8 12 16 INCHES

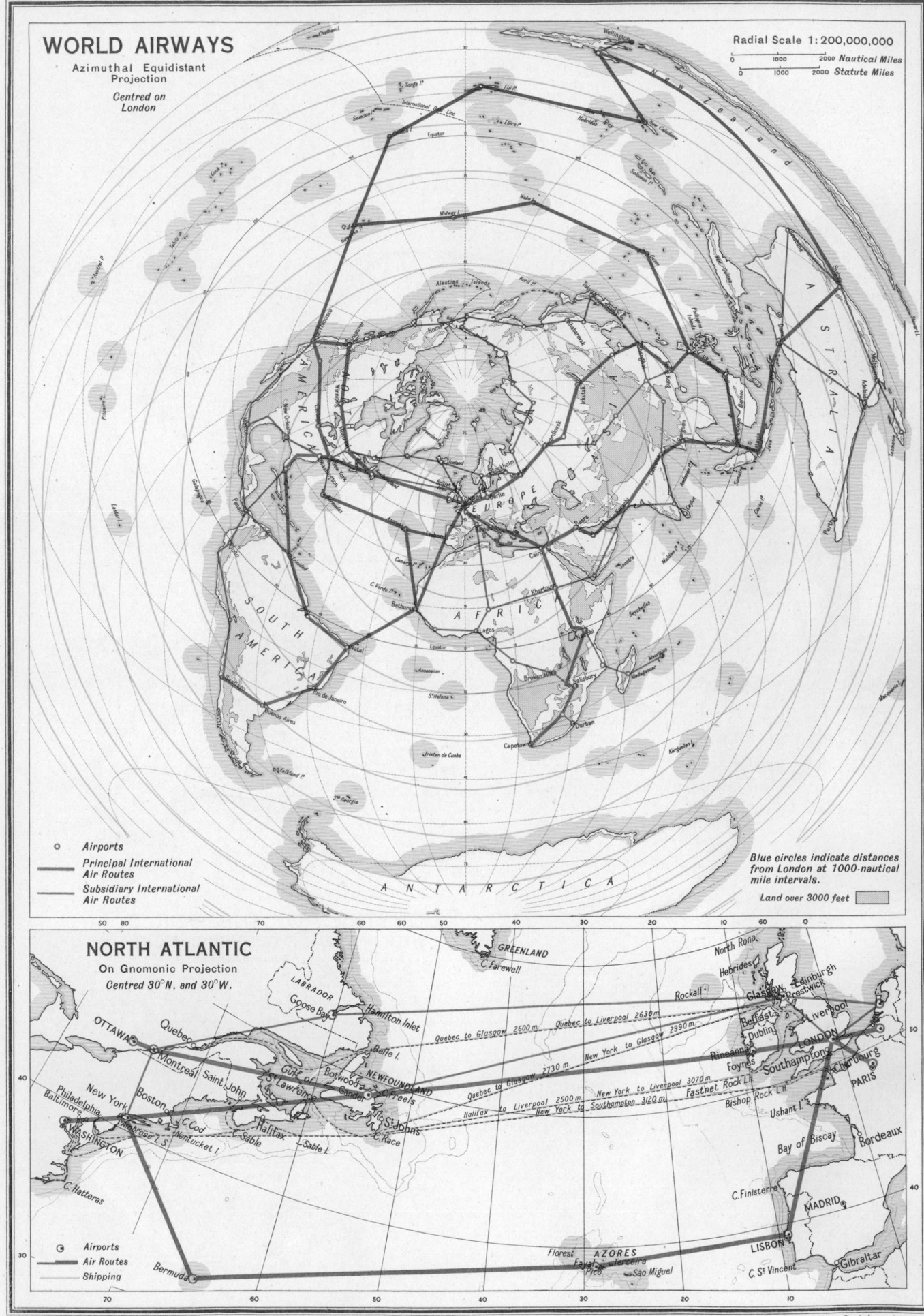

WORLD AIRWAYS

Azimuthal Equidistant
Projection

Centred on
London

Radial Scale 1:200,000,000

	Nautical Miles
	Statute Miles

○   Airports

──   Principal International
Air Routes

──   Subsidiary International
Air Routes

Blue circles indicate distances
from London at 1000-nautical
mile intervals.

Land over 3000 feet

NORTH ATLANTIC

On Gnomonic Projection
Centred 30°N. and 30°W.

Quebec to Glasgow 2600 m.   Quebec to Liverpool 2630 m.
New York to Glasgow 2990 m.
Quebec to Glasgow 2730 m.
Quebec to Glasgow 2500 m.   New York to Liverpool 3070 m.
Halifax to Liverpool 2500 m.
New York to Southampton 3120 m.

○   Airports

──   Air Routes

──   Shipping

Copyright John Bartholomew & Son, Ltd.

ARCTIC LANDS

1:14,000,000

English Miles

Kilometres

Heights in feet

Above 6000	
3000 to 6000	
1500 to 3000	
600 to 1500	
Sea Level to 600	

SPITSBERGEN

GREENLAND

GREENLAND SEA

NORWEGIAN SEA

NORWAY

SWEDEN

ICELAND

Hekla 6763

Vatnajökull

Öraefa-Jökull

Reykjavik

Jan Mayen

Beeren Berg

Denmark Strait

Scoresby Land

Scoresbysund

Franz Josef Fjord

King William Land

Queen Louise Ld.

King Frederick VIII Land

Peary Land

Crown Prince Christian Land

Washington Land

Hall Land

Inglefield Land

Prudhoe Ld.

Humboldt Glacier

BAFFIN BAY

DAVIS STRAIT

King Christian IX Land

King Frederick VI Land

C. Farewell

Arctic Circle

Meridian of Greenwich

Longitude West 20 of Greenwich

Copyright- John Bartholomew & Son, Ltd.

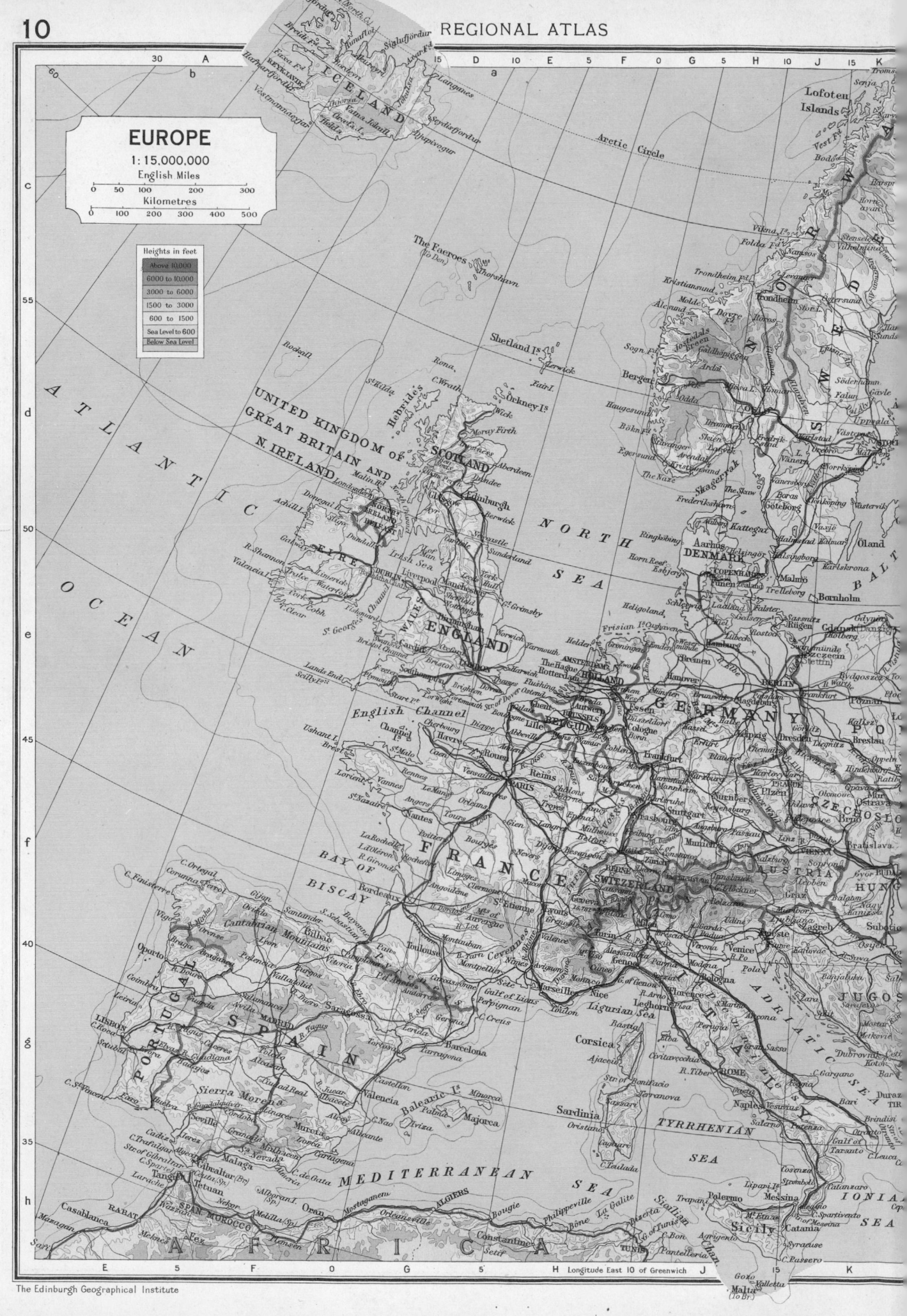

EUROPE
1:15,000,000
English Miles

Kilometres

Heights in feet
Above 10,000
6000 to 10,000
3000 to 6000
1500 to 3000
600 to 1500
Sea Level to 600
Below Sea Level

Copyright - John Bartholomew & Son Ltd.

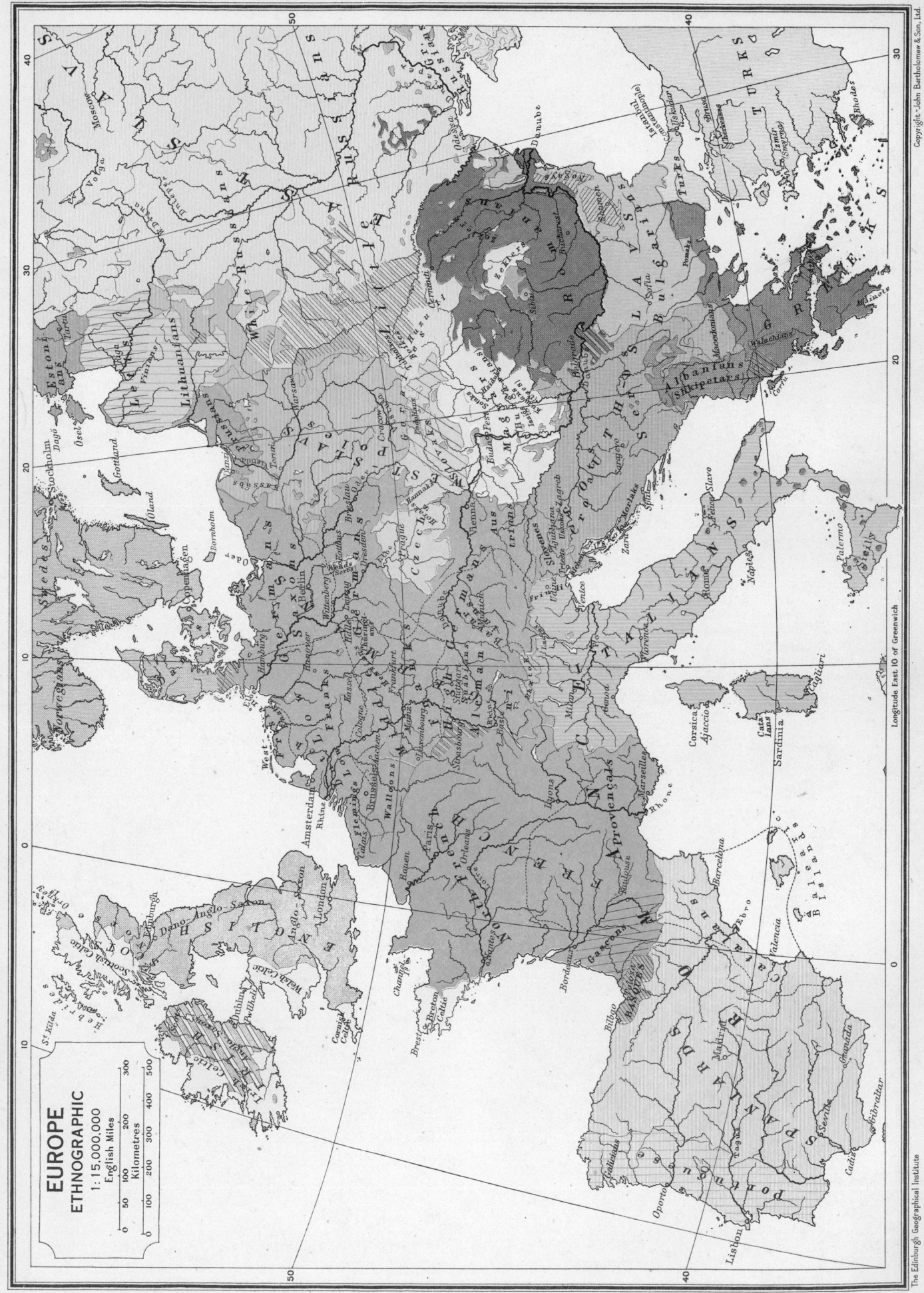

EUROPE
ETHNOGRAPHIC

1:15,000,000

English Miles

Kilometres

The Edinburgh Geographical Institute

Copyright. John Bartholomew & Son, Ltd.

BRITISH ISLES

1 : 5,300,000

English Miles

0 20 40 60 80 100 120

Kilometres

0 20 40 60 80 100 120 140 160 180

The Edinburgh Geographical Institute

Copyright—John Bartholomew & Son, Ltd.

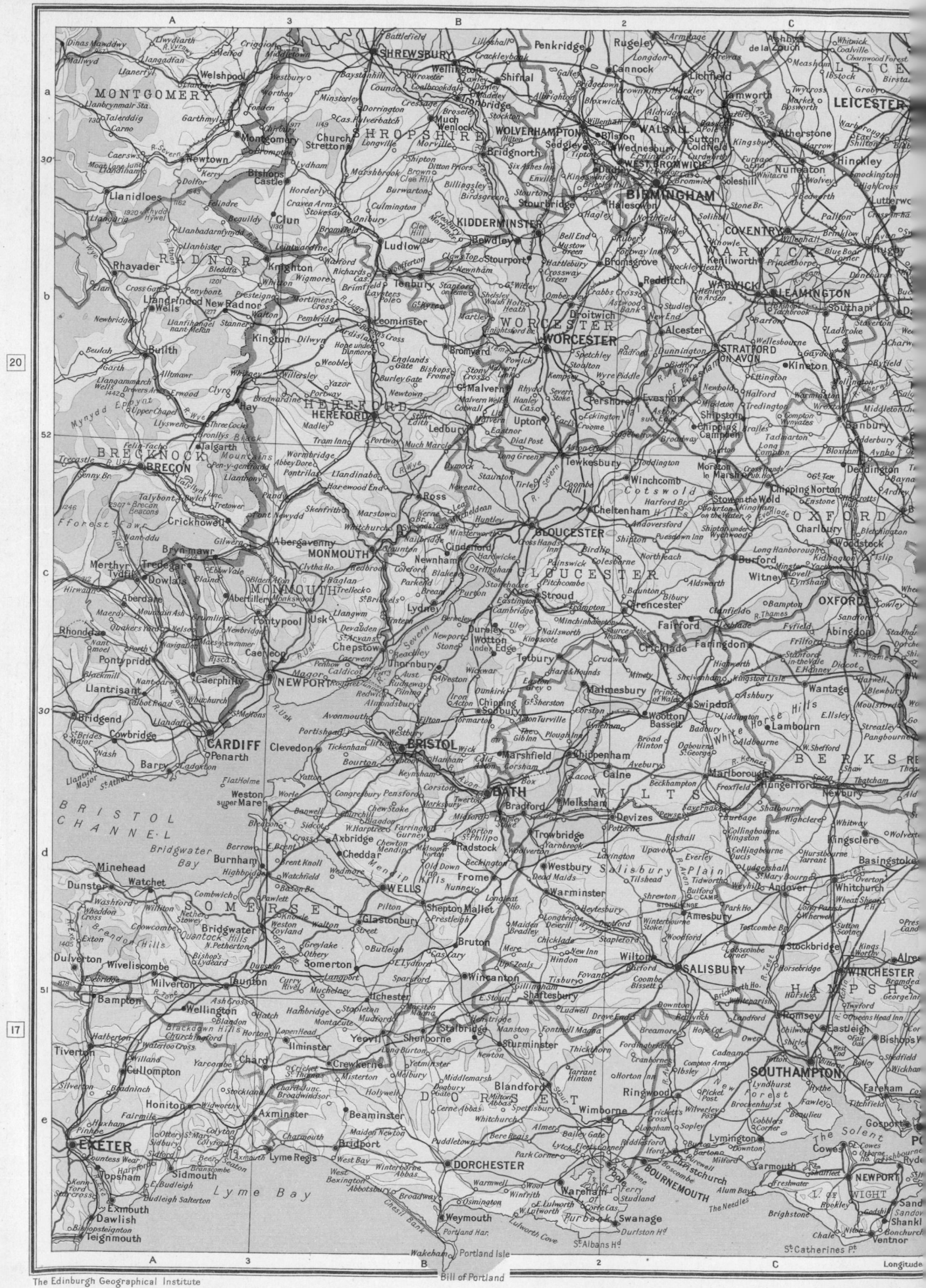

MONTGOMERY
SHROPSHIRE
RADNOR
WORCESTER
WARWICK
HEREFORD
BRECKNOCK
MONMOUTH
GLOUCESTER
OXFORD
BERKS
WILTS
SOMERSET
DORSET
HAMPSH
LEICESTER
BRISTOL CHANNEL
Lyme Bay
The Solent
I. of WIGHT
SHREWSBURY
WOLVERHAMPTON
WALSALL
WEST BROMWICH
BIRMINGHAM
KIDDERMINSTER
COVENTRY
WARWICK
LEAMINGTON
STRATFORD ON AVON
WORCESTER
HEREFORD
BRECON
MONMOUTH
GLOUCESTER
NEWPORT
CARDIFF
BRISTOL
BATH
OXFORD
SALISBURY
WINCHESTER
SOUTHAMPTON
BOURNEMOUTH
DORCHESTER
EXETER
Welshpool
Montgomery
Newtown
Llanidloes
Rhayader
Knighton
Ludlow
Leominster
Bewdley
Stourport
Tenbury
Bromsgrove
Redditch
Evesham
Pershore
Ledbury
Ross
Tewkesbury
Cheltenham
Cirencester
Stroud
Chepstow
Abergavenny
Pontypool
Merthyr Tydfil
Pontypridd
Caerphilly
Llantrisant
Bridgend
Cowbridge
Barry
Penarth
Clevedon
Weston super Mare
Burnham
Bridgwater
Taunton
Wellington
Minehead
Watchet
Dunster
Dulverton
Tiverton
Cullompton
Honiton
Axminster
Chard
Yeovil
Sherborne
Shaftesbury
Blandford
Wimborne
Wareham
Swanage
Weymouth
Bridport
Lyme Regis
Sidmouth
Exmouth
Dawlish
Teignmouth
Topsham
Wells
Glastonbury
Frome
Trowbridge
Westbury
Warminster
Devizes
Chippenham
Calne
Marlborough
Swindon
Malmesbury
Faringdon
Abingdon
Wantage
Hungerford
Newbury
Andover
Romsey
Lymington
Ringwood
Christchurch
Cowes
Newport
Portland Isle
Bill of Portland
St. Albans Hd.
St. Catherines Pt.
A
3
B
2
C
a
b
c
d
e
30'
52
51
20
17
Longitude

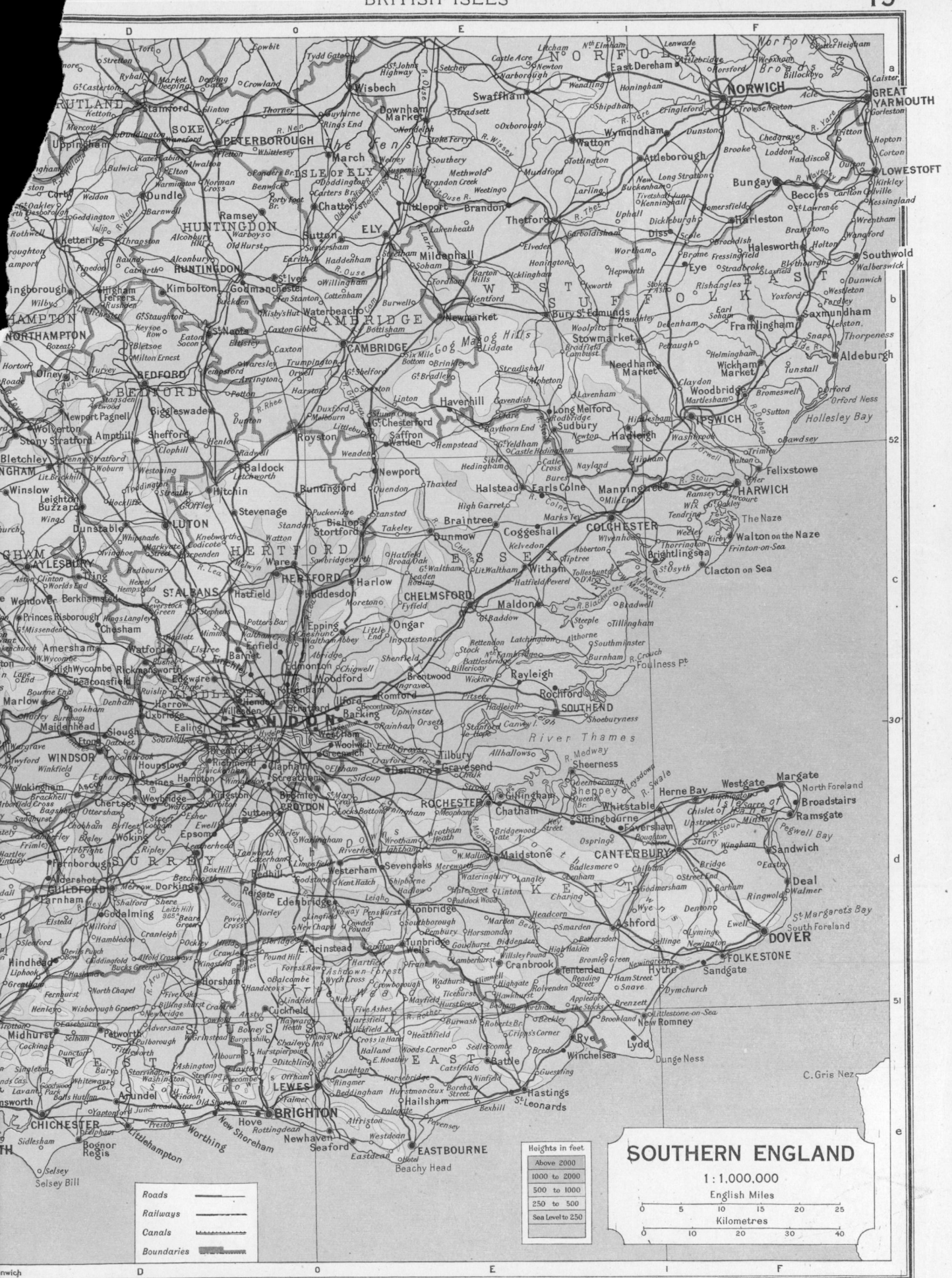

SOUTHERN ENGLAND

1 : 1,000,000

English Miles

Kilometres

Heights in feet

| Above 2000 |
| 1000 to 2000 |
| 500 to 1000 |
| 250 to 500 |
| Sea Level to 250 |

Roads
Railways
Canals
Boundaries

Copyright - John Bartholomew & Son Ltd.

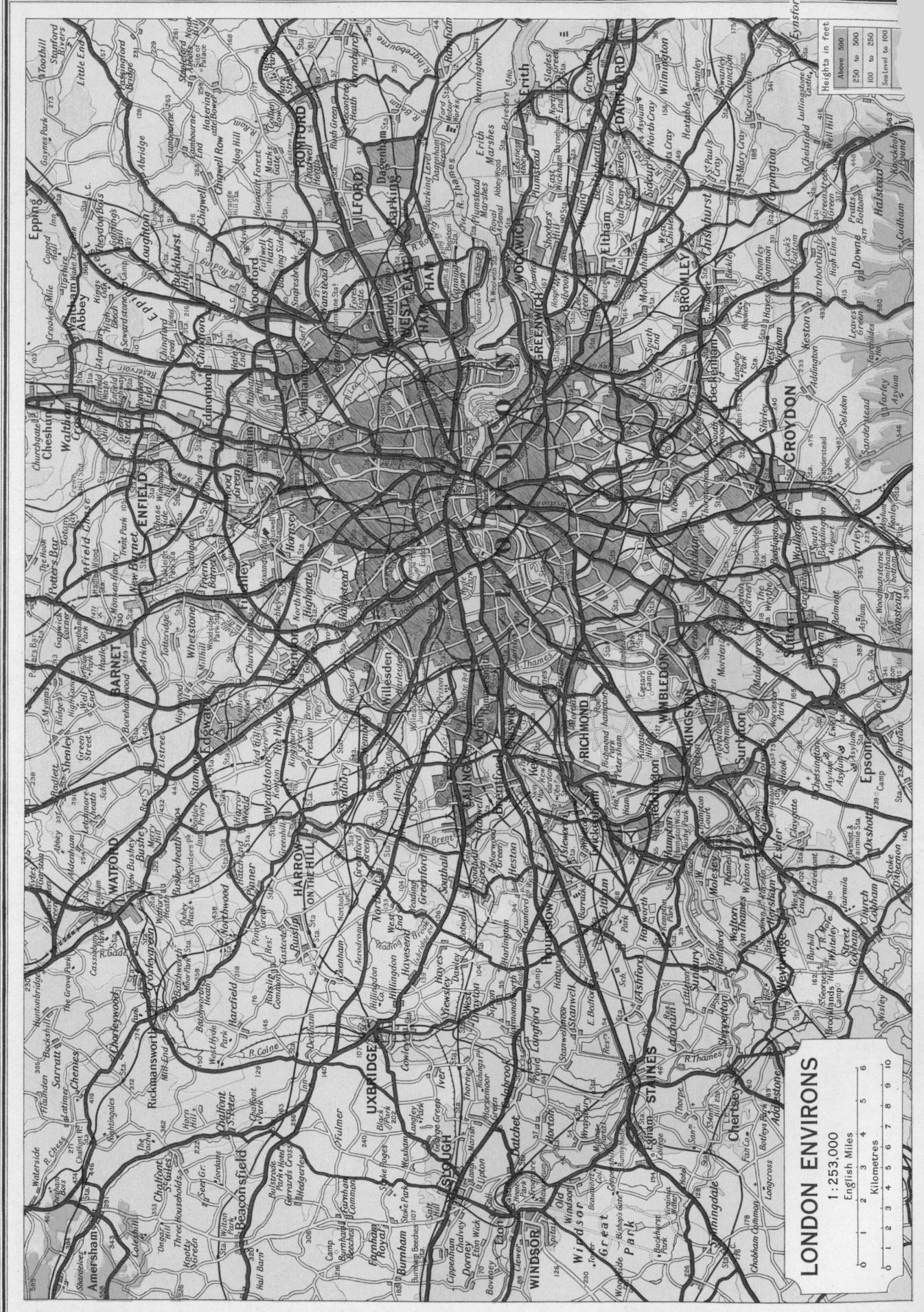
LONDON ENVIRONS
1:253,000
English Miles
0 1 2 3 4 5 6
Kilometres
0 1 2 3 4 5 6 7 8 9 10
Heights in feet
Above 500
250 to 500
100 to 250
Sea Level to 100
LONDON
ROMFORD
ILFORD
Barking
Dagenham
WEST HAM
EAST HAM
WOOLWICH
GREENWICH
Erith
DARTFORD
BROMLEY
CROYDON
ENFIELD
BARNET
WATFORD
HARROW ON THE HILL
EALING
RICHMOND
WIMBLEDON
KINGSTON
UXBRIDGE
SLOUGH
WINDSOR
STAINES
Epping
Amersham
Beaconsfield
Epsom
Chertsey
R. Thames
R. Colne
R. Brent
The Edinburgh Geographical Institute

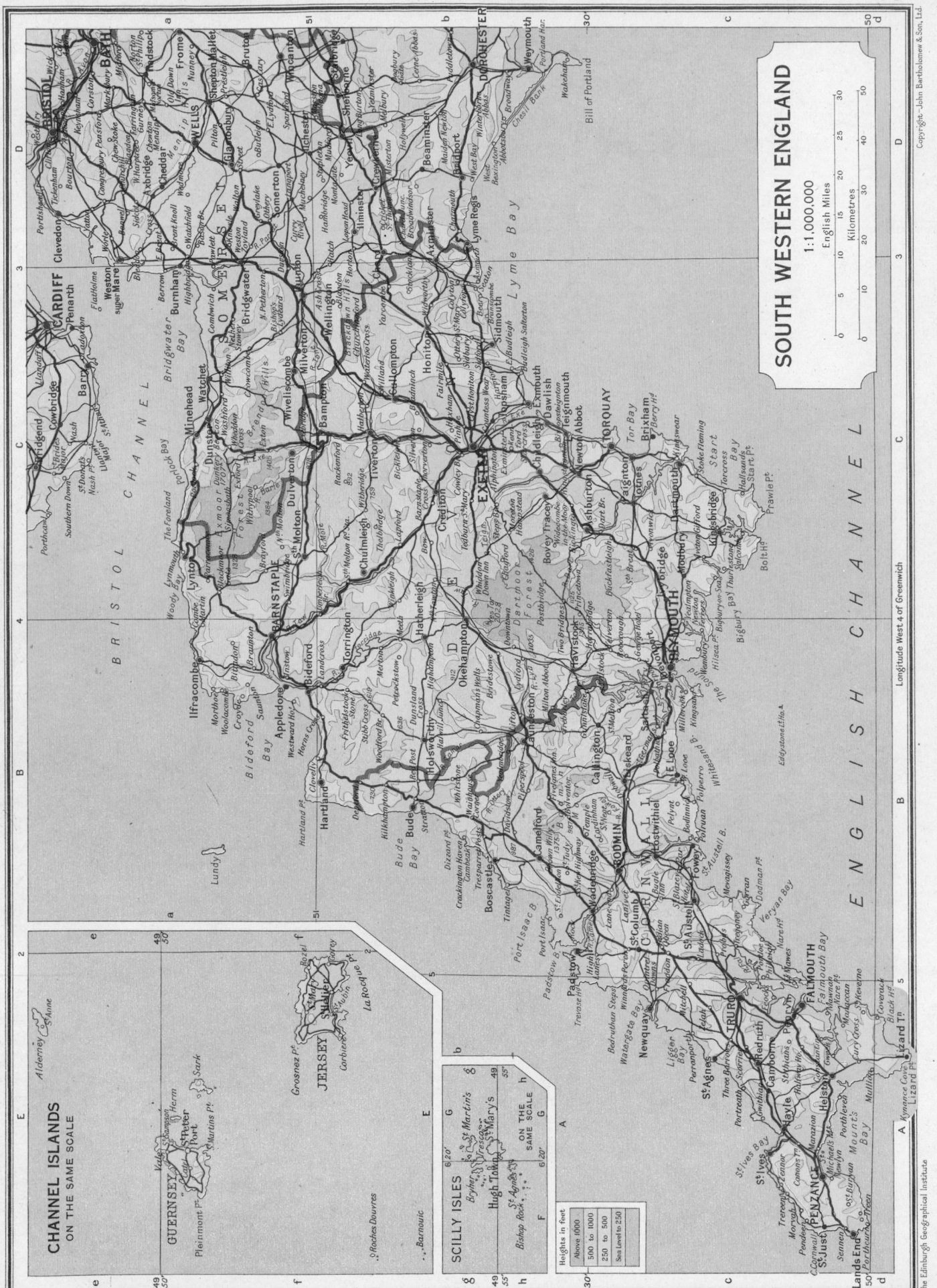

SOUTH WESTERN ENGLAND

1:1,000,000

English Miles

Kilometres

CHANNEL ISLANDS
ON THE SAME SCALE

GUERNSEY

JERSEY

SCILLY ISLES   ON THE SAME SCALE

Heights in Feet

Above 1000	
500 to 1000	
250 to 500	
Sea Level to 250	

BRISTOL CHANNEL

ENGLISH CHANNEL

Lyme Bay

Bridgwater Bay

Bideford Bay

Bude Bay

Copyright—John Bartholomew & Son, Ltd.

The Edinburgh Geographical Institute

Longitude West 4 of Greenwich

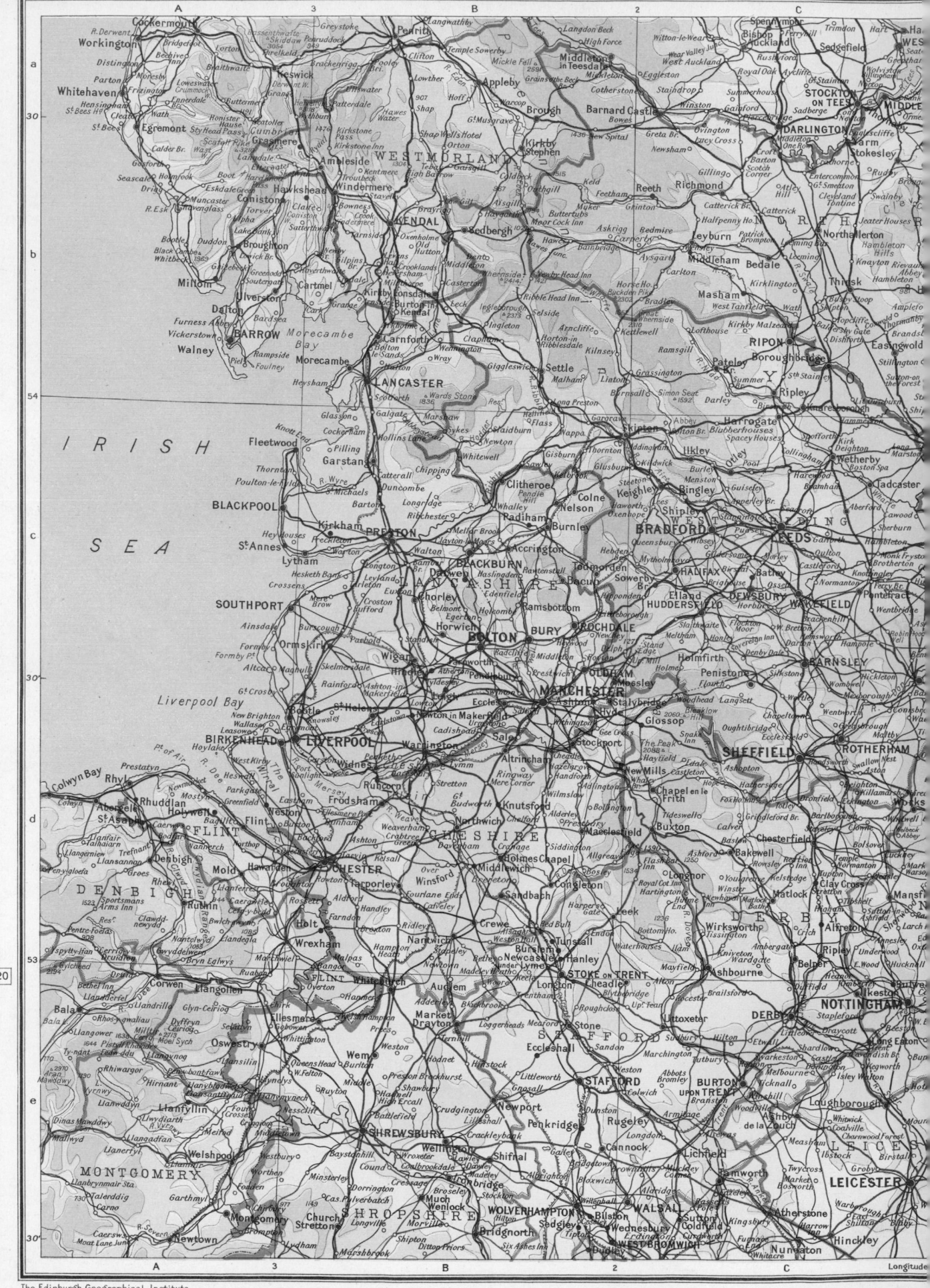

N. CENTRAL ENGLAND
1:1,000,000

ISLE OF MAN

Copyright- John Bartholomew & Son, Ltd.

WALES

1:1,000,000

English Miles

Kilometres

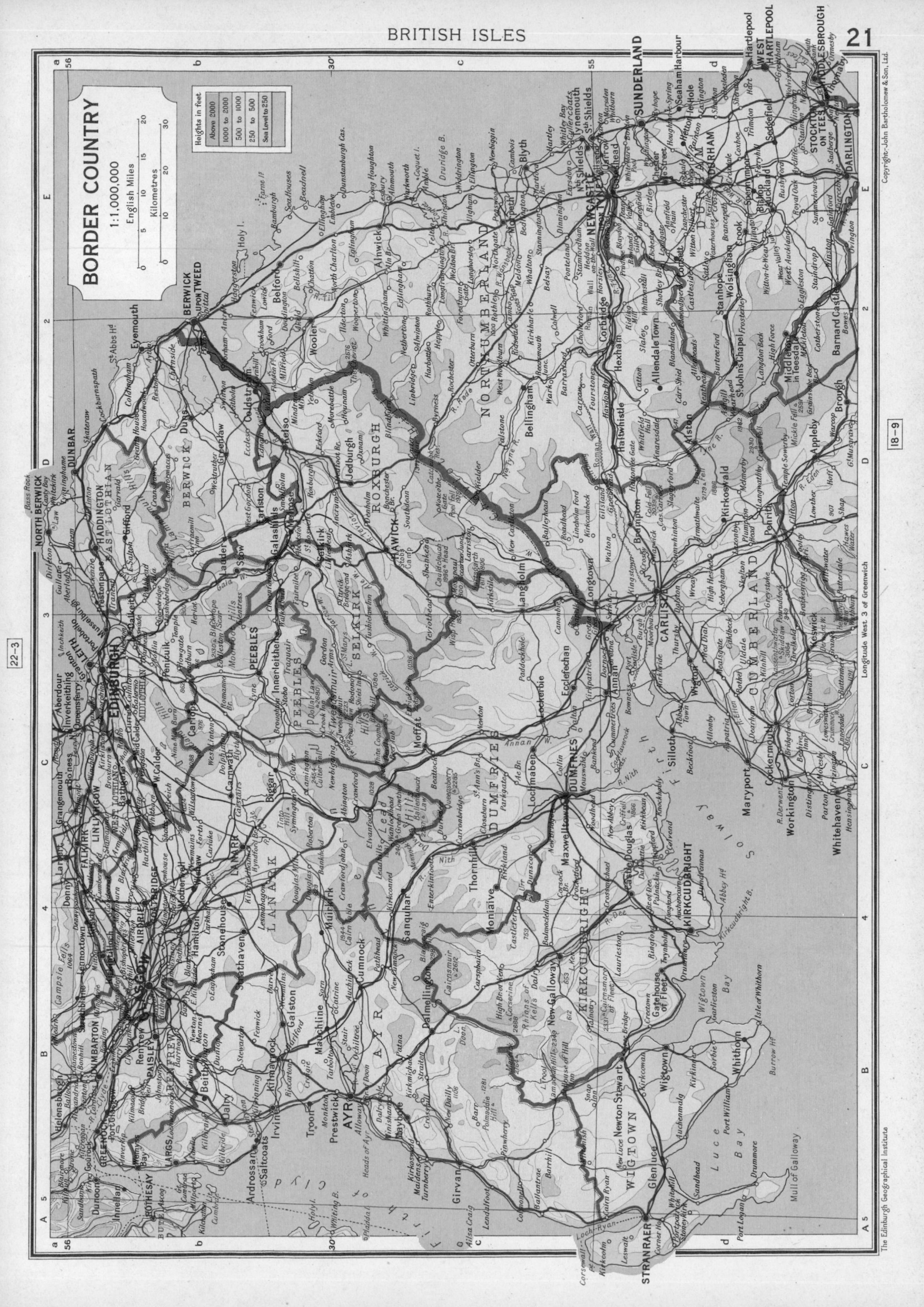

BORDER COUNTRY

1:1,000,000

English Miles

Kilometres

Heights in feet
Above 2000
1000 to 2000
500 to 1000
250 to 500
Sea Level to 250

Copyright–John Bartholomew & Son, Ltd.

SCOTTISH
HIGHLANDS

1 : 1,000,000

English Miles

Kilometres

Heights in feet

Above 2000

1000 to 2000

500 to 1000

250 to 500

Sea Level to 250

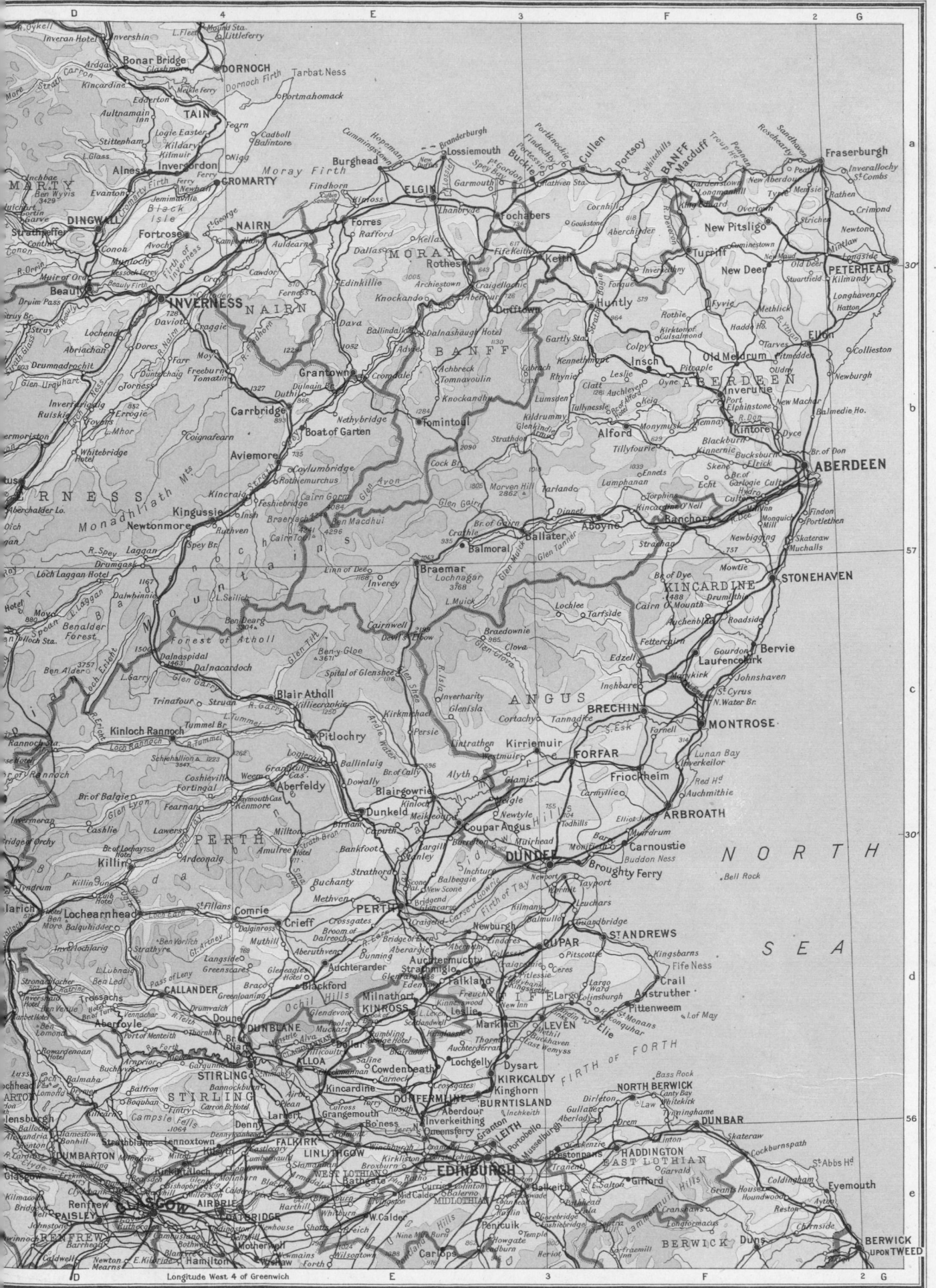

Longitude West 4 of Greenwich

Copyright—John Bartholomew & Son Ltd.

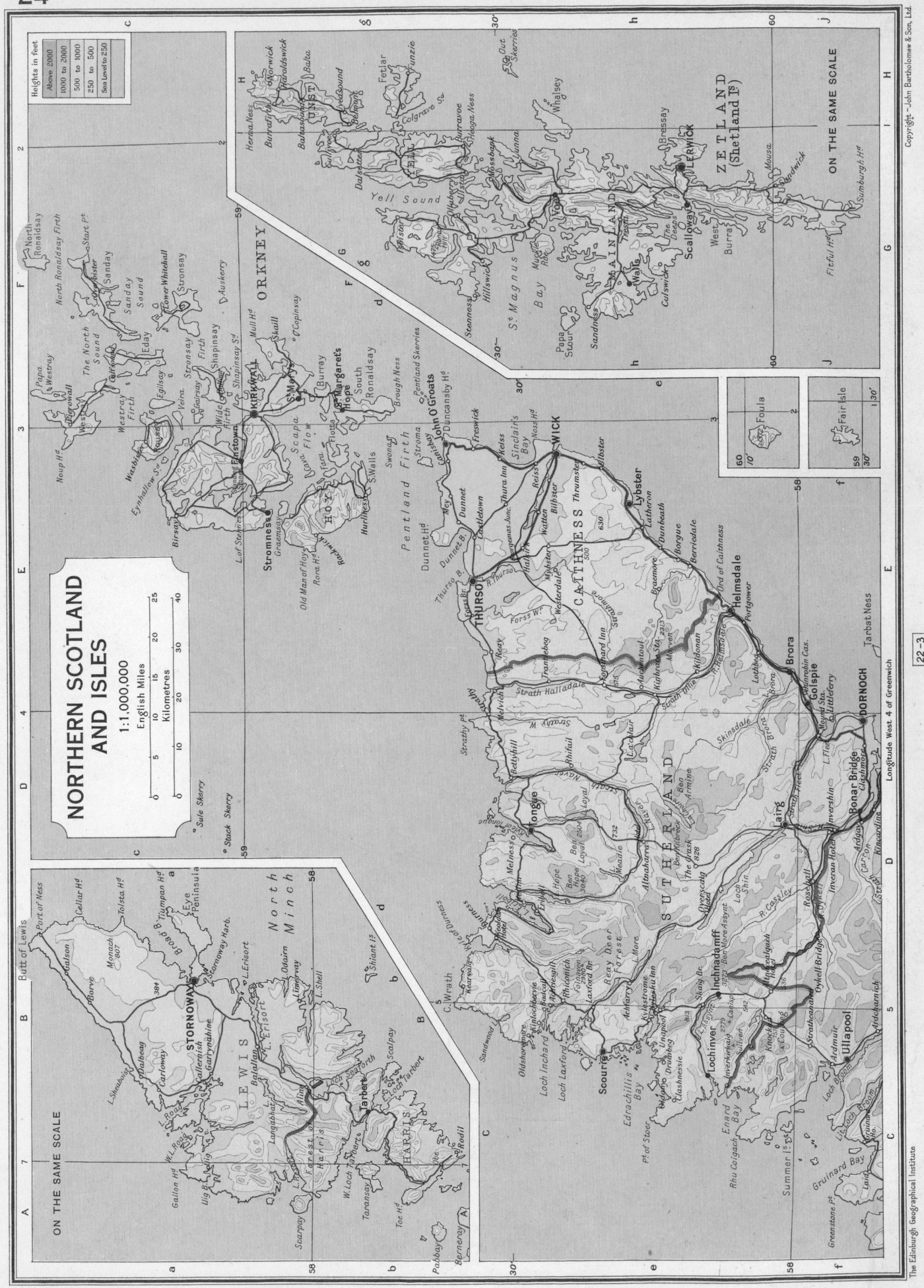

NORTHERN SCOTLAND
AND ISLES

1:1,000,000

English Miles

Kilometres

Copyright—John Bartholomew & Son, Ltd.

The Edinburgh Geographical Institute

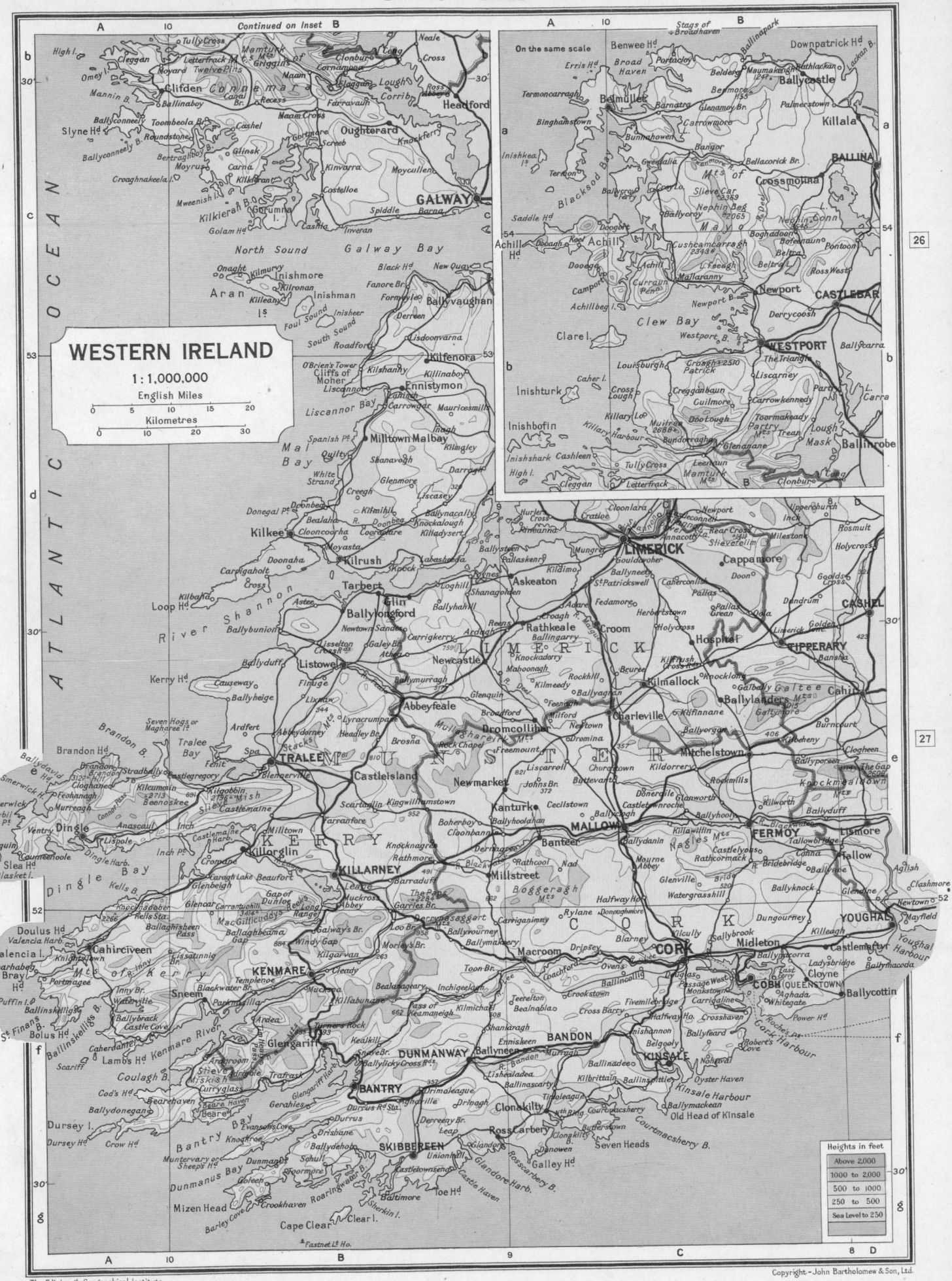

WESTERN IRELAND

1 : 1,000,000

English Miles

Kilometres

On the same scale

Copyright – John Bartholomew & Son, Ltd.

The Edinburgh Geographical Institute

Heights in feet

| Above 2,000 |
| 1000 to 2,000 |
| 500 to 1000 |
| 250 to 500 |
| Sea Level to 250 |

NORTHERN AND CENTRAL IRELAND

1 : 1,000,000

English Miles

Kilometres

Heights in feet

	Above 2000
	1000 to 2000
	500 to 1000
	250 to 500
	Sea Level to 250

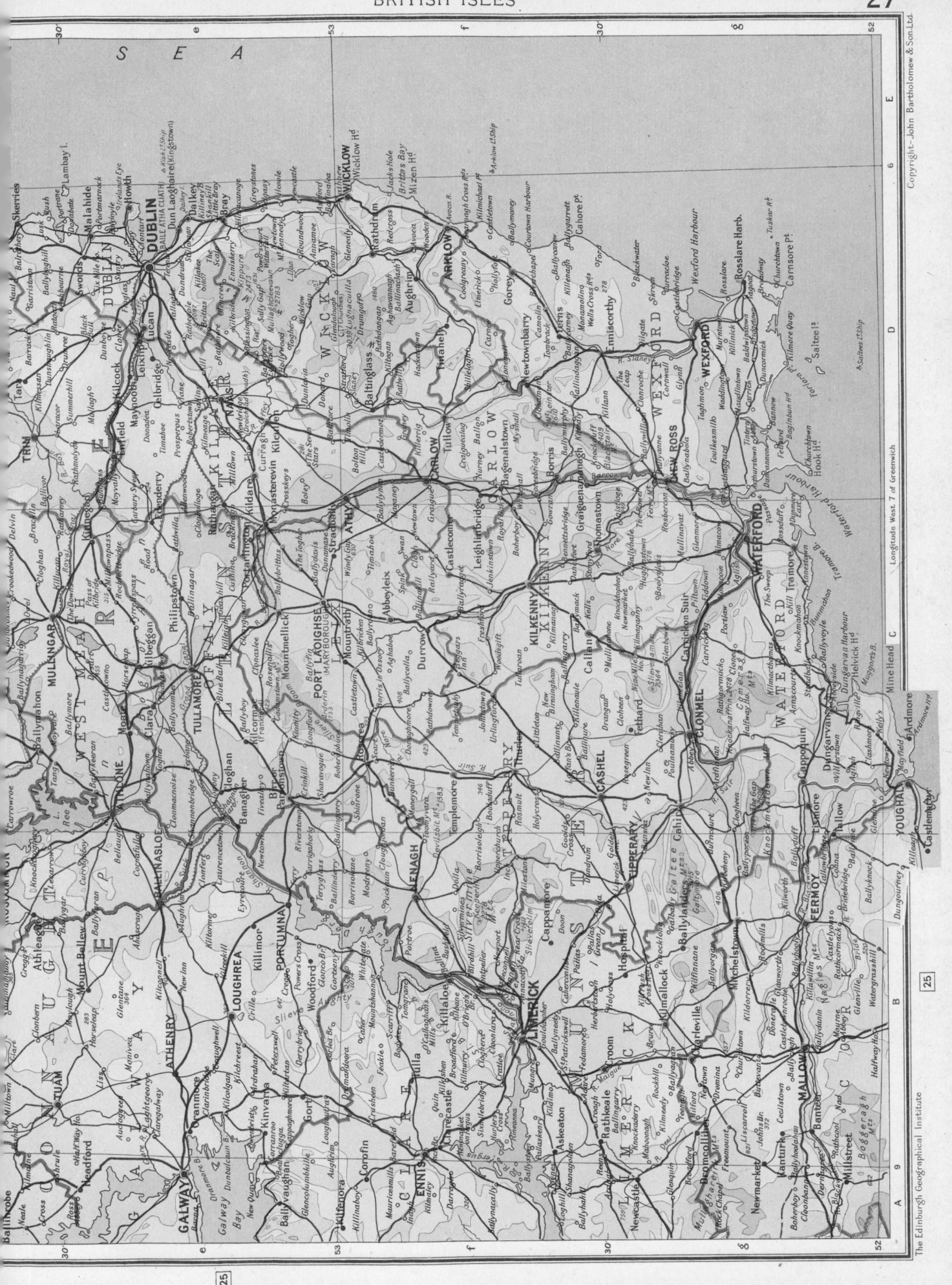

Copyright- John Bartholomew & Son.Ltd.

The Edinburgh Geographical Institute

WESTERN EUROPE

1 : 8,000,000

English Miles

0   50   100   150   200

Kilometres

0   100   200   300

Copyright - John Bartholomew & Son, Ltd.

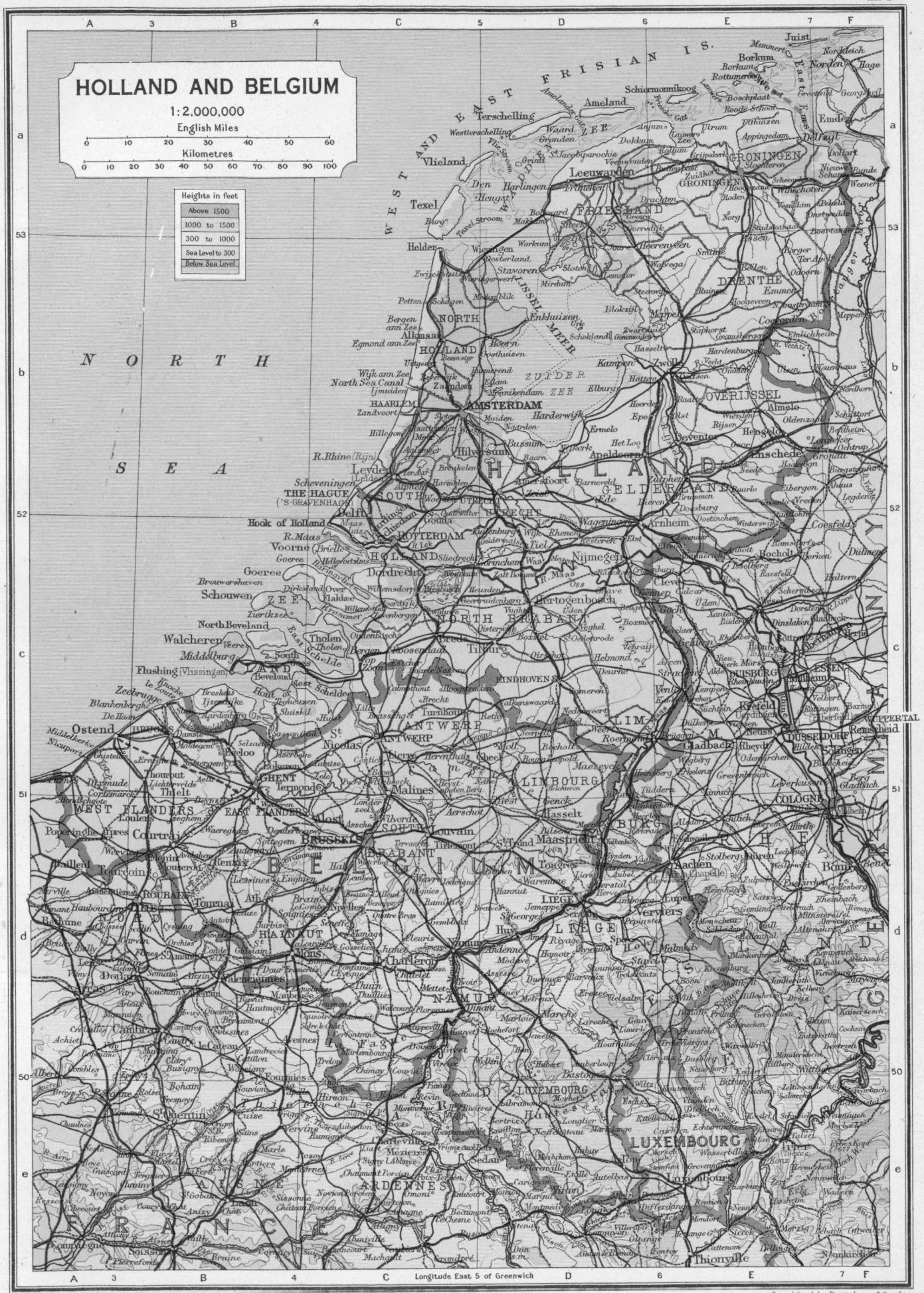

HOLLAND AND BELGIUM

1:2,000,000

English Miles

Kilometres

Heights in feet
Above 1500
1000 to 1500
300 to 1000
Sea Level to 300
Below Sea Level

NORTH SEA

WEST AND EAST FRISIAN IS.

HOLLAND
GELDERLAND
NORTH BRABANT
LIMBOURG
BELGIUM
BRABANT
HAINAUT
NAMUR
LUXEMBOURG
ARDENNES
FRANCE

Longitude East 5 of Greenwich

Copyright John Bartholomew & Son Ltd.

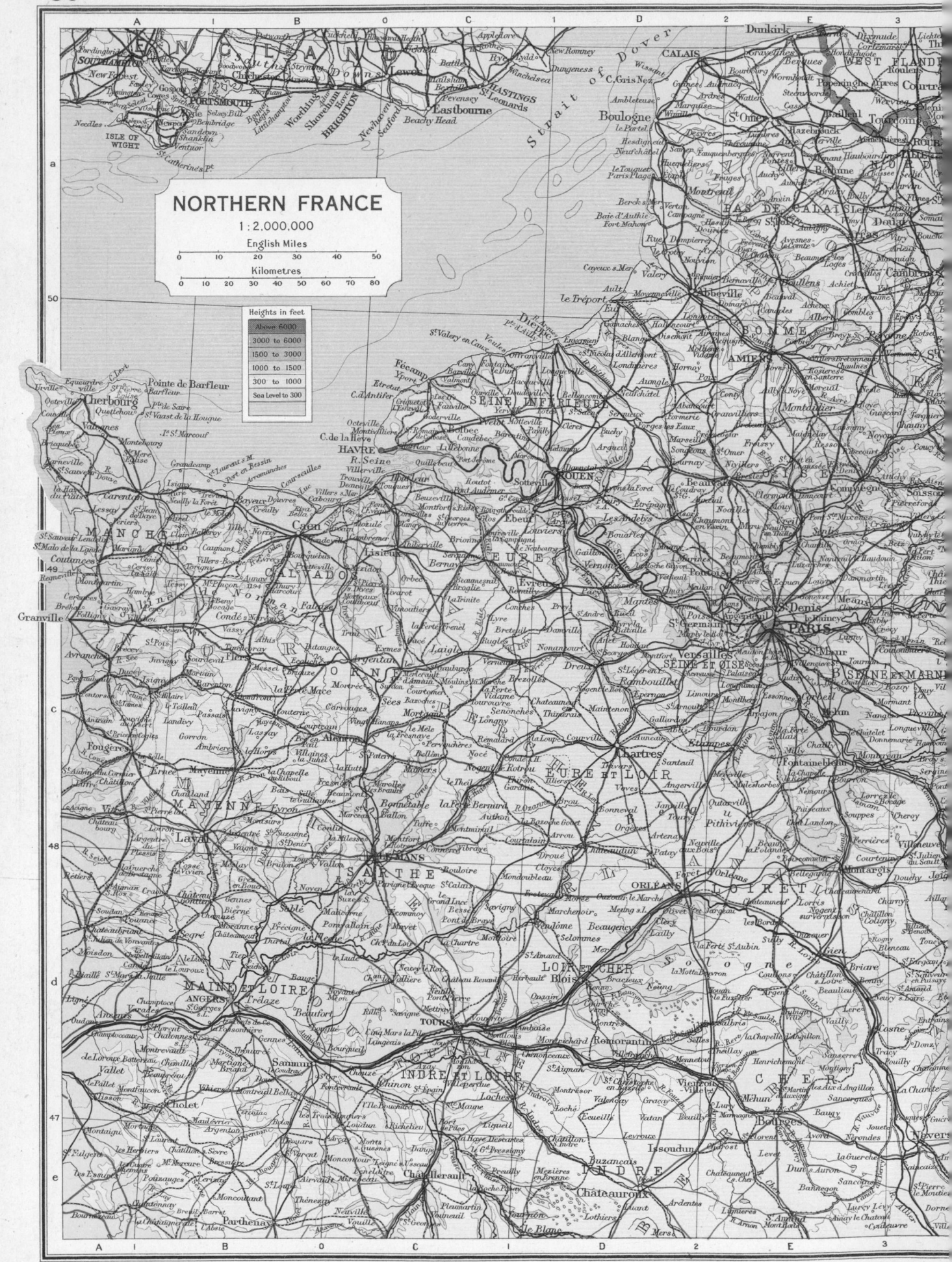

NORTHERN FRANCE

1 : 2,000,000

English Miles

0   10   20   30   40   50

Kilometres

0 10 20 30 40 50 60 70 80

Heights in feet

Above 6000
3000 to 6000
1500 to 3000
1000 to 1500
300 to 1000
Sea Level to 300

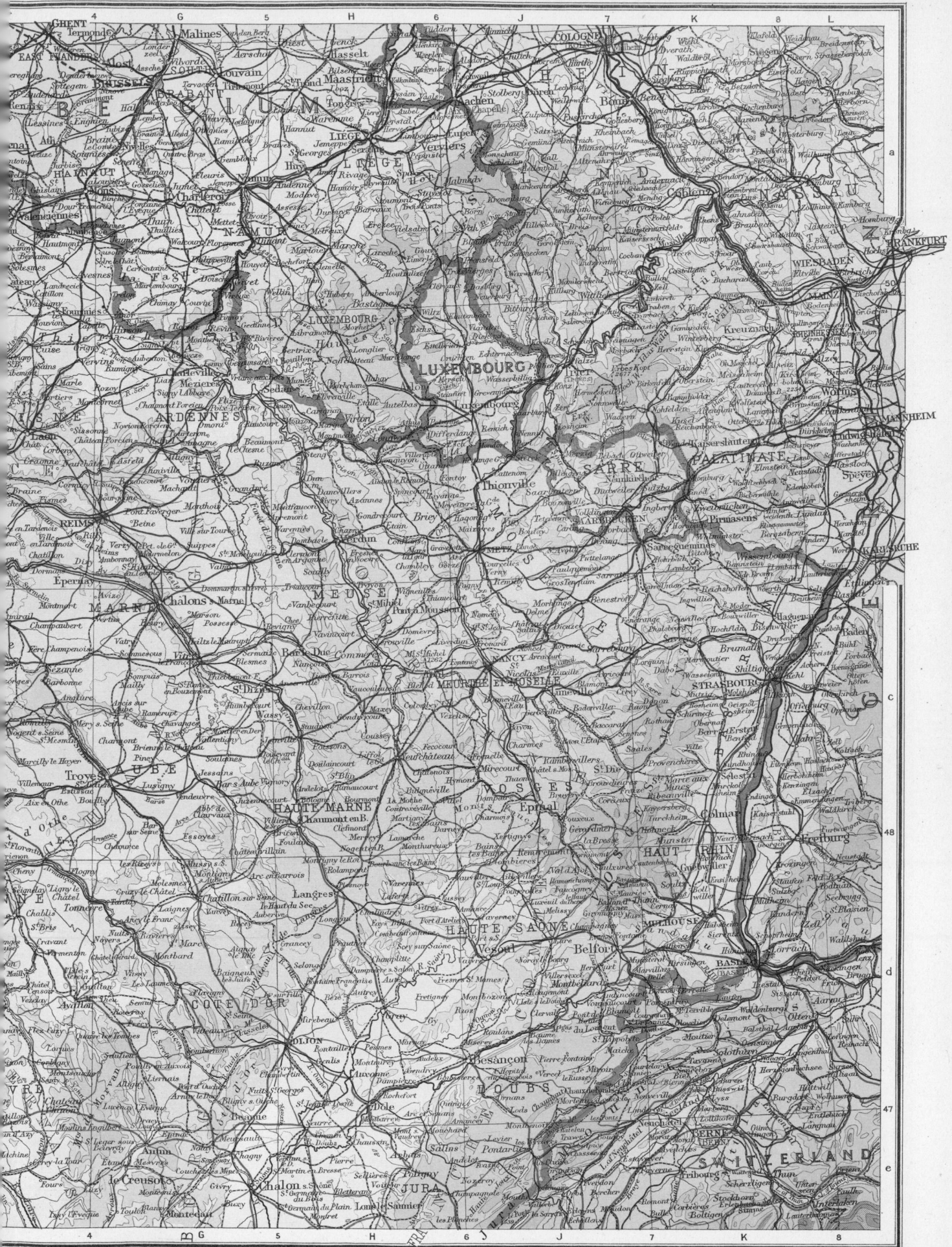

Copyright- John Bartholomew & Son.Ltd.

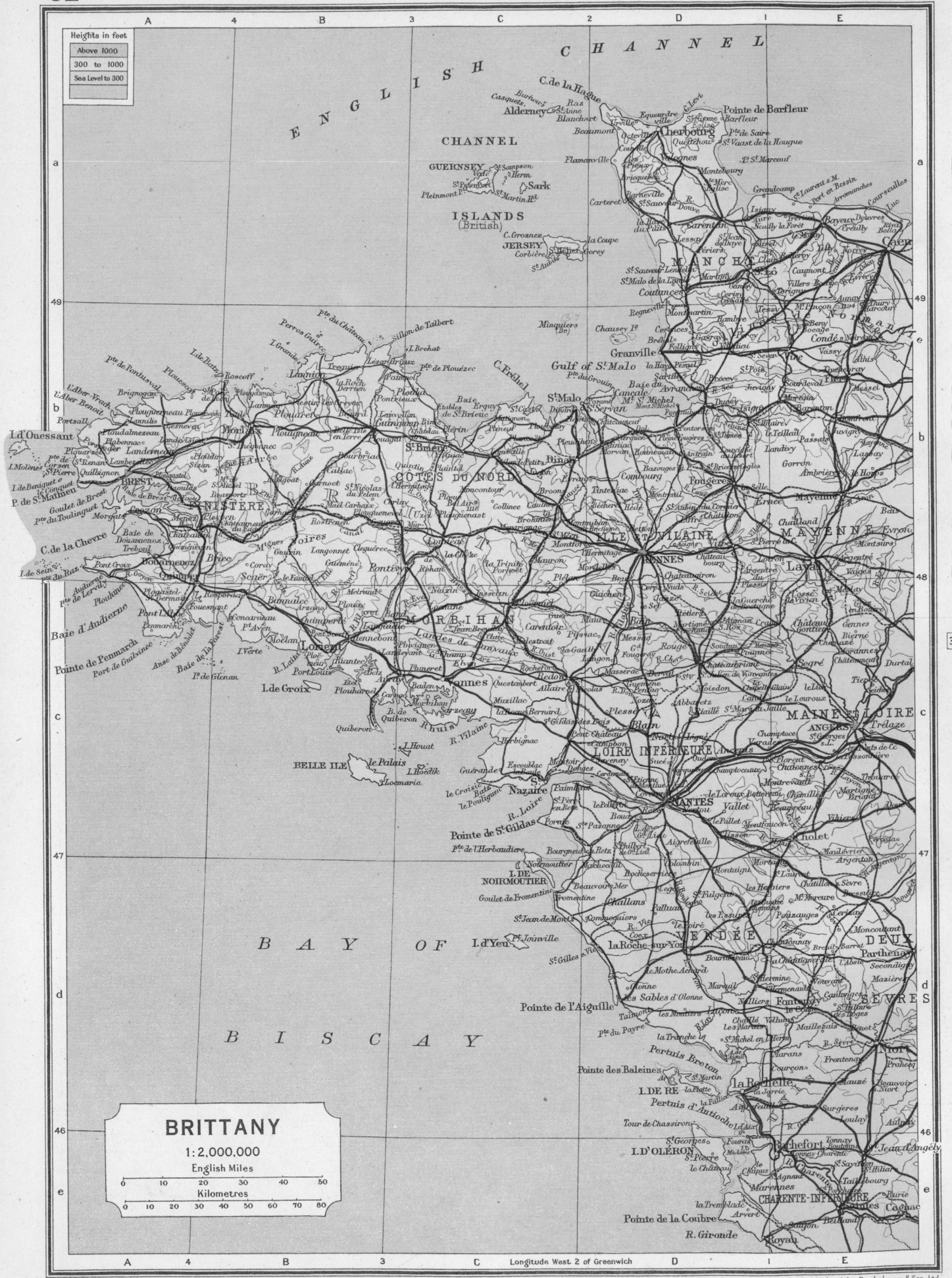

Heights in feet
Above 1000
300 to 1000
Sea Level to 300

BRITTANY
1:2,000,000
English Miles
0   10   20   30   40   50
Kilometres
0 10 20 30 40 50 60 70 80

Copyright John Bartholomew & Son Ltd.

Longitude West 2 of Greenwich

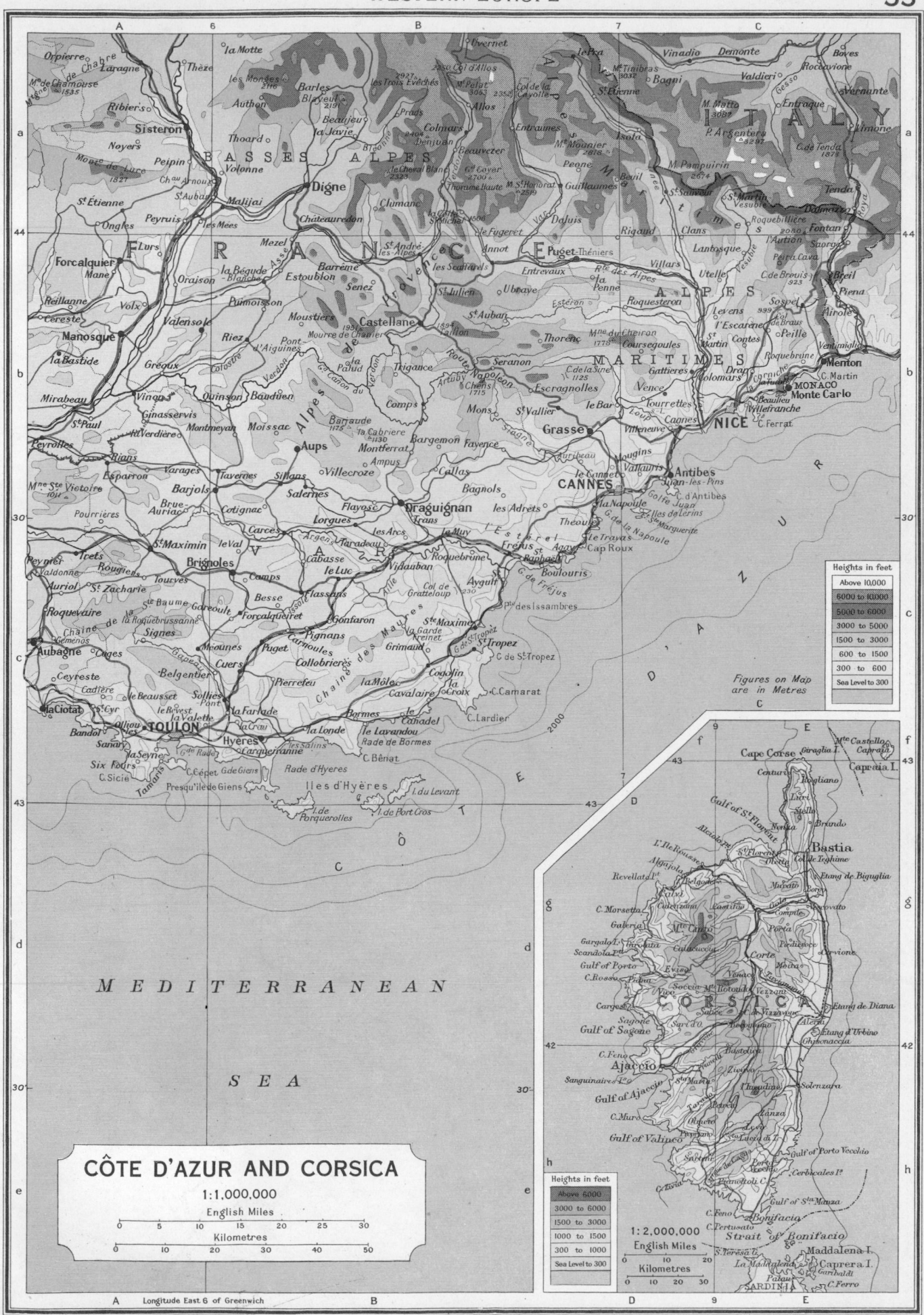

CÔTE D'AZUR AND CORSICA

1:1,000,000

English Miles

0 5 10 15 20 25 30

Kilometres

0 10 20 30 40 50

MEDITERRANEAN

SEA

Heights in feet

Above 10,000
6000 to 10,000
5000 to 6000
3000 to 5000
1500 to 3000
600 to 1500
300 to 600
Sea Level to 300

Figures on Map
are in Metres

Heights in feet

Above 6000
3000 to 6000
1500 to 3000
1000 to 1500
300 to 1000
Sea Level to 300

1:2,000,000
English Miles

0 10 20

Kilometres

0 10 20 30

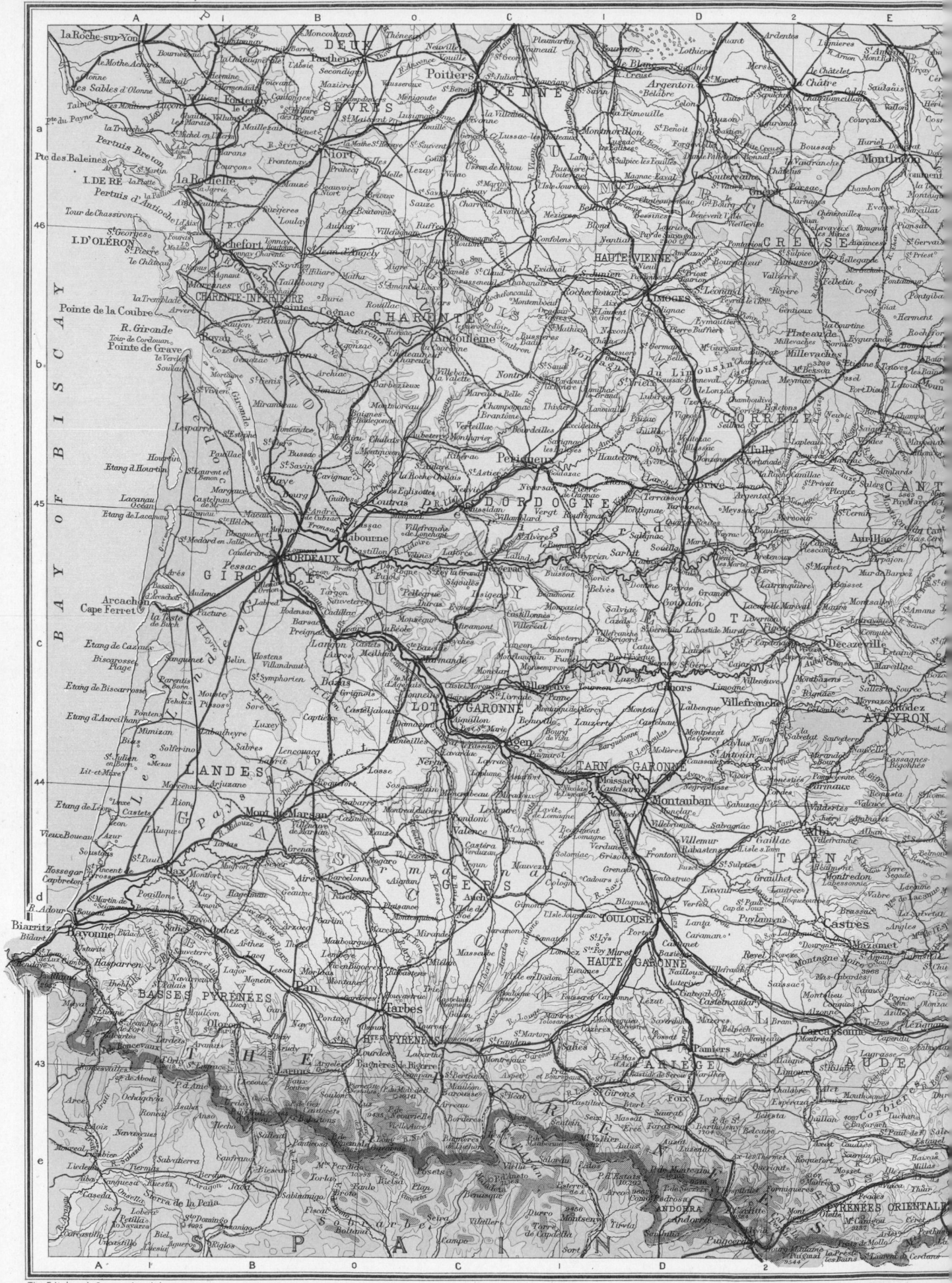

BAY OF BISCAY
DEUX SÈVRES
VIENNE
CHARENTE-INFÉRIEURE
CHARENTE
HAUTE VIENNE
CREUSE
CORRÈZE
DORDOGNE
GIRONDE
LOT
LOT ET GARONNE
TARN ET GARONNE
LANDES
GERS
AVEYRON
TARN
HAUTE GARONNE
BASSES PYRÉNÉES
HTES PYRÉNÉES
ARIÈGE
AUDE
PYRÉNÉES ORIENTALES
ANDORRA
I. DE RÉ
I. D'OLÉRON
Pertuis Breton
Pertuis d'Antioche
Pointe de la Coubre
Pointe de Grave
Cape Ferret
Poitiers
Niort
la Rochelle
Rochefort
Angoulême
Limoges
Périgueux
Bordeaux
Arcachon
Agen
Cahors
Montauban
Toulouse
Mont de Marsan
Dax
Bayonne
Biarritz
Pau
Tarbes
Foix
Carcassonne
Castres
Albi
Rodez
Aurillac
Tulle
Brive
Guéret
Montluçon
Argenton
la Châtre
Bergerac
Libourne
Marmande
Auch
Montagne Noire
Corbières
Sierra de la Peña

SOUTHERN FRANCE

1 : 2,000,000

English Miles

Kilometres

Heights in feet

| Above 10,000 |
| 6000 to 10,000 |
| 3000 to 6000 |
| 1500 to 3000 |
| 1000 to 1500 |
| 300 to 1000 |
| Sea Level to 300 |

Roads
Railways
Canals
Boundaries

Copyright—John Bartholomew & Son.Ltd.

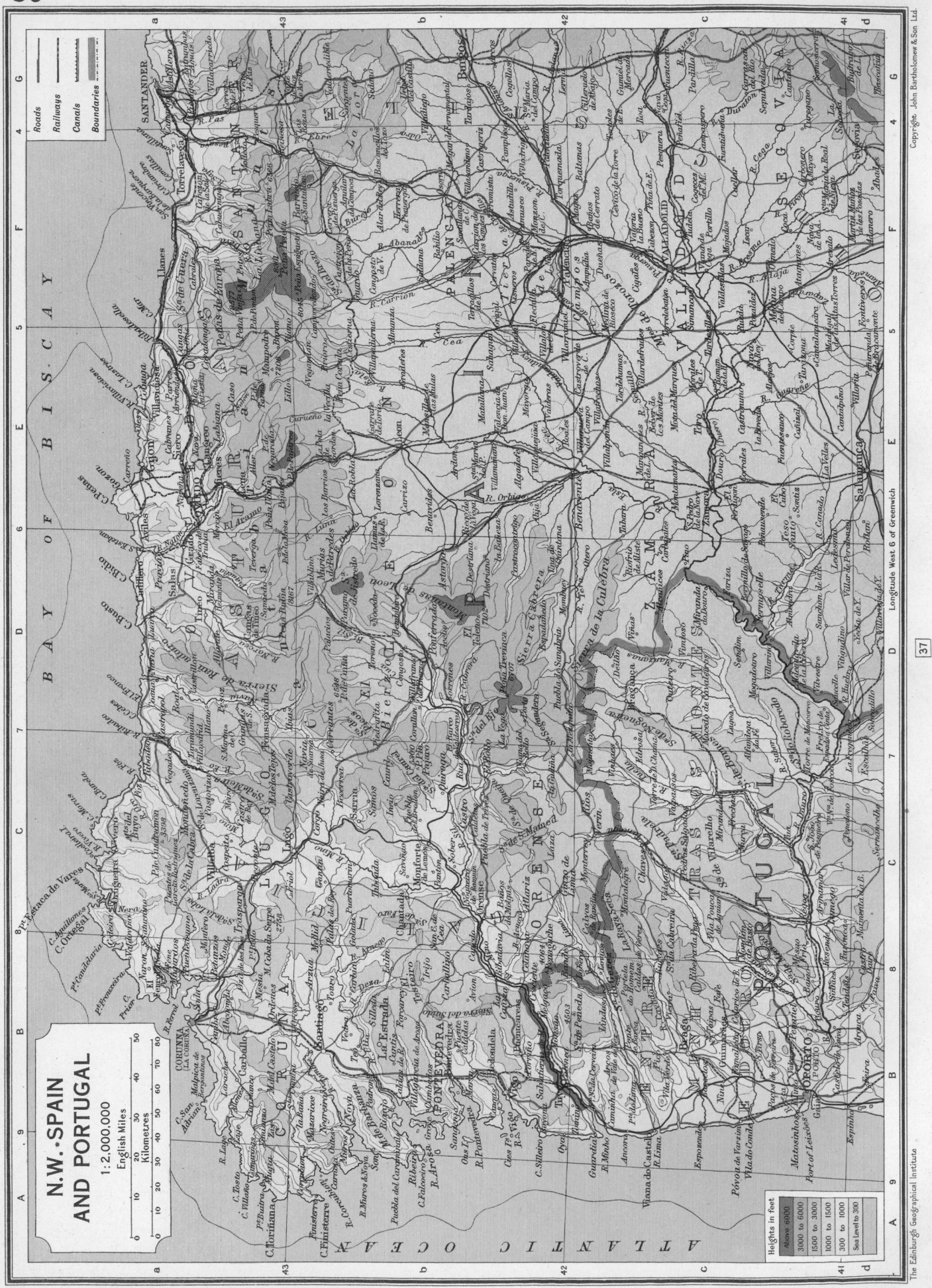

N.W. SPAIN AND PORTUGAL

1 : 2,000,000

English Miles

Kilometres

Copyright. John Bartholomew & Son Ltd.

The Edinburgh Geographical Institute

Heights in feet

| Above 6000 |
| 3000 to 6000 |
| 1500 to 3000 |
| 1000 to 1500 |
| 300 to 1000 |
| Sea Level to 300 |

Roads
Railways
Canals
Boundaries

37

WESTERN SPAIN AND PORTUGAL

1 : 2,000,000

English Miles

Kilometres

Heights in feet

| Above 6000 |
| 3000 to 6000 |
| 1500 to 3000 |
| 1000 to 1500 |
| 300 to 1000 |
| Sea Level to 300 |

PORTUGAL

SPAIN

ATLANTIC OCEAN

Bay of Setúbal

OPORTO (PORTO)

LISBON (LISBOA)

SALAMANCA

BADAJOZ

Longitude West 7 of Greenwich

Copyright.—John Bartholomew & Son, Ltd.

The Edinburgh Geographical Institute

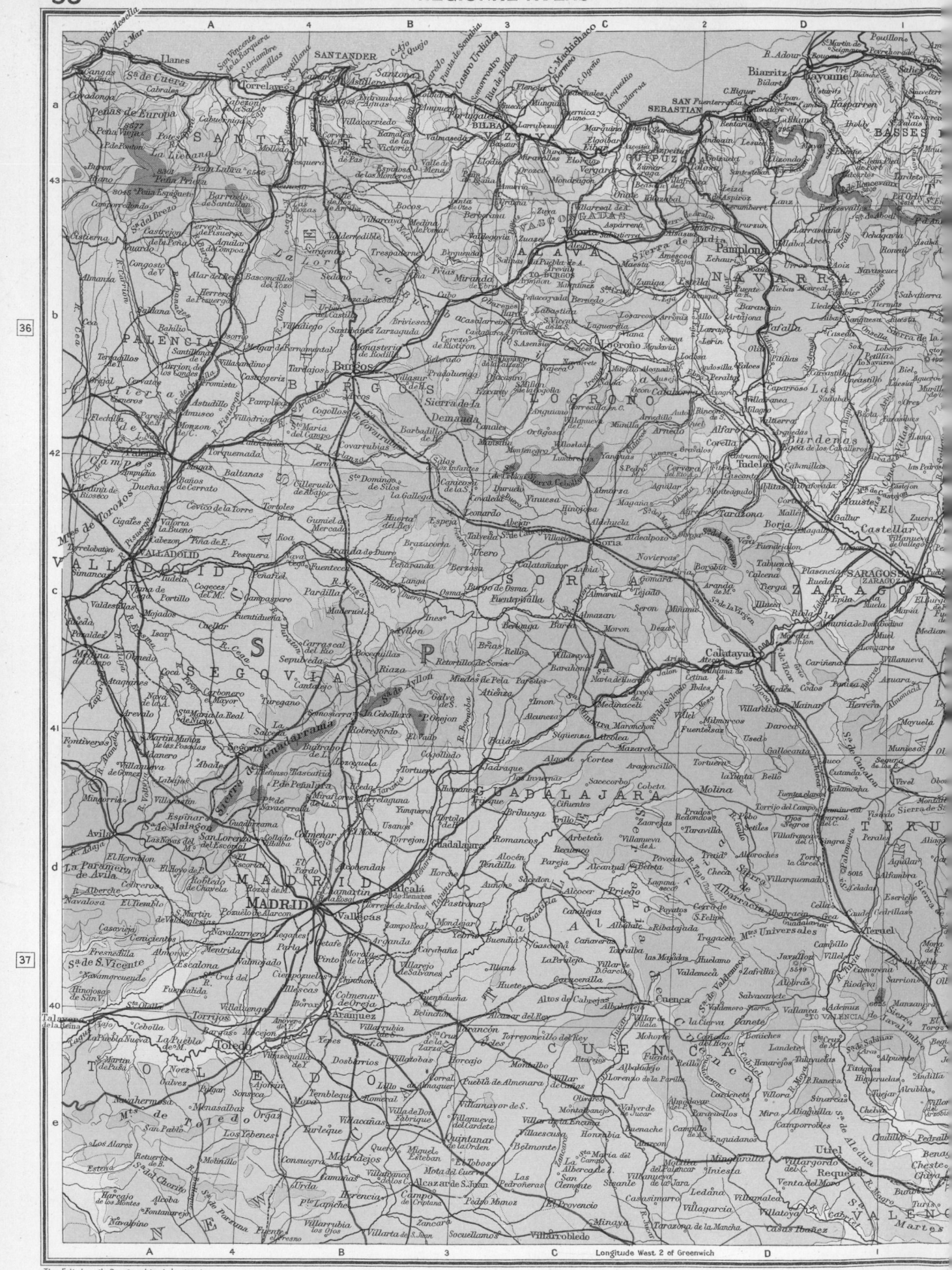

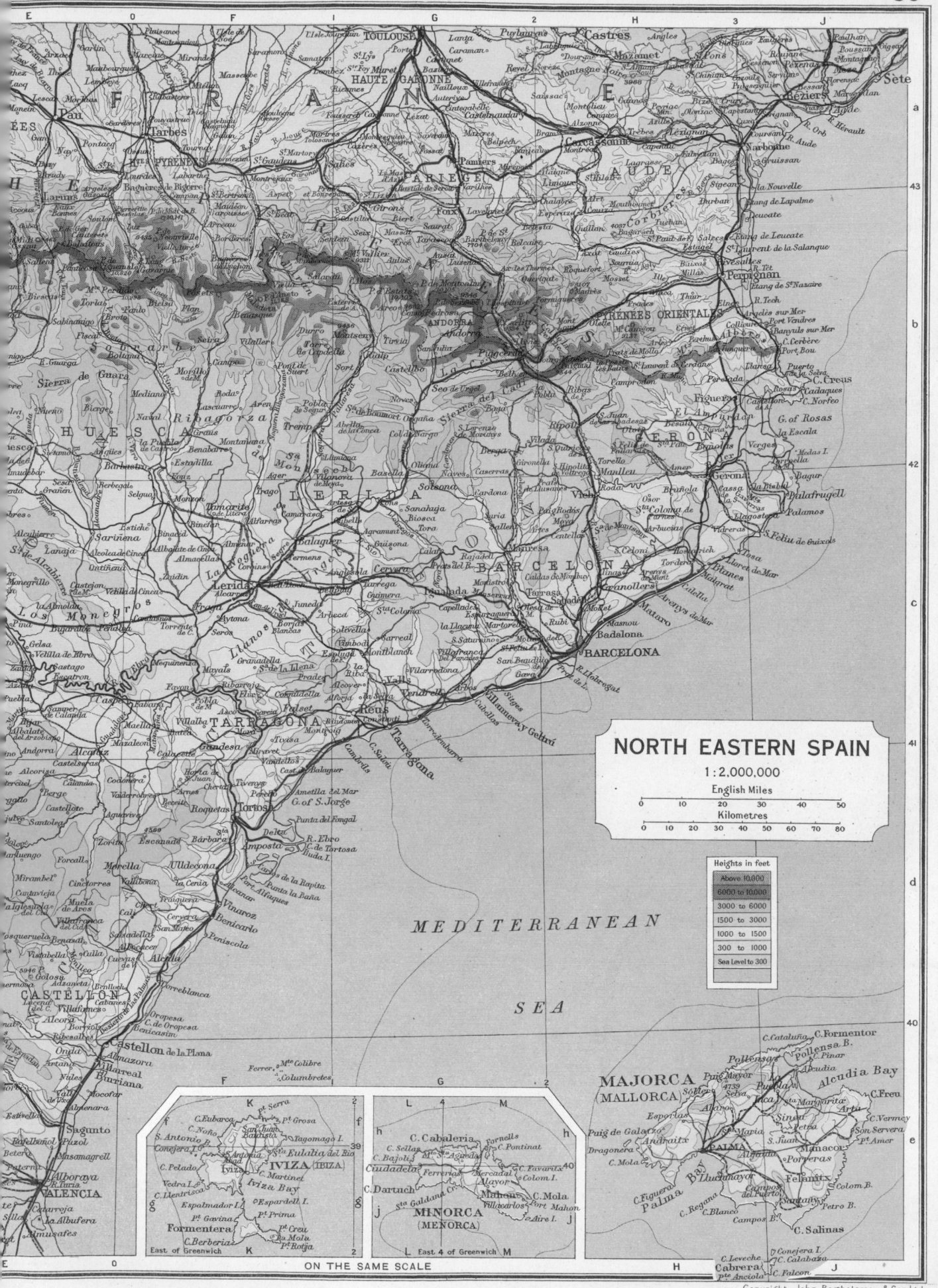

NORTH EASTERN SPAIN

1 : 2,000,000

English Miles

Kilometres

Heights in feet

Above 10,000
6000 to 10,000
3000 to 6000
1500 to 3000
1000 to 1500
300 to 1000
Sea Level to 300

IVIZA (IBIZA)

MINORCA (MENORCA)

MAJORCA
MALLORCA

MEDITERRANEAN

SEA

ON THE SAME SCALE

Copyright- John Bartholomew & Son. Ltd.

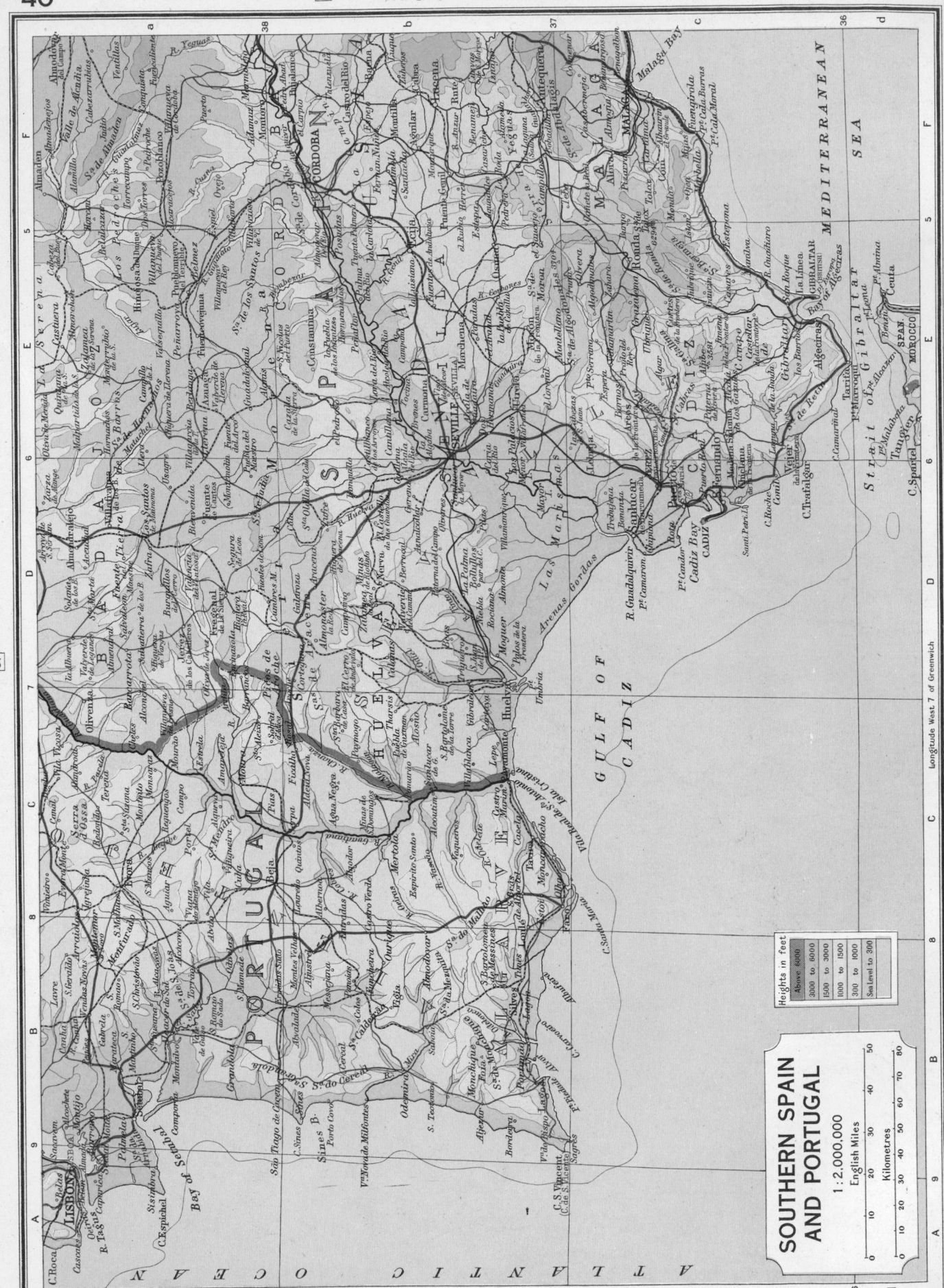

SOUTHERN SPAIN
AND PORTUGAL
1 : 2,000,000

English Miles

Kilometres

Heights in feet

Above 6000		
3000 to 6000		
1500 to 3000		
1000 to 1500		
300 to 1000		
Sea Level to 300		

Longitude West 7 of Greenwich

Copyright—John Bartholomew & Son,Ltd.

The Edinburgh Geographical Institute

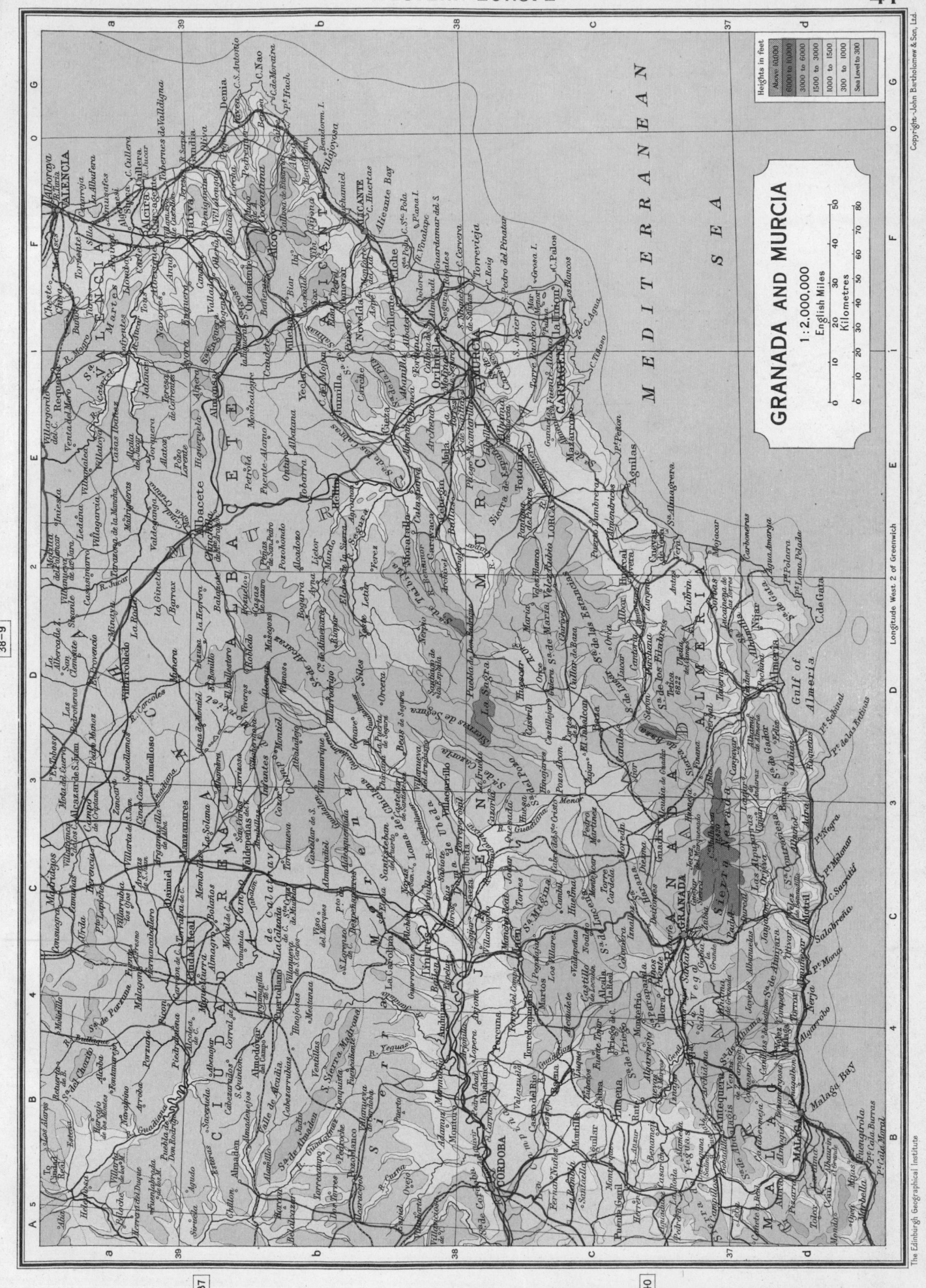

GRANADA AND MURCIA
1 : 2,000,000
English Miles

Copyright John Bartholomew & Son, Ltd.

The Edinburgh Geographical Institute

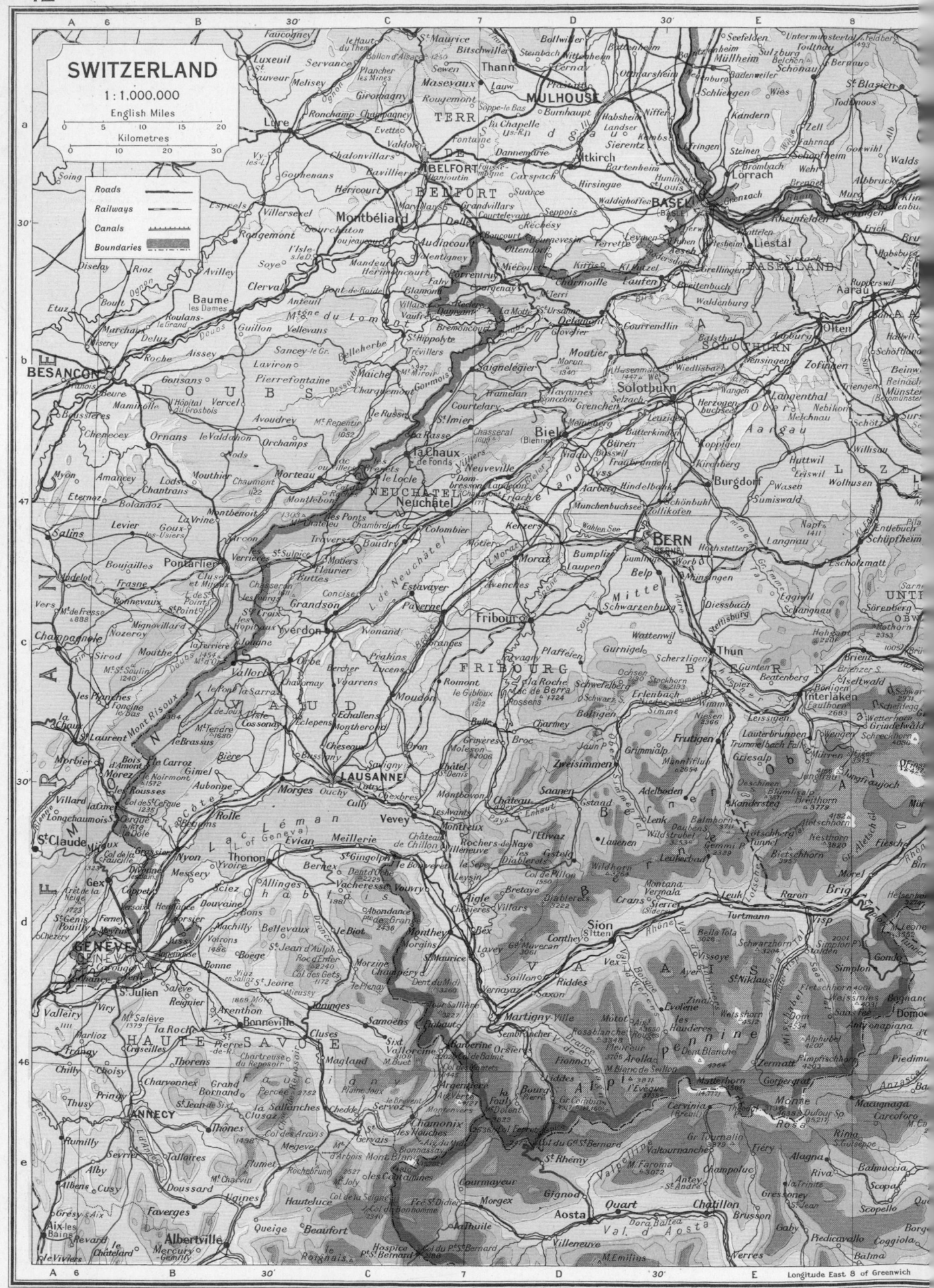

SWITZERLAND

1 : 1,000,000

English Miles

0   5   10   15   20

Kilometres

0   10   20   30

Roads
Railways
Canals
Boundaries

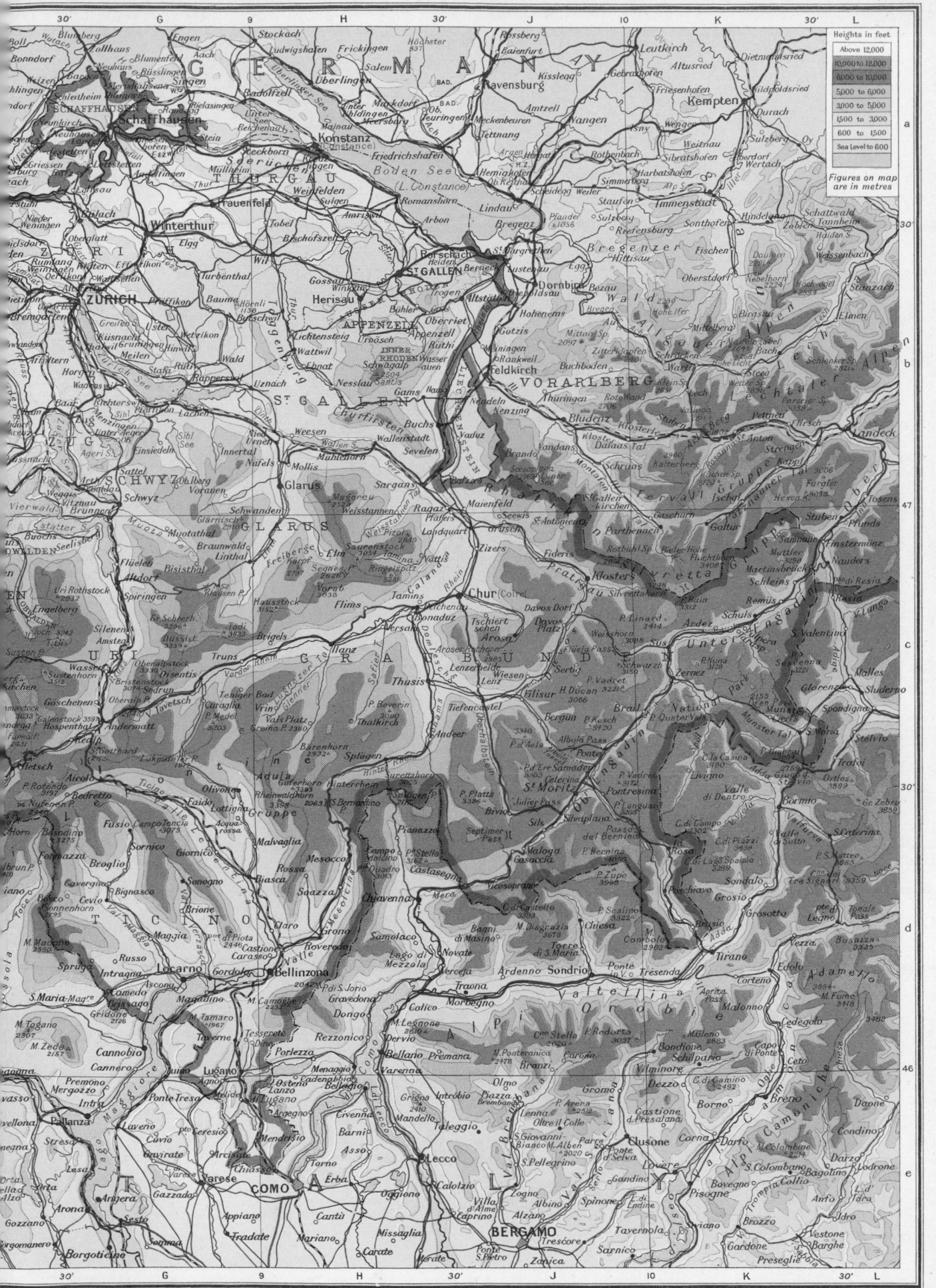

Copyright—John Bartholomew & Son, Ltd.

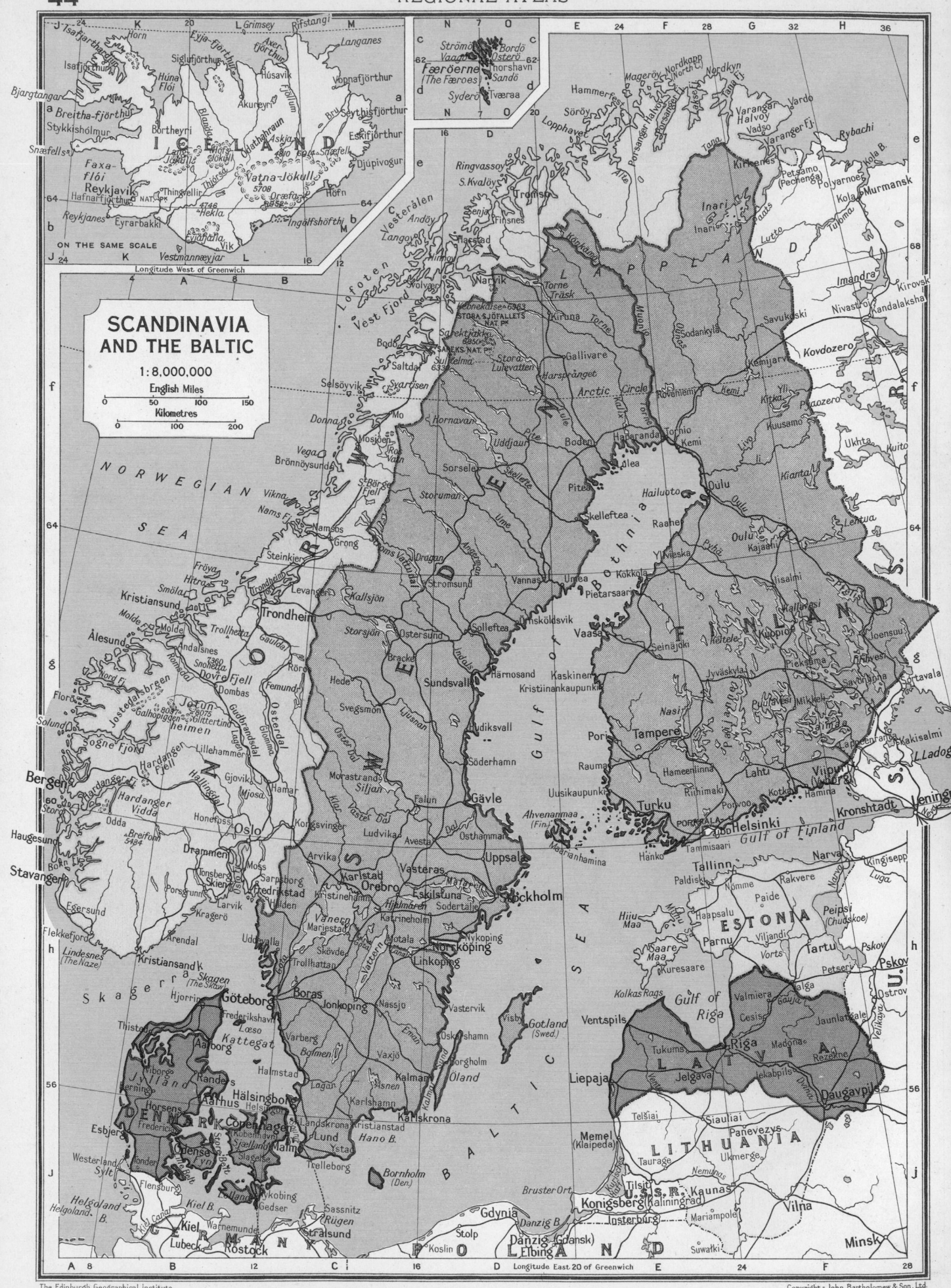

SCANDINAVIA AND THE BALTIC
1: 8,000,000

English Miles
0   50   100   150

Kilometres
0   100   200

Copyright - John Bartholomew & Son, Ltd.

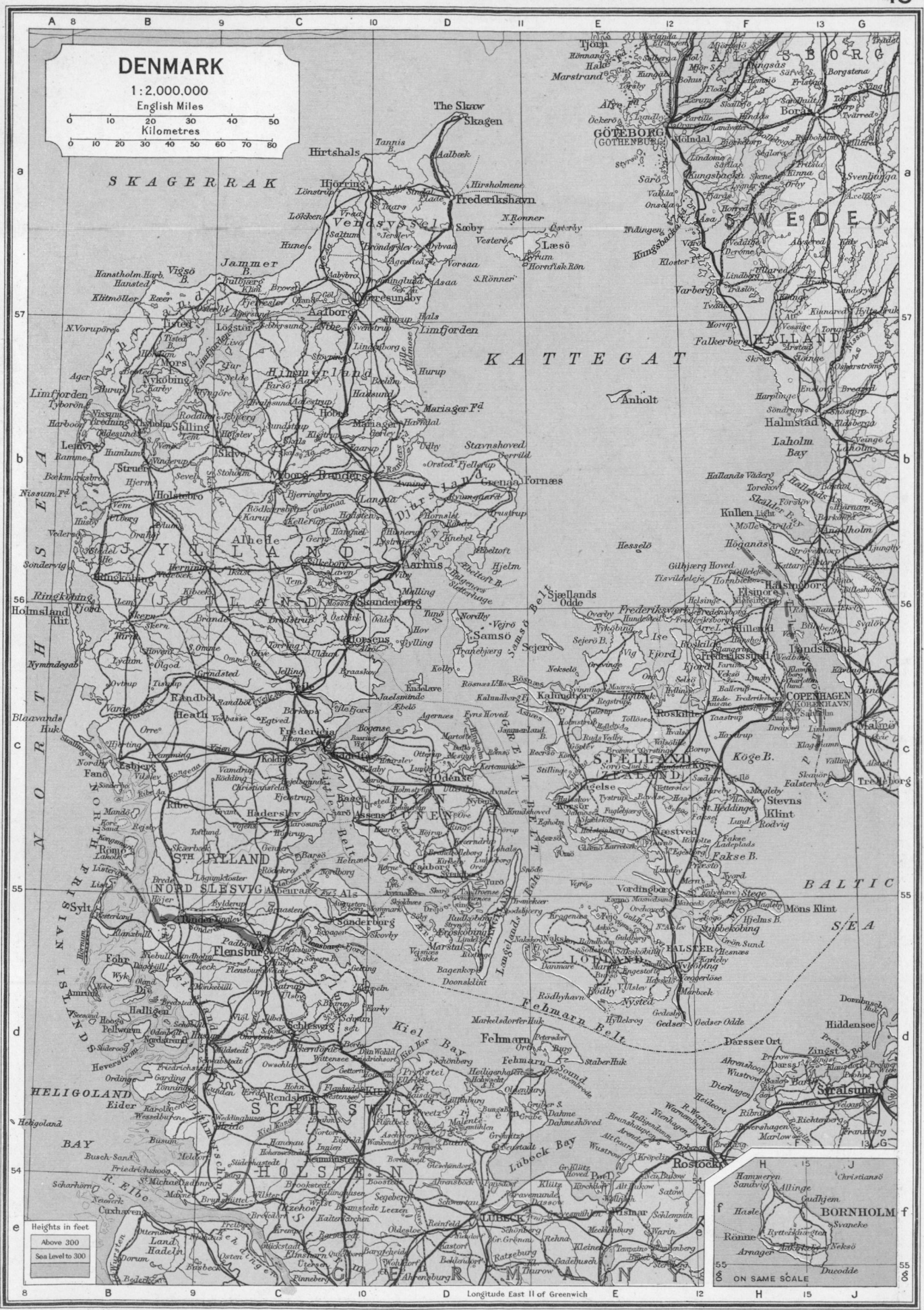

DENMARK

1:2,000,000

English Miles

Kilometres

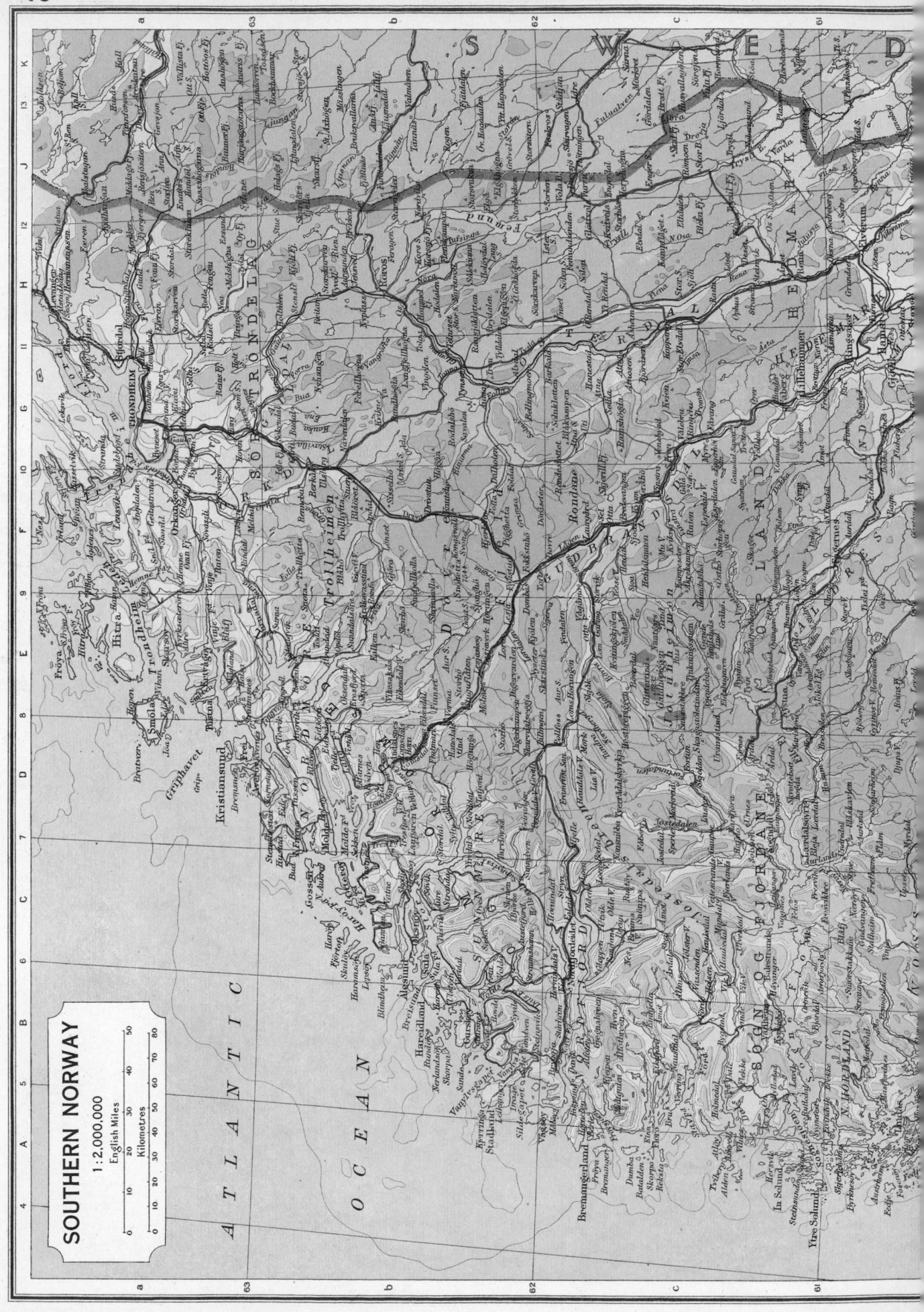
SOUTHERN NORWAY
1:2,000,000
English Miles
Kilometres
ATLANTIC
OCEAN
SWEDEN
TRONDHEIM
Kristiansund
Ålesund
Røros
Rondane
Jotunheimen
Trollheimen
Dovrefjell
Jostedalsbre
SOGN OG FJORDANE
HEDMARK
OPLAND
NORDMØRE
SUNNMØRE
NORDFJORD
N. HORDLAND

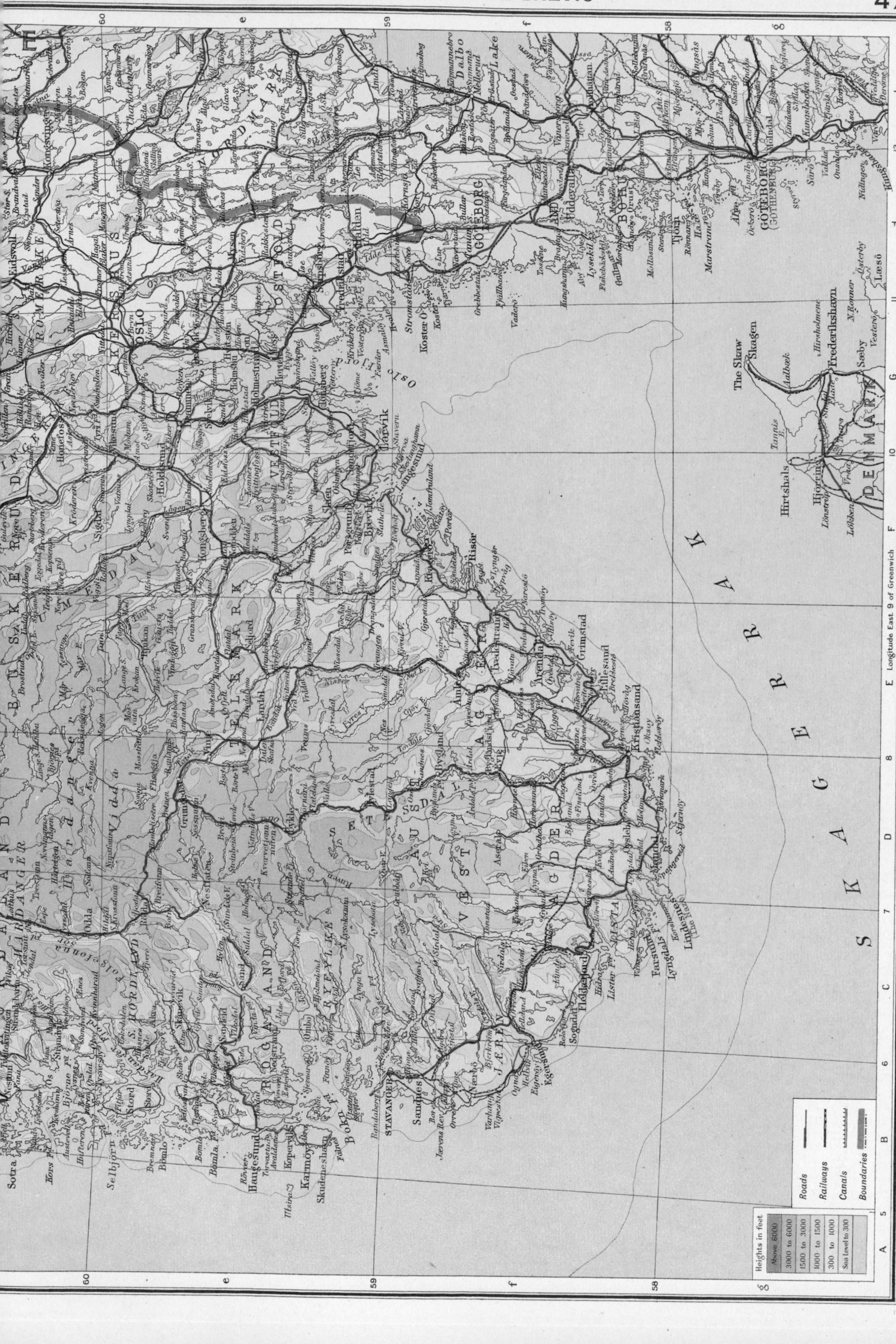

SKAGER RAK

KATTEGAT

DENMARK

GÖTEBORG (GOTHENBURG)

BOHUS

OSLO

AKERSHUS

SMAALENENE

ØSTFOLD

BUSKERUD

TELEMARK

VESTFOLD

AUST AGDER

VEST AGDER

ROGALAND

Skagen

The Skaw

Frederikshavn

Hirtshals

Hjørring

Læsø

Stavanger

Haugesund

Kristiansand

Arendal

Grimstad

Larvik

Risør

Heights in feet	
Above 6000	
3000 to 6000	
1500 to 3000	
1000 to 1500	
300 to 1000	
Sea Level to 300	

Roads
Railways
Canals
Boundaries

Copyright–John Bartholomew & Son, Ltd.

The Edinburgh Geographical Institute

E Longitude East 9 of Greenwich

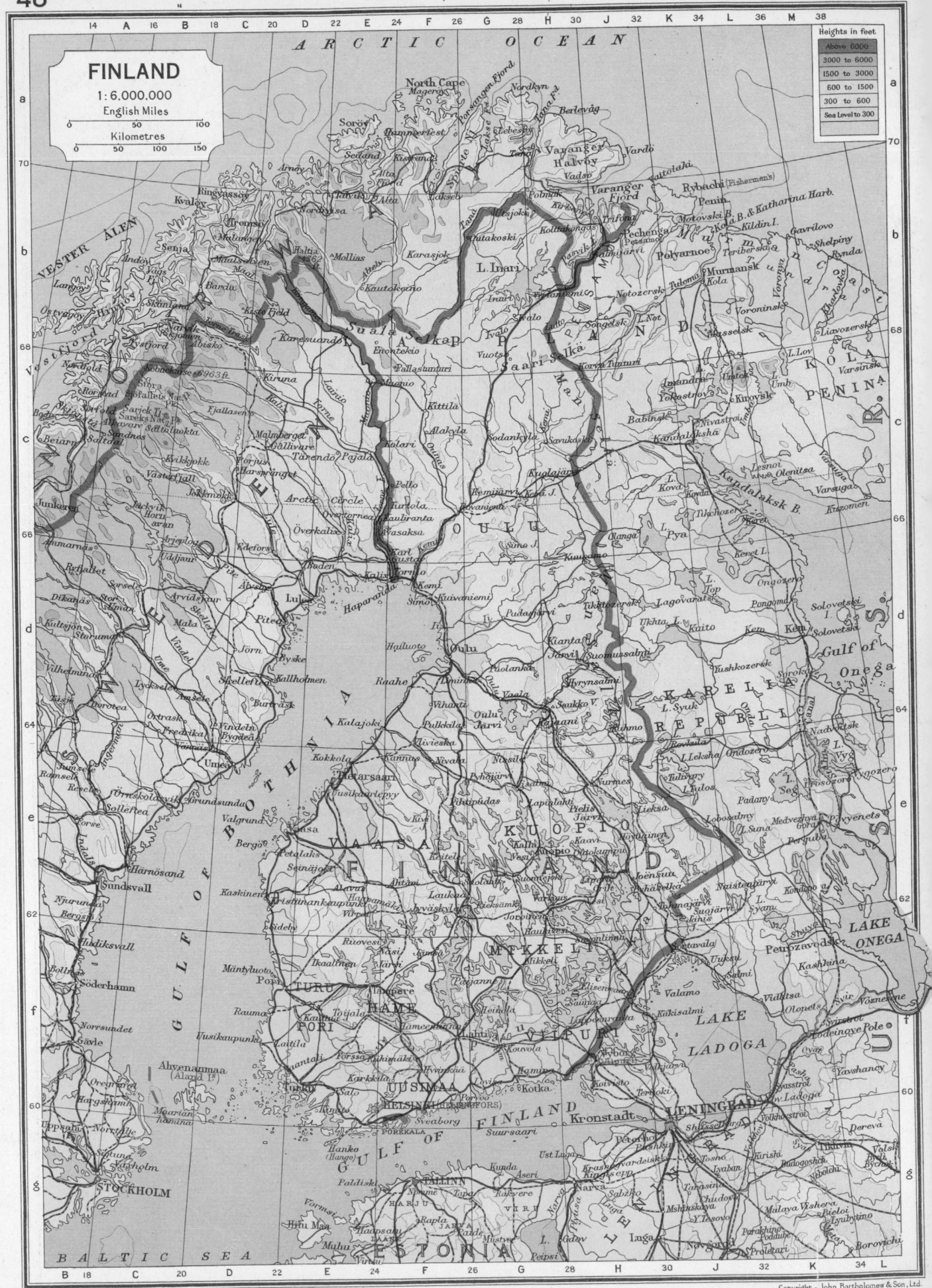

FINLAND

1 : 6,000,000

English Miles

Kilometres

Heights in feet

The Edinburgh Geographical Institute   Copyright · John Bartholomew & Son, Ltd.

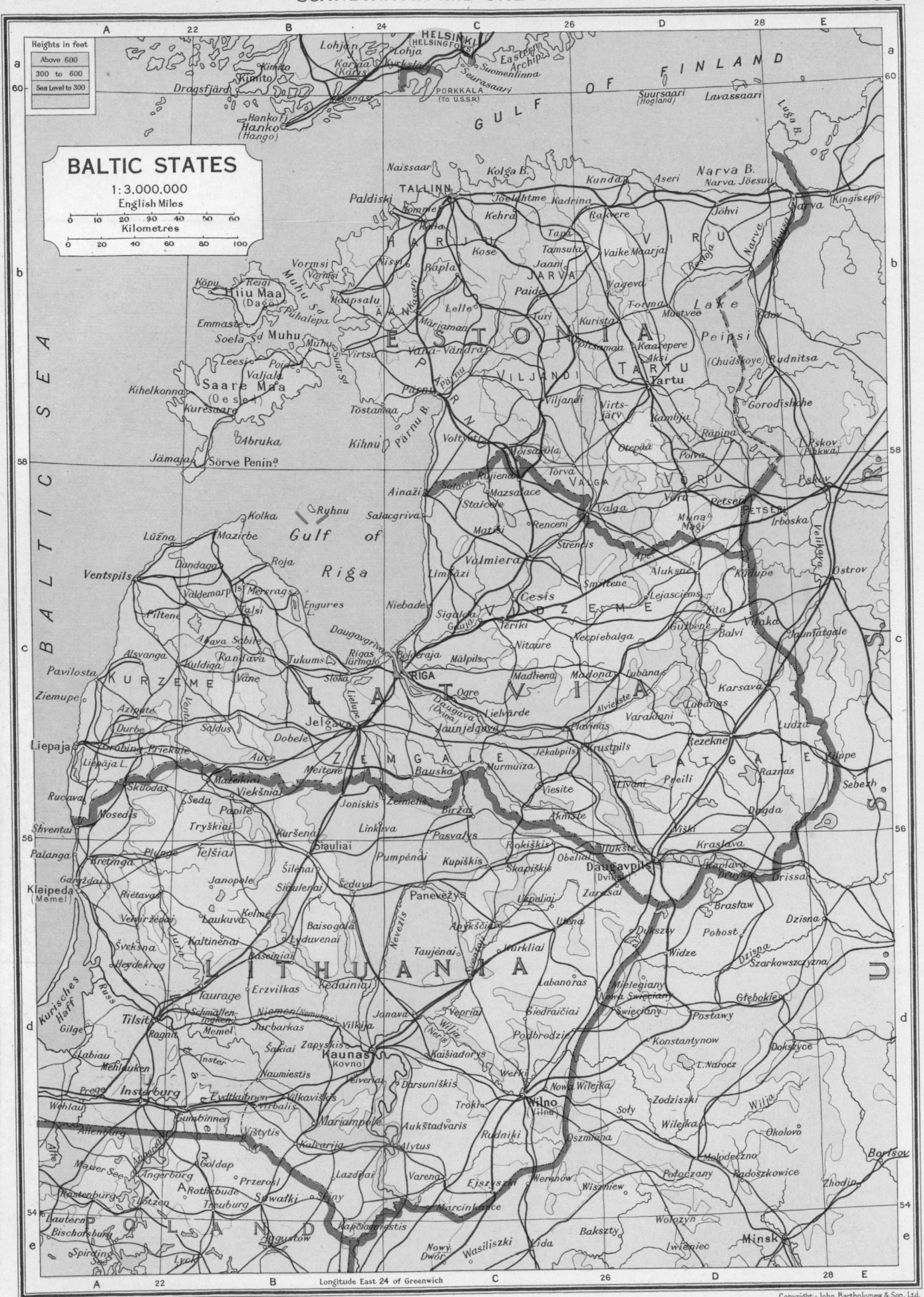

BALTIC STATES

1:3,000,000

English Miles

Kilometres

Heights in feet
Above 600
300 to 600
Sea Level to 300

GULF OF FINLAND

HELSINKI
(HELSINGFORS)

BALTIC SEA

Gulf of Riga

ESTONIA

Lake Peipsi
(Chudskoye)

TALLINN

Tartu

LATVIA

RIGA

KURZEME

VIDZEME

LATGALE

ZEMGALE

Liepaja

Daugavpils
(Dvinsk)

LITHUANIA

KAUNAS
(Kovno)

Klaipeda
(Memel)

Wilno
(Vilna)

Tilsit

POLAND

Minsk

The Edinburgh Geographical Institute

Copyright-John Bartholomew & Son, Ltd.

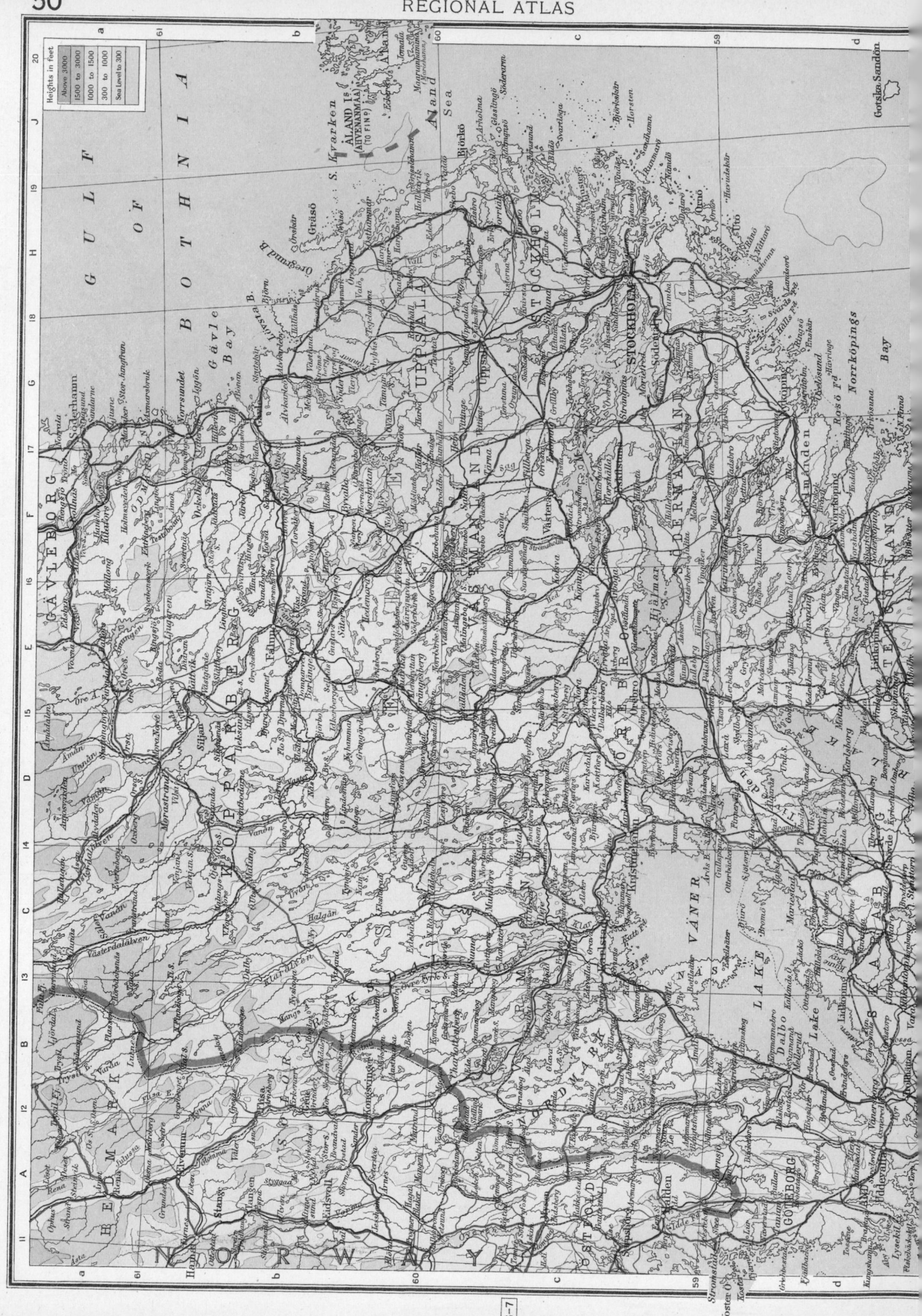
Heights in feet
Above 3000
1500 to 3000
1000 to 1500
300 to 1000
Sea Level to 300
GULF OF BOTHNIA
Gävle Bay
Åland Sea
ÅLAND IS. (AHVENANMAA) (TO FIN.)
Norrköpings Bay
NORWAY
STOCKHOLM
UPPSALA
GÄVLEBORG
KOPPARBERG
VÄSTMANLAND
ÖREBRO
SÖDERMANLAND
VÄRMLAND
LAKE VÄNER
Hjälmar
GÖTEBORG
HEDMARK
ÖSTFOLD

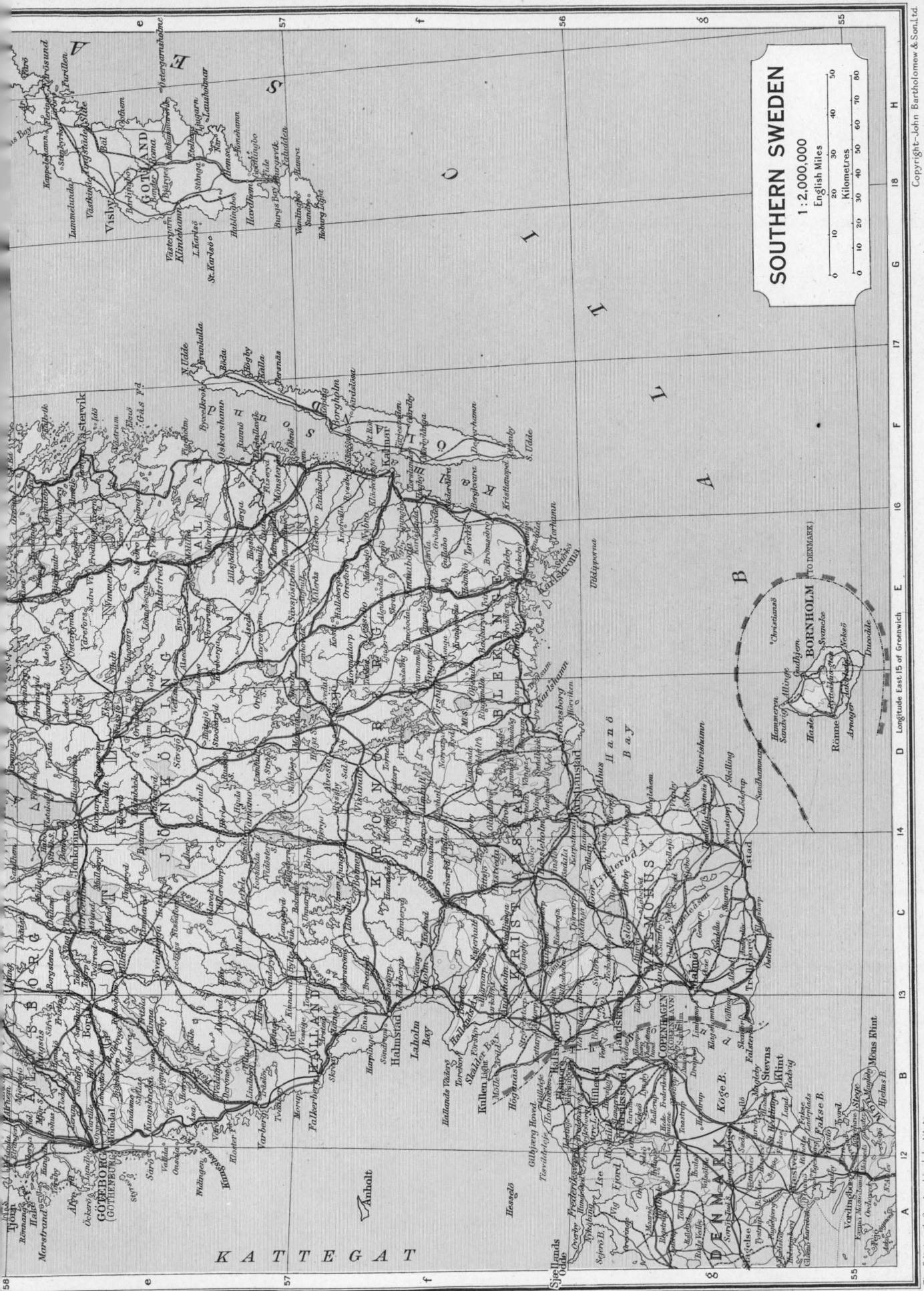

SOUTHERN SWEDEN
1 : 2,000,000
English Miles

Kilometres

Copyright–John Bartholomew & Son, Ltd.

KATTEGAT

A 24   B   Straumnes   Horn(Nord Cap)   C   20   D   18   E   Rifstangi   16   Ranfarhöfn   F   14   G

Látrar   Horn   Blikalón   Langanes

a   Hesteyri   Jökulfirdhir   Kópasker   Thistilfj.   Skálar   a

Bolungavik   Ísafjardhardjúp   H. Drangaj   Axarfj.   Krossavik   Thorshöfn

Ísafjördhur   Flateyri   Sudhavik   Hraun   Siglufjördhur   Ólafsfjördhur   Flatey   Skjálfandi   Lón   NORDHUR   Bakkaflói

66   Dýrafjördhur   Thingeyri   Ritsnes   Kálfshamsrvik   Hrisey   Húsavik   THINGEYJAR   Bakkafjördhur   66

Kópanes   Arnarfj.   Gláma   Nautevri   Arnes   Kúvikur   Húna-   Skagaströnd   Hofsós   Dalvik   SUDHUR   Vopnafj.   Kollumúli

Patreksfj.   Bildudalur   flói   SKAGAFJARDHAR   Akureyri   Godhafoss   Grímsstadhir   Heradhsflói

Kollsvik   Vatneyri   BARDHASTRANDAR   Sandhárkrókur   Tungnahryggsj.   THINGEYJAR   NORDHUR   Bakkagerdhi   Glettinganes

Bjargtangar   Hamar   Skalmarnesmuli   Blönduós   Mývatn   Fossvellir

Raudhasandur   Hjaltevri   Seydhisfjördhur

Flatey   Gilsfjördhur   HÚNAVATNS   Gilja   Blanda   Blafjall 4009 ft   MULA   Neskaupsstadhur

Breidha-   Stadharhólskirkja   Hvammstangi   Grímstunga   Jökulsá á Brú   Eskifjördhur

b   fjordhur   Dagverdharn.   Asgardhur   Bordheyri   Fnjóská   Odádhahraun   Herdhubreidh 5518 ft   Reydhar fj.   Budhir   b

Stykkisholmur   Hvammsfj.   Budhardalur   Skjálfandafljót   Askja   Breidhdalsvík

Setberg   Hvammsfj.   Snæfell 6014 ft   Thrandarj.

Sandur   Olafsvik   SNÆFELLSNES   HNAPPADALS   Hofsjökull   Snæfell   Djúpivogur

Snæfells   Budhir   Tungnafellsj.   Dyngjuj.   Brúarj.   Papey   Eystrahorn

Hafursfjördhur   Langjökull   VATNAJOKULL   Eyjabakkaj.   Hofsj.

Ferjukot   Ok 3830 ft   Ulvitárvatn   Grímsvötn   Lónsvik

Faxa-   Borgarnes   BORGARFJARDHAR   Thórisj.   SKAFTAFELLS   Heinabergsj.   Vesturhorn

Borgarfj.   Skorradalsvatn   Hvitá   Kjálkaversfoss   Thórdharhyrna 5446 ft   Höfn   Hornafj.

flói   Saurbær   Gullfoss   AUSTUR   Breidhamerkurj. 6952   Hvannadalshnukur

Akranes   Hvalfjördhur   Torfastadhir   Thórisvatn   Langi-   Skaftári   Skeidharárj.   (Öræfaj.)

64   Skagaflös   KJÓSAR   Thingvalla-   Lagafell   Thingvellir   Thjórsá   sjór   Skaftá   Skeidharársandur   Ingólfshöfdhi   64

Reykjavik   vatn   Hekla 4746 ft   Breidhabólsstadhur

Keflavik   Hafnarfjördhur   GULLBRINGU   Laugarvelir   Torfaj.   Skaftáós

Grindavik   Eyrarbakki   RANGARVALLA   Tindfjallaj.

Reykjanes   Stokkseyri   Myrdalsj.   Katla 3445 ft   SKAFTAFELLS

c   Fuglasker   Störólfshvoll   Thykkvibær   Eyjafjallaj.   VESTUR   Vik   c

Vestmanna-   Kaupstadhur   Kötlutangi

eyjar

B   22   C   Longitude West 20 of Greenwich   D   18   E   16   F   14

Heights in feet

| Above 5000 |
| 3000 to 5000 |
| 1500 to 3000 |
| 600 to 1500 |
| Sea Level to 600 |

ICELAND

1 : 2,000,000

English Miles

0   10   20   30   40

Kilometres

0   10   20   30   40   50   60

The Edinburgh Geographical Institute   Copyright. John Bartholomew & Son Ltd

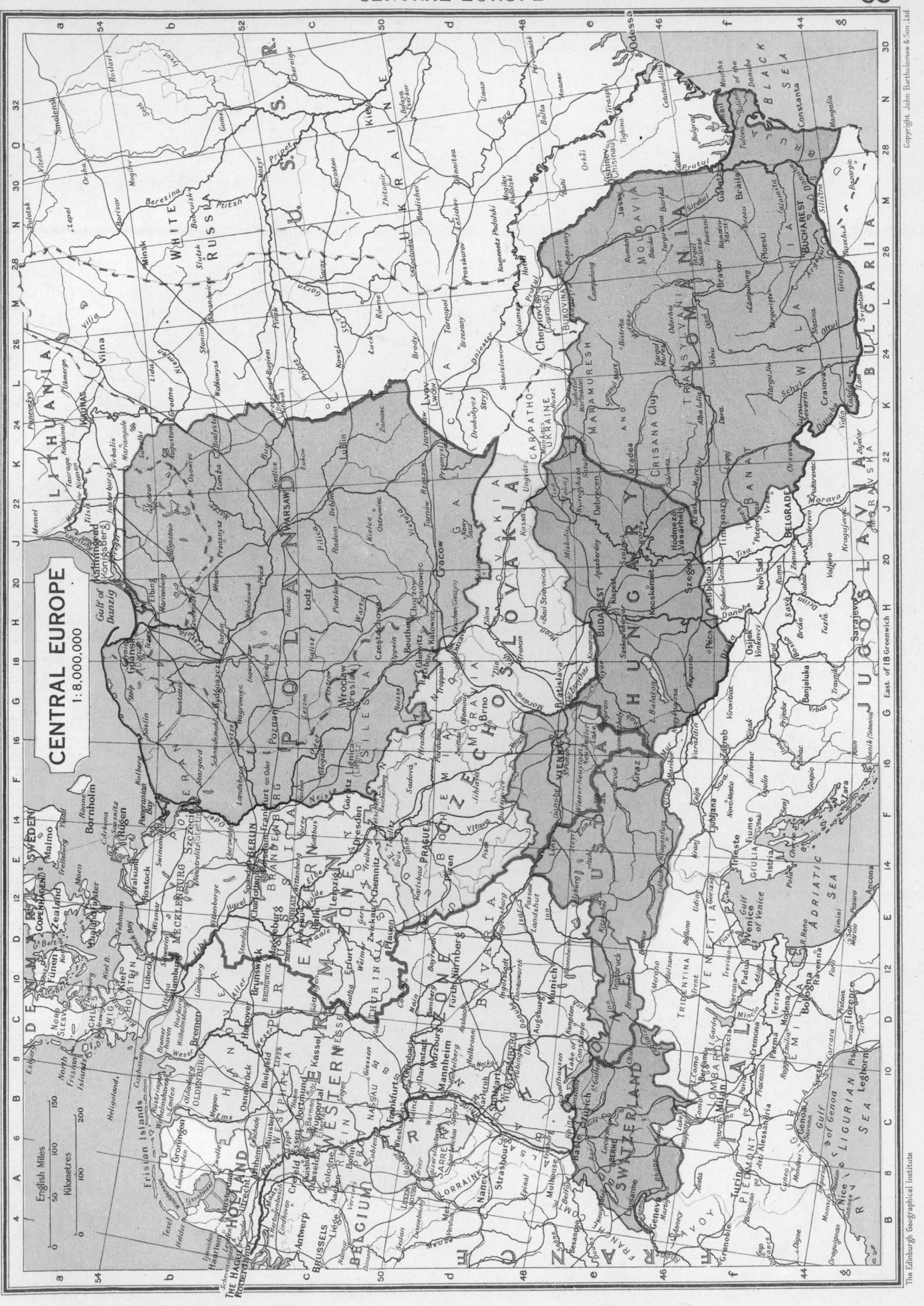

CENTRAL EUROPE
1 : 8,000,000

Copyright. John Bartholomew & Son, Ltd.

The Edinburgh Geographical Institute

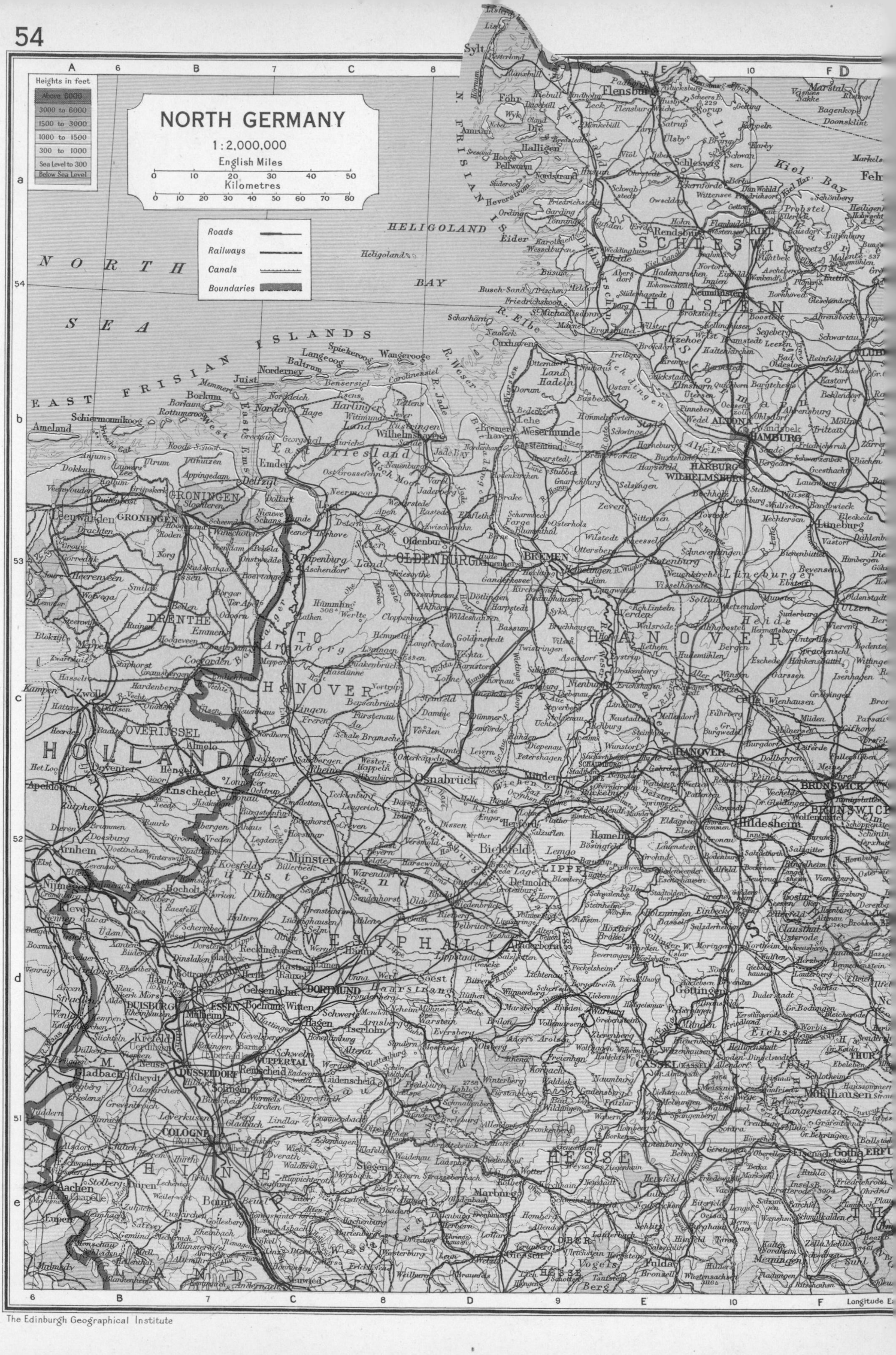

NORTH GERMANY

1 : 2,000,000

English Miles

Kilometres

Roads
Railways
Canals
Boundaries

Heights in feet

Above 6000
3000 to 6000
1500 to 3000
1000 to 1500
300 to 1000
Sea Level to 300
Below Sea Level

NORTH SEA

HELIGOLAND BAY

EAST FRISIAN ISLANDS

NORTH FRISIAN IS.

SCHLESWIG HOLSTEIN

HAMBURG

HOLLAND

HANOVER

WESTPHALIA

RHINE

HESSE

COLOGNE

DORTMUND

BRUNSWICK

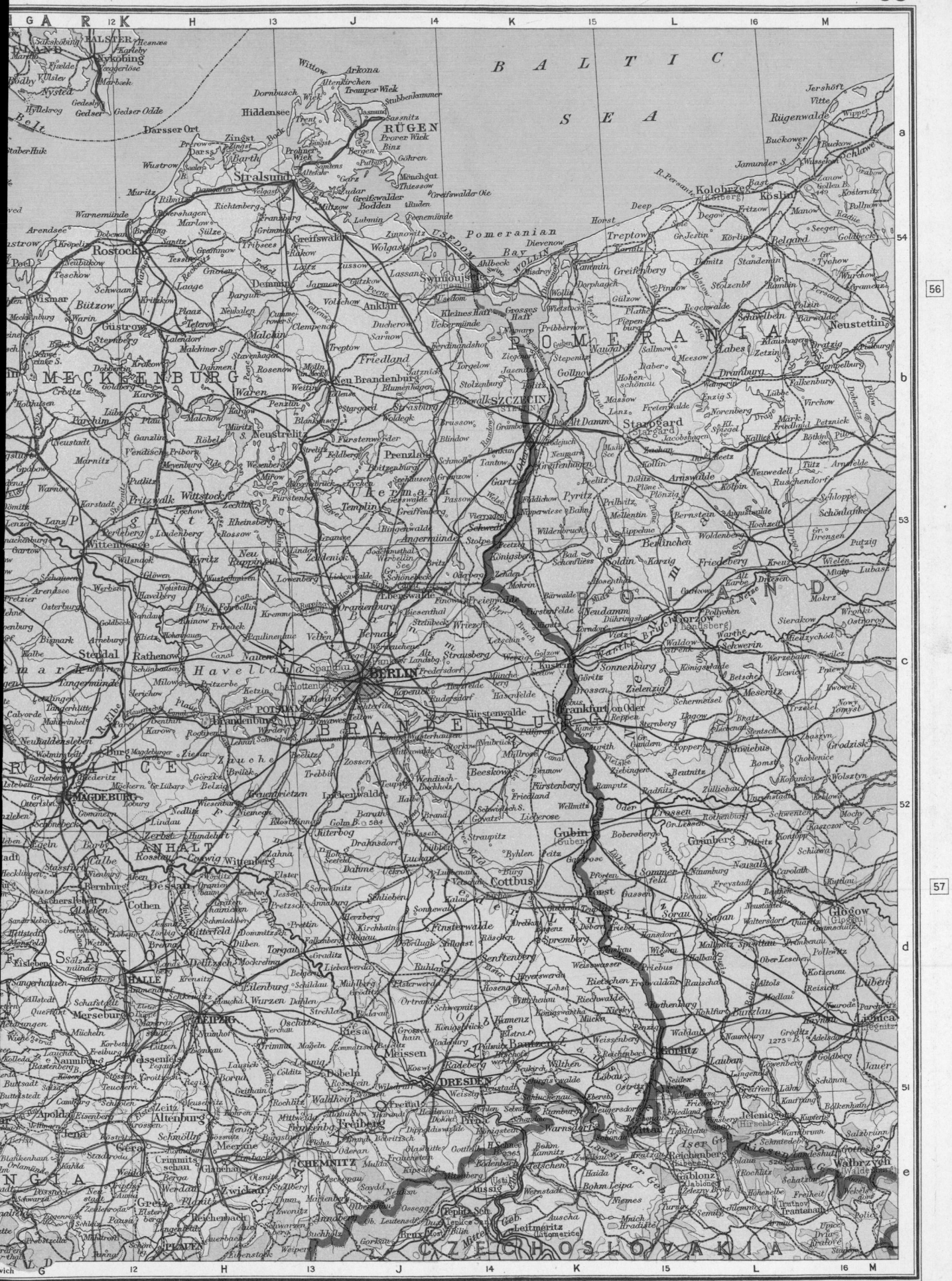

Copyright- John Bartholomew & Son, Ltd.

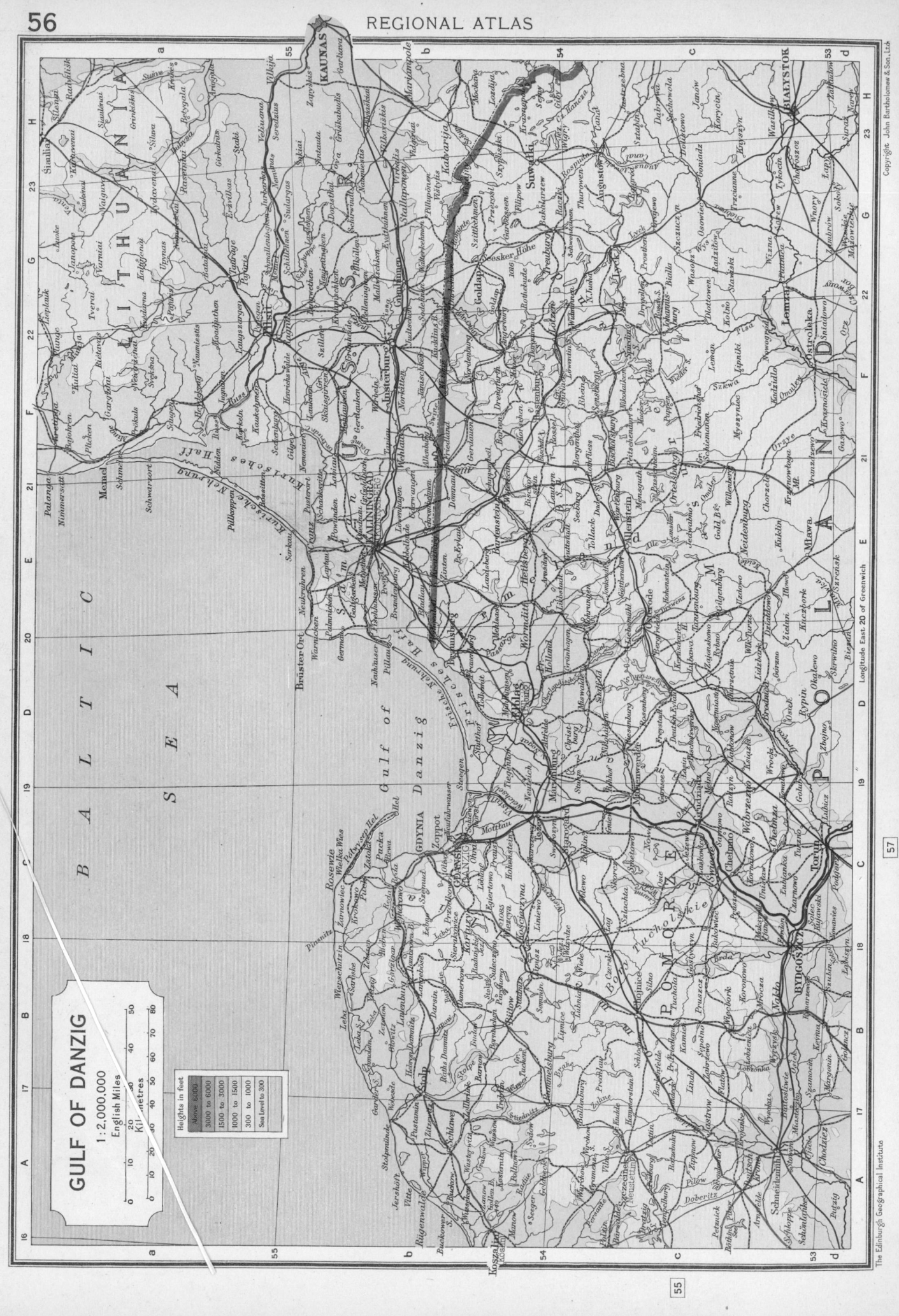

GULF OF DANZIG
1:2,000,000
English Miles

Heights in feet

Above 6000
3000 to 6000
1500 to 3000
1000 to 1500
300 to 1000
Sea Level to 300

Copyright. John Bartholomew & Son, Ltd.

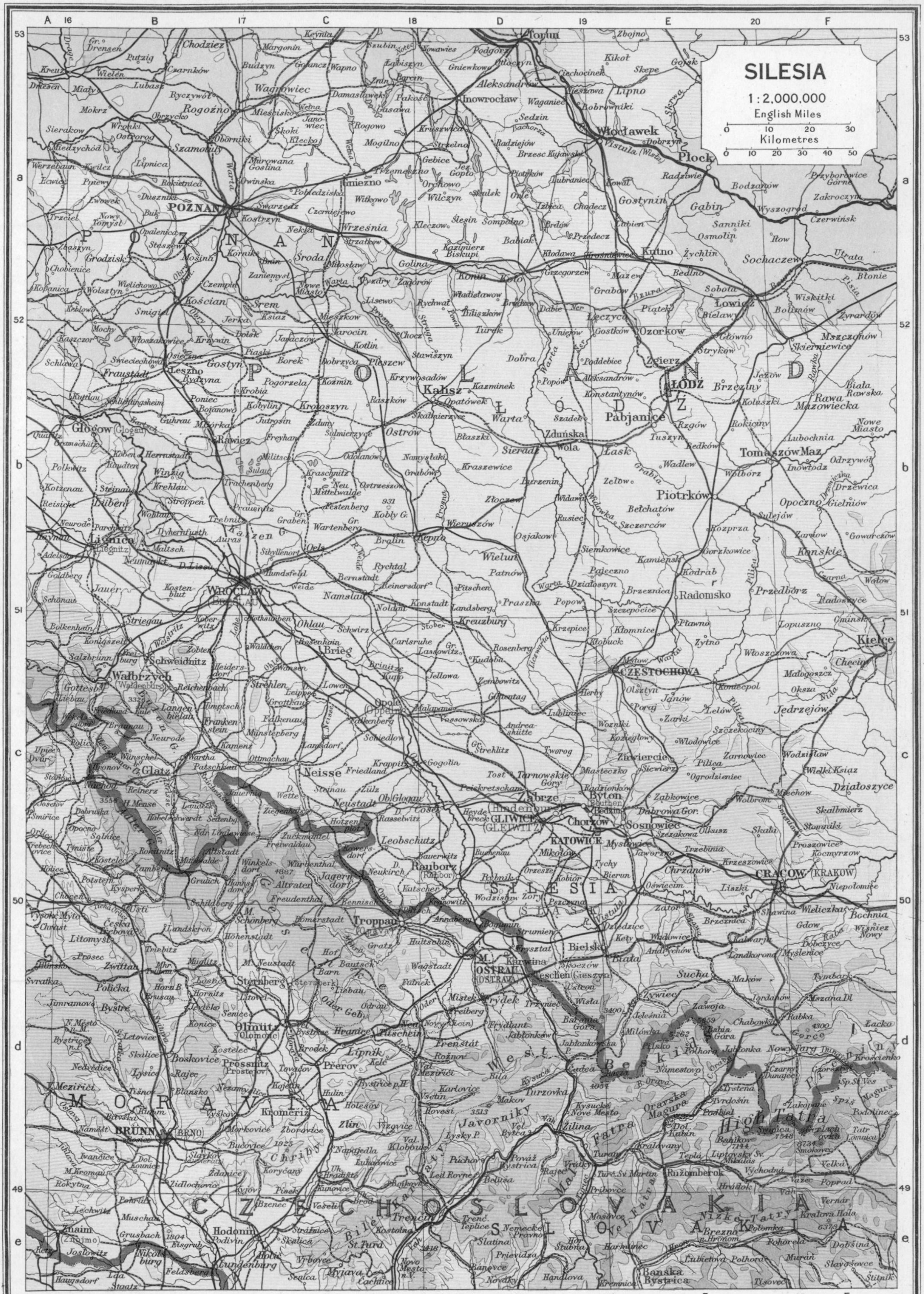

SILESIA

1 : 2,000,000

English Miles

0   10   20   30

Kilometres

0   10   20   30   40   50

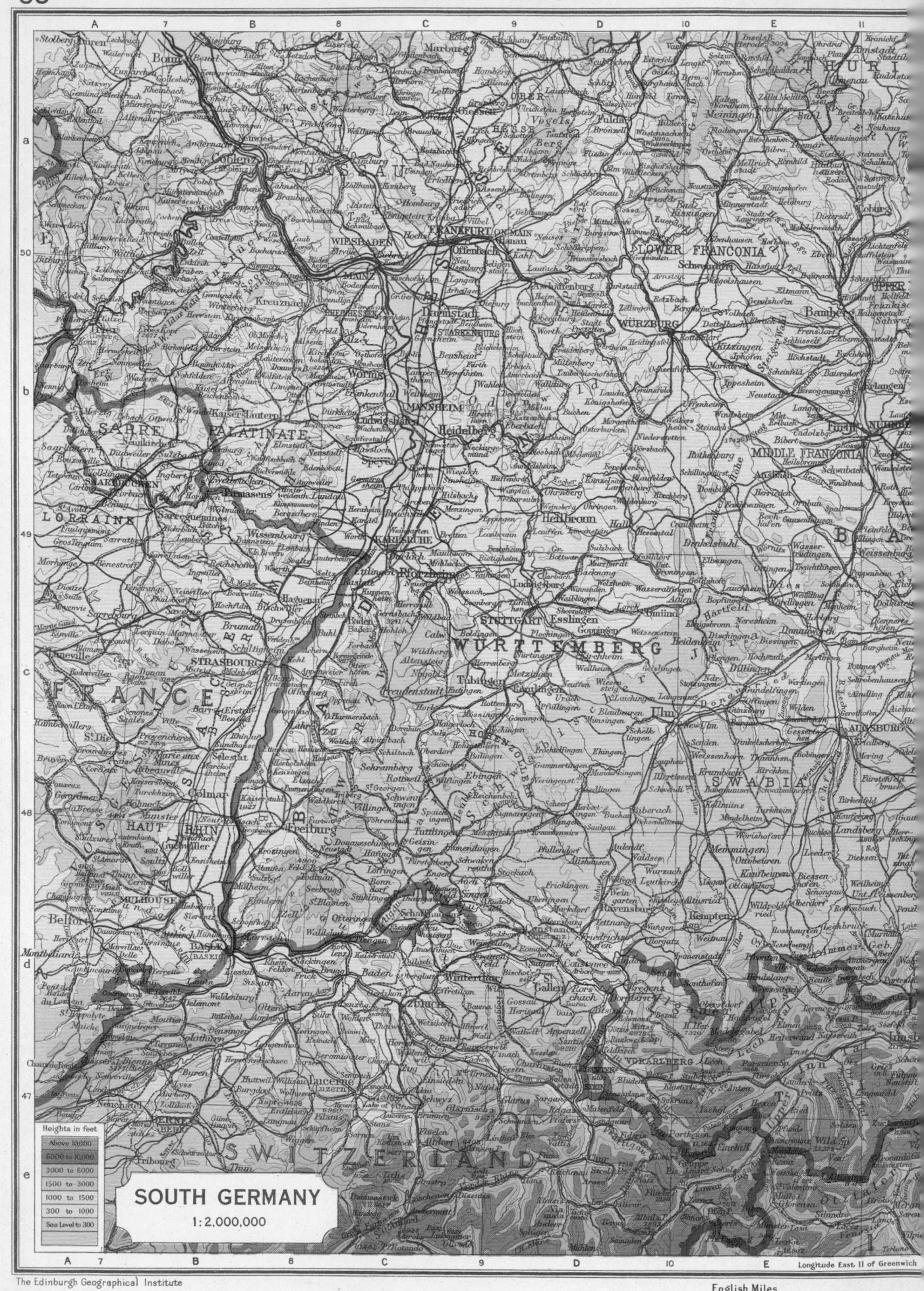

SOUTH GERMANY

1:2,000,000

Heights in feet

Above 10000
6000 to 10000
3000 to 6000
1500 to 3000
1000 to 1500
300 to 1000
Sea Level to 300

Longitude East 11 of Greenwich

English Miles

0   10   20   30   40   50

Copyright-John Bartholomew & Son, Ltd.

Kilometres

0 10 20 30 40 50 60 70 80

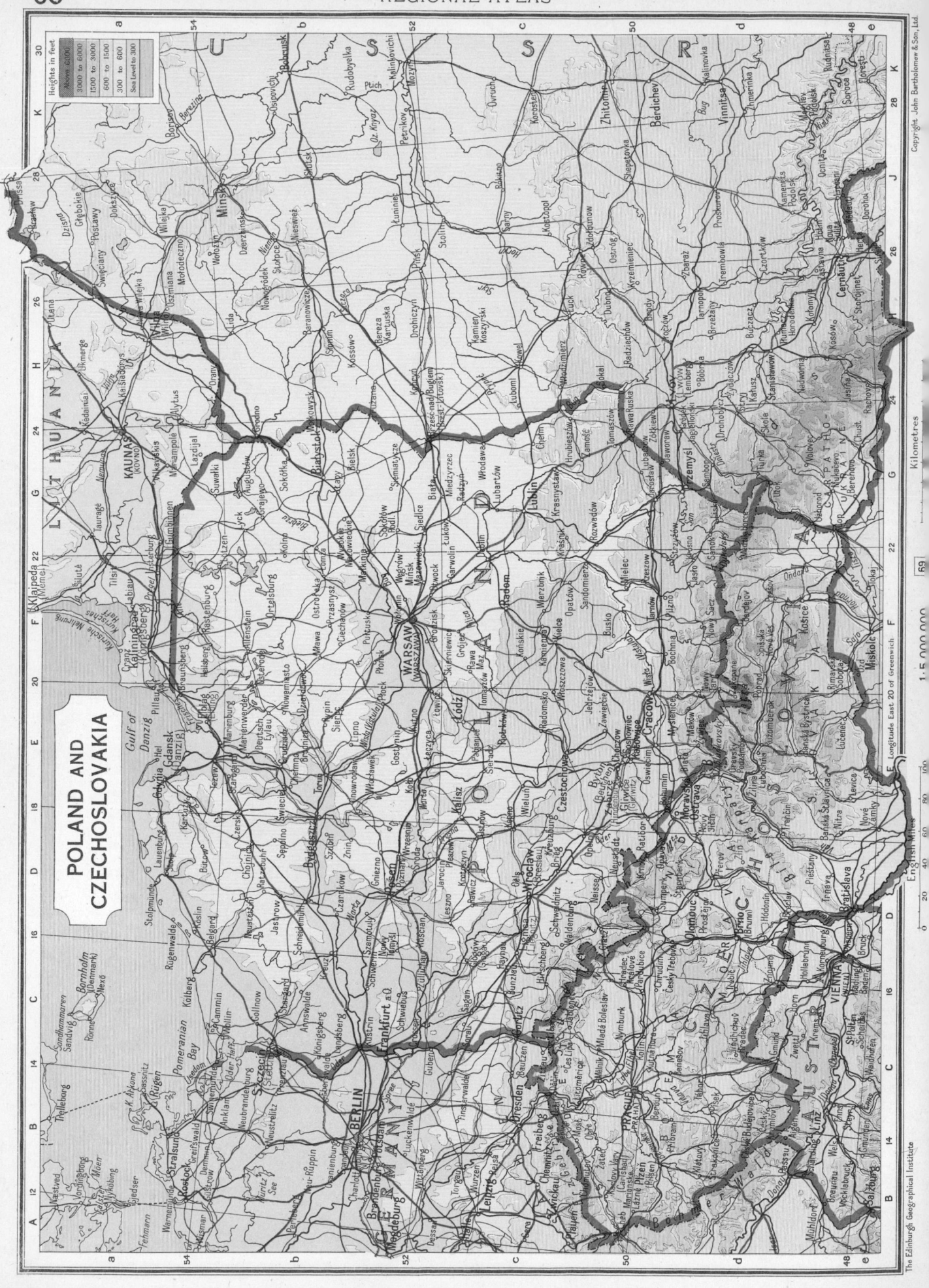

POLAND AND
CZECHOSLOVAKIA

Heights in feet
Above 6000
3000 to 6000
1500 to 3000
600 to 1500
300 to 600
Sea Level to 300

1:5,000,000

Copyright. John Bartholomew & Son, Ltd.

The Edinburgh Geographical Institute

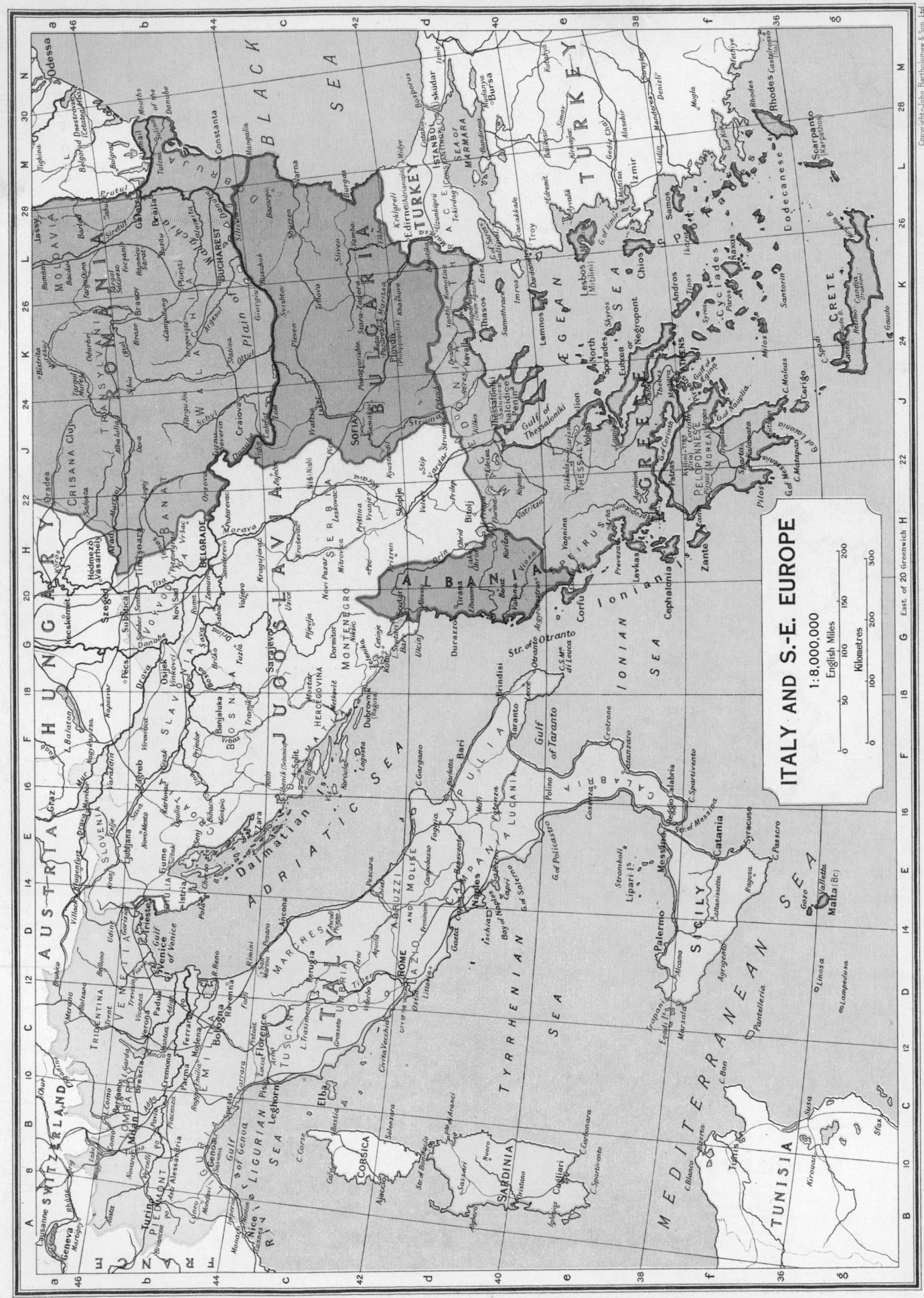

ITALY AND S.-E. EUROPE

1:8,000,000

English Miles

Kilometres

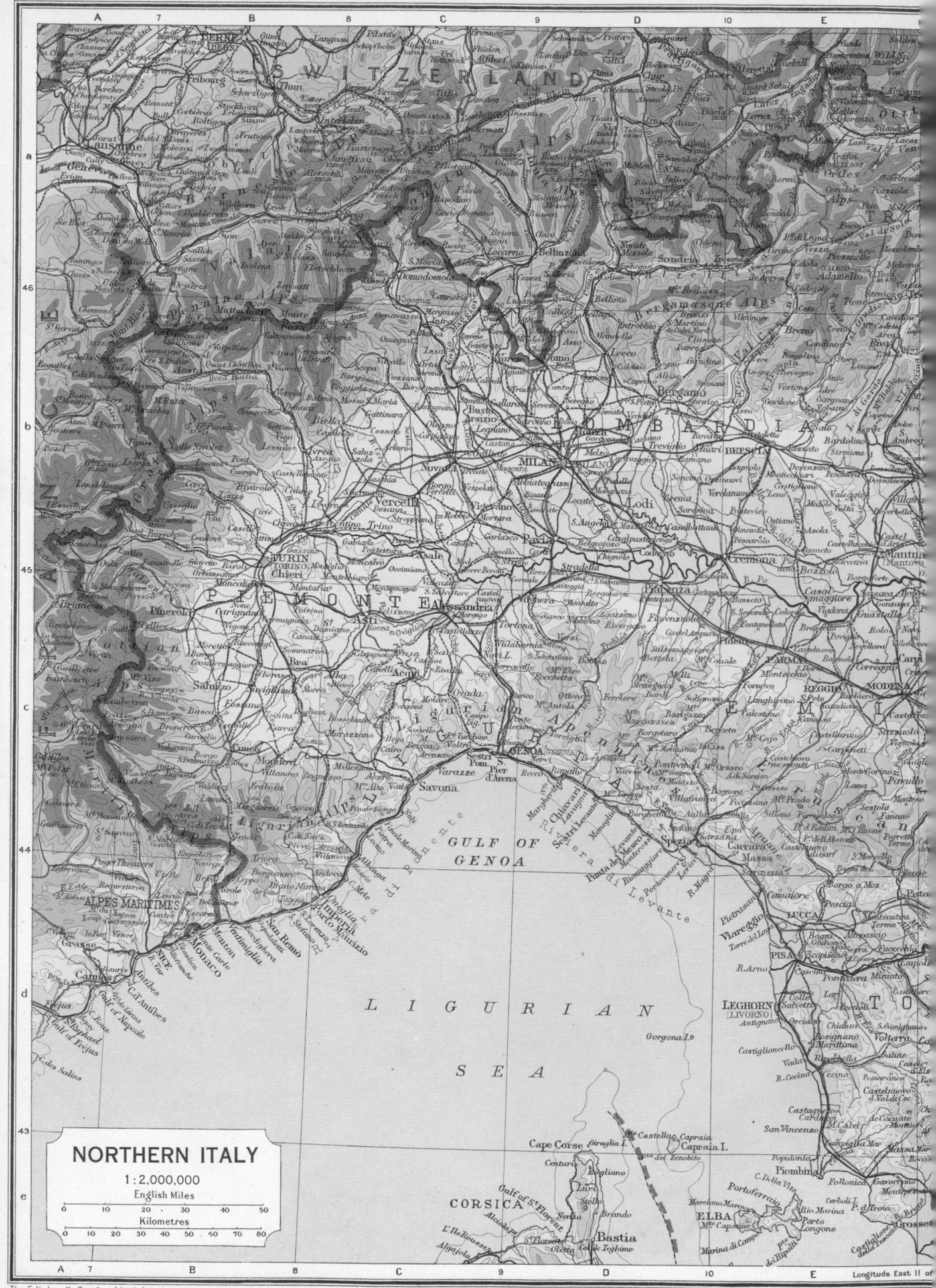

NORTHERN ITALY

1 : 2,000,000

English Miles

Kilometres

Copyright- John Bartholomew & Son, Ltd.

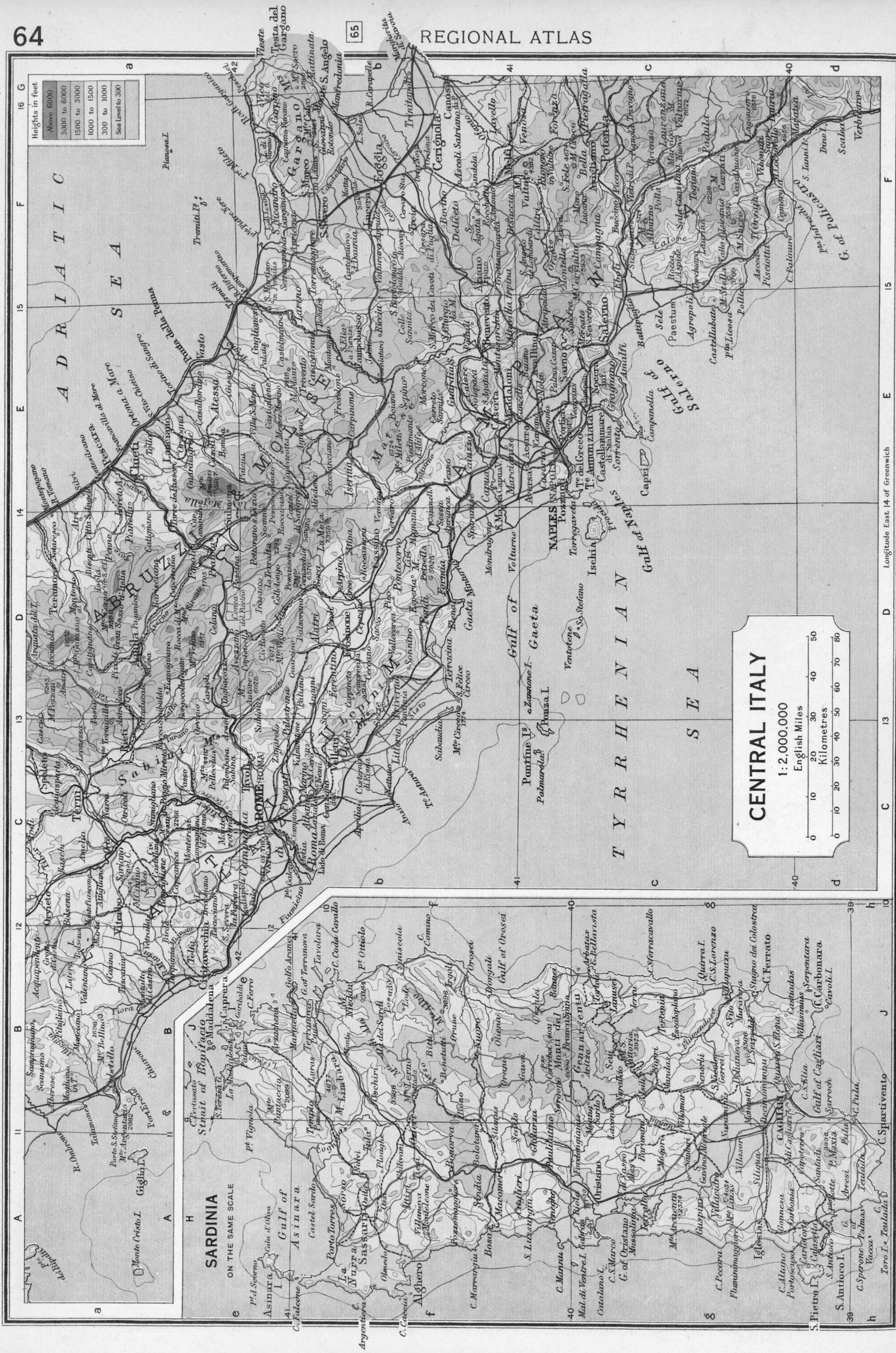

CENTRAL ITALY
1:2,000,000
English Miles
Kilometres

SARDINIA
ON THE SAME SCALE

Heights in feet

Above 6000
3000 to 6000
1500 to 3000
1000 to 1500
300 to 1000
Sea Level to 300

ADRIATIC SEA

TYRRHENIAN SEA

ABRUZZI

MONTE

ROME
Roma

NAPLES

Gulf of Gaeta

Gulf of Naples

Gulf of Salerno

Gulf of Policastro

Gulf of Cagliari

Gulf of Oristano

Gulf of Orosei

Gulf of Asinara

Strait of Bonifacio

Longitude East 14 of Greenwich

Copyright · John Bartholomew & Son, Ltd.

The Edinburgh Geographical Institute

SOUTHERN ITALY

1:2,000,000

English Miles

0 10 20 30 40 50

Kilometres

0 10 20 30 40 50 60 70 80

G. of Policastro

LUCANIA (BASILICATA)

CALABRIA

Gulf of S. Eufemia

Gulf of Gioia

Aspromonte

Gulf of Squillace

Cape Rizzuto

C. Colonne

Gulf of Taranto

Stromboli I.

Messina

REGGIO CALABRIA

Barletta

Andria

Molfetta

BARI

TARANTO

Brindisi

Lecce

Otranto

S. Maria di Leuca

Eolie or Lipari Is.

Alicudi I.   Salina   Salina

Filicudi I.   Lipari I.   Lipari

Vulcano I.   La Fabrica   Palmi

Egadi Is.   Trapani

Levanzo I.

Marettimo I.

Favignana I.

Marsala

Mazara del Vallo

Castelvetrano

Sciacca

Agrigento

Porto Empedocle

Licata

Gela

PALERMO

G. of Castellammare

Monreale

Termini Imerese

Cefalù

Nebrodi

M. Etna

CATANIA

Gulf of Catania

Caltanissetta

Enna

Caltagirone

Modica

Ragusa

Noto

Avola

Syracuse (Siracusa)

MESSINA

Strait of Messina

Taormina

Acireale

Riposto

Punta del Faro

Milazzo

Pantelleria I.

Sicilian Channel

SICILY

ON THE SAME SCALE

MALTA

(TO GT BRITAIN)

ON SAME SCALE

Gozo

Victoria

Comino

VALLETTA

Citta Vecchia

Notabile

Longitude East 15 of Greenwich

Heights in feet	
Above 6000	
3000 to 6000	
1500 to 3000	
1000 to 1500	
300 to 1000	
Sea Level to 300	

The Edinburgh Geographical Institute

Copyright - John Bartholomew & Son, Ltd.

289

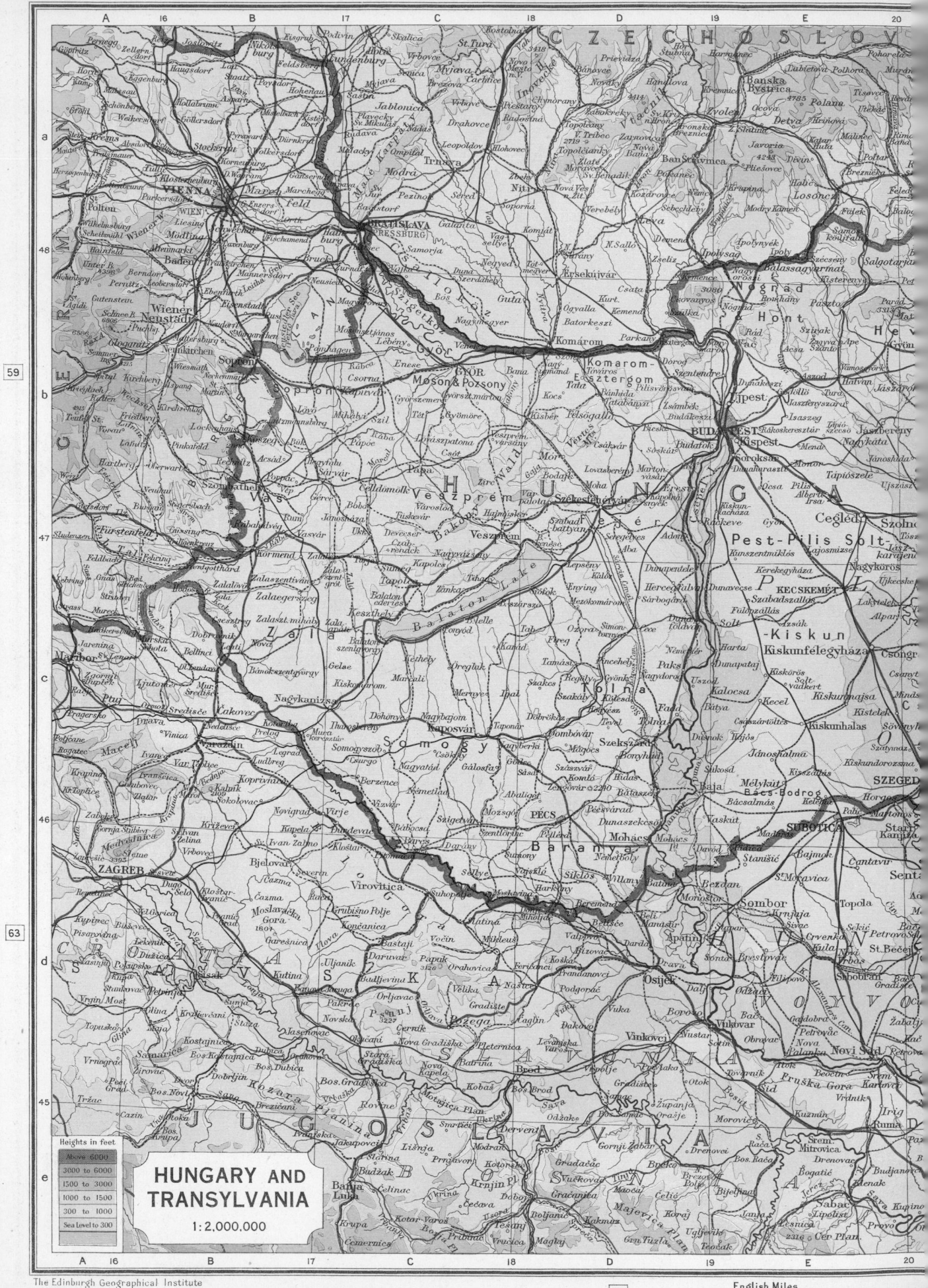

HUNGARY AND
TRANSYLVANIA

1:2,000,000

Heights in feet

Above 6000
3000 to 6000
1500 to 3000
1000 to 1500
300 to 1000
Sea Level to 300

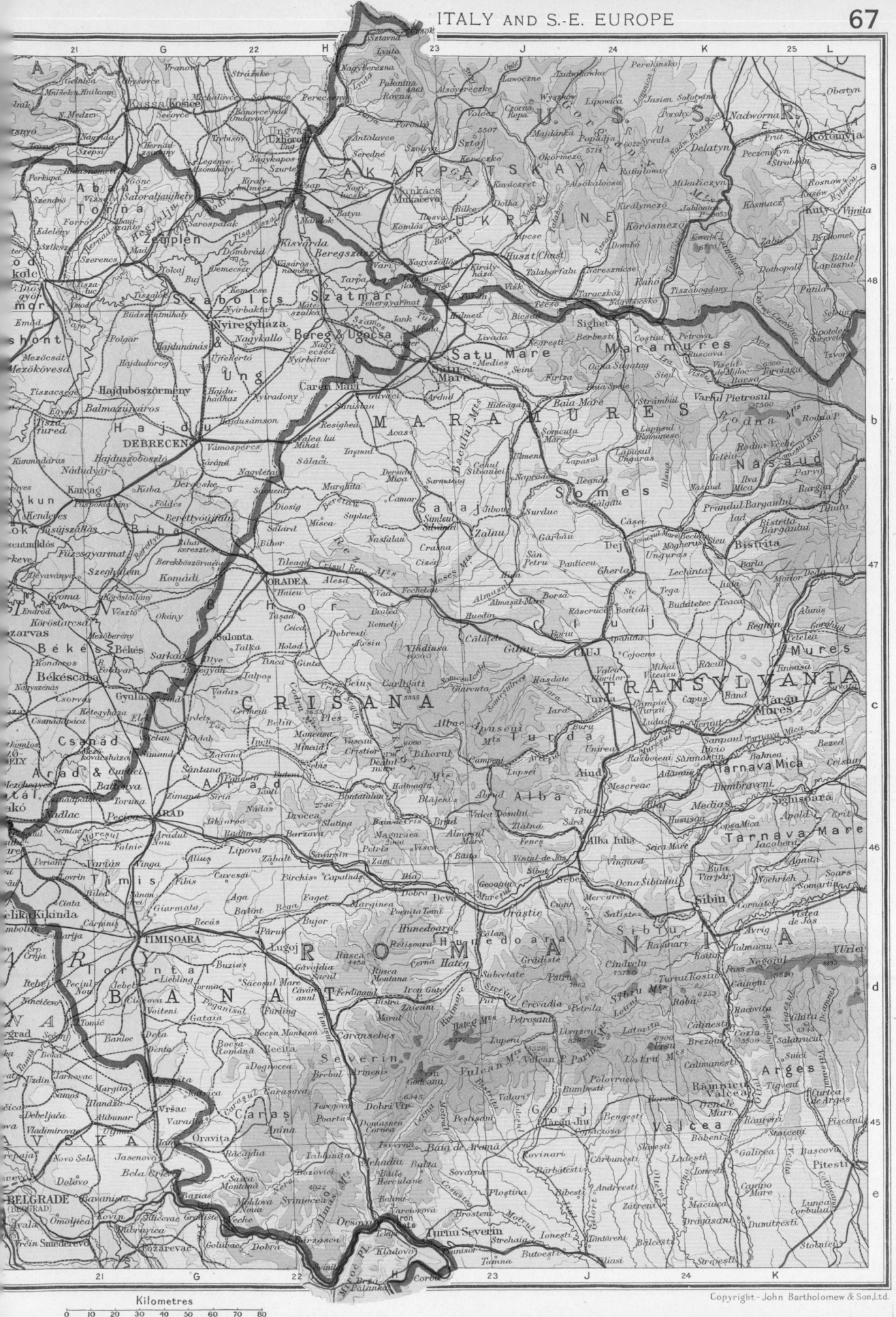

Kilometres

0 10 20 30 40 50 60 70 80

Copyright–John Bartholomew & Son, Ltd.

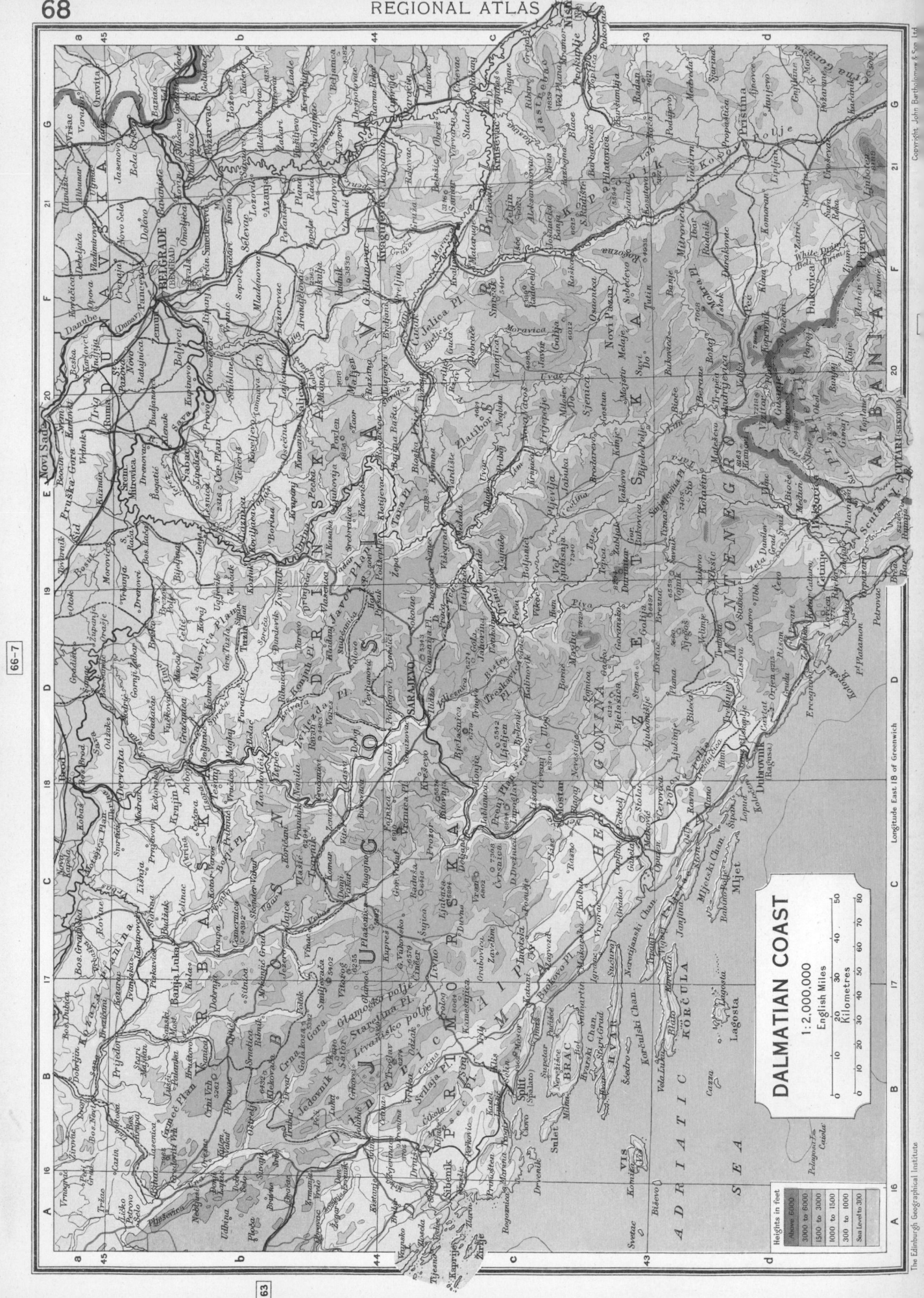

DALMATIAN COAST

1:2,000,000

English Miles

Kilometres

Copyright John Bartholomew & Son Ltd

The Edinburgh Geographical Institute

BLACK SEA

Sea of Marmara

ADRIATIC SEA

LOWER DANUBE LANDS

1:5,000,000

English Miles

Kilometres

Heights in feet

Above 6000	
3000 to 6000	
1500 to 3000	
600 to 1500	
300 to 600	
Sea Level to 300	

Copyright—John Bartholomew & Son, Ltd.

The Edinburgh Geographical Institute

Longitude East 22 of Greenwich

GREECE AND ALBANIA

1:2,000,000

English Miles

0 10 20 30 40 50

Kilometres

0 10 20 30 40 50 60 70 80

CRETE
(KRITI)
ON THE SAME SCALE

IONIAN SEA

IONIAN ISLANDS

CEPHALONIA (KEFALLINIA)

ZANTE (ZAKINTHOS)

AKARNANIA AND AITOLIA

GREECE

FOKIS

EUBOEA (EVVOIA)

ATTICA

PELOPONNESE

AKHAÏA

KORINTHIA

ARGOLIS

ARKADHIA

ILIA

MESSINIA

LAKONIA

MIRTÓON SEA

Gulf of Corinth

Gulf of Patras

Patras (Patrai)

ATHENS (ATHINAI)

PIRAEUS (PIRAIEVS)

Salamis

Saronic Gulf

Tripolis

Sparta (Sparti)

Kalamai (Kalamata)

Gulf of Messinia

Gulf of Kiparissia

Gulf of Argolis

Gulf of Lakonia

C. Matapan (Tainaron)

Kithira (Cerigo)

Andikithira (Cerigotto)

Milos

Sérifos

Kithnos (Thermiá)

Kéa

Hydra (Idhra)

Spetsopoula

Longitude East 25 of Greenwich

Heights in feet

Above 10000
6000 to 10000
3000 to 6000
1500 to 3000
1000 to 1500
300 to 1000
Sea Level to 300

KHANIA

Canea (Khania)

RETHIMNI

Réthimnon

IRAKLION

Candia (Iraklion)

LASITHI

Mesará Bay

The Edinburgh Geographical Institute

Copyright - John Bartholomew & Son, Ltd.

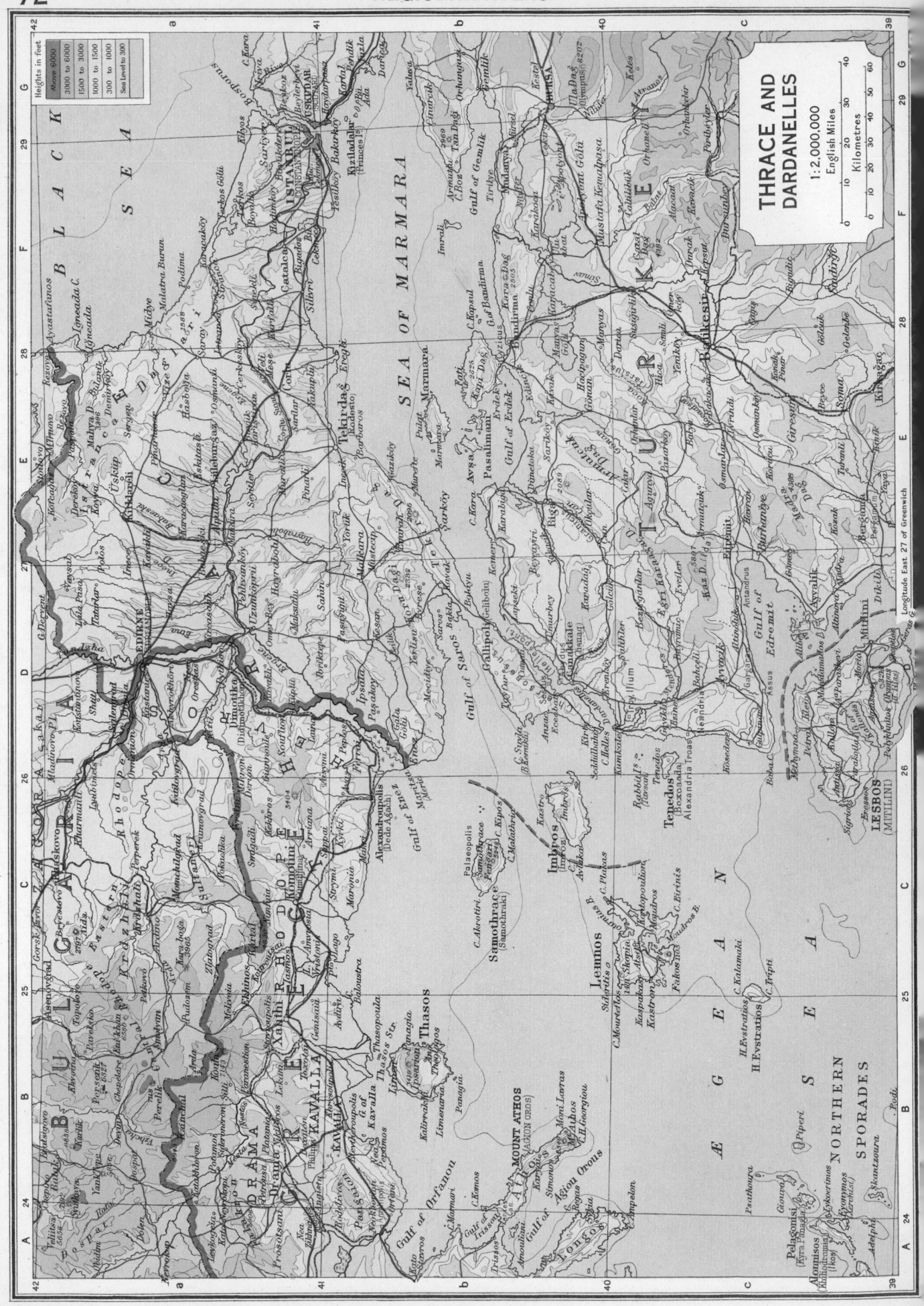
THRACE AND DARDANELLES
1:2,000,000
English Miles
0 10 20 30 40
Kilometres
0 10 20 30 40 50 60
Heights in feet
Above 6000
3000 to 6000
1500 to 3000
1000 to 1500
300 to 1000
Sea Level to 300
BLACK SEA
SEA OF MARMARA
ÆGEAN SEA
NORTHERN SPORADES
BULGARIA
GREECE
TURKEY
ISTANBUL (CONSTANTINOPLE)
EDIRNE (ADRIANOPLE)
Gallipoli (Gelibolu)
Dardanelles
Bosporus
MOUNT ATHOS (AGION OROS)
Thasos
Samothrace (Samothraki)
Imbros (Imroz)
Lemnos
Tenedos (Bozcaada)
LESBOS (MITILINI)
Longitude East 27 of Greenwich

70

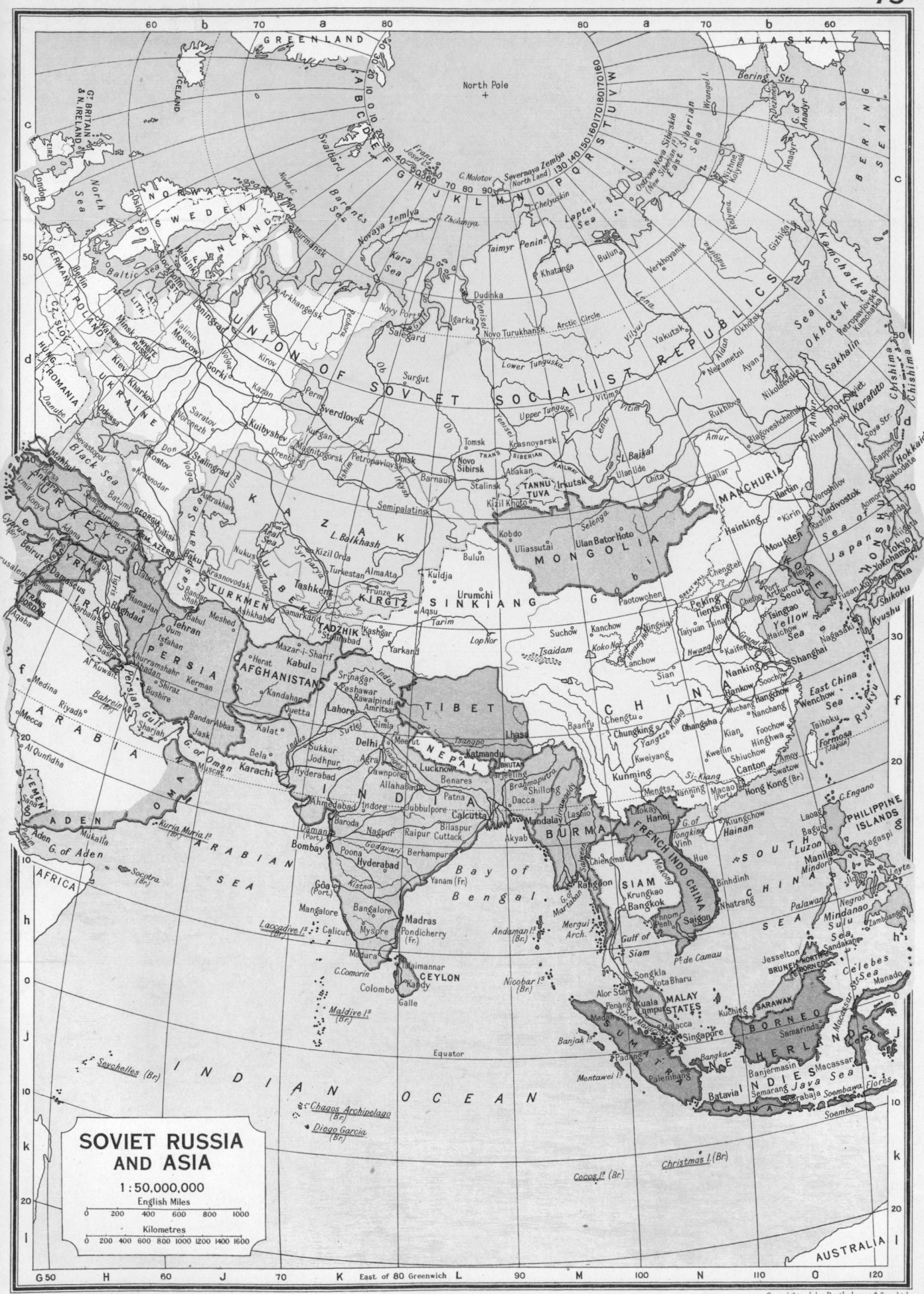

SOVIET RUSSIA
AND ASIA

1 : 50,000,000

English Miles

Kilometres

Copyright - John Bartholomew & Son, Ltd.

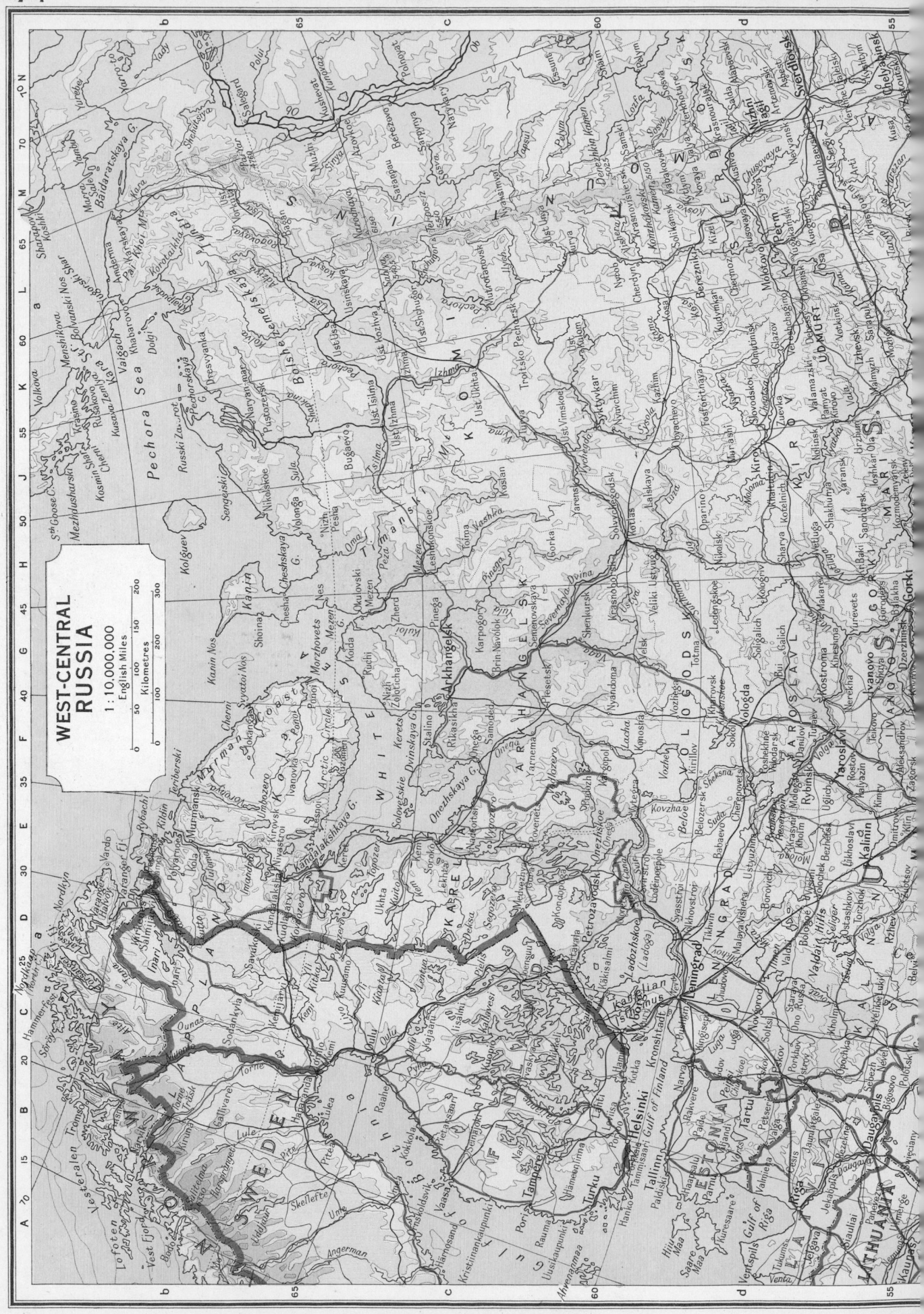

WEST-CENTRAL
RUSSIA

1 : 10,000,000
English Miles
0   50   100   150   200   300
Kilometres
0   50   100   200   300

Heights in feet

Above 9000	
6000 to 9000	
3000 to 6000	
1500 to 3000	
600 to 1500	
300 to 600	
Sea Level to 300	
Below Sea Level	

Copyright–John Bartholomew & Son, Ltd.

The Edinburgh Geographical Institute

Longitude East 40 of Greenwich

THE SOVIET UNION
1:35,000,000
Heights in feet
Above 12,000
6000 to 12,000
3000 to 6000
1500 to 3000
600 to 1500
Sea Level to 600
Below Sea Level
English Miles
Kilometres
East of 90 Greenwich
ARCTIC OCEAN
Barents Sea
Kara Sea
Laptev Sea
East Siberian Sea
Bering Sea
Sea of Okhotsk
Sea of Japan
Norwegian Sea
North Sea
Baltic Sea
Black Sea
Caspian Sea
Western Siberian Plain
Central Siberian Plateau
MONGOLIA
MANCHURIA
KOREA
JAPAN (NIPPON)
CHINA
AFGHANISTAN
PERSIA
The Edinburgh Geographical Institute
Copyright - John Bartholomew & Son Ltd.

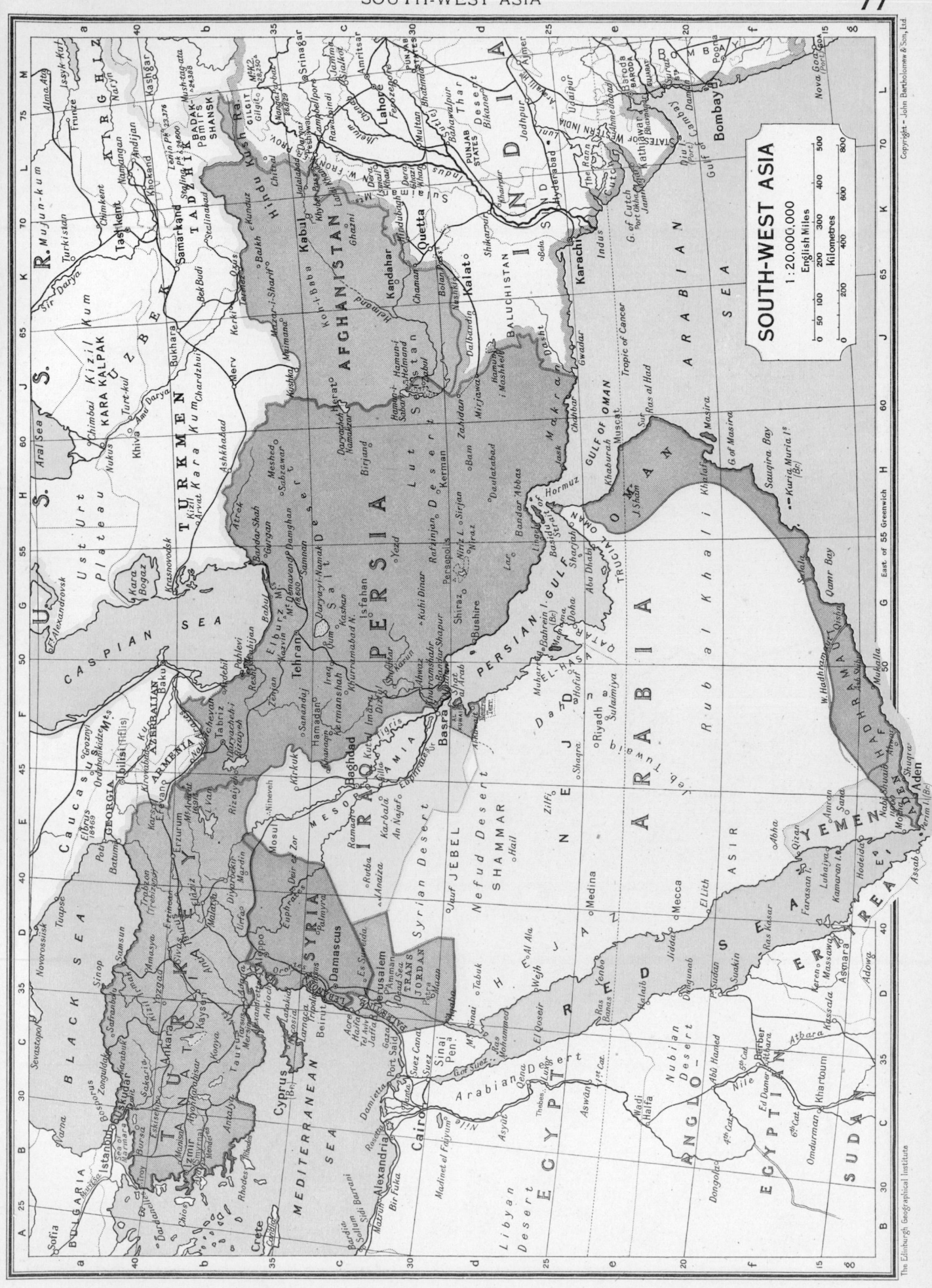

SOUTH-WEST ASIA
1:20,000,000
English Miles

The Edinburgh Geographical Institute

Copyright - John Bartholomew & Son, Ltd.

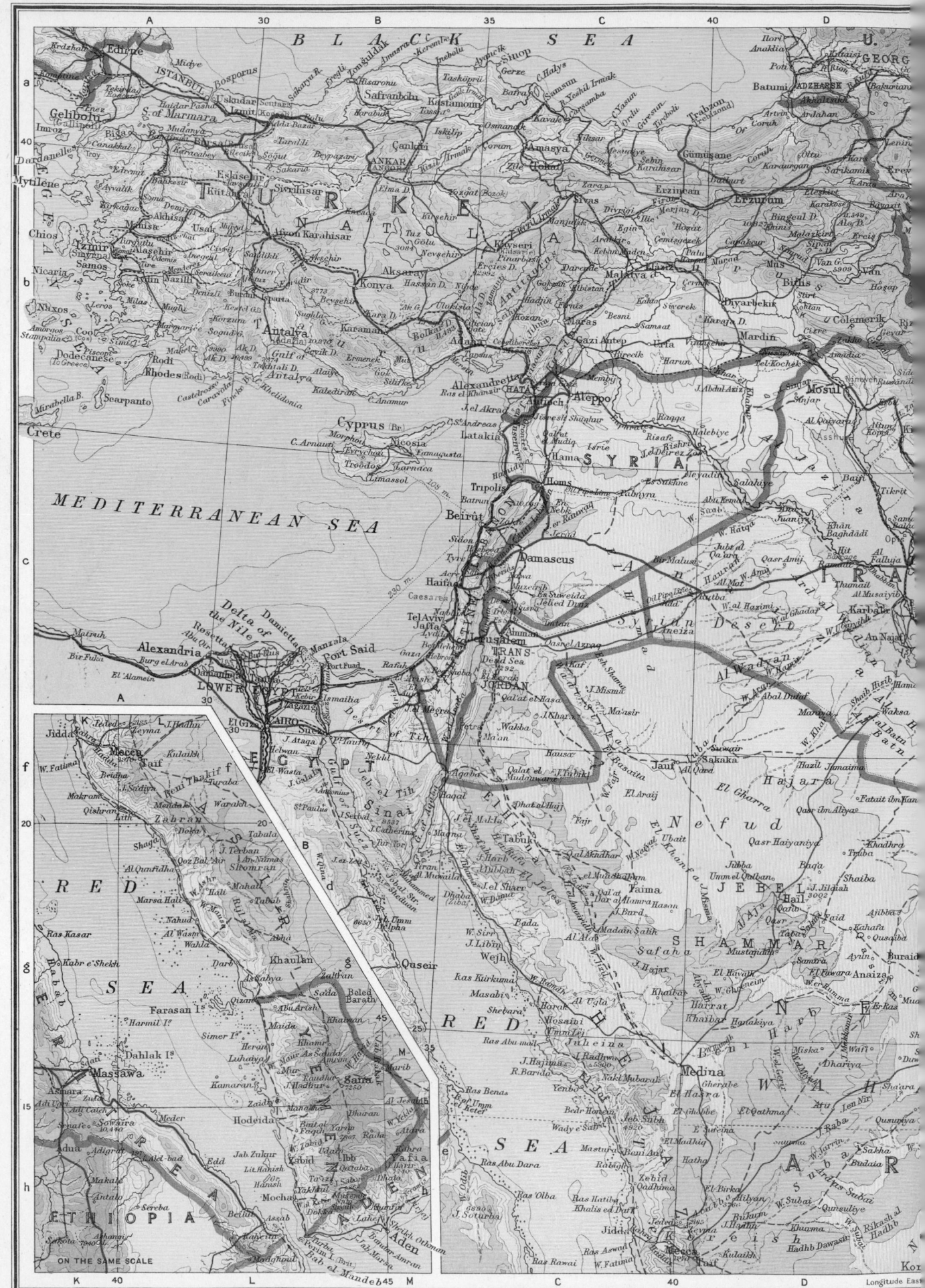

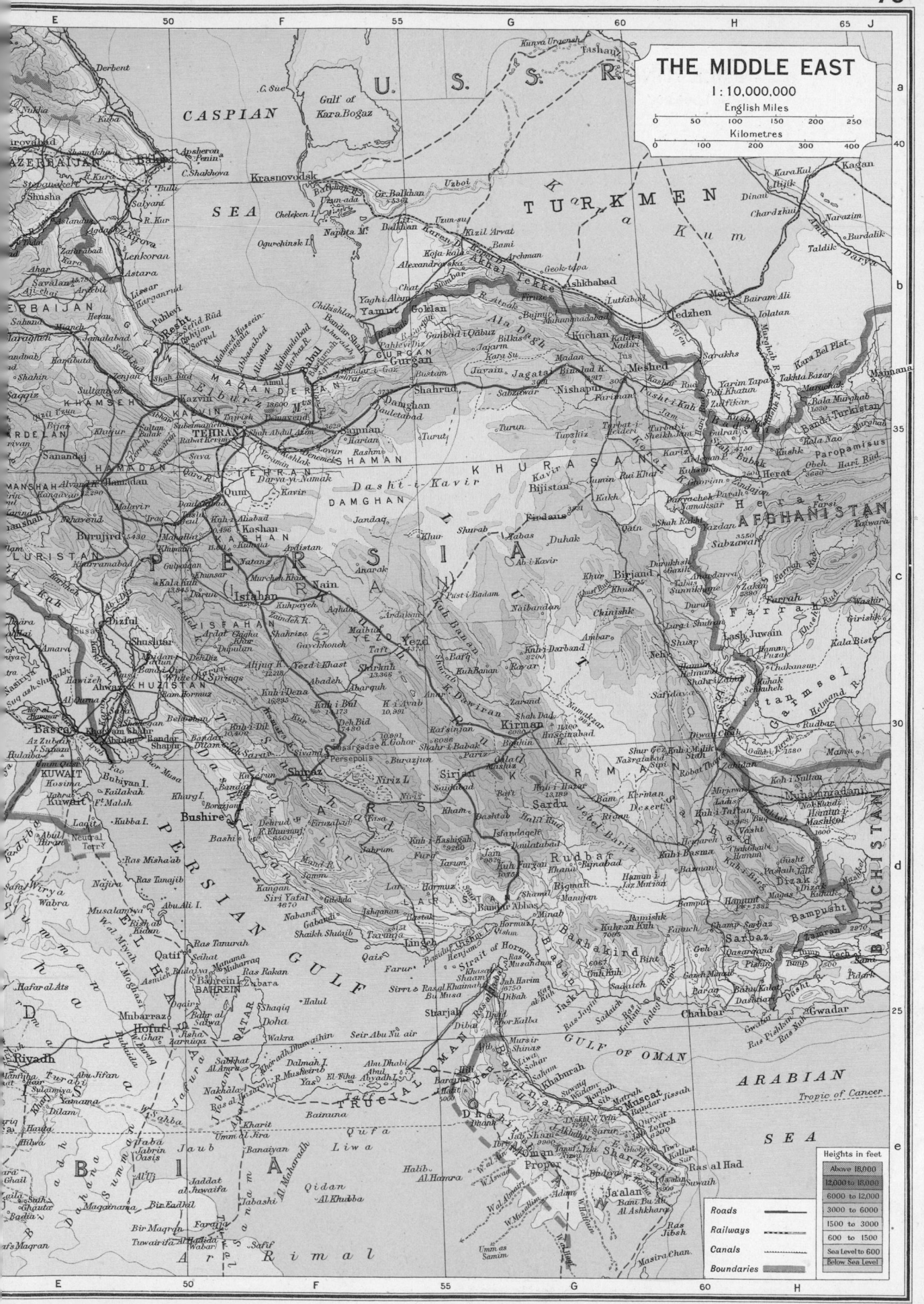

THE MIDDLE EAST

1 : 10,000,000

English Miles

| 0 | 50 | 100 | 150 | 200 | 250 |

Kilometres

| 0 | 100 | 200 | 300 | 400 |

Heights in feet

| Above 18,000 |
| 12,000 to 18,000 |
| 6000 to 12,000 |
| 3000 to 6000 |
| 1500 to 3000 |
| 600 to 1500 |
| Sea Level to 600 |
| Below Sea Level |

Roads
Railways
Canals
Boundaries

Copyright - John Bartholomew & Son. Ltd.

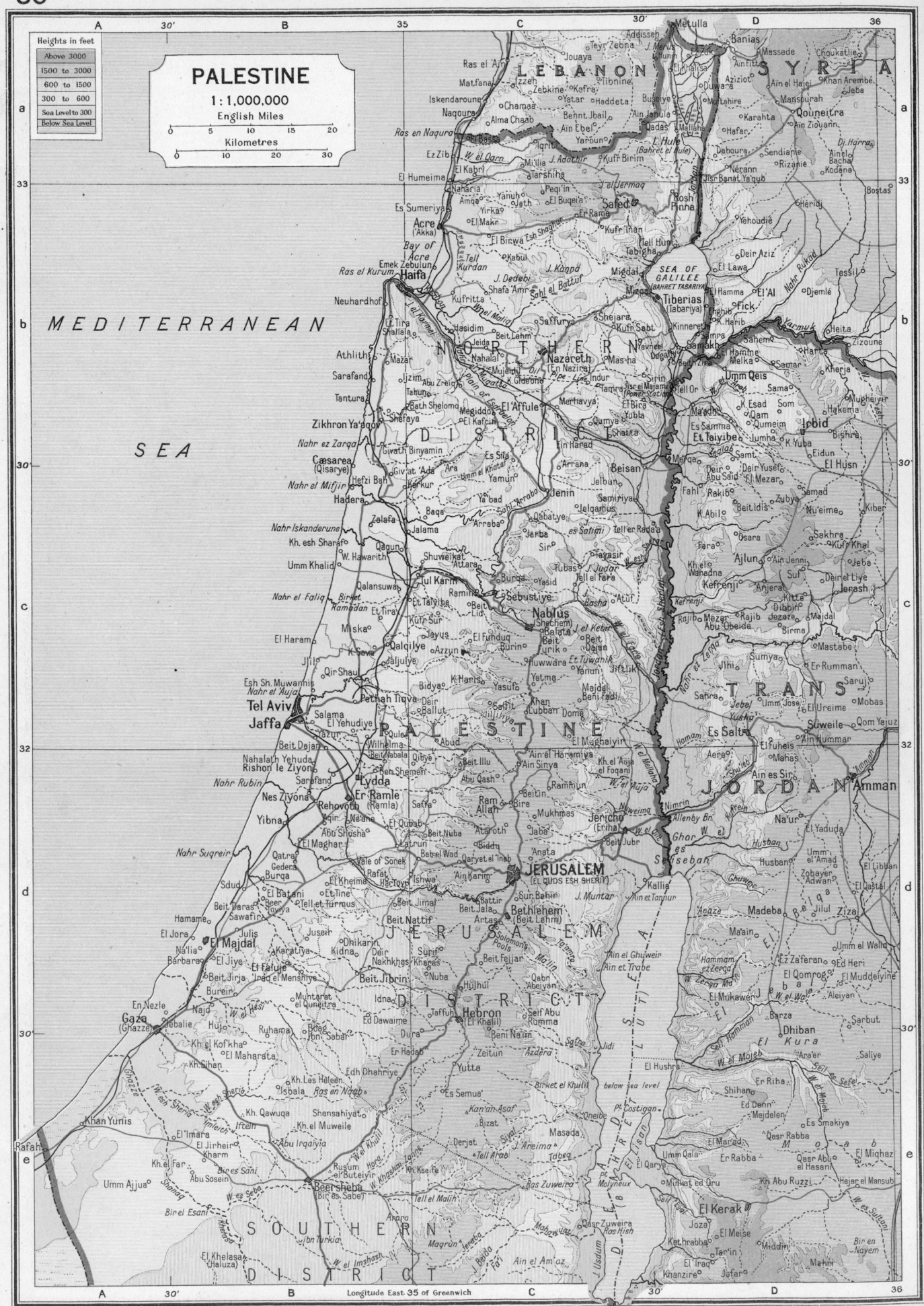

PALESTINE

1 : 1,000,000

English Miles

Heights in feet
Above 3000
1500 to 3000
600 to 1500
300 to 600
Sea Level to 300
Below Sea Level

MEDITERRANEAN

SEA

LEBANON

SYRIA

NORTHERN

DISTRICT

PALESTINE

JERUSALEM

DISTRICT

SOUTHERN

DISTRICT

TRANS-

JORDAN

Acre ('Akka)
Haifa
Nazareth (En Nazira)
Tiberias (Tabariya)
SEA OF GALILEE (BAHRET TABARIYA)
Safed
Jenin
Beisan
Irbid
Nablus (Shechem)
Tul Karm
Tel Aviv
Jaffa
Lydda
Er Ramle (Ramla)
Rehovoth
JERUSALEM (EL QUDS ESH SHERIF)
Bethlehem (Beit Lehm)
Hebron (El Khalil)
Gaza (Ghazze)
Beersheba (Bir es Saba)
Amman
El Kerak

Longitude East 35 of Greenwich

The Edinburgh Geographical Institute

Copyright - John Bartholomew & Son, Ltd.

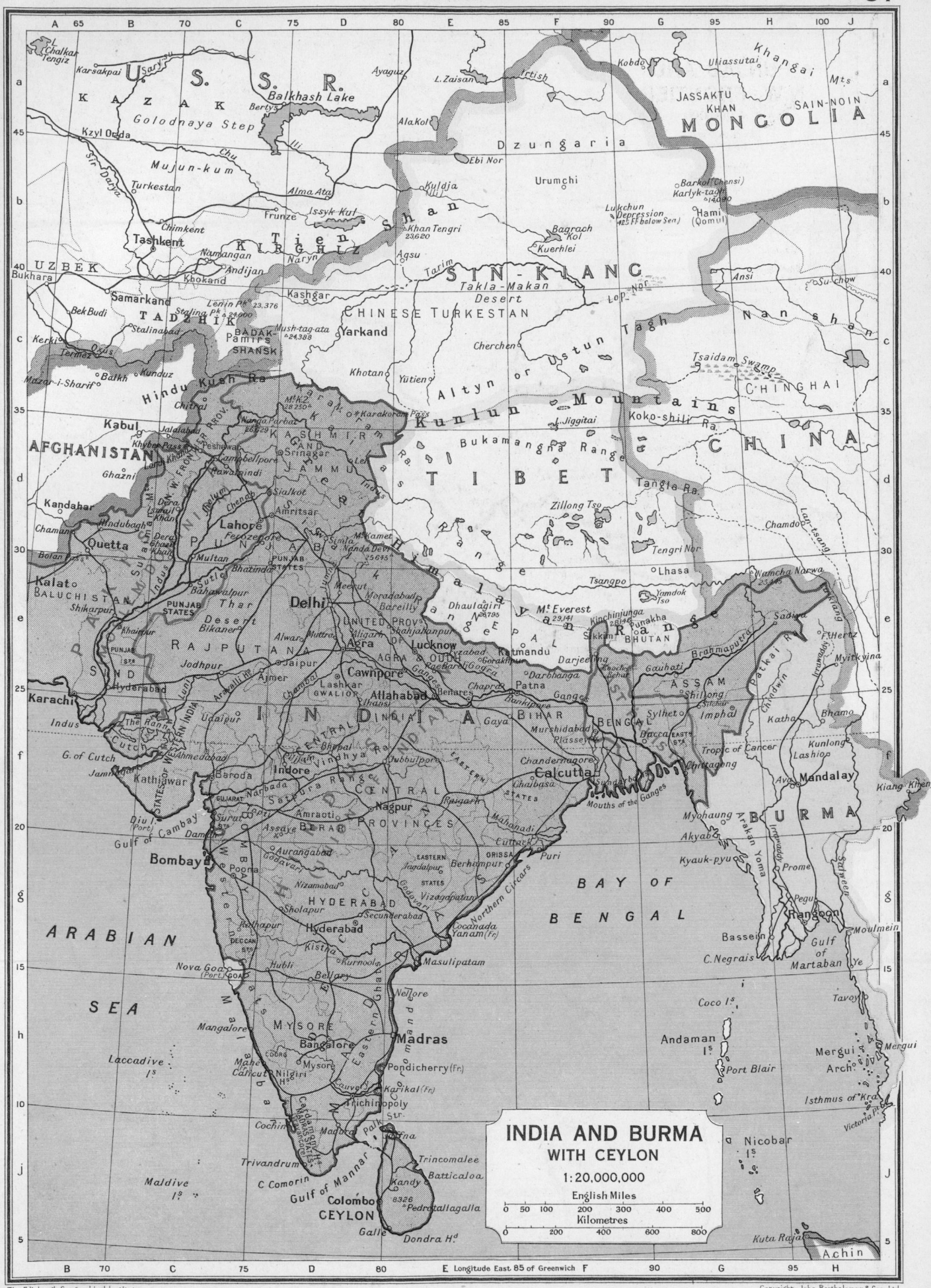

INDIA AND BURMA
WITH CEYLON
1:20,000,000
English Miles
0 50 100   200   300   400   500
Kilometres
0   200   400   600   800

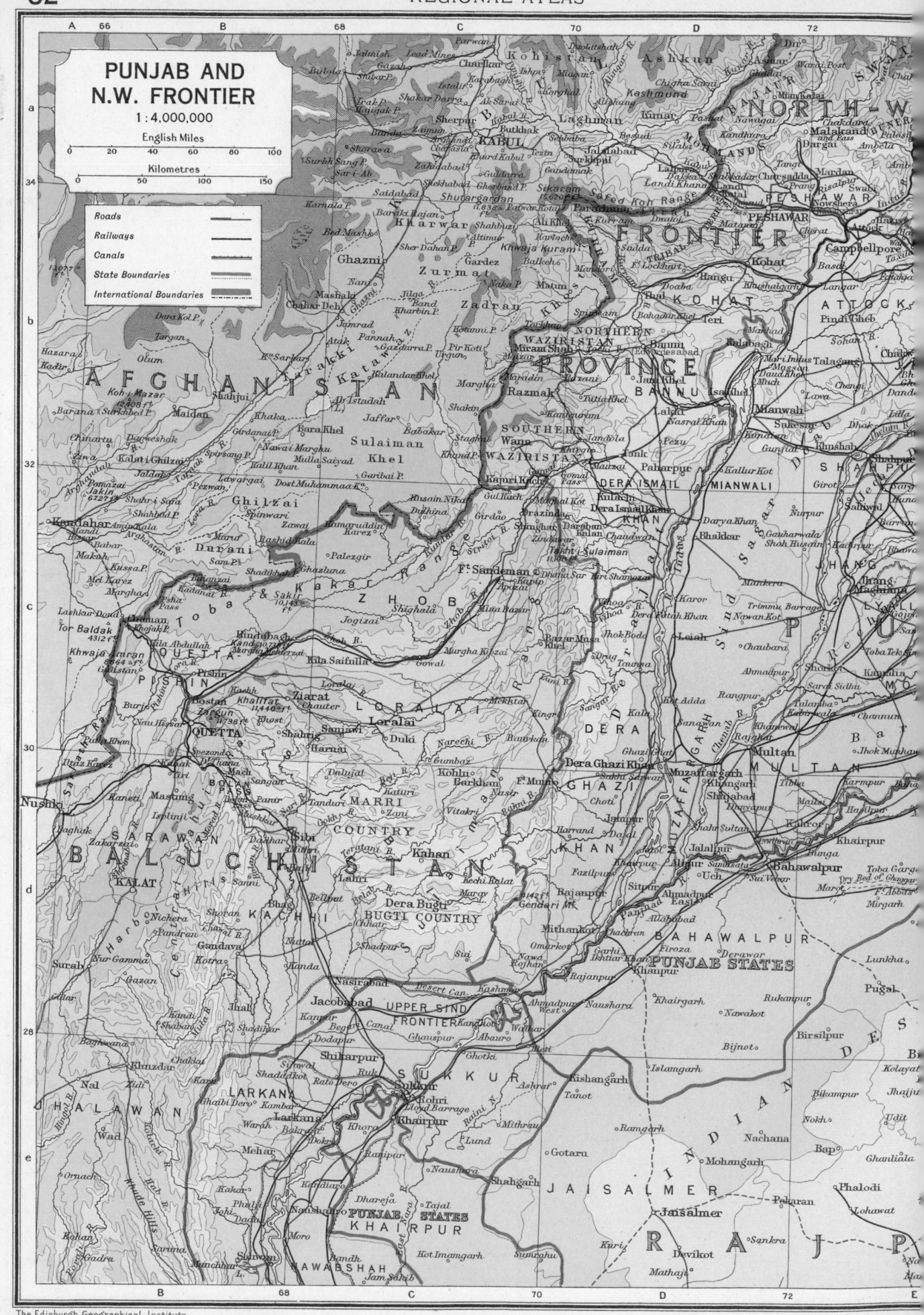

PUNJAB AND
N.W. FRONTIER
1 : 4,000,000

English Miles

Kilometres

Roads
Railways
Canals
State Boundaries
International Boundaries

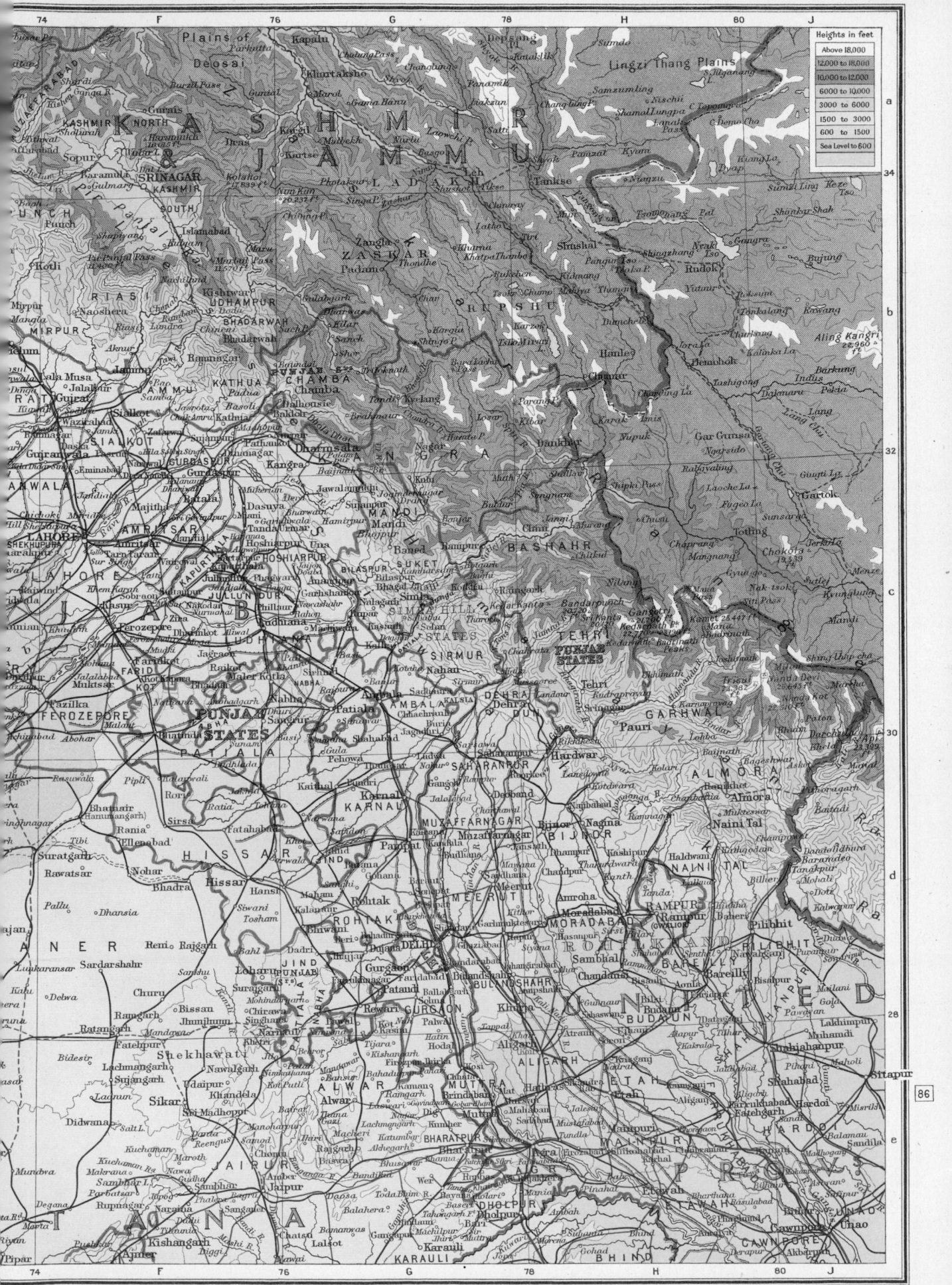

Heights in feet

Above 18,000	
12,000 to 18,000	
10,000 to 12,000	
6000 to 10,000	
3000 to 6000	
1500 to 3000	
600 to 1500	
Sea Level to 600	

Copyright—John Bartholomew & Son, Ltd.

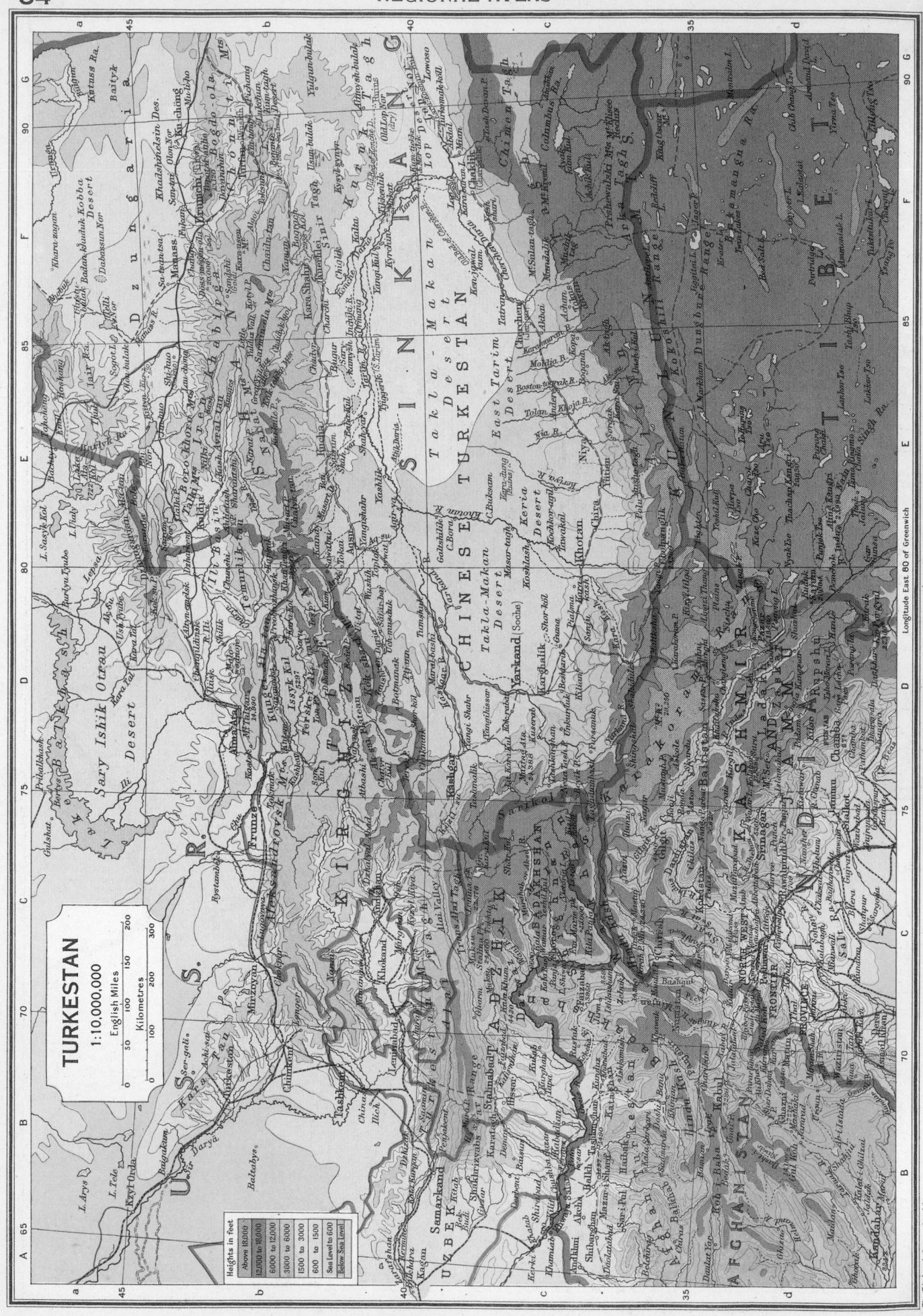

TURKESTAN

1:10,000,000

English Miles

50   100   150   200

Kilometres

0   100   200   300

Heights in Feet.

	Above 18,000
	12,000 to 18,000
	6000 to 12,000
	3000 to 6000
	1500 to 3000
	600 to 1500
	Sea Level to 600
	Below Sea Level

Longitude East 80 of Greenwich

WESTERN INDIA
1:4,000,000
English Miles

Heights in feet	
Above 3000	
1500 to 3000	
600 to 1500	
Sea level to 600	

ARABIAN SEA

Tropic of Cancer

Longitude East, 72 of Greenwich

Copyright - John Bartholomew & Son, Ltd.

The Edinburgh Geographical Institute

UNITED PROVINCES
AND CENTRAL INDIA

1 : 4,000,000

English Miles

Kilometres

Copyright-John Bartholomew & Son, Ltd.

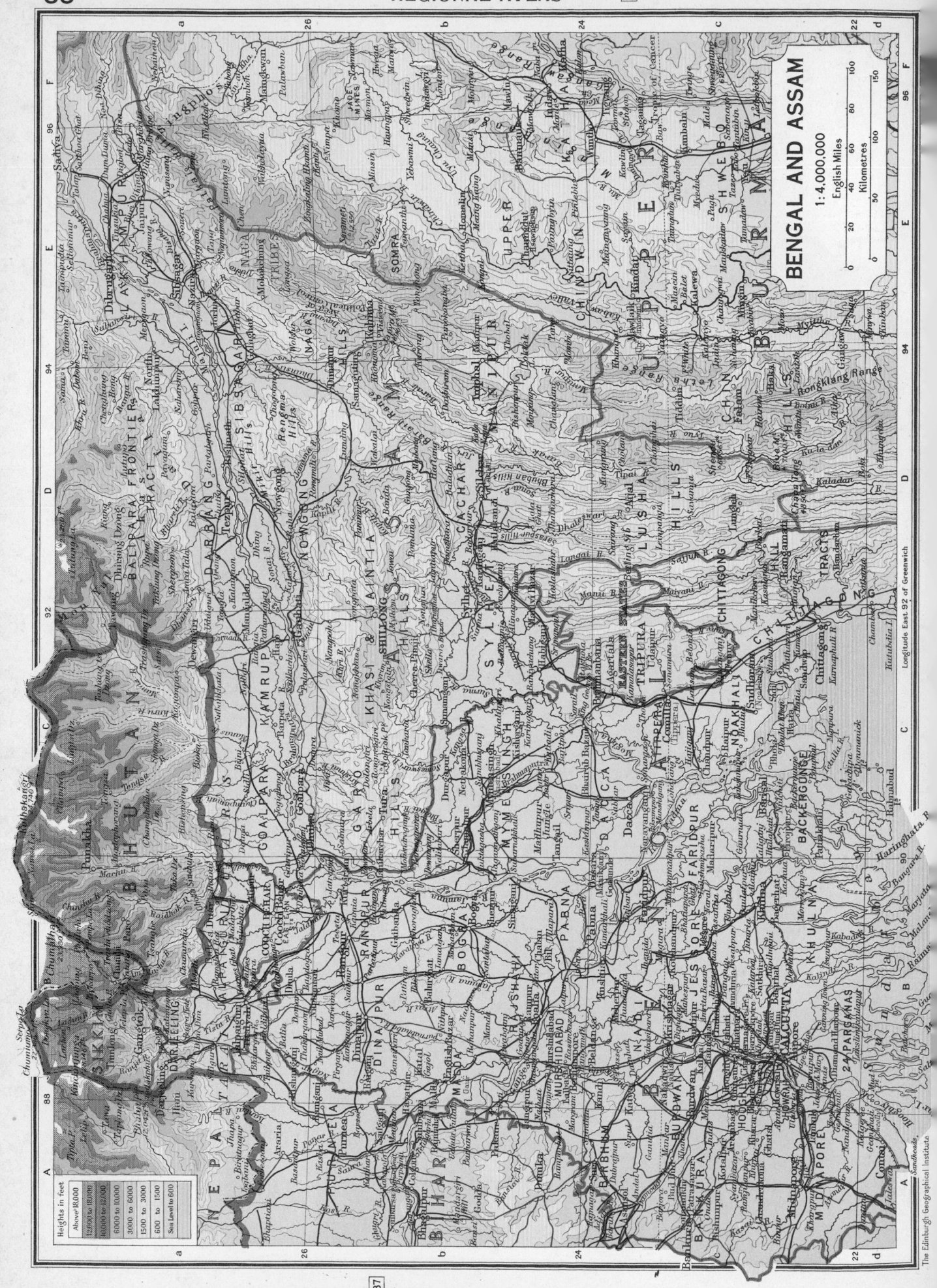

BENGAL AND ASSAM
1:4,000,000

English Miles
Kilometres

Heights in feet
Above 18,000
12,000 to 18,000
10,000 to 12,000
6000 to 10,000
3000 to 6000
1500 to 3000
600 to 1500
Sea Level to 600

The Edinburgh Geographical Institute

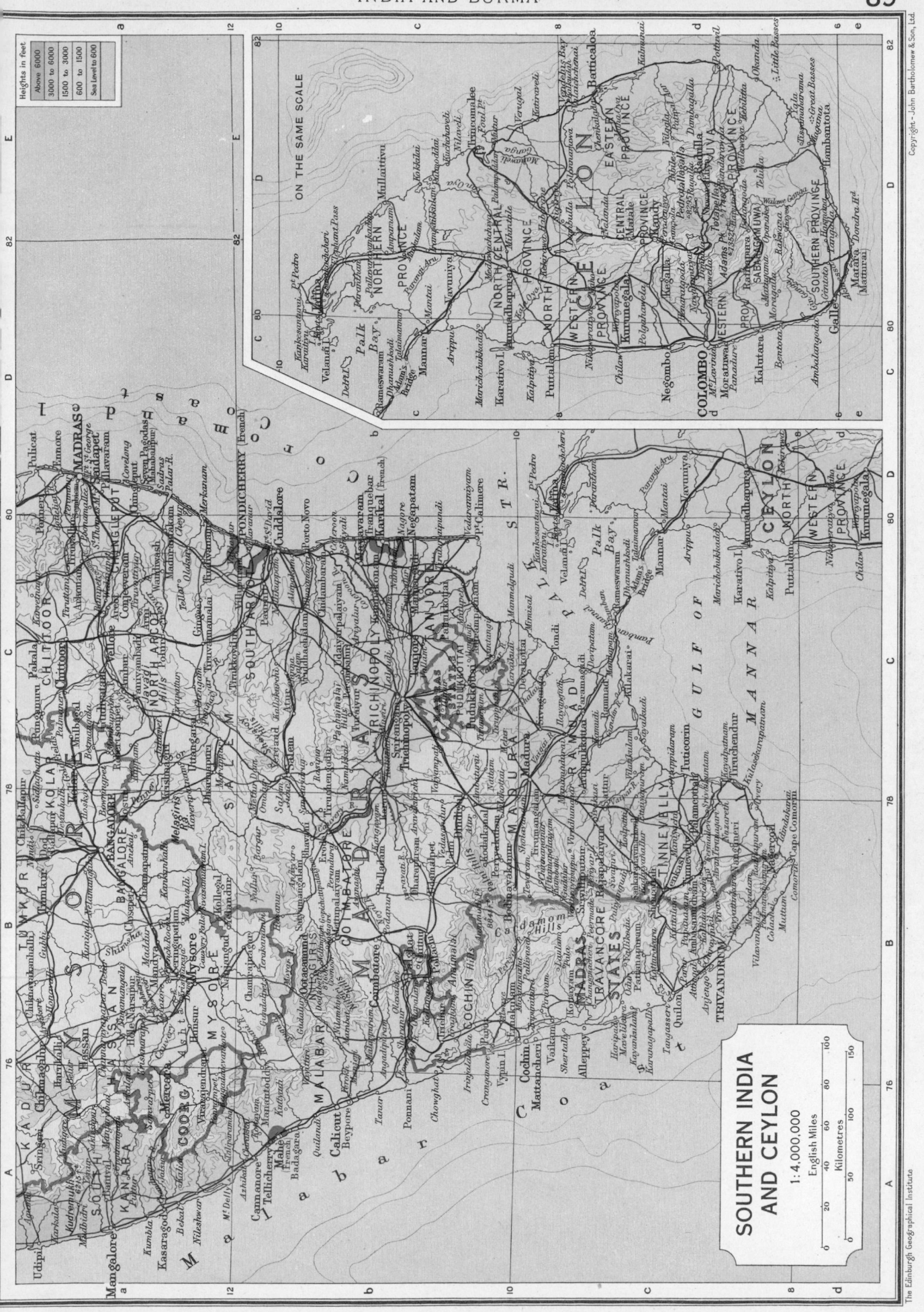

ON THE SAME SCALE

SOUTHERN INDIA
AND CEYLON

1 : 4,000,000

English Miles

Kilometres

Copyright—John Bartholomew & Son, Ltd.

The Edinburgh Geographical Institute

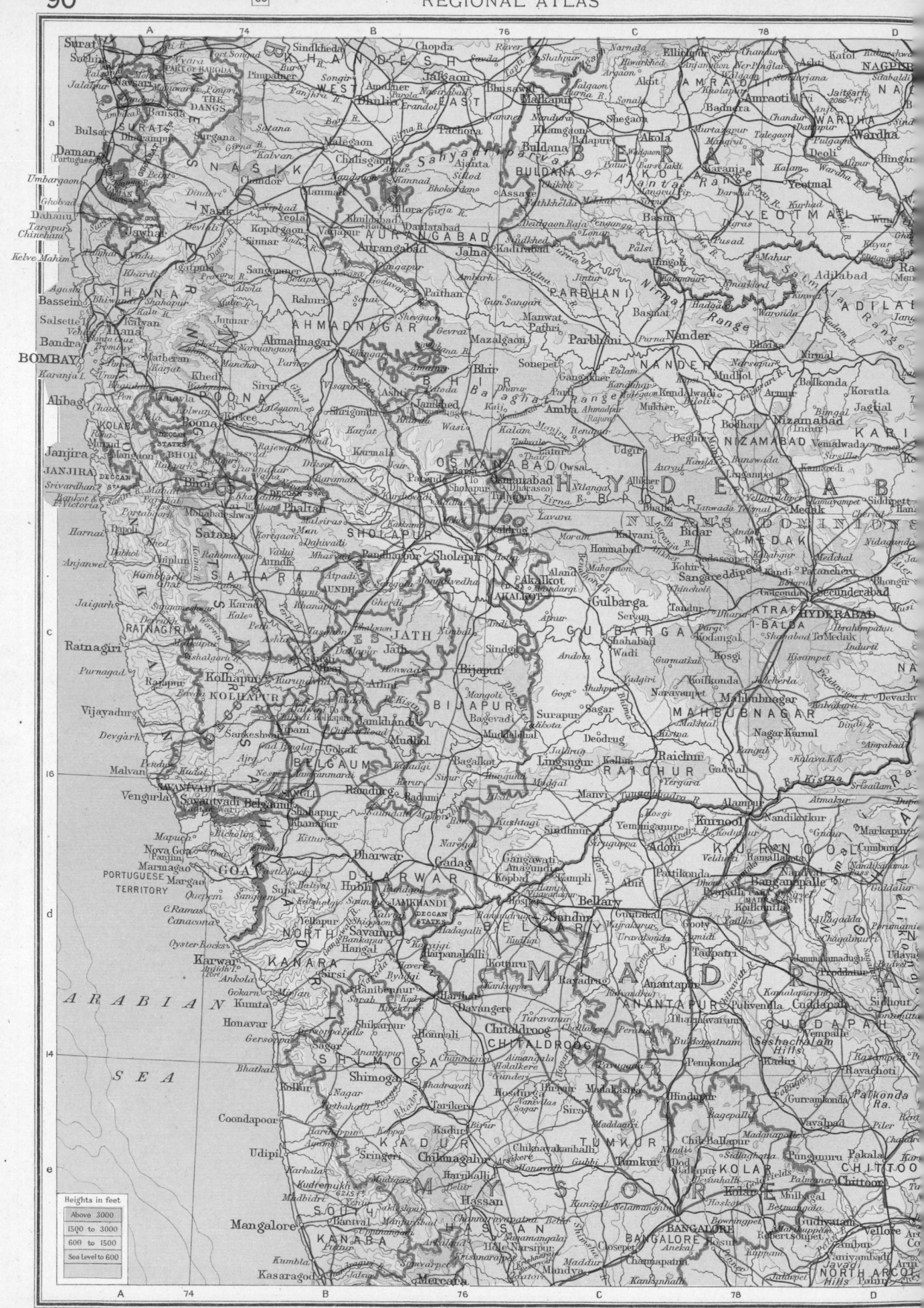
Heights in feet
Above 3000
1500 to 3000
600 to 1500
Sea Level to 600
ARABIAN SEA
BOMBAY
Surat
Daman
Bassein
Bandra
Alibag
Janjira
Ratnagiri
Vengurla
Nova Goa
PORTUGUESE TERRITORY
GOA
Karwar
Honavar
Coondapoor
Udipi
Mangalore
Kasaragod
KHANDESH
NASIK
THANA
POONA
AHMADNAGAR
AURANGABAD
SATARA
SHOLAPUR
KOLHAPUR
BELGAUM
DHARWAR
BIJAPUR
NORTH KANARA
SOUTH KANARA
SHIMOGA
KADUR
HASSAN
MYSORE
BANGALORE
TUMKUR
KOLAR
CHITALDROOG
BELLARY
ANANTAPUR
CUDDAPAH
KURNOOL
NORTH ARCOT
BERAR
BULDANA
AKOLA
AMRAOTI
YEOTMAL
WARDHA
NAGPUR
ADILABAD
PARBHANI
NANDER
BHIR
OSMANABAD
BIDAR
NIZAMABAD
MEDAK
GULBARGA
RAICHUR
MAHBUBNAGAR
HYDERABAD
Secunderabad
Poona
Nasik
Ahmadnagar
Aurangabad
Jalna
Sholapur
Bijapur
Belgaum
Dharwar
Hubli
Gadag
Bellary
Kurnool
Shimoga
Hassan
Mercara
Cuddapah
Chittoor
Vellore
NIZAM'S DOMINIONS
A, B, C, D
a, b, c, d, e
74, 76, 78
16, 14

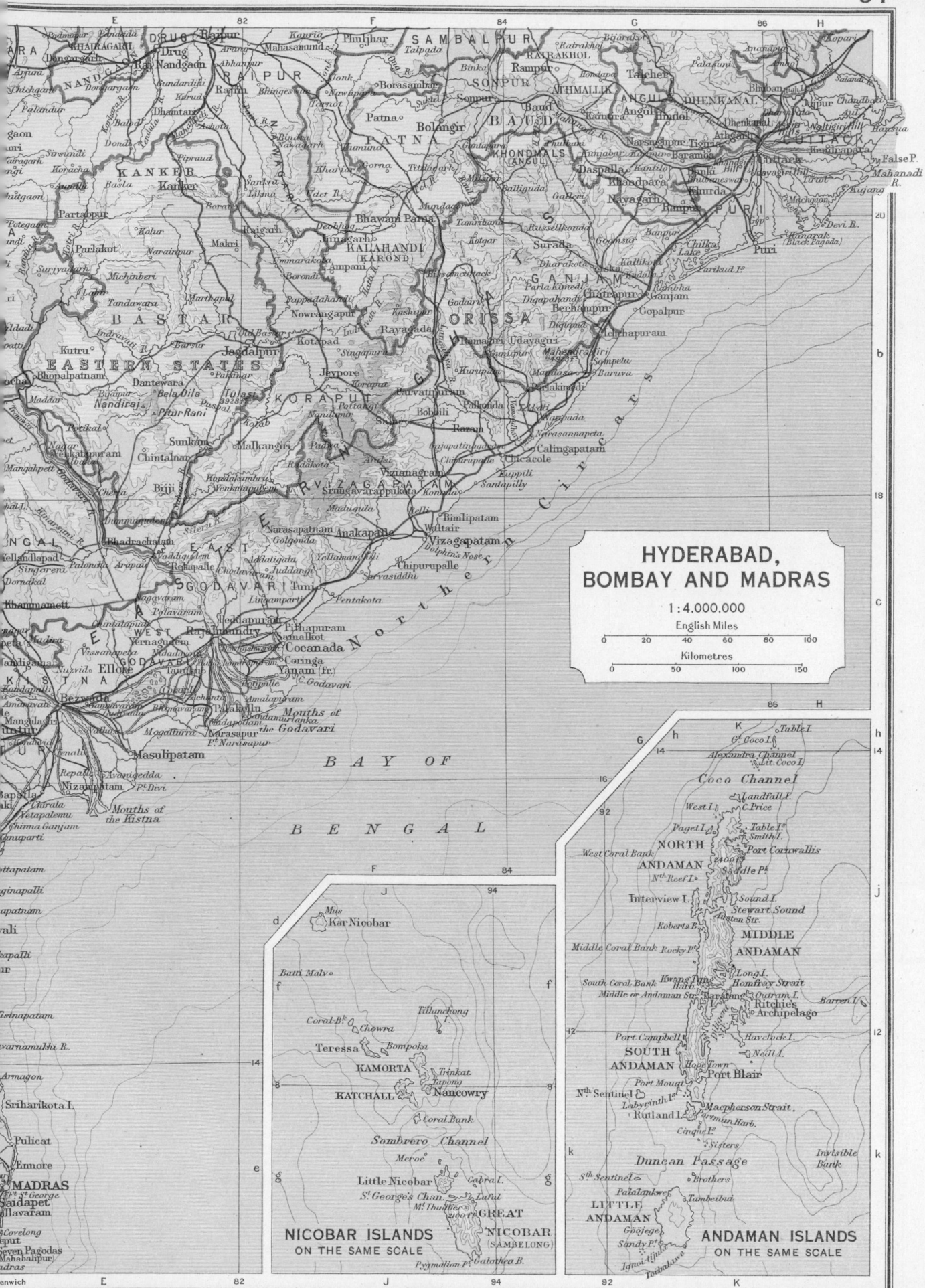

HYDERABAD,
BOMBAY AND MADRAS

1:4,000,000

English Miles

Kilometres

BAY OF

BENGAL

NICOBAR ISLANDS
ON THE SAME SCALE

ANDAMAN ISLANDS
ON THE SAME SCALE

Copyright–John Bartholomew & Son, Ltd.

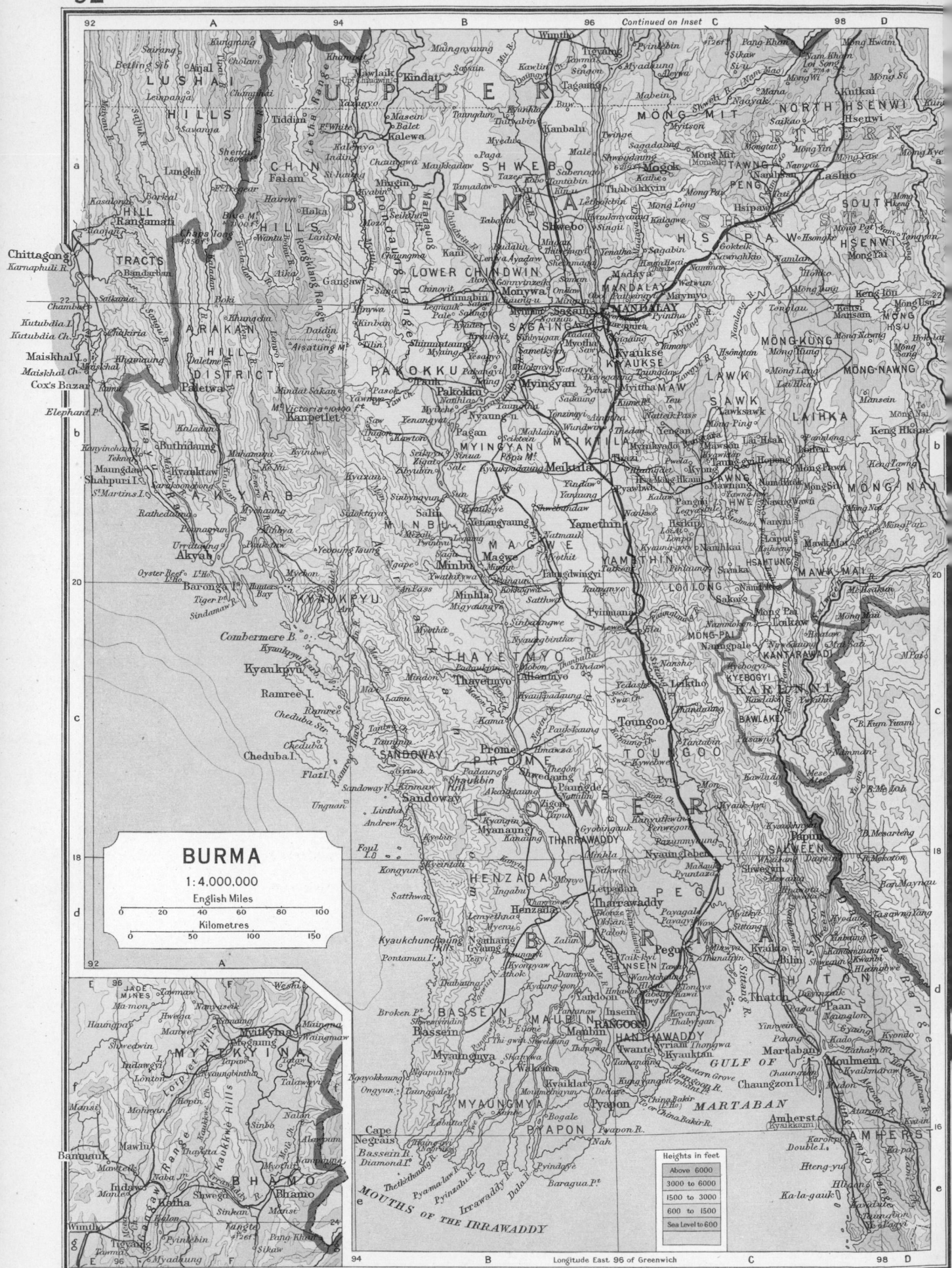

BURMA

1 : 4,000,000

English Miles

Kilometres

Heights in feet

| Above 6000 |
| 3000 to 6000 |
| 1500 to 3000 |
| 600 to 1500 |
| Sea Level to 600 |

Longitude East 96 of Greenwich

MOUTHS OF THE IRRAWADDY

The Edinburgh Geographical Institute

Copyright - John Bartholomew & Son, Ltd

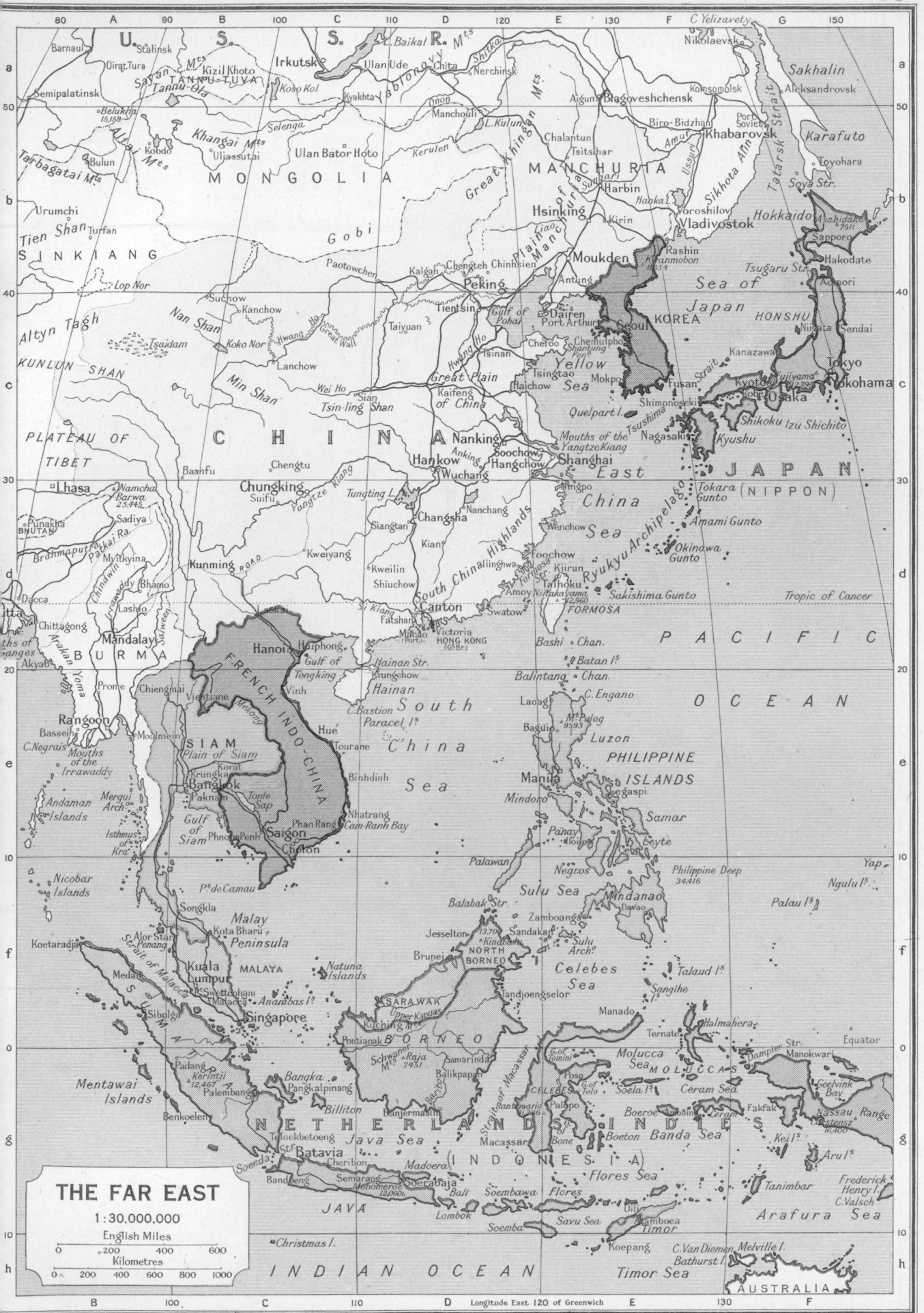

THE FAR EAST

1:30,000,000

English Miles

0   200   400   600

Kilometres

0   200   400   600   800   1000

The Edinburgh Geographical Institute

Copyright-John Bartholomew & Son, Ltd.

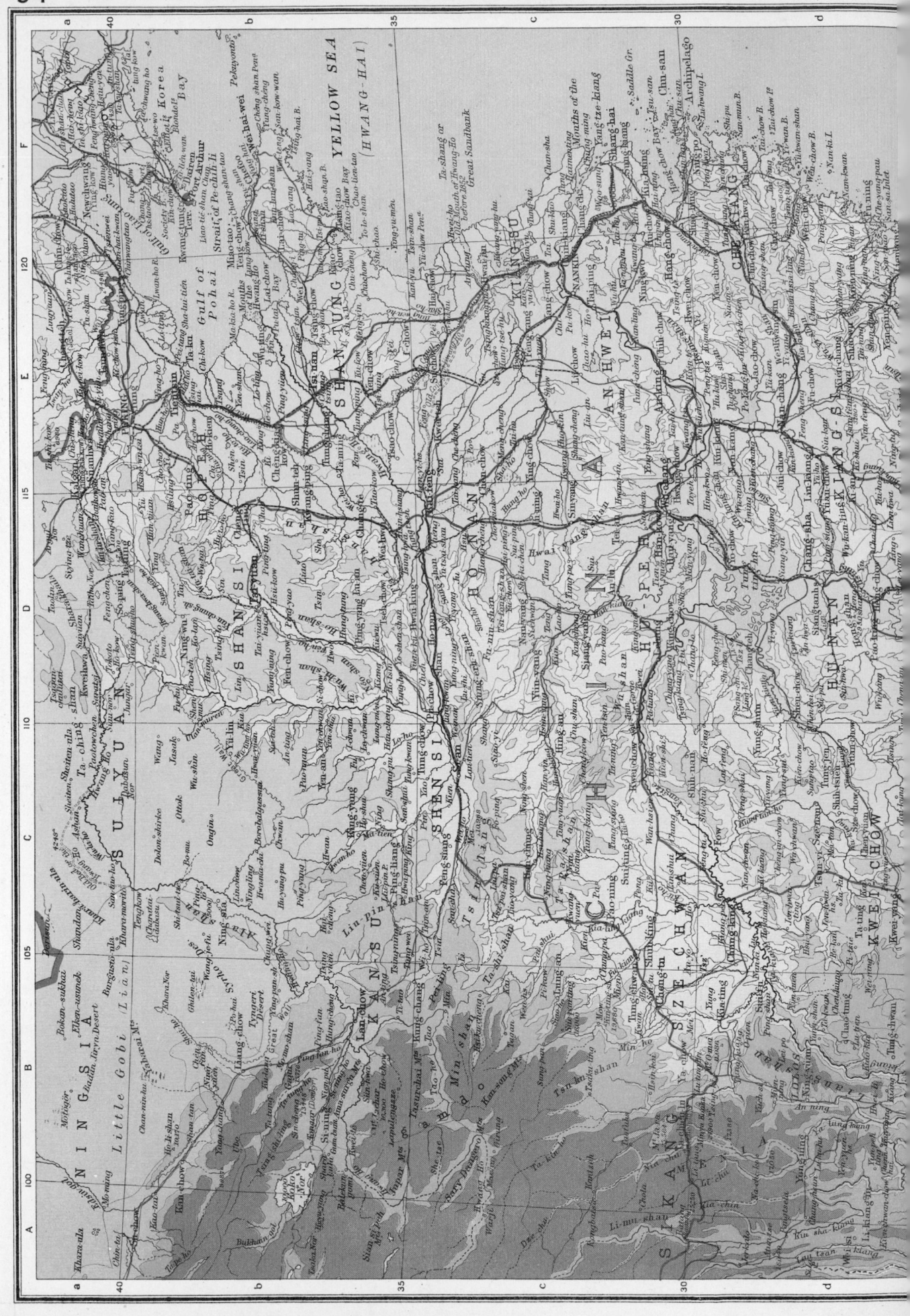
YELLOW SEA
(HWANG-HAI)
Gulf of Pohai
Strait of Pe-chih-li
Korea Bay
SHAN TUNG
HO PEH
SHAN SI
HO NAN
SHEN SI
KAN SU
SUIYUAN
NINGSIA
Little Gobi
CHINA
HU PEH
AN HWEI
KIANG SU
CHE KIANG
KIANG SI
HU NAN
SZECHWAN
KWEI CHOW
SIKANG
Chu-san Archipelago
Great Sandbank

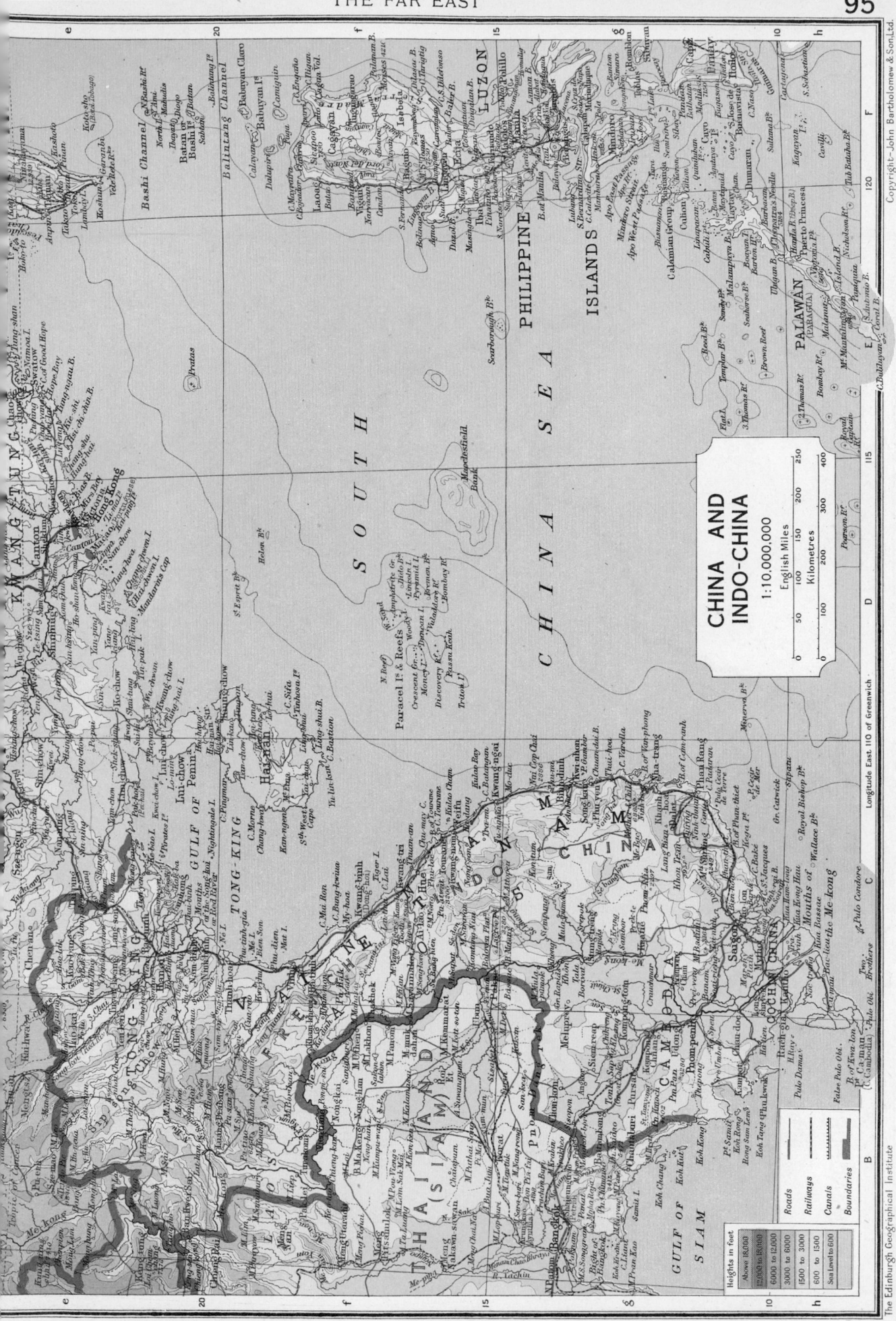

CHINA AND
INDO-CHINA

1:10,000,000

English Miles

Kilometres

Copyright-John Bartholomew & Son,Ltd.

MANCHURIA

1:10,000,000

English Miles

Heights in feet

| Above 6000 |
| 3000 to 6000 |
| 1500 to 3000 |
| 600 to 1500 |
| Sea Level to 600 |

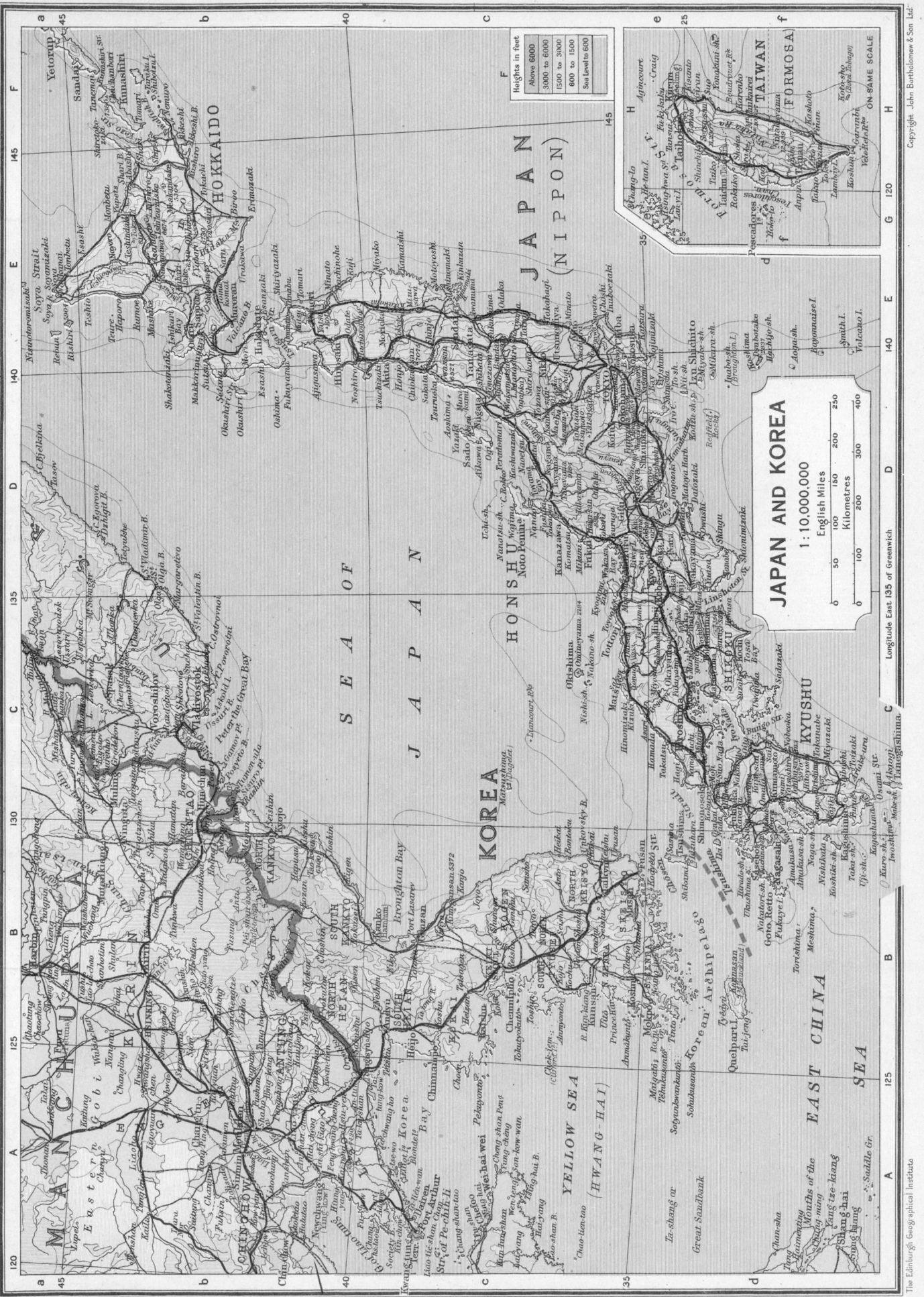

JAPAN AND KOREA
1:10,000,000

English Miles

Kilometres

TAIWAN (FORMOSA) ON-SAME SCALE

JAPAN (NIPPON)

HOKKAIDO

HONSHU

SHIKOKU

KYUSHU

KOREA

MANCHURIA

KIRIN

EAST CHINA SEA

YELLOW SEA (HWANG-HAI)

SEA OF JAPAN

Copyright. John Bartholomew & Son Ltd.

94

Longitude East 135 of Greenwich

INDONESIA

1 : 10,000,000

English Miles

Kilometres

Heights in feet

Above 12,000
6000 to 12,000
3000 to 6000
1500 to 3000
600 to 1500
Sea Level to 600

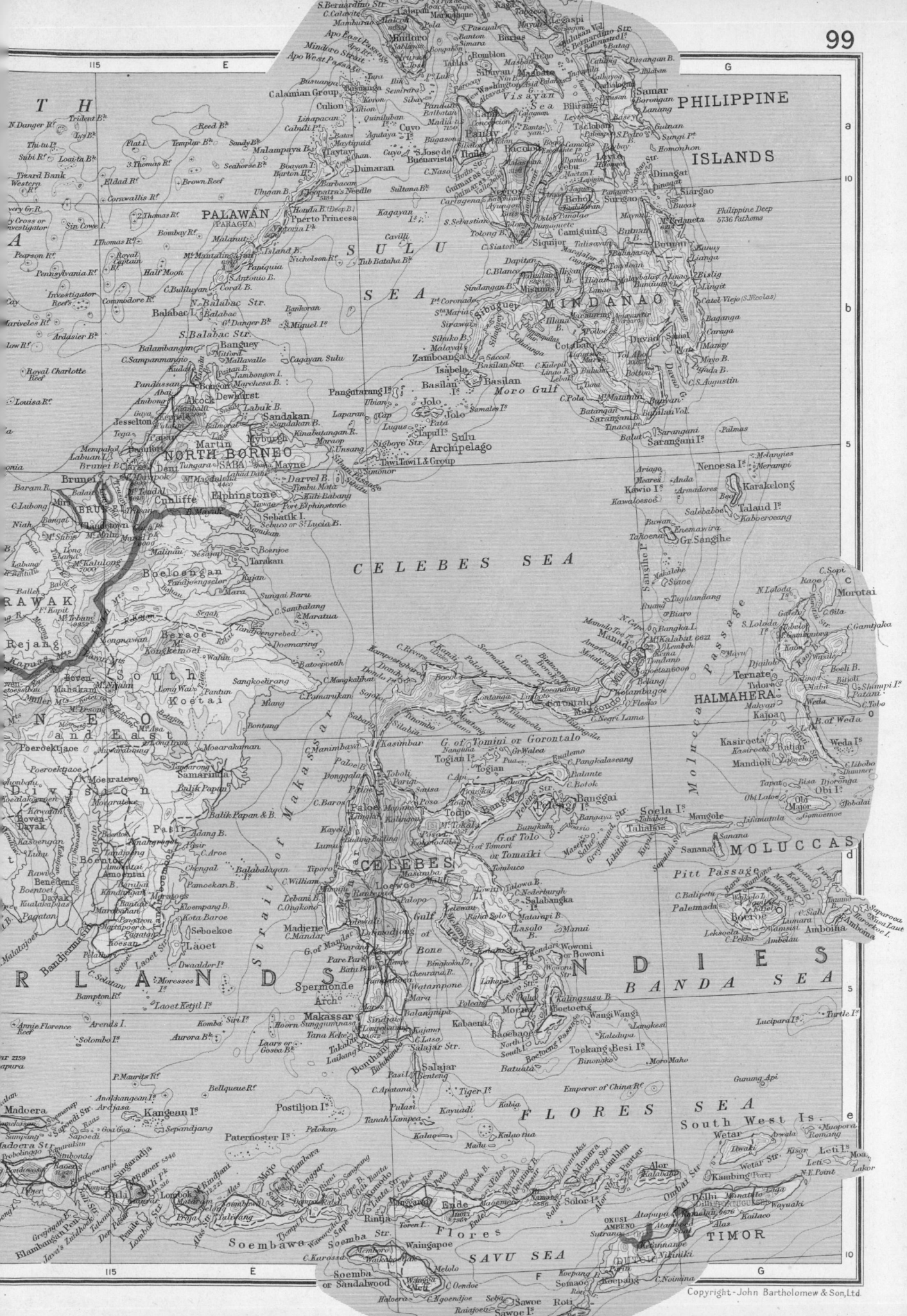

PHILIPPINE

ISLANDS

CELEBES SEA

MOLUCCAS

HALMAHERA

CELEBES

BANDA SEA

FLORES SEA

South West Is.

SAVU SEA

TIMOR

Copyright - John Bartholomew & Son, Ltd.

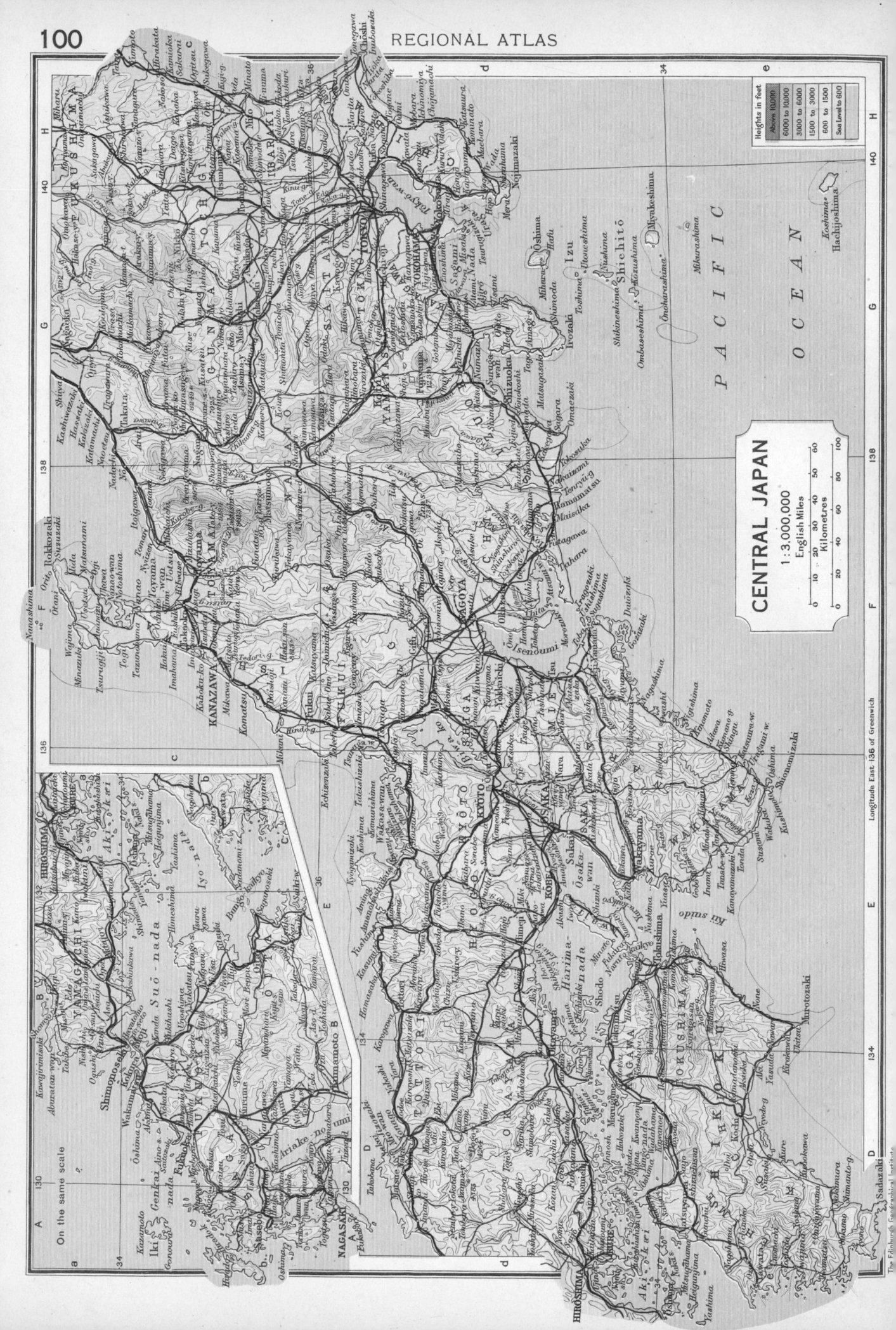

CENTRAL JAPAN
1:3,000,000
English Miles
Kilometres

PACIFIC OCEAN

On the same scale

Longitude East 136 of Greenwich

The Edinburgh Geographical Institute

Heights in feet
Above 10,000
6000 to 10,000
3000 to 6000
1500 to 3000
600 to 1500
Sea Level to 600

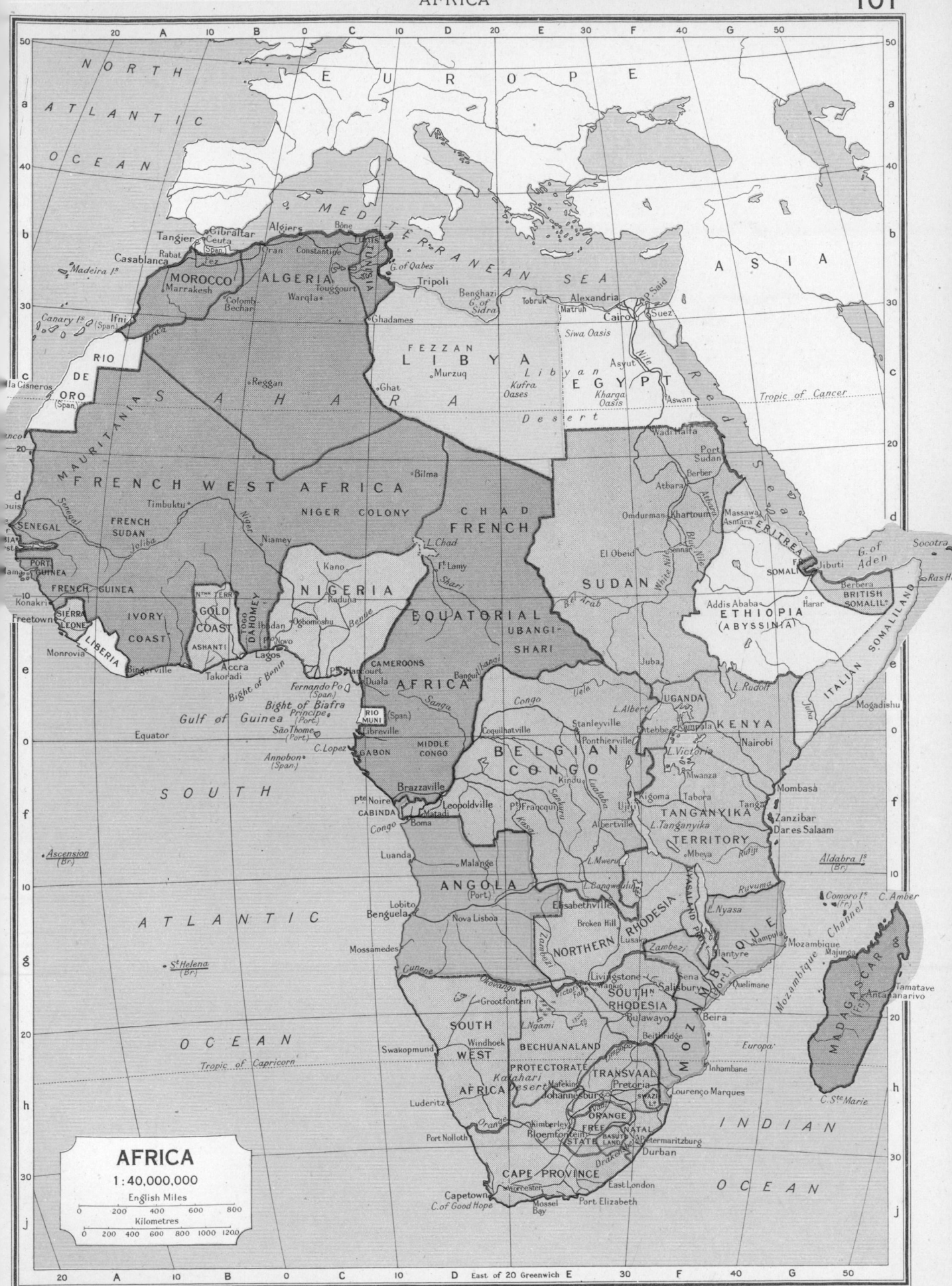

AFRICA
1:40,000,000
English Miles
0   200   400   600   800
Kilometres
0   200 400 600 800 1000 1200

The Edinburgh Geographical Institute

Copyright – John Bartholomew & Son, Ltd.

NORTH AFRICA

1 : 5,000,000

English Miles

| 0 | 20 | 40 | 60 | 80 | 100 |

Kilometres

| 0 | 20 | 40 | 60 | 80 | 100 | 120 | 140 | 160 |

Longitude West 4 of Greenwich

The Edinburgh Geographical Institute

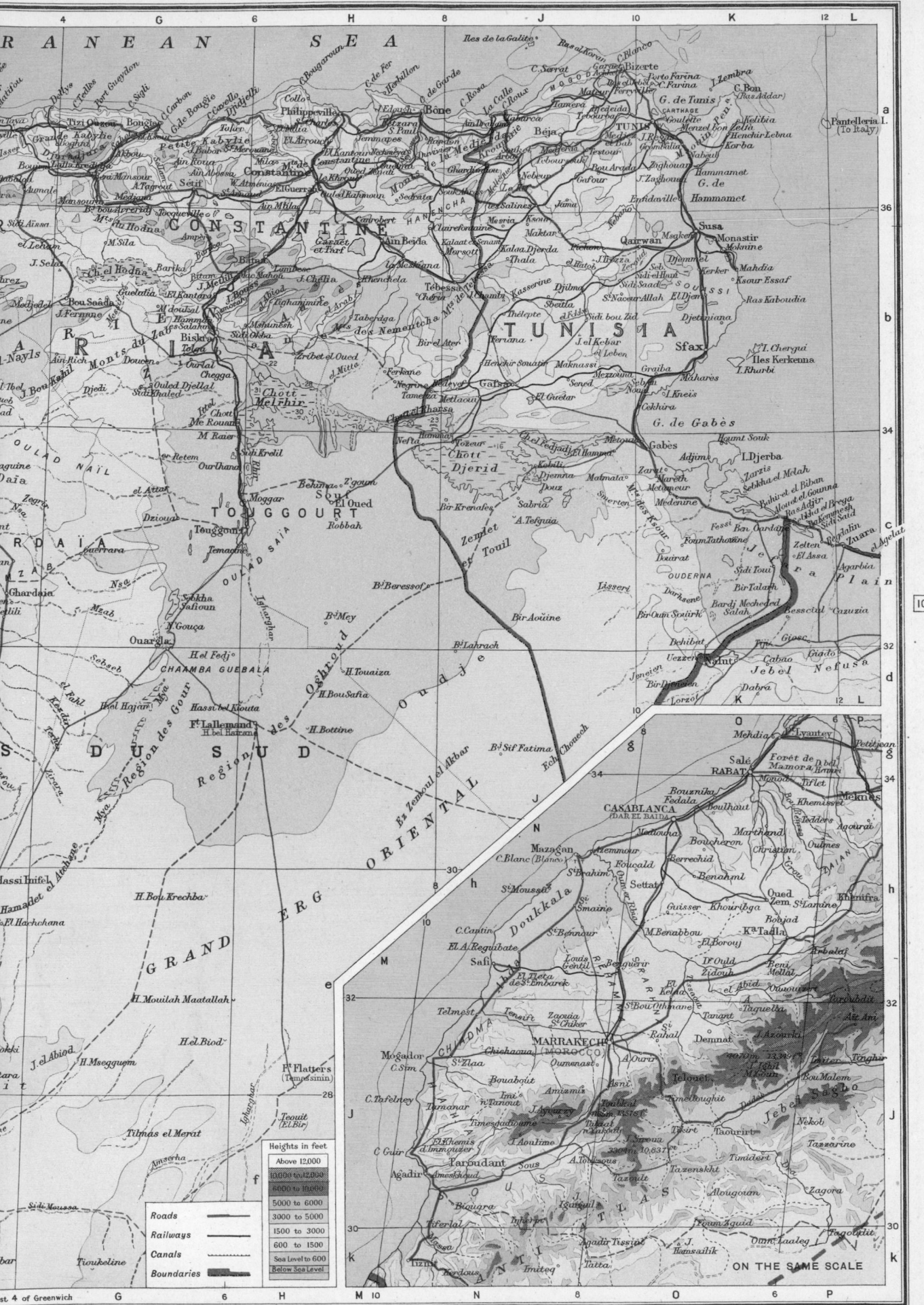

Copyright-John Bartholomew & Son,Ltd.

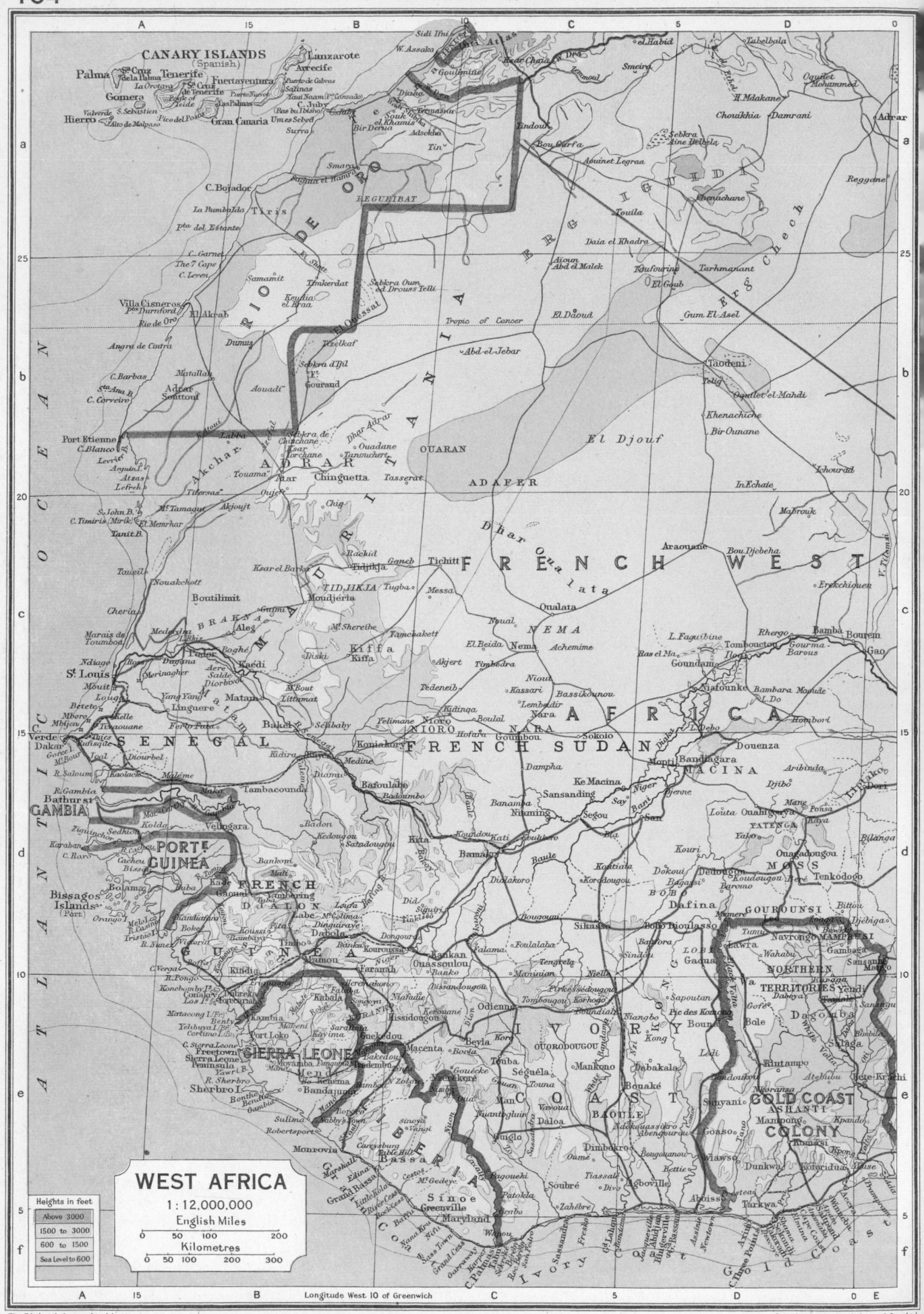

Copyright.-John Bartholomew & Son, Ltd.

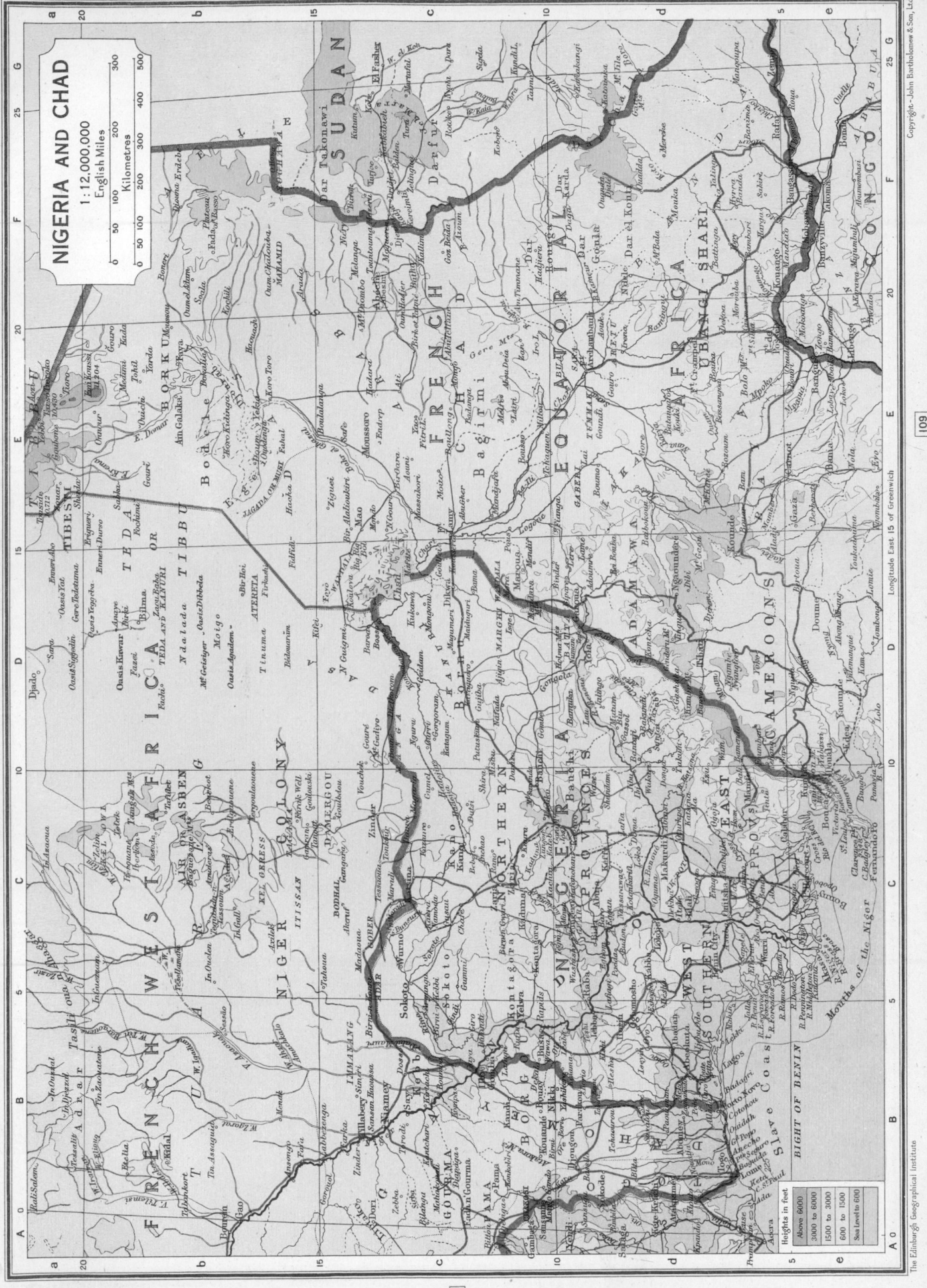

NIGERIA AND CHAD
1 : 12,000,000
English Miles

Copyright-John Bartholomew & Son, Ltd.

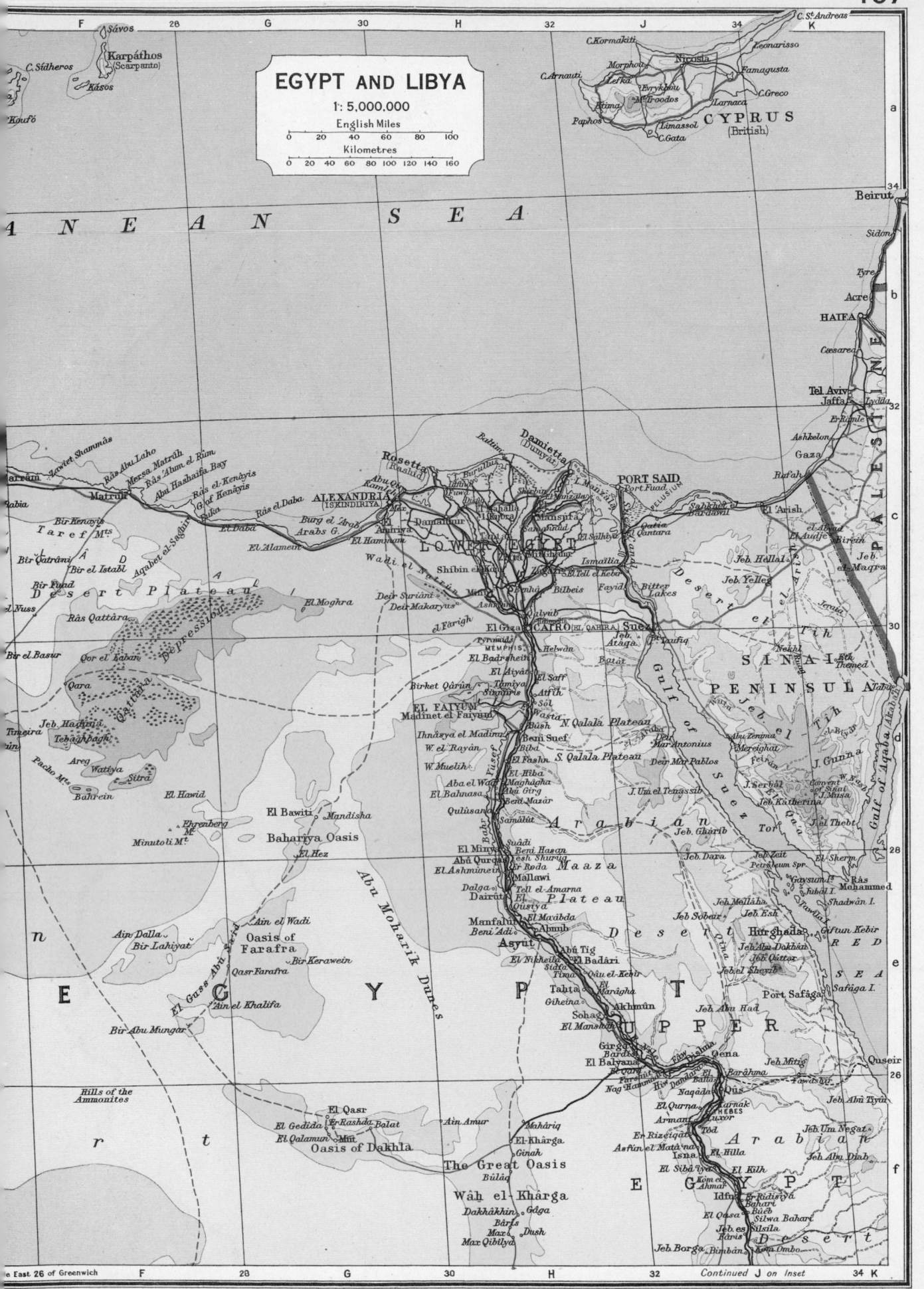

EGYPT AND LIBYA

1 : 5,000,000

English Miles

0 20 40 60 80 100

Kilometres

0 20 40 60 80 100 120 140 160

MEDITERRANEAN SEA

CYPRUS (British)

C. St. Andreas
C. Kormakiti
Leonarisso
Morphou
Nicosia
Famagusta
C. Arnauti
Lefka
Evrykhou
Troodos
Larnaca
C. Greco
Kima
Paphos
Limassol
C. Gata

Beirut
Sidon
Tyre
Acre
HAIFA
Cæsarea
Tel Aviv
Jaffa
Lydda
Er Ramle
Ashkelon
Gaza
Rafah
PALESTINE

Karpáthos (Scarpanto)
C. Sídheros
Kásos
Koufó
Sávos

LOWER EGYPT
Matruh
Jawlet Shammâs
Râs Abu Laho
Mersa Matrûh
Râs 'Alum el Rûm
Abu Hashaifa Bay
Râs el-Kenâyis
Gl. of Kenâyis
Duka
Râs el Daba
El Daba
El 'Alamein
El Hammân
El Amariya
Rosetta (Rashid)
Abu Qir
Kom
ALEXANDRIA (ISKINDIRIYA)
Max
Damanhûr
Wadi el Natrûn
Shibin el Kôm
Damietta (Dumyat)
Baltim
L. Burullus
Fuwa
Dikirs
Mahalla
El Mansra
Samanûd
Mit Ghamr
L. Manzala
Shirbin
PORT SAID
Port Fuad
Jeb. Hellal
El 'Arish
Sabkhet el Bardawil
Qatia
Qantara
El Audje
Bireïn
Jeb. Yelleg

Deir Suriâni
Deir Makaryus
el Fârigh
El Moghra
Deir Abu Maqraus
Ashmun
Benha
Senha
Bilbeis
Fayid
Bitter Lakes
Ismaïlia
El Tell el Kebir
Faqus
Jeb. Maghra
Jerula
SINAI PENINSULA
Jebel el Tih
Nekhl
Eth Themed
Tâba

Taref Mts
Bir Qatrâni
Bir el Istabl
Aqabet el-Seghir
Bir Fuad
El Nuss
Bir el Basur
Ras Qattâra
Qara
Qor el Laban
Qattâra Depression
Jeb. Hashnia
Tebaghbagh
Tingra
Areg
Watiya
Pacho Mt.
Bahrein
Minuto li Mt.
Sitra
El Hawid
Ehrenberg Mt.

Desert Plateau
El Gizah
CAIRO (EL QAHIRA)
Pyramids MEMPHIS
El Badrsheit
El Aiyât
El Saff
Atfih
Birket Qârûn
Tamiya
Sinnûris
Bûsh
N Qalala Plateau
Helwân
Batât
Suez
Jeb. Ataqa
Pt Taufiq
Mar Antonius
Abu Zenîma
Mereighat
Feirân
J. Serbâl
Convent of Sinai
Jeb. Katherina
J. Musa
J. Um el Tenassib
Tor
Gulf of Suez
El Thebt
W. Sudr
Wann Qaa

EL FAIYÛM
Madinet el Faiyûm
Ihnâsya el Madîna
W. el Rayân
W. Muelih
El Fashn
El Hîba
Maghâgha
Abu Girg
Beni Mazâr
Samalût
Aba el Wadi
El Bahnasa
Qulûsana
Suâdi
Beni Hasan
Esh Shurya
Maza
Abu Qurqas
El Ashmunein
Dalga
Er Roda
Mallawi
Tell el-Amarna
Dairût
El Qusiya
El Maabda
Manfalut
Beni Adi
Abnub
Asyut
Abu Tig
El Badâri
El Nukheila
Sidfa
Tima
Qau el-Kebir
Tahta
El Maragha
Giheina
Akhmûn
Sohag
El Manshah
Jeb. Gharib
Jeb. Dara
Jeb. Zeit
Petroleum Spr.
El Sherm
Gaysum I.
Jubal I.
Shadwân I.
Ras Mohammed
Jawlat I.
Hurghada
Giftun Kebir
Jeb. Abu Dakhân
Jeb. Qattar
Jebel Sheyib
Port Safâga
Safâga I.
RED SEA
Quseir

Arabian Desert
Qena
Maaza Plateau
Maaza Desert

Ain Dalla
Bir Lahiyat
Ain el Wadi
Oasis of Farafra
Bir Kerawein
Qasr Farafra
Ain el Khalifa
Bir Abu Mungar
Hills of the Ammonites
El Gass Abu Nord
El Bawiti
Mandisha
Baharîya Oasis
El Hez
El Minya
Abu Moharik Dunes

EGYPT
El Qasr
El Gedida
Er Rashda
Balat
El Qalamun
Mut
Oasis of Dakhla
Ain Amur
Mahâriq
El-Khârga
Ginah
The Great Oasis
Bûlâq
Wâh el-Khârga
Dakhâkhin
Gdga
Bâris
Max
Max Qiblîya
Dush

Girga
Bardis
El Balyana
Baliana
Farshût
Nag Hamadi
Hiw
Dendora
El Waqf
Barahma
Naqâda
Qûs
El Qurna
THEBES
Luxor
Karnak
Armant
Tôd
Er Rizeiqat
Asfûn el Matâ'na
El Hilla
Isna
El Sibâ'iya
El Kilh
Idfu
Kôm el Ahmar
El Qasa
El Ridisiya Bahari
Bueb
Silwa Bahari
Jeb. Kâris
Jeb. Borga
Bimbân
Kom Ombo
UPPER EGYPT
Arabian Desert
Jeb. Mitiq
Jeb. Abu Tiyûr
Jeb. Um Negat
Jeb. Abu Diab

Copyright—John Bartholomew & Son, Ltd.

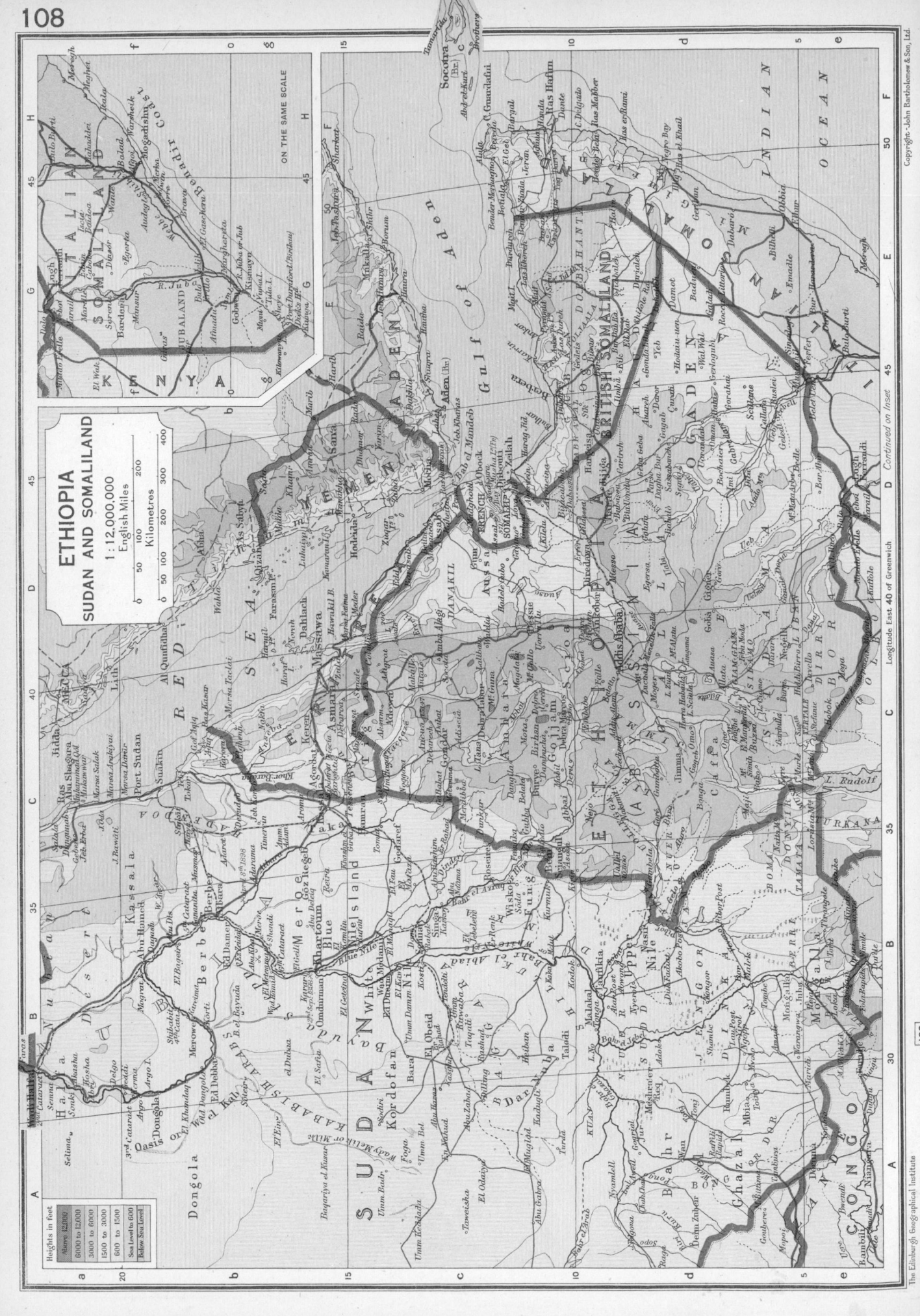

ETHIOPIA
SUDAN AND SOMALILAND
1:12,000,000
English Miles
Kilometres

Copyright. John Bartholomew & Son, Ltd.

The Edinburgh Geographical Institute

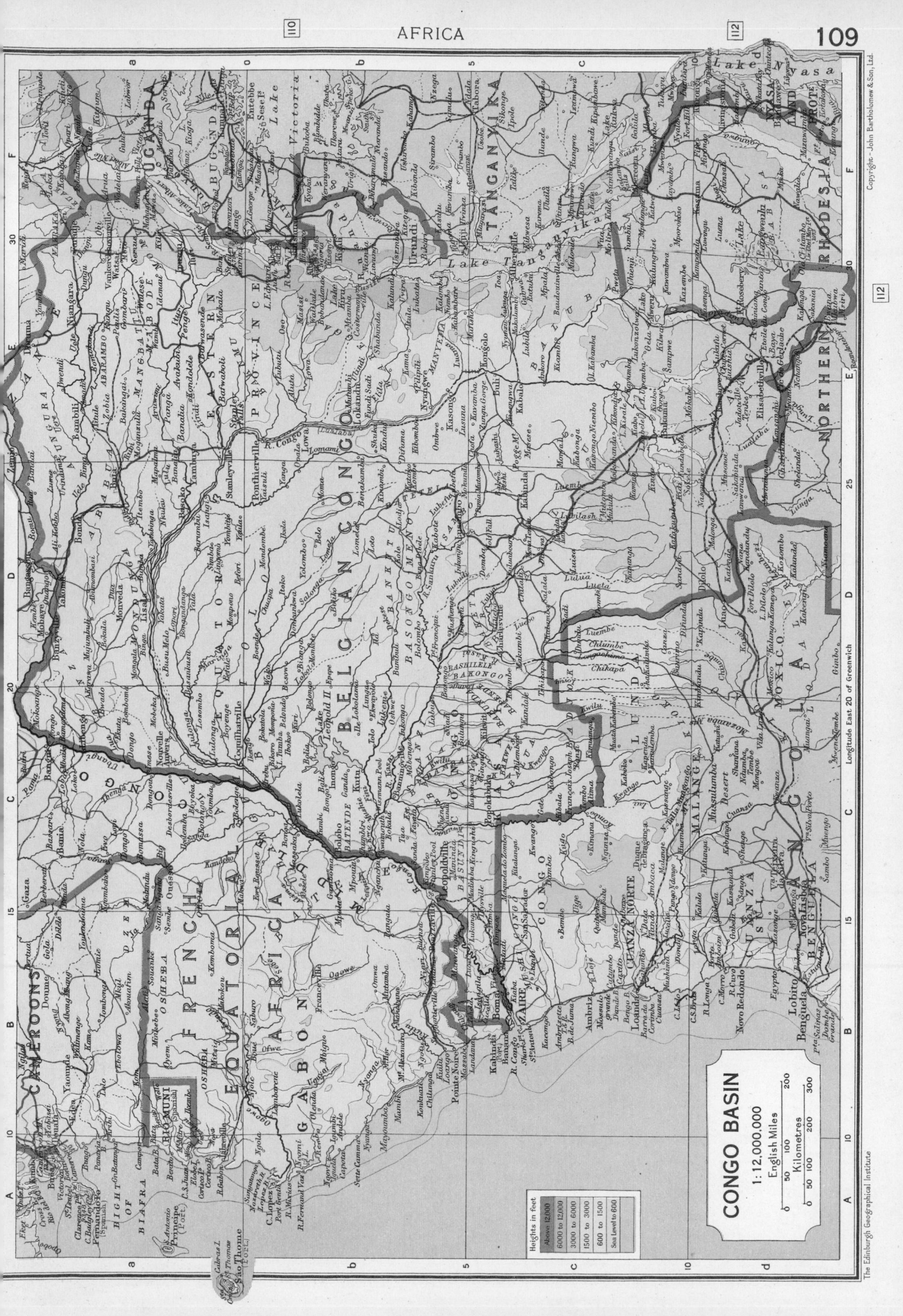

CONGO BASIN

1:12,000,000

English Miles

Kilometres

Heights in feet

| Above 12000 |
| 6000 to 12000 |
| 3000 to 6000 |
| 1500 to 3000 |
| 600 to 1500 |
| Sea Level to 600 |

Copyright - John Bartholomew & Son, Ltd.

The Edinburgh Geographical Institute

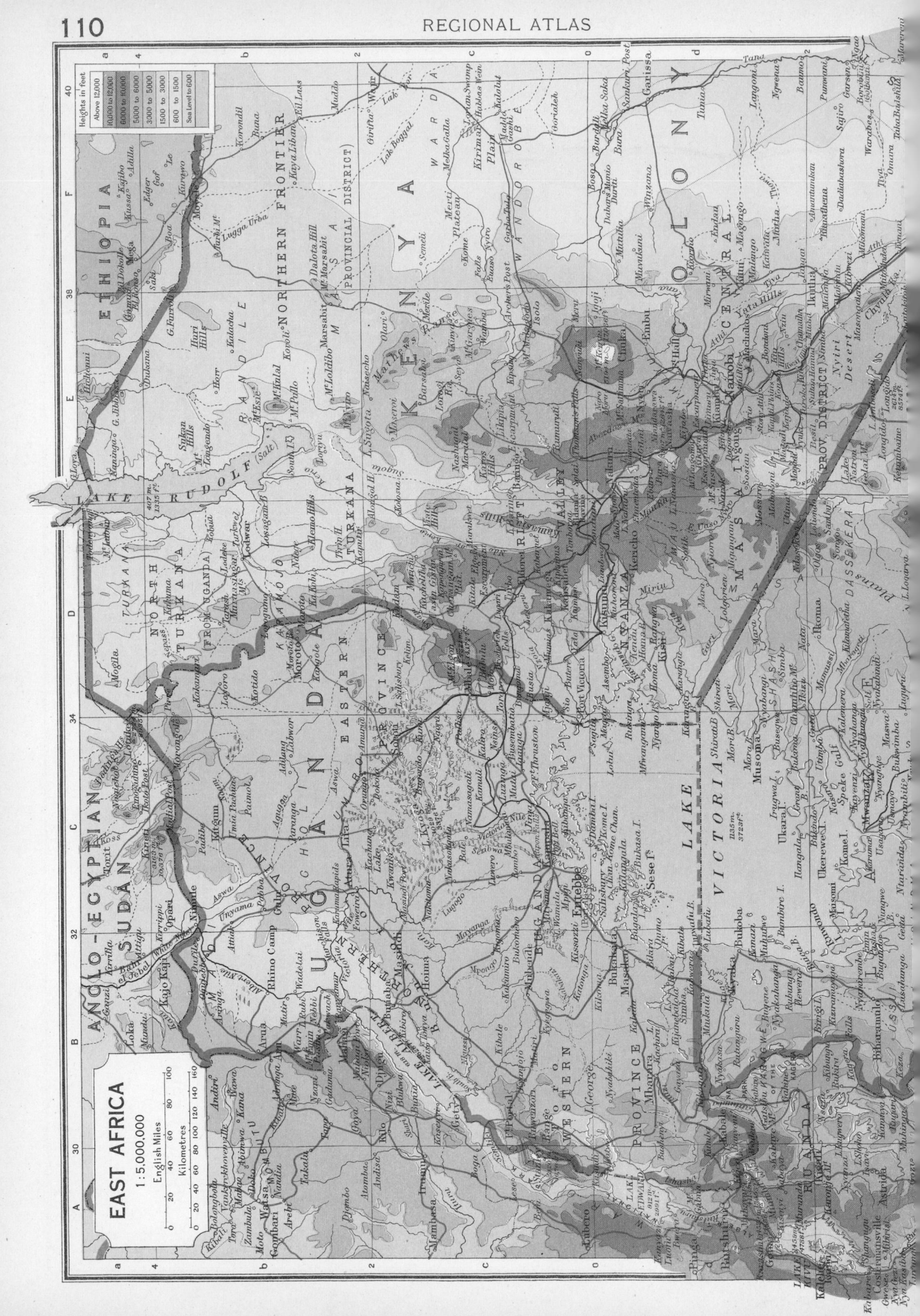
EAST AFRICA
1:5,000,000
English Miles
0 20 40 60 80 100
Kilometres
0 20 40 60 80 100 120 140 160
Heights in feet
Above 12,000
10,000 to 12,000
6000 to 10,000
5000 to 6000
3000 to 5000
1500 to 3000
600 to 1500
Sea Level to 600
ANGLO-EGYPTIAN SUDAN
ETHIOPIA
UGANDA
KENYA COLONY
NORTHERN FRONTIER (PROVINCIAL DISTRICT)
NORTH TURKANA (FROM UGANDA)
TURKANA
LAKE RUDOLF (Salt)
EASTERN PROVINCE
NORTHERN PROVINCE
WESTERN PROVINCE
BUGANDA
NYANZA
RIFT VALLEY
MASAI PROV. DISTRICT
CENTRAL
LAKE VICTORIA
LAKE ALBERT
LAKE EDWARD
LAKE KIVU
RUANDA
Kampala
Entebbe
Nairobi
Kisumu
Mombasa

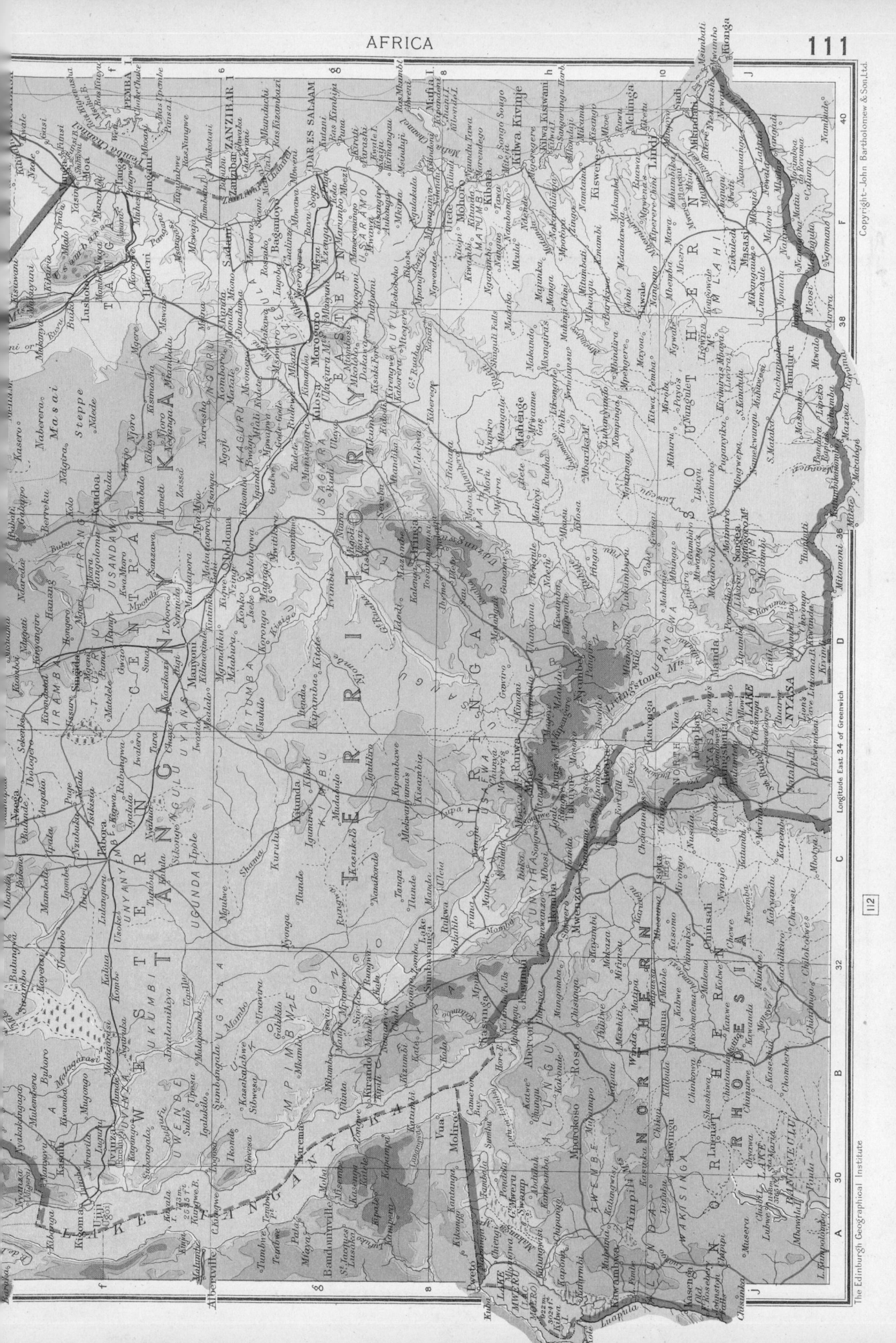

Copyright–John Bartholomew & Son, Ltd.

The Edinburgh Geographical Institute

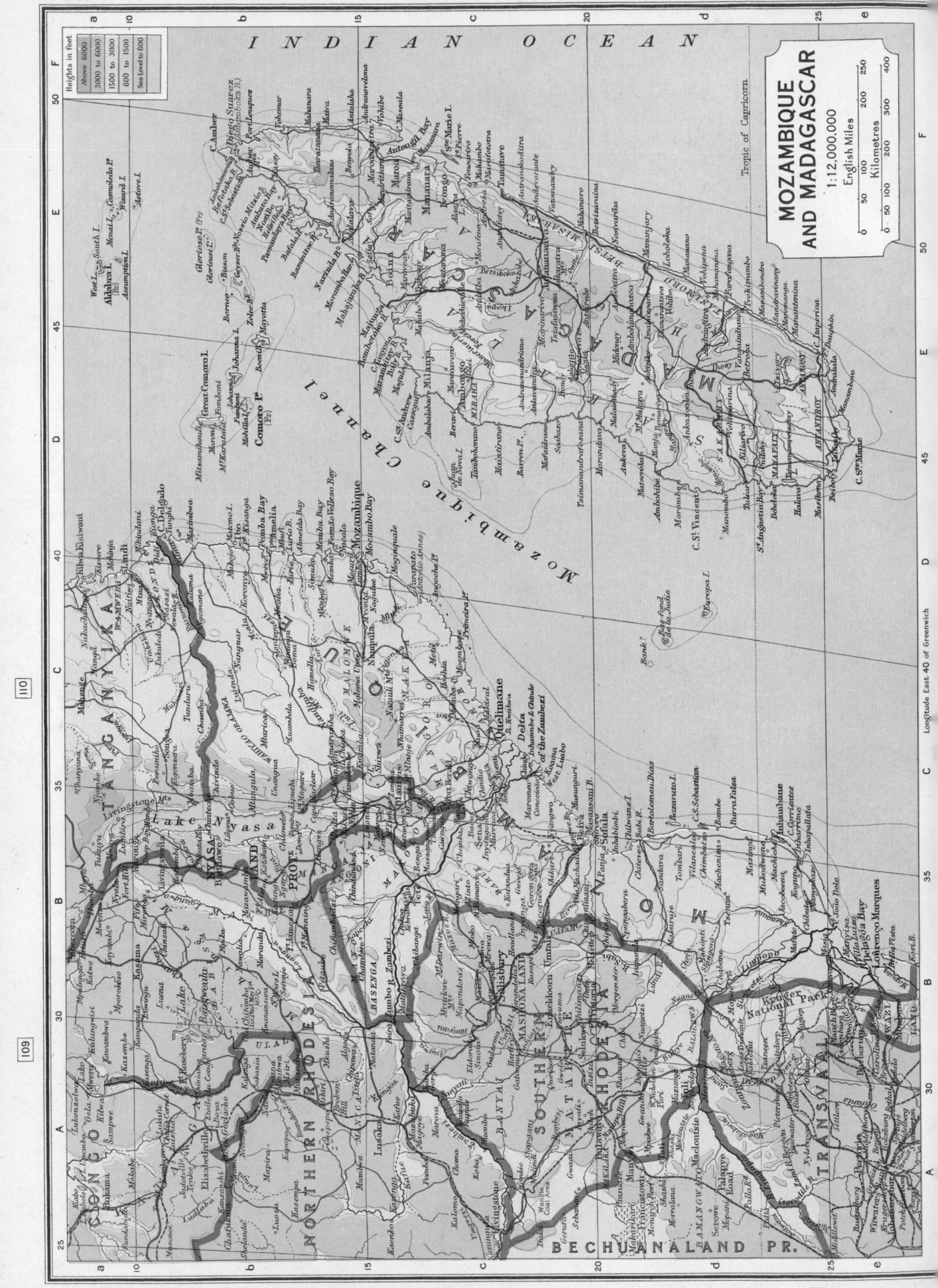

MOZAMBIQUE
AND MADAGASCAR

1:12,000,000
English Miles
Kilometres

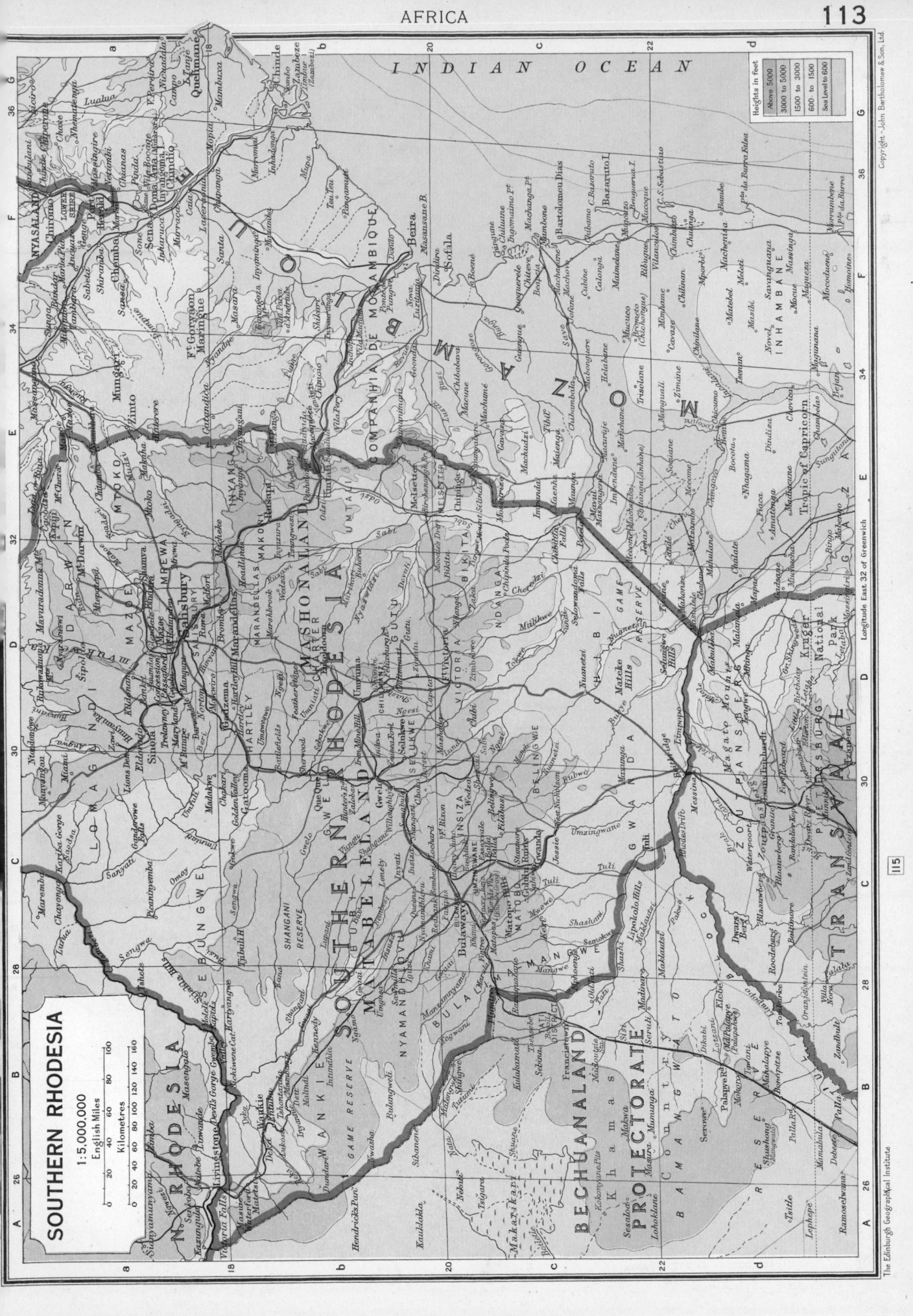

INDIAN OCEAN

SOUTHERN RHODESIA
1:5,000,000
English Miles

Kilometres

SOUTHERN RHODESIA

MASHONALAND

MATABELELAND

BECHUANALAND PROTECTORATE

TRANSVAAL

COMPANHIA DE MOÇAMBIQUE

Tropic of Capricorn

Beira

Sofala

INHAMBANE

Bulawayo

Salisbury

Victoria Falls

Copyright-John Bartholomew & Son, Ltd.

The Edinburgh Geographical Institute

115

BECHU

PROTE

SOUTH-WEST

GREAT NAMA LAND

AFRICA

Maltahöhe

MALTAHÖHE

Nanansib Gibeon
Plateau

Hanam
Plateau
Gt'Bruckarez

Tiraz
Mts

Bethanie

Sylvia H.

Lüderitz

Elizabeth Pt.
Elizabeth B.
Possession I.
Prinzenbucht.
Pomona
Granitberg
Bogenfels

Angraz
Yuldaz

Chamais B.
C. Dernberg

Kolmanskop
Grasplatz
Wüstenkönig

Keetmanshoop

KEETMANSHOOP

BETHANIE

Little
Karaz
Berg
Haloog

Richtberg

S. Namiziz

Chamaites
Churutabis

Kleinkarus

Grunau

Karasburg

WARMBAD

Warmbad

Haib

Hogeis

ATLANTIC

OCEAN

Sendeling's Drift

Annis Fontein

Alexander B.

Port Nolloth
McDougall Bay

Little
Nama Land

Little
Bushman Land

Steinkopf

Anenous

Nababeep
Concordia
O'Okiep

Springbok
Vogel Klip

NAMA

LAND

Buffels

Naas Naas Pt.

Kamieskroon

Leliefontein
Komies Sector B.

Gamoep

Hondeklip
Baai

Wallekraal

Garies

Lange
berg

Kreefte B.

Kotzerust

CALVINIA

Loeriesfontein

Bitterfontein
Bokkeveld B.
Nieuwrust

VAN RHYNSDORP

Koekenaap

Vanrhynsdorp

Olifants

Klipraz Kop

Lamberts Bay

Graauwater

Clanwilliam

CLANWILLIAM

Cedarberg

Whuppertal

Redelinghuis

St. Helena Fontein

Citrusdal

Cold
Bokkeveld

C. Columbine
Vredenburg

St. Helena

C.S'Martin

Aurora

PIQUETBERG

Hoedjes Bay
Saldanha B.

Piquetberg

Porterville

Winterhoek

CERES

Moorreesburg

Hopefield
Bridgetown

MALMESBURY

Darling

Malmesbury

Mamre

Kalabas
Philadelphia

Hottentots

Table Bay

Tulbagh

Wellington

WORCESTER

Hex Riv.

MONTAGU

PAARL

Paarl

Worcester

Robertson

CAPETOWN

Table Mt.
Hout B.

Stellenbosch

Somerset W.

Strand

Zwart B.

Simonstown

False B.

Cape of Good Hope

Sandown Bay

Hangklip

CAPE

FRASERBURG

Fraserburg

Middelpost

Sutherland

SUTHERLAND

Komsberg Mts.

Merweville

Prince Albert Rd.

Laingsburg

LAINGSBURG

Prince Albert

Kl. Swartberg

BEAUFORT WEST

Beaufort West

Nieuwveld Range

Great Karro

Little Karoo

GEORGE

Oudtshoorn

Uniondale

Swart
berg

Mossel Bay

Riversdale

RIVERSDALE

Swellendam

SWELLENDAM

Heidelberg

Port Beaufort

Bredasdorp

C. Agulhas

English B.
North Pt.
Porpoise Pt.
North East B.

Clarence B.
Georgetown
Cross Sisters Peak
Hill 1460
White
Hills
Settlement Green Mt. 2817
The Peak

Boatswain-bird
I.

S.E. Head

Portland Pt.

Red Hills
Site or
1786
Obs?

South Pt.

ASCENSION

1:400,000

Jamestown

Ruperts B.

Sugar-loaf Pt.

The Barn
2019

Lemon Valley

Prosperous B.
Longwood

Half Moon Battery
High Knoll

The Briars
Goldfast
Tom
New Longwood

Saddle
Pt.

Plantation Ho.
Cathedral

Napoleon's
Tomb

Gill Pt.

Egg I.
Casons

2704
Diana's
Peak

George I.

West Lodge

Lot's Wife

Long Range Pt.

Manatee B.
Castle Rock Pt.

ST. HELENA

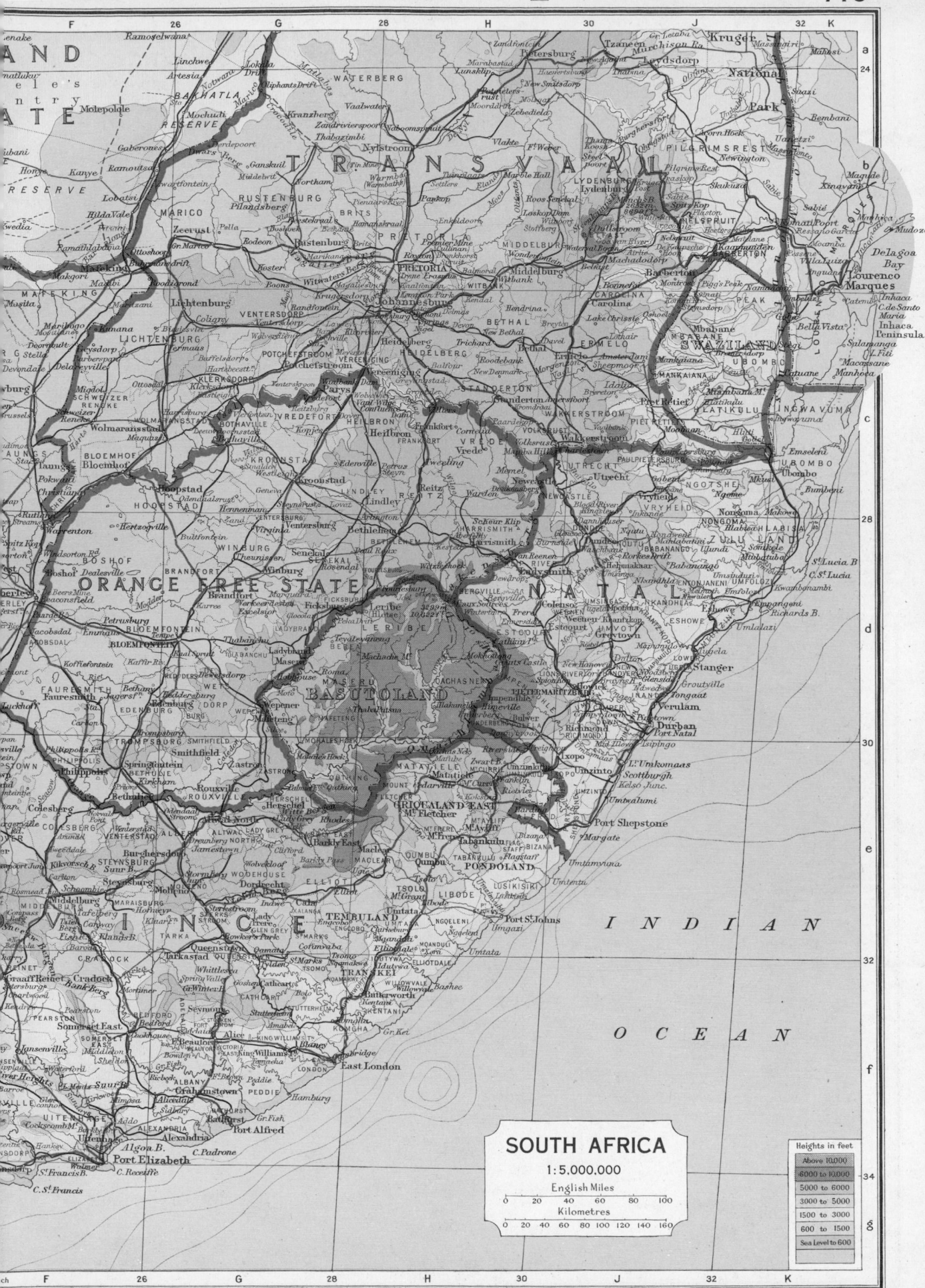

SOUTH AFRICA

1:5,000,000

English Miles

| 0 | 20 | 40 | 60 | 80 | 100 |

Kilometres

| 0 | 20 | 40 | 60 | 80 | 100 | 120 | 140 | 160 |

Heights in feet

Above 10,000
6000 to 10,000
5000 to 6000
3000 to 5000
1500 to 3000
600 to 1500
Sea Level to 600

Copyright-John Bartholomew & Son, Ltd.

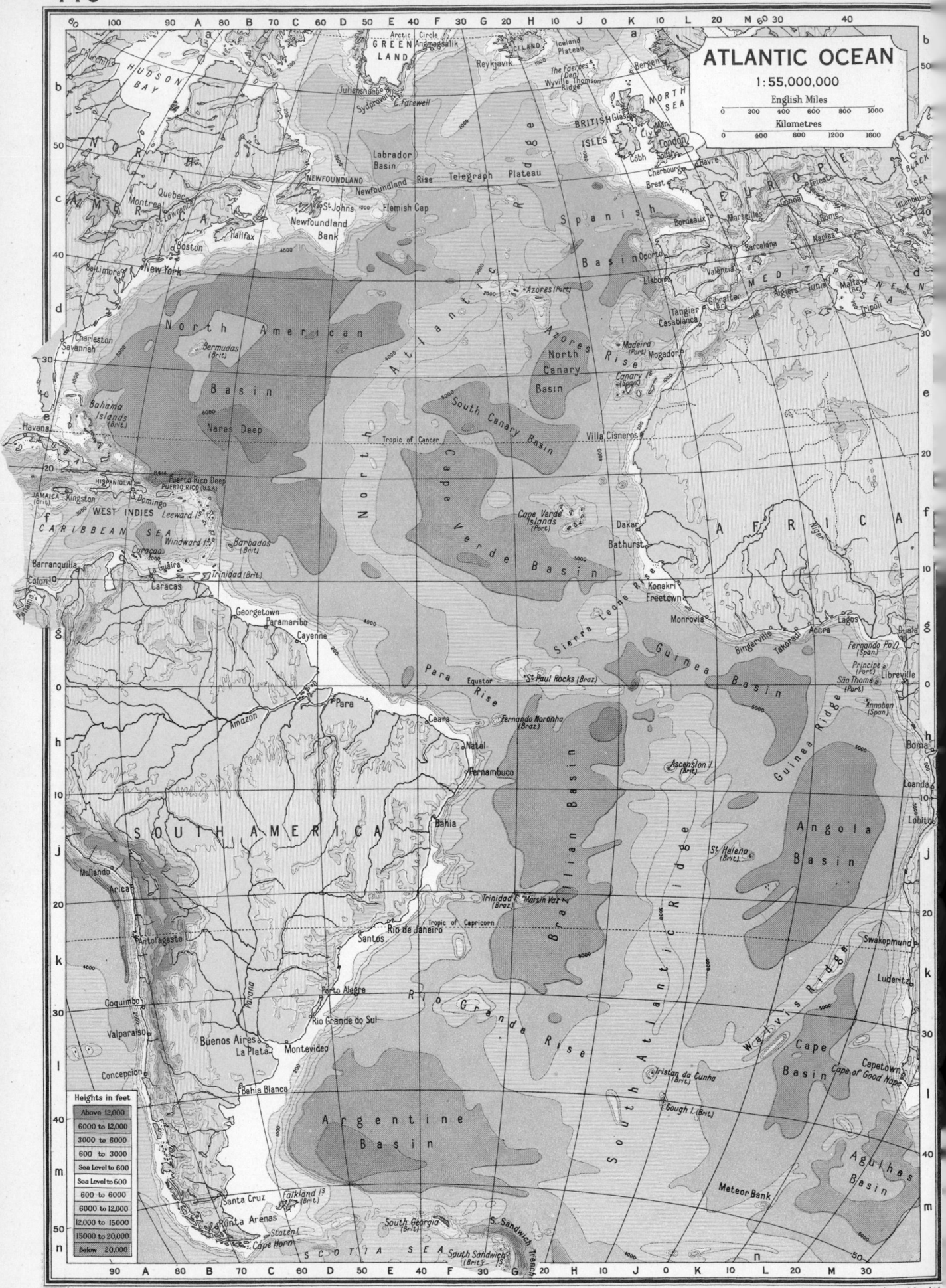

ATLANTIC OCEAN
1:55,000,000

English Miles

| 0 | 200 | 400 | 600 | 800 | 1000 |

Kilometres

| 0 | 400 | 800 | 1200 | 1600 |

GREENLAND

HUDSON BAY

NORTH AMERICA

Labrador Basin

NEWFOUNDLAND

Newfoundland Rise   Telegraph Plateau

Newfoundland Bank

Flemish Cap

Spanish Basin

BRITISH ISLES

NORTH SEA

EUROPE

MEDITERRANEAN SEA

North American Basin

Bermudas (Brit.)

Nares Deep

Bahama Islands (Brit.)

Tropic of Cancer

Azores (Port.)

Azores Rise

North Canary Basin

South Canary Basin

Canary Is.

AFRICA

Puerto Rico Deep
PUERTO RICO (U.S.A.)

HISPANIOLA

JAMAICA (Brit.)   Kingston

WEST INDIES   Leeward Is.

CARIBBEAN SEA

Barbados (Brit.)

Windward Is.

Trinidad (Brit.)

Caracas

Cape Verde Islands (Port.)

Dakar

Bathurst

Cape Verde Basin

Sierra Leone Rise

Konakri
Freetown

Monrovia

Guinea Basin

Georgetown
Paramaribo

Cayenne

Para Rise

Equator   São Paulo Rocks (Braz.)

St Paul Rocks (Braz.)

Fernando Noronha (Braz.)

SOUTH AMERICA

Amazon

Para

Ceara

Natal

Pernambuco

Bahia

Ascension I. (Brit.)

Guinea Ridge

Brazilian Basin

Angola Basin

St Helena (Brit.)

Trinidad (Braz.)   Martin Vaz

Tropic of Capricorn

Rio de Janeiro
Santos

Porto Alegre

Rio Grande do Sul

Rio Grande Rise

South Atlantic Ridge

Walvis Ridge

Swakopmund

Cape Basin

Cape of Good Hope
Capetown

Buenos Aires
La Plata   Montevideo

Bahia Blanca

Argentine Basin

Tristan da Cunha

Gough I. (Brit.)

Agulhas Basin

Heights in feet
Above 12,000
6000 to 12,000
3000 to 6000
600 to 3000
Sea Level to 600
Sea Level to 600
600 to 6000
6000 to 12,000
12,000 to 15000
15000 to 20,000
Below 20,000

Santa Cruz   Falkland Is. (Brit.)

Punta Arenas

Staten I.

Cape Horn   South Georgia (Brit.)

SCOTIA SEA   South Sandwich (Brit.)

S. Sandwich Trench

Meteor Bank

The Edinburgh Geographical Institute   Copyright - John Bartholomew & Son Ltd.

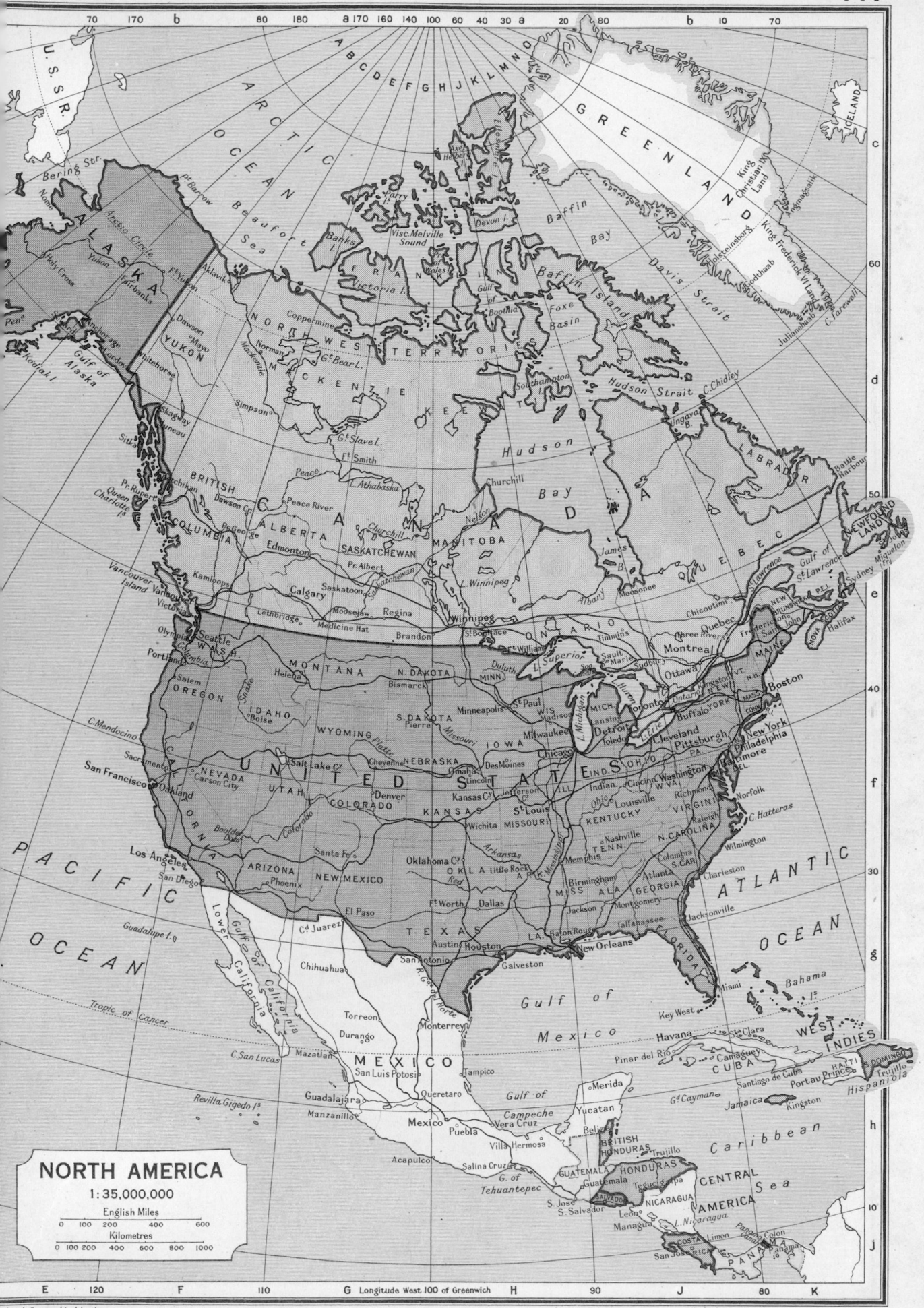

NORTH AMERICA

1 : 35,000,000

English Miles

0 100 200 400 600

Kilometres

0 100 200 400 600 800 1000

Edinburgh Geographical Institute

Copyright - John Bartholomew & Son, Ltd.

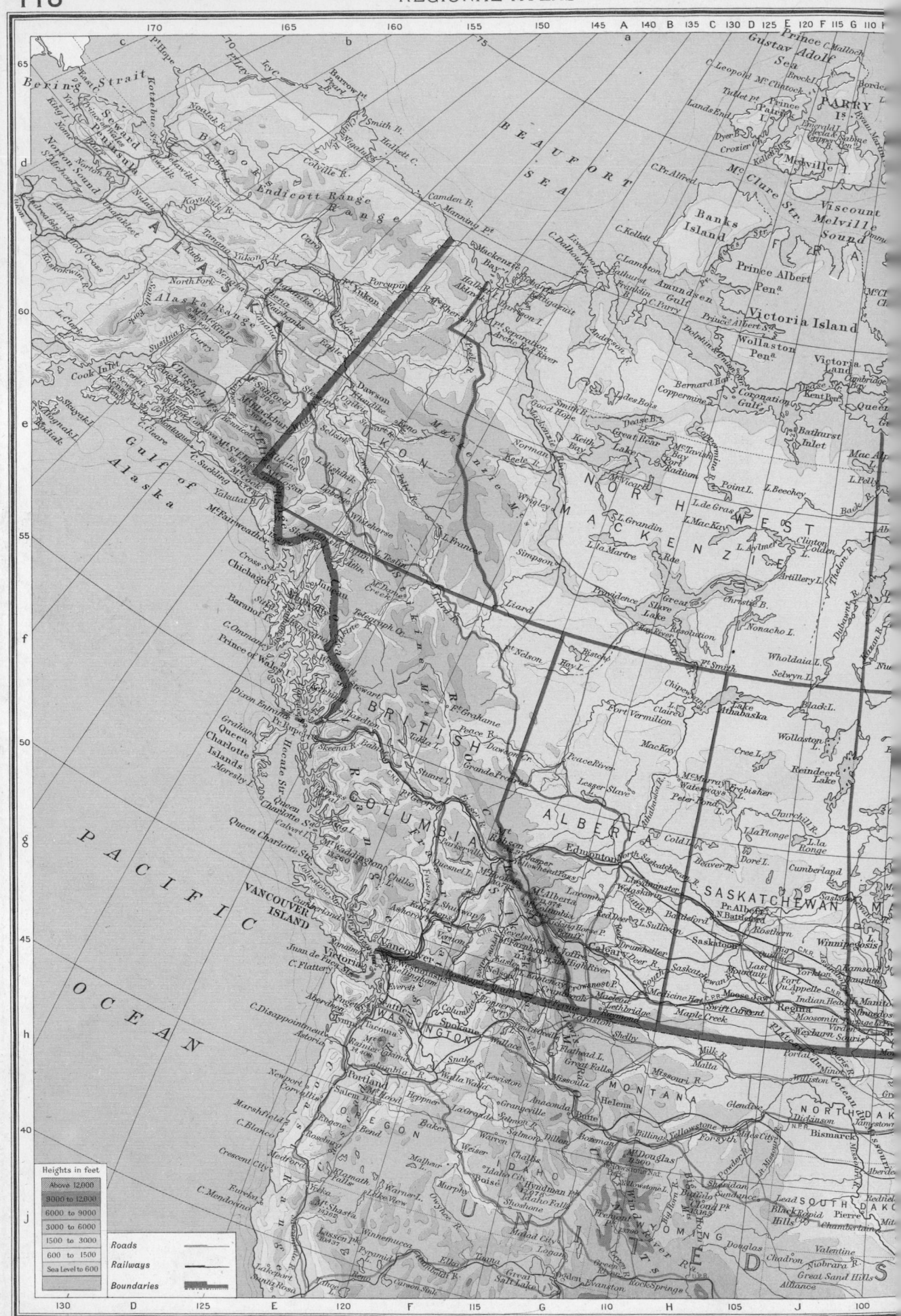
Heights in feet
Above 12,000
9000 to 12,000
6000 to 9000
3000 to 6000
1500 to 3000
600 to 1500
Sea Level to 600
Roads
Railways
Boundaries
PACIFIC OCEAN
BEAUFORT SEA
Gulf of Alaska
ALASKA
YUKON
BRITISH COLUMBIA
ALBERTA
SASKATCHEWAN
NORTH WEST
MACKENZIE
VANCOUVER ISLAND
WASHINGTON
OREGON
IDAHO
MONTANA
WYOMING
Bering Strait
Seward Peninsula
Norton Sound
Brooks Range
Endicott Range
Alaska Range
Mt McKinley
Yukon R.
Mackenzie Mts
Great Bear Lake
Great Slave Lake
Lake Athabaska
Banks Island
Victoria Island
Prince Albert Sd
Amundsen Gulf
Coronation Gulf
Melville I.
Viscount Melville Sound
Prince Gustav Adolf Sea
PARRY Is.
Queen Charlotte Islands
Prince of Wales I.
Dawson
Whitehorse
Juneau
Fairbanks
Anchorage
Prince Rupert
Edmonton
Calgary
Vancouver
Victoria
Seattle
Spokane
Portland
Saskatoon
Regina
Moose Jaw
Medicine Hat
Helena
Butte
Great Falls
Bismarck
Great Salt Lake
Yellowstone R.
Missouri R.
Peace R.
Fraser R.
Columbia R.
Snake R.
130
125
120
115
110
105
100
D
E
F
G
H
J
40
45
50
55
60
65

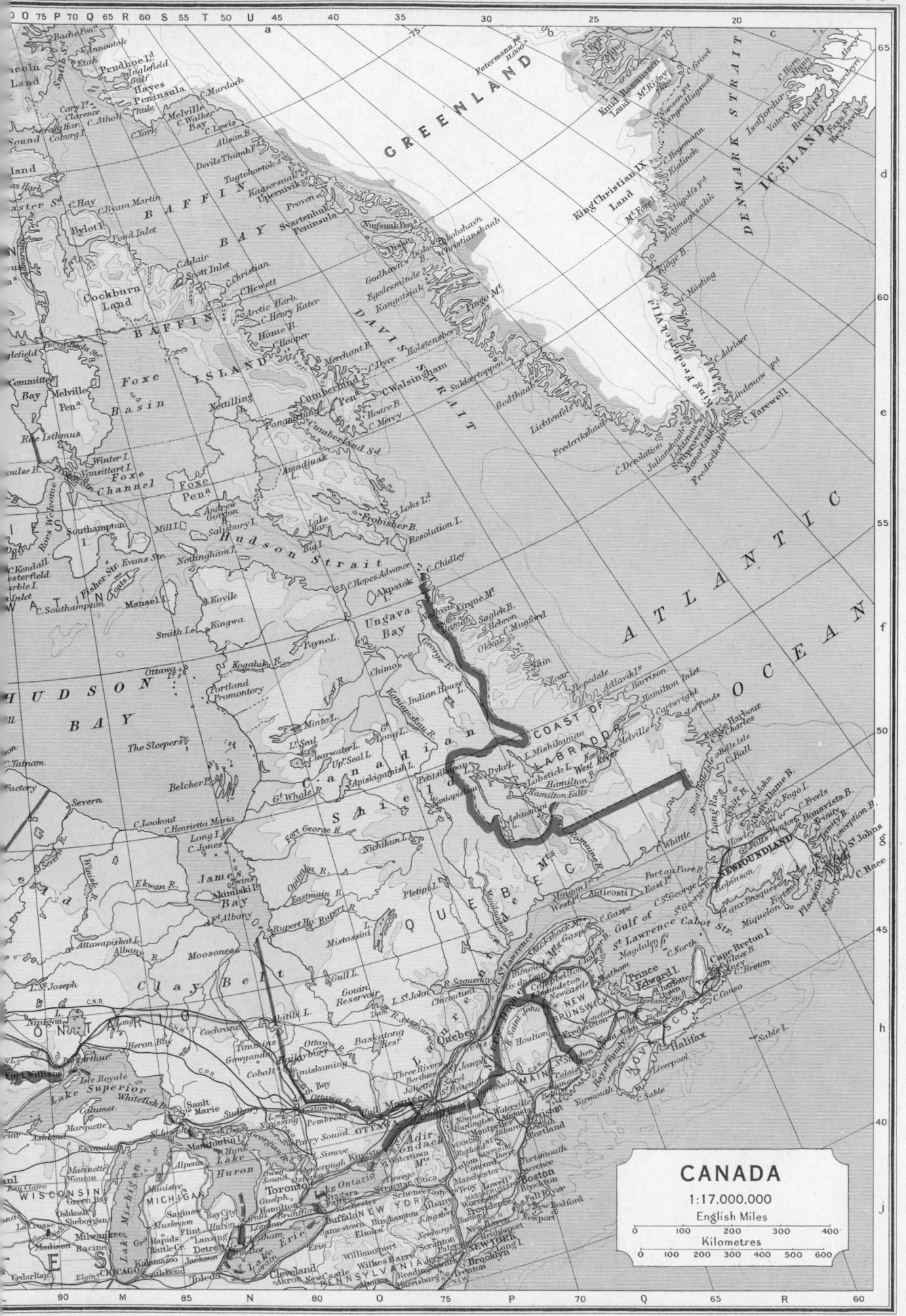

CANADA

1:17,000,000

English Miles

Kilometres

Copyright- John Bartholomew & Son, Ltd.

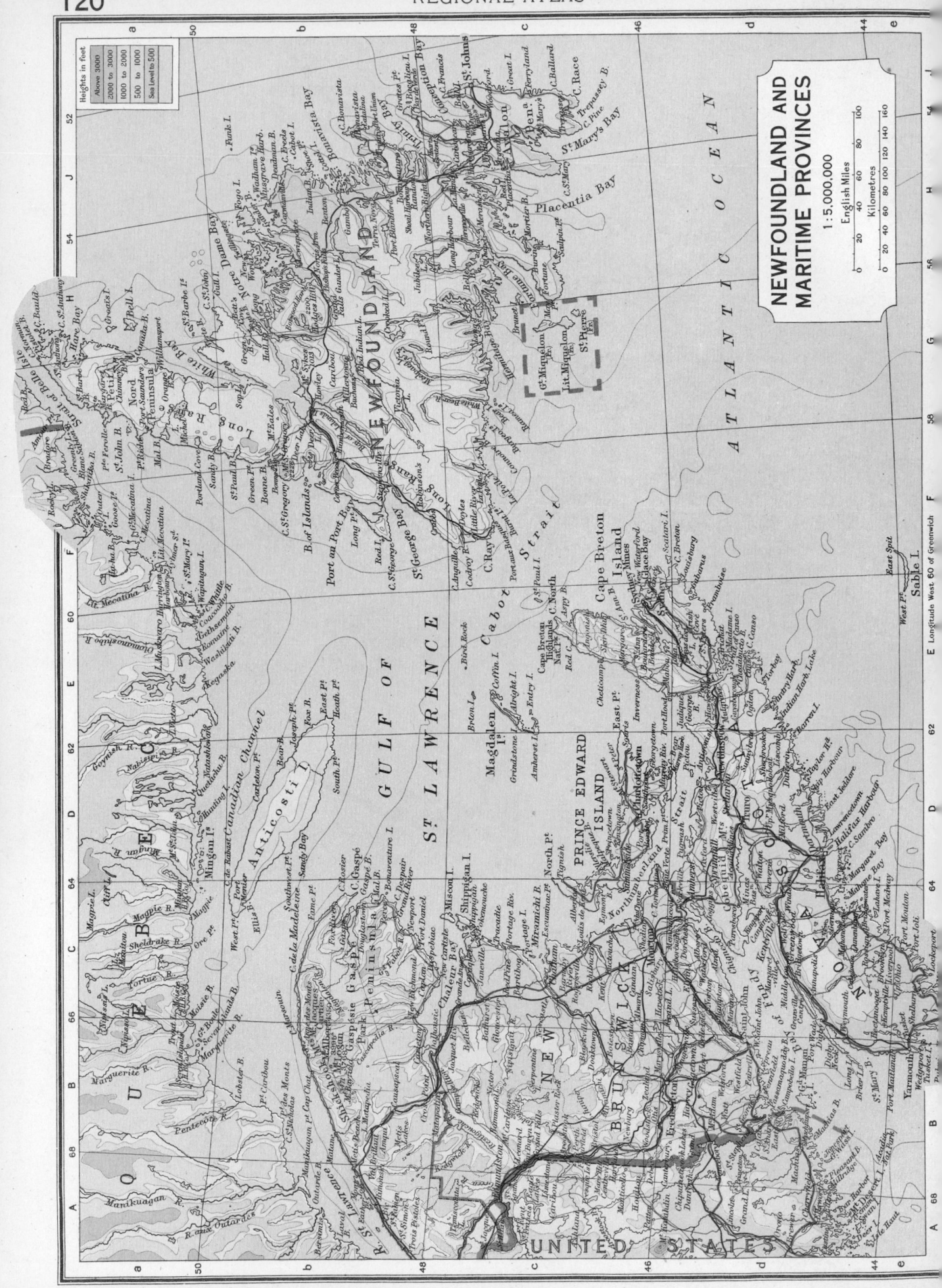

NEWFOUNDLAND AND
MARITIME PROVINCES
1:5,000,000
English Miles
Kilometres

Heights in feet.
Above 3000
2000 to 3000
1000 to 2000
500 to 1000
Sea Level to 500

ATLANTIC OCEAN

NEWFOUNDLAND

GULF OF ST. LAWRENCE

Cabot Strait

Cape Breton Island

PRINCE EDWARD ISLAND

QUEBEC

Anticosti I.

Magdalen Is.

NEW BRUNSWICK

NOVA SCOTIA

UNITED STATES

UPPER ST LAWRENCE

1 : 2,500,000

English Miles

Kilometres

Heights in Feet
Above 3000
2000 to 3000
1000 to 2000
500 to 1000
Sea Level to 500

Copyright—John Bartholomew & Son, Ltd.

Longitude West 76 of Greenwich

LAKE ONTARIO

246 Feet above Sea Level

The Edinburgh Geographical Institute

128

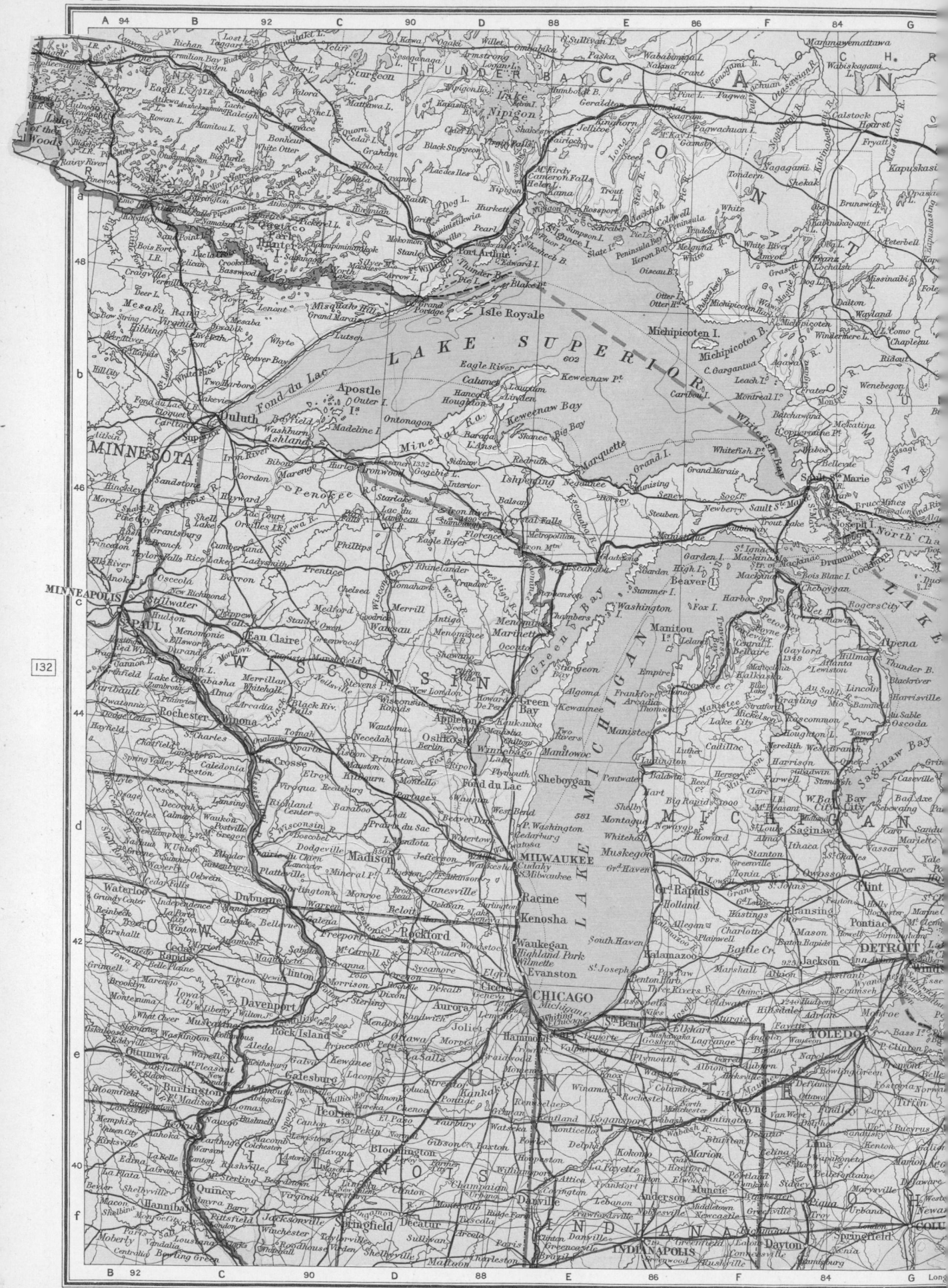

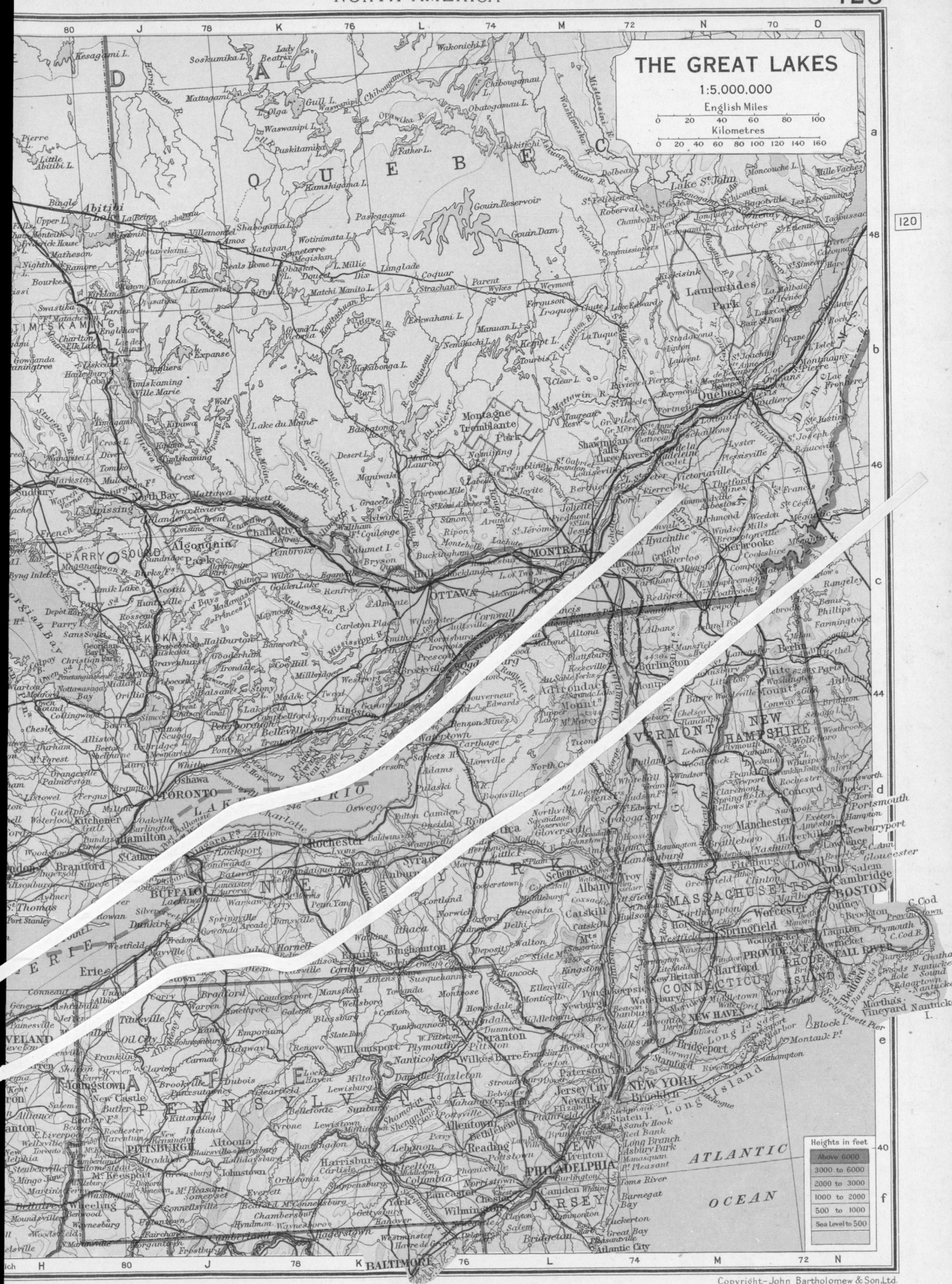

THE GREAT LAKES

1:5,000,000

English Miles

Kilometres

Copyright—John Bartholomew & Son, Ltd.

WESTERN CANADA

1:12,500,000

English Miles

Kilometres

Heights in feet

| Above 12,000 |
| 9000 to 12,000 |
| 6000 to 9000 |
| 3000 to 6000 |
| 1500 to 3000 |
| 600 to 1500 |
| Sea Level to 600 |

The Edinburgh Geographical Institute

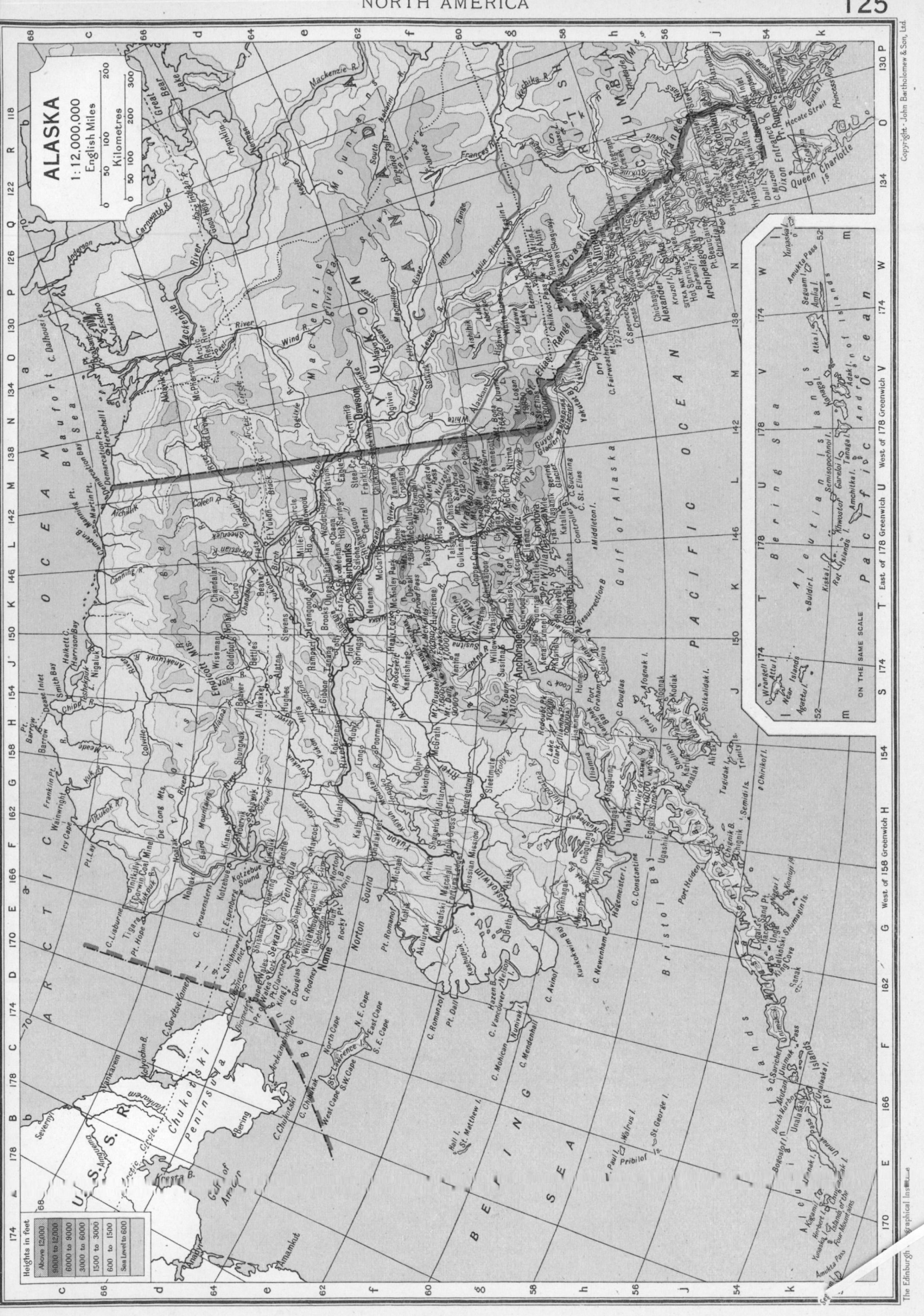

ALASKA
1:12,000,000
English Miles

Copyright. John Bartholomew & Son, Ltd.

The Edinburgh Geographical Institute

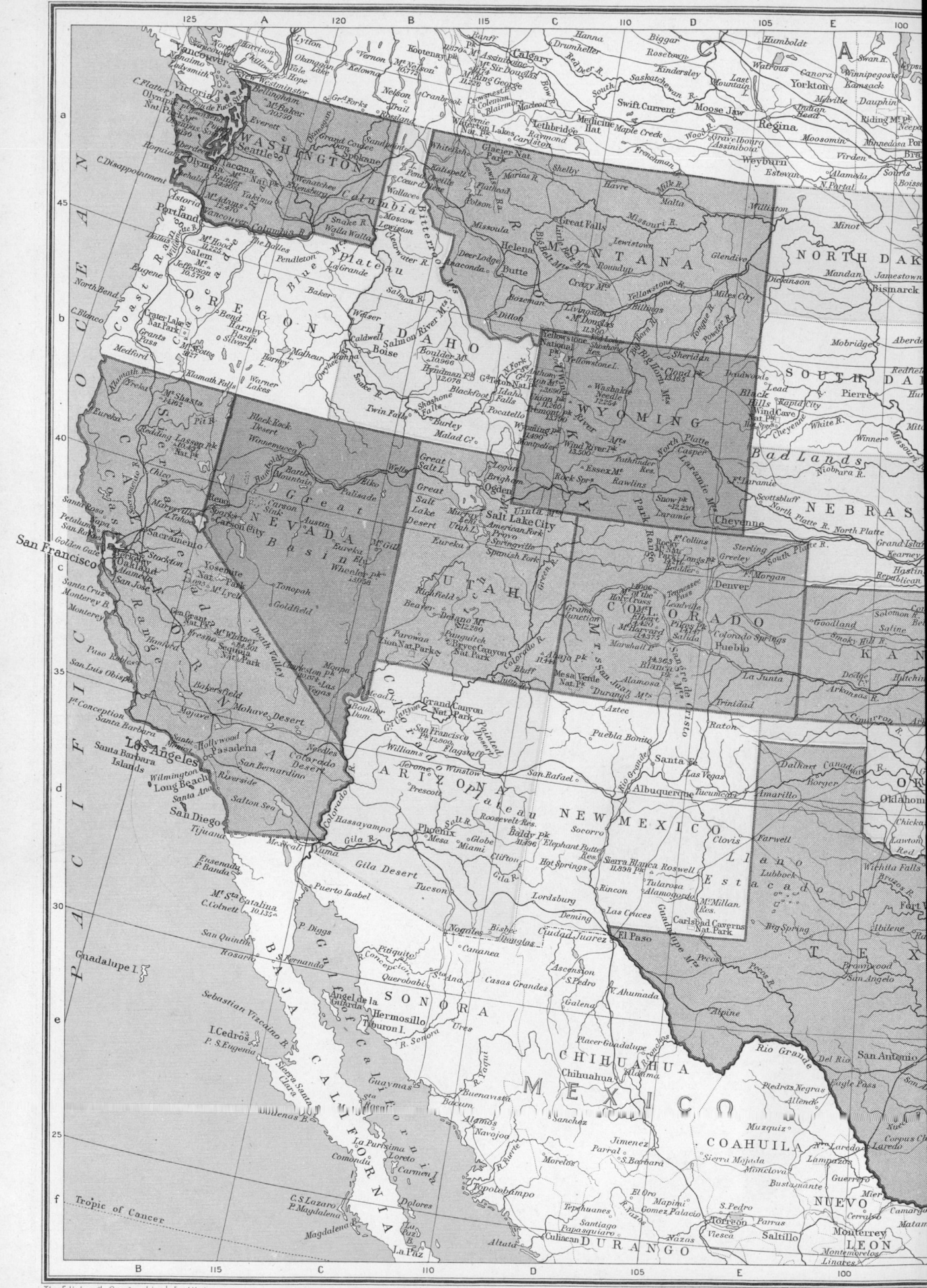

UNITED STATES

1:12,500,000

English Miles

0   50   100   200   300

Kilometres

0   50 100   200   300   400   500

Copyright-John Bartholomew & Son,Ltd.

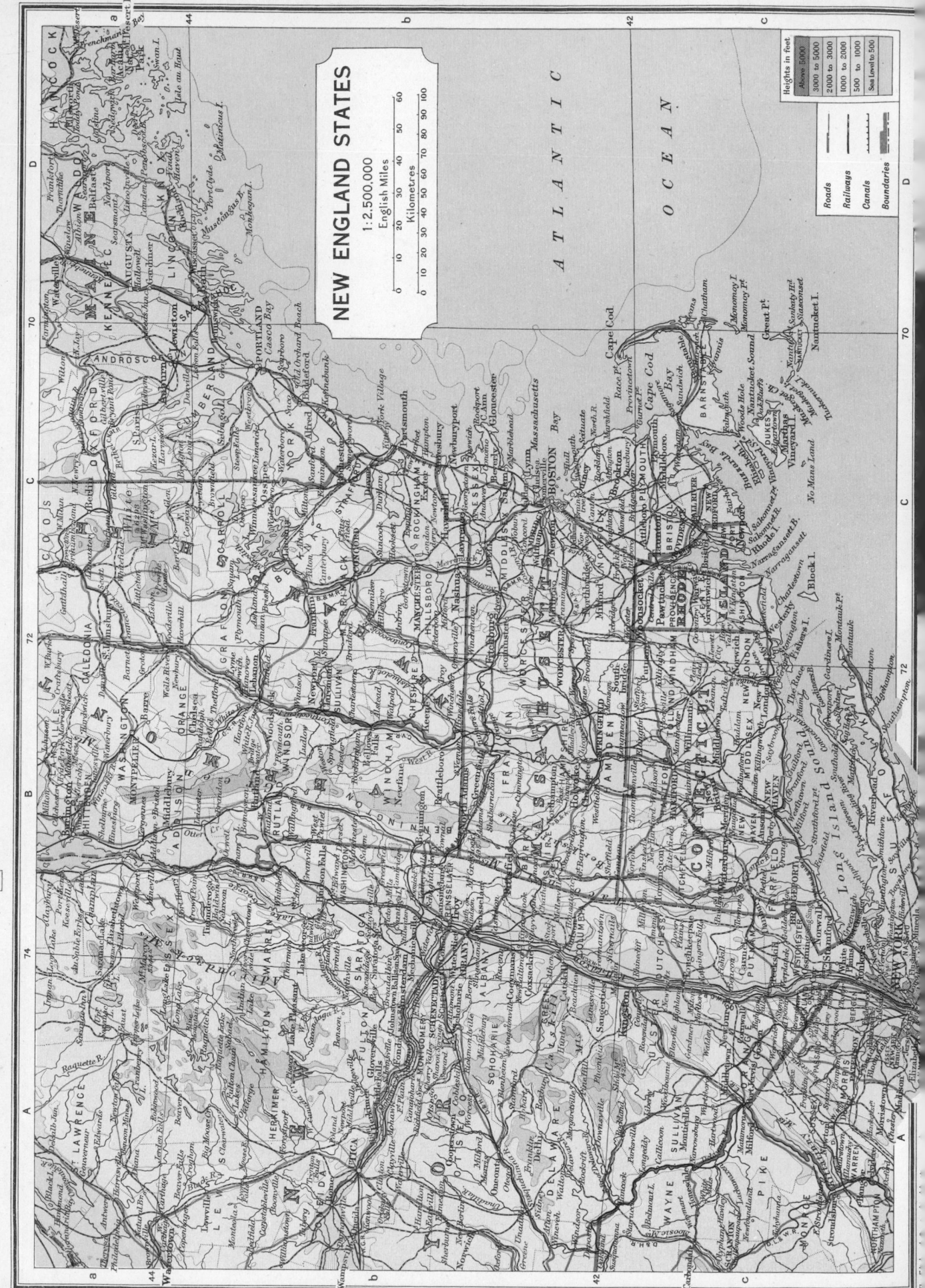
NEW ENGLAND STATES
1:2,500,000
English Miles
0 10 20 30 40 50 60
Kilometres
0 10 20 30 40 50 60 70 80 90 100
ATLANTIC
OCEAN
Heights in feet
Above 5000
3000 to 5000
2000 to 3000
1000 to 2000
500 to 1000
Sea Level to 500
Roads
Railways
Canals
Boundaries
MAINE
MASSACHUSETTS
CONNECTICUT
RHODE ISLAND
BOSTON
NEW YORK
PORTLAND
Cape Cod
Cape Cod Bay
Massachusetts Bay
Long Island Sound
Nantucket Sound
121

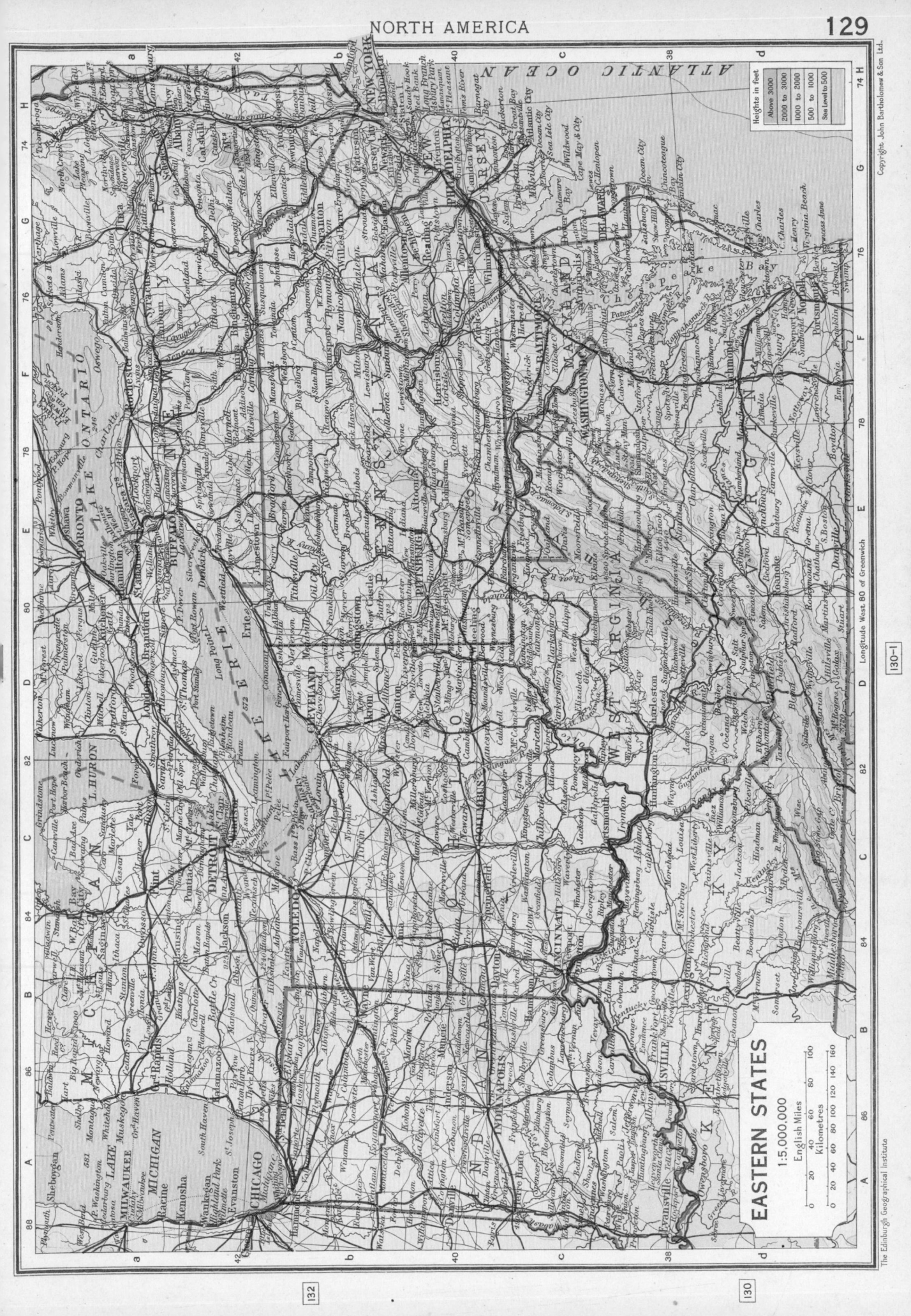

EASTERN STATES
1:5,000,000
English Miles
0 20 40 60 80 100
Kilometres
0 20 40 60 80 100 120 140 160

Heights in feet
Above 3000
2000 to 3000
1000 to 2000
500 to 1000
Sea Level to 500

Copyright. John Bartholomew & Son Ltd.

The Edinburgh Geographical Institute

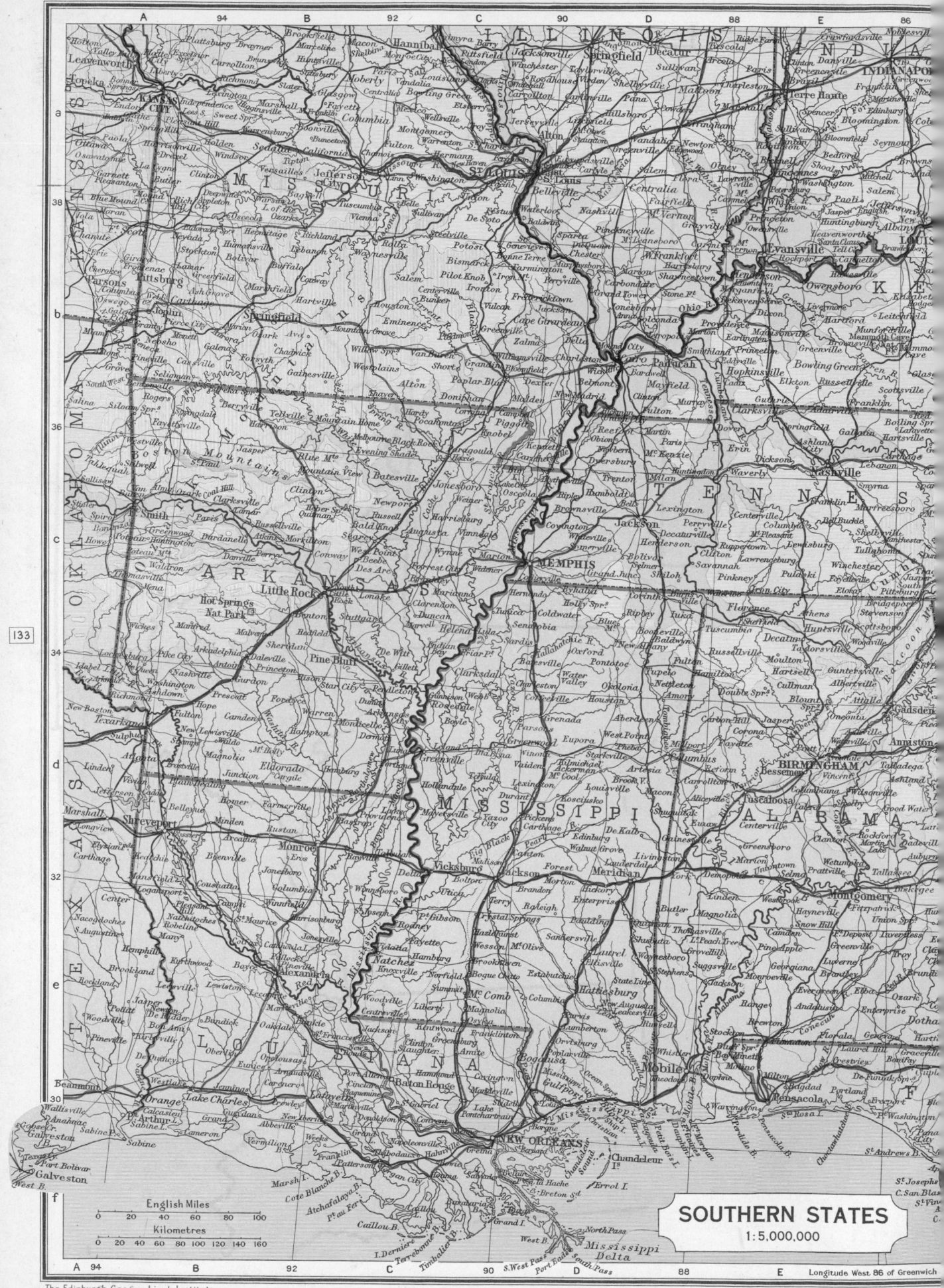

SOUTHERN STATES
1:5,000,000

English Miles
0 20 40 60 80 100

Kilometres
0 20 40 60 80 100 120 140 160

Longitude West 86 of Greenwich

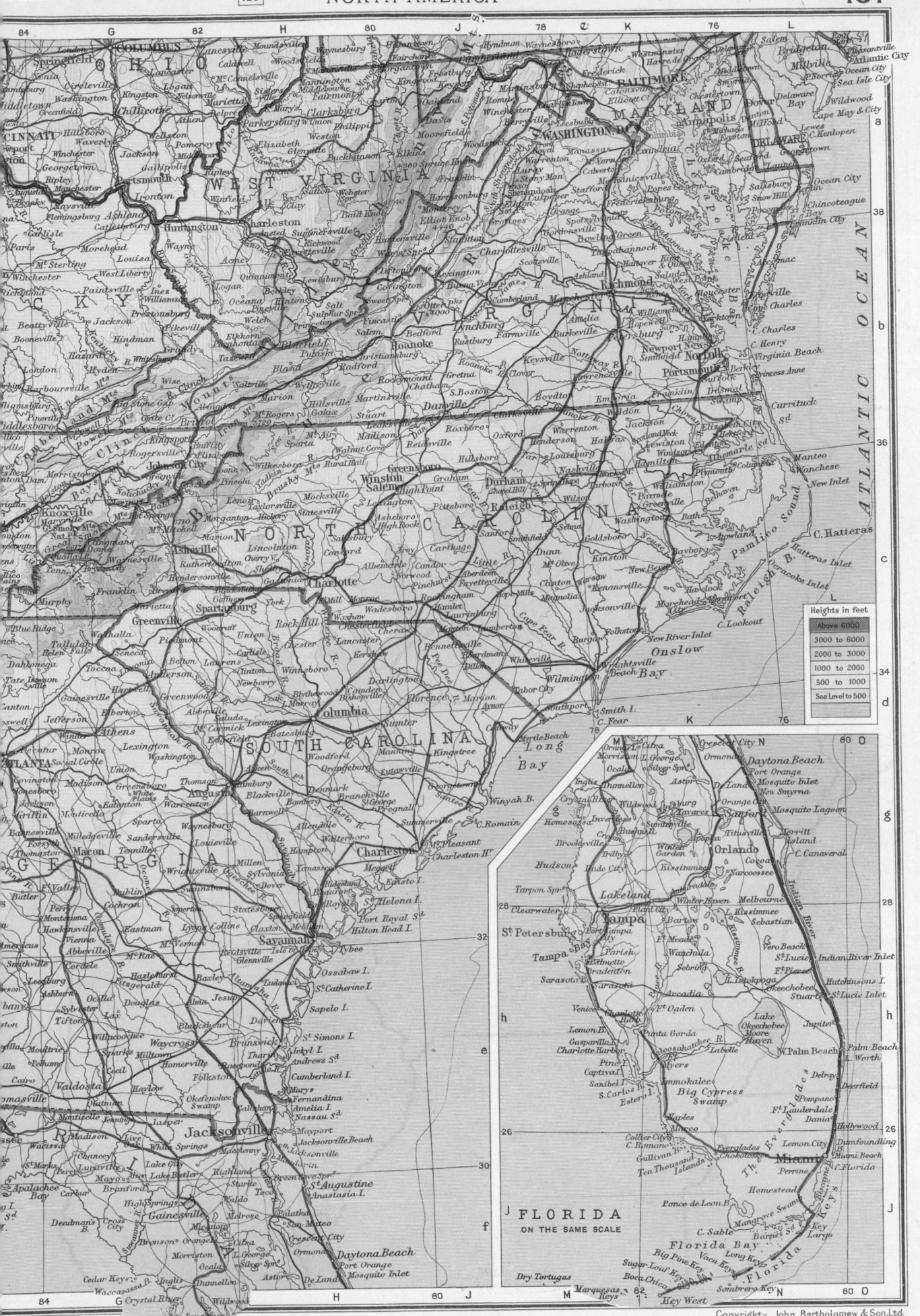

FLORIDA
ON THE SAME SCALE

Heights in feet

Above 6000
3000 to 6000
2000 to 3000
1000 to 2000
500 to 1000
Sea Level to 500

Continued on Inset

Copyright- John Bartholomew & Son, Ltd.

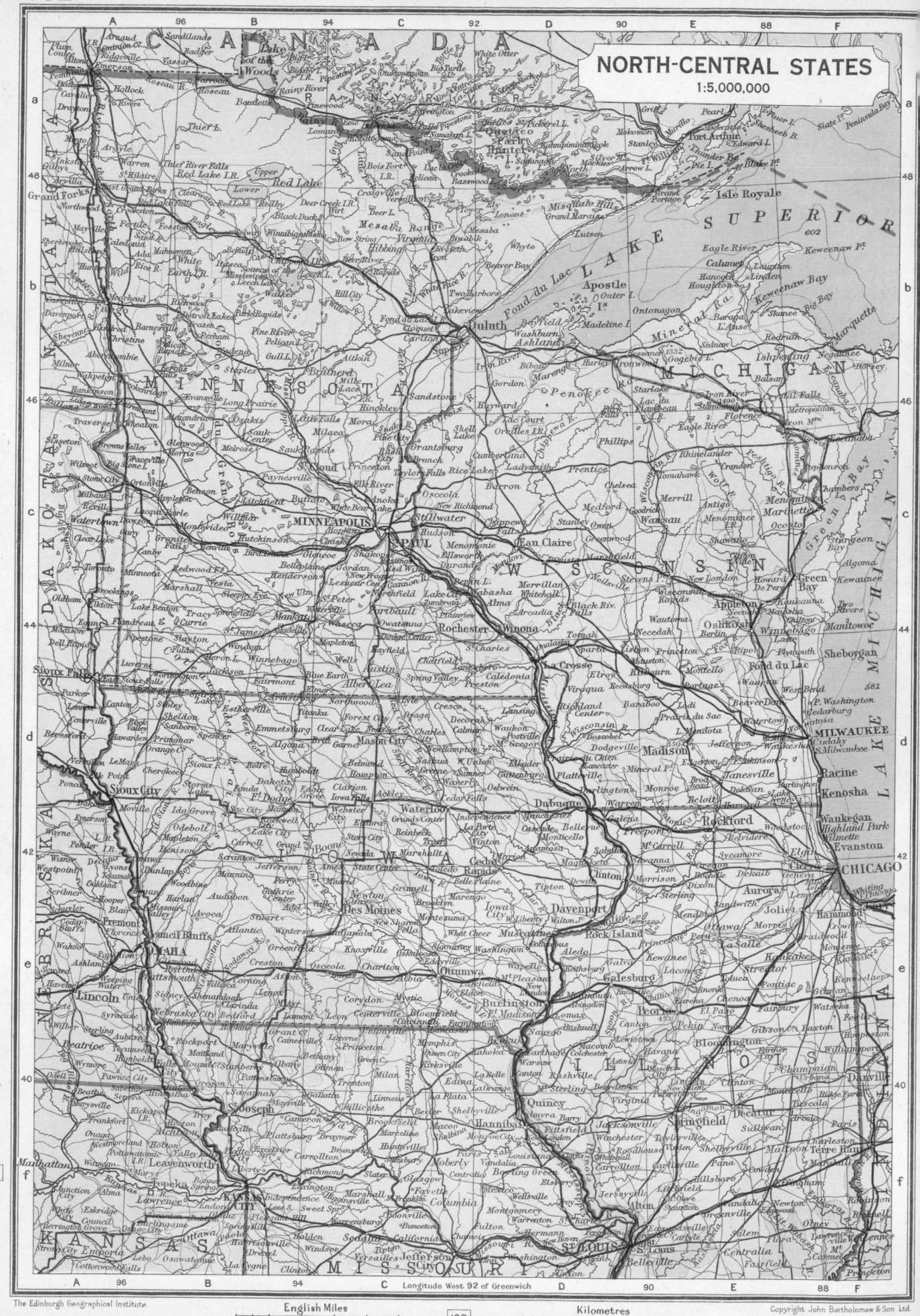

NORTH-CENTRAL STATES
1:5,000,000

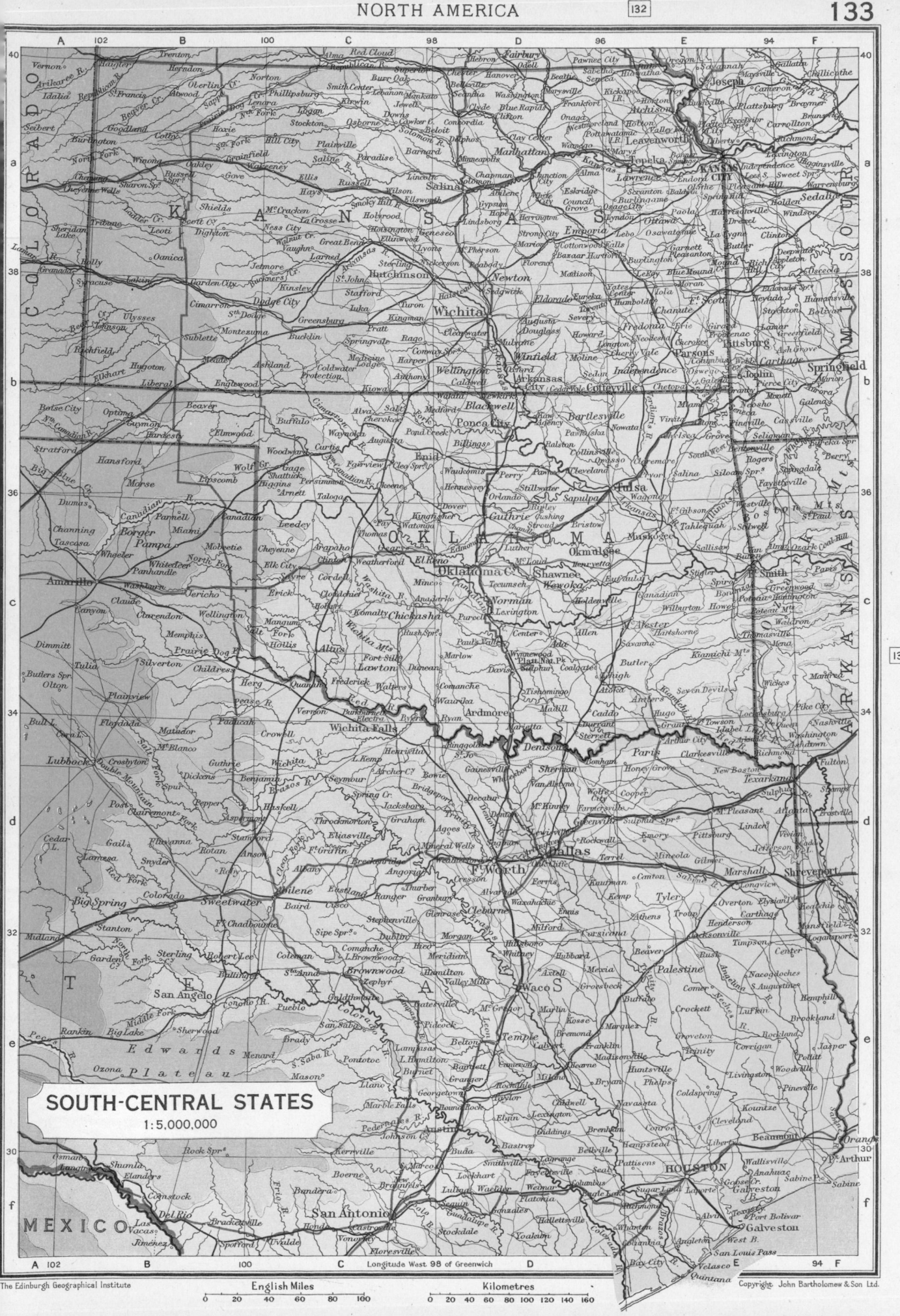

SOUTH-CENTRAL STATES
1:5,000,000

English Miles

Kilometres

Longitude West 98 of Greenwich

Copyright John Bartholomew & Son Ltd.

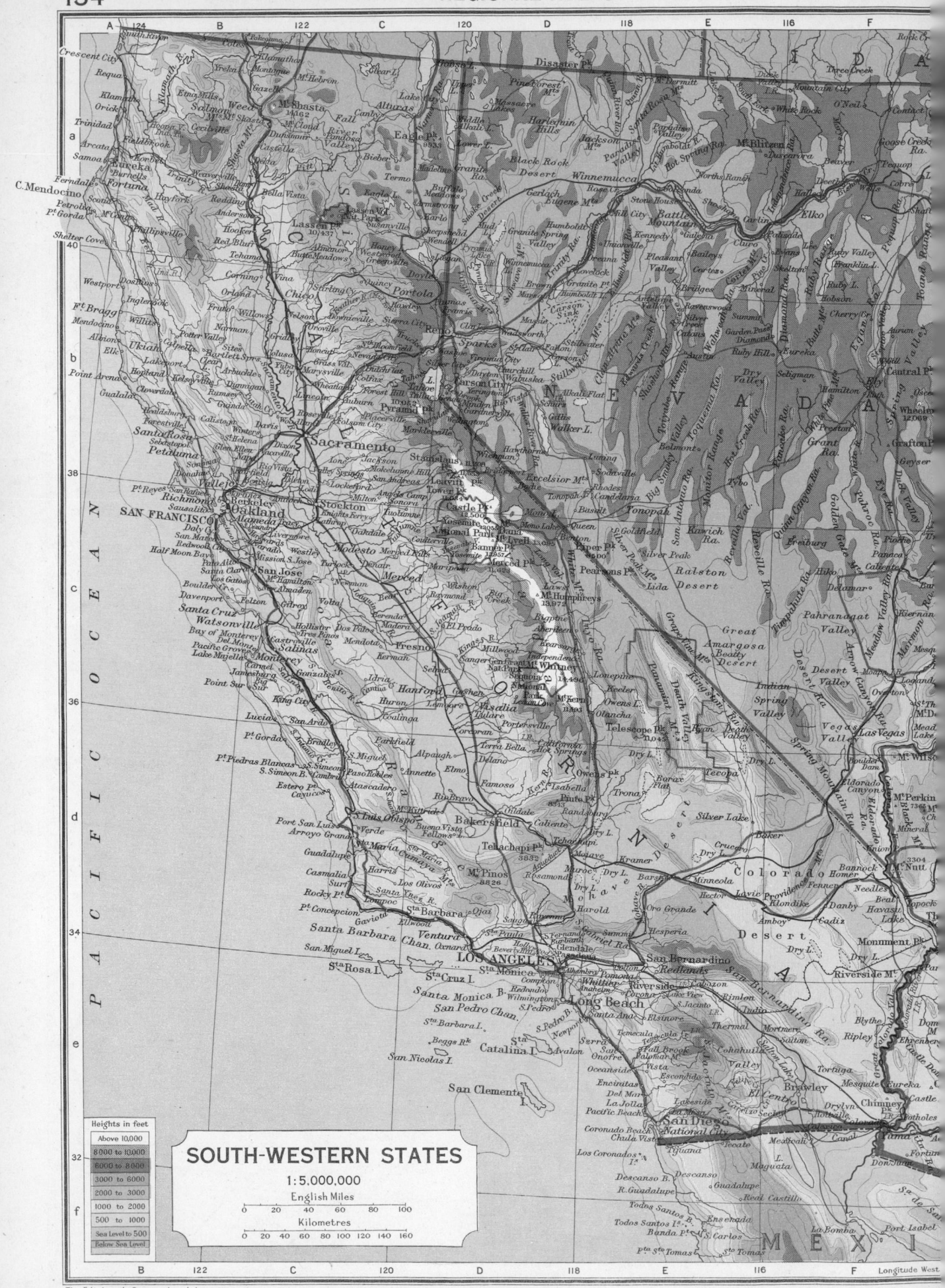

SOUTH-WESTERN STATES

1:5,000,000

English Miles

Kilometres

Heights in feet

Above 10,000
8000 to 10,000
6000 to 8000
3000 to 6000
2000 to 3000
1000 to 2000
500 to 1000
Sea Level to 500
Below Sea Level

The Edinburgh Geographical Institute

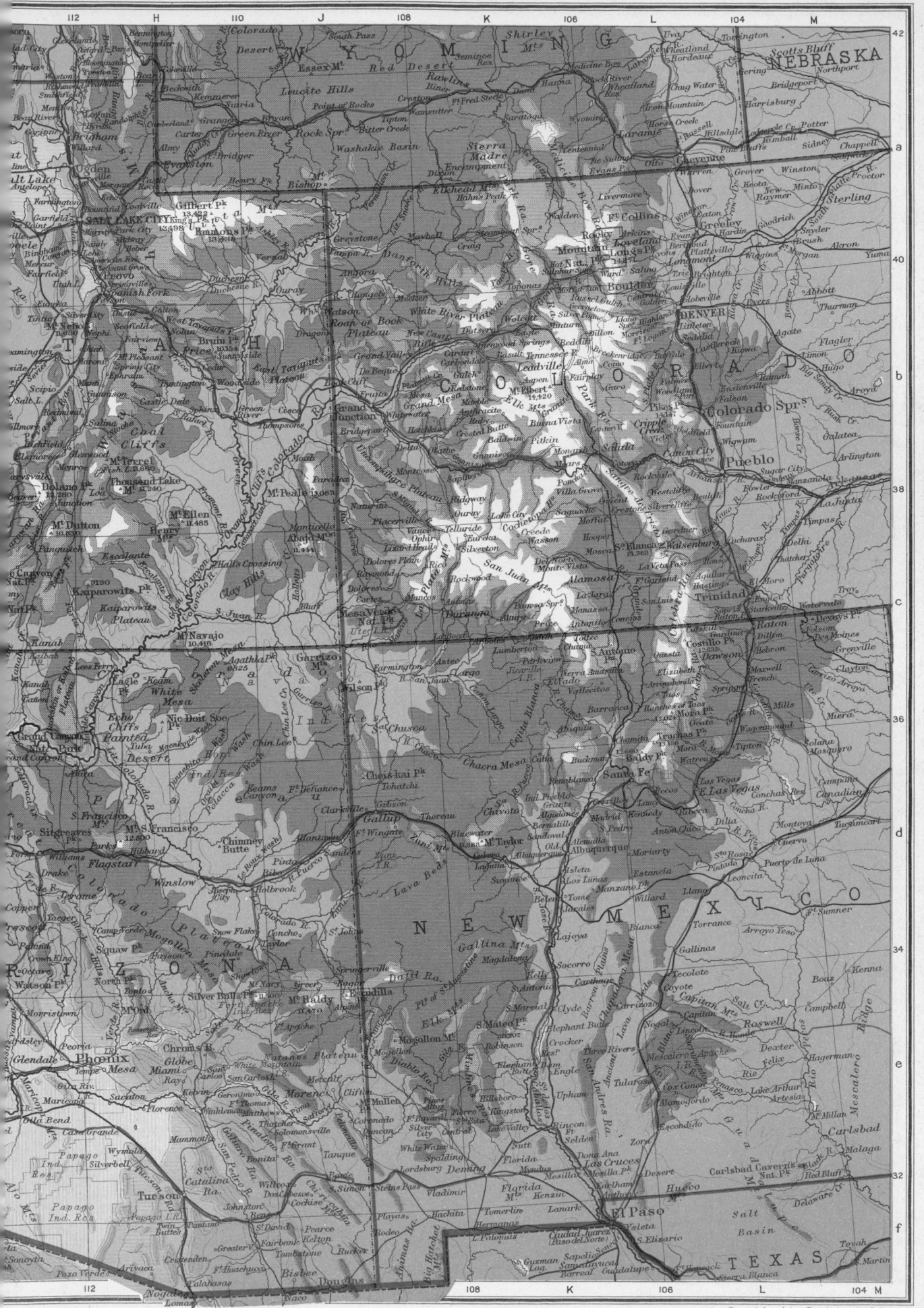

Copyright—John Bartholomew & Son, Ltd.

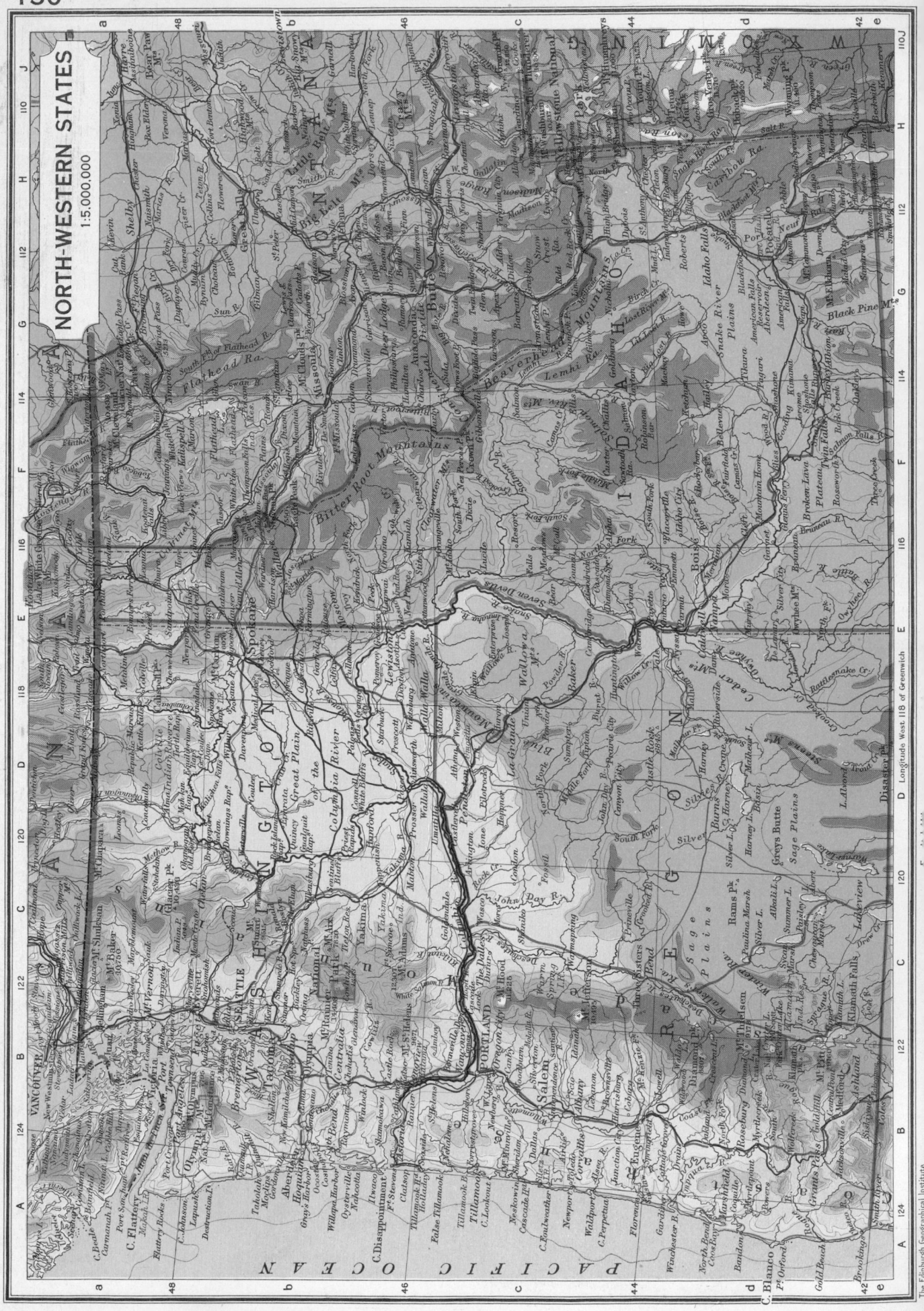

NORTH-WESTERN STATES
1:5,000,000

PACIFIC OCEAN

The Edinburgh Geographical Institute

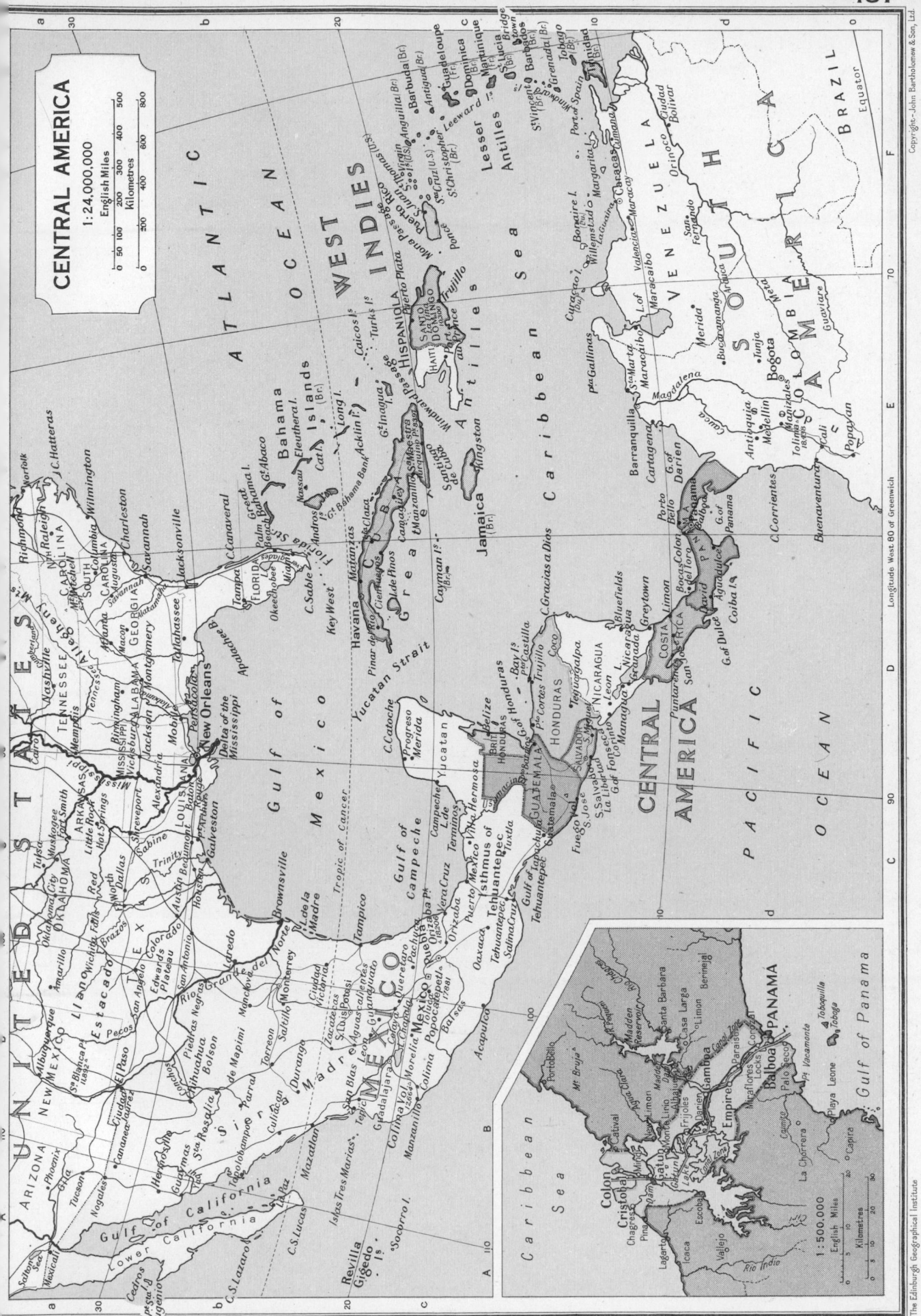

CENTRAL AMERICA
1:24,000,000
English Miles
0 50 100 200 300 400 500
Kilometres
0 200 400 600 800

Copyright–John Bartholomew & Son, Ltd.

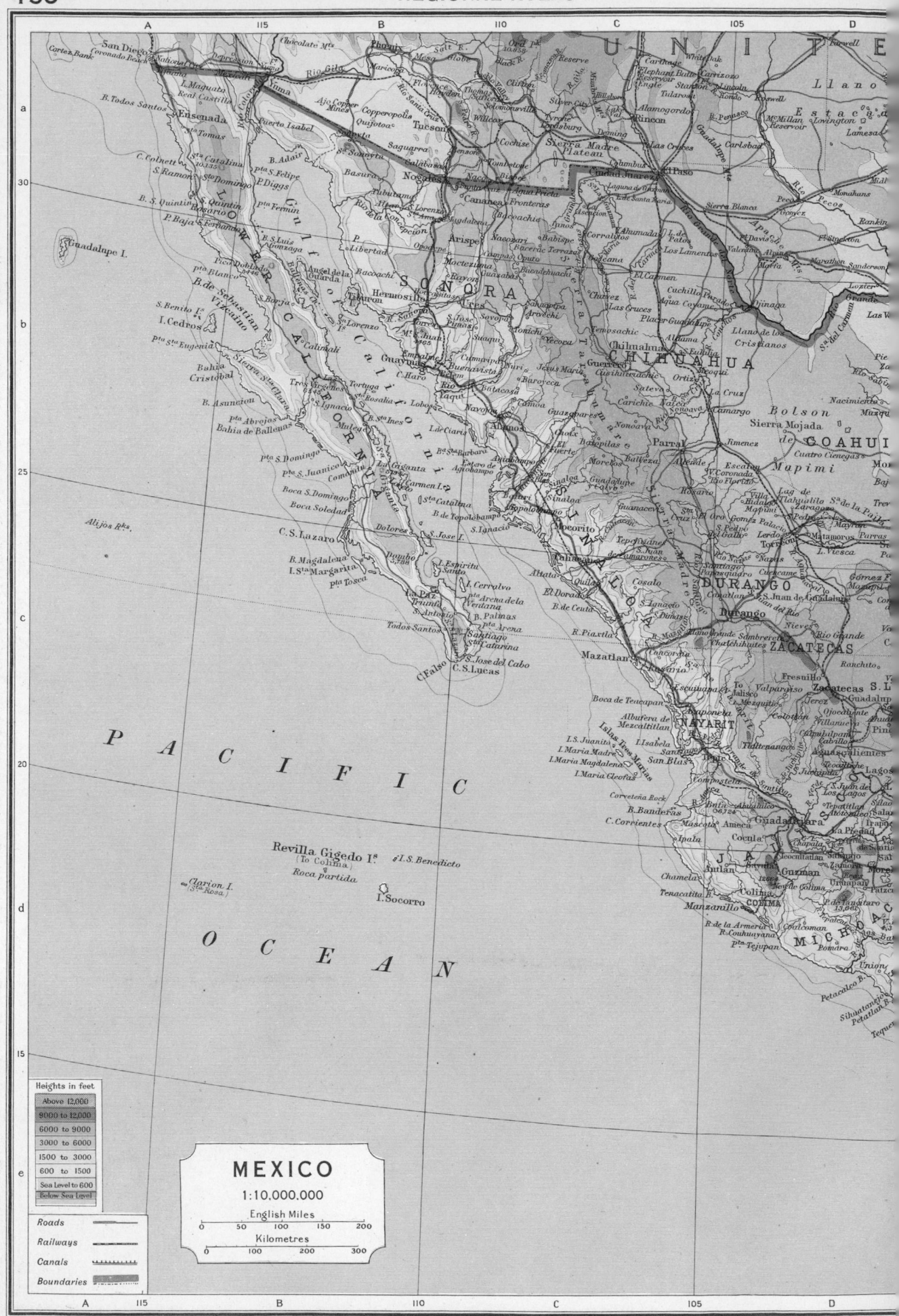

MEXICO

1:10,000,000

English Miles

0   50   100   150   200

Kilometres

0   100   200   300

Heights in feet

Above 12,000
9000 to 12,000
6000 to 9000
3000 to 6000
1500 to 3000
600 to 1500
Sea Level to 600
Below Sea Level

Roads
Railways
Canals
Boundaries

The Edinburgh Geographical Institute

Copyright-John Bartholomew & Son,Ltd.

WEST INDIES

& CENTRAL AMERICAN STATES

1:10,000,000

English Miles

Kilometres

Longitude West 85 of Greenwich

The Edinburgh Geographical Institute

Copyright-John Bartholomew & Son, Ltd.

SOUTH AMERICA

1:30,000,000

English Miles

Kilometres

Copyright-John Bartholomew & Son, Ltd.

Edinburgh Geographical Institute

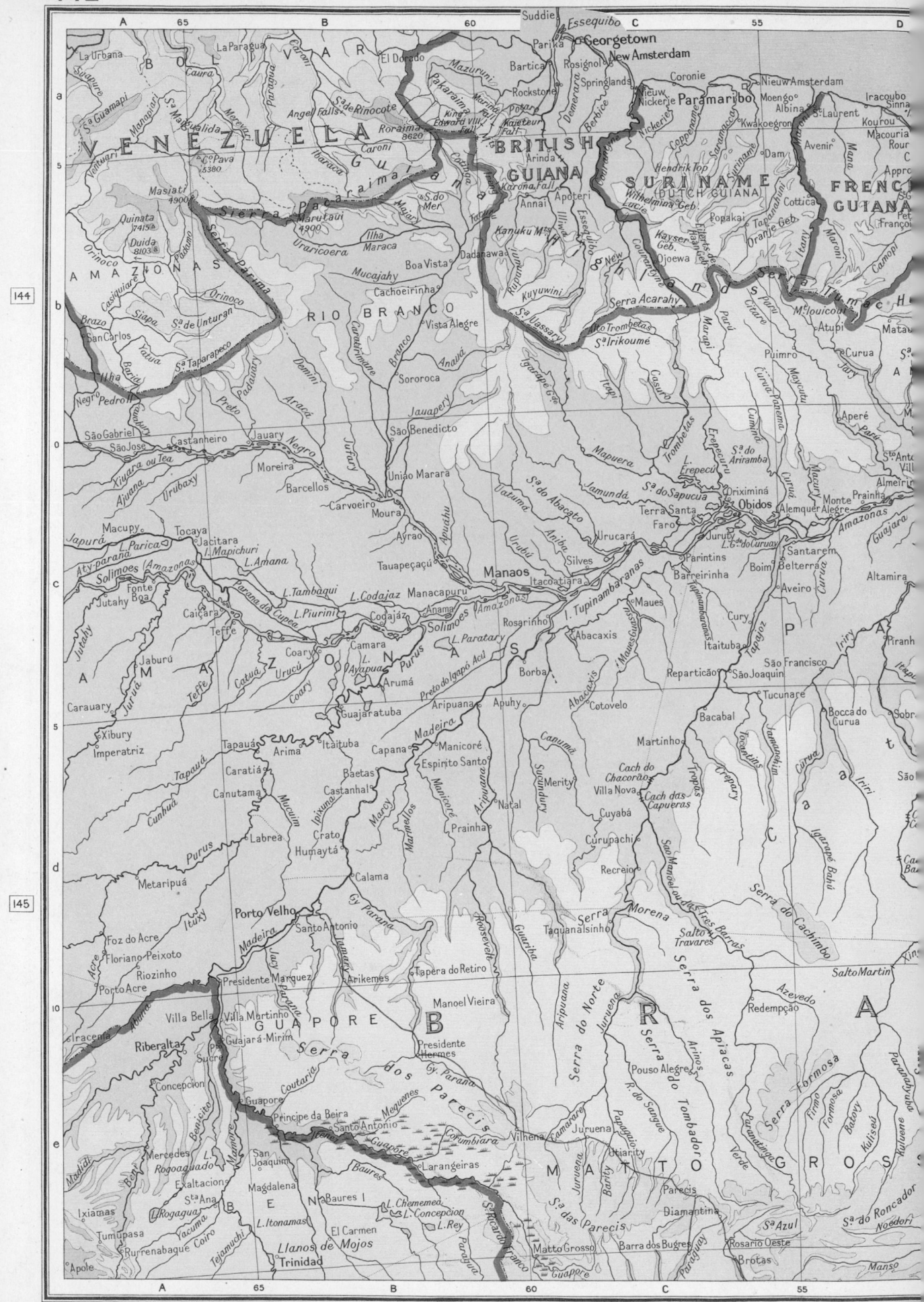

LOWER AMAZON

1:10,000,000

English Miles

0   50   100   150   200   250

Kilometres

0   100   200   300   400

Roads
Railways
Canals
Boundaries

A T L A N T I C

Equator

O C E A N

Heights in feet

| Above 6000 |
| 3000 to 6000 |
| 1500 to 3000 |
| 600 to 1500 |
| Sea Level to 600 |

Copyright- John Bartholomew & Son,Ltd.

COLOMBIA AND VENEZUELA

1:10,000,000

English Miles

Kilometres

Heights in feet

| Above 18,000 |
| 12,000 to 18,000 |
| 10,000 to 12,000 |
| 6000 to 10,000 |
| 3000 to 6000 |
| 1500 to 3000 |
| 600 to 1500 |
| Sea Level to 600 |

CARIBBEAN SEA

VENEZUELA

BRITISH GUIANA

BRAZIL

COLOMBIA

PERU

ECUADOR

PANAMA

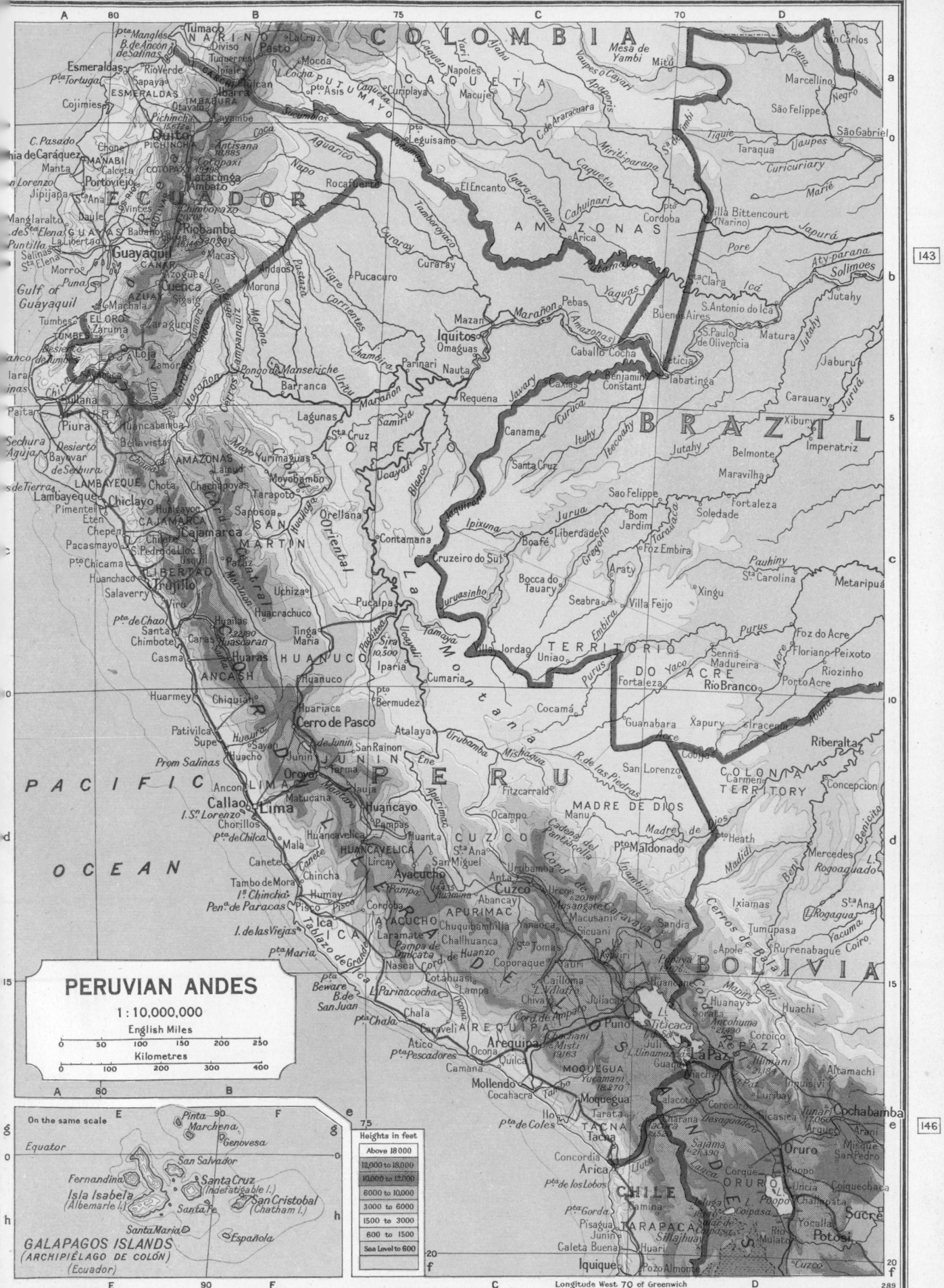

SOUTH AMERICA

COLOMBIA

ECUADOR

BRAZIL

PERU

BOLIVIA

PACIFIC

OCEAN

CHILE

PERUVIAN ANDES

1 : 10,000,000

English Miles

0   50   100   150   200   250

Kilometres

0   100   200   300   400

On the same scale

GALAPAGOS ISLANDS
(ARCHIPIÉLAGO DE COLÓN)
(Ecuador)

Heights in feet	
Above 18,000	
12,000 to 18,000	
10,000 to 12,000	
6000 to 10,000	
3000 to 6000	
1500 to 3000	
600 to 1500	
Sea Level to 600	

Longitude West 70 of Greenwich

The Edinburgh Geographical Institute

Copyright—John Bartholomew & Son, Ltd.

145

142

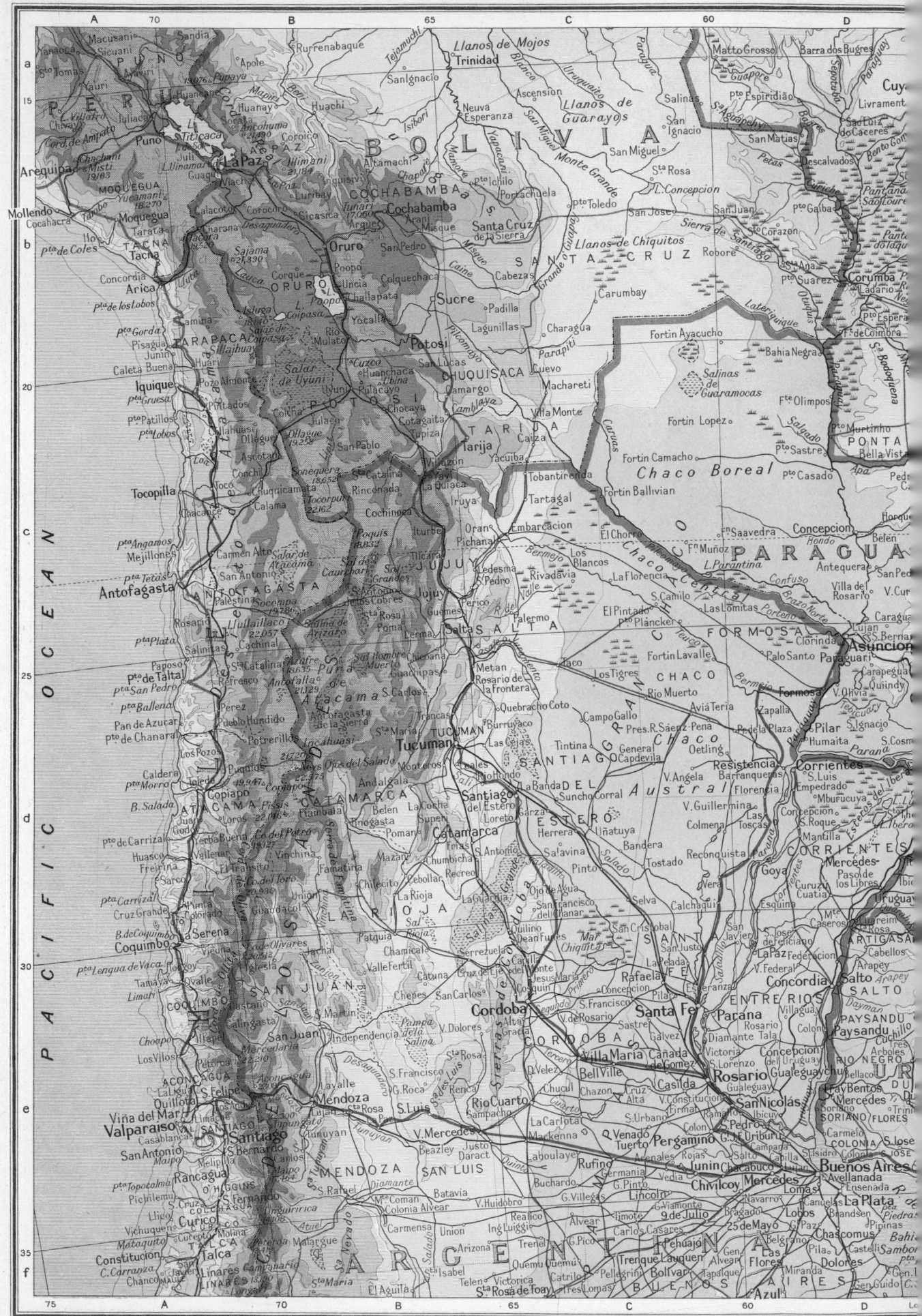
PACIFIC OCEAN
PERU
BOLIVIA
PARAGUAY
ARGENTINA
Chaco Boreal
Llanos de Mojos
Llanos de Guarayos
Llanos de Chiquitos
Puna de Atacama
Chaco Austral
PUNO
LA PAZ
COCHABAMBA
ORURO
POTOSI
CHUQUISACA
TARIJA
SANTA CRUZ
TACNA
TARAPACA
ANTOFAGASTA
ATACAMA
COQUIMBO
ACONCAGUA
SANTIAGO
O'HIGGINS
COLCHAGUA
TALCA
LINARES
JUJUY
SALTA
TUCUMAN
CATAMARCA
SANTIAGO DEL ESTERO
LA RIOJA
SAN JUAN
CORDOBA
SANTA FE
ENTRE RIOS
CORRIENTES
MENDOZA
SAN LUIS
BUENOS AIRES
FORMOSA
CHACO
La Paz
Cochabamba
Oruro
Sucre
Potosi
Tarija
Arequipa
Puno
Tacna
Arica
Iquique
Antofagasta
Tocopilla
Copiapo
Coquimbo
La Serena
Valparaiso
Santiago
Rancagua
Talca
Mendoza
San Juan
Cordoba
Tucuman
Salta
Jujuy
Catamarca
Santa Fe
Parana
Rosario
Corrientes
Resistencia
Asuncion
Concepcion
Buenos Aires
La Plata
Concordia
Paysandu
Salto
Villa Maria
Rio Cuarto
A
B
C
D
a
b
c
d
e
f
70
65
60
75
15
20
25
30
35

148

MID SOUTH AMERICA

1:10,000,000

English Miles

0   50   100   150   200   250   300

Kilometres

0   100   200   300   400   500

1:500,000

Miles

Copyright—John Bartholomew & Son, Ltd.

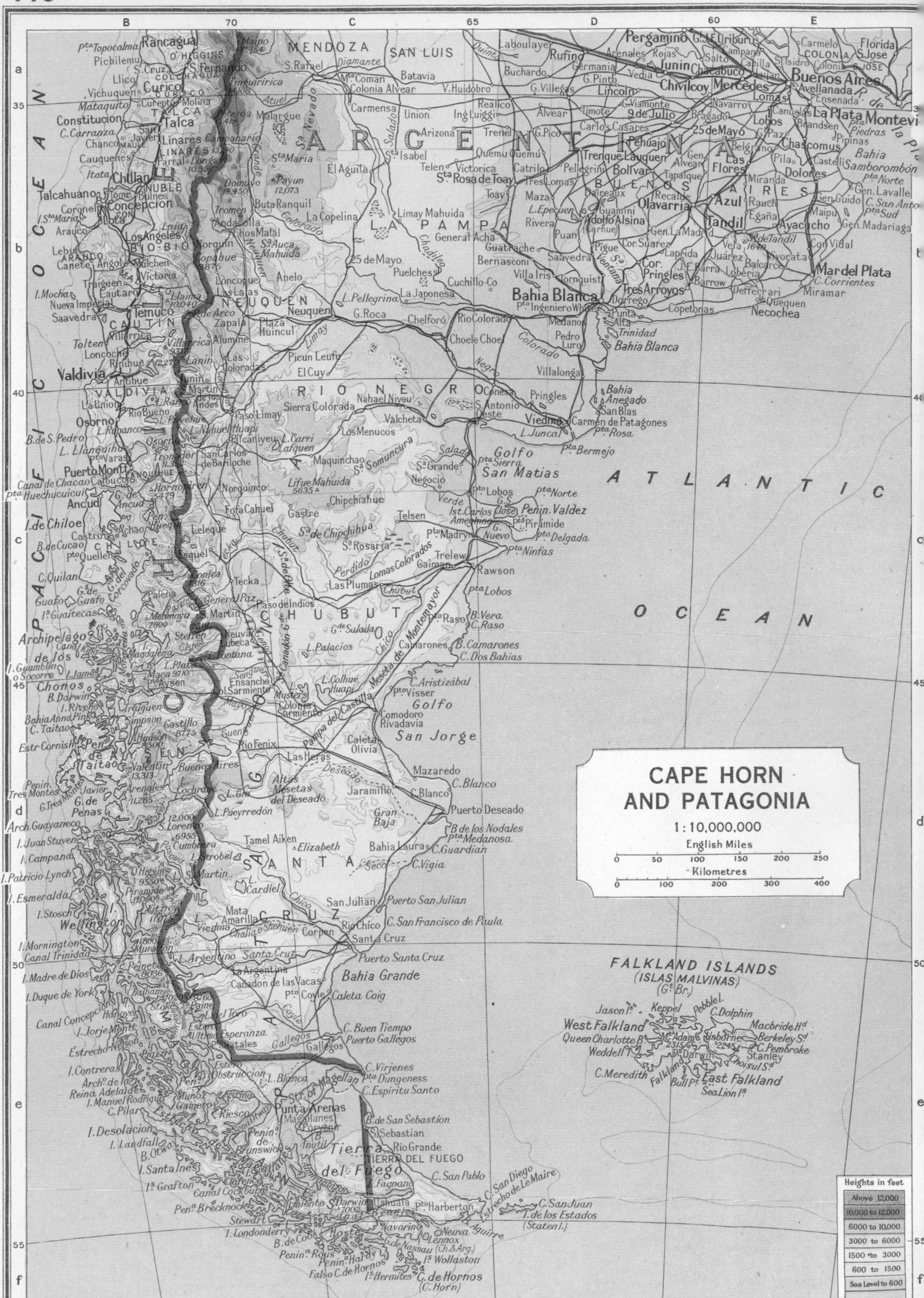

CAPE HORN AND PATAGONIA

1:10,000,000

English Miles

0 50 100 150 200 250

Kilometres

0 100 200 300 400

FALKLAND ISLANDS
(ISLAS MALVINAS)
(Gt. Br.)

Heights in feet

| Above 12,000 |
| 10,000 to 12,000 |
| 6000 to 10,000 |
| 3000 to 6000 |
| 1500 to 3000 |
| 600 to 1500 |
| Sea Level to 600 |

The Edinburgh Geographical Institute

Copyright-John Bartholomew & Son, Ltd.

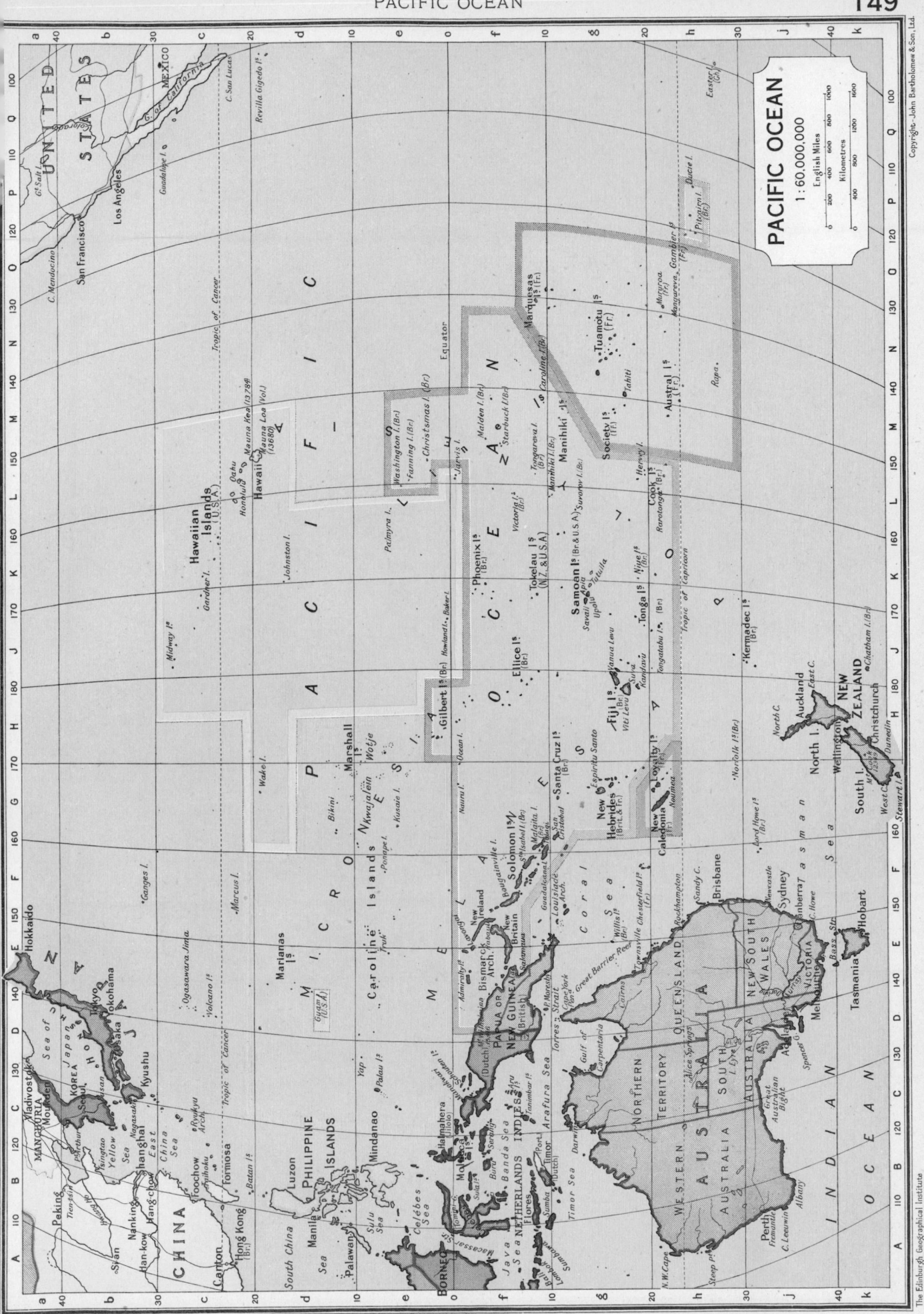

PACIFIC OCEAN
1:60,000,000
English Miles
Kilometres

Copyright - John Bartholomew & Son, Ltd.

The Edinburgh Geographical Institute

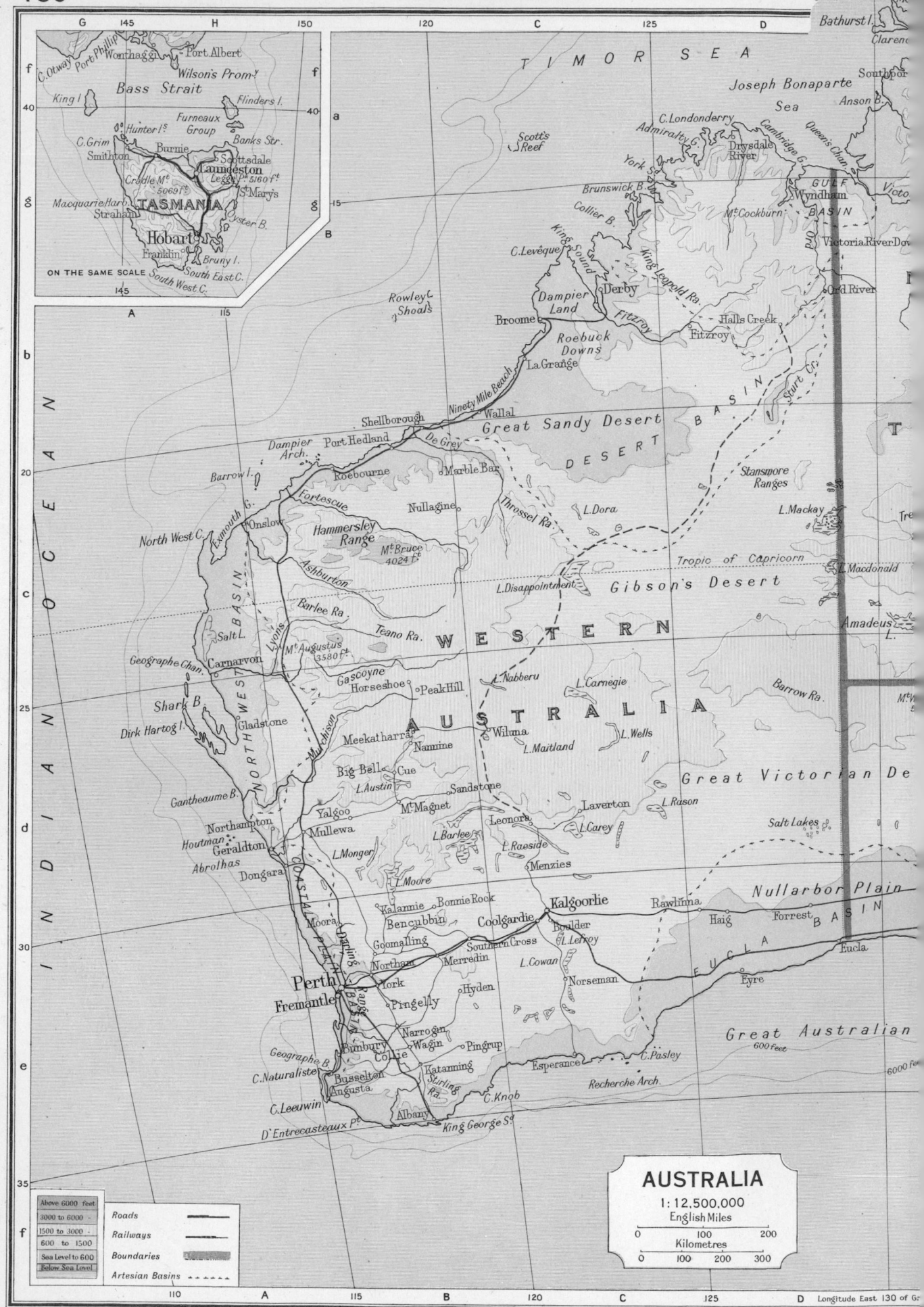

TASMANIA
ON THE SAME SCALE

AUSTRALIA
1: 12,500,000
English Miles

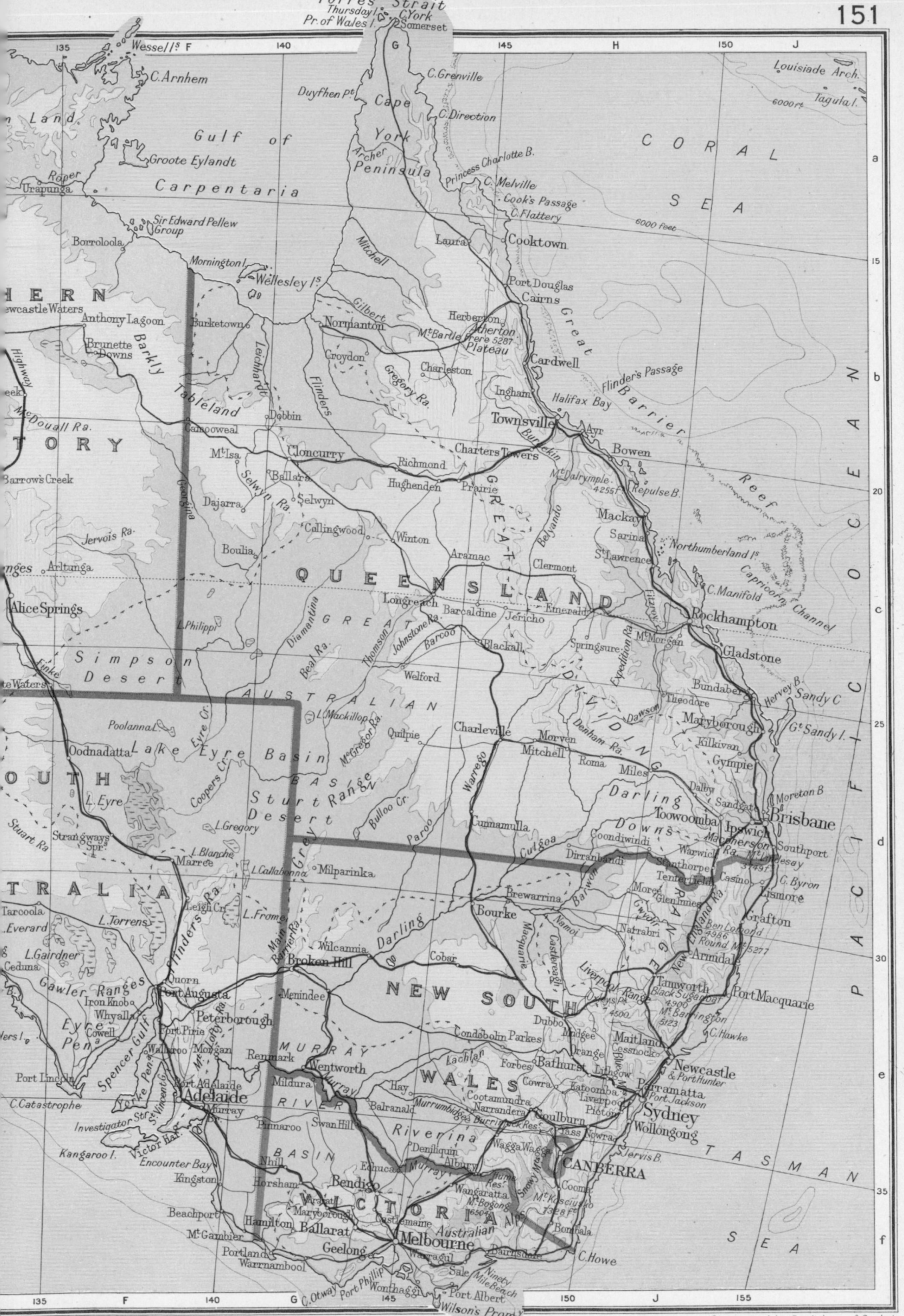

Copyright—John Bartholomew & Son, Ltd.

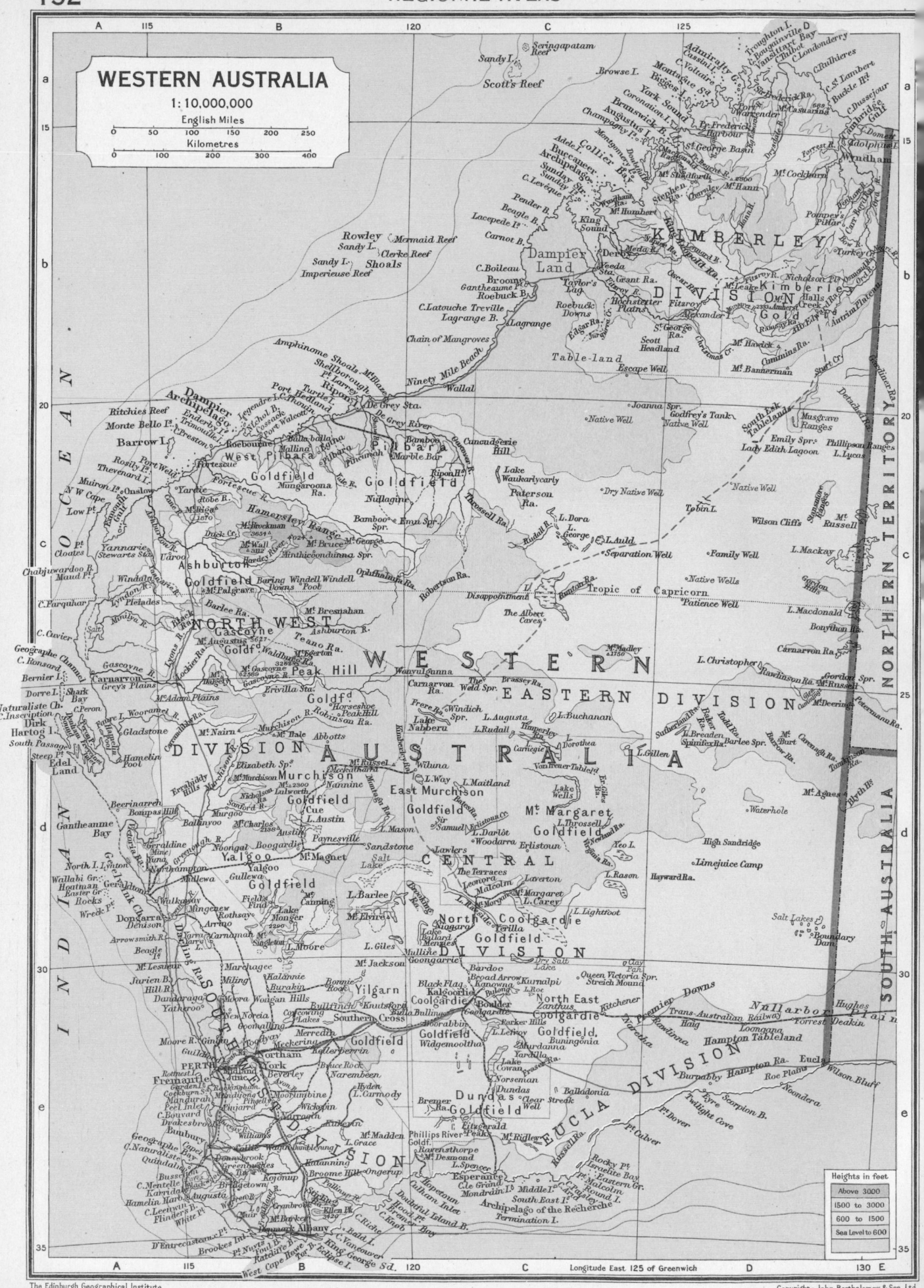

WESTERN AUSTRALIA

1 : 10,000,000

English Miles

Kilometres

Copyright—John Bartholomew & Son, Ltd.

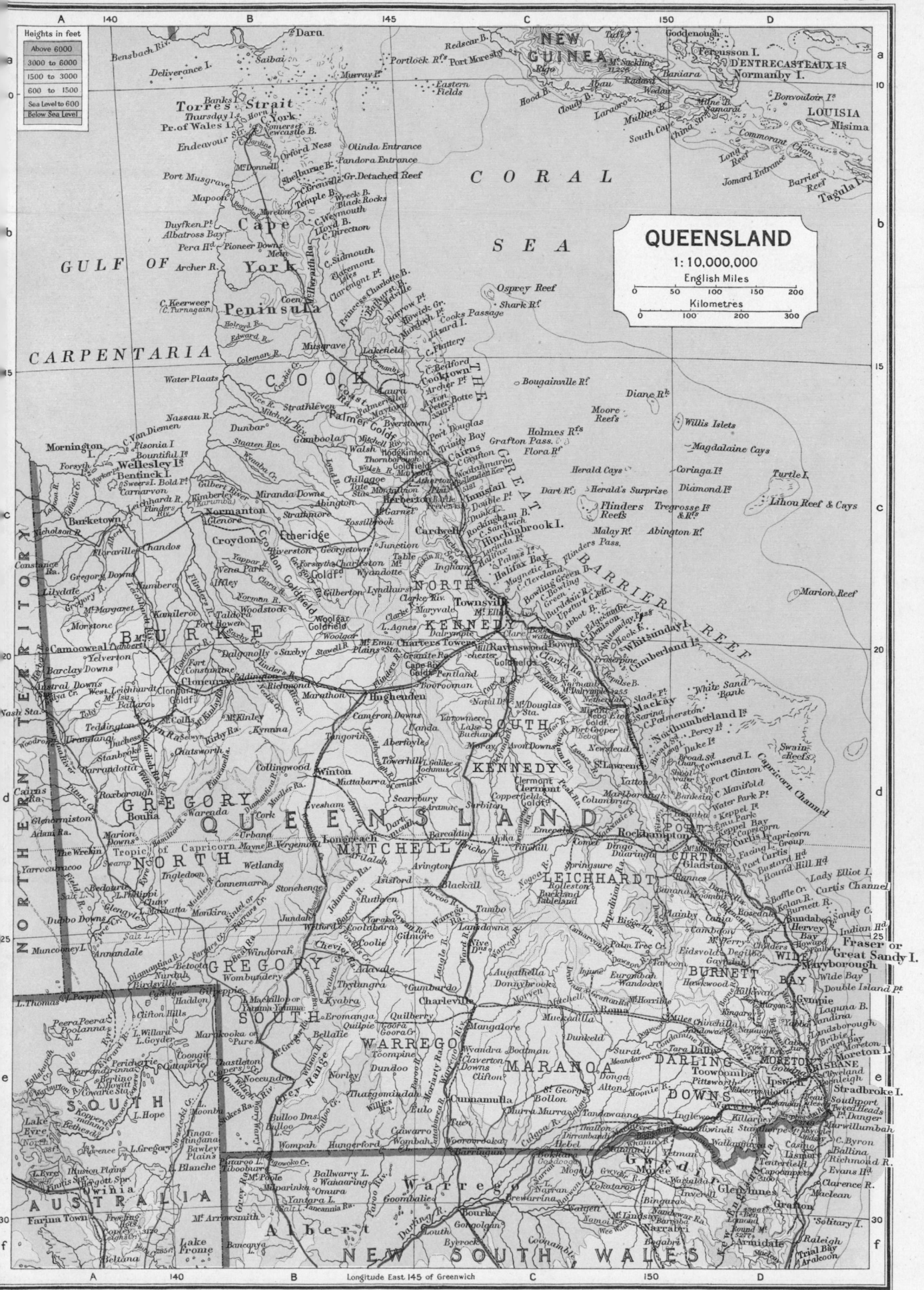

QUEENSLAND
1 : 10,000,000
English Miles

Edinburgh Geographical Institute

Copyright-John Bartholomew & Son, Ltd.

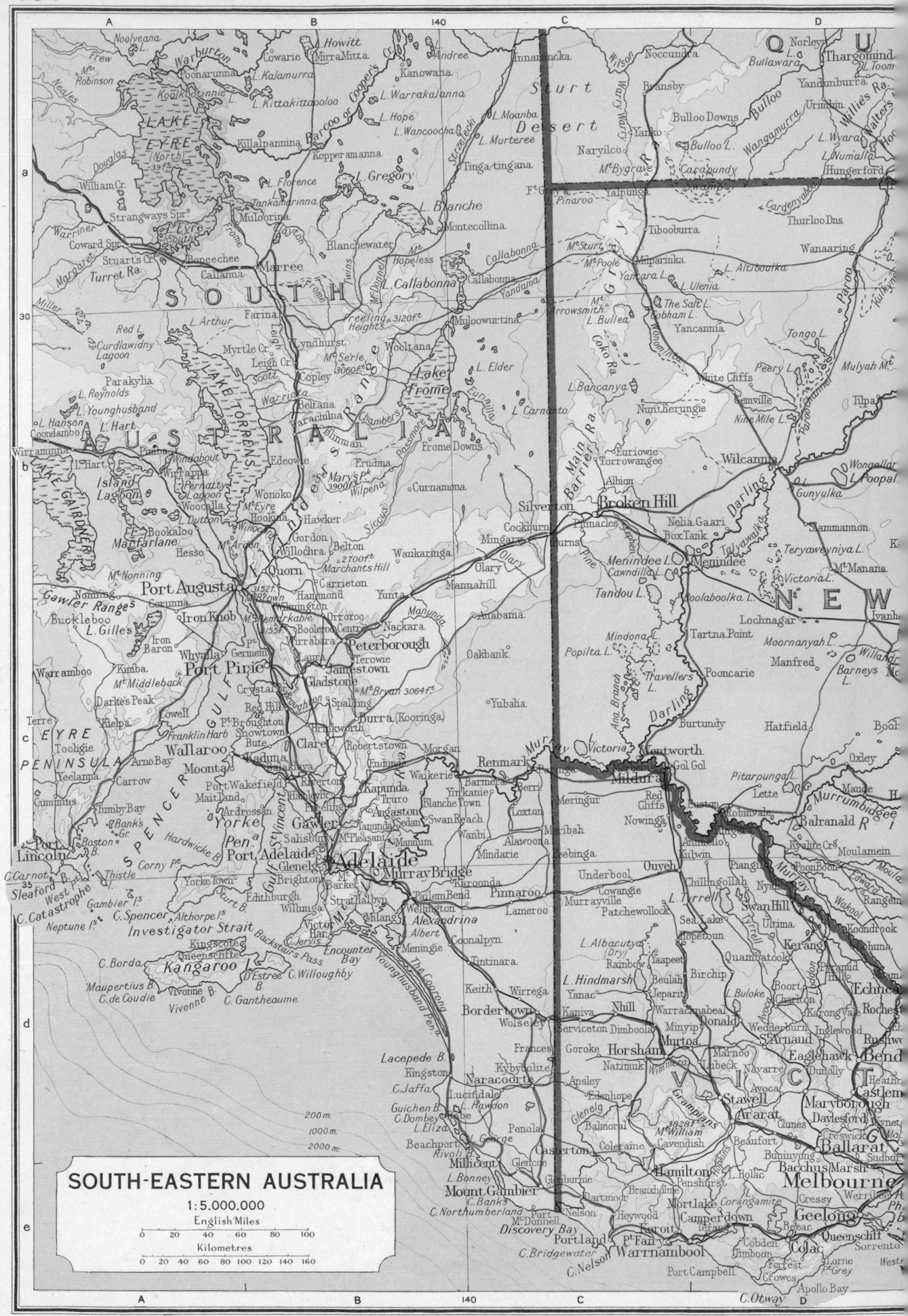

SOUTH-EASTERN AUSTRALIA

1:5.000.000

English Miles

0   20   40   60   80   100

Kilometres

0   20 40 60 80 100 120 140 160

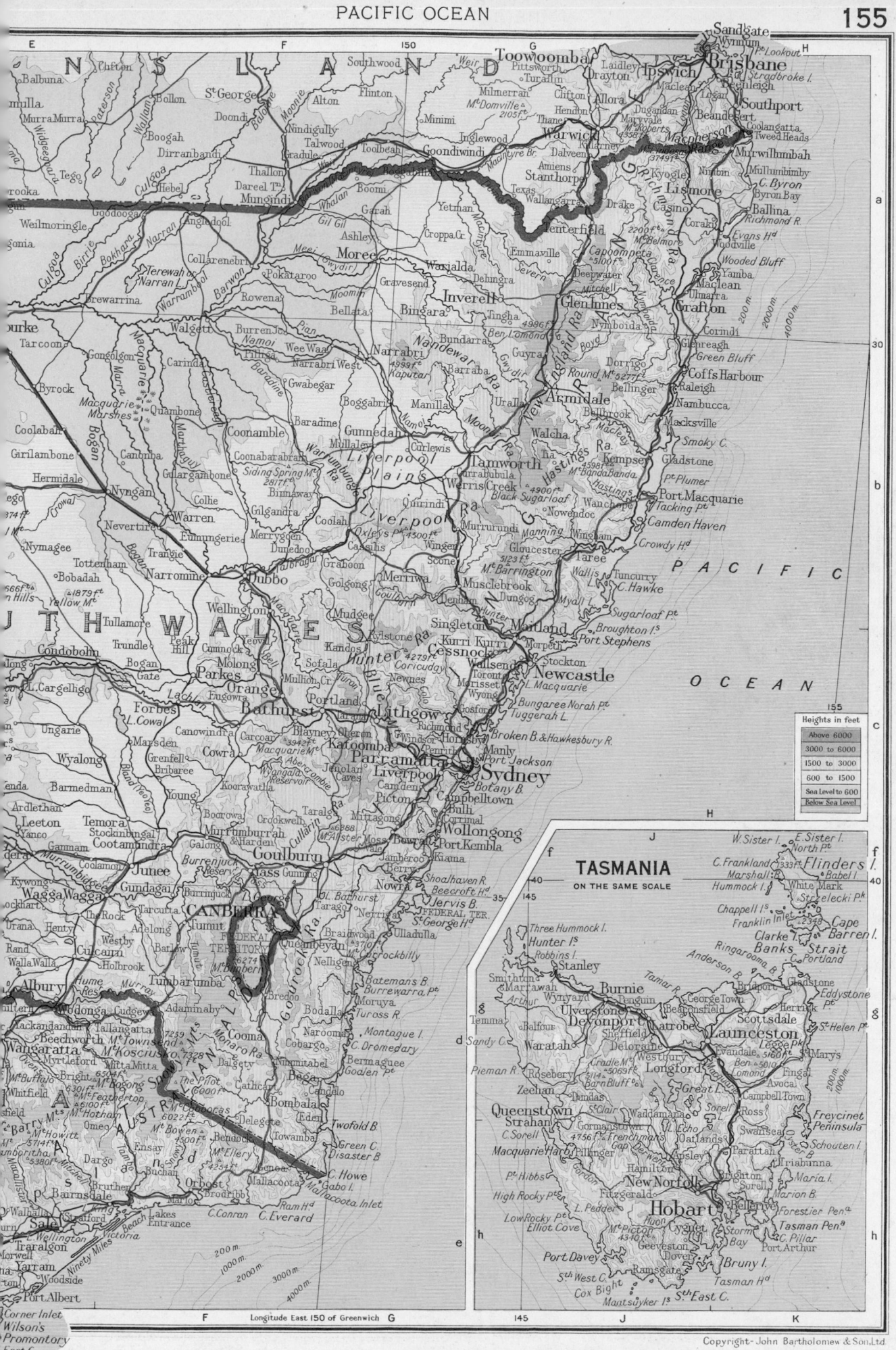

TASMANIA
ON THE SAME SCALE

Heights in feet	
Above 6000	
3000 to 6000	
1500 to 3000	
600 to 1500	
Sea Level to 600	
Below Sea Level	

Copyright-John Bartholomew & Son, Ltd.

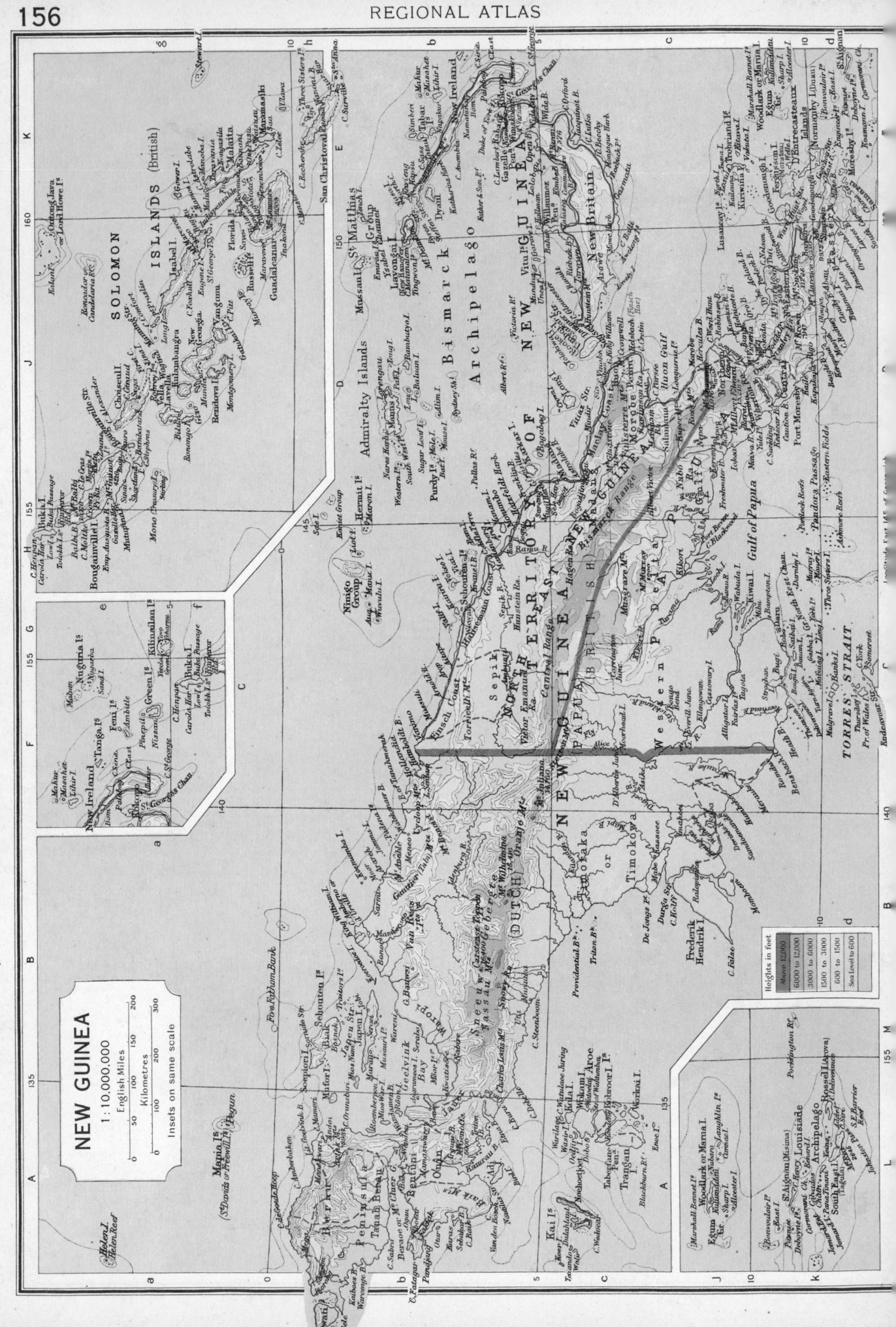

NEW GUINEA
1:10,000,000
English Miles
50   100   150   200
0
Kilometres
100   200   300
0
Insets on same scale

Heights in feet
Above 12,000
6000 to 12,000
3000 to 6000
1500 to 3000
600 to 1500
Sea Level to 600

SOLOMON
ISLANDS (British)

Admiralty Islands

St Matthias
Group

Bismarck   Archipelago

NEW BRITAIN

New Ireland

NORTH EAST NEW GUINEA
TERRITORY OF

DUTCH   NEW GUINEA

PAPUA BRITISH

Gulf of Papua

Western P.   Eastern P.

TORRES STRAIT

ISLANDS OF THE PACIFIC

1:40,000,000

English Miles

Kilometres

Heights in feet

Above 12,000	
6000 to 12,000	
3000 to 6000	
1500 to 3000	
600 to 1500	
Sea Level to 600	

HAWAII   1:6,000,000   English Miles   Kilometres

West of 156 Greenwich

MAUI   Lanai   Molokai   Kahoolawe

OAHU   Honolulu   Pearl Harbor   Waipahu

HAWAII   Mauna Kea   Mauna Loa   Hilo   Kilauea

VITI LEVU (FIJI GROUP)   1:6,000,000   Suva   Ovalau   Levuka   East 178 of Greenwich

WAKE I.   Scale 1:500,000

GUAM   1:2,000,000   Agana   Port Apra

Marianas Islands   Marcus   Los Jardines   Saipan   Tinian   Guam (U.S.A.)

Caroline Islands   Yap   Truk   Ponape

Marshall Islands   Bikini   Ralik   Radak   Jaluit I.

Gilbert Islands   Ocean I. (Banaba)   Tarawa   Makin

Ellice Islands (Brit.)   Nanumea   Funafuti

Phoenix Is.   Canton (Br. & U.S.A.)   Enderbury

Howland I.   Baker I.

Tropic of Cancer

Equator

Hawaiian Islands   Kauai   Oahu   Maui   Hawaii   Honolulu

Johnston I. (U.S.A.)

Palmyra I.   Washington (Br.)   Fanning I. (Br.)   Christmas I. (Brit.)

Jarvis I. (Br.)   Malden I. (Br.)   Starbuck I.   Penrhyn I.   Caroline I.

Marquesas Is.   Nukuhiva   Hiva Oa

Tuamotu or Low Archipelago (Fr.)

Society Is. (Fr.)   Tahiti   Leeward Is.

Cook Islands (Brit.)   Rarotonga

Samoa   Savaii   Upolu   Tutuila (U.S.A.)

Tokelau Is. (N.Z.)

Tonga or Friendly Is.

Fiji Is.   Viti Levu   Vanua Levu

New Hebrides (Fr. & Brit.)   Espiritu Santo   Malekula   Efate

New Caledonia (Fr.)   Noumea   Loyalty Is. (Fr.)

Solomon Islands   Bougainville I.   New Georgia   Guadalcanal   Malaita   San Cristobal

New Ireland   New Britain   Bismarck Arch.

NEW GUINEA   PAPUA   Port Moresby   Lae   Hollandia

AUSTRALIA   Gulf of Carpentaria   Cape York   Townsville

Coral Sea   Great Barrier Reef

Ogasawara Jima   Kazan Retto (Volcano) (Jap.)   Iwojima

Copyright — John Bartholomew & Son, Ltd.

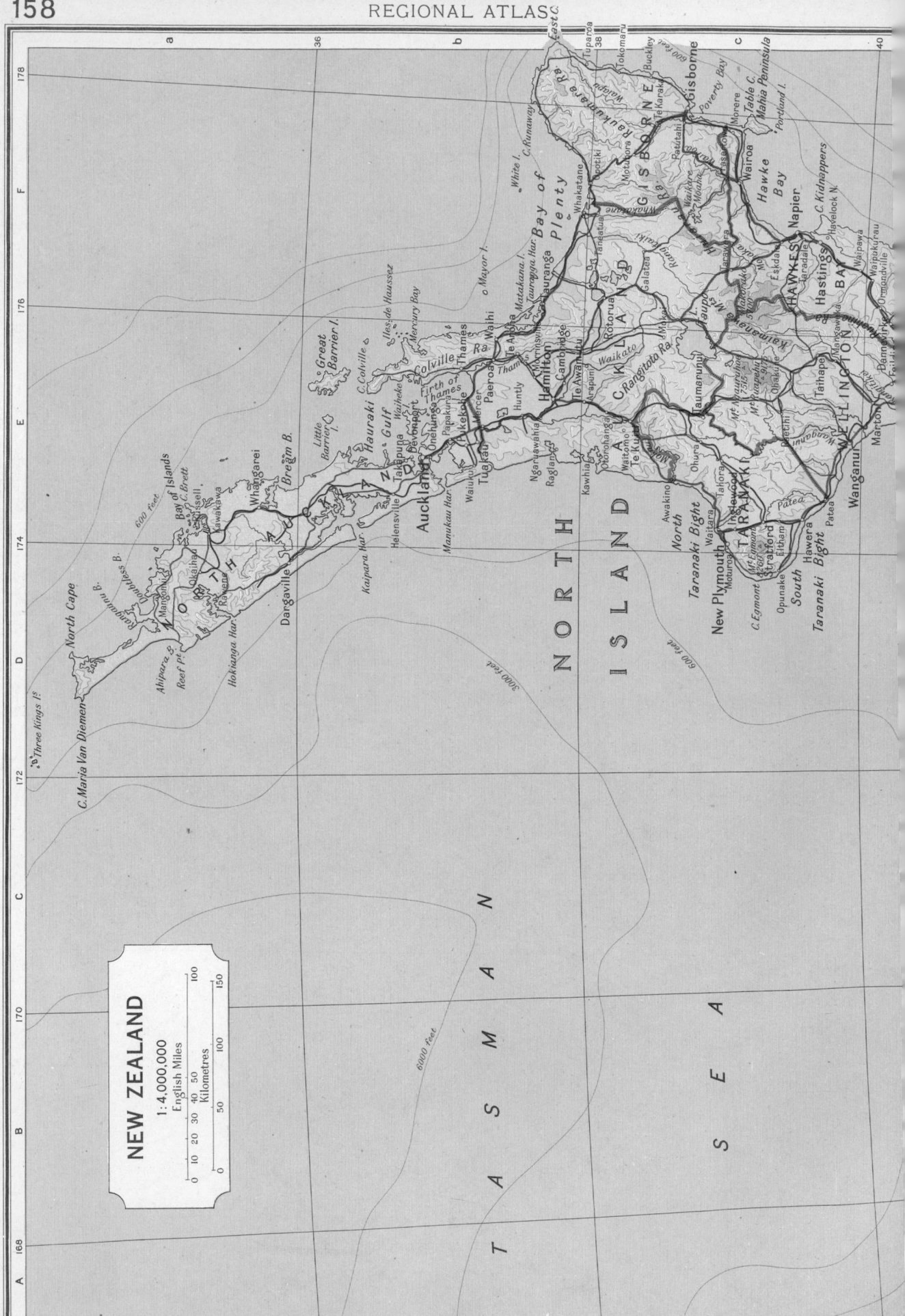

NEW ZEALAND

1 : 4,000,000

English Miles

Kilometres

NORTH ISLAND

TASMAN SEA

Copyright-John Bartholomew & Son, Ltd.

The Edinburgh Geographical Institute

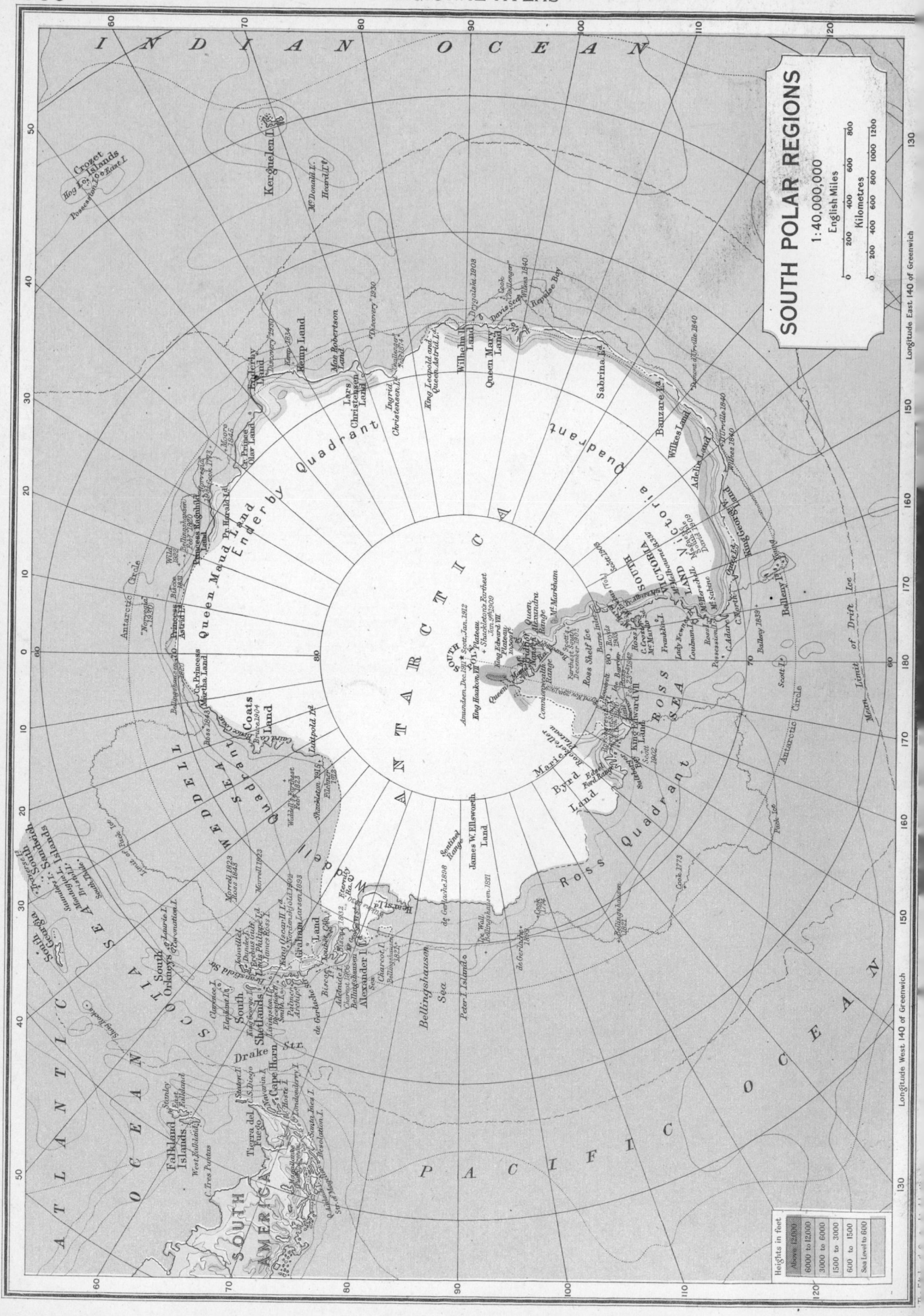
SOUTH POLAR REGIONS
1:40,000,000
English Miles
0 200 400 600 800
Kilometres
0 200 400 600 800 1000 1200
Heights in feet
Above 12,000
6000 to 12,000
3000 to 6000
1500 to 3000
600 to 1500
Sea Level to 600
Longitude West 140 of Greenwich
Longitude East 140 of Greenwich
ATLANTIC OCEAN
INDIAN OCEAN
PACIFIC OCEAN
ANTARCTICA
SOUTH AMERICA
SCOTIA SEA
WEDDELL SEA
ROSS SEA
Bellingshausen Sea
Drake Str.
Antarctic Circle
Mean Limit of Drift Ice
Limit of Pack Ice
Weddell Quadrant
Enderby Quadrant
Victoria Quadrant
Ross Quadrant
Falkland Islands
South Georgia
South Sandwich Islands
South Orkneys
South Shetlands
Graham Land
Tierra del Fuego
Cape Horn
Alexander I. Ld.
Peter I. Island
Coats Land
Luitpold Ld.
Queen Maud Land
Princess Astrid Ld.
Princess Ragnhild Land
Cr. Princess Martha Land
Pr. Harald Ld.
Cr. Prince Olav Land
Enderby Land
Kemp Land
Mac Robertson Land
Lars Christensen Land
Ingrid Christensen Ld.
King Leopold and Queen Astrid Ld.
Wilhelm II. Land
Queen Mary Land
Sabrina Ld.
Banzare Ld.
Wilkes Land
Adelie Land
King George V. Land
Oates Ld.
SOUTH VICTORIA LAND
James W. Ellsworth Land
Marie Byrd Land
Rockefeller Plateau
King Edward VII Land
Ross Shelf Ice
Queen Alexandra Range
Commonwealth Range
Mt. Markham
Mt. Melbourne
C. Adare
Balleny Is.
Scott I.
Kerguelen I.
Crozet Islands
Mc Donald I.
Heard I.
Sentinel Range
Amundsen, Dec. 1911
Scott, Jan. 1912
King Haakon VII Plateau
Shackleton's Farthest Jan. 9th 1909
King Edward VII Plateau
Magnetic South Pole David 1909

Regional Atlas

GENERAL INDEX

For the speedy finding of a place, the rectangles formed on the maps by the intersection of the lines of latitude and longitude are indicated by capital letters along the top and bottom margins of the maps and by small letters down the sides. The number immediately following the names and preceding the marginal letters is that of the page of the atlas in which the place will be found. For example, the name **Aachen** will be found on page **54** of the atlas, under the top marginal letter **B** and along from the side letter **e**.

ABBREVIATIONS

A.-E., Anglo-Egyptian; **Arch**, Archipelago; **Aust.**, Australia; **B.**, Bay, Bahia; **B.C.**, British Columbia; **C.**, Cape, Cabo; **C.A.**, Central America; **Can.**, Canal; **Cent.**, Central; **Chan.**, Channel; **C.I.**, Central India; **Co.**, County; **Col.**, Colony; **Cord.**, Cordillera; **C.P.**, Central Provinces; **Cr.**, Creek; **Dep.**, Department; **Des.**, Desert; **Dist.**, District; **Div.**, Division; **E.**, East, Eastern; **E.I.**, East Indies; **Equat.**, Equatorial; **F.E.A.**, Far Eastern Area; **Fd.**, Fjord; **F.M.S.**, Federated Malay States; **Fr.**, French; **G.**, Gulf, Golfo; **Geb.**, Gebirge; **G.F.**, Goldfield; **Gov.**, Government; **Gt.**, Great; **Harb.**, Harbour; **Hd.**, Head; **I.**, **Is.**, Island, Islands; **Ital.**, Italian; **Junc.**, Junction; **L.**, Lake, Lac, Lago, Loch, Lough; **Lit.**, Little; **Lr.**, Lower; **Mt.**, **Mte.**, Mount, Mont, Monte; **N.**, North, Northern; **N.B.**, New Brunswick; **Nfd.**, Newfoundland; **N.I.**, Netherlands Indies; **N. Ire.**, Northern Ireland; **N.S.**, Nova Scotia; **N.S.W.**, New South Wales; **N.-W.F.P.**, North-West Frontier Province; **N.-W.T.**, North-West Territory; **N.Z.**, New Zealand; **O.F.S.**, Orange Free State; **Pk.**, Peak; **P.E.I.**, Prince Edward Island; **Pen.**, Peninsula; **Plat.**, Plateau; **Prot.**, Protectorate; **Prov.**, Province; **Pt.**, **Pta.**, **Pte.**, Point, Punta, Pointe; **R.**, River; **Ra.**, Range; **Rep.**, Republic; **Res.**, Reservoir; **S.**, South, Southern; **Sa.**, Serra, Sierra; **Sask.**, Saskatchewan; **Sd.**, Sound; **Set.**, Settlement; **St.**, **Ste.**, Saint, Sainte; **Sta.**, Station; **Str.**, Strait; **Terr.**, Territory; **Up.**, Upper; **U.P.**, United Provinces; **U.S.S.R.**, Union of Soviet Socialist Republics (Russia); **Val.**, Valley; **Vol.**, Volcano; **W.**, West, Western; **W.I.**, West Indies.

Aabenraa & Fjord, *Denm'k* 45 Cc
Aabybro, *Denmark* 45 Ca
Aachen (Aix la Chapelle), *Prussia* 54 Be
Aakirkeby, *Bornholm I.* 45 Hf
Aalbæk, *Denmark* 45 Da
Aalborg, *Denmark* 45 Ca
Aalen, *Württemberg* 58 Dc
Aalestrup, *Denmark* 45 Cb
Aarau, *Switzerland* 42 Fb
Aarberg, *Switzerland* 42 Db
Aarburg, *Switzerland* 42 Eb
Aardenburg, *Holland* 29 Bc
Aare, R., *Switzerland* 42 Eb
Aargau, canton, *Switz.* 42 Fb
Aarhus, *Denmark* 45 Db
Aarö, *Denmark* 45 Cc
Aars, *Denmark* 45 Cb
Aba, *Hungary* 66 Db
Aba, *Nigeria* 105 Cd
Abacato, Sa. do, *Brazil* 142 Cc
Abacaxis and R., *Brazil* 142 Cc
Abadan, *Persia* 79 Ec
Abadeh, *Persia* 79 Fc
Abadla, *Algeria* 102 Cd
Aba el Waqf, *Egypt* 107 Hd
Abaete, *Brazil* 143 Ec
Abai, *N. Borneo* 99 Eb
Abaiang, Is., *Gilbert Is.* 157 Ec
Abajo Mts., *Utah* 135 Jc
Abakaliki, *Nigeria* 105 Cd
Abakan, *U.S.S.R.* 76 Kd
Abancay, *Peru* 145 Cd
Abanilla, *Spain* 41 Eb
Abarquh, *Persia* 79 Fc
Abasa, *China* 96 Ac
Abashiri, *Japan* 97 Eb
Abaswein, *Br. Somaliland* 108 Dc
Abau, *New Guinea* 156 Dd
Abauj-Torna, *Hungary* 67 Ga
Abbadia San Salvatore, *Italy* 63 Fe
Abbaretz, *France* 32 Dc
Abbasabad, *Persia* 79 Fb
Abbazia 63 Jb
Abbeville, *Alabama* 130 Fe
Abbeville, *France* 30 Da
Abbeville, *Georgia* 131 Gd
Abbeville, *Louisiana* 130 Bf
Abbeville, *S. Carolina* 131 Gc
Abbey Dore, *England* 14 Bc
Abbeydorney, *Eire* 25 Be
Abbeyfeale, *Eire* 25 Be
Abbeyleix, *Eire* 27 Cf
Abbeyside, *Eire* 27 Cg
Abbey Town, *England* 21 Cd
Abbia, R., *Ethiopia* 108 Cc
Abbiategrasso, *Italy* 62 Db
Abbots Bromley, *England* 18 Ce
Abbotsford, *Quebec* 121 Db
Abbottabad, *N.-W.F.P.* 82 Ea
Abbots, *W. Australia* 152 Bd
Abdal, *Sinkiang* 84 Fc
Abdalagis, Sa. de, *Spain* 40 Fc
Abdelliat, El, *Libya* 106 Ql
Abdulino, *U.S.S.R.* 75 Je
Abéche (Abeshr), *French Equat. Africa* 105 Fc
Abejar, *Spain* 38 Cc
Abemama, I., *Gilbert Is.* 157 Ec
Abengourou, *Fr. W. Afr.* 104 De
Abeokuta, *Nigeria* 105 Bd
Aberavon, *Wales* 20 Cd
Aberayron, *Wales* 20 Bc
Abercorn, *N. Rhodesia* 112 Ba
Abercrombie, *N. Dakota* 132 Ab
Aberdare, *Wales* 20 Cd
Aberdare Mts., *Kenya* 110 Ed
Aberdaron, *Wales* 20 Bb
Aberdeen, *California* 134 Dc
Aberdeen, *Cape Prov.* 114 Ef
Aberdeen, *Idaho* 136 Gd
Aberdeen, *Mississippi* 130 Dd
Aberdeen, *N. Carolina* 131 Jc
Aberdeen, *S. Dakota* 126 Fa
Aberdeen, *Washington* 136 Ab
Aberdeen and co., *Scot.* 23 Fb
Aberdeen L., *N.-W. Terr.* 118 Jd
Aberdour, *Scotland* 23 Ed
Aberdovey, *Wales* 20 Bb
Aberfeldy, *O.F.S.* 115 Hd
Aberfeldy, *Scotland* 23 Ec
Aberffraw, *Wales* 20 Ba
Aberford, *England* 18 Cc
Aberfoyle, *Queensland* 153 Bd
Aberfoyle, *Scotland* 23 Dd
Abergavenny, *England* 14 Bc
Abergele, *Wales* 20 Ca
Abernethy, *Greenland* 9 Cb
Aber Rhiwlech, *Wales* 20 Cb
Aber Soch, *Wales* 20 Bb
Abertillery, *England* 14 Ac
Aberystwyth, *Wales* 20 Bc
Abeshr (Abéche), *French Equat. Africa* 105 Fc
Abha, *Arabia* 78 Lg
Abidjan, *Fr. W. Africa* 104 Df
Abilene, *Kansas* 133 Da
Abilene, *Texas* 133 Cd
Abingdon, *England* 14 Cc
Abingdon, *Illinois* 132 De
Abingdon, *Virginia* 129 Cd
Abington, *Queensland* 153 Bc
Abington, *Scotland* 21 Cc
Abinsi, *Nigeria* 105 Cd
Abiodh Si Cheikh, El, *Algeria* 102 Ec
Abiquiu, *New Mexico* 135 Kc
Abisko, *Sweden* 48 Cb
Abitibi L., *Ontario* 123 Ja
Abitibi R., *Ontario* 123 Ha
Abkhazsk, *Georgia* 75 Gg
Ablitas, *Spain* 38 Dc
Abnub, *Egypt* 107 He
Aboisso, *Fr. W. Africa* 104 De
Abomey, *Fr. W. Africa* 105 Bd
Abondance, *France* 35 Ja
Abong Mbang, *Fr. Equat. Africa* 105 De
Abou Deia, *Fr. Eq. Afr.* 105 Ec
Aboyne, *Scotland* 23 Fb
Abrantes, *Portugal* 37 Bc
Abri, *A.-E. Sudan* 108 Ba
Abrud, *Romania* 67 Jc
Abruka, *Estonia* 49 Bb
Abruzzi & Molise, *Italy* 64 Da
Absaroka Ra., *Montana* 136 Hc
Absdorf, *Austria* 59 Kc
Abtenau, *Austria* 59 Hd
Abu, *Rajputana* 85 Db
Abu Ali I., *Persian Gulf* 79 Ed
Abu Arish, *Yemen* 78 Lg
Abu Deleiq, *A.-E. Sudan* 108 Bb
Abu Dhabi, *Arabia* 79 Fe
Abu Diab, Jeb., *Egypt* 107 Jf
Abu Dis, *A.-E. Sudan* 108 Bb
Abu Gabra, *A.-E. Sudan* 108 Ac
Abu Gher, *Fr. Eq. Afr.* 105 Ec
Abu Girg, *Egypt* 107 Hd
Abu Hamed, *A.-E. Sudan* 108 Bb
Abu Haraz, *A.-E. Sudan* 108 Ac
Abu Hashaifa B., *Egypt* 107 Fc
Abu Hashim, *A.-E. Sudan* 108 Bc
Abu Hôr, *Egypt* 106 Mh
Abuja, *Nigeria* 105 Cd
Abu Kemal, *Syria* 78 Dc
Abul Hiran, *Arabia* 79 Ed
Abu Moharik Dunes, *Egypt* 107 Ge
Abumombasi, *Belg. Congo* 109 Da
Abu Na'ama, *A.-E. Sudan* 108 Bc
Abu Qash, *Palestine* 80 Cd
Abu Qir, *Egypt* 107 Gc
Abû Qurqas, *Egypt* 107 He
Abu Road, *Rajputana* 85 Db
Abu Simbil, *Egypt* 106 Lh
Abu Sosein, *Palestine* 80 Be
Abu Telfane, mt., *Fr. Equat. Africa* 105 Ec
Abû Tig, *Egypt* 107 He
Abu Zabad, *A.-E. Sudan* 108 Ac
Abu Zenima, *Egypt* 107 Jd
Abwong, *A.-E. Sudan* 108 Bd
Abyadh I., *Arabia* 79 Fe
Abyssinia (Ethiopia), *E. Africa* 101 Fe
Acadia Mines, *Nova Scotia* 120 Dd
Acadia Nat. Park, *Maine* 128 Da
Acajutla, *Salvador* 140 Ee
Acambaro, *Mexico* 138 Dc
Acaponeta, *Mexico* 138 Cc
Acapulco, *Mexico* 138 Dd
Acara and R., *Brazil* 143 Ec
Acarigua, *Venezuela* 144 Cb
Acas, *Transylvania* 67 Hb
Acatlan, *Mexico* 139 Ed
Acceglio, *Italy* 62 Bc
Accomac, *Virginia* 129 Gd
Accous, *France* 34 Be
Accra, *Gold Coast* 104 De
Accrington, *England* 18 Bc
Acerra, *Italy* 64 Ec
Achaguas, *Venezuela* 144 Cb
Achao, *Chile* 148 Bc
Acheng, *Manchuria* 96 Db
Achikulak, *U.S.S.R.* 75 Gg
Achill I. and Hd., *Eire* 25 Ab
Achnasheen, *Scotland* 22 Ca
Achray, *Ontario* 121 Bb
Aci Catena, *Sicily* 65 Jg
Acireale, *Sicily* 65 Jg
Ackerman, *Mississippi* 130 Dd
Ackley, *Iowa* 132 Cd
Acklin I., *Bahamas* 140 Cb
Aclare, *Eire* 26 Bc
Acle, *England* 15 Fa
Acme, *W. Virginia* 129 Dc
Aconcagua, mt., *Argent.* 146 Be
Aconcagua, prov., *Chile* 146 Ae
Acorn Hoek, *Transvaal* 115 Jb
Acoyapa, *Nicaragua* 140 Fe
Acquapendente, *Italy* 63 Fe
Acqui, *Italy* 62 Cc
Acre, R., *Brazil* 145 Dc
Acre, Terr. do, *Brazil* 145 Dc
Acre (Akka), & B., *Palestine* 80 Cb
Acroma, *Libya* 106 Db
Acsa, *Hungary* 66 Eb
Actaeon Is., *Tuamotu Arch.* 157 Kf
Actium (Aktion), *Greece* 71 Be
Acton Turville, *England* 14 Bc
Actonvale, *Quebec* 121 Db
Ada, *Gold Coast* 104 Ee
Ada, *Minnesota* 132 Ab
Ada, *Oklahoma* 133 Dc
Ada, *Voyvodina* 66 Fd
Ada-Bazar, *Turkey* 78 Ba
Adair, B., *Mexico* 138 Ba
Adair C., *N.-W. Terr.* 119 Pb
Adairsville, *Georgia* 131 Fc
Adairville, *Kentucky* 130 Eb
Adaja, R., *Spain* 38 Ac
Adak I., *Aleutian Is.* 125 Vm
Adalia (Antalya), *Turkey* 78 Bb
Adam, *Oman* 79 Ge
Adam, Mt., *Falkland Is.* 148 Ee
Adamello, *Italy* 62 Ea
Adaminaby, *N. S. Wales* 155 Fd
Adams, *New York* 123 Ld
Adam's Bridge, *India-Ceylon* 89 Cc
Adams, Mt., *Washington* 136 Cb
Adam's Pk., *Ceylon* 89 Dd
Adămus, *Transylvania* 67 Kc
Adana, *Turkey* 78 Bb
Adanero, *Spain* 38 Ad
Adang B., *Borneo* 99 Ed
Adarama, *A.-E. Sudan* 108 Cb
Adare, *Eire* 27 Bf
Adarot, *A.-E. Sudan* 108 Cb
Adaua, *Ital. Somaliland* 108 Fc
Adavale, *Queensland* 153 Be
Adda, R., *Italy* 62 Db
Addanki, *Madras* 91 Ed
Addis Ababa, *Ethiopia* 108 Cd
Addis Alem, *Ethiopia* 108 Cd
Addison, *New York* 123 Kd
Addison, *Vermont* 128 Ba
Addo, *Cape Prov.* 115 Ff
Addyston, *Ohio* 129 Bc
Adegaon, *Central Provs.* 86 Cd
Adeisseh, *Lebanon* 80 Ca
Adel, *Iowa* 132 Be
Adelaide, *Cape Prov.* 115 Gf
Adelaide, *S. Australia* 154 Bc
Adelaide I., *Antarctica* 160 —
Adelaide Pen., *N.-W. T.* 118 Jc
Adelie Land, *Antarctica* 160 —
Adelong, *New S. Wales* 155 Fd
Adelsheim, *Baden* 58 Db
Ademuz, *Spain* 38 Dd
Aden and colony, *Arabia* 77 Fg
Aden, Gulf of, *Arabia, etc.* 108 Ec
Adhéres, *Greece* 71 Ef
Adi I., *Dutch New Guinea* 156 Ab
Adige, R., *Italy* 62 Ea
Adigrat, *Ethiopia* 108 Cc
Adilabad, *Hyderabad* 90 Db
Adirampatnam, *Madras* 89 Cb
Adirondack Mts., *New York* 123 Lc
Adiscia, *Ethiopia* 108 Cc
Adjim, *Tunisia* 103 Kc
Adjudu-Nou, *Romania* 69 Gb
Adlavik Is., *Labrador* 119 Se
Adler, *U.S.S.R.* 75 Gg
Adler Geb., *Moravia* 57 Bc
Admiralty G., *W. Aust.* 152 Da
Admiralty Is., *Bismarck Ar.* 156 Db
Admiralty Sd., *N.-W. T.* 119 Mb
Adok, *A.-E. Sudan* 108 Bd
Adolfo Alsina (Carhue), *Argentina* 148 Db
Adolphus I., *W. Aust.* 152 Db
Adonara, I., *Nether. Indies* 99 Fe
Adonde, *Arizona* 134 Fe
Adoni, *Madras* 90 Cd
Adony, *Hungary* 66 Db
Adoumre, *Fr. Eq. Africa* 105 Dd
Adour, R., *France* 34 Ad
Adowa, *Ethiopia* 108 Cc
Adra, *Spain* 41 Cd
Adrano, *Sicily* 65 Hg
Adrar, *Algeria* 102 Df
Adrar Souttouf, *Rio de Oro* 104 Ab
Adria, *Italy* 63 Gb
Adrian, *Michigan* 122 Fe
Adrianople (Edirne), *Turkey* 72 Da
Adriatic Sea, *S. Europe* 61 Ec
Adsokha, *Rio de Oro* 104 Ba
Adula Mts., *Switzerland* 43 Hc
Adygeisk, *U.S.S.R.* 75 Fg
Adzaneta, *Spain* 39 Ed
Adzharsk, *Georgia* 75 Gg
Æbeltoft & B., *Denmark* 45 Db
Æbelö, *Denmark* 45 Dc
Ægean Sea, *Greece-Turkey* 61 Ke
Aegina (Aiyina), I., *Greece* 71 Ef
Aere, *Trans-Jordan* 80 Dd
Aërinón, *Greece* 70 Dd
Ærö, *Denmark* 45 Dd
Æröskōbing, *Denmark* 45 Dd
Aerschot, *Belgium* 29 Cd
Aesch, *Switzerland* 42 Eb
Aetós, *Greece* 71 Cf
Affoltern, *Switzerland* 43 Fb
Affreville, *Algeria* 102 Fa
Affric L. and Glen, *Scotland* 22 Cb
Affroun, El, *Algeria* 103 Fa
Affua, *Brazil* 143 Dc
Afghanistan, *S.-W. Asia* 77 Jc
Afghan Turkestan, *Afghan.* 84 Bc
Afgoi, *Ital. Somaliland* 108 Hf
Afidnai, *Greece* 71 Ee
Afikpo, *Nigeria* 105 Cd
Aflenz, *Austria* 59 Kd
Afleu, *Algeria* 102 Fb
Afmadu, *Ital. Somaliland* 108 Gf
Afogados de Ingazeira, *Brazil* 143 Gd
Afognak and I., *Alaska* 125 Jg
Afton, *Iowa* 132 Be
Afton, *Oklahoma* 133 Eb
Afyon Karahisar, *Turkey* 78 Bb
Aga, *Romania* 67 Gd
Agades, *Fr. W. Africa* 105 Cb
Agadir, *Morocco* 103 Nj
Agana, *Marianas Is.* 157 Ql
Agano, R., *Japan* 97 Dc
Agar, *Gwalior* 86 Bd
Agarbiceni, *Transylvania* 69 Eb

Agartala, Eastern States 88 Cc
Agat, Marianas Is. - 157 Ql
Agate, Colorado - 135 Mb
Agathla Pk., Arizona - 135 Hc
Agattu I., Aleutian Is. - 125 Sl
Agawa, Ontario - 122 Fb
Agazzano, Italy - 62 Dc
Agboville, Fr. W. Africa 104 De
Agdam, Azerbaijan - 75 Hg
Agdash, Azerbaijan - 75 Hh
Agde, France - 35 Fd
Agedabia, Libya - 106 Cc
Agelat, el, Libya - 106 Ok
Agen, France - 34 Cc
Agersö, Denmark - 45 Ec
Agersund, Denmark - 45 Ca
Aghda, Persia - 79 Fc
Agiabampo, Mexico - 138 Cb
Agiassos, Lesbos I., Greece 72 Dc
Agira, Sicily - 65 Hg
Agnanda, Greece - 70 Bd
Agnes, Mt., W. Aust. - 152 Dd
Agnita, Romania - 67 Kd
Agno, Philippines - 95 Ef
Agnone, Italy - 64 Eb
Agoes, Texas - 133 Dd
Agordat, Eritrea - 108 Cb
Agordo, Italy - 63 Ga
Agouraï, Morocco - 102 Bc
Agra, United Provs. - 83 He
Agrafa, Greece - 71 Cd
Agrakhanski, U.S.S.R. 75 Hg
Agramunt, Spain - 39 Gc
Agreda, Spain - 38 Dc
Agri, R., Italy - 65 Cb
Agrigento, Sicily - 65 Gg
Agrihan, I., Marianas Is. 157 Bb
Agrínion, Greece - 71 Ce
Agropoli, Italy - 64 Ec
Agua Amarga, Spain - 41 Ed
Agua Clara, Brazil - 147 Ec
Aguadas, Colombia - 144 Ab
Aguadilla, Puerto Rico - 140 Jg
Aguadulce, Panama - 140 Gf
Agua Limpa, Brazil - 143 Dc
Aguanaval, R., Mexico - 138 Dc
Agua Negra, Portugal - 40 Cb
Aguapehy, Sa., Brazil - 146 Db
Agua Prieta, Mexico - 138 Ca
Aguarico, R., Ecuador - 145 Bb
Aguascalientes, Mexico - 138 Dc
Aguaviva, Spain - 39 Ed
Agudos, Brazil - 147 Fc
Aguila, El, Argentina - 148 Cb
Aguilar, Colorado - 135 Lc
Aguilar, Spain - 40 Fb
Aguilas, Spain - 41 Ec
Agulhas, C., Cape Prov. 114 Dg
Agunya, Turkey - 72 Ec
Ahar, Persia - 79 Eb
Ahar, United Provs. - 83 Hd
Ahaus, Prussia - 54 Cc
Ahermoumou, Morocco - 102 Bc
Ahiri, Cent. Provs. - 91 Eb
Ahlen, Prussia - 54 Cd
Ahlhorn, Oldenburg - 54 Dc
Ahmadabad, Bombay - 85 Dc
Ahmadnagar, Bombay - 90 Bb
Ahmadnagar, W. India 85 Dc
Ahmadpur, Punjab - 82 Dc
Ahmadpur, East, Punjab States - 82 Dd
Ahmadpur, West, Punjab States - 82 Dd
Ahmedabad, Bombay - 85 Dc
Ahraura, United Provs. - 87 Ec
Ahrensburg, Prussia - 54 Fb
Ähtäri, Finland - 48 Fe
Ahuachapan, Salvador - 140 Ee
Ahualulco, Mexico - 138 Dc
Ahun, France - 34 Ea
Ahus, Sweden - 51 Dg
Ahvenanmaa (Aland Is.), Finland - 48 Cf
Ahwar, Aden - 77 Fg
Ahwaz, Persia - 79 Ec
Aidone, Sicily - 65 Hg
Aidussina - 63 Hb
Aigle, Switzerland - 42 Dd
Aignan, France - 34 Cd
Aigrefeuille, Loire Inférieure, France - 32 Dc
Aigrefeuille, Charente Inférieure, France - 32 Dd
Aigues-Mortes, France - 35 Gd
Aiguilles, France - 35 Jc
Aiguillon, France - 34 Cc
Aigun (Heilung Kiang), Manchuria - 96 Db
Aigurande, France - 34 Da
Aijal, Assam - 88 Dc
Aika, Burma - 92 Aa
Aikawa, Japan - 97 Dc
Aiken, S. Carolina - 131 Hd
Ai-lao, Annam - 95 Cf
Ailinglapalap Is., Marshall Is. - 157 Dc
Aillant, France - 30 Fd
Ailly-sur-Noye, France - 30 Eb
Ailsa Craig, Scotland - 21 Bc
Aime, France - 35 Jb
Ain, dep., France - 35 Ha
Ain Abessa, Algeria - 103 Ga
Ain Amur, Egypt - 107 Hf
Ainaži, Latvia - 49 Cc
Aïn Beïda, Algeria - 103 Hb
Ain Draham, Tunisia - 103 Ja
Ain Ebel, Lebanon - 80 Ca
Ain el Abd, Libya - 106 Bd
Aïn el Hajel, Syria - 80 Da
Ain el Haramiya, Palestine 80 Cd
Ain-el-Ibel, Algeria - 103 Fb
'Ain es Sir, Trans-Jordan 80 Dd
Ain Galaka, Fr. Eq. Afr. 105 Eb
'Ain Hummar, Trans-Jordan 80 Dc
Ainif, Morocco - 102 Bd
Aïn Madhi, Algeria - 102 Fc
Ain Melfa, Egypt - 106 Ed
Ain Mlila, Algeria - 103 Ha
Ain-Rich, Algeria - 103 Gb
Ain Roua, Algeria - 103 Ga
Ain Sefra, Algeria - 102 Dc
'Ain Sinya, Palestine - 80 Cd
Ain Souf, Algeria - 102 Fe
Ainsworth, Washington - 136 Db
Ain Tagrout, Algeria - 103 Ga
Ain Taya, Algeria - 103 Fa
Ain Temouchent, Algeria 102 Db
Aïoun, El, Morocco - 102 Cb
Aïr (Asben), Fr. W. Afr. 105 Cb
Airabu, I., Nether. Indies 98 Cc
Aird of Sleat, Scotland - 22 Bb
Airdrie, Scotland - 23 De
Aire, Landes, France - 34 Bd
Aire, Pas-de-Calais, France 30 Ea
Aire, R., England - 18 Cc
Airlie, Oregon - 136 Bc
Airlie, Transvaal - 115 Jb
Airole, Italy - 62 Bd
Airolo, Switzerland - 43 Gc
Airvault, France - 30 Be
Aisatung Mt., Burma - 92 Ab
Ai-shan, China - 94 Fb
Aishihik L., Yukon - 124 Bb
Aisne, R. & dep., France 31 Fb
Aït Ani, Morocco - 102 Bd
Aitape, New Guinea - 156 Cb
Aitkin, Minnesota - 132 Cb
Aitolikón, Greece - 71 Ce
Aït Ourir, Morocco - 103 Oj
Aitutaki, I., Cook Is. - 157 He
Aiud, Transylvania - 67 Jc
Aix, France - 35 Hd
Aix, Mt., Washington - 136 Cb
Aix la Chapelle (Achen), Prussia - 54 Be
Aix-les-Bains, France - 35 Hb
Aiyina (Aegina), I., Greece 71 Ef
Aíyion, Greece - 71 De
Ajaccio and G., Corsica 33 Dh
Ajaigarh, Central India - 86 Dc
Ajanta, Hyderabad - 90 Ba
Ajanta Ra., Berar, C.P. 86 Be
Ajib, Oman - 79 Ge
Ajibba, Arabia - 78 Dd
Ajigawasa, Japan - 97 Db
Ajigin, Nigeria - 105 Dc
Ajlun, Trans-Jordan - 80 Dc
Ajmer, Ajmer-Merwara - 85 Ea
Ajmer-Merwara, prov., India - 85 Ea
Ajo and Mts., Arizona - 135 Ge
Akabli, Algeria - 102 Ef
Akalkot, Deccan States - 90 Cc
Akaroa, New Zealand - 159 De
Akas, Assam - 88 Da
Akasa, Nigeria - 105 Ce
Akasha, A.-E. Sudan - 108 Ba
Akashi, Japan - 100 Ed
Akbarpur, United Provs. 83 Je
Akbou, Algeria - 103 Ga
Akcha, Afghanistan - 84 Bc
Ak Dagh, Turkey - 78 Bb
Akershus, fylke, Norway 47 Ge
Akeruf, Fr. W. Africa - 105 Cc
Akhalkalaki, Georgia - 75 Gg
Akhaltsikhe, Georgia - 75 Gg
Akharnaí, Greece - 71 Ee
Akhdhar, Jeb., Oman - 79 Ge
Akhelóos (Aspropótamos), R., Greece - 71 Ce
Akhinós, Greece - 70 Ec
Akhisar, Turkey - 78 Ab
Akhladherí, Greece - 71 Fe
Akhladhokambos, Greece 71 Df
Akhladhokhórion, Greece 70 Eb
Akhmûn, Egypt - 107 He
Akhty, U.S.S.R. - 75 Hg
Akhtyrka Krasnokutsk, Ukraine - 75 Ee
Aki, Japan - 100 De
Akiak, Alaska - 125 Gf
Akimiski I., James B., Canada - 119 Nf
Akita, Japan - 97 Dc
Akjert, Fr. W. Africa - 104 Cc
Akjoujt, Fr. W. Africa - 104 Bc
Akka (Acre), Palestine - 80 Cb
Akkemir, Kazak - 75 Kf
Akkeshi and B., Japan - 97 Fb
Aklavik, N.-W. Terr. - 118 Bc
Akmolinsk, Kazak - 76 Hd
Akniste, Latvia - 49 Cc
Aknoul, Morocco - 102 Cb
Akola, Berar, C.P. - 86 Be
Akot, Berar, C.P. - 86 Be
Akouafim, Fr. Eq. Africa 109 Ba
Akpatok I., N.-W. Terr. 119 Qd
Akra, Norway - 47 Ce
Akra, Jeb. el, Turkey - 78 Cb
Akrála, Greece - 71 De
Akranes, Iceland - 52 Bb
Akrítas, C., Greece - 71 Cg
Akron, Colorado - 135 Ma
Akron, Ohio - 129 Db
Akrotíri Pen., Crete - 71 Hj
Ak-sai Plat., Kirghiz - 84 Db
Aksaray, Turkey - 78 Bb
Akşehir, Turkey - 78 Bb
Aksi, Estonia - 49 Db
Aksum, Ethiopia - 108 Cc
Aktyubinsk, Kazak - 75 Ke
Akulurak, Alaska - 125 Fe
Akune, Japan - 97 Cd
Akureyri, Iceland - 52 Db
Akuse, Gold Coast - 104 Ee
Akutan I., Aleutian Is. - 125 Ej
Akyab, Burma - 92 Ab
Ål, Norway - 46 Ed
Ala, Monti di, Sardinia 64 Jf
Alabama, state, U.S.A. 127 Hd
Alabama R., Alabama - 130 Ee
Alabama City, Alabama 130 Ed
Alaçaat, Turkey - 72 Fc
Ala Dagh, Persia - 79 Gb
Ala dei Sardi, Sardinia - 64 Jf
Alaganik, Alaska - 125 Lf
Alagna, Italy - 62 Bb
Alagoas and state, Brazil 143 Gd
Alagoinhas, Brazil - 143 Ge
Alagon, R., Spain - 37 Dc
Alahanpanjang, Sumatra 98 Bd
Alai Tagh, Kirghiz - 84 Cc
Alaiye, Turkey - 78 Bb
Alajuela, Costa Rica - 140 Ge
Alakylä, Finland - 48 Fc
Al'Ala, Arabia - 78 Cd
Alameda, California - 134 Bc
Alameda, Saskatchewan - 124 Je
Alamogordo, New Mexico 135 Le
Alamos, Mexico - 138 Cb
Alamosa, Colorado - 135 Kc
Alampur, Hyderabad - 90 Cd
Aland, Hyderabad - 90 Cc
Aland Is. (Ahvenanmaa), Finland - 48 Cf
Alandroal, Portugal - 37 Cd
Alaotra L., Madagascar 112 Ec
Alapaevsk, U.S.S.R. 74 Ld
Alarcon, Spain - 38 Ce
Alar del Rey, Spain - 38 Ab
Alas, Timor I., N.I. - 99 Ge
Alas Str., Nether. Indies 99 Ee
Alasehir, Turkey - 78 Ab
Ala-shan, China - 94 Cb
Al Ashkhara, Oman - 79 Ge
Alaska, terr., N. America 118 Da
Alaska, Gulf of, Alaska 125 Lg
Alaska Pen., Alaska - 125 Fj
Alassio, Italy - 62 Cd
Alati, Fr. Equat. Africa 109 Ba
Alatna, Alaska - 125 Jc
Alatri, Italy - 64 Db
Alatyr, U.S.S.R. - 75 He
Alava, prov., Spain - 38 Cb
Alavus, Finland - 48 Ee
Alawoona, S. Australia - 154 Cc
Alayor, Balearic Is. - 39 Mj
Alba, Italy - 62 Cc
Albac, Transylvania - 67 Hc
Albacete & prov., Spain 41 Eb
Alba de Tormes, Spain - 37 Eb
Alba Iulia, Romania - 67 Jc
Albaladejo, Spain - 38 Ce
Albalate, Spain - 38 Cd
Albalate del Arzobispo, Spain 39 Ec
Albania, S.-E. Europe - 61 Hd
Albano, Mte., Italy - 62 Ed
Albany, Georgia - 131 Fe
Albany, Kentucky - 130 Fb
Albany, Missouri - 132 Be
Albany, New York - 123 Ld
Albany, Oregon - 136 Bc
Albany, Texas - 133 Cd
Albany, W. Australia - 152 Be
Albany R., Ontario - 119 Mf
Albarracin & Sa. de, Spain 38 Dd
Al Batn and Jeb., Iraq - 78 Dc
Albemarle, N. Carolina - 131 Hc
Albemarle I. (Isla Isabela), Galapagos Is. - 145 Eh
Albemarle Sd., N. Carolina 131 Kb
Albenga, Italy - 62 Cc
Alberese, Italy - 62 Fe
Albergaria, Portugal - 37 Bb
Alberigue, Spain - 41 Fa
Alberobello, Italy - 65 Db
Albert, France - 30 Ea
Albert, New Brunswick - 120 Cd
Albert L., Oregon - 136 Cd
Albert, L., S. Australia 154 Bd
Albert, L., Uganda-Belg. Congo - 110 Bc
Albert, Mt., Quebec - 120 Bb
Alberta, Mt., Alberta - 124 Fd
Alberta, prov., Canada - 118 Ff
Albert Edward, Mt., New Guinea - 156 Dc
Albert Edward Ra., W. Australia - 152 Db
Albertinia, Cape Prov. - 114 Dg
Albert Lea, Minnesota - 132 Cd
Albert Nat. Park, Belg. Congo - 109 Eb
Albert Nile, R., Uganda 110 Bb
Alberton, Prince Edward I. 120 Cc
Alberton, Victoria - 155 Ee
Albertville, Alabama - 130 Ec
Albertville, Belg. Congo 109 Ec
Albertville, France - 35 Jb
Albi, France - 34 Ed
Albia, Iowa - 132 Ce
Albina, Suriname - 142 Da
Albino, Italy - 62 Db
Albion, California - 134 Bb
Albion, Idaho - 136 Gd
Albion, Indiana - 129 Bb
Albion, Michigan - 122 Fd
Albion, New S. Wales - 154 Cb
Albion, New York - 123 Jd
Albion, Pennsylvania - 129 Db
Albocacer, Spain - 39 Fd
Albona - 63 Jb
Alboran I., Mediterr. Sea 102 Cb
Alboraya, Spain - 39 Ee
Albrighton, England - 14 Ba
Albufeira, Portugal - 40 Bb
Albufera de Mezcaltitlan, Mexico - 138 Cc
Albuquerque, New Mexico 135 Kd
Alburquerque, Spain - 37 Dc
Albury, New S. Wales - 155 Ed
Alby, France - 35 Jb
Alcacer do Sal, Portugal 37 Bd
Alcala, Spain - 39 Fd
Alcalá de Henares, Spain 38 Bd
Alcala de la Selva, Spain 38 Ed
Alcala del Jucar, Spain - 41 Ea
Alcala la Real, Spain - 41 Cc
Alcamo, Sicily - 65 Fg
Alcanar, Spain - 39 Fd
Alcañiz, Spain - 39 Ec
Alcantara, Brazil - 143 Ec
Alcantara, Spain - 37 Dc
Alcantarilla, Spain - 41 Ec
Alcaraz and Sa. de, Spain 41 Db
Alcarraz, Spain - 39 Fc
Alcarria, Spain - 38 Cd
Alcazar del Rey, Spain - 38 Cd
Alcazar de San Juan, Spain 38 Be
Alcazarquivir, Sp. Morocco 102 Bb
Alcester, England - 14 Cb
Alcira, Spain - 41 Fa
Alcobaça, Brazil - 143 Dc
Alcocer, Spain - 38 Cd
Alcochete, Portugal - 37 Bd
Alcolea de Cinca, Spain 39 Ec
Alconbury, England - 15 Db
Alconbury Hill, England 15 Db
Alconchel, Spain - 37 Cd
Alcora, Spain - 39 Ed
Alcoutim, Portugal - 40 Cb
Alcoy, Spain - 41 Fb
Alcubierre and Sa. de, Spain - 39 Ec
Alcublas, Spain - 38 Ee
Alcudia & B., Balearic Is. 39 Je
Alcuescar, Spain - 37 Dc
Alcuneza, Spain - 38 Cc
Aldabra, I., Indian Oc. - 112 Ea
Aldama, Chihuahua, Mexico 138 Cb
Aldama, Tamaulipas, Mexico - 139 Ec
Aldeadavila de la Ribera, Spain - 37 Da
Aldeaquemada, Spain - 41 Cb
Aldeburgh, England - 15 Fb
Aldeia Cumare, Brazil - 142 De
Alder, Montana - 136 Gc
Alderley Edge, England 18 Bd
Aldermaston, England - 14 Cd
Alderney, I., Channel Is. 17 Ee
Aldershot, England - 15 Dd
Aldrea, Quebec - 121 Da
Aldridge, England - 14 Ca
Aldridge, Montana - 136 Hc
Aledo, Illinois - 132 De
Aledua, Sa. de, Spain - 38 De
Aleg, Fr. W. Africa - 104 Bc
Alegrete, Brazil - 146 Dd
Alegria, Spain - 38 Cb
Aleksandrov, U.S.S.R. - 74 Fd
Aleksandrovac, Serbia - 68 Fc
Aleksandrov Gai, U.S.S.R. 75 He
Aleksandrovo, Serbia - 70 Ca
Aleksandrovsk, U.S.S.R. 93 Ga
Aleksandrovsk Mts., Kirghiz - 84 Db
Aleksandrow, Poland - 57 Da
Alekseevka, U.S.S.R. - 75 Fe
Aleksinac, Serbia - 69 Dd
Ålem, Sweden - 51 Ff
Alemalla, New Mexico - 135 Kd
Alemquer, Brazil - 142 Dc
Alençon, France - 30 Bc
Alenquer, Portugal - 37 Ac
Alentejo, prov., Portugal 40 Bb
Aleppo, Syria - 78 Cb
Aleria, Corsica - 33 Eg
Alés, France - 35 Gc
Alesd, Transylvania - 67 Hb
Alessandria, Italy - 62 Cc
Alessio (Lesh), Albania - 70 Ab
Aletschhorn, Switzerland 42 Ed
Aleutian Is., Bering Sea 125 Dk
Aleutian Ra., Alaska - 125 Gh
Alexander Arch., Alaska 125 Nh
Alexander, C., Greenland 9 Bb
Alexander I., W. Aust. - 152 Db
Alexander I. Land, Antarctica - 160 —
Alexandra, New Zealand 159 Bf
Alexandra, Mt., Fr. Eq. Africa - 109 Bb
Alexandretta, Turkey - 78 Cb
Alexandria, Cape Prov. - 115 Gf
Alexandria, Louisiana - 130 Be
Alexandria, Minnesota - 132 Bc
Alexandria, Ontario - 121 Cb
Alexandria, Romania - 69 Fc
Alexandria, Scotland - 23 De
Alexandria, Victoria - 154 Ed
Alexandria, Virginia - 129 Fc
Alexandria Bay, New York 128 Aa
Alexandria (Iskindiriya), Egypt - 107 Gc
Alexandrina, L., S. Aust. 154 Bd
Alexandroupolis (Dede Agach), Greece - 72 Cb
Aléxia, Greece - 70 Db
Al Falluja, Iraq - 78 Dc
Alfaro, Spain - 38 Db
Alfarras, Spain - 39 Fc
Alfatar - 69 Gd
Alfedena, Italy - 64 Eb
Alfeizerao, Portugal - 37 Ac
Alfeld, Prussia - 54 Ed
Alfios, R., Greece - 71 Cf
Alfonsine, Italy - 63 Gc
Alford, Scotland - 23 Fb
Alfotbreen, mt., Norway 46 Bc
Alfred, Maine - 128 Cb
Alfredo Chaves, Brazil - 147 Ed
Alfreton, England - 18 Cd
Alfta, Sweden - 50 Fa
Alga, Kazak - 75 Ke
Algadefe, Spain - 36 Eb
Algaida, Balearic Is. - 39 He
Algarås, Sweden - 50 Dd
Algard, Norway - 47 Bf
Algarinejo, Spain - 41 Bc
Algarve, prov., Portugal 40 Bb
Algauer Alps, Austria - 58 Dd
Algeciras & B., Spain - 40 Ec
Alger and dep., Algeria 102 Fa
Alger B. d', Algeria - 103 Fa
Algeria, N. Africa - 101 Cb
Alghero, Sardinia - 64 Hf
Algiers (Alger), Algeria 102 Fa
Alginet, Spain - 38 Ee

Algoa, N. Rhodesia - 112 Ab
Algoa B., Cape Prov. - 115 Ff
Algodonales & Sa. de, Spain - - - - 40 Ec
Algodones, New Mexico 135 Kd
Algoma, Ontario - - 122 Gb
Algoma, Wisconsin - 132 Fc
Algona, Iowa - - 132 Bd
Algonquin Park, Ontario 121 Ab
Algyö, Hungary - - 66 Fc
Alhama, Sa. de, Spain - 41 Bd
Alhama de Aragón, Spain 38 Dc
Alhambra, California - 134 Dd
Alhambra, Spain - - 41 Cb
Alhamilla, Sa., Spain - 41 Dd
Alhandra, Portugal - 37 Bd
Alia, Sicily - - - 65 Gg
Alia, Spain - - - 37 Ec
Aliabad, Persia - - 79 Fb
Aliákmon, R., Greece - 70 Cc
Alibag, Bombay - - 90 Ab
Alibey, Turkey - - 72 Dc
Alibunar, Voyvodina - 67 Gd
Alicante and B., Spain - 41 Fb
Alicante, prov., Spain - 41 Fb
Alice, Cape Prov. - - 115 Gf
Alice, Ontario - - 121 Bb
Alicedale, Cape Prov. - 115 Gf
Alice Springs, N. T., Aust. 151 Ec
Aliceville, Alabama - 130 Dd
Alicudi I., Italy - - 65 Hf
Aliganj, United Provs. - 83 He
Aligarh, Rajputana - 86 Bc
Aligarh, United Provs. - 83 He
Aligarh (Koil), Unit. Provs. 83 Ge
Alika, Greece - - - 71 Dg
Ali Khel, Afghanistan - 82 Cb
Ali Kobbo, Belg. Congo - 109 Da
Alimena, Sicily - - 65 Hg
Aling Kangri, Tibet - 84 Ed
Alingsas, Sweden - - 51 Be
Alipore, Bengal - - 88 Bc
Alipur, Bengal - - 88 Ba
Alipur, Punjab - - 82 Dd
Alipura, Central India - 86 Cc
Alirajpur, Central India 85 Ec
Aliuş, Romania - - 67 Gc
Aliverion, Greece - - 71 Fe
Aliwal, Punjab - - 83 Fc
Aliwal North, Cape Prov. 115 Ge
Al Jazira, Iraq - - 78 Db
Aljustrel, Portugal - 40 Bb
Alkali L., Oregon - - 136 Cd
Alkavare, Sweden - - 48 Bc
Alkionídhes Is., Greece - 71 De
Alkmaar, Holland - - 29 Cb
Allada, Fr. W. Africa - 105 Bd
Allahabad, United Provs. 86 Dc
Allakaket, Alaska - - 125 Jc
Allanmyo, Burma - - 92 Bc
Allantown, Arizona - 135 Jd
Allariz, Spain - - 36 Cb
Allas, Sumatra - - 98 Bd
Allata, Ethiopia - - 108 Cd
Alle, R. - - - 56 Eb
Alleg, Jeb., Algeria - 102 Eb
Alleghany R., Pennsyl. - 129 Eb
Alleghe, Italy - - 63 Ga
Allegheny Mts., U.S.A. 129 Ed
Allègre, France - - 35 Fb
Allen, Oklahoma - - 133 Dc
Allen, Bog of, Eire - 27 Ce
Allenburg - - - 56 Fb
Allenby Bridge, Trans-Jordan - - - 80 Dd
Allendale, South Carolina 131 Hd
Allendale Town, England 21 Dd
Allende, Mexico - - 138 Db
Allende, Mexico - - 138 Cb
Allendorf, Prussia - - 54 Ed
Allenstein - - - 56 Ec
Allentown, Pennsylvania 129 Gb
Alleppey, Madras States 89 Bc
Aller, R., Prussia - - 54 Ec
Alliance, Ohio - - 129 Db
Allier R. & dep., France 35 Fa
Alligny, France - - 31 Gd
Allikher, Hyderabad - 90 Cb
Alliston, Ontario - - 123 Hc
Alloa, Scotland - - 23 Ed
Allora, Queensland - - 153 De
Allos, France - - 33 Ba
All Pines, Br. Honduras 140 Fd
Allumette I., Quebec - 121 Bb
Allur, Madras - - 91 Ed
Alma, Arkansas - - 130 Ac
Alma, Georgia - - 131 Ge
Alma, Kansas - - 133 Da
Alma, Michigan - - 122 Fd
Alma, Washington - 136 Da
Alma, Wisconsin - - 132 Dc
Alma Ata, Kazak - - 76 He
Alma Chaab, Lebanon - 80 Ca
Almaden & Sa. de, Spain 37 Fd
Almagrera, Sa., Spain - 41 Ec
Almagro, Spain - - 41 Cb
Almansa, Spain - - 41 Eb
Almanzor, Pico de, Spain 37 Eb
Almarail, Spain - - 38 Cc
Almaraz, Spain - - 37 Ec
Almarza, Spain - - 38 Cc
Almas Mts., Romania - 67 He
Almasul Mare, Romania 67 Hc
Almaville, Quebec - - 121 Da
Almazan, Spain - - 38 Cc
Almazora, Spain - - 39 Ee
Älmeboda, Sweden - 51 Ef
Almeida, Portugal - - 37 Db
Almeida B., Mozambique 112 Db
Almeirim, Brazil - - 142 Dc
Almeirim, Portugal - 37 Bc
Almelo, Holland - - 29 Eb
Almenar, Spain - - 39 Fc
Almenara, Sa. de, Spain 41 Ec
Almendra, Spain - - 36 Dc
Almendralejo, Spain - 37 Dd
Almendricos, Spain - 41 Ec
Almeria, prov., Spain - 41 Dc
Almeria & Gulf of, Spain 41 Dd
Älmhult, Sweden - - 51 Df
Almijara, Sa. de, Spain 41 Cd
Almina, Pta., Sp. Morocco 102 Bb
Almirante, Panama - 140 Gf
Almirós, Greece - - 70 Dd
Almirós, B. of, Crete - 71 Hj
Almodovar, Portugal - 40 Bb
Almodovar del Campo, Spain - - - 41 Bb
Almodovar del Rio, Spain 40 Eb
Almolda, la, Spain - 39 Ec
Almonaster la Real, Spain 40 Db
Almondsbury, England - 14 Bc
Almonte, Ontario - - 121 Bb
Almonte, Spain - - 40 Db
Almora, United Provs. - 83 Hd
Almorox, Spain - - 38 Ad
Almudebar, Spain - - 39 Eb
Almuñecar, Spain - - 41 Cd
Almunia de Doña Godina, la, Spain - - - 38 Dc
Almusafes, Spain - - 39 Ee
Al Musaiyib, Iraq - - 78 Dc
Al Muwaila, Arabia - 78 Bd
Almy, Wyoming - - 135 Ha
Alness, Scotland - - 23 Da
Alnmouth, England - 21 Ec
Alnwick, England - - 21 Ec
Alobras, Spain - - 38 Dd
Alon, Burma - - - 92 Ba
Alón (Iliodhromia), I., Greece - - - 70 Ed
Alor, I., Nether. Indies - 99 Fe
Alora, Spain - - - 40 Fc
Alor Star, Malay States 98 Bb
Alos, Spain - - - 39 Gb
Alosno, Spain - - 40 Cb
Alost, Belgium - - 29 Cd
Alouet el Gounna, Tunisia 103 Kc
Alougoum, Morocco - 103 Oj
Alpar, Hungary - - 66 Ec
Alpena, Michigan - - 122 Gc
Alpes Maritimes & dep., France - - - 33 Ba
Alpha, Idaho - - 136 Fc
Alpha, Queensland - - 153 Cd
Alphen, Holland - - 29 Cb
Alpheton, England - 15 Eb
Alpuente, Spain - - 38 Ee
Alpujarras, Las, Spain - 41 Cd
Alpullu, Turkey - - 72 Ea
Al Qaiyara, Iraq - - 78 Db
Al Qara, Arabia - - 78 Dd
Al Qunfidha, Arabia - 78 Lg
Al Qurna, Iraq - - 79 Ec
Alresford, England - 14 Cd
Alrewas, England - - 14 Ca
Als and Fjord, Denmark 45 Cc
Alsasua, Spain - - 38 Cb
Alsea R., Oregon - - 136 Bc
Alsenz, Saar Palatinate - 58 Bb
Alsfeld, Hesse - - 58 Da
Alsleben, Prussia - - 55 Gd
Alstead, New Hampshire 128 Bb
Alsterbro, Sweden - - 51 Ef
Alston, England - - 21 Dd
Alsvanga, Latvia - - 49 Ac
Alta, Norway - - 48 Eb
Alta Fjord, Norway - 48 Ea
Alta Gracia, Argentina - 146 Ce
Altagracia, Venezuela - 144 Ba
Altagracia de Orituco, Venezuela - - - 144 Cb
Altai Mts., Mongolia - 93 Bb
Altamachi, Bolivia - 146 Bb
Altamaha R., Georgia - 131 He
Altamira, Brazil - - 142 Dc
Altamont, New York - 128 Ab
Altamura, Italy - - 65 Cb
Altar, Mexico - - 138 Ba
Altas Mesetas del Deseado, Argentina - - 148 Bd
Altata, Mexico - - 138 Cc
Altavas, Philippines - 99 Fa
Altavilla Irpina, Italy - 64 Eb
Alt Damm - - - 55 Kb
Altdorf, Switzerland - 43 Gc
Alte, R., Norway - - 44 Ee
Alte Land, Prussia - 54 Eb
Altea, Spain - - - 41 Fb
Altena, Prussia - - 54 Cd
Altenberg, Saxony - - 55 Je
Altenburg, Thuringia - 55 He
Altenglan, Saar Palatinate 58 Bb
Altenkirchen, Prussia - 55 Ja
Altenmarkt, Austria - 59 Lc
Alter de Chão, Portugal 37 Cc
Althorpe, England - 19 Dc
Altinoluk, Turkey - - 72 Dc
Altkirch, France - - 31 Kd
Alt Landsberg, Prussia - 55 Jc
Altmark, dist., Prussia - 55 Gc
Altmuhl, R., Bavaria - 59 Fc
Altnaharra, Scotland - 24 De
Altömunster, Bavaria - 58 Fc
Alton, England - - 15 Dd
Alton, Florida - - 131 Ge
Alton, Illinois - - 132 Df
Alton, Missouri - - 130 Cb
Alton, New Hampshire - 128 Cb
Alton, Queensland - - 153 Ce
Altona, Hamburg - - 54 Eb
Altona, New York - - 123 Mc
Altoona, Pennsylvania - 129 Eb
Altopascio, Italy - - 62 Ed
Altrincham, England - 18 Bd
Altshausen, Württemberg 58 Dd
Altstadt, Moravia - - 57 Bc
Altstätten, Switzerland - 43 Jb
Altstetten, Switzerland - 43 Gb
Altun Köpri, Iraq - - 78 Db
Altura, Colorado - - 135 Kc
Altura - - - - 63 Hc
Altura, Spain - - 38 Ee
Alturas, California - 134 Ca
Altus, Oklahoma - - 133 Cc
Altvater, Moravia - - 57 Cc
Alty Kara Su, Kazak - 75 Kf
Altyn Tagh, Sinkiang - 84 Ec
Al Ugla, Arabia - - 78 Cd
Aluksne, Latvia - - 49 Dc
Alula, Ital. Somaliland - 108 Fc
Alumine, Argentina - 148 Bb
Alunis, Transylvania - 67 Kc
Alur, Madras - - 90 Cd
Alushta, Crimea - - 75 Eg
Aluta, Belgian Congo - 109 Eb
Alva, Oklahoma - - 133 Cb
Alvand Kuh, Persia - 79 Ec
Alvarado, California - 134 Bc
Alvarado, Mexico - - 139 Ed
Alvarado, Texas - - 133 Dd
Älvdalen, Sweden - - 50 Da
Älve Fd., Sweden - - 51 Ae
Alvear, Argentina - 148 Db
Alverca, Portugal - - 37 Ad
Alversund, Norway - 46 Bd
Alvesta, Sweden - - 51 Df
Alveston, England - 14 Bc
Älvik, Norway - - 47 Cd
Alvin, Texas - - 133 Ef
Alvito, Portugal - - 40 Ba
Alvord, L., Oregon - 136 Dd
Älvsborg, län, Sweden - 51 Be
Älvsby, Sweden - - 48 Dd
Älvsered, Sweden - - 51 Be
Älvsjö, Sweden - - 50 Hc
Al Wadyan, Arabia, etc. 78 Dc
Alwalton, England - 15 Da
Alwar, Rajputana - - 83 Ge
Alward, New Brunswick 120 Cc
Al Wasm, Arabia - - 78 Lg
Alyaty, Azerbaijan - 75 Hh
Alyth, Scotland - - 23 Ec
Alytus, Lithuania - - 49 Cd
Alzey, Hesse - - 58 Cb
Alzonne, France - - 34 Ed
Amabele, Cape Prov. - 115 Gf
Amacuro, Terr., Venezuela 144 Db
Amadeus L., N.T., Aust. 150 Dc
Amadi, A.-E. Sudan - 108 Bd
Amadi, Belgian Congo - 109 Ea
Amadia, Iraq - - - 78 Db
Amadjuak L., N.-W. Terr. 119 Qd
Amager I., Denmark - 45 Fc
Amagne, France - - 31 Gb
Amakusa Nada, Japan - 97 Bd
Amakusa-shima, Japan - 97 Bd
Åmål, Sweden - - 50 Bc
Amalfi, Italy - - - 64 Ec
Amalga, Alaska - - 125 Ng
Amalias, Greece - - 71 Cf
Amalner, Bombay - - 90 Ba
Amami Gunto, Japan - 93 Ed
Amanalco, Mexico - - 138 Dd
Amandas, S. Rhodesia - 113 Da
Amandola, Italy - - 63 He
Amantea, Italy - - 65 Bc
Amantumkan, Kenya - 110 Fe
Amapala, Honduras - 140 Fe
Amapa, terr., Brazil - 142 Db
'Amara, Iraq - - 79 Ec
Amaramba, Mozambique 112 Cb
Amarante, Brazil - - 143 Fd
Amarapura, Burma - 92 Cb
Amargosa, Brazil - - 143 Fe
Amarillo, Texas - - 133 Ac
Amaro, Mte., Italy - 64 Ea
Amarracão, Brazil - - 143 Fc
Amasra, Turkey - - 78 Ba
Ama-surgu Mts., China 94 Bb
Amasya, Turkey - - 78 Ca
Amatique, Gulf, Guatemala 140 Fd
Amatitlan, Guatemala - 140 Ee
Amatonga, Mozambique - 113 Ed
Amayantir (Vergara), Philippines - - - 99 Fb
Amazon, Mths. R., Brazil 143 Eb
Amazonas, Colombia - 144 Bd
Amazonas, dep., Peru - 145 Bc
Amazonas R. and state, Brazil - - - 142 Bc
Amazonas, terr., Venez. 144 Cc
Amba, Hyderabad - - 90 Cb
Amba Alagi, mt., Ethiopia 108 Cc
Ambaca, Angola - - 109 Cc
Ambala, Punjab - - 83 Gc
Ambalabao, Madagascar 112 Dc
Ambaro B., Madagascar 112 Eb
Ambasamudram, Madras 89 Bc
Ambato, Ecuador - - 145 Bb
Ambazac, France - - 34 Db
Ambelákia, Greece - - 70 Dd
Ambelau, I., Nether. Indies 99 Gd
Ambelon, Greece - - 70 Dd
Ambelos, C., Greece - 70 Ed
Amber, Rajputana - - 83 Fe
Amber, C., Madagascar 112 Eb
Amber Mts., Madagascar 112 Eb
Amberg, Bavaria - - 59 Fb
Ambergris Cay, Bahamas 140 Cb
Ambergris Cay, British Honduras - - - 140 Fd
Ambert, France - - 35 Fb
Ambgaon, Central Provs. 86 De
Ambikapur, Eastern States 87 Ed
Amble, England - - 21 Ec
Ambleside, England - 18 Bb
Ambohibé, Madagascar 112 Dd
Ambohimahasoa, Madag. 112 Ed
Amboina, I., Nether. Indies 99 Gd
Amboise, France - - 30 Dd
Ambong, N. Borneo - 99 Eb
Ambongo, Madagascar - 112 Dc
Ambonnay, France - - 31 Gb
Ambositra, Madagascar 112 Ed
Amboy, California - - 134 Fd
Amboy, New Jersey - 129 Gb
Amboy, Washington - 136 Bc
Ambridge, Pennsylvania 129 Db
Ambrières, France - - 32 Eb
Ambrim, I., New Hebrides 157 De
Ambriz, Angola - - 109 Bc
Ambrizette & R., Angola 109 Bc
Ambunti, New Guinea - 156 Cb
Ambur, Madras - - 90 De
Amchitka I., Aleutian Is. 125 Um
Amderma, U.S.S.R. - 74 Lb
Ameca, Mexico - - 138 Dc
Ameca, R., Mexico - 138 Cc
Ameland, I., Holland - 29 Da
Amelia, Italy - - 64 Ca
Amelia, Virginia - - 129 Fd
Amelia I., Florida - 131 He
Amendolara, Italy - 65 Cc
Amenia, New York - 128 Bc
Amer, Spain - - - 39 Hb
American Falls & Reservoir, Idaho - - - 136 Gd
Americus, Georgia - 131 Fd
Amersfoort, Holland - 29 Db
Amersfoort, Transvaal - 115 Hc
Amersham, England - 15 Dc
Ames, Iowa - - 132 Ce
Amesbury, England - 14 Cd
Amesbury, Massachusetts 128 Cb
Ameskhoud, Morocco - 103 Nj
Amet, Rajputana - - 85 Eb
Amethi, United Provs. - 86 Db
Ametlla del Mar, Spain - 39 Fd
Amfiklia, Greece - - 71 De
Amfilokhía, Greece - 71 Ce
Amfipolis, Greece - - 70 Ec
Amfissa, Greece - - 71 De
Amfreville, France - 30 Cb
Amgun, R., U.S.S.R. - 96 Fa
Amhara, Ethiopia - - 108 Cc
Amherst, Massachusetts - 128 Bb
Amherst, Nova Scotia - 120 Cd
Amherst I., Ontario - 121 Bb
Amherst, Mt., W. Aust. 152 Db
Amherst (Kyaikkami), Burma - - - 92 Cd
Amherstburg, Ontario - 122 Gd
Amiens, France - - 30 Eb
Amigdhala, Greece - 70 Cc
Amik Lake, Ontario - 123 Jc
Amíndaion, Greece - 70 Cc
Aming, Japan - - 100 Ed
Aminwiz, S.-W. Africa - 114 Ca
Amite, Louisiana - - 130 Ce
Amizmiz, Morocco - - 103 Nj
Amjhera, Gwalior - - 85 Ec
Åmli, Norway - - 47 Ef
Amlia I., Aleutian Is. - 125 Wl
Amlwch, Wales - - 20 Ba
'Amm Adam, A.-E. Sudan 108 Cb
Amman, Trans-Jordan - 80 Dd
Ammanford, Wales - 20 Cd
Ammarnäs, Sweden - 48 Ad
Ammendorf, Prussia - 55 Hd
Ammer Geb., Bavaria - 58 Ed
Ammer See, Bavaria - 58 Fd
Ammi Mussa, Algeria - 102 Eb
Ammouliani, Greece - 70 Ec
Amoentai, Borneo - - 99 Ed
Amoerang, Celébes - - 99 Fc
Amorgos, I., Ægean Sea 78 Ab
Amory, Mississippi - 130 Dc
Amos, Quebec - - 123 Ka
Åmot, Norway - - 46 Cc
Åmot, Norway - - 46 Hc
Åmot, Sweden - - 50 Bc
Amotsdal, Norway - 47 Ee
Amour, Jeb., Algeria - 102 Ec
Amoy, China - - - 95 Ee
Ampani, Eastern States - 91 Fb
Amparo, Bahia, Brazil - 143 Ge
Amparo, São Paulo, Brazil 147 Fc
Ampato, Cord. de, Peru 145 Ce
Ampere, Algeria - - 103 Gb
Ampezzo, Italy - - 63 Ga
Ampleforth, England - 18 Cb
Amplepuis, France - 35 Gb
Amposta, Spain - - 39 Fd
Ampthill, England - 15 Db
Ampudia, Spain - - 38 Ac
Ampuero, Spain - - 38 Ba
Ampurdan, El, Spain - 39 Hb
Amqui, Quebec - - 120 Bb
Amran, Yemen - - 78 Lg
Amraoti, Berar, C.P. - 86 Be
Amrapur, Western India 85 Bd
Amreli, Baroda - - 85 Cd
Amriswil, Switzerland - 43 Ha
Amritsar, Punjab - - 83 Fc
Amroha, United Provs. - 83 Hd
Amrum, I., Prussia - 54 Da
Amsele, Sweden - - 48 Cd
Amsterdam, Holland - 29 Cb
Amsterdam, New York - 123 Md
Amsterdam, Transvaal - 115 Jc
Amsterdam I., Svalbard 9 Kb
Amstetten, Austria - 59 Jc
Am Timmane, Fr. Equat. Africa - - - 105 Ec
Amu Darya, Turkmen - 76 Gf
Amul, Persia - - 79 Fb
Amulree, Scotland - 23 Ed
Amund Ringnes I., N.-W. Terr. - - - 118 Ka
Amundsen Gulf, N.-W. T. 118 Eb
Amungen, L., Sweden - 50 Ea
Amur R., Manchuria-U.S.S.R. - - - 96 Fa
Amuria, Uganda - - 110 Cb
Amurrio, Spain - - 38 Ca
Amusco, Spain - - 38 Ab
Amvrakía L. & G., Greece 71 Ce
Amvrosia, Greece - - 72 Ca
Amyot, Ontario - - 122 Fa
'Ana, Iraq - - - 78 Dc
Anaa Is., Tuamotu Arch. 157 Je
Anabama, S. Australia - 154 Cc
Anaconda, Montana - 136 Gb
Anacortes, Washington - 136 Ba
Anadarko, Oklahoma - 133 Cc
Anadyr & Mts., U.S.S.R. 76 Sc
Anadyr, G. of, U.S.S.R. 76 Sc
Anagni, Italy - - 64 Db
Anagundi, Hyderabad - 90 Cd

Anahauc, Texas 133 Ef
Anaheim, California 134 Ee
Anaimalai Hills, Madras States 89 Bb
Anaiza, Arabia 78 Dd
Anaiza, Jeb., Iraq 78 Dc
Anakapalle, Madras 91 Fc
Analalava, Madagascar 112 Eb
Anama, Brazil 142 Bc
Anambas Is., Nether. Indies 98 Cc
Anamosa, Iowa 132 Dd
Anand, Bombay 85 Dc
Anandpur, Punjab 83 Gc
Ananev, Moldavia 75 Ef
Anantapur, Madras 90 Cd
Anapa, U.S.S.R. 75 Ff
Anar, Persia 79 Gc
Anarak, Persia 79 Fc
Anardarra, Afghanistan 79 Hc
Anascaul, Eire 25 Ae
Anastasia I., Florida 131 Hf
'Anata, Palestine 80 Cd
Anatahan, I., Marianas Is. 157 Bb
Anatolia, Turkey 78 Bb
Anatone, Washington 136 Eb
Anávissos, Greece 71 Ef
Anavrití, Greece 71 Df
Ancash, dep., Peru 145 Bc
Ancenis, France 32 Dc
Ancerville, France 31 Hc
Ancha Mts., Arizona 135 Hd
Anchao, Nigeria 105 Cc
Anchieta, Brazil 147 Gc
Anchorage, Alaska 125 Jf
Ancião, Portugal 37 Bc
Ancohuma, Bolivia 146 Bb
Ancon, Peru 145 Bd
Ancona, Italy 63 Hd
Ancon de Salinas B., Ecuador 145 Ba
Ancrum, Scotland 21 Db
Ancua, mt., Ethiopia 108 Cc
Ancuaze, Mozambique 113 Fa
Ancud and G. de, Chile 148 Bc
Ancy-le-Franc, France 31 Gd
Andacolla, Argentina 148 Bb
Andai, New Guinea 156 Ab
Andal, Bengal 88 Ac
Andalgala, Argentina 146 Bd
Andalsnes, Norway 46 Db
Andalusia, Alabama 130 Ee
Andalusia, div., Spain 40 Eb
Andaman Is., Bay of Bengal 91 Kk
Andaos, Peru 145 Bb
Andelfingen, Switzerland 43 Ga
Andenne, Belgium 29 Dd
Andere, Sinkiang 84 Ec
Andermatt, Switzerland 43 Gc
Andernack, Prussia 54 Ce
Anders, Oklahoma 133 Ec
Anderson, California 134 Ba
Anderson, Indiana 129 Ab
Anderson, South Carolina 131 Gc
Anderson R., N.-W. T. 118 Dc
Andes, Cord. de los, S. America 146 Bd
Andevorante, Madagascar 112 Ec
Andia, Sa. de, Spain 38 Cb
Andíkira, B. of, Greece 71 De
Andikíthira (Cerigotto), I., Greece 71 Eh
Andimilos, I., Greece 71 Fg
Andizhan, Uzbek 84 Cb
Andkhui, Afghanistan 84 Bc
Andoain, Spain 38 Da
Andora, Italy 62 Cd
Andorra, Spain 39 Ec
Andorra & rep., Pyrenees 39 Gb
Andover, England 14 Cd
Andoversford, England 14 Cc
Andöy, Norway 44 Ce
Andraitx, Balearic Is. 39 He
Andrakala, Madagascar 112 Ee
Andranomalaza, Madag. 112 Eb
Andranovelona, Madag. 112 Fc
Andravidha, Greece 71 Cf
Andreafski, Alaska 125 Fe
Andreanof Is., Aleutian Is. 125 Vm
Andreevka, U.S.S.R. 75 Je
Andrew Gordon B., N.-W. Terr. 119 Od
Andrews Sd., Georgia 131 He
Andria, Italy 65 Ca
Andrijevica, Montenegro 68 Ed
Andros I., Bahamas 140 Bb
Andros, I., Greece 61 Kf
Androscoggin R., Maine 128 Ca
Androúsa, Greece 71 Cf
Andujár, Spain 41 Bb
Anduze, France 35 Fc
Andyû, Korea 97 Bc
Anecho, Fr. W. Africa 105 Bd
Anegada, Virgin Is. 140 Kg
Anegado, B., Argentina 148 Dc
Aneityum, I., New Hebrides 157 Df
Anelo, Argentina 148 Cb
Anenous, Cape Prov. 114 Bd
Anet, France 30 Dc
Anfo, Italy 62 Eb
Angadipuram, Madras 89 Bb
Angalia, Tanganyika Terr. 111 Cf
Angamos, Pta., Chile 146 Ac
Angangneo, Mexico 138 Dd
Angaston, S. Australia 154 Bc
Angel de la Guarda, Mexico 138 Bb
Angel Falls, Venezuela 144 Db
Angelholm, Sweden 51 Bf
Angelina R., Texas 133 Ee
Angeln, Prussia 54 Ea
Angelókastron, Greece 71 Ef
Angelokastron, Akarnania and Aitolia, Greece 71 Ce
Angels Camp, California 134 Cb
Angerburg 56 Fb
Angerman, R., Sweden 44 Df
Angermünde, Prussia 55 Jb
Angers, France 32 Ec
Angerville, France 30 Dc
Angikuni L., N.-W. Terr. 124 Kb
Angísta, Greece 70 Fb
Angístri, I., Greece 71 Ef
Angkor, Siam 95 Bg
Angledool, New S. Wales 155 Fa
Anglesey, co., Wales 20 Ba
Anglesola, Spain 39 Gc
Angleton, Texas 133 Ef
Angliers, Quebec 123 Jb
Anglo-Egyptian Sudan, N.-E. Africa 101 Ed
Angmagssalik, Greenland 9 Fd
Angoche Is., Mozambique 112 Dc
Angola, Indiana 129 Bb
Angola, col., S.-W. Afr. 101 Dg
Angora, Colorado 135 Ja
Angora (Ankara), Turkey 78 Ba
Angoria, Texas 133 Cd
Angoulême, France 34 Cb
Angoumois, France 34 Cb
Angra, Brazil 147 Gc
Angraz Yuntaz, S.-W. Afr. 114 Ac
Anguane, Mozambique 115 Kb
Anguilla, I., Leeward Is. 140 Kg
Angul, Orissa 87 Fe
Angus, co., Scotland 23 Ee
Angvik, Norway 46 Db
Anhalt, state, Germany 55 Hd
Anholt, I., Denmark 45 Eb
An-hwa, China 94 Dd
An-hwei, prov., China 94 Ec
Anina, Romania 67 Gd
Aninuz, S.-W. Africa 114 Ce
Anita, Arizona 135 Gd
Anizy, France 31 Fb
Anjer, Java 98 Ce
Anjha, Baroda 85 Dc
Anjou, old prov., France 30 Bd
Ankara (Angora), Turkey 78 Ba
Ankaratra Mts., Madagas. 112 Ec
Ankavandra, Madagascar 112 Ec
Ankazoaba, Madagascar 112 Dd
Ankazobé, Madagascar 112 Ec
Ankeva, Madagascar 112 Dd
An-khe, Annam 95 Cg
An-king, China 94 Ec
Ankiriky, Madagascar 112 Ed
Anklan, Prussia 55 Jb
Anklesvar, Bombay 85 Dd
Ankober, Ethiopia 108 Cd
Ankor & Pk., Br. Somalil'd 108 Ec
Ankoro, Belg. Congo 109 Ec
Ankwang, Manchuria 96 Cb
An-lu, China 94 Dc
Anmâkunto, Korea 97 Bc
Anmyonto, Korea 97 Bc
Ann, C., Massachusetts 128 Cb
Anna, Illinois 130 Db
Annaberg, Saxony 55 Je
Annacotty, Eire 27 Bf
Anna Creek, S. Australia 154 Aa
Annagassan, Eire 26 Dd
Annai, Brit. Guiana 144 Ec
An Najaf, Iraq 78 Dc
Annaka, Japan 100 Gc
Annam, Fr. Indo-China 95 Cf
An-nan, China 94 Cd
Annan, Scotland 21 Cd
Annandale, Queensland 153 Ae
Anna Pink B., Chile 148 Ad
Annapolis, Brazil 147 Fb
Annapolis, Maryland 129 Fc
Annapolis, Nova Scotia 120 Cd
Ann Arbor, Michigan 122 Gd
An Nasiriya, Iraq 79 Ec
Annatok, Greenland 9 Cb
Annecy, France 35 Hb
Annefors, Sweden 50 Db
Annemasse, France 35 Ja
Annfield Plain, England 21 Ed
Annis Fontein, Cape Prov. 114 Bd
Anniston, Alabama 130 Fd
Annobon, I., Gulf of Guinea 101 Cf
Annonay, France 35 Gb
Annot, France 33 Bb
Annuello, Victoria 154 Dc
An Numas, Arabia 78 Lg
Anoka, Minnesota 132 Cc
Ano Palaioxári, Greece 71 Ce
Ano Theologos, Greece 70 Fc
Anoual, Morocco 102 Cc
Ano Váthia, Greece 71 Ee
Añover del Tajo, Spain 38 Be
Ano Viánnos, Crete 71 Jj
Anpin, Taiwan 97 Gf
Ansbach, Bavaria 58 Eb
An shan chan, Manchuria 96 Cc
An-shun, China 94 Cd
Ansi, China 81 Hb
Anson, Texas 133 Cd
Anson B., N. T., Aust. 150 Da
Ansongo, Fr. W. Africa 105 Bb
Ansonia, Connecticut 128 Bc
Ansted, W. Virginia 129 Dc
Anstruther, Scotland 23 Fd
Anta, Manchuria 96 Db
Anta, Peru 145 Cd
Antalaha, Madagascar 112 Fb
Antalo, Ethiopia 108 Cc
Antalya (Adalia), Turkey 78 Bb
Antalya, Gulf of, Turkey 78 Bb
Antananarivo, Madagas. 112 Ec
Antarctica, S. Polar Regions 160 —
Antelat, Libya 106 Cc
Antelope Val., Nevada 134 Eb
Antequera, Paraguay 146 Dc
Antequera, Spain 40 Fb
Anterselva, Italy 63 Ga
Anthony, Kansas 133 Cb
Anthony, New Mexico 135 Ke
Anthony Lagoon, N. T., Aust. 151 Fb
Anthracite, Colorado 135 Kb
Anti Atlas, mts., Algeria 104 Ca
Antibes & C. d', France 33 Cb
Anticosti I., Quebec 119 Rg
Antigo, Wisconsin 132 Ec
Antigonish, Nova Scotia 120 Dd
Antigua, I., Leeward Is. 140 Kg
Antihue, Chile 148 Bb
Anti Lebanon, Syria 78 Cc
Antilla, Cuba 140 Bb
Antilles, Greater, W. Indies 137 Ec
Antilles, Lesser, W. Indies 137 Fc
An-ting, Kan-su, China 94 Bb
An-ting, China 94 Cb
Antioch, California 134 Cc
Antioch, Turkey 78 Cb
Antioquia & dep., Colombia 144 Ab
Antisana, mt., Ecuador 145 Bb
Antitaurus, mts., Turkey 78 Cb
Anto, Korea 97 Bc
Antofagasta & prov., Chile 146 Ac
Antofagasta de la Sierra, Argentina 146 Bd
Antofalla, mt., Argentina 146 Bd
Antoine, Arkansas 130 Bc
Antola, Mte., Italy 62 Dc
Antomboka B., Madagas. 112 Eb
Anton Chico, New Mexico 135 Ld
Antongil B., Madagascar 112 Fc
Antonina, Brazil 147 Fd
Antonito, Colorado 135 Kc
Antranokoditra, Madagas. 112 Ec
Antrim, New Hampshire 128 Cb
Antrim & co., N. Ireland 26 Db
Antrim Mts., N. Ireland 26 Da
Antrodoco, Italy 64 Da
Ants, I., Caroline Is. 157 Cc
Antsirabe, Madagascar 112 Ec
Antu, Manchuria 96 Dc
An-tung, China 94 Ec
An-tung & prov., Manchuria 96 Cc
Antwerp, New York 128 Aa
Antwerp & prov., Belgium 29 Cc
An Uaimh (Navan), Eire 26 Dd
Anupgarh, Rajputana 82 Ed
Anupshahr, United Provs. 83 Hd
Anuradhapura, Ceylon 89 Cc
Anvik, Alaska 125 Ge
Anykščiai, Lithuania 49 Cd
An-yo, China 94 Cc
Anzac, Turkey 72 Db
Anzeglouf, Algeria 102 Ef
Anzoategui, state, Venezuela 144 Db
Aoiz, Spain 38 Db
Aomori, Japan 97 Eb
Aonla, United Provs. 83 Hd
Aosta, Italy 62 Bb
Aouderas, Fr. W. Africa 105 Cb
Aoufous, Morocco 102 Bd
Aouk, Fr. Eq. Africa 105 Ed
Aoulef el Arab, Algeria 102 Ef
Aouni, Fr. Eq. Africa 105 Ec
Apahida, Transylvania 67 Jc
Apalachee B., Florida 131 Ff
Apalachicola and R., Florida 130 Ff
Apalachicola B., Florida 130 Ff
Apam, Gold Coast 104 De
Apaporis, Colombia 144 Bc
Aparri, Philippines 95 Ff
Apatin, Voyvodina 66 Dd
Ape, Hungary 66 Eb
Apeldoorn, Holland 29 Db
Aperé, Brazil 142 Dc
Apex, Montana 136 Gc
Api, C., Borneo 98 Cc
Apiacas, Sa. dos, Brazil 142 Ce
Apiahy, Brazil 147 Fc
Apidhiá, Greece 71 Dg
Apiskigamish L., Quebec 119 Pe
Apo Passage, E. and W., Philippines 99 Ea
Apo Vol., Philippines 99 Gb
Apody, Brazil 143 Gd
Apold, Romania 67 Kc
Apolda, Thuringia 55 Ge
Apollo Bay, Victoria 154 De
Apollonia, Libya 106 Cb
Apolyont & Gölü, Turkey 72 Fb
Apopka L., Florida 131 Ng
Apostle Is., Wisconsin 132 Db
Apostoles, Argentina 146 Dd
Apoteri, British Guiana 144 Ec
Apozai, Baluchistan 82 Cc
Appalachian, U.S.A. 127 Jc
Äppelbo, Sweden 50 Cb
Appenzell and canton, Switzerland 43 Hb
Appleby, England 18 Ba
Applecross, Scotland 22 Cb
Appledore, England 17 Ba
Appleton, Minnesota 132 Bc
Appleton, Wisconsin 132 Ec
Appleton City, Missouri 130 Aa
Approuague, Fr. Guiana 142 Db
Aprica, Col. de, Italy 62 Ea
Apricena, Italy 64 Fb
Aprigliano, Italy 65 Cc
Aprilia, Italy 64 Cb
Apsalos, Greece 70 Cc
Apsley, Victoria 154 Cd
Apt, France 35 Hd
Apuane Alps, Italy 62 Ec
Apucarana ou Lagarto, Sa., Brazil 147 Ec
Apuhy, Brazil 142 Cd
Apure, R. & state, Venezu. 144 Cb
Apurimac, dep. and R., Peru 145 Cd
Apuseui Mts., Transylva. 67 Jc
Aputaiuitsok, Greenland 9 Ee
Aqaba, Trans-Jordan 78 Cd
Aqaba, G. of, Egypt-Arabia 78 Bd
Aqaba, Jeb. el, Libya 106 Dc
'Aqiq & Gulf, A.-E. Sudan 108 Cb
Aqir, Palestine 80 Bd
Aqsu, Sinkiang 84 Eb
Aqua Coyame, Mexico 138 Cb
Aquedal, Algeria 102 De
Aquidauana, Brazil 146 Dc
Aquila, Italy 64 Da
Aquin, Haiti 140 Cc
Arabatskaya, Crimea 75 Ff
Arabia, S.-W. Asia 77 Fe
Arabian Des., Egypt 107 Hd
Arabian Sea, S.-W. Asia 73 Jg
Arabkir, Turkey 78 Cb
Arabs Gulf, Egypt 107 Gc
Aracajú, Brazil 143 Ge
Araçatuba, Brazil 147 Ec
Aracaty, Brazil 143 Gc
Aracena, Sas. de, Spain 40 Db
Arad, Romania 67 Gc
Aradul Nou, Romania 67 Gc
Arafura Sea, Australasia 149 Df
Aragon, Spain 38 Ec
Aragon R., Spain 38 Db
Aragona, Sicily 65 Gg
Aragua, state, Venezuela 144 Cb
Aragua de Barcelona, Venezuela 144 Db
Araguary, Brazil 147 Fb
Araguaya, R., Brazil 143 Ed
Arahoab, S.-W. Africa 114 Cb
Arai, Japan 100 Fd
Arakaka, Brit. Guiana 144 Db
Arakan Hill Dist., Burma 92 Ab
Arakan Yoma, Burma 92 Bc
Arákhova, Greece 71 De
Arákinthos, mt., Greece 71 Ce
Aral Sea, Kazak, etc. 76 Fe
Aralsk, Kazak 76 Ge
Aramac, Queensland 153 Cd
Arambagh, Bengal 88 Ac
Aramon, France 35 Gd
Aran I., Eire 26 Bb
Aran Is., Eire 25 Bc
Aranda de Duero, Spain 38 Bc
Aranda de Moncayo, Spain 38 Dc
Arandjelovac, Serbia 68 Fb
Arani, Bolivia 146 Bb
Aranjuez, Spain 38 Bd
Araouane, Fr. W. Africa 104 Dc
Arapaho, Oklahoma 133 Cc
Arapey and R., Uruguay 146 De
Arapuni, New Zealand 158 Ec
Araracuara, Cord. de, Colombia 144 Bc
Araraquara, Brazil 147 Fc
Ararat, Armenia 75 Gh
Ararat, Victoria 154 Dd
Ararat, mt., Turkey 78 Db
Arareh, New Guinea 156 Bb
Araria, Bihar 87 Gb
Arassuahy, Brazil 147 Gb
Araty, Brazil 145 Cc
Arauca & R., Colombia 144 Bb
Arauco and prov., Chile 148 Bb
Aravalli Ra., Rajputana 85 Db
Arawe, New Britain 156 Dc
Araxa, Brazil 147 Fb
Araxes, R., Persia, etc. 79 Eb
Araxos (Pápas), C., Greece 71 Ce
Arba, R., Spain 38 Dc
Arba Foukani, Algeria 102 Ec
Arbala, Morocco 102 Bc
Arba Tahtani, Algeria 102 Ec
Arboga, Sweden 50 Ec
Arbois, France 31 He
Arboles, Colorado 135 Kc
Arbos, Spain 39 Gc
Arbroath, Scotland 23 Fc
Arbuckle, California 134 Bb
Arcachon, France 34 Ac
Arcade, New York 123 Jd
Arcadia, Florida 131 Nh
Arcadia, Louisiana 130 Bd
Arcadia, Michigan 122 Ec
Arcadia, Wisconsin 132 Dc
Arcata, California 134 Aa
Arçay, France 30 Ce
Arce, Italy 64 Db
Archena, Spain 41 Eb
Archer Pt., Queensland 153 Ce
Archer R., Queensland 153 Bb
Archer City, Texas 133 Cd
Archer's Post, Kenya 110 Ec
Arcidosso, Italy 63 Fe
Arcila, Span. Morocco 102 Ab
Arcis-sur-Aube, France 31 Gc
Arcizul 69 Hc
Arco, Idaho 136 Gd
Arco, Italy 62 Eb
Arcola, Illinois 132 Ef
Arcos, Spain 38 Bb
Arcos de la Frontera, Spain 40 Ec
Arcot, Madras 90 De
Arcot, N. and S., Madras 89 Ca
Arctic Harbour, N.-W. T. 119 Qc
Arctic Red River, N.-W. T. 118 Cc
Ardahan, Turkey 78 Da
Ardakan, Persia 79 Fc
Ardal, Norway 46 Dc
Ardal, Norway 47 Ce
Ardal, Persia 79 Fc
Ardalov, U.S.S.R. 75 He
Ard al Wadian, Iraq 78 Dc
Ardara, Eire 26 Bb
Ardbeg, Scotland 22 Be
Ardebil, Persia 79 Eb
Ardeche, dep., France 35 Gc
Ardee, Eire 26 Dd
Ardeiş, Transylvania 67 Gc
Ardelan, Persia 79 Eb
Ardennes, Belgium, etc. 29 Ce
Ardennes, dep., France 31 Gb
Ardez, Switzerland 43 Kc
Ardfinnan, Eire 27 Cg
Ardglass, N. Ireland 26 Ec
Ardgroom, Eire 25 Bf
Ardistan, Persia 79 Fc
Ardmore, Eire 27 Cg
Ardmore, Oklahoma 133 Dc
Ardnamurchan and Pt., Scotland 22 Bc
Ardon, Spain 36 Eb
Ardore, Italy 65 Cd
Ardrahan, Eire 27 Be

Atlas Saharie, mts., Alger. 102 Dc
Atlin, Brit. Columbia 124 Cc
Atmakur, Madras 90 Dd
Atna and R., Norway 46 Gc
Atner, Central Provs. 86 Be
Atoka, Oklahoma 133 Dc
Atokos, I., Greece 71 Be
Atotonileo, Mexico 138 Dc
Atoyac, R., Mexico 139 Ed
Atraf-i-Balda, Hyderabad 90 Dc
Atrak, R., Persia 79 Fb
Atranos, R., Turkey 72 Gc
Atrato, R., Colombia 144 Ab
Atrauli, United Provs. 83 He
Atri, Italy 64 Da
Atripalda, Italy 64 Ec
Atsiki, Greece 72 Cc
Atsuta, Japan 100 Fd
Attalla, Alabama 130 Ec
Attawapiskat L., Ontario 119 Mf
Attica, Indiana 129 Ab
Attigliano, Italy 64 Ca
Attingal, Madras States 89 Bc
Attleboro, Massachusetts 128 Cc
Attleborough, England 15 Fa
Attlebridge, England 15 Fa
Attnang, Austria 59 Hc
Attock, Punjab 82 Eb
Attu I., Aleutian Is. 125 Sl
Atun-tse, China 94 Ad
Atupi, Brazil 142 Db
Atur, Madras 89 Cb
Atura, Uganda 110 Cb
Atures, Venezuela 144 Cb
Atvidaberg, Sweden 50 Fd
Atwood, Kansas 133 Ba
Atzas, Fr. W. Africa 104 Ab
Auareh, Ethiopia 108 Dd
Aubagne, France 33 Ac
Aube, R. & dep., France 31 Gc
Aubenas, France 35 Gc
Aubigny, France 30 Ea
Aubin, France 34 Ec
Aubonne, Switzerland 42 Bd
Aubrac, Mtgnes, d', France 35 Fc
Aubrey, Quebec 121 Db
Auburn, Alabama 130 Fd
Auburn, California 134 Cb
Auburn, Indiana 129 Bb
Auburn, Maine 128 Ca
Auburn, Nebraska 127 Fb
Auburn, New York 123 Kd
Auburndale, Florida 131 Ng
Aubusson, France 34 Eb
Auca Mahuida, Sa., Argentina 148 Cb
Auce, Latvia 49 Bc
Auch, France 34 Cd
Auchterarder, Scotland 23 Ed
Auchtermuchty, Scotland 23 Ed
Auckland and prov., New Zealand 158 Eb
Aude, dep., France 34 Ed
Aude, R., France 35 Fd
Audegle, Ital. Somaliland 108 Gf
Audenarde, Belgium 29 Bd
Audierne and B., France 32 Ac
Audincourt, France 31 Jd
Audlem, England 18 Be
Audrada, Mozambique 113 Eb
Audruicq, France 30 Da
Audubon, Iowa 132 Be
Aue, Saxony 55 He
Augathella, Queensland 153 Ce
Augher, N. Ireland 26 Cc
Aughnacloy, N. Ireland 26 Dc
Aughrim, Galway, Eire 27 Be
Aughrim, Wicklow, Eire 27 Df
Augila, Libya 106 Cd
Augsburg, Bavaria 58 Ec
Augusta, Arkansas 130 Cc
Augusta, Georgia 131 Gd
Augusta, Kansas 133 Db
Augusta, Kentucky 131 Fa
Augusta, Maine 128 Da
Augusta, Oklahoma 133 Cb
Augusta, Sicily 65 Jg
Augusta, W. Australia 152 Be
Augusta, Wisconsin 132 Dc
Augustenborg, Denmark 45 Cd
Augustów, Poland 60 Gb
Augustus I., W. Aust. 152 Ca
Augustus, Mt., W. Aust. 152 Bc
Aukanga, Tanganyika Ter. 111 Fg
Aukštadvaris, Lithuania 49 Cd
Aulla, Italy 62 Dc
Aultbea, Scotland 22 Ca
Aultsville, Ontario 121 Cb
Auma, Norway 46 Gb
Aumale, Algeria 103 Fa
Aumgle, France 30 Db
Aumont, France 35 Fc
Aunay, France 32 Ea
Aundh, Deccan States 90 Bc
Aunis, old prov., France 32 Ed
Auñon, Spain 38 Cd
Aups, France 33 Bb
Auraiya, United Provs. 83 He
Aurangabad, Bihar 87 Fc
Aurangabad, Hyderabad 90 Bb
Auray, France 32 Bc
Aurdal, Norway 46 Fd
Aure, Norway 46 Ea
Aurillac, France 34 Ec
Aurisina 63 Hb
Aurland, Norway 46 Dd
Auronza, Italy 63 Ga
Aurora, Cape Prov. 114 Cf
Aurora, Illinois 132 Ee
Aurora, Indiana 129 Bc
Aurora, Missouri 130 Bb
Aurora, Ontario 123 Jd
Aus, S.-W. Africa 114 Bc
Au Sable & R., Michigan 122 Gc
Au Sable Forks, New York 123 Lc
Ausangate, mt., Peru 145 Cd
Ausivit, Greenland 9 Ee
Ausser-Rhoden, Switz. 43 Hb
Aust-Agder, fylke, Norway 47 Df
Austerlitz (Slavkov), Moravia 57 Bd
Austin, Minnesota 132 Cd
Austin, Nevada 134 Eb
Austin, Texas 133 De
Austin & L., W. Aust. 152 Bd
Austral Is., Pacific Oc. 149 Mh
Australian Alps, Victoria 155 Fd
Austrheim, Norway 46 Ad
Austria, state, Germany 59 Jd
Autel, France 31 Hd
Authon, France 33 Ba
Autlan, Mexico 138 Dd
Autry, France 31 Hd
Autun, France 31 Ge
Auvergne, France 35 Fb
Auxerre, France 31 Fd
Auxi-le-Château, France 30 Ea
Auxonne, France 31 Hd
Auzances, France 34 Ea
Auzon, France 35 Fb
Ava, Burma 92 Bb
Avakubi, Belg. Congo 109 Ea
Avala, mt., Serbia 68 Fb
Avallon, France 31 Fd
Avalon, California 134 De
Avalon Pen., Newfoundl'd 120 Jc
Avare, Brazil 147 Fc
Avasaksa, Finland 48 Ec
Avdira, Greece 72 Bb
Avebury, England 14 Cd
Aveiro, Brazil 142 Dc
Aveiro, Portugal 37 Bb
Avellanada, Argentina 148 Ea
Avellino, Italy 64 Ec
Avenches, Switzerland 42 Dc
Avenir, Fr. Guiana 142 Db
Avernakö, I., Denmark 45 Dc
Averöy, I., Norway 46 Da
Aversa, Italy 64 Ec
Avesnes, France 31 Fa
Avesnes-le-Comte, France 30 Ea
Avesta, Sweden 50 Fb
Aveyron, dep. & R., France 34 Ec
Avezzano, Italy 64 Da
Aviano, Italy 63 Ga
Aviá Teria, Argentina 146 Cd
Aviemore, Scotland 23 Eb
Avigliano, Italy 64 Fc
Avignon, France 35 Gd
Avila, Spain 38 Ad
Aviles, Spain 36 Ea
Avington, Queensland 153 Cd
Aviz, Portugal 37 Cc
Avlídhos (Vathi), Greece 71 Ee
Avlón, Greece 71 Ee
Avlonárion, Greece 71 Ee
Avning, Denmark 45 Db
Avoca, Eire 27 Df
Avoca, Iowa 132 Be
Avoca, Tasmania 155 Kg
Avoca, Victoria 154 Dd
Avola, Sicily 65 Jh
Avon, Montana 136 Gb
Avon, R., Glos., etc., Eng. 14 Bd
Avon R., Hants, England 14 Ce
Avon, R., Warwicks, etc., England 14 Cb
Avondale, Alabama 130 Ed
Avon Downs, Queensland 153 Cd
Avonmouth, England 14 Bc
Avontuur, Cape Prov. 114 Ef
Avral-tau, Sinkiang 84 Eb
Avranches, France 32 Db
Avricourt, France 31 Jc
Avrig, Romania 67 Kd
Avsa, I., Turkey 72 Eb
Awaji, I., Japan 97 Cd
Awakino, New Zealand 158 Ec
Awasib Mts., S.-W. Africa 114 Ab
Awe, L., Scotland 22 Cd
Aweil, A.-E. Sudan 108 Ad
Axat, France 34 Ee
Axbridge, England 14 Bd
Axel Heiberg, I., N.-W.T. 117 Ha
Axilek, Fr. W. Africa 105 Cb
Axim, Gold Coast 104 Df
Ax-les-Thermes, France 34 De
Axminster, England 14 Be
Axtell, Texas 133 De
Ayabaca, Peru 145 Bb
Ayabe, Japan 100 Ed
Ayacucho, Argentina 148 Eb
Ayacucho & dep., Peru 145 Cd
Ayamonte, Spain 40 Cb
Ayan, U.S.S.R. 76 Od
Ayancik, Turkey 78 Ba
Ayaviri, Peru 145 Cd
Aydin, Turkey 78 Ab
Ayer Bangis, Sumatra 98 Ac
Ayerbe, Spain 38 Eb
Ayiá, Greece 70 Dd
Ayia Triás, Crete 71 Gj
Ayioi Dhéka, Crete 71 Hj
Ayion Oros (Mount Athos), Greece 70 Fc
Ayion Órous, G. of, Greece 70 Fc
Áyios Ioánnis, Greece 71 Df
Áyios Nikolaos, Crete 71 Jj
Aylesbury, England 15 Dc
Ayllon, Spain 38 Bc
Aylmer, Ontario 123 Hd
Aylmer, Quebec 121 Bb
Aylmer L., N.-W. Terr. 124 Hb
Aylmer Sd., Quebec 120 Fa
Aylsham, England 19 Fe
Aylwin, Quebec 121 Ba
Aymores and Sa., Brazil 147 Gb
Aynho, England 14 Cb
Aynor, S. Carolina 131 Jc
Ayora, Spain 41 Ea
Ayr, Queensland 153 Cc
Ayr and co., Scotland 21 Bc
Ayrao, Brazil 142 Bc
Aysen, prov., Chile 148 Bd
Aysgarth, England 18 Cb
Ayton, Queensland 153 Cc
Aytona, Spain 39 Fc
Ayun, Arabia 78 Dd
Ayungon, Philippines 99 Fb
Ayuthia (Krungkao), Siam 95 Bg
Ayutla, Guatemala 140 Ee
Ayutla, Mexico 139 Ed
Ayvacik, Turkey 72 Dc
Ayvalik, Turkey 72 Dc
Azamgarh, United Provs. 87 Eb
Azanja, Serbia 68 Fb
Azanovskoe, U.S.S.R. 96 Ea
Azemmour, Morocco 103 Nh
Azerbaijan, Persia 79 Eb
Azerbaijan, rep., U.S.S.R. 75 Hg
Azipute, Latvia 49 Ac
Azizia, el, Libya 106 Ok
Azogues, Ecuador 145 Bb
Azores, Is., N. Atlantic Oc. 116 Gd
Azourki, Jeb., Morocco 102 Ad
Azov & Sea of, U.S.S.R. 75 Ff
Azovkoe, U.S.S.R. 74 Lc
Azpeitia, Spain 38 Ca
Aztec, New Mexico 135 Kc
Azua, Santo Domingo 140 Cc
Azuaga, Spain 37 Ed
Azuay, prov., Ecuador 145 Bb
Azul, Argentina 148 Eb
Az Zubair, Iraq 79 Ec
Baagö, Denmark 45 Cc
Baanfu (Batang), China 94 Ac
Baar, Switzerland 43 Fb
Babadag, Romania 69 Hc
Babaeski, Turkey 72 Da
Babaevo, U.S.S.R. 74 Fd
Babahoya, Ecuador 145 Bb
Babai, Central Provs. 86 Bd
Babanango, Natal 115 Jd
Babel I., Tasmania 155 Kf
Bab el Mandeb, str., Red Sea 108 Dc
Babeni, Romania 67 Ke
Baberu, United Provs. 86 Dc
Babine L., Br. Columbia 124 Dc
Babinsk, U.S.S.R. 48 Jc
Babispe, Mexico 138 Ca
Babo, New Guinea 156 Ab
Babul (Barfurush), Persia 79 Fb
Babuyan Is., Philippines 95 Ff
Babuyan Claro, Philippines 95 Ff
Babylon, Iraq 78 Dc
Bacabal, Brazil 142 Cd
Bacadehuachi, Mexico 138 Cb
Bacalar, Mexico 139 Gd
Bacău, Romania 69 Gb
Bacau Vol., Philippines 99 Fb
Bacchus Marsh, Victoria 154 De
Bacerac, Mexico 138 Ca
Bac Gradiste, Voyvodina 66 Ed
Bachau, Western India 85 Cc
Baciu, Translyvania 67 Jc
Backergunge, Bengal 88 Cc
Backstairs Pass., S. Aust. 154 Bd
Bac-lieu, Cochin-China 95 Ch
Bac-ninh, Tong-king 95 Ce
Bacoachi, Mexico 138 Bb
Bacoachie, Mexico 138 Ca
Bacolod, Philippines 99 Fa
Bacolor, Philippines 95 Ff
Bac Petrovo Selo, Voyvodina 66 Fd
Bacs-Bodrog, Hungary 66 Ec
Bacului Mts., Transylvan. 67 Jb
Bacup, England 18 Bc
Badagara, Madras 89 Ab
Badagri, Nigeria 105 Bd
Badajoz, Brazil 143 Ec
Badajoz & prov., Spain 37 Dd
Badakhshan, Afghanistan 84 Bc
Badakhshan, Tadzhik 84 Cc
Badalona, Spain 39 Hc
Badami, Bombay 90 Bd
Badan-khuduk, Sinkiang 84 Fa
Badarpur, Assam 88 Db
Bad Axe, Michigan 122 Gd
Baddeck, Nova Scotia 120 Ec
Baden, Austria 59 Ld
Baden, Switzerland 43 Fb
Baden, state, Germany 58 Cc
Baden-Baden, Baden 58 Cc
Badenoch, Scotland 22 Dc
Badenwerder, Brunswick 54 Ed
Badia, Arabia 79 Ee
Badia, Italy 63 Fa
Badia, Venetia, Italy 63 Fb
Badin, Sind 85 Bb
Badinh, Mt., Cochin-China 95 Cg
Bad Ischl, Austria 59 Hd
Badiya, Oman 79 Ge
Bad Kissingen, Bavaria 58 Da
Bad Lands, Nebraska 126 Eb
Badnera, Berar, C.P. 86 Be
Badnur, Central Provs. 86 Be
Bad Oldesloe, Prussia 54 Fb
Badon, Fr. W. Africa 104 Bd
Badoumbo, Fr. W. Afr. 104 Bd
Badrinath, United Provs. 83 Hc
Badrinath Peaks, U.P. 83 Hc
Baduen, Ital. Somaliland 108 Ed
Badulla, Ceylon 89 Dd
Bad Wildungen, Prussia 54 Dd
Badzhal, U.S.S.R. 96 Ea
Bækmarksbro, Denmark 45 Bb
Baena, Spain 40 Fb
Baetas, Brazil 142 Bd
Baeza, Spain 41 Cc
Baffa, Liberia 104 Cf
Baffin B., Greenland-N.-W. Terr. 119 Qb
Baffin I., N.-W. Terr. 119 Oc
Bafoulabe, Fr. W. Africa 104 Bd
Bafra, Turkey 78 Ca
Baft, Persia 79 Gd
Bafwaboli, Belg. Congo 109 Ea
Bafwasende, Belg. Congo 109 Ea
Baga, Spain 39 Gb
Bagalkot, Bombay 90 Bc
Bagamoyo, Tanganyika Terr. 111 Fg
Bagan, U.S.S.R. 74 Lb
Baganga, Philippines 99 Gb
Bagan-Siapiapi, Sumatra 98 Bc
Bagassi, Fr. W. Africa 104 Dd
Bagdad, Florida 130 Ee
Bagdogra, Bengal 88 Ba
Bagé, Brazil 147 Ee
Bagenalstown, Eire 27 Df
Bagenkop, Denmark 45 Dd
Bagepalli, Mysore 90 Ce
Bagerhat, Bengal 88 Bc
Bageshwar, United Provs. 83 Hd
Bagevadi, Bombay 90 Bc
Bagh, Gwalior 85 Ec
Baghdad, Iraq 78 Dc
Baghelkhand, Cent. India 86 Dc
Bagheria, Sicily 65 Gf
Baghin, Persia 79 Gc
Baghpat, United Provs. 83 Gd
Bagirmi, Fr. Eq. Africa 105 Ec
Bagley, Minnesota 132 Bb
Bagn, Norway 46 Fd
Bagnacavallo, Italy 63 Gc
Bagnell, Missouri 130 Ba
Bagnères-de-Bigorre, France 34 Cd
Bagnères-de-Luchon, France 34 Ce
Bagno di Rom, Italy 63 Fd
Bagnolo, Italy 62 Eb
Bagnols, France 35 Gc
Bagnone, Italy 62 Ec
Bagodar, Bihar 87 Fc
Bagolino, Italy 62 Eb
Bagotville, Quebec 123 Na
Bagrach Kol, Sinkiang 84 Fb
Baguezane Mts., Fr. W. Africa 105 Cb
Baguida, Fr. W. Africa 105 Bd
Baguio, Philippines 95 Ff
Bagur, Spain 39 Jc
Bah, United Provs. 83 He
Bahadurgarh, Punjab 83 Gd
Bahama Bank, Gt., Bahamas 140 Bb
Bahama Is., W. Indies 137 Eb
Bahardipur, Sind 85 Bb
Baharîya Oasis, Egypt 107 Gd
Baha Solo, Celébes 99 Fd
Bahawalnagar, Punjab States 82 Ed
Bahawalpur, Punjab States 82 Dd
Bahbah, Algeria 103 Fb
Bahçeli, Turkey 72 Dc
Bahera, Bihar 87 Gb
Baheri, United Provs. 83 Hd
Bahia, state, Brazil 143 Fe
Bahia (São Salvador), Brazil 143 Ge
Bahia Blanca, Argentina 148 Db
Bahia de Caráquez, Ecuador 145 Ab
Bahia Honda, Cuba 140 Ab
Bahia Laura, Argentina 148 Cd
Bahia Negra, Paraguay 146 Dc
Bahia Solano, Colombia 144 Ab
Bahindi, Nigeria 105 Bc
Bahnea, Transylvania 67 Kc
Bahra, Arabia 78 Ce
Bahraich, United Provs. 86 Db
Bahrein & I., Persian Gulf 79 Fd
Bahr el Abiad (White Nile), A.-E. Sudan 108 Bc
Bahr el Azraq (Blue Nile), A.-E. Sudan 108 Bc
Bahr el Ghazal, A.-E. Sudan 108 Ad
Bahr el Jebel, A.-E. Sudan 108 Bd
Bahret Lut (Dead Sea), Pal.-Trans-Jordan 80 Ce
Bahret Tabariya (Galilee, Sea of), Palestine 80 Db
Bahr Yûsef, Egypt 107 Hd
Bahu, New Britain 156 Dc
Bahu Kalat, Persia 79 Hd
Bahus, Brazil 147 Eb
Baia de Aramă, Romania 67 He
Baia-de-Cris, Romania 67 Hc
Baia-Mare, Transylvania 67 Jb
Baiano, Italy 64 Ec
Baiao, Brazil 143 Ec
Baibokoun, Fr. Eq. Africa 105 Ed
Baiburt, Turkey 78 Da
Baidaratskaya Gulf, U.S.S.R. 74 Mb
Baides, Spain 38 Cc
Baiersdorf, Bavaria 58 Eb
Baie St Paul, Quebec 123 Nb
Baie Verte, New Brunswick 120 Cc
Baignes-Ste Radegonde, France 34 Bb
Baigneux-les-Juifs, France 31 Gd
Baiji, Iraq 78 Dc
Baik Mts., New Guinea 156 Ab
Baikal Mts. & L., U.S.S.R. 76 Ld
Baile Atha Claith (Dublin), Eire 27 De
Baile Herculane, Romania 67 He
Bailen, Spain 41 Cb
Băileşti, Romania 69 Ec
Baileys, Neveda 134 Ea
Bailieborough, Eire 26 Dd
Bailleul, France 30 Ea
Baimak Tanalykovo, U.S.S.R. 74 Ke
Bain, France 32 Dc
Bainbridge, Georgia 131 Fe
Bairat, Rajputana 83 Ge
Baird, Texas 133 Cd
Baird Mts., Alaska 125 Gc
Bairnsdale, Victoria 155 Ee
Bais, Philippines 99 Fb
Baisogala, Lithuania 49 Bd
Baisun, Uzbek 84 Bc
Baja, Hungary 66 Dc
Bajan, Mexico 138 Db
Bajaur, N.-W. F.P. 82 Da
Bajkovo, Serbia 70 Db
Bajranggarh, Gwalior 86 Bc

Betwa R., United Provs. 86 Cc
Beuel, Prussia 54 Ce
Beulah, Victoria 154 Cd
Beunitz 55 Lc
Beurkot, Fr. W. Africa 105 Cb
Beuthen 55 Ld
Beuthen (Byton), Poland 57 Dc
Beveland, N. & S., Holland 29 Bc
Bevensen, Prussia 54 Fb
Beverley, England 19 Dc
Beverley, W. Australia 152 Be
Beverly, Massachusetts 128 Cb
Beverly Hills, California 134 Dd
Beverungen, Prussia 54 Ed
Bevier, Missouri 132 Cf
Bewdley, England 14 Bb
Bex, Switzerland 42 Dd
Bexhill, England 15 Ee
Beyçayiri, Turkey 72 Db
Beykoz, Turkey 72 Ga
Beyla, Fr. W. Africa 104 Ce
Beylerbeyi, Turkey 72 Ga
Beypazari, Turkey 78 Ba
Beypore, Madras 89 Ab
Beyşehir & Gölu, Turkey 78 Bb
Bezdan, Voyvodina 66 Dd
Bezhetsk, U.S.S.R. 74 Fd
Béziers, France 35 Fd
Bezirganlar, Turkey 72 Dc
Bezwada, Madras 91 Ec
Bhabua, Bihar 87 Ec
Bhachbar, Rajputana 85 Cb
Bhadarwah, Kashmir 83 Fb
Bhadaur, Punjab States 83 Fc
Bhadaura, Gwalior 86 Bc
Bhadohi, Gwalior 87 Ec
Bhadra, Rajputana 83 Fd
Bhadrachalam, Madras 91 Ec
Bhadrajan, Rajputana 85 Db
Bhadrakh, Orissa 87 Ge
Bhadreswar, Bengal 88 Bc
Bhag, Baluchistan 82 Bd
Bhagal, Punjab States 83 Gc
Bhagalpur, Bihar 87 Gc
Bhagirath R., Bengal 88 Bc
Bhainsdehi, Central Provs. 86 Be
Bhainsror, Rajputana 85 Eb
Bhairab Bazar, Bengal 88 Cb
Bhaisa, Hyderabad 90 Cb
Bhakkar, Punjab 82 Dc
Bhalki, Hyderabad 90 Cb
Bhamo, Burma 92 Ff
Bhandara, Central Provs. 86 Ce
Bhangor, Western India 85 Bc
Bhanpura, Central India 85 Eb
Bhanrer Ra., Central Provs. 86 Cd
Bharatpur, Eastern States 86 Dd
Bharatpur, Rajputana 83 Ge
Bharwain, Punjab 83 Gc
Bhatgaon, Nepal 87 Fb
Bhatgarh L., Deccan States 90 Ab
Bhatinda, Punjab States 83 Fc
Bhatnair (Hanumangarh), Rajputana 83 Fd
Bhatpara, Bengal 88 Bc
Bhaun, Punjab 82 Eb
Bhavani, Madras 89 Bb
Bhavnagar, Western India 85 Dd
Bhawani-Patna, Eastern States 91 Fb
Bhera, Punjab 82 Eb
Bheri, R., Nepal 86 Da
Bhilsa, Gwalior 86 Bd
Bhilwara, Rajputana 85 Eb
Bhima R., Bombay 90 Bb
Bhind, Gwalior 86 Cb
Bhindar, Rajputana 85 Eb
Bhinmal, Rajputana 85 Db
Bhir, Hyderabad 90 Bb
Bhiwani, Punjab 83 Gd
Bhojpur, Bihar 87 Fc
Bhojpur, Nepal 87 Gb
Bhojpur, Punjab States 83 Gc
Bhola, Bengal 88 Cc
Bhongir, Hyderabad 90 Dc
Bhongra, Rajputana 85 Ec
Bhopal, Central India 86 Bd
Bhopalpatnam, Eastern States 91 Eb
Bhor, Deccan States 90 Ab
Bhuban, Eastern States 87 Fe
Bhuban Hills, Assam 88 Db
Bhuj, Western India 85 Bc
Bhusawal, Bombay 90 Ba
Bhutan, state, Himalaya 81 Ge
Biafra, Bight of, W. Afr. 109 Aa
Biak, I., Du. New Guinea 156 Bb
Biała, Poland 60 Gb
Biała, Poland 60 Ed
Białośliwie, Poland 56 Ac
Białystok, Poland 60 Gb
Bianca, New Mexico 135 Ld
Biancavilla, Sicily 65 Hg
Bianco, Italy 65 Cd
Bianga, Belgian Congo 109 Db
Biaora, Central India 86 Bd
Biaro, I., Nether. Indies 99 Gc
Biarritz, France 34 Ad
Bias B., China 95 De
Biasca, Switzerland 43 Hd
Bia Uoraba, Ethiopia 108 Dd
Biba, Egypt 107 Hd
Biban, Bahiret el, Tunisia 103 Kc
Bibbiena, Italy 63 Fd
Biberach, Württemberg 58 Dc
Bibert, Bavaria 58 Eb
Bibest, Romania 67 Je
Bibo, Arizona 135 Jd
Bibon, Wisconsin 132 Db
Bic, Quebec 120 Ab
Bicester, England 14 Cc
Bichabhera, Rajputana 85 Db
Bichl, Bavaria 58 Fd
Bickleigh, England 17 Cb
Bicknell, Indiana 129 Ac
Bicsad, Transylvania 67 Jb
Bicske, Hungary 66 Db
Bida, Nigeria 105 Cd
Bidar, Hyderabad 90 Cc
Biddeford, Maine 128 Cb
Bideford & B., England 17 Ba
Bidford, England 14 Cb
Bidya, Palestine 80 Cc
Bidzhan, U.S.S.R. 96 Eb
Bieber, California 134 Ca
Biebrich, Prussia 58 Ca
Biel (Bienne), Switz. 42 Db
Bielefeld, Prussia 54 Dc
Bieler See, Switzerland 42 Db
Biella, Italy 62 Bb
Bieloi, U.S.S.R. 48 Kg
Bielsa, Spain 39 Fb
Bielsk, Poland 60 Gb
Bielsko, Poland 57 Dd
Bien-hoa, Cochin-China 95 Cg
Bienville, Louisiana 130 Bd
Bière, Switzerland 42 Bc
Bierne, France 32 Ec
Biesbosch, Holland 29 Cc
Biessenhofen, Bavaria 58 Ed
Big I., N.-W. Terr. 119 Pd
Big I., Ontario 122 Aa
Big L., Arkansas 130 Cc
Biga, Turkey 72 Eb
Bigados, Turkey 72 Fa
Big Bay, Michigan 122 Eb
Big Belt Mts., Montana 136 Ha
Big Black R., Mississippi 130 Cd
Big Blue R., Nebraska 132 Ae
Big Blue Creek, R., Texas 133 Ab
Big Creek, California 134 Dc
Big Cypress Swamp, Florida 131 Nh
Bigelow, Maine 123 Nc
Big Fork, R., Minnesota 132 Ca
Biggar, Saskatchewan 124 Hd
Biggar, Scotland 21 Cb
Bigges I., W. Australia 152 Ca
Biggleswade, England 15 Db
Big Hatchet Mts., New Mexico 135 Jf
Big Hole R. and Pass, Montana 136 Gc
Big Horn Mts., Wyoming 126 Db
Big Lake, Texas 133 Be
Big Moose Creek, New York 128 Ab
Bigosovo, White Russia 74 Dd
Big Pine Key, Florida 131 Nj
Big Rapids, Michigan 122 Fd
Big Sandy R., Ky.-W. Va. 131 Ga
Bigsby I., Ontario 122 Aa
Big Sioux R., S. Dakota 132 Ac
Big Smoky Val., Nevada 134 Eb
Big Snowy Mts., Montana 136 Jb
Big Spring, Texas 133 Bd
Big Stone L., Minnesota 132 Ac
Big Stone City, S. Dakota 132 Ac
Big Stone Gap, Virginia 129 Cd
Big Sur, California 134 Bc
Bigtimber, Montana 136 Jc
Bihac, Bosnia 68 Ab
Bihar, Bihar 87 Fc
Bihar, Hungary 67 Gb
Bihar, prov., India 81 Ff
Biharamulo, Tanganyika Terr. 110 Be
Biharkeresztes, Hungary 67 Gb
Bihor, Transylvania 67 Gb
Bihor Mts., Transylvania 67 Hc
Bijacaboba, Ethiopia 108 Dc
Bijapur, Bombay 90 Bc
Bijar, Persia 79 Eb
Bijawar, Central India 86 Cc
Bijeljinar, Bosnia 68 Eb
Bijelo Polje, Montenegro 68 Ec
Bijistan, Persia 79 Gc
Bijji, Eastern States 91 Eb
Bijna, Central India 86 Cc
Bijnabad, Persia 79 Gd
Bijnor, United Provs. 83 Hd
Bijolia, Rajputana 85 Eb
Bikampur, Rajputana 82 Ee
Bikaner, Rajputana 82 Ed
Bikar Is., Marshall Is. 157 Eb
Bikin, U.S.S.R. 96 Eb
Bikini I., Pacific Oc. 157 Dc
Bikira, Uganda 110 Bd
Bikita, S. Rhodesia 113 Dc
Bikoro, Belgian Congo 109 Cb
Bilanga, Fr. W. Africa 104 Ed
Bilara, Rajputana 85 Da
Bilari, United Provs. 83 Hd
Bilaspur, Central Provs. 86 Dd
Bilaspur, Punjab States 83 Gc
Bilbao, Spain 38 Ba
Bilbeis, Egypt 107 Hc
Bildudalur, Iceland 52 Bb
Bileća, Hercegovina 68 Dd
Bilecik, Turkey 78 Aa
Bilé Karpaty, Czechoslov. 60 Dd
Bilhaur, United Provs. 83 He
Bilhelli, Ital. Somaliland 108 Ed
Bilin, Burma 92 Cd
Biliran, I., Philippines 99 Fa
Bilkis, Persia 79 Gb
Billerbeck, Prussia 54 Cd
Billericay, England 15 Ec
Billesdon, England 15 Da
Billings, Oklahoma 133 Db
Billiton, I., Nether. Indies 98 Cd
Bilma, Fr. W. Africa 105 Db
Bilo Gora, Jugoslavia 66 Cd
Bilongala, Celébes 99 Fc
Biloxi, Mississippi 130 De
Bilsi, United Provs. 83 Hd
Bilston, England 14 Ba
Bilunbaevski, U.S.S.R. 74 Kd
Bima, Belg. Congo 109 Da
Bima, Soembawa I., N.I. 99 Ee
Bimbân, Egypt 107 Jf
Bimberi, Mt., N. S. Wales 155 Fd
Bimlipatam, Madras 91 Fc
Binder, Fr. Eq. Africa 105 Dd
Bindjai, Sumatra 98 Ac
Bindki, United Provs. 86 Db
Bindura, S. Rhodesia 113 Da
Binga, Belg. Congo 109 Da
Bingara, New S. Wales 155 Ga
Bingen, Hesse 58 Bb
Bingerville, Fr. W. Africa 104 Df
Bingeul Dagh, Turkey 78 Db
Bingham, England 19 De
Bingham Canyon, Utah 135 Ga
Binghampton, New York 123 Kd
Binghamstown, Eire 25 Aa
Bingle, Ontario 123 Ha
Bingley, England 18 Cc
Binh-dinh, Annam 95 Cg
Binn, Switzerland 42 Fd
Binnaway, New S. Wales 155 Fb
Binongko, I., Neth. Indies 99 Fd
Bint, Persia 79 Gd
Bintan, I., Nether. Indies 98 Bc
Bintoehan, Sumatra 98 Bd
Bintulu, Sarawak 99 Dc
Bio, Fr. Eq. Africa 109 Ca
Bio-Bio, prov., Chile 148 Bb
Bioče, Montenegro 68 Ed
Biod, El, Algeria 102 Dc
Biograd, Dalmatia 63 Kd
Bioka, Bhutan 88 Ca
Biokovo Planina, Dalmatia 68 Bc
Bioska, Serbia 68 Ec
Biota, Spain 38 Db
Biougra, Morocco 103 Nj
Bira, U.S.S.R. 96 Eb
Birakan, U.S.S.R. 96 Eb
Bir Alaloukiri, Fr. Eq. Afr. 105 Ec
Biratnagur, Nepal 87 Gb
Bir Bescer, Libya 106 Bc
Birbhum, Bengal 88 Ac
Bird I., Hawaiian Is. 157 Ga
Bird Island, Minnesota 132 Bc
Birdsville, Queensland 153 Ae
Birdum, N. Terr., Aust. 151 Eb
Birtley, England 21 Ed
Birecik, Turkey 78 Cb
Bir el Merduna, Libya 106 Ac
Bir es Sabe (Beersheba), Palestine 80 Be
Bireuen, Sumatra 98 Ab
Bir Giofer, Libya 106 Bc
Biri, Norway 46 Gd
Birigi L., Tangan. Terr. 110 Be
Birjand, Persia 79 Gc
Birka, U.S.S.R. 96 Ba
Bir Kelab, Libya 106 Ol
Birkendale, Ontario 121 Ab
Birkenes, Norway 47 Ef
Birkenhead, England 18 Ad
Birket Qârûn, Egypt 107 Hd
Birma, Trans-Jordan 80 Dc
Birmingham, Alabama 130 Ed
Birmingham, England 14 Cb
Birmingham, Michigan 122 Gd
Birmingham Corporation Res., Wales 20 Cc
Birni, Fr. W. Africa 105 Bc
Birnie I., Phoenix Is. 157 Fd
Birnin Gwari, Nigeria 105 Cc
Birni-n-Kebbi, Nigeria 105 Bc
Biro Bidzhan, U.S.S.R. 96 Eb
Biroo, Japan 97 Eb
Birr (Parsonstown), Eire 27 Ce
Bir Rabalou, Algeria 103 Fa
Bir Rissam, Libya 106 Bc
Birrok, A.-E. Sudan 105 Fc
Birsay, Orkney Is. 24 Ec
Birsilpur, Rajputana 82 Ed
Birsk, U.S.S.R. 74 Kd
Birstall, England 14 Ca
Birthday, Transvaal 113 Dd
Biržai, Lithuania 49 Cc
Bisa, Assam 88 Ea
Bisa, I., Nether. Indies 99 Gd
Bisaccia, Italy 64 Fb
Bisacquino, Sicily 65 Gg
Bisalpur, United Provs. 83 Hd
Bisauli, United Provs. 83 Hd
Bisbal, la, Spain 39 Jc
Bisbee, Arizona 135 Jf
Biscay, B. of, France 32 Bd
Biscayne B., Florida 131 Nj
Bisceglie, Italy 65 Ca
Bischofsburg 56 Fc
Bischofsgrun, Bavaria 59 Fa
Bischofshofen, Austria 59 Gd
Bischofswerda, Saxony 55 Kd
Bischofswerder, Poland 56 Dc
Bischwiller, France 31 Kc
Biscia, Eritrea 108 Cb
Biscoe Is., Antarctica 160 —
Biscotasing, Ontario 122 Gb
Biševo, I., Dalmatia 68 Ad
Bishenpur, Assam 88 Db
Bishensing, Bhutan 88 Ca
Bishnath, Assam 88 Da
Bishnupur, Bengal 88 Ac
Bishop, Mt., Wyoming 135 Ja
Bishop Auckland, Eng. 18 Ca
Bishop's Castle, England 14 Ab
Bishop's Falls, Newfound. 120 Hb
Bishop's Frome, England 14 Bb
Bishop's Stortford, Eng. 15 Ec
Bishop's Tachbrook, Eng. 14 Cb
Bishop's Waltham, Eng. 14 Ce
Bishopville, S. Carolina 131 Hc
Bishra, Trans-Jordan 80 Db
Bishri, Jeb. el, Syria 78 Cb
Biskra, Algeria 103 Gb
Bisley, England 15 Dd
Bislig, Philippines 99 Gb
Bismarck, Missouri 130 Cb
Bismarck, N. Dakota 126 Ea
Bismarck Arch., Pac. Oc. 156 Db
Bismarck, Mt., Mozamb. 112 Bc
Bismarck Ra., New Guinea 156 Cc
Bispberg, Sweden 50 Eb
Bissagos Is., Port. Guinea 104 Ad
Bissau, Port. Guinea 104 Ad
Bissau, Rajputana 83 Fd
Bissett, Quebec 123 Jb
Bistrita, Transylvania 67 Kb
Bistrita, R., Romania 69 Fb
Bistrita Bargaului, Transylvania 67 Kb
Bitburg, Prussia 58 Ab
Bithur, United Provs. 83 Je
Bitlis, Turkey 78 Db
Bitolj (Monastir), Serbia 70 Cb
Bitonto, Italy 65 Ca
Bitter Ls., Egypt 107 Jc
Bitter Creek, Wyoming 135 Ja
Bitterfeld, Prussia 55 Hd
Bitterfontein, Cape Prov. 114 Ce
Bitter Root Mts., Idaho 136 Fb
Bitterroot R., Montana 136 Fb
Bivona, Sicily 65 Gg
Biwa L., Japan 97 Dc
Biwabik, Minnesota 132 Cb
Biyadh, Arabia 79 Ee
Bizana, Cape Prov. 115 He
Bizerte, Tunisia 103 Ja
Bizovac, Slavonia 66 Dd
Bjelašnica, mt., Bosnia 68 Dc
Bjelemić, Hercegovina 68 Dc
Bjelland, Norway 47 Df
Bjelovar, Croatia 66 Bd
Björbo, Sweden 50 Db
Bjordal, Norway 46 Bc
Bjorkelangen, Norway 47 He
Björkhult, Sweden 51 Ee
Björkö, Sweden 50 Jc
Björkvik, Sweden 50 Fd
Björne Fd., Norway 47 Bd
Björne Sd., Greenland 9 De
Björneborg, Sweden 50 Dc
Bjorsäter, Sweden 50 Fd
Blaauwberg and mt., Transvaal 113 Cd
Blaavands Huk, Denmark 45 Ac
Blaby, England 14 Ca
Blace, Serbia 68 Gc
Blackall, Queensland 153 Cd
Blackburn, England 18 Bc
Blackburn, Mt., Alaska 125 Lf
Black Drin, R., Albania 70 Bb
Black Duck, Minnesota 132 Bb
Black B., Ontario 122 Da
Black Belt, Alabama 130 Ed
Black Hills, Wyo.-S. Dak. 126 Eb
Black Mts., Arizona 134 Fd
Black Mts., N.-W.F.P. 82 Ea
Black Mts., Eng.-Wales 14 Ab
Black Ra., W. Australia 152 Bc
Black R., Missouri, etc. 130 Cb
Black R., New York 128 Ab
Black R. (Song-bo), Tong-king 95 Ce
Black Sea, Europe-Asia 75 Eg
Black Flag, W. Aust. 152 Ce
Blackfoot, Idaho 136 Gd
Blackfoot Mts., Idaho 136 Hd
Blackford, Scotland 23 Bd
Blackhead, New Zealand 158 Fd
Black Isle, Scotland 23 Da
Black Pine Mts., Idaho 136 Gd
Blackpool, England 18 Ac
Black River, Jamaica 140 Bc
Blackriver, Michigan 122 Gc
Black River Falls, Wisconsin 132 Dc
Black Rock, Arkansas 130 Cb
Black Rock Des., Nevada 134 Da
Blacksburg, S. Carolina 131 Hc
Blackshear, Georgia 131 Ge
Blacksod B., Eire 25 Aa
Black Sturgeon L., Ontario 122 Da
Blackville, New Brunswick 120 Bc
Blackville, S. Carolina 131 Hd
Black Warrior R., Alaba. 130 Ed
Blackwater, R., Eire 27 Bg
Blackwater, R., England 15 Ec
Blackwell, Oklahoma 133 Db
Blackwood R., W. Aust. 152 Be
Bladgrond, Cape Prov. 114 Cd
Blaen Afon, England 14 Ac
Blaenau-Ffestiniog, Wales 20 Cb
Blagaj, Hercegovina 68 Cc
Blagdon, England 14 Bd
Blagodarnoe, U.S.S.R. 75 Gf
Blagoveshchensk, U.S.S.R. 96 Da
Blain, France 32 Dc
Blaina, England 14 Ac
Blaine, Washington 136 Ba
Blair, Nebraska 132 Ae
Blair Atholl, Scotland 23 Ec
Blairgowrie, Scotland 23 Ec
Blairmore, Alberta 124 Ge
Blairsville, Pennsylvania 129 Eb
Blaj, Romania 67 Jc
Blăjeni, Romania 67 Hc
Blakely, Georgia 131 Fe
Blaker, Norway 47 Hd
Blamangan Pen., Java 99 De
Blamont, France 31 Jd
Blanc, le, France 30 De
Blanc, Mt., France 35 Jb
Blanc (Blanco), C., Moroc. 103 Nh
Blanca, Sa., Colorado 135 Lc
Blanca, Sa., New Mexico 135 Le
Blanche, L., S. Aust. 154 Ba
Blanchester, Ohio 129 Bc
Blanche Town, S. Aust. 154 Bc
Blanchewater, S. Aust. 154 Ba
Blanco, Cape Prov. 114 Ef
Blanco, C., Fr. W. Africa 104 Ab
Blanco, C., Oregon 136 Ad
Blanco, C., Tunisia 103 Ja
Bland, Virginia 129 Dd
Blandford, England 14 Be
Blandford, Quebec 121 Da
Blanes, Spain 39 Hc
Blaney, Cape Prov. 115 Gf
Blangy, France 30 Db
Blankenberghe, Belgium 29 Ac
Blankenburg, Brunswick 54 Fd
Blankenheim, Prussia 54 Be
Blanquefort, France 34 Bc

Blanquilla, I., Venezuela 144 Da
Blantyre, Nyasaland - 112 Cc
Blasket I., Gt., Eire - 25 Ae
Błaszke, Poland - - 57 Db
Blato, Dalmatia - - 68 Bd
Blaufelden, Württemberg 58 Db
Blavet, R., France - 32 Bc
Blaydon, England - - 21 Ed
Blaye, France - - 34 Bb
Blayney, New S. Wales 155 Fc
Bleckede, Prussia - - 54 Fb
Bled, Slovenia - - 63 Ja
Bleiburg, Austria - - 59 Je
Blekinge, län, Sweden - 51 Df
Bleneau, France - - 30 Ed
Blenheim, New Zealand 159 Dd
Blenheim, Ontario - 123 Hd
Blessington, Eire - - 27 De
Bletchington, England - 14 Cc
Bletchley, England - 15 Db
Bletsoe, England - - 15 Db
Bletterman, Cape Prov. - 115 Fe
Blida, Algeria - - 103 Fa
Blinden Horn, Switz. - 42 Ed
Blind River, Ontario - 122 Gb
Blinman, S. Australia - 154 Bb
Bliss Wood R., Idaho - 136 Fd
Blisworth, England - 15 Db
Blita, Fr. W. Africa - 105 Bd
Blitar, Java - - - 98 De
Blitzen Mt., Nevada - 134 Ea
Blliçaj, Albania - - 70 Bb
Block I., New York - 123 Ne
Bloemfontein, O.F.S. - 115 Fd
Bloemhof, Cape Prov. - 115 Fc
Blois, France - - 30 Dd
Blomberg, Lippe - - 54 Dd
Blonde Is., Kwang-tung T. 97 Ac
Blönduós, Iceland - - 52 Cb
Blood River, Natal - 115 Jc
Bloody Foreland, Eire - 26 Ba
Bloomfield, Indiana - 129 Ac
Bloomfield, Iowa - - 132 Ce
Bloomfield, Missouri - 130 Cb
Bloomfield, New Jersey - 128 Ac
Bloomfield, Ontario - 121 Bc
Bloomington, Idaho - 136 Hd
Bloomington, Illinois - 132 Ee
Bloomington, Indiana - 129 Ac
Blossburg, Montana - 136 Gb
Blossburg, Pennsylvania 129 Fb
Blountstown, Florida - 130 Fe
Blovice, Bohemia - - 59 Hb
Bloxwich, England - 14 Ba
Bludenz, Austria - - 58 Dd
Blue Mts., Arkansas - 130 Bc
Blue Mts., Jamaica - 140 Bc
Blue Mts., New S. Wales 155 Gc
Blue Mts., Oregon - 136 Dc
Blue Earth, Minnesota - 132 Bd
Bluefield, W. Virginia - 129 Dd
Bluefields, Nicaragua - 140 Ge
Blue Island, Illinois - 132 Fe
Blue Mound City, Kansas 133 Ea
Blue Mount, Mississippi 130 Dc
Blue Nile, R., A.-E. Sudan 108 Bc
Blue Rapids, Kansas - 133 Da
Blue Ridge, Georgia - 131 Fc
Blue Ridge, mts., U.S.A. 127 Jc
Bluewater, New Mexico - 135 Kd
Bluff, Alaska - - 125 Fd
Bluff, New Zealand - 159 Bg
Bluff, Utah - - - 135 Jc
Bluff Springs, Alabama 130 Ee
Bluffton, Indiana - - 129 Bb
Blumenau, Brazil - - 147 Fd
Blumenhagen, Prussia - 55 Jb
Blumenthal, Prussia - 54 Db
Blunt Springs, Alabama 130 Ec
Blyth, Northumb., Eng. 21 Ec
Blyth, Notts, England - 18 Cd
Blythe, California - - 134 Fe
Blytheville, Arkansas - 130 Dc
Blythewood, S. Carolina 131 Hc
Bo, Sierra Leone - - 104 Be
Boafé, Brazil - - 145 Cc
Boag, Philippines - - 99 Fa
Boag Ibn Sabar, Palestine 80 Be
Boal, Spain - - - 36 Da
Boa-lam, Tong-king - 95 Ce
Boano, I., Nether. Indies 99 Gd
Boardman, N. Carolina 131 Jc
Boatman, Queensland - 153 Ce
Boat of Garten, Scotland 23 Eb
Boa Vista, Amazonas,
Brazil - - - 142 Bb
Boa Vista, Pernambuco,
Brazil - - - 143 Fd
Boa Vista Tocantins, Brazil 143 Ed
Boaz, New Mexico - 135 Le
Bobadah, New S. Wales 155 Eb
Bobawaba, Queensland - 153 Cc
Bobbili, Madras - - 91 Fb
Bobbio, Italy - - 62 Dc
Bobi, Paraguay - - 146 Dd
Bobingen, Bavaria - 58 Ec
Bobo Dioulasso, Fr. W.
Africa - - - 104 Dd
Boboshevo, Bulgaria - 70 Da
Bobrka - - - 60 Hd
Bobrov, U.S.S.R. - 75 Fe
Bobruisk, White Russia 75 De
Boca Chica, Florida - 131 Nj
Boca de Teacapan, Mexico 138 Cc
Boca San Domingo, Mexico 138 Bb
Bocas del Toro, Panama 140 Gf
Boca Soledad, Mexico - 138 Bb
Bocayuva, Brazil - - 147 Gb
Bocca do Curua, Brazil 142 Dd
Bocca do Tauary, Brazil 145 Cc
Bochaier, Ethiopia - 108 Dd
Bochnia, Poland - - 60 Fd
Bocholt, Belgium - - 29 Dc
Bocholt, Prussia - - 54 Bd
Bochum, Prussia - - 54 Cd
Bocşa, Romania - - 67 Gd
Bocşa Montană, Romania 67 Gd
Bocşa Română, Romania 67 Gd
Böda, Sweden - - 51 Ge
Bodalla, New S. Wales 155 Fd
Bodby, Denmark - - 45 Ed
Boden, Sweden - - 44 Ef
Boden See (Constance,
L.), Switzerland - 43 Ha
Bodenbach, Bohemia - 59 Ja
Bodenburg, Prussia - 54 Ec
Bodenheim, Hesse - 58 Cb
Boderg, L., Eire - - 26 Cd
Bodhan, Hyderabad - 90 Cb
Bodinayakanur, Madras 89 Bb
Bodmin, England - - 17 Bc
Bodö, Norway - - 44 Cf
Bodoquena, Sa., Brazil 146 Dc
Boeli B., Halmahera, N.I. 99 Gc
Boende, Belg. Congo - 109 Db
Boene, I., Mozambique - 113 Fc
Boenjoe, I., Neth. Indies 99 Ec
Boenoet, Borneo - - 99 Dc
Boentoei, Borneo - - 99 Dd
Boentok, Borneo - - 99 Dd
Boeol, Celébes - - 99 Fc
Boerne, Texas - - 133 Cf
Boeroe, I., Nether. Indies 99 Gd
Boetoeng I. and Pass,
Netherlands Indies - 99 Fe
Boffa, Fr. W. Africa - 104 Bd
Bofors, Sweden - - 50 Dc
Bogadjim, New Guinea - 156 Dc
Bogalusa, Louisiana - 130 De
Bogana, Sinkiang - - 84 Ec
Bogan Gate, New S. Wales 155 Fc
Bogdo-ola, Sinkiang - 84 Fb
Bogenfels, S.-W. Africa 114 Ac
Bogense, Denmark - 45 Dc
Boggabri, New S. Wales 155 Fb
Boggeragh Mts., Eire - 25 Ce
Boghari, Algeria - - 102 Fb
Boghé, Fr. W. Africa - 104 Bc
Boghni, Algeria - - 103 Ga
Bognor Regis, England 15 De
Bogö, Denmark - - 45 Fd
Bogo, Philippines - - 99 Fa
Bogodukhov, Ukraine - 75 Fe
Bogomila, Serbia - - 70 Cb
Bogong, Mt., Victoria - 155 Ed
Bogoslof I., Aleutian Is. 125 Ej
Bogota, Colombia - - 144 Bc
Bogra, Bengal - - 88 Bb
Boguchar, U.S.S.R. - 75 Ff
Bogue Chitto, Mississippi 130 Ce
Bogumin, Moravia - 57 Dd
Bohain, France - - 30 Fb
Bohemia, Czechoslovakia 60 Cd
Bohinjska Bistrica, Slovenia 63 Ha
Bohmer Wald, Bavaria-
Bohemia - - - 59 Gb
Bohol, I., Philippines - 99 Fb
Bohotleh, Br. Somaliland 108 Ed
Bohumin, Moravia - 60 Ed
Boiana, Italy - - 64 Eb
Boiboly, Madagascar - 112 De
Boiestown, New Bruns. 120 Bc
Boim Brazil - - 142 Cc
Boina, Madagascar - 112 Ec
Bois, L. des, N.-W. T. 118 Ec
Bois Blanc I., Michigan 122 Fc
Boisé, Idaho - - 136 Ed
Boise R., Idaho - - 136 Fd
Boise City, Oklahoma - 133 Ab
Bois Fort, Minnesota - 132 Ca
Boissevain, Manitoba - 124 Ke
Boitzenburg, Prussia - 55 Jb
Boizenburg, Mecklenburg 54 Fb
Bojador, C., Rio de Oro 104 Aa
Bojeador, C., Philippines 95 Ff
Boka, Voyvodina - - 67 Fd
Bokala, Belg. Congo - 109 Cb
Bokan-sukhai, China - 94 Ba
Bokatola, Belg. Congo - 109 Cb
Boke, Fr. W. Africa - 104 Bd
Bokn Fd., Norway - 47 Be
Boksburg, Transvaal - 115 Hc
Bokula, Belg. Congo - 109 Da
Bol, Fr. Eq. Africa - 105 Dc
Bolama, Port. Guinea - 104 Ad
Bolangir, Eastern States 87 Ee
Bolano, Celébes - - 99 Fc
Bolan Pass, Baluchistan 82 Bd
Bolayu, Turkey - - 72 Db
Bolbec, France - - 30 Cb
Bolderaja, Latvia - - 49 Cc
Bole, Gold Coast - - 104 De
Bole, Sinkiang - - 84 Ea
Bolia, Belg. Congo - 109 Cb
Boliko, Belgian Congo - 109 Db
Bolinao, Philippines - 95 Ef
Bolivar, Argentina - 148 Db
Bolivar, Colombia - - 144 Ac
Bolivar, Missouri - - 130 Bb
Bolivar, Tennessee - - 130 Dc
Bolivar, dep., Colombia 144 Ab
Bolivar, prov., Ecuador 145 Bb
Bolivar, state, Venezuela 144 Cb
Bolivia, rep., S. America 141 Cd
Boljanic, Bosnia - - 68 Db
Boljanići, Montenegro - 68 Ec
Bolkar Dagh, Turkey - 78 Bb
Bolkesjo, Norway - - 47 Fe
Bolkhov, U.S.S.R. - 75 Fe
Bollebygd, Sweden - 51 Be
Bollène, France - - 35 Gc
Bollnäs, Sweden - - 50 Fa
Bollon, Queensland - 153 Ce
Bolmen and L., Sweden 51 Cf
Bolo Mts., Fr. Eq. Afr. 105 Ed
Bolobo, Belgian Congo - 109 Cb
Bologna, Italy - - 63 Fc
Bologoe, U.S.S.R. - 74 Ed
Bolombo, Belgian Congo 109 Db
Bolon, L., U.S.S.R. - 96 Fb
Boloncheticul, Mexico - 139 Fc
Bolongo, Belg. Congo - 109 Cb
Bolotana, Sardinia - 64 Hf
Bolsena L., Italy - - 64 Ba
Bolshezemelskaya Tundra,
U.S.S.R. - - - 74 Kb
Bolshoy Tokmak, Ukraine 75 Ef
Bolson de Mapimi, Mexico 138 Db
Bolsover, England - 18 Cd
Boltana, Spain - - 39 Eb
Boltigen, Switzerland - 42 Dc
Bolton, England - - 18 Bc
Bolton, Mississippi - 130 Cd
Bolton, Philippines - 99 Gb
Bolton-le-Sands, England 18 Bb
Bolu, Turkey - - 78 Ba
Bolzano, Italy - - 63 Fa
Bom, New Ireland - 156 Eb
Boma, Belgian Congo - 109 Bc
Bomassa, Fr. Eq. Africa 109 Ca
Bomba, Italy - - 64 Ea
Bomba & G. di, Libya - 106 Db
Bombala, New S. Wales 155 Fd
Bombay, Bombay - - 90 Ab
Bombay, presidency,
India - - - 81 Cf
Bombetoke B., Madag. - 112 Ec
Bombo, Uganda - - 110 Cc
Bomboma, Belg. Congo - 109 Ca
Bomfim, Bahia, Brazil - 143 Fe
Bomfim, Goyaz, Brazil - 147 Fb
Bom Jardim, Amazonas,
Brazil - - - 145 Cc
Bom Jardim, Bahia, Brazil 143 Ge
Bom Jesus da Lapa, Brazil 143 Fe
Bom Jesus do Gurgueia,
Brazil - - - 143 Fd
Bömlo, Norway - - 47 Be
Bon, C., Tunisia - - 103 Ka
Bona, Mt., Alaska - 125 Mf
Bonaberi, Fr. Eq. Africa 105 Ce
Bonaduz, Switzerland - 43 Hc
Bonai, Eastern States 87 Fe
Bonaigarh, Eastern States 87 Fe
Bonaire I., Caribbean Sea 137 Fc
Bon Ami, Louisiana - 130 Be
Bonapitse, Bechuanaland 113 Bd
Bonar Bridge, Scotland 23 Da
Bonaventure, Newfoundl'd 120 Hb
Bonavista, Newfoundland 120 Jb
Bonavista, B. and C.,
Newfoundland - - 120 Jb
Bondeno, Italy - - 63 Fc
Bondo, Belgian Congo - 109 Da
Bondoni, Kenya - - 110 Ed
Bondowoso, Java - - 99 De
Bône, Algeria - - 103 Ha
Bone, Gulf of, Celébes - 99 Fd
Bo'ness, Scotland - - 23 Ed
Bonfield, Ontario - - 121 Aa
Bonga, Ethiopia - - 108 Cd
Bonga, Fr. Eq. Africa - 109 Cb
Bongabon, Philippines - 99 Fa
Bongandanga, Belg. Congo 109 Da
Bongo, Belg. Congo - 109 Cb
Bongon, N. Borneo - 99 Eb
Bonham, Texas - - 133 Dd
Bonheur, Ontario - - 122 Ca
Bonifacio and Str. of,
Corsica - - - 33 Eh
Bonifay, Florida - - 130 Fe
Bonita, Arizona - - 135 He
Bonn, Prussia - - 54 Ce
Bonnat, France - - 34 Da
Bonndorf, Baden - - 58 Cd
Bonne Bay, Newfoundland 120 Fb
Bonnefoi, Transvaal - 115 Jb
Bonner, Montana - - 136 Gb
Bonners Ferry, Idaho - 136 Ea
Bonner Springs, Kansas 133 Ea
Bonnetable, France - 30 Cc
Bonne Terre, Missouri - 130 Cb
Bonneval, France - - 30 Dc
Bonneville, France - 35 Ja
Bonneville Dam,
Washington - - 136 Bc
Bonnie Rock, W. Aust. 152 Be
Bonnievale, Cape Prov. - 114 Cg
Bonny, Nigeria - - 105 Ce
Bono, Sardinia - - 64 Jf
Bonoi, New Guinea - 156 Bb
Bonorva, Sardinia - 64 Hf
Bontafalau, Romania - 67 Hc
Bontang, Borneo - - 99 Ec
Bonteberg Mts., Cape Pr. 114 Cf
Bontekoe I., Greenland - 9 Gc
Bonthain, Celébes - - 99 Ee
Bonthe, Sierra Leone - 104 Be
Bontida, Transylvania - 67 Jc
Bontoc, Philippines - 95 Ff
Bontoku, Korea - - 97 Bc
Bonyhád, Hungary - 66 Dc
Boogardie, W. Aust. - 152 Bd
Boogtu, China - - 96 Ac
Bookaloo, S. Australia - 154 Ab
Book Cliff, Colorado - 135 Jb
Booleroo Centre, S. Aust. 154 Bc
Booligal, New S. Wales 154 Dc
Boomi, New S. Wales - 155 Fa
Boone, Iowa - - - 132 Cd
Boone, N. Carolina - 131 Hb
Booneville, Kentucky - 131 Fb
Booneville, Mississippi - 130 Dc
Boons, Transvaal - - 115 Gb
Boonville, Missouri - 130 Ba
Booneville, New York - 123 Ld
Boorabbin, W. Aust. - 152 Ce
Boorcoon, New S. Wales 155 Eb
Boorindal, New S. Wales 155 Eb
Boorooman, Queensland 153 Cd
Booroorban, N. S. Wales 154 Dc
Boostedt, Prussia - - 54 Fb
Boothia Isthmus, N.-W.T. 119 Lc
Boothia Pen. and Gulf,
N.-W. Terr. - - 119 Lb
Bootle, England - - 18 Ad
Bopeechee, S. Australia 154 Aa
Bopfingen, Württemberg 58 Ec
Boporo, Liberia - - 104 Be
Boppard, Prussia - - 58 Ba
Boquete, Panama - - 140 Gf
Bor, A.-E. Sudan - - 108 Bd
Bör, L., Manchuria - 96 Bb
Boras, Sweden - - 51 Be
Borasamber, Orissa - 87 Ee
Borazjan, Persia - - 79 Fd
Borba, Brazil - - 142 Cc
Borborema, Planalto da,
Brazil - - - 143 Gd
Borca, Romania - - 69 Fb
Bordeaux, France - - 34 Bc
Bordeaux, Wyoming - 135 La
Borden I., N.-W. Terr. 118 Ha
Bordertown, S. Aust. - 154 Cd
Bordes, les, France - 30 Ed
Bordheyri, Iceland - 52 Cb
Bordighera, Italy - - 62 Bd
Bordj Beressof, Algeria 103 Hc
Bordj d'Ain Guettara,
Algeria - - - 102 Fe
Bordj Lahrach, Tunisia 103 Jc
Bordj May, Algeria - 103 Hc
Bordj Viollette, Algeria 102 Cf
Bordö, Færoe Is. - - 44 Oc
Borga, Jeb., Egypt - 107 Jf
Borgarfjördhur, Iceland 52 Bb
Borgarnes, Iceland - 52 Cb
Borger, Texas - - 133 Bc
Borghetto, Italy - - 62 Dc
Borgholm, Sweden - 51 Ff
Borghorst, Prussia - 54 Cc
Borgne, Haiti - - 140 Cc
Borgne, L., Mississippi - 130 De
Borgo a Moz, Italy - 62 Ed
Borgoforte, Italy - - 62 Eb
Borgomanero, Italy - 62 Cb
Borgomaro, Italy - - 62 Bd
Borgo San Dalmazzo, Italy 62 Bc
Borgo San Lorenzo, Italy 63 Fd
Borgosesia, Italy - - 62 Cb
Borgotaro, Italy - - 62 Dc
Borgou, Fr. W. Africa - 105 Bc
Borgo Vercelli, Italy - 62 Cb
Borgvik, Sweden - - 50 Bc
Bori, Central Provs. - 86 Ce
Bori, Fr. W. Africa - 105 Bd
Borina, Serbia - - 68 Eb
Borio, Fr. W. Africa - 105 Bd
Borisoglebsk, U.S.S.R. 75 Ge
Borisov, White Russia - 75 De
Borisovgrad, Bulgaria - 69 Fe
Borja, Spain - - - 38 Dc
Borja Planina, Bosnia - 68 Cb
Borjas Blancas, Spain - 39 Fc
Borken, Prussia - - 54 Bd
Börkop, Denmark - - 45 Cc
Borlänge, Sweden - - 50 Eb
Bormida, R , Italy - 62 Cc
Borna, Saxony - - 55 Hd
Borneo, I., E. Indies - 98 Dc
Bornes, Sa. de, Portugal 36 Cc
Bornholm, I., Denmark - 45 Hf
Borntuchen - - - 56 Bb
Bornu, Nigeria - - 107 Ha
Borobini (Golbanti), Kenya 110 Fe
Boro-khoro Mts., Sinkiang 84 Eb
Boroko, Celébes - - 99 Fc
Borongan, Philippines - 99 Ga
Boroughbridge, England 18 Cb
Borouj, El, Morocco - 103 Oh
Borove, Albania - - 70 Bb
Borovichi, U.S.S.R. - 74 Ed
Borovo, Slavonia - - 66 Dd
Borox, Spain - - 38 Bd
Borriol, Spain - - 39 Ed
Borris, Eire - - 27 Df
Borrisokane, Eire - - 27 Bf
Borroloola, N. T., Aust. 151 Fb
Borsa, Transylvania - 67 Kb
Borsad, Bombay - - 85 Dc
Borsod, Hungary - - 67 Fa
Borup, Denmark - - 45 Fc
Bory Tucholskie, Poland 56 Bc
Borzhom, Georgia - - 75 Gg
Bosa, Sardinia - - 64 Hf
Bosanska Gradiška, Bosnia 68 Ca
Bosanska Krupa, Bosnia 68 Bb
Bosanska Rača, Bosnia - 68 Eb
Boscastle, England - 17 Bb
Boscobel, Wisconsin - 132 Dd
Boscombe, England - 14 Ce
Boshoek, Transvaal - 115 Gb
Boshof, O.F.S. - - 115 Fd
Bosiljgrad, Serbia - - 69 Ed
Boskovice, Moravia - 57 Bd
Bosna, R., Bosnia - 68 Db
Bosnia, Jugoslavia - 68 Cb
Boso, Kenya - - - 110 Fd
Bosoli, Bechuanaland - 113 Bc
Bosporus, Turkey - - 72 Ga
Bosquet, Algeria - - 102 Ea
Bossangoa, Fr. Eq. Africa 105 Ed
Bossier City, Louisiana - 130 Bd
Bosso, Fr. W. Africa - 105 Dc
Bostan, Baluchistan - 82 Bc
Boston, England - - 19 Ee
Boston, Massachusetts - 128 Cb
Boston Mts., Arkansas - 130 Ac
Botany B., New S. Wales 155 Gc
Botchawana, Ontario - 122 Fb
Botevgrad, Bulgaria - 69 Ed
Bothaville, O.F.S. - 115 Gc
Bothnia, Gulf of, Sweden-
Finland - - - 44 Dg
Botiala, Ital. Somaliland 108 Ec
Botley, England - - 14 Ce
Botmanak, Sinkiang - 84 Db
Botongo, Fr. Eq. Africa 109 Ca
Botosani, Romania - 69 Gb
Botter Kloof Pass, Cape
Province - - - 114 Ce
Bottesford, England - 19 De
Bottisham, England - 15 Eb
Bottrop, Prussia - - 54 Bd
Botucatu, Brazil - - 147 Fc
Botun, Serbia - - 70 Bb
Botwood Harbour, New-
foundland - - - 120 Hb
Bouabout, Morocco - 103 Nj
Bou Aïech, Algeria - 102 Dd

BOU **Regional Atlas** BRO

Bouaké, *Fr. W. Africa* - 104 De
Bou Anane, *Morocco* - 102 Cc
Bouar, *Fr. Eq. Africa* - 105 Ed
Bou Arada, *Tunisia* - 103 Ja
Bou Arfa, *Morocco* - 102 Dc
Bouay, *Fr. W. Africa* - 105 Bc
Bouaye, *France* - 32 Dc
Bou Cedraïa, *Algeria* - 102 Fb
Boucheron, *Morocco* - 103 Oh
Bouches-du-Rhône, dep., *France* - 35 Gd
Bouchette, *Quebec* - 121 Ca
Bou Denib, *Morocco* - 102 Cd
Bou Djebeha, *Fr. W. Afr.* 104 Dc
Boudoukou, *Fr. W. Afr.* 104 De
Boudry, *Switzerland* - 42 Cc
Boué, *Fr. Eq. Africa* - 109 Bb
Bouea, *Nigeria* - 105 Ce
Boufarik, *Algeria* - 102 Fa
Bougainville, C., *W. Aust.* 152 Da
Bougainville I., *Solomon Is.* 157 Cd
Bou Garfa, *Algeria* - 104 Ca
Bougaroun, C., *Algeria* 103 Ha
Bougie & G. de, *Algeria* 103 Ga
Bougouni, *Fr. W. Africa* 104 Cd
Bou Guezoul, *Algeria* - 103 Fb
Bouira, *Algeria* - 103 Fa
Boujad, *Morocco* - 102 Ac
Bouka, *Fr. Eq. Africa* - 105 Ed
Boulal, *Fr. W. Africa* - 104 Cc
Boulalanga, *Fr. Eq. Afr.* 105 Ec
Boularderie I., *Nova Scotia* 120 Ec
Boulay, *France* - 31 Jb
Boulder, *Colorado* - 135 Lb
Boulder, *Montana* - 136 Gb
Boulder, *W. Aust.* - 152 Ce
Boulder Creek, *California* 134 Bc
Boulder Dam, *Nevada* - 134 Fd
Boulhaut, *Morocco* - 103 Oh
Boulia, *Queensland* - 153 Ad
Boulogne, *France* - 30 Da
Boulogne, R., *France* - 32 Dd
Boulogne-Gesse, *France* 34 Cd
Bou Malem, *Morocco* - 102 Bd
Boumba, *Fr. W. Africa* 105 Bc
Boumo, *Fr. Eq. Africa* - 105 Ed
Bouna, *Fr. W. Africa* - 104 De
Boundary, *Br. Columbia* 124 Cc
Boundiali, *Fr. W. Africa* 104 Ce
Bouné, *Fr. W. Africa* - 105 Dc
Bountiful, *Utah* - 135 Ha
Bourbon-Lancy, *France* 35 Fa
Bourbonnais, prov., *France* 34 Ea
Bourbriac, *France* - 32 Bb
Bourdeilles, *France* - 34 Cb
Bourem, *Fr. W. Africa* 104 Dc
Bourg, *France* - 35 Ha
Bourg, le, *France* - 35 Jb
Bourganeuf, *France* - 34 Db
Bourges, *France* - 30 Ed
Bourgogne, *France* - 31 Gb
Bourgoin, *France* - 35 Hb
Bourg St Andéol, *France* 35 Gc
Bourg-St Maurice, *France* 35 Jb
Bourg, St Pierre, *Switzer.* 42 De
Bourke, *New S. Wales* - 155 Eb
Bourkes, *Ontario* - 123 Ha
Bourne, *England* - 19 De
Bournemouth, *England* 14 Ce
Bourron, *France* - 30 Ec
Bourtanger Moor, *Prussia* 54 Cc
Bourton, *England* - 14 Cb
Bourton-on-the-Water, *England* - 14 Cc
Bou Saâda, *Algeria* - 103 Gb
Bousquet, *Quebec* - 121 Da
Bouss, Jeb., *Algeria* - 103 Gb
Boussac, *France* - 34 Ea
Boussières, *France* - 31 Hd
Bousso, *Fr. Eq. Africa* - 105 Ec
Boutilimit, *Fr. W. Africa* 104 Bc
Bouveret, le, *Switzerland* 42 Cd
Bouxwiller, *France* - 31 Kc
Bouznika, *Morocco* - 103 Oh
Bouzonville, *France* - 31 Jb
Bovalino Marina, *Italy* - 65 Cd
Bovegno, *Italy* - 62 Eb
Boven-Dayak, *Borneo* - 99 Dd
Böverdal, *Norway* - 46 Ec
Boves, *Italy* - 62 Bc
Bovey Tracey, *England* 17 Cb
Bovine, *Utah* - 134 Ga
Bovino, *Italy* - 64 Fb
Bow R., *Alberta* - 124 Gd
Bowden, *Cape Prov.* - 115 Gf
Bowen, *Queensland* - 153 Cd
Bowie, *Arizona* - 135 Je
Bowie, *Louisiana* - 130 Cf
Bowie, *Texas* - 133 Cd
Bowker's Park, *Cape Prov.* 115 Ge
Bowling Green, *Kentucky* 130 Eb
Bowling Green, *Missouri* 130 Ca
Bowling Green, *Ohio* - 129 Cb
Bowling Green, *Virginia* 129 Fc
Bowling Green B. & C., *Queensland* - 153 Cc
Bowmanville, *Ontario* - 121 Ac
Bowoni (Wowoni), I., *Netherlands Indies* - 99 Fd
Bowral, *New S. Wales* - 155 Gc
Bowser, *Victoria* - 155 Ed
Bow String, *Minnesota* - 132 Cb
Boxcaada (Tenedos) I., *Turkey* - 72 Cc
Box Elder, *Montana* - 136 Ha
Box Hill, *England* - 15 Dd
Boxstel, *Holland* - 29 Dc
Box Tank, *New S. Wales* 154 Cb
Boyacá, dep., *Colombia* - 144 Bb
Boyce, *Louisiana* - 130 Be
Boydton, *Virginia* - 129 Ed
Boyenge, *Belg. Congo* - 109 Ca
Boyer, *Iowa* - 132 Be
Boyle, *Eire* - 26 Bd
Boyle, *Mississippi* - 130 Cd
Boyne, R., *Eire* - 26 Dd
Boyne City, *Michigan* - 122 Fc
Boynton, *Quebec* - 121 Db
Boyoka, *Fr. Eq. Africa* 109 Ca
Bozava, *Dalmatia* - 63 Jc
Bozel, *France* - 35 Jb
Bozeman, *Montana* - 136 Hc
Boževac, *Serbia* - 68 Gb
Bozhigrad, *Albania* - 70 Bc
Bozoum, *Fr. Eq. Africa* 105 Ed
Bozzolo, *Italy* - 62 Eb
Bra, *Italy* - 62 Bc
Brac, I., *Dalmatia* - 68 Bc
Bracadale & L., *Scotland* 22 Bb
Bracciano & L., *Italy* - 64 Ca
Bracebridge, *Ontario* - 121 Ab
Bracke, *Sweden* - 44 Cg
Brackettville, *Texas* - 133 Bf
Brackley, *England* - 14 Cb
Braco Maior, R., *Brazil* 143 De
Braco Menor, R., *Brazil* 143 De
Brad, *Romania* - 67 Hc
Bradano, R., *Italy* - 65 Cb
Braddock, *Pennsylvania* 129 Eb
Bradenton, *Florida* - 131 Mh
Bradfield Combust, *Eng.* 15 Eb
Bradford, *Wilts, Eng.* - 14 Bd
Bradford, *Yorks, Eng.* - 18 Cc
Bradford, *New Hampshire* 128 Cb
Bradford, *Pennsylvania* - 129 Eb
Bradley, *California* - 134 Cd
Bradore B., *Quebec* - 120 Ga
Bradwell, *England* - 15 Ec
Brady, *Texas* - 133 Ce
Braemar, *Scotland* - 23 Ec
Braga, *Portugal* - 36 Bc
Bragado, *Argentina* - 148 Db
Bragança, *Para, Brazil* 143 Ec
Bragança, *São Paulo, Brazil* - 147 Fc
Bragança, *Portugal* - 36 Dc
Brahmanbaria, *Bengal* - 88 Cc
Brahmaputra R., *Assam* 88 Ca
Brahmaur, *Punjab States* 83 Gb
Braidwood, *Illinois* - 132 Fe
Braidwood, *New S. Wales* 155 Fd
Brail, *Switzerland* - 43 Jc
Brăila, *Romania* - 69 Gc
Braine, *France* - 31 Fb
Braine-le-Comte, *Belgium* 29 Cd
Brainerd, *Minnesota* - 132 Bb
Braintree, *England* - 15 Ec
Brállos, *Greece* - 71 De
Bramhapuri, *Central Provs.* 86 Ce
Bramming, *Denmark* - 45 Bc
Brampton, *Cumb., England* 21 Dd
Brampton, *Suffolk, Eng.* 15 Fb
Brampton, *Ontario* - 123 Jd
Bramsche, *Prussia* - 54 Cc
Bramstedt, *Prussia* - 54 Eb
Branchville, *S. Carolina* 131 Hd
Branco, R., *Brazil* - 142 Bb
Brande, *Denmark* - 45 Bc
Brandenberg, *Kentucky* 129 Ac
Brandenburg - 56 Eb
Brandenburg and prov., *Prussia* - 55 Hc
Brandfort, *O.F.S.* - 115 Gd
Brandon, *Eire* - 25 Ae
Brandon, *England* - 15 Eb
Brandon, *Manitoba* - 124 Ke
Brandon, *Mississippi* - 130 Dd
Brandon B. & Hd., *Eire* 25 Ae
Brandsen, *Argentina* - 148 Eb
Brandval, *Norway* - 47 Hd
Brandvlei, *Cape Prov.* - 114 De
Branford City, *Florida* - 131 Gf
Bransfield Str., *Antarctica* 160 —
Branston, *England* - 19 Dd
Brantford, *Ontario* - 123 Hd
Brantley, *Alabama* - 130 Ee
Branxholme, *Victoria* - 154 Ce
Bras dor L., *Nova Scotia* 120 Ed
Brasław - 60 Ja
Braşov, *Romania* - 69 Fc
Brass and R., *Nigeria* - 105 Ce
Brassac, *France* - 34 Ed
Brassus, le, *Switzerland* 42 Bc
Brastad, *Sweden* - 50 Ad
Bratea, *Transylvania* - 67 Hc
Bratislava (Pressburg), *Slovakia* - 66 Ca
Bratsigovo, *Bulgaria* - 70 Fb
Brattleboro, *Vermont* - 128 Bb
Braubach, *Prussia* - 58 Ba
Braunau, *Austria* - 59 Hc
Braunsberg 56 Db
Braunwald, *Switzerland* 43 Gc
Brava, *It. Somaliland* - 108 Gf
Brawley, *California* - 134 Fe
Brawny, *Ontario* - 121 Bb
Bray, *Eire* - 27 De
Bray, *Ontario* - 121 Cb
Bray Hd., *Eire* - 25 Af
Braymer, *Missouri* - 130 Ba
Bray-sur-Seine, *France* - 30 Fc
Bray-sur-Somme, *France* 30 Eb
Brazil, *Indiana* - 129 Ac
Brazil, rep., *S. America* 141 Dd
Brazilia, *Brazil* - 147 Gb
Brazos R., *Texas* - 133 Dd
Brazzaville, *Fr. Eq. Afr.* 109 Bb
Brca, *Dalmatia* - 68 Dd
Brdjani, *Serbia* - 68 Fc
Brdów, *Poland* - 57 Da
Brea, La, *Honduras* - 140 Fe
Breadalbane, *Scotland* - 23 Dd
Breadalbin, *New York* - 123 Ld
Breaker B., *Sarawak* - 99 Dc
Bream, *England* - 14 Bc
Bream B., *New Zealand* 158 Ea
Brebul, *Romania* - 67 Hd
Brechin, *Scotland* - 23 Fc
Breckenridge, *Colorado* - 135 Lb
Breckenridge, *Minnesota* 132 Ab
Breckenridge, *Texas* - 133 Cd
Brecknock, co., *Wales* - 20 Cd
Brecknock Pen., *Chile* - 148 Be
Breclav, *Moravia* - 6C Dd
Brecon, *Wales* - 20 Cd
Brecon Beacons, *Wales* 20 Cd
Breda, *Holland* - 29 Cc
Bredasdorp, *Cape Prov.* 114 Cg
Brede, *Denmark* - 45 Bc
Bredevangen, *Norway* - 46 Fc
Bredoo, *New S. Wales* - 155 Fd
Bredstrup, *Denmark* - 45 Cc
Bredwardine, *England* - 14 Ab
Breenagh, *Eire* - 26 Cb
Bregalnica, R., *Serbia* - 70 Db
Bregenz, *Austria* - 58 Dd
Breidhabolsstadhur, *Iceland* - 52 Ec
Breidhafjördhur, *Iceland* 52 Bb
Breim and Vatn, *Norway* 46 Cc
Breisgau, dist., *Baden* - 58 Bd
Brejó, *Brazil* - 143 Fc
Brekke, *Norway* - 46 Bd
Brekken, *Norway* - 46 Hb
Brěko, *Bosnia* - 68 Db
Bremangerland, *Norway* 46 Ac
Bremen & state, *Germany* 54 Db
Bremerhaven, *Bremen* - 54 Db
Bremersdorp, *Swaziland* 115 Jc
Bremerton, *Washington* 136 Bb
Bremervorde, *Prussia* - 54 Eb
Bremgarten, *Switzerland* 43 Fb
Bremond, *Texas* - 133 De
Brendon Hills, *England* 14 Ad
Brenham, *Texas* - 133 De
Brennar Pass, *Austria-Italy* 59 Fd
Breno, *Italy* - 62 Eb
Brent, *Ontario* - 121 Aa
Brenta, R., *Italy* - 63 Gb
Brentford, *England* - 15 Dd
Brentwood, *England* - 15 Ec
Brescello, *Italy* - 62 Ec
Brescia, *Italy* - 62 Eb
Breslau (Wroclaw), *Poland* 57 Bb
Bresles, *France* - 30 Eb
Bressay, I., *Scotland* - 24 Gh
Bressuire, *France* - 32 Ed
Brest, *France* - 32 Ab
Brest (Brzesc-nad Bugiem), *White Russia* - 60 Gb
Brestovac, *Voyvodina* - 66 Ed
Breteuil, *France* - 30 Eb
Breton, C., *Nova Scotia* 120 Fd
Breton Sd., *Louisiana* - 130 Df
Breuëh, *Sumatra* - 98 Ab
Brevard, *N. Carolina* - 131 Gc
Breves, *Brazil* - 143 Dc
Brevik, *Norway* - 47 Fe
Brewarrina, *New S. Wales* 155 Ea
Brewer, *Maine* - 120 Ad
Brewster, C., *Greenland* 9 Gc
Brewton, *Alabama* - 130 Ee
Breyton, *Transvaal* - 115 Hc
Brezičani, *Bosnia* - 68 Ba
Brezice, *Slovenia* - 63 Kb
Brézina, *Algeria* - 102 Ec
Brezna, *Montenegro* - 68 Dd
Březnice, *Bohemia* - 59 Jb
Brezno, *Slovenia* - 63 Ka
Brezno-nad-Hronom, *Slovakia* - 57 Ee
Brezolles, *France* - 30 Cc
Brezova, *Slovakia* - 66 Ca
Bria, *Fr. Eq. Africa* - 105 Fd
Briançon, *France* - 35 Jc
Briare, *France* - 30 Ed
Brias, *Spain* - 38 Cc
Briatico, *Italy* - 65 Bd
Bricquebec, *France* - 32 Da
Bridgehampton, *New York* 128 Bc
Bridgend, *Scotland* - 22 Be
Bridgend, *Wales* - 20 Ce
Bridge of Allan, *Scotland* 23 Ed
Bridge of Earn, *Scotland* 23 Ed
Bridgeport, *Alabama* - 130 Ec
Bridgeport, *California* - 134 Db
Bridgeport, *Colorado* - 135 Jb
Bridgeport, *Connecticut* - 128 Bc
Bridgeport, *Texas* - 133 Cd
Bridgeport, *Nebraska* - 135 Ma
Bridgeport, *Washington* 136 Db
Bridges, *Nevada* - 134 Ea
Bridgeton, *New Jersey* - 129 Gc
Bridgetown, *Cape Prov.* 114 Cf
Bridgetown, *England* - 14 Ba
Bridgetown, *Nova Scotia* 120 Cd
Bridgetown, *W. Australia* 152 Be
Bridgetown, *Windward Is.* 140 Kh
Bridgewater, *Massachus.* 128 Cb
Bridgewater, *Nova Scotia* 120 Cd
Bridgman, C., *Greenland* 9 Fa
Bridgnorth, *England* - 14 Ba
Bridgton, *Maine* - 128 Ca
Bridgwater & B., *England* 14 Ad
Bridlington & B., *England* 19 Db
Bridport, *England* - 14 Be
Bridport, *Tasmania* - 155 Kg
Brie, *France* - 30 Ec
Briec, *France* - 32 Ab
Brieg - 57 Cc
Brielle, *Holland* - 29 Cc
Brienne-le-Château, *France* 31 Gc
Brienz, *Switzerland* - 42 Fc
Brienza, *Italy* - 64 Fc
Brier I., *Nova Scotia* - 120 Bd
Brierley Hill, *England* - 14 Bb
Briey, *France* - 31 Hb
Brig, *Switzerland* - 42 Ed
Brigels, *Switzerland* - 43 Hc
Brigg, *England* - 19 Dc
Brigham, *Utah* - 135 Ha
Bright, *Victoria* - 155 Ed
Brightlingsea, *England* - 15 Fc
Brighton, *Colorado* - 135 La
Brighton, *England* - 15 De
Brighton, *Ontario* - 121 Bb
Brighton, *S. Australia* - 154 Bd
Brighton, *Tasmania* - 155 Jh
Brignoles, *France* - 33 Ac
Brihuega, *Spain* - 38 Cd
Brimfield, *England* - 14 Bb
Brindaban, *United Provs.* 83 Ge
Brindisi, *Italy* - 65 Db
Brinje, *Croatia* - 63 Kb
Brinkene, *Algeria* - 102 De
Brinkley, *Arkansas* - 130 Cc
Brinkley, *England* - 15 Eb
Brinklow, *England* - 14 Cb
Brinkworth, *S. Australia* 154 Bc
Brin Navolok, *U.S.S.R.* 74 Gc
Brintbodarne, *Sweden* - 50 Db
Brione, *Switzerland* - 43 Gd
Briones, *Spain* - 38 Cb
Brioni I. - 63 Hc
Brionne, *France* - 30 Cb
Brioude, *France* - 35 Fb
Briouze, *France* - 30 Bc
Brisbane, *Queensland* - 153 De
Brisighella, *Italy* - 63 Fc
Brissago, *Switzerland* - 43 Gd
Bristol, *Connecticut* - 128 Bc
Bristol, *England* - 14 Bd
Bristol, *Florida* - 130 Fe
Bristol, *New Brunswick* 120 Bc
Bristol, *Quebec* - 121 Bb
Bristol, *Rhode I.* - 128 Cc
Bristol, *Vermont* - 128 Ba
Bristol, *Virginia* - 129 Cd
Bristol B., *Alaska* - 125 Gh
Bristol Chan., *Eng.-Wales* 17 Ca
Bristow, *Oklahoma* - 133 Dc
Britannia, *Ontario* - 121 Cb
British Columbia, prov., *Canada* - 118 De
British Guiana, *S. Amer.* 141 Db
British Honduras, *Cent. America* - 140 Fd
British Isles, *W. Europe* 10 —
British Somaliland, *E. Africa* - 101 Ge
Brito, *Nicaragua* - 140 Fe
Briton Ferry, *Wales* - 20 Cd
Britstown, *Cape Prov.* - 114 Ee
Britt, *Iowa* - 132 Cd
Brittany, old prov., *France* 32 Bb
Britz, *Prussia* - 55 Jc
Brive, *France* - 34 Db
Brixham, *England* - 17 Cc
Brno (Brunn), *Moravia* 60 Dd
Broach, *Bombay* - 85 Dd
Broad B., *Scotland* - 24 Ba
Broad Pass, *Alaska* - 125 Ke
Broad R., *S. Carolina* - 131 Hc
Broad Sd., *Queensland* - 153 Cd
Broadalbin, *New York* - 129 Ha
Broad Arrow, *W. Aust.* 152 Ce
Broadford, *Eire* - 27 Ag
Broadford, *Scotland* - 22 Cb
Broad Haven, *Eire* - 25 Ba
Broad Haven, *Wales* - 20 Ad
Broad Hinton, *England* 14 Cd
Broadstairs, *England* - 15 Fd
Broadway, *England* - 14 Cb
Brochet, *Quebec* - 121 Da
Brock I., *N.-W. Terr.* - 118 Fa
Brockman, Mt., *W. Aust.* 152 Bc
Brockton, *Massachusetts* 128 Cb
Brockville, *Ontario* - 121 Cb
Brod, *Serbia* - 70 Cb
Brod, *Slavonia* - 66 Dd
Brodear Pen., *N.-W. T.* 119 Mb
Brodhead, *Wisconsin* - 132 Ed
Brodick, *Scotland* - 22 Ce
Brodnica, *Poland* - 60 Eb
Brody - 60 Hc
Broer Ruys, C., *Greenland* 9 Hc
Broglio, *Switzerland* - 43 Gd
Broken B., *New S. Wales* 155 Gc
Broken Hill, *New S. Wales* 154 Cb
Broken Hill, *N. Rhodesia* 112 Ab
Broken Lava Plateau, *Idaho* - 136 Fd
Brokind, *Sweden* - 50 Ed
Brome, *England* - 15 Fb
Brome, *Quebec* - 121 Db
Brometo (Chichongue), *Mozambique* - 113 Fc
Bromfield, *England* - 14 Bb
Bromley, *England* - 15 Dd
Bromley, *S. Rhodesia* - 113 Db
Bromme, *Denmark* - 45 Ec
Brompton, *England* - 14 Aa
Bromptonville, *Quebec* - 121 Db
Bromsgrove, *England* - 14 Bb
Bromyard, *England* - 14 Bb
Brönderslev, *Denmark* - 45 Ca
Brönnöysund, *Norway* - 44 Bf
Bronson, *Florida* - 131 Gf
Bronte, *Sicily* - 65 Hg
Bronzell, *Prussia* - 54 Ee
Bronzolo, *Italy* - 63 Fa
Brooke, *England* - 15 Fa
Brookes Inlet, *W. Aust.* 152 Be
Brookfield, *Massachusetts* 128 Bb
Brookfield, *Missouri* - 130 Ba
Brookhaven, *Mississippi* 130 Ce
Brookings, *Oregon* - 136 Ad
Brookings, *S. Dakota* - 126 Fb
Brookland, *Texas* - 133 Fe
Brooklin, *Ontario* - 121 Ac
Brooklyn, *Iowa* - 132 Ce
Brooklyn, *New York* - 123 Me
Brooklyn, *Nova Scotia* - 120 Cd
Brookport, *Quebec* - 121 Db
Brooks, *Alaska* - 125 Kd
Brooks Ra., *Alaska* - 125 Gb
Brooksville, *Florida* - 131 Mg
Brookville, *Kentucky* - 131 Fa
Brookville, *Mississippi* - 130 Dd
Brookville, *Pennsylvania* 129 Eb
Broom, L., *Scotland* - 22 Ca
Broome, *W. Aust.* - 152 Cb
Broome Hill, *W. Aust.* - 152 Be
Brora, *Scotland* - 24 Ee
Brosteni, *Romania* - 67 He
Brostrud, *Norway* - 47 Ed
Brotas, *Brazil* - 146 Db
Brough, *Lancs, England* 19 Dc
Brough, *Westmorland, Eng.* 18 Ba
Broughton, *Lancs, Eng.* 18 Ab

Byske, *Sweden* 48 Dd
Bystré, *Moravia* 57 Bd
Bystřice, *Bohemia* 59 Jb
Byton (Beuthen), *Poland* 57 Dc
Byvalla, *Sweden* 50 Fb
Bzéma, *Libya* 106 Df
Bzenec, *Moravia* 57 Ce
Caaguazu, *Paraguay* 146 Dd
Caatinga, *Brazil* 142 Dd
Caazapa, *Paraguay* 146 Dd
Cabaleria, C., *Balearic Is.* 39 Mh
Caballeros, *Spain* 38 Db
Caballo Cocha, *Peru* 145 Cb
Caballos, Sa. de los, *New Mexico* 135 Ke
Cabanas, *Cuba* 140 Ab
Cabanatuan, *Philippines* 95 Ff
Cabanes, *Spain* 39 Ed
Cabao, *Libya* 103 Kd
Cabar, *Slovenia* 63 Jb
Cabazon, *California* 134 Ee
Cabedell, *Brazil* 143 Hd
Cabellos, *Uruguay* 146 De
Cabeza del Buey, *Spain* 37 Ed
Cabezas, *Bolivia* 146 Cb
Cabezon de la Sal, *Spain* 38 Aa
Cabezuela del Valle, *Spain* 37 Eb
Cabinet & Mts., *Montana* 136 Fa
Cabo Frio, *Brazil* 147 Gc
Caboolture, *Queensland* 153 De
Cabo Roxo, *Mexico* 139 Ec
Cabot Hd., *Ontario* 123 Hc
Cabot Str., *Newfoundland* 120 Ec
Cabra, *Spain* 40 Fb
Cabra, Sa. de la, *Spain* 36 Ca
Cabras, *Sardinia* 64 Hg
Cabras, Sa. de las, *Spain* 41 Eb
Cabrejas, Sa. de, *Spain* 38 Cc
Cabrera, I., *Balearic Is.* 39 He
Cabrera, Sierra, *Spain* 36 Db
Cabrial, R., *Spain* 38 De
Cabrobo, *Brazil* 143 Gd
Cabuli Pt., *Philippines* 99 Ea
Cabure, *Venezuela* 144 Ba
Čačak, *Serbia* 68 Fc
Caçapava, *Brazil* 147 Ee
Caccamo, *Sicily* 65 Gg
Caccia, C., *Sardinia* 64 Hf
Cacequy, *Brazil* 147 Ee
Caceres & prov., *Spain* 37 Dc
Cachar, *Assam* 88 Db
Cache R., *Arkansas* 130 Cc
Cacheu & R., *Port. Guinea* 104 Ad
Cachimbo, Sa. do, *Brazil* 142 Cd
Cachinal, *Chile* 146 Bc
Cachoeira, *Bahia, Brazil* 143 Ge
Cachoeira, *Rio Grande do Sul, Brazil* 147 Ee
Cachoeirinha, *Brazil* 142 Bb
Cadaques, *Spain* 39 Jb
Cadaval, *Portugal* 37 Ac
Caddo, *Oklahoma* 133 Dc
Caddo L., *Louisiana* 130 Bd
Cadena del Pantiacolla, *Peru* 145 Cd
Cadereyta, *Mexico* 139 Eb
Cader Idris, *Wales* 20 Cb
Cadi, Sa. del, *Spain* 39 Gb
Cadillac, *France* 34 Bc
Cadillac, *Michigan* 122 Fc
Cadiz, *California* 134 Fd
Cadiz, *Kentucky* 130 Eb
Cadiz and B., *Spain* 40 Dc
Cadiz, Gulf of, *Spain-Portugal* 40 Cc
Cadiz, prov., *Spain* 40 Ec
Cadots Pass, *Montana* 136 Gb
Caen, *France* 32 Ea
Caerleon, *England* 14 Ac
Caernarvon, *Wales* 20 Ba
Caernarvon, co. and B., *Wales* 20 Ba
Caerphilly, *Wales* 20 Cd
Caersws, *Wales* 20 Cb
Cæsarea (Qisarye), *Palestine* 80 Bb
Caetite, *Brazil* 143 Fe
Cagayan, *Mindanao, Philippines* 99 Fb
Cagayan & R., *Philippines* 95 Ff
Cagayan Sulu, *Philippines* 99 Eb
Cagli, *Italy* 63 Gd
Cagliari & G., *Sardinia* 64 Jg
Caglin, *Slavonia* 66 Dd
Cagnes, *France* 33 Cb
Cagollo, *Italy* 63 Fb
Cagua Vol., *Philippines* 95 Ff
Caguas, *Puerto Rico* 140 Jg
Caha Mts., *Eire* 25 Bf
Cahir, *Eire* 27 Cg
Cahirciveen, *Eire* 25 Af
Cahore Pt., *Eire* 27 Df
Cahors, *France* 34 Dc
Cahul 69 Hc
Caia, *Mozambique* 113 Fa
Caiazzo, *Italy* 64 Eb
Caibarien, *Cuba* 140 Bb
Caiçara, *Amazonas, Brazil* 142 Ac
Caiçara, *Rio Grande do Norte, Brazil* 143 Gc
Caicara, *Bolivar; Venez.* 144 Cb
Caicara, *Monagos, Venez.* 144 Db
Caicos Is. and Pass, *Bahamas* 140 Cb
Cailloma, *Peru* 145 Ce
Caillou B., *Louisiana* 130 Cf
Caillou L., *Louisiana* 130 Cf
Caimanera, *Cuba* 140 Bc
Câineni, *Romania* 67 Kd
Cainesville, *Missouri* 132 Be
Cairn Gorm, mt., *Scot.* 23 Eb
Cairns, *Queensland* 153 Cc
Cairn Toul, *Scotland* 23 Eb
Cairo, *Georgia* 131 Fe
Cairo, *Illinois* 130 Db
Cairo, *Italy* 62 Cc
Cairo (El Qahira), *Egypt* 107 Hc
Caisole 63 Jb
Caister, *England* 15 Fa
Caistor, *England* 19 Dc
Caivano, *Italy* 64 Ec
Caiwarro, *Queensland* 153 Be
Caiza, *Bolivia* 146 Cc
Cajamarca & dep., *Peru* 145 Bc
Cajazeiras, *Brazil* 143 Gd
Cajo, Mte., *Italy* 62 Ec
Čakovec, *Croatia* 66 Bc
Cala, *Cape Prov.* 115 Ge
Calabar, *Nigeria* 105 Cd
Calabasas, *Arizona* 135 Hf
Calabogie, *Ontario* 121 Bb
Calabozo, *Venezuela* 144 Cb
Calabria, *Italy* 65 Cc
Calacoto, *Bolivia* 146 Bb
Calaf, *Spain* 39 Gc
Calafat, *Romania* 69 Ed
Calagnan Is., *Philippines* 99 Fa
Calahorra, *Spain* 38 Cb
Calais, *France* 30 Da
Calais, *Maine* 120 Bd
Calama, *Brazil* 142 Bd
Calama, *Chile* 146 Bc
Calamar, *Colombia* 144 Ba
Calamar, *Vaupes, Colombia* 144 Bc
Calamian Group, *Philippines* 99 Ea
Calamocha, *Spain* 38 Dd
Călan, *Romania* 67 Jd
Calañas, *Spain* 40 Db
Calapan, *Philippines* 99 Fa
Călăraşi 69 Hb
Călăraşi, *Romania* 69 Gc
Calasetta, *Sardinia* 64 Hg
Calasparra, *Spain* 41 Eb
Calatañazor, *Spain* 38 Cc
Calatayud, *Spain* 38 Dc
Călăţele, *Transylvania* 67 Jc
Calatrava, Campo de, *Spain* 41 Cb
Calava, C., *Sicily* 65 Hf
Calayan, I., *Philippines* 95 Ff
Calbayog, *Philippines* 99 Fa
Calbe, *Prussia* 55 Gd
Calbuco, *Chile* 148 Bc
Calcasieu, *Louisiana* 130 Bf
Calceta, *Ecuador* 145 Ab
Calchaqui, *Argentina* 146 Cd
Calcutta, *Bengal* 88 Bc
Caldas, dep., *Colombia* 144 Ab
Caldas da Rainha, *Portugal* 37 Ac
Caldas de Reyes, *Spain* 36 Bb
Caldeirão, Sa., *Portugal* 40 Bb
Caldera, *Chile* 146 Ad
Caldercruix, *Scotland* 23 Ee
Caldicot, *England* 14 Bc
Caldwell, *Idaho* 136 Ed
Caldwell, *Kansas* 133 Db
Caldwell, *Ohio* 129 Dc
Caldwell, *Texas* 133 De
Calebra Ra., *Colorado* 135 Lc
Caledon, *Cape Prov.* 114 Cg
Caledonia, *Minnesota* 132 Dd
Caledonia, *N. Dakota* 132 Ab
Caledonia, *Nova Scotia* 120 Cd
Calera, *Alabama* 130 Ed
Calestano, *Italy* 62 Ec
Caleta Buena, *Chile* 146 Ab
Caleta Olivia, *Argentina* 148 Cd
Calexico, *California* 134 Fe
Calgary, *Alberta* 124 Gd
Calhoun, *Georgia* 131 Fc
Cali, *Colombia* 144 Ac
Caliacra, C. 69 Hd
Calicut, *Madras* 89 Ab
Caliente, *California* 134 Dd
Caliente, *Nevada* 134 Fc
California, *Missouri* 130 Ba
California, state, *U.S.A.* 126 Ac
California, G. of, *Mexico* 138 Bb
California Hot Springs, *California* 134 Dd
Calimali, *Mexico* 138 Bb
Calimanesti, *Romania* 67 Kd
Calimere Pt., *Madras* 89 Cb
Calinesti, *Romania* 67 Kd
Calingapatam, *Madras* 91 Gb
Calingasta, *Argentina* 146 Ae
Calispell Pk., *Washington* 136 Ea
Calistoga, *California* 134 Bb
Calitri, *Italy* 64 Fc
Calitzdorp, *Cape Prov.* 114 Df
Callabonna, L., *S. Aust.* 154 Ba
Callac, *France* 32 Bb
Callafa, *Ethiopia* 108 Dd
Callahan, *Florida* 131 He
Callan, *Eire* 27 Cf
Callander, *Scotland* 23 Dd
Callander, *Ontario* 121 Aa
Callanna, *S. Australia* 154 Ba
Callao, *Peru* 145 Bd
Callas, *France* 33 Bb
Calle, La., *Algeria* 103 Ja
Calliano, *Italy* 62 Fb
Callington, *England* 17 Bc
Calmar, *Iowa* 132 Cd
Calmon, *Brazil* 147 Ed
Calne, *England* 14 Cd
Caloosahatchee R., *Florida* 131 Nh
Calpe, *Spain* 41 Gb
Calpella, *California* 134 Bb
Calpulalpam, *Mexico* 138 Dc
Calstock, *Ontario* 122 Ga
Caltabellotta, *Sicily* 65 Gg
Caltagirone, *Sicily* 65 Hg
Caltanissetta, *Sicily* 65 Hg
Caltavuturo, *Sicily* 65 Gg
Calumbo, *Angola* 109 Bc
Calumet, *Michigan* 122 Db
Calumet I., *Quebec* 121 Bb
Caluso, *Italy* 62 Bb
Calvados, dep., *France* 30 Bb
Calvert, *Texas* 133 De
Calverton, *Virginia* 129 Fc
Calvi, *Corsica* 33 Dg
Calvi, Mt., *Italy* 62 Ed
Calvillo, *Mexico* 138 Dc
Calvin, *Montana* 136 Gb
Calvinia, *Cape Prov.* 114 Ce
Calw, *Württemberg* 58 Cc
Calzada, La, *Spain* 41 Cb
Cam, R., *England* 15 Eb
Camagüey & Islas de, *Cuba* 140 Bb
Camaiore, *Italy* 62 Ed
Camana, *Peru* 145 Ce
Camar, *Transylvania* 67 Hb
Camara, *Brazil* 142 Bc
Camargo, *Bolivia* 146 Bc
Camargo, *Chihuahua, Mexico* 138 Db
Camargo, *Tamaulipas, Mexico* 139 Eb
Camargo, *Spain* 38 Ba
Camargue I., *France* 35 Gd
Camarillos, *Spain* 38 Ed
Camariñas, *Spain* 36 Aa
Camaron, C., *Honduras* 140 Gd
Camarones & B., *Argent.* 148 Cc
Camas, *Washington* 136 Bc
Ca-mau, Pt., *Cochin-China* 95 Bh
Cambay, *Gujarat States* 85 Dc
Camberley, *England* 15 Dd
Cambodia, *Fr. Indo-China* 95 Bg
Cambodia, C., *Cochin-China* 95 Bh
Camboon, *Queensland* 153 De
Camborne, *England* 17 Ac
Cambrai, *France* 30 Fa
Cambre, *Spain* 36 Ba
Cambria, *California* 134 Cd
Cambrian Mts., *Wales* 20 Cc
Cambridge, *Cape Prov.* 115 Gf
Cambridge, *Glos., Eng.* 14 Bc
Cambridge, *Idaho* 136 Ec
Cambridge, *Maryland* 129 Gc
Cambridge, *Massachusetts* 128 Cb
Cambridge, *New Zealand* 158 Eb
Cambridge, *Ohio* 129 Db
Cambridge & co., *Eng.* 15 Eb
Cambridge B., *N.-W. T.* 118 Jc
Cambridge G., *W. Aust.* 152 Da
Cambrils, *Spain* 39 Gc
Cambronde, *France* 35 Fb
Camburg, *Thuringia* 55 Gd
Cambuslang, *Scotland* 23 De
Camden, *Alabama* 130 Ee
Camden, *New Jersey* 129 Gc
Camden, *New York* 123 Ld
Camden, *S. Carolina* 131 Hc
Camelford, *England* 17 Bb
Camerino, *Italy* 63 Hd
Cameron, *Louisiana* 130 Bf
Cameron, *Missouri* 132 Bf
Cameron, *Texas* 133 De
Cameron Mts., *New Zeal.* 159 Ag
Cameron Downs, *Queensl'd* 153 Bd
Cameron Falls, *Ontario* 122 Da
Cameroon Mt., *Nigeria* 105 Ce
Cameroons, *W. Africa* 105 Dd
Camerota, *Italy* 64 Fc
Cameroun B., *Fr. Eq. Afr.* 105 Ce
Cameta, *Brazil* 143 Ec
Camiguin, I., *Philippines* 99 Fb
Camilla, *Georgia* 131 Fe
Camina, *Chile* 146 Bb
Caminha, *Portugal* 36 Bc
Cammarata, *Sicily* 65 Gg
Cammin 55 Kb
Camoa, *Mexico* 138 Cb
Camocin, *Brazil* 143 Fc
Camonica, Val, *Italy* 62 Eb
Camooweal, *Queensland* 153 Ac
Camotes Is., *Philippines* 99 Fa
Campagna, *Italy* 64 Fc
Campagna di Roma, *Italy* 64 Cb
Campana, *Argentina* 148 Ea
Campana, *New Mexico* 135 Md
Campana, I., *Chile* 148 Ad
Campanario, *Spain* 37 Ed
Campanario, mt., *Chile* 148 Bb
Campanella, Pta., *Italy* 64 Ec
Campania, *Italy* 64 Eb
Campanquiz, Cerros, *Peru* 145 Bb
Campaspero, *Spain* 38 Ac
Campbell, *Cape Prov.* 114 Ed
Campbell, *Missouri* 130 Cb
Campbell, *New Mexico* 135 Le
Campbell, *Ohio* 129 Db
Campbell, Mt., *Yukon* 124 Bb
Campbellford, *Ontario* 121 Bb
Campbellpore, *Punjab* 82 Eb
Campbellsville, *Kentucky* 130 Fb
Campbellton, *New Bruns.* 120 Bc
Campbelltown, *N.S.W.* 155 Gc
Campbell Town, *Tasmania* 155 Kg
Campbeltown, *Scotland* 22 Cf
Campeche & state, *Mexico* 139 Fd
Campeche, Bank of, *Mexico* 139 Fc
Campeche, Gulf of, *Mexico* 139 Fd
Campeni, *Transylvania* 67 Jc
Camperdown, *Natal* 115 Jd
Camperdown, *Victoria* 154 De
Campia Turzii, *Transylv.* 67 Jc
Campillos, *Spain* 40 Fb
Câmpina, *Romania* 69 Fc
Campina, La, *Spain* 40 Fb
Campina Grande, *Brazil* 143 Gd
Campinas, *Brazil* 147 Fc
Campinas ou Ararangua, *Brazil* 147 Fd
Campine, *Belgium* 29 Cc
Campi Salentina, *Italy* 65 Eb
Campo, *Fr. Eq. Africa* 109 Aa
Campo, *Mozambique* 113 Ga
Campobasso, *Italy* 64 Eb
Campo Bello, *Brazil* 147 Fc
Campobello I., *New Brunswick* 120 Bd
Campobello di Licata, *Sicily* 65 Gg
Campo de Criptana, *Spain* 38 Be
Campo de Gibraltar, *Spain* 40 Db
Campo Formosa, *Brazil* 143 Fe
Campo Formoso, *Brazil* 147 Fb
Campo Gallo, *Argentina* 146 Cd
Campo Largo, *Brazil* 143 Fe
Campo Maior, *Brazil* 143 Fc
Campo Maior, *Portugal* 37 Cc
Campo Mare, *Romania* 67 Ke
Camporeale, *Sicily* 65 Gg
Camporrobles, *Spain* 38 De
Camport, *Eire* 25 Ab
Campos, *Brazil* 147 Ed
Campos, *Brazil* 147 Gc
Campos, Tierra de, *Spain* 38 Ab
Campo Salles, *Brazil* 143 Fd
Camposanpiero, *Italy* 63 Gb
Campos del Puerto, *Balearic Is.* 39 He
Campos Novos, *Brazil* 147 Ed
Campo Tures, *Italy* 63 Fa
Camprodon, *Spain* 39 Hb
Campsie Fells, *Scotland* 23 Dd
Campti, *Louisiana* 130 Be
Campul Lung, *Romania* 69 Fb
Câmpulung, *Bucegi, Rom.* 69 Fc
Camp Verde, *Arizona* 135 Hd
Camrose, *Alberta* 124 Gd
Camsell, Mt., *N.-W. T.* 124 Eb
Camuñas, *Spain* 38 Be
Canaan, *New Brunswick* 120 Cc
Canaan, *New Hampshire* 128 Cb
Canada, *N. America* 117 Fd
Canada B., *Newfoundl'd* 120 Ha
Cañada de Gomez, *Argent.* 146 Ce
Cañada del Hoyo, *Spain* 38 De
Canadian, *New Mexico* 135 Md
Canadian, *Oklahoma* 133 Ec
Canadian & R., *Texas* 133 Bc
Canadian Shield, *Canada* 118-9 Kd
Canadón Grande, Sa., *Argentina* 148 Cc
Cañadon de las Vacas, *Argentina* 148 Be
Canakkale (Chanaq), *Turkey* 72 Db
Canale 63 Ha
Canale, Mte., *Italy* 62 Dc
Canale, Val, *Italy* 63 Ha
Canal San Bovo, *Italy* 63 Fa
Canama, *Brazil* 145 Cc
Canandaigua, *New York* 123 Kd
Cananea, *Brazil* 147 Fd
Cananea, *Mexico* 138 Ba
Canaples, *France* 30 Ea
Canar, prov., *Ecuador* 145 Bb
Canarreos, Arch. de los, *Cuba* 140 Ab
Canary Is., *N. Atlan. Oc.* 104 Aa
Canatlan, *Mexico* 138 Dc
Canaveral C., *Florida* 131 Ng
Cañaveras, *Spain* 38 Cd
Canbelego, *New S. Wales* 155 Eb
Canberra (Fed. Cap.), *Australia* 155 Fd
Canby, *California* 134 Ca
Canby, *Minnesota* 132 Ac
Canby, *Oregon* 136 Bc
Cancale, *France* 32 Db
Cancello, *Italy* 64 Ec
Cande, *France* 32 Dc
Candé, *Mozambique* 113 Ed
Candela, *Italy* 64 Fb
Candelaria, *Nevada* 134 Db
Candelo, *Italy* 62 Cb
Candelo, *New S. Wales* 155 Fd
Candia, *Italy* 62 Cb
Candia (Iráklion), *Crete* 71 Jj
Candle, *Alaska* 125 Gd
Candon, *Philippines* 95 Ff
Candor, *N. Carolina* 131 Jc
Canea and B., *Crete* 71 Gj
Canella, *Brazil* 147 Ed
Canelli, *Italy* 62 Cc
Canelones & dep., *Uruguay* 146 De
Canete, *Peru* 145 Bd
Canete, *Spain* 38 Dd
Cañete la Real, *Spain* 40 Fc
Cangas de Onis, *Spain* 36 Ea
Cangas de Tineo, *Spain* 36 Da
Canha & R., *Portugal* 37 Bd
Cania, *Queensland* 153 Dd
Canicatti, *Sicily* 65 Gg
Canicosa de la Sierra, *Spain* 38 Bc
Caniles, *Spain* 41 Dc
Canin, Mte., *Italy* 63 Ha
Canisbay, *Scotland* 24 Ed
Canisty, *France* 32 Da
Caniza, La, *Spain* 36 Bb
Çankiri, *Turkey* 78 Ba
Canna, I., *Scotland* 22 Bb
Cannanore, *Madras* 89 Ab
Cannavieiras, *Brazil* 147 Hb
Cannelton, *Indiana* 129 Ad
Cannes, *France* 33 Bb
Canning, *Nova Scotia* 120 Cd
Canning, Mt., *W. Aust.* 152 Bd
Cannobio, *Italy* 62 Ca
Cannock, *England* 14 Ba
Cannon R., *Minnesota* 132 Cc
Canoa, La, *Venezuela* 144 Db
Canonba, *New S. Wales* 155 Eb
Canon City, *Colorado* 135 Lb
Canora, *Saskatchewan* 124 Jd
Canosa di Puglia, *Italy* 64 Fb
Canossa, *Italy* 62 Ec
Canourgue, la, *France* 35 Fc
Canrobert, *Algeria* 103 Hb
Canrobert, *Quebec* 121 Db
Canso & C., *Nova Scotia* 120 Ed
Canso, Str. of, *Nova Scotia* 120 Ed
Cantabrian Mts., *Spain* 36 Da
Cantal, dep. & Mtgne. du, *France* 34 Eb
Cantalpino, *Spain* 37 Ea
Cantavir, *Voyvodina* 66 Ed
Canterbury, *England* 15 Ed
Canterbury, *New Bruns.* 120 Bd
Canterbury, *New Hamps.* 128 Cb
Canterbury, prov., *New Zealand* 159 Ce
Canterbury Bight, *New Zealand* 159 Df

Catalina, *Newfoundland* 120 Jb
Catalonia, *Spain* 39 Fc
Catamarca and prov., *Argentina* 146 Bd
Catandica, *Mozambique* 113 Ea
Catania & Gulf, *Sicily* 65 Jg
Catanzaro, *Italy* 65 Cd
Catarina la Grande, *Mexico* 139 Fd
Catarro (Kotor), *Dalmatia* 68 Dd
Catastrophe, C., *S. Aust.* 154 Ad
Catawba R., *N. Carolina* 131 Hc
Catbalogan, *Philippines* 99 Fa
Cateau, le, *France* 31 Fa
Catel Viejo, *Philippines* 99 Gb
Cathcart, *Cape Prov.* 115 Gf
Cathcart, *New S. Wales* 155 Fd
Cathkin Pk., *Natal* 115 Hd
Cathlamet, *Washington* 136 Bb
Catillon, *France* 31 Fa
Catingueiro, *Brazil* 143 Ee
Catlettsburg, *Kentucky* 131 Ga
Catoche, C., *Mexico* 139 Gc
Catons, *Nevada* 134 Eb
Catonsville, *Maryland* 129 Fc
Catorce, *Mexico* 138 Dc
Catria, Mte., *Italy* 63 Gd
Catrilo, *Argentina* 148 Db
Catskill, *New Mexico* 135 Lc
Catskill & Mts., *New York* 123 Ld
Catterick, *England* 18 Cb
Cattolica, *Italy* 63 Gd
Catuane, *Mozambique* 115 Kc
Catubig, *Philippines* 99 Fa
Catumbo, *Angola* 109 Bc
Catuna, *Argentina* 146 Be
Catworth, *England* 15 Db
Cauca, R. and dep., *Colombia* 144 Ac
Caucasus, mts., *U.S.S.R.* 75 Gg
Caude, *Spain* 38 Dd
Caudete, *Spain* 41 Eb
Caudry, *France* 30 Fa
Caulonia, *Italy* 65 Cd
Caumont, *France* 32 Ea
Cauquenes, *Chile* 148 Bb
Căuşani 69 Hb
Causapscal, *Quebec* 120 Bb
Cautin, prov., *Chile* 148 Bb
Cauvery R. and Falls, *Mysore* 89 Ba
Caux, *Fr. Guiana* 142 Db
Cavaignac, *Algeria* 102 Ea
Cavaillon, *France* 35 Hd
Cavalcante, *Brazil* 143 Ee
Cavalese, *Italy* 63 Fa
Cavalier, *N. Dakota* 132 Aa
Cavallermaggiore, *Italy* 62 Bc
Cavallo, Mte., *Italy* 63 Ga
Cavan and co., *Eire* 26 Cd
Cavarna 69 Hd
Cavarzere, *Italy* 63 Gb
Cavazuccherine, *Italy* 63 Gb
Cave, *New Zealand* 159 Cf
Cavedine, *Italy* 62 Eb
Cavenagh Ra., *W. Aust.* 152 Dd
Cavendish, *England* 15 Eb
Cavendish, *Victoria* 154 Ce
Caviana, I., *Brazil* 143 Db
Cavite, *Philippines* 95 Fg
Cavoli I., *Sardinia* 64 Jg
Cavtat, *Dalmatia* 68 Dd
Cawker City, *Kansas* 133 Ca
Cawnpore, *United Provs.* 83 Je
Caxias, *Amazonas, Brazil* 145 Cb
Caxias, *Maranhão, Brazil* 143 Fc
Caxias, *Rio Grande do Sul, Brazil* 147 Ed
Caxito, *Angola* 109 Bc
Caxton, *England* 15 Db
Cayambe, *Ecuador* 145 Ba
Cayan, *Philippines* 95 Ff
Cayenne, *Fr. Guiana* 142 Db
Cayes, *Haiti* 140 Cc
Cayman, I., Grand and Lit., *West Indies* 140 Ac
Cayo, *Brit. Honduras* 140 Fd
Cayuga, *Ontario* 123 Jd
Cayuga L., *New York* 123 Kd
Cazères, *France* 34 Dd
Cazma and R., *Croatia* 66 Bd
Cazorla, *Spain* 41 Cc
Cazoulès, *France* 34 Dc
Cea and R., *Spain* 36 Eb
Ceanannus Mor (Kells), *Eire* 26 Dd
Ceara, state, *Brazil* 143 Fd
Ceará (Fortaleza), *Brazil* 143 Gc
Ceara Mirim, *Brazil* 143 Gd
Cebaco, I., *Panama* 140 Gf
Cebollar, *Argentina* 146 Bd
Cebolo, *Texas* 133 Cf
Cebreros, *Spain* 38 Ad
Cebu and I., *Philippines* 99 Fa
Ceccano, *Italy* 64 Db
Cecil, *Georgia* 131 Ge
Cecilville, *California* 134 Ba
Cecina, R., *Italy* 62 Ed
Ceclavin, *Spain* 37 Dc
Cedar, *Utah* 135 Hb
Cedar Berg, *Cape Prov.* 114 Cf
Cedar L., *Texas* 133 Ad
Cedar Mts., *Oregon* 136 Ed
Cedar Ra., *Utah* 135 Ga
Cedar R., *Iowa* 132 De
Cedar Bluffs, *Nebraska* 132 Ae
Cedarburg, *Wisconsin* 132 Fd
Cedar City, *Utah* 135 Gc
Cedar Falls, *Iowa* 132 Cd
Cedar Keys, *Florida* 131 Gf
Cedar Point, *Ohio* 129 Cb
Cedar Rapids, *Iowa* 132 Dd
Cedar Springs, *Michigan* 122 Fd
Cedartown, *Georgia* 130 Fd
Cedar Vale, *Kansas* 133 Db
Cedarville, *Cape Prov* 115 He
Cedegolo, *Italy* 62 Ea
Cedral, *Mexico* 138 Dc
Cedros I., *Mexico* 138 Ab
Ceduna, *S. Australia* 151 Ee
Cefalu, *Sicily* 65 Gf
Cega, R., *Spain* 38 Ac
Cegléd, *Hungary* 66 Eb
Ceglie, *Italy* 65 Db
Cehegin, *Spain* 41 Eb
Ceiba, *Honduras* 140 Fd
Ceiba, La, *Venezuela* 144 Bb
Cekhira, *Tunisia* 103 Kb
Cekirge, *Turkey* 72 Fb
Celano, *Italy* 64 Da
Celanova, *Spain* 36 Bb
Celaya, *Mexico* 138 Dc
Celbridge, *Eire* 27 De
Celébes, I, & Sea, *Nether. Indies* 99 Fd
Celestum, *Mexico* 139 Fc
Čelić, *Bosnia* 68 Db
Celina, *Ohio* 129 Bb
Čelinac, *Bosnia* 68 Cb
Celje, *Slovenia* 63 Ka
Celldömölk, *Hungary* 66 Cb
Celle, *Prussia* 54 Fc
Celles, *France* 34 Ba
Cembra, *Italy* 63 Fa
Çemisgezek, *Turkey* 78 Cb
Cemmaes Rd., *Wales* 20 Cb
Cencenighe, *Italy* 63 Fa
Cenicientos, *Spain* 38 Ad
Ceno, R., *Italy* 62 Dc
Centallo, *Italy* 62 Bc
Centennial, *Wyoming* 135 Ka
Center, *Alabama* 130 Fc
Center, *Oklahoma* 133 Dc
Center, *Texas* 133 Ee
Centerville, *Alabama* 130 Ed
Center Ville, *Colorado* 135 Kb
Centerville, *Iowa* 132 Ce
Centerville, *Missouri* 130 Cb
Centerville, *S. Dakota* 132 Ad
Centerville, *Tennessee* 130 Ec
Cento, *Italy* 63 Fc
Central, *Alaska* 125 Ld
Central, *New Mexico* 135 Je
Central, Cord., *Colombia* 144 Ab
Central, Cord., *Peru* 145 Bc
Central Pk., *Nevada* 134 Fb
Central Ra., *New Guinea* 156 Cb
Central America 137 Dc
Central City, *Colorado* 135 Lb
Central Div., *W. Aust.* 152 Cd
Central Falls, *Rhode I.* 128 Cc
Centralia, *Illinois* 132 Ef
Centralia, *Washington* 136 Bb
Central India, agency, *India* 81 Df
Central Lake, *Michigan* 122 Fc
Central Plain, *Eire* 26 Bd
Central Point, *Oregon* 136 Bd
Central Prov., *Ceylon* 89 Dd
Central Provs. & Berar, *India* 81 Df
Central Russian Uplands, *U.S.S.R.* 74 Ed
Central Siberian Plat., *U.S.S.R.* 76 Kc
Centreville, *Mississippi* 130 Ce
Centreville, *New Bruns.* 120 Ac
Centuripe, *Sicily* 65 Hg
Cephalonia (Kefallinía), I., *Greece* 71 Be
Ceprano, *Italy* 64 Db
Ceracero, *Spain* 38 Cb
Cercy-la-Tour, *France* 31 Fe
Cerdana, La, *Spain* 39 Gb
Cère, R., *France* 34 Dc
Cereal, Sa. do, *Portugal* 40 Bb
Ceres, *Cape Prov.* 114 Cf
Ceres, *Italy* 62 Bb
Ceret, *France* 34 Ee
Cerignola, *Italy* 64 Fb
Cerigo (Kíthira), I., *Greece* 71 Eg
Cerigotto (Andikíthira), I., *Greece* 71 Eh
Cerizay, *France* 32 Ed
Çerkesköy, *Turkey* 72 Ea
Cerknica, *Slovenia* 63 Jb
Cermeiu, *Transylvania* 67 Gc
Çermik, *Turkey* 78 Cb
Cernauti (Chernovtsy), *Ukraine* 69 Fa
Cernavoda, *Romania* 69 Hc
Cernik, *Slavonia* 66 Cd
Cerovica, *Hercegovina* 68 Cd
Cerralvo, *Mexico* 139 Eb
Cerralvo, I., *Mexico* 138 Cc
Cerrillos, *New Mexico* 135 Kd
Cerro de Pasco, *Peru* 145 Bd
Cerro Largo, dep., *Uruguay* 147 Ee
Cerros de Bala, *Bolivia* 145 Dd
Cervantes, *Spain* 36 Cb
Cervaro, *Italy* 64 Db
Cervaro, R., *Italy* 64 Fb
Cervate, Mte., *Italy* 64 Fc
Cervera, *Castellon, Spain* 39 Fd
Cervera, *Lerida, Spain* 39 Gc
Cervera del Rio Alhama, *Spain* 38 Cb
Cervera de Pisuerga, *Spain* 38 Ab
Cervia, *Italy* 63 Gc
Cervialto, Mte., *Italy* 64 Fc
Cervignano del Friuli, *Italy* 63 Hb
Cesena, *Italy* 63 Gc
Cesis, *Latvia* 49 Cc
České Budějovice, *Bohemia* 60 Bd
Český Krumlov, *Bohemia* 60 Cd
Český Třebova, *Bohemia* 60 Cd
Ces Lipa, *Bohemia* 60 Cc
Cespedosa, *Spain* 37 Eb
Cessnock, *New S. Wales* 155 Gc
Cetatea Alba (Belgorod Dnestrovski), *Ukraine* 60 Gb
Cetina & R., *Dalmatia* 68 Bc
Cetinje, *Montenegro* 68 Dd
Ceto, *Italy* 62 Ea
Cetraro, *Italy* 65 Bc
Ceuta, *Span. Morocco* 102 Bb
Ceuta, B. de, *Mexico* 138 Cc
Cevennes, Les, *France* 35 Fd
Cevico de la Torre, *Spain* 38 Ac
Čevljanovic, *Bosnia* 68 Db
Čevo, *Montenegro* 68 Dd
Ceylon, I., *Indian Oc.* 89 Dd
Ceyreste, *France* 33 Ac
Ceyzeriat, *France* 35 Ha
Chabane, *Mozambique* 112 Bd
Chabjuwardoo B., *W. Australia* 152 Ac
Chablais, *France* 35 Ja
Chabounia, *Algeria* 102 Fb
Chabowka, *Poland* 57 Ed
Chacabuco, *Argentina* 148 Da
Chacahua B., *Mexico* 139 Ed
Chacance, *Chile* 146 Ac
Chacao, Canal de, *Chile* 148 Bc
Chachani, mt., *Peru* 145 Ce
Chachapoyas, *Peru* 145 Bc
Chachro, *Sind* 85 Cb
Chaco, terr., *Argentina* 146 Cd
Chaco Boreal, *Paraguay* 146 Cc
Chacon, C., *Alaska* 125 Oj
Chacra Mesa, *New Mexico* 135 Kd
Chactowhatchee B., *Florida* 130 Ee
Chad, col., *Fr. Eq. Afri.* 105 Ec
Chad, L., *Fr. Eq. Afr.* 105 Dc
Chadder, el, *Libya* 106 Bd
Chadileo, R., *Argentina* 148 Cb
Chadwick, *Missouri* 130 Bb
Chadyr, *Sinkiang* 84 Eb
Chafe, *Nigeria* 105 Cc
Chagford, *England* 17 Cb
Chagny, *France* 31 Ge
Chagos Arch., *Indian Oc.* 73 Kj
Chahar, prov., *China* 96 Bc
Chahar Deh, *Afghanistan* 82 Bb
Chahbar, *Persia* 79 Hd
Chai, R., *Manchuria* 96 Db
Chaibasa, *Bihar* 87 Fd
Chaidu-tau, *Sinkiang* 84 Fb
Chaikowpu, *China* 94 Da
Chaillé-les-Marais, *France* 32 Dd
Cha Kalumba, *Angola* 109 Dc
Chakansur, *Afghanistan* 79 Hc
Chakari, *S. Rhodesia* 113 Cb
Chak Chak, *A.-E. Sudan* 108 Ad
Chakdaha, *Bengal* 88 Bc
Chakdara, *N.-W.F.P.* 82 Ea
Chakia, *Gwalior* 87 Ec
Chakiria, *Bengal* 92 Ab
Chakku, *Baluchistan* 82 Be
Chaklik, *Sinkiang* 84 Fc
Chakmak, *Sinkiang* 84 Db
Chakwal, *Punjab* 82 Eb
Chala, *Tanganyika Terr.* 111 Bg
Chala and Pta., *Peru* 145 Ce
Chalabre, *France* 34 Ee
Chalainoerh, *Manchuria* 96 Bb
Chalamont, *France* 35 Hb
Chalan Bil, *Bengal* 88 Bb
Chalang, I., *Siam* 98 Ab
Chalantun, *Manchuria* 96 Cb
Chalate, *Mozambique* 113 Ed
Chalchihuites, *Mexico* 138 Dc
Chalcis (Khalkís), *Greece* 71 Ee
Chaleur B., *New Bruns.* 120 Cc
Chalgali, *Eastern States* 87 Ed
Chalham, I., *Chile* 148 Be
Chalindrey, *France* 31 Hd
Chalinze, *Tangan. Terr.* 111 Fg
Chalisgaon, *Bombay* 90 Ba
Challans, *France* 32 Dd
Challapata, *Bolivia* 146 Bb
Challhuanca, *Peru* 145 Cd
Challis, *Idaho* 136 Fc
Chalonnes-sur-Loire, *France* 32 Ec
Châlons-sur Marne, *France* 31 Gc
Chalons-sur-Saone, *France* 31 Ge
Chalyk-tau, *Sinkiang* 84 Eb
Cham, *Switzerland* 43 Fb
Chama, *New Mexico* 135 Kc
Chamaa, *Lebanon* 80 Ca
Chamaites, *S.-W. Africa* 114 Bc
Chaman, *Baluchistan* 82 Bc
Chamartin de la Rosa, *Spain* 38 Bd
Chamba, *Punjab States* 83 Gb
Chamba, *Tangany. Terr.* 111 Ej
Chambal, *Bengal* 88 Cd
Chambal R., *Rajputana* 86 Bc
Chambalo, *Tangan. Terr.* 111 Ef
Chambersburg, *Pennsyl.* 129 Ec
Chambéry, *France* 35 Hb
Chambi Jeb., *Tunisia* 103 Jb
Chambivas, *Brazil* 143 Ed
Chambly, *Quebec* 121 Db
Chambon, le, *France* 35 Gb
Chambord, *Quebec* 123 Ma
Chambre, la, *France* 35 Jb
Chambwe, *Mozambique* 112 Bb
Chamdo, *China* 81 Hd
Chamela, *Mexico* 138 Cd
Chamelecon, R., *Honduras* 140 Fd
Chamical, *Argentina* 146 Be
Chamita, *New Mexico* 135 Kc
Chamlang, mt., *Nepal* 87 Gb
Chamliho Mt., *Tang. T.* 110 Cd
Chamois, *Missouri* 130 Ba
Chamonix, *France* 35 Jb
Champ, *Persia* 79 Hd
Champa, *Bhutan* 88 Ca
Champa, *Cent. Provs.* 87 Ee
Champagne, *France* 35 Hb
Champagne, dist., *France* 31 Gc
Champagney, *France* 31 Jd
Champagnole, *France* 31 Je
Champagny Is., *W. Aust.* 152 Ca
Champaign, *Illinois* 132 Ee
Champaran, *Bihar* 87 Fb
Champerico, *Guatemala* 140 Ee
Champlain, *Quebec* 121 Da
Champlain L., *New York-Vermont* 123 Mc
Champlitte, *France* 31 Hd
Champoton, *Mexico* 139 Fd
Champtoceaux, *France* 32 Dc
Chamrajnagar, *Mysore* 89 Bb
Chamusca, *Portugal* 37 Bc
Chanac, *France* 35 Fc
Chanaq (Canakkale), *Turkey* 72 Db
Chancey, *Florida* 131 Ge
Chanco, *Chile* 148 Bb
Chancy, *Switzerland* 42 Bd
Chanda, *Cent. Provs.* 90 Db
Chandalar & R., *Alaska* 125 Kc
Chandausi, *United Provs.* 83 Hd
Chandeleur Is. and Sd., *Louisiana* 130 Df
Chanderi, *Gwalior* 86 Bc
Chandernagore, *Bengal* 88 Bc
Chandler, *Oklahoma* 133 Dc
Chandod, *Gujarat States* 85 Dd
Chandor, *Bombay* 90 Ba
Chandos, *Queensland* 153 Bc
Chandpur, *Bengal* 88 Cc
Chandpur, *United Provs.* 83 Hd
Chandrakona, *Bengal* 88 Ac
Chanduria, *Bengal* 88 Bc
Chang Bhakar, *Eastern States* 86 Dd
Chang-chow, *Fu-kien, China* 95 Ee
Chang-chow, *Kiang-su, China* 94 Fc
Chang-chwen I., *China* 95 De
Chang-hsing tao, *Manchuria* 96 Cd
Chang-hwa, *China* 95 Cf
Chang-i, *China* 94 Eb
Changi, *Sinkiang* 84 Fb
Chang-kia-kow (Kalgan), *China* 94 Ea
Chang-kwan-tsai, *Manchuria* 96 Dc
Changlani, *Assam* 88 Db
Changling, *Manchuria* 96 Cc
Chang-lo, *Fu-kien, China* 94 Ed
Chang-lo, *Hu-peh, China* 94 Dc
Chang-lo, *Kwang-tung, China* 95 Ee
Chang-ning, *China* 95 Ee
Chang-pai-shan, *Manchuria* 96 Dc
Chang-ping, *Hopeh, China* 94 Ea
Chang-ping, *Fu-kien, China* 94 Ed
Chang-pu, *China* 95 Ee
Chang-sha, *Hu-nan, China* 94 Dd
Chang-sha, *Kwang-tung, China* 95 Ee
Chang-tê, *China* 94 Db
Chang-teh, *China* 94 Dd
Chang-tsing, *China* 94 Eb
Chang-tu, *Manchuria* 96 Cc
Chang-yang, *China* 94 Dc
Channapatna, *Mysore* 90 Ce
Channel Is., *English Chan.* 32 Ca
Channing, *Texas* 133 Ac
Chan-sha, *China* 94 Fc
Chantaburi, *Siam* 95 Bg
Chantada, *Spain* 36 Cb
Chantonnay, *France* 32 Ed
Chanute, *Kansas* 133 Eb
Chanyu, *Manchuria* 96 Cc
Chao, *China* 94 Db
Chaochow, *China* 94 Ad
Chao-chow, *China* 95 Ee
Chaochow, *Manchuria* 96 Db
Chao-hu, *China* 94 Ec
Chao-lien-tao, *China* 94 Fb
Chaotung, *Manchuria* 96 Db
Chao-yang, *China* 95 Ee
Chao-yang, *Manchuria* 96 Bc
Chao-yang-chen, *Manchuria* 96 Dc
Chapaca, Mt., *Washington* 136 Ca
Chapaev, *Kazak* 76 Fe
Chapaevsk, *U.S.S.R.* 75 He
Chapala L., *Mexico* 138 Dc
Chapchachi, *Kazak* 75 Hf
Chapel I., *Newfoundl'd* 120 Hc
Chapel-en-le-Frith, *Eng.* 18 Cd
Chapel Hill, *N. Carolina* 131 Jc
Chapelle-au-Riboul, la, *France* 30 Bc
Chapleau, *Ontario* 122 Gb
Chapman, *Kansas* 133 Da
Chapman, Mt., *New Guinea* 156 Dc
Chappell, *Nebraska* 135 Ma
Chapra, *Bihar* 87 Fc
Chaprang, *Tibet* 83 Hc
Charagua, *Bolivia* 146 Cb
Charambira, Pta., *Colombia* 144 Ac
Charana, *Bolivia* 146 Bb
Charara, *Paraguay* 146 Dd
Charchi, *Sinkiang* 84 Fb
Charco Azul, B., *Panama* 140 Gf
Charcot I., *Antarctica* 160 —
Chard, *England* 14 Be
Chardzhui, *Turkmen* 77 Jb
Charef, *Algeria* 102 Fb
Charente, R. & dep., *France* 34 Bb
Charente-Inférieure, dep., *France* 32 Ee
Chargalik, *Sinkiang* 84 Fc
Chari R., *Fr. Eq. Africa* 105 Dc
Charikar, *Afghanistan* 82 Ca
Charing, *England* 15 Ed
Charité, La, *France* 30 Fd
Chariton, *Iowa* 132 Ce
Chariton R., *Missouri* 132 Ce
Charkhari, *Cent. India* 86 Cc
Charlbury, *England* 14 Cc
Charlemagne, *Quebec* 121 Db
Charleroi, *Belgium* 29 Cd
Charles, C., *Virginia* 129 Gd
Charles City, *Iowa* 132 Cd
Charleston, *Illinois* 132 Ff
Charleston, *Mississippi* 130 Dc
Charleston, *Missouri* 130 Db
Charleston, *Queensland* 153 Bc
Charleston, *S. Carolina* 131 Hd

Charleston, W. Virginia 129 Dc
Charleston Harb., S. Carolina - 131 Jd
Charleston L., Ontario - 121 Cb
Charlestown, Eire - 26 Bd
Charlestown, Natal - 115 Hc
Charlestown, New Hamps. 128 Bb
Charlestown, N. Ireland 26 Dc
Charlestown, W. Virginia 129 Fc
Charlesville, Belg. Congo 109 Dc
Charleville, Eire - - 27 Bg
Charleville, France - 31 Gb
Charleville, Queensland - 153 Ce
Charlevoix, Michigan - 122 Fc
Charlieu, France - - 35 Ga
Charlos, Montana - - 136 Gb
Charlotte, Michigan - 122 Fd
Charlotte, New York - 123 Kd
Charlotte, N. Carolina - 131 Hc
Charlotte Amalie, Virgin Is. - - - 140 Kg
Charlotte Harbor, Florida 131 Mh
Charlottenberg, Sweden 50 Bc
Charlottenburg, Prussia 55 Hc
Charlottesville, Virginia 129 Ec
Charlottetown, Prince Edward I. - - - 120 Dc
Charlotte Waters, N. Terr., Australia - - - 151 Ed
Charlton, Ontario - - 123 Hb
Charlton, Victoria - - 154 Dd
Charlwood, Cape Prov. - 115 Ff
Charmes, France - - 31 Jc
Charnwood Forest, Eng. 14 Ca
Charny, Meuse, France - 31 Hb
Charny, Yonne, France - 30 Fd
Charolais, Mts. du, France 35 Ga
Charolles, France - - 35 Ga
Charouîne, Algeria - 102 De
Charsadda, N.-W.F.P. - 82 Da
Charters Towers, Queensl'd 153 Cd
Chartre, la, France - 30 Cd
Chartres, France - - 30 Dc
Chascomus, Argentina - 148 Eb
Chashiniza Mts., U.S.S.R. 96 Eb
Chaska, Minnesota - 132 Cc
Chasse, France - - 35 Gb
Chassov, U.S.S.R. - 96 Ba
Chastleton, Queensland - 153 Be
Châtaigneraie, la, France 32 Ed
Chatanika, Alaska - 125 Kd
Châteaubourg, France - 32 Db
Châteaubriant, France - 32 Dc
Château Chinon, France 31 Fd
Château d'Oex, Switz. - 42 Dd
Château-du-Loir, France 30 Cd
Châteaudun, France - 30 Dc
Chateaugay, New York - 123 Lc
Château-Giron, France - 32 Db
Château-Gontier, France 32 Ec
Chateauguay, Quebec - 121 Db
Château-la-Vallière, France 30 Cd
Châteaulin, France - 32 Ab
Châteauneuf-sur-Charente, France - - 34 Cb
Châteauneuf-sur-Cher, France - - - 30 Ee
Châteauponsac, France 34 Da
Châteauredon, France - 33 Ba
Châteaurenard, Bouches-du-Rhône, France - 35 Gd
Châteaurenard, Loiret, France - - - 30 Ed
Château Renault, France 30 Cd
Châteauroux, France - 30 De
Château-Salins, France - 31 Jc
Château Thierry, France 30 Fb
Châteauvillain, France - 31 Gc
Châtel Censoir, France - 31 Fd
Châteldon, France - 35 Fb
Chatelet, Belgium - - 29 Cd
Châtelet, le, France - 30 Ec
Chatellerault, France - 30 Ce
Châtel-St-Denis, Switz. 42 Cc
Châtenois, France - - 31 Hc
Chatfield, Minnesota - 132 Cd
Chatham, Alaska - - 125 Nh
Chatham, England - - 15 Ed
Chatham, New Bruns. - 120 Cc
Chatham, New York - 128 Bb
Chatham, Ontario - - 122 Gd
Chatham, Virginia - 129 Ed
Chatham I. (San Cristobal), Galapagos Is. - - 145 Fh
Châtillon, Italy - - 62 Bb
Châtillon Coligny, France 30 Ed
Châtillon-en-Bazois, France 31 Fd
Châtillon-sur-Indre, France 30 De
Châtillon-sur-Loire, France 30 Ed
Châtillon-sur-Marne, France 31 Fb
Châtillon-sur-Seine, France 31 Gd
Chatra, Bihar - - 87 Fc
Chatra, Nepal - - 87 Gb
Chatrapur, Orissa - - 91 Gb
Châtre, la, France - 34 Ea
Chatsu, Rajputana - 83 Ge
Chatsworth, Queensland 153 Bd
Chattahoochee R., Georgia 131 Fd
Chattanooga, Tennessee - 131 Fc
Chatteris, England - 15 Eb
Chaudesaigues, France - 34 Ec
Chaudiere, Quebec - - 121 Ea
Chaudiere R., Quebec - 123 Nb
Chau-doc, Cambodia - 95 Bg
Chauka R., United Provs. 86 Db
Chaulnes, France - - 30 Eb
Chaumont-en-Bassigny, France - - - 31 Hc
Chaumont-Porcien, France 31 Gb
Chaungma, Burma - 92 Ba
Chaungzon I., Burma - 92 Cd
Chauny, France - - 30 Fb
Chaussin, France - - 31 He
Chaux de Fonds, la, Switz. 42 Cb
Chavanges, France - 31 Gc
Chavantes, Sa., Brazil - 143 Ee
Chave, Mozambique - 113 Fa
Chaves, Brazil - - 143 Ec
Chaves, Portugal - - 36 Cc
Chavez, México - - 138 Cb
Chaya, Tanganyika Terr. 111 Cf
Chazelles, France - - 35 Gb
Chazon, Argentina - 146 Ce
Cheadle, England - - 18 Be
Cheat R., W. Virginia - 129 Ec
Cheb, Bohemia - - 60 Bc
Cheboksary, U.S.S.R. - 74 Hd
Cheboygan, Michigan - 122 Fc
Ché-chêng, China - - 94 Ec
Checheno Ingushsk, U.S.S.R. - - 75 Hg
Checmu, Mexico - - 139 Gc
Chedabucto B., Nova Scotia - - - 120 Ed
Cheddar, England - 14 Bd
Chedgrave, England - 15 Fa
Cheduba I., Burma - 92 Ac
Chefoo, China - - 94 Fb
Chegga, Algeria - - 103 Gb
Chehalis & R., Washington 136 Bb
Che-kiang, China - - 94 Ed
Chekunda, U.S.S.R. - 96 Ea
Chelan, Washington - 136 Db
Chelan, L., Washington 136 Ca
Chelforó, Argentina - 148 Cb
Chélia, Jeb., Algeria - 103 Hb
Cheliff, R., Algeria - 102 Ea
Che-ling Pass, China - 94 Dd
Chełm, Poland - - 60 Gc
Chelmer, R., England - 15 Ec
Chełmno, Poland - - 60 Eb
Chelmsford, England - 15 Ec
Chelsea, Massachusetts - 128 Cb
Chelsea, Oklahoma - 133 Eb
Chelsea, Quebec - - 121 Cb
Chelsea, Vermont - - 128 Bb
Chelsea, Wisconsin - 132 Dc
Cheltenham, England - 14 Bc
Chelva, Spain - - 38 De
Chelyabinsk, U.S.S.R. - 74 Ld
Chelyuskin, C., U.S.S.R. 76 Mb
Chemba, Mozambique - 112 Bc
Chembar, U.S.S.R. - 75 Ge
Chem-hoa-chow, Tong-king 95 Ce
Chemille, France - - 32 Ec
Chemnitz, Saxony - - 55 He
Chemulpho, Korea - 97 Bc
Chena, Alaska - - 125 Kd
Chenab R., Punjab - 82 Ec
Chenachane, Algeria - 104 Da
Chena Hot Springs, Alaska 125 Ld
Chen-an, China - - 95 Ce
Chên-chow, Ho-nan, China 94 Dc
Chen-chow, Hu-nan, China 94 Dd
Cheney, Washington - 136 Eb
Chên-fan, China - - 94 Bb
Chengal, Borneo - - 99 Ed
Cheng-an-chow, China - 94 Cd
Chengfeng, China - - 94 Bd
Cheng-kia-kow, China - 94 Eb
Cheng-kiang, China - 95 Be
Cheng-kow, China - 94 Cc
Cheng-pu, China - - 94 Dd
Cheng-teh (Jehol), Manchuria - - - 96 Bc
Cheng-ting, China - 94 Db
Cheng-tu, China - - 94 Bc
Chengtung, Manchuria - 96 Cb
Chen-hiung, China - 94 Bd
Chên-hsi, China - - 94 Dd
Chen-nan-chow, China - 94 Bd
Chenoa, Illinois - - 132 Ee
Chenpien, China - - 95 Ae
Chên-ping, China - - 95 Ee
Cheny, France - - 31 Fd
Chen-yüan, Kwei-chow, China - - - 94 Cd
Chen-yüan, Yun-nan, China 95 Be
Chen-yüen, China - 94 Cb
Cheochi Mts., Nigeria - 105 Dd
Chepen, Peru - - 145 Bc
Chepepo, N. Rhodesia - 112 Ab
Chepes, Argentina - 146 Be
Chepino, Bulgaria - 70 Eb
Chepon, Laos - - 95 Cf
Chepsta, R., U.S.S.R. - 74 Jd
Chepstow, England - 14 Bc
Cher, dep., France - 30 Ed
Cher, R., France - - 30 Cd
Cherangani Mt., Kenya 110 Dc
Cheraw, S. Carolina - 131 Hc
Cherbourg, France - 32 Da
Cherchel, Algeria - - 102 Fa
Cherchen, Sinkiang - 84 Fc
Cherchen Daria, Sinkiang 84 Fc
Cherdyn, U.S.S.R. - 74 Kc
Cherepovets, U.S.S.R. - 74 Fd
Cheria, Algeria - - 103 Hb
Cheria, Fr. W. Africa - 104 Ac
Cheribon, Java - - 98 Ce
Cherkassy, Ukraine - 75 Ef
Cherkessk, U.S.S.R. - 75 Gg
Cherla, Madras - - 91 Eb
Chermoz, U.S.S.R. - 74 Kd
Cherni, U.S.S.R. - - 74 Ja
Chernigov, Ukraine - 75 Ee
Chernigovka, U.S.S.R. 96 Ec
Chernikovka, U.S.S.R. 74 Ke
Chernovtsy (Cernauti), Ukraine - - - 69 Fa
Chernyi Yar, U.S.S.R. 75 Hf
Cherokee, Iowa - - 132 Bd
Cherokee, Kansas - - 133 Eb
Cherokee, Oklahoma - 133 Cb
Cherra Punji, Assam - 88 Cb
Cherry I., Pacific Oc. - 157 Ee
Cherry Creek, Nevada - 134 Fb
Cherryfield, Maine - 120 Ad
Cherry Vale, Kansas - 133 Eb
Cherry Valley, New York 128 Ab
Cherry Ville, N. Carolina 131 Hc
Cherskogo Mts., U.S.S.R. 76 Pc
Cherso and I. - - 63 Jc
Cherta, Spain - - 39 Fd
Chertkovo, U.S.S.R. - 75 Gf
Chertsey, England - 15 Dd
Cherwell, R., England - 14 Cb
Chesapeake B., Maryland 129 Fc
Chesha, U.S.S.R. - 74 Gb
Chesham, England - 15 Dc
Cheshire, co., England - 18 Bd
Cheshire Plain, England 18 Bd
Cheshskaya Gulf, U.S.S.R. 74 Hb
Cheshunt, England - 15 Dc
Chesil Bank, England - 14 Be
Chesley, Ontario - - 123 Hc
Cheste, Spain - - 38 Ee
Chester, England - - 18 Bd
Chester, Idaho - - 136 Hd
Chester, Illinois - - 130 Db
Chester, Montana - - 136 Ha
Chester, Nebraska - - 133 Da
Chester, Pennsylvania - 129 Gb
Chester, S. Carolina - 131 Hc
Chesterfield, England - 18 Cd
Chesterfield, S. Carolina 131 Hc
Chesterfield and Inlet, N.-W. Terr. - - 124 Lb
Chesterfield Is., Pac. Oc. 149 Fg
Chester-le-Street, Eng. - 21 Ed
Chestertown, Maryland 129 Fc
Chestertown, New York 128 Bb
Chesterville, Ontario - 121 Cb
Chestnut, Montana - 136 Hc
Chetco R., Oregon - 136 Ad
Cheticamp, Nova Scotia 120 Ec
Chetopa, Kansas - - 133 Eb
Chetumal Pen. & B. Mexico 139 Gd
Cheurhkanho, Manchuria 96 Ca
Chevagnes, France - 35 Fa
Cheverie, Nova Scotia - 120 Cd
Cheviot, New Zealand - 159 De
Cheviot Hills, Scot.-Eng. 21 Dc
Cheviot Ra., Queensland 153 Be
Chevre, C. de la, France 32 Ab
Chewaucan Marsh, Oregon 136 Cd
Che-we-lah, Washington 136 Ea
Chew Stoke, England - 14 Bd
Chewton Mendip, Eng. 14 Bd
Che-yang-pau, China - 94 Fd
Cheyenne, Oklahoma - 133 Cc
Cheyenne, Wyoming - 135 La
Cheyenne R., S. Dakota 126 Eb
Cheylard, le, France - 35 Gc
Cheze, la, France - - 32 Cb
Chhabra, Rajputana - 86 Bc
Chhachrauli, Punjab States 83 Gc
Chhata, United Provs. - 83 Ge
Chhatarpur, Cent. India 86 Cc
Chhibramau, United Prvs. 83 He
Chhindwara, Central Provs. 86 Cd
Chhoti Sadri, Rajputana 85 Eb
Chhuikhadan, Eastern States 86 De
Chi, China - - - 94 Eb
Chiamussu, Manchuria - 96 Eb
Chiana, Valle de, Italy - 63 Fd
Chianas, Mozambique - 113 Fa
Chianavalle, Italy - - 63 Hd
Chianni, Italy - - 62 Ed
Chianti, Mt., Italy - 63 Fd
Chiapas and R., Mexico 139 Fd
Chiapas, state, Mexico - 139 Fd
Chiapovano - - 63 Ha
Chiaramonte Gulfi, Sicily 65 Hg
Chiaravalle Centrale, Italy 65 Cd
Chiari, Italy - - 62 Db
Chiarone, Italy - - 64 Ba
Chiavari, Italy - - 62 Dc
Chiavenna, Italy - - 62 Da
Chiba, Japan - - 97 Ec
Chibabava, Mozambique 113 Gb
Chibambala, Mozambique 113 Ec
Chibamo, Mozambique - 113 Fc
Chibi, S. Rhodesia - 113 Dc
Chibougamau L. and R., Quebec - - - 123 La
Chibuto, Mozambique - 112 Bd
Chicacole, Madras - 91 Gb
Chicago, Illinois - - 132 Fe
Chichagof, Alaska - 125 Nh
Chichaoua, Morocco - 103 Nj
Chi-cheng, China - - 94 Ea
Chichen-itza, Mexico - 139 Gc
Chichester, England - 15 De
Chichoki, Punjab - - 83 Ec
Chickaloon, Alaska - 125 Kf
Chickasha, Oklahoma - 133 Cc
Chicken, Alaska - - 125 Ld
Chicklade, England - 14 Bd
Chicla, Libya - - 106 Ok
Chiclana de la Frontera, Spain - - - 40 Dc
Chiclayo, Peru - - 145 Bc
Chico, California - - 134 Cb
Chico, R., Argentina - 148 Cc
Chicoana, Argentina - 146 Bd
Chicopee & R., Mass. - 128 Bb
Chicoutimi, Quebec - 123 Na
Chidambaram, Madras - 89 Cb
Chidley, C., N.-W. Terr. 119 Rd
Chieh, China - - 94 Dc
Chiem See, Bavaria - 59 Gd
Chienchang, Manchuria 96 Cc
Chieng, China - - 94 Dc
Chieng-kan, Siam - - 95 Bf
Chieng-khuang, Laos - 95 Bf
Chieng-kong, Siam - 95 Ae
Chieng-Rai, Siam - - 95 Af
Chienji, N. Rhodesia - 109 Ec
Chienping, Manchuria - 96 Bc
Chientao, prov., Manchuria 96 Dc
Chieri, Italy - - - 62 Bb
Chiesa, Lombardia, Italy 62 Da
Chiesa, Tridentina, Italy 63 Fa
Chiese, R., Italy - - 62 Eb
Chifumbadzi, Mozambique 112 Bb
Chig, Fr. W. Africa - 104 Bc
Chigha Khur, Persia - 79 Fc
Chiglik, Sinkiang - - 84 Fb
Chignecto B., New Bruns.-Nova Scotia - - 120 Cd
Chignik & B., Alaska - 125 Gh
Chignolo, Italy - - 62 Db
Chigwell, England - 15 Ec
Chih-chow, China - - 94 Ec
Chihfeng, Manchuria - 96 Bc
Chihi, Tanganyika Terr. 111 Eh
Chihuahua & state, Mexico 138 Cb
Chikalda, Berar, C.P. - 86 Be
Chikan, Manchuria - 96 Ca
Chik-Ballapur, Mysore - 90 Ce
Chikmagalur, Mysore - 90 Be
Chiknayakanhalli, Mysore 90 Ce
Chikoa, Mozambique - 112 Bc
Chi-kow, China - - 94 Eb
Chikreng, Cambodia - 95 Bg
Chikusi, Mozambique - 112 Bb
Chilapa, Mexico - - 139 Ed
Chilas, Kashmir - - 84 Cc
Childers, Queensland - 153 De
Childress, Texas - - 133 Bc
Chile, rep., S. America - 141 Bf
Chilecito, Argentina - 146 Bd
Chilete, Peru - - 145 Bc
Chilia Noua - - 69 Hc
Chilimanzi, S. Rhodesia 113 Db
Chilinan, Mozambique - 113 Fd
Chilka L., Orissa - - 91 Gb
Chilko L. & R., Br. Col. 124 Ed
Chilkoot Pass, B.C.-Alaska - - - 125 Ng
Chillagoe, Queensland - 153 Bc
Chillan, Chile - - 148 Bb
Chillicothe, Illinois - 132 Ee
Chillicothe, Missouri - 132 Cf
Chillicothe, Ohio - - 129 Cc
Chilliwack, Br. Columbia 124 Ee
Chiloe I. &-prov., Chile 148 Bc
Chilpancingo, Mexico - 139 Ed
Chiltern, Victoria - - 155 Ed
Chiltern Hills, England 15 Dc
Chilton, Wisconsin - 132 Ec
Chilunga, Fr. Eq. Africa 109 Bb
Chilwane I., Mozambique 112 Cd
Chimanimani, Mozambique 112 Bc
Chimay, Belgium - - 29 Cd
Chimbai, Uzbek - 77 Ja
Chimborazo, mt. & prov., Ecuador - - - 145 Bb
Chimbote, Peru - - 145 Bc
Chimbutzo, Mozambique 112 Bd
Chimen Tagh, Sinkiang 84 Fc
Chimney Butte, Arizona 135 Hd
Chimney Pk., California 134 Fe
Chimo, Quebec - - 119 Qe
Chimoio, Mozambique - 112 Bc
Chimray, Kashmir - 83 Gb
China, Asia - - - 93 Cc
Chinandega, Nicaragua 140 Fe
Chincha and Is., Peru - 145 Bd
Chinchilla, Queensland - 153 De
Chinchilla de Mte. Aragon, Spain - - - 41 Eb
Chinchon, Spain - - 38 Bd
Chincoteague B., Maryl'd 129 Gc
Chinde, Mozambique - 112 Ce
Chindie, Mozambique - 113 Fa
Chindio, Mozambique - 112 Cc
Chindundo, Mozambique 112 Bb
Chindwin R., Burma - 92 Ba
Chinese Turkestan, Sinkiang - - - 84 Dc
Chingcheng, Manchuria 96 Db
Chingchishanchun, Manchuria - - - 96 Da
Chinghow & prov. Manchur. 96 Cc
Chingleput, Madras - 91 Ee
Chingping, Manchuria - 96 Bc
Chingshanchen, Manchur. 96 Da
Chinguetta, Fr. W. Africa 104 Bb
Chin-hai, China - - 94 Fc
Chin Hills, dist., Burma 92 Aa
Chini, Punjab States - 83 Hc
Chiniot, Punjab - - 82 Ec
Chinishk, Persia - - 79 Gc
Chin-kiang, China - - 94 Ec
Chin Lee, Arizona - - 135 Jc
Chinnampo, Korea - - 97 Ac
Chinna Salem, Madras - 89 Cb
Chinnur, Hyderabad - 90 Db
Chino, Arizona - - 135 Gd
Chinon, France - - 30 Cd
Chinsali, N. Rhodesia - 112 Bb
Chinsura, Bengal - - 88 Bc
Chin-ta, China - - 94 Aa
Chintai, China - - 96 Ac
Chintalnar, Eastern States 91 Eb
Chinwangtao, China - 94 Eb
Chioggia, Italy - - 63 Gb
Chiokai-san, Japan - 97 Dc
Chios, I., Ægean Sea - 78 Ab
Chipawa, N. Rhodesia - 112 Ab
Chipchiahue, Argentina 148 Cc
Chipchihua, Sa. de, Argen. 148 Cc
Chiperone, Mt., Mozamb. 113 Fa
Chipewyan, Alberta - 124 Gc
Chipinda Pools, S. Rhod. 113 Dc
Chipinga, S. Rhodesia - 113 Ec
Chipiona, Spain - - 40 Dc
Chiplun, Bombay - - 90 Ac
Chipman, New Brunswick 120 Bc
Chippenham, England - 14 Bd
Chippewa, Minnesota - 132 Bb
Chippewa Falls, Wisconsin 132 Dc
Chippewa R., Wisconsin 132 Dc
Chipping Campden, Eng. 14 Cb
Chipping Norton, England 14 Cc
Chipping Sodbury, Eng. 14 Bc
Chipurupalle, Madras - 91 Fc
Chiputneticook Ls., Maine-New Brunswick 120 Ad
Chiquian, Peru - - 145 Bd
Chiquimula, Guatemala 140 Ee
Chiquinquira, Colombia 144 Bb
Chira, Sinkiang - - 84 Ec
Chirawa, Rajputana - 83 Fd
Chirayinkil, Madras States 89 Bc
Chirbury, England - 14 Aa
Chiriqui, Lag. de, Panama 140 Gf
Chiriqui Grande, Panama 140 Gf

2

Chiromo, Nyasaland - 112 Bc
Chirpan, Bulgaria - 69 Fd
Chisana, Alaska - 125 Me
Chishima (Kuril Is.), Japan 76 Pe
Chishmy, U.S.S.R. - 75 Je
Chisinau(Kishinev)Moldavia 69 Hb
Chistochina, Alaska - 125 Le
Chistopol, U.S.S.R. - 74 Jd
Chita, U.S.S.R. - 76 Md
Chitadi, Belg. Congo - 109 Dc
Chitaldroog, Mysore - 90 Cd
Chitalwana, Rajputana - 85 Cb
Chitanga (Ahane), Mozambique - 113 Ec
Chiteve, Mozambique - 112 Bd
Chitina & R., Alaska - 125 Lf
Chitor, Rajputana - 85 Eb
Chitral, N.-W. F.P. - 84 Cc
Chitre, Panama - 140 Gf
Chittagong, Bengal - 88 Cc
Chittagong Hill Tracts, Bengal - 88 Dc
Chittoor, Madras - 90 De
Chittur, Madras States - 89 Bb
Chiusdino, Italy - 62 Fd
Chiusi, Italy - 63 Fd
Chiuta, L., Mozambique 112 Cb
Chiva, Spain - 38 Ee
Chivasso, Italy - 62 Bb
Chivay, Peru - 145 Ce
Chivilcoy, Argentina - 148 Da
Chivinde, Mozambique - 112 Cb
Chivoto, Sa., New Mexico 135 Kd
Chiwongo, Mozambique - 112 Cc
Chixoy, R., Guatemala - 140 Ed
Chizu, Japan - 100 Ed
Chkalov (Orenburg), U.S.S.R. - 75 Je
Choapam, Mexico - 139 Ed
Chocaya, Bolivia - 146 Bc
Cho-chow, China - 94 Eb
Choco & Cord. de, Colombia 144 Ab
Choconta, Colombia - 144 Bb
Chocz, Poland - 57 Cb
Chodau, Bohemia - 59 Ga
Chodziez, Poland - 57 Ba
Choele Choel, Argentina 148 Cb
Choen, Korea - 97 Ac
Chofa, Belg. Congo - 109 Ec
Chogiung, Alaska - 125 Gg
Choiseul I., Solomon Is. 157 Cd
Chois-kai Pk., New Mexico 135 Jd
Choisy-le-Roi, France - 30 Ec
Choix, Mexico - 138 Cb
Chojnice, Poland - 60 Db
Choko, mt., S. Rhodesia 113 Cb
Chokoloskee, Florida - 131 Nj
Chola, China - 94 Bc
Cholet, France - 32 Ec
Cho-lon, Cochin-China - 95 Cg
Cholpanglik, mt., Kashmir 84 Ec
Choluteca, Honduras - 140 Fe
Choma, N. Rhodesia - 112 Ac
Chomu, Rajputana - 83 Fe
Chomutov, Bohemia - 60 Bc
Chone, Ecuador - 145 Ab
Chon-kon, Siam - 95 Bg
Chonn-ti Mts., Sinkiang 84 Fb
Chonos, Arch. de los, Chile 148 Ac
Choo-tung, China - 94 Bd
Chopda, Bombay - 90 Ba
Chorges, France - 35 Jc
Chorillos, Peru - 145 Bd
Chorley, England - 18 Bc
Chorrera, Panama - 140 Hf
Chorro, El, Argentina - 146 Cc
Chorzow, Poland - 60 Ec
Chosen Str., Japan - 97 Bd
Chosen (Korea), Japan - 97 Bc
Choshi, Japan - 97 Ec
Choshin, Korea - 97 Bb
Chos Malal, Argentina - 148 Bb
Chota, Peru - 145 Bc
Chotan, Rajputana - 85 Cb
Chota Nagpur, Bihar - 87 Ed
Chota Sinchula, Bhutan 88 Ba
Chota Udaipur, Gujarat States - 85 Dc
Choteau, Montana - 136 Gb
Choti, Punjab - 82 Dd
Chotila, Western India - 85 Cc
Chott Djerid, Tunisia - 103 Jc
Chott ech Chergui, Algeria 102 Db
Chott el Rharsa, Tunisia 103 Hb
Chott Melrhir, Algeria - 103 Hb
Chouzé, France - 30 Cd
Chowan R., N. Carolina 131 Kb
Chowkiakow, China - 94 Dc
Chow-tsun, China - 94 Eb
Chrast, Bohemia - 59 Kb
Chrast, Bohemia - 59 Hb
Chriby, mts., Moravia - 57 Cd
Christchurch, England - 14 Ce
Christchurch, New Zeal'd 159 De
Christian, Morocco - 103 Oh
Christian, C., N.-W. Terr. 119 Qb
Christian I., Ontario - 123 Hc
Christian Sd., Alaska - 125 Nh
Christiana, Transvaal - 115 Fc
Christiansburg, Virginia 129 Dd
Christiansfeld, Denmark 45 Cc
Christianshaab, Greenland 9 Dd
Christie B., N.-W. Terr. 118 Gd
Christie, Mt., Yukon - 124 Db
Christina B., Cape Prov. 114 Eg
Christine, N. Dakota - 132 Ab
Christmas I., Line Is. - 157 Hc
Christmas I., Indian Oc. 93 Ch
Chriutnea - 69 Hb
Chroms Berg, Arizona - 135 He
Chrudim, Bohemia - 60 Cd
Chrzanów, Poland - 57 Ec
Chuan-chow, China - 94 Dd
Chüan-chow & B., China 95 Ed
Chubut, terr. & R., Argent. 148 Cc
Chu-cheng, China - 94 Eb
Chu-chow, Che-kiang, China - 94 Ed
Chuchow, Shan-tung, China 94 Eb
Chü-chow-fu, China - 94 Ed
Chucul, Argentina - 146 Ce
Chudleigh, England - 17 Cb
Chudovo, U.S.S.R. - 74 Ed
Chudskoe (Peipsi), L., U.S.S.R. - 74 Dd
Chugach Mts., Alaska - 125 Kf
Chuginadak I., Aleutian Is. 125 Ek
Chuguev, Ukraine - 75 Ff
Chug Water, Wyoming - 135 La
Chuka, Kenya - 110 Ed
Chukairei, Mt., Taiwan 97 Hf
Chu-ki, China - 94 Ed
Chukotski Pen., U.S.S.R. 76 Sc
Chukwani, Zanzibar - 111 Fg
Chula Vista, California - 134 Ee
Chulilla, Spain - 38 Ee
Chulmleigh, England - 17 Cb
Chumar, Kashmir - 83 Hb
Chumbicha, Argentina - 146 Bd
Chumbiri, Belg. Congo - 109 Cb
Chumiumo, mt., Sikkim 88 Ba
Chunar, United Provs. - 87 Ec
Chung, China - 94 Cc
Chung-an, China - 94 Ed
Chung-king, China - 94 Cd
Chung-ming, China - 94 Fc
Chung-pa, China - 94 Cc
Chunian, Punjab - 83 Ec
Chunya, Tang. Terr. - 111 Ch
Chupadera Mesa, New Mexico - 135 Ke
Chupanga, Mozambique 113 Fb
Chuquibambilla, Peru - 145 Cd
Chuquicamata, Chile - 146 Bc
Chuquisaca, dep., Bolivia 146 Cc
Chur (Coire), Switzerland 43 Jc
Churab, Tadzhik - 84 Cb
Churchill, Nevada - 134 Db
Churchill & C., Manitoba 124 Lc
Churchill L., Saskatch. - 124 Hc
Churchill R., Manitoba - 124 Kc
Church Stretton, Eng. - 14 Ba
Churfirsten, Switzerland 43 Hb
Churia Ghati Hills, Nepal 87 Fb
Churu, Rajputana - 83 Fd
Churutabis, S.-W. Africa 114 Bc
Chu-san I., China - 94 Fc
Chu-san Arch., China - 94 Fc
Chusca, Sa., New Mexico 135 Jc
Chu-shan, China - 94 Cc
Chusovaya & R., U.S.S.R. 74 Kd
Chust, Carpatho Ukraine 60 Gd
Chutes Cornet, Belg. Congo 109 Ed
Chuvash, U.S.S.R. - 74 Hd
Chwan, China - 94 Cb
Chynov, Bohemia - 59 Jb
Chyula Ra., Kenya - 110 Ee
Ciacova, Romania - 67 Gd
Ciampino, Italy - 64 Cb
Cianciana, Sicily - 65 Gg
Ciaris, I. de, Mexico - 138 Bb
Ciata, Romania - 67 Fd
Cibao, Cord. de, Santo Domingo - 140 Cc
Cicero, Illinois - 132 Ee
Ciechanów, Poland - 60 Fb
Ciempozuelos, Spain - 38 Bd
Cienaga, Colombia - 144 Ba
Cienfuegos, Cuba - 140 Ab
Cieszyn (Teschen), Poland 57 Dd
Cieza, Spain - 41 Eb
Cifuentes, Spain - 38 Cd
Cigales, Spain - 38 Ac
Cilician Gate, Turkey - 78 Bb
Cimaltepec, Mexico - 139 Ed
Cimarron, Kansas - 133 Bb
Cimarron R., Oklahoma 133 Cb
Ciminna, Sicily - 65 Gg
Cimone, Mte., Italy - 62 Ec
Çinarcik, Turkey - 72 Gb
Cinat, Spain - 39 Ed
Cinca, R., Spain - 39 Fb
Cinçer, mt., Bosnia - 68 Cc
Cincinnati, Iowa - 132 Ce
Cincinnati, Ohio - 129 Bc
Cinclare, Louisiana - 130 Ce
Cinco Casas, Spain - 41 Ca
Cinderford, England - 14 Bc
Cingoli, Italy - 63 Hd
Cinisi, Sicily - 65 Gf
Cinquefrondi, Italy - 65 Cd
Cinto, Mte., Corsica - 33 Dg
Ciotat, la, France - 33 Ac
Ciovo, Dalmatia - 68 Bc
Circle, Alaska - 125 Ld
Circleville, Ohio - 129 Cc
Cirenaica, Libya - 106 Cc
Cirencester, England - 14 Cc
Cirene, Libya - 106 Cb
Ciria, Spain - 38 Cc
Ciriè, Italy - 62 Bb
Ciro, Italy - 65 Dc
Cirque Mt., Labrador - 119 Re
Cisco, Texas - 133 Cd
Cisco, Utah - 135 Jb
Cisterna di Roma, Italy 64 Cb
Cistierna, Spain - 36 Eb
Citra, Florida - 131 Hf
Citrusdal, Cape Prov. - 114 Cf
Cittadella, Italy - 63 Fb
Citta della Pieve, Italy - 63 Ge
Citta di Castello, Italy - 63 Gd
Cittanova, Italy - 65 Bd
Citta San Angelo, Italy 64 Da
Citta Vecchia (Notabile), Malta - 65 Kk
Ciudad Bolivar, Venezuela 144 Db
Ciudadela, Balearic Is. - 39 Lj
Ciudad Juarez, Mexico - 138 Ca
Ciudad Real & prov., Spain 41 Cb
Ciudad Rodrigo, Spain - 37 Db
Ciudad Victoria, Mexico 139 Ec
Cividale del Friuli, Italy 63 Ha
Civita Castellana, Italy 64 Ca
Civitavecchia, Italy - 64 Ba
Civitella dell Tronto, Italy 63 He
Civray, France - 34 Ca
Civril, Turkey - 78 Ab
Clackmannan and co., Scotland - 23 Ed
Clacton-on-Sea, England 15 Fc
Claggan, Eire - 26 Da
Claire L., Alberta - 124 Gc
Clairefontaine, Algeria - 103 Hb
Clairemont, Texas - 133 Bd
Clairvaux, France - 35 Ha
Clamecy, France - 31 Fd
Clan Alpine Mts., Nevada 134 Eb
Clancey, Montana - 136 Hb
Clanton, Alabama - 130 Ed
Clanwilliam, Cape Prov. 114 Cf
Clapham, England - 15 Dd
Clara, Eire - 27 Ce
Clare, England - 15 Eb
Clare, Michigan - 122 Fd
Clare, Queensland - 153 Cc
Clare, S. Australia - 154 Bc
Clare, co., Eire - 27 Af
Clare I., Eire - 25 Ab
Clarecastle, Eire - 27 Bf
Claregalway, Eire - 27 Be
Claremont, New Hamps. 128 Bb
Claremont Isles and Pt., Queensland - 153 Bb
Claremore, Oklahoma - 133 Eb
Claremorris, Eire - 26 Bd
Clarence C., Greenland - 9 Ha
Clarence, C., N.-W. Terr. 119 Oa
Clarence I., Chile - 148 Be
Clarence Pk., Fernando Po 105 Ce
Clarence Pt., Alaska - 125 Ed
Clarence R., New S. Wales 155 Ha
Clarence Str., N.T., Aust. 150 Ea
Clarendon, Arkansas - 130 Cc
Clarendon, Texas - 133 Bc
Clarinda, Iowa - 132 Be
Clarion, Iowa - 132 Cd
Clarion, Pennsylvania - 129 Eb
Clarion I. (Santa Rosa), Mexico - 138 Bd
Clark, Nevada - 134 Db
Clark L., Alaska - 125 Hf
Clarke I., Tasmania - 155 Kg
Clarke Ra., Queensland - 153 Cd
Clarkebury, Cape Prov. - 115 He
Clarke River, Queensland 153 Cc
Clarkesville, Tennessee - 130 Eb
Clarkesville, Texas - 133 Ed
Clarksburg, W. Virginia 129 Dc
Clarksdale, Mississippi - 130 Cc
Clarksville, Arkansas - 130 Bc
Clarksville, Missouri - 132 Df
Clarksville, Virginia - 129 Ed
Clashmore, Eire - 27 Cg
Clatsop, Oregon - 136 Ab
Claude, Texas - 133 Bc
Claudetown, Sarawak - 99 Dc
Claudy, N. Ireland - 26 Cb
Claushavn, Greenland - 9 Dd
Clausthal, Prussia - 54 Fd
Claveria, Philippines - 95 Ff
Clavering I., Greenland - 9 Hc
Claverton Downs, Queensland - 153 Ce
Claxton, Georgia - 131 Hd
Clay, W. Virginia - 129 Dc
Clay Center, Kansas - 133 Da
Clay Cross, England - 18 Cd
Claydon, England - 15 Fb
Clay Hills, Utah - 135 Hc
Clayton, Alabama - 130 Fe
Clayton, Idaho - 136 Fc
Clayton, New Jersey - 129 Gc
Clayton, New Mexico - 135 Mc
Clayton, New York - 123 Kc
Clayville, New York - 128 Ab
Cleady, Eire - 25 Bf
Clear I. and C., Eire - 25 Bg
Clear L., California - 134 Bb
Clearfield, Pennsylvania 129 Eb
Clear Lake, Iowa - 132 Cd
Clear Lake, S. Dakota - 132 Ac
Clear Streak Well, W. Aust. 152 Ce
Clearwater, Kansas - 133 Db
Clearwater, Florida - 131 Mh
Clearwater L., Quebec - 119 Pe
Clearwater Mts. and R., Idaho - 136 Fb
Clearwater R., Minnesota 132 Bb
Cleburne, Texas - 133 Dd
Clee Hill, England - 14 Bb
Cle Elum, Washington - 136 Cb
Cleethorpes, England - 19 Dc
Clefmont, France - 31 Hc
Cleft, Idaho - 136 Fd
Cleggan, Eire - 25 Ab
Cleguérec, France - 32 Bb
Clempenow, Prussia - 55 Jb
Cleobury Mortimer, Eng. 14 Bb
Cleopatra's Needle, Philippines - 99 Ea
Cleo Springs, Oklahoma 133 Cb
Clères, France - 30 Db
Clermont, Hérault, France 35 Fd
Clermont, Oise, France - 30 Eb
Clermont and Goldfield, Queensland - 153 Cd
Clermont-en-Argonne, France - 31 Hb
Clermont-Ferrand, France 35 Fb
Clerval, France - 31 Jd
Clervaux, Luxembourg - 29 Dd
Clery, France - 30 Dd
Clevedon, England - 14 Bd
Cleveland, Idaho - 136 Gd
Cleveland, Ohio - 129 Db
Cleveland, Oklahoma - 133 Db
Cleveland, Queensland - 153 De
Cleveland, Tennessee - 131 Fc
Cleveland, Texas - 133 Ee
Cleveland Hills, England 18 Cb
Cleveland, Mt., Montana 136 Fa
Clew B., Eire - 25 Bb
Clifden, Eire - 25 Ac
Clifford, Cape Prov. - 115 Ge
Cliffs of Moher, Eire - 25 Bd
Clifton, Arizona - 135 Je
Clifton, England - 14 Bd
Clifton, Kansas - 133 Da
Clifton, Queensland - 153 Ce
Clifton, Tennessee - 130 Dc
Clifton Forge, Virginia 129 Ed
Cliftonville, Wisconsin - 132 Ec
Clinch Mts., Tennessee - 131 Gb
Clingmans Dome, N. Carolina - 131 Gc
Clinton, Arkansas - 130 Bc
Clinton, Illinois - 132 Ee
Clinton, Indiana - 129 Ac
Clinton, Iowa - 132 De
Clinton, Kentucky - 130 Db
Clinton, Louisiana - 130 Ce
Clinton, Missouri - 130 Aa
Clinton, Montana - 136 Gb
Clinton, N. Carolina - 131 Jc
Clinton, Oklahoma - 133 Cc
Clinton, Ontario - 123 Hd
Clinton, S. Carolina - 131 Hc
Clinton Dam, Tennessee 131 Fb
Clinton Golden L., N.-W. Terr. - 124 Hb
Clio, Alabama - 130 Fe
Clisson, France - 32 Dc
Clitheroe, England - 18 Bc
Cloche I., Ontario - 123 Hb
Cloghan, Eire - 27 Ce
Clogher, Eire - 26 Dd
Clogher, N. Ireland - 26 Cc
Clonakilty, Eire - 25 Cf
Cloncurry & Goldfield, Queensland - 153 Bd
Clonee, Eire - 27 De
Clones, Eire - 26 Cc
Clonmel, Eire - 27 Cg
Clontarf, Eire - 27 De
Cloone, Eire - 26 Cd
Cloppenburg, Oldenburg 54 Cc
Cloquet, Minnesota - 132 Cb
Clorinda, Argentina - 146 Dd
Closepet, Mysore - 90 Ce
Cloud Pk., Wyoming - 126 Db
Cloudchief, Oklahoma - 133 Cc
Cloughjordan, Eire - 27 Bf
Clover, Virginia - 129 Ed
Cloverdale, California - 134 Bb
Clovis, New Mexico - 126 Ed
Cloyes, France - 30 Dd
Cloyne, Eire - 25 Cf
Cluj, Transylvania - 67 Jc
Clun, England - 14 Ab
Clunes, Victoria - 154 Dd
Cluny, France - 35 Ga
Cluny, Queensland - 153 Ad
Cluro, Nevada - 134 Ea
Cluse, la, France - 35 Ha
Cluses, France - 35 Ja
Clusone, Italy - 62 Db
Clwyd, R., Wales - 20 Ca
Clydach, Wales - 20 Cd
Clyde, Kansas - 133 Da
Clyde, New Mexico - 135 Ke
Clyde, New Zealand - 159 Bf
Clyde, Firth of, Scotland 21 Bb
Clyde, R., Scotland - 21 Cb
Clydebank, Scotland - 23 De
Clydesdale, Ontario - 121 Ab
Coachford, Eire - 25 Cf
Coahuila, state, Mexico - 138 Db
Coal Cliffs, Utah - 135 Hb
Coalcoman, Mexico - 138 Dd
Coalgate, Oklahoma - 133 Dc
Coal Harbor, Alaska - 125 Gj
Coal Hill, Arkansas - 130 Bc
Coalville, England - 14 Ca
Coalville, Utah - 135 Ha
Coamo, Puerto Rico - 140 Jg
Coary, Brazil - 142 Bc
Coast Ra., Queensland - 153 Bc
Coast Ra., U.S.A.-Canada 124 Dd
Coatbridge, Scotland - 23 De
Coatepeque, Guatemala - 140 Ee
Coaticook, Quebec - 121 Eb
Coats I., N.-W. Terr. - 119 Nd
Coats Land, Antarctica - 160 —
Coatzintla, Mexico - 139 Ec
Coba, L., Mexico - 139 Gc
Cobalt, Ontario - 123 Jb
Coban, Guatemala - 140 Ed
Cobar, New S. Wales - 155 Eb
Cobargo, New S. Wales 155 Fd
Cobden, Ontario - 121 Bb
Cobequid Mts., Nova Scot. 120 Cd
Cobh (Queenstown), Eire 25 Cf
Cobija, Bolivia - 145 Dd
Coblenz (Koblenz), Prussia 58 Ba
Cobleskill, New York - 128 Ab
Coboconk, Ontario - 121 Ab
Cobourg, Ontario - 121 Ac
Cobram, New S. Wales 155 Ed
Cobre, Nevada - 134 Fa
Cobue, Mozambique - 112 Bb
Coburg, Bavaria - 58 Fa
Coburg, Oregon - 136 Bc
Coburg I., N.-W. Terr. 119 Oa
Coburg Pen., N.T., Aust. 150 Ea
Coca, Spain - 38 Ac
Cocahacra, Peru - 145 Ce
Cocamá, Peru - 145 Cd
Cocanada, Madras - 91 Fc
Cocentaina, Spain - 41 Fb
Cocha, La, Argentina - 146 Bd
Cochabamba and dep., Bolivia - 146 Bb
Cochin, Madras States - 89 Bc
Cochin-China, Fr. Indo-China - 95 Cg
Cochinoca, Argentina - 146 Bc
Cochise, Arizona - 135 Je
Cochran, Georgia - 131 Gd
Cochrane, Ontario - 123 Ha

Cochrane, L., *Argentina-Chile* - 148 Bd
Cockburn, *S. Australia* - 154 Cb
Cockburn I., *Ontario* - 122 Gc
Cockburn Land, *N.-W.T.* 119 Ob
Cockburn, Mt., *W. Aust.* 152 Db
Cockburn Sd., *W. Aust.* 152 Be
Cockermouth, *England* - 18 Aa
Cocking, *England* - 15 De
Cockscomb Mt., *Cape Prov.* - 115 Ff
Cockscomb Mts., *Brit. Honduras* - 140 Fd
Coco Chan. and Is., *Andaman Is.* - 91 Kj
Cocoa, *Florida* - 131 Ng
Cocopara Ra., *N.S.W.* - 155 Ec
Cocos I., *Marianas Is.* - 157 Qm
Cocos Is., *Indian Oc.* - 73 Mk
Cocula, *Mexico* - 138 Dc
Cocuy, *Colombia* - 144 Bb
Cod, C., *Massachusetts* - 128 Cb
Codajaz and L., *Brazil* - 142 Bc
Codogno, *Italy* - 62 Db
Codosera, la, *Spain* - 37 Cc
Codróipo, *Italy* - 63 Hb
Codroy R., *Newfoundland* 120 Fc
Codru Mts., *Transylvania* 67 Hc
Codú, *Brazil* - 143 Fc
Coen, *Queensland* - 153 Bb
Cœur d' Alene, *Idaho* - 136 Eb
Coevorden, *Holland* - 29 Eb
Coeymans, *New York* - 128 Ab
Coffeeville, *Mississippi* - 130 Dd
Coffeyville, *Kansas* - 133 Eb
Coff's Harbour, *N.S.W.* 155 Hb
Cofimvaba, *Cape Prov.* - 115 Ge
Cogeces del Monte, *Spain* 38 Ac
Coggeshall, *England* - 15 Ec
Coggiola, *Italy* - 62 Cb
Coghinas, R., *Sardinia* - 64 Hf
Cognac, *France* - 32 Ee
Cohoes, *New York* - 123 Md
Cohuna, *Victoria* - 154 Dd
Coiba, I., *Panama* - 140 Gf
Coimbatore, *Madras* - 89 Bb
Coimbra, *Portugal* - 37 Bb
Coin, *Spain* - 40 Fc
Coipasa L. & Salar de, *Bolivia* - 146 Bb
Coire (Chur), *Switzerland* 43 Jc
Cojedes, state, *Venezuela* 144 Cb
Cojimies, *Ecuador* - 145 Aa
Cojocna, *Transylvania* - 67 Jc
Cokeville, *Wyoming* - 135 Ha
Colac, *Victoria* - 154 De
Colair L., *Madras* - 91 Ec
Colby, *Kansas* - 133 Ba
Colcha, *Bolivia* - 146 Bc
Colchagua, prov., *Chile* 146 Ae
Colchester, *England* - 15 Ec
Colchester, *Illinois* - 132 De
Colchester, *Vermont* - 128 Ba
Cold Aston, *England* - 14 Bd
Cold Bokkeveld, *Cape Prov.* 114 Cf
Col de Nargo, *Spain* - 39 Gb
Coldfoot, *Alaska* - 125 Jc
Coldingham, *Scotland* - 23 Fe
Coldspring, *Texas* - 133 Ee
Coldstream, *Scotland* - 21 Db
Coldwater, *Kansas* - 133 Cb
Coldwater, *Michigan* - 122 Fe
Coldwater, *Mississippi* - 130 Dc
Coldwell, *Ontario* - 122 Ea
Colebrook, *New Hamps.* 123 Nc
Coleman, *Alberta* - 124 Ge
Coleman, *Texas* - 133 Ce
Colemerik, *Turkey* - 78 Db
Colenso, *Natal* - 115 Hd
Coleraine, *N. Ireland* - 26 Da
Coleraine, *Quebec* - 121 Eb
Coleraine, *Victoria* - 154 Ce
Coleridge L., *New Zealand* 159 Ce
Coleroon R., *Madras* - 89 Cb
Coles, Pta. de, *Peru* - 145 Ce
Colesberg, *Cape Prov.* - 115 Fe
Coleshill, *England* - 14 Cb
Colfax, *California* - 134 Cb
Colfax, *Iowa* - 132 Ce
Colfax, *Louisiana* - 130 Be
Colfax, *Washington* - 136 Eb
Colfiorito, *Italy* - 63 Gd
Colgong, *Bihar* - 87 Gc
Colhué Huapi, L., *Argent.* 148 Cd
Colico, *Italy* - 62 Da
Coligny, *France* - 35 Ha
Coligny, *Transvaal* - 115 Gc
Colima & state, *Mexico* - 138 Dd
Colinas, *Honduras* - 140 Fd
Coll, I., *Scotland* - 22 Bc
Collahuasi, *Chile* - 146 Bc
Collalto, mt., *Italy* - 63 Ga
Colle, *Italy* - 62 Fd
Colle Isarco, *Italy* - 63 Fa
Collelongo, *Italy* - 64 Db
Colle Salvetti, *Italy* - 62 Ed
Collie, *W. Australia* - 152 Be
Collier B., *W. Australia* 152 Cb
Collier City, *Florida* - 131 Nj
Collierville, *Tennessee* - 130 Dc
Collingbourne Kingston, *England* - 14 Cd
Collingwood, *Ontario* - 123 Hc
Collingwood, *Queensland* 153 Bd
Collingwood B., *New Guinea* - 156 Dc
Collins, *Georgia* - 131 Gd
Collins, *Montana* - 136 Ha
Collinstown, *Eire* - 26 Cd
Collinsville, *Oklahoma* - 133 Db
Collo, *Algeria* - 103 Ha
Collo, Mt., *Ethiopia* - 108 Cc
Collobrières, *France* - 33 Bc
Collooney, *Eire* - 26 Bc
Colmar, *France* - 31 Kc
Colmars, *France* - 33 Ba
Colmena, *Argentina* - 146 Cd
Colmenar de Oreja, *Spain* 38 Bd
Colmenar Viejo, *Spain* - 38 Bd
Colmi, *Honduras* - 140 Fd
Colnbrook, *England* - 15 Dd
Colne, *England* - 18 Bc
Colne, R., *England* - 15 Ec
Colnett, C., *Mexico* - 138 Aa
Cologna, *Italy* - 63 Fb
Cologne (Koln), *Prussia* 54 Be
Colomb Bechar, *Algeria* 102 Cd
Colombey, *France* - 31 Hc
Colombia, *Brazil* - 147 Fc
Colombia, rep., *S. Amer.* 141 Bb
Colombier, *Switzerland* - 42 Cc
Colombo, *Ceylon* - 89 Cd
Colon, *Buenos Aires, Argentina* - 146 Ce
Colon, *Entre Rios, Argent.* 146 De
Colon, *Cuba* - 140 Ab
Colon, *Venezuela* - 144 Bb
Colon (Aspinwall), *Panama* 140 Gf
Colonel Fer. Gomez, *Braz.* 143 Db
Colonelganj, *United Provs.* 86 Db
Colonia & dep., *Uruguay* 146 De
Colonia Terr., *Bolivia* - 145 Dd
Colonia Alvear, *Argentina* 146 Be
Colonia Sarmiento, *Argent.* 148 Cd
Colonne, C., *Italy* - 65 Dc
Colonnella, *Italy* - 63 He
Colonsay, I., *Scotland* - 22 Bd
Colorado, *California* - 134 Fe
Colorado, *Texas* - 133 Bd
Colorado Des., *California* 134 Ed
Colorado Des., *Wyoming* 135 Ja
Colorado, Grand Canyon of the, *Arizona* - 135 Gc
Colorado Plat., *Arizona* 135 Hc
Colorado, R., *Argentina* 148 Db
Colorado R., *U.S.A.* - 135 Jb
Colorado R., Little, *Ariz.* 135 Hc
Colorado, state, *U.S.A.* 126 Dc
Colorado Springs, *Colorado* 135 Lb
Colorno, *Italy* - 62 Ec
Colotlan, *Mexico* - 138 Dc
Colquechaca, *Bolivia* - 146 Bb
Coltishall, *England* - 19 Fe
Colton, *Utah* - 135 Hb
Colulli, *Eritrea* - 108 Cc
Columbia, *Alabama* - 130 Fe
Columbia, *Indiana* - 129 Bb
Columbia, *Kentucky* - 130 Fb
Columbia, *Louisiana* - 130 Bd
Columbia, *Mississippi* - 130 De
Columbia, *Missouri* - 130 Ba
Columbia, *N. Carolina* - 131 Kc
Columbia, *Pennsylvania* 129 Fb
Columbia, *S. Carolina* - 131 Hc
Columbia, *Tennessee* - 130 Ec
Columbia, *Texas* - 133 Ef
Columbia, Mt., *Alberta* 124 Fd
Columbia R., *Br. Columbia* 124 Fd
Columbia R., *Washington-Oregon* - 136 Cc
Columbia Falls, *Montana* 136 Fa
Columbiana, *Alabama* - 130 Ed
Columbria, *Queensland* - 153 Cd
Columbus, *Georgia* - 131 Fd
Columbus, *Indiana* - 129 Bc
Columbus, *Iowa* - 132 De
Columbus, *Kansas* - 133 Eb
Columbus, *Mississippi* - 130 Dd
Columbus, *Nebraska* - 126 Fb
Columbus, *Ohio* - 129 Cc
Columbus, *Texas* - 133 Df
Columbus Ra., *Sinkiang* 84 Fc
Colunga, *Spain* - 36 Ea
Colusa, *California* - 134 Cb
Colville, *Washington* - 136 Ea
Colville Ra. and C., *New Zealand* - 158 Eb
Colville R., *Alaska* - 125 Hb
Colwall, *England* - 14 Bb
Colwyn Bay, *Wales* - 20 Ca
Colyton, *England* - 14 Ae
Comacchio, *Italy* - 63 Gc
Comacchio Valli de, *Italy* 63 Fc
Comanche, *Oklahoma* - 133 Dc
Comanche, *Texas* - 133 Ce
Comayagua, *Honduras* - 140 Fe
Combermere B., *Burma* 92 Ac
Combourg, *France* - 32 Db
Comeglians, *Italy* - 63 Ga
Comer, *Texas* - 133 Ee
Comeragh Mts., *Eire* - 27 Gg
Comet, *Queensland* - 153 Cd
Comilla, *Bengal* - 88 Cc
Comiso, *Sicily* - 65 Hh
Comitan, *Mexico* - 139 Fd
Commentry, *France* - 34 Ea
Commercy, *France* - 31 Hc
Committee B., *N.-W.T.* 119 Mc
Commonwealth Ra., *Antarctica* - 160 —
Como, L., *Italy* - 62 Db
Comodoro Rivadavia, *Argentina* - 148 Cd
Comondu, *Mexico* - 138 Bb
Comorin & C., *Madras States* - 89 Bc
Comoro Is., *Indian Oc.* - 112 Db
Compass Berg, *Cape Prov.* 115 Fe
Compiegne, *France* - 30 Eb
Compomarino, *Italy* - 64 Fb
Comporta, *Portugal* - 40 Ba
Compostela, *Mexico* - 138 Dc
Comps, *France* - 33 Bb
Compton, *California* - 134 De
Compton, *Quebec* - 123 Nc
Compton Wynyates, *England* - 14 Cb
Comrie, *Scotland* - 23 Ed
Comstock, *Texas* - 133 Bf
Comunanza, *Italy* - 63 He
Conakry, *Fr. W. Africa* 104 Be
Concarneau, *France* - 32 Bc
Conceicão, *Mozambique* - 112 Cc
Conceiçao da Barra, *Brazil* 147 Hb
Conceicão do Araguaya, *Brazil* - 143 Dd
Conceicao do Arroio, *Brazil* - 147 Ed
Concepcion, *Córdoba, Argentina* - 146 Ce
Concepcion, *Corrientes, Argentina* - 146 Dd
Concepcion, *Bolivia* - 145 Dd
Concepcion, *Paraguay* - 146 Dc
Concepcion, *Philippines* 99 Fa
Concepción & prov., *Chile* 148 Bb
Concepcion Can., *Chile* 148 Ae
Concepcion, Rio de la, *Mexico* - 138 Ba
Concepcion del Oro, *Mexico* 138 Dc
Concepcion del Uruguay, *Argentina* - 146 De
Conception, La, *Quebec* - 121 Ca
Conception B., *Newfoundland* - 120 Jc
Conception I., *Bahamas* 140 Bb
Concession, *S. Rhodesia* 113 Da
Conches, *France* - 30 Cc
Conchi, *Chile* - 146 Bc
Concho, *Arizona* - 135 Jd
Concho R., *Texas* - 133 Be
Conchos, R., *Mexico* - 138 Cb
Conconully, *Washington* 136 Da
Concord, *New Hampshire* 128 Cb
Concord, *N. Carolina* - 131 Hc
Concordia, *Argentina* - 146 De
Concordia, *Cape Prov.* - 114 Cd
Concordia, *Kansas* - 133 Da
Concordia, *Mexico* - 138 Cc
Concordia, *Peru* - 145 Ce
Condamine R., *Queensl'd* 153 De
Condat, *France* - 34 Eb
Conde, *Brazil* - 143 Ge
Conde-sur-Noireau, *France* 32 Eb
Condino, *Italy* - 62 Eb
Condobolin, *New S. Wales* 155 Ec
Condom, *France* - 34 Cd
Condon, *Oregon* - 136 Cc
Condor, Cord. del, *Peru* 145 Bb
Condrieu, *France* - 35 Gb
Conecuh R., *Alabama* - 130 Ee
Conegliano, *Italy* - 63 Gb
Conejos, *Colorado* - 135 Lc
Conesa, *Argentina* - 148 Dc
Coney I., *New York* - 128 Bc
Conflans, *France* - 31 Hb
Confolens, *France* - 34 Ca
Confusa, R., *Paraguay* - 146 Dc
Confusion Ra., *Utah* - 134 Gb
Congleton, *England* - 18 Bd
Congo, R., *W. Africa* - 109 Cb
Congresbury, *England* - 14 Bd
Conil, *Spain* - 40 Dc
Coningsby, *England* - 19 Dd
Coniston & Water, *Eng.* 18 Ab
Conjeeveram, *Madras* - 90 De
Conlic, *France* - 30 Bc
Conliege, *France* - 35 Ha
Conlu, *Turkey* - 72 Fb
Conn, L., *Eire* - 25 Ba
Connaught, prov., *Eire* 26 Ad
Conneaut, *Ohio* - 129 Db
Connecticut, state, *U.S.A.* 127 Lb
Connecticut R., *Connecticut* 128 Bc
Connell, *Washington* - 136 Db
Connellsville, *Pennsylva.* 129 Ec
Connelly, *New York* - 128 Ac
Connemara, Mts., *Eire* - 25 Bc
Connemarra, *Queensland* 153 Bd
Connerre, *France* - 30 Cc
Connersville, *Indiana* - 129 Bc
Connoire B., *Newfoundl'd* 120 Fc
Conquet, le, *France* - 32 Ab
Conquista, *Spain* - 41 Bb
Conrad, *Montana* - 136 Ga
Conroe, *Texas* - 133 Ee
Consecon, *Ontario* - 121 Bc
Consett, *England* - 21 Ed
Constable, *Cape Prov.* - 114 Df
Constance (Konstanz), *Baden* - 58 Dd
Constance, L. (Boden See), *Switzerland* - 43 Ha
Constance, Mt., *Washing'n* 136 Bb
Constanţa, *Romania* - 69 Hc
Constantina, *Spain* - 40 Eb
Constantine & Mts. de, *Algeria* - 103 Ha
Constantine, dep., *Algeria* 103 Gb
Constantine, C., *Alaska* 125 Gg
Constantinople (Istanbul), *Turkey* - 72 Fa
Constitucion, *Chile* - 148 Bb
Consuegra, *Spain* - 38 Be
Contact, *Nevada* - 134 Fa
Contai, *Bengal* - 88 Ad
Contamana, *Peru* - 145 Cc
Contes, *France* - 33 Cb
Conthey, *Switzerland* - 42 Dd
Continental Divide, *Montana* - 136 Gc
Contreras, I., *Chile* - 148 Ae
Contres, *France* - 30 Dd
Convent, *Louisiana* - 130 Ce
Conversano, *Italy* - 65 Da
Convoy, *Eire* - 26 Cb
Conway, *Arkansas* - 130 Bc
Conway, *Cape Prov.* - 115 Fe
Conway, *Missouri* - 130 Bb
Conway, *S. Carolina* - 131 Jd
Conway and R., *Wales* - 20 Ca
Conway Springs, *Kansas* 133 Cb
Coo (Cos), I., *Ægean Sea* 78 Ab
Cooch Behar, *Eastern States* 88 Ba
Cook Chan., *Philippines* 99 Ea
Cook Inlet, *Alaska* - 125 Jf
Cook Is., *Pacific Oc.* - 157 Ge
Cook Mt., *New Zealand* 159 Ce
Cook Str., *New Zealand* 159 Ed
Cookeville, *Tennessee* - 130 Fb
Cookham, *England* - 15 Dc
Cookhouse, *Cape Prov.* - 115 Ff
Cookshire, *Quebec* - 121 Eb
Cookstown, *N. Ireland* - 26 Db
Cooktown, *Queensland* - 153 Cc
Coolabah, *New S. Wales* 155 Eb
Coolabara, *Queensland* - 153 Be
Coolah, *New S. Wales* - 155 Fb
Coolamon, *New S. Wales* 155 Ec
Coole, *Eire* - 26 Cd
Coolgardie & Goldfield, *W. Australia* - 152 Ce
Coolgreany, *Eire* - 27 Df
Coolie, *Queensland* - 153 Be
Cooma, *New S. Wales* - 155 Fd
Coombe Bissett, *England* 14 Cd
Coombe Hill, *England* - 14 Bc
Coonabarabran, *New S. Wales* - 155 Fb
Coonalpyn, *S. Aust.* - 154 Bd
Coonamble, *New S. Wales* 155 Fb
Coondambo, *S. Aust.* - 154 Ab
Coondapoor, *Madras* - 90 Be
Cooper, *Texas* - 133 Ed
Coopers (Barcoo) Cr., *S. Australia* - 154 Ba
Cooperstown, *New York* 123 Ld
Coorg, prov., *S. India* - 89 Aa
Coorong, The, *S. Aust.* 154 Bd
Coos Bay, *Oregon* - 136 Ad
Coosa R., *Alabama* - 130 Ed
Cootamundra, *New S. Wales* - 155 Ec
Cootehall, *Eire* - 26 Bd
Cootehill, *Eire* - 26 Cc
Cop, *Slovakia* - 60 Gd
Copăciósa, *Romania* - 67 Jd
Copeland, *Idaho* - 136 Ea
Copelina, La, *Argentina* 148 Cb
Copenhagen, *New York* 128 Ab
Copenhagen (Köbenhavn), *Denmark* - 45 Fc
Copetonas, *Argentina* - 148 Db
Copiapo, *Chile* - 146 Ad
Copiapo, mt., *Chile* - 146 Bd
Copley, *S. Australia* - 154 Bb
Coporaque, *Peru* - 145 Cd
Copparo, *Italy* - 63 Fc
Coppename, R., *Suriname* 142 Cb
Copper, *Arizona* - 135 Gd
Copper R., *Alaska* - 125 Lf
Copper Center, *Alaska* - 125 Ke
Copper Cliff, *Ontario* - 123 Hb
Copperfield, *Queensland* 153 Cd
Coppermine and R., *N. W. Terr.* - 118 Fc
Coppet, *Switzerland* - 42 Bd
Copsa Mica, *Romania* - 67 Kc
Coquar, *Quebec* - 123 La
Coquilhatville, *Belg. Congo* 109 Ca
Coquille, *Oregon* - 136 Bd
Coquimbo, prov., *Chile* - 146 Ae
Coquimbo and B., *Chile* 146 Ad
Cora L., *Texas* - 133 Ad
Corabia, *Romania* - 69 Fd
Coraçoes, *Brazil* - 147 Fc
Coraki, *New S. Wales* - 155 Ha
Coral B., *Philippines* - 99 Eb
Coral Sea, *Queensland, etc.* 153 Cb
Corangamite, L., *Victoria* 154 De
Corato, *Italy* - 65 Ca
Corbeil, *France* - 30 Ec
Corbie, *France* - 30 Eb
Corbin, *Kentucky* - 131 Fb
Corbins, *Spain* - 39 Fc
Corbridge, *England* - 21 Dd
Corby, *Lincs, England* - 19 De
Corby, *Northants, Eng.* 15 Db
Corcoran, *California* - 134 Dc
Corcovado, G. del, *Chile* 148 Bc
Cordele, *Georgia* - 131 Ge
Cordell, *Oklahoma* - 133 Cc
Cordoba, *Mexico* - 139 Ed
Córdoba, *Peru* - 145 Cd
Córdoba & prov., *Argent.* 146 Ce
Cordoba & prov., *Spain* 40 Fb
Cordoba, Sierra de, *Spain* 40 Fb
Córdoba, Sas. de, *Argent.* 146 Ce
Cordova, *Alaska* - 125 Lf
Corella, *Spain* - 38 Db
Corfu (Kérkira), I., *Greece* 70 Ad
Corfu & Str. of, *Greece* - 70 Ad
Corgo, *Spain* - 36 Cb
Cori, *Italy* - 64 Cb
Coria, *Spain* - 37 Db
Corigliano Calabro, *Italy* 65 Cc
Corinaldo, *Italy* - 63 Hd
Coringa, *Madras* - 91 Fc
Corinne, *Utah* - 135 Ga
Corinth, *Mississippi* - 130 Dc
Corinth, *New York* - 128 Bb
Corinth, G. of, *Greece* - 71 De
Corinth (Kórinthos), *Greece* 71 Df
Corintho, *Brazil* - 147 Gb
Corinto, *Nicaragua* - 140 Fe
Corisco B., *Fr. Eq. Afr.* 109 Aa
Coristine, *Ontario* - 123 Jb
Cork, *Queensland* - 153 Bd
Cork and co., *Eire* - 25 Cf
Cork Harb., *Eire* - 25 Cf
Corleone, *Sicily* - 65 Gg
Corleto Perticaro, *Italy* 65 Cb
Corlu, *Turkey* - 72 Ea
Corlu Suyu, *Turkey* - 72 Ea
Cormons, *Italy* - 63 Hb
Cornatel, *Romania* - 67 Kd
Cornelia, *O.F.S.* - 115 Hc
Corner Brook, *Newfound.* 120 Fb
Corning, *Arkansas* - 130 Cb
Corning, *California* - 134 Bb
Corning, *Iowa* - 132 Be
Corning, *New York* - 123 Kd
Cornwall, *New York* - 128 Ac
Cornwall, *Ontario* - 121 Cb
Cornwall, co., *England* - 17 Bc
Cornwall I., *N.-W. Terr.* 118 La
Cornwallis I., *N.-W. T.* 118 Ka
Coro, *Venezuela* - 144 Ca
Coroata, *Brazil* - 143 Fc
Corocoro, *Bolivia* - 146 Bb

Corofin, *Eire* - - 27 Af
Coroico, *Bolivia* - - 146 Bb
Coromandel Coast, *Madras* 89 Db
Coron (Koroni), *Greece* - 71 Cg
Corona, *Alabama* - - 130 Ed
Corona, *California* - 134 Ee
Coronada, *Spain* - - 37 Ed
Coronada, B., *Costa Rica* 140 Gf
Coronado, *Arizona* - 135 Je
Coronado, *California* - 134 Ee
Coronation Gulf, *N.-W.T.* 118 Gc
Coronation I., *W. Aust.* 152 Ca
Coronel, *Chile* - - 148 Bb
Coronel Pringles, *Argent.* 148 Db
Coronel Suarez, *Argent.* 148 Db
Coronel Vidal, *Argentina* 148 Eb
Coronie, *Suriname* - 142 Ca
Corovodë, *Albania* - 70 Bc
Corowa, *New S. Wales* 155 Ed
Corozal, *Br. Honduras* - 140 Fd
Corpen, *Argentina* - 148 Cd
Corpie, *Spain* - - 36 Ec
Corque, *Bolivia* - - 146 Bb
Corral de Almaguer, *Spain* 38 Be
Corrales, *Spain* - - 36 Ec
Corrales, *Uruguay* - 146 De
Corralitos, *Mexico* - - 138 Ca
Correggio, *Italy* - - 62 Ec
Corrèze, dep., *France* - 34 Db
Corrib, L., *Eire* - - 25 Bc
Corrientes and prov., *Argentina* - - - 146 Dd
Corrientes, C., *Argentina* 148 Eb
Corrientes, C., *Colombia* 144 Ab
Corrientes, C., *Mexico* - 138 Cc
Corrientes, C., *Mozamb.* 112 Cd
Corrigan, *Texas* - - 133 Ee
Corry, *Pennsylvania* - 129 Eb
Corse, C., *Corsica* - 33 Ef
Corsham, *England* - 14 Bd
Corsica, I., *France* - 61 Bc
Corsicana, *Texas* - - 133 Dd
Corston, *England* - - 14 Bc
Corte, *Corsica* - - 33 Eg
Cortegana, *Spain* - - 40 Db
Cortes, G. de, *Cuba* - 140 Ab
Cortes de la Frontera, *Spain* - - - 40 Ec
Cortez, *Colorado* - - 135 Jc
Cortez, & Mts., *Nevada* 134 Ea
Cortimo I., *Sierra Leone* 104 Be
Cortina, *Italy* - - 63 Ga
Cortland, *New York* - 123 Kd
Corton, *England* - - 15 Fa
Cortona, *Italy* - - 63 Gd
Coruche, *Portugal* - 37 Bd
Coruh & R., *Turkey* - 78 Da
Çorum, *Turkey* - - 78 Ca
Corumba, *Goyaz, Brazil* 147 Fb
Corumba, *Matto Grosso, Brazil* - - - 146 Db
Coruña and prov., *Spain* 36 Ba
Corunna, *S. Australia* - 154 Ac
Corunna (La Coruña), *Spain* - - - 36 Ba
Corvallis, *Oregon* - - 136 Bc
Corwen, *Wales* - - 20 Cb
Corydon, *Iowa* - - 132 Ce
Cos (Coo), I., *Ægean Sea* 78 Ab
Cosalo, *Mexico* - - 138 Cc
Coseguina Vol., *Nicaragua* 140 Fe
Cosel - - - - 57 Dc
Coseley, *England* - - 14 Ba
Cosenza, *Italy* - - 65 Cc
Coshocton, *Ohio* - - 129 Cb
Cosina - - - - 63 Jb
Cosmoledo Is., *Indian Oc.* 112 Ea
Cosmopolis, *Washington* 136 Ab
Cosne, *Allier, France* - 34 Ea
Cosne, *Nievre, France* - 30 Ed
Cospeito, *Spain* - - 36 Ca
Cospić, *Croatia* - - 63 Kc
Cosquin, *Argentina* - 146 Ce
Cossack, *W. Australia* - 152 Bc
Cosse-le-Vivien, *France* 32 Ec
Cossonay, *Switzerland* - 42 Bc
Costa Rica, rep., *Cent. America* - - - 140 Ge
Costermansville, *Belgian Congo* - - - 109 Eb
Costillo Pk., *New Mexico* 135 Lc
Coswig, *Anhalt* - - 55 Hd
Cotabato, *Philippines* - 99 Fb
Cotagaita, *Bolivia* - - 146 Bc
Cotahuasi, *Peru* - - 145 Ce
Côteau, *Quebec* - - 121 Cb
Coteau des Prairies, *Minnesota, etc.* - - 132 Bd
Coteau du Grand Bois, *Minnesota* - - 132 Bb
Cote Blanche B., *Louisiana* 130 Cf
Côte D'Azur, *France* - 33 Bd
Cote-d-Or, dep., *France* 31 Gd
Cotes-du-Nord, dep., *France* 32 Cb
Cothen, *Anhalt* - - 55 Hb
Cotherstone, *England* - 18 Ba
Cotignac, *France* - - 33 Bb
Cotonou, *Fr. W. Africa* 105 Bd
Cotopaxi, *Colorado* - 135 Lb
Cotopaxi, mt. and prov., *Ecuador* - - - 145 Bb
Cotovelo, *Brazil* - - 142 Cd
Cotronei, *Italy* - - 65 Cc
Cotswold Hills, *England* 14 Cc
Cottage Grove, *Oregon* - 136 Bd
Cottbus, *Prussia* - - 55 Kd
Cottel I., *Newfoundland* 120 Jb
Cottesmore, *England* - 15 Da
Cottian Alps, *France-Italy* 35 Jc
Cottica, *Suriname* - - 142 Db
Cottingham, *England* - 19 Dc
Cottonwood, *Idaho* - 136 Eb
Cottonwoods Falls, *Kansas* 133 Da
Couches-les-Mines, *France* 31 Ge
Coudersport, *Pennsylvania* 129 Eb
Couga Mts., *Cape Prov.* 114 Ef
Couhuayana, R., *Mexico* 138 Dd
Coulagh B., *Eire* - - 25 Af
Coulanges, *France* - 31 Fd
Coulanges-la-Vineuse, *France* - - - 31 Fd
Coulee, *Washington* - 136 Db
Couleuvre, *France* - - 35 Ea
Coulman I., *Antarctica* - 160 —
Coulommiers, *France* - 30 Ec
Coulonge, R., *Quebec* - 121 Ba
Coulterville, *California* - 134 Cc
Council, *Alaska* - - 125 Fd
Council, *Idaho* - - 136 Ec
Council Bluffs, *Iowa* - 132 Be
Council Grove, *Kansas* - 133 Da
Cound, *England* - - 14 Ba
Country Harbour, *Nova Scotia* - - - 120 Ed
Coupar Angus, *Scotland* 23 Ec
Coupeville, *Washington* 136 Ba
Couptrain, *France* - 30 Bc
Courantyne, R., *Brit. Guiana* - - - 144 Ec
Courçon, *France* - - 32 Ed
Courgenay, *Switzerland* 42 Db
Courgne, *Italy* - - 62 Bb
Couronne, C., *France* - 35 Gd
Coursegoules, *France* - 33 Cb
Courseulles, *France* - 32 Ea
Courtalain, *France* - 30 Cc
Courtmacsherry & B., *Eire* 25 Cf
Courtomer, *France* - 30 Cc
Courtrai, *Belgium* - - 29 Bd
Cousance, *France* - - 35 Ha
Coushatta, *Louisiana* - 130 Bd
Coutances, *France* - - 32 Da
Coutras, *France* - - 34 Bb
Covadonga, *Spain* - - 36 Ea
Covaledo, *Spain* - - 38 Bc
Covarrubias and Sa. de, *Spain* - - - 38 Bb
Coventry, *England* - 14 Cb
Coventry, *Rhode I.* - 128 Cc
Coveron, *France* - - 32 Dc
Covilha, *Portugal* - - 37 Cb
Covington, *Georgia* - 131 Fd
Covington, *Indiana* - 129 Ab
Covington, *Kentucky* - 131 Fa
Covington, *Louisiana* - 130 Ce
Covington, *Tennessee* - 130 Dc
Covington, *Virginia* - 129 Ed
Cowal, *Scotland* - - 22 Cd
Cowan, L., *W. Aust.* - 152 Ce
Cowangie, *Victoria* - 154 Cd
Cowansville, *Quebec* - 121 Db
Coward Springs, *S. Aust.* 154 Aa
Cowarie, *S. Australia* - 154 Ba
Cowbit, *England* - - 15 Da
Cowbridge, *Wales* - - 20 Ce
Cowden, *Illinois* - - 132 Ef
Cowdenbeath, *Scotland* - 23 Ed
Cowell, *S. Australia* - 154 Ac
Cowes, *I. of Wight, Eng.* 14 Ce
Cowley, *England* - - 14 Cc
Cowlitz Pass, *Washington* 136 Cb
Cowlitz R., *Washington* 136 Bb
Cowra, *New S. Wales* - 155 Fc
Cox Canon, *New Mexico* 135 Le
Coxim, *Brazil* - - 147 Eb
Coxsackie, *New York* - 123 Ld
Cox's Bazar, *Bengal* - 92 Ab
Coyote, *New Mexico* - 135 Le
Coyuca, *Mexico* - - 138 Dd
Cozumel, I., *Mexico* - 139 Gc
Crabbs, *Newfoundland* - 120 Fb
Cracow, *Poland* - - 60 Ec
Cradle Mt., *Tasmania* - 155 Jg
Cradock, *Cape Prov.* - 115 Ff
Craftsbury, *Vermont* - 128 Ba
Craig, *Alaska* - - 125 Oj
Craig, *Colorado* - - 135 Ka
Craig Harbour, *N.-W.T.* 119 Oa
Craigville, *Minnesota* - 132 Cb
Crail, *Scotland* - - 23 Fd
Craiova, *Romania* - - 69 Ec
Cranbrook, *Br. Columbia* 124 Fe
Cranbrook, *England* - 15 Ed
Cranbrook, *W. Aust.* - 152 Be
Crandon, *Wisconsin* - 132 Ec
Crane, *Idaho* - - 136 Ec
Crane, R., *Oregon* - 136 Dd
Cranleigh, *England* - 15 Dd
Crans, *Switzerland* - 42 Dd
Cranz - - - - 56 Eb
Craponne, *France* - - 35 Fb
Crasna, *Transylvania* - 67 Hb
Crater Lake, *Oregon* - 136 Bd
Cratheus, *Brazil* - - 143 Fd
Crathorne, *England* - 18 Cb
Crati, R., *Italy* - - 65 Cc
Crato, *Brazil* - - 143 Gd
Crato, *Brazil* - - 142 Bd
Crato, *Portugal* - - 37 Cc
Crauchmar, *Cambodia* - 95 Cg
Craughwell, *Eire* - - 27 Be
Craven Arms, *England* - 14 Bb
Cravo, *Colombia* - - 144 Bb
Crawfordsville, *Indiana* 129 Ac
Crawfordville, *Florida* - 131 Fe
Crazy Mts., *Montana* - 136 Hb
Crécy, *France* - - 30 Da
Crediton, *England* - 17 Cb
Cree L. & R., *Saskatch.* 124 Hc
Creede, *Colorado* - - 135 Kc
Creeslough, *Eire* - - 26 Ba
Creighton, *Natal* - - 115 He
Creil, *France* - - 30 Eb
Crema, *Italy* - - 62 Db
Cremona, *Italy* - - 62 Eb
Crepaja, *Voyvodina* - 67 Fe
Crescent L., *Oregon* - 136 Bd
Crescent City, *California* 134 Aa
Crescent City, *Florida* - 131 Hf
Crescintino, *Italy* - - 62 Cb
Cresco, *Iowa* - - 132 Cd
Cressage, *England* - 14 Ba
Cresson, *Texas* - - 133 Dd
Cressy, *Victoria* - - 154 De
Crest, *France* - - 35 Hc
Crest, *Quebec* - - 121 Aa
Crestline, *Nevada* - 134 Fc
Creston, *Iowa* - - 132 Be
Creston, *Wyoming* - 135 Ka
Crestone, *Colorado* - 135 Lb
Crestview, *Florida* - 130 Ee
Creswick, *Victoria* - 154 Dd
Crete, *Nebraska* - - 132 Ae
Crete (Kríti), I., *Greece* - 71 —
Creto, *Italy* - - 62 Eb
Creus, C., *Spain* - - 39 Jb
Creuse, dep. & R., *France* 34 Da
Creusot, le, *France* - 31 Ge
Crevalcore, *Italy* - - 62 Fc
Crevillente, *Spain* - 41 Fb
Crewe, *England* - - 18 Bd
Crewkerne, *England* - 14 Be
Crianlarich, *Scotland* - 23 Dd
Criccieth, *Wales* - - 20 Bb
Crich, *England* - - 18 Cd
Crick, *England* - - 14 Cb
Crickhowell, *Wales* - 20 Cd
Cricklade, *England* - 14 Cc
Cridola, Mte., *Italy* - 63 Ga
Crieff, *Scotland* - - 23 Ed
Crikvenica, *Croatia* - 63 Jb
Crillon, Mt., *Alaska* - 125 Ng
Crimea, *U.S.S.R.* - - 75 Ef
Crimmitsschau, *Saxony* - 55 He
Cringleford, *England* - 15 Fa
Cripple Creek, *Colorado* 135 Lb
Crisana, *Romania* - - 69 Db
Crisfield, *Virginia* - 129 Gd
Cristior, *Transylvania* - 67 Hc
Cristobal, *Panama* - 140 Hf
Cristobal, B., *Mexico* - 138 Ab
Crittenden, *Arizona* - 135 Hf
Crivadia, *Romania* - 67 Jd
Crivitz, *Mecklenburg* - 55 Gb
Crna Gora, *Serbia* - 68 Gd
Crni Drim, R., *Serbia* - 70 Bb
Crni Vrh, mt., *Bosnia* - 68 Bb
Croagh Patrick, *Eire* - 25 Bb
Croatia, *Jugoslavia* - 66 Ad
Crocker, *New Mexico* - 135 Ke
Crockett, *Texas* - - 133 Ee
Crodo, *Italy* - - 62 Ca
Croix, Lac la, *Minnesota* 132 Ca
Cromane, *Eire* - - 25 Be
Cromarty & Firth, *Scot.* 23 Da
Cromer, *England* - - 19 Fe
Cromwell, *New Zealand* 159 Bf
Crook, *England* - - 21 Ed
Crooked I., *Bahamas* - 140 Cb
Crooked L., *Newfoundl'd* 120 Gb
Crooked L., *Ont.-Minn.* 132 Ca
Crooked R., *Idaho* - 136 Fc
Crooked R., *Oregon* - 136 Cc
Crookston, *Minnesota* - 132 Ab
Crookstown, *Eire* - - 25 Cf
Croom, *Eire* - - - 27 Bf
Croom, *Florida* - - 131 Mg
Cropalati, *Italy* - - 65 Cc
Cropani, *Italy* - - 65 Cd
Crosby, *England* - - 21 Dd
Crosbyton, *Texas* - - 133 Bd
Cross, R., *Nigeria* - 105 Ce
Cross Sd., *Alaska* - - 125 Ng
Crossakeel, *Eire* - - 26 Dd
Cross City, *Florida* - 131 Gf
Crossdoney, *Eire* - - 26 Cd
Crossen - - - - 55 Lc
Crossgar, *N. Ireland* - 26 Ec
Crosshaven, *Eire* - - 25 Cf
Crosskeys, *Eire* - - 27 De
Crossmoline, *Eire* - - 25 Ba
Cross Point, *Quebec* - 120 Bb
Croston, *England* - - 18 Bc
Crotone, *Italy* - - 65 Dc
Crotoy, le, *France* - - 30 Da
Crouch, R., *England* - 15 Ec
Crowell, *Texas* - - 133 Cd
Crowes, *Victoria* - - 154 De
Crowland, *England* - 15 Da
Crowle, *England* - - 19 Dc
Crowley, *Louisiana* - 130 Be
Crown Pk., *Idaho* - - 136 Fc
Crown King, *Arizona* - 135 Gd
Crown Point, *Indiana* - 129 Ab
Crown Prince Christian Land, *Greenland* - - 9 Ha
Crown Prince Frederiks Mts., *Greenland* - - 9 Fd
Crown Prince Olav Ld., *Antarctica* - - - 160 —
Crown Princess Martha Land, *Antarctica* - 160 —
Crows Foot Pass, *Montana* 136 Gc
Croydon, *England* - 15 Dd
Croydon and Goldfield, *Queensland* - - - 153 Bc
Crozet Is., *Indian Oc.* - 160 —
Crozier Chan., *N.-W.T.* 118 Ea
Crozon, *France* - - 32 Ab
Cruces, Pta., *Colombia* - 144 Ab
Crummock Water, *Eng.* 18 Aa
Cruz, *Utah* - - - 135 Gb
Cruz, La, *Colombia* - 144 Ac
Cruz, C. de, *Cuba* - 140 Bc
Cruz Alta, *Argentina* - 146 Ce
Cruz Alta, *Brazil* - - 147 Ed
Cruz del Eje, *Argentina* 146 Be
Cruzeiro do Sul, *Brazil* 145 Cc
Cruz Grande, *Chile* - 146 Ad
Cruz Grande, *Mexico* - 139 Ed
Crvenka, *Voyvodina* - 66 Ed
Crymmych Arms, *Wales* 20 Bd
Crysler, *Ontario* - - 121 Cb
Crystal Bridge, *S. Aust.* 154 Bc
Crystal Falls, *Michigan* 122 Db
Crystal River, *Florida* - 131 Gf
Crystal Springs, *Mississippi* 130 Ce
Csákvár, *Hungary* - 66 Db
Csallóköz, *Slovakia* - 66 Ca
Csanádapáca, *Hungary* - 67 Fc
Csanád Arad & Torontal, *Hungary* - - - 67 Fc
Csata, *Slovakia* - - 66 Db
Csenger, *Hungary* - - 67 Hb
Csepel I., *Hungary* - 66 Db
Csongrád, *Hungary* - 66 Ec
Csorna, *Hungary* - - 66 Cb
Csorvás, *Hungary* - - 67 Fc
Cuanza, R., *Angola* - 109 Bc
Cua-rao, *Annam* - - 95 Bf
Cuareim, *Brazil* - - 146 De
Cuatro Cienegas, *Mexico* 138 Db
Cuba - - - - 69 Hc
Cuba, *New Mexico* - 135 Kd
Cuba, *New York* - - 123 Jd
Cuba, *Portugal* - - 40 Ca
Cuba, I., *West Indies* - 140 Ab
Cubero, *New Mexico* - 135 Kd
Cucalon, Sa. de, *Spain* - 38 Dd
Cucharas, *Colorado* - 135 Lc
Cuchillo, *Argentina* - 148 Cb
Cuchillo Parado, *Mexico* 138 Cb
Cuckfield, *England* - 15 Dd
Cucuta, *Colombia* - - 144 Bb
Cudahy, *Wisconsin* - 132 Fd
Cuddalore, *Madras* - 89 Cb
Cuddapah, *Madras* - 90 Dd
Cudillero, *Spain* - - 36 Da
Cue, *W. Australia* - 152 Bd
Cuéllar, *Spain* - - 38 Ac
Cuenca, *Ecuador* - - 145 Bb
Cuenca & prov., *Spain* - 38 Cd
Cuencame, *Mexico* - 138 Dc
Cuengue, *Mozambique* - 112 Bc
Cuera, Sa. de, *Spain* - 38 Aa
Cuernavaca, *Mexico* - 139 Ed
Cuervo, *New Mexico* - 135 Ld
Cuevas de Vera, *Spain* - 41 Ec
Cuevo, *Bolivia* - - 146 Cc
Cuglieri, *Sardinia* - - 64 Hf
Cuillin Hills, *Scotland* - 22 Bb
Cuise, *France* - - 31 Fb
Culcairn, *New S. Wales* 155 Ed
Culdaff, *Eire* - - 26 Ca
Culdesac, *Idaho* - - 136 Eb
Culebra, G. de la, *Costa Rica* - - - 140 Fe
Culebra, I., *Puerto Rico* 140 Kg
Culebra, Sierra de la, *Spain* - - - 36 Dc
Culgoa, R., *N. S. Wales-Queensland* - - 155 Ea
Culham Inlet, *W. Aust.* 152 Ce
Culiacan, *Mexico* - - 138 Cc
Culiacan, R., *Mexico* - 138 Cb
Culion, I., *Philippines* - 99 Ea
Culla, *Spain* - - - 39 Ed
Cullar de Baza, *Spain* - 41 Da
Cullen, *Scotland* - - 23 Fc
Cullera and C., *Spain* - 41 Fa
Cullman, *Alabama* - 130 Ec
Cullompton, *England* - 14 Ae
Cully, *Switzerland* - 42 Cd
Culpeper, *Virginia* - 129 Ec
Cults, *Scotland* - - 23 Fb
Culverden, *New Zealand* 159 De
Cumana, *Venezuela* - 144 Da
Cumaria, *Peru* - - 145 Cc
Cu-mau, *Cochin-China* - 95 Ch
Cumaya Mts., *California* 134 Dd
Cumberland, *Br. Columbia* 124 De
Cumberland, *Maryland* - 129 Ec
Cumberland, *Ontario* - 121 Cb
Cumberland, *Virginia* - 129 Ed
Cumberland, *Wisconsin* 132 Dc
Cumberland, co., *Eng.* - 21 Cd
Cumberland I., *Georgia* 131 He
Cumberland Is., *Queensl'd* 153 Cd
Cumberland Mts., *Tennes.* 131 Gb
Cumberland Pen. & Sd., *N.-W. Terr.* - - 119 Qc
Cumberland Plateau, *Tennessee* - - - 130 Fc
Cumberland R., *Kentucky* 130 Db
Cumbernauld, *Scotland* - 23 Ee
Cumbrian Mts., *England* 18 Ab
Cumbum, *Madras* - - 90 Dd
Cummertrees, *Scotland* - 21 Cd
Cummington, *Mass.* - 128 Bb
Cummins, *S. Australia* - 154 Ac
Cummins Ra., *W. Aust.* 152 Db
Cumnock, *New S. Wales* 155 Fc
Cumnock, *Scotland* - 21 Bc
Cumpas, *Mexico* - - 138 Ca
Cumuripa, *Mexico* - 138 Cb
Cuncudgerie Hill, *W. Australia* - - 152 Cc
Cundinamarca, dep., *Colombia* - - - 144 Bc
Cuneo, *Italy* - - - 62 Bc
Cunnamulla, *Queensland* 153 Ce
Cupar, *Scotland* - - 23 Fd
Cupica & B. de, *Colombia* 144 Ab
Çupley, *Florida* - - 130 Fe
Cuprija, *Serbia* - - 68 Gc
Cura, *Venezuela* - - 144 Ca
Curaça, *Brazil* - - 143 Gd
Curaçao I., *Caribbean Sea* 137 Ec
Curaray and R., *Peru* - 145 Cb
Curati, *Ethiopia* - - 108 Dd
Curdworth, *England* - 14 Ca
Curepto, *Chile* - - 148 Bb
Curiapo, *Venezuela* - 144 Db
Curico and prov., *Chile* 146 Ae
Curiplaya, *Colombia* - 144 Ac
Curityba, *Brazil* - - 147 Ed
Curitybanos, *Brazil* - 147 Ed
Curnamona, *S. Aust.* - 154 Bb
Curraes Novos, *Brazil* - 143 Gd
Curragh, The, *Eire* - 27 De
Curralinho, *Brazil* - 143 Dc
Curraun Pen., *Eire* - 25 Bb
Currie, *Minnesota* - - 132 Bc
Currie, *Scotland* - - 23 Ee
Currie, Mt., *Cape Prov.* 115 He
Currituck Sd., *N. Carolina* 131 Kb
Curry, *Alaska* - - 125 Ke
Curtea de Arges, *Romania* 67 Kd
Curtis, *Oklahoma* - - 133 Cb
Curtis, *Queensland* - 153 Dd

De Kalb, *Mississippi* - 130 Dd
Dekese, *Belg. Congo* - 109 Db
De Keur, *Cape Prov.* - 114 Cf
Dekina, *Nigeria* - 105 Cd
Dekoa, *Fr. Eq. Africa* - 105 Ed
Dekoven, *Kentucky* - 130 Db
Deksa, *U.S.S.R.* - 74 Ec
Delagoa B., *Mozambique* 115 Kb
De Lamar, *Idaho* - 136 Ed
Delamar, *Nevada* - 134 Fc
De Land, *Florida* - 131 Hf
Delano, *California* - 134 Dd
Delareyville, *Transvaal* 115 Fc
Delavan, *Wisconsin* - 132 Ed
Delaware, *Ohio* - 129 Cb
Delaware B., *Delaware-New Jersey* - 129 Gc
Delaware, state and R., *U.S.A.* - 127 Kc
Delaware City, *Delaware* 129 Gc
Delbrück, *Prussia* - 54 Dd
Delegete, *New S. Wales* 155 Fd
Délélé, *Fr. Eq. Africa* - 109 Ba
Delemont, *Switzerland* - 42 Db
Delft, *Holland* - 29 Cb
Delft I., *Ceylon* - 89 Cc
Delfzijl, *Holland* - 29 Ea
Delgado, C., *It. Somal.* - 108 Fd
Delgado, C., *Mozambique* 112 Db
Delgo, *A.-E. Sudan* - 108 Ba
Delhi, *Colorado* - 135 Mc
Delhi, *New York* - 123 Ld
Delhi (Dilli), *Timor I., Netherlands Indies* - 99 Ge
Delhi, *India* - 83 Gd
Deliceto, *Italy* - 64 Fb
Delitzsch, *Prussia* - 55 Hd
Dellenhaugh, Mt., *Arizona* 134 Gc
Dell Rapids, *S. Dakota* - 132 Ad
Dellys, *Algeria* - 103 Fa
Del Mar, *California* - 134 Ee
Delmenhorst, *Oldenburg* 54 Db
Del Monte, *California* - 134 Bc
Delnice, *Croatia* - 63 Jb
Del Norte, *Colorado* - 135 Kc
De Long Mts., *Alaska* - 125 Gb
Deloraine, *Tasmania* - 155 Jg
Delphi, *Indiana* - 129 Ab
Delphos, *Kansas* - 133 Da
Delphos, *Ohio* - 129 Bb
Delray, *Florida* - 131 Nh
Del Rio, *Mexico* - 138 Db
Del Rio, *Texas* - 133 Bf
Delta, *California* - 134 Ba
Delta, *Colorado* - 135 Jb
Delta, *Louisiana* - 130 Cd
Delta, *Missouri* - 130 Db
Delta, terr., *Venezuela* - 144 Db
Delungra, *New S. Wales* 155 Ga
Delvinákion, *Greece* - 70 Bd
Delvine, *Albania* - 70 Bd
Delwara, *Rajputana* - 85 Db
Demanda, Sa. de la, *Spain* 38 Bb
Demarcation B. and Pt., *Alaska* - 125 Mb
Demavend, mt., *Persia* - 79 Fb
Demba, *Belg. Congo* - 109 Dc
Demchok, *Tibet* - 84 Dd
Deming, *New Mexico* - 135 Je
Demirji Dagh, *Turkey* - 78 Ab
Demir Kapija, *Serbia* - 70 Db
Demirköy, *Turkey* - 72 Ea
Demmin, *Prussia* - 55 Hb
Demnat, *Morocco* - 103 Oj
Demopolis, *Alabama* - 130 Ed
Dempo, Mt., *Sumatra* - 98 Bd
Denain, *France* - 31 Fa
Denair, *California* - 134 Cc
Denali, *Alaska* - 125 Ke
Denan, *Uzbek* - 84 Bc
Denbigh and co., *Wales* 20 Ca
Dender, R., *Belgium* - 29 Bd
Dendura, *Libya* - 106 Ee
Denemek, *Persia* - 79 Fb
Denham, *New S. Wales* 155 Gb
Denham Ra., *Queensland* 153 Cd
Denham Sd., *W. Aust.* - 152 Ad
Denia, *Spain* - 41 Gb
Deniliquin, *New S. Wales* 154 Ed
Denison, *Iowa* - 132 Bd
Denison, *Texas* - 133 Dd
Denison, *W. Australia* - 152 Ad
Denizli, *Turkey* - 78 Ab
Denmark, *S. Carolina* - 131 Hd
Denmark, *W. Australia* 152 Be
Denmark, *W. Europe* - 44 Bj
Denmark Str., *Greenland* 9 Fe
Denno, *Italy* - 62 Ea
Denny, *Scotland* - 23 Ed
Den Pasar, *Bali I., N.I.* 99 Ee
Denta, *Romania* - 67 Gd
Dent Blanche, *Switz.* - 42 Ed
Denton, *Maryland* - 129 Gc
Denton & R., *Texas* - 133 Dd
D'Entrecasteaux Is., *New Guinea* - 156 Ec
D'Entrecasteaux Pt., *W. Australia* - 150 Ae
Denver, *Colorado* - 135 Lb
Deoband, *United Provs.* 83 Gd
Deobhog, *Cent. Provs.* - 91 Fb
Deodar, *Western India* - 85 Cb
Deodrug, *Hyderabad* - 90 Cc
Deogarh, *Central Provs.* 86 Ce
Deogarh, *Eastern States* 87 Fe
Deogarh Pk., *Eastern States* 86 Ed
Deoghar, *Bihar* - 87 Gc
Deoli, *Ajmer-Merwara* - 85 Eb
Deoli, *Central Provs.* - 86 Ce
Deolia, *Rajputana* - 85 Eb
Deori, *Central Provs.* - 86 Cd
De Pere, *Wisconsin* - 132 Ec
Deposit, *New York* - 123 Ld
Depot Harbour, *Ontario* 123 Hc
Deptford, *England* - 14 Cd
De Queen, *Arkansas* - 130 Ad
De Quincy, *Louisiana* - 130 Be
Dera, *Trans-Jordan* - 78 Cc
Dera Bugti, *Baluchistan* 82 Cd
Dera Fatah Khan, *Punjab* 82 Dc
Dera Ghazi Khan, *Punjab* 82 Dc
Dera Ismail Khan and dist., *N.-W.F.P.* - 82 Dc
Derajat, *Punjab* - 82 Dc
Dera Nanak, *Punjab* - 83 Fb
Derbent, *U.S.S.R.* - 75 Hg
Derbent, *Uzbek* - 84 Bc
Derby, *Connecticut* - 128 Bc
Derby, *W. Australia* - 152 Cb
Derby and co., *England* 18 Ce
Derecske, *Hungary* - 67 Gb
Derenberg, *Prussia* - 54 Fd
Dereva, *U.S.S.R.* - 48 Lg
Derg, L., *Eire* - 27 Bf
De Ridder, *Louisiana* - 130 Be
Derisun, *China* - 94 Ca
Dermott, *Arkansas* - 130 Cd
Derna & prov., *Libya* - 106 Db
Derniere, I., *Louisiana* - 130 Cf
Derravaragh, L., *Eire* - 26 Cd
Derrynasaggart Mts., *Eire* 25 Bf
Derryveagh Mts., *Eire* - 26 Bb
Dersida Mica, *Transylva.* 67 Hb
Deru, *Ethiopia* - 108 Cc
Derudeb, *A.-E. Sudan* - 108 Cb
De Rust, *Cape Prov.* - 114 Ef
Deruta, *Italy* - 63 Ge
Derval, *France* - 32 Dc
Dervéni, *Greece* - 71 De
Derventa, *Bosnia* - 68 Cb
Derviziana, *Greece* - 70 Bd
Derwent R., *Cumberland, England* - 18 Aa
Derwent, R., *Derby, Eng.* 18 Cd
Derwent, R., *Yorks, Eng.* 19 Db
Derwent Water, *England* 18 Aa
Desaguadero, R., *Argent.* 146 Be
Desaguadero, R., *Bolivia* 146 Bb
Des Arc, *Arkansas* - 130 Cc
Desbordesville, *Fr. Eq. Africa* - 109 Ca
Desborough, *England* - 15 Db
Descalvados, *Brazil* - 146 Db
Deschaillons, *Quebec* - 121 Da
Deschutes, R., *Oregon* - 136 Cc
Desenzano, *Italy* - 62 Eb
Deseret, *Utah* - 135 Gb
Deseronto, *Ontario* - 121 Bb
Desert, *New Mexico* - 135 Ke
Desert Ra. & Val., *Nevada* 134 Fc
Deshamboult L., *Saskatch.* 124 Hd
Deshnok, *Rajputana* - 83 Ee
Desierto de las Palmas, *Spain* - 39 Ed
De Smet, *Montana* - 136 Fb
Des Moines, *New Mexico* 135 Mc
Des Moines & R., *Iowa* 132 Ce
Desmond, Mt., *W. Aust.* 152 Ce
Desolacion, I., *Chile* - 148 Ae
Desordem, Sa. da, *Brazil* 143 Ed
De Soto, *Missouri* - 130 Ca
Despeñaperros, Pto. de, *Spain* - 41 Cb
Dessau, *Anhalt* - 55 Hd
Dessie, *Ethiopia* - 108 Cc
Destruction I., *Washing'n* 136 Ab
Desyres, *France* - 30 Da
Deta, *Romania* - 67 Gd
Detmold, *Lippe* - 54 Dd
Detroit, *Michigan* - 122 Gd
Detroit Lakes, *Minnesota* 132 Bb
Dett, *S. Rhodesia* - 113 Bb
Dettelbach, *Bavaria* - 58 Eb
Dettifos, *Iceland* - 52 Eb
Detva, *Slovakia* - 66 Ea
Deutsch Eylau - 56 Dc
Deutsch Krone - 56 Ac
Deutschlandsberg, *Austria* 59 Ke
Deux Rivières, *Ontario* - 121 Aa
Deux-Sevres, dep., *France* 32 Ed
Deva, *Romania* - 67 Hd
Deva, *Spain* - 38 Ca
Devakottai, *Madras* - 89 Cc
Devarkonda, *Hyderabad* 90 Dc
Devdelija, *Serbia* - 70 Db
Deventer, *Holland* - 29 Eb
Devikot, *Rajputana* - 82 De
Devil's Lake, *N. Dakota* 126 Fa
Devin, *Bulgaria* - 70 Fb
Devipatam, *Madras* - 89 Cc
Devizes, *England* - 14 Cd
Devoluy, *France* - 35 Hc
Devon, co., *England* - 17 Cb
Devon I., *N.-W. Terr.* - 119 Ma
Devondale, *Cape Prov.* - 115 Fc
Devonport, *England* - 17 Bc
Devonport, *New Zealand* 158 Eb
Devonport, *Tasmania* - 155 Jg
Devoys Pk., *New Mexico* 135 Mc
Devrukh, *Bombay* - 90 Ac
Dewanganj, *Bengal* - 88 Bb
Dewangiri, *Assam* - 88 Ca
Dewas, *Central India* - 86 Bd
Dewetsdorp, *O.F.S.* - 115 Gd
De Witt, *Arkansas* - 130 Cc
Dewitt, *Iowa* - 132 De
Dewsbury, *England* - 18 Cc
Dexter, *Missouri* - 130 Cb
Dexter, *New Mexico* - 135 Le
Dhaba (Ziba), *Arabia* - 78 Cd
Dhabban, *Iraq* - 78 Dc
Dháfni, *Greece* - 71 Cf
Dhala, *Aden* - 78 Lh
Dhalbhum, *Bihar* - 87 Gd
Dhaleswari R., *Assam* - 88 Db
Dhamasi, *Greece* - 70 Dd
Dhampur, *United Provs.* 83 Hd
Dhamra, *Orissa* - 87 Ge
Dhamtari, *Central Provs.* 86 De
Dhandhuka, *Bombay* - 85 Cc
Dhandi, *Sind* - 85 Bb
Dhang Ra., *Nepal* - 86 Da
Dhangain, *Bihar* - 87 Fc
Dhangarhi, *Nepal* - 86 Da
Dhank, *Oman* - 79 Ge
Dhankuta, *Nepal* - 87 Gb
Dhansua, *Central Provs.* 86 De
Dhanushkodi, *Madras* - 89 Cc
Dhar, *Central India* - 85 Ec
Dharampur, *Gujarat States* 90 Aa
Dharapuram, *Madras* - 89 Bb
Dharaseo, *Hyderabad* - 90 Cb
Dhariya, *Arabia* - 78 De
Dharmapuri, *Madras* - 89 Ca
Dharmavaram, *Madras* - 90 Cd
Dharmjaygarh (Rabkob), *Eastern States* - 87 Ed
Dharmkot, *Punjab* - 83 Fc
Dharmsala, *Punjab* - 83 Gb
Dharnaoda, *Gwalior* - 86 Bc
Dharwar, *Bombay* - 90 Bd
Dharwas, *Punjab States* 83 Gb
Dhasa, *Western India* - 85 Cd
Dhat al-Hajj, *Arabia* - 78 Cd
Dhaulagiri, mt., *Nepal* 87 Ea
Dhebar L., *Rajputana* - 85 Eb
Dhélfi (Dhírfis), mts., *Greece* - 71 Ee
Dhelfoí, *Greece* - 71 De
Dhenkanal, *Eastern States* 87 Fe
Dhesfína, *Greece* - 71 De
Dheskáti, *Greece* - 70 Cd
Dhía (Día), *Crete* - 71 Jj
Dhiakópi, *Greece* - 71 De
Dhiapória Is., *Greece* - 71 Ef
Dhiavolítsi, *Greece* - 71 Cf
Dhiban, *Trans-Jordan* - 80 De
Dhídhimoi, I., *Greece* - 71 Ef
Dhídhimon, mt., *Greece* 71 Ef
Dhíkti Ori (Lasithi Mts.), *Crete* - 71 Jj
Dhimitsana, *Greece* - 71 Df
Dhing, *Assam* - 88 Da
Dhirang Dzong, *Assam* - 88 Da
Dhírfis (Dhélfi), *Greece* - 71 Ee
Dhístos, L., *Greece* - 71 Fe
Dhístraton, *Greece* - 70 Cc
Dhola, *Western India* - 85 Cd
Dholera, *Bombay* - 85 Dc
Dholka, *Bombay* - 85 Dc
Dholpur, *Rajputana* - 83 Ge
Dhomokós, *Greece* - 71 Dd
Dhond, *Bombay* - 90 Bb
Dhoraji, *Western India* - 85 Cd
Dhouka, *Greece* - 71 Cf
Dhoxáton, *Greece* - 70 Fb
Dhragonera Is., *Greece* - 71 Be
Dhrangadhra, *Western India* 85 Cc
Dhrápanon, C., *Crete* - 71 Hj
Dhrol, *Western India* - 85 Cc
Dhrovjan, *Albania* - 70 Bd
Dhubri, *Assam* - 88 Ca
Dhudial, *Punjab* - 82 Eb
Dhulia, *Bombay* - 90 Ba
Dhuran, *Yemen* - 78 Lh
Dhurwai, *Central India* - 86 Cc
Día (Dhía), *Crete* - 71 Jj
Diable, I. du (Devils I.), *Fr. Guiana* - 142 Da
Diablerets, *Switzerland* - 42 Dd
Diablo Ra., *New Mexico* 135 Je
Diaha *Rio de Oro* - 104 Ba
Dialakoro, *Fr. W. Africa* 104 Cd
Diamante, *Argentina* - 146 Ce
Diamantina, *Matto Grosso, Brazil* - 142 Ce
Diamantina, *Minas Geraes, Brazil* - 147 Gb
Diamond, *Nevada* - 134 Eb
Diamond L., *Oregon* - 136 Bd
Diamond Pk., *Oregon* - 136 Bd
Diamond Ra., *Nevada* - 134 Fb
Diamond Harbour, *Bengal* 88 Bc
Diamond Springs, *Idaho* 136 Ec
Diamu, *Fr. W. Africa* - 104 Bd
Diana, *New York* - 128 Aa
Diana, *Wyoming* - 135 Ka
Diano Marina, *Italy* 62 Bd
Diapaga, *Fr. W. Africa* 105 Bc
Dibah, *Arabia* - 79 Gd
Dibai, *Arabia* - 79 Gd
Dibbah, Jeb., *Arabia* - 78 Cd
Dibbin, *Trans-Jordan* - 80 Dc
Dibi, *Fr. Eq. Africa* - 105 Dd
Dibrugarh, *Assam* - 88 Ea
Dicio Sânmartin, *Transyl.* 67 Kc
Dickens, *Texas* - 133 Bd
Dickinson, *N. Dakota* - 126 Ea
Dickinson, *Ontario* - 121 Cb
Dickson, *Tennessee* - 130 Eb
Dickson I., *U.S.S.R.* - 76 Hb
Didcot, *England* - 14 Cc
Didikhaosu, *Manchuria* - 96 Bb
Didimotikhon (Dimotika), *Greece* - 72 Da
Didwana, *Rajputana* - 83 Fe
Die, *France* - 35 Hc
Die, I., *Prussia* - 54 Da
Dieburg, *Hesse* - 58 Cb
Diego Garcia, *Indian Oc.* 73 Kj
Die Hitzacker, *Prussia* - 54 Fb
Diepholz, *Prussia* - 54 Dc
Dieppe, *France* - 30 Cb
Diest, *Belgium* - 29 Dd
Dietfurt, *Bavaria* - 59 Fb
Dietikon, *Switzerland* - 43 Fb
Dietkorom, *Fr. W. Afr.* 105 Dc
Dieuze, *France* - 31 Jc
Diezma, *Spain* - 41 Cc
Difuma, *Belg. Congo* - 109 Eb
Difunda, *Belgian Congo* 109 Dc
Dig, *Rajputana* - 83 Ge
Digboi, *Assam* - 88 Ea
Digby, *Nova Scotia* - 120 Bd
Digby Neck, *Nova Scotia* 120 Bd
Dighton, *Kansas* - 133 Ba
Dignano d'I. - 63 Hc
Digne, *France* - 33 Ba
Digoel R., *New Guinea* - 156 Cc
Digoin, *France* - 35 Fa
Dihmit, *Egypt* - 106 Mh
Dijon, *France* - 31 Hd
Dikabi, *Bechuanaland* - 113 Bd
Dikaia, *Greece* - 72 Da
Dikanäs, *Sweden* - 48 Ad
Dikgatlon, *Cape Prov.* - 114 Ec
Dikwa, *Nigeria* - 105 Dc
Dila, *Ethiopia* - 108 Dd
Dilam, *Arabia* - 79 Ee
Dilemba, *Belg. Congo* - 109 Cc
Dilia, *New Mexico* - 135 Ld
Dillenburg, *Prussia* - 54 De
Dilling, *A.-E. Sudan* - 108 Ac
Dillingen, *Bavaria* - 58 Ec
Dillingham, *Alaska* - 125 Gg
Dillon, *Colorado* - 135 Kb
Dillon, *Montana* - 136 Gc
Dillon, *New Mexico* - 135 Lc
Dillon, *S. Carolina* - 131 Jc
Dilman, *Persia* - 78 Db
Dilolo, *Belg. Congo* - 109 Dd
Dilwyn, *England* - 14 Bb
Dimapur, *Assam* - 88 Db
Dimbokro, *Fr. W. Africa* 104 Ce
Dimboola, *Victoria* - 154 Cd
Dimbula, *Ceylon* - 89 Dd
Dimla, *Bengal* - 88 Ba
Dimmitt, *Texas* - 133 Ac
Dimotika (Didimotikhon), *Greece* - 72 Da
Dinagat, I., *Philippines* 99 Ga
Dinajpur, *Bengal* - 88 Bb
Dinan, *France* - 32 Cb
Dinanagar, *Punjab* - 83 Fb
Dinant, *Belgium* - 29 Cd
Dinapore, *Bihar* - 87 Fc
Dinard, *France* - 32 Cb
Dinaric Alps, *Jugoslavia* 69 Bc
Dinas Mawddwy, *Wales* 20 Cb
Dinder, R., *A.-E. Sudan* 108 Bc
Dindi R., *Hyderabad* - 90 Dc
Dindigul, *Madras* - 89 Bb
Dindira, *Mozambique* - 113 Fc
Dindori, *Central Provs.* - 86 Dd
Diner, *Turkey* - 78 Bb
Dingalan B., *Philippines* 95 Ff
Dingle and B., *Eire* - 25 Ae
Dingo, *Queensland* - 153 Cd
Dinguiraye, *Fr. W. Afr.* 104 Bd
Dingwall, *Scotland* - 23 Da
Dinkelsbuhl, *Bavaria* - 58 Eb
Dinorwic, *Ontario* - 122 Ba
Dinslaken, *Prussia* - 54 Bd
Dinsor, *Ital. Somaliland* 108 Gf
Diombo, Mt., *Fr. Eq. Afr.* 105 Ec
Diorbivol, *Fr. W. Africa* 104 Bc
Diosgyor, *Hungary* - 67 Fa
Diouna, *Fr. Eq. Africa* - 105 Fb
Diourbel, *Fr. W. Africa* 104 Ad
Dipalpur, *Punjab* - 83 Ec
Dipton, *New Zealand* - 159 Bf
Diquis R., *Costa Rica* - 140 Gf
Dir, *N.-W.F.P.* - 82 Da
Dirdal, *Norway* - 47 Cf
Direction, C., *Queensland* 153 Bb
Diredawa, *Ethiopia* - 108 Dd
Diriamba, *Nicaragua* - 140 Fe
Dirjaj, *Aden* - 78 Mh
Dirk Hartog I., *W. Aust.* 152 Ad
Dirranbandi, *Queensland* 153 Ce
Dirri, *Ital. Somaliland* - 108 Ee
Disappointment, C., *Washington* - 136 Ab
Disappointment, L., *W. Australia* - 152 Cc
Disaster B., *New S. Wales* 155 Gd
Disaster Pk., *Nevada* - 134 Da
Disaster Pk., *Oregon* - 136 Dd
Discord C., *Greenland* - 9 Ee
Discovery B., *Victoria* - 154 Ce
Disentis, *Switzerland* - 43 Gc
Disgrazia, *Italy* - 62 Da
Dishna, *Egypt* - 107 Je
Diski, *Fr. W. Africa* - 104 Bc
Disko I. & B., *Greenland* 9 Dd
Dismal Swamp, *Virginia* 129 Fd
Diss, *England* - 15 Fb
Disûq, *Egypt* - 107 Hc
Dithmarschen, *Prussia* - 54 Ea
Dittaino, R., *Sicily* - 65 Hg
Ditton Priors, *England* - 14 Ba
Diu (Portuguese), *Western India* - 85 Cd
Diver, *Ontario* - 123 Jb
Divide, *Montana* - 136 Gc
Divin, *Slovakia* - 66 Ea
Diviso, *Colombia* - 144 Ac
Divnoe, *U.S.S.R.* - 75 Gf
Divrigi, *Turkey* - 78 Cb
Diwan Chah, *Persia* - 79 Hc
Diwanganj, *Bengal* - 88 Cc
Diwaniya, *Iraq* - 78 Dc
Dix, *Quebec* - 123 Ka
Dixcove, *Gold Coast* - 104 Df
Dixie, *Idaho* - 136 Fc
Dixmude, *Belgium* - 29 Ac
Dixon, *California* - 134 Cb
Dixon, *Illinois* - 132 Ee
Dixon, *Kentucky* - 130 Eb
Dixon, *Montana* - 136 Fb
Dixon, *Wyoming* - 135 Ka
Dixon Entrance, *Br. Col.* 124 Cd
Dixville, *Quebec* - 121 Eb
Diyarbekir, *Turkey* - 78 Db
Dizak, *Persia* - 79 Hd
Dizful, *Persia* - 79 Ec
Djado, *Fr. W. Africa* - 105 Da
Djafou, *Algeria* - 102 Ff
Djaid, *Arabia* - 79 Gd
Djailolo, *Halmahera, N.I.* 99 Gc
Djalica e Lumës, *Albania* 70 Bb
Djalon, *Fr. W. Africa* - 104 Bd
Djambi, *Sumatra* - 98 Bd
Djapara, *Java* - 98 De
Djébiga, *Fr. W. Africa* - 104 Ed
Djedeida, *Tunisia* - 103 Ja
Djelfa, *Algeria* - 103 Fb
Djemlé, *Syria* - 80 Db
Djemmel, *Tunisia* - 103 Kb
Djemna, *Tunisia* - 103 Jc

Dunchurch, England - 14 Cb
Duncormick, Eire - - 27 Dg
Dundaga, Latvia - - 49 Bc
Dundalk, Eire - - 26 Dc
Dundalk B., Eire - - 26 Dd
Dundari, S. Rhodesia - 113 Ab
Dundas, Ontario - - 123 Hd
Dundas, Tasmania - 155 Jg
Dundas, W. Australia - 152 Ce
Dundas Goldfield, W. Aust. 152Ce
Dundas Harbour, N.-W. Terr. - - 119 Mb
Dundee, Natal - - 115 Jd
Dundee, Quebec - - 121 Cb
Dundee, Scotland - - 23 Ed
Dundoo, Queensland - 153 Be
Dundrum, Eire - - 27 De
Dundrum & B., N. Ire. 26 Ec
Dundu, Angola - - 109 Dc
Dunduma, Tangany. Terr. 111 Eg
Dundwa Ra., Nepal - 87 Eb
Dunedin, New Zealand - 159 Cf
Dunfermline, Scotland - 23 Ed
Dungannon, N. Ireland 26 Db
Dungarpur, Rajputana - 85 Dc
Dungarvan & Harb., Eire 27 Cg
Dungbure Ra., Tibet - 84 Ec
Dungeness, England - 15 Ee
Dungeness, Pta., Argent. 148 Ce
Dungiven, N. Ireland - 26 Db
Dungloe, Eire - - 26 Bb
Dungog, New S. Wales 155 Gb
Dungunab, A.-E. Sudan 108 Ca
Dunju, Belg. Congo - 109 Ea
Dunk I., Queensland - 153 Cc
Dunkeld, Queensland - 153 Ce
Dunkeld, Scotland - 23 Ec
Dunkerrin, Eire - - 27 Cf
Dunkirk, England - 14 Bc
Dunkirk, France - - 30 Ea
Dunkirk, Indiana - - 129 Bb
Dunkirk, New York - 123 Jd
Dunkur, Ethiopia - - 108 Cc
Dunkwa, Gold Coast - 104 De
Dun Laoghaire (Kingstown), Eire - - 27 De
Dunlap, Iowa - - 132 Be
Dunlap, Tennessee - - 130 Fc
Dunlavin, Eire - - 27 De
Dunleer, Eire - - 26 Dd
Dunmanus & B., Eire - 25 Bf
Dunmanway, Eire - - 25 Bf
Dunmore, Eire - - 26 Bd
Dunmore, Pennsylvania 129 Gb
Dunmow, England - 15 Ec
Dunn, N. Carolina - 131 Jc
Dunnellon, Florida - 131 Mg
Dunnet Hd. & B., Scot. 24 Ed
Dunnigan, California - 134 Bb
Dunnington, England - 14 Cb
Dunoon, Scotland - - 22 Ce
Dunowen, Eire - - 25 Cf
Duns, Scotland - - 23 Fe
Dunsmuir, California - 134 Ba
Dunstable, England - 15 Dc
Dunster, England - - 14 Ad
Dunston, England - 15 Fa
Dun-sur-Auron, France - 30 Ee
Dun-sur-Meuse, France 31 Hb
Dunvegan, Scotland - 22 Bb
Dunwich, England - 15 Fb
Duperre Is., Nether. Indies 98 Cc
Dupleix, Algeria - - 102 Ea
Dupnitza, Bulgaria - 69 Ed
Dupulan, Persia - - 79 Fc
Dupuyer, Montana - 136 Ga
Du Quoin, Illinois - 130 Da
Duque de Bragança, Angola - - 109 Cc
Duque de York, I., Chile 148 Ae
Dura, Palestine - - 80 Be
Durak, Turkey - - 72 Fc
Durakovac, Montenegro 68 Fd
Durance R., France - 35 Jc
Durand, Wisconsin - 132 Cc
Durango, Colorado - 135 Kc
Durango, Spain - - 38 Ca
Durango & state, Mexico 138 Dc
Durant, Mississippi - 130 Cd
Durazno & dep., Uruguay 146 De
Durazzo (Durrës), Albania 70 Ab
Durazzo, B. of, Albania 70 Ab
Durban, Natal - - 115 Jd
Durbe, Latvia - - 49 Ac
Durdevac, Croatia - 66 Cc
Durdureh, Brit. Somalil'd 108 Ec
Düren, Prussia - - 54 Be
Durga Str., New Guinea 156 Bc
Durgapur, Bengal - 88 Cb
Durham, N. Carolina - 131 Jc
Durham, Ontario - - 121 Ab
Durham & co., England 21 Ed
Durhamville, New York 128 Ab
Durlach, Baden - - 58 Cc
Durmitor, mt., Montenegro 68 Dc
Durness & Kyle of, Scot. 24 Dd
Durnford, Pta., Rio de Oro 104 Ab
Durrant, Oklahoma - 133 Dd
Durrës (Durazzo), Albania 70 Ab
Durrow, Eire - - 27 Cf
Dursey I., Eire - - 25 Af
Dursley, England - - 14 Bc
Dursunbey, Turkey - 72 Fc
Durtal, France - - 30 Bd
Duruelo, Spain - - 38 Cc
Duruh, Persia - - 79 Hc
Durukhsh, Persia - - 79 Gc
D'Urville I., New Zealand 159 Dd
Dush, Egypt - - - 107 Hf
Dushar, Albania - - 70 Bc
Dusnok, Hungary - - 66 Dc
Dusse-Alin, U.S.S.R. - 96 Ea
Dussejour, C., W. Aust. 152 Da
Dusseldorf, Prussia - 54 Bd
Dutchflat, California - 134 Cb
Dutch Guiana (Surinam), S. America - - 141 Db
Dutch Harbor, Aleutian Is. 125 Ej
Duthumi, Tangan. Terr. 111 Eg
Dutsi, Nigeria - - 105 Cc
Dutton Mt., Utah - - 135 Gb
Duveyrier, Algeria - 102 Dc
Duvivier, Algeria - - 103 Ha
Duvno, Bosnia - - 68 Cc
Duwara, Palestine - - 80 Da
Duxbury, Massachusetts 128 Cd
Duxford, England - - 15 Eb
Duzica, Croatia - - 66 Bd
Dvina R., White Russia 74 Dd
Dvina (Daugava), R., Latvia - - - 49 Cc
Dvinsk (Daugavpils), Latvia - - - 49 Dd
Dvinskaya Gulf, U.S.S.R. 74 Fb
Dvor, Croatia - - 66 Bd
Dwarka, Baroda - - 85 Bc
Dwars River, Transvaal 113 Cd
Dwyka, Cape Prov. - 114 Df
Dyaul, I., Bismarck Arch. 156 Eb
Dybvad, Denmark - - 45 Da
Dyce, Scotland - - 23 Fb
Dyer B., N.-W. Terr. - 118 Ea
Dyer I., Cape Prov. - 114 Cg
Dyersburg, Tennessee - 130 Db
Dyhernfurth - - - 57 Bb
Dyke L., Labrador - 119 Qf
Dyke Acland B., New Guinea - - - 156 Dc
Dymchurch, England - 15 Fd
Dymock, England - - 14 Bc
Dysart, Scotland - - 23 Ed
Džepa, Serbia - - 69 Ed
Dzerzhinsk, U.S.S.R. - 74 Gd
Dzhalingda, Manchuria 96 Ca
Dzhalyal Abad, Kirghiz 84 Cb
Dzhankoi, Crimea - - 75 Ef
Dzhizak, Uzbek - - 84 Bb
Dzhlfa, Nakhichevan - 75 Hh
Dzhubga, U.S.S.R. - 75 Fg
Dzhugdzhur Mts., U.S.S.R. - - - 76 Od
Dzhusaly, Kazak - - 75 Je
Działdowo, Poland - 60 Eb
Działoszyce, Poland - 57 Fc
Działoszyn, Poland - 57 Db
Dziedzice, Poland - - 57 Ed
Dzioua, Algeria - - 103 Gc
Dzungaria, Sinkiang - 84 Fa
Eagar, Arizona - - 135 Jd
Eagle, Alaska - - 125 Ld
Eagle, Colorado - - 135 Kb
Eagle L., Ontario - - 122 Ba
Eagle Ls., Maine - - 120 Ac
Eagle Pk., Arizona - 135 Hc
Eagle Pk., California - 134 Ca
Eagle Grove, Iowa - 132 Bd
Eaglehawk, Victoria - 154 Dd
Eagle Lake, Texas - 133 Df
Eagle Peak, Idaho - 136 Fb
Eagle River, Michigan - 122 Db
Eagle River, Wisconsin 132 Ec
Eales, Mt., Newfoundland 120 Gb
Ealing, England - - 15 Dc
Eardisland, England - 14 Bb
Earith, England - - 15 Db
Earlham, New Mexico - 135 Ke
Earlington, Kentucky - 130 Eb
Earls Colne, England - 15 Ec
Earl Shilton, England - 14 Ca
Earl Soham, England - 15 Fb
Earlston, Scotland - - 21 Db
Earlstown, England - 18 Bd
Earlville, New York - 128 Ab
Earn, L., Scotland - 23 Dd
Earn, R., Scotland - 23 Ed
Earsdon, England - - 21 Ec
Easingwold, England - 18 Cb
Easky, Eire - - - 26 Bc
East C., New Zealand - 158 Gb
East Pt., Pr. Edward I. 120 Ec
East Aurora, New York 123 Jd
Eastbourne, England - 15 Ee
Eastbourne, New Zealand 159 Ed
East Brent, England - 14 Bd
East Chicago, Indiana - 129 Ab
East China Sea, China-Japan - - - 93 Ed
East Cleveland, Ohio - 129 Db
East Dereham, England 15 Ea
Easter I., Pacific Oc. - 149 Ph
Eastern Div., W. Aust. 152 Cd
Eastern Gobi, Manchuria 96 Cc
Eastern Group, W. Aust. 152 Ce
Eastern Prov., Ceylon - 89 Dd
Eastern States, India - 81 Ef
East Grand Forks, Minnesota - - 132 Ab
East Grinstead, England 15 Dd
East Helena, Montana - 136 Gb
East Ilsley, England - 14 Cc
Eastington, England - 14 Bc
East Jeddore, Nova Scotia 120 Dd
Eastland, Texas - - 133 Cd
East Las Vegas, New Mexico - - - 135 Ld
Eastleigh, England - 14 Ce
Eastleigh, Transvaal - 115 Gc
East Liverpool, Ohio - 129 Db
East London, Cape Prov. 115 Hf
East Lothian, co., Scot. 23 Fe
East Lydford, England - 14 Bd
Eastman, Georgia - - 131 Gd
Eastman, Quebec - - 121 Db
Eastmain R., Quebec - 119 Of
East Murchison Goldfd., W. Australia - - 152 Cd
Eastnor, England - - 14 Bb
Easton, Colorado - - 135 La
Easton, Maryland - - 129 Gc
Easton, Pennsylvania - 129 Gb
Eastonville, Colorado - 135 Lb
East Port, Georgia - 131 Fd
Eastport, Maine - - 120 Bd
East Raynham, England - 19 Ee
East Retford, England - 19 Dd
East Riding, Yorks, Eng. 19 Dc
East St Louis, Illinois - 132 Ef
East Siberian Sea, U.S.S.R. 76Rb
East Sioux Falls, S. Dakota 132Ad
East Tarim Des., Sinkiang 84 Ec
Eastville, Virginia - 129 Gd
Eaton, Ohio - - - 129 Bc
Eaton Socon, England - 15 Db
Eatonton, Georgia - - 131 Gd
Eau Claire, Ontario - 121 Aa
Eau Claire, Wisconsin - 132 Dc
Eauripik, I., Caroline Is. 157 Bc
Eauze, France - - 34 Cd
Ebbw Vale, England - 14 Ac
Ebchester, England - 21 Ed
Ebenau Reichenau, Austria 59He
Ebenfurth, Austria - 66 Bb
Ebenhausen, Bavaria - 58 Ea
Ebensburg, Pennsylvania 129 Eb
Eberbach, Baden - - 58 Db
Ebermannstadt, Bavaria 58 Eb
Eberswalde, Prussia - 55 Jc
Ebeuf, France - - 30 Cb
Ebi, Japan - - - 100 Dd
Ebingen, Württemberg - 58 Cc
Ebi Nor, Sinkiang - 84 Ea
Eboli, Italy - - - 64 Fc
Ebolowa, Fr. Eq. Africa 109 Ba
Ebon I., Marshall Is. - 157 Dc
Ebrach, Bavaria - - 58 Eb
Ebro, R., Spain - - 39 Fd
Ebstorf, Prussia - - 54 Fb
Eburru, Kenya - - 110 Ed
Ebute Metta, Nigeria - 105 Bd
Ecclefechan, Scotland - 21 Cc
Eccles, England - - 18 Bd
Ecclesfield, England - 18 Cd
Eccleshall, England - 18 Be
Eceabat, Turkey - - 72 Db
Echallens, Switzerland - 42 Cc
Echo, Utah - - - 135 Ha
Echo Cliffs, Arizona - 135 Hc
Echuca, Victoria - - 154 Dd
Ecija, Philippines - - 95 Ff
Ecija, Spain - - - 40 Eb
Ecka, Voyvodina - - 67 Fd
Eckernförde, Prussia - 54 Ea
Eckington, Derby, Eng. 18 Cd
Eckington, Worcs, Eng. 14 Bb
Eckmond, mt., Cape Prov. 115 Fd
Ecos, France - - - 30 Db
Ecuador, rep., S. Amer. 141 Bc
Ecueillé, France - - 30 Dd
Eda, Sweden - - - 50 Bc
Edain Caboba, It. Somal'd 108 Gf
Eday, I., Orkney Is. - 24 Fc
Edd, Eritrea - - - 108 Dc
Ed Damer, A.-E. Sudan 108 Bb
Ed Dawaime, Palestine - 80 Bd
Ed Debba, A.-E. Sudan 108 Bb
Eddington, Queensland - 153 Bd
Ed Dueim, A.-E. Sudan 108 Bc
Eddystone Lt. Ho., Eng. 17 Bc
Eddystone Pt., Tasmania 155 Kg
Eddyville, Iowa - - 132 Ce
Eddyville, Kentucky - 130 Eb
Ede, Holland - - 29 Db
Edea, Fr. Eq. Africa - 105 De
Edefors, Sweden - - 48 Dc
Edelény, Hungary - 67 Fa
Edel Land, W. Aust. - 152 Ad
Eden, Maine - - - 120 Ad
Eden, New S. Wales - 155 Fd
Eden, Nicaragua - - 140 Ge
Eden, R., England - 21 Dd
Edenbridge, England - 15 Dd
Edenburg, O.F.S. - - 115 Fd
Edendale, New Zealand 159 Bg
Edenderry, Eire - - 27 Ce
Edenhope, Victoria - 154 Cd
Edenton, N. Carolina - 131 Kb
Edenville, O.F.S. - - 115 Gc
Edeowie, S. Australia - 154 Bb
Edgar Ra., W. Australia 152 Cb
Edgartown, Massachusetts 128 Cc
Edge I., Svalbard - - 9 Mb
Edgefield, S. Carolina - 131 Hd
Edgerton, Wisconsin - 132 Ed
Edgewood, Illinois - 132 Ef
Edgeworthstown, Eire - 26 Cd
Edgware, England - 15 Dc
Edhessa (Vodená), Greece 70 Cc
Edh Dhahriye, Palestine 80 Be
Edina, Liberia - - 104 Be
Edina, Missouri - - 132 Ce
Edinburg, Indiana - 129 Ac
Edinburg, Mississippi - 130 Dd
Edinburgh, Scotland - 23 Ee
Edirne (Adrianople), Turkey 72Da
Edisto I., S. Carolina - 131 Hd
Edisto R., S. Carolina - 131 Hd
Edith, Colorado - - 135 Kc
Edithburgh, S. Australia 154 Bd
Edith Cavell, Mt., Alberta 124 Fd
Edmeston, New York - 128 Ab
Edmond, Oklahoma - 133 Dc
Edmonds, Washington - 136 Bb
Edmonton, Alberta - 124 Gd
Edmonton, Cape Prov. - 114 Ef
Edmonton, England - 15 Dc
Edmundston, New Bruns. 120 Ac
Edolo, Italy - - - 62 Ea
Edrachillis B., Scotland 24 Ce
Edremit, Turkey - - 72 Ec
Edremit, G. of, Turkey - 72 Dc
Edsbro, Sweden - - 50 Hc
Edsbyn, Sweden - - 50 Ea
Edsel Ford Ra., Antarctica 160 —
Edson, Alberta - - 124 Fd
Edsvalla, Sweden - - 50 Cc
Eduni, N.-W. Terr. - 124 Db
Edward, L., Belg. Congo-Uganda - - - 110 Ad
Edwardesabad (Bannu), N.-W.F.P. - - 82 Db
Edwards, New York - 123 Lc
Edwards Creek, S. Aust. 154 Aa
Edwards Plateau, Texas 133 Be
Edwardsville, Illinois - 132 Ef
Edzell, Scotland - - 23 Fc
Eecloo, Belgium - - 29 Bc
Eek, Alaska - - - 125 Gf
Eel R., California - - 134 Ba
Efate, I., New Hebrides 157 De
Effingham, Illinois - 132 Ef
Egadi Is., Italy - - 65 Ff
Egan, S. Dakota - - 132 Ac
Egan Ra., Nevada - 134 Fb
Egaña, Argentina - - 148 Eb
Eganville, Ontario - - 121 Bb
Egbom, Nigeria - - 105 Cd
Egea de los Caballeros, Spain - - - 38 Db
Egedesminde, Greenland 9 Dd
Egegik, Alaska - - 125 Hg
Egeln, Prussia - - 55 Gd
Eger, Hungary - - 66 Fb
Egersa, Ethiopia - - 108 Dd
Egersund, Norway - 47 Bf
Egerta, Ital. Somaliland 108 Gf
Eggan, Nigeria - - 105 Cd
Egge Geb., Prussia - 54 Dd
Eggedal, Norway - - 47 Fd
Egg Harbor, New Jersey 129 Gc
Eggiwil, Switzerland - 42 Ec
Eggmuhl, Bavaria - 59 Gc
Egham, England - - 15 Dd
Egin, Turkey - - - 78 Cb
Egina, W. Australia - 152 Bc
Egmont B., Pr. Edward I. 120 Cc
Egmont, Mt., New Zeal'd 158 Dc
Egna, Italy - - - 63 Fa
Egremont, England - 18 Ab
Egridir & Gölu, Turkey - 78 Bb
Egri Karaagac Dag, Turkey 72 Dc
Egton, England - - 19 Db
Egum Group, New Guinea 156 Ec
Eguzon, France - - 34 Da
Egyek, Hungary - - 67 Fb
Egypt, N. Africa - - 101 Ec
Egypto, Angola - - 109 Bd
Ehingen, Württemberg - 58 Dc
Ehrenberg, Arizona - 134 Fe
Ehrenberg Mt., Egypt - 107 Fd
Eiao, I., Marquesas Is. - 157 Kd
Eibar, Spain - - - 38 Ca
Eibenstock, Saxony - 59 Ga
Eichsfeld, Prussia - 54 Fd
Eichstätt, Bavaria - 58 Fc
Eidanger, Norway - - 47 Fe
Eide, Hordaland, Norway 47 Cd
Eide, More-og-Romsdal, Norway - - - 46 Db
Eider, R., Prussia - 54 Da
Eidfjord, Norway - - 47 Dd
Eidsbugaren, Norway - 46 Ec
Eidsfoss, Norway - - 47 Fe
Eidsvold, Queensland - 153 De
Eidsvoll, Norway - - 47 Hd
Eidun, Trans-Jordan - 80 Db
Eifel, mts., Prussia - 58 Aa
Eigg, I., Scotland - - 22 Bc
Eik, Brit. Somaliland - 108 Ed
Eikefjord, Norway - 46 Bc
Eikesdals Vatn, Norway 46 Eb
Eiko, Korea - - - 97 Bc
Eil, It. Somaliland - 108 Ed
Eil, L., Scotland - - 22 Cc
Eil Dab, Br. Somaliland 108 Ed
Eilenburg, Prussia - 55 Hd
Eil Lass, Kenya - - 110 Fb
Eilsleben, Prussia - - 55 Gc
Eina, Norway - - 46 Gd
Einbeck, Prussia - - 54 Ed
Eindhoven, Holland - 29 Dc
Ein Harad, Palestine - 80 Cb
Einöd Riegel, Bavaria - 59 Hc
Eire, British Isles - - 13 Ce
Eisenach, Thuringia - 54 Fe
Eisenberg, Thuringia - 55 Ge
Eisenstadt, Austria - 66 Bb
Eisern, Prussia - - 54 De
Eisleben, Prussia - - 55 Gd
Ejutla, Mexico - - 139 Ed
Ekeby, Sweden - - 50 Hb
Eket, Nigeria - - 105 Ce
Eketahuna, New Zealand 158 Ed
Ekhinadhes Is., Greece - 71 Be
Ekhinos, Greece - - 72 Ba
Ekimchan, U.S.S.R. - 96 Ea
Eklingji, Rajputana - 85 Db
Ekne, Norway - - 46 Ga
Eksjö, Sweden - - 51 De
Ekuta, Belg. Congo - 109 Ca
Ekwayolo, Belg. Congo - 109 Cb
El Abiar, Libya - - 106 Cb
El Adem, Libya - - 106 Dc
El' Affule, Palestine - 80 Cb
Elafónisi Str., Greece - 71 Dg
Elafos, I., Greece - - 71 Dg
El Agheila, Libya - - 106 Bc
El' Aiyât, Egypt - - 107 Hd
El' Al, Syria - - 80 Db
El Alamein, Egypt - 107 Gc
El Allaqi, Egypt - - 106 Mh
El Amiriya, Egypt - 107 Gc
Elanders, Texas - - 133 Bf
Elands Berg, Cape Prov. 114 De
Elands Berg, Cape Prov. 115 Fe
Elandsvlei, Cape Prov. - 114 Cf
El Arbaa du Rharb, Morocco - - - 102 Bb
El Arba de Tissa, Morocco 102 Bb
El 'Arish, Egypt - - 107 Jc
El Ashmûnein, Egypt - 107 He
Elassön, Greece - - 70 Dd
Elátia, Greece - - 71 De
Elatiás, Greece - - 70 Fb
Elaziz, Turkey - - 78 Cb
Elba, Alabama - - 130 Ee
Elba, I., Italy - - 62 Ee
El Badâri, Egypt - - 107 He
El Badrshein, Egypt - 107 Hd
El Bageir, A.-E. Sudan 108 Bb
El Bahnasa, Egypt - 107 Hd

Eriskay, I., *Scotland* - 22 Ab
Erith, *England* - - 15 Ed
Erithraí, *Greece* - - 71 Ee
Eritrea, *N.-E. Africa* - 101 Fd
Erivilla Sta., *W. Aust.* - 152 Bd
Erlach, *Switzerland* 42 Db
Erlangen, *Bavaria* - 58 Fb
Erlenbach, *Switzerland* 42 Dc
Erlistoun, *W. Australia* 152 Cd
Ermakovo, *U.S.S.R.* - 96 Da
Erman Mts., *U.S.S.R.* - 96 Aa
Ermeland - - - 56 Eb
Ermelo, *Transvaal* - 115 Hc
Ermenek, *Turkey* - - 78 Bb
Ermióni, *Greece* - - 71 Ef
Ernakulam, *Madras States* 89 Bb
Erne, L., *N. Ireland* - 26 Cc
Erne, L., Upper, *N. Ire.* 26 Cc
Erne, R., *Eire* - - 26 Bb
Ernée, *France* - - 32 Db
Erode, *Madras* - - 89 Bb
Eromanga, *Queensland* - 153 Be
Eromanga, I., *New Hebrid.* 157De
Eros, *Louisiana* - - 130 Bd
Errabiddy Hills, *W. Aust.* 152 Bd
Er Rahad, *A.-E. Sudan* 108 Bc
Erramala Ra., *Madras* - 90 Cd
Er Rame, *Palestine* - 80 Cd
Er Ramle, *Palestine* - 80 Bd
Er Ras, *Arabia* - - 78 Dd
Er Rashda, *Egypt* - 107 Gf
Er Renk, *A.-E. Sudan* - 108 Bc
Errer, *Ethiopia* - - 108 Dd
Er Ridisîya Bahari, *Egypt* 107 Jf
Erris Hd., *Eire* - - 25 Aa
Er Rizeiqât, *Egypt* - 107 Jf
Er Roda, *Egypt* - - 107 He
Errol I., *Louisiana* - 130 Df
Er Rumman, *Trans-Jordan* 80 Dc
Ersekë, *Albania* - - 70 Bc
Érsekújvár, *Slovakia* - 66 Da
Erstein, *France* - - 31 Kc
Ertvågöy, *Norway* - 46 Ea
Erudina, *S. Australia* - 154 Bb
Ervalla, *Sweden* - - 50 Ec
Ervy, *France* - - 31 Fc
Erz Geb., *Bohemia, etc.* 59 Ga
Erzincan, *Turkey* - - 78 Cb
Erzurum, *Turkey* - - 78 Db
Erzvilkas, *Lithuania* - 49 Bd
Esashi, *Japan* - - 97 Eb
Esbjerg, *Denmark* - - 45 Bc
Esbly, *France* - - 30 Ec
Escada, *Brazil* - - 143 Gd
Escalante, *Philippines* - 99 Fa
Escalante, *Utah* - - 135 Hc
Escalon, *Mexico* - - 138 Db
Escalona, *Spain* - - 38 Ad
Escanaba & R., *Michigan* 122 Ec
Escarpment, *Kenya* - 110 Ed
Escatron, *Spain* - - 39 Ec
Esch, *Luxembourg* - - 29 Ee
Escholzmatt, *Switzerland* 42 Ec
Eschwege, *Prussia* - 54 Ed
Eschweiler, *Prussia* - 54 Be
Escondido, *California* - 134 Ee
Escondido, *New Mexico* 135 Le
Escondido B., *Mexico* - 139 Ed
Escoumains, Les, *Quebec* 123 Oa
Escudilla Pk., *Arizona* - 135 Je
Escudo de Veragua, *Panama* - - - 140 Gf
Escuinapa, *Mexico* - - 138 Cc
Escuintla, *Guatemala* - 140 Ee
Escuminac Pt., *New Bruns.* 120Cc
Esdraelon, Plain of, *Palestine* - - - 80 Cb
Esh, Jeb., *Egypt* - - 107 Je
Esher, *England* - - 15 Dd
Eshogbo, *Nigeria* - - 105 Bd
Eshowe, *Natal* - - 115 Jd
Esh Shama, *Arabia* - 78 Cc
Esh Sheria (Jordan, R.), *Palestine, etc.* - - 80 Dc
Esino, R., *Italy* - - 63 Hd
Eskdale, *New Zealand* - 158 Fc
Eskifjordhur, *Iceland* - 52 Gb
Eskilstuna, *Sweden* - 50 Fc
Eskisehir, *Turkey* - - 78 Ab
Eskítaşli, *Turkey* - - 72 Ea
Eskridge, *Kansas* - - 133 Da
Eslöv, *Sweden* - - 51 Cg
Esmeralda, I., *Chile* - 148 Ad
Esmeraldas and prov., *Ecuador* - - - 145 Aa
Espa, *Norway* - - 46 Hd
Espada, Pta., *Venezuela* 144 Ba
Espadan, Sa. de, *Spain* 39 Ee
Espalion, *France* - - 34 Ec
Española, *Galapagos Is.* 145 Fh
Española, *Ontario* - - 123 Hb
Espe, *Norway* - - 47 Cd
Espedalen, *Norway* - 46 Fc
Espeja, *Spain* - - 38 Bc
Esperance, *W. Australia* 152 Ce
Esperanza, *Argentina* - 146 Ce
Esperanza, La, *Honduras* 140 Fe
Espichel, C., *Portugal* - 37 Ad
Espiel, *Spain* - - 40 Ea
Espinar, *Spain* - - 38 Ad
Espirito Santo, *Brazil* - 142 Bd
Espirito Santo, state, *Brazil* - - - 147 Gb
Espiritu Santo, *New Hebrid.* 157De
Espiritu Santo, B., *Mexico* 139 Gd
Espiritu Santo, I., *Mexico* 138 Cc
Espita, *Mexico* - - 139 Gc
Espluga de Francoli, *Spain* 39 Gc
Espuna, Sa. de, *Spain* - 41 Ec
Esquel, *Argentina* - - 148 Bc
Esquimalt, *Br. Columbia* 124 Ee
Esquina, *Argentina* - 146 Dd
Es Salt, *Trans-Jordan* - 80 Dc
Es Samma, *Trans-Jordan* 80 Db
Es Semua, *Palestine* - 80 Ce
Essen, *Oldenburg* - - 54 Cc
Essen, *Prussia* - - 54 Bd
Essequibo, R., *Br. Guiana* 144 Eb
Essex, *Ontario* - - 122 Gd
Essex, co., *England* - 15 Ec
Essex Mt., *Wyoming* - 135 Ja
Essexvale, *S. Rhodesia* - 113 Cc
Esslingen, *Württemberg* 58 Dc
Essoyes, *France* - - 31 Gc
Es Sukhne, *Syria* - - 78 Cc
Essunt, *U.S.S.R.* - - 74 Lc
Es Suweida, *Syria* - 78 Cc
Estabutchie, *Mississippi* 130 De
Estados, I. de los (Staten I.), *Argentina* - - 148 De
Estagel, *France* - - 34 Ee
Estaing, *France* - - 34 Ec
Estancias, Sa. de las, *Spain* 41 Dc
Estats, Pic d', *France-Spain* - - - 39 Gb
Estavayer, *Switzerland* - 42 Cc
Estcourt, *Natal* - - 115 Hd
Este, *Italy* - - - 63 Fb
Estella, *Spain* - - 38 Cb
Estepa, *Spain* - - 40 Fb
Estepona, *Spain* - - 40 Ec
Ester, *Alaska* - - 125 Kd
Estercuel, *Spain* - - 39 Ed
Estero I., *Florida* - - 131 Mh
Estero de Agiabampo, *Mexico* - - - 138 Cb
Esteros del Ibera, *Argent.* 146 Dd
Esterri de Aneu, *Spain* - 39 Gb
Estevan, *Saskatchewan* - 124 Je
Est Fayala, *Belg. Congo* - 109 Cb
Estherville, *Iowa* - - 132 Bd
Estiche, *Spain* - - 39 Fc
Estivella, *Spain* - - 39 Ee
Estonia, *Europe* - - 49 Cb
Estrecho Nelson, *Chile* - 148 Ae
Estrées-St. Denis, *France* 30 Eb
Estreito, *Brazil* - - 147 Ee
Estrêla, Sa., de, *Portugal* 37 Cb
Estremadura, prov., *Portugal* - - - 37 Bd
Estremoz, *Portugal* - 37 Cd
Estrondo, Sa. des, *Brazil* 143 Ed
Esztergom, *Hungary* - 66 Db
Etah, *Greenland* - - 9 Bb
Etah, *United Provs.* - 83 He
Etain, *France* - - 31 Hb
Etampes, *France* - - 30 Dc
Etang, *France* - - 31 Ge
Étaples, *France* - - 30 Da
Etawah, *United Provs.* - 83 He
Etawney, *Manitoba* - 124 Kc
Etelia, *Fr. W. Africa* - 105 Bb
Eten, *Peru* - - - 145 Ac
Eternity Ra., *Antarctica* 160 —
Et Faluje, *Palestine* - 80 Bd
Etheridge Goldfield, *Queensland* - - 153 Bc
Ethiopia (Abyssinia), *E. Africa* - - - 101 Fe
Eth Themed, *Egypt* - 107 Kd
Etivaz, l', *Switzerland* - 42 Dd
Etive L. & Glen, *Scotland* 22 Cc
Etna, Mt., *China* - - 95 Cf
Etna, Mt., *Sicily* - - 65 Hg
Etne, *Norway* - - 47 Be
Etnedal, *Norway* - - 46 Fd
Etoile du Congo, *Belg. Congo* - - - 109 Ed
Eton, *England* - - 15 Dd
Eton, *Queensland* - - 153 Cd
Etowa R., *Georgia* - 131 Fc
Etrépagny, *France* - 30 Db
Etruscan Alps, *Italy* - 62 Ec
Et Taiyibe, *Palestine* - 80 Cc
El Taiyibe, *Trans-Jordan* 80 Db
Ettington, *England* - 14 Cb
Et Tira, *Palestine* - - 80 Bc
Et Tira Shallala, *Palestine* 80 Bb
Ettlingen, *Baden* - - 58 Cc
Ettrick, *New Zealand* - 159 Bf
Eua, I., *Tonga Is.* - 157 Ff
Euabalong, *New S. Wales* 155 Ec
Euboea (Évvoia), *Greece* 71 Fe
Eucla & Div., *W. Aust.* 152 De
Eudunda, *S. Australia* - 154 Bc
Eufaula, *Alabama* - - 130 Fe
Eufaula, *Oklahoma* - 133 Ec
Eugene, *Oregon* - - 136 Bc
Eugene Mts., *Nevada* - 134 Da
Euka, *Egypt* - - - 107 Gc
Eulen Geb. - - - 57 Bc
Eulo, *Queensland* - - 153 Ce
Eunice, *Louisiana* - - 130 Be
Eupen, *Belgium* - - 29 Ed
Euphrates, R., *Iraq, etc.* 78 Ec
Eupora, *Mississippi* - 130 Dd
Eure, dep. & R., *France* 30 Cb
Eure-et-Loir, dep., *France* 30 Dc
Eureka, *Arizona* - - 134 Fe
Eureka, *California* - 134 Aa
Eureka, *Colorado* - - 135 Kc
Eureka, *Illinois* - - 132 Ee
Eureka, *Kansas* - - 133 Db
Eureka, *Montana* - - 136 Fa
Eureka, *Nevada* - - 134 Fb
Eureka, *Transvaal* - 115 Jb
Eureka, *Utah* - - 135 Ga
Eureka Sd., *N.-W. Terr.* 119 Ma
Eureka Springs, *Arkansas* 130 Bb
Euriowie, *New S. Wales* 154 Cb
Euroa, *Victoria* - - 155 Ed
Europa I., *Mozambique Channel* - - - 112 Dd
Europa, Penas de, *Spain* 38 Aa
Euskirchen, *Prussia* - 54 Be
Euston, *New S. Wales* - 154 Dc
Eutaw, *Alabama* - - 130 Dd
Eutawville, *S. Carolina* - 131 Hd
Eutin, *Prussia* - - 54 Fa
Eutsuk L., *Br. Columbia* 124 Dd
Evandale, *Tasmania* - 155 Jg
Evanger, *Norway* - - 46 Cd
Evans, *Colorado* - - 135 La
Evans, *Nevada* - - 134 Ea
Evans Str., *N.-W. Terr.* 119 Nd
Evanston, *Illinois* - - 132 Fd
Evanston, *Wyoming* - 135 Ha
Evansville, *Indiana* - 129 Ac
Evansville, *Minnesota* - 132 Bb
Eveleth, *Minnesota* - 132 Cb
Evening Shade, *Arkansas* 130 Cb
Evenlode, R., *England* - 14 Cc
Everard, C., *Victoria* - 155 Fe
Everard, L., *S. Aust.* - 151 Ee
Everest, *Nepal-Tibet* - 87 Ga
Everett, *Pennsylvania* - 129 Eb
Everett, *Washington* - 136 Bb
Everglades, *Florida* - 131 Nj
Evergreen, *Alabama* - 130 Ee
Everöd, *Sweden* - - 51 Dg
Eversberg, *Prussia* - 54 Dd
Evesham, *Queensland* - 153 Bd
Evesham & Vale of, *Eng.* 14 Cb
Evje, *Norway* - - 47 Df
Evo, *Fr. Eq. Africa* - 105 Ee
Evolène, *Switzerland* - 42 Ed
Evora, *Portugal* - - 37 Cd
Evora Monte, *Portugal* - 37 Cd
Evoron L. & R., *U.S.S.R.* 96 Fa
Evran, *France* - - 32 Cb
Evrecy, *France* - - 32 Ea
Evreše, *Turkey* - - 72 Db
Evreux, *France* - - 30 Cb
Evron, *France* - - 30 Bc
Evrons, *France* - - 32 Eb
Évropos, *Greece* - - 70 Db
Evrótas, R., *Greece* - 71 Dg
Evrychou, *Cyprus* - - 78 Bb
Évvoia (Euboea), *Greece* 71 Fe
Évvoia, G. of, *Greece* - 71 Ee
Ewarton, *Jamaica* - - 140 Bc
Ewe, L., *Scotland* - - 22 Ca
Exaltacion, *Bolivia* - 142 Ae
Excelsior, *O.F.S.* - - 115 Gd
Excelsior Mts., *Nevada* - 134 Db
Excelsior Springs, *Missouri* 130Aa
Exe, R., *England* - - 17 Cb
Exebridge, *England* - 14 Ad
Exeter, *England* - - 14 Ae
Exeter, *New Hampshire* 128 Cb
Exilles, *Italy* - - 62 Ab
Exmoor Forest, *England* 17 Ca
Exmouth, *England* - 14 Ae
Exmouth G., *W. Australia* 152 Ac
Expanse, L., *Quebec* - 123 Jb
Expedition Ra., *Queensl'd* 153 Cd
Extremadura, *Spain* - 37 Dd
Exuma Is. & Sd., *Bahamas* 140Bb
Eyak, *Alaska* - - 125 Lf
Eyasi, L., *Tangany. Terr.* 111 De
Eye, *Northants, Eng.* - 15 Da
Eye, *Suffolk, England* - 15 Fb
Eye Pen., *Scotland* - 24 Ba
Eye Ra., *Nevada* - - 134 Fb
Eyemouth, *Scotland* - 23 Fe
Eygurande, *France* - 34 Eb
Eymet, *France* - - 34 Cc
Eymoutiers, *France* - 34 Db
Eynsham, *England* - 14 Cc
Eyrarbakki, *Iceland* - 52 Cc
Eyre, *W. Australia* - 152 De
Eyre Cr., *Queensland* - 153 Ad
Eyre, Ls. *S. Australia* - 154 Aa
Eyre, Mt., *S. Australia* - 154 Bb
Eyrecourt, *Eire* - - 27 Be
Eysden, *Holland* - - 29 Dd
Eystrup, *Prussia* - - 54 Ec
Ezine, *Turkey* - - 72 Dc
Ezu, *Nigeria* - - 105 Cd
Ezvonoi, *Greece* - - 70 Db
Ez Zeidab, *A.-E. Sudan* 108 Bb
Ez Zib, *Palestine* - - 80 Ca
Ez Zuetina, *Libya* - 106 Cc
Ez Zuk, *Palestine* - - 80 Da
Faaborg, *Denmark* - 45 Dc
Faarup, *Denmark* - - 45 Cb
Fabara, *Spain* - - 39 Fc
Fåberg, *Norway* - - 46 Gc
Fabrezan, *France* - - 34 Ed
Fabriano, *Italy* - - 63 Gd
Fabrizia, *Italy* - - 65 Cd
Facatativa, *Colombia* - 144 Bc
Fachi, *Fr. W. Africa* - 105 Db
Fada, *Fr. Eq. Africa* - 105 Fb
Fadalto, *Italy* - - 63 Ga
Fada n'Gourma, *Fr. W. Africa* - - - 105 Bc
Fadd, *Hungary* - - 66 Dc
Fæmö, *Denmark* - - 45 Ed
Faenza, *Italy* - - 63 Fc
Færöerne (Færoes, The), *N. Atlantic* - - 44 Nd
Fafa, *Fr. W. Africa* - 105 Bb
Fafe, *Portugal* - - 36 Bc
Fagăras, *Romania* - - 69 Fc
Fagernes, *Norway* - 46 Fd
Faget, *Romania* - - 67 Hd
Fagnano, L., *Argentina* 148 Ce
Fagne, La, *Belgium* - 29 Cd
Fagre, *Sweden* - - 50 Cd
Fahl, *Trans-Jordan* - 80 Dc
Faid, *Arabia* - - 78 Dd
Faido, *Switzerland* - 43 Gd
Fair Hd., *N. Ireland* - 26 Da
Fair Isle, *Zetland* - - 24 —
Fairbank, *Arizona* - 135 Hf
Fairbanks, *Alaska* - 125 Kd
Fairburn, *Georgia* - - 131 Fd
Fairbury, *Illinois* - - 132 Ee
Fairbury, *Nebraska* - 126 Fb
Fairchance, *Pennsylvania* 129 Ec
Fairfield, *California* - 134 Bb
Fairfield, *Idaho* - - 136 Fd
Fairfield, *Illinois* - - 132 Ef
Fairfield, *Iowa* - - 132 Ce
Fairfield, *Utah* - - 135 Ga
Fairford, *England* - 14 Cc
Fairhaven, *Massachusetts* 128 Cc
Fairlie, *New Zealand* - 159 Cf
Fairloch, *Ontario* - - 122 Ea
Fairmont, *Minnesota* - 132 Bd
Fairmont, *W. Virginia* - 129 Dc
Fairmount, *N. Dakota* - 132 Ac
Fairport Harbor, *Ohio* - 129 Db
Fairview, *Alberta* - - 124 Fc
Fairview, *Oklahoma* - 133 Cb
Fairview, *Utah* - - 135 Hb
Fairville, *New Brunswick* 120 Bd
Fairweather Mt. and C., *Alaska* - - - 125 Mg
Faizabad, *Afghanistan* - 84 Cc
Faizabad, *Tadzhik* - 84 Bc
Fajr, *Arabia* - - 78 Cd
Fakaofi I., *Tokelau Is.* - 157 Fd
Fakaraya, I., *Tuamotu Arch.* - - - 157 Je
Fakenham, *England* - 19 Ee
Fakfak, *New Guinea* - 156 Ab
Faković, *Bosnia* - - 68 Eb
Fakse & B., *Denmark* - 45 Fc
Fakumen, *Manchuria* - 96 Cc
Falaba, *Sierra Leone* - 104 Be
Falaise, *France* - - 30 Bc
Falam, *Burma* - - 92 Aa
Falama, *Fr. W. Africa* - 104 Cd
Falcon, *Colorado* - - 135 Lb
Falcon, state, *Venezuela* 144 Ba
Falcone, C., *Sardinia* - 64 Hf
Fălești - - - - 69 Gb
Falkenau, *Bohemia* - 59 Ga
Falkenau - - - - 57 Cc
Falkenberg - - - 57 Cc
Falkenburg - - - 55 Mb
Falkenstein, *Bavaria* - 59 Gb
Falkenstein, *Saxony* - 59 Ga
Falkerberg, *Sweden* - 51 Bf
Falkirk, *Scotland* - - 23 Ee
Falkland, *Scotland* - 23 Ed
Falkland, East, *Falkland Islands* - - - 148 Ee
Falkland, West, *Falkland Islands* - - - 148 De
Falkland Is. (Islas Malvinas), *S. Atlantic Oc.* 148 De
Falkland Sd., *Falkland Is.* 148 De
Falkoping, *Sweden* - 50 Cd
Fall Brook, *California* - 134 Ee
Falle, *Ethiopia* - - 108 Cd
Fallingbostel, *Prussia* - 54 Ec
Fallon, *Nevada* - - 134 Db
Fallowfield, *Ontario* - 121 Cb
Fall River, *Massachusetts* 128 Cc
Fall River Valley, *Calif.* 134 Ca
Falls, *Idaho* - - - 136 Ec
Falls City, *Nebraska* - 127 Eb
Falmouth, *Jamaica* - 140 Bc
Falmouth, *Kentucky* - 131 Fa
Falmouth, *Massachusetts* 128 Cc
Falmouth & B., *England* 17 Ac
Falnic, *Romania* - - 67 Gc
False B., *Cape Prov.* - 114 Cg
False, C., *New Guinea* - 156 Bc
False Pt., *Orissa* - - 91 Ha
Falset, *Spain* - - 39 Fc
False Tillamook, *Oregon* 136 Ac
Falso, C., *Mexico* - - 138 Bc
Falster, I., *Denmark* - 45 Ed
Falsterbo, *Sweden* - - 51 Bg
Falterona, Mte., *Italy* - 63 Fd
Fălticeni, *Romania* - 69 Fb
Falun, *Sweden* - - 50 Eb
Famagusta, *Cyprus* - 78 Bb
Famaka, *A.-E. Sudan* - 108 Bc
Famalicão, *Portugal* - 36 Bc
Famatina & Sa., *Argent.* 146 Bd
Famoso, *California* - 134 Dd
Fan, *China* - - - 94 Eb
Fanári, *Greece* - - 71 Ef
Fan chêng, *China* - - 94 Dc
Fangcheng, *Manchuria* - 96 Db
Fanghina, I., *Tuamotu Arch.* - - - 157 Ke
Fannich, *Scotland* - - 22 Ca
Fanning I., *Line Is.* - 157 Hc
Fano, *Italy* - - - 63 Hd
Fanö, I., *Denmark* - 45 Bc
Fanos (Othonoi), I., *Greece* 70 Ad
Fanueh, *Persia* - - 79 Gd
Fao, *Iraq* - - - 79 Ed
Fara, *Arabia* - - - 79 Ee
Faradje, *Belgian Congo* 109 Ea
Farafangana, *Madagascar* 112 Ed
Farafra, Oasis of, *Egypt* 107 Ge
Farak Well, *Fr. W. Afr.* 105 Cb
Farallon de Pajaros, I., *Marianas Is.* - - 157 Ba
Faranah, *Fr. W. Africa* 104 Bd
Farasan Is., *Red Sea* - 78 Lg
Faraulep, I., *Caroline Is.* 157 Bc
Fareham, *England* - 14 Ce
Farewell, C., *Greenland* 9 Ef
Farewell, C., *New Zealand* 158Dd
Farge, *Prussia* - - 54 Db
Fargo, *N. Dakota* - - 126 Fa
Faribault, *Minnesota* - 132 Cc
Faridabad, *Punjab* - 83 Gd
Faridkot, *Punjab States* - 83 Fc
Faridpur, *Bengal* - - 88 Bc
Faridpur, *United Provs.* 83 Hd
Fariman, *Persia* - - 79 Gb
Farina, *S. Australia* - 154 Bb
Farina, C., *Tunisia* - 103 Ka
Faringdon, *England* - 14 Cc
Faringe, *Sweden* - - 50 Gc
Fâris, *Egypt* - - - 107 Jf
Farka, *Fr. W. Africa* - 105 Bc
Farlade, la, *France* - 33 Bc
Farmer City, *Illinois* - 132 Ee
Farmersville, *Texas* - 133 Dd
Farmerville, *Louisiana* - 130 Bd
Farmington, *Idaho* - 136 Eb
Farmington, *Iowa* - - 132 Ce
Farmington, *Maine* - 128 Ca
Farmington, *Missouri* - 130 Cb
Farmington, *New Mexico* 135 Jc
Farmington, *Utah* - - 135 Ga
Farmville, *Virginia* - 129 Ed
Farnborough, *England* - 15 Dd
Farne Is., *England* - 21 Eb
Farnes, *Norway* - - 46 Dc

FAR General Index FOR

Farnham, England - 15 Dd
Farnham, Quebec - 121 Db
Farningham, England - 15 Ed
Farnworth, England - 18 Bc
Faro, Brazil - 142 Cc
Faro, Portugal - 40 Cb
Fårön, Sweden - 51 Jd
Fårösund, Sweden - 51 Je
Farquhar, C., W. Aust. 152 Ac
Farrah, Afghanistan - 79 Hc
Farrars Cr., Queensland 153 Be
Farrell, Pennsylvania - 129 Db
Farrellton, Quebec - 121 Bb
Farrington, Ontario - 122 Ba
Farrington Gurney, Eng. 14 Bd
Farrukhabad, United Prs. 83 He
Farrukhnagar, Punjab - 83 Gd
Fars, Persia - 79 Fd
Fársala, Greece - 70 Dd
Farshût, Egypt - 107 Hf
Farsi, Afghanistan - 79 Hc
Farsö, Denmark - 45 Cb
Farso, Ethiopia - 108 Dd
Farsund, Norway - 47 Cf
Fartura, Sa., Brazil - 147 Ed
Farwell, Michigan - 122 Fd
Fasano, Italy - 65 Db
Fassa, Val di, Italy - 63 Fa
Fassett, Quebec - 121 Cb
Fastnet Lt. Ho., Eire - 25 Bg
Fastov, Ukraine - 75 De
Fatagar, C., New Guinea 156 Ab
Fatahabad, Punjab - 83 Fd
Fatait ibn Kanat, Arabia 78 Dd
Fatehgarh, United Provs. 83 He
Fatehpur, Rajputana - 83 Fe
Fatehpur, United Provs. 86 Dc
Fatezh, U.S.S.R. - 75 Fe
Father L., Quebec - 123 La
Fati, Turkey - 72 Eb
Fat-shan, China - 95 De
Fatu Hiva, I., Marquesas Islands - 157 Ke
Faucigny, France - 35 Jb
Faucilles, Mts., France - 31 Jc
Faucogney, France - 31 Jd
Faurei, Romania - 69 Gc
Fauresmith, O.F.S. - 115 Fd
Fauro, I., Solomon Is. - 156 Jg
Faust, New York - 128 Aa
Fåvang, Norway - 46 Gc
Favara, Sicily - 65 Gg
Faverges, France - 35 Jb
Faversham, England - 15 Ed
Favignana I., Italy - 65 Fg
Fâw, Egypt - 107 Je
Faxaflói, Iceland - 52 Bb
Faxina, Brazil - 147 Fc
Fay, Oklahoma - 133 Cc
Faya, Fr. Eq. Africa - 105 Eb
Fayence, France - 33 Bb
Fayette, Alabama - 130 Ed
Fayette, Mississippi - 130 Ce
Fayette, Missouri - 130 Ba
Fayette, Ohio - 129 Cb
Fayetteville, Arkansas - 130 Ab
Fayetteville, N. Carolina 131 Jc
Fayetteville, Tennessee - 130 Ec
Fayetteville, Texas - 133 Df
Fayetteville, W. Virginia 129 Dc
Fayid, Egypt - 107 Jc
Fayon, Spain - 39 Fc
Fazeley, England - 14 Ca
Fazilka, Punjab - 83 Fc
Feale R., Eire - 25 Be
Fear, C., N. Carolina - 131 Kd
Fear R., N. Carolina - 131 Jc
Featherstone, S. Rhodesia 113 Db
Feathertop, Mt., Victoria 155 Ed
Fécamp, France - 30 Cb
Fechetau, Transylvania 67 Hc
Fedala, Morocco - 103 Oh
Federacion, Argentina - 146 De
Fedje, Norway - 46 Ad
Fehergyarmat, Hungary 67 Ha
Fehmarn, I. & Sd., Prussia 54 Fa
Fehrbellin, Prussia - 55 Hc
Fehring, Austria - 66 Bc
Féi, China - 94 Eb
Feifu, Annam - 95 Cf
Feilding, New Zealand - 158 Ed
Feilnbach, Bavaria - 59 Gd
Feira, Portugal - 37 Bb
Feira Santa Ana, Brazil 143 Ge
Fejér, Hungary - 66 Db
Fejö, Denmark - 45 Ed
Felanitx, Balearic Is. - 39 Je
Feldbach, Austria - 59 Ke
Feldkirch, Austria - 58 Dd
Felicia - 63 Jb
Felixburg Road, S. Rhod. 113 Db
Felixstowe, England - 15 Fc
Fella Tarvisio, R., Italy 63 Ha
Felletin, France - 34 Eb
Felsögalla, Hungary - 66 Db
Feltre, Italy - 63 Fa
Femund, L., Norway - 46 Hb
Fen-chow, China - 94 Db
Fenelon Falls, Ontario - 121 Ab
Fénétrange, France - 31 Kc
Feng-chen, China - 94 Da
Feng-chêng, China - 94 Ed
Feng-chow, China - 94 Dd
Feng-hwa, China - 94 Fd
Fenghwa, Manchuria - 96 Cc
Feng-hwang-cheng, Manchuria - 96 Cc
Feng-ning, Manchuria - 96 Bc
Feng-Siang, China - 94 Cc
Fengtien, prov., Manchuria 96 Cc
Feng-tu, China - 94 Cd
Feng-yang, China - 94 Ec
Fên-ho, China - 94 Db
Feni Is., Pacific Oc. - 156 Fe
Fenner, California - 134 Fd
Fenny and R., Bengal - 88 Cc
Fenny Stratford, England 15 Db
Fenoarivo, Madagascar - 112 Ec
Fens, The, England - 15 Ea
Fens Fd, Norway - 46 Ad
Fen Stanton, England - 15 Db
Fenua Ura, I., Society Is. 157 He
Fer, C. de, Algeria - 103 Ha
Ferbane, Eire - 27 Ce
Ferdinand, Romania - 67 Hd
Ferdinand (Yumruk Chal), Bulgaria - 69 Fd
Ferentino, Italy - 64 Db
Ferfer, It. Somaliland - 108 Ee
Fergus, Ontario - 123 Hd
Fergus R., Eire - 27 Bf
Fergus Falls, Minnesota 132 Bb
Ferguson, Missouri - 130 Ca
Ferguson, Quebec - 123 Mb
Fergusson (Moratau) I., New Guinea - 156 Ec
Feriana, Tunisia - 103 Jb
Ferkane, Algeria - 103 Hb
Ferlo Futa, Fr. W. Afr. 104 Bc
Fermanagh, N. Ireland - 26 Cc
Fermo, Italy - 63 Hd
Fermoselle, Spain - 36 Dc
Fermoy, Eire - 27 Bg
Fernandina, Florida - 131 He
Fernandina, Galapagos Is. 145 Eh
Fernando Noronha, I., Brazil - 116 Gh
Fernando Po, I., W. Afr. 105 Ce
Fernão Velleso B., Mozambique - 112 Db
Ferndale, California - 134 Aa
Fernie, Brit. Columbia - 124 Fe
Ferns, Eire - 27 Df
Feronia, Ontario - 121 Aa
Ferozepore, Punjab - 83 Fc
Ferrai, Greece - 72 Db
Ferrandina, Italy - 65 Cb
Ferrara, Italy - 63 Fc
Ferrât, C., Algeria - 102 Db
Ferrato, C., Sardinia - 64 Jg
Ferret, C., France - 34 Ac
Ferriere, Italy - 62 Dc
Ferrières, France - 30 Ec
Ferris, Texas - 133 Dd
Ferro, C., Sardinia - 64 Je
Ferros, Brazil - 147 Gb
Ferryland, Newfoundland 120 Jc
Ferryville, Tunisia - 103 Ja
Ferté, la, France - 30 Fc
Ferté Alais, le, France - 30 Ec
Ferté Bernard, la, France 30 Cc
Ferté Mace, la, France - 30 Bc
Fertile, Minnesota - 132 Ab
Ferté-Milon, la, France - 30 Fb
Ferto Tava (Neusiedler See), Austria - 66 Bb
Fès (Fez), Morocco - 102 Bb
Feshiebridge, Scotland - 23 Eb
Festenberg - 57 Cb
Festus, Missouri - 130 Ca
Fethard, Eire - 27 Cg
Fetlar, I., Zetland - 24 Hg
Fetzara, L., Algeria - 103 Ha
Feuchtwangen, Bavaria 58 Eb
Feudatory States, Eastern States - 87 Fe
Fez (Fès), Morocco - 102 Bb
Fezzou, Morocco - 102 Bd
Ffestiniog, Wales - 20 Cb
Fiambala, Argentina - 146 Bd
Fiamignano, Italy - 64 Da
Fianarantsoa, Madagascar 112 Ed
Fianga, Fr. Eq. Africa - 105 Ed
Fianona - 63 Jb
Fibis, Romania - 67 Gd
Fichtel Geb., Bavaria - 59 Fa
Fichtelberg, Bavaria - 59 Fb
Fick, Syria - 80 Db
Ficksburg, O.F.S. - 115 Gd
Fidenza, Italy - 62 Ec
Fideris, Switzerland - 43 Jc
Fieldbrook, California - 134 Ba
Field's Find, W. Aust. - 152 Bd
Fiemme, Val di, Italy - 63 Fa
Fiera, Albania - 70 Ac
Fiera di Primiero, Italy 63 Fa
Fierro, New Mexico - 135 Je
Fiesch, Switzerland - 42 Fd
Fife, N. Rhodesia - 112 Bb
Fife, co., Scotland - 23 Ed
Figeac, France - 34 Dc
Figline, Italy - 63 Fd
Figtree, S. Rhodesia - 113 Cc
Figueira da Foz, Portugal 37 Bb
Figueira de Castello Rodrigo, Portugal - 37 Cb
Figueiro dos Vinhos, Portugal - 37 Bc
Figueras, Spain - 39 Hb
Figuig, Morocco - 102 Dc
Fiji Is., Pacific Oc. - 157 Ee
Fíkhtia, Greece - 71 Df
Filabres, Sa. de los, Spain 41 Dc
Filabusi, S. Rhodesia - 113 Cc
Filadelfia, Italy - 65 Cd
File Fjeld, Norway - 46 Dc
Filey, England - 19 Db
Fflia, Greece - 71 Df
Filiasi, Romania - 67 Je
Filiátes, Greece - 70 Bd
Filiatrá, Greece - 71 Cf
Filicudi I., Italy - 65 Hf
Filipow, Poland - 56 Gb
Filipstad, Sweden - 50 Cc
Filisur, Switzerland - 43 Jc
Fillmore, Utah - 135 Gb
Filton, England - 14 Bc
Finale, Italy - 63 Fc
Finale Marina, Italy - 62 Cc
Fincastle, Virginia - 129 Dd
Finch, Ontario - 121 Cb
Finchley, England - 15 Dc
Findhorn, Scotland - 23 Ea
Findhorn, R., Scotland - 23 Eb
Findlay, Ohio - 129 Cb
Findlay Is., N.-W. Terr. 118 Ja
Finedon, England - 15 Db
Fingal, Tasmania - 155 Kg
Finglas, Eire - 27 De
Finhaut, Switzerland - 42 Cd
Finistère, dep., France - 32 Ab
Finisterre & C., Spain - 36 Ab
Finisterre Mts., New Guinea - 156 Dc
Finland, W. Europe - 44 Fg
Finland, G. of, Finland 48 Gf
Finlay R., Brit. Columbia 124 Ec
Finley, New S. Wales - 154 Ed
Finn, Montana - 136 Hb
Finne Berg, Prussia - 55 Gd
Finnerödja, Sweden - 50 Dd
Finnöy, Norway - 47 Be
Finnskog, Norway - 46 Jd
Finntown, Eire - 26 Bb
Finsch Coast, New Guinea 156 Cb
Finse, Norway - 46 Dd
Finsnes, Norway - 44 De
Finspang, Sweden - 50 Ed
Finsteraarhorn, Switz. - 42 Fc
Finsterwalde, Prussia - 55 Jd
Finstown, Orkney Is. - 24 Ec
Fintona, N. Ireland - 26 Cc
Finucane Ra., Queensland 153 Bd
Fionnay, Switzerland - 42 Dd
Fiordland, New Zealand 159 Af
Fiorenzuola, Italy - 62 Dc
Firdaus, Persia - 79 Gc
Firenze (Florence), Italy 63 Fd
Firmat, Argentia - 146 Ce
Firminy, France - 35 Gb
Firnis, Turkey - 78 Cb
Firozabad, United Provs. 83 He
Firozpur Jhirka, Punjab 83 Ge
First Cataract (Aswân Dam), Egypt - 106 Mg
Firuzabad, Persia - 79 Fd
Firuze, Persia - 79 Gb
Fischamend, Austria - 66 Ba
Fischhausen - 56 Eb
Fish B., Cape Prov. - 114 Eg
Fisher Str., N.-W. Terr. 119 Nd
Fishers I., New York - 128 Cc
Fishguard, Wales - 20 Bd
Fish River, Cape Prov. - 115 Fe
Fiskenæsset & Lichtenfels, Greenland - 9 De
Fismes, France - 31 Fb
Fitchburg, Massachusetts 128 Cb
Fitzcarrald, Peru - 145 Cd
Fitzgerald, Alberta - 124 Gc
Fitzgerald, Georgia - 131 Ge
Fitzgerald, Tasmania - 155 Jh
Fitzgerald Pks., W. Aust. 152 Ce
Fitzpatrick, Alabama - 130 Ed
Fitzroy & R., W. Aust. 152 Db
Fitzroy, mt., Chile - 148 Bd
Fitzroy Harbour, Ontario 121 Bb
Fitzwilliam I., Ontario - 122 Gc
Fiume and G. - 63 Jb
Fiumefreddo Bruzio, Italy 65 Bc
Fiumicino, Italy - 64 Cb
Fivemiletown, N. Ireland 26 Cc
Fjallasen, Sweden - 48 Cc
Fjerreslev, Denmark - 45 Ca
Fjœre, Norway - 47 Ce
Fjotland, Norway - 47 Cf
Flå, Norway - 47 Fd
Flaga, Iceland - 52 Dc
Flagstaff, Arizona - 135 Hd
Flagstaff, Cape Prov. - 115 He
Flåm, Norway - 46 Dd
Flamborough Hd., Eng. 19 Db
Fläming, mts., Prussia - 55 Hc
Flanders, E. & W., provs., Belgium - 29 Bd
Flandreau, Minnesota - 132 Ac
Flannan Is., Scotland - 13 Cb
Flat, Alaska - 125 He
Flatey, Iceland - 52 Bb
Flathead & L., Montana 136 Fb
Flathead Range, Montana 136 Ga
Flatmark, Norway - 46 Db
Flatonia, Texas - 133 Df
Flatow - 56 Bc
Flattery, C., Queensland 153 Cb
Flattery, C., Washington 136 Aa
Flattery Rocks, Washing'n 136Aa
Flavigny, France - 31 Gd
Flavy-le-Martel, France 30 Fb
Fleche, la, France - 30 Bd
Fleetwood, England - 18 Ac
Flekkefjord, Norway - 47 Cf
Flekkeröy, Norway - 47 Ef
Flemingsburg, Kentucky 131 Ga
Flen, Sweden - 50 Fc
Flensburg, Prussia - 54 Ea
Flenskampan, mt., Norway 46Hb
Flers, France - 32 Eb
Flesberg, Norway - 47 Fe
Fletton, England - 15 Da
Fleurieu (Hunter) I., Tasmania - 155 Jg
Fleuris, Belgium - 29 Cd
Flims, Switzerland - 43 Hc
Flinders B., W. Australia 152 Ae
Flinders I., S. Australia 151 Ee
Flinders I., Tasmania - 155 Kf
Flinders Ra., S. Aust. - 154 Bb
Flinders Reefs & Pass, Queensland - 153 Cc
Flinders R., Queensland 153 Bc
Flin-Flon, Manitoba - 124 Jd
Flint, Michigan - 122 Gd
Flint and co., Wales - 20 Ca
Flint I., Line Is. - 157 He
Flint R., Georgia - 131 Fd
Flisa, Norway - 46 Jd
Flix, Spain - 39 Fc
Flogny, France - 31 Fd
Flomaton, Alabama - 130 Ee
Flora, Illinois - 132 Ef
Flora, Norway - 46 Ha
Flora, Tennessee - 130 Ec
Florac, France - 35 Fc
Florala, Alabama - 130 Ee
Floraville, Queensland - 153 Ac
Florence, Alabama - 130 Ec
Florence, Arizona - 135 He
Florence, Colorado - 135 Lb
Florence, Kansas - 133 Da
Florence, Nebraska - 132 Ae
Florence, Oregon - 136 Ac
Florence, S. Carolina - 131 Jc
Florence, Wisconsin - 132 Ec
Florence (Firenze), Italy 63 Fd
Florencia, Argentina - 146 Dd
Florencia, Colombia - 144 Ac
Florencia, La, Argentina 146 Cc
Flores, Guatemala - 140 Ed
Flores, dep., Uruguay - 146 De
Flores I. & Sea, Nether. Indies - 99 Fe
Floreşti - 69 Hb
Floresville, Texas - 133 Cf
Floriano, Brazil - 143 Fd
Floriano Peixoto, Brazil 145 Dc
Florianopolis, Brazil - 147 Fd
Florida, Transvaal - 115 Gc
Florida, state, U.S.A. - 127 Je
Florida & dep., Uruguay 146 De
Florida and Mts., New Mexico - 135 Ke
Florida B. & C., Florida 131 Nj
Florida Is., Solomon Is. 156 Jg
Florida Keys, Florida - 131 Nj
Floridia, Sicily - 65 Jg
Flórina, Greece - 70 Cc
Floro, Norway - 46 Ac
Flotta, Orkney Is. - 24 Eb
Floweree, Montana - 136 Ha
Floyd Pk., Arizona - 135 Gd
Floydada, Texas - 133 Bd
Fluberg, Norway - 46 Gd
Flüelen, Switzerland - 43 Gc
Flushing, New York - 128 Bc
Flushing (Vlissingen), Holland - 29 Bc
Fluvanna, Texas - 133 Bd
Fly R., New Guinea - 156 Cc
Foča, Bosnia - 68 Dc
Fochabers, Scotland - 23 Ea
Focsani, Romania - 69 Gc
Fofa Cahuel, Argentina 148 Bc
Foga, A.-E. Sudan - 108 Ac
Foggaret ez Zoua, Algeria 102 Ff
Foggia, Italy - 64 Fb
Fogo I., Newfoundland - 120 Jb
Föhr, I., Prussia - 54 Da
Foix, France - 34 De
Fojnica, Bosnia - 68 Cc
Fojnica, Hercegovina - 68 Dc
Fokstua, Norway - 46 Fb
Foldal, Norway - 46 Fb
Foleyet, Ontario - 122 Ga
Folgefonna, Norway - 47 Ce
Foligno, Italy - 63 Ge
Folkston, Georgia - 131 Ge
Folkstone, England - 15 Fd
Folkestone, N. Carolina 131 Kc
Follina, Italy - 63 Gb
Follinica, Italy - 62 Ee
Folsom, New Mexico - 135 Mc
Folsom City, California 134 Cb
Fo-lu, Tong-king - 95 Be
Fomboni, Comoro Is. - 112 Db
Fonda, Iowa - 132 Bd
Fonda, New York - 128 Ab
Fondak, Span. Morocco - 102 Bb
Fond du Lac, Minn.-Wis. 132 Db
Fond du Lac, Minnesota 132 Cb
Fond du Lac, Saskatch. 124 Hc
Fond du Lac, Wisconsin 132 Ed
Fondi, Italy - 64 Db
Fondo, Italy - 62 Fa
Fonsagrada, Spain - 36 Ca
Fonseca, Gulf of, Honduras 140Fe
Fontainebleau, France - 30 Ec
Fontaine-le-Dun, France 30 Cb
Fontane - 63 Hb
Fonte Boa, Brazil - 142 Ac
Fontenay-le-Comte, France 32 Ed
Fontiveros, Spain - 37 Fb
Fonyód, Hungary - 66 Cc
Fonz, Spain - 39 Fb
Foochow, China - 94 Ed
Fo-ping, China - 94 Ce
Foraker, Mt., Alaska - 125 Jc
Forbach, France - 31 Jb
Forbes, New S. Wales - 155 Fc
Forbes, Mt., Alberta - 124 Fd
Forcados & R., Nigeria 105 Bd
Forcalquier, France - 33 Ab
Forcuza, Italy - 64 Fc
Förde, Norway - 46 Bc
Forde, Norway - 47 Be
Fordham, England - 15 Eb
Fordingbridge, England 14 Ce
Fordley, England - 15 Fb
Fordon, Poland - 56 Cc
Ford's Bridge, N. S. W. 154 Ea
Fordyce, Arkansas - 130 Bd
Forecariah, Fr. W. Africa 104 Be
Foreland, N. & S., Eng. 15 Fd
Forellhogna, Norway - 46 Gb
Forest, Mississippi - 130 Dd
Forest, Ontario - 122 Gd
Forest City, Iowa - 132 Cd
Forest Hall, Cape Prov. 114 Ef
Forest Hill, California - 134 Cb
Forestier's Pen. & Hd., Tasmania - 155 Kh
Forestport, New York - 128 Ab
Forestville, California - 134 Bb
Forez, Mts. du, France 35 Fb
Forfar, Scotland - 23 Fc
Forgevielle, France - 34 Da
Forlie, Italy - 63 Gc
Formazzo, Italy - 62 Ca
Formby, England - 18 Ac
Formentera, I., Balearic Is. 39 Kg

FUJ

General Index

GEN

Fujiyama, Japan - - 97 Dc
Fukan, Sinkiang - - 84 Fb
Fu-kang, China - - 95 De
Fukaye I., Japan - - 97 Bd
Fu-kiang, China - - 94 Bc
Fu-kien, prov., China - 94 Ed
Fu-ki-kaku, Taiwan - - 97 He
Fu-ku, China - - 94 Db
Fukuchiyama, Japan - 100 Ed
Fukui, Japan - - 97 Dc
Fukuoka, Japan - - 97 Cd
Fukushima, Japan - 97 Ec
Fukuyama, Hokkaido, Japan - - - 97 Db
Fukuyama, Honshu, Japan 97 Cd
Fulda, Minnesota - - 132 Bd
Fulda, Prussia - - 54 Ee
Fulda, R., Prussia - 54 Ed
Fülek, Slovakia - - 66 Ea
Fu-li, Tong-king - - 95 Ce
Fullarton, Cape Prov. - 114 Ef
Fulpmes, Austria - - 58 Fd
Fulton, Arkansas - - 130 Bd
Fulton, Illinois - - 132 De
Fulton, Kentucky - - 130 Db
Fulton, Mississippi - 130 Dc
Fulton, Missouri - - 130 Ca
Fulton, New York - - 123 Kd
Fultonville, New York - 128 Ab
Fumay, France - - 31 Gb
Fumbuni, Comoro Is. - 112 Db
Fumel, France - - 34 Cc
Funabashi, Japan - - 100 Gd
Funafuto, I., Ellice Is. - 157 Ed
Funatsu, Japan - - 100 Fc
Funcheira, Portugal - 40 Bb
Fundi Sadi, Belg. Congo 109 Eb
Fundy, B. of, Nova Scotia 120 Cd
Funen (Fyn), Denmark - 45 Dc
Fu-ning, China - - 94 Fd
Fu-niu-shan, China - 94 Dc
Funsi & B., Kenya - 111 Ff
Funter, Alaska - - 125 Ng
Furbara, la, Italy - - 64 Ca
Furg, Persia - - - 79 Fd
Furgan, Kuh, Persia - 79 Gd
Furliug, Romania - - 67 Gd
Furnace End, England 14 Ca
Furneaux Group, Tasman. 151 Hg
Furnes, Belgium - - 29 Ac
Furnes, Norway - - 46 Hd
Furness Abbey, England 18 Ab
Fursanuk, Sinkiang - 84 Dc
Fürstenberg, Prussia - 55 Kc
Furstenfeld, Austria - 59 Kd
Fürstenwalde, Prussia - 55 Kc
Fürstenwerder, Mecklenburg 55 Jb
Fürth, Mid. Franconia, Bavaria - - - 58 Eb
Fürth, Upper Palatinate, Bavaria - - - 59 Gb
Furue, Japan - - 97 Cd
Fury and Hecla Str., N.-W. Terr. - - 119 Nc
Fusa, Norway - - 47 Bd
Fusagasuga, Colombia - 144 Bc
Fusan, Korea - - 97 Bc
Fuscaldo, Italy - - 65 Bc
Fu-shan, China - - 94 Fb
Fushiki, Japan - - 97 Dc
Fushimi, Japan - - 100 Ed
Fushun, Manchuria - 96 Cc
Fusio, Switzerland - 43 Gd
Fusung, Manchuria - 96 Dc
Futagawa, Japan - - 100 Fd
Futai, Japan - - 100 Gc
Fu-tsing, China - - 94 Ed
Fuwa, Egypt - - 107 Hc
Fuyu (Petuna), Manchuria 96 Cb
Füzesabony, Hungary - 67 Fb
Fuzesgyarmat, Hungary 67 Fb
Fyeodosiya, Crimea - 75 Fg
Fyfield, England - - 14 Cc
Fyn (Funen), Denmark - 45 Dc
Fyne, L., Scotland - 22 Cd
Fyres Vatn, Norway - 47 Ee
Fyresdal, Norway - - 47 Ee
Fyzabad, United Provs. - 86 Eb
Gabandi, Persia - - 79 Fd
Gabarret, France - - 34 Bd
Gabarus, Nova Scotia - 120 Ed
Gabela, Angola - - 109 Bd
Gabela, Hercegovina - 68 Cc
Gaberones, Bechuanal'd 115 Fb
Gabès & G. de, Tunisia 103 Kc
Gabin, Poland - - 57 Ea
Gabon, col., Fr. Eq. Afr. 109 Bb
Gabon, R., Fr. Eq. Afr. 109 Aa
Gabredarre, Ethiopia - 108 Dd
Gabrovo, Bulgaria - 69 Fd
Gacé, France - - 30 Cc
Gacko, Hercegovina - 68 Dc
Gadag, Bombay - - 90 Bd
Gadarwara, Cent. Provs. 86 Cd
Gadeana, Mexico - - 138 Ca
Gadensberg, Prussia - 54 Ed
Gadhada, Western India 85 Cc
Gadhap, Sind - - 85 Ab
Gadhia, Baroda - - 85 Cd
Gadhka, Western India - 85 Bc
Gador and Sa. de, Spain 41 Dd
Gadsane, Mozambique - 113 Dd
Gadsden, Alabama - 130 Fd
Gadwal, Hyderabad - 90 Cc
Gadzema, S. Rhodesia - 113 Db
Gaerwen, Wales - - 20 Ba
Găeşti, Romania - - 69 Fc
Gaeta & Gulf, Italy - 64 Db
Gaffney, S. Carolina - 131 Hc
Gafour, Tunisia - - 103 Ja
Gafsa, Tunisia - - 103 Jb
Gâga, Egypt - - 107 Hf
Gagab, Ethiopia - - 108 Dd
Gage, Oklahoma - - 133 Cb
Gagetown, New Bruns. - 120 Bd
Gagliano Castelferrato, Sicily - - - 65 Hg
Gagry, Georgia - - 75 Fg
Gaia, Portugal - - 37 Ba
Gaibanda, Bengal - - 88 Bb
Gail, Texas - - - 133 Bd
Gail Tal, Austria - - 59 He
Gaillac, France - - 34 Dd
Gaillon, France - - 30 Db
Gaiman, Argentina - 148 Cc
Gainesboro, Tennessee - 130 Fb
Gainesville, Alabama - 130 Dd
Gainesville, Florida - 131 Gf
Gainesville, Georgia - 131 Gc
Gainesville, Missouri - 130 Bb
Gainesville, Texas - - 133 Dd
Gainsborough, England 19 Dd
Gaiole, Italy - - - 63 Fd
Gairdner, L., S. Aust. - 154 Ab
Gairloch, Scotland - 22 Ca
Gaisin, Ukraine - - 75 Df
Gaitzabiz, S.-W. Africa 114 Bb
Gajdobra, Voyvodina - 66 Ed
Gajur, mt., China - - 94 Bb
Gala Water, Scotland - 21 Db
Galadi, Ethiopia - - 108 Ed
Galag, Persia - - 79 Gd
Galam, I., Nether. Indies 98 Cd
Galamo, Fr. Somaliland 108 Dc
Galan, France - - 34 Cd
Galanita, Slovakia - - 66 Ca
Galapagos Is. (Archipiélago de Colón), Pac. Oc. 145 Eh
Galappo, Tanganyika Terr. 111 Df
Galashiels, Scotland - 21 Db
Galatea, New Zealand - 158 Fc
Galati, Romania - - 69 Gc
Galatina, Italy - - 65 Eb
Galatone, Italy - - 65 Db
Galax, Virginia - - 129 Dd
Galaxídhion, Greece - 71 De
Galdhöpiggen, mt., Norway 46 Ec
Galeana, Mexico - - 138 Dc
Galeata, Italy - - 63 Fc
Galela, Halmahera, N.I. 99 Gc
Galena, Illinois - - 132 Dd
Galena, Kansas - - 133 Eb
Galena, Missouri - - 130 Bb
Galena, Nevada - - 134 Ea
Galesburg, Illinois - 132 De
Galeton, Pennsylvania - 129 Fb
Gâlgău, Transylvania - 67 Jb
Galich, U.S.S.R. - - 74 Gd
Galicia, Spain - - 36 Cb
Galilee, L., Queensland - 153 Cd
Galilee, Sea of, Palestine 80 Db
Galion, Ohio - - 129 Cb
Galişte, Serbia - - 70 Cb
Galite, Iles de la, Mediterranean Sea - - 103 Ja
Galiuro Ra., Arizona - 135 He
Gallarate, Italy - - 62 Cb
Gallardon, France - - 30 Dc
Gallatin, Missouri - - 132 Cf
Gallatin, Tennessee - 130 Eb
Galle, Ceylon - - 89 Dd
Gallego, R., Spain - 38 Eb
Gallegos & Puerto, Argent. 148 Ce
Galley Hd., Eire - - 25 Cf
Galliate, Italy - - 62 Cb
Gallina, Italy - - 65 Bd
Gallina Mts., New Mexico 135 Kd
Gallinas, New Mexico - 135 Ld
Gallinas, Pta., Colombia 144 Ba
Gallipoli, Italy - - 65 Db
Gallipoli (Gelibolu), Turkey 72 Db
Gallipolis, Ohio - - 129 Cc
Gallivare, Sweden - - 44 Ef
Galloway, Mull of, Scot. 21 Bd
Gallup, New Mexico - 135 Jd
Gallur, Spain - - 38 Dc
Gálosfa, Hungary - - 66 Cc
Galt, Ontario - - 123 Hd
Galtee Mts., Eire - - 27 Bg
Galukilo, Tangany. Terr. 111 Bg
Galva, Illinois - - 132 De
Galveston and B., Texas 133 Ef
Galvez, Argentina - 146 Ce
Galway and co., Eire - 27 Ae
Galway B., Eire - - 27 Ae
Gama Hanu, Kashmir - 83 Ga
Gambaga, Gold Coast - 104 Dd
Gambela, Ethiopia - 108 Bd
Gambia, Sierra Leone - 104 Be
Gambia, col., N.-W. Afr. 101 Ad
Gambia, R., Fr. W. Afr. 104 Bd
Gambier Is., Pacific Oc. 149 Nh
Gambo, Newfoundland - 120 Hb
Gamboma, Fr. Eq. Africa 109 Cb
Gamboola, Queensland - 153 Bc
Gambotta, Ethiopia - 108 Cd
Gaming, Austria - - 59 Kd
Gamkonora, Mt., Halmahera, N.I. - - 99 Gc
Gamleby, Sweden - - 51 Fe
Gamoep, Cape Prov. - 114 Cd
Gamran, Fr. W. Africa 105 Cb
Gams, Switzerland - 43 Hb
Gamsby, Ontario - - 122 Ea
Gan R., Manchuria - 96 Ba
Gananita, A.-E. Sudan - 108 Bb
Gananoque, Ontario - 121 Bb
Ganda, Belgian Congo - 109 Cb
Gandak R., Bihar - 87 Fb
Gandava, Baluchistan - 82 Bd
Gander B. & L., Newfoundland - - - 120 Hb
Ganderowe Falls, S. Rhod. 113 Ca
Gandesa, Spain - - 39 Fc
Gandia, Spain - - 41 Fb
Gandino, Italy - - 62 Db
Gando, Fr. W. Africa - 105 Bc
Gando, Nigeria, etc. - 105 Bc
Ganeb, Fr. W. Africa - 104 Bc
Gangakhér, Hyderabad - 90 Cb
Gangapur, Rajputana - 83 Ge
Gangara, Fr. W. Africa 105 Cc
Gangaw, Burma - - 92 Aa
Gangaw Ra., Burma - 88 Fb
Gangawati, Hyderabad - 90 Cd
Ganges, France - - 35 Fd
Ganges I., Pacific Oc. - 149 Fb
Ganges R., India - - 81 Ee
Gangi, Sicily - - 65 Hg
Gangkofen, Bavaria - 59 Gc
Gangoh, United Provs. - 83 Gd
Gangotri, mt., Punjab States 83 Hc
Gangpur, Eastern States 87 Fd
Gangrar, Rajputana - 85 Ec
Gangtok, Sikkim - - 88 Ba
Ganh-rai B., Cochin-China 95 Cg
Ganjam, Orissa - - 91 Gb
Ganmam, New S. Wales 155 Ec
Gannat, France - - 35 Fa
Gannavaram, Madras - 91 Ec
Ganora, Rajputana - 85 Ec
Ganskuil, Transvaal - 115 Gb
Gantheaume B., W. Aust. 152 Ad
Gao, Fr. W. Africa - 104 Ec
Gaoua, Fr. W. Africa - 104 Dd
Gaoual, Fr. W. Africa - 104 Bd
Gap, France - - - 35 Jc
Gapan, Philippines - 95 Ff
Gara, L., Eire - - 26 Bd
Garachine, Panama - 140 Hf
Garaet et Tarf, Algeria 103 Hb
Garanhuns, Brazil - 143 Gd
Garba Tula, Kenya - 110 Fc
Garboldisham, England 15 Eb
Garcia, Spain - - 39 Fc
Gard, dep., France - 35 Gc
Garda, L. di, Italy - 62 Eb
Gardby, Sweden - - 51 Ff
Garde, C. de, Algeria - 103 Ha
Gardelegen, Prussia - 55 Gc
Garden, Michigan - - 122 Ec
Garden City, Kansas - 133 Bb
Garden City, Texas - 133 Be
Garden Pass, Nevada - 134 Eb
Gardez, Afghanistan - 82 Cb
Gardhíki, Greece - - 70 Bd
Gardiner, Maine - - 128 Da
Gardiner, Montana - 136 Hc
Gardiner, New Mexico - 135 Lc
Gardiner, New York - 128 Ac
Gardiner, Oregon - - 136 Ad
Gardiner I., Hawaiian Is. 157 Ga
Gardiners I. and B., New York - - - 128 Bc
Gardner, Colorado - - 135 Lc
Gardner I., Pacific Oc. - 149 Jc
Gardner I., Phœnix Is. - 157 Fd
Gardnerville, Nevada - 134 Db
Gardone, Italy - - 62 Eb
Gardulla, Ethiopia - 108 Cd
Garelochhead, Scotland 22 Dd
Gareloi I., Aleutian Is. - 125 Um
Garfield, Utah - - 135 Ga
Garfield, Washington - 136 Eb
Gargaliánoi, Greece - 71 Cf
Gargano Mts., Italy - 64 Fb
Gargaon, Assam - - 88 Ea
Gargnano, Italy - - 62 Eb
Gargues, Mt., Kenya - 110 Ec
Gar Gunsa, Tibet - - 84 Ed
Gargzdai, Lithuania - 49 Ad
Garha, Gwalior - - 86 Cc
Garhakota, Cent. Provs. 86 Cd
Garhmuktesar, United Provs. - - - 83 Gd
Garhshankar, Punjab - 83 Gc
Garhwa, Bihar - - 87 Ec
Garhwal, United Provs. - 83 Hc
Garian, Libya - - 106 Ok
Garibaldi, Brazil - - 147 Ed
Garibaldi, Sardinia - 64 Je
Garibaldi Park, Br. Columb. 124 Ed
Garies, Cape Prov. - 114 Be
Garissa, Kenya - - 110 Fd
Garlasco, Italy - - 62 Cb
Garli, Norway - - 46 Gb
Garlieston, Scotland - 21 Bd
Garmo, Norway - - 46 Ec
Garmsel, Afghanistan - 79 Hc
Garneill, Montana - - 136 Jb
Garner, Iowa - - 132 Cd
Garnes, Norway - - 47 Bd
Garnet, Idaho - - 136 Fd
Garnett, Kansas - - 133 Ea
Garo Hills, Assam - 88 Cb
Garoet, Java - - 98 Ce
Garola, Central Provs. - 86 Cc
Garonne, R., France - 34 Bc
Garoua, Fr. Eq. Africa 105 Dd
Garrafe de Torio, Spain 36 Eb
Garrauli, Central India - 86 Cc
Garraway, Liberia - 104 Cf
Garrett, Indiana - - 129 Bb
Garrigues, Mts., France 35 Fd
Garrison, Montana - 136 Gb
Garrizo Mts., Arizona - 135 Jc
Garrovillas, Spain - - 37 Dc
Garry, L., N.-W. Terr. 124 Ka
Garry L. & Glen, Scot. - 22 Cb
Garry R., Scotland - 23 Ec
Garsen, Kenya - - 110 Fe
Garstang, England - 18 Bc
Garth, Wales - - 20 Cc
Garthby, Quebec - - 121 Eb
Gartok, Tibet - - 83 Jc
Garton-on-the-Wolds, England - - - 19 Db
Gartow, Prussia - - 55 Gc
Gartz, Prussia - - 55 Kb
Garub, S.-W. Africa - 114 Bc
Garvagh, N. Ireland - 26 Db
Garwolin, Poland - - 60 Fc
Gary, Indiana - - 129 Ab
Gary, S. Dakota - - 132 Ac
Garza, Argentina - - 146 Cd
Garzigar - - - 56 Bb
Garzon, Colombia - - 144 Ac
Gas, Indiana - - - 129 Bb
Gas Fd., Sweden - - 51 Fe
Gascony, France - - 34 Bd
Gascoyne Mt. & Goldfield, W. Aust. - - 152 Bc
Gascoyne R., W. Aust. 152 Ac
Gasi, Kenya - - - 111 Ff
Gasimursk, U.S.S.R. - 96 Ba
Gasmata, New Britain - 156 Ec
Gasparilla L., Florida - 131 Mh
Gaspé, Quebec - - 119 Qg
Gaspé B., Quebec - - 120 Cb
Gaspé C. & Pen., Quebec 120 Cb
Gasper Str., Nether. Indies 99 Cd
Gaspésie Park, Quebec - 120 Bb
Gasr el Brega, Libya - 106 Bc
Gasr el Mugtar, Libya - 106 Bc
Gasr Ghiranghedi, Libya 106 Cf
Gasr Zoabi, Libya - 106 Cd
Gassol, Nigeria - - 105 Dd
Gastonia, N. Carolina - 131 Hc
Gastoúni, Greece - - 71 Cf
Gastouri, Corfu I. - - 70 Ad
Gastre, Argentina - - 148 Cc
Gata, Sa. & C. de, Spain 41 Dd
Gataia, Romania - - 67 Gd
Gate City, Virginia - 129 Cd
Gatehouse of Fleet, Scot. 21 Bd
Gateshead, England - 21 Ed
Gatesville, Texas - - 133 Ce
Gatineau R., Quebec - 121 Cb
Gatooma, S. Rhodesia - 113 Cb
Gattinara, Italy - - 62 Cb
Gaucin, Spain - - 40 Ec
Gaud-i-Zirreh, Afghan. 79 Hd
Gauguaretama, Brazil - 143 Hd
Gauhati, Assam - - 88 Ca
Gauldel, Norway - - 46 Gb
Gauri Ghat, Nepal - 86 Da
Gaurihar, Central India 86 Dc
Gauripur, Assam - - 88 Ba
Gauri Sankar, Nepal-Tibet 87 Ga
Gausta, mt., Norway - 47 Ee
Gauttier Mts., New Guinea 156 Bb
Gava, Spain - - - 39 Gc
Gavaza, Mozambique - 113 Ec
Gavião, Portugal - - 37 Cc
Gaviota, California - 134 Cd
Gavirate, Italy - - 62 Cb
Gävle and B., Sweden - 50 Gb
Gävleborg, län, Sweden 50 Ea
Gavoi, Sardinia - - 64 Jf
Găvojdia, Romania - 67 Hd
Gavorrano, Italy - - 62 Ee
Gavray, France - - 32 Db
Gavrilovo, U.S.S.R. - 48 Mb
Gávros, Greece - - 70 Cc
Gawachab, S.-W. Africa 114 Bc
Gawilgarh and Hills, Berar, C.P. - - 86 Be
Gawler, S. Australia - 154 Bc
Gaya, Bihar - - - 87 Fc
Gaya, Fr. W. Africa - 105 Bc
Gayaza, Uganda - - 110 Bd
Gaydon, England - - 14 Cb
Gaylord, Michigan - 122 Fc
Gayndah, Queensland - 153 De
Gaysum Is., Egypt - 107 Je
Gaza, Fr. Eq. Africa - 105 Ee
Gaza (Ghazze), Palestine 80 Ad
Gazeh Manzil, Persia - 79 Hd
Gazelle, California - 134 Ba
Gazelle Pen., New Britain 156 Eb
Gazi Antep, Turkey - 78 Cb
Gazik, Persia - - 79 Hc
Gdansk (Danzig), Poland 56 Cb
Gdov, U.S.S.R. - - 74 Dd
Gdynia, Poland - - 60 Ea
Gea, Spain - - - 38 Dd
Geary, Oklahoma - - 133 Cc
Geba Geba, Ethiopia - 108 Dd
Gebeit, A.-E. Sudan - 108 Ca
Gedaref, A.-E. Sudan - 108 Cc
Geddi, A.-E. Sudan - 108 Bb
Geddington, England - 15 Db
Gedeis, Br. Somaliland - 108 Ed
Gediyo, Mt., Fr. W. Afr. 105 Dc
Gedser, Denmark - - 45 Ed
Geelong, Victoria - - 154 De
Geelvink B., New Guinea 156 Bb
Geelvink Chan., W. Aust. 152 Ad
Geestemünde, Prussia - 54 Db
Geevagh, Eire - - 26 Bc
Geeveston, Tasmania - 155 Jh
Gefara, Libya - - 106 Ok
Gegab, Libya - - 106 Db
Geh, Persia - - - 79 Hd
Geidam, Nigeria - - 105 Dc
Geilo, Norway - - 47 Ed
Geiranger, Norway - 46 Db
Geita, Tangany. Terr. - 110 Be
Gela, Belg. Congo - - 109 Ec
Gela, Sicily - - 65 Hg
Gelderland, Holland - 29 Db
Geldern, Prussia - - 54 Bd
Geledi, Ethiopia - - 108 Dd
Gelendzhik, U.S.S.R. - 75 Fg
Gelert, Ontario - - 121 Ab
Gelibolu (Gallipoli), Turkey 72 Db
Gelse, Hungary - - 66 Cc
Gelsenkirchen, Prussia - 54 Cd
Gemas, Malay States - 98 Bc
Gemlik, Turkey - - 72 Gb
Gemlik, Gulf, Turkey - 72 Fb
Gemmi Pass, Switzerland 42 Ed
Gemono, Italy - - 63 Ha
Gemünd, Prussia - - 54 Be
Gemünden, Bavaria - 58 Da
Gemville, New S. Wales 154 Db
Genck, Belgium - - 29 Dd
Genderu Mt., Fr. Eq. Afr. 105 Dd
General Acha, Argentina 148 Cb
General Alvear, Argent. 148 Db
General Capdevila, Argent. 146 Cd
General Carneiro, Brazil 147 Eb
General Grant Nat. Park, California - - - 134 Dc
General Guido, Argentina 148 Eb
General la Madrid, Argent. 148 Db
General Lavalle, Argent. 148 Eb
General Madariaga, Argent. 148 Eb
General Paz, Argentina 148 Eb
General Pico, Argentina 148 Db

General Pinto, *Argentina* 148 Da
General Roca, *Argentina* 148 Cb
General Uriburu, *Argent.* 148 Ea
General Viamonte, *Argent.* 148 Db
General Villegas, *Argent.* 148 Da
Genesa, *Cape Prov.* 115 Fc
Genesee, *Idaho* 136 Eb
Geneseo, *Illinois* 132 Ee
Geneseo, *Kansas* 133 Da
Geneva, *Alabama* 130 Ee
Geneva, *Illinois* 132 Ee
Geneva, *New York* 123 Kd
Geneva, *Ohio* 129 Db
Geneva (Geneve), *Switz.* 42 Bd
Geneva, L. of (Léman, Lac), *France-Switz.* 42 Bd
Geneve & canton, *Switz.* 42 Bd
Genge, *Mozambique* 113 Fa
Genipapo, *Brazil* 143 Ec
Genisaia, *Greece* 72 Ba
Genkai Nada, *Japan* 97 Cd
Genlis, *France* 31 Hd
Gennargentu, Monti del, *Sardinia* 64 Jg
Gennep, *Holland* 29 Dc
Genner, *Denmark* 45 Cc
Genoa, *Nevada* 134 Db
Genoa, *Victoria* 155 Fd
Genoa (Genova), & G., *Italy* 62 Cc
Genoffa, Mt., *New Guinea* 156 Ab
Genovesa, *Galapagos Is.* 145 Fg
Genshu, *Korea* 97 Bc
Genthin, *Prussia* 55 Hc
Genzan, *Korea* 97 Bc
Genzano, *Italy* 65 Cb
Genzano di Roma, *Italy* 64 Cb
Geographe B., *W. Aust.* 152 Ae
Geographe Chan., *W. Aust.* 152 Ac
Geokchai, *Azerbaijan* 75 Hg
Geonkhali, *Bengal* 88 Bc
George, *Cape Prov.* 114 Ef
George B., *Nova Scotia* 120 Ed
George L., *Florida* 131 Hf
George, L., *New S. Wales* 155 Fd
George L., *New York* 129 Ha
George, L., *Uganda* 110 Bc
George R., *Quebec* 119 Qe
Georgetown, *Alaska* 125 He
Georgetown, *Ascension I.* 114 Lh
Georgetown, *Br. Guiana* 144 Eb
Georgetown, *Colorado* 135 Kb
Georgetown, *Delaware* 129 Gc
Georgetown, *Georgia* 131 Fe
Georgetown, *Kentucky* 131 Fa
Georgetown, *Massachusetts* 128 Cb
Georgetown, *Ohio* 129 Cc
Georgetown, *Penang I., Malay States* 98 Ab
Georgetown, *Pr. Edward I.* 120 Dc
Georgetown, *Queensland* 153 Bc
Georgetown, *S. Carolina* 131 Jd
George Town, *Tasmania* 155 Jg
Georgetown, *Texas* 133 De
Georgia, rep., *U.S.S.R.* 75 Gg
Georgia, state, *U.S.A.* 127 Jd
Georgia, Str., *Br. Columb.* 118 Eg
Georgian B., *Ontario* 123 Hc
Georgian Bay Is. Nat. Pk., *Ontario* 123 Hc
Georgiana, *Alabama* 130 Ee
Georgievsk, *U.S.S.R.* 75 Gg
Gera, *Thuringia* 55 Ge
Geral, Sa., *Brazil* 147 Gb
Geraldine, *New Zealand* 159 Cf
Geraldine, *W. Australia* 152 Ad
Geraldton, *Ontario* 122 Ea
Geraldton, *W. Aust.* 152 Ad
Gérardmer, *France* 31 Jc
Gerbéviller, *France* 31 Jc
Gérce, *Hungary* 66 Bb
Gerdauen 56 Fb
Gerdes, *Libya* 106 Cb
Geremoabo, *Brazil* 143 Ge
Gergal, *Spain* 41 Dc
Geriban, *It. Somaliland* 108 Ed
Gering, *Nebraska* 135 Ma
Gerlach, *Nevada* 134 Da
Gerlache, de, Str., *Antarctica* 160 —
Gerlache, Pic de, *Belg. Congo* 109 Ed
Gerlachovka, *Slovakia* 57 Fd
Gerlogubi, *Ethiopia* 108 Ed
Germania, *Argentina* 148 Da
Germania Land, *Greenl'd* 9 Hb
Germantown, *New York* 128 Bb
German Volga, *U.S.S.R.* 75 He
Germany, *Cent. Europe* 53 Cc
Germiston, *Transvaal* 115 Hc
Gernsheim, *Hesse* 58 Cb
Gerolstein, *Prussia* 58 Aa
Gerona and prov., *Spain* 39 Hc
Geronimo, *Arizona* 135 He
Gers, dep., *France* 34 Cd
Gersoppa, *Bombay* 90 Bd
Gerswalde, *Prussia* 55 Jb
Géryville, *Algeria* 102 Ec
Gerze, *Turkey* 78 Ca
Gesenke, *Moravia* 57 Cd
Gessertshausen, *Bavaria* 58 Ec
Getafe, *Spain* 38 Bd
Gete, *Belg. Congo* 109 Cc
Gethsemani, *Quebec* 120 Ea
Gettysburg, *Pennsylvania* 129 Fc
Gety, *Belg. Congo* 110 Bc
Gevar, *Turkey* 78 Db
Gevelsberg, *Prussia* 54 Cd
Geyikli, *Turkey* 72 Dc
Geysdorp, *Transvaal* 115 Fc
Geyser, *Nevada* 134 Fb
Ghail, *Arabia* 79 Ee
Ghanen, El, *Libya* 106 Ok
Ghantwar, *Baroda* 85 Cd
Ghar, *Arabia* 79 Ed
Ghardaia, *Algeria* 103 Fc
Ghardimaou, *Tunisia* 103 Ja
Ghârib, Jeb., *Egypt* 107 Jd
Gharm, *Tadzhik* 84 Cc
Gharo, *Sind* 85 Ab
Ghassoul, *Algeria* 102 Ec
Ghat, *Arabia* 78 Dd
Ghatal, *Bengal* 88 Ac
Ghatampur, *United Provs.* 86 Db
Ghatghat, *Arabia* 79 Ee
Ghats, Eastern, *S. India* 90 Dd
Ghats, Western, *S. India* 90 Aa
Ghauta, *Arabia* 79 Ee
Ghaziabad, *United Provs.* 83 Gd
Ghazipur, *United Provs.* 87 Ec
Ghazni & R., *Afghanistan* 82 Cb
Gheddahia, el, *Libya* 106 Pl
Gheel, *Belgium* 29 Dc
Ghemines, *Libya* 106 Bc
Ghent, *Belgium* 29 Bc
Gheorgheni, *Transylvania* 69 Fb
Gherabe, *Arabia* 78 De
Gherla, *Transylvania* 67 Jb
Ghilarza, *Sardinia* 64 Hf
Ghilianwala, *Punjab* 83 Eb
Ghirza, *Libya* 106 Pl
Ghobreh, *Oman* 79 Ge
Ghora, *Central India* 85 Ec
Ghorabari, *Sind* 85 Ab
Ghor es Seiseban, *Trans-Jordan* 80 Dd
Ghorian, *Afghanistan* 79 Hc
Ghotki, *Sind* 82 Ce
Giado, *Libya* 106 Nl
Gialo Oasi, *Libya* 106 Cd
Giano dell' Umbria, *Italy* 63 Ge
Giant's Castle, *Natal* 115 Hd
Giant's Causeway, *N. Ire.* 26 Da
Gianyar, *Bali I., N.I.* 99 Ee
Giarabub, *Libya* 106 Ed
Giardina, *Libya* 106 Cc
Giarmata, *Romania* 67 Gd
Giarre, *Sicily* 65 Jg
Gibara, *Cuba* 140 Bb
Gibbonsville, *Idaho* 136 Fc
Gibeon, *S.-W. Africa* 114 Bb
Gibraltar, *Spain* 40 Ec
Gibraltar, Str. of, *Spain-Africa* 40 Ed
Gibson, *New Mexico* 135 Jd
Gibson City, *Illinois* 132 Ee
Giddings, *Texas* 133 De
Giedraičiai, *Lithuania* 49 Cd
Gielniów, *Poland* 57 Fb
Gien, *France* 30 Ed
Giengen, *Württemberg* 58 Ec
Giessen, *Hesse* 58 Ca
Gifford, *Scotland* 23 Fe
Gifhorn, *Prussia* 54 Fc
Giftun Kebir, *Egypt* 107 Ke
Gifu, *Japan* 97 Dc
Gigant, *U.S.S.R.* 75 Gf
Giganta, Sierra, *Mexico* 138 Bb
Gigha I., *Scotland* 22 Ce
Giglio I., *Italy* 64 Aa
Gigner, *Ethiopia* 108 Dd
Giheina, *Egypt* 107 He
Gijnokaster (Argyrokastron), *Albania* 70 Ac
Gijon, *Spain* 36 Ea
Gila Ra., *Arizona* 134 Fe
Gila R., *Arizona* 134 Ge
Gila Bend, *Arizona* 135 Ge
Gilan, *Persia* 79 Eb
Gilău, *Transylvania* 67 Jc
Gilbert Is., *Pacific Oc.* 157 Ec
Gilbert Pk., *Utah* 135 Ha
Gilbert R., *Queensland* 153 Bc
Gilberton, *Queensland* 153 Bc
Gilbertville, *Maine* 128 Ca
Gilbjærg Hoved, *Denmark* 45 Eb
Gilbués, *Brazil* 143 Fd
Gilby, *N. Dakota* 132 Aa
Gildessa, *Ethiopia* 108 Dd
Gilead, *Maine* 128 Ca
Gilehdar, *Persia* 79 Fd
Gilgandra, *New S. Wales* 155 Fb
Gilge 56 Fa
Gilgenburg 56 Ec
Gilgil, *Kenya* 110 Ed
Gilgit and R., *Kashmir* 84 Cc
Gilgunnia, *New S. Wales* 155 Eb
Gill, L., *Eire* 26 Bc
Gilles, L., *S. Australia* 154 Ac
Gillett, *Arkansas* 130 Cc
Gillingham, *Dorset, Eng.* 14 Bd
Gillingham, *Kent, Eng.* 15 Ed
Gillis, *Nevada* 134 Db
Gilly, *France* 35 Fa
Gilman, *Illinois* 132 Fe
Gilman, *Missouri* 132 Ce
Gilman, *Montana* 136 Gb
Gilman, *Washington* 136 Bb
Gilmer, *Texas* 133 Ed
Gilmore, *Idaho* 136 Gc
Gilmore, *Queensland* 153 Be
Gilpeppie, *Queensland* 153 Be
Gilroy, *California* 134 Cc
Gilvaci, *Transylvania* 67 Hb
Gimaj, *Albania* 70 Aa
Gimbo, *Angola* 109 Dd
Gimel, *Switzerland* 42 Bc
Gimigliano, *Italy* 65 Cd
Gimo, *Sweden* 50 Hb
Gimont, *France* 34 Cd
Ginah, *Egypt* 107 Hf
Gingee, *Madras* 89 Ca
Gingin, *W. Australia* 152 Be
Gingugi, *Belg. Congo* 109 Cc
Ginta, *Transylvania* 67 Hc
Ginzo de Limea, *Spain* 36 Cb
Gioia, G. of, *Italy* 65 Bd
Gioia del Colle, *Italy* 65 Cb
Giornico, *Switzerland* 43 Gd
Giosc, *Libya* 106 Nk
Gippsland, *Victoria* 155 Ee
Gir Forest, *W. India* 85 Cd
Giran, *Taiwan* 97 Hf
Girard, *Kansas* 133 Eb
Girardot, *Colombia* 144 Bc
Giraud, *France* 35 Gd
Gird Gwalior, *Gwalior* 86 Cb
Girdwood, *Alaska* 125 Kf
Giresun, *Turkey* 72 Ec
Girga, *Egypt* 107 He
Giridih, *Bihar* 87 Gc
Girifta, *Kenya* 110 Fc
Girilambone, *N. S. W.* 155 Eb
Girishk, *Afghanistan* 79 Hc
Giro, *Nigeria* 105 Bc
Gironde, dep., *France* 34 Bc
Gironde, R., *France* 34 Aa
Gironella, *Spain* 39 Gb
Girung, *China* 94 Bc
Girvan, *Scotland* 21 Bc
Gisborne & prov., *New Zealand* 158 Gc
Gisors, *France* 30 Db
Giudicarie, Val, *Italy* 62 Eb
Giulianova, *Italy* 63 He
Giurgiu, *Romania* 69 Fd
Give, *Denmark* 45 Cc
Givet, *France* 31 Ga
Givors, *France* 35 Gb
Givry, *France* 31 Ge
Gizhiga, *U.S.S.R.* 76 Qc
Gjegnabreen, mt., *Norway* 46 Bc
Gjerstad, *Norway* 47 Ef
Gjövdal, *Norway* 47 Ef
Gjövik, *Norway* 46 Gd
Glace Bay, *Nova Scotia* 120 Fc
Glacier, *Brit. Columbia* 124 Fd
Glacier, *Washington* 136 Ca
Glacier B., *Greenland* 9 Hb
Glacier Nat. Pk., *Montana* 136 Ga
Glacier Pk., *Washington* 136 Ca
Glacier Bay Nat. Mon., *Alaska* 125 Ng
Gladbeck, *Prussia* 54 Bd
Gladstone, *Michigan* 122 Ec
Gladstone, *New S. Wales* 155 Hb
Gladstone, *New Zealand* 159 Bf
Gladstone, *Queensland* 153 Dd
Gladstone, *S. Aust.* 154 Bc
Gladstone, *Tasmania* 155 Kg
Gladstone, *W. Aust.* 152 Ad
Gladstone, Mt., *New Guin.* 156 Dc
Gladwin, *Michigan* 122 Fd
Glænö, *Denmark* 45 Ec
Glaf Fd., *Sweden* 50 Bc
Glamoč, *Bosnia* 68 Bb
Glamocko polje, *Bosnia* 68 Bb
Glamorgan, co., *Wales* 20 Cd
Glandore & Harb., *Eire* 25 Bf
Glarus & canton, *Switz.* 43 Hb
Glasgow, *Kentucky* 130 Fb
Glasgow, *Missouri* 130 Ba
Glasgow, *Scotland* 23 De
Glaslough, *Eire* 26 Dc
Glassdrummond, *N. Ire.* 26 Ec
Glastonbury, *England* 14 Bd
Glatz 57 Bc
Glauchau, *Saxony* 55 He
Glazov, *U.S.S.R.* 74 Jd
Gleason, *Montana* 136 Gb
Głębokie 60 Ja
Gleisdorf, *Austria* 59 Kd
Gleiwitz (Gliwice), *Poland* 57 Dc
Glen, *Eire* 26 Ca
Glen, *Montana* 136 Gb
Glen, *Montana* 136 Gc
Glen, *New Hampshire* 128 Ca
Glenamaddy, *Eire* 27 Bd
Glenanane, *Eire* 25 Bb
Glenarm, *N. Ireland* 26 Eb
Glenavon, *Washington* 136 Bb
Glenavy, *N. Ireland* 26 Db
Glenbrook, *Nevada* 134 Db
Glenburnie, *S. Australia* 154 Ce
Glencoe, *Minnesota* 132 Bc
Glencoe, *Natal* 115 Hd
Glen Coe, *Scotland* 22 Dc
Glencoe, *S. Australia* 154 Ce
Glenconner, *Cape Prov.* 115 Ff
Glendale, *Arizona* 135 Ge
Glendale, *California* 134 Dd
Glendale, *S. Rhodesia* 113 Da
Glendalough, *Eire* 27 De
Glendaruel, *Scotland* 22 Cd
Glenealy, *Eire* 27 Df
Glenelg, *Scotland* 22 Cb
Glenelg, *S. Australia* 154 Bc
Glenelg, R., *Victoria* 154 Cd
Glen Ellen, *California* 134 Bb
Glengariff, *Eire* 25 Bf
Glengyle, *Queensland* 153 Ad
Glenharry, *Cape Prov.* 115 Ff
Glenhope, *New Zealand* 159 Dd
Glen Innes, *New S. Wales* 155 Ga
Glenluce, *Scotland* 21 Bd
Glenmore, *Eire* 25 Bd
Glen More, *Scotland* 22 Db
Glen Moriston, *Scotland* 22 Db
Glenns Ferry, *Idaho* 136 Fd
Glenore, *Queensland* 153 Bc
Glenormiston, *Queensland* 153 Ad
Glenreagh, *New S. Wales* 155 Hb
Glen Robertson, *Ontario* 121 Cb
Glenrose, *Texas* 133 Dd
Glen Shee, *Scotland* 23 Ec
Glens Falls, *New York* 123 Md
Glenside, *Natal* 115 Jd
Glen Tay, *Ontario* 121 Bb
Glenties, *Eire* 26 Bb
Glen Urquhart, *Scotland* 23 Db
Glenville, *Georgia* 131 He
Glenville, *W. Virginia* 129 Dc
Glenwood, *Iowa* 132 Be
Glenwood, *Minnesota* 132 Bc
Glenwood, *Utah* 135 Hb
Glenwood Springs, *Colorado* 135 Kb
Gletsch, *Switzerland* 43 Fc
Glin, *Eire* 25 Bd
Glina, *Croatia* 66 Bd
Glinsk, *Eire* 25 Bc
Glinton, *England* 15 Da
Glittertind, mt., *Norway* 46 Ec
Gliwice (Gleiwitz), *Poland* 57 Dc
Globe, *Arizona* 135 He
Glogau 55 Md
Gloggnitz, *Austria* 59 Kd
Glomma, R., *Norway* 46 Gb
Gloppen, *Norway* 46 Cc
Glorenza, *Italy* 62 Ea
Glorioso Is., *Madagascar* 112 Eb
Glossa, C., *Albania* 70 Ac
Glossop, *England* 18 Cd
Gloucester, *Massachusetts* 128 Cb
Gloucester, *New Bruns.* 120 Bc
Gloucester, *New S. Wales* 155 Gb
Gloucester, *Virginia* 129 Fd
Gloucester & co., *Eng.* 14 Bc
Gloversville, *New York* 123 Ld
Gloveville, *Colorado* 135 Lb
Główno, *Poland* 57 Eb
Glukhov, *Ukraine* 75 Ee
Glyngöre, *Denmark* 45 Bb
Glynn, *Eire* 27 Dg
Glynn, *N. Ireland* 26 Eb
Gmund, *Austria* 59 Jc
Gmünd, *Württemberg* 58 Dc
Gmunden, *Austria* 59 Hd
Gnas, *Austria* 66 Ac
Gnesta, *Sweden* 50 Gc
Gniew, *Poland* 56 Cc
Gniezno, *Poland* 60 Db
Gnjilane, *Serbia* 68 Gd
Gnoien, *Mecklenburg* 55 Hb
Goa (Portuguese), *Bombay* 90 Bd
Goajira, dep., *Colombia* 144 Ba
Goalpara, *Assam* 88 Ca
Goalundo, *Bengal* 88 Bc
Goaso, *Gold Coast* 104 De
Goba, *Ethiopia* 108 Cd
Goba, *Mozambique* 115 Kc
Gobad, *Fr. Somaliland* 108 Dc
Gobas, *S.-W. Africa* 114 Cc
Gobeni, *Natal* 115 Jc
Gobi Des., *Mongolia* 76 Ke
Gobindpur, *Bihar* 87 Gd
Gobo, *Japan* 100 Ee
Gobwen, *It. Somaliland* 108 Gg
Goch, *Prussia* 54 Bd
Godalming, *England* 15 Dd
Godavari, E. & W., *Madras* 91 Ec
Godavari R., *Madras, etc.* 91 Eb
Godda, *Bihar* 87 Gc
Gode-Gode, *Tang. Terr.* 111 Eg
Goderich, *Ontario* 122 Gd
Goderville, *France* 30 Cb
Godesberg, *Prussia* 54 Ce
Godhavn, *Greenland* 9 Dd
Godhra, *Bombay* 85 Dc
Godmanchester, *England* 15 Db
Gödöllö, *Hungary* 66 Eb
Gods L. & R., *Manitoba* 124 Kd
Godthaab, *Greenland* 9 De
Godwar, *Rajputana* 85 Db
Goede Hope, C. of, *New Guinea* 156 Ab
Goenoengsahilan, *Sumatra* 98 Bc
Goenoengsitoli, *Nias I., Nether. Indies* 98 Ac
Goenoengsoegih, *Sumatra* 98 Cd
Goeree, *Holland* 29 Bc
Goes, *Holland* 29 Bc
Gofe, *Gold Coast* 104 De
Gogama, *Ontario* 123 Hb
Gog Magog Hills, *Eng.* 15 Eb
Gogolin 57 Dc
Gogra R., *United Provs.* 87 Eb
Gogri, *Bihar* 87 Gc
Gogrial, *A.-E. Sudan* 108 Ad
Gogunda, *Rajputana* 85 Db
Gohana, *Punjab* 83 Gd
Goil, L., *Scotland* 22 Dd
Gois, *Portugal* 37 Bb
Gojjam, *Ethiopia* 108 Cc
Gojo, *Japan* 100 Ed
Gojra, *Punjab* 82 Ec
Gokak, *Bombay* 90 Bc
Gokcha (Sevan), L., *Armenia* 75 Hg
Gokhaz, *S.-W. Africa* 114 Cb
Go-kong, *Cochin-China* 95 Cg
Göksun, *Turkey* 78 Cb
Gokwe, *S. Rhodesia* 113 Cb
Gol, *Norway* 46 Ed
Gola, *United Provs.* 83 Jd
Golaghat, *Assam* 88 Ea
Golbanti (Borobini), *Kenya* 110 Fe
Golconda, *Hyderabad* 90 Dc
Golconda, *Illinois* 130 Db
Golconda, *Nevada* 134 Ea
Golčuv Jenikov, *Bohemia* 59 Kb
Goldap & R. 56 Gb
Gold Beach, *Oregon* 136 Ad
Goldberg 55 Ld
Goldburg, *Idaho* 136 Gc
Gold Coast, col., *W. Afr.* 101 Be
Golden, *Colorado* 135 Lb
Goldenbridge, *New York* 128 Bc
Goldendale, *Washington* 136 Cb
Goldene Aue, *Prussia* 54 Fd
Golden Gate Mts., *Nevada* 134 Fb
Golden Lake, *Ontario* 121 Bb
Golden Vale, *Eire* 27 Bf
Golden Valley, *S. Rhod.* 113 Cb
Goldfield, *Colorado* 135 Lb
Goldfield, *Nevada* 134 Ec
Gold Hill, *Oregon* 136 Bd
Goldsboro, *N. Carolina* 131 Kc
Goldshöfe, *Württemberg* 58 Ec
Goldthwaite, *Texas* 133 Ce
Golega, *Portugal* 37 Bc
Golfo Aranci, *Sardinia* 64 Je
Gol Gol, *New S. Wales* 154 Cc
Golgonda, *Madras* 91 Fc
Golgong, *New S. Wales* 155 Fb
Goli, I., *Dalmatia* 63 Jc
Golija, mt., *Serbia* 68 Fc
Golina, *Poland* 57 Ca
Gollel, *Transvaal* 115 Jc
Gollnow 55 Kb
Golovin, *Alaska* 125 Fd

General Index

Greenfield, Iowa - - 132 Be
Greenfield, Massachusetts 128 Bb
Greenfield, Missouri - 130 Bb
Greenfield, Ohio - - 129 Cc
Greenland, N. America - 117 Nb
Greenlaw, Scotland - 21 Db
Greenock, Scotland - 22 De
Greenore, Eire - - 26 Dc
Greenport, New York - 123 Me
Green River, Utah - 135 Hb
Green River, Wyoming - 135 Ja
Greensboro, Alabama - 130 Ed
Greensboro, Georgia - 131 Gd
Greensboro, N. Carolina 131 Jb
Greensburg, Indiana - 129 Bc
Greensburg, Kansas - 133 Cb
Greensburg, Kentucky - 130 Fb
Greensburg, Louisiana - 130 Ce
Greensburg, Pennsylvania 129 Eb
Greenville, Alabama - 130 Ee
Greenville, California - 134 Ca
Greenville, Georgia - 131 Fd
Greenville, Illinois - 132 Ef
Greenville, Kentucky - 130 Eb
Greenville, Liberia - 104 Ce
Greenville, Michigan - 122 Fd
Greenville, Mississippi - 130 Cd
Greenville, Missouri - 130 Cb
Greenville, N. Carolina 131 Kc
Greenville, Ohio - - 129 Bb
Greenville, Pennsylvania 129 Db
Greenville, S. Carolina - 131 Gc
Greenville, Tennessee - 131 Gb
Greenville, Texas - - 133 Dd
Greenwich, Connecticut - 128 Bc
Greenwich, England - 15 Ed
Greenwich, New York - 128 Bb
Greenwich, Rhode Island 128 Cc
Greenwood, Arkansas - 130 Ac
Greenwood, Indiana - 129 Ac
Greenwood, Mississippi 130 Dd
Greenwood, Nova Scotia 120 Cd
Greenwood, S. Carolina 131 Gc
Greenwood, Wisconsin - 132 Dc
Greer, Arizona - - 135 Jd
Gregory, L., S. Australia 154 Ba
Gregory Ra., Queensland 153 Bc
Gregory R., Queensland 153 Ac
Gregory Downs, Queensl'd 153 Ac
Greifenberg, Austria - 59 He
Greifenberg - - - 55 Lb
Greifenhagen - - 55 Kb
Greifswald, Prussia - 55 Ja
Greifswalder Bodden, Prussia - - - 55 Ja
Greiner Wald, Austria - 59 Jc
Greipstad, Norway - 47 Df
Greiz, Thuringia - - 55 He
Grejač, Serbia - - 68 Gc
Grenaa, Denmark - - 45 Db
Grenada, Mississippi - 130 Dd
Grenada, Windward Is. 140 Kh
Grenade, France - - 34 Bd
Grenadines, Windward Is. 140 Kh
Grenfell, New S. Wales - 155 Fc
Grenoble, France - - 35 Hb
Grenville, New Mexico - 135 Mc
Grenville, Quebec - - 121 Cb
Grenville, C., Queensland 153 Bb
Gressoney la Trinite, Italy 62 Bb
Gretna, Louisiana - - 130 Cf
Gretna, Virginia - - 129 Ed
Gretna Green, Scotland 21 Cc
Greve, Italy - - - 63 Fd
Grevená, Greece - - 70 Cc
Grevesmühlen, Mecklenb'g 55 Gb
Grevinge, Denmark - 45 Ec
Grey Ra., Queensland - 153 Be
Greycliff, Montana - 136 Jc
Greyhound Str., Nether. Indies - - - 99 Fd
Greylake, England - 14 Bd
Greylingstad, Transvaal 115 Hc
Greylock, Mt., Mass. - 128 Bb
Greymouth, New Zealand 159 Ce
Greys Butte, mt., Oregon 136 Dd
Greystone, Colorado - 135 Ja
Greyton, Cape Prov. - 114 Cg
Greytown, Natal - - 115 Jd
Greytown, New Zealand 159 Ed
Greytown (San Juan del Norte), Nicaragua - 140 Ge
Gridley, California - 134 Cb
Gries Pass, Switzerland 43 Ed
Griesalp, Switzerland - 42 Ec
Griff, Ontario - - 122 Da
Griffin, Georgia - - 131 Fd
Griffith, New S. Wales - 155 Ec
Griffith, Ontario - - 121 Bb
Grijalva, R., Mexico - 139 Fd
Grim, C., Tasmania - 155 Jg
Grimari, Fr. Eq. Africa 105 Ed
Grimaud, France - - 33 Bc
Grimes I., Caroline Is. - 157 Bc
Grimma, Saxony - - 55 Hd
Grimo, Norway - - 47 Cd
Grimstad, Norway - - 47 Ef
Grimstunga, Iceland - 52 Cb
Grindavik, Iceland - 52 Bc
Grindelwald, Switz. - 42 Fc
Grindsted, Denmark - 45 Bc
Grindstone, Michigan - 122 Gc
Grinnell, Iowa - - 132 Ce
Grinnell Pen., N.-W. T. 118 Ka
Gripenberg, Sweden - 51 De
Griphavet, Norway - 46 Da
Griqualand East, Cape Prov. - - - - 115 He
Griqualand West, Cape Prov. - - - - 114 Ed
Griquatown, Cape Prov. 114 Ed
Gris Nez, C., France - 30 Da
Grisolles, France - - 34 Dd
Grmeč Planina, Bosnia - 68 Bb
Groai's I., Newfoundland 120 Ha
Grobing, Latvia - - 49 Ac
Grobyo, England - - 14 Ca
Gródek Jagiellonski - 60 Gd
Grodekovo, U.S.S.R. - 96 Ec
Grodno, - - - 60 Gb
Grodzisk, Poland - - 60 Fb
Grodzisk, Poland - - 57 Ba
Groenlo, Holland - - 29 Eb
Groesbeck, Texas - - 133 De
Grohnde, Prussia - - 54 Ec
Groix, I. de, France - 32 Bc
Grójec, Poland - - 60 Fc
Grombalia, Tunisia - 103 Ka
Grön Sd., Denmark - 45 Fd
Gronau, Prussia - - 54 Cc
Grondines, Quebec - - 121 Da
Grong, Norway - - 44 Cf
Groningen & prov., Holland 29 Ea
Grono, Switzerland - 43 Hd
Grootdoorn, Cape Prov. 114 Ed
Groote Eylandt, N.Terr., Australia - - - 151 Fa
Groote, R., Cape Prov. - 115 Ff
Groote River Heights, Cape Prov. - - - 115 Ff
Grootfontein, S.-W. Afr. 101 Dg
Groot Marico, Transvaal 115 Gb
Groppi, Mte., Italy - 62 Dc
Grossenhain, Saxony - 55 Jd
Grossenkneten, Oldenburg 54 Dc
Grosses Haff - - 55 Kb
Grosseto, Italy - - 62 Ee
Gross Glockner, Austria 59 Gd
Gross Schiemanen, Poland - - - 56 Fc
Gross Schönebeck, Prussia 55 Jc
Gross Strehlitz - - 57 Dc
Gross Sturlack - - 56 Fb
Gross Venediger, Austria 59 Gd
Grosuplje, Slovenia - 63 Jb
Gros Ventre Pk., Wyoming 136 Hd
Groth, Norway - - 46 Db
Groton, Connecticut - 128 Bc
Groton, Vermont - - 128 Ba
Grottaglie, Italy - - 65 Db
Grottammare, Italy - 63 Hd
Grotte, Sicily - - 65 Gg
Grotte di Castro, Italy - 63 Fe
Grottkau - - - 57 Cc
Grottoes, Virginia - 129 Ec
Groutville, Natal - - 115 Jd
Grouz, Jeb., Morocco - 102 Dc
Grovane, Norway - - 47 Df
Grove, Oklahoma - - 133 Eb
Grove Hill, Alabama - 130 Ee
Grover, Colorado - - 135 La
Groveton, New Hamps. 128 Ca
Groveton, Texas - - 133 Ee
Groznyi, U.S.S.R. - - 75 Gg
Grubišno Polje, Croatia 66 Cd
Gruda, Dalmatia - - 68 Dd
Grudziadz, Poland - - 60 Eb
Grue, Norway - - 47 Jd
Gruinard B., Scotland - 22 Ca
Grulich, Moravia - - 57 Bc
Grumo Appula, Italy - 65 Ca
Grunau, S.-W. Africa - 114 Cc
Grünberg, Hesse - - 58 Ca
Grunberg - - - 55 Ld
Grundsunda, Sweden - 48 Ce
Grundy, Virginia - - 129 Cd
Grundy Center, Iowa - 132 Cd
Grungedal, Norway - 47 De
Grünheide - - - 56 Fb
Grunsfeld, Baden - - 58 Db
Grusch, Switzerland - 43 Jc
Gruyeres, Switzerland - 42 Dc
Gruž, Dalmatia - - 68 Dd
Gruža, Serbia - - 68 Fc
Gryazi, U.S.S.R. - - 75 Ge
Grycksbo, Sweden - - 50 Eb
Gryt, Sweden - - 50 Ed
Gsteig, Switzerland - 42 Dd
Guacanayabo, G. de, Cuba 140Bb
Guachipas, Argentina - 146 Bd
Guadalajara, Mexico - 138 Dc
Guadalajara and prov., Spain - - - 38 Bd
Guadalaviar, R., Spain - 38 Dd
Guadalcanal, Spain - 40 Ea
Guadalcanal, I., Solomon Is. - - - - 157 Cd
Guadalcazar, Mexico - 139 Ec
Guadalimar R., Spain - 41 Cb
Guadalope, R., Spain - 38 Ed
Guadalquivir, R., Spain 40 Dc
Guadalupe, California - 134 Cd
Guadalupe, Mexico - 138 Dc
Guadalupe & Sa. de, Spain 37 Ec
Guadalupe I., Mexico - 138 Ab
Guadalupe Mts., New Mexico-Texas - - 135 Le
Guadalupe R., Texas - 133 Df
Guadalupe-y-Calvo, Mexico138Cb
Guadarrama & Sa. de, Spain - - - 38 Ad
Guadeloupe, I., Leeward Is. 140Kg
Guadiana, R., Spain - 37 Ec
Guadiana Menor R., Spain 41 Cc
Guadix, Spain - - 41 Cc
Guafo, G. de & I., Chile 148 Bc
Guaira, La, Venezuela - 144 Ca
Guaitecas Is., Chile - 148 Bc
Guajará-Mirim, Brazil - 142 Ae
Guajaratuba, Brazil - 142 Bd
Gualala, California - 134 Bb
Gualdo Tadino, Italy - 63 Gd
Gualeguay, Argentina - 146 Ce
Gualeguaychu, Argentina 146 De
Gualpit Rapids, Wash. - 136 Db
Guam, I., Marianas Is. 157 Bb
Guamapi, Sa., Venezuela 144 Cb
Guamini, Argentina - 148 Db
Guamo, Colombia - - 144 Ac
Guanabacoa, Cuba - 140 Ab
Guanabara, Brazil - 145 Cd
Guanacevi, Mexico - 138 Cb
Guanajuato, Mexico - 138 Dc
Guanamby, Brazil - 143 Fe
Guanare & R., Venezuela 144 Cb
Guanarito, Venezuela - 144 Cb
Guandacol, Argentina - 146 Bd
Guane, Cuba - - 140 Ab
Guanica, Puerto Rico - 140 Jg
Guanta, Venezuela - 144 Da
Guantanamo & B., Cuba 140 Bb
Guapi, Colombia - - 144 Ac
Guapiles, Costa Rica - 140 Ge
Guapore, Brazil - - 147 Ed
Guapore & terr., Brazil 142 Be
Guaqui, Bolivia - - 146 Bb
Guara, Sa. de, Spain - 39 Eb
Guarapuava, Brazil - 147 Ed
Guaratuba, Brazil - 147 Fd
Guarayos, Llanos de, Bolivia - - - 146 Cb
Guarda, Portugal - - 37 Cb
Guardafui, C., It. Somal. 108 Fc
Guardia, Portugal - - 36 Bc
Guardia, La, Argentina 146 Bd
Guardiagrele, Italy - 64 Ea
Guardia Sanframondi, Italy - - - 64 Eb
Guardo, Spain - - 38 Ab
Guardunha, Sa., Portugal 37 Cb
Guareña, Spain - - 37 Ed
Guarico, state & R., Venez. 144Cb
Guasbas, Mexico - - 138 Cb
Guasdualito, Venezuela - 144 Bb
Guasipati, Venezuela - 144 Db
Guastalla, Italy - - 62 Ec
Guatemala and rep., Cent. America - - 140 Ee
Guatrache, Argentina - 148 Db
Guaviare, R., Colombia 144 Cc
Guaxupe, Brazil - - 147 Fc
Guayabal, Venezuela - 144 Cb
Guayama, Puerto Rico - 140 Jg
Guayaneco, Arch., Chile 148 Ad
Guayaquil and G. of, Ecuador - - - 145 Bb
Guayas, prov., Ecuador 145 Ab
Guaymas, Mexico - - 138 Bb
Guazapares, Mexico - 138 Cb
Gubba, Ethiopia - - 108 Cc
Gubbio, Italy - - 63 Gd
Guben, - - - 55 Kd
Gubwa, Belg. Congo - 109 Ec
Gudalur, Madras - - 89 Bc
Gudar, Sa. de, Spain - 38 Ed
Gudbrandsdal, Norway - 46 Fc
Gudermes, U.S.S.R. - 75 Hg
Gudhjem, Bornholm I. - 45 Jf
Gudiyatam, Madras - 90 De
Gudur, Madras - - 91 Dd
Gudvangen, Norway - 46 Cd
Guebwiller, France - 31 Kd
Guecho, Spain - - 38 Ca
Guefait, Morocco - - 102 Cb
Guejar Sierra, Spain - 41 Cc
Guekedou, Fr. W. Africa 104 Be
Guelalia, Algeria - - 103 Gb
Guelma, Algeria - - 103 Ha
Guelph, Ontario - - 123 Hd
Guemes, Argentina - 146 Bc
Guerehe, la, France - 30 Ee
Guerche de Bretagne, la, France - - - 32 Dc
Guercif, Morocco - - 102 Cb
Gueret, France - - 34 Da
Guernsey, I., Channel Is. 17 Ef
Guerrah, El, Algeria - 103 Ha
Guerrara, Algeria - - 103 Gc
Guerrero, Chihuahua, Mexico - - - 138 Cb
Guerrero, Tamaulipas, Mexico - - - 139 Eb
Guerrero, state, Mexico 138 Dd
Guerzim, Algeria - - 102 De
Guetar, El, Tunisia - 103 Jb
Gueydan, Louisiana - 130 Be
Gugera, Punjab - - 83 Ec
Guglionesi, Italy - - 64 Eb
Guiana Highlands, S. America - - 142 Bb
Guichen, France - - 32 Dc
Guiglo, Fr. W. Africa - 104 Ce
Guildford, England - 15 Dd
Guildford, W. Australia 152 Be
Guildhall, Vermont - 128 Ca
Guilford, Connecticut - 128 Bc
Guilia, dep., Italy - 63 Jb
Guillaumes, France - 33 Ba
Guimaraes, Brazil - 143 Ec
Guimarães, Portugal - 36 Bc
Guimaras & Str., Philippines 99Fa
Guinan, Philippines - 99 Ga
Guinda, California - 134 Bb
Guinea, Gulf of, W. Afr. 101 Be
Guinea Fowl, S. Rhod. - 113 Db
Guines, Cuba - - 140 Ab
Guingamp, France - 32 Bb
Guipuzcoa, prov., Spain 38 Ca
Guir, C., Morocco - - 103 Nj
Guisborough, England - 18 Ca
Guisser, Morocco - - 103 Oh
Gujarat, reg., Bombay-Western India - - 85 Cc
Gujarat States, Western India - - - 85 Dd
Gujar Khan, Punjab - 82 Eb
Gujiba, Nigeria - - 105 Dc
Gujranwala, Punjab - 83 Fb
Gujrat, Punjab - - 83 Fb
Gul Koh, Afghanistan - 84 Bd
Gulargambone, N.S.W. 155 Fb
Gulbarga, Hyderabad - 90 Cc
Gulbene, Latvia - - 49 Dc
Gulch, Colorado - - 135 Kb
Guldborg & Sd., Denmark 45 Ed
Gulfport, Mississippi - 130 De
Gulkana, Alaska - - 125 Ke
Gull L., Minnesota - 132 Bb
Gull L., Quebec - - 123 Ka
Gullane, Scotland - - 23 Fd
Gullewa, W. Australia - 152 Bd
Gullfoss, Iceland - - 52 Cb
Gullivan B., Florida - 131 Nj
Gullmars Fd., Sweden - 50 Ad
Gulpaigan, Persia - - 79 Ec
Gulpinar, Turkey - - 72 Dc
Gulran, Afghanistan - 79 Hb
Gulu, Uganda - - 110 Cb
Gulwe, Tang. Terr. - 111 Eg
Gum, Ethiopia - - 108 Dc
Guma, Sinkiang - - 84 Dc
Gumbardo, Queensland - 153 Be
Gumbinnen - - - 56 Gb
Gumbiro, Tang. Terr. - 111 Dj
Gum-bum, China - - 94 Bb
Gumel, Nigeria - - 105 Cc
Gumiel de Mercado, Spain 38 Bc
Gummersbach, Prussia - 54 Cd
Gummi, Nigeria - - 105 Cc
Gumti R., United Provs. 86 Db
Gümüljina (Komotini), Greece - - - 72 Ca
Gümüşane, Turkey - 78 Ca
Guna, Gwalior - - 86 Bc
Guna, Mt., Ethiopia - 108 Cc
Guname, Tang. Terr. - 111 Dh
Gunbar, New S. Wales - 154 Ec
Gundagai, New S. Wales 155 Fd
Gundelfingen, Bavaria - 58 Ec
Gunderson, Montana - 136 Gb
Gundlakamma R., Madras 91 Dd
Gunisao R., Manitoba - 124 Kd
Gunna, Jeb., Egypt - 107 Kd
Gunnaur, United Provs. 83 Hd
Gunnedah, New S. Wales 155 Fb
Gunning, New S. Wales 155 Fc
Gunnislake, England - 17 Bb
Gunnison, Mississippi - 130 Cd
Gunnison, Utah - - 135 Hb
Gunnison & R., Colorado 135 Kb
Gunong Tahan, Malay States - - - 98 Bc
Guntersville, Alabama - 130 Ec
Guntur, Madras - - 91 Ec
Gunupur, Orissa - - 91 Fb
Günzburg, Bavaria - 58 Ec
Gunzenhausen, Bavaria 58 Eb
Gura, Pk., Borneo - - 99 Ec
Gura Galbena - - 69 Hb
Gurais, Kashmir - - 83 Fa
Gurdaspur, Punjab - 83 Fb
Gurdon, Arkansas - 130 Bd
Gurgan, Persia - - 79 Fb
Gurgan, R., Persia - 79 Gb
Gurgaon, Punjab - - 83 Gd
Gurha, Rajputana - - 85 Cb
Guriev (Chapaev), Kazak 75 Jf
Gurkha, Nepal - - 87 Fa
Gurnigel, Switzerland - 42 Dc
Gurramkonda, Madras - 90 De
Gurri, Nigeria - - 105 Dc
Gurskøy, I., Norway - 46 Bb
Gurupa and I., Brazil - 142 Dc
Gurupy, B., R. & Sa., Brazil - - - 143 Ec
Guru Sikhar, Rajputana 85 Db
Gurzalla, Madras - - 90 Dc
Gusau, Nigeria - - 105 Cc
Gusht, Persia - - 79 Hd
Gusinje, Montenegro - 68 Ed
Güstrow, Mecklenburg - 55 Gb
Guta, Slovakia - - 66 Cb
Guta, Tang. Terr. - - 110 Ce
Gutannen, Switzerland - 42 Fc
Gütersloh, Prussia - 54 Dd
Guthrie, Kentucky - - 130 Eb
Guthrie, Oklahoma - 133 Dc
Guthrie, Texas - - 133 Bd
Guthrie Center, Iowa - 132 Be
Guttenburg, Iowa - - 132 Dd
Guttstadt - - - 56 Ec
Gutu, S. Rhodesia - - 113 Db
Guveja, Mozambique - 112 Bc
Guyandot R., W. Virg. 129 Dd
Guyenne, France - - 34 Bc
Guyhirne, England - 15 Ea
Guymon, Oklahoma - 133 Bb
Guyot Glacier, Alaska - 125 Mf
Guyra, New S. Wales - 155 Gb
Guysborough, Nova Scotia 120Ed
Guzar, Uzbek - - 84 Bc
Guzman, Mexico - - 138 Dd
Gwa, Burma - - - 92 Bd
Gwaai & R., S. Rhod. - 113 Bb
Gwabegar, New S. Wales 155 Fb
Gwadar, Baluchistan - 79 Hd
Gwalior & state, India - 86 Cb
Gwanda, S. Rhodesia - 113 Cc
Gwao, Tanganyika Terr. 111 Df
Gwatar, Persia - - 79 He
Gwebi, S. Rhodesia - 113 Da
Gweebarra B., Eire - 26 Bb
Gweedore, Eire - - 26 Ba
Gweesalia, Eire - - 25 Ba
Gwelo & R., S. Rhod. - 113 Cb
Gwembe Val., N.-S. Rhod. 113Ba
Gydanski Pen., U.S.S.R. 76 Hb
Gylling, Denmark - - 45 Dc
Gympie, Queensland - 153 De
Gyoma, Hungary - - 67 Fc
Gyöngyös, Hungary - 66 Eb
Gyönk, Hungary - - 66 Dc
Györ, Hungary - - 66 Cb
Gyorszentmárton, Hungary 66 Cb
Gy Parana, R., Brazil - 142 Bd
Gypsum, Kansas - - 133 Da
Gypsumville, Manitoba - 124 Kd
Gysinge, Sweden - - 50 Fb
Gyueshevo, Bulgaria - 70 Da
Gyula, Hungary - - 67 Gc
Gyun-go, Tibet - - 83 Hc
Haabai Group, Tonga Is. 157 Fe
Haag, Austria - - 59 Jc
Haapamäki, Finland - 48 Ee
Haapsalu, Estonia - 49 Bb
Haarlem, Cape Prov. - 114 Ef
Haarlem, Holland - - 29 Cb
Haarstrang, Prussia - 54 Cd
Habarane, Ceylon - - 89 Dc
Habbas Wein, Kenya - 110 Fc

Hastings, *Nebraska* - 126 Fb
Hastings, *New Zealand* - 158 Fc
Hastings, *Ontario* - 121 Bb
Hastings, co., *Ontario* - 121 Bb
Hastings R. and Ra., *New S. Wales* - 155 Gb
Hästveda, *Sweden* - 51 Cf
Hatay, *Turkey* - 78 Cb
Hateg & Mts., *Romania* 67 Hd
Hatfield, *Hertford, Eng.* 15 Dc
Hatfield, *Yorks, Eng.* - 19 Dc
Hatfield, *New S. Wales* 154 Dc
Hatfield Broad Oak, *Eng.* 15 Ec
Hatfield Peverel, *England* 15 Ec
Hatha, *Arabia* - 78 De
Hatherleigh, *England* - 17 Bb
Hathras, *United Provs.* - 83 He
Hatia I., *Bengal* - 88 Cc
Ha-tien, *Cambodia* - 95 Bg
Ha-tinh, *Annam* - 95 Cf
Hatta, *Cent. Provs.* - 86 Cc
Hatteras, C. and Inlet, *N. Carolina* - 131 Lc
Hattiesburg, *Mississippi* 130 De
Hatvan, *Hungary* - 66 Eb
Hatzfeldt Harbour, *New Guinea* - 156 Db
Haughley, *England* - 15 Eb
Hauijen, *Manchuria* - 96 Cc
Haukeliseter, *Norway* - 47 De
Haukesdal, *Norway* - 46 Cc
Haukivesi, *Finland* - 48 Ge
Haungpa, *Burma* - 88 Eb
Hauraki Gulf, *New Zeal.* 158 Eb
Haurangi Mts., *N.Z.* - 159 Ed
Hauroko, L., *New Zeal'd* 159 Af
Hausach, *Baden* - 58 Cc
Hauser, *Idaho* - 136 Eb
Hausruck, mts., *Austria* 59 Hc
Haut, I. au, *Maine* - 128 Da
Hauta, *Arabia* - 79 Ee
Hautefort, Fork, *France* - 34 Db
Haute-Garonne, dep., *France* - 34 Dd
Haute-Loire, dep., *France* 35 Fb
Haute-Marne, dep., *France* 31 Hc
Hautes-Alpes, dep., *France* 35 Jc
Haute-Saone, dep., *France* 31 Jd
Haute-Savoie, dep., *France* 35 Ja
Hautes Fagnes, *Belgium* 29 De
Hautes-Pyrénees, dep., *France* - 34 Cd
Haute-Vienne, dep., *France* 34Db
Hauteville, *France* - 35 Hb
Hautmont, *France* - 31 Fa
Haut-Rhin, dep., *France* 31 Kd
Hauts Plateaux, *Algeria* 102 Dc
Havana, *Cuba* - 140 Ab
Havana, *Illinois* - 132 Ee
Havant, *England* - 15 De
Havasu L., *California* - 134 Fd
Havdhem, *Sweden* - 51 He
Havel, R., *Prussia* - 55 Hc
Havelberg, *Prussia* - 55 Hc
Havelland, dist., *Prussia* 55 Hc
Havelock, *Nebraska* - 132 Ae
Havelock, *New Brunswick* 120 Cc
Havelock, *N. Carolina* - 131 Kc
Havelock, *Ontario* - 121 Ab
Havelock North, *N.Z.* - 158 Fc
Haverfordwest, *Wales* - 20 Ad
Haverhill, *England* - 15 Eb
Haverhill, *Massachusetts* 128 Cb
Haverhill, *New Hamps.* 128 Ca
Haverstraw, *New York* - 123 Le
Havndal, *Denmark* - 45 Db
Havran, *Turkey* - 72 Ec
Havre, *France* - 30 Bb
Havre, *Montana* - 136 Ja
Havre de Grace, *Maryland* 129 Fc
Havsa, *Turkey* - 72 Da
Hawaii, I., *Hawaiian Is.* 157 Mh
Hawaiian Is., *Pacific Oc.* 157 Ga
Hawakil B., *Eritrea* - 108 Db
Hawarden, *Iowa* - 132 Ad
Hawarden, *Wales* - 20 Ca
Hawera, *New Zealand* - 158 Ec
Hawesville, *Kentucky* - 130 Eb
Hawick, *Scotland* - 21 Dc
Hawizeh, *Persia* - 79 Ec
Hawke B., *New Zealand* 158 Fc
Hawker, *S. Australia* - 154 Bb
Hawke's Bay, prov., *New Zealand* - 158 Fc
Hawkesbury, *Ontario* - 121 Cb
Hawkesbury R., *N.S.W.* 155 Gc
Hawkinsville, *Georgia* - 131 Gd
Hawkshead, *England* - 18 Ab
Hawkwood, *Queensland* 153 De
Hawley, *California* - 134 Cb
Hawston, *Cape Prov.* - 114 Cg
Hawthorne, *Nevada* - 134 Db
Hay, *England* - 14 Ab
Hay, *New S. Wales* - 154 Dc
Hay, C., *N.-W. Terr.* - 119 Ob
Hay R., *Alberta* - 124 Fc
Hayatpur, *Bengal* - 88 Bb
Haycock, *Alaska* - 125 Gd
Haydon Bridge, *England* 21 Dd
Haye-Descartes, la, *France* 30 Ce
Hayes, Mt., *Alaska* - 125 Ke
Hayes Pen., *Greenland* - 9 Cb
Hayfield, *England* - 18 Cd
Hayfield, *Minnesota* - 132 Cd
Hayfork, *California* - 134 Ba
Hayle, *England* - 17 Ac
Hayling I., *England* - 15 De
Haylow, *Georgia* - 131 Ge
Haynau - 55 Ld
Hayneville, *Alabama* - 130 Ed
Hayrabolu, *Turkey* - 72 Da
Hay River, *N.-W. Terr.* 124 Fb
Hays, *Kansas* - 133 Ca
Hayward, *Wisconsin* - 132 Db
Haywards, *California* - 134 Cc
Haywards Heath, *Eng.* 15 De
Hazara, dist., *N.-W.F.P.* 82 Ea
Hazard, *Kentucky* - 131 Gb
Hazaribagh, *Bihar* - 87 Fd
Hazaribagh Ra., *Eastern States* - 87 Ed
Hazebrouck, *France* - 30 Ea
Hazen B., *Alaska* - 125 Ff
Hazlehurst, *Georgia* - 131 Ge
Hazlehurst, *Mississippi* - 130 Ce
Hazleton, *Br. Columbia* 124 Dc
Hazleton, *Pennsylvania* - 129 Gb
Hazpo, *Punjab* - 82 Eb
Hazuur, *S.-W. Africa* - 114 Cc
Headford, *Eire* - 27 Ae
Headlands, *S. Rhodesia* - 113 Db
Healdsburg, *California* - 134 Bb
Healesville, *Victoria* - 154 Ee
Healy Fork, *Alaska* - 125 Je
Heanor, *England* - 18 Cd
Heany Junction, *S. Rhod.* 113 Cc
Heard I., *Antarctica* - 160 —
Hearne, *Texas* - 133 De
Hearst, *Ontario* - 122 Ga
Hearst Land, *Antarctica* 160 —
Hearts Content, *Newf'd.* 120 Jc
Heath B., *New Guinea* - 156 Cc
Heathcote, *Victoria* - 154 Dd
Hebden Bridge, *England* 18 Bc
Hebel, *Queensland* - 153 Ce
Heber, *Utah* - 135 Ha
Heber Springs, *Arkansas* 130 Bc
Hebertville, *Quebec* - 123 Na
Hebron, *Labrador* - 119 Re
Hebron, *Maine* - 128 Ca
Hebron, *New Mexico* - 135 Lc
Hebron (El Khalil), *Palestine* 80Cd
Heby, *Sweden* - 50 Fc
Hecate Str., *Br. Columbia* 124 Cd
Hecelchacan, *Mexico* - 139 Fc
Hechingen, *Prussia* - 58 Cc
Hecho, *Spain* - 38 Eb
Heckington, *England* - 19 De
Hecla and Gripper B., *N.-W. Terr.* - 118 Ga
Hectanooga, *Nova Scotia* 120 Cd
Hedalen, *Norway* - 46 Fd
Heddal, *Norway* - 47 Fe
Hede, *France* - 32 Db
Hede, *Sweden* - 44 Cg
Hedemora, *Sweden* - 50 Eb
Hedmark, *Norway* - 46 Gc
Hedmark, fylke, *Norway* 46 Hc
Hedon, *England* - 19 Dc
Heerde, *Holland* - 29 Db
Heerenveen, *Holland* - 29 Db
Heerlen, *Holland* - 29 Dd
Heflin, *Alabama* - 130 Fd
Hefzi Bah, *Palestine* - 80 Bc
Hegyalja, *Hungary* - 67 Ga
Heiban, *A.-E. Sudan* - 108 Bc
Heidal, *Norway* - 46 Fc
Heide, *Prussia* - 54 Ea
Heidelberg, *Baden* - 58 Cb
Heidelberg, *Cape Prov.* - 114 Dg
Heidelberg, *Transvaal* - 115 Hc
Heiden, *Switzerland* - 43 Hb
Heidenheim, *Württemberg* 58 Ec
Heidenreichstein, *Austria* 59 Jc
Heidersdorf - 57 Bc
Heiho & prov., *Manchuria* 96 Da
Heijo, *Korea* - 97 Bc
Heikai, *Korea* - 97 Bc
Heilbron, *O.F.S.* - 115 Gc
Heilbronn, *Württemberg* 58 Db
Heiligenbeil - 56 Db
Heiligenhafen, *Prussia* - 54 Fa
Heiligenkreuz, *Austria* - 66 Bb
Heiligenstadt, *Bavaria* - 58 Fb
Heiligenstadt, *Prussia* - 54 Fd
Heilsberg - 56 Eb
Heimbuchenthal, *Bavaria* 58 Da
Heinola, *Finland* - 48 Gf
Heishan, *Manchuria* - 96 Cc
Heita, *Syria* - 80 Db
Heizan, *Korea* - 97 Bc
Hejaz, *Arabia* - 78 Ce
Hekla, mt., *Iceland* - 52 Db
Hel, *Poland* - 60 Ea
Helabane, *Mozambique* - 113 Ec
Helder, *Holland* - 29 Cb
Helechosa, *Spain* - 37 Ec
Helen, *Georgia* - 131 Gc
Helena, *Arkansas* - 130 Cc
Helena, *Montana* - 136 Hb
Helensburgh, *Scotland* - 23 Dd
Helensville, *New Zealand* 158 Eb
Helga Sjö, *Sweden* - 51 Df
Helicon (Elikón), mt., *Greece* - 71 De
Heligoland & B., *Germany* 54 Ca
Heliopolis, *Egypt* - 107 Hc
Hell, *Norway* - 46 Ga
Hellespont (Dardanelles), *Turkey* - 72 Db
Hellesylt, *Norway* - 46 Cb
Hellin, *Spain* - 41 Eb
Hellville, *Madagascar* - 112 Eb
Helmand R., *Afghanistan* 79 Hc
Helmingham, *England* - 15 Fb
Helmond, *Holland* - 29 Dc
Helmsdale & R., *Scotland* 24 Ee
Helmsley, *England* - 18 Cb
Helmstedt, *Brunswick* - 54 Fc
Helnæs, *Denmark* - 45 Cc
Helpmakaar, *Natal* - 115 Jd
Helsbach, *New Guinea* - 156 Dc
Helsinge, *Denmark* - 45 Fb
Helsingör (Elsinore), *Denmark* - 45 Fb
Helsinki, *Finland* - 48 Ff
Helston, *England* - 17 Ac
Helvellyn, *England* - 18 Aa
Helwân, *Egypt* - 107 Hd
Hemel Hempstead, *Eng.* 15 Dc
Hemelingen, *Bremen* - 54 Db
Hemmelte, *Oldenburg* - 54 Cc
Hemmingford, *Quebec* - 121 Db
Hemne, *Norway* - 46 Fa
Hemnes, *Norway* - 47 He
Hemphill, *Texas* - 133 Fe
Hempstead, *England* - 15 Eb
Hempstead, *Texas* - 133 Ee
Hemse, *Sweden* - 51 He
Hemsedal, *Norway* - 46 Ed
Hemsworth, *England* - 18 Cc
Henares, R., *Spain* - 38 Bd
Henchir Lebna, *Tunisia* 103 Ka
Henchir Souatir, *Tunisia* 103 Jb
Hendaye, *France* - 34 Ad
Henderson, *Kentucky* - 130 Eb
Henderson, *Minnesota* - 132 Bc
Henderson, *New York* - 123 Kd
Henderson, *N. Carolina* 131 Jb
Henderson, *Tennessee* - 130 Dc
Henderson, *Texas* - 133 Ed
Hendersonville, *N. Carolina* 131Gc
Hendon, *England* - 15 Dc
Hendrick's Pan, *Bechuanaland* - 113 Ab
Hendrik Top, *Suriname* 142 Cb
Hendrina, *Transvaal* - 115 Hc
Heng-chow, *Hu-nan, China* 94 Dd
Heng-chow, *Kwang-si, China* - 95 Ce
Hengelo, *Holland* - 29 Eb
Heng-shan, *China* - 94 Dd
Henin Lietard, *France* - 30 Ea
Henjareh, *Persia* - 79 Hd
Henley-in-Arden, *Eng.* - 14 Cb
Henley-on-Thames, *Eng.* 15 Dc
Henlopen, C., *Delaware* 129 Gc
Hennebont, *France* - 32 Bc
Hennenman, *O.F.S.* - 115 Gc
Hennessey, *Oklahoma* - 133 Db
Henniker, *New Hamps.* 128 Cb
Henrichemont, *France* - 30 Ed
Henrietta, *Texas* - 133 Cd
Henrietta Maria C., *Ont.* 119 Ne
Henry, C., *Virginia* - 129 Gd
Henry L., *Idaho* - 136 Hc
Henry Mts., *Utah* - 135 Hb
Henryetta, *Oklahoma* - 133 Dc
Henty, *New S. Wales* - 155 Ed
Henzada, *Burma* - 92 Bd
Heppner, *Oregon* - 136 Dc
Hepworth, *England* - 15 Eb
Heradhsflói, *Iceland* - 52 Fb
Heran, *Yemen* - 78 Lg
Herat, *Afghanistan* - 79 Hc
Herau, *Persia* - 79 Eb
Hérault, R. & dep., *France* 35 Fd
Herbert, *Queensland* - 153 Dd
Herbert I., *Aleutian Is.* 125 Dk
Herbertingen, *Württemberg* 58 Dc
Herberton, *Queensland* - 153 Bc
Herbertsdale, *Cape Prov.* 114 Df
Herbertville, *New Zeal'd* 158 Fd
Herbiers, les, *France* - 32 Dd
Herbillon, *Algeria* - 103 Ha
Herborn, *Prussia* - 54 De
Herby, *Poland* - 57 Dc
Hercegfalva, *Hungary* - 66 Dc
Hercegovina, *Jugoslavia* 68 Cc
Heredia, *Costa Rica* - 140 Ge
Hereford and co., *Eng.* 14 Bb
Herefoss, *Norway* - 47 Ef
Herehretue, I., *Tuamotu Arch.* - 157 Je
Heremakono, *Fr. W. Afr.* 104 Be
Herencia, *Spain* - 38 Be
Herenthals, *Belgium* - 29 Cc
Herford, *Prussia* - 54 Dc
Herg, *Texas* - 133 Cc
Hergatz, *Bavaria* - 58 Dd
Héridj, *Syria* - 80 Db
Heriot, *New Zealand* - 159 Bf
Herisau, *Switzerland* - 43 Hb
Herjehogna, mt., *Norway* 46 Jc
Herkimer, *New York* - 123 Ld
Hermann, *Missouri* - 130 Ca
Hermanus, *Cape Prov.* - 114 Cg
Herment, *France* - 34 Eb
Hermidale, *New S. Wales* 155 Eb
Hermit Is, *Pacific Oc.* - 156 Db
Hermitage, *Missouri* - 130 Bb
Hermitage B., *Newfoun'd* 120 Gc
Hermites Is., *Chile* - 148 Cf
Hermon, *Cape Prov.* - 114 Cf
Hermon, mt., *Syria* - 78 Cc
Hermosillo, *Mexico* - 138 Bb
Hernando, *Mississippi* - 130 Dc
Herndon, *Kansas* - 133 Ba
Herne, *Prussia* - 54 Cd
Herne Bay, *England* - 15 Fd
Herning, *Denmark* - 45 Bb
Heron, *Montana* - 136 Eb
Heron L., *Minnesota* - 132 Bd
Heron Bay, *Ontario* - 122 Ea
Herrera, *Argentina* - 146 Cd
Herrera, *Spain* - 38 Dc
Herrera del Duque, *Spain* 37 Ec
Herrera de Pisuerga, *Spain* 38 Ab
Herrero, Pta., *Mexico* - 139 Gd
Herrhult, *Sweden* - 50 Dc
Herrick, *Tasmania* - 155 Kg
Herrington, *Kansas* - 133 Da
Herrljunga, *Sweden* - 51 Cd
Herrnstadt - 57 Bb
Hersbruck, *Bavaria* - 58 Fb
Herschel, *Cape Prov.* - 115 Ge
Herschell, Mt., *Antarctica* 160 —
Hersey, *Michigan* - 122 Fd
Herstal, *Belgium* - 29 Dd
Herţa, *Romania* - 69 Ga
Hertford, *N. Carolina* - 131 Kb
Hertford & co., *England* 15 Dc
's Hertogenbosch, *Holland* 29 Dc
Hertzogville, *O.F.S.* - 115 Fd
Herval, *Brazil* - 147 Ee
Herval, *Santa Catharina, Brazil* - 147 Ed
Hervas, *Spain* - 37 Eb
Hervey B., *Queensland* - 153 Dd
Hervey Is., *Cook Is.* - 157 Ge
Hervey Junction, *Quebec* 121 Da
Herzberg, *Hanover, Prussia* 54 Fd
Herzberg, *Saxony, Prussia* 55 Jd
Herzfeld, *Prussia* - 54 Ee
Herzogenbuchsee, *Switz.* 42 Eb
Heskestad, *Norway* - 47 Cf
Hesnæs, *Denmark* - 45 Fd
Hesperia, *California* - 134 Ed
Hesse, state, *Germany* - 58 Cb
Hesselö, *Denmark* - 45 Eb
Hesse-Nassau, prov., *Prussia* - 54 Ee
Hessental, *Württemberg* 58 Db
Hesso, *S. Australia* - 154 Ab
Hesteyri, *Iceland* - 52 Ba
He-tan I., *China* - 94 Ed
Hetton-le-Hole, *England* 21 Ed
Hève, Cap de la, *France* 30 Cb
Heves, *Hungary* - 67 Fb
Hewett, C., *N.-W. Terr.* 119 Qb
Hexham, *England* - 21 Dd
Heydebreck - 57 Dc
Heydekrug, *Lithuania* - 49 Ad
Heysham, *England* - 18 Bb
Heywood, *Victoria* - 154 Ce
Hiang-chêng, *China* - 94 Dc
Hiangyao, *Manchuria* - 96 Cc
Hiawassee R., *Tennessee* 131 Fc
Hiawatha, *Kansas* - 133 Ea
Hibbard, *Arizona* - 135 Hd
Hibbing, *Minnesota* - 132 Cb
Hickman, *Kentucky* - 130 Db
Hickory, *Mississippi* - 130 Dd
Hickory, *N. Carolina* - 131 Hc
Hicksville, *Indiana* - 129 Bb
Hico, *Texas* - 133 Ce
Hida, *Transylvania* - 67 Jb
Hidaka Mts., *Japan* - 97 Eb
Hidalgo, *Mexico* - 138 Db
Hidalgo, state, *Mexico* - 139 Ec
Hiddensee, *Prussia* - 55 Ha
Hiddi Birro, *Ethiopia* - 108 Cd
Hideaga, *Transylvania* - 67 Jb
Hidra, *Norway* - 47 Cf
Hieflau, *Austria* - 59 Jd
Hierro, I., *Canary Is.* - 104 Aa
Higgins, *Texas* - 133 Cb
Higginsville, *Missouri* - 130 Ba
Higham, *England* - 15 Ec
Higham Ferrers, *England* 15 Db
Highbridge, *England* - 14 Ad
High Bridge, *Idaho* - 136 Hc
Highclere, *England* - 14 Cd
Highland, *Florida* - 131 Ge
Highland Park, *Illinois* 132 Fd
Highlands, *Colorado* - 135 Lb
High Point, *N. Carolina* 131 Jc
High Rock L., *N. Carolina* 131Hc
High Springs, *Florida* - 131 Gf
Highwood Mts., *Montana* 136 Ha
Highworth, *England* - 14 Cc
High Wycombe, *England* 15 Dc
Higuera la Real, *Spain* - 40 Da
Hiiu Maa (Dagö), *Estonia* 49 Bb
Hijar, *Spain* - 39 Ec
Hikeda, *Japan* - 100 Ed
Hiko, *Nevada* - 134 Fc
Hikone, *Japan* - 100 Fd
Hilda Vale, *Bechuanaland* 115 Fb
Hildburg, *Thuringia* - 58 Ea
Hildesheim, *Prussia* - 54 Fc
Hili, *Oman* - 79 Ge
Hilla, *Iraq* - 78 Dc
Hillared, *Sweden* - 51 Ce
Hill City, *Kansas* - 133 Ca
Hill City, *Minnesota* - 132 Cb
Hillerod, *Denmark* - 45 Fc
Hillesheim, *Prussia* - 58 Aa
Hillman, *Michigan* - 122 Gc
Hillsboro, *Illinois* - 132 Ef
Hillsboro, *New Mexico* - 135 Ke
Hillsboro, *N. Carolina* - 131 Jb
Hillsboro, *N. Dakota* - 132 Ab
Hillsboro, *Ohio* - 129 Cc
Hillsboro, *Oregon* - 136 Bc
Hillsboro, *Texas* - 133 De
Hillsborough, *N. Ireland* 26 Dc
Hillsborough, *New Bruns.* 120 Cd
Hillsdale, *Michigan* - 122 Fe
Hillsdale, *Wyoming* - 135 La
Hillston, *New S. Wales* 155 Ec
Hillsville, *Virginia* - 129 Dd
Hillswick, *Zetland* - 24 Gg
Hilo, *Hawaiian Is.* - 157 Nh
Hilongos, *Philippines* - 99 Fa
Hilpoltstein, *Bavaria* - 58 Fb
Hilsbach, *Baden* - 58 Cb
Hilton, *England* - 14 Ba
Hilton Hd. I., *S. Carolina* 131 Hd
Hilversum, *Holland* - 29 Cb
Hilwase, *Japan* - 100 Fc
Hilyan, *Arabia* - 78 De
Himalayan Ra., *N. India* 81 Ed
Himarë, *Albania* - 70 Ac
Himeji, *Japan* - 97 Cd
Himeville, *Natal* - 115 Hd
Himi, *Japan* - 100 Fc
Himmerland, *Denmark* - 45 Cb
Hinchinbrook I., *Queensl'd* 153 Cc
Hinckley, *England* - 14 Ca
Hinckley, *Minnesota* - 132 Cb
Hindaun, *Rajputana* - 83 Ge
Hindenburg (Zabrze) *Poland* 57Dc
Hindhead, *England* - 15 Dd
Hindley, *England* - 18 Bc
Hindman, *Kentucky* - 131 Gb
Hindmarsh L., *Victoria* 154 Cd
Hindol, *Eastern States* - 87 Fe
Hindon, *England* - 14 Bd
Hindubagh, *Baluchistan* 82 Bc
Hindu Kush Mts., *Afghanistan* - 84 Bc
Hindupur, *Madras* - 90 Ce
Hinesburg, *Vermont* - 128 Ba
Hing-an, *China* - 94 Cc
Hinganghat, *Cent. Provs.* 86 Ce
Hingham, *Montana* - 136 Ha
Hing-hwa, *China* - 94 Ed
Hing-king, *Manchuria* - 96 Cc
Hing-kwo, *China* - 94 Dd

Hingoli, *Hyderabad* 90 Cb
Hing-yi, *China* 95 Cd
Hinna, *Norway* 47 Bf
Hinnöy, *Norway* 44 Ce
Hino, *Japan* 100 Gd
Hinojosa del Duque, *Spain* 37 Ed
Hinsdale, *New Hampshire* 128 Bb
Hinsholm, pen., *Denmark* 45 Dc
Hinton, *W. Virginia* 129 Dd
Hinwil, *Switzerland* 43 Gb
Hirado-shima, *Japan* 97 Bd
Hiriyur, *Mysore* 90 Ce
Hirnant, *Wales* 20 Cb
Hirosaki, *Japan* 97 Db
Hiroshima, *Japan* 97 Cd
Hirschberg 55 Le
Hirsingen, *France* 31 Kd
Hirson, *France* 31 Gb
Hirtshals, *Denmark* 45 Ca
Hirwaun, *Wales* 20 Cd
Hisaronu, *Turkey* 78 Ba
Hispaniola, I., *W. Indies* 140 Cc
Hissa, *Libya* 106 Pl
Hissar, *Punjab* 83 Fd
Hissar & Ra., *Tadzhik* 84 Bc
Hisua, *Bihar* 87 Fc
Hit, *Iraq* 78 Dc
Hitchin, *England* 15 Dc
Hitoyoshi, *Japan* 97 Cd
Hitra, I., *Norway* 46 Ea
Hiva Oa, I., *Marquesas Is.* 157 Kd
Hiw, *Egypt* 107 Jf
Hiwasa, *Japan* 97 Cd
Hjalmar Sjö, *Sweden* 50 Ec
Hjartdal, *Norway* 47 Ee
Hjelle, *Norway* 46 Dc
Hjelmeland, *Norway* 47 Ce
Hjelms B., *Denmark* 45 Fd
Hjerkinn, *Norway* 46 Fb
Hjö, *Sweden* 50 Dd
Hjorring, *Denmark* 45 Ca
Hlabisa, *Natal* 115 Jd
Hlaing R., *Burma* 92 Bd
Hlakanelo, *Basutoland* 115 Hd
Hlatikulu, *Swaziland* 115 Jc
Hluti, *Swaziland* 115 Jc
Ho, *China* 94 Cc
Hoa-binh, *Tong-king* 95 Ce
Hoachanas, *S.-W. Africa* 114 Ca
Hoare B., *N.-W. Terr.* 119 Rc
Hoback Pk., *Wyoming* 136 Hd
Hobart, *Oklahoma* 133 Cc
Hobart, *Tasmania* 155 Jh
Hobhouse, *O.F.S.* 115 Gd
Hobok, *Ethiopia* 108 Ce
Hobro, *Denmark* 45 Cb
Hobson, *Nevada* 134 Fa
Hoch Alpe, *Austria* 59 Kd
Hoch Moor, *Prussia* 54 Cb
Hoch Wald, *Prussia* 58 Bb
Ho-chow, *China* 94 Bb
Hochschwab, *Austria* 59 Kd
Hochst, *Prussia* 58 Ca
Hochstadt, *Bavaria* 58 Ed
Hochstetter Plains, *W. Australia* 152 Cb
Hochvogel, *Austria* 58 Ed
Hochwald, *Bohemia* 59 Jc
Hochzeit 55 Lb
Hockliffe, *England* 15 Dc
Hodaiu-uen, *Ethiopia* 108 Ed
Hodal, *Punjab* 83 Ge
Hodalen, *Norway* 46 Hb
Hoddesdon, *England* 15 Ec
Hodeida, *Yemen* 78 Lh
Hodgenville, *Kentucky* 130 Fb
Hodges Hill, *Newfoundl'd* 120 Hb
Hodgkinson Goldfield, *Queensland* 153 Bc
Hodgson, *Manitoba* 124 Kd
Hódmezövásárhély, *Hung.* 67 Fc
Hodna, Mts. du, *Algeria* 103 Gb
Hódonín, *Moravia* 60 Dd
Hodos, *Slovenia* 66 Bc
Hoedjes Bay, *Cape Prov.* 114 Bf
Hof, *Bavaria* 59 Fa
Hofara, *Fr. W. Africa* 104 Cd
Ho-feng, *China* 94 Cd
Hofgastein, *Austria* 59 Hd
Hofmeyr, *Cape Prov.* 115 Fe
Höfn, *Iceland* 52 Ba
Hofn, *Iceland* 52 Fb
Hofsjökull, *Iceland* 52 Db
Hofsos, *Iceland* 52 Db
Hofuf, *Arabia* 79 Ed
Hogan, *Alaska* 125 Le
Höganäs, *Sweden* 51 Bf
Hogansville, *Georgia* 131 Fd
Högby, *Sweden* 51 Ge
Hogeis, *S.-W. Africa* 114 Cd
Högyész, *Hungary* 66 Dc
Hohenau, *Austria* 66 Ba
Höhenstadt, *Moravia* 57 Bd
Hohenstein 56 Ec
Hohenwart, *Austria* 59 Jd
Hohenzollern, *Prussia* 58 Cc
Hohe Tauern, *Austria* 59 Fd
Hohe Venn, *Belgium* 29 Dd
Hoi-hang, *China* 95 Ce
Hoi-how, *China* 95 Ce
Hoima, *Uganda* 110 Bc
Hoisington, *Kansas* 133 Ca
Hoi-tung, *China* 95 Df
Hōjō, *Japan* 100 Ed
Ho-kiang, *China* 94 Cd
Hokianga Harb., *N.Z.* 158 Da
Ho-kien, *China* 94 Eb
Hokitika, *New Zealand* 159 Ce
Hokkaido, I., *Japan* 97 Eb
Hokksund, *Norway* 47 Fe
Hokoda, *Japan* 100 Hc
Ho-kow, *China* 94 Da
Hokusei, *Korea* 97 Bb
Hol, *Norway* 46 Ed
Holaveden, *Sweden* 51 Dd
Holbæk, *Denmark* 45 Ec
Holbeach, *England* 19 De
Holbrook, *Arizona* 135 Hd
Holbrook, *New S. Wales* 155 Ed
Holden, *Missouri* 130 Ba
Holdenville, *Oklahoma* 133 Dc
Holderness, *England* 19 Dc
Hole Narsipur, *Mysore* 90 Ce
Holguin, *Cuba* 140 Bb
Holič, *Slovakia* 66 Ca
Holing, *Manchuria* 96 Dc
Ho-li-shan, *China* 94 Bb
Holladay, *Oregon* 136 Ac
Holland, *Michigan* 122 Ed
Holland, country, *W. Europe* 28 Ja
Holland, Parts of, *Lincs, England* 19 De
Hollandale, *Mississippi* 130 Cd
Hollandia, *New Guinea* 156 Cb
Hollidaysburg, *Pennsyla.* 129 Eb
Hollis, *Oklahoma* 133 Cc
Holly, *Michigan* 122 Gd
Hollymount, *Eire* 26 Ad
Hollywood, *California* 134 Dd
Hollywood, *Florida* 131 Oh
Holma Mts., *Nigeria* 105 Dd
Hólmavik, *Iceland* 52 Cb
Holmes Chapel, *England* 18 Bd
Holmestrand, *Norway* 47 Ge
Holmfirth, *England* 18 Cc
Holmsbu, *Norway* 47 Ge
Holmsjö, *Sweden* 51 Ef
Holmsland Klit, *Denmark* 45 Ac
Holmstrup, *Denmark* 45 Ec
Holod, *Transylvania* 67 Hc
Holoog, *S.-W. Africa* 114 Bc
Holöydal, *Norway* 46 Hb
Holsenöy, *Norway* 46 Bd
Holstebro, *Denmark* 45 Bb
Holsteinsborg, *Greenland* 9 Dd
Holston R., *Tennessee* 131 Gb
Holsworthy, *England* 17 Bb
Holt, *England* 19 Fe
Holt, *Wales* 20 Da
Holtålen, *Norway* 46 Hb
Holt Heath, *England* 14 Bb
Holthusen, *Mecklenburg* 55 Gb
Holton, *England* 15 Fb
Holton, *Kansas* 133 Ea
Holtville, *California* 134 Fe
Holum, *Norway* 47 Df
Holy I., *England* 21 Eb
Holy I., *Wales* 20 Ba
Holy Cross, *Alaska* 125 Ge
Holyhead, *Wales* 20 Ba
Holyoke, *Massachusetts* 128 Bb
Holyrood, *Kansas* 133 Ca
Holy Springs, *Mississippi* 130 Dc
Holywell, *Wales* 20 Ca
Holzkirchen, *Bavaria* 59 Fd
Holzminden, *Brunswick* 54 Ed
Homa and B., *Kenya* 110 Dd
Homalig, I., *Philippines* 95 Fg
Homalin, *Burma* 88 Eb
Homberg, *Hesse* 58 Ca
Homburg, *Prussia* 58 Ca
Home B., *N.-W. Terr.* 119 Qc
Homer, *Alaska* 125 Jg
Homer, *California* 134 Fd
Homer, *Louisiana* 130 Bd
Homer, *New York* 123 Kd
Homersfield, *England* 15 Fb
Homerville, *Georgia* 131 Ge
Homestead, *Florida* 131 Nj
Homestead, *Pennsylvania* 129 Db
Homnabad, *Hyderabad* 90 Cc
Homonhon, I., *Philippines* 99 Ga
Homosassa, *Florida* 131 Gf
Homs, *Libya* 106 Pk
Homs, *Syria* 78 Cc
Ho-nan & prov., *China* 94 Dc
Honavar, *Bombay* 90 Bd
Honda, *Colombia* 144 Bb
Honda, *Philippines* 99 Eb
Hondagua, *Philippines* 95 Fg
Hondeklip Baai, *Cape Pr.* 114 Be
Hondo, *Mexico* 138 Db
Hondo, *Texas* 133 Cf
Honduras, rep. & Gulf, *Cent. America* 140 Fd
Hönefoss, *Norway* 47 Gd
Honesdale, *Pennsylvania* 129 Gb
Honey L., *California* 134 Ca
Honey Grove, *Texas* 133 Ed
Honfleur, *France* 30 Cb
Hongay, *Tong-king* 95 Ce
Hongero, *Tang. Terr.* 111 Df
Hong-kong (Brit.), *China* 95 De
Hongo, *Japan* 100 Hd
Hongū, *Japan* 100 Ee
Honingham, *England* 15 Fa
Honington, *England* 15 Eb
Honiton, *England* 14 Ae
Honjo, *Japan* 97 Dc
Honnali, *Mysore* 90 Bd
Honnef, *Prussia* 54 Ce
Honolulu, *Hawaiian Is.* 157 La
Honshu, I., *Japan* 97 Cc
Hood C., *Washington* 136 Bb
Hood, Mt., *Oregon* 136 Cc
Hood Pt., *W. Australia* 152 Be
Hood River, *Oregon* 136 Cc
Hooge, *Prussia* 54 Da
Hoogeveen, *Holland* 29 Eb
Hooghly, *Bengal* 88 Bc
Hooghly R., *Bengal* 88 Bd
Hook Hd., *Eire* 27 Dg
Hook I., *Queensland* 153 Cd
Hooker, *California* 134 Ba
Hook of Holland, *Holland* 29 Bc
Hooksett, *New Hampshire* 128 Cb
Hoonah, *Alaska* 125 Nh
Hooper, *Colorado* 135 Kc
Hooper, *Nebraska* 132 Ae
Hoopstad, *O.F.S.* 115 Fc
Höör, *Sweden* 51 Cg
Hoorn, *Holland* 29 Db
Hoorn Is., *Pacific Oc.* 157 Fe
Hoosick Falls, *New York* 128 Bb
Hope, *Alaska* 125 Jf
Hope, *Arkansas* 130 Bd
Hope, *Br. Columbia* 124 Ee
Hope, *Idaho* 136 Ea
Hope, *Kansas* 133 Da
Hope B., *China* 95 Ee
Hope I., *Svalbard* 9 Mb
Hope Pk., *Arizona* 135 Gd
Hope Pt., *Alaska* 125 Eb
Hopedale, *Labrador* 119 Re
Hopefield, *Cape Prov.* 114 Cf
Hopeh, prov., *China* 94 Db
Hopelchen, *Mexico* 139 Fd
Hope Mills, *N. Carolina* 131 Jc
Hopetoun, *W. Australia* 152 Ce
Hope Town, *Andaman Is.* 91 Kk
Hopetown, *Cape Prov.* 114 Ed
Hope-under-Dinmore, *England* 14 Bb
Hopewell, *Virginia* 129 Fd
Hopfgarten, *Austria* 59 Gd
Hopkins, *Minnesota* 132 Cc
Hopkins, *Missouri* 132 Be
Hopkins, R., *Victoria* 154 De
Hopkinsville, *Kentucky* 130 Eb
Hopland, *California* 134 Bb
Hopong, *Burma* 92 Cb
Hopton, *England* 15 Fa
Hoquiam, *Washington* 136 Ab
Hor al Hammar, *Iraq* 79 Ec
Hörby, *Sweden* 51 Cg
Horcasitas, *Mexico* 138 Bb
Hordaland, fylke, *Norway* 47 Cd
Hordland, N., *Norway* 46 Bd
Hordland, S., *Norway* 47 Ce
Horez, *Romania* 67 Jd
Horg, *Norway* 46 Ga
Horgen, *Switzerland* 43 Gb
Hořice, *Bohemia* 59 Ka
Horitz, *Bohemia* 59 Jc
Horken, *Sweden* 50 Db
Hormuz, *Persia* 79 Fd
Hormuz I. & Str., *Persia* 79 Gd
Horn, *Austria* 59 Kc
Horn (Nord Cap), *Iceland* 52 Ba
Horn I., *Mississippi* 130 De
Horn I., *Queensland* 153 Bb
Horn Mts., *N.-W. Terr.* 124 Fb
Hornachos, Sa. de, *Spain* 37 Ed
Hornafjordur, *Iceland* 52 Fb
Hornavan, *Sweden* 44 Df
Hornbæk, *Denmark* 45 Fb
Horncastle, *England* 19 Dd
Horne, *Denmark* 45 Dc
Hornell, *New York* 123 Kd
Hornesund, *Norway* 47 Df
Hornindal & Vatn, *Norway* 46 Cc
Hornitz, *Moravia* 57 Bd
Hornnes, *Norway* 47 Df
Hornos, C., *Chile* 148 Cf
Hornsby, *New S. Wales* 155 Gc
Hornsea, *England* 19 Dc
Horodenka 60 Hd
Hořovice, *Bohemia* 59 Hb
Horqueta, *Paraguay* 146 Dc
Horred, *Sweden* 51 Be
Hor Sanniya, *Iraq* 79 Ec
Horse Creek, *Wyoming* 135 La
Horsens, *Denmark* 45 Cc
Horseshoe, *W. Australia* 152 Bd
Horsford, *England* 15 Fa
Horsham, *England* 15 Dd
Horsham, *Victoria* 154 Cd
Horstmar, *Prussia* 54 Cc
Horten, *Norway* 47 Ge
Horton, *Kansas* 133 Ea
Horwich, *England* 18 Bc
Horyn, R. 60 Jc
Hosdurga, *Mysore* 90 Ce
Ho-shan, *Kwang-tung, China* 95 De
Ho-shan, *Shan-si, China* 94 Db
Hoshang, *Sinkiang* 84 Ea
Hoshangabad, *Cent. Provs.* 86 Bd
Hoshia, *Mozambique* 112 Cc
Hoshiarpur, *Punjab* 83 Fc
Ho-shui, *China* 94 Cb
Hospenthal, *Switzerland* 43 Fc
Hospet, *Madras* 90 Cd
Hospital, *Eire* 27 Bg
Hostalrich, *Spain* 39 Hc
Hoste, I., *Chile* 148 Cf
Hostomice, *Bohemia* 59 Jb
Hosur, *Madras* 90 Ce
Hotatun, *Manchuria* 96 Cb
Hotchkiss, *Colorado* 135 Jb
Hot Creek Ra., *Nevada* 134 Eb
Hotgi, *Hyderabad* 90 Cc
Ho-tsin, *China* 94 Db
Hot Spring, *Nevada* 134 Ea
Hot Springs, *Alaska* 125 Jd
Hot Springs, *Alaska* 125 Nh
Hot Springs, *N. Carolina* 131 Gc
Hot Springs, *S. Dakota* 126 Eb
Hot Springs, *Washington* 136 Cb
Hot Springs Nat. Park, *Arkansas* 130 Bc
Hot Sulphur Springs, *Colorado* 135 Ka
Houghton, *Michigan* 122 Db
Houghton L., *Michigan* 122 Fc
Houghton-le-Spring, *Eng.* 21 Ed
Houlton, *Maine* 120 Ac
Houma, *Louisiana* 130 Cf
Houmt Souk, *Tunisia* 103 Kc
Hounslow, *England* 15 Dd
Hourtin and Etang d', *France* 34 Aa
Housatonic R., *Connecticut* 128 Bc
House Ra., *Utah* 135 Gb
Houston, *Mississippi* 130 Dd
Houston, *Missouri* 130 Cb
Houston, *Texas* 133 Ef
Houtkraal, *Cape Prov.* 114 Ee
Houtman Rocks, *W. Aust.* 152 Ad
Houwater, *Cape Prov.* 114 Ee
Hovde, *Norway* 47 De
Hove, *England* 15 De
Hovgaard I., *Greenland* 9 Hb
Howard, *Kansas* 133 Db
Howard, *Michigan* 122 Fd
Howard, *Queensland* 153 De
Howard Fort, *Wisconsin* 132 Ec
Howden, *England* 19 Dc
Howe, *Idaho* 136 Gd
Howe, *Oklahoma* 133 Ec
Howe, C., *Victoria* 155 Fd
Howick, *Natal* 115 Jd
Howitt, L., *S. Aust.* 154 Ba
Howland I., *Pacific Oc.* 149 Je
Howley, *Newfoundland* 120 Gb
Howrah, *Bengal* 88 Bc
Howth, *Eire* 27 De
Hoxie, *Arkansas* 130 Cb
Hoxie, *Kansas* 133 Ba
Höxter, *Prussia* 54 Ed
Hoy, I., *Orkney Is.* 24 Ed
Hoya, *Prussia* 54 Ec
Höyanger, *Norway* 46 Cc
Hoyas, *Spain* 37 Db
Hoyerswerda, *Prussia* 55 Kd
Hoylake, *England* 18 Ad
Hoyo de Pinares, El, *Spain* 38 Ad
Hoyt, *New Brunswick* 120 Bd
Höytiäinen, *Finland* 48 He
Ho-yuen, *China* 95 De
Hozat, *Turkey* 78 Cb
Hradec Králové, *Bohemia* 60 Cc
Hrádok, *Slovakia* 57 Ed
Hranice, *Moravia* 57 Cd
Hraun, *Iceland* 52 Ca
Hron, *Slovakia* 66 Da
Hron, R., *Slovakia* 57 Ee
Hronska Breznica, *Slovakia* 66 Da
Hrubieszów, *Poland* 60 Gc
Hrustovo, *Bosnia* 68 Bb
Hrütafjördhur, *Iceland* 52 Cb
Hsahtung, *Burma* 92 Cb
Hsa-Möng-Hkam, *Burma* 92 Cb
Hsawnghsup, *Burma* 88 Eb
Hsenwi, *Burma* 92 Da
Hsenwi, N. & S., *Burma* 92 Da
Hsiang-chow, *China* 95 Ce
Hsiao Hsingan Shan, *Manchuria* 96 Db
Hsi-hsiang, *China* 94 Cc
Hsikip, *Burma* 92 Cb
Hsiku-cheng, *China* 94 Bc
Hsiling, *China* 94 Db
Hsing, *China* 94 Db
Hsingan, prov., *Manchuria* 96 Cb
Hsingan Mts., *Manchuria* 96 Cb
Hsing-hwa, *China* 94 Ed
Hsingshanchen, *Manchuria* 96 Db
Hsing-ye, *China* 95 Ce
Hsin-hsiang, *China* 94 Db
Hsin-kai, *China* 94 Bc
Hsinking, *Manchuria* 96 Dc
Hsipaw, *Burma* 92 Ca
Hsi-ping, *China* 94 Dc
Hsiu-yen, *Manchuria* 96 Cc
Hsu, *China* 94 Dc
Hsü-kow, *China* 94 Db
Hsum Hsai, *Burma* 92 Ca
Hsun, R., *Manchuria* 96 Db
Hsün-yang, *China* 94 Cc
Hsü-yang, *China* 94 Cd
Hteng-yu, *Burma* 92 Ce
Huachi, *Bolivia* 146 Bb
Huacho, *Peru* 145 Bd
Huacrachuco, *Peru* 145 Bc
Huailas, *Peru* 145 Bc
Hualgayoc, *Peru* 145 Bc
Huallaga, R., *Peru* 145 Bc
Hualpai Ra., *Arizona* 134 Gd
Huamina, mt., *Peru* 145 Cd
Huanay, *Bolivia* 146 Bb
Huancabamba, *Peru* 145 Bc
Huancane, *Peru* 145 De
Huancavelica and dep., *Peru* 145 Bd
Huancayo, *Peru* 145 Cd
Huanchaca, *Bolivia* 146 Bc
Huanchaco, *Peru* 145 Bc
Huanta, *Peru* 145 Cd
Huanuco & dep., *Peru* 145 Bc
Huanzo, Cord. de, *Peru* 145 Cd
Huaras, *Peru* 145 Bc
Huari, *Chile* 146 Bb
Huariaca, *Peru* 145 Bd
Huarmey, *Peru* 145 Bd
Huarte, *Spain* 38 Db
Huascaran, *Peru* 145 Bc
Huasco, *Chile* 146 Ad
Huatusco, *Mexico* 139 Ed
Hubbard, *Texas* 133 De
Huberdeau, *Quebec* 121 Ca
Hubli, *Bombay* 90 Bd
Hu-chow, *China* 94 Ec
Huchting, *Bremen* 54 Db
Hucknall, *England* 18 Cd
Huddersfield, *England* 18 Cc
Hude, *Oldenburg* 54 Db
Hudemühlen, *Prussia* 54 Ec
Hudiksvall, *Sweden* 44 Dg
Hudson, *Florida* 131 Mg
Hudson, *New York* 123 Md
Hudson, *Ontario* 122 Ba
Hudson, *Quebec* 121 Cb
Hudson, *Wisconsin* 132 Cc
Hudson B., *Canada* 119 Me
Hudson R., *New York* 123 Me
Hudson Str., *N.-W. T.* 119 Pd
Hudson Falls, *New York* 123 Md
Hue, *Annam* 95 Cf
Huedin, *Transylvania* 67 Jc
Huehuetenango, *Guatemala* 140 Ed
Huejutla, *Mexico* 139 Ec
Huelamo, *Spain* 38 Dd
Huelgoat, *France* 32 Bb
Huelva & prov., *Spain* 40 Cb
Huelva, R., *Spain* 40 Db
Huemba, *Angola* 109 Cc
Huequi, Pen., *Chile* 148 Bc

Huercal Overa, *Spain* 41 Dc
Huerhhula, *Manchuria* 96 Cb
Huerta del Rey, *Spain* 38 Bc
Huesca & prov., *Spain* 39 Eb
Huescar, *Spain* 41 Dc
Huete, *Spain* 38 Cd
Hugginstown, *Eire* 27 Cg
Hughenden, *Queensland* 153 Bd
Hughes, *Alaska* 125 Jc
Hugh Town, *Scilly Is.* 17 Fg
Hugo, *Colorado* 135 Mb
Hugo, *Oklahoma* 133 Ec
Hugoton, *Kansas* 133 Bb
Huhi, *Mexico* 139 Gc
Huiarau Ra., *New Zeal'd* 158 Fc
Hui-fa-ho, *Manchuria* 96 Dc
Huila, dep. and mt., *Colombia* 144 Ac
Hui-tau B., *China* 95 Ee
Hu-kow, *China* 94 Ed
Hukuntsi, *Bechuanaland* 114 Db
Hulanfu, *Manchuria* 96 Db
Hule, L., *Palestine* 80 Da
Hulhul, *Palestine* 80 Cd
Hulin, *Manchuria* 96 Eb
Hull, *Massachusetts* 128 Cb
Hull, *Quebec* 121 Cb
Hull & R., *England* 19 Dc
Hull I., *Phœnix Is.* 157 Fd
Hultschin, *Moravia* 57 Dd
Hultsfred, *Sweden* 51 Ee
Hulutao, *Manchuria* 96 Cc
Huma, *Manchuria* 96 Da
Humacao, *Puerto Rico* 140 Jg
Humaita, *Paraguay* 146 Dd
Humansdorp, *Cape Prov.* 115 Fg
Humansville, *Missouri* 130 Bb
Humay, *Peru* 145 Bd
Humaytá, *Brazil* 142 Bd
Humber, R., *England* 19 Ec
Humbermouth, *Newfound.* 120 Gb
Humboldt, *Iowa* 132 Bd
Humboldt, *Kansas* 133 Eb
Humboldt, *Nebraska* 132 Ae
Humboldt, *Saskatchewan* 124 Jd
Humboldt, *Tennessee* 130 Dc
Humboldt & R., *Nevada* 134 Da
Humboldt B., *New Guinea* 156 Cb
Humboldt Glacier, *Greenl'd* 9 Cb
Humbuti, *Tangan. Terr.* 111 Dj
Hume Res., *N. S. W.* 155 Ed
Hummock I., *Tasmania* 155 Jg
Humphrey, *Idaho* 136 Hc
Humphreys, Mt., *Calif.* 134 Dc
Humphreys, Mt., *Wyoming* 136 Hc
Humpolec, *Bohemia* 59 Kb
Hunáflói, *Iceland* 52 Cb
Hu-nan, prov., *China* 94 Dd
Hun-chun, *Manchuria* 96 Ec
Hundested, *Denmark* 45 Ec
Hundewali, *Punjab* 82 Ec
Hundsfeld 57 Cb
Hunedoara, *Romania* 67 Hd
Hungary, *Cent. Europe* 53 Ge
Hungary, Plain of, *Cent. Europe* 66 Ec
Hung-cheng, *China* 94 Bb
Hungerford, *England* 14 Cd
Hungerford, *Queensland* 153 Be
Hung-hai, B., *China* 95 Ee
Hung-hoa, *Tong-king* 95 Be
Hung-tsê-hu, *China* 94 Ec
Hung-tung, *China* 94 Db
Hun-ho, R., *Manchuria* 96 Cc
Hunmanby, *England* 19 Db
Huns Mts., *S.-W. Africa* 114 Bc
Hunsrück, *Prussia* 58 Bb
Hunstanton, *England* 19 Ee
Hunsur, *Mysore* 89 Ba
Hunter, *N. Dakota* 132 Ab
Hunter I., *Ontario* 122 Ca
Hunter Is., *Tasmania* 155 Jg
Hunter's Road, *S. Rhod.* 113 Cb
Huntersville, *W. Virginia* 129 Ec
Huntingburg, *Indiana* 129 Ac
Huntingdon, *Pennsylva.* 129 Fb
Huntingdon, *Quebec* 121 Cb
Huntingdon, *Tennessee* 130 Db
Huntingdon & co., *Eng.* 15 Db
Huntington, *Arkansas* 130 Ac
Huntington, *Indiana* 129 Bb
Huntington, *New York* 128 Bc
Huntington, *Oregon* 136 Ec
Huntington, *Utah* 135 Hb
Huntington, *W. Virginia* 129 Dc
Huntly, *New Zealand* 158 Eb
Huntly, *Scotland* 23 Fb
Huntsville, *Alabama* 130 Ec
Huntsville, *Missouri* 130 Ba
Huntsville, *Ontario* 121 Ab
Huntsville, *Tennessee* 131 Fb
Huntsville, *Texas* 133 Ee
Hunucma, *Mexico* 139 Fc
Hun-yüan, *China* 94 Db
Huo-kin, *China* 94 Ec
Huon Gulf & Pen., *New Guinea* 156 Dc
Huon Is., *Pacific Oc.* 157 De
Huon, R., *Tasmania* 155 Jh
Hu-peh, prov., *China* 94 Dc
Hurdal Sjoen, *Norway* 47 Gd
Hurghada, *Egypt* 107 Je
Hurgnian, *Ontario* 122 Ca
Hurkett, *Ontario* 122 Da
Hurley, *England* 15 Dc
Hurley, *Wisconsin* 132 Db
Huron, *California* 134 Cc
Huron, *Oregon* 136 Dc
Huron, *S. Dakota* 126 Fb
Huron, L., *Canada-U.S.A.* 122 Gc
Hurricane, *Alaska* 125 Ke
Hurstbourne Tarrant, *Eng.* 14 Cd
Hurth, *Prussia* 54 Be
Hurtsboro, *Alabama* 130 Fd
Hurup, *Aalborg, Denmark* 45 Db
Hurup, *Thisted, Denmark* 45 Bb
Húsavik, *Iceland* 52 Ea
Husavik, *Iceland* 52 Cb
Husban, *Trans-Jordan* 80 Dd
Husbands Bosworth, *Eng.* 14 Cb
Huseinabad Kuh, *Persia* 79 Gc
Husi, *Romania* 69 Gb
Huskvarna, *Sweden* 5 De
Hussytar, Mt., *Manchuria* 96 Cb
Husum, *Prussia* 54 Da
Hususau, *Romania* 67 Kc
Hutchinson, *Cape Prov.* 114 Ee
Hutchinson, *Kansas* 133 Ca
Hutchinson, *Minnesota* 132 Bc
Hutchinsons I., *Florida* 131 Nh
Huttwil, *Switzerland* 42 Eb
Huwwara, *Palestine* 80 Cc
Huy, *Belgium* 29 Dd
Hu-yang-pu, *China* 94 Cb
Hvaler, *Norway* 47 Ge
Hvalfjördhur, *Iceland* 52 Bb
Hvammsfjördhur, *Iceland* 52 Bb
Hvannadalshnukur, *Iceland* 52 Eb
Hvar & I., *Dalmatia* 68 Bc
Hvarski Chan., *Dalmatia* 68 Bc
Hvitsten, *Norway* 47 Ge
Hvittingfoss, *Norway* 47 Fe
Hvvinkaa, *Finland* 48 Ff
Hwa, *China* 95 De
Hwachwan, *Manchuria* 96 Eb
Hwai-an, *China* 94 Ec
Hwai-king, *China* 94 Db
Hwailai, *China* 94 Ea
Hwai-te, *Manchuria* 96 Cc
Hwai-yang-shan, *China* 94 Dc
Hwai-yüan, *China* 94 Cb
Hwai-yüen, *China* 94 Cd
Hwa-ma-chi, *China* 94 Cb
Hwan, *China* 94 Cb
Hwang, *China* 94 Fb
Hwang-an, *China* 94 Dc
Hwang-chow, *China* 94 Dc
Hwang-Ho, *China* 94 Ca
Hwang-hwa-shan, *China* 94 Db
Hwang-shan, *China* 94 Ec
Hwa-ping, *China* 94 Cb
Hwatien, *Manchuria* 96 Dc
Hwega, *Burma* 88 Fb
Hwei-chang, *China* 94 Ed
Hwei-chow, *China* 94 Ec
Hwei-ho, R., *China* 94 Fc
Hwei-li, *China* 94 Bd
Hwo, *China* 94 Db
Hyannis, *Massachusetts* 128 Cc
Hydaburg, *Alaska* 125 Oj
Hyde, *England* 18 Bd
Hyden, *Kentucky* 131 Gb
Hyden, *W. Australia* 152 Be
Hyde Park, *Vermont* 128 Ba
Hyder, *Alaska* 125 Oj
Hyderabad, *Hyderabad* 90 Dc
Hyderabad, *Sind* 85 Bb
Hyderabad, state, *India* 81 Dg
Hydra & I., *Greece* 71 Ef
Hyères & Iles d', *France* 33 Bc
Hylestad, *Norway* 47 De
Hyllekrog, *Denmark* 45 Ed
Hyllestad, *Norway* 46 Bc
Hyltebruk, *Sweden* 51 Ce
Hyndman, *Pennsylvania* 129 Ec
Hyrra Banda, *Fr. Eq. Afr.* 105 Fd
Hyrum, *Utah* 135 Ha
Hyrynsalmi, *Finland* 48 Hd
Hythe, *England* 14 Ce
Hythe, *England* 15 Ed
Iablaniţa, *Romania* 67 He
Iad, *Transylvania* 67 Kb
Ialomiţa, *Romania* 69 Gc
Iam, *Romania* 67 Gd
Iasi, *Romania* 69 Gb
Iasmos, *Greece* 72 Ca
Iavello, *Ethiopia* 108 Ce
Iba, *Philippines* 95 Ef
Ibadan, *Nigeria* 105 Bd
Ibague, *Colombia* 144 Ac
Ibanda, *Tangan. Terr.* 111 Cf
Ibanshi, *Belg. Congo* 109 Db
Ibaraca, R., *Venezuela* 144 Dc
Ibarra, *Ecuador* 145 Ba
Ibb, *Yemen* 78 Lh
Ibbenbüren, *Prussia* 54 Cc
Iberkom, *Fr. W. Africa* 105 Cb
Iberville, *Quebec* 121 Db
Ibi, *Nigeria* 105 Cd
Ibicuhy, *Brazil* 146 Dd
Ibicuy, *Argentina* 146 De
Ibo, I., *Mozambique* 112 Db
Iboear, *New Guinea* 156 Ab
Ibokakule, *Tang. Terr.* 111 Ce
Iboko, *Belg. Congo* 109 Cb
Ibologero, *Tang. Terr.* 111 Cf
Ibrahimpatan, *Hyderabad* 90 Dc
Ibri, *Oman* 79 Ge
Ibros, *Spain* 41 Cb
Ibstock, *England* 14 Ca
Iburg, *Prussia* 54 Cc
Ica and dep., *Peru* 145 Bd
Icatu, *Brazil* 143 Fe
Iceland, I., *N. Atlantic Oc.* 9 Ge
Ichak, *Bihar* 87 Fc
I-chang, *China* 94 Dc
Ichchapuram, *Madras* 91 Gb
I-chow, *China* 94 Eb
I-chow, *Manchuria* 96 Cc
I-chwan, *China* 94 Cb
Icy C., *Alaska* 125 Fa
Ida (Psiloritis) Mt., *Crete* 71 Hj
Idabel, *Oklahoma* 133 Ed
Ida Grove, *Iowa* 132 Bd
Idah, *Nigeria* 105 Cd
Idaho, state, *U.S.A.* 126 Bb
Idaho City, *Idaho* 136 Fd
Idaho Falls, *Idaho* 136 Gd
Idaho Springs, *Colorado* 135 Lb
Idalia, *Transvaal* 115 Jc
Idanah, *Oregon* 136 Bc
Idar, *Western India* 85 Dc
Idar Wald, *Prussia* 58 Bb
Idd, *Norway* 47 He
Idemau, *Belg. Congo* 109 Ea
Idenburg R., *New Guinea* 156 Bb
Idfina, *Egypt* 107 Hc
Idfu, *Egypt* 107 Jf
Idhra (Hydra), I., *Greece* 71 Ef
Idi, *Sumatra* 98 Ab
Iditarod, *Alaska* 125 He
Idria, *California* 134 Cc
Idro, *Italy* 62 Eb
Idutywa, *Cape Prov.* 115 Hf
Ierápetra (Yirápetra), *Crete* 71 Jk
Iérax, C., *Greece* 71 Eg
Ierissós & G. of, *Greece* 70 Ec
Ifakara, *Tanganyika Terr.* 111 Eh
Ifassy, *Madagascar* 112 Fb
Iferouane, *Fr. W. Africa* 105 Cb
Iffley, *Queensland* 153 Bc
Ifni, *N.-W. Africa* 104 Ba
Igal, *Hungary* 66 Cc
Igamba, *Tang. Terr.* 111 Ch
Igan, *Sarawak* 98 Dc
Igandu, *Tanganyika Terr.* 111 Eg
Iganga, *Uganda* 110 Cc
Igarka, *U.S.S.R.* 76 Jc
Igatpuri, *Bombay* 90 Ab
Igherm, *Morocco* 103 Nj
Iglesias, *Sardinia* 64 Hg
Iglesla, *Argentina* 146 Be
Iglesuela del Cid, la, *Spain* 39 Ed
Igli, *Algeria* 102 Cd
Ignace, *Ontario* 122 Ca
Iğneada & C., *Turkey* 72 Fa
Igoji, *Kenya* 110 Ed
Igombe, *Tang. Terr.* 111 Cf
Igoumenítsa, *Greece* 70 Bd
Iguala, *Mexico* 139 Ed
Igualada, *Spain* 39 Gc
Iguapé, *Brazil* 147 Fc
Iguassu and R., *Brazil* 147 Ed
Iguassu, terr., *Brazil* 147 Ed
Iguatu, *Brazil* 143 Gd
Iguiguil, Jeb., *Morocco* 103 Nj
Igumira, *Tang. Terr.* 111 Cg
Ihanda, *Tang. Terr.* 111 Ch
Ihnâsya el Madina, *Egypt* 107 Hd
Ihosy & R., *Madagascar* 112 Ed
Ii and R., *Finland* 48 Fd
Iisalmi, *Finland* 48 Ge
Iiyama, *Japan* 100 Gc
Ijebu Ode, *Nigeria* 105 Bd
Ijssel Meer, *Holland* 29 Db
Ijssel, R., *Holland* 29 Eb
Ijuhy, *Brazil* 147 Ed
Ikaalinen, *Finland* 48 Ef
Ikagogda, mt., *Manchuria* 96 Ca
Ikebara, *Japan* 100 Ed
Ikeda, *Japan* 100 Dd
Ikela, *Belgian Congo* 109 Db
Ikelemba, *Fr. Eq. Africa* 109 Ca
Ikembe, *Rio Muni* 109 Ba
Ikeminan, *Manchuria* 96 Db
Ikhin-elesu, *Mongolia* 96 Ab
Ikhtman, *Bulgaria* 69 Ed
Iki, I., *Japan* 97 Bd
Ikizu, *Tanganyika Terr.* 110 Dd
Ikom, *Nigeria* 105 Cd
Ikoma, *Tang. Terr.* 110 De
Ikomba, *Tang. Terr.* 111 Ch
Ikombe, *Tang. Terr.* 111 Dh
Ikonde, *Tang. Terr.* 111 Bg
Ikungi, *Tang. Terr.* 111 Df
Ikuno, *Japan* 100 Ed
Ikutha, *Kenya* 110 Ee
Ilam, *Nepal* 87 Gb
Ilam, *Persia* 79 Ec
Ilandza, *Voyvodina* 67 Fd
Ilangala, *Tangan. Terr.* 110 Cd
Ilanz, *Switzerland* 43 Hc
Ilaro, *Nigeria* 105 Bd
Ilchester, *England* 14 Bd
Ile-a-la, L., *Saskatch.* 124 Hc
Ileanda, *Transylvania* 67 Jb
Ilĕk, *U.S.S.R.* 75 Je
Ilesha, *Nigeria* 105 Bd
Iletskaya Zashchita, *U.S.S.R.* 75 Ke
Ilewera, *Tang. Terr.* 110 Bd
Ilfeld, *Prussia* 54 Fd
Ilford, *England* 15 Ec
Ilfracombe, *England* 17 Ba
Ilhavo, *Portugal* 37 Bb
Ilhéos, *Brazil* 143 Ge
Ilia, *Romania* 67 Hd
Iliamna & L., *Alaska* 125 Hg
Iliamna Pk., *Alaska* 125 Jf
Ilidža, *Bosnia* 68 Dc
Ilie, *Turkey* 78 Cb
Iligan & B., *Philippines* 99 Fb
Ilikotu, *Manchuria* 96 Cb
Ilin, I., *Philippines* 99 Fa
Iliódhrómia (Alon) I., *Greece* 70 Ed
Ilkeston, *England* 18 Ce
Ilkley, *England* 18 Cc
Ilkuri Shan, *Manchuria* 96 Ca
Ill, R., *France* 31 Kd
Illana B., *Philippines* 99 Fb
Illapel, *Chile* 146 Ab
Illasi, *Italy* 63 Fb
Ille-et-Vilaine, *France* 32 Db
Iller, R., *Bavaria, etc.* 58 Ec
Illig, *It. Somaliland* 108 Ed
Illimani, mt., *Bolivia* 146 Bb
Illinois R., *Oklahoma, etc.* 133 Ec
Illinois, state, *U.S.A.* 127 Gc
Illo, *Nigeria* 105 Bc
Illora, *Spain* 41 Cc
Illye, *Transylvania* 67 Gc
Ilmen, L., *U.S.S.R.* 74 Ed
Ilmenau, *Thuringia* 54 Fe
Ilminster, *England* 14 Be
Ilo, *Peru* 145 Ce
Iloa, *Fr. W. Africa* 104 Dc
Iloilo & Str., *Philippines* 99 Fa
Ilorin, *Nigeria* 105 Bd
Ilovlinsk, *U.S.S.R.* 75 Gf
Ilsenburg, *Prussia* 54 Fd
Ilukste, *Latvia* 49 Dd
Ilunde, *Tangan. Terr.* 111 Bf
Ilunde, *Tangan. Terr.* 111 Cg
Ilva Mica, *Transylvania* 67 Kb
Ilwaco, *Washington* 136 Ab
Imahazoarivo, *Madagascar* 112 Ed
Imaichi, *Japan* 100 Dd
Imaichi, *Japan* 100 Gc
Imalamihiya, *Tang. Terr.* 111 Bf
Iman & R., *U.S.S.R.* 96 Eb
Imandra, L., *U.S.S.R.* 74 Eb
Imasho, *Japan* 100 Fd
Imatara, Sa. de, *Venezuela* 144 Db
Imazu, *Japan* 100 Ed
Imbabura, prov., *Ecuador* 145 Ba
Imbendane, *Mozambique* 113 Ec
Imbituba, *Brazil* 147 Fd
Imbros & I., *Turkey* 72 Cb
Imenau R., *Prussia* 54 Fb
Imese, *Belgian Congo* 109 Ca
Imi, *Ethiopia* 108 Dd
Imi n'Tanout, *Morocco* 103 Nj
Imiteq, *Morocco* 103 Nk
Imiter, *Morocco* 102 Bd
Immeln, *Sweden* 51 Df
Immenstadt, *Bavaria* 58 Ed
Immokalee, *Florida* 131 Nh
Imnaha R., *Oregon* 136 Ec
Imola, *Italy* 63 Fc
Imon, *Spain* 38 Cc
Imotski, *Dalmatia* 68 Cc
Impanda, *Mozambique* 112 Bd
Impendhle, *Natal* 115 Hd
Imperatriz, *Amazonas, Brazil* 145 Dc
Imperatriz, *Maranhao, Brazil* 143 Ed
Imperia, *Italy* 62 Cd
Imphal, *Assam* 88 Db
Imrali, I., *Turkey* 72 Fb
Imroz (Imbros), I., *Turkey* 72 Cb
Inagua I., Gt. and Lit., *Bahamas* 140 Cb
Inami, *Japan* 100 Ee
Inari & L., *Finland* 48 Gb
Incahuasi, *Argentina* 146 Bd
Inchkeith, *Scotland* 23 Ed
Inchnadamff, *Scotland* 24 De
Inchôpe, *Mozambique* 113 Eb
Incisa Valdarno, *Italy* 63 Fd
Indals, R., *Sweden* 44 Dg
Indargarh, *Rajputana* 86 Bc
Indaw, *Burma* 88 Fb
Indawgyi L., *Burma* 88 Fb
Indaya, *Brazil* 147 Fb
Indefatigable I. (Santa Cruz), *Galapagos Is.* 145 Eh
Independence, *California* 134 Dc
Independence, *Idaho* 136 Gd
Independence, *Iowa* 132 Cd
Independence, *Kansas* 133 Eb
Independence, *Missouri* 130 Aa
Independence, *Oregon* 136 Bc
Independence B., *Greenland* 9 Fa
Independence Ra., *Nevada* 134 Ea
Independencia, *Argentina* 146 Be
Inderborstroi, *Kazak* 75 Jf
India, *Asia* 73 Kf
Indian Desert, *Rajputana* 82 De
Indian Hd., *Queensland* 153 Dd
Indian L., *New York* 128 Ab
Indiana, *Pennsylvania* 129 Eb
Indiana, state, *U.S.A.* 127 Hb
Indianapolis, *Indiana* 129 Ac
Indian Bay, *Arkansas* 130 Cc
Indian Harbour Lake, *Nova Scotia* 120 Ed
Indian Head, *Saskatch.* 124 Jd
Indian House L., *Quebec* 119 Qe
Indianola, *Iowa* 132 Ce
Indian River Inlet, *Florida* 131 Nh
Indio, *California* 134 Ee
Indispensable Str., *Solomon Is.* 156 Jg
Indiva, *S. Rhodesia* 113 Db
Indjija, *Slavonia* 66 Fd
Indore, *Central India* 86 Bd
Indramajoe, *Java* 98 Ce
Indrapoera, *Sumatra* 98 Bd
Indravati R., *Eastern States* 91 Eb
Indre, R. & dep., *France* 30 Dd
Indre-et, Loire, *France* 30 Cd
Indur (Nizamabad), *Hyderabad* 90 Db
Indus R., *N.-W. India* 81 Ce
Indus, Mouths of the, *Sind* 85 Ab
Indwe, *Cape Prov.* 115 Ge
Inebolu, *Turkey* 78 Ba
Inece, *Turkey* 72 Da
Inegeul, *Turkey* 78 Ab
Ineri, mt., *Flores I., N.I.* 99 Fe
Ines, *Spain* 38 Bc
Ineu, *Transylvania* 67 Gc
Inez, *Kentucky* 131 Gb
Infanta C., *Cape Prov.* 114 Dg
Infantes, *Spain* 41 Cb
Infiesta (Pilona), *Spain* 36 Ea
Ingabu, *Burma* 92 Bd
In Gall, *Fr. W. Africa* 105 Cb
Ingatestone, *England* 15 Ec
Ingeniero Luiggi, *Argent.* 148 Cb
Ingersoll, *Ontario* 123 Hd
Ingham, *Queensland* 153 Cc
Ingledoon, *Queensland* 153 Bd
Inglefield Land, *Greenland* 9 Cb
Inglenook, *California* 134 Bb
Inglewood, *New Zealand* 158 Ec
Inglewood, *Queensland* 153 De
Inglewood, *Victoria* 154 Dd
Inglis, *Florida* 131 Gf
Ingolf, *Ontario* 122 Aa
Ingólfshöfdhi, *Iceland* 52 Ec
Ingolstadt, *Bavaria* 58 Fc
Ingonish, *Nova Scotia* 120 Ec
Ingrave, *England* 15 Ec
Ingrid Christensen Land, *Antarctica* 160 —
Ingwavuma, *Natal* 115 Kc
Inhabimbi, *Mozambique* 112 Bd

Inhaca I. and Pen., Mozambique - - 115 Kc
Inhadonga, Mozambique 113 Fb
Inhambane, Mozambique 112 Cd
Inhapallata, Mozambique 112 Cd
Inharrime, Mozambique 112 Cd
Inharuca, Mozambique - 113 Fa
I-ning, China - - 94 Dd
Inirida, R., Colombia - 144 Cc
Inishannon, Eire - - 25 Cf
Inishbofin, Eire - - 25 Ab
Inishkea Is., Eire - - 25 Aa
Inishman, Eire - - 25 Bc
Inishmore, Eire - - 25 Bc
Inishowen, Eire - - 26 Ca
Inishturk I., Eire - - 25 Ab
Initkilly (Corwin Coal Mine), Alaska - - 125 Fb
Inkermann, Algeria - 102 Eb
Inkom, Idaho - - 136 Gd
Inkongo, Belg. Congo - 109 Cb
Inkongu, Belg. Congo - 109 Db
Inkster, N. Dakota - 132 Aa
Inman, New York - - 128 Aa
Inn, R., Bavaria - - 59 Gd
Inn Tal, Lower, Austria 58 Ed
Inn Tal, Upper, Austria 58 Ed
Innamincka, S. Aust. - 154 Ca
Innellan, Scotland - - 22 Ce
Innerleithen, Scotland - 21 Cb
Inner-Rhoden, Switz. - 43 Hb
Innertkirchen, Switz. - 42 Fc
Innisfail, Queensland - 153 Cc
Innokentevka, U.S.S.R. 96 Eb
Innsbruck, Austria - 58 Fd
Inongo, Belg. Congo - 109 Cb
In Ouelen, Fr. W. Africa 105 Cb
Inowłodz, Poland - - 57 Fb
Inowrocław, Poland - - 60 Eb
Inquisivi, Bolivia - 146 Bb
In Rhar, Algeria - - 102 Ef
Ins, Switzerland - - 42 Db
In Salah, Algeria - - 102 Ff
Insar, U.S.S.R. - - 75 Ge
Insch, Scotland - - 23 Fb
Insein, Burma - - 92 Cd
Insiza, S. Rhodesia - 113 Cb
Inster R. - - - 56 Fb
Insterburg - - - 56 Fb
Interbergerovka, U.S.S.R. 96 Eb
Interior, Michigan - 122 Db
Interlaken, Switzerland 42 Ec
International Falls, Minnesota - - 132 Ca
Interview I., Andaman Is. 91 Kj
Intra, Italy - - - 62 Cb
Intragna, Switzerland - 43 Gd
Introbbio, Italy - - 62 Db
Intundhla, S. Rhodesia - 113 Bb
Inuboezaki, Japan - 97 Ec
Inveraray, Scotland - 22 Cd
Invercargill, New Zealand 159 Bg
Inverell, New S. Wales - 155 Ga
Inverfarigaig, Scotland - 23 Db
Invergordon, Scotland - 23 Da
Inverkeithing, Scotland 23 Ed
Invermoriston, Scotland 23 Db
Inverness, Alabama - 130 Fe
Inverness, Florida - 131 Gf
Inverness, Nova Scotia - 120 Ec
Inverness & co., Scotland 23 Db
Inverness, Firth of, Scot. 23 Da
Invershin, Scotland - 24 Df
Inverurie, Scotland - 23 Fb
Investigator Str., S. Aust. 154 Ad
Inwood, New York - 128 Bc
Inyaminga, Mozambique 113 Fb
Inyanga, S. Rhodesia - 113 Eb
Inyangoma I., Mozambique 112 Bc
Inyantue, S. Rhodesia - 113 Bb
Inyati, S. Rhodesia - 113 Cb
Inyauranga, Mozambique 113 Fb
Inyazura, S. Rhodesia - 113 Eb
Inyo Ra., California - 134 Dc
Inza, U.S.S.R. - - 75 He
Inzegmir, Algeria - - 102 Df
Ioánnina (Yannina), Greece 70 Bd
Iokanga, U.S.S.R. - - 74 Fb
Iokea, New Guinea - 156 Dc
Iola, Kansas - - 133 Eb
Ioma, New Guinea - 156 Dc
Iona, Nova Scotia - 120 Ed
Iona, I., Scotland - 22 Bd
Ione, California - 134 Cb
Ione, Oregon - - 136 Dc
Ioneşti, Romania - - 67 Je
Ionia, Michigan - - 122 Fd
Ionian Is., Greece - - 70 Ad
Ionian Sea, S.-E. Europe 61 Ge
Ioshkar Ola, U.S.S.R. - 74 Hd
Iowa, state, U.S.A. - 127 Gb
Iowa R., Iowa - - 132 Ce
Iowa City, Iowa - - 132 De
Iowa Falls, Iowa - - 132 Cd
Ipala, Mexico - - 138 Cc
Ipala, Tanganyika Terr. 111 Cf
Ipamery, Brazil - - 147 Fb
Iparia, Peru - - 145 Cc
Ipáti, Greece - - 71 De
Ipiales, Colombia - 144 Ac
Ipoeh, Sumatra - - 98 Bd
Ipoh, Malay States - 98 Bc
Ipolysag, Slovakia - 66 Da
Ippy, Fr. Eq. Africa - 105 Fd
Ipsala, Turkey - - 72 Db
Ipsili, Greece - - 71 Df
Ipsili, I., Greece - - 71 Ef
Ipsoús, Greece - - 71 Df
Ipswich, England - - 15 Fb
Ipswich, Queensland - 153 De
Iquique, Chile - - 146 Ac
Iquitos, Peru - - 145 Cb
Iracema, Brazil - - 145 Dd
Iracoubo, Fr. Guiana - 142 Da
Iragozaki, Japan - - 97 Dd
Iráklion (Candia), Crete 71 Jj
Iran Mts., Borneo - - 99 Dc
Irapa, Venezuela - 144 Da
Irapuato, Mexico - - 138 Dc
Iraq, Persia - - 79 Ec
Iraq, S.-W. Asia - - 77 Ec
Irara, Brazil - - 143 Ge
Irba Moda, Ethiopia - 108 Cd
Irbid, Trans-Jordan - 80 Db
Irboska, Estonia - - 49 Dc
Irebu, Belg. Congo - 109 Cb
Iremel, mt., U.S.S.R. - 74 Ke
Irena, Fr. Eq. Africa - 105 Ed
Iren-Khabirga, Sinkiang 84 Eb
Irgoli, Sardinia - - 64 Jf
Irig, Slavonia - - 66 Ed
Irikoumé, Sa., Brazil - 142 Cb
Iringa, Tanganyika Terr. 111 Dg
Iriomoto-shima, Japan - 95 Fe
Iriry, R., Brazil - - 142 Dc
Irish Cove, Nova Scotia 120 Ed
Irish Sea, British Isles - 13 De
Iriva, Turkey - - 72 Ga
Irkutsk, U.S.S.R. - - 76 Ld
Iro C., Japan - - 97 Dd
Iron, Minnesota - - 132 Cb
Iron Mt., Missouri - 130 Cb
Iron Acton, England - 14 Bc
Iron Baron, S. Australia 154 Ac
Ironbridge, England - 14 Ba
Iron City, Tennessee - 130 Ec
Irondale, Ontario - - 121 Ab
Iron Gate, Romania - 67 He
Iron Gate Pass, Romania 67 Hd
Iron Knob, S. Australia 154 Ac
Iron Mine Hill, S. Rhod. 113 Db
Iron Mountain, Michigan 122 Ec
Iron Mountain, Montana 136 Fb
Iron Mountain, Wyoming 135 La
Iron River, Michigan - 122 Db
Iron River, Wisconsin - 132 Db
Ironton, Missouri - - 130 Cb
Ironton, Ohio - - 129 Cc
Ironwood, Michigan - 122 Cb
Iroquois, Ontario - - 121 Cb
Iroquois Falls, Ontario - 123 Ha
Irrawaddy R., Burma - 92 Bb
Irtysh, R., Kazak - - 76 Hd
Irumu, Belgian Congo - 109 Ea
Irun, Spain - - - 38 Da
Irurun, Philippines - 99 Fa
Iruya, Argentina - - 146 Bc
Irvine, Scotland - - 21 Bb
Irvinestown, N. Ireland 26 Cc
Isabela, Basilan, Philippines - - - - 99 Fb
Isabela, Luzon, Philippines 95 Ff
Isabela, I., Mexico - 138 Cc
Isabella, California - 134 Dd
Isafjardhardjup, Iceland 52 Ba
Isafjordhur, Iceland - 52 Ba
Isagarh, Gwalior - - 86 Bc
Isaichi, Japan - - 100 Ba
Isakaya, Japan - - 100 Bb
Isa Khel, Punjab - - 82 Db
Isangi, Belgian Congo - 109 Da
Isangila, Belgian Congo 109 Bc
Isar, R., Bavaria - - 59 Fd
Isarco, Val di, Italy - 63 Fa
Ísari, Greece - - - 71 Df
Ischia, I., Italy - - 64 Dc
Iscia Baidoa, It. Somal'd 108 Gf
Ise B., Japan - - 97 Dd
Ise Fjord, Denmark - 45 Ec
Iseo & L. d', Italy - 62 Eb
Iser Geb., Bohemia - 59 Ka
Isère R. & dep., France 35 Hb
Iserlohn, Prussia - - 54 Cd
Isernia, Italy - - 64 Eb
Iseyin, Nigeria - - 105 Bd
Isfahan, Persia - - 79 Fc
Isfandaqeh, Persia - 79 Gd
Isfjord, Spitsbergen - 9 Lb
Ishibe, Japan - - 100 Ed
Ishigaki-shima, Japan - 95 Fe
Ishikari B. & R., Japan 97 Eb
Ishim, R., Kazak - - 76 Gd
Ishimbai, U.S.S.R. - 74 Ke
Ishinomaki & B., Japan 97 Ec
Ishioka, Japan - - 100 Hc
Ishm & R., Albania - 70 Ab
Ishpeming, Michigan - 122 Db
Ishqanan, Persia - - 79 Fd
Ishwa, Palestine - - 80 Cd
Isigny, France - - 32 Da
Isili, Sardinia - - 64 Jg
Isiolo, Kenya - - 110 Ec
Isipengo, Natal - - 115 Je
Isisford, Queensland - 153 Bd
Isker, R., Bulgaria - 69 Ed
Iskilip, Turkey - - 78 Ba
Iskindiriya (Alexandria), Egypt - - - 107 Gc
Isla Isabela (Albemarle I.), Galapagos Is. - - 145 Eh
Islamabad, Kashmir - 83 Fb
Island Lag., S. Australia 154 Ab
Island L., Manitoba - 124 Ld
Island Magee, N. Ireland 26 Eb
Island Pond, Vermont - 123 Mc
Islands, B. of, Newfound. 120 Fb
Islands, Bay of, N.Z. - 158 Ea
Islas Malvinas (Falkland Is.), S. Atlantic Oc. - 148 De
Islas Tres Marias, Mexico 138 Cc
Islay, I. & Sd., Scotland 22 Be
Isle of Hope, Georgia - 131 He
Isleta, New Mexico - 135 Kd
Isleton, California - 134 Cb
Islip, England - - 14 Cc
Isluga, mt., Chile - - 146 Bb
Ismail - - - - 69 Hc
Ismailia, Egypt - - 107 Hc
Isna, Egypt - - - 107 Jf
Isola - - - - 63 Hb
Isola d' Scala, Italy - 62 Fb
Ísoma, Greece - - 70 Eb
Isparta, Turkey - - 78 Bb
Isselberg, Prussia - - 54 Bd
Issoire, France - - 35 Fb
Issoudun, France - - 30 De
Issyk Kul, Kirghiz - 84 Db
Ist I., Dalmatia - - 63 Jc
Istanbul (Constantinople), Turkey - - - 72 Fa
Isthmia, Greece - - 71 Ef
Istia, Italy - - - 62 Fe
Istiaia (Xirokhóri), Greece 71 Ee
Istmina, Colombia - - 144 Ab
Istok, Montenegro - - 68 Fd
Istokpoga, Florida - 131 Nh
Istrana, Italy - - 63 Gb
Istranca, Turkey - - 72 Fa
Istres, France - - 35 Gd
Istria - - - - 63 Hb
Itabaianna, Brazil - 143 Gd
Itaberaba, Brazil - - 143 Fe
Itabira, Brazil - - 147 Gb
Itabuna, Brazil - - 143 Ge
Itacoatiara, Brazil - 142 Cc
Itaete, Brazil - - 143 Fe
Itaituba, Amazonas, Brazil 142 Bd
Itaituba, Para, Brazil - 142 Cc
Itajahy, Brazil - - 147 Fd
Itako, Japan - - 100 Hd
Italian Somaliland, E. Africa - - 101 Ge
Italy, S. Europe - - 61 Cc
Itamos, mt., Greece - 71 Cd
Itapecuru, R. and Sa., Brazil - - - 143 Fd
Itapecurúmirim, Brazil 143 Fc
Itaperina, C., Madagascar 112 Ed
Itaperuna, Brazil - - 147 Gc
Itapetininga, Brazil - 147 Fc
Itapira, Brazil - - 143 Ge
Itapocoroy, Brazil - 147 Fd
Itapura, Brazil - - 147 Ec
Itaqui, Brazil - - 146 Dd
Itasca L., Minnesota - 132 Bb
Itatiaya, mt., Brazil - 147 Gc
Itauna, Brazil - - 147 Gc
Itaúnas, Brazil - - 147 Hb
Itcani, Romania - - 69 Gb
Itéa, Greece - - - 71 De
Itebej, Voyvodina - - 67 Fd
Itembo, Belgian Congo - 109 Da
Ithaca, Michigan - - 122 Fd
Ithaca, New York - 123 Kd
Ithaca (Itháki), Greece - 71 Be
Ithaca & Str., Greece - 71 Be
Itiés, Greece - - - 70 Cc
Itiquira, Brazil - - 147 Eb
Itivdliarsuk, Greenland - 9 Dc
Itobe, Nigeria - - 105 Cd
Itoko, Belgian Congo - 109 Db
Itta Bena, Mississippi - 130 Cd
I-tu, China - - - 94 Dc
Ituassú, Brazil - - 143 Fe
Itung, Manchuria - - 96 Dc
Iturbe, Argentina - - 146 Bc
Iturbide, Mexico - - 139 Gd
Itzawisis, S.-W. Africa 114 Cc
Itzehoe, Prussia - - 54 Eb
Itzer, Morocco - - 102 Bc
Iuda, Transylvania - 67 Kc
Iuka, Kansas - - 133 Cb
Iuka, Mississippi - - 130 Dc
Ivalo & R., Finland - 48 Gb
Ivanec, Croatia - - 66 Bc
Ivanhoe, New S. Wales 154 Dc
Ivanjica, Serbia - - 68 Fc
Ivanjska, Bosnia - - 68 Bb
Ivanovka, U.S.S.R. - 74 Fb
Ivanovo, U.S.S.R. - 74 Gd
Ivanteevka, U.S.S.R. - 75 He
Ives Pk., Arizona - - 135 Gd
Iveşti, Romania - - 69 Gc
Ivigtiit, Greenland - - 9 Ee
Ivinghoe, England - 15 Dc
Iviza & B., Balearic Is. 39 Kg
Iviza (Ibiza), I., Balearic Is. 39 Kg
Ivohitrambo, Madagascar 112 Ed
Ivory Coast, col., Fr. W. Africa - - - 104 Ce
Ivrea, Italy - - - 62 Bb
Ivrindi, Turkey - - 72 Ec
Ivry-la-Bataille, France 30 Dc
Ivybridge, England - 17 Cc
Iwabuchi, Japan - - 100 Gd
Iwakuni, Japan - - 100 Ca
Iwamatsu, Japan - - 100 De
Iwanuma, Japan - - 97 Ec
Iwoshima, Japan - - 97 Bd
Ixiamas, Bolivia - - 145 Dd
Ixopo, Natal - - 115 Je
Ixtlan, Mexico - - 139 Ed
Ixworth, England - - 15 Eb
Iyo Nada, Japan - - 97 Cd
Iz, Dalmatia - - - 63 Kc
Izabel & L., Guatemala 140 Fd
Izamal, Mexico - - 139 Gc
Izhevsk, U.S.S.R. - 74 Jd
Izhma & R., U.S.S.R. - 74 Jc
Izki, Oman - - - 79 Je
Izmir (Smyrna), Turkey 78 Ab
Izmit (Kocaeli), Turkey 78 Aa
Iznajar, Spain - - 40 Fb
Iztapa, Guatemala - - 140 Ee
Izu Shichitō, Japan - 97 Dd
Izvor, Serbia - - 70 Cb
Izyum, Ukraine - - 75 Ff
Jaab, Utah - - 135 Hb
Ja'alen & Jeb., Oman - 79 Ge
Jaani, Estonia - - 49 Cb
Jabal, Ras al, Arabia - 79 Gd
Jablanac, Croatia - - 63 Jc
Jablanica, Hercegovina - 68 Cc
Jablonec, Bohemia - 60 Cc
Jablonica, Slovakia - 66 Ca
Jabłonka, Poland - - 57 Ed
Jabłonow, Poland - - 56 Dc
Jablunkovsky, pass, Czech. 60 Ed
Jaburu, Brazil - - 145 Db
Jaca, Spain - - - 39 Eb
Jacarary, Brazil - - 143 Fe
Jacarezinho, Brazil - 147 Ec
Jachal, Argentina - - 146 Be
Jachar, Mt., China - 94 Bb
Jacitara, Brazil - - 142 Ac
Jackfish, Ontario - - 122 Ea
Jacksboro, Tennessee - 131 Fb
Jacksboro, Texas - - 133 Cd
Jackson, Alabama - - 130 Ee
Jackson, California - 134 Cb
Jackson, Georgia - - 131 Fd
Jackson, Kentucky - - 131 Gb
Jackson, Louisiana - 130 Ce
Jackson, Michigan - - 122 Fd
Jackson, Minnesota - 132 Bd
Jackson, Mississippi - 130 Cd
Jackson, Missouri - - 130 Db
Jackson, Montana - - 136 Gc
Jackson, N. Carolina - 131 Kb
Jackson, Ohio - - 129 Cc
Jackson, Tennessee - 130 Dc
Jackson & L., Wyoming 136 Hd
Jackson Mts., Nevada - 134 Da
Jacksonboro, Ontario - 122 Ga
Jacksonville, Florida - 131 Ge
Jacksonville, Illinois - 132 Df
Jacksonville, N. Carolina 131 Kc
Jacksonville, Oregon - 136 Bd
Jacksonville, Texas - 133 Ed
Jacksonville Beach, Florida 131 He
Jacmel, Haiti - - 140 Cc
Jacobabad, Sind - - 82 Cd
Jacobecua, Mozambique 112 Bd
Jacobina, Brazil - - 143 Fe
Jacobsdal, O.F.S. - - 115 Fd
Jacobshagen - - - 55 Lb
Jacques Cartier, Mt., Quebec - - - 120 Cb
Jacques Cartier R., Quebec 123 Nb
Jacquet River, New Bruns. 120 Bc
Jacqueville, Fr. W. Africa 104 Df
Jacuhy, R., Brazil - 147 Ee
Jade B. & R., Oldenburg 54 Db
Jade Mines, Burma - 88 Fb
Jaderberg, Oldenburg - 54 Db
Jadotville, Belg. Congo - 109 Ed
Jadraque, Spain - - 38 Cd
Jaelsminde, Denmark - 45 Dc
Jaén and prov., Spain - 41 Cc
Jæren, Norway - - 47 Bf
Jaffa, Palestine - - 80 Bc
Jaffna, Ceylon - - 89 Dc
Jagadhri, Punjab - - 83 Gc
Jagdalpur, Eastern States 91 Eb
Jagdispur, Bihar - - 87 Fc
Jagerndorf, Moravia - 57 Cc
Jagersfontein, O.F.S. - 115 Fd
Jaggayyapeta, Madras - 91 Ec
Jagodina, Serbia - - 68 Gc
Jagraon, Punjab - - 83 Fc
Jagtial, Hyderabad - 90 Db
Jagua, Philippines - - 99 Fa
Jaguarão, Brazil - - 147 Ee
Jaguariahyva, Brazil - 147 Ec
Jaguaribe, R., Brazil - 143 Gd
Jaguaruna, Brazil - 147 Fd
Jaguary, Brazil - - 146 Dd
Jahangirabad, United Prs. 83 Gd
Jahazpur, Rajputana - 85 Eb
Jahra, Kuwait - - 79 Ed
Jahrum, Persia - - 79 Fd
Jahu, Brazil - - 147 Fc
Jaicós, Brazil - - 143 Fd
Jaintiapur, Assam - - 88 Db
Jaipur, Assam - - 88 Ea
Jaipur, Rajputana - - 83 Fe
Jair Ra., Sinkiang - 84 Ea
Jais, United Provs. - 86 Db
Jaisalmer, Rajputana - 82 De
Jaitgarh, mt., Cent. Provs. 86 Ce
Jaitpur, United Provs. - 86 Cc
Jajarkot, Nepal - - 86 Da
Jajarm, Persia - - 79 Gb
Jajce, Bosnia - - 68 Cb
Jajpur, Orissa - - 87 Ge
Jakhau, Western India - 85 Bc
Jakobshavn, Greenland - 9 Dd
Jakupovci, Bosnia - - 68 Cb
Jalalabad, Afghanistan - 82 Da
Jalalabad, Punjab - - 83 Fc
Jalalabad, United Provs. 83 Gd
Jalalpur, Punjab - - 83 Fb
Jalalpur, Punjab - - 82 Dd
Jalalpur, United Provs. - 87 Eb
Jalama, Palestine - - 80 Cc
Jalance, Spain - - 41 Ea
Jalapa, Mexico - - 139 Ed
Jalapa, Nicaragua - 140 Fe
Jalaun, United Provs. - 86 Cb
Jaleswar, Nepal - - 87 Gb
Jalgaon, Bombay - - 90 Ba
Jaligny, France - - 35 Fa
Jalingo, Nigeria - - 105 Dd
Jalisco, state, Mexico - 138 Dc
Jaljulye, Palestine - 80 Bc
Jalk, Persia - - 79 Hd
Jalla, Nigeria - - 105 Bd
Jalna, Hyderabad - 90 Bb
Jalon, R., Spain - - 38 Dc
Jalor, Rajputana - - 85 Db
Jalpaiguri, Bengal - 88 Ba
Jalpan, Mexico - - 139 Ec
Jalpes, Bengal - - 88 Ba
Jaluit Is., Marshall Is. - 157 Ec
Jama, Tunisia - - 103 Ja
Jamaica B., New York - 128 Bc
Jamaica, I., West Indies 140 Bc
Jämaja, Estonia - - 49 Ab
Jamalabad, Persia - 79 Eb
Jamalpur, Bengal - - 88 Cb
Jamalpur, Bihar - - 87 Gc
Jamberoo, New S. Wales 155 Gc
Jambongon I., E. Indies 99 Eb
James B., Canada - - 119 Nf
James I., Chile - - 148 Bc
James Ras., N. Terr., Australia - - 150 Ec
James R., S. Dakota - 126 Fb
James R., Virginia - 129 Ed
Jamesburg, California - 134 Cc

Jameson Land, *Greenland* 9 Gc
James Ross I., *Antarctica* 160 —
Jamestown, *Cape Provs.* 115 Ge
Jamestown, *Eire* - - 26 Bd
Jamestown, *New York* - 123 Jd
Jamestown, *N. Dakota* - 126 Ea
Jamestown, *St Helena I.* 114 Nj
Jamestown, *S. Australia* 154 Bc
James W. Ellsworth Ld., *Antarctica* - - - 160 —
Jamiltepec, *Mexico* - 139 Ed
Jamkhandi, *Deccan States* 90 Bc
Jamkhed, *Bombay* - - 90 Bb
Jamm, *Persia* - - 79 Fd
Jammalamadugu, *Madras* 90 Dd
Jammer B., *Denmark* - 45 Ca
Jammerland B., *Denmark* 45 Dc
Jammu, *Kashmir* - - 83 Fb
Jamnagar, *Western India* 85 Cc
Jampur, *Punjab* - - 82 Dd
Jämsä, *Finland* - - 48 Ff
Jam Sahib, *Sind* - - 85 Ba
Jamshedpur, *Bihar* - 87 Gd
Jamtara, *Bihar* - - 87 Gc
Jamui, *Bihar* - - 87 Gc
Jamuna R., *Bengal* - 88 Bb
Jamundi, *Colombia* - 144 Ac
Jandiala, *Punjab* - - 83 Fc
Janesville, *Wisconsin* - 132 Ed
Janeville, *New Brunswick* 120 Cc
Jangi, *Punjab States* - 83 Hc
Jangipur, *Bengal* - - 88 Ab
Jani Khel, *N.-W.F.P.* - 82 Db
Janja, *Bosnia* - - 68 Eb
Janjevo, *Serbia* - - 68 Gd
Janjina, *Dalmatia* - - 68 Cd
Janjira, *Deccan States* - 90 Ab
Jank, *Hungary* - - 67 Hb
Jankaria, *Assam* - - 88 Cb
Jan Mayen, I., *Arctica* - 9 Jc
Janopole, *Lithuania* - 49 Bd
Janos, *Mexico* - - 138 Ca
Jánoshalma, *Hungary* - 66 Ec
Jánosháza, *Hungary* - 66 Cb
Janovice, *Bohemia* - 59 Hb
Janów, *Poland* - - 57 Ec
Jansath, *United Provs.* - 83 Gd
Jansenville, *Cape Prov.* - 115 Ff
Januaria, *Brazil* - - 147 Gb
Janze, *France* - - 32 Dc
Jao-chow, *China* - - 94 Ed
Jaoho, *Manchuria* - - 96 Eb
Jaora, *Central India* - 85 Ec
Japan (Nippon), and Sea of, *E. Asia* - - 93 Fc
Japen I. and Str., *Dutch New Guinea* - - 156 Bb
Japonesa, La, *Argentina* 148 Cb
Japura, R., *Brazil* - 145 Db
Jaquila, *Mexico* - - 139 Ed
Jara, La, *Colorado* - 135 Kc
Jara, La, *Spain* - - 37 Ec
Jaragua, *Goyaz, Brazil* - 147 Fb
Jaragua, *Santa Catharina, Brazil* - - - 147 Fd
Jarales, *New Mexico* - 135 Kd
Jaramillo, *Argentina* - 148 Cd
Jaranwala, *Punjab* - 83 Ec
Jarba, *Palestine* - - 80 Cc
Järbo, *Sweden* - - 50 Fb
Jardim, *Brazil* - - 143 Gd
Jardines de la Reina, *Cuba* 140 Bb
Jaren, *Norway* - - 47 Gd
Jargeau, *France* - - 30 Ed
Jarkovac, *Voyvodina* - 67 Fd
Järna, *Sweden* - - 50 Db
Järnskog, *Sweden* - - 50 Bc
Jarocin, *Poland* - - 60 Dc
Jaromer, *Bohemia* - - 59 Ka
Jarosław, *Poland* - - 60 Gc
Jarrow, *England* - - 21 Ed
Jarvis I., *Line Is.* - - 157 Hd
Jary, R., *Brazil* - - 142 Db
Jasak, *China* - - 94 Cb
Jasenica, *Bosnia* - - 68 Bb
Jasenovac, *Slavonia* - 66 Bd
Jashpur, *Eastern States* - 87 Ed
Jashpurnagar, *Eastern States* - - - 87 Ed
Jasiña, *Carpatho-Ukraine* 60 Hd
Jask, *Persia* - - 79 Gd
Jasło, *Poland* - - 60 Fd
Jaso, *Central India* - 86 Dc
Jason Is., *Falkland Is.* - 148 De
Jasper, *Alabama* - - 130 Ed
Jasper, *Arkansas* - - 130 Bc
Jasper, *Florida* - - 131 Ge
Jasper, *Georgia* - - 131 Fc
Jasper, *Indiana* - - 129 Ac
Jasper, *Tennessee* - - 130 Fc
Jasper, *Texas* - - 133 Fe
Jasper and Park, *Alberta* 124 Fd
Jastrebarsko, *Croatia* - 63 Kb
Jastrow - - - 56 Ac
Jászárokszállás, *Hungary* 66 Eb
Jászberény, *Hungary* - 66 Eb
Jászfenyszaru, *Hungary* 66 Eb
Jaszkarajeno, *Hungary* - 66 Eb
Jaszkisér, *Hungary* - 66 Fb
Jászladány, *Hungary* - 66 Fb
Jász-Nagykun, *Hungary* 67 Fb
Jatahy, *Brazil* - - 147 Ec
Jath, *Deccan States* - 90 Bc
Jativa, *Spain* - - 41 Fb
Jatoba, *Brazil* - - 143 Gd
Jauary, *Brazil* - - 142 Bc
Jauer - - - - 55 Md
Jauf, *Arabia* - - - 78 Cd
Jauja, *Peru* - - 145 Bd
Jaunjelgava, *Latvia* - 49 Cc
Jaunlatgale, *Latvia* - 49 Dc
Jaunpur, *United Provs.* - 87 Ec
Java I. and Sea, *Borneo* 98 Ce
Javadi Hills, *Madras* - 90 De
Javalambre, Sa de, *Spain* 38 Ed
Javary, R., *Peru* - - 145 Cb
Javea, *Spain* - - - 41 Gb
Javie, la, *France* - - 35 Jc
Javor Planina, *Bosnia* - 68 Db
Javorniky, mts., *Slovakia* 57 Dd
Jawad, *Gwalior* - - 85 Eb
Jawalamukhi, *Punjab* - 83 Gc
Jawhar, *Gujarat States* - 90 Ab
Jaworaw - - - 60 Gd
Jaynagar, *Bihar* - - 87 Gb
Jayus, *Palestine* - - 80 Cc
Jeba, *Syria* - - - 80 Da
Jebalie, *Palestine* - - 80 Ad
Jebba, *Nigeria* - - 105 Bd
Jebel, *Romania* - - 67 Gd
Jebjerg, *Denmark* - - 45 Cb
Jech Doab, *Punjab* - 82 Eb
Jedburgh, *Scotland* - 21 Dc
Jedede, *Arabia* - - 78 Ce
Jędrzejów, *Poland* - - 60 Ec
Jedwabno - - - 56 Ec
Jefara Plain, *Tunisia-Libya* - - - 103 Kc
Jefferson, *Georgia* - - 131 Gc
Jefferson, *Iowa* - - 132 Be
Jefferson, *Ohio* - - 129 Db
Jefferson, *Texas* - - 133 Ed
Jefferson, *Wisconsin* - 132 Ed
Jefferson, Mt., *Idaho* - 136 Hc
Jefferson, Mt., *Oregon* - 136 Cc
Jefferson R., *Montana* - 136 Gc
Jefferson City, *Missouri* 130 Ba
Jeffersonville, *Indiana* - 129 Ac
Jefren, *Libya* - - 106 Ok
Jehol, prov., *Manchuria* 96 Bc
Jekabpils, *Latvia* - - 49 Cc
Jekyl I., *Georgia* - - 131 He
Jelgava, *Latvia* - - 49 Bc
Jelib, *Ital. Somaliland* - 108 Gf
Jelica Planina, *Serbia* - 68 Fc
Jellicoe, *Ontario* - - 122 Ea
Jellico, *Tennessee* - - 131 Fb
Jelling, *Denmark* - - 45 Cc
Jellowa - - - 57 Dc
Jelse, *Norway* - - 47 Ce
Jemelle, *Belgium* - - 29 Dd
Jemeppe, *Belgium* - - 29 Dd
Jemmapes, *Algeria* - 103 Ha
Jena, *Thuringia* - - 55 Ge
Jenas, *Mozambique* - 113 Ec
Jenbach, *Austria* - - 59 Fd
Jenchu, *Korea* - - 97 Bc
Jen-hwai-hsien, *China* - 94 Cd
Jen-hwai-ting, *China* - 94 Cd
Jenin, *Palestine* - - 80 Cc
Jennings, *Florida* - - 131 Ge
Jennings, *Louisiana* - 130 Be
Jennings, *Montana* - - 136 Fa
Jensvoll, *Norway* - - 46 Hb
Jeparit, *Victoria* - - 154 Cd
Jequie, *Brazil* - - 143 Fe
Jeran, *Ital. Somaliland* - 108 Fc
Jerash, *Trans-Jordan* - 80 Dc
Jeremie, *Haiti* - - 140 Cc
Jerez, *Mexico* - - 138 Dc
Jerez de la Frontera, *Spain* 40 Dc
Jerez de los Caballeros, *Spain* - - - 37 Dd
Jericho, *Queensland* - 153 Cd
Jericho, *Texas* - - 133 Bc
Jericho, *Vermont* - - 128 Ba
Jericho (Eriha), *Palestine* 80 Cd
Jerilderie, *New S. Wales* 155 Ed
Jerome, *Arizona* - - 135 Gd
Jerome, *Idaho* - - 136 Fd
Jerruck, *Sind* - - 85 Bb
Jersey, I., *Channel Is.* - 17 Ef
Jersey City, *New Jersey* 129 Gb
Jerseyville, *Illinois* - 132 Df
Jerusalem (El Quds Esh Sherif), *Palestine* - 80 Cd
Jervis, *New S. Wales* - 155 Gd
Jesenice, *Croatia* - - 63 Kb
Jesenice, *Slovenia* - - 63 Ha
Jesi, *Italy* - - - 63 Hd
Jesselton, *N. Borneo* - 99 Eb
Jessie, *S. Rhodesia* - 113 Cc
Jessore, *Bengal* - - 88 Bc
Jesup, *Georgia* - - 131 Ge
Jesus, I., *Quebec* - - 121 Db
Jesus, Sa. de, *Paraguay* 146 Dd
Jesus Maria, *Argentina* - 146 Ce
Jesus Maria, *Mexico* - 138 Cb
Jetmore, *Kansas* - - 133 Ca
Jevicko, *Moravia* - - 57 Bd
Jevnaker, *Norway* - - 47 Gd
Jewell, *Kansas* - - 133 Ca
Jewett City, *Connecticut* 128 Cc
Jeypore, *Orissa* - - 91 Fb
Jezero, *Bosnia* - - 68 Cb
Jhabua, *Central India* - 85 Ec
Jhajjar, *Punjab* - - 83 Gd
Jhal, *Baluchistan* - - 82 Bd
Jhalakati, *Bengal* - - 88 Cc
Jhalawan, *Baluchistan* - 82 Be
Jhalrapatan Chhaoni, *Rajputana* - - - 86 Bc
Jhang-Maghiana, *Punjab* 82 Ec
Jhansi, *United Provs.* - 86 Cc
Jhanzi R., *Assam* - - 88 Ea
Jharia, *Bihar* - - 87 Gd
Jhelum, *Punjab* - - 83 Eb
Jhelum R., *Punjab* - - 82 Eb
Jhingergacha, *Bengal* - 88 Bc
Jhinjhuvada, *W. India* - 85 Cc
Jhudo, *Sind* - - - 85 Bb
Jhumra, *Punjab* - - 82 Ec
Jhunjhunu, *Rajputana* - 83 Fd
Jiabalo, *Ethiopia* - - 108 Dd
Jianpur, *United Provs.* - 87 Eb
Jibou, *Transylvania* - 67 Jb
Jibu, *Nigeria* - - 105 Cd
Jicaro, *Nicaragua* - - 140 Fe
Jičin, *Bohemia* - - 59 Ka
Jidbaleh, *Br. Somaliland* 108 Ed
Jidd, *Iraq* - - - 78 Cc
Jidda, *Arabia* - - 78 Ce
Jiggitai L., *Tibet* - - 84 Fc
Jigni, *Central India* - 86 Cc
Jihlava, *Moravia* - - 60 Cd
Jihlava, R., *Moravia* - 60 Dd
Jijiga, *Ethiopia* - - 108 Dd
Jiljiliya, *Palestine* - - 80 Cc
Jiloca, R., *Spain* - - 38 Dc
Jimaja, I., *Nether. Indies* 98 Cc
Jimba, *Br. Somaliland* - 108 Dd
Jimbolia, *Romania* - 67 Fd
Jimenez, *Chihuahua, Mexico* 138 Db
Jimenez, *Caohuila, Mexico* 138 Db
Jimenez, *Tamaulipas, Mexico* - - 139 Ec
Jimma, *Ethiopia* - - 108 Cd
Jind, *Punjab States* - 83 Gd
Jindřichův Hradec, *Bohemia* - - - 60 Cd
Jinja, *Uganda* - - 110 Cc
Jinotega, *Nicaragua* - 140 Fe
Jipijapa, *Ecuador* - - 145 Ab
Jisha, *Arabia* - - 79 Ed
Jisresh Shughur, *Syria* - 78 Cb
Jiul, R., *Romania* - - 67 Je
Joachimsthal, *Prussia* - 55 Jc
Joal, *Fr. W. Africa* - 104 Ad
Joanna Spring, *W. Aust.* 152 Cc
João Pessoa, *Brazil* - 143 Gd
João Pinheiro, *Brazil* - 147 Fb
Joazeira, *Brazil* - - 143 Fd
Jobat, *Central India* - 85 Ec
Jodar, *Spain* - - - 41 Cc
Jodhpur, *Rajputana* - 85 Da
Jodiya, *Western India* - 85 Cc
Jöelehtme, *Estonia* - 49 Cb
Joënsuu, *Finland* - - 48 Je
Jofane, *Mozambique* - 113 Fe
Joffre, Mt., *Br. Columbia* 118 Ff
Joggins, *Nova Scotia* - 120 Cd
Jogindernagar, *Punjab States* - - - 83 Gc
Jogjakarta, *Java* - - 98 De
Johanna & I., *Comoro Is.* 112 Db
Johannesburg, *Transvaal* 115 Hc
Johannisburg - - 56 Fc
John Day R., *Oregon* - 136 Cc
John O'Groats, *Scotland* 24 Ed
Johnson, *Kansas* - - 133 Bb
Johnson, C., *Washington* 136 Ab
Johnsonburg, *Pennsylva.* 129 Eb
Johnson City, *New York* 123 Ld
Johnson City, *Tennessee* 131 Gb
Johnson City, *Texas* - 133 Ce
Johnston I., *Pacific Oc.* 157 Gb
Johnston City, *New York* 129 Ga
Johnstone, *Scotland* - 23 De
Johnstone Ra., *Queensland* 153 Bd
Johnstown, *New York* - 123 Ld
Johnstown, *Pennsylvania* 129 Eb
Johore, *Malay States* - 98 Bc
Johore Bharu, *Malay States* - - - 98 Bc
Johvi, *Estonia* - - 49 Db
Joigny, *France* - - 30 Fd
Joinville, *Brazil* - - 147 Fd
Joinville I., *Antarctica* - 160 —
Jokkmokk, *Sweden* - 48 Cc
Jokulfirdhir, *Iceland* - 52 Ba
Jökulsá á Brú, *Iceland* - 52 Fb
Jokulsá á Fjöllum, *Iceland* 52 Eb
Joliet, *Illinois* - - 132 Ee
Joliette, *Quebec* - - 121 Da
Jolo & I., *Philippines* - 99 Fb
Jölster Vatn, *Norway* - 46 Cc
Jolsva, *Slovakia* - - 66 Fa
Jombongs, *Fr. Eq. Africa* 105 De
Jomfruland, *Norway* - 47 Ff
Jonava, *Lithuania* - - 49 Cd
Jondal, *Norway* - - 47 Cd
Jones Sd., *N.-W. Terr.* - 119 Ma
Jonesboro, *Arkansas* - 130 Cc
Jonesboro, *Georgia* - 131 Fd
Jonesboro, *Illinois* - 130 Db
Jonesboro, *Louisiana* - 130 Bd
Jonesport, *Maine* - - 120 Bd
Jonesville, *Vermont* - 128 Ba
Joniskis, *Lithuania* - 49 Bc
Jönköping & län, *Sweden* 51 Ce
Jonquière, *Quebec* - - 123 Na
Jonuta, *Mexico* - - 139 Fd
Jonzac, *France* - - 34 Bb
Joplin, *Missouri* - - 130 Ab
Jordan, *Minnesota* - - 132 Cc
Jordan R., *Oregon* - - 136 Ed
Jordan, R., *Syria-Palestine* 80 Db
Jordan R., *Utah* - - 135 Ga
Jorhat, *Assam* - - 88 Ea
Jorge Montt, I., *Chile* - 148 Ae
Jörn, *Sweden* - - - 48 Dd
Joroinen, *Finland* - - 48 Ge
Jorullo, Vol., *Mexico* - 138 Dd
Jos, *Nigeria* - - - 105 Cd
Jošanicka Banja, *Serbia* 68 Fc
Josen Fd., *Norway* - 47 Ce
Joseph, *Oregon* - - 136 Ec
Joseph Bonaparte Sea, *W. Australia* - - 150 Da
Joseph City, *Arizona* - 135 Hd
Joshin, *Korea* - - 97 Bb
Josipdol, *Croatia* - - 63 Kb
Josselin, *France* - - 32 Cc
Jostedal, *Norway* - - 46 Dc
Jostedalen, *Norway* - 46 Dc
Jostedalsbreen, *Norway* - 46 Cc
Jotunheimen, *Norway* - 46 Ec
Jouaya, *Lebanon* - - 80 Ca
Joyo, *Korea* - - - 97 Bc
Joza, *Trans-Jordan* - 80 De
Juamave, *Mexico* - - 139 Ec
Juan de Fuca Str., *Can.-U.S.A.* - - - 124 Ee
Juan de Nova I., *Indian Ocean* - - - 112 Dc
Juan Fernandez Is., *Chile* 141 Af
Juan Godoy, *Chile* - 146 Ad
Juaniye, *Iraq* - - 78 Dc
Juan-les-Pins, *France* - 33 Cb
Juan Stuven, I., *Chile* - 148 Ad
Juárez, *Argentina* - - 148 Eb
Juarez, *Mexico* - - 139 Gd
Juba, *A.-E. Sudan* - 108 Bd
Juba, R., *It. Somaliland* 108 Gf
Jubâl I., *Egypt* - - 107 Je
Juban, *Albania* - - 70 Aa
Jubba, *Arabia* - - 78 Dd
Jubbulpore, *Central Provs.* 86 Dd
Jubilee L., *Newfoundland* 120 Hb
Jucar R., *Spain* - - 41 Fa
Juchipila & R., *Mexico* - 138 Dc
Juchitan, *Mexico* - - 139 Fd
Judenburg, *Austria* - 59 Jd
Judique, *Nova Scotia* - 120 Ed
Judith, *Montana* - - 136 Jb
Judtschen - - - 56 Fb
Jugoslavia, *S.-E. Europe* 61 Fc
Jui-chow, *China* - - 94 Dd
Juillac, *France* - - 34 Db
Juiz de Fora, *Brazil* - 147 Gc
Juja, *Kenya* - - - 110 Ed
Jujuy & prov., *Argentina* 146 Bc
Juli, *Peru* - - - 145 De
Juliaca, *Peru* - - 145 Ce
Juliana, Mt., *New Guinea* 156 Cb
Julianehaab, *Greenland* - 9 Ee
Jülich, *Prussia* - - 54 Be
Julio de Castilhos, *Brazil* 147 Ed
Jullundur, *Punjab* - - 83 Fc
Jumbo, *Ital. Somaliland* 108 Gf
Jumeaux, *France* - - 35 Fb
Jumentos Is., *Bahamas* - 140 Bb
Jumilla, *Spain* - - 41 Eb
Jumin, *Persia* - - 79 Gc
Jumna R., *United Provs.* 86 Dc
Jumsele, *Sweden* - - 48 Be
Junagarh, *Eastern States* 91 Fb
Junagarh, *Western India* 85 Cd
Junction, *Arkansas* - 130 Bd
Junction, *Queensland* - 153 Bc
Junction, *Utah* - - 135 Gb
Junction City, *Kansas* - 133 Da
Junction City, *Oregon* - 136 Bc
Jundah, *Queensland* - 153 Bd
Jundiahy, *Brazil* - - 147 Fc
Juneau, *Alaska* - - 125 Ng
Junee, *New S. Wales* - 155 Fc
Jungar, *China* - - 94 Da
Jungfrau, mt., *Switzerland* 42 Ec
Jungshahi, *Sind* - - 85 Ab
Jungtseh, *China* - - 94 Db
Junin, *Buenos Aires, Argentina* - - - 148 Da
Junin, *Neuquen, Argentina* 148 Bb
Junin, *Chile* - - - 146 Ab
Junin and L., *Peru* - 145 Bd
Junin, dep., *Peru* - - 145 Bd
Ju-ning, *China* - - 94 Dc
Juniper, *New Brunswick* 120 Bc
Juniper Mts., *Arizona* - 135 Gd
Junkerath, *Prussia* - 58 Aa
Junnar, *Bombay* - - 90 Ab
Junta, La, *Colorado* - 135 Mc
Junyo, *Korea* - - 97 Bc
Jupar Mts., *China* - - 94 Bb
Jupia, *Brazil* - - 147 Ec
Jupiter, *Florida* - - 131 Nh
Juquia, *Brazil* - - 147 Fc
Jura, dep., *France* - 31 He
Jura I. and Sd., *Scotland* 22 Ce
Jura, Mts. du, *France-Switz.* 42 Db
Jurbarkas, *Lithuania* - 49 Bd
Jurua, R., *Brazil* - - 145 Cc
Juruena and R., *Brazil* - 142 Ce
Juruty, *Brazil* - - 142 Cc
Jussy, *Switzerland* - 42 Bd
Justlahuaco, *Mexico* - 139 Ed
Justo Daract, *Argentina* 146 Be
Jutahy and R., *Brazil* - 145 Db
Jüterbog, *Prussia* - - 55 Jd
Juticalpa, *Honduras* - 140 Fe
Juwain, *Afghanistan* - 79 Hc
Jylland (Jutland), *Denmark* 45 Bb
Jyväskylä, *Finland* - 48 Fe
K2, Mt., *Kashmir* - - 84 Dc
Kaap Plat., *Cape Prov.* - 114 Ed
Kaapmuiden, *Transvaal* 115 Jb
Kaarepere, *Estonia* - 49 Db
Kaavi, *Finland* - - 48 He
Kaba, *Hungary* - - 67 Gb
Kabadak R., *Bengal* - 88 Bc
Kabadian, *Tadzhik* - 84 Bc
Kabaena, I., *Nether. Indies* 99 Fe
Kabakovsk, *U.S.S.R.* - 74 Kd
Kabala, *Sierra Leone* - 104 Be
Kabale, *Uganda* - - 110 Bd
Kabalo, *Belgian Congo* - 109 Ec
Kabambare, *Belg. Congo* 109 Eb
Kabardino Balkarsk, *U.S.S.R.* - - 75 Gg
Kabarnet, *Kenya* - - 110 Dc
Kabatogama L., *Minnesota* 132 Ca
Kabba, *Nigeria* - - 105 Cd
Kabinda, *Angola* - - 109 Bc
Kabinda, *Belg. Congo* - 109 Dc
Kabkabieh, *A.-E. Sudan* 105 Fc
Kaboeroeang, I., *Nether. Indies* - - - 99 Gc
Kaboko, *Angola* - - 109 Cc
Kabonga, *Belgian Congo* 109 Ec
Kabongo, *Belgian Congo* 109 Cc
Kabote, *Belgian Congo* - 109 Db
Kabul, *Palestine* - - 80 Cb
Kabul & R., *Afghanistan* 82 Ca
Kabula, *Uganda* - - 110 Bd
Kabwera, *Uganda* - - 110 Bd
Kabylie, Gde. & Petite, *Algeria* - - - 103 Ga
Kač, *Voyvodina* - - 66 Fd
Kačanik, *Serbia* - - 68 Gd
Kachalinsk. *U.S.S.R.* - 75 Gf
Kachek, *China* - - 95 Cf
Kacheliba, *Kenya* - - 110 Dc
Kachia, *Nigeria* - - 105 Cc
Kachung, *Uganda* - - 110 Cc
Kacongo, *Angola* - - 109 Bc
Kadan hatala ahn, *Manchur.* 96 Eb
Kadaura, *Central India* - 86 Cb
Kade, *Fr. W. Africa* - 104 Bd
Kadi, *Baroda* - - 85 Dc

Karatagh, *Tadzhik*	- 84	Bc
Karatala, Mt., *Comoro Is.*	112	Db
Karativo I., *Ceylon*	- 89	Cc
Karatiya, *Palestine*	- 80	Bd
Karatsu, *Japan*	- 97	Cd
Karauli, *Rajputana*	- 83	Dd
Karaurgan, *Turkey*	- 78	Da
Karawa, *Belgian Congo*	109	Ca
Karbala, *Iraq*	- 78	Dc
Karby, *Denmark*	- 45	Bb
Karcag, *Hungary*	- 67	Fb
Kardhamili, *Greece*	- 71	Dg
Kardhítsa, *Greece*	- 70	Cd
Kareima, *A.-E. Sudan*	108	Bb
Karelia, *U.S.S.R.*	- 74	Ec
Karema, *Tanganyika Terr.*	111	Bg
Karenko, *Taiwan*	- 97	Hf
Karenni, states, *Burma*	92	Cc
Karesuando, *Sweden*	- 48	Db
Karganrud, *Persia*	- 79	Eb
Karghalik, *Sinkiang*	- 84	Dc
Kargil, *Kashmir*	- 83	Ga
Kargopol, *U.S.S.R.*	- 74	Fc
Karhal, *United Provs.*	83	He
Kariá, *Greece*	- 71	De
Kariaí, *Greece*	- 71	Df
Karikal (French), *Madras*	89	Cb
Karimata Arch., *Nether.*		
Indies	- 98	Cd
Karimata I. and Str.,		
Netherlands Indies	- 98	Cd
Karimganj, *Assam*	- 88	Db
Karimi, *Belgian Congo*	109	Ea
Karimnagar, *Hyderabad*	90	Cc
Karimon Java Is., *Nether.*		
Indies	- 98	Ce
Karind, *Persia*	- 79	Ec
Káristos, *Greece*	- 71	Fe
Karítaina, *Greece*	- 71	Df
Kariyangwe, *S. Rhodesia*	113	Bb
Kariz, *Persia*	- 79	Hc
Karjat, *Bombay*	- 90	Ab
Karkar I., *New Guinea*	156	Db
Karkar Mts., *Br. Soma-*		
liland	- 108	Ec
Karkheh, R., *Persia*	79	Ec
Karkinitski G., *Ukraine*	75	Ef
Karkkila, *Finland*	- 48	Ef
Karkoj, *A.-E. Sudan*	108	Bc
Karlá (Voiviís), L., *Greece*	70	Dd
Karleby, *Denmark*	- 45	Fd
Karl Gustav, *Sweden*	- 48	Ec
Karlo, *California*	- 134	Ca
Karlobag, *Croatia*	- 63	Kc
Karlovac, *Croatia*	- 63	Kb
Karlovice, *Moravia*	- 57	Cd
Karlovo, *Bulgaria*	- 69	Fd
Karlovy Vary (Carlsbad),		
Bohemia	- 60	Bc
Karlsborg, *Sweden*	- 50	Dd
Karlshamn, *Sweden*	- 51	Df
Karlskoga, *Sweden*	- 50	Dc
Karlskrona, *Sweden*	- 51	Ef
Karlsruhe, *Baden*	- 58	Cb
Karlstad, *Sweden*	- 50	Cc
Karluk, *Alaska*	- 125	Hh
Karmala, *Bombay*	- 90	Bb
Karmöÿ, *Norway*	- 47	Ae
Karmpur, *Punjab*	- 82	Ed
Karnak, *Egypt*	- 107	Jf
Karnal, *Punjab*	- 83	Gd
Kar Nicobar, *Nicobar Is.*	91	Jf
Karnobat, *Bulgaria*	- 69	Gd
Karokpi, *Burma*	- 92	Ce
Karona Fall, *Br. Guiana*	144	Ec
Karond (Kalahandi),		
Eastern States	- 91	Fb
Karong, *Assam*	- 88	Eb
Karonga, *Nyasaland*	- 112	Bb
Karong Vale, *Victoria*	155	Bd
Karonje Mt., *Belg. Congo*	110	Ae
Karoonda, *S. Australia*	154	Bd
Karor, *Punjab*	- 82	Dc
Karora, *Eritrea*	- 108	Cb
Karos Hills, *Kenya*	- 110	Ec
Karousádhes, *Corfu I.*	70	Ad
Karow, *Mecklenburg*	- 55	Hb
Karpenísion, *Greece*	- 71	Ce
Karperón, *Greece*	- 70	Cd
Karpogory, *U.S.S.R.*	- 74	Gc
Karras Mts., Gt., *S.-W.*		
Africa	- 114	Cc
Karrebæk, *Denmark*	- 45	Ec
Karree Bergen, *Cape Prov.*	114	De
Karridale, *W. Australia*	152	Ae
Karrin, *Br. Somaliland*	108	Ec
Karroo, Gt. and Lit.,		
Cape Prov.	- 114	Df
Kars, *Turkey*	- 78	Da
Karsakpai, *Kazak*	- 76	Ge
Karsava, *Latvia*	- 49	Dc
Karskaya, *U.S.S.R.*	- 74	Lb

Kårsta, *Sweden*	- 50	Hc
Karsun, *U.S.S.R.*	- 75	He
Kartal, *Turkey*	- 72	Gb
Kartarpur, *Punjab*	- 83	Fc
Kartse, *Kashmir*	- 83	Ga
Kartuzy, *Poland*	- 60	Da
Karuizawa, *Japan*	- 100	Gc
Karuma, *Tangan. Terr.*	110	Ce
Karumba (Kimberley),		
Queensland	- 153	Bc
Karumwa, *Tangan. Terr.*	110	Ce
Karun, R., *Persia*	- 79	Ec
Karungu & B., *Kenya*	110	Dd
Karup, *Denmark*	- 45	Cb
Karur, *Madras*	- 89	Bb
Karwar, *Bombay*	- 90	Bd
Karwendel Geb., *Austria*	58	Fd
Karwi, *United Provs.*	- 86	Dc
Karwina, *Moravia*	- 57	Dd
Kasai, R., *Belg. Congo*	109	Cb
Kasakalabwe, *Tangan.*		
Terr.	- 111	Bg
Kasama, *Japan*	- 100	Hc
Kasama, *N. Rhodesia*	112	Bb
Kasanda, *Tangan. Terr.*	110	Be
Kasanga, *Tangan. Terr.*	111	Bh
Kasaoka, *Japan*	- 100	Dd
Kasaragod, *Madras*	- 90	Be
Kasauli, *Punjab*	- 83	Gc
Kasba L., *N.-W. Terr.*	124	Jb
Kasba Tadla, *Morocco*	102	Ac
Kasempa, *N. Rhodesia*	112	Ab
Kasenga, *N. Rhodesia*	112	Ac
Kasero, *Tanganyika Terr.*	111	Cf
Kasganj, *United Provs.*	83	He
Kash, *Sinkiang*	- 84	Eb
Kashan, *Persia*	- 79	Ec
Kashgar & R., *Sinkiang*	84	Dc
Kashima, *Japan*	- 100	Hc
Kashipur, *Eastern States*	91	Fb
Kashipur, *United Provs.*	83	Hd
Kashira, *U.S.S.R.*	- 75	Ce
Kashiwazaki, *Japan*	- 97	Dc
Kashkina, *U.S.S.R.*	- 48	Kf
Kashmir & Jammu, *India*	81	Dd
Kashpir, *U.S.S.R.*	- 75	He
Kasilof, *Alaska*	- 125	Jf
Kasimbar, *Celébes*	- 99	Fd
Kasimov, *U.S.S.R.*	- 75	Gd
Kasiroeta, I., *Nether. Indies*	99	Gd
Kaskaskia R., *Illinois*	132	Ef
Kaskinen, *Finland*	- 48	Ec
Kasonge, *Angola*	- 109	Bd
Kasongo, *Belg. Congo*	109	Eb
Kasongo Niembo, *Belg.*		
Congo	- 109	Ec
Kassala, *A.-E. Sudan*	108	Cb
Kassan, *Alaska*	- 125	Oj
Kassándra, *Greece*	- 70	Ec
Kassándra (Toróni), G.		
of, *Greece*	- 70	Ed
Kassanga, *Angola*	- 109	Cc
Kassari, *Fr. W. Africa*	104	Cc
Kassel (Cassel), *Prussia*	54	Ed
Kasserine, *Tunisia*	- 103	Jb
Kassidhiáris, mt., *Greece*	70	Dd
Kassoee, *New Guinea*	- 156	Bc
Kastamonu, *Turkey*	- 78	Ba
Kastaniá, *Greece*	- 70	Cd
Kastaniá, *Greece*	- 71	Df
Kastanies, *Greece*	- 72	Da
Kastélli, *Crete*	- 71	Gj
Kastéllion, *Crete*	- 71	Jj
Kastel Lukšić, *Dalmatia*	68	Bc
Kastorf, *Prussia*	- 54	Fb
Kastoría & L., *Greece*	- 70	Cc
Kastós, I., *Greece*	- 71	Be
Kastron, *Greece*	- 72	Bc
Kastrop Rauxel, *Prussia*	54	Cd
Kastrosikiá, *Greece*	- 71	Bd
Kasukelo, *Tangan. Terr.*	111	Cg
Kasulu, *Tangan. Terr.*	- 111	Bf
Kasumi, *Japan*	- 100	Ed
Kasungu, *Nyasaland*	- 112	Bb
Kasur, *Punjab*	- 83	Fc
Kata, *Japan*	- 100	Ed
Kataghan, *Afghanistan*	- 84	Bc
Katagum, *Nigeria*	- 105	Dc
Katahdin, Mt., *Maine*	120	Ad
Katakami, *Japan*	- 100	Dd
Katákhloron, *Greece*	- 70	Fb
Katako Kombe, *Bel. Congo*	109	Db
Katákolon, *Greece*	- 71	Cf
Kata Kurgan, *Uzbek*	- 84	Bc
Katal, *Bengal*	- 88	Bb
Katalla, *Alaska*	- 125	Lf
Katamachi, *Japan*	- 100	Cc
Katandua, *Mozambique*	112	Bc
Katangi, *Central Provs.*	- 86	Ce
Katanning, *W. Australia*	152	Be
Katarnian Ghat, *United*		
Provs.	- 86	Da

Katawaz, *Afghanistan*	- 82	Cb
Katchall, *Nicobar Is.*	91	Jg
Katerere, *S. Rhodesia*	- 113	Ea
Katerini, *Greece*	- 70	Dc
Katha, *Burma*	- 88	Fb
Katharina Harb., *U.S.S.R.*	48	Lb
Katherina, Jeb., *Egypt*	107	Jd
Katherine, *N. Terr., Aust.*	150	Ea
Kathiawar, *Western India*	85	Cd
Kathu, *Cape Prov.*	- 114	Ec
Kathua, *Kashmir*	- 83	Fb
Kati, *Fr. W. Africa*	- 104	Cc
Katkop, *Cape Prov.*	- 114	De
Katkop Hills, *Cape Prov.*	114	Ce
Katmandu, *Nepal*	- 87	Fb
Kato Akhaΐa, *Greece*	- 71	Ce
Kato Alissós, *Greece*	- 71	Ce
Kato Figalía, *Greece*	- 71	Cf
Katokhi, *Greece*	- 71	Ce
Katol, *Central Provs.*	- 86	Ce
Katoomba, *New S. Wales*	155	Fc
Káto Stavros, *Greece*	- 70	Ec
Katouaka, *A.-E. Sudan*	- 105	Fd
Katowice, *Poland*	- 60	Ec
Katrine, L., *Scotland*	- 23	Dd
Katrineholm, *Sweden*	- 50	Ed
Katsina, *Nigeria*	- 105	Cc
Katsura, *Japan*	- 97	Ec
Kattegat, *Denmark-Sweden*	45	Eb
Kattinge, *Sweden*	- 50	Fd
Katumbi, *N. Rhodesia*	- 112	Bb
Katumbikanombo, *Tang-*		
anyika Terr.	- 111	Ej
Katunga, *Angola*	- 109	Cd
Katunga, *Nyasaland*	- 112	Bc
Katuni, *Dalmatia*	- 68	Bc
Katushi, *Angola*	- 109	Cd
Katwa, *Bengal*	- 88	Bc
Katwe, *Uganda*	- 110	Ad
Katwe, *N. Rhodesia*	- 112	Ba
Katzen Geb.	- 57	Cb
Katzhutte, *Thuringia*	- 58	Fa
Kauai, I., *Hawaiian Is.*	157	Ga
Kaufbeuren, *Bavaria*	- 58	Ed
Kaufering, *Bavaria*	- 58	Ec
Kaufman, *Texas*	- 133	Dd
Kaukauna, *Wisconsin*	- 132	Ec
Kaukkwe Hills, *Burma*	- 92	Ff
Kauklakla, *Bechuanaland*	113	Ac
Kaukluft Mts., *S.-W. Afr.*	114	Ab
Kauliranta, *Finland*	- 48	Ec
Kaunas (Kovno), *Lithuania*	49	Bd
Kauoo, *Hawaiian Is..*	- 157	Mg
Kaura, *Nigeria*	- 105	Cc
Kaura Namoda, *Nigeria*	105	Cc
Kautokeino, *Norway*	- 48	Eb
Kauttua, *Finland*	- 48	Ef
Kau-yu, *China*	- 94	Ec
Kavadarci, *Serbia*	- 70	Db
Kavajë, *Albania*	- 70	Bb
Kavak, *Turkey*	- 78	Ca
Kavakli, *Turkey*	- 72	Ea
Kavali, *Madras*	- 91	Ed
Kaválla & G. of, *Greece*	70	Fc
Kavamba, *Belgian Congo*	109	Ec
Kavieng, *New Ireland*	156	Eb
Kavirondo Gulf, *Kenya*	- 110	Dd
Kävlinge, *Sweden*	- 51	Bg
Kaw Agency, *Oklahoma*	133	Db
Kawagoe, *Japan*	- 100	Gd
Kawaguchi, *Japan*	- 100	Gd
Kawakawa, *New Zealand*	158	Ea
Kawambwa, *N. Rhodesia*	112	Aa
Kawanoe, *Japan*	- 100	Dd
Kawara, *Japan*	- 100	Ed
Kawardha, *Eastern States*	86	Dd
Kawar Oasis, *Fr. W. Afr.*	105	Db
Kawartha Ls., *Ontario*	- 121	Ab
Kawasaki, *Japan*	- 97	Dc
Kawatan, *Borneo*	- 99	Dd
Kawhia, *New Zealand*	- 158	Ec
Kawich Ra., *Nevada*	- 134	Ec
Kawio Is., *Nether. Indies*	99	Gc
Kaw Peunan, *Siam*	- 98	Bb
Kaw Samui, *Siam*	- 98	Bb
Kawton, *Burma*	- 92	Bb
Kaya, *Fr. W. Africa*	- 104	Dd
Kaya Lahan, *Kenya*	- 110	Fb
Kayalpatnam, *Madras*	- 89	Cc
Kayambi, *N. Rhodesia*	- 112	Ba
Kayeli, *Celébes*	- 99	Ed
Kayenzi, *Tangan. Terr.*	110	Ce
Kayes, *Fr. W. Africa*	- 104	Bd
Kayima, *Sierra Leone*	- 104	Be
Ka-ying, *China*	- 95	Ee
Ka Yoshida, *Japan*	- 100	Fd
Kayser Geb., *Suriname*	- 142	Cb
Kayseri (Kaisarie), *Turkey*	78	Cb
Kaysville, *Utah*	- 135	Ha
Kayumba, *Belgian Congo*	109	Ec
Kazabazua, *Quebec*	- 121	Bb
Kazak, *U.S.S.R.*	- 76	Ge

Kazakh, *Azerbaijan*	- 75	Gg
Kazan, *U.S.S.R.*	- 74	Hd
Kazan R., *N.-W. Terr.*	118	Jd
Kazanlik, *Bulgaria*	- 69	Fd
Kazatin, *Ukraine*	- 75	Df
Kazaure, *Nigeria*	- 105	Cc
Kazbek, mt., *U.S.S.R.*	- 75	Gg
Kazembe, *N. Rhodesia*	112	Aa
Kazerun, *Persia*	- 79	Fd
Kazhim, *U.S.S.R.*	- 74	Jc
Kazi Ahmad, *Sind*	- 85	Ba
Kazikazi, *Tangan. Terr.*	111	Df
Kaztalovka, *Kazak*	- 75	Hf
Kazungula, *N. Rhodesia*	112	Ac
Kazvin, *Persia*	- 79	Fb
Kéa I. & Str., *Greece*	- 71	Ff
Keady, *N. Ireland*	- 26	Dc
Keam, *Arizona*	- 135	Hc
Keams Canyon, *Arizona*	135	Hd
Kearney, *Nebraska*	- 126	Fb
Kearney, *Ontario*	- 121	Ab
Kearsarge, *California*	- 134	Dc
Keatchie, *Louisiana*	- 130	Bd
Keban Maden, *Turkey*	- 78	Cb
Ke-bao I., *Tong-king*	- 95	Ce
Kebili, *Tunisia*	- 103	Jc
Kebir, Jeb. el, *Palestine*	80	Cc
Kebnekaise, mt., *Sweden*	44	Df
Keboemen, *Java*	- 98	Ce
Kecel, *Hungary*	- 66	Ec
Kechi Kalat, *Baluchistan*	82	Cd
Kecskemét, *Hungary*	- 66	Ec
Kedah, *Malay States*	- 98	Bb
Kedainiai, *Lithuania*	- 49	Bd
Kedarnath and Pk.,		
United Provs.	- 83	Hc
Kedgeree, *Bengal*	- 88	Ad
Kedgwick and R., *New*		
Brunswick	- 120	Bc
Kediri, *Java*	- 98	De
Kedougou, *Fr. W. Africa*	104	Bd
Kedu, *Manchuria*	- 96	Bb
Keele Pk. & R., *N.-W.*		
Terr.	- 124	Db
Keeler, *California*	- 134	Ec
Keelung (Kürun), *Taiwan*	97	He
Keene, *New Hampshire*	- 128	Bd
Keeseville, *New York*	- 123	Mc
Keetmanshoop, *S.-W. Afr.*	114	Cc
Keewatin, *Ontario*	- 122	Aa
Keewatin, dist., *N.-W.T.*	119	Ld
Keewong, *New S. Wales*	154	Db
Kefallinia (Cephalonia)		
I., *Greece*	- 71	Be
Kéfannanoe, *Timor I., E.I.*	99	Fe
Kefermarkt, *Austria*	- 59	Jc
Keffi, *Nigeria*	- 105	Cd
Keflavik, *Iceland*	- 52	Bb
Kega Pt., *Annam*	- 95	Cg
Kegalla, *Ceylon*	- 89	Dd
Kegaska, *Quebec*	- 120	Ea
Kegworth, *England*	- 18	Cc
Kehl, *Baden*	- 58	Bc
Kehra, *Estonia*	- 49	Cb
Kehsi Mansam, *Burma*	- 92	Cb
Keighley, *England*	- 18	Cc
Keil Berg, *Bohemia*	- 59	Ga
Keila, *Estonia*	- 49	Cb
Keimoes, *Cape Prov.*	- 114	Dd
Keishu, *Korea*	- 97	Bc
Keitele, *Finland*	- 48	Fe
Keith, *Scotland*	- 23	Fa
Keith S., *Australia*	- 154	Cc
Keith B., *N.-W. Terr.*	124	Ea
Keithsburg, *Illinois*	- 132	De
Kekhros, *Greece*	- 72	Ca
Kekri, *Ajmer-Merwara*	- 85	Eb
Keku, *New Guinea*	- 156	Bc
Kelaa, El, *Morocco*	- 103	Oh
Kelang, I., *Nether. Indies*	99	Gd
Kelantan, *Malay States*	- 98	Bb
Kelcyre, *Albania*	- 70	Bc
Kelheim, *Bavaria*	- 59	Fc
Kelibia, *Tunisia*	- 103	Ka
Kelle, *Fr. W. Africa*	- 104	Ac
Kellerberrin, *W. Aust.*	- 152	Be
Kellerup, *Denmark*	- 45	Cb
Kellett, C., *N.-W. Terr.*	118	Db
Kellett Str., *N.-W. Terr.*	118	Fa
Kellinghusen, *Prussia*	- 54	Eb
Kellmünz, *Bavaria*	- 58	Ec
Kells, *Éire*	- 27	Cf
Kells (Ceanannus Mor),		
Éire	- 26	Dd
Kells, *N. Ireland*	- 26	Db
Kelly, *New Mexico*	- 135	Kd
Kelmarsh, *England*	- 15	Db
Kelme, *Lithuania*	- 49	Bd
Kelowna, *Br. Columbia*	- 124	Fe
Kelseyville, *California*	- 134	Bb
Kelso, *Scotland*	- 21	Db

Kelso, *Washington*	- 136	Bb
Kelton, *Arizona*	- 135	Jf
Kelton, *Utah*	- 135	Ga
Kelvedon, *England*	- 15	Ec
Kelvin, *Arizona*	- 135	He
Kelwara, *Rajputana*	- 85	Db
Kem and R., *U.S.S.R.*	- 74	Ec
Kema, *Celébes*	- 99	Gc
Ke Macina, *Fr. W. Africa*	104	Cd
Kemal Pasa, *Turkey*	- 78	Ab
Kemboma, *Fr. Eq. Africa*	109	Ba
Kemecse, *Hungary*	- 67	Ga
Kemer, *Turkey*	- 72	Db
Kemerovo, *U.S.S.R.*	- 76	Jd
Kemi and R., *Finland*	- 48	Fd
Kemijärvi, *Finland*	- 48	Gc
Kemmerer, *Wyoming*	- 135	Ha
Kemp, *Texas*	- 133	Dd
Kemp, L., *Texas*	- 133	Cd
Kempen, *Prussia*	- 54	Bd
Kemp Land, *Antarctica*	160	—
Kempsey, *England*	- 14	Bb
Kempsey, *New S. Wales*	155	Gb
Kempt L., *Quebec*	- 123	Lb
Kempten, *Bavaria*	- 58	Ed
Kempton Park, *Transvaal*	115	Hc
Kemptville, *Nova Scotia*	120	Cb
Kemptville, *Ontario*	- 121	Cb
Kemu, *Nigeria*	- 105	Bd
Kenadsa, *Algeria*	- 102	Cd
Kenai Mts., *Alaska*	- 125	Jg
Kenai Tunnel, *Alaska*	- 125	Jf
Kenali, *Serbia*	- 70	Cc
Kenansville, *N. Carolina*	131	Kc
Kenâyis, G. of, *Egypt*	- 107	Gc
Kendal, *England*	- 18	Bb
Kendal, *Transvaal*	- 115	Hc
Kendari, *Celébes*	- 99	Fd
Kendawangan, *Borneo*	- 98	Dd
Kenderes, *Hungary*	- 67	Fb
Kendrapara, *Orissa*	- 87	Ge
Kendrew, *Cape Prov.*	- 115	Ff
Kendrick, *Idaho*	- 136	Eb
Kendu, *Kenya*	- 110	Dd
Kenema, *Sierra Leone*	- 104	Be
Keng Hkam, *Burma*	- 92	Db
Keng-Hung, *China*	- 95	Be
Keng-lön, *Burma*	- 92	Da
Kenhardt, *Cape Prov.*	- 114	Dd
Kenilworth, *England*	- 14	Cb
Kenmare and R., *Eire*	- 25	Bf
Kenna, *New Mexico*	- 135	Me
Kennebec R., *Maine*	- 128	Da
Kennebunk, *Maine*	- 128	Cb
Kennecott, *Alaska*	- 125	Lf
Kennedy, *Nevada*	- 134	Ea
Kennedy, *New Mexico*	- 135	Ld
Kennedy, *S. Rhodesia*	- 113	Bb
Kenner, *Louisiana*	- 130	Ce
Kennet R., *England*	- 14	Cd
Kennett, *Missouri*	- 130	Cb
Keno City, *Yukon*	- 124	Bb
Kenogami & L., *Quebec*	123	Na
Kenora, *Ontario*	- 122	Aa
Kenosha, *Wisconsin*	- 132	Ed
Kensington, *Pr. Edward I.*	120	Dc
Kent, *New Brunswick*	- 120	Cc
Kent, *Ohio*	- 129	Db
Kent, *Washington*	- 136	Bb
Kent, co., *England*	- 15	Ed
Kent Pen., *N.-W. Terr.*	118	Hc
Kentani, *Cape Prov.*	- 115	Hf
Ken-tao, *Siam*	- 95	Bf
Kentei-alin, *Manchuria*	- 96	Ec
Kentland, *Indiana*	- 129	Ab
Kenton, *Ohio*	- 129	Cb
Kentucky, state, *U.S.A.*	127	Hc
Kentucky R., *Kentucky*	131	Fa
Kentville, *Nova Scotia*	- 120	Cd
Kentwood, *Louisiana*	- 130	Ce
Kenwood, *New York*	- 128	Ab
Kenya, col., *E. Africa*	101	Dd
Kenya, Mt., *Kenya*	- 110	Ed
Kenzin, *New Mexico*	- 135	Kc
Keokuk, *Iowa*	- 132	De
Keonjhar (Nijgarh),		
Eastern States	- 87	Fe
Kéos (Tziá, Kéa), I.,		
Greece	- 71	Ff
Kepler Mts., *New Zealand*	159	Af
Kępno, *Poland*	- 60	Ec
Keppel, *Falkland Is.*	- 148	De
Keppel Is. & B., *Queens'ld*	153	Dd
Kepsut, *Turkey*	- 72	Fc
Kerak, *U.S.S.R.*	- 96	Ca
Keramídhi, *Greece*	- 70	Dd
Kerang, *Victoria*	- 154	Cd
Kerassón, *Greece*	- 71	Cd
Keratea, *Greece*	- 71	Ef
Kerch, *Crimea*	- 75	Ff
Kerchenski, *Crimea*	- 75	Ff
Kerdous, *Morocco*	- 103	Nk

King Haakon VII. Plat., *Antarctica* - - - 160 —
Kingham, *England* - 14 Cc
Kinghorn, *Ontario* - 122 Ea
Kinghorn, *Scotland* - 23 Ed
Kingisepp, *U.S.S.R.* - 74 Dd
King Leopold Ra., *W. Australia* - - 152 Cb
King Leopold & Queen Astrid Land, *Antarctica* 160 —
Kingman, *Arizona* - 134 Gd
Kingman, *Kansas* - - 133 Cb
King-men, *China* - - 94 Dc
King Oscar Mt., *Tibet* - 84 Fc
King Oscar II. Land, *Antarctica* - - - 160 —
Kings Pk., *Utah* - - 135 Ha
Kingsand, *England* - 17 Bc
Kingsbridge, *England* - 17 Cc
Kingsbury, *England* - 14 Ca
Kingsclere, *England* - 14 Cd
Kingscote, *England* - 14 Bc
Kingscote, *S. Australia* - 154 Ad
Kingscourt, *Eire* - - 26 Dd
Kingsey, *Quebec* - - 121 Db
Kingsingchen, *Manchuria* 96 Cb
Kings Langley, *England* 15 Dc
Kingsley, *Natal* - - 115 Jc
Kings Lynn, *England* - 19 Ee
Kingsport, *Nova Scotia* - 120 Cd
Kingsport, *Tennessee* - 131 Gb
Kingston, *England* - 15 Dd
Kingston, *Jamaica* - 140 Bc
Kingston, *New Mexico* - 135 Ke
Kingston, *New York* - 123 Le
Kingston, *New Zealand* 159 Bf
Kingston, *Ohio* - - 129 Cc
Kingston, *Ontario* - - 121 Bb
Kingston, *S. Australia* - 154 Bd
Kingston Ra., *California* 134 Ec
Kingston Lisle, *England* 14 Cc
Kingstown, *Windward Is.* 140 Kh
Kingstown (Dun Laoghaire), *Eire* - - 27 De
Kingstree, *S. Carolina* - 131 Jd
Kingswear, *England* - 17 Cc
Kingswinford, *England* - 14 Bb
King-teh-chen, *China* - 94 Ed
Kington, *England* - 14 Ab
King-tung, *China* - - 95 Be
Kingushi, *Belgian Congo* 109 Cc
Kingussie, *Scotland* - 23 Db
Kingwa, *Quebec* - - 119 Od
King William I., *New Guinea* - - - 156 Bb
King William I., *N.-W. Terr.* - - - - 118 Kc
King William I. Land, *Greenland* - - - 9 Gb
King William's Town, *Cape Prov.* - - - 115 Gf
Kingwilliamstown, *Eire* 25 Be
Kingwood, *W. Virginia* 129 Ec
King-yang, *China* - - 94 Cb
King-yüan, *China* - - 95 Ce
Kinhi, *Central Provs.* - 86 De
Kin-hwa, *China* - - 94 Ed
Kin-kiang, *China* - - 94 Ed
Kinlochewe, *Scotland* - 22 Ca
Kinlochleven, *Scotland* - 22 Dc
Kinlochmoidart, *Scotland* 22 Cc
Kinloch Rannoch, *Scot.* 23 Dc
Kinna, *Sweden* - - 51 Be
Kinne B., *Sweden* - - 50 Cd
Kinnegad, *Eire* - - 27 Ce
Kinnereth, *Palestine* - 80 Db
Kinnilty, *Eire* - - 27 Ce
Kinomoto, *Japan* - - 100 Fd
Kinomoto, *Japan* - - 100 Fe
Kinross and co., *Scotland* 23 Ed
Kinsale and Harb., *Eire* 25 Cf
Kinsale, Old Hd. of, *Eire* 25 Cf
Kin-sha-kiang, *China* - 94 Bd
Kinsley, *Kansas* - - 133 Cb
Kinston, *N. Carolina* - 131 Kc
Kintampo, *Gold Coast* - 104 De
Kintinku, *Tangan. Terr.* 111 Df
Kintore, *Scotland* - - 23 Fb
Kintyre & Mull of, *Scot.* 22 Cf
Kinvarra, *Eire* - - 27 Be
Kinya, *Kenya* - - 110 Ec
Kinyangiri, *Tangan. Terr.* 111 Df
Kiomboi, *Tangan. Terr.* 111 Df
Kionga, *Mozambique* - 112 Db
Kiormo, *Kenya* - - 110 Fd
Kiowa, *Kansas* - - 133 Cb
Kipamba, *Tangan. Terr.* 111 Dg
Kiparissi, *Greece* - - 71 Eg
Kiparíssia & Gulf, *Greece* 71 Cf
Kipawa & L., *Quebec* - 121 Aa
Kipengere, *Tangan. Terr.* 111 Dh
Kipkabus, *Kenya* - - 110 Dc
Kipouryió, *Greece* - - 70 Cd
Kippford, *Scotland* - 21 Cd
Kipsing, *Kenya* - - 110 Ec
Kipumbwe, *Tangan. Terr.* 111 Ff
Kirando, *Tangan. Terr.* 111 Bg
Kirá Panayia (Pélagos), I., *Greece* - - - 70 Ed
Kirati, *Tangan. Terr.* - 111 Fg
Kirby, *England* - - 15 Fc
Kirby Moorside, *England* 19 Db
Kircasalih, *Turkey* - 72 Da
Kirchberg, *Prussia* - 58 Bb
Kirchhain, *Prussia* - 54 De
Kirchheim, *Württemberg* 58 Dc
Kirchschlag, *Austria* - 66 Bb
Kirchweyne, *Prussia* - 54 Dc
Kircubbin, *N. Ireland* - 26 Ec
Kirengwe, *Tangan. Terr.* 111 Eg
Kirgiz, rep., *U.S.S.R.* - 76 He
Kirgiz Steppe, *Kazak* - 76 Ge
Kiri, *Belgian Congo* - 109 Cb
Kirillov, *U.S.S.R.* - 74 Fc
Kirimai Plain, *Kenya* - 110 Fc
Kirimira's Mbaya, *Tanganyika Terr.* - 111 Ej
Kirin, *Ethiopia* - - 108 Bc
Kirin & prov., *Manchuria* 96 Dc
Kirishi, *U.S.S.R.* - 48 Kg
Kirishima, *Japan* - - 97 Cd
Kiriwina I., *New Guinea* 156 Ec
Kirkağaç, *Turkey* - - 72 Ec
Kirkbride, *England* - 21 Cd
Kirkby Lonsdale, *England* 18 Bb
Kirkby Stephen, *England* 18 Bb
Kirkcaldy, *Scotland* - 23 Ed
Kirkcudbright & co., *Scot.* 21 Bd
Kirkee, *Bombay* - - 90 Ab
Kirkenes, *Norway* - - 44 Ge
Kirkham, *England* - 18 Bc
Kirkham, *O.F.S.* - - 115 Fe
Kirkintilloch, *Scotland* - 23 De
Kirklareli, *Turkey* - - 72 Ea
Kirkley, *England* - - 15 Fb
Kirkmichael, *I. of Man* - 19 Gf
Kirkoswald, *England* - 21 Dd
Kirkpatrick, *Scotland* - 21 Cc
Kirksville, *Missouri* - 132 Ce
Kirkuk, *Iraq* - - 78 Db
Kirkwall, *Orkney Is.* - 24 Fd
Kirkwood, *Cape Prov.* - 115 Ff
Kirman, *Persia* - - 79 Gc
Kirn, *Prussia* - - 58 Bb
Kirn, *Scotland* - - 22 De
Kirong Dzong, *Nepal* - 87 Fa
Kirov, *U.S.S.R.* - - 74 Hd
Kirov, *Smolensk, U.S.S.R.* 75 Ee
Kirovabad, *Azerbaijan* - 75 Hg
Kirovakan, *Armenia* - 75 Gg
Kirovograd, *Ukraine* - 75 Ef
Kirovsk, *U.S.S.R.* - 74 Eb
Kirriemuir, *Scotland* - 23 Ec
Kirsanov, *U.S.S.R.* - 75 Ge
Kirşehir, *Turkey* - - 78 Bb
Kirtach, *Fr. W. Africa* - 105 Bc
Kirte, *Turkey* - - 72 Db
Kirthar Ra., *Sind* - - 85 Ab
Kirton, *Holland Lincs, England* - - - 19 De
Kirton, *Lindsey Lincs, England* - - - 19 Dd
Kiruna, *Sweden* - - 44 Ef
Kirwin, *Kansas* - - 133 Ca
Kisa, *Sweden* - - 51 Ee
Kisaki Fort, *Tangan. Terr.* 111 Eg
Kisambia, *Tangan. Terr.* 111 Cg
Kisamos, G. of, *Crete* - 71 Gj
Kisango, *Tangan. Terr.* 111 Fh
Kisar I., *Nether. Indies* - 99 Ge
Kisbér, *Hungary* - - 66 Db
Kisen, *Korea* - - 97 Bb
Kisengwa, *Belg. Congo* - 109 Ec
Kisenyi, *Belg. Congo* - 109 Eb
Kishanganj, *Bihar* - 87 Hb
Kishangarh, *Alwar, Rajputana* - - - 83 Ge
Kishangarh, *Jaipur, Rajputana* - - - 83 Fe
Kishangarh, *Jaisalmar, Rajputana* - - 82 De
Kishi, *Nigeria* - - 105 Bd
Kishinev (Chisinau) *Moldavia* 69 Hb
Kishiwada, *Japan* - - 100 Ed
Kishlak, *Persia* - - 79 Fb
Kishon, R., *Palestine* - 80 Cb
Kishorganj, *Bengal* - 88 Cb
Kishtwar, *Kashmir* - 83 Fb
Ki-shui, *China* - - 94 Ed
Kisigao Mt., *Kenya* - 111 Fe
Kisii, *Kenya* - - 110 Dd
Kisiju, *Tanganyika Terr.* 111 Fg
Kisilwa, *Tang. Terr.* - 111 Dg
Kiska I., *Aleutian Is.* - 125 Tl
Kiskisink, *Quebec* - - 123 Mb
Kiskomarom, *Hungary* - 66 Cc
Kiskörös, *Hungary* - 66 Ec
Kiskundorozsma, *Hungary* 66 Ec
Kiskunfélegyháza, *Hung.* 66 Ec
Kiskunhalas, *Hungary* - 66 Ec
Kiskunmajsa, *Hungary* - 66 Ec
Kislovodsk, *U.S.S.R.* - 75 Gg
Kismayu, *It. Somaliland* 108 Gg
Kispest, *Hungary* - - 66 Eb
Kissangiro, *Tang. Terr.* 111 Ee
Kíssavos (Ossa), mt., *Greece* 70 Dd
Kisshu, *Korea* - - 97 Bb
Kissidougou, *Fr. W. Afr.* 104 Ce
Kissimmee, *Florida* - 131 Ng
Kissimmee, L. and R., *Florida* - - - 131 Nh
Kissozzi, *Uganda* - - 110 Bc
Kistelek, *Hungary* - 66 Ec
Kistna, *Madras* - - 91 Ec
Kistna, Mouths of the, *Madras* - - - 91 Ed
Kistrand, *Norway* - - 48 Fa
Kisújszallás, *Hungary* - 67 Fb
Kisumu, *Kenya* - - 110 Dd
Kisuwani, *Tang. Terr.* - 111 Ff
Kisvarda, *Hungary* - 67 Ha
Kiswere, *Tang. Terr.* - 111 Fh
Kita, *Fr. W. Africa* - 104 Cd
Kitalanga, *Angola* - - 109 Cc
Kitale, *Kenya* - - 110 Dc
Kitate, *Tanganyika Terr.* 111 Dg
Kitchener, *Ontario* - 123 Hd
Kitchener, *W. Australia* 152 Ce
Kitega, *Belg. Congo* - 109 Fb
Kitere, *Tanganyika Terr.* 111 Fj
Kitgum, *Uganda* - - 110 Cb
Kithairón, *Greece* - - 71 Ee
Kithira, *Greece* - - 71 Dg
Kíthira (Cerigo), I., *Greece* 71 Eg
Kithirai Str., *Greece* - 71 Eh
Kíthnos (Thermia), I., *Greece* - - - 71 Ff
Kitigan, *Ontario* - - 122 Ga
Kitros, *Greece* - - 70 Dc
Kitsuki, *Japan* - - 100 Bb
Kítta, *Greece* - - - 71 Dg
Kittanning, *Pennsylvania* 129 Eb
Kittatinny Mts., *New Jersey* 128 Ac
Kitteny, *Maine* - - 128 Cb
Kittha-reng I.' *Burma* - 98 Aa
Kittigazuit, *N.-W. Terr.* 118 Cc
Kittilä, *Finland* - - 48 Fc
Kitui, *Kenya* - - 110 Fd
Kitunda, *Tang. Terr.* - 111 Fh
Kitunda, *Tang. Terr.* - 111 Cg
Kitzbühel, *Austria* - 59 Gd
Kitzingen, *Bavaria* - 58 Eb
Kiu, *Kenya* - - - 110 Ed
Kiu Hills, *Kenya* - - 110 Ed
Kiu-kiang, *China* - - 94 Ed
Kiu-kung-shan, *China* - 94 Dd
Kiung-chow, *China* - 95 Df
Kiuyaping, *China* - - 94 Bd
Kivi Järvi, *Finland* - 48 Fe
Kivindi, *Tang. Terr.* - 111 Dj
Kivu, L., *Belg. Congo* - 109 Eb
Kiwai I., *New Guinea* - 156 Cc
Kiwalik, *Alaska* - - 125 Gc
Kiwamba, *Tang. Terr.* - 111 Dh
Kiwambi, *Tang. Terr.* - 111 Fh
Kiwanda, *Tang. Terr.* - 111 Dj
Kizel, *U.S.S.R.* - - 74 Kd
Kiziladalar (Princes Is.), *Turkey* - - - 72 Fb
Kizil Arvat, *Turkmen* - 77 Hb
Kizil Irmak, *Turkey* - 78 Ba
Kizil Khoto, *Tannu-Tuva* 93 Ba
Kizil Orda, *Kazak* - 76 Ge
Kizil Rabat, *Tadzhik* - 84 Cc
Kizilski, *U.S.S.R.* - 75 Ke
Kizlyar, *U.S.S.R.* - 75 Hg
Kizuki, *Japan* - - 97 Cc
Kizyl Jilga, *Kashmir* - 84 Dc
Kjoli Fjeld, *Norway* - 46 Hb
Klaarstroom, *Cape Prov.* 114 Ef
Kladanj, *Bosnia* - - 68 Db
Kladno, *Bohemia* - - 59 Ja
Kladovo, *Serbia* - - 69 Ec
Klagenfurt, *Austria* - 59 Je
Klaipeda (Memel) *Lithuania* 49 Ad
Klamath, *California* - 134 Aa
Klamath Pk., *Oregon* - 136 Bd
Klamath R., *California* - 134 Ba
Klamath Falls, *Oregon* - 136 Cd
Klamathon, *California* - 134 Ba
Klang, *Malay States* - 98 Bc
Klarälven, *Sweden* - 50 Cb
Klarija, *Voyvodina* - 67 Fd
Klatovy, *Bohemia* - - 60 Bd
Klaus, *Austria* - - 59 Jd
Klaushagen, *Prussia* - 55 Lb
Klaver, *Cape Prov.* - 114 Ce
Klavreström, *Sweden* - 51 Ee
Kleifar, *Iceland* - - 52 Cb
Kleinbegin, *Cape Prov.* - 114 Dd
Kleines Haff, *Prussia* - 55 Kb
Kleinkaras, *S.-W. Africa* 114 Cc
Kleio, *Lesbos I., Greece* - 72 Dc
Klembotsárion, *Greece* - 71 Ee
Klenak, *Slavonia* - - 66 Ee
Klepp, *Norway* - - 47 Bf
Klerksdorp, *Transvaal* - 115 Gc
Kletsk, *U.S.S.R.* - - 75 Gf
Kleve, *Prussia* - - 54 Bd
Klidhí, *Greece* - - 70 Eb
Klikitat R., *Washington* 136 Cc
Klim, *Denmark* - - 45 Ca
Klimovichi, *White Russia* 75 Ee
Klin, *U.S.S.R.* - - 74 Fd
Klina, *Montenegro* - - 68 Fd
Klingnau, *Switzerland* - 42 Fa
Klintehamn, *Sweden* - 51 Ge
Klipdam, *S.-W. Africa* - 114 Cc
Klippan, *Sweden* - - 51 Cf
Klipplaat, *Cape Prov.* - 115 Ff
Kliprivier, *Transvaal* - 115 Gc
Kliprug Kop, *Cape Prov.* 114 Ce
Klipsdale, *Cape Prov.* - 114 Cg
Klis, *Dalmatia* - - 68 Bc
Klisoúra, *Greece* - - 70 Cc
Klitmöller, *Denmark* - 45 Ba
Kljake, *Dalmatia* - - 68 Bc
Ključ, *Bosnia* - - 68 Bb
Klobuk, *Hercegovina* - 68 Cc
Kłodawa, *Poland* - - 57 Da
Kloempang B., *Borneo* - 99 Ed
Klondike, *California* - 134 Fd
Klondike, *Yukon* - - 118 Bd
Klondike R., *Yukon* - 124 Bb
Klonga, Mt., *Angola* - 109 Cd
Klos, *Albania* - - 70 Bb
Kloştar, *Croatia* - - 66 Cd
Klosterneuburg, *Austria* 59 Lc
Klosters, *Switzerland* - 43 Jc
Klost Zinna, *Prussia* - 55 Hc
Kloten, *Sweden* - - 50 Ec
Klotijevac, *Bosnia* - 68 Eb
Klötze, *Prussia* - - 54 Gc
Klouto, *Fr. W. Africa* - 105 Bd
Kluane and L., *Yukon* - 124 Bb
Knaby, *Sweden* - - 50 Hb
Knared, *Sweden* - - 51 Cf
Knaresborough, *England* 18 Cb
Kneïs I., *Tunisia* - - 103 Kb
Knighton, *Wales* - - 20 Cc
Knights Ferry, *California* 134 Cc
Knights Town, *Eire* - 25 Af
Knin, *Dalmatia* - - 68 Bb
Knittelfeld, *Austria* - 59 Jd
Knivsta, *Sweden* - - 50 Gc
Knjazevac, *Serbia* - - 69 Ed
Knob, C., *W. Australia* 152 Be
Knobel, *Arkansas* - - 130 Cb
Knockalough, *Eire* - - 25 Bd
Knockferry, *Eire* - - 25 Bc
Knockmealdown Mts., *Eire* 27 Cg
Knockroe, *Eire* - - 25 Bf
Knottingley, *England* - 18 Cc
Knowle, *Somerset, England* 14 Bd
Knowle, *Warwicks, Eng.* 14 Cb
Knox, *Indiana* - - 129 Ab
Knoxville, *Illinois* - - 132 De
Knoxville, *Iowa* - - 132 Ce
Knoxville, *Mississippi* - 130 Ce
Knoxville, *Tennessee* - 131 Gc
Knud Rasmussen Land, *Greenland* - - - 9 Fd
Knutby, *Sweden* - - 50 Hc
Knutsford, *England* - 18 Bd
Knutsford, *W. Australia* 152 Be
Knysna and Harb., *Cape Prov.* - - 114 Eg
Koba, *N. Rhodesia* - - 112 Ac
Kobba Des., *Sinkiang* - 84 Fa
Kobbelbude - - - 56 Eb
Kobdo, *Mongolia* - - 93 Bb
Kobe, *A.-E. Sudan* - - 105 Fc
Kobe, *Japan* - - 97 Cd
Kobelyaki, *Ukraine* - 75 Ef
København (Copenhagen), *Denmark* - - - 45 Fc
Kobior, *Poland* - - 57 Dc
Koblenz (Coblenz), *Prussia* 58 Ba
Kobon, *A.-E. Sudan* - 105 Fc
Kobroor I., *Aroe Is., N.I.* 156 Ac
Kobryn - - - - 60 Hb
Kobuk R., *Alaska* - - 125 Gc
Kobungo, *Angola* - - 109 Cd
Kobylin, *Poland* - - 57 Cb
Kocaeli (Izmit), *Turkey* - 78 Aa
Kočane, *Serbia* - - 70 Db
Koceljevo, *Serbia* - - 68 Eb
Kočevje, *Slovenia* - - 63 Jb
Koch Fd., *Greenland* - 9 Ea
Kocherinovo, *Bulgaria* - 70 Ea
Kochi, *Japan* - - 97 Cd
Ko-chow, *China* - - 95 De
Kochu, *Korea* - - 97 Bc
Kodaikanal, *Madras* - 89 Bb
Kodana, *Syria* - - 80 Da
Kodangal, *Hyderabad* - 90 Cc
Kodiak and I., *Alaska* - 125 Jh
Kodok, *A.-E. Sudan* - 108 Bc
Kodrab, *Poland* - - 57 Eb
Kodyêtô, *Korea* - - 97 Bd
Koealakoeroen, *Borneo* - 99 Dd
Koeandang, *Celébes* - 99 Fc
Koeboe, *Borneo* - - 98 Cd
Koedoes Mts., *Cape Prov.* 114 Df
Koegas, *Cape Prov.* - 114 Ed
Koegrabie, *Cape Prov.* - 114 Dd
Koekenaap, *Cape Prov.* - 114 Be
Koemai and B., *Borneo* - 98 Dd
Koendoer, *Nether. Indies* 98 Bc
Koepang, *Timor I., E.I.* 99 Fe
Koesfeld, *Prussia* - - 54 Bd
Koeteradja, *Sumatra* - 98 Ab
Koez, *S.-W. Africa* - 114 Cb
Kofcağaz, *Turkey* - - 72 Ea
Koffiefontein, *O.F.S.* - 115 Fd
Koforidua, *Gold Coast* - 104 De
Kofu, *Japan* - - - 97 Dc
Koga, *Japan* - - - 100 Gc
Kogaluk R., *Quebec* - 119 Oe
Köge and B., *Denmark* - 45 Fc
Koggiung, *Alaska* - - 125 Hg
Koguno, *Mozambique* - 112 Bd
Kohan, *Baluchistan* - 82 Be
Kohat, *N.-W.F.P.* - 82 Db
Koh Chang, *Siam* - 95 Bg
Koh-i-Baba, *Afghanistan* 84 Bd
Kohima, *Assam* - - 88 Eb
Kohir, *Hyderabad* - - 90 Cc
Kohistan, *N.-W.F.P.* - 84 Cc
Koh-i-Sultan, *Baluchistan* 79 Hd
Koh Kong, I., *Fr. Indo-China* - - - 95 Bg
Koh Kut, *Siam* - - 95 Bg
Kohlfurt - - - 55 Ld
Kohlu, *Baluchistan* - 82 Cd
Koh Rong, I., *Fr. Indo-China* - - - 95 Bg
Koida, *U.S.S.R.* - - 74 Gb
Koidejima, *Japan* - - 100 Gc
Koilkonda, *Hyderabad* - 90 Cc
Koilkuntla, *Madras* - 90 Dd
Koilpatti, *Madras* - - 89 Bc
Köinge, *Sweden* - - 51 Be
Koivisto - - - - 48 Hf
Kojetin, *Moravia* - - 57 Cd
Kojo, *Korea* - - - 97 Bc
Kojonup, *W. Australia* - 152 Be
Koka, *Korea* - - - 97 Bc
Kokai, *Korea* - - 97 Bb
Kokai, *Korea* - - 97 Bc
Kokerboom, *S.-W. Africa* 114 Cd
Kokkinoplós, *Greece* - 70 Dc
Kokkogwa, *Burma* - 92 Bc
Kokkola, *Finland* - - 48 Ee
Kokoda, *New Guinea* - 156 Dc
Kokomo, *Indiana* - - 129 Ab
Koko Nor, *China* - - 94 Bb
Kokonyane Pits, *Bechuanaland* - - - 113 Ac
Kokopo, *New Britain* - 156 Eb
Kokoskill Ra., *Tibet* - 84 Ec
Kokrines, *Alaska* - - 125 Hd
Kok-Shaal Mt., *Kirghiz-Sinkiang* - - - 84 Db
Kokstad, *Cape Prov.* - 115 He
Kokura, *Japan* - - 97 Cd
Kok Zhar (Oil), *Kazak* - 75 Jf
Kola, *Tanganyika Terr.* 111 Fg
Kola, *U.S.S.R.* - - 74 Eb
Kola I., *Aroe Is., N.I.* - 156 Ac
Kolaba, *Bombay.* - - 90 Ab
Kolabira, *Orissa* - - 87 Fe
Ko-lan, *China* - - 94 Db
Kolar, *Mysore* - - 90 Ce
Kolari, *Finland* - - 48 Fc
Kolašin, *Montenegro* - 68 Ed
Kolbe, *Prussia* - - 54 De
Kolberg (Kolobrzeg) *Poland* 55 La
Kolda, *Fr. W. Africa* - 104 Ad
Koldewey I., *Greenland* - 9 Hb
Kolding, *Denmark* - - 45 Cc
Kole, *Belg. Congo* - - 109 Db
Kolea, *Algeria* - - 102 Fa
Kölesd, *Hungary* - - 66 Dc
Kolga B., *Estonia* - - 49 Cb
Kolguev, I., *U.S.S.R.* - 74 Hb
Kolhan, *Bihar* - - 87 Fd
Kolhapur, *Deccan States* 90 Bc
Kolin, *Bohemia* - - 60 Cc
Kolindrós, *Greece* - - 70 Dc

Kucklins Berg - - 56 Fb
Kudat, *N. Borneo* - - 99 Eb
Kudremukh, mt., *Madras* 90 Be
Kudupe, *Latvia* - - 49 Dc
Kudus, *Java* - - - 98 De
Kudymkar, *U.S.S.R.* - 74 Jd
Kuerhlei, *Sinkiang* - 84 Fb
Ku-fow, *China* - - 94 Eb
Kufra, Oasi di, *Libya* - 106 Df
Kufr Birim, *Palestine* - 80 Ca
Kufr 'Inan, *Palestine* - 80 Cb
Kufritta, *Palestine* - 80 Cb
Kufr Sabt, *Palestine* - 80 Cb
Kufstein, *Austria* - 59 Gd
Kuga, *Japan* - - - 100 Ca
Kuhak, *Persia* - - 79 Hd
Kuh-i-Aliabad, *Persia* - 79 Fc
Kuh-i-Darband, *Persia* - 79 Gc
Kuh-i-Dena, *Persia* - 79 Fc
Kuh-i-Dil, *Persia* - 79 Fc
Kuh-i-Hazar, *Persia* - 79 Gd
Kuh-i-Kashigah, *Persia* - 79 Fd
Kuh-i-Taftan, *Persia* - 79 Hd
Kuhmo, *Finland* - 48 Hd
Kuhn I., *Greenland* - 9 Hc
Kuhpayeh, *Persia* - - 79 Fc
Kuhrua, *Persia* - - 79 Fc
Kuh Rud, *Persia* - - 79 Fc
Küibis, *S.-W. Africa* - 114 Bc
Kuibyshev, *U.S.S.R.* - 75 Je
Kuibyshevka, *U.S.S.R.* 96 Da
Kuilenburg, *Holland* - 29 Dc
Kuilu, R., *Fr. Eq. Africa* 109 Bb
Kuito, L., *U.S.S.R.* - 74 Eb
Kuivaniemi, *Finland* - 48 Fd
Kuiz, *S.-W. Africa* - 114 Bb
Kuji, *Japan* - - - 97 Eb
Kuju San, *Japan* - - 97 Cd
Kukan, *Siam* - - 95 Bg
Kukatush, *Ontario* - 122 Ga
Kukawa, *Nigeria* - - 105 Dc
Kukerin, *W. Australia* - 152 Be
Kukës, *Albania* - - 70 Ba
Kukshi, *Central India* - 85 Ec
Kuku L., *Manchuria* - 96 Bb
Kula, *Bulgaria* - - 69 Ed
Kula, *Voyvodina* - - 66 Ed
Kulab, *Tadzhik* - - 84 Bc
Kulachi, *N.-W.F.P.* - 82 Dc
Kulaikh, *Arabia* - - 78 De
Kulakamati, *Bechuanaland* 113 Bc
Kulal, Mt., *Kenya* - - 110 Eb
Kulama, *Nigeria* - - 105 Ce
Kulambangra, I., *Solomon Is.* - - 156 Jg
Ku-lang, *China* - - 94 Bb
Kuldiga, *Latvia* - - 49 Bc
Kuldja, *Sinkiang* - - 84 Eb
Kulebaki, *U.S.S.R.* - 75 Gd
Kulen Vakuf, *Bosnia* - 68 Bb
Kulgam, *Kashmir* - - 83 Fb
Kuli Babang, *E. Indies* - 99 Ec
Kullen, *Sweden* - - 51 Bf
Kulmbach, *Bavaria* - 58 Fa
Kulu, *Punjab* - - 83 Gc
Kulun, L., *Manchuria* - 96 Bb
Kuma, *Japan* - - 100 Bb
Kuma R. & G., *U.S.S.R.* 75 Hg
Kumagaya, *Japan* - - 100 Gc
Kumamoto, *Japan* - - 97 Cd
Kumane, *Voyvodina* - 66 Fd
Kumanicevo, *Serbia* - 70 Db
Kumanovo, *Serbia* - 70 Ca
Kumara, *New Zealand* - 159 Ce
Kumara, *U.S.S.R.* - 96 Da
Kumara, R., *Manchuria* 96 Ca
Kumasi, *Gold Coast* - 104 De
Kumba, *Nigeria* - - 105 Ce
Kumba, *Uganda* - - 110 Ad
Kumbakonam, *Madras* - 89 Cb
Kumbeke, *New Guinea* - 156 Bc
Kumbher, *Nepal* - - 86 Da
Kumgansan, mt., *Korea* 97 Bc
Kumher, *Rajputana* - 83 Ge
Kumi, *Uganda* - - 110 Cc
Kumihama, *Japan* - - 100 Ed
Kumkale, *Turkey* - - 72 Dc
Kums, *S.-W. Africa* - 114 Cd
Kumta, *Bombay* - - 90 Bd
Kün, *China* - - - 94 Dc
Kunana, *Transvaal* - 115 Fc
Kunar & R., *Afghanistan* 82 Da
Kunashiri, I. & Str., *Japan* 97 Fb
Kunch, *United Provs.* - 86 Cc
Kunda, *Estonia* - - 49 Db
Kundian, *Punjab* - - 82 Db
Kundla, *Western India* - 85 Cd
Kunduz, *Afghanistan* - 84 Bc
Kung-chang, *China* - 94 Bc
Kungei Alta-tau, *Kirghiz* 84 Db
Kungrad, *Uzbek* - - 76 Fe
Kungsbacka, *Sweden* - 51 Be
Kungsbacka Fd., *Sweden* 51 Ae
Kung-tan-ho, *China* - 94 Cd
Kungur, *U.S.S.R.* - 74 Kd
Kun-kiang, R., *Korea* - 97 Bc
Kunlong, *Burma* - - 92 Da
Kunlun Mts., *Sinkiang* - 84 Ec
Kun-lun-shan, *China* - 94 Fb
Kunming, *China* - - 94 Bd
Kunsan, *Korea* - - 97 Bc
Kunszentmiklós, *Hungary* 66 Eb
Kuolajärvi, *Finland* - 48 Hc
Kuopio, *Finland* - - 48 Ge
Kupinec, *Croatia* - - 66 Ad
Kupiškis, *Lithuania* - 49 Cd
Kupp - - - - 57 Cc
Kupyansk, *Ukraine* - 75 Ff
Kura, R., *Azerbaijan* - 75 Hh
Kurd Dagh, *Turkey* - 78 Cb
Kurdistan, *Turkey* - - 78 Db
Kure, *Japan* - - - 97 Cd
Kuresaare, *Estonia* - 49 Bb
Kurfalli, *Turkey* - - 72 Fa
Kurgan, *U.S.S.R.* - 76 Gd
Kuria Muria Is., *Arabian Sea* - - - - 77 Hf
Kurigram, *Bengal* - - 88 Bb
Kuril Is. (Chishima), *Japan* 76 Pe
Kuřim, *Moravia* - - 57 Bd
Kurio, I., *Gilbert Is.* - 157 Ec
Kurisches Haff - - 56 Fa
Kurista, *Estonia* - - 49 Db
Kurkliai, *Lithuania* - 49 Cd
Kurleya, *U.S.S.R.* - 96 Ba
Kurmuk, *A.-E. Sudan* - 108 Bc
Kurnalpi, *W. Australia* 152 Ce
Kurnool, *Madras* - - 90 Cd
Kuroe, *Japan* - - 100 Ed
Kurosaka, *Japan* - - 100 Dd
Kurow, *New Zealand* - 159 Cf
Kurram, *N.-W.F.P.* - 82 Db
Kurri Kurri, *N. S. Wales* 155 Gc
Kursk, *U.S.S.R.* - - 75 Fe
Kuršumlija, *Serbia* - 68 Gc
Kurt, *Slovakia* - - 66 Db
Kurthwood, *Louisiana* - 130 Be
Kuru, *Tanganyika Terr.* 110 Ce
Kuruk Tagh, *Sinkiang* - 84 Fb
Kurulu, *Tanganyika Terr.* 111 Cg
Kurum, Ras el, *Palestine* 80 Bb
Kuruman, *Cape Prov.* - 114 Ec
Kurume, *Japan* - - 97 Cd
Kürun (Keelung), *Taiwan* 97 He
Kurunegala, *Ceylon* - 89 Cd
Kurupam, *Madras* - - 91 Fb
Kurusku, *Egypt* - - 106 Mh
Kurya, *U.S.S.R.* - - 74 Kc
Kusa, *U.S.S.R.* - - 74 Kd
Kusaie I., *Caroline Is.* - 157 Dc
Kusatsu, *Japan* - - 100 Fd
Kusava Zemlya, *U.S.S.R.* 74 Ja
Kuserab, *Sinkiang* - - 84 Dc
Kushchevsk, *U.S.S.R.* - 75 Ff
Kushevat, *U.S.S.R.* - 74 Mb
Kushimoto, *Japan* - - 100 Ee
Kushiro & L., *Japan* - 97 Eb
Kushk, *Afghanistan* - 79 Hc
Kushka, *Turkmen* - - 77 Jb
Kushtia, *Bengal* - - 88 Bc
Kushva, *U.S.S.R.* - 74 Kd
Kušiljevo, *Serbia* - - 68 Gb
Kuskokwim, R. and B., *Alaska* - - - - 125 Gf
Kusma, *Nepal* - - 87 Ea
Küsnacht, *Switzerland* - 43 Gb
Küssnacht, *Switzerland* - 43 Fb
Kustanai, *Kazak* - - 76 Gd
Kustrin, *Prussia* - - 55 Kc
Kütahya, *Turkey* - - 78 Ab
Kutaisi, *Georgia* - - 75 Gg
Kut-al-Hai, *Iraq* - - 79 Ec
Kut-al-Imara, *Iraq* - 79 Ec
Kutani, *Tangan. Terr.* - 111 Fg
Kutem, *Kirghiz* - - 84 Db
Kutina, *Croatia* - - 66 Bd
Kutkai, *Burma* - - 92 Da
Kutná Hora, *Bohemia* - 60 Cd
Kutno, *Poland* - - 60 Eb
Kutru, *Eastern States* - 91 Eb
Ku-tsing, *China* - - 94 Bd
Kutu, *Belgian Congo* - 109 Cb
Kutum, *A.-E. Sudan* - 105 Fc
Kutuss Ra., *Sinkiang* - 84 Ga
Kuusamo, *Finland* - 48 Hc
Kuvikur, *Iceland* - - 52 Cb
Kuwait & state, *Persian Gulf* - - - - 79 Ed
Kuwana, *Japan* - - 97 Dc
Ku-wu, *China* - - 94 Db
Ku-yüen, *China* - - 94 Cb
Kuzmin, *Slavonia* - - 66 Ed
Kuznetsk, *U.S.S.R.* - 75 He
Kuzomen, *U.S.S.R.* - 74 Fb
Kværndrup, *Denmark* - 45 Dc
Kvalöy, Sth., *Norway* - 44 De
Kvam, *Norway* - - 46 Fc
Kvarkeno, *U.S.S.R.* - 75 Ke
Kvarnerolo, *Dalmatia* - 63 Jc
Kvikkjokk, *Sweden* - 48 Bc
Kvillinge, *Sweden* - 50 Ed
Kvinesdal, *Norway* - 47 Cf
Kviteseid, *Norway* - 47 Ee
Kwainei, *Korea* - - 97 Bb
Kwai-tsi, *China* - - 95 De
Kwajalem Is., *Marshall Is.* 157 Dc
Kwakoegron, *Suriname* - 142 Ca
Kwale, *Kenya* - - 111 Ff
Kwa-lon, B., *Cochin-China* 95 Bh
Kwamba, *Mozambique* - 112 Cb
Kwamouth, *Belg. Congo* 109 Cb
Kwan, *China* - - 94 Bc
Kwang, *China* - - 94 Ec
Kwang-binh (Donghoi), *Annam* - - - 95 Cf
Kwang-chow, I., *China* - 95 De
Kwang-hai, *China* - - 95 De
Kwang-nam, *Annam* - 95 Cf
Kwang-nan, *China* - 95 Be
Kwang-ngai, *Annam* - 95 Cf
Kwango, *Angola* - - 109 Cc
Kwango, R., *Belg. Congo* 109 Cb
Kwang-ping, *China* - 94 Db
Kwang-si, *China* - - 95 Be
Kwang-si, prov., *China* - 95 Ce
Kwang-sin, *China* - - 94 Ed
Kwang-tê, *China* - - 94 Ec
Kwang-tri, *Annam* - 95 Cf
Kwang-tsi, *China* - - 94 Ec
Kwang Tung Harb., *Andaman Is.* - - 91 Kj
Kwang-tung, prov., *China* 95 De
Kwang-tung Terr., *Japan* 97 Ac
Kwang-yen, *Tong-king* - 95 Ce
Kwang-yuen, *China* - 94 Cc
Kwania, L., *Uganda* - 110 Cc
Kwannonji, *Japan* - - 100 Dd
Kwan-tien, *Manchuria* - 96 Cc
Kwanyinshan, *Manchuria* 96 Db
Kwanza, *Angola* - - 109 Cd
Kwatisore, *New Guinea* - 156 Bb
Kwedia, *Bechuanaland* - 115 Fb
Kwei, *China* - - - 94 Dc
Kwei, *China* - - - 95 Ce
Kwei-chow, *China* - 94 Cc
Kwei-chow I., *China* - 95 Ce
Kwei-chow, prov., *China* 94 Cd
Kweihwa, *China* - - 94 Da
Kwei-lin, *China* - - 94 Dd
Kwei-te, *China* - - 94 Bb
Kwei-teh, *China* - - 94 Ec
Kwei-tung, *China* - - 94 Dd
Kwei-yang, *China* - - 94 Cd
Kwi-chu, *Annam* - - 95 Cf
Kwijwi I., *Belgian Congo* 110 Ae
Kwi-nhon, *Annam* - 95 Cg
Kwui-nhai Chow, *Tong-king* - - - - 95 Be
Kyabra & Cr., *Queensland* 153 Be
Kyaiklat, *Burma* - - 92 Bd
Kyaikto, *Burma* - - 92 Cd
Kyaka, *Tangan. Terr.* - 110 Bd
Kyakhta, *U.S.S.R.* - 76 Ld
Kyanjojo, *Uganda* - 110 Bc
Kyaukchunchaung Hills, *Burma* - - - 92 Bd
Kyaukpyu & Harb., *Burma* 92 Ac
Kyaukse, *Burma* - - 92 Cb
Kyauktan, *Burma* - - 92 Cd
Kyauktaw, *Burma* - - 92 Ab
Kyauk-yè, *Burma* - - 92 Bb
Kybybolite, *S. Australia* 154 Cd
Kyebogyi, *Burma* - - 92 Cc
Kyelang, *Punjab* - - 83 Gb
Kyneton, *Victoria* - - 154 Dd
Kynuna, *Queensland* - 153 Bd
Kyo, *Korea* - - - 97 Bc
Kyoga, L., *Uganda* - 110 Cc
Kyogamizaki, *Japan* - 97 Cc
Kyogle, *New S. Wales* - 155 Ha
Kyojo, *Korea* - - 97 Bb
Kyong, *Burma* - - 92 Cb
Kyoto, *Japan* - - 97 Dd
Kyrchin, *Sinkiang* - 84 Fb
Kyritz, *Prussia* - - 55 Hc
Kyrki, *Greece* - - 72 Cb
Kyrkjebo, *Norway* - 46 Bc
Kyshtym, *U.S.S.R.* - 74 Ld
Kysperk, *Bohemia* - - 59 La
Kysucké Nové Mesto, *Slovakia* - - - 57 Dd
Kytlym, *U.S.S.R.* - 74 Kd
Kyunglung, *Tibet* - - 83 Jc
Kyunhla, *Burma* - - 92 Ba
Kyushu, I., *Japan* - 97 Cd
Kyustendil, *Bulgaria* - 69 Ed
Kywong, *New S. Wales* 155 Ed
Kyzyl Kiya, *Kirghiz* - 84 Cb
Kyzyl Kum, *U.S.S.R.* - 76 Ge
Laa, *Austria* - - - 66 Ba
Laage, *Mecklenburg* - 55 Hb
La Asencion, *Mexico* - 138 Ca
Laasphe, *Prussia* - - 54 De
Labang, *Sarawak* - - 99 Dc
Labanoras, *Lithuania* - 49 Cd
Labarthe, *France* - - 34 Cd
Labastida, *Spain* - - 38 Cb
Labba, *Fr. W. Africa* - 104 Bb
Labbezenga, *Fr. W. Africa* 105Bc
Labe, *Fr. W. Africa* - 104 Bd
Labe (Elbe), R., *Bohemia* 60 Cc
Labelle, *Florida* - - 131 Nh
La Belle, *Missouri* - 132 De
Labelle, *Quebec* - - 121 Ca
Laberge L., *Yukon* - 124 Bb
Labes - - - - 55 Lb
Labiana, *Spain* - - 36 Ea
Labiau - - - 56 Eb
Laboehanbatoe, *Sumatra* 98 Bc
Laboehan Bilik, *Sumatra* 98 Bc
Laboehandeli, *Sumatra* - 98 Ac
Laboehanroekoe, *Sumatra* 98 Ac
Laboulaye, *Argentina* - 148 Da
Labpak, *Mexico* - - 139 Gd
Labrador, Coast of, *Canada* - - - 119 Rf
Labrea, *Brazil* - - 142 Bd
Labuan I., *N. Borneo* - 99 Db
Labuk B., *N. Borneo* - 99 Eb
Labwor, *Uganda* - - 110 Cb
Lac à la Tortue, *Quebec* 121 Da
Lacantun, R., *Mexico* - 139 Fd
Lacaune & Mts., *France* 34 Ed
Laccadive Is., *Arabian Sea* 81 Ch
Lac Court, *Wisconsin* - 132 Dc
Lac du Flambeau, *Wisconsin* - - - 132 Eb
Lacepede B., *S. Australia* 154 Bd
Lacepede Is., *W. Aust.* 152 Cb
Laceraonia, *Mozambique* 113 Fa
Laces, *Italy* - - 62 Ea
Lac Frontiere, *Quebec* - 123 Nb
Lachen, *Switzerland* - 43 Gb
Lachen and R., *Sikkim* - 88 Ba
Lachine, *Quebec* - - 121 Db
Lachlan, R., *N. S. W.* - 154 Ec
Lachmangarh, *Rajputana* 83 Fe
Lachung, *Sikkim* - - 88 Ba
Lachute, *Quebec* - - 121 Cb
Lackawanna, *New York* 123 Jd
Lac la Croix, *Minnesota* 132 Ca
Lacock, *England* - - 14 Bd
Lacolle, *Quebec* - - 121 Db
Lacombe, *Alberta* - - 124 Gd
Lacon, *Illinois* - - 132 Ee
La Concordia, *Salvador* 140 Fe
Laconia, *New Hampshire* 128 Cb
La Connor, *Washington* 136 Ba
Lacoste, *Quebec* - - 121 Ca
Lacqui Parle, *Minnesota* 132 Ac
La Crosse, *Kansas* - 133 Ca
La Crosse, *Wisconsin* - 132 Dd
La Cruz, *Mexico* - - 138 Cb
La Cygne, *Kansas* - 133 Ea
Ladakh, *Kashmir* - - 83 Ga
Ladario, *Brazil* - - 146 Db
Ladbroke, *England* - 14 Cb
Ladesti, *Romania* - - 67 Ke
Ladis, *Persia* - - 79 Hd
Ladismith, *Cape Prov.* - 114 Df
Ladispoli, *Italy* - - 64 Cb
Ladoga, L. (Ladozhskoe), *Finland-U.S.S.R.* - 74 Ec
Ladwa, *Punjab* - - 83 Gd
Ladybank, *Scotland* - 23 Ed
Lady Beatrix L., *Quebec* 123 Ka
Ladybrand, *O.F.S.* - 115 Gd
Lady Frere, *Cape Prov.* 115 Ge
Lady Grey, *Cape Prov.* - 115 Ge
Lady Newnes B., *Antarctica* 160—
Ladysmith, *Br. Columbia* 124 Ee
Ladysmith, *Natal* - - 115 Hd
Ladysmith, *Wisconsin* - 132 Dc
Lae, *New Guinea* - - 156 Dc
Lærdalsöyri, *Norway* - 46 Dc
Læsö, I., *Denmark* - 45 Ea
La Estrada, *Spain* - 36 Bb
Lafagu, *Nigeria* - - 105 Bc
Lafayette, *Alabama* - 130 Fd
La Fayette, *Georgia* - 130 Fc
La Fayette, *Indiana* - 129 Ab
Lafayette, *Louisiana* - 130 Ce
Lafayette, *Tennessee* - 130 Fb
Lafia, *Nigeria* - - 105 Cd
Lafiagi, *Nigeria* - - 105 Cd
Laforce, *France* - - 34 Cc
Laga, *Timor I., N.I.* - 99 Ge
Lagan, *U.S.S.R.* - - 75 Hf
Lagan Ålv, *Sweden* - 51 Cf
Lagarfljöt, *Iceland* - 52 Fb
Lagarina, Val, *Italy* - 62 Eb
Lagartos, Pt., *Mexico* - 139 Gc
Lage, *Lippe* - - 54 Dd
Lågen, R., *Norway* - 46 Fc
Lages, *Rio Grande do Norte, Brazil* - - 143 Gd
Lages, *Santa Catharina, Brazil* - - 147 Ed
Laggan, L., *Scotland* - 23 Dc
Lagheia, *Libya* - 106 Cd
Laghouat, *Algeria* - 103 Fc
Lago, *Idaho* - - 136 Hd
Lagonegro, *Italy* - 64 Fc
Lagor, *France* - - 34 Bd
Lagos, *Mexico* - - 138 Dc
Lagos, *Nigeria* - - 105 Bd
Lagos, *Portugal* - 40 Bb
Lagovaratsk, *U.S.S.R.* 48 Jd
La Grande, *Oregon* - 136 Dc
Lagrange, *Georgia* - 130 Fd
Lagrange, *Indiana* - 129 Bb
Lagrange, *Kentucky* - 130 Fa
La Grange, *Missouri* - 132 De
Lagrange, *Texas* - 133 Df
Lagrange & B., *W. Aust.* 152 Cb
Lagrasse, *France* - - 34 Ed
Lagree Pk., *Laos* - 95 Cf
Laguna, *Brazil* - - 147 Fd
Laguna, *New Mexico* - 135 Kd
Laguna B., *Queensland* - 153 De
Lagunas, *Peru* - - 145 Bc
Lagunillas, *Bolivia* - 146 Cb
Lahad Datu, *N. Borneo* 99 Ec
Lahai, *Sumatra* - - 98 Bd
Laharpur, *United Provs.* 86 Db
Laha-shan, *Manchuria* - 96 Cb
Lahave I., *Nova Scotia* - 120 Cd
Lahej, *Aden* - - - 78 Lh
Lahijan, *Persia* - - 79 Fb
Laholm, *Sweden* - - 51 Cf
Laholm B., *Sweden* - 51 Bf
Lahore, *Punjab* - - 83 Fc
Lahr, *Baden* - - 58 Bc
Lahri, *Baluchistan* - 82 Cd
Lahti, *Finland* - - 48 Ff
Lahuta, *Tang. Terr.* - 111 Fj
Lai, *Fr. Eq. Africa* - 105 Ed
Lai-chau, *Tong-king* - 95 Be
Lai-chow, *China* - - 94 Fb
Lai-chow B., *China* - 94 Eb
Lai-feng, *China* - - 94 Cd
Laigle, *France* - - 30 Cc
Laignes, *France* - - 31 Gd
Laihka, *Burma* - - 92 Cb
Lai-Hsak, *Burma* - 92 Cb
Laila, *Arabia* - - 79 Ee
Laina, *Greece* - - 72 Da
Laingsburg, *Cape Prov.* 114 Df
Lairg, *Scotland* - - 24 De
Lairi, *Fr. Eq. Africa* - 105 Ec
Lais, *Sumatra* - - 98 Bd
Laïsta, *Greece* - - 70 Bd
Lai-Thui, *Annam* - 95 Cf
Laitila, *Finland* - - 48 Df
Laitokitok, *Kenya* - 110 Ee
Lajão, *Brazil* - - 147 Gb
Lajkovac, *Serbia* - - 68 Eb
La Jolla, *California* - 134 Ee
Lajoya, *New Mexico* - 135 Kd
Lakara, *Celebes* - - 99 Fd
Lake Arthur, *New Mexico* 135 Le
Lake Benton, *Minnesota* 132 Ac
Lake Butler, *Florida* - 131 Ge
Lake Cargelligo, *N.S.W.* 155 Ec
Lake Charles, *Louisiana* 130 Be
Lake Chrissie, *Transvaal* 115 Jc
Lake City, *Arkansas* - 130 Cc
Lake City, *California* - 134 Ca
Lake City, *Colorado* - 135 Kb
Lake City, *Florida* - 131 Ge
Lake City, *Iowa* - - 132 Bd
Lake City, *Michigan* - 122 Fc
Lake City, *Minnesota* - 132 Cc
Lake Edward, *Quebec* - 123 Mb
Lakefield, *Queensland* - 153 Bb
Lake Geneva, *Wisconsin* 132 Ed
Lake George, *New York* 123 Md
Lake Harbour, *N.-W. T.* 119 Qd
Lakeland, *Florida* - - 131 Mg
Lake Majella, *California* 134 Bc
Lakenheath, *England* - 15 Eb
Lake Pleasant, *New York* 128 Ab
Lake Point, *Utah* - - 135 Ga
Lakeport, *California* - 134 Bb
Lake Providence, *Louisiana* 130Cd
Lakes Entrance, *Victoria* 155 Fe
Lakeside, *California* - 134 Ee
Lake Valley, *New Mexico* 135 Ke
Lake View, *California* - 134 Ee
Lakeview, *Minnesota* - 132 Cb

Ledesma, Argentina - 146 Cc
Ledesma, Spain - 37 Da
Ledo, C., Angola - 109 Bc
Lee, Nevada - 134 Fa
Lee, R., Eire - 25 Cf
Leech Lake, Minnesota - 132 Bb
Leeder, Bavaria - 58 Ed
Leedey, Oklahoma - 133 Cc
Leeds, England - 18 Cc
Leeds Junction, Maine - 128 Ca
Leek, England - 18 Bd
Leer, Prussia - 54 Cb
Leesburg, Florida - 131 Ng
Leesburg, Georgia - 131 Fe
Leesburg, Virginia - 129 Fc
Lees Ferry, Arizona - 135 Hc
Leesi, Estonia - 49 Bb
Leeston, New Zealand - 159 De
Leesville, Louisiana - 130 Be
Leeton, New S. Wales - 155 Ec
Leeuwarden, Holland - 29 Da
Leeuwin, C., W. Aust. - 152 Ae
Leeward Is., W. Indies - 140 Kg
Lefreh, Fr. W. Africa - 104 Ab
Lefroy, L., W. Aust. - 152 Ce
Leganes, Spain - 38 Bd
Legaspi, Philippines - 99 Fa
Legendre I., W. Aust. - 152 Bc
Legge Pk., Tasmania - 155 Kg
Leghorn (Livorno), Italy 62 Ed
Legnago, Italy - 63 Fb
Legnano, Italy - 62 Cb
Le Grau-du-Roi, France 35 Gd
Leh, Kashmir - 83 Ga
Lehe, Prussia - 54 Db
Lehi, Utah - 135 Ha
Lehigh, Oklahoma - 133 Dc
Lehrte, Prussia - 54 Ec
Leiah, Punjab - 82 Dc
Leibnitz, Austria - 59 Ke
Leicester, Vermont - 128 Bb
Leicester & co., England 14 Ca
Leichhardt Ra., Queensl'd 153 Cd
Leichhardt R., Queensland 153 Ac
Leigh, Essex, England - 15 Ec
Leigh, Lancs, England - 18 Bd
Leigh, Idaho - 136 Hd
Leigh Creek, S. Aust. - 154 Bb
Leighlinbridge, Eire - 27 Cf
Leighton Buzzard, Eng. 15 Dc
Leikanger, Norway - 46 Cc
Leiksa, Finland - 48 Je
Leiktho, Burma - 92 Cc
Leinefelde, Prussia - 54 Fd
Leinster, prov., Eire - 27 Ce
Leintwardine, England - 14 Bb
Lei-po, China - 94 Bd
Leiptig - 69 Hb
Leipzig, Saxony - 55 Hd
Leiria, Portugal - 37 Bc
Leisnig, Saxony - 55 Hd
Leissigen, Switzerland - 42 Ec
Leiston, England - 15 Fb
Leitchfield, Kentucky - 130 Eb
Leith, Scotland - 23 Ee
Leitrim, co., Eire - 26 Bc
Leix, co., Eire - 27 Ce
Leixlip, Eire - 27 De
Lei-yang, China - 94 Dd
Lejasciems, Latvia - 49 Dc
Lekáni, Greece - 70 Fb
Le Kef, Tunisia - 103 Ja
Lekenik, Croatia - 66 Bd
Lekhainá, Greece - 71 Cf
Lekhta, U.S.S.R. - 74 Ec
Lekki, Nigeria - 105 Bd
Leksand, Sweden - 50 Db
Leksvik, Norway - 46 Ga
Leland, Michigan - 122 Fc
Leland, Mississippi - 130 Cd
Lelei, Halmahera, N.I. - 99 Gd
Leleque, Argentina - 148 Bc
Leliefontein, Cape Prov. 114 Ce
Lelle, Estonia - 49 Cb
Lem, Denmark - 45 Bb
Léman, Lac (Geneva, L. of), France-Switz. - 42 Bd
Le Mars, Iowa - 132 Ad
Lembeh, I., Nether. Indies 99 Gc
Lemberg (Lwów) - 60 Hd
Lemförde, Prussia - 54 Dc
Lemgo, Lippe - 54 Dc
Lemhi Pass, Montana - 136 Gc
Lemhi Ra. & R., Idaho 136 Gc
Lemieux, Quebec - 121 Da
Lemmer, Holland - 29 Db
Lemnos, I., Greece - 72 Cb
Lemon B., Florida - 131 Mh
Lemon City, Florida - 131 Nj
Lemont, Illinois - 132 Ee
Lemoore, California - 134 Dc
Lempa R., Salvador - 140 Fe
Lemro R., Burma - 92 Ab
Lemvig, Denmark - 45 Bb
Lena, Spain - 36 Ea
Lena, R., U.S.S.R. - 76 Nc
Lendinara, Italy - 63 Fb
Lengerich, Prussia - 54 Cc
Lenggries, Bavaria - 59 Fd
Lengwethen - 56 Gb
Lenina Pk., Kirghiz - 84 Cc
Leninabad, Tadzhik - 84 Bb
Leninakan, Armenia - 75 Gg
Leningrad, U.S.S.R. - 74 Ed
Leninsk, U.S.S.R. - 76 Jd
Leninskoe, U.S.S.R. - 75 Hf
Lenkoran, Azerbaijan - 75 Hh
Lennep, Montana - 136 Ha
Lennox, Massachusetts - 128 Bb
Lennox, S. Dakota - 132 Ad
Lennoxtown, Scotland - 23 De
Lennoxville, Quebec - 121 Eb
Leno, Italy - 62 Eb
Lenoir, N. Carolina - 131 Hc
Lenora, Kansas - 133 Ba
Lenox, Iowa - 132 Be
Lens, France - 30 Ea
Lensvik, Norway - 46 Fa
Lenti, Hungary - 66 Bc
Lentini, Sicily - 65 Jg
Lenwade, England - 15 Fa
Lenya, Burma - 98 Aa
Lenzburg, Switzerland - 42 Fb
Lenzen, Prussia - 55 Gb
Leo, Fr. W. Africa - 104 Dd
Leoben, Austria - 59 Kd
Leobersdorf, Austria - 59 Ld
Leobschutz - 57 Cc
Leominster, England - 14 Bb
Leominster, Massachusetts 128Bb
Leon, Iowa - 132 Ce
Leon, Mexico - 138 Dc
Leon, Nicaragua - 140 Fe
Leon and prov., Spain - 36 Eb
Leon R., Texas - 133 De
Leonardo, Spain - 38 Bc
Leoncita, New Mexico - 135 Ld
Leondári, Greece - 71 Dd
Leondarion, Greece - 71 Df
Leonforte, Sicily - 65 Hg
Leongatha, Victoria - 155 Ee
Leonia, Idaho - 136 Ea
Leonídhion, Greece - 71 Df
Leonora, W. Australia - 152 Cd
Leopold McClintock C., N.-W. Terr. - 118 Da
Leopold II., L., Belg. Congo - 109 Cb
Leopoldville, Belg. Congo 109 Cb
Leoti, Kansas - 133 Ba
Leova - 69 Hb
Lepar I., Nether. Indies 98 Cd
Lepel, White Russia - 74 De
Lephepe, Bechuanaland 113 Ad
Lepini Mts., Italy - 64 Db
L'Epiphanie, Quebec - 121 Db
Lepontine Alps, Switz.-Italy - 62 Ca
Lepreau, New Brunswick 120 Bd
Lepseny, Hungary - 66 Dc
Lercara Friddi, Sicily - 65 Gg
Lerdo, Mexico - 138 Db
Lere, France - 30 Ed
Lere, Fr. Eq. Africa - 105 Dd
Leribe (Hlotse), Basutoland - 115 Hd
Lerici, Italy - 62 Dc
Lerida and prov., Spain 39 Fc
Lerma, Argentina - 146 Bc
Lermoos, Austria - 58 Ed
Lerno, Mte., Sardinia - 64 Jf
Leros, I., Ægean Sea - 78 Ab
Leroy, Illinois - 132 Ee
Le Roy, Kansas - 133 Ea
Leroy, New York - 123 Jd
Lerum, Sweden - 51 Be
Lerwick, Zetland - 24 Gh
Lesa, Italy - 62 Cb
Les Andelys, France - 30 Db
Lesbos (Mitilini), I., Greece 72 Cc
Lescar, France - 34 Bd
Leseru, Kenya - 110 Dc
Lesh (Alessio), Albania - 70 Ab
Leshukonskoe, U.S.S.R. 74 Hc
Lesja, Norway - 46 Eb
Lesjaskog, Norway - 46 Eb
Lesjofors, Sweden - 50 Dc
Leskovac, Serbia - 69 Dd
Leskoviq, Albania - 70 Bc
Leslie, Scotland - 23 Ed
Lesneven, France - 32 Ab
Lesnica, Serbia - 68 Eb
Lesnoi, U.S.S.R. - 74 Eb
Lesparre, France - 34 Aa
Lessay, France - 32 Da
Lessebo, Sweden - 51 Ef
Lesser Slave L., Alberta 124 Fc
Lessini, Mt., Italy - 62 Fb
Lesueur, Minnesota - 132 Cc
Leszno, Poland - 60 Dc
Letchworth, England - 15 Dc
Let Elv, Sweden - 50 Dc
Letha Ra., Burma - 92 Aa
Lethbridge, Alberta - 124 Ge
Leti Is., Nether. Indies - 99 Ge
Leticia, Colombia - 145 Db
Letjesbosch, Cape Prov. 114 Ef
Letovica, Serbia - 70 Ca
Letpadan, Burma - 92 Bd
Lette, New S. Wales - 154 Dc
Letterkenny, Eire - 26 Cb
Leuchars, Scotland - 23 Fd
Leucite Hills, Wyoming 135 Ja
Leuk, Switzerland - 42 Ed
Leukerbad, Switzerland 42 Ed
Leun, Prussia - 54 De
Leuser, mt., Sumatra - 98 Ac
Leuzigen, Switzerland - 42 Db
Leva, Slovakia - 66 Da
Levadhia, Greece - 71 De
Levan, Albania - 70 Ac
Levanger, Norway - 46 Ha
Levanto, Italy - 62 Dc
Levanzo I., Italy - 65 Fg
Leven, Scotland - 23 Fd
Levenna, mt., Italy - 62 Bb
Levens, France - 33 Cb
Leventina, Valle, Switz. 43 Gd
Leverkusen, Prussia - 54 Bd
Levice, Slovakia - 60 Ed
Levico, Italy - 63 Fa
Levídhi, Greece - 71 Df
Levin, New Zealand - 158 Ed
Levis, Quebec - 121 Ea
Levkás and I., Greece - 71 Be
Levrier B., Fr. W. Africa 104 Ab
Levroux, France - 30 Dd
Lev-Tolstoi, U.S.S.R. - 75 Fe
Levuka, Fiji Is. - 157 Pk
Lewes, Delaware - 129 Gc
Lewes, England - 15 De
Lewes R., Yukon - 124 Bb
Lewis, I., Scotland - 24 Ba
Lewis and Clarke Pass, Montana - 136 Gb
Lewisburg, Pennsylvania 129 Fb
Lewisburg, Tennessee - 130 Ec
Lewisburg, W. Virginia 129 Dd
Lewisporte, Newfoundl'd 120 Hb
Lewiston, Louisiana - 130 Be
Lewiston, Maine - 128 Ca
Lewiston, N. Carolina - 131 Kb
Lewistone, Washington - 136 Eb
Lewistown, Illinois - 132 De
Lewistown, Montana - 136 Jb
Lewistown, Pennsylvania 129 Fb
Lewisville, Texas - 133 Dd
Lexington, Georgia - 131 Gd
Lexington, Kentucky - 131 Fb
Lexington, Mississippi - 130 Dd
Lexington, Missouri - 130 Ba
Lexington, N. Carolina - 131 Hc
Lexington, Oklahoma - 133 Dc
Lexington, S. Carolina - 131 Hd
Lexington, Tennessee - 130 Dc
Lexington, Texas - 133 De
Lexington, Virginia - 129 Ed
Lexos, France - 34 Dc
Leyburn, England - 18 Cb
Leyden (Leiden), Holland 29 Cb
Leydsdorp, Transvaal - 115 Ja
Leyland, England - 18 Bc
Leysdown, England - 15 Ed
Leyte & I., Philippines - 99 Fa
Lezay, France - 34 Ca
Lézignan, France - 34 Ed
Lgov, U.S.S.R. - 75 Fe
Lhasa, Tibet - 81 Ge
Lho' Seumawe, Sumatra 98 Ab
Liákoura, Greece - 71 De
Liancourt, France - 30 Eb
Lianga, Philippines - 99 Gb
Liang-chow, China - 94 Bb
Liang-shan, China - 94 Bd
Liaochung, Manchuria - 96 Cc
Liao-ho, Manchuria - 96 Cc
Liaoho, R., Manchuria - 96 Cc
Liaohsi, Manchuria - 96 Cc
Liao-tié-shan Chan., Kwang-tung Terr. - 97 Ac
Liao yang, Manchuria - 96 Cc
Liaoyuan, Manchuria - 96 Cc
Liard & R., N.-W. T. - 124 Eb
Liatorp, Sweden - 51 Df
Liavozersk, U.S.S.R. - 48 Mb
Libby, Montana - 136 Fa
Libenge, Belg. Congo - 109 Ca
Liberal, Kansas - 133 Bb
Liberdade, Brazil - 145 Cc
Liberec, Bohemia - 60 Gc
Liberia, Costa Rica - 140 Fe
Liberia, rep., W. Africa 101 Ae
Libertad, Mexico - 138 Bb
Libertad, dep., Peru - 145 Bc
Liberty, Mississippi - 130 Ce
Liberty, Missouri - 130 Aa
Liberty, New York - 128 Ac
Liberty, Texas - 133 Ee
Libode, Cape Prov. - 115 He
Libohovë, Albania - 70 Bc
Libourne, France - 34 Bc
Libramont, Belgium - 29 De
Librazhd, Albania - 70 Bb
Libreville, Fr. Eq. Africa 109 Aa
Libya, N. Africa - 101 Dc
Libyan Des., Libya-Egypt 106 Ce
Libyan Des. Plat., Egypt 106 Ec
Licata, Sicily - 65 Gg
Lichfield, England - 14 Ca
Lichtenburg, Transvaal 115 Gc
Lichtenfels, Bavaria - 58 Fa
Liciro, Mozambique - 113 Ga
Licking R., Kentucky - 131 Fa
Lički Osik, Croatia - 63 Kc
Licodia Eubea, Sicily - 65 Hg
Lida, Nevada - 134 Ec
Lida - 60 Hb
Liddington, England - 14 Cc
Lidgate, England - 15 Eb
Lidgerwood, N. Dakota 132 Ab
Lidingo, Sweden - 50 Hc
Lidköping, Sweden - 50 Bd
Lido di Roma, Italy - 64 Cb
Liebach, Austria - 59 Ke
Liebana, La, Spain - 38 Aa
Liebemühl - 56 Dc
Liebenau (Lubrza), Poland - 55 Lc
Liebenau, Hanover, Prussia 54 Dc
Liebenwerda, Prussia - 55 Jd
Liebling, Romania - 67 Gd
Liebstadt, - 56 Eb
Liechtenstein, state, Europe 43 Jb
Liedena, Spain - 38 Db
Liegan, California - 134 Ca
Liége & prov., Belgium - 29 Dd
Liegnitz (Lignica), Poland 55 Md
Lielvārde, Latvia - 49 Cc
Lien-hwa, China - 94 Dd
Lienkong, China - 94 Ed
Lienz, Austria - 59 Ge
Liepaja and L., Latvia - 49 Ac
Lier, Norway - 47 Ge
Lierre, Belgium - 29 Cc
Liestal, Switzerland - 42 Eb
Lieşti, Romania - 69 Gc
Lièvre R., Quebec - 121 Ca
Lifamatula, I., Neth. Indies 99 Gd
Liffey, R., Eire - 27 De
Lifford, Eire - 26 Cb
Lifou, I., Loyalty Is. - 157 Df
Ligné, France - 32 Dc
Lignica (Liegnitz), Poland 55 Md
Ligny-en-Barrios, France 31 Hc
Ligoudhísta (Khóra), Greece 71 Cf
Ligua, La, Chile - 146 Ae
Liguria, dep., Italy - 62 Cc
Ligurian Alps, Italy - 62 Cc
Ligurian Apennines, Italy 62 Cc
Ligurian Sea, Italy - 62 Cd
Ligwira Mt., Tang. Terr. 111 Ej
Likhoslavl, U.S.S.R. - 74 Fd
Likhvin, U.S.S.R. - 75 Fe
Li-kiang-fu, China - 94 Ad
Likódhimos, mt., Greece 71 Cg
Likongole, Tang. Terr. - 111 Eh
Likorema, Greece - 70 Fd
Likuyu, Tang. Terr. - 111 Ej
Likuyu, Tang. Terr. - 111 Dj
Lille, France - 30 Fa
Lillebonne, France - 30 Cb
Lillehammer, Norway - 46 Gc
Lillers, France - 30 Ea
Lillesand, Norway - 47 Ef
Lilleshall, England - 14 Ba
Lillestrom, Norway - 47 He
Lille Vildmose, Denmark 45 Db
Lillooet, Brit. Columbia 124 Ed
Lilongwe, Nyasaland - 112 Bb
Lilydale, Queensland - 153 Ac
Lim, R., Serbia, etc. - 68 Ec
Lima, Montana - 136 Gc
Lima, Ohio - 129 Bb
Lima and dep., Peru - 145 Bd
Li-ma Is., China - 95 De
Lima, R., Portugal - 36 Bc
Limache, Chile - 146 Ae
Liman, Ukraine - 75 Ff
Limassol, Cyprus - 78 Bc
Limavady, N. Ireland - 26 Da
Limay, R., Argentina - 148 Cb
Limay Mahuida, Argent. 148 Cb
Limback, Saxony - 55 He
Limbara, Mti, Sardinia 64 Jf
Limbazi, Latvia - 49 Cc
Limbdi, Western India - 85 Cc
Limboto, Celébes - 99 Fc
Limbourg and prov., Belgium - 29 Dc
Limburg, Prussia - 58 Ca
Limburg, prov., Holland 29 Dc
Lim-chow, China - 95 Ce
Limeira, Brazil - 147 Fc
Limejuice Camp, W. Aust. 152 Dd
Limerick and co., Eire - 27 Bf
Limestone, Maine - 120 Ac
Limfjorden, Denmark - 45 Bb
Liminka, Finland - 48 Fd
Limmared, Sweden - 51 Ce
Límni, Greece - 71 Ee
Limoges, France - 34 Db
Limon, Colorado - 135 Mb
Limon, Costa Rica - 140 Ge
Limone, Lombardy, Italy 62 Eb
Limone, Piemonte, Italy 62 Bc
Limousin, Mtgns. du, France - 34 Db
Limousin, old prov., France 34Db
Limoux, France - 34 Ed
Limpley Stoke, England 14 Bd
Limpopo, R., Mozambique 112 Bd
Limuru, Kenya - 110 Ed
Li-ma-shan, China - 94 Ac
Lin, Albania - 70 Bb
Lin-an, China - 95 Be
Linao L., Philippines - 99 Gb
Linapacan, I., Philippines 99 Ea
Linares, Mexico - 139 Ec
Linares, Jaen, Spain - 41 Cb
Linares, Teruel, Spain - 38 Ed
Linares and prov., Chile 148 Bb
Linas, Mte., Sardinia - 64 Hg
Linchow, China - 94 Cb
Lin-chow, China - 95 De
Linchwe, Bechuanaland 115 Ga
Lincoln, Argentina - 148 Da
Lincoln, California - 134 Cb
Lincoln, Illinois - 132 Ee
Lincoln, Kansas - 133 Ca
Lincoln, Maine - 120 Ad
Lincoln, Michigan - 122 Gc
Lincoln, Nebraska - 126 Fb
Lincoln, New Mexico - 135 Le
Lincoln, New Zealand - 159 De
Lincoln and co., Eng. - 19 Dd
Lincoln Land, N.-W.T. 119 Na
Lincolnton, N. Carolina 131 Hc
Lincoln Wolds, England 19 Dd
Lindås, Norway - 46 Bd
Lindau, Anhalt - 55 Hc
Lindau, Bavaria - 58 Dd
Linden, Alabama - 130 Ed
Linden, Prussia - 54 Ec
Linden, Texas - 133 Ed
Lindenberg, Mecklenburg 55 Hb
Lindenborg, Denmark - 45 Cb
Linderod Ås, Sweden - 51 Cg
Lindesberg, Sweden - 50 Dc
Lindesnes (The Naze), Norway - 47 Cg
Lindi, Tanganyika Terr. 111 Fh
Lindley, O.F.S. - 115 Hc
Lindow, Prussia - 55 Jc
Lindsay, Ontario - 121 Ab
Lindsborg, Kansas - 133 Da
Lindsey, Parts of, Lincs, England - 19 Dd
Line Is., Pacific Oc. - 157 Gc
Linevska, U.S.S.R. - 75 Je
Ling, China - 94 Dd
Lingampet, Hyderabad - 90 Cb
Lingayen & B., Philippines 95 Ff
Lingbo, Sweden - 50 Fa
Lingeh, Persia - 79 Fd
Lingen, Prussia - 54 Cc
Lingga, I. and Arch., Netherlands Indies - 98 Bd
Linghed, Sweden - 50 Eb
Lingit, Philippines - 99 Gb
Lingomo, Belg. Congo - 109 Da
Ling-shui & B., China - 95 Cf
Lingsugur, Hyderabad - 90 Cc
Lingtsi Dzong, Bhutan - 88 Ca
Ling-tsing, China - 94 Eb
Linguere, Fr. W. Africa 104 Ac
Lingyuan, Manchuria - 96 Bc
Lin-kiang, China - 94 Dd
Linkiang, Manchuria - 96 Dc
Linköping, Sweden - 50 Ed
Linkuva, Lithuania - 49 Bc

Loray, *Nevada* - - 134 Fa
Lorca, *Spain* - - 41 Ec
Lord Howe Is., *Pacific Oc.* 149 Gj
Lordsburg, *New Mexico* 135 Je
Loreno, *Brazil* - 147 Gc
Lorenzana, Sa. de, *Spain* 36 Ca
Loreo, *Italy* - - 63 Gb
Loreto, *Argentina* - 146 Cd
Loreto, *Brazil* - 143 Ed
Loreto, *Mexico* - 138 Bb
Loreto, dep., *Peru* - 145 Bc
Loreto Aprutino, *Italy* - 64 Da
Lorette, *Quebec* - 121 Ea
Lorgues, *France* - 33 Bc
Lorica, *Colombia* - 144 Ab
Lorient, *France* - 32 Bc
L'Orignal, *Ontario* - 121 Cb
Loriyu, *Kenya* - 110 Eb
Lorne, Firth of, *Scotland* 22 Cd
Lorne, *Victoria* - 154 De
Lorogi Ra., *Kenya* - 110 Ec
Lorogumo, *Kenya* - 110 Db
Loros, *Chile* - - 146 Bd
Lorrach, *Baden* - 58 Bd
Lorraine, old prov., *France* 31 Hb
Los Is., *Fr. W. Africa* - 104 Be
Los Andes, *Chile* - 146 Ae
Los Andes, terr., *Argentina* 146Bc
Los Angeles, *California* 134 Dd
Los Angeles, *Chile* - 148 Bb
Losap, I., *Caroline Is.* - 157 Cc
Los Blancos, *Argentina* - 146 Cc
Los Blancos, *Spain* - 41 Fc
Los Gatos, *California* - 134 Bc
Losheim, *Prussia* - 58 Ab
Los Jardines, I., *Pac. Oc.* 157 Ba
Los Lamentos, *Mexico* - 138 Ca
Los Lunas, *New Mexico* 135 Kd
Los Menucos, *Argentina* 148 Cc
Losombo, *Belg Congo* - 109 Ca
Los Palacios, *Spain* - 40 Eb
Los Pedroches, *Spain* - 37 Ed
Los Pozos, *Chile* - 146 Ad
Los Rios, prov., *Ecuador* 145 Bb
Los Roques, *Venezuela* - 144 Ca
Los Santos, *Panama* - 140 Gf
Los Santos de Maimona, *Spain* - - - 37 Dd
Lossiemouth, *Scotland* - 23 Ea
Lost R., *Oregon* - 136 Cd
Los Teques, *Venezuela* - 144 Ca
Los Testigos, *Windward Is.* 140Kh
Los Tigres, *Argentina* - 146 Cd
Lost River Mts., *Idaho* - 136 Gd
Lostwithiel, *England* - 17 Bc
Los Vilos, *Chile* - 146 Ae
Lot, R. & dep., *France* - 34 Dc
Lota, *Chile* - - 148 Bb
Lotbinière, *Quebec* - 121 Ea
Lot-et-Garonne, *France* 34 Cc
Lothair, *Transvaal* - 115 Jc
Lo-ting, *China* - 95 De
Loto, *Belg. Congo* - 109 Db
Lotru Mts., *Romania* - 67 Jd
Lotui, I., *Uganda* - 110 Cd
Lotzen - - - 56 Fb
Loudeac, *France* - 32 Cb
Loudes, *France* - 35 Fb
Loudon, *Tennessee* - 131 Fc
Louga, *Fr. W. Africa* - 104 Ac
Loughborough, *England* 18 Ce
Lougheed I., *N.-W. T.* 118 Ja
Loughor and R., *Wales* 20 Bd
Loughrea, *Eire* - 27 Be
Louhans, *France* - 35 Ha
Louisa, *Kentucky* - 131 Ga
Louisberg, *N. Carolina* - 131 Jb
Louisburg, *Nova Scotia* 120 Fd
Louisburgh, *Eire* - 25 Bb
Louiseville, *Quebec* - 121 Da
Louis Gentil, *Morocco* - 103 Nh
Louisiade Arch., *New Guin.* 156Lk
Louisiana, *Missouri* - 130 Ca
Louisiana, state, *U.S.A.* 127 Gd
Louis Philippe Land *Antarctica* - - 160 —
Louis Trichardt, *Transvaal* 113Cd
Louisville, *Colorado* - 135 Lb
Louisville, *Georgia* - 131 Gd
Louisville, *Kentucky* - 130 Fa
Louisville, *Mississippi* - 130 Dd
Loulay, *France* - 32 Ed
Loule, *Portugal* - 40 Bb
Louny, *Bohemia* - 59 Ha
Loup, R. de, *Quebec* - 121 Da
Loupe, la, *France* - 30 Dc
Lourdes, *France* - 34 Bd
Lourenço Marques, *Mozambique* - 115 Kb
Louriçal, *Portugal* - 37 Bb
Lourinha, *Portugal* - 37 Ac
Loúron, *Greece* - - 71 Bd
Louta, *Fr. W. Africa* - 104 Dd
Louth, *England* - 19 Dd
Louth, *New S. Wales* - 154 Eb
Louth and co., *Eire* - 26 Dd
Loutraki, *Greece* - 71 Df
Louvain, *Belgium* - 29 Cd
Louviers, *France* - 30 Db
Louvres, *France* - 30 Eb
Louwsburg, *Natal* - 115 Jc
Louza & Sa. de, *Portugal* 37 Bb
Lovászpatona, *Hungary* 66 Cb
Lovech, *Bulgaria* - 69 Fd
Loveland, *Colorado* - 135 La
Lovell, *England* - 14 Cc
Lovelock, *Nevada* - 134 Da
Lovisa, *Finland* - 48 Gf
Lövö, *Hungary* - 66 Bb
Lovrin, *Romania* - 67 Fd
Lövsta B., *Sweden* - 50 Gb
Lovur, *Persia* - 79 Fb
Low, *Quebec* - 121 Bb
Low (Midai) I., *Neth. Indies* 98 Cc
Lowa, *Belg. Congo* - 109 Eb
Lowell, *Massachusetts* - 128 Cb
Lowell, *Michigan* - 122 Fd
Lowell, *Oregon* - 136 Bd
Lowenberg, *Brandenburg, Prussia* - - - 55 Hc
Löwenberg - - 55 Ld
Löwenhagen - - 56 Eb
Löwentin See - 56 Fc
Lower California, state, *Mexico* - - 138 Bb
Lower Chindwin, *Burma* 92 Ba
Lower Egypt, *Egypt* - 107 Hc
Lower Peach Tree, *Alabama* - - 130 Ee
Lower Umkomaas, *Natal* 115 Je
Lowestoft, *England* - 15 Fb
Łowicz, *Poland* - 60 Eb
Lowland, *N. Carolina* - 131 Kc
Lowville, *New York* - 123 Ld
Loxton, *Cape Prov.* - 114 Ee
Loxton, *S. Australia* - 154 Cc
Loya Ada, *Br. Somaliland* 108 Dc
Loyalty Is., *Pacific Oc.* - 149 Gh
Loyoro, *Uganda* - 110 Db
Lo-yung, *China* - 95 Ce
Lozère, dep., *France* - 35 Fc
Lozère, Mt., *France* - 35 Fc
Loznica, *Serbia* - 68 Eb
Lozovaya, *Ukraine* - 75 Ff
Lu, *China* - - 94 Cd
Luambala, *Mozambique* - 112 Cb
Lu-an, *China* - 94 Db
Luang Prabang, *Laos* - 95 Bf
Luao, *Angola* - 109 Dd
Lubaczów, *Poland* - 60 Gc
Lubafu, *Tangan. Terr.* - 110 Bd
Lubaña, *Latvia* - 49 Dc
Lubanas L., *Latvia* - 49 Dc
Lubang, I., *Philippines* - 95 Eg
Lubartow, *Poland* - 60 Gc
Lubasz, *Poland* - 57 Ba
Lübben, *Prussia* - 55 Jd
Lubbock, *Texas* - 133 Ad
Lubeck, *Prussia* - 54 Fb
Lubeck, *Victoria* - 154 Dd
Lübeck B., *Prussia* - 54 Fa
Lubefa, *Belg. Congo* - 109 Db
Lüben - - - 55 Md
Lubenz, *Bohemia* - 59 Ha
Lubero, *Belg. Congo* - 110 Ac
Lubia, *Spain* - 38 Cc
Lubile, *Belg. Congo* - 109 Ec
Lublin, *Poland* - 60 Gc
Lubliniec, *Poland* - 57 Dc
Lubnia, *Poland* - 56 Bc
Lubny, *Ukraine* - 75 Ef
Lubochna, *Slovakia* - 60 Ed
Luboml - - 60 Hc
Lubraniec, *Poland* - 57 Da
Lubrin, *Spain* - 41 Dc
Lubu, *Borneo* - 99 Dd
Lubue, *Belg. Congo* - 109 Cb
Lubumba, *Tang. Terr.* - 111 Bf
Lubur, Mt., *Kenya* - 110 Da
Lubutu, *Belg. Congo* - 109 Eb
Luc, le, *France* - 33 Bc
Lucan, *Eire* - 27 De
Lucania (Basilicata), *Italy* 65 Cb
Lucar and Sa. de, *Spain* 41 Dc
Lucas, *Iowa* - 132 Ce
Lucca, *Italy* - 62 Ed
Lucch, *Libya* - 106 Ec
Luce B., *Scotland* - 21 Bd
Lucen, Sa. de, *Spain* - 41 Cc
Lucena, *Philippines* - 95 Fg
Lucena, *Spain* - 40 Fb
Lucena del Cid, *Spain* - 39 Ed
Lucenay-l'Evêque, *France* 31 Gd
Lucenec, *Slovakia* - 60 Ed
Lucera, *Italy* - 64 Fb
Lucerne, *Missouri* - 132 Ce
Lucerne (Luzern), *Switz.* 42 Fb
Lü-chow, *China* - 94 Ec
Lüchow, *Prussia* - 55 Gc
Lucia, *California* - 134 Cc
Lucile, *Idaho* - 136 Ec
Lucinda Pt., *Queensland* 153 Cc
Lucindale, *S. Australia* - 154 Bd
Lucipara Is., *Nether. Indies* 99 Ge
Łuck, (Lutsk), *Ukraine* - 60 Hc
Luckau, *Prussia* - 55 Jd
Luckenwalde, *Prussia* - 55 Jc
Luckhoff, *O.F.S.* - 115 Fd
Lucknow, *Ontario* - 123 Hd
Lucknow, *United Provs.* 86 Db
Luco, *Spain* - 38 Dd
Luçon, *France* - 32 Dd
Ludawici, *Georgia* - 131 He
Ludbreg, *Croatia* - 66 Bc
Lüdenscheid, *Prussia* - 54 Cd
Lüderitz, *S.-W. Africa* - 114 Ac
Ludgershall, *England* - 14 Cd
Ludhiana, *Punjab* - 83 Fc
Ludima, *Fr. Eq. Africa* - 109 Bb
Lüdinghausen, *Prussia* - 54 Cd
Ludington, *Michigan* - 122 Ec
Ludlow, *England* - 14 Bb
Ludlow, *Vermont* - 128 Bb
Ludus, *Transylvania* - 67 Jc
Ludvika, *Sweden* - 50 Eb
Ludwigsburg, *Württemberg* 58 Dc
Ludwigshafen, *Saar Palatinate* - - 58 Cb
Ludwigslust, *Mecklenburg* 55 Gb
Ludza, *Latvia* - 49 Dc
Luebo, *Belg. Congo* - 109 Dc
Luena, *N. Rhodesia* - 112 Bb
Lu-feng, *China* - 95 Ee
Lufkin, *Texas* - 133 Ee
Luga and R., *U.S.S.R.* 74 Dd
Lugano and L., *Switz.* - 43 Gd
Lugari, *Kenya* - 110 Dc
Lugasi, *Central India* - 86 Cc
Lugg, R., *England* - 14 Bb
Lugh Ferrandi, *Ital. Somaliland* - - 108 De
Lugny, *France* - 35 Ga
Lugo, *Italy* - 63 Fc
Lugo and prov., *Spain* - 36 Ca
Lugoj, *Romania* - 67 Gd
Lugufu, *Tang. Terr.* - 111 Bf
Luguru, *Tang. Terr.* - 110 De
Lugus, I., *Philippines* - 99 Fb
Luhaiya, *Yemen* - 78 Lg
Lu-hwang I., *China* - 94 Fd
Lui-chow & Pen., *China* 95 Ce
Luis, Sa. des, *Argentina* 146 Be
Luisa, *Belgian Congo* - 109 Dc
Luishia, *Belgian Congo* - 109 Ed
Lujan, *Argentina* - 146 Be
Lujan, *Argentina* - 148 Ea
Lujan, *Paraguay* - 146 Dd
Luka, *Bosnia* - 68 Bb
Lukafu, *Belgian Congo* - 109 Ed
Lukata, *Belgian Congo* - 109 Eb
Lukchun, *Sinkiang* - 84 Fb
Lukenie, R., *Belg. Congo* 109 Cb
Lukolela, *Belgian Congo* 109 Cb
Lukonzolwa, *Belg. Congo* 109 Ec
Lukosi, *S. Rhodesia* - 113 Bb
Lukovit, *Bulgaria* - 69 Fd
Łuków, *Poland* - 60 Gc
Lukoyanov, *U.S.S.R.* - 75 Gd
Lukumburu, *Tang. Terr.* 111 Dh
Lukunga, *Belg. Congo* - 109 Bc
Lula, *Mississippi* - 130 Cc
Lulanguru, *Tang. Terr.* 111 Cf
Luleå, *Sweden* - 44 Ef
Lüleburgaz, *Turkey* - 72 Ea
Luling, *Texas* - 133 Df
Lulonga & R., *Belg. Congo* 109 Ca
Lulua, R., *Belg. Congo* - 109 Dc
Luluabourg, *Belg. Congo* 109 Dc
Lulworth, Mt., *W. Aust.* 152 Bd
Lumara, *Boeroe I., N.I.* 99 Gd
Lumberton, *Mississippi* - 130 De
Lumberton, *New Mexico* 135 Kd
Lumberton, *N. Carolina* 131 Jc
Lumbi, *Angola* - 109 Bc
Lumbier, *Spain* - 38 Db
Lumbo, *Mozambique* - 112 Db
Lumbres, *France* - 30 Ea
Lumbwa, *Kenya* - 110 Dd
Lumding, *Assam* - 88 Db
Lumesule, *Tang. Terr.* - 111 Fj
Lumpkin, *Georgia* - 131 Fd
Lumsden, *New Zealand* 159 Bf
Lumtong, *Burma* - 88 Ea
Lumu, *Celébes* - 99 Ed
Luna, *Arkansas* - 130 Cd
Luna, *Spain* - - 38 Eb
Lunavada, *Gujarat States* 85 Dc
Lund, *Sweden* - 51 Cg
Lundby, *Denmark* - 45 Ec
Lündenburg, *Moravia* - 57 Be
Lundi, R., *S. Rhodesia* - 113 Dc
Lundy, I., *England* - 17 Ba
Lune, R., *England* - 18 Bb
Lüneburg, *Prussia* - 54 Fb
Lüneburger Heide, *Prussia* 54 Eb
Lunel, *France* - 35 Gd
Lunen, *Prussia* - 54 Cd
Lunenburg, *Nova Scotia* 120 Cd
Luneville, *France* - 31 Jc
Lunga, *Belg. Congo* - 109 Cb
Lung-an, *China* - 94 Bc
Lungau, dist., *Austria* - 59 Hd
Lung-chow, *China* - 95 Ce
Lunghua, *Manchuria* - 96 Bc
Lungkiang, prov., *Manchuria* - - 96 Db
Lungleh, *Assam* - 88 Dc
Lung-mên, pass, *China* - 94 Cb
Lungmenchen, *Manchuria* 96 Db
Lungro, *Italy* - 65 Cc
Luning, *Nevada* - 134 Db
Łuniniec - - 60 Jb
Lunsklip, *Transvaal* - 115 Hb
Lunz, *Austria* - 59 Kd
Luofu, *Belgian Congo* - 109 Eb
Luoza, *N. Rhodesia* - 112 Ab
Luozi, *Belgian Congo* - 109 Bc
Lupei, *Manchuria* - 96 Cc
Lupembe, *Tang. Terr.* - 111 Dh
Lupiro, *Tang. Terr.* - 111 Eh
Luras, *Sardinia* - 64 Jf
Luraville, *Florida* - 131 Ge
Luray, *Virginia* - 129 Ec
Lure, *France* - 31 Jd
Lurgan, *N. Ireland* - 26 Dc
Luribay, *Bolivia* - 146 Bb
Lurio & B., *Mozambique* 112 Db
Luristan, *Persia* - 79 Ec
Lury, *France* - 30 Ed
Lusahunga, *Tang. Terr.* 110 Be
Lusaka, *N. Rhodesia* - 112 Ac
Lusambo, *Belg. Congo* - 109 Db
Lusancay Is., *New Guinea* 156 Dc
Lusên, *Albania* - 70 Bb
Lushai Hills, *Assam* - 88 Dc
Lu-shi, *China* - 94 Dc
Lushnjë, *Albania* - 70 Ac
Lushoto, *Tang. Terr.* - 111 Ef
Lusikisiki, *Cape Prov.* - 115 He
Luso, *Portugal* - 37 Bb
Lussac-les-Chateaux, *France* 34Ca
Lussac-les-Eglises, *France* 34 Da
Lussin - - - 63 Jc
Lussino, C. di - 63 Jc
Lussinpiccolo - 63 Jc
Luster, *Norway* - 46 Dc
Lusuna, *Belg. Congo* - 109 Eb
Luther, *Oklahoma* - 133 Dc
Lu-tien, *China* - 94 Bd
Luton, *England* - 15 Dc
Lutsen, *Minnesota* - 132 Db
Lutsk (Łuck), *Ukraine* - 60 Hc
Lutterworth, *England* - 14 Cb
Luverne, *Alabama* - 130 Ee
Luverne, *Minnesota* - 132 Ad
Luvungi, *Belg. Congo* - 109 Eb
Luwero, *Uganda* - 110 Cc
Luwingu, *N. Rhodesia* - 112 Bb
Luxembourg, prov., *Belg.* 29 De
Luxembourg, *Luxembourg* 29 Ee
Luxembourg, Grand Duchy of, *Europe* - - 29 De
Luxor, *Egypt* - 107 Jf
Luz, *France* - 34 Ce
Luzarches, *France* - 30 Eb
Luzern (Lucerne), and canton, *Switzerland* - 42 Fb
Luzinga, *Uganda* - 110 Cc
Lūžna, *Latvia* - 49 Ac
Luzon, I., *Philippines* - 95 Ff
Luzy, *France* - 31 Fe
Luzzi, *Italy* - 65 Cc
Lvov (Lwów), *Ukraine* - 60 Hd
Lwan, *China* - 94 Eb
Lwan-ho, R., *Manchuria* 96 Bc
Lwów (Lvov), *Ukraine* - 60 Hd
Lyallpur, *Punjab* - 82 Ec
Lybster, *Scotland* - 24 Ee
Lyck & R. - - 56 Gc
Lyckeby, *Sweden* - 51 Ef
Lycksele, *Sweden* - 48 Bd
Lydd, *England* - 15 Ee
Lydda, *Palestine* - 80 Bd
Lydenburg, *Transvaal* - 115 Jb
Lydham, *England* - 14 Ba
Lydney, *England* - 14 Bc
Lyduvenai, *Lithuania* - 49 Bd
Lye, *England* - - 14 Bb
Lyell, Mt., *Brit. Columbia* 124 Fd
Lyell, Mt., *California* - 134 Dc
Lyell Ra., *New Zealand* 159 Dd
Lyle, *Minnesota* - 132 Cd
Lyme B., *England* - 14 Ae
Lyme Regis, *England* - 14 Be
Lymington, *England* - 14 Ce
Lynchburg, *Virginia* - 129 Ed
Lynden, *Washington* - 136 Ba
Lyndhurst, *England* - 14 Ce
Lyndhurst, *Queensland* - 153 Bc
Lyndhurst, *S. Australia* 154 Bb
Lyndon, *Kansas* - 133 Ea
Lyngby, *Denmark* - 45 Fc
Lyngdal, *Norway* - 47 Df
Lyngör, *Norway* - 47 Ff
Lynn, *Massachusetts* - 128 Cb
Lynton, *England* - 17 Ca
Lyö, I., *Denmark* - 45 Dc
Lyon, *Montana* - 136 Hc
Lyonnais, prov., *France* 35 Fb
Lyonnais, Mts. du, *France* 35 Gb
Lyons, *Colorado* - 135 La
Lyons, *France* - 35 Gb
Lyons, *Georgia* - 131 Gd
Lyons, *Kansas* - 133 Ca
Lyons, *Nebraska* - 133 Ae
Lyons, *New York* - 123 Kd
Lyons-la-Foret, *France* - 30 Db
Lys, R., *Belgium* - 29 Bd
Lysebota, *Norway* - 47 Ce
Lysekil, *Sweden* - 50 Ad
Lyss, *Switzerland* - 42 Db
Lystrup, *Denmark* - 45 Db
Lysva, *U.S.S.R.* - 74 Kd
Lytham St Annes, *Eng.* 18 Ac
Lyttelton, *New Zealand* 159 De
Lytton, *Brit. Columbia* - 124 Ed
Ma'adh, *Trans-Jordan* - 80 Db
Ma'ain, *Trans-Jordan* - 80 Dd
Maalselven, *Norway* - 48 Cb
Ma'an, *Trans-Jordan* - 78 Cc
Maas, *Eire* - - 26 Bb
Maas, R., *Holland* - 29 Bc
Maastricht, *Holland* - 29 Dd
Maaza Plat., *Egypt* - 107 He
Maba, *Halmahera, N.I.* 99 Gc
Mabe, *New Guinea* - 156 Bc
Mabein, *Burma* - 92 Ca
Mabenga, *Belg. Congo* - 109 Cb
Mabil, *Ethiopia* - 108 Cc
Mablethorpe, *England* - 19 Ed
Mabokoni, *Kenya* - 110 Dd
Mabonguere, *Mozambique* 113 Ec
Mabou, *Nova Scotia* - 120 Ec
Mabrouk, *Fr. W. Africa* 104 Dc
Mabton, *Washington* - 136 Cb
Mabuli, *Cape Prov.* - 115 Fb
Macaaca, *Eritrea* - 108 Dc
McAdam, *New Brunswick* 120 Bd
Macahe, *Brazil* - 147 Gc
Macahyba, *Brazil* - 143 Gd
Macajalar B., *Philippines* 99 Fb
McAlester, *Oklahoma* - 133 Ec
MacAlpine L., *N.-W.T.* 118 Jc
Macao (Portuguese), *China* 95 De
Macapa, *Brazil* - 142 Db
Macas, *Ecuador* - 145 Bb
Macassane, *Mozambique* 115 Kc
Macaturing, mt., *Philippines* 99Fb
Macáu, *Brazil* - 143 Gd
Macaza, *Quebec* - 121 Ca
McCall, *Idaho* - 136 Ec
McCallum, *Alaska* - 125 Le
McCammon, *Idaho* - 136 Gd
McCann, *California* - 134 Aa
McCarthy, *Alaska* - 125 Lf
MacCarthy, *Gambia* - 104 Ab
McCarty, *Alaska* - 125 Kd
Macclenny, *Florida* - 131 Ge
Macclesfield, *England* - 18 Bd
Macclesfield Str., *N.I.* - 98 Cd
McClintock Chan., *N.-W. Terr.* - 118 Jb
McCloud, *California* - 134 Ba
McClouds Pk., *Montana* 136 Gb
McClure Str., *N.-W. T.* 118 Fb
McComb, *Mississippi* - 130 Ce
McConnellsburg, *Pennsyl.* 129 Fc
McConnelsville, *Ohio* - 129 Dc
McConnico, *Arizona* - 134 Gd
McCool, *Mississippi* - 130 Dd
McCormick, *S. Carolina* 131 Gd
McCracken, *Kansas* - 133 Ca
McDermitt, *Nevada* - 134 Ea
McDonald I., *Antarctica* 160 —
McDonald L., *Montana* 136 Fa
Macdonald, L., *W. Aust.* 152 Dc
Macdonald Ra., *W. Aust.* 152 Cb
McDonnell, *Queensland* - 153 Bb
Macdonnell Ras., *N. Terr., Australia* - - 150 Ec

Maladeta, Mte., *Spain* 39 Fb
Mala Fatra, *Slovakia* 57 Dd
Malaga, *New Mexico* 135 Me
Malaga & prov., *Spain* 40 Fc
Malaga B., *Spain* 40 Fc
Malagarasi, *Tang. Terr.* 111 Bf
Malagas, *Cape Prov.* 114 Dg
Malagon, *Spain* 41 Ca
Malagon, Sa. de, *Spain* 38 Ad
Malahide, *Eire* 27 De
Malaimbady, *Madagascar* 112 Dd
Malaita, I., *Solomon Is.* 157 Dd
Malakal, *A.-E. Sudan* 108 Bd
Malakand, *N.-W.F.P.* 82 Ea
Mala Kavela, *Croatia* 63 Kc
Malakoff, *Algeria* 102 Ea
Malakou, *Manchuria* 96 Dc
Mala Krsna, *Serbia* 68 Fb
Malalaling, *Bechuanaland* 114 Eb
Malamala, *Mozambique* 113 Dd
Malamocco, *Italy* 63 Gb
Malampaya B., *Philippines* 99 Ea
Malangali, *Tang. Terr.* 111 Dh
Malange, *Angola* 109 Cc
Malangen, *Norway* 48 Cb
Malango, *Kenya* 110 Fd
Malanut, *Philippines* 99 Eb
Malapamba, *Tang. Terr.* 111 Bf
Malapane 57 Dc
Malar L., *Sweden* 50 Fc
Malargue, *Argentina* 148 Cb
Malaspina, mt., *Philippines* 99 Fa
Malathriá, *Greece* 70 Dc
Malatya, *Turkey* 78 Cb
Malaut, *Punjab* 83 Fc
Malayagiri Mt., *Eastern States* 87 Fe
Malayal, *Philippines* 99 Fb
Malaya Vishera, *U.S.S.R.* 74 Ed
Malaybalay, *Philippines* 99 Gb
Malayir, *Persia* 79 Ec
Malay States, *Asia* 98 Bc
Malazkirt, *Turkey* 78 Db
Malbaie, La, *Quebec* 123 Nb
Malchin, *Mecklenburg* 55 Hb
Malchow, *Mecklenburg* 55 Hb
Malcolm, *W. Australia* 152 Cd
Malda, *Bengal* 88 Bb
Malden, *Massachusetts* 128 Cb
Malden, *Missouri* 130 Cb
Malden I., *Line Is.* 157 Hd
Maldive Is., *Indian Oc.* 81 Cj
Mal di Ventre I., *Sardinia* 64 Hg
Maldon, *England* 15 Ec
Maldonado and dep., *Uruguay* 146 De
Male, *Italy* 62 Ea
Maléa C., *Greece* 71 Eg
Malegaon, *Bombay* 90 Ba
Malek, *A.-E. Sudan* 108 Bd
Malé Karpaty, *Slovakia* 66 Ca
Malekula, I., *New Hebrides* 157De
Malema Utete, *Mozambique* 112Cb
Malemba, *Kenya* 110 Ee
Maleme, *Crete* 71 Gj
Máléme, *Fr. W. Africa* 104 Ad
Målerås, *Sweden* 51 Ef
Maler Kotla, *Punjab States* 83 Fc
Malesherbes, *France* 30 Ec
Malesína, *Greece* 71 Ee
Malestroit, *France* 32 Cc
Malevon Mts., *Greece* 71 Df
Malgrat, *Spain* 39 Hc
Malhargarh, *Gwalior* 85 Eb
Malheur L., *Oregon* 136 Dd
Malheur R., *Oregon* 136 Ed
Mali, *Fr. W. Africa* 104 Bd
Maliaic Gulf, *Greece* 71 De
Mal'i Cikës, *Albania* 70 Ac
Malicorne, *France* 30 Bd
Mali Jablanices, *Albania* 70 Bb
Malijai, *France* 33 Ba
Malik, L., *Albania* 70 Bc
Malili, *Celébes* 99 Fd
Målilla, *Sweden* 51 Ee
Malin and Hd., *Eire* 26 Ca
Malinau, *Borneo* 99 Ec
Malindang, mt., *Philippines* 99 Fb
Malindi, *Kenya* 110 Fe
Malindi, *S. Rhodesia* 113 Bb
Malines, *Belgium* 29 Cc
Malingping, *Java* 98 Ce
Malingsbo, *Sweden* 50 Ec
Malin More, *Eire* 26 Bb
Malinyi, *Tang. Terr.* 111 Eh
Malkangiri, *Orissa* 91 Fb
Malkapur, *Berar, C.P.* 86 Be
Malkara, *Turkey* 72 Db
Małkinia, *Poland* 60 Fb
Malko Trnovo, *Bulgaria* 69 Gd
Mallacoota and Inlet, *Victoria* 155 Fe
Mallaig, *Scotland* 22 Cb
Mallani, *Rajputana* 85 Cb
Mallaranny, *Eire* 25 Bb
Mallavalle, *E. Indies* 99 Eb
Mallawi, *Egypt* 107 He
Malleco, prov., *Chile* 148 Bb
Malles, *Italy* 62 Ea
Mallia, G. of, *Crete* 71 Jj
Mallina, *W. Australia* 152 Bc
Malling, *Denmark* 45 Db
Mallmitz 55 Ld
Malloch, C., *N.-W.T.* 118 Ga
Mallorca (Majorca), I., *Balearic Is.* 39 He
Mallow, *Eire* 27 Bg
Mallwischken 56 Gb
Malmbäck, *Sweden* 51 De
Malmberget, *Sweden* 48 Dc
Malmedy, *Belgium* 29 Ed
Malmesbury, *Cape Prov.* 114 Cf
Malmesbury, *England* 14 Bc
Malmö, *Sweden* 51 Cg
Malmohus, län, *Sweden* 51 Cg
Malmyshsk, *U.S.S.R.* 96 Fb
Malmyzh, *U.S.S.R.* 74 Jd
Malo Arkhangelsk, *U.S.S.R.* 75Fe
Maloelap Is., *Marshall Is.* 157 Ec
Maloga, *Switzerland* 43 Jd
Malolo, I., *Fiji Is.* 157 Ok
Malolos, *Philippines* 95 Fg
Malomwe, *Mozambique* 112 Cb
Malone, *New York* 123 Lc
Malonga, *Belgian Congo* 109 Dd
Målöy, *Norway* 46 Ac
Malpartida de Caceres, *Spain* 37 Dc
Malpeque B., *Prince Edward I.* 120 Dc
Malpica de Bergantinos, *Spain* 36 Ba
Mālpils, *Latvia* 49 Cc
Malprabha R., *Bombay* 90 Bd
Malpura, *Rajputana* 85 Ea
Malta, I., *Mediterranean* 61 Eg
Maltahohe, *S.-W. Africa* 114 Bb
Malters, *Switzerland* 42 Fb
Malton, *England* 19 Db
Malu, Mt., *Sarawak* 99 Dc
Malung, *Sweden* 50 Cb
Malvaglia, *Switzerland* 43 Hd
Malvan, *Bombay* 90 Ac
Malvern, *Arkansas* 130 Bc
Malvern, Gt. and Little, *England* 14 Bb
Malvern Link, *England* 14 Bb
Malvern Wells, *England* 14 Bb
Malvina, *Quebec* 121 Eb
Malzieu, le, *France* 35 Fc
Mamabula, *Bechuanaland* 113 Bd
Mamadysh, *U.S.S.R.* 74 Jd
Mamantel, *Mexico* 139 Fd
Mamasiware, *New Guinea* 156 Ab
Mamba, *Tang. Terr.* 111 Bg
Mambali, *Tang. Terr.* 111 Cf
Mambanje, *S. Rhodesia* 113 Bb
Mambasa, *Belg. Congo* 110 Ac
Mambat, *Madras* 89 Bb
Mambi, *Fr. Eq. Africa* 109 Bb
Mambone, *Mozambique* 113 Fc
Mambrui, *Kenya* 110 Fe
Mambulu, *Angola* 109 Bc
Mamburao, *Philippines* 99 Ea
Mambuxa, *Mozambique* 113 Gb
Mamdot, *Punjab* 83 Fc
Mamers, *France* 30 Cc
Mamfe, *Nigeria* 105 Cd
Mammawemattawa, *Ontario* 122 Fa
Mammola, *Italy* 65 Cd
Mammoth, *Arizona* 135 He
Mammoth Cave, *Kentucky* 130 Fb
Mammoth Cave Nat. Park, *Kentucky* 130 Eb
Mammoth Hot Springs, *Wyoming* 136 Hc
Mamora, Foret de, *Morocco* 102Ab
Mamou, *Fr. W. Africa* 104 Bd
Mampawa, *Borneo* 98 Cc
Mampong, *Gold Coast* 104 De
Mamre, *Cape Prov.* 114 Cf
Mamturk Mts., *Eire* 25 Bb
Mamu, *Afghanistan* 79 Hd
Mamuju, *Celébes* 99 Ed
Man, *Fr. W. Africa* 104 Ce
Man, Isle of, *Irish Sea* 19 Gf
Mana, *Burma* 92 Ca
Mana, *Sumatra* 98 Bd
Manabi, prov., *Ecuador* 145 Ab
Manacapuru, *Brazil* 142 Bc
Manacor, *Balearic Is.* 39 Je
Manado, *Celébes* 99 Fc
Manage, *Belgium* 29 Cd
Managua & L., *Nicaragua* 140 Fe
Manama, *Bahrein I.* 79 Fd
Manamadurai, *Madras* 89 Cc
Manambondro, *Madagas'r* 112Ed
Mananano, *Madagascar* 112 Ed
Mananara, *Madagascar* 112 Fc
Mananjary, *Madagascar* 112 Ed
Manantenina, *Madagascar* 112 Ed
Manantoddy, *Madras* 89 Ab
Manaos, *Brazil* 142 Bc
Manapouri L., *New Zeal'd* 159 Af
Manasquan, *New Jersey* 129 Hb
Manass & R., *Sinkiang* 84 Fb
Manassa, *Colorado* 135 Kc
Manassas, *Virginia* 129 Fc
Manatuto, *Timor I., N.I.* 99 Ge
Manay, *Philippines* 99 Gb
Manbhum, *Bihar* 87 Gd
Mancelona, *Michigan* 122 Fc
Mancha, La, *Spain* 41 Cb
Mancha Real, *Spain* 41 Cc
Manche, *France* 32 Da
Manchester, *Connecticut* 128 Bc
Manchester, *England* 18 Bc
Manchester, *Iowa* 132 Dd
Manchester, *New Hamps.* 128 Cb
Manchester, *Ohio* 129 Cc
Manchester, *Tennessee* 130 Ec
Manchester, *Vermont* 128 Bb
Manchester, *Virginia* 129 Fd
Manchouli, *Manchuria* 96 Bb
Manchuria, *Asia* 93 Eb
Manciano, *Italy* 64 Ba
Mancos, *Colorado* 135 Jc
Manda, *Iringa, Tang. Terr.* 111Cg
Manda, *Southern, Tang. Terr.* 111 Dj
Mandagiri Hills, *Bihar* 87 Gc
Mandal, *Norway* 47 Df
Mandal Pass, *Afghanistan* 84 Cc
Mandalay, *Burma* 92 Cb
Mandalgarh, *Rajputana* 85 Eb
Mandalik, *Sinkiang* 84 Fc
Mandamados, *Lesbos I., Greece* 72 Dc
Mandan, *N. Dakota* 126 Ea
Mandapam, *Madras* 89 Cc
Mandar, C. & Gulf, *Celébes* 99 Ed
Mandara Mts., *Fr. Eq. Afr.* 105Dc
Mandarin, *Florida* 131 He
Mandas, *Sardinia* 64 Jg
Mandasor, *Gwalior* 85 Eb
Mandav Hills, *Western India* 85Cc
Mandawar, *Rajputana* 83 Ge
Mandello, *Italy* 62 Db
Mandera, *Tang. Terr.* 111 Fg
Mandeville, *Louisiana* 130 Ce
Mandhili, *Greece* 71 Ff
Mandi, *Punjab States* 83 Gc
Mandi, *Tibet* 83 Jc
Mandi Hissar, *Afghanistan* 82 Bc
Mandinga, *Panama* 140 Hf
Mandioli, I., *Nether. Indies* 99 Gd
Mandira, *Turkey* 72 Ea
Mandisha, *Egypt* 107 Gd
Mandjafa, *Fr. Eq. Africa* 105 Ec
Mandla, *Central Provs.* 86 Dd
Mandling, *Austria* 59 Hd
Mandö, I., *Denmark* 45 Bc
Mandor, *Rajputana* 82 Ee
Mándra, *Greece* 71 Ee
Mandra, *Punjab* 82 Eb
Mandritsara, *Madagascar* 112 Ec
Mandsaur, *Gwalior* 85 Eb
Mandurah, *W. Aust.* 152 Be
Manduria, *Italy* 65 Db
Mandvi, *Western India* 85 Bc
Mandya, *Mysore* 90 Ce
Manermiut, *Greenland* 9 Dd
Manetin, *Bohemia* 59 Hb
Manfalût, *Egypt* 107 He
Manfred, *Arkansas* 130 Bc
Manfred, *New S. Wales* 154 Dc
Manfredonia, *Italy* 64 Fb
Manfuha, *Arabia* 79 Ee
Manga, *Tang. Terr.* 111 Bg
Manga, *Tang. Terr.* 111 Fh
Mangabeiras, Sa. das, *Brazil* 143 Ed
Mangaia, I., *Cook Is.* 157 Hf
Mangalagiri, *Madras* 91 Ec
Mangaldai, *Assam* 88 Ca
Mangalia, *Romania* 69 Hd
Mangalore, *Madras* 90 Be
Mangalore, *Queensland* 153 Ce
Mangaon, *Bombay* 90 Ab
Mangareva, *Pacific Oc.* 149 Nh
Mangaweka, *New Zeal'd* 158 Ec
Manger, *Norway* 46 Ad
Mangfall Geb., *Bavaria* 59 Fd
Manggar, *Billiton I., N.I.* 98 Cd
Mangkalihat, C., *Borneo* 99 Ec
Mangla, *Kashmir* 83 Eb
Manglaralto, *Ecuador* 145 Ab
Mangles, Pta., *Colombia* 144 Ac
Mangnang, *Tibet* 83 Hc
Mango, *Tang. Terr.* 111 De
Mangoky R., *Madagascar* 112Dd
Mangole, I., *Nether. Indies* 99 Gd
Mangoloma, *Tang. Terr.* 111 Df
Mangonui, *New Zealand* 158 Da
Mangoupa, *Fr. Eq. Africa* 105 Fd
Mangrol, *Western India* 85 Bd
Mangrove Swamp, *Florida* 131 Nj
Manguali, *Mozambique* 113 Ed
Mangueira, L., *Brazil* 147 Ee
Mangum, *Oklahoma* 133 Cc
Mangura, *S. Rhodesia* 113 Da
Mangyshlak, pen., *Kazak* 75 Jg
Man-hao, *China* 95 Be
Manhattan, *Kansas* 133 Da
Manhiça, *Mozambique* 115 Kb
Manhoca, *Mozambique* 115 Kc
Manhuassu, *Brazil* 147 Gc
Maniago, *Italy* 63 Ga
Manicoré, *Brazil* 142 Bd
Manihari, *Bihar* 87 Gc
Manihiki, I., *Cook Is.* 157 He
Manikarchar, *Assam* 88 Bb
Manikganj (Dasara), *Bengal* 88Bc
Manikgarh (Rajura), *Hyderabad* 90 Db
Manikuagan R., *Quebec* 120 Aa
Manila & B., *Phillipines* 95 Fg
Manilla, *New S. Wales* 155 Gb
Manimbaya, C., *Çelébes* 99 Ed
Maninda, *Belg. Congo* 109 Cb
Maninian, *Fr. W. Africa* 104 Cd
Manipa I. and Str., *Netherlands Indies* 99 Gd
Manipur and R., *Assam* 88 Db
Manisa, *Turkey* 78 Ab
Manises, *Spain* 38 Ee
Manistee, *Michigan* 122 Ec
Manistique, *Michigan* 122 Eb
Manitoba, prov., *Canada* 118 Kf
Manitoba L., *Manitoba* 124 Kd
Manitou Is., *Michigan* 122 Ec
Manitou L., *Ontario* 122 Ba
Manitoulin I., *Ontario* 122 Gc
Manitowoc, *Wisconsin* 132 Fc
Maniwaki, *Quebec* 121 Ca
Maniyachi, *Madras* 89 Bc
Manizales, *Colombia* 144 Ab
Manja, *Madagascar* 112 Dd
Manjhand, *Sind* 85 Ab
Manjra R., *Hyderabad* 90 Cb
Manjulik, *Turkey* 78 Cb
Mank, *Austria* 59 Kc
Mankaiana, *Swaziland* 115 Jc
Mankarnacha, mt., *Eastern States* 87 Fe
Mankato, *Kansas* 133 Ca
Mankato, *Minnesota* 132 Bc
Mankheri, *Bihar* 87 Fd
Mankono, *Fr. W. Africa* 104 Ce
Mankovo, *U.S.S.R.* 96 Ba
Mankulam, *Ceylon* 89 Dc
Manle, *Burma* 88 Eb
Manlleu, *Spain* 39 Hb
Manly, *New S. Wales* 155 Gc
Manmad, *Bombay* 90 Ba
Mannahill, *S. Australia* 154 Cc
Mannar, *Ceylon* 89 Cc
Mannar, Gulf of, *Madras-Ceylon* 89 Cc
Mannargudi, *Madras* 89 Cb
Mannheim, *Baden* 58 Cb
Mannin B., *Eire* 25 Ac
Manning, *Iowa* 132 Be
Manning, *S. Carolina* 131 Hd
Mannington, *W. Virginia* 129 Dc
Manningtree, *England* 15 Ec
Mannu, C., *Sardinia* 64 Hf
Mannu, R., *Sardinia* 64 Hg
Mannum, *S. Australia* 154 Bc
Mano, *Sierra Leone* 104 Be
Manoel Vieira, *Brazil* 142 Be
Manoharpur, *Rajputana* 83 Fe
Manohar Thana, *Rajputana* 86Bc
Manokwari, *New Guinea* 156 Ab
Manolás, *Greece* 71 Ce
Manombo, *Madagascar* 112 Dd
Manor Hamilton, *Eire* 26 Bc
Manosque, *France* 33 Ab
Manpur, *Central India* 85 Ec
Manpura I., *Bengal* 88 Cc
Manresa, *Spain* 39 Gc
Mans, Le, *France* 30 Cc
Man Salka, *Finland* 48 Hd
Mansehra, *N.-W.F.P.* 82 Ea
Mansel I., *N.-W. Terr.* 119 Nd
Man Selkä, *Finland* 48 Hc
Mansfield, *England* 18 Cd
Mansfield, *Louisiana* 130 Bd
Mansfield, *Massachusetts* 128 Cb
Mansfield, *Ohio* 129 Cb
Mansfield, *Pennsylvania* 129 Fb
Mansfield, *Victoria* 155 Ed
Mansfield Mt., *Vermont* 128 Ba
Mansilla, *Spain* 38 Cb
Mansle, *France* 34 Cb
Manson, *Iowa* 132 Bd
Mansour, El, *Algeria* 102 Df
Mansoura, *Algeria* 103 Ga
Mansourah, *Syria* 80 Da
Mansur, *Ital.Somaliland* 108 Gf
Manta, *Ecuador* 145 Ab
Mantaro, R., *Peru* 145 Bd
Manteo, *N. Carolina* 131 Lc
Mantes, *France* 30 Dc
Manthani, *Hyderabad* 90 Db
Manti, *Utah* 135 Hb
Mantilla, *Argentina* 146 Dd
Mantua (Mantova), *Italy* 62 Eb
Mäntyluoto, *Finland* 48 Df
Manu, *Peru* 145 Cd
Manua Is., *Samoa Is.* 157 Ge
Manuel Rodrigue, I., *Chile* 148 Ae
Manui, I., *Neth. Indies* 99 Fd
Manujan, *Persia* 79 Gd
Manus, I., *Admiralty Is.* 156 Db
Manvanga, *Belg. Congo* 109 Bb
Manvi, *Hyderabad* 90 Cd
Manwat, *Hyderabad* 90 Cb
Manwe, *Burma* 88 Fb
Many, *Louisiana* 130 Be
Manyakaze, *Mozambique* 112 Bd
Manyangau, mt., *S. Rhod.* 113 Ca
Manyara, L., *Tang. Terr.* 110 Ee
Manyas & Golü, *Turkey* 72 Eb
Manych, L. & R., *U.S.S.R.* 75 Gf
Manyisa, *Mozambique* 112 Be
Manyoni, *Tang. Terr.* 111 Df
Manyovu, *Tang. Terr.* 111 Af
Manzai, *N.-W.F.P.* 82 Db
Manzala L., *Egypt* 107 Hc
Manzanares, *Spain* 41 Ca
Manzanera, *Spain* 38 Ed
Manzanillo, *Cuba* 140 Bb
Manzanillo, *Mexico* 138 Cd
Manzano Pk., *New Mexico* 135 Kd
Manzanola, *Colorado* 135 Mb
Manzat, *France* 34 Eb
Manze L., *Mozambique* 112 Bc
Mao, *Fr. Eq. Africa* 105 Ec
Maoemere, *Flores I., N.I.* 99 Fe
Maopa, *New Guinea* 156 Dd
Maopora I., *Nether. Indies* 99 Ge
Maouin Pen., *Tunisia* 103 Ka
Mapae, *Mozambique* 113 Dd
Mapalma, *Belg. Congo* 109 Da
Mapia Is., *Pacific Oc.* 156 Aa
Mapimi, *Mexico* 138 Db
Mapira, *N. Rhodesia* 112 Ab
Mapire, *Venezuela* 144 Cb
Maple Creek, *Saskatch.* 124 He
Mapleton, *Iowa* 132 Bd
Mapleton, *Minnesota* 132 Cd
Mapleton, *N. Dakota* 132 Ab
Mapoon, *Queensland* 153 Bb
Mapuera, R., *Brazil* 142 Cc
Mapumulo, *Natal* 115 Jd
Maqainama, *Arabia* 79 Ee
Maqna, *Arabia* 78 Bd
Maquassi, *Transvaal* 115 Fc
Maquela do Zombo, *Angola* 109Cc
Maquinchao, *Argentina* 148 Cc
Maquoketa, *Iowa* 132 Dd
Mar, Sa. do, *Brazil* 147 Fd
Mara, *Borneo* 99 Ec
Mara, *Celébes* 99 Fd
Mara, *Kenya* 110 Dd
Marab, R., *Eritrea* 108 Cc
Maraba, *Brazil* 143 Ed
Marabahan, *Borneo* 99 Dd
Maracá, I. de, *Brazil* 143 Db
Maracaibo and L. de, *Venezuela* 144 Ba
Maracaju, Sa. de, *Paraguay* 146Dc
Maracana, *Brazil* 143 Ec
Maracassume, *Brazil* 143 Ec
Maracay, *Venezuela* 144 Ca
Marada, *Libya* 106 Bd
Maradi, *Fr. W. Africa* 105 Cc
Maragheh, *Persia* 79 Eb
Maragogy, *Brazil* 143 Gd
Marahu, *Brazil* 143 Ge
Maraile, *Ital. Somaliland* 108 De
Maraisburg, *Cape Prov.* 115 Fe
Marajo, I., *Brazil* 143 Dc
Maraker, *Sweden* 50 Ga
Marakwet, *Kenya* 110 Dc
Maralal, *Kenya* 110 Ec
Maral-bashi, *Sinkiang* 84 Dc
Maramasiki, I., *Solomon Is.* 156Kg

Maramba, *Tang. Terr.* 111 Ff
Marambitsy B., *Madag'r* 112 Ec
Maramures, *Transylvania* 67 Hb
Maranchon, *Spain* 38 Cc
Marand, *Persia* 79 Eb
Maranda, *N. Rhodesia* 112 Bb
Marandellas, *S. Rhodesia* 113 Db
Maranguape, *Brazil* 143 Gc
Maranhão, state, *Brazil* 143 Ec
Marano L., *Italy* 63 Hb
Marañon (Amazonas), R., *Peru* 145 Cb
Marans, *France* 32 Ed
Maraop, *N. Borneo* 99 Eb
Marapi, Mt., *Sumatra* 98 Bd
Marapok, Mt., *N. Borneo* 99 Ec
Maras, *Turkey* 78 Cb
Mărăşeşti, *Romania* 69 Gc
Maratea, *Italy* 64 Fd
Marathón, *Greece* 71 Ee
Marathon, *Queensland* 153 Bd
Marathon I., *Greece* 71 Dg
Maravilha, *Brazil* 145 Dc
Marawa, *Libya* 106 Cb
Marazion, *England* 17 Ac
Marbæk, *Denmark* 45 Ed
Marbau, *Sumatra* 98 Ac
Marbella, *Spain* 40 Fc
Marble, *Colorado* 135 Kb
Marble Bar, *W. Australia* 152 Bc
Marble Canyon, *Arizona* 135 Hc
Marble Falls, *Texas* 133 Ce
Marble Hall, *Transvaal* 115 Hb
Marblemount, *Washington* 136 Ca
Marble Rocks, *Cent. Provs.* 86 Cd
Marbleton, *Quebec* 121 Eb
Marburg, *Prussia* 54 De
Marcali, *Hungary* 66 Cc
Marceline, *Missouri* 130 Ba
Marcellino, *Brazil* 145 Da
Marcenat, *France* 34 Eb
March, *England* 15 Ea
Marchagee, *W. Australia* 152 Be
Marche, *Belgium* 29 Dd
Marche, *Italy* 63 Gd
Marche, old prov., *France* 34 Da
Marchena, *Galapagos Is.* 145 Eg
Marchena, *Spain* 40 Eb
Mar Chica, *Span. Morocco* 102 Cb
Mar Chiquita, *Argentina* 146 Ce
Marcianise, *Italy* 64 Eb
Marco, *Florida* 131 Nh
Marcoing, *France* 30 Fa
Marcus, *Washington* 136 Da
Marcus I., *Pacific Oc.* 157 Ca
Marcy, Mt., *New York* 123 Lc
Mardan, *N.-W.F.P.* 82 Ea
Mar del Plata, *Argentina* 148 Eb
Mardin, *Turkey* 78 Db
Mardis, *Egypt* 107 He
Maré, I., *Loyalty Is.* 157 Df
Maree, L., *Scotland* 22 Ca
Mareeba, *Queensland* 153 Bc
Marekta, *Manchuria* 96 Ca
Marenberg, *Slovenia* 63 Ka
Marendego, *Tang. Terr.* 111 Fh
Marengo, *Algeria* 102 Fa
Marengo, *Iowa* 132 Ce
Marengo, *Wisconsin* 132 Db
Marennes, *France* 32 De
Marereni, *Kenya* 110 Fe
Mareth, *Tunisia* 103 Kc
Marettimo I., *Italy* 65 Fg
Mareuil, *France* 32 Dd
Margao, *Goa* 90 Ad
Margaree, *Nova Scotia* 120 Ec
Margaretivo, *U.S.S.R.* 96 Ec
Margaretville, *Nova Scotia* 120Cd
Margarita, *Venezuela* 144 Da
Margarítes (Elouthorna), *Crete* 71 Hj
Margate, *England* 15 Fd
Margate, *Natal* 115 Je
Margelan, *Uzbek* 84 Cb
Margeride, Mtgne de la, *France* 35 Fc
Margha, *Afghanistan* 82 Cb
Margherita, *Assam* 88 Ea
Margherita, *It. Somaliland* 108 Gf
Margherita, Sta., *Italy* 62 Dc
Margherita di Savoia, *Italy* 64 Gb
Marghita, *Transylvania* 67 Hb
Marginea, *Romania* 67 Hd
Margita, *Voyvodina* 67 Gd
Marguareis, Pta., *Italy* 62 Bc
Marhoum, *Algeria* 102 Db
Mari, *U.S.S.R.* 74 Hd
Maria, *Spain* 38 Ec
Maria & Sa. de, *Spain* 41 Dc
Maria I., *Tasmania* 155 Kh
Maria Is., *Pacific Oc.* 157 Hf
Maria Cleofas, I., *Mexico* 138 Cc
Mariager, *Denmark* 45 Cb
Mariager Fd., *Denmark* 45 Db
Mariakani, *Kenya* 111 Fe
Maria Madre, I., *Mexico* 138 Cc
Maria Magdalena, I., *Mexico* 138 Cc
Mariampole, *Lithuania* 49 Bd
Mariana, *Cuba* 140 Ab
Marianas Is., *Pacific Oc.* 157 Bb
Marianna, *Arkansas* 130 Cc
Marianna, *Florida* 130 Fe
Marianské Lázně, *Bohemia* 60 Bc
Maria Pia, *Mozambique* 113 Fa
Marias and R., *Montana* 136 Ha
Marias Pass, *Montana* 136 Ga
Mariato, Pta., *Panama* 140 Gf
Maria Van Diemen, C., *New Zealand* 158 Da
Marib, *Yemen* 78 Lg
Maribo, *Denmark* 45 Ed
Maribor, *Slovenia* 66 Ac
Marichi, *Kenya* 110 Dc
Maricopa & Mts., *Arizona* 135 Ge
Maridi, *A.-E. Sudan* 108 Ae
Marie Byrd Ld., *Antarctica* 160 —
Mariefred, *Sweden* 50 Gc
Marie Galante, I., *Leeward Is.* 140 Kg
Mariel, *Cuba* 140 Ab
Marienberg, *New Guinea* 156 Cb
Marienberg, *Saxony* 55 Je
Marienburg 56 Db
Mariental, *S.-W. Africa* 114 Cb
Marienwerder 56 Cc
Mariestad, *Sweden* 50 Cd
Marietta, *Georgia* 131 Fd
Marietta, *Ohio* 129 Dc
Marietta, *Oklahoma* 133 Dd
Marietta, *S. Carolina* 131 Gc
Marieville, *Quebec* 121 Db
Mariguana, I., *Bahamas* 140 Cb
Mariha, *Brazil* 147 Ec
Mari Indus, *Punjab* 82 Db
Marille, *Ital. Somaliland* 108 Gf
Marin, *Spain* 36 Bb
Marina, *Dalmatia* 68 Bc
Marina de Ravenna, *Italy* 63 Gc
Marina Fall, *Br. Guiana* 144 Eb
Marinduque, I., *Philippines* 99 Fa
Marine City, *Michigan* 122 Gd
Marinella, *Sardinia* 64 Jf
Marineo, *Sicily* 65 Gg
Marines, *France* 30 Db
Marinette, *Wisconsin* 132 Ec
Maringues, *France* 35 Fb
Marinha Grande, *Portugal* 37 Ac
Marino, *Italy* 64 Cb
Marino di Campo, *Italy* 62 Ee
Marion, *Alabama* 130 Ed
Marion, *Arkansas* 130 Cc
Marion, *Illinois* 130 Db
Marion, *Indiana* 129 Bb
Marion, *Iowa* 132 Dd
Marion, *Kansas* 133 Da
Marion, *Kentucky* 130 Db
Marion, *Montana* 136 Fa
Marion, *N. Carolina* 131 Gc
Marion, *Ohio* 129 Cb
Marion, *S. Carolina* 131 Jc
Marion, *Virginia* 129 Dd
Marion Downs, *Queensl'd* 153 Ad
Marionville, *Missouri* 130 Bb
Mariposa, *California* 134 Dc
Maritsa, R., *Greece, etc.* 72 Cb
Maritzani, *Cape Prov.* 115 Fc
Mariupol, *Ukraine* 75 Ff
Marivan, *Persia* 79 Eb
Mâriya, *Egypt* 106 Mh
Märjamaa, *Estonia* 49 Cb
Marka, *Mozambique* 113 Fa
Markapur, *Madras* 90 Dd
Markaryd, *Sweden* 51 Cf
Market Bosworth, *Eng.* 14 Ca
Market Deeping, *Eng.* 15 Da
Market Drayton, *Eng.* 18 Be
Market Harborough, *Eng.* 15 Db
Markethill, *N. Ireland* 26 Dc
Market Rasen, *England* 19 Dd
Market Weighton, *Eng.* 19 Dc
Märk Friedland 55 Mb
Markham, *Ontario* 121 Ac
Markham, Mt., *Antarctica* 160 —
Markham Ra., *New Guinea* 156Dc
Markinch, *Scotland* 23 Ed
Markleeville, *California* 134 Cb
Markópoulon, *Greece* 71 Ef
Marksbury, *England* 14 Bd
Marksshtadt, *U.S.S.R.* 75 He
Markstay, *Ontario* 123 Hb
Marks Tey, *England* 15 Ec
Marksville, *Louisiana* 130 Be
Markt, *Bavaria* 58 Db
Marktbreit, *Bavaria* 58 Eb
Markt Erlbach, *Bavaria* 58 Eb
Marktl, *Bavaria* 59 Gc
Marlboro, *Massachusetts* 128 Cb
Marlborough, *England* 14 Cd
Marlborough, *Queensland* 153 Cd
Marlborough, prov., *New Zealand* 159 Dd
Marle, *France* 31 Fb
Marlette, *Michigan* 122 Gd
Marlin, *Texas* 133 De
Marlo, *Victoria* 155 Fe
Marloie, *Belgium* 29 Dd
Marlow, *England* 15 Dc
Marlow, *Oklahoma* 133 Dc
Marly-le-Roi, *France* 30 Dc
Marmagao, *Goa* 90 Ad
Marmande, *France* 34 Cc
Marmara & I., *Turkey* 72 Eb
Marmara, Sea of, *Turkey* 72 Fb
Marmarica, *Libya* 106 Dc
Marmarice, *Turkey* 78 Ab
Mar Menor, *Spain* 41 Fc
Marmolada, mt., *Italy* 63 Fa
Marmolejo, *Spain* 40 Fa
Marnay, *France* 31 Hd
Marne, dep. & R., *France* 31 Gc
Marnia, *Algeria* 102 Db
Marnoo, *Victoria* 154 Dd
Maroa, *Madagascar* 112 Ec
Maroantsetra, *Madagascar* 112 Fc
Marofototra, *Madagascar* 112 Ec
Marol, *Kashmir* 83 Ga
Maromanga, *Madagascar* 112 Ed
Maromeu, *Mozambique* 112 Cc
Maroni, *Comoro Is.* 112 Db
Maroni, R., *Fr. Guiana-Suriname* 142 Db
Maronia, *Greece* 72 Cb
Maros, *Celébes* 99 Ed
Maroua, *Fr. Eq. Africa* 105 Dc
Marova, *N. Rhodesia* 112 Ac
Marquesas Is., *Pacific Oc.* 157 Kd
Marquesas Keys, *Florida* 131 Mj
Marquette, *Michigan* 122 Eb
Marquez, *Texas* 133 De
Marquise, *France* 30 Da
Marra, Jeb., *A.-E. Sudan* 105 Fc
Marrakech (Morocco), *Morocco* 103 Nj
Marrawah, *Tasmania* 155 Jg
Marree, *S. Australia* 154 Ba
Marri Country, *Baluchistan* 82 Cd
Marromeu, *Mozambique* 113 Fb
Marsa Arakiyai, *A.-E. Sudan* 108 Ca
Marsabit & Mt., *Kenya* 110 Eb
Marsa Fatma, *Eritrea* 108 Dc
Marsa Hali, *Arabia* 78 Lg
Marsala, *Nevada* 134 Db
Marsala, *Sicily* 65 Fg
Marsberg, *Prussia* 54 Dd
Marsciano, *Italy* 63 Ge
Marsden, *New S. Wales* 155 Fc
Marseilles, *France* 35 Hd
Marsh I., *Louisiana* 130 Cf
Marshall, *Illinois* 132 Ff
Marshall, *Liberia* 104 Be
Marshall, *Michigan* 122 Fd
Marshall, *Minnesota* 132 Bc
Marshall, *Missouri* 130 Ba
Marshall, *Texas* 133 Ed
Marshall Is., *Pacific Oc.* 157 Dc
Marshall (Fortuna Ledge), *Alaska* 125 Ge
Marshalltown, *Iowa* 132 Cd
Marshbrook, *S. Rhodesia* 113 Db
Marshfield, *Missouri* 130 Bb
Marshfield, *Oregon* 136 Ad
Marshfield, *Wisconsin* 132 Dc
Mars Hill, *Maine* 120 Ac
Marsico Nuovo, *Italy* 64 Fc
Marstal, *Denmark* 45 Dd
Marstow, *England* 14 Bc
Marstrand, *Sweden* 51 Ae
Martaban & G. of, *Burma* 92 Cd
Martafal, *A.-E. Sudan* 105 Fc
Martanesh, *Albania* 70 Bb
Martapoera, *Borneo* 99 Dd
Martélos, C., *Crete* 71 Jk
Marthand, *Morocco* 103 Oh
Marthapal, *Eastern States* 91 Eb
Martha's Vineyard I., *Massachusetts* 128 Cc
Martiago, *Spain* 37 Db
Martigne-Briand, *France* 32 Ec
Martigny-le-Bains, *France* 31 Hc
Martigny-Ville, *Switz.* 42 Dd
Martigues, *France* 35 Hd
Martin, *Tennessee* 130 Db
Martin L., *Alabama* 130 Ed
Martina Franca, *Italy* 65 Db
Martinez, *California* 134 Bc
Martinho, *Brazil* 142 Cd
Martinique, *Windward Is.* 140 Kh
Martin Muñoz de las Posados, *Spain* 38 Ad
Martínon, *Greece* 71 Ee
Martinsbruck, *Switzerland* 43 Kc
Martinsburg, *Maryland* 129 Ec
Martin's Ferry, *Ohio* 129 Db
Martinsville, *Indiana* 129 Ac
Martinsville, *Virginia* 129 Ed
Martley, *England* 14 Bb
Martoffe, *Denmark* 45 Dc
Marton, *New Zealand* 158 Ed
Martonos, *Voyvodina* 66 Ec
Martonvásár, *Hungary* 66 Db
Martorell, *Spain* 39 Gc
Martos, *Spain* 41 Cc
Martre, Lac la, *N.-W.T.* 124 Fb
Martres-Tolosane, *France* 34 Cd
Martuba, *Libya* 106 Db
Marua (Woodlark) I., *New Guinea* 156 Ec
Marudu B., *N. Borneo* 99 Eb
Maruf, *Afghanistan* 82 Bc
Marugame, *Japan* 97 Cd
Marula, *S. Rhodesia* 113 Cc
Marumbo, *Tang. Terr.* 111 Fg
Marünsk, *U.S.S.R.* 96 Ga
Marutaui, mt., *Venez.-Brazil* 144 Dc
Marvejols, *France* 35 Fc
Marvell, *Arkansas* 130 Cc
Marvillars, *France* 31 Jd
Marwar Junc., *Rajputana* 85 Db
Maryborough, *Queensland* 153 De
Maryborough, *Victoria* 154 Dd
Maryborough (Port Laoighse), *Eire* 27 Ce
Marydale, *Cape Prov.* 114 Dd
Maryland, *S. Rhodesia* 113 Da
Maryland, state, *U.S.A.* 127 Kc
Maryport, *England* 21 Cd
Marysvale, *Utah* 135 Gb
Marysville, *California* 134 Cb
Marysville, *Kansas* 133 Da
Marysville, *Montana* 136 Gb
Marysville, *New Bruns.* 120 Bc
Marysville, *Ohio* 129 Cb
Marysville, *Washington* 136 Ba
Maryvale, *Queensland* 153 Cc
Maryville, *Missouri* 132 Be
Maryville, *Tennessee* 131 Gc
Masada, *Palestine* 80 Ce
Masagulu, *Tang. Terr.* 111 Fj
Masai Steppe, *Tang. Terr.* 111 Ef
Masaka, *Uganda* 110 Bd
Masamba, *Celébes* 99 Fd
Masan, *Korea* 97 Bc
Masansane B., *Mozambique* 113Fb
Masansani B., *Mozambique* 112 Cc
Masara, *Mozambique* 113 Fb
Masasi, *Tang. Terr.* 111 Fj
Masaya, *Nicaragua* 140 Fe
Masbate, I., *Philippines* 99 Fa
Mascara, *Algeria* 102 Eb
Mascota, *Mexico* 138 Cc
Masepe, I., *Nether. Indies* 99 Fd
Maseroi, *Kenya* 110 Ec
Maseru, *Basutoland* 115 Gd
Masese, *Belgian Congo* 109 Ec
Masfjordnes, *Norway* 46 Bd
Mas-ha, *Palestine* 80 Cb
Mashaba, *S. Rhodesia* 113 Dc
Mashaki, *Afghanistan* 82 Cb
Masham, *England* 18 Cb
Mashike, *Japan* 97 Eb
Mashonaland, *S. Rhodesia* 113 Db
Masia, *Mozambique* 112 Bd
Masiati, mt., *Venezuela* 144 Cc
Masikona, *Madagascar* 112 Dd
Masindi, *Uganda* 110 Bc
Masindi Port, *Uganda* 110 Cc
Masinga, *Mozambique* 112 Bd
Masira I. & Gulf, *Arabia* 77 He
Masisi, *Belgian Congo* 109 Eb
Mask, L., *Eire* 25 Bb
Masker, Jeb., *Morocco* 102 Bc
Maskinongé & R., *Quebec* 121 Da
Mason, *Michigan* 122 Fd
Mason, *Texas* 133 Ce
Mason City, *Illinois* 132 Ee
Mason Springs, *Iowa* 132 Cd
Masrar, Jeb., *Egypt* 106 Mh
Massa, *Italy* 63 Fc
Massa, *Italy* 62 Ec
Massa, *Italy* 62 Ed
Massabi, *Fr. Eq. Africa* 109 Bb
Massachusetts B., *Mass.* 128 Cb
Massachusetts, state, *U.S.A.* 127 Lb
Massade, *Syria* 80 Da
Massafra, *Italy* 65 Db
Massaka, *Fr. Eq. Africa* 109 Cb
Massakori, *Fr. Eq. Africa* 105 Ec
Massangano, *Mozambique* 112 Bc
Massangena, *Mozambique* 113 Ec
Massawa, *Eritrea* 108 Cb
Massawippi & L., *Quebec* 121 Eb
Masselsk, *U.S.S.R.* 48 Kb
Massena, *New York* 123 Lc
Massey, *Ontario* 123 Hb
Massiac, *France* 35 Fb
Massie, *Nevada* 134 Db
Massillon, *Ohio* 129 Db
Massinga, *Mozambique* 113 Fd
Massingire, *Mozambique* 113 Fa
Masson, *Quebec* 121 Cb
Mastabe, *Trans-Jordan* 80 Dc
Mastardas, *Brazil* 147 Ee
Masterton, *New Zealand* 159 Ed
Mastulele, *Mozambique* 113 Dd
Mastung, *Baluchistan* 82 Bd
Mastura, *Arabia* 78 Ce
Masuie, *S. Rhodesia* 113 Ab
Masulipatam, *Madras* 91 Ec
Masumbwe, *Tang. Terr.* 111 Be
Masura, *Bechuanaland* 113 Bc
Masurenland 56 Ec
Maswa, *Tanganyika Terr.* 110 Ce
Mat, *United Provs.* 83 Ge
Mata Amarilla, *Argentina* 148 Bd
Matabeleland, *S. Rhod.* 113 Cb
Matadi, *Belgian Congo* 109 Bc
Matador, *Texas* 133 Bd
Matagalpa, *Nicaragua* 140 Fe
Matak, I., *Nether. Indies* 98 Cc
Matakenya, *Mozambique* 112 Bc
Matale, *Ceylon* 89 Dd
Matale, *Tanganyika Terr.* 111 Eg
Matallah, *Rio de Oro* 104 Ab
Matam, *Fr. W. Africa* 104 Bc
Matamoros, *Mexico* 139 Eb
Matamoros, *Mexico* 138 Db
Matan, *Borneo* 98 Dd
Matanda, *N. Rhodesia* 112 Ac
Matane, *Quebec* 120 Bb
Matang, *Malay States* 98 Bc
Matanuska, *Alaska* 125 Kf
Matanzas, *Cuba* 140 Ab
Matapan (Taínaron), C., *Greece* 71 Dg
Matapedia & L., *Quebec* 120 Bb
Matara, *Ceylon* 89 De
Mataram, *Lombok I., N.I.* 99 Ee
Matarka, *Morocco* 102 Cc
Mataro, *Spain* 39 Hc
Mataruge, *Serbia* 68 Fc
Matatiele, *Cape Prov.* 115 He
Mataule, *Brazil* 142 Db
Mataura, *New Zealand* 159 Bg
Matehuala, *Mexico* 138 Dc
Matelica, *Italy* 63 Gd
Matemo I., *Mozambique* 112 Db
Matera, *Italy* 65 Cb
Matese, mts., *Italy* 64 Eb
Mateševo, *Montenegro* 68 Ed
Mátészalka, *Hungary* 67 Ha
Matetsi, *S. Rhodesia* 113 Ab
Mateur, *Tunisia* 103 Ja
Matfana, *Lebanon* 80 Ca
Matheran, *Bombay* 90 Ab
Matheson, *Ontario* 123 Ha
Mathew's Ra., *Kenya* 110 Ec
Mathráki (Samothráki), I., *Greece* 70 Ad
Mati, *Philippines* 99 Gb
Matiakouali, *Fr. W. Afr.* 105 Bc
Matiari, *Sind* 85 Bb
Matifou, C., *Algeria* 103 Fa
Matimira, *Tang. Terr.* 111 Dj
Matiri, *Uganda* 110 Bc
Matisi, *Latvia* 49 Cc
Matjesfontein, *Cape Prov.* 114 Df
Matla R., *Bengal* 88 Bd
Matlock, *England* 18 Cd
Matlock Bath, *England* 18 Cd
Matmata, *Tunisia* 103 Jc
Matoewa, *Borneo* 98 Dd
Matogoro Mt., *Tang. Terr.* 111 Dj
Matope, *Nyasaland* 112 Bc
Matopo Hills, *S. Rhodesia* 113 Cc
Matopos, *S. Rhodesia* 113 Cc
Matora, *Tangan. Terr.* 111 Fj
Matosinhos, *Portugal* 37 Ba
Matour, *France* 35 Ga
Matoya Harb., *Japan* 97 Dd
Matra, mt., *Hungary* 66 Fb
Matra, R., *Italy* 62 Bc
Matrah, *Oman* 79 Ge
Matrand, *Norway* 47 Hd
Matredal, *Norway* 46 Bd
Matrei, *Austria* 59 Fd
Matrûh, *Egypt* 107 Fc

Matsaida, *Japan* 100 Gc
Matseroka, *Madagascar* 112 Dd
Matsue, *Japan* 97 Cc
Matsugasaki, *Japan* 100 Fd
Matsumoto, *Japan* 100 Fc
Matsushima, *Japan* 97 Cc
Matsushiro, *Japan* 100 Gc
Matsuyama, *Japan* 97 Cd
Matsużaka, *Japan* 100 Fd
Matsuzaki, *Japan* 100 Dd
Mattagami, L., *Quebec* 123 Ja
Mattagami R., *Ontario* 122 Ga
Mattancheri, *Madras States* 89 Bc
Mattão, Sa., *Brazil* 143 Dd
Mattawa & R., *Ontario* 121 Aa
Mattawa L., *Ontario* 122 Ca
Mattawin R., *Quebec* 121 Da
Matterhorn, *Switz.-Italy* 42 Ee
Mattersburg, *Austria* 66 Bb
Matthews, *Arizona* 135 He
Mattighofen, *Austria* 59 Gc
Mattinata, *Italy* 64 Gb
Matto Grosso and state, *Brazil* 142 Ce
Matto Grosso, Planalto de, *Brazil* 147 Eb
Mattoon, *Illinois* 132 Ef
Mattuglie 63 Jb
Matturai, *Ceylon* 89 De
Matucana, *Peru* 145 Bd
Matun, *Afghanistan* 82 Cb
Matura, *Brazil* 145 Db
Maturin, *Venezuela* 144 Db
Matzambo, *Mozambique* 113 Ed
Mau, *Central Provs.* 86 Dd
Mau, *Azamgarh, United Provs.* 87 Ec
Mau, *United Provs.* 86 Dc
Mau Ra., *Kenya* 110 Dd
Mau Aimma, *United Provs.* 86 Dc
Maubeuge, *France* 31 Fa
Maubin, *Burma* 92 Bd
Mauchline, *Scotland* 21 Bb
Mauchs Berg, *Transvaal* 115 Jb
Maudaha, *United Provs.* 86 Dc
Maude, *New S. Wales* 154 Dc
Mauer See 56 Fb
Maues, *Brazil* 142 Cc
Mauganj, *Central India* 86 Dc
Maugerville, *New Bruns.* 120 Bd
Maui, I., *Hawaiian Is.* 157 Mg
Maujhi, *Bihar* 87 Fc
Maule, prov., *Chile* 148 Bb
Mauléon, *France* 34 Bd
Maumee R., *Ohio* 129 Bb
Maun I., *Dalmatia* 63 Jc
Mauna Kea, *Hawaii* 157 Nh
Mauna Loa, *Hawaii* 157 Nh
Maunga, *Mozambique* 113 Ec
Maungdaw, *Burma* 92 Ab
Maungu, *Kenya* 111 Fe
Mau Ranipur, *United Prs.* 86 Cc
Maurawan, *United Provs.* 86 Db
Mauriac, *France* 34 Eb
Maurienne, *France* 35 Jb
Mauritania, col., *Fr. W. Africa* 104 Bc
Mauron, *France* 32 Cb
Maurs, *France* 34 Ec
Mauset, *Norway* 47 Dd
Mauston, *Wisconsin* 132 Ec
Mautern, *Austria* 59 Kc
Mauvezin, *France* 34 Cd
Mavréli, *Greece* 70 Cd
Mavrolithárion, *Greece* 71 De
Mavrovoúm (Karadág), *Greece* 70 Dd
Mavrovoúni, mt., *Greece* 70 Dd
Mavul, *Mozambique* 113 Ec
Mavuradonna Mts., *S. Rhodesia* 113 Da
Maw, *Burma* 92 Cb
Mawk Mai, *Burma* 92 Cb
Mawlaik, *Burma* 92 Ba
Mawlu, *Burma* 88 Fb
Mawnang, *Burma* 92 Cb
Mawson, *Burma* 92 Cb
Mawteik, *Burma* 88 Eb
Max, *Egypt* 107 Hf
Maxcanu, *Mexico* 139 Fc
Maxey, *France* 31 Hc
Max Qibilya, *Egypt* 107 Hf
Maxton, *N. Carolina* 131 Jc
Maxwell, *New Mexico* 135 Lc
Maxwelltown, *Scotland* 21 Cc
May, C., *New Jersey* 129 Gc
May, I. of, *Firth of Forth, Scotland* 23 Fd
Mayaguez, *Puerto Rico* 140 Jg
Mayang, *Borneo* 98 Dc
Mayari, *Cuba* 140 Bb
Mayavaram, *Madras* 89 Cb
Maybell, *Colorado* 135 Ka
Maybole, *Scotland* 21 Bc
Mayen, *Prussia* 58 Ba
Mayenne & dep., *France* 32 Eb
Mayersville, *Mississippi* 130 Cd
Mayfield, *Kentucky* 130 Db
Maymyo, *Burma* 92 Ca
Maynooth, *Eire* 27 De
Maynooth, *Ontario* 121 Bb
Mayo, *Florida* 131 Ge
Mayo, co., *Eire* 26 Ad
Mayo, Mts. of, *Eire* 25 Ba
Mayo, R., *Mexico* 138 Cb
Mayoa, *Tanganyika Terr.* 111 Eh
Mayotta, I., *Madagascar* 112 Eb
Mayoumba, *Fr. Eq. Africa* 109 Ab
Mayport, *Florida* 131 He
Mayran, L., *Mexico* 138 Db
Maysi, C., *Cuba* 140 Cb
Maysville, *Kentucky* 131 Ga
Maysville, *Missouri* 132 Bf
Maytown, *Queensland* 153 Bc
Mayu, I., *Nether. Indies* 99 Gc
Mayu Ra., *Burma* 92 Ab
Mayumi, *Japan* 100 Fd
Mayurbhanj, *Eastern States* 87 Ge
Mayville, *New York* 123 Jd
Mayville, *N. Dakota* 132 Ab
Maza, *Argentina* 148 Db
Mazabuka, *N. Rhodesia* 112 Ac
Mazagan, *Morocco* 103 Nh
Mazaganopolis, *Brazil* 142 Dc
Mazalgaon, *Hyderabad* 90 Bb
Mazamba, *Mozambique* 113 Fb
Mazamet, *France* 34 Ed
Mazan, *Argentina* 146 Bd
Mazan, *Peru* 145 Cb
Mazanderan, *Persia* 79 Fb
Mazanova, *U.S.S.R.* 96 Da
Mazapil, *Mexico* 138 Dc
Mazar, *Palestine* 80 Bb
Mazara del Vallo, *Sicily* 65 Fg
Mazaraki, mt., *Greece* 71 Df
Mazarakia, *Greece* 70 Bd
Mazarate, *Spain* 38 Cc
Mazaredo, *Argentina* 148 Cd
Mazar-i-Sharif, *Afghan.* 84 Bc
Mazarron, *Spain* 41 Ec
Mazatenango, *Guatemala* 140 Ec
Mazatlan & R., *Mexico* 138 Cc
Mazawamba, *N. Rhodesia* 112 Bb
Mažeikiai, *Lithuania* 49 Bc
Mazelsfontein, *Cape Prov.* 114 Ed
Mazeras, *Kenya* 111 Fe
Mazeru, *A.-E. Sudan* 105 Fc
Mazimbwa, *Mozambique* 112 Db
Mazirbe, *Latvia* 49 Bc
Mazoe, *S. Rhodesia* 113 Da
Mazoe & R., *Mozambique* 113 Ea
Mazombe, *Tang. Terr.* 111 Dg
Mazsalace, *Latvia* 49 Cc
Mazunga, *S. Rhodesia* 113 Cc
Mazuruni, *Brit. Guiana* 144 Db
Mazzarino, *Sicily* 65 Hg
Mazzer, *Algeria* 102 Cd
Mbabane, *Swaziland* 115 Jc
M'Bala, *Fr. Eq. Africa* 105 Fd
Mbale, *Uganda* 110 Dc
Mbamba Bay, *Tang. Terr.* 111 Dj
Mbarara, *Uganda* 110 Bd
Mbemba, *Tang. Terr.* 111 Fj
Mbengga, *Fiji Is.* 157 Pk
Mbeya & Mt., *Tang. Terr.* 111 Ch
Mbia, *A.-E. Sudan* 108 Ad
Mbigu, *Fr. Eq. Africa* 109 Bb
Mbindira, *Tang. Terr.* 111 Eh
M'Bittima, *A.-E. Sudan* 108 Ad
Mboro, *Fr. W. Africa* 104 Ac
Mbosi, *Tangan. Terr.* 111 Ch
Mbululu, *Kenya* 110 Fe
Mbungo, *Kenya* 111 Fe
Mburucuya, *Argentina* 146 Dd
Mbweni, *Tang. Terr.* 111 Fg
Mchinga, *Tang. Terr.* 111 Fh
M'conta, *Mozambique* 112 Cc
Mdabura, *Tang. Terr.* 111 Dg
Mead L., *Nevada, etc.* 134 Fc
Meade, *Kansas* 133 Bb
Meadows, *Idaho* 136 Ec
Meadow Valley Ra., *Nevada* 134 Fc
Meadville, *Pennsylvania* 129 Db
Meaford, *Ontario* 123 Hc
Mealhada, *Portugal* 37 Bb
Meandarra, *Queensland* 153 Ce
Meano Sardo, *Sardinia* 64 Jg
Mearim R., *Brazil* 143 Ed
Mears, *Colorado* 135 Kb
Measham, *England* 14 Ca
Meaux, *France* 30 Ec
Me-Bac, *Annam* 95 Cg
Mecatina, I., Gt. & Lit., *Quebec* 120 Fa
Mecca, *Arabia* 78 Ce
Mechanicsville, *Maryland* 129 Fc
Mechanicsville, *New York* 128 Bb
Mecheria, *Algeria* 102 Dc
Mechra bel Ksiri, *Morocco* 102 Bb
Mechra Benabbou, *Morocco* 103 Oh
Mecissi, *Morocco* 102 Bd
Meckering, *W. Australia* 152 Be
Mecklenburg, and state, *Germany* 55 Gb
Mecome (Machamba), *Mozambique* 113 Ec
Meda R., *W. Australia* 152 Cb
Medaguine, *Algeria* 103 Fc
Medak, *Croatia* 63 Kc
Medak, *Hyderabad* 90 Db
Medan, *Sumatra* 98 Ac
Medanos, *Argentina* 148 Db
Medchal, *Hyderabad* 90 Dc
Médéa, *Algeria* 103 Fa
Mededa, *Bosnia* 68 Ec
Medellin, *Colombia* 144 Ab
Medellin, *Spain* 37 Dd
Medenine, *Tunisia* 103 Kc
Meder, *Eritrea* 108 Dc
Medford, *Oklahoma* 133 Db
Medford, *Oregon* 136 Bd
Medford, *Wisconsin* 132 Dc
Medgidia, *Romania* 69 Hc
Mediana, *Spain* 38 Ec
Medias, *Romania* 67 Kc
Medical Lake, *Washington* 136 Db
Medicina, *Italy* 63 Fc
Medicine Bow, *Wyoming* 135 La
Medicine Bow Ra., *Wyoming* 135 Ka
Medicine Hat, *Alberta* 124 Ge
Medicine Lodge, *Kansas* 133 Cb
Medies, *Transylvanaia* 67 Jb
Medina, *Arabia* 78 De
Medina, *Ohio* 129 Cb
Medinaceli, *Spain* 38 Cc
Medina del Campo, *Spain* 38 Ac
Medina de Pomar, *Spain* 38 Bb
Medina de Rioseco, *Spain* 38 Ac
Medina Sidonia, *Spain* 40 Ec
Medine, *Fr. W. Africa* 104 Bd
Mediterranean Sea, *Europe-Africa* 101 Cb
Medjana, *Algeria* 103 Ga
Medjedel, *Algeria* 103 Fb
Medjerda, *Tunisia* 103 Ja
Medjerda, Mts. de la, *Algeria* 103 Ha
Medjez el Bab, *Tunisia* 103 Ja
Medoc, *France* 34 Ab
Medole, *Italy* 62 Eb
Medun, *Montenegro* 68 Ed
Meduna, R., *Italy* 63 Gb
Meduno, *Italy* 63 Ga
Medveda, *Serbia* 68 Gd
Medveđitsa, R., *U.S.S.R.* 75 Ge
Medvednica, mts., *Croatia* 66 Ad
Medvezhya Gora, *U.S.S.R.* 74 Ec
Medway, R., *England* 15 Ed
Medyn, *U.S.S.R.* 74 Fd
Medzilaborce, *Slovakia* 60 Fd
Meehan, *Alaska* 125 Kd
Meekatharra, *W. Aust.* 152 Bd
Meelpaeg L., *Newfoundl'd* 120 Gb
Meerane, *Saxony* 55 He
Meersburg, *Baden* 58 Dd
Meerut, *United Provs.* 83 Gd
Meesow 55 Lb
Meester Cornelis, *Java* 98 Ce
Mega, *Ethiopia* 108 Ce
Mega, *New Guinea* 156 Ab
Megalópolis, *Greece* 71 Cf
Meganísi, I., *Greece* 71 Be
Megantic & L., *Quebec* 123 Nc
Megaplátanon, *Greece* 70 Cc
Mégara, *Greece* 71 Ee
Megárkhi, *Greece* 70 Cd
Megatokhóri, *Greece* 71 Ef
Meggett, *S. Carolina* 131 Hd
Meghasani Hill, *Eastern States* 87 Ge
Meghna R., *Bengal* 88 Cc
Megiddo, *Palestine* 80 Cb
Megiskan, *Quebec* 123 Ka
Megsem Drâa, *Algeria* 102 Ce
Meguic, *Quebec* 121 Da
Mehabad, *Persia* 79 Eb
Mehadia, *Romania* 67 He
Mehar, *Sind* 82 Be
Mehdia, *Morocco* 102 Ab
Mehede, *Sweden* 50 Gb
Meherpur, *Bengal* 88 Bc
Mehidpur, *Central India* 85 Ec
Mehitia, I., *Tuamotu Arch.* 157 Je
Mehlauken 56 Fb
Mehmadabad, *Bombay* 85 Dc
Mehndawal, *United Provs.* 87 Eb
Mehsana, *Baroda* 85 Dc
Méhun, *France* 30 Ed
Mei, *Shen-si, China* 94 Cc
Mei, *Sze-chwan, China* 94 Bc
Mei-kiang, *China* 95 Ee
Meiktila, *Burma* 92 Bb
Meilen, *Switzerland* 43 Gb
Mein, *Queensland* 153 Bb
Meiningen, *Thuringia* 54 Fe
Meira, Sa. de, *Spain* 36 Ca
Meiringen, *Switzerland* 42 Fc
Meissen, *Saxony* 55 Jd
Mei-tan, *China* 94 Cd
Meitene, *Latvia* 49 Bc
Mejillones, *Chile* 146 Ac
Mekalis, *Algeria* 102 Dc
Mekatina, *Ontario* 122 Gb
Mekhtar, *Baluchistan* 82 Cc
Mekili, *Libya* 106 Db
Mekleta, *U.S.S.R.* 75 Hf
Meknes, *Morocco* 102 Bc
Meko, *Nigeria* 105 Bd
Mekong R., *Siam, etc.* 95 Bf
Me-kong, Mths. of the, *Cochin-China* 95 Ch
Mekongga Mts., *Celébes* 99 Fd
Melagiris Ra., *Madras* 89 Ba
Mélambes, *Crete* 71 Hj
Melanesia, div., *Pacific Oc.* 157 Bc
Melanga, *Fr. Eq. Africa* 105 Fc
Melapis Is., *Nether. Indies* 98 Cd
Melawi and R., *Borneo* 98 Dd
Melbourne, *Arkansas* 130 Cb
Melbourne, *England* 18 Ce
Melbourne, *Florida* 131 Ng
Melbourne, *Quebec* 121 Db
Melbourne, *Victoria* 154 De
Meldal, *Norway* 46 Fa
Meldola, *Italy* 63 Gc
Meldrim, *Georgia* 131 Hd
Mele, C., *Italy* 62 Cd
Melédi, *Greece* 70 Ed
Melegnano, *Italy* 62 Db
Melekes, *U.S.S.R.* 75 He
Melenci, *Voyvodina* 67 Fd
Melenki, *U.S.S.R.* 74 Gd
Meleti, *Mozambique* 113 Fd
Meleuz, *U.S.S.R.* 74 Ke
Melfa, *Libya* 106 Pl
Melfi, *Fr. Eq. Africa* 105 Ec
Melfi, *Italy* 64 Fb
Melfort, *Saskatchewan* 124 Jd
Melfort, *S. Rhodesia* 113 Da
Melgar de Fernamental, *Spain* 38 Ab
Melgund, *Ontario* 122 Ea
Melhus, *Norway* 46 Ga
Meliau, *Borneo* 98 Dd
Melíki, *Greece* 70 Dc
Melilla, *Span. Morocco* 102 Cb
Melilli, *Sicily* 65 Jg
Melipilla, *Chile* 146 Ae
Meliti, *Greece* 70 Cc
Melito di Porto Salvo, *Italy* 65 Be
Melitopol, *Ukraine* 75 Ef
Melivaia, *Greece* 72 Ba
Melk, *Austria* 59 Kc
Melka, *Trans-Jordan* 80 Db
Melka Saka, *Kenya* 110 Fd
Melksham, *England* 14 Bd
Mella, R., *Italy* 62 Eb
Melle, *France* 34 Ba
Mellendorf, *Prussia* 54 Ec
Mellerud, *Sweden* 50 Bd
Mell Fryk Sjö, *Sweden* 50 Cc
Melli, *Italy* 62 Dc
Mellingen, *Switzerland* 43 Fb
Mellrichstadt, *Bavaria* 58 Ea
Melmerby, *England* 21 Dd
Melnik, *Bohemia* 60 Cc
Mĕlnik, *Bulgaria* 70 Eb
Melo, *Uruguay* 147 Ee
Melo I., *Port. Guinea* 104 Ad
Melrose, *Florida* 131 Gf
Melrose, *Minnesota* 132 Bc
Melrose, *Scotland* 21 Db
Melsetter, *S. Rhodesia* 113 Eb
Melshogna, mt., *Norway* 46 Ha
Melsungen, *Prussia* 54 Ed
Melton Mowbray, *England* 19 De
Melun, *France* 30 Ec
Meluprey, *Siam* 95 Bg
Melvich, *Scotland* 24 Ed
Melville, *Saskatchewan* 124 Jd
Melville B., *Greenland* 9 Cb
Melville, C., *Queensland* 153 Bb
Melville I., *N. Terr., Aust.* 150 Ea
Melville I., *N.-W. Terr.* 118 Ga
Melville, L., *Labrador* 119 Sf
Melville Pen., *N.-W. T.* 119 Nc
Melvin, L., *Eire* 26 Bc
Mélykút, *Hungary* 66 Ec
Melzo, *Italy* 62 Db
Memba & B., *Mozambique* 112 Db
Membij, *Syria* 78 Cb
Memboro, *Soemba I., N.I.* 99 Ee
Memel (Klaipeda) *Lithuania* 49 Ad
Memel, *O.F.S.* 115 Hc
Memel R. 56 Gb
Memere, *Fr. W. Africa* 104 Dd
Memmingen, *Bavaria* 58 Ed
Mempakol, *N. Borneo* 99 Db
Memphis, *Egypt* 107 Hd
Memphis, *Missouri* 132 Ce
Memphis, *Tennessee* 130 Dc
Memphis, *Texas* 133 Bc
Memphremagog L., *Quebec* 121 Db
Memramcook, *New Bruns.* 120 Cd
Mena, *Arkansas* 130 Ac
Menaggio, *Italy* 62 Da
Menai Bridge, *Wales* 20 Ba
Menai I., *Indian Oc.* 112 Ea
Menai Str., *Wales* 20 Ba
Menak, *Fr. W. Africa* 105 Bb
Menan, *Idaho* 136 Hd
Me-nan, R., *Siam* 95 Bf
Menard, *Texas* 133 Ce
Menasalbas, *Spain* 38 Ae
Menasha, *Wisconsin* 132 Ec
Menat, *France* 34 Ea
Mendak, *Arabia* 78 Lf
Mendanau, I., *Nether. Indies* 98 Cd
Mendawe & R., *Borneo* 99 Dd
Mende, *France* 35 Fc
Menderes, R., *Turkey* 72 Dc
Mendhenítsa, *Greece* 71 De
Mendif, *Fr. Eq. Africa* 105 Dc
Mendig, *Prussia* 58 Ba
Mendip Hills, *England* 14 Bd
Mendocino, C., *California* 134 Aa
Mendon, *Utah* 135 Ga
Mendota, *California* 134 Cc
Mendota, *Illinois* 132 Ee
Mendota, L., *Wisconsin* 132 Ed
Mendoza & prov., *Argent.* 146 Be
Mendrisio, *Switzerland* 43 He
Mendro, Sa., *Portugal* 40 Ca
Menegosa, Mte., *Italy* 62 Dc
Menelik Falls, *Ethiopia* 108 Cd
Meneo, *New Guinea* 156 Bb
Menerville, *Algeria* 103 Fa
Menez Hom, *France* 32 Ab
Menfi, *Sicily* 65 Fg
Meng Aran Pratet, *Siam* 95 Bg
Meng Chai Nat, *Siam* 95 Bf
Meng-cheng, *China* 94 Ec
Meng Chumforn, *Siam* 98 Aa
Meng Det, *Siam* 95 Bg
Mengen, *Württemberg* 58 Dc
Menggala, *Sumatra* 98 Cd
Meng-hwa-hsien, *China* 94 Bd
Meng Kalamasai, *Siam* 95 Bf
Meng Kemmarat, *Siam* 95 Bf
Meng Kon-ken, *Siam* 95 Bf
Meng Krabin, *Siam* 95 Bg
Meng Krat, *Siam* 95 Bg
Meng Kumpu-wapi, *Siam* 95 Bf
Meng-La, *China* 95 Be
Meng Lakhon, *Siam* 95 Bf
Meng Leo, *China* 95 Be
Meng Liep, *Siam* 95 Bf
Meng Lim, *Siam* 95 Bf
Meng-loi, *Siam* 95 Bf
Meng Lom Sak Mai, *Siam* 95 Bf
Meng Lop-buri, *Siam* 95 Bg
Meng-mukdahan, *Siam* 95 Bf
Meng Mula-pumok, *Siam* 95 Cg
Meng Nakawn-sawan, *Siam* 95 Bf
Meng nan, *Siam* 95 Bf
Meng Nang-rong, *Siam* 95 Bg
Mengoub, *Morocco* 102 Cc
Meng Panom, *Siam* 95 Bf
Meng Pase, *Siam* 95 Bg
Meng Phrayow, *Siam* 95 Af
Meng Pichai, *Siam* 95 Bf
Meng Pitsanulok, *Siam* 95 Bf
Meng Pou-Vieng, *Siam* 95 Bf
Meng Prachuabkhirikun, *Siam* 98 Aa
Meng Pran-Kao, *Siam* 95 Bg
Meng Puthai Song, *Siam* 95 Bf
Meng Rayong, *Siam* 95 Bg
Meng Samut Songgram, *Siam* 95 Bg
Meng Saniabury, *Siam* 95 Bf
Meng Sara-buri, *Siam* 95 Bg
Meng Shajeungtrao (Petriu), *Siam* 95 Bg
Meng Tien-tuk, *Siam* 95 Bg
Mengtsz, *China* 95 Be
Meng Utaradit, *Siam* 95 Bf

Mineral Wells, *Texas* 133 Cd
Minerbio, *Italy* 63 Fc
Minersville, *Utah* 135 Gb
Minervino Murge, *Italy* 65 Ca
Minety, *England* 14 Cc
Mineville, *New York* 128 Ba
Mingan, *Quebec* 120 Ca
Mingan & R., *Quebec* 120 Ca
Mingan Is., *Quebec* 119 Qf
Mingary, *S. Australia* 154 Cb
Mingenew, *W. Australia* 152 Bd
Mingin, *Burma* 92 Ba
Mingin Ra., *Burma* 88 Eb
Minglanilla, *Spain* 38 De
Mingoyo, *Tang. Terr.* 111 Fj
Mingshui, *Manchuria* 96 Db
Mingun, *Burma* 92 Ba
Mingwepa, *Tang. Terr.* 111 Ej
Minhla, *Burma* 92 Bc
Min-ho, *China* 94 Bc
Minho, R., *Portugal* 36 Bc
Ministra, Sierra, *Spain* 38 Cc
Minkat ed Dru, *Trans-Jord.* 80 De
Minkebe, *Fr. Eq. Africa* 109 Ba
Min-kiang, *China* 94 Ed
Minna, *Nigeria* 105 Cd
Minneapolis, *Kansas* 133 Da
Minneapolis, *Minnesota* 132 Cc
Minnedosa, *Manitoba* 124 Jd
Minneola, *California* 134 Ed
Minneota, *Minnesota* 132 Ac
Minnesota, state and R., *U.S.A.* 127 Fa
Minnesund, *Norway* 47 Hd
Minnitaki L., *Ontario* 122 Ca
Mino, R., *Spain* 36 Cb
Minonk, *Illinois* 132 Ee
Minorca (Menorca), I., *Balearic Is.* 39 Lj
Minot, *N. Dakota* 126 Ea
Min-shan, *China* 94 Bc
Minsk, *White Russia* 75 De
Minsk Mazowiecki, *Poland* 60 Fb
Minster, *England* 15 Fd
Minsterley, *England* 14 Ba
Minsterworth, *England* 14 Bc
Minthicoondunna Spring, *W. Australia* 152 Bc
Minto, *Colorado* 135 Ma
Minto, *N. Dakota* 132 Aa
Minto L., *Quebec* 119 Pe
Min-tsing, *China* 94 Ed
Minturn, *Colorado* 135 Kb
Minturno, *Italy* 64 Db
Minuf, *Egypt* 107 Hc
Minwya, *Burma* 92 Cd
Minyip, *Victoria* 154 Cd
Minywa, *Burma* 92 Bb
Mio, *Michigan* 122 Fc
Mionica, *Serbia* 68 Eb
Miquelon, I., Gt. & Lit., *Atlantic Oc.* 120 Gc
Mira, *Portugal* 37 Bb
Mira, *Spain* 38 De
Mira, R., *Portugal* 40 Bb
Mirabel, *France* 35 Gb
Mirabel, *Spain* 37 Dc
Mirabella Imbaccari, *Sicily* 65 Hg
Mirador, *Brazil* 143 Ed
Miraflores, *Colombia* 144 Bb
Miraj, *Deccan States* 90 Bc
Miramar, *Argentina* 148 Eb
Mirambel, *Spain* 39 Ed
Miramichi R., *New Bruns.* 120 Bc
Miramont, *France* 34 Cc
Miram Shah, *N.-W.F.P.* 82 Cb
Miranda, *Argentina* 148 Eb
Miranda, *Venezuela* 144 Ca
Miranda (Belmonte), *Spain* 36 Da
Miranda and R., *Brazil* 146 Dc
Miranda de Ebro, *Spain* 38 Bb
Miranda do Corvo, *Portugal* 37 Bb
Miranda do Douro, *Portugal* 36 Dc
Miranda Downs, *Queensl'd* 153 Bc
Mirande, *France* 34 Cd
Mirandela, *Portugal* 36 Cc
Mirandilla, *Spain* 37 Dc
Mirandola, *Italy* 62 Fc
Mirandol-Bourg, *France* 34 Ec
Mirani, *Queensland* 153 Cd
Mirano, *Italy* 63 Gb
Miravalles, *Spain* 38 Ca
Miravet, *Spain* 39 Fc
Mirebeau, *Cote-d'Or, France* 31 Hd
Mirebeau, *Vienne, France* 30 Ce
Mirecourt, *France* 31 Jc
Mirepoix, *France* 34 Dd
Mirgorod, *Ukraine* 75 Ef
Miri, *Sarawak* 99 Dc
Mirim, L., *Uruguay-Brazil* 147 Ee
Mirjawa, *Persia* 79 Hd
Mirola, *Tang. Terr.* 111 Ej
Mirongo, *N. Rhodesia* 112 Bb
Mirosi, *Romania* 69 Fc
Mirovce, *Serbia* 70 Db
Mirovice, *Bohemia* 59 Hb
Mirpur, *Kashmir* 83 Eb
Mirpur Khas, *Sind* 85 Bb
Mirpur Sakro, *Sind* 85 Ab
Mirs B., *China* 95 De
Mirtia, *Greece* 71 Cf
Mirtóön Sea, *Greece* 71 Ef
Mírtos, *Crete* 71 Jk
Mirtos B., *Greece* 71 Be
Mirwani, *Kenya* 110 Ed
Mirzapur, *United Provs.* 87 Ec
Mirzawala, *Rajputana* 83 Ed
Misaki, *Japan* 100 Gd
Misakubo, *Japan* 100 Fd
Misamis, *Philippines* 99 Fb
Misau, *Nigeria* 105 Cc
Mischabel, *Switzerland* 42 Ed
Miscou I., *New Brunswick* 120 Cc
Mishan, *Manchuria* 96 Eb
Mishawaka, *Indiana* 129 Ab
Mishikamau, L., *Labrador* 119 Rf
Misima (St Aignan), *Louisiade Arch.* 156 Lk
Misiones, terr., *Argentina* 147 Ed
Miska, *Arabia* 78 De
Miška, *Palestine* 80 Bc
Miskolc, *Hungary* 67 Fa
Misquah Hills, *Minnesota* 132 Db
Misque, *Bolivia* 146 Bb
Missinaibi L., *Ontario* 122 Ga
Mission San José, *Californ.* 134 Cc
Missis, *Turkey* 78 Cb
Mississagi R., *Ontario* 122 Gb
Mississippi, state, *U.S.A.* 127 Gd
Mississippi Delta, *Louisiana* 130 Df
Mississippi, L. & R., *Ont.* 121 Bb
Mississippi R., *U.S.A.* 127 Gc
Mississippi Sd., *Mississippi* 130 De
Mississippi City, *Miss.* 130 De
Missolonghi (Mesolóngian), *Greece* 71 Ce
Missoula, *Montana* 136 Gb
Missoula, R., *Montana* 136 Fb
Missour, *Morocco* 102 Cc
Missouri, state and R., *U.S.A.* 127 Gc
Missouri Valley, *Iowa* 132 Be
Mistassini, *Quebec* 119 Of
Mistassini R., *Quebec* 123 Ma
Mistelbach, *Austria* 66 Ba
Misterbianco, *Sicily* 65 Hg
Misti, mt., *Peru* 145 Ce
Mistrás, *Greece* 71 Df
Mistretta, *Sicily* 65 Hg
Misumi, *Japan* 97 Cd
Misurata & C., *Libya* 106 Pk
Misurata, prov., *Libya* 106 Ac
Miswalde 56 Dc
Mitajiri, *Japan* 100 Ba
Mitcheldean, *England* 14 Bc
Mitchell, *Indiana* 129 Ac
Mitchell, *Ontario* 123 Hd
Mitchell, *Queensland* 153 Ce
Mitchell, *S. Dakota* 126 Fb
Mitchell, Mt., *N. Carolina* 131 Gc
Mitchell R., *Queensland* 153 Bc
Mitchelstown, *Eire* 27 Bg
Mit Ghamr, *Egypt* 107 Hc
Mithankot, *Punjab* 82 Dd
Mitiero, I., *Cook Is.* 157 He
Mítikas, *Greece* 71 Be
Mitilini, *Lesbos I., Greece* 72 Dc
Mitilini (Lesbos), I., *Greece* 72 Cc
Mitla, *Mexico* 139 Ed
Mito, *Japan* 97 Ec
Mitondo, *Mozambique* 113 Fa
Mitre, Mt., *Rio Muni* 109 Aa
Mitrovica, *Serbia* 68 Fd
Mitsamihouli, *Comoro Is.* 112 Db
Mitsig, *Fr. Eq. Africa* 109 Ba
Mitsikéli, mts., *Greece* 70 Bd
Mitsuishi, *Japan* 100 Ed
Mittag Spitze, *Austria* 58 Dd
Mittagong, *New S. Wales* 155 Gc
Mitta Mitta, *Victoria* 155 Ed
Mittel Geb., *Bohemia* 59 Ha
Mittelland, *Switzerland* 42 Dc
Mittenwald, *Bavaria* 58 Fd
Mittenwalde, *Prussia* 55 Jc
Mitterndorf, *Austria* 59 Hd
Mitter-Pinzgau, *Austria* 59 Gd
Mittersill, *Austria* 59 Gd
Mittweida, *Saxony* 55 He
Mitu, *Colombia* 144 Bc
Mityana, *Uganda* 110 Cc
Miyajima, *Japan* 100 Ca
Miyakeshima, *Japan* 100 Gd
Miyako, *Japan* 97 Ec
Miyanduab, *Persia* 79 Eb
Miyanoshita, *Japan* 97 Dc
Miyasu, *Japan* 97 Cc
Miyazaki, *Japan* 97 Cd
Miyoshi, *Japan* 100 Dd
Mi-yün, *China* 94 Ea
Mizda, *Libya* 106 Ol
Mizen Hd., *Cork, Eire* 25 Bg
Mizen Hd., *Wicklow, Eire* 27 Df
Mizil, *Romania* 69 Gc
Mizilmeri, *Sicily* 65 Gf
Mizpa, *Palestine* 80 Cb
Mizuhashi, *Japan* 100 Fc
Mizukaido, *Japan* 100 Gc
Mizusawa, *Japan* 97 Ec
Mjanji, *Uganda* 110 Dc
Mjölby, *Sweden* 50 Ed
Mjor Sjö, *Sweden* 51 Be
Mjösa, L., *Norway* 46 Gd
Mkalama, *Tang. Terr.* 111 Df
Mkamba, *Tang. Terr.* 111 Bg
Mkangira's, *Tang. Terr.* 111 Eh
Mkasu, *Tang. Terr.* 111 Dh
Mkata, *Tang. Terr.* 111 Eg
Mkima, *Tang. Terr.* 111 Fg
Mkoe, *Tang. Terr.* 111 Fh
Mkokotoni, *Zanzibar* 111 Ff
Mkololo, *Tang. Terr.* 111 Eg
Mkondaji, *Tang. Terr.* 111 Fh
Mkonja, *Tang. Terr.* 111 Fj
Mkufi, *Mozambique* 112 Db
Mkul, *Fr. Eq. Africa* 109 Ba
Mkunduchi, *Zanzibar* 111 Fg
Mkunse, *Tang. Terr.* 111 De
Mkushi, *N. Rhodesia* 112 Ab
Mkusi, *Natal* 115 Jc
Mkwaja, *Tang. Terr.* 111 Ff
Mláda Boleslav, *Bohemia* 60 Cc
Mláda Vožice, *Bohemia* 59 Jb
Mladenovac, *Serbia* 68 Fb
Mlale, *Tanganyika Terr* 110 Ce
Mlali, *Tanganyika Terr.* 111 Eg
Mlangali Milo, *Tang. Terr.* 111 Dh
Mlanje, *Nyasaland* 112 Ce
Mlanje, mt., *Mozambique* 112 Cc
Mława, *Poland* 60 Fb
Mlekwanyuma's, *Tang. Terr.* 111 Cg
Mljet, I., *Dalmatia* 68 Cd
Mljetski Chan., *Dalmatia* 68 Cd
Mnisek, *Bohemia* 59 Jb
Mo, *Norway* 44 Cf
Mo, *Norway* 47 De
Moa, *Tanganyika Terr.* 111 Ff
Moa, I., *Netherlands Indies* 99 Ge
Moab, *Utah* 135 Jb
Moama, *New S. Wales* 154 Dd
Moamba, *Mozambique* 115 Kb
Moate, *Eire* 27 Ce
Moba, *Belg. Congo* 109 Ec
Mobara, *Japan* 100 Hd
Mobas, *Trans-Jordan* 80 Dc
Mobaye, *Fr. Eq. Africa* 105 Fe
Mobeetie, *Texas* 133 Bc
Mobeka, *Belgian Congo* 109 Ca
Moberly, *Missouri* 130 Ba
Mobile & B., *Alabama* 130 De
Mobile R., *Alabama* 130 Ee
Mobon, *Burma* 92 Bc
Mobridge, *S. Dakota* 126 Ea
Mocajuba, *Brazil* 143 Ec
Mocambo B., *Mozambique* 112 Dc
Mocejon, *Spain* 38 Be
Mocha, *Yemen* 78 Lh
Mochudi, *Bechuanaland* 115 Gb
Möckern, *Prussia* 55 Gc
Mocksville, *N. Carolina* 131 Hc
Moclips, *Washington* 136 Ab
Mocoa, *Colombia* 144 Ac
Mocorito, *Mexico* 138 Cb
Moctezuma, *San Luis Potosi, Mexico* 138 Dc
Moctezuma, *Sonora, Mexico* 138 Bb
Moctezuma, R., *Mexico* 139 Ec
Modane, *France* 35 Jb
Modasa, *Bombay* 85 Dc
Modbury, *England* 17 Cc
Modder R., *O.F.S.* 115 Fd
Modder River, *Cape Prov.* 115 Fd
Modena, *Italy* 62 Ec
Modesto, *California* 134 Cc
Modica, *Sicily* 65 Hh
Modigliana, *Italy* 63 Fc
Mödling, *Austria* 59 Lc
Modon (Methóni), *Greece* 71 Cg
Modrá, *Slovakia* 66 Ca
Modran, *Bosnia* 68 Cb
Modrie, *Bosnia* 68 Db
Modry Kamen, *Slovakia* 66 Ea
Mo-duc, *Annam* 95 Cg
Modugno, *Italy* 65 Ca
Modzbah, *Algeria* 102 Db
Moe, *Victoria* 155 Ee
Moearaaman, *Sumatra* 98 Bd
Moearadoea, *Sumatra* 98 Bd
Moearaenim, *Sumatra* 98 Bd
Moearakaman, *Borneo* 99 Ed
Moearalaboeh, *Sumatra* 98 Bd
Moearaoepit, *Sumatra* 98 Bd
Moearatebo, *Sumatra* 98 Bd
Moearatewe, *Borneo* 99 Dd
Moekomoeko, *Sumatra* 98 Bd
Mœl, *Norway* 47 Ee
Moembaze, *Mozambique* 112 Cc
Moena, *Italy* 63 Fa
Moena, I., *Neth. Indies* 99 Fe
Moengo, *Suriname* 142 Da
Moerdijk, *Holland* 29 Cc
Moesala, I., *Nether. Indies* 98 Ac
Moffat, *Colorado* 135 Kc
Moffat, *Scotland* 21 Cc
Mofo, *Basutoland* 115 Gd
Mofu, *Tanganyika Terr.* 111 Eh
Mogacha, *U.S.S.R.* 96 Ba
Mogadishu, *It. Somaliland* 108 Hf
Mogador, *Morocco* 103 Mj
Mogadouro, *Portugal* 36 Dc
Moganzulu, *Belg. Congo* 109 Ea
Mogaung, *Burma* 92 Ff
Mogen, *Norway* 47 Ed
Moger, *Ethiopia* 108 Cd
Moggar, *Algeria* 103 Hc
Moggio Ud, *Italy* 63 Ha
Moghar Foukeni, *Algeria* 102 Dc
Moghasi, Jeb., *Arabia* 79 Ed
Mogilev, *White Russia* 75 De
Mogilev Podolski, *Ukraine* 75 Df
Mogilno, *Poland* 57 Ca
Moginquale, *Mozambique* 112 Dc
Mogliano, *Italy* 63 Gb
Moglicë, *Albania* 70 Bc
Mogok, *Burma* 92 Ca
Mogollon and Mts., *New Mexico* 135 Je
Mogollon Mesa, *Arizona* 135 Hd
Mogoro, *Sardinia* 64 Hg
Moguer, *Spain* 40 Db
Mogy-das-Cruzes, *Brazil* 147 Fc
Moha, *Hungary* 66 Db
Mohacs, *Hungary* 66 Dc
Mohale's Hoek, *Basutol'd* 115 Ge
Mohangarh, *Rajputana* 82 De
Mohari, *Central Provs.* 86 Ce
Mohave Des., *California* 134 Ed
Mohawk, *New York* 128 Ab
Mohawk & Mts., *Arizona* 134 Ge
Mohawk R., *New York* 123 Ld
Moheda, *Sweden* 51 De
Mohedas de la Jura, *Spain* 37 Ec
Mohgaon, *Central Provs.* 86 Ce
Mohill, *Eire* 26 Cd
Mohilla I., *Comoro Is.* 112 Db
Möhne See, *Prussia* 54 Dd
Mohnyin, *Burma* 88 Fb
Moho, *Manchuria* 96 Ca
Moholm, *Sweden* 50 Dd
Mohoro, *Tang. Terr.* 111 Fh
Mohrungen 56 Ec
Moi, *Norway* 47 Cf
Moi, Col. del, *Italy* 63 Ga
Moikabanda, *Belg. Congo* 109 Dc
Moine, du, L. & R., *Quebec* 123 Kb
Moira, *N. Ireland* 26 Dc
Moirans, *France* 35 Ha
Môisaküla, *Estonia* 49 Cb
Moisie, *Quebec* 120 Ca
Moissac, *France* 34 Dc
Moito, *Fr. Eq. Africa* 105 Ec
Möja, *Sweden* 50 Hc
Mojave, *California* 134 Dd
Mojeb, Wady el, *Trans-Jordan* 80 De
Moji, *Japan* 97 Cd
Mojo, I., *Nether. Indies* 99 Ee
Mokabe, *Belg. Congo* 109 Ec
Mokai, *New Zealand* 158 Ec
Mokameh, *Bihar* 87 Fc
Mokelumne Hill, *California* 134 Cb
Mokhós, *Crete* 71 Jj
Mokhotlong, *Basutoland* 115 Hd
Moknine, *Tunisia* 103 Kb
Mokoange, *Belgian Congo* 109 Ca
Mokokchung, *Assam* 88 Ea
Mokomon, *Ontario* 122 Da
Mokoro, *Bechuanaland* 113 Bd
Mokpo, *Korea* 97 Bd
Mokra Planina, *Montenegro* 68 Fd
Mokrin, *Voyvodina* 67 Fd
Mokuba, *Mozambique* 112 Cc
Mol, *Voyvodina* 66 Fd
Mola di Bari, *Italy* 65 Da
Moláoi, *Greece* 71 Dg
Molar, El, *Spain* 38 Bd
Molare, *Italy* 62 Cc
Molat, *Dalmatia* 63 Jc
Molay, le, *France* 32 Ea
Mold, *Wales* 20 Ca
Moldavia, *Ukraine* 75 Df
Molde & Fjord, *Norway* 46 Db
Moldova, *Romania* 69 Gb
Moldova Noua, *Romania* 67 Ge
Molepolole, *Bechuanaland* 115 Fb
Môle St Nicolas, *Haiti* 140 Cc
Molesmes, *France* 31 Gd
Molfetta, *Italy* 65 Ca
Molina, *Chile* 148 Bb
Molina, *Spain* 38 Dd
Molina de Segura, *Spain* 41 Eb
Molinatico, Mte., *Italy* 62 Dc
Moline, *Illinois* 132 De
Moline, *Kansas* 133 Db
Molinella, *Italy* 63 Fc
Molino, *Florida* 130 Ee
Molins de Rey, *Spain* 39 Gc
Moliterno, *Italy* 65 Bb
Moll, *Belgium* 29 Dc
Möll Tal, *Austria* 59 He
Molledo, *Spain* 38 Aa
Mollendo, *Peru* 145 Ce
Mollet, *Spain* 39 Hc
Molliens Vidame, *France* 30 Db
Mölln, *Prussia* 54 Fb
Mölme, *Norway* 46 Eb
Mölndal, *Sweden* 51 Be
Molo, *Kenya* 110 Dd
Molo, *Uganda* 110 Dc
Mołodeczno 60 Ja
Mologa & R., *U.S.S.R.* 74 Fd
Molokai, I., *Hawaiian Is.* 157 Mg
Moloma, R., *U.S.S.R.* 74 Hd
Molong, *New S. Wales* 155 Fc
Molopo, R., *Cape Prov.* 114 Ec
Molotova, C., *U.S.S.R.* 76 La
Molotovo, *U.S.S.R.* 74 Kd
Molsheim, *France* 31 Kc
Molteno, *Cape Prov.* 115 Ge
Molucca Pass, *Neth. Indies* 99 Gd
Moluccas, Is., *Neth. Indies* 99 Gd
Molundu, *Fr. Eq. Africa* 109 Ca
Moma, *Belgian Congo* 109 Db
Mombasa, *Kenya* 111 Ff
Mombo, *Tanganyika Terr.* 111 Ff
Momboem, *New Guinea* 156 Bc
Mombuey, *Spain* 36 Db
Momchilgrad, *Bulgaria* 69 Fe
Momeik (Mong Mit), *Burma* 92 Ca
Momence, *Illinois* 132 Fe
Mo-ming, *China* 94 Aa
Mo-mo-shan, *China* 94 Bb
Mompona, *Belg. Congo* 109 Cb
Mompono, *Belg. Congo* 109 Da
Mompós, *Colombia* 144 Bb
Mön, I., *Denmark* 45 Fd
Mona I. & Pass, *West Indies* 140 Jg
Monach Is. & Sd., *Scotland* 22 Aa
Monaco, principality, *S. Europe* 33 Cb
Monadhliath Mts., *Scot.* 23 Db
Monagas, state, *Venezuela* 144 Db
Monaghan & co., *Eire* 26 Dc
Monarch, *Colorado* 135 Kb
Monarch, *Montana* 136 Ha
Monasterevin, *Eire* 27 Ce
Monasterio de Rodilla, *Spain* 38 Bb
Monastir, *Sardinia* 64 Jg
Monastir, *Tunisia* 103 Kb
Monastir (Bitolj), *Serbia* 70 Cb
Mona Tenda, *Belg. Congo* 109 Dc
Monbetu, *Japan* 97 Eb
Moncalieri, *Italy* 62 Bc
Moncalvo, *Italy* 62 Cb
Moncayo, Sa. del, *Spain* 38 Dc
Monchique and Sa. de, *Portugal* 40 Bb
Monclova, *Mexico* 138 Db
Moncontour, *Cotes-du-Nord, France* 32 Cb
Moncontour, *Vienne, France* 30 Ce
Moncoutant, *France* 32 Ed
Moncrabeau, *France* 34 Cc
Moncton, *New Brunswick* 120 Cc
Mondego C. & R., *Portugal* 37 Bb
Mondejar, *Spain* 38 Bd
Mondim de Basto, *Portugal* 36 Cc
Mondo, *Fr. Eq. Africa* 105 Ec
Mondombe, *Belg. Congo* 109 Db
Mondoñedo, *Spain* 36 Ca
Mondoubleau, *France* 30 Cd
Mondovi, *Italy* 62 Bc
Mondovi, *Wisconsin* 132 Dc
Mondragone, *Italy* 64 Db
Mondrain I., *W. Australia* 152 Ce
Mondsee, *Austria* 59 Hd
Mondul, *Tang. Terr.* 110 Ee
Monea, *N. Ireland* 26 Cc
Moneglia, *Italy* 62 Dc

Mosan, *Korea* 97 Bb
Mosbach, *Baden* 58 Db
Mosby, *Norway* 47 Df
Mosca, *Colorado* 135 Kc
Moscow, *Idaho* 136 Eb
Moscow (Moskva), *U.S.S.R.* 74 Fd
Moseć Planina, *Dalmatia* 68 Bc
Mosedis, *Lithuania* 49 Ac
Moselle, dep., *France* 31 Jb
Moselle, R., *Prussia* 58 Ba
Mosgiel, *New Zealand* 159 Cf
Moshi, *Tanganyika Terr.* 110 Ee
Mosina, *Poland* 57 Ba
Mosita, *Cape Prov.* 115 Fc
Mositlane, *Cape Prov.* 115 Fc
Mosjoen, *Norway* 44 Cf
Moskva (Moscow), *U.S.S.R.* 74 Fd
Moslavacka Gora, *Croatia* 66 Bd
Moson, Pozsony & Gyor, *Hungary* 66 Cb
Mosonsztjános, *Hungary* 66 Cb
Mosovce, *Slovakia* 57 De
Mosqueiro, *Brazil* 143 Ec
Mosquera, *Colombia* 144 Ac
Mosquero, *New Mexico* 135 Md
Mosquito Bank, *Nicaragua* 140 Ge
Mosquito Cays, *Nicaragua* 140 Ge
Mosquito Inlet, *Florida* 131 Hf
Mosquito Lagoon, *Florida* 131 Ng
Moss, *Norway* 47 Ge
Mossamedes, *Angola* 101 Dg
Mossbank, *Zetland* 24 Gg
Mossburn, *New Zealand* 159 Af
Mossel B., *Spitzbergen* 9 La
Mossel Bay, *Cape Prov.* 114 Eg
Mossgiel, *New S. Wales* 154 Dc
Mossiro, *Kenya* 110 Dd
Mossley, *England* 18 Bc
Mossoro, *Brazil* 143 Gd
Mosso San Maria, *Italy* 62 Cb
Mossulogrande, *Angola* 109 Bc
Mossurize, *Mozambique* 113 Ec
Moss Vale, *New S. Wales* 155 Gc
Most, *Bohemia* 60 Bc
Mostaganem, *Algeria* 102 Eb
Mostar, *Hercegovina* 68 Cc
Mösting C., *Greenland* 9 Fe
Mostyn, *Wales* 20 Ca
Mosul, *Iraq* 78 Db
Mosuril, *Mozambique* 112 Db
Mös-vatn, *Norway* 47 Ee
Mota, *Ethiopia* 108 Cc
Mota del Marques, *Spain* 36 Ec
Motagua, R., *Guatemala* 140 Fd
Motajica Planina, *Bosnia* 68 Ca
Motala, *Sweden* 50 Dd
Motaling, *Celébes* 99 Fc
Motatan, *Venezuela* 144 Bb
Mother and Child, mt., *Annam* 95 Cg
Motherwell, *Scotland* 23 Ee
Motihari, *Bihar* 87 Fb
Motilla del Palancar, *Spain* 38 De
Motiton, *Cape Prov.* 114 Ec
Motnik, *Slovenia* 63 Ja
Moto, *Belgian Congo* 109 Ea
Mötögör, *China* 94 Ba
Motoyoshi, *Japan* 97 Ec
Motril, *Spain* 41 Cd
Motta, *Italy* 63 Gb
Motte Beuvron, *France* 30 Dd
Motueka, *New Zealand* 159 Dd
Motuhora, *New Zealand* 158 Fc
Motul, *Mexico* 139 Gc
Motu One, I., *Society Is.* 157 He
Moturoa, *New Zealand* 158 Dc
Mouchard, *France* 31 He
Moudjeria, *Fr. W. Africa* 104 Bc
Moudon, *Switzerland* 42 Cc
Moudros & B., *Greece* 72 Cc
Mouit, *Fr. W. Africa* 104 Ac
Mouka, *Fr. Eq. Africa* 105 Fd
Moukden (Fengtienfu), *Manchuria* 96 Cc
Moulamein & R., *N.S.W.* 154 Dd
Moulay bou Selham, *Morocco* 102 Ab
Moul el Bacha, *Morocco* 102 Cb
Moulins, *France* 35 Fa
Moulmein, *Burma* 92 Cd
Moulouya, R., *Morocco* 102 Cc
Moulsford, *England* 14 Cc
Moulton, *Alabama* 130 Ec
Moultrie, *Georgia* 131 Fe
Mound, *Kansas* 133 Ea
Mound City, *Illinois* 130 Db
Mound City, *Missouri* 132 Be
Moundsville, *W. Virginia* 129 Dc
Mouni, *Kenya* 110 Fe
Mountain, *Ontario* 121 Cb
Mountain Ash, *Wales* 20 Cd
Mountain City, *Nevada* 134 Fa
Mountain Grove, *Missouri* 130 Bb
Mountain Home, *Arkansas* 130 Bb
Mountain Home, *Idaho* 136 Fd
Mountain View, *Arkansas* 130 Bc
Mount Airy, *N. Carolina* 131 Hb
Mount Athos (Áyion Óros), *Greece* 70 Fc
Mount Ayliff, *Cape Prov.* 115 He
Mount Ayr, *Iowa* 132 Be
Mount Barker, *S. Aust.* 154 Bd
Mount Barker, *W. Aust.* 152 Be
Mount Bellew, *Eire* 27 Be
Mount Blanco, *Texas* 133 Bd
Mount Blaze, *W. Aust.* 152 Bb
Mount Carmel, *Illinois* 132 Ff
Mount Carroll, *Illinois* 132 Dd
Mount Charles, *Eire* 26 Bb
Mount Collis, *Queensland* 153 Bd
Mount Cuthbert, *Queensl'd* 153 Ac
Mount Darwin, *S. Rhod.* 113 Da
Mount Desert, *Maine* 128 Da
Mount Desert I., *Maine* 120 Ad
Mount Douglas Sta., *Queensland* 153 Cd
Mount Drysdale, *N.S.W.* 154 Eb
Mount Fletcher, *Cape Pr.* 115 He
Mount Forest, *Ontario* 123 Hc
Mount Frere, *Cape Prov.* 115 He
Mount Gambier, *S. Aust.* 154 Ce
Mount Garnet, *Queensland* 153 Bc
Mount Gilead, *Ohio* 129 Cb
Mount Hamilton, *Calif.* 134 Cc
Mount Hamilton, *N. Ire.* 26 Cb
Mount Hebron, *California* 134 Ca
Mount Holly, *Arkansas* 130 Bd
Mount Hope, *N.S.W.* 155 Ec
Mount Idaho, *Idaho* 136 Ec
Mount Isa, *Queensland* 153 Ad
Mount Lofty Ra., *S. Aust.* 154 Bd
Mount McKinley Nat. Park, *Alaska* 125 Je
Mount Magnet, *W. Aust.* 152 Bd
Mount Manana, *N.S.W.* 154 Db
Mount Margaret, *Queensl'd* 153 Ac
Mount Margaret, *W. Aust.* 152 Cd
Mount Margaret Goldfield, *W. Australia* 152 Cd
Mountmellick, *Eire* 27 Ce
Mount Morgan, *Queensl'd* 153 Dd
Mount Morgan, *W. Aust.* 152 Cd
Mount Morris, *New York* 123 Kd
Mount Murray, *Alberta* 124 Gc
Mount Nugent, *Eire* 26 Cd
Mount Olive, *Illinois* 132 Ef
Mount Olive, *Mississippi* 130 De
Mount Olive, *N. Carolina* 131 Jc
Mount Perry, *Queensland* 153 De
Mount Pleasant, *Iowa* 132 De
Mount Pleasant, *Michigan* 122 Fd
Mount Pleasant, *Pennsylva.* 129 Eb
Mount Pleasant, *S. Aust.* 154 Bc
Mount Pleasant, *S. Carolina* 131 Jd
Mount Pleasant, *Tennessee* 130 Ec
Mount Pleasant, *Texas* 133 Ed
Mount Pleasant, *Utah* 135 Hb
Mountrath, *Eire* 27 Cf
Mount Robson Park, *Brit. Columbia* 124 Ed
Mount's B., *England* 17 Ac
Mountshannon, *Eire* 27 Bf
Mount Shasta, *California* 134 Ba
Mount Silinda, *S. Rhod.* 113 Ec
Mountsorrel, *England* 14 Ca
Mount Sterling, *Illinois* 132 De
Mount Sterling, *Kentucky* 131 Ga
Mount Stewart, *Prince Edward I.* 120 Dc
Mount Vernon, *Georgia* 131 Gd
Mount Vernon, *Illinois* 130 Da
Mount Vernon, *Kentucky* 131 Fb
Mount Vernon, *New York* 128 Bc
Mount Vernon, *Ohio* 129 Cb
Mount Vernon, *Virginia* 129 Fc
Mount Vernon, *Washington* 136 Ba
Moura, *Brazil* 142 Bc
Moura, *Portugal* 40 Ca
Mourão, *Portugal* 37 Cd
Mourne Mts., *N. Ireland* 26 Dc
Mourne Abbey, *Eire* 27 Bg
Mouscron, *Belgium* 29 Bd
Moussoro, *Fr. Eq. Africa* 105 Fc
Moussou, *Fr. Eq. Africa* 105 Eb
Moustiers, *France* 33 Bb
Moutier, *Switzerland* 42 Db
Moutiers, *France* 35 Jb
Moutong, *Celébes* 99 Fc
Moville, *Eire* 26 Ca
Moville, *Iowa* 132 Ad
Mow, *China* 94 Bc
Moxico, *Angola* 109 Dd
Moy, *N. Ireland* 26 Dc
Moy, R., *Eire* 26 Ac
Moyale, *Kenya* 110 Fb
Moyamba, *Sierra Leone* 104 Be
Moyenneville, *France* 30 Da
Moyobambo, *Peru* 145 Bc
Moyvally, *Eire* 27 De
Mozamba Mts., *Angola* 109 Cd
Mozambique, *Mozambique* 112 Db
Mozambique, col., *S. Africa* 101 Fh
Mozambique Channel, *Mozambique* 112 Dc
Mozdok, *U.S.S.R.* 75 Gg
Mozhaisk, *U.S.S.R.* 74 Fd
Mozhga, *U.S.S.R.* 74 Jd
Mozsgó, *Hungary* 66 Cc
Mozyr, *White Russia* 75 De
Mpala, *Belg. Congo* 109 Ec
Mpanga, *Tang. Terr.* 111 Fg
Mpanganya, *Tang. Terr.* 111 Fg
Mpengere, *Tang. Terr.* 111 Eh
Mphoengs, *S. Rhodesia* 113 Cc
Mpigi, *Uganda* 110 Cc
Mpika, *N. Rhodesia* 112 Bb
Mpimbwe, *Tang. Terr.* 111 Bg
Mpitimbi, *Tang. Terr.* 111 Dj
Mpofana, *Natal* 115 Jd
Mporbi, *Mozambique* 113 Fd
Mporokoso, *N. Rhodesia* 112 Ba
Mpouia, *Fr. Eq. Africa* 109 Cb
Mpui, *Tanganyika Terr.* 111 Bh
Mpulungu, *N. Rhodesia* 112 Ba
Mpwapwa, *Tang. Terr.* 111 Eg
M'Raier, *Algeria* 103 Gc
Mrakovo, *U.S.S.R.* 74 Ke
Mramor, *Serbia* 68 Gc
Mrewa, *S. Rhodesia* 113 Da
Mrežičko, *Serbia* 70 Cb
M'Rumpe, mt., *S. Rhod.* 113 Da
Msaken, *Tunisia* 103 Kb
Msalalo, *Tang. Terr.* 111 Df
Mšeno, *Bohemia* 59 Ja
Mshinskaya, *U.S.S.R.* 48 Jg
Mshiri, *N. Rhodesia* 112 Ab
Mshunesh, *Algeria* 103 Hb
M'Sila, *Algeria* 103 Gb
Msimbati, *Tang. Terr.* 111 Fj
Msiri, *N. Rhodesia* 112 Ab
Msoun, *Morocco* 102 Cb
Msowero, *Tang. Terr.* 111 Eg
Mstislavl, *White Russia* 75 Ee
Mstow, *Poland* 57 Ec
Msua, *Tanganyika Terr.* 111 Fg
Msus, *Libya* 106 Cc
Msuva, *Mozambique* 112 Cc
Mswa, *Belg. Congo* 109 Fa
Mszczonow, *Poland* 57 Fb
Mtama, *Tanganyika Terr.* 111 Fj
Mtamba, *Belg. Congo* 109 Eb
Mtambalu, *Tang. Terr.* 111 Ef
Mtambana Mt., *Swazil'd* 115 Jc
Mtanganvika, *Kenya* 111 Fe
Mtangula, *Mozambique* 112 Cb
Mtarica, *Mozambique* 112 Cb
Mtegere, *Tang. Terr.* 111 Eg
Mtepatepa, *S. Rhodesia* 113 Da
Mtito Andei, *Kenya* 110 Fe
Mtoakordi, *Tang. Terr.* 111 Dj
Mtoko, *S. Rhodesia* 113 Ea
Mtombosi, *Tang. Terr.* 111 Eg
Mtoni, *Ital. Somaliland* 108 Gg
Mtsensk, *U.S.S.R.* 75 Fe
Mtua, *Tanganyika Terr.* 111 Fj
Mtubatuba, *Natal* 115 Jd
Muangai, *Angola* 109 Cd
Muang Chaiya, *Siam* 98 Ab
Muang Chana, *Siam* 98 Bb
Muang Langsuan, *Siam* 98 Aa
Muang Palien, *Siam* 98 Ab
Muang Patalung, *Siam* 98 Ab
Muang Patana, *Siam* 98 Bb
Muang Saiburi, *Siam* 98 Bb
Muang Songkla (Singora), *Siam* 98 Bb
Muani, *Kenya* 110 Ee
Muarotembesi, *Sumatra* 98 Bd
Muata Kabembo, *Angola* 109 Cc
Muazzam, *Punjab* 83 Ec
Mubarakpur, *Punjab States* 82 Ed
Mubarraz, *Arabia* 79 Ed
Mubende, *Uganda* 110 Bc
Mubur, I., *Neth. Indies* 98 Cc
Muccia, *Italy* 63 Hd
Muchacha, *Mozambique* 113 Ed
Muchikan shan, *Manchuria* 96 Ca
Muchkat, *U.S.S.R.* 75 Ge
Much Wenlock, *England* 14 Ba
Muck, I., *Scotland* 22 Bc
Mücka, *Prussia* 55 Kd
Muckadilla, *Queensland* 153 Ce
Muckross Abbey, *Eire* 25 Be
Mucoque, *Mozambique* 113 Fc
Mud L., *Idaho* 136 Gd
Mudabulo, *Tang. Terr.* 111 Cg
Mudanya, *Turkey* 72 Fb
Mudau, *Baden* 58 Db
Muddebihal, *Bombay* 90 Cc
Müden, *Prussia* 54 Fc
Mudgee, *New S. Wales* 155 Fc
Mudhnib, *Arabia* 78 Dd
Mudhol, *Deccan States* 90 Bc
Mudhol, *Hyderabad* 90 Cb
Mudoza, *Mozambique* 115 Kb
Muel, *Spain* 38 Dc
Muemba, *N. Rhodesia* 112 Ac
Muëne Kundi, *Belg. Congo* 109 Cb
Muengo, *Angola* 109 Cd
Mufisho, *Belgian Congo* 109 Ec
Mufor I., *Du. New Guinea* 156 Ab
Muga, *Japan* 100 Ed
Mugan, *Burma* 92 Ba
Mugardos, *Spain* 36 Ba
Mugford, C., *Labrador* 119 Re
Mughalbhin, *Sind* 85 Bb
Mughal Kot, *Baluchistan* 82 Cc
Mugia, *Spain* 36 Aa
Mugla, *Turkey* 78 Ab
Mugodzhanskie, *Kazak* 75 Kf
Mugongo, *Tang. Terr.* 111 Bf
Mugonzo, *Mozambique* 113 Fc
Mugron, *France* 34 Bd
Muhamdi, *United Provs.* 83 Je
Muhammadabad, *Persia* 79 Gb
Muhammadani, *Baluchistan* 79 Hd
Muhammadgarh, *Cent. India* 86 Bd
Muhammad Qol, *A.-E. Sudan* 108 Ca
Muhesa, *Tang. Terr.* 111 Ff
Muhinji Chini, *Tang. Ter.* 111 Eh
Mühlacker, *Württemberg* 58 Cc
Mühlberg, *Prussia* 55 Jd
Mühldorf, *Bavaria* 59 Gc
Mühlehorn, *Switzerland* 43 Hb
Mühlhausen 56 Db
Mühlhausen, *Prussia* 54 Fd
Muhoroni, *Kenya* 110 Dd
Muhu I. & Sd., *Estonia* 49 Bb
Muhumbika, *Tang. Terr.* 111 Fj
Muhutwe, *Tang. Terr.* 110 Bd
Muiden, *Holland* 29 Db
Muir Glacier, *Alaska* 125 Ng
Muirkirk, *Scotland* 21 Bb
Mui-Ron, C., *Annam* 95 Cf
Muiron Is., *W. Australia* 152 Ac
Muiskraal, *Cape Prov.* 114 Df
Mujeidil, *Palestine* 80 Cb
Mujumbuli, *Belg. Congo* 109 Da
Muka, *Sarawak* 99 Dc
Mukačevo, *Carpatho-Ukraine* 60 Gd
Mukhmas, *Palestine* 80 Cd
Mukalla, *Arabia* 77 Fg
Mukher, *Hyderabad* 90 Cb
Mukodwene, *Mozambique* 112 Bd
Mukojo, *Mozambique* 112 Db
Muktinath, *Nepal* 87 Ea
Muktsar, *Punjab* 83 Fc
Mul, *Central Provs.* 90 Da
Mula, *Spain* 41 Eb
Mulan, *Manchuria* 96 Db
Mula-pumok, *Cambodia* 95 Cg
Mulatas, Arch., *Panama* 140 Hf
Mulbagal, *Mysore* 90 De
Mulchatna R., *Alaska* 125 Hf
Mulchen, *Chile* 148 Bb
Mulde, R., *Anhalt, etc.* 55 Hd
Mulege, *Mexico* 138 Bb
Mulembera, *Tang. Terr.* 111 Bf
Mulgrave, *Nova Scotia* 120 Ed
Mulhacen, Cerro, *Spain* 41 Cc
Mulheim, *Baden* 58 Bd
Mülheim, *Prussia* 54 Ce
Mülheim, *Prussia* 54 Bd
Mulhouse, *France* 31 Kd
Muling, *Manchuria* 96 Ec
Muling, R., *Manchuria* 96 Eb
Mull, I. & Sd., *Scotland* 22 Cd
Mullagh, *Eire* 27 De
Mullaghareirk Mts., *Eire* 25 Be
Mullaghmore, *Eire* 26 Bc
Mullaittivu, *Ceylon* 89 Dc
Mullaley, *New S. Wales* 155 Fb
Mullan, *Idaho* 136 Fb
Müller Mts., *Borneo* 99 Dc
Mullet L., *Michigan* 122 Fc
Mullewa, *W. Australia* 152 Bd
Mullinavat, *Eire* 27 Cg
Mullingar, *W. Australia* 152 Cd
Mullingar, *Eire* 27 Cd
Mullion Creek, *N.S.W.* 155 Fc
Müllrose, *Prussia* 55 Kc
Mullsjö, *Sweden* 51 Ce
Mulock, *Ontario* 123 Jb
Mulonde, *Belg. Congo* 109 Ec
Muloorina, *S. Australia* 154 Ba
Muloowurtina, *S. Aust.* 154 Cb
Multan, *Punjab* 82 Dc
Mulvane, *Kansas* 133 Db
Mumbles, *Wales* 20 Cd
Mumbwa, *N. Rhodesia* 112 Ab
Mumford, *Ontario* 121 Ab
Mumia's, *Kenya* 110 Dc
Mumtrak, *Alaska* 125 Gg
Mumunga, *Bechuanaland* 113 Bc
Münchberg, *Bavaria* 59 Fa
Munchen (Munich), *Bavaria* 59 Fc
Munchen-Gladbach, *Prussia* 54 Bd
Muncie, *Indiana* 129 Bb
Mundagor, *Eastern States* 91 Fa
Münden, *Prussia* 54 Ed
Mundford, *England* 15 Ea
Mundijong, *W. Australia* 152 Be
Mundo, R., *Spain* 41 Eb
Mundo Novo, *Brazil* 143 Fe
Mundra, *Western India* 85 Bc
Mundwa, *Rajputana* 83 Ee
Munela, mt., *Albania* 70 Ba
Muner R., *Hyderabad* 91 Ec
Munfordville, *Kentucky* 130 Eb
Mungari, *Mozambique* 112 Bc
Mungaroona Ra., *W. Aust.* 152 Bc
Mungeli, *Cent. Provs.* 86 Dd
Mungindi, *New S. Wales* 155 Fa
Munich (Munchen), *Bavaria* 59 Fc
Munilla, *Spain* 38 Cb
Munisagara, *Tang. Terr.* 111 Eg
Munising, *Michigan* 122 Eb
Munkedal, *Sweden* 50 Ad
Munkfors, *Sweden* 50 Cc
Münnerstadt, *Bavaria* 58 Ea
Munnik, *Transvaal* 113 Cd
Munoz Gamers Pen., *Chile* 148 Be
Münsingen, *Switzerland* 42 Ec
Munster, *France* 31 Kc
Münster, *Prussia* 54 Cd
Munster, *Switzerland* 43 Kc
Münster, *Switzerland* 42 Fd
Munster, prov., *Eire* 25 Ce
Munster Tal, *Switzerland* 43 Kc
Münster (Beromünster), *Switzerland* 42 Fb
Münstereifel, *Prussia* 54 Be
Münsterland, *Prussia* 54 Cd
Muntarat el Quneitra, *Palestine* 80 Bd
Muntenia (Walachia), *Romania* 69 Fc
Muntok, *Bangka I., N.I.* 98 Cd
Muong Attopeu, *Laos* 95 Cg
Muong Borikan, *Laos* 95 Bf
Muong Falan, *Laos* 95 Cf
Muong Het, *Laos* 95 Be
Muong Hiem, *Laos* 95 Be
Muong Hua-muong, *Laos* 95 Be
Muong Hu-neua, *Laos* 95 Be
Muong Hung, *Tong-king* 95 Be
Muong Khat, *Laos* 95 Bf
Muong Koung, *Laos* 95 Bf
Muong Kwa, *Laos* 95 Be
Muong La, *Tong-king* 95 Be
Muong Luong, *Laos* 95 Be
Muong Mohasay, *Laos* 95 Bf
Muong Ngoi, *Laos* 95 Be
Muong-Nong, *Laos* 95 Cf
Muong Sai, *Laos* 95 Be
Muong Sapat, *Laos* 95 Cf
Muong Saravan, *Laos* 95 Cf
Muong Savannaket, *Laos* 95 Bf
Muong Sen, *Annam* 95 Bf
Muong Sen, *Laos* 95 Bf
Muong Sing, *Laos* 95 Be
Muong Son, *Laos* 95 Be
Muong Song-kon, *Laos* 95 Cf
Muong Sui, *Laos* 95 Bf
Muong Theng, *Tong-king* 95 Be
Muong Vang, *Laos* 95 Cf
Muonio & Elv, *Finland* 48 Ec
Muonio, R., *Swed.-Finland* 44 Ef
Muqatta, Nahr el, *Palestine* 80 Cb
Mur, *Yemen* 78 Lg
Mur, R., *Austria* 59 Ke
Mur Tal, *Austria* 59 Hd
Murad Dagh, *Turkey* 78 Ab
Murakami, *Japan* 97 Dc
Murang, *Punjab States* 83 Hc
Murano, *Italy* 63 Gb
Murashi, *U.S.S.R.* 74 Hd
Murat, *France* 34 Eb
Muratli, *Turkey* 72 Ea
Murau, *Austria* 59 Jd
Murauka, *New Guinea* 156 Bb
Murazzano, *Italy* 62 Cc
Murcheh Khur, *Persia* 79 Fc
Murchison, Mt., *W. Aust.* 152 Bd
Murchison Mts., *N. Z.* 159 Af
Murchison Ra., *Transvaal* 115 Ja

Narrandera, *New S. Wales* 155 Ec
Narromine, *New S. Wales* 155 Fb
Narrowsburg, *New York* 128 Ac
Narsinghgarh, *Cent. India* 86 Bd
Narsinghpur, *Cent. Provs.* 86 Cd
Narsinghpur, *Eastern States* 87 Fe
Nartës, L., *Albania* - 70 Ac
Narthakion Hills, *Greece* 70 Dd
Narubis, *S.-W. Africa* - 114 Cc
Narva, *Estonia* - - 49 Eb
Narva B. & R., *Estonia* 49 Db
Narvacan, *Philippines* - 95 Ff
Narva Jõesu, *Estonia* - 49 Db
Narvik, *Norway* - - 44 De
Narwar, *Gwalior* - - 86 Bc
Naryan-mar, *U.S.S.R.* - 74 Jb
Narykary, *U.S.S.R.* - 74 Lc
Narynsk, *Kirghiz* - - 84 Db
Nas, *Sweden* - - 50 Db
Nasaro, *Tang. Terr.* - 110 Ce
Nasaud, *Transylvania* - 67 Kb
Nasbinals, *France* - - 35 Fc
Nasca, *Peru* - - - 145 Cd
Naseby, *New Zealand* - 159 Cf
Nashua, *Iowa* - - 132 Cd
Nashua, *New Hampshire* 128 Cb
Nashugal, *Kenya* - - 110 Ec
Nashville, *Arkansas* - 130 Bd
Nashville, *Illinois* - - 130 Da
Nashville, *N. Carolina* - 131 Jb
Nashville, *Tennessee* - 130 Eb
Našice, *Slavonia* - - 66 Cd
Nasi Järvi, *Finland* - 48 Ff
Nasik, *Bombay* - - 90 Aa
Nasir, *A.-E. Sudan* - 108 Bd
Nasirabad, *Ajmer-Merwara* 85 Ea
Nasirabad, *Baluchistan* - 82 Cd
Nasirabad (Mymensingh), *Bengal* - - - 88 Cb
Naso, C., *Philippines* - 99 Fa
Nasriganj, *Bihar* - - 87 Fc
Nassarawa, *Nigeria* - 105 Cd
Nassau, *Bahamas* - - 140 Ba
Nassau, I., *Cook Is.* - 157 Ge
Nassau Mts., *New Guinea* 156 Bb
Nassau Sd., *Florida* - 131 He
Nässjö, *Sweden* - - 51 De
Nata, *Panama* - - 140 Gf
Nata, *Tanganyika Terr.* 110 Dd
Natagan, *Quebec* - - 123 Ka
Natal, *Amazonas, Brazil* 142 Bd
Natal, *Brazil* - - 143 Gd
Natal, *Sumatra* - - 98 Ac
Natal, prov., *S. Africa* - 101 Eh
Natanz, *Persia* - - 79 Fc
Natashkwan, *Quebec* - 120 Da
Natchess Pass, *Washington* 136Cb
Natchez, *Mississippi* - 130 Ce
Natchitoches, *Louisiana* 130 Be
Nathdwara, *Rajputana* - 85 Db
Nathia Gali, *N.-W.F.P.* 82 Ea
Natimuk, *Victoria* - - 154 Cd
Nation, *Alaska* - - 125 Ld
National City, *California* 134 Ee
Natividade, *Brazil* - 143 Ee
Natoena, Gt. (Bunguran) I., *Netherlands Indies* - 98 Cc
Natoena Is., N. and S., *Netherlands Indies* - 98 Cc
Natron, L., *Tang. Terr.* 110 Ee
Natrûn, Wadi el, *Egypt* 107 Hc
Nattalin, *Burma* - - 92 Bc
Naturaliste, C., *W. Aust.* 152 Ae
Naturaliste Channel, *W. Australia* - - 152 Ad
Naturawit L., *N.-W.T.* 124 Kb
Naturita, *Colorado* - 135 Jb
Naubinway, *Michigan* - 122 Fb
Naucelle, *France* - - 34 Ec
Nauchas, *S.-W. Africa* - 114 Ba
Nauders, *Austria* - - 58 Ee
Nauen, *Prussia* - - 55 Hc
Naugard - - - 55 Kb
Naugatuck, *Connecticut* - 128 Bc
Nau Hissar, *Baluchistan* 82 Bc
Naumburg, *Hesse-Nassau, Prussia* - - - 54 Ed
Naumburg, *Prov. of Saxony, Prussia* - - - 55 Gd
Naumburg - - - 55 Ld
Naumiestis, *Lithuania* - 49 Bd
Naundu Tawa, *Tang. Ter.* 111 Fh
Naungpale, *Burma* - 92 Cc
Nauplia (Návplion), *Greece* 71 Df
Na'ur, *Trans-Jordan* - 80 Dd
Nauru, I., *Pacific Oc.* - 157 Dd
Naushahra (Nowshera), *N.-W.F.P.* - - 82 Ea
Naushahro, *Sind* - - 82 Ce
Naushara, *Punjab States* 82 Ce
Naustdal, *Norway* - - 46 Bc
Nauta, *Peru* - - 145 Cb
Nauteyri, *Iceland* - - 52 Bb
Nautgars Tind, *Norway* 46 Ec
Nautla, *Mexico* - - 139 Ec
Nauvoo, *Illinois* - - 132 De
Nava de la Asunción, *Spain* 38 Ac
Nava del Rey, *Spain* - 36 Ec
Navahermosa, *Spain* - 38 Ae
Navajo, Mt., *Utah* - 135 Hc
Navalcarnero, *Spain* - 38 Ad
Navalmoral de la Mota, *Spain* - - - 37 Ec
Navan (An Uaimh), *Eire* 26 Dd
Navanagar, *Western India* 85 Bc
Navarino, I., *Chile* - 148 Cf
Navarínon B., *Greece* - 71 Cg
Navarra, prov., *Spain* - 38 Db
Navarre, *Victoria* - - 154 Dd
Navarre, old prov., *France* 34 Ad
Navarrenx, *France* - 34 Bd
Navarro, *Argentina* - 148 Eb
Navas del Marqués, Las, *Spain* - - - 38 Ad
Navas del Modrono, *Spain* 37 Dc
Navasota, *Texas* - - 133 Ee
Naver, L. & Strath, *Scot.* 24 De
Näverdalen, *Norway* - 46 Gb
Navia and R., *Spain* - 36 Da
Navia de Suarna, *Spain* 36 Cb
Navlakhi, *Western India* 85 Cc
Navojoa, *Mexico* - - 138 Cb
Návpaktos, *Greece* - - 71 Ce
Návplion (Nauplia), *Greece* 71 Df
Navrongo, *Gold Coast* - 104 Dd
Navsari, *Baroda* - - 90 Aa
Nawa, *Rajputana* - - 83 Fe
Nawa, *Syria* - - - 78 Cc
Nawab Basoda, *Cent. India* 86 Cd
Nawabganj, *Bengal* - - 88 Bb
Nawabganj, *United Provs.* 87 Eb
Nawabganj, *United Provs.* 86 Db
Nawabshah, *Sind* - - 85 Ba
Nawada, *Bihar* - - 87 Fc
Nawagarh, *Cent. Provs.* 91 Fa
Nawahganj, *United Provs.* 83 Hd
Nawalgarh, *Rajputana* - 83 Fe
Nawalia, *N. Rhodesia* - 112 Bb
Nawng Wawn, *Burma* - 92 Cb
Naxos, *Ægean Sea* - 78 Ab
Nay, *France* - - - 34 Bd
Nayagarh, *Eastern States* 91 Ga
Nayarit, state, *Mexico* - 138 Cc
Nayarit, Sierra de, *Mexico* 138 Dc
Nayaro, *Japan* - - 97 Eb
Nayland, *England* - 15 Ec
Nazare, *Portugal* - - 37 Ac
Nazareth, *Bahia, Brazil* 143 Ge
Nazareth, *Pernambuco, Brazil* - - - 143 Gd
Nazareth, *Madras* - - 89 Bc
Nazareth (En Nazira), *Palestine* - - - 80 Cb
Nazareth B., *Fr. Eq. Afr.* 109 Ab
Nazas and R., *Mexico* - 138 Db
Naze, The, *England* - 15 Fc
Naze, The (Lindesnes), *Norway* - - - 47 Cg
Nazilli, *Turkey* - - 78 Ab
Nazira, *Assam* - - 88 Ea
Nchanga, *N. Rhodesia* - 112 Ab
Ncheu, *Nyasaland* - 112 Bb
Ncomi L., *Fr. Eq. Africa* 109 Ab
N'Dala Tando, *Angola* - 109 Bc
Ndanga, *S. Rhodesia* - 113 Dc
Ndege, *Kenya* - - 110 Db
N'dele, *Fr. Eq. Africa* - 105 Fd
Ndende, *Tang. Terr.* - 111 Fh
Ndeni, I., *Santa Cruz Is.* 157 De
Nderfande, *Albania* - 70 Ab
Ndiago, *Fr. W. Africa* - 104 Ac
Ndokouassikro, *Fr. W. Africa* - - 104 De
Ndola, *N. Rhodesia* - 112 Ab
Ndundu, *Tang. Terr.* - 111 Fg
Né I., *Annam* - - 95 Cf
Néa Epídhavros, *Greece* - 71 Ef
Néa Filippias, *Greece* - 71 Bd
Neagh L., *N. Ireland* - 26 Db
Néa Mádhitos, *Greece* - 70 Ec
Neá Mikhaniόna, *Greece* 70 Dc
Nea Moudhania, *Greece* 70 Ec
Neamţu, *Romania* - - 69 Gb
Néa Orestias, *Greece* - 72 Da
Néa Péramos, *Greece* - 70 Fc
Neápolis, *Crete* - - 71 Jj
Neapolis, *Greece* - - 71 Eg
Neápolis (Lipsísta), *Greece* 70 Cc
Néa Psara (Erétria), *Greece* 71 Ee
Near Is., *Aleutian Is.* - 125 Sl
Neath and R., *Wales* - 20 Cd
Néa Zikhna, *Greece* - 70 Eb
Nebbi, *Uganda* - - 110 Bb
Nebeur, *Tunisia* - - 103 Ja
Nebo, Mt., *Utah* - - 135 Gb
Nebo (Fort Cooper), *Queensland* - - 153 Cd
Nebolchi, *U.S.S.R.* - 48 Kg
Nebraska, state, *U.S.A.* 126 Eb
Nebraska City, *Nebraska* 132 Be
Nebrodi Mts., *Sicily* - 65 Hg
Nebtjusi, *Croatia* - - 68 Ab
Necedah, *Wisconsin* - 132 Ec
Neches R., *Texas* - - 133 Ee
Nechmeya, *Algeria* - 103 Ha
Neckar, R., *Württemberg* 58 Cc
Necker I., *Hawaiian Is.* 157 Ga
Necochea, *Argentina* - 148 Eb
Neddich, *Libya* - - 106 Bd
Nederburgh, C., *Celébes* 99 Fd
Nederweert, *Holland* - 29 Dc
Nedroma, *Algeria* - - 102 Db
Nedstrand, *Norway* - 47 Be
Needham Market, *Eng.* 15 Eb
Needle Ra., *Utah* - - 134 Gb
Needles, *California* - 134 Fd
Needles, *Arizona* - - 134 Fd
Needles, The, *I. of Wight, England* - - - 14 Ce
Neemuch, *Gwalior* - 85 Eb
Neenah, *Wisconsin* - 132 Ec
Neepawa, *Manitoba* - 124 Kd
Nefta, *Tunisia* - - 103 Hc
Neftegorsk, *U.S.S.R.* - 75 Fg
Nefud, des., *Arabia* - 78 Dd
Nefud Dahi, *Arabia* - 78 De
Nefusa, Jeb., *Libya* - 103 Kd
Negapatam, *Madras* - 89 Cb
Negaunee, *Michigan* - 122 Eb
Negbina, *Serbia* - - 68 Ec
Negelli, *Ethiopia* - - 108 Cd
Negocio, *Argentina* - 148 Cc
Negoiul, *Romania* - - 67 Kd
Negombo, *Ceylon* - - 89 Cd
Negoroloye, *White Russia* 75 De
Negotin, *Serbia* - - 69 Ec
Negotino, *Serbia* - - 70 Db
Negra, Sa., *Brazil* - 143 Ed
Negrais, C., *Burma* - 92 Be
Negreira, *Spain* - - 36 Bb
Negrepelisse, *France* - 34 Dc
Negrine, *Algeria* - - 103 Hb
Negri Sembilan, *Malay States* - - - 98 Bc
Negro, B., *It. Somaliland* 108 Fd
Negro, R., *Argentina* - 148 Db
Negro, R., *Brazil* - - 142 Bc
Negro, R., *Uruguay* - 146 De
Negros I., *Philippines* - 99 Fa
Negyed, *Slovakia* - - 66 Ca
Neh, *Persia* - - - 79 Gc
Nehalem, *Oregon* - - 136 Bc
Nehavend, *Persia* - - 79 Ec
Neibull, *Prussia* - - 54 Da
Neidenburg - - - 56 Ec
Neihart, *Montana* - - 136 Ha
Neihen, *Korea* - - 97 Bc
Neilsville, *Wisconsin* - 132 Dc
Neisse - - - - 57 Cc
Neiva, *Colombia* - - 144 Ac
Nejd, *Arabia* - - 78 Dd
Nejo, *Ethiopia* - - 108 Cd
Nekati, *Bechuanaland* - 113 Ac
Nekhl, *Egypt* - - 107 Jd
Nekob, *Morocco* - - 102 Bd
Nekrila, *Morocco* - - 102 Cb
Neksö, *Bornholm I.* - 45 Jf
Nelas, *Portugal* - - 37 Cb
Nelia Gaari, *New S. Wales* 154 Cb
Nelligen, *New S. Wales* 155 Fd
Nellikuppam, *Madras* - 89 Cb
Nellore, *Madras* - - 91 Dd
Nelson, *Arizona* - - 135 Gd
Nelson, *Brit. Columbia* - 124 Fe
Nelson, *California* - 134 Cb
Nelson, *England* - - 18 Bc
Nelson, *Victoria* - - 154 Ce
Nelson and prov., *New Zealand* - - - 159 Dd
Nelson I., *Alaska* - - 125 Ff
Nelson L., *Manitoba* - 124 Kc
Nelson, Mt., *Br. Columbia* 124 Fd
Nelson R., *Manitoba* - 124 Lc
Nelsonville, *Ohio* - - 129 Cc
Nelspoort, *Cape Prov.* - 114 Ef
Nelspruit, *Transvaal* - 115 Jb
Nema, *Fr. W. Africa* - 104 Cc
Nemawar, *Central India* 86 Bd
Neméa, *Greece* - - 71 Df
Nemecky Brod, *Bohemia* 59 Kb
Nementcha, Mts. des, *Algeria* - - - 103 Hb
Nemer R., *Manchuria* - 96 Db
Némétlad, *Hungary* - 66 Cc
Nemetsko Khaginskoe, *U.S.S.R.* - - - 75 Gf
Nemi, *Italy* - - - 64 Cb
Nemikachi L., *Quebec* - 123 Lb
Nemila, *Bosnia* - - 68 Cb
Nemonien - - - 56 Fb
Nemours, *Algeria* - - 102 Cb
Nemours, *France* - - 30 Ec
Nemunas (Niemen), R., *Lithuania* - - 49 Bd
Nemuro, *Japan* - - 97 Fb
Nen, R., *England* - 15 Db
Nenagh, *Eire* - - 27 Bf
Nenana, *Alaska* - - 125 Kd
Nendeln, *Liechtenstein* - 43 Jb
Nengonengo, I., *Tuamotu Arch.* - - - - 157 Je
Nenndorf, *Prussia* - 54 Ec
Neno, *Nyasaland* - - 112 Bc
Nenoesa Is., *Neth. Indies* 99 Gc
Neodesha, *Kansas* - - 133 Eb
Néon Petrítsi, *Greece* - 70 Eb
Neosho, *Missouri* - - 130 Ab
Neosho R., *Oklahoma* - 133 Eb
Nepa, *New Guinea* - 156 Dc
Nepal, *Asia* - - - 81 Ee
Nepalganj, *Nepal* - - 86 Da
Nephi, *Utah* - - - 135 Hb
Nephin Beg, mt., *Eire* - 25 Ba
Nepomuk, *Bohemia* - 59 Hb
Nérac, *France* - - 34 Cc
Nérann, *Syria* - - 80 Da
Nerchinsk, *U.S.S.R.* - 76 Md
Nerekha, *U.S.S.R.* - 74 Gd
Neretva, R., *Hercegovina* 68 Cc
Nerja, *Spain* - - - 41 Cd
Nerokoúron, *Crete* - - 71 Gj
Nerpio, *Spain* - - 41 Db
Nerriga, *New S. Wales* - 155 Gd
Nerva, *Spain* - - 40 Db
Nervesa, *Italy* - - 63 Gb
Nervi, *Italy* - - - 62 Dc
Nes, *Norway* - - - 46 Fa
Nes, *U.S.S.R.* - - 74 Gb
Nesbyen, *Norway* - - 46 Fd
Nesflaten, *Norway* - - 47 Ce
Neskaupsstadhur, *Iceland* 52 Fb
Neskowin, *Oregon* - - 136 Ac
Ness, L., *Scotland* - 23 Db
Ness City, *Kansas* - - 133 Ca
Neston, *England* - - 18 Ad
Nestórion, *Greece* - - 70 Bc
Nesttun, *Norway* - - 47 Bd
Nes Ziyona, *Palestine* - 80 Bd
Netherdale, *Queensland* - 153 Cd
Netherlands Indies, *S.-E. Asia* - - - 93 Bg
Nethybridge, *Scotland* - 23 Eb
Netolice, *Bohemia* - - 59 Jb
Netrakona, *Bengal* - 88 Cb
Nettilling L., *N.-W. Terr.* 119 Pc
Nettleton, *Mississippi* - 130 Dc
Nettuno, *Italy* - - 64 Cb
Netumbi, *Mozambique* - 113 Fa
Neu Brandenburg, *Mecklenburg* - - 55 Jb
Neuburg, *Bavaria* - - 58 Fc
Neuchâtel and canton, *Switzerland* - - 42 Cb
Neuchâtel, L., *Switz.* - 42 Cc
Neudamm - - - 55 Kc
Neudeck, *Bohemia* - 59 Ga
Neuenburg, *Oldenburg* - 54 Cb
Neuenhaus, *Prussia* - 54 Bc
Neuenkirchen, *Prussia* - 54 Eb
Neufahrwasser - - 56 Cb
Neufchâteau, *Belgium* - 29 De
Neufchâteau, *France* - 31 Hc
Neufchâtel, *France* - 30 Db
Neufelden, *Austria* - 59 Jc
Neugersdorf, *Saxony* - 55 Ke
Neuhaldensleben, *Prussia* 55 Gc
Neuhardhof, *Palestine* - 80 Bb
Neuhaus, *Prussia* - - 54 Fb
Neuhaus, *Hanover, Prussia* 54 Eb
Neuhausen, *Switzerland* 43 Ga
Neuillé-Pont-Pierre, *France* 30 Cd
Neuilly-St Front, *France* 30 Fb
Neu Isenburg, *Hesse* - 58 Ca
Neukruhren - - - 56 Eb
Neumagen, *Prussia* - 58 Ab
Neumark - - - 55 Lc
Neumarkt, *Bavaria* - 59 Fb
Neuminster, *Prussia* - 54 Ea
Neu Mittelwalde - - 57 Cb
Neung, *France* - - 30 Dd
Neung-ju, *Korea* - - 97 Bd
Neunkirch, *Switzerland* 43 Fa
Neunkirchen, *Austria* - 66 Bb
Neunkirchen, *Saar Palatin.* 58 Ab
Neuquen & terr., *Argent.* 148 Cb
Neuquen, R., *Argentina* 148 Cb
Neusalz - - - - 55 Ld
Neuse R., *N. Carolina* - 131 Kc
Neusiedl, *Austria* - - 66 Bb
Neusiedler See (Fertö Tava), *Austria* - - 66 Bb
Neusorg, *Bavaria* - - 59 Fb
Neuss, *Prussia* - - 54 Bd
Neustadt, *Baden* - - 58 Cd
Neustadt, *Bavaria* - 59 Fc
Neustadt, *Bavaria* - 58 Eb
Neustadt, *Mecklenburg* - 55 Gb
Neustadt, *Brandenburg, Prussia* - - - 55 Hc
Neustadt, *Schleswig-Holstein, Prussia* - 54 Fa
Neustadt - - - - 57 Cc
Neustadt, *Saar Palatinate* 58 Bb
Neustadt, *Saxony* - - 55 Kd
Neustettin - - - 55 Mb
Neustrelitz, *Mecklenberg* 55 Hb
Neuteich - - - 56 Cb
Neuva Esperanza, *Bolivia* 146 Cb
Neuva Lubeca, *Argentina* 148 Bc
Neuveville, *Switzerland* 42 Db
Neuville-aux-Bois, *France* 30 Dc
Neuvy-le-Roi, *France* - 30 Cd
Neuvy-St Sepulchre, *France* 34Da
Neuwedell - - - 55 Lb
Neuwied, *Prussia* - - 54 Ce
Nevada, *Iowa* - - 132 Cd
Nevada, *Missouri* - - 130 Ab
Nevada, state, *U.S.A.* - 126 Bc
Nevada, Sa., *California* 134 Dc
Nevada, Sa., *Spain* - 41 Cc
Nevada City, *California* 134 Cb
Nevada de Santa Marta, Sa., *Colombia* - - 144 Ba
Nevado, Sa., *Argentina* 148 Cb
Nevel, *U.S.S.R.* - - 74 Dd
Nevers, *France* - - 30 Fd
Nevertire, *New S. Wales* 155 Eb
Nevesinje, *Hercegovina* - 68 Dc
Nevin, *Wales* - - 20 Bb
Nevinnomyssk, *U.S.S.R.* 75 Gg
Nevis, I., *Leeward Is.* - 140 Kg
Nevis, L., *Scotland* - 22 Cb
Nevrokop, *Bulgaria* - 69 Ee
Nevşehir, *Turkey* - - 78 Bb
Nevyansk, *U.S.S.R.* - 74 Kd
New R., *N. Carolina* - 131 Hb
Newala, *Tang. Terr.* - 111 Fj
New Albany, *Indiana* - 129 Bc
New Albany, *Mississippi* 130 Dc
New Almaden, *California* 134 Cc
New Amsterdam, *Brit. Guiana* - - - 144 Eb
New Amsterdam, *Holland* 29 Eb
Newark, *England* - - 19 Dd
Newark, *New Jersey* - 129 Gb
Newark, *Ohio* - - 129 Cb
New Augusta, *Mississippi* 130 De
Newaygo, *Michigan* - 122 Ed
New Baltimore, *New York* 128 Ab
New Bedford, *Massachus.* 128 Cc
Newberg, *Oregon* - - 136 Bc
New Berlin, *New York* - 128 Ab
New Bern, *N. Carolina* - 131 Kc
Newbern, *Tennessee* - 130 Db
Newberry, *Michigan* - 122 Fb
Newberry, *S. Carolina* - 131 Hc
New Bethal, *Transvaal* - 115 Hc
New Bethesda, *Cape Prov.* 115 Fe
Newbiggin, *England* - 21 Ec
Newbliss, *Eire* - - 26 Cc
Newbold, *England* - 14 Cb
Newboro & L., *Ontario* - 121 Bb
New Boston, *Texas* - 133 Ed
New Braunfels, *Texas* - 133 Cf
Newbridge, *England* - 14 Ac
Newbridge, *Wales* - 20 Cc
Newbridge (Droichead Nuadh), *Eire* - - 27 De
New Brighton, *New York* 128 Ac
New Britain, *Connecticut* 128 Bc
New Britain I., *Bismarck Arch.* - - - 156 Dc
New Brunswick, *New Jersey* 129Gb
New Brunswick, prov., *Canada* - - - 119 Qg
New Buckenham, *Eng.* 15 Fb
Newburg, *New Brunswick* 120 Bc
Newburgh, *New York* - 123 Le
Newburgh, *Ontario* - 121 Bb
Newburgh, *Scotland* - 23 Ed
Newbury, *England* - 14 Cd
Newburyport, *Mass.* - 128 Cb
New Caledonia I., *Pac. Oc.* 157 Df
New Carlisle, *Quebec* - 120 Cc
New Carlow, *Ontario* - 121 Bb
New Castle, *Colorado* - 135 Jb
Newcastle, *Delaware* - 129 Gc
Newcastle, *Dublin, Eire* 27 De
Newcastle, *Limerick, Eire* 27 Ag
Newcastle, *Indiana* - 129 Bb

NEW
General Index
NOM

Newcastle, *Natal* - - 115 Hc
Newcastle, *New Bruns.* - 120 Cc
Newcastle, *New S. Wales* 155 Gc
Newcastle, *N. Ireland* - 26 Ec
New Castle, *Pennsylvania* 129 Db
Newcastle Emlyn, *Wales* 20 Bc
New Castleton, *Scotland* 21 Dc
Newcastle-under-Lyme, *England* - - - 18 Bd
Newcastle-upon-Tyne, *England* - - - 21 Ec
Newcastle Waters, *N. Terr., Australia* - 151 Eb
Newchang (Ying-kow), *Manchuria* - - - 96 Cc
New City, *New York* - 128 Bc
New Cumberland, *W. Virginia* - - 129 Db
New Deer, *Scotland* - 23 Fa
New Denmark, *Transvaal* 115 Hc
New England Ra., *New S. Wales* - - - 155 Gb
Newent, *England* - - 14 Bc
Newfane, *Vermont* - 128 Bb
New Forest, *England* - 14 Ce
Newfoundland, I., *N. America* - - - 119 Sg
Newgale, *Wales* - - 20 Ad
New Galloway, *Scotland* 21 Bc
New Georgia, I., *Solomon Islands* - - - 157 Cd
New Germany, *Nova Scotia* 120Cd
New Glasgow, *Nova Scotia* 120Dd
New Guinea (Papua), *Pacific Oc.* - - - 156 Cc
New Guinea, Terr. of, *Pacific Oc.* - - - 156 Cb
New Hampshire, state, *U.S.A.* - - - 127 Lb
New Hampton, *Iowa* - 132 Cd
New Hanover, *Natal* - 115 Jd
New Hanover (Lavongai I.), *Bismarck Arch.* - 156 Db
New Hartford, *Connecticut* 128 Bc
New Haven, *Connecticut* 128 Bc
Newhaven, *England* - 15 De
New Haven, *Missouri* - 130 Ca
New Hebrides Is., *Pac. Oc.* 157De
New Iberia, *Louisiana* - 130 Ce
Newington, *Transvaal* - 115 Jb
New Inlet, *N. Carolina* - 131 Lc
New Ireland, I., *Bismarck Arch.* - - - 156 Eb
New Jersey, state, *U.S.A.* 127 Lb
New Kamilche, *Washing'n.* 136Bb
New Kensington, *Penns.* 129 Eb
New Kent, *Virginia* - 129 Fd
Newkirk, *Oklahoma* - 133 Db
Newland, *Nevada* - - 134 Fb
New Lewisville, *Arkansas* 130 Bd
New Liskeard, *Ontario* - 123 Jb
New London, *Connecticut* 128 Bc
New London, *Iowa* - 132 De
New London, *Missouri* - 130 Ca
New London, *Wisconsin* 132 Ec
Newlyn, *England* - - 17 Ac
New Madrid, *Missouri* - 130 Db
Newmarket, *Eire* - - 27 Ag
Newmarket, *England* - 15 Eb
Newmarket, *New Hamps.* 128 Cb
Newmarket, *Ontario* - 123 Jc
Newmarket-on-Fergus, *Eire* - - - - 27 Bf
New Mexico, state, *U.S.A.* 126Dd
New Milford, *Connecticut* 128 Bc
New Milford, *Wales* - 20 Bd
New Mills, *England* - 18 Cd
Newnan, *Georgia* - - 131 Fd
Newnes, *New S. Wales* - 155 Gc
Newnham, *England* - 14 Bc
New Norcia, *W. Aust.* - 152 Be
New Norfolk, *Tasmania* 155 Jh
New Orleans, *Louisiana* 130 Df
Newpaltz, *New York* - 128 Ac
New Philadelphia, *Ohio* 129 Db
New Pitsligo, *Scotland* - 23 Fa
New Plymouth, *New Zeal.* 158 Dc
Newport, *Arkansas* - 130 Cc
Newport, *California* - 134 De
Newport, *Eire* - - 25 Bb
Newport, *Essex, England* 15 Ec
Newport, *I. of Wight, Eng.* 14 Ce
Newport, *Monmouth, Eng.* 14 Bc
Newport, *Salop, Eng.* - 18 Be
Newport, *Kentucky* - 131 Fa
Newport, *New Hamps.* - 128 Bb
Newport, *Oregon* - - 136 Ac
Newport, *Quebec* - - 120 Cb
Newport, *Rhode Island* - 128 Cc
Newport, *Scotland* - 23 Fd
Newport, *Vermont* - - 123 Mc
Newport, *Washington* - 136 Ea
Newport and B., *Wales* 20 Bc
Newport News, *Virginia* 129 Fd
Newport Pagnell, *England* 15 Db
New Prague, *Minnesota* - 132 Cc
New Providence, I., *Bahamas* - - - 140 Bb
New Quay, *Eire* - - 27 Ae
Newquay, *England* - 17 Ac
New Quay, *Wales* - - 20 Bc
New Radnor, *Wales* - 20 Cc
New Richmond, *Quebec* 120 Cb
New Richmond, *Wisconsin* 132 Cc
New River Inlet, *N. Carolina* - - - 131 Kc
New Roads, *Louisiana* - 130 Ce
New Rochelle, *New York* 128 Bc
New Romney, *England* 15 Ee
New Ross, *Eire* - - 27 Dg
Newry, *N. Ireland* - 26 Dc
New Salem, *Illinois* - 132 Ee
New Sharon, *Iowa* - 132 Ce
New Shoreham, *England* 15 De
New Smitsdorp, *Transvaal* 115Hb
New Smyrna, *Florida* - 131 Ng
New South Wales, state, *Australia* - - - 151 He
Newstead, *Queensland* - 153 Cd
Newton, *Norfolk, Eng.* - 15 Ea
Newton, *Suffolk, Eng.* - 15 Eb
Newton, *Illinois* - - 132 Ef
Newton, *Iowa* - - 132 Ce
Newton, *Kansas* - - 133 Da
Newton, *Massachusetts* - 128 Cb
Newton, *New Jersey* - 129 Gb
Newton Abbot, *England* 17 Cb
Newton Ferrers, *England* 17 Bc
Newton-in-Makerfield, *England* - - - 18 Bd
Newtonmore, *Scotland* - 23 Db
Newton Stewart, *Scotland* 21 Bd
Newtonville, *Ontario* - 121 Ac
Newtown, *Fr. W. Africa* 104 Df
Newtown, *Eire* - - 27 Be
Newtown, *England* - 14 Bb
Newtown, *Wales* - - 20 Cb
Newtownards, *N. Ireland* 26 Eb
Newtownbarry, *Eire* - 27 Df
Newtown Butler, *N. Ire.* 26 Cc
Newtown Forbes, *Eire* - 26 Cd
Newtown Gore, *Eire* - 26 Cc
Newtown Hamilton, *N. Ire.* 26Dc
Newtown Mt. Kennedy, *Eire* - - - - 27 De
Newtown Stewart, *N. Ire.* 26 Cb
New Ulm, *Bavaria* - 58 Ec
New Ulm, *Minnesota* - 132 Bc
New Washington, *Philippines* - - - 99 Fa
New Waterford, *Nova Scotia* - - - 120 Fc
New Westminster, *Brit. Columbia* - - - 124 Ee
New World I., *Newfld.* 120 Hb
New York, *New York* - 123 Me
New York, state, *U.S.A.* 127 Kb
Nexon, *France* - - 34 Db
Nezametni, *U.S.S.R.* - 76 Nd
Nezhin, *Ukraine* - - 75 Ee
Nez Perce, *Idaho* - - 136 Eb
Nez Perces Pass, *Idaho* - 136 Fc
Ngabang, *Borneo* - - 98 Cc
Ngambe-Nyangforo, *Fr. Eq. Africa* - - - 105 Dd
Ngamdo, *China* - - 94 Bb
Ngamo, *S. Rhodesia* - 113 Bb
Nganchu, *Fr. Eq. Afr.* - 109 Cb
Ngao, *Kenya* - - - 110 Fe
Ngaoundere, *Fr. Eq. Afr.* 105 Dd
Ngapara, *New Zealand* - 159 Cf
Ngara, *Nyasaland* - - 112 Bb
Ngarambi, *Tang. Terr.* - 111 Fh
Ngaruawahia, *New Zeal.* 158 Eb
Ngathaing Gyaung, *Burma* 92 Bd
Ngazun, *Burma* - - 92 Bb
Ngerengere, *Tang. Terr.* 111 Fg
Ngola, *Fr. Eq. Africa* - 109 Ab
Ngoma, *Belgian Congo* - 109 Eb
Ngomano, *Mozambique* - 112 Cb
Ngombako, *Fr. Eq. Afr.* 105 Ee
Ngome, *Natal* - - 115 Jc
Ngong, *Kenya* - - 110 Ed
Ngongo, *Tang. Terr.* - 111 Bg
Ngopp, *A.-E. Sudan* - 108 Bd
Ngora, *Uganda* - - 110 Cc
Ngorongoro Crater, *Tanganyika Terr.* - 110 De
Ngotu, *Fr. Eq. Africa* - 109 Bb
N'Gouça, *Algeria* - - 103 Gc
N'Gouri, *Fr. Eq. Africa* 105 Ec
Ngovi, *Fr. Eq. Africa* - 109 Ab
Ngqeleni, *Cape Prov.* - 115 He
Ngudu, *Tang. Terr.* - 110 Ce
N'Guigmi, *Fr. W. Africa* 105 Dc
Nguila, *Fr. Eq. Africa* - 105 De
Ngulu Is., *Caroline Is.* - 157 Ac
Ngunza, *Angola* - - 109 Cc
Nguru, *Nigeria* - - 105 Dc
Ngutu, *Natal* - - 115 Jd
Ngwena, *Kenya* - - 110 Fd
Nhagama, *Mozambique* - 113 Ed
Nhamarroi, *Mozambique* 112 Cc
Nha-trang, *Annam* - 95 Cg
Nhematenga, *Mozambique* 113 Fa
Nhill, *Victoria* - - 154 Cd
Niadi, *Belg. Congo* - 109 Cb
Niafadie, *Fr. W. Africa* 104 Ce
Niafounke, *Fr. W. Africa* 104 Dc
Niagara, *Ontario* - - 123 Jd
Niagara Falls, *New York* 123 Jd
Niah, *Sarawak* - - 99 Dc
Niamey, *Fr. W. Africa* - 105 Bc
Niaming, *Fr. W. Africa* 104 Cd
Niamoana, *Angola* - 109 Dd
Niandarawa, mt., *Kenya* 110 Ed
Niangara, *Belg. Congo* - 109 Ea
Niangbo, *Fr. W. Africa* 104 De
Nianza, *Belg. Congo* - 109 Eb
Nias I., *Nether. Indies* - 98 Ac
Niáta, *Greece* - - 71 Dg
Nibbiano, *Italy* - - 62 Dc
Nibe, *Denmark* - - 45 Cb
Niblock, *Ontario* - - 122 Ca
Nicaragua, rep. and L., *Nicaragua* - - - 140 Fe
Nicaria, *Ægean Sea* - 78 Ab
Nicastro, *Italy* - - 65 Cd
Nic Doit Soe Pk., *Arizona* 135 Hc
Nice, *France* - - 33 Cb
Nichikun L., *Quebec* - 119 Pf
Nichol B., *W. Australia* 152 Bc
Nicholia, *Idaho* - - 136 Gc
Nicholson Ra., *W. Aust.* 152 Bd
Nicholson R., *Queensland* 153 Ac
Nickerson, *Kansas* - 133 Ca
Nicobar, Gt. and Lit., *Nicobar Is.* - - 91 Jg
Nicobar Is., *Bay of Bengal* 91 Jg
Nicolas Chan., *Cuba* - 140 Ab
Nicolet, *Quebec* - - 121 Da
Nicopolis, *Greece* - - 71 Bd
Nicosia, *Cyprus* - - 78 Bb
Nicosia, *Sicily* - - 65 Hg
Nicotera, *Italy* - - 65 Bd
Nicoya, *Costa Rica* - 140 Fe
Nicoya Pen. and Gulf, *Costa Rica* - - - 140 Ff
Nictheroy, *Brazil* - - 147 Gc
Nicuadala, *Mozambique* - 113 Ga
Nidau, *Switzerland* - 42 Db
Nidda, *Hesse* - - - 58 Da
Nidden - - - - 56 Fa
Nidwalden, *Switzerland* 43 Fc
Niebade, *Latvia* - - 49 Cc
Niedere Tauern, *Austria* 59 Hd
Nieder Lausitz, *Prussia* 55 Jd
Nieheim, *Prussia* - - 54 Ed
Niekerkshope, *Cape Prov.* 114 Ed
Niembo, *Belg. Congo* - 109 Eb
Niemen, R. - - - 60 Jb
Niemen (Nemunas), R., *Lithuania* - - - 49 Bd
Nienburg, *Prussia* - 54 Ec
Nien-pu, *China* - - 94 Bb
Nientzeshan, *Manchuria* 96 Cb
Niéry, *Fr. Eq. Africa* - 105 Fc
Niesky, *Prussia* - - 55 Kd
Nieswież - - - - 60 Jb
Nieuport, *Belgium* - 29 Ac
Nieuw Amsterdam, *Suriname* - - - - 142 Da
Nieuwerust, *Cape Prov.* - 114 Ce
Nieuw Nickerie, *Suriname* 142 Ca
Nieuwoudtville, *Cape Pr.* 114 Ce
Nieuwveld Ra., *Cape Pr.* 114 Df
Nieves, *Mexico* - - 138 Dc
Nièvre, dep., *France* - 31 Fd
Nifa, *Liberia* - - - 104 Cf
Nigaluk, *Alaska* - - 125 Ja
Nigde, *Turkey* - - 78 Bb
Nigel, *Transvaal* - - 115 Hc
Niger, R., *Nigeria, etc.* 107 Fe
Niger Colony, *Fr. W. Afr.* 105 Cb
Nigeria, terr., *W. Africa* 101 Cd
Nigg, *Scotland* - - 23 Ea
Nighasan, *United Provs.* 86 Da
Nighthawk L., *Ontario* - 123 Ha
Nigishima, *Japan* - - 100 Fe
Nigrita, *Greece* - - 70 Ec
Nihiru Is., *Tuamotu Arch.* 157 Je
Niigata, *Japan* - - 97 Dc
Niishima, *Japan* - - 97 Dd
Niitaka Ra., *Taiwan* - 97 Hf
Niitakayama, mt., *Taiwan* 97 Hf
Nijaan, Mt., *Borneo* - 99 Dc
Nijar, *Spain* - - - 41 Dd
Nijkerk, *Holland* - - 29 Db
Nijmegen, *Holland* - 29 Dc
Nikifóros, *Greece* - - 70 Fb
Nikiniki, *Timor I., E.I.* 99 Fe
Nikki, *Fr. W. Africa* - 105 Bc
Nikko, *Japan* - - 97 Dc
Nikolaev, *Ukraine* - - 75 Ef
Nikolaevsk, *U.S.S.R.* - 75 Hf
Nikolaievsk, *U.S.S.R.* - 96 Ga
Nikolaiken - - - 56 Dc
Nikolsburg, *Moravia* - 57 Be
Nikolsk, *U.S.S.R.* - 74 Hd
Nikolskoe, *U.S.S.R.* - 74 Hb
Nikopol, *Bulgaria* - - 69 Fd
Nikopol, *Ukraine* - - 75 Ef
Niksar, *Turkey* - - 78 Ca
Nikšic, *Montenegro* - 68 Dd
Nilakottai, *Madras* - 89 Bb
Nilambur, *Madras* - 89 Bb
Nile, R., *Egypt* - - 107 Je
Niles, *Michigan* - - 122 Ee
Niles, *Ohio* - - - 129 Db
Nileshwar, *Madras* - 89 Aa
Nilgiri, *Eastern States* - 87 Ge
Nilgiri Hills, *Madras* - 89 Bb
Nilgiris, *Madras* - - 89 Bb
Nili, *Algeria* - - - 103 Fc
Nilki, *Sinkiang* - - 84 Eb
Nilphamari, *Bengal* - 88 Bb
Nimach, *Gwalior* - - 85 Eb
Nimar, *Cent. Provs.* - 86 Be
Nimbahera, *Rajputana* - 85 Eb
Nimbi, *Nigeria* - - 105 Ce
Nimbin, *New S. Wales* - 155 Ha
Nîmes, *France* - - 35 Gd
Nimfaia, *Greece* - - 72 Ca
Nimmitabel, *New S. Wales* 155Fd
Nimpa, *Burma* - - 88 Eb
Nimrin, R., *Trans-Jordan* 80 Dd
Nimrod, *Montana* - - 136 Ga
Nimule, *A.-E. Sudan* - 108 Be
Nin, *Dalmatia* - - 63 Kc
Ninčevo, *Voyvodina* - 67 Fd
Nine de Julio, *Argentina* 148 Db
Ninety Mile Beach, *W. Australia* - - 152 Cb
Ninety Mile Beach, *Vict.* 155 Ee
Nineveh, *New York* - 128 Ab
Ninfas, Pta., *Argentina* - 148 Dc
Ning, *China* - - - 94 Cb
Ning-hai, *China* - - 94 Fb
Ning-ho, *China* - - 94 Eb
Ning-hwa, *China* - - 94 Ed
Ning-kiang, *China* - - 94 Cc
Ning-kwo, *China* - - 94 Ec
Ning-kwo, *China* - - 94 Ec
Ningling, *China* - - 94 Cb
Ningnienchan, *Manchuria* 96 Cb
Ning-po, *China* - - 94 Fd
Ning-shen, *China* - - 94 Cc
Ning-sia, *China* - - 94 Cb
Ningsia, prov., *China* - 94 Ba
Ning-te, *China* - - 94 Ed
Ning-tu, *China* - - 94 Ed
Ninguta, *Manchuria* - 96 Dc
Ning-wu, *China* - - 94 Db
Ning-yüan, *Manchuria* - 96 Bc
Ning-yüan, *China* - - 94 Bd
Ning-yuen, *China* - - 94 Bb
Ninh-binh, *Tong-king* - 95 Ce
Ninh-hoa, *Annam* - - 95 Cg
Ninh-thuan, *Annam* - 95 Cg
Ninigo Group, *Pac. Oc.* 156 Cb
Nioac, *Brazil* - - 146 Dc
Niobrara R., *Nebraska* - 126 Eb
Nioche, *Utah* - - 135 Hb
Niogara, *W. Australia* - 152 Cd
Niokhóri, *Greece* - - 70 Cd
Nioro, *Fr. W. Africa* - 104 Cc
Niort, *France* - - 32 Ed
Niout, *Fr. W. Africa* - 104 Cc
Nipani, *Bombay* - - 90 Bc
Nipe, B. de, *Cuba* - - 140 Bb
Nipigon & L., *Ontario* - 122 Da
Nipigon R. & B., *Ontario* 122 Da
Nipigon House, *Ontario* 122 Da
Nipisiguit R., *New Bruns.* 120 Bc
Nipissing, L., *Ontario* - 123 Hb
Nipisso L., *Quebec* - 120 Ba
Nirazaki, *Japan* - - 100 Gd
Niriz & L., *Persia* - - 79 Fd
Nirmal, *Hyderabad* - 90 Db
Nirmal Ra., *Hyderabad* 90 Cb
Niš (Nish), *Serbia* - - 68 Gc
Nisarpur, *Central India* - 85 Ec
Niscemi, *Sicily* - - 65 Hg
Nish (Niš), *Serbia* - - 68 Gc
Nishapur, *Persia* - - 79 Gb
Nishikata, *Japan* - - 97 Bd
Nishio, *Japan* - - 100 Fd
Nishnabotna, R., *Iowa* - 132 Be
Nisporeni - - - 69 Gb
Nissa Ålv, *Sweden* - 51 Cf
Nissedal, *Norway* - - 47 Ee
Nisser Vatn, *Norway* - 47 Ee
Nissi, *Estonia* - - 49 Cb
Nissilo, *Finland* - - 48 Ge
Nissum Bredning, *Denmark* 45 Bb
Nith, R., *Scotland* - 21 Cd
Nithpur, *Bengal* - - 88 Bb
Nitra, *Slovakia* - - 60 Ed
Niu, I., *Ellice Is.* - - 157 Ed
Niuafoo, I., *Pacific Oc.* 157 Fe
Niuatobutabu, I., *Pac. Oc.* 157 Fe
Niue Is., *Pacific Oc.* - 149 Kg
Niutao, I., *Ellice Is.* - 157 Ed
Nivala, *Finland* - - 48 Fe
Nivastroi, *U.S.S.R.* - 74 Eb
Nive Downs, *Queensland* 153 Ce
Nivelles, *Belgium* - - 29 Cd
Niverna, *France* - - 31 Fd
Niversac, *France* - - 34 Cb
Niya, *Sinkiang* - - 84 Ec
Niza, *Portugal* - - 37 Cc
Nizamabad, *Hyderabad* - 90 Db
Nizampatam, *Madras* - 91 Ed
Nizhne Baskunchak, *U.S.S.R.* - - - 75 Hf
Nizhne Chirskaya, *U.S.S.R.* 75Gf
Nizhne Elton, *U.S.S.R.* 75 Hf
Nizhne Kolymsk, *U.S.S.R.* 76 Rc
Nizhne Lomov, *U.S.S.R.* 75 Ge
Nizhne Pesha, *U.S.S.R.* 74 Hb
Nizhne Sergi, *U.S.S.R.* 74 Kd
Nizhne Troitski, *U.S.S.R.* 75 Je
Nizhne Udinsk, *U.S.S.R.* 76 Ld
Nizhne Zoloticha, *U.S.S.R.* 74Gb
Nizhni Tagil, *U.S.S.R.* 74 Ld
Nizina, *Alaska* - - 125 Lf
Nizwa, *Oman* - - 79 Ge
Njango B., *Kenya* - - 110 Cd
Njiorro, *Kenya* - - 110 Dd
Njole, *Fr. Eq. Africa* - 109 Bb
Njombe, *Tang. Terr.* - 111 Dh
Njoro, *Kenya* - - 110 Dd
Njoro, *Tanganyika Terr.* 111 Ef
Njoro Neganga, *Tang. Ter.* 111Ef
Njurunda, *Sweden* - 48 Be
Nkata Bay, *Nyasaland* - 112 Bb
Nkoranza, *Gold Coast* - 104 De
Nkandhla, *Natal* - - 115 Jd
Noakhali, *Bengal* - - 88 Cc
Noanama, *Colombia* - 144 Ac
Noatak & R., *Alaska* - 125 Fc
Nobeoka, *Japan* - - 97 Cd
Noblesville, *Indiana* - 129 Ab
Noccundra, *Queensland* - 153 Be
Nocera, *Italy* - - 65 Ce
Nocera Inferiore, *Italy* - 64 Ec
Nocera Umbria, *Italy* - 63 Gd
Nochistlan, *Mexico* - 139 Ed
Nodaway R., *Iowa* - 132 Be
Nœröy & Fjord *Norway* 46 Cd
Nogal, *New Mexico* - 135 Le
Nogales, *Arizona* - - 135 Hf
Nogaro, *France* - - 34 Cd
Nogat, R. - - - 56 Db
Nogent, *France* - - 30 Fc
Nogent-en-Bassigny, *France* - - - 31 Hc
Nogent-le-Roi, *France* - 30 Dc
Nogent-le-Rotrou, *France* 30 Cc
Nogent-sur-Seine, *France* 31 Fc
Noggara, *Ethiopia* - 108 Cc
Noginsk, *Moskva, U.S.S.R.* - - 74 Fd
Noginsk, *Tulsk, U.S.S.R.* - - 75 Fe
Nógrád and Hont, *Hung.* 66 Eb
Nogueira, Sa. de, *Portugal* 36 Dc
Noguera, La, *Spain* - 39 Fc
Noguera Pallaresa, *Spain* 39 Fb
Noguera Ribagorzana, *Spain* - - - 39 Fb
Nohar, *Rajputana* - 83 Fd
Nohaval, *Eire* - - 25 Cf
Noho, *Manchuria* - - 96 Cb
Noires, mtgnes, *France* 32 Bb
Noirmoutier, and I. de, *France* - - - 32 Cd
Nokata, *Japan* - - 100 Bb
Nokrek Pk., *Assam* - 88 Cb
Nola, *Fr. Equat. Africa* 105 Ee
Nola, *Italy* - - 64 Ec
Nolan, *Alaska* - - 125 Kc
Nolan, *Utah* - - 135 Hb
Noldau - - - - 57 Cb
Noli, *Italy* - - - 62 Cc
Nolichucky R., *Tenness.* 131 Gb
Nolinsk, *U.S.S.R.* - 74 Hd
Nome *Alaska,* - - 125 Fd
Nomeny, *France* - 31 Jc
Nomining Ls., *Quebec* - 123 Lb

Nom-kwan, *China* - 94 Fd
Nomme, *Estonia* - 49 Cb
Nomoi I., *Caroline Is.* - 157 Cc
Non, Val di, *Italy* - 62 Fa
Nonacho L., *N.-W. Terr.* 124 Hb
Nonancourt, *France* - 30 Dc
Nondweni, *Natal* - 115 Jd
None, *Italy* - 62 Bc
None, *Japan* - 100 Ee
Nong-han, *Siam* - 95 Bf
Nongjuri, *Assam* 88 Cb
Nong-kai, *Siam* - 95 Bf
Nongoma, *Natal* - 115 Jc
Nong-son, *Annam* - 95 Cf
Nonni R., *Manchuria* 96 Ca
Nonning & Mt., *S. Aust.* 154 Ab
Nonnweiler, *Prussia* - 58 Ab
Nonoava and R., *Mexico* - 138 Cb
Nonouti I., *Gilbert Is.* 157 Ed
Nontron, *France* - 34 Cb
Noodsberg, *Natal* - 115 Jd
Noojee, *Victoria* - 155 Ee
Noondera, *W. Australia* 152 De
Noongal, *W. Australia* 152 Bd
Noorvik, *Alaska* - 125 Gc
Nootka I., *Br. Columbia* 124 De
Nor, *Norway* - 47 Jd
Norah I., *Eritrea* - 108 Db
Noranda, *Quebec* - 123 Ja
Nora Springs, *Iowa* - 132 Cd
Norcia, *Italy* - 63 He
Nord, dep., *France* - 30 Ea
Nord Fjord, *Norway* - 46 Bc
Nordborg, *Denmark* - 45 Cc
Nordby, *Fanö I., Denmark* 45 Bc
Nordby, *Samsö I., Den.* 45 Dc
Norddal, *Norway* - 46 Db
Nordelph, *England* - 15 Ea
Norden, *Prussia* - 54 Cb
Nordenburg - 56 Fb
Nordenham, *Oldenburg* 54 Db
Norderney I., *Prussia* 54 Cb
Nordfjord, *Norway* - 46 Bc
Nordfjordeidet, *Norway* 46 Cc
Nordfold, *Norway* - 48 Ac
Nordhausen, *Prussia* - 54 Fd
Nordkapp (North C.), *Norway* - 44 Fe
Nordkyn, *Norway* - 44 Fe
Nordlingen, *Bavaria* - 58 Ec
Nordmark, *Sweden* - 50 Cc
Nordmark, *Sweden* - 50 Bc
Nordmore, *Norway* - 46 Db
Nordreisa, *Norway* - 48 Db
Nord Slesvig (South Jylland), *Denmark* - 45 Bc
Nordstrand, *Prussia* - 54 Da
Nore, *Norway* - 47 Ed
Nore Fjell, *Norway* - 47 Fd
Norfield, *Mississippi* - 130 Ce
Norfolk, *Nebraska* - 126 Fb
Norfolk, *Virginia* - 129 Fd
Norfolk Broads, *Eng.* - 15 Fa
Norfolk I., *Pacific Oc.* 149 Gh
Norheimsund, *Norway* 47 Bd
Norkitten - 56 Fb
Norley, *Queensland* - 153 Be
Normal, *Illinois* - 132 Ee
Norman, *California* - 134 Bb
Norman, *N.-W. Terr.* - 124 Db
Norman, *Oklahoma* - 133 Dc
Normanby, *England* - 19 Db
Normanby, *Queensland* 153 Cd
Normanby (Duau) I., *New Guinea* - 156 Ed
Norman Cross, *England* 15 Da
Normandy, old prov., *France* - 30 Bc
Normanton, *England* - 18 Cc
Normanton, *Queensland* 153 Bc
Norman Wells, *N.-W. Terr.* - 124 Da
Norquin, *Argentina* - 148 Bb
Norquinco, *Argentina* - 148 Bc
Norrarya, *Sweden* - 51 Df
Nörresundby, *Denmark* 45 Ca
Norris, *Montana* - 136 Hc
Norris Arm, *Newfoundland* - 120 Hb
Norristown, *Pennsylv.* 129 Gb
Norrköping, *Sweden* - 50 Fd
Norrköpings B., *Sweden* 50 Gd
Norrsundet, *Sweden* - 50 Gb
Norrtälje, *Sweden* - 50 Hc
Norseman, *W. Aust.* - 152 Ce
Norsholm, *Sweden* - 50 Fd
Nor Sjo, *Norway* - 47 Fe
Nort, *France* - 32 Dc
Norte, Cord. del, *Philippines* - 95 Ff
Norte, Sa. do, *Brazil* - 142 Ce
Norte de Sandander, dep., *Colombia* - 144 Bb
North C., *New Zealand* 158 Da
North C., *Nova Scotia* 120 Ec
North Chan., *Netherlands Indies* - 98 Ac
North Chan., *Ontario* - 122 Gb
North I., *Netherlands Indies* - 99 Fe
North I., *New Zealand* 158 Db
North Pk, *Arizona* - 135 Hd
North Pt., *Pr. Edward I.* 120 Dc
North Sd., *Eire* - 25 Bc
North Adams, *Mass.* - 128 Bb
Northallerton, *England* 18 Cb
Northam, *Transvaal* - 115 Gb
Northam, *W. Australia* 152 Be
Northampton, *Mass* - 128 Bb
Northampton, *W. Aust.* 152 Ad
Northampton and co., *England* - 15 Db
North Auckland, prov., *New Zealand* - 158 Da
North Battleford, *Saskatchewan* - 124 Hd
North Bay, *Ontario* - 121 Aa
North Bend, *Oregon* - 136 Ad
North Berwick, *Scotland* 23 Fd
North Bloomfield, *California* - 134 Cb
North Borneo (Brit.), *E. Indies* - 99 Eb
North Brabant, prov., *Holland* - 29 Cc
North Branch, *Minnesota* 132 Cc
Northbridge, *Mass.* - 128 Cb
North Canadian R., *Oklahoma* - 133 Ab
North Central Prov., *Ceylon* - 89 Dc
North Coates, *England* 19 Ed
North Creek, *New York* 123 Ld
North Downs, *England* 15 Dd
North-East Foreland, *Greenland* - 9 Ha
North-East Land, *Arctic Ocean* - 76 Cb
Northeim, *Prussia* - 54 Fd
North Elmham, *England* 15 Ea
Northern Bight, *Newfoundland* - 120 Hb
Northern Circars, *Madras* - 91 Fc
Northern Ireland, *British Isles* - 13 Cd
Northern Prov., *Ceylon* 89 Dc
Northern Provs., *Nigeria* - 105 Cc
Northern Territory, *Australia* - 150 Eb
Northfield, *England* - 14 Cb
Northfield, *Minnesota* - 132 Cc
North Holland, prov., *Holland* - 29 Cb
North Lake, *Ontario* - 122 Ca
North Lakhimpur, *Assam* - 88 Da
Northleach, *England* - 14 Cc
North Lisbon, *Wisconsin* 132 Dd
North Manchester, *Indiana* - 129 Bb
North Martinsville, *W. Virginia* - 129 Dc
North Minch, *Scotland* 24 Ba
North Pass, *Louisiana* 130 Df
North Platte, *Nebraska* 126 Eb
North Platte R., *Neb.-Wyo.* - 126 Eb
Northport, *Maine* - 128 Da
Northport, *Nebraska* - 135 Ma
Northport, *Washington* 136 Ea
North Portal, *Sask.* - 124 Je
North Powder, *Oregon* 136 Dc
North Riding, *Yorks, England* - 18 Cb
Norths Ranch, *Nevada* 134 Ea
North Sydney, *Nova Scotia* - 120 Ec
North Tawton, *England* - 17 Cb
North Tonawanda, *New York* - 123 Jd
Northumberland, *New Hampshire* - 128 Ca
Northumberland, *Ontario* - 121 Ab
Northumberland, co., *England* - 21 Dc
Northumberland I., *Queensland* - 153 Cd
Northumberland Str., *New Brunswick, etc.* 120 Cc
North Vancouver, *Brit. Columbia* - 124 Ee
North Vernon, *Indiana* 129 Bc
Northville, *New York* - 123 Ld
North Walsham, *England* - 19 Fe
North-West C., *W. Australia* - 152 Ac
North-West Div., *W. Australia* - 152 Bc
North Western Prov., *Ceylon* - 89 Dc
North-West Frontier Prov., *India* - 81 Cd
North-West Highlands, *Scotland* - 22 Cb
North-West River, *Labrador* - 119 Rf
North-West Territories, *Canada* - 118-119
Northwich, *England* - 18 Bd
North Wood, *Iowa* - 132 Cd
Northwood, *N. Dakota* 132 Ab
Norton, *Kansas* - 133 Ba
Norton, *New Brunswick* 120 Cd
Norton, *S. Rhodesia* - 113 Da
Norton B., *Alaska* - 125 Gd
Norton Sd., *Alaska* - 125 Fe
Norton St. Philip, *England* - 14 Bd
Norwalk, *Connecticut* - 128 Bc
Norwalk, *Ohio* - 129 Cb
Norway, *Michigan* - 122 Ec
Norway, *Ontario* - 121 Ac
Norway, *W. Europe* - 44 Bg
Norwegian B., *N.-W. Terr.* - 118 La
Norwich, *Connecticut* - 128 Bc
Norwich, *England* - 15 Fa
Norwich, *New York* - 123 Ld
Norwich, *Vermont* - 128 Bb
Norwood, *Massachusetts* 128 Cb
Norwood, *New York* - 123 Lc
Norwood, *N. Carolina* 131 Jc
Noshiro, *Japan* - 97 Db
Nosi Be I., *Madagascar* 112 Eb
Nosivarika, *Madagascar* 112 Ed
Notabile (Citta Vecchia), *Malta* - 65 Kk
Nótia, *Greece* - 70 Db
Noto, *Sicily* - 65 Jh
Noto Pen., *Japan* - 97 Dc
Notodden, *Norway* - 47 Fe
Notoshima, *Japan* - 100 Fc
Notozersk, *U.S.S.R.* - 48 Jb
Notre Dame B., *Newfoundland* - 120 Hb
Notre Dame Mts., *Quebec* - 123 Nb
Nottawasaga B., *Ontario* - 123 Hc
Nötteröy, *Norway* - 47 Ge
Nottingham and co., *England* - 18 Ce
Nottingham I., *N.-W. Terr.* - 119 Od
Nottoway R., *Virginia* 129 Fd
Nouakchott, *Fr. W.Africa* 104Ac
Noual, *Fr. W. Africa* - 104 Cc
Noua Sulita - 69 Ga
Nouatja, *Fr. W. Africa* 105 Bd
Noumea, *New Caledonia* 157 Df
Nouvelle Anvers, *Belgian Congo* - 109 Ca
Nouvion, *France* - 30 Da
Nouvion, Le, *France* - 31 Fb
Nova, *Hungary* - 66 Bc
Nová Baňa, *Slovakia* - 66 Da
Nova Cruz, *Brazil* - 143 Gd
Nova Friburgo, *Brazil* 147 Gc
Nova Goa (Panjim), *Goa* 90 Ad
Nova Gradiska, *Slavonia* 66 Cd
Nova Granada, *Brazil* - 147 Ec
Nova Kapela, *Slavonia* 66 Cd
Nóváky, *Slovakia* - 57 De
Nova Levante, *Italy* - 63 Fa
Nova Lisboa, *Angola* - 109 Bd
Nova Luzitania, *Mozambique* - 113 Fb
Nova Palanka, *Voyvodina* - 66 Ed
Nova Pava, *Bohemia* - 59 Ka
Novara, *Italy* - 62 Cb
Novara di Sicilia, *Sicily* 65 Jg
Nova Scotia, prov., *Canada* - 119 Qh
Nová Surány, *Slovakia* 66 Da
Novate Mezzola, *Italy* - 62 Da
Nova Varos, *Serbia* - 68 Ec
Nova Venecia, *Brazil* - 147 Gb
Novaya Lyalya, *U.S.S.R.* 74 Kd
Novaya Zemlya I., *U.S.S.R.* - 76 Fb
Nova York, *Brazil* - 143 Fd
Nova Zagora, *Bulgaria* 69 Gd
Novel, *Mozambique* - 113 Fd
Novelda, *Spain* - 41 Fb
Novene, *Idaho* - 136 Hd
Noventa, *Italy* - 63 Gb
Nové Zámky, *Slovakia* 60 Ed
Novgorod, *U.S.S.R.* - 74 Ed
Novgorod-Severski, *Ukraine* - 75 Ee
Novi, *Croatia* - 63 Jb
Novi, *Italy* - 62 Ec
Novi Bečej, *Voyvodina* 66 Fd
Novigrad, *Croatia* - 66 Bc
Novigrad, *Dalmatia* - 63 Kc
Novi Ligure, *Italy* - 62 Cc
Novi Marof, *Croatia* - 66 Bc
Novion Porcien, *France* 31 Gb
Novi Pazar, *Bulgaria* - 69 Gd
Novi Pazar, *Serbia* - 68 Fc
Novi Sad, *Voyvodina* - 66 Ed
Novi Vrbas, *Voyvodina* 66 Ed
Novocherkassk, *U.S.S.R.* 75 Ff
Novograd Volynsk, *Ukraine* - 75 De
Novo Kazanka, *Kazak* 75 Hf
Novokhoperski, *U.S.S.R.* 75 Ge
Novo Mesto, *Slovenia* - 63 Kb
Novo Moskovsk, *Ukraine* 75 Ef
Novo Orsk, *U.S.S.R.* - 75 Ke
Novo Redondo, *Angola* 109 Bd
Novorossiisk, *U.S.S.R.* 75 Fg
Novo Selo, *Serbia* - 70 Db
Novo Selo, *Voyvodina* - 67 Fe
Novoseltsi, *Bulgaria* - 69 Ed
Novo Sibirsk, *U.S.S.R.* 76 Jd
Novosil, *U.S.S.R.* - 75 Fe
Novo Ukrainka, *Ukraine* - 75 Ef
Novouzensk, *U.S.S.R.* 75 He
Novozybkov, *U.S.S.R.* 75 Ee
Novska, *Slavonia* - 66 Cd
Nový Bydžov, *Bohemia* 59 Ka
Novy Jičin (Neu Titschein), *Moravia* - 60 Ed
Novy Port, *U.S.S.R.* - 76 Hc
Nowata, *Oklahoma* - 133 Eb
Nowawes, *Prussia* - 55 Jc
Nowa Wilejka - 60 Ha
Nowe, *Poland* - 56 Cc
Nowe Miasto, *Poland* - 57 Ca
Nowemiasto, *Poland* - 60 Eb
Nowendoc, *N. S. Wales* 155 Gb
Nowgong, *Assam* - 88 Da
Nowgong, *United Provs.* 86 Cc
Nowogród, *Poland* - 56 Fc
Nowogródek - 60 Hb
Nowra, *New S. Wales* - 155 Gc
Nowrangapur, *Orissa* - 91 Fb
Nowshera (Naushahra), *N.-W.F.P.* - 82 Ea
Nowy Sacz, *Poland* - 60 Fd
Nowy Targ, *Poland* - 60 Fd
Nowy Tomysl, *Poland* 60 Db
Noya, *Spain* - 36 Bb
Noyen, *France* - 30 Bd
Noyers, *France* - 33 Aa
Noyon, *France* - 30 Eb
Nozay, *France* - 32 Dc
Nqamakwe, *Cape Prov.* 115 Gf
Nsinse, *Uganda* - 110 Cc
Ntaranda, *Tang. Terr.* 110 Ce
Ntendatshi, *Tang. Terr.* 111 Fj
Ntondongwe, Mt., *S. Rhodesia* - 113 Da
Nuanetsi, *S. Rhodesia* - 113 Dc
Nuantogluin, *French W. Africa* - 104 Ce
Nuba, *Palestine* - 80 Cd
Nubia, *A.-E. Sudan* - 108 Ba
Nubian Des., *A.-E. Sudan* - 108 Ba
Nuble, prov., *Chile* - 148 Bb
Nueltin L., *N.-W. Terr.* 124 Jb
Neuva Esparte, state, *Venezuela* - 144 Da
Nueva Imperial, *Chile* 148 Bb
Nuevitas, *Cuba* - 140 Bb
Nuevo Laredo, *Mexico* 138 Db
Nuevo Leon, state, *Mexico* - 139 Eb
Nûgsuak and Penin., *Greenland* - 9 Dc
Nugaria I., *Pacific Oc.* 156 Fe
Nuits, *France* - 31 Gd
Nukha, *Azerbaijan* - 75 Hg
Nukufetau I., *Ellice Is.* 157 Ed
Nukuhiva I., *Marquesas Is.* - 157 Kd
Nukulaelae, I., *Ellice Is.* 157 Ed
Nukunana I., *Tokelau Is.* 157 Fd
Nukunau I., *Gilbert Is.* 157 Ed
Nukuoro I., *Caroline Is.* 157 Cc
Nukus, *Uzbek* - 76 Gd
Nulato, *Alaska* - 125 Gd
Nullagine, *W. Australia* 152 Bc
Nullarbor Plain, *W. Aust.* 152 De
Nullur, *Madras* - 89 Bb
Nulvi, *Sardinia* - 64 Hf
Numan, *Nigeria* - 105 Dd
Numata, *Japan* - 100 Gc
Numazu, *Japan* - 100 Gd
Numberg, *Queensland* - 153 Bc
Numedal, *Norway* - 47 Ed
Numin, Mt., *Manchuria* 96 Ca
Numurkah, *Victoria* - 154 Ed
Nunchia, *Colombia* - 144 Bb
Nuneaton, *England* - 14 Ca
Nungan, *Manchuria* - 96 Cc
Nunivak I., *Alaska* - 125 Ef
Nunkiang (Mergen), *Manchuria* - 96 Db
Nun Kun, Mt., *Kashmir* 83 Ga
Nuntherungie, *N. S. W.* 154 Cb
Nuoro, *Sardinia* - 64 Jf
Nuqui, *Colombia* - 144 Ab
Nurakita I., *Ellice Is.* 157 Ed
Nurallo, *Sardinia* - 64 Jg
Nurdah, *Queensland* - 153 Ae
Nuri, *Mexico* - 138 Cb
Nuristan, *Afghanistan* - 84 Cc
Nurmes, *Finland* - 48 He
Nurnberg, *Bavaria* - 58 Fb
Nurpur, *Punjab* - 83 Fb
Nurra, La, *Sardinia* - 64 Hf
Nurri, *Sardinia* - 64 Jg
Nürtingen, *Württemberg* 58 Dc
Nuseiriye, Jeb. en, *Syria* 78 Cb
Nushagak & R., *Alaska* 125 Gg
Nushki, *Baluchistan* - 82 Ad
Nustar, *Slavonia* - 66 Dd
Nutria, *Wyoming* - 135 Ha
Nutrias, *Venezuela* - 144 Cb
Nutt, *New Mexico* - 135 Ke
Nutt, Mt., *Arizona* - 134 Fd
Nutzotin Mts., *Alaska* 125 Le
Nuwara Eliya, *Ceylon* - 89 Dd
Nwasha, *S. Rhodesia* - 113 Bb
Nyabangi, *Tang. Terr.* 110 Cd
Nyabuhiki, *Uganda* - 110 Bd
Nyack, *New York* - 123 Le
Nyah, *Victoria* - 154 Dd
Nyahanga, *Tang. Terr.* 110 Ce
Nyahua, *Tang. Terr.* 111 Cf
Nyakabindi, *Tanganyika Terr.* - 110 De
Nyakahanga, *Tanganyika Terr.* - 110 Bd
Nyakasa, *Tang. Terr.* - 110 Bd
Nyaksimvol, *U.S.S.R.* 74 Kc
Nyala, *A.-E. Sudan* - 105 Fc
Nyala, *N. Rhodesia* - 112 Ba
Nyamandhlovu, *S. Rhodesia* - 113 Cb
Nyambhara, Mt., *S. Rhodesia* - 113 Ea
Nyambiti, *Tang.Terr.* - 110 Ce
Nyamgee, *N. S. W.* - 155 Eb
Nyamirembe, *Tang.Terr.* 110 Be
Nyamlell, *A.-E. Sudan* 108 Ad
Nyandoma, *U.S.S.R.* - 74 Gc
Nyanga, *Fr. Eq. Africa* 109 Ab
Nyange, *Tang. Terr.* - 111 Bf
Nyangwe, *Belg.Congo* - 109 Eb
Nyangwo, *Mozambique* 112 Cc
Nyarasuswi, *S. Rhodesia* 113 Da
Nyasa, L., *Nyasaland* - 112 Bb
Nyasaland Protectorate, *E. Africa* - 101 Fg
Nyaungbintha, *Burma* 92 Bc
Nyaungleben, *Burma* 92 Cc
Nyaung-u, *Burma* - 92 Bb
Nyborg, *Denmark* - 45 Dc
Nybro, *Sweden* - 51 Ef
Nye, *Montana* - 136 Hc
Nyeri, *Kenya* - 110 Ed
Nyerol, *A.-E. Sudan* - 108 Bd
Nygard, *Norway* - 47 Dd
Nyiradony, *Hungary* - 67 Gb
Nyirbákta, *Hungary* - 67 Gb
Nyirbátor, *Hungary* - 67 Hb
Nyiregyháza, *Hungary* 67 Gb
Nyiri Des., *Kenya* - 110 Ee
Nyiro, Mt., *Kenya* - 110 Eb
Nyköbing, *Falster I., Denmark* - 45 Ed
Nyköbing, *Mors I., Denmark* - 45 Bb

Nykøbing, *Sjælland, Denmark* 45 Ec
Nyköping, *Sweden* 50 Gd
Nykroppa, *Sweden* 50 Dc
Nylstroom, *Transvaal* 115 Gb
Nymboida, *N. S. Wales* 155 Ga
Nymburk, *Bohemia* 60 Cc
Nymindegab, *Denmark* 45 Ac
Nyngan, *New S. Wales* 155 Eb
Nyombi, *S. Rhodesia* 113 Db
Nyon, *Switzerland* 42 Bd
Nyons, *France* 35 Hc
Nyplass, *Norway* 46 Hb
Nyrob, *U.S.S.R.* 74 Kc
Nyseter, *Norway* 46 Eb
Nyssa, *Oregon* 136 Ed
Nysted, *Denmark* 45 Ed
Nystua, *Norway* 46 Ec
Nyuki, *Kenya* 110 Ed
Nyunzu, *Belgian Congo* 109 Ec
Nyudvchim, *U.S.S.R.* 74 Jc
Nyūzen, *Japan* 100 Fc
Nzega, *Tang. Terr.* 111 Cf
Nzérékoré, *Fr. W. Africa* 104 Ce
Nzima, *Tang. Terr.* 110 Ce
Nzinge, *Tang. Terr.* 111 Dg
Nziu, *Kenya* 110 Ed
Nzole, *Kenya* 111 Ff
Nzubuku, *Tang. Terr.* 111 Cf
Oadweina, *Brit. Somaliland* 108 Dd
Oahu, *Hawaiian Is.* 157 La
Oakbank, *S. Australia* 154 Cc
Oak Cliffe, *Texas* 133 Dd
Oakdale, *California* 134 Cc
Oakdale, *Louisiana* 130 Be
Oakesdale, *Washington* 136 Eb
Oakham, *England* 15 Da
Oakland, *California* 134 Bc
Oakland, *Maryland* 129 Ec
Oakland, *Nebraska* 132 Ae
Oakland, *Oregon* 136 Bd
Oakley, *Idaho* 136 Fd
Oakley, *Kansas* 133 Ba
Oakville, *Ontario* 123 Jd
Oamaru, *New Zealand* 159 Cf
Oami, *Japan* 100 Hd
Oanica, *Kansas* 133 Ba
Oates Land, *Antarctica* 160
Oatlands, *Tasmania* 155 Jg
Oaxaca, and state, *Mexico* 139 Ed
Ob, Gulf of, *U.S.S.R.* 76 Hc
Ob, R., *U.S.S.R.* 76 Gc
Oba, *Ontario* 122 Fa
Obama, *Japan* 100 Ed
Oban, *New Zealand* 159 Ag
Oban, *Scotland* 22 Cd
Obashing L., *Quebec* 121 Aa
Obbia, *It. Somaliland* 108 Ed
Obdash, *Austria* 59 Jd
Obeh, *Afghanistan* 79 Hc
Obeliai, *Lithuania* 49 Cd
Ober Aargau, *Switz.* 42 Eb
Ober Ammergau, *Bavaria* 58 Fd
Oberdorf, *Bavaria* 58 Ed
Ober Glogau 57 Cc
Oberhausen, *Prussia* 54 Bd
Oberhesse, *Hesse* 58 Da
Oberkirch, *Baden* 58 Cc
Ober Lausitz, *Saxony* 55 Kd
Oberlin, *Kansas* 133 Ba
Oberlin, *Louisiana* 130 Be
Oberlin, *Ohio* 129 Cb
Obernburg, *Bavaria* 58 Da
Obernkirchen, *Schaumburg-Lippe* 54 Ec
Oberon, *New S. Wales* 155 Fc
Ober Pfalz (Upper Palatinate), *Bavaria* 59 Fb
Oberriet, *Switzerland* 43 Hb
Oberstdorf, *Bavaria* 58 Ed
Oberstein, *Prussia* 58 Bb
Oberwald, *Switzerland* 42 Fc
Oberwart, *Austria* 66 Bb
Ober Wesel, *Prussia* 58 Ba
Obi Is., *Nether. Indies* 99 Gd
Obidos, *Brazil* 142 Cc
Obidos, *Portugal* 37 Ac
Obihiro, *Japan* 97 Eb
Obi Latoe, I., *Netherlands Indies* 99 Gd
Obi Major, I., *Netherlands Indies* 99 Gd
Obion, *Tennessee* 130 Db
Objat, *France* 34 Db
Obo, *Burma* 92 Ba
Obock, *Fr. Somaliland* 108 Dc
Oborniki, *Poland* 57 Ba
Obovan, *U.S.S.R.* 75 Fe
Obrenovac, *Serbia* 68 Fb
Obrež, *Serbia* 68 Gc
Obrovac, *Dalmatia* 68 Ab
Obwalden, *Switzerland* 43 Fc
Obyachevo, *U.S.S.R.* 74 Hc
Ocala, *Florida* 131 Gf
Ocampo, *Mexico* 139 Ec
Ocampo, *Peru* 145 Cd
Ocana, *Colombia* 144 Bb
Ocaña, *Spain* 38 Be
Ocate, *New Mexico* 135 Lc
Occhiobello, *Italy* 63 Fc
Occidental, Cord., *Colombia* 144 Ab
Ocean I., *Gilbert Is.* 157 Dd
Ocean I., *Hawaiian Is.* 157 Fa
Oceana, *W. Virginia* 129 Dd
Ocean City, *Maryland* 129 Gc
Ocean City, *New Jersey* 129 Gc
Oceanside, *California* 134 Ee
Ocean Springs, *Mississippi* 130 De
Ochagavia, *Spain* 38 Db
Ochakov, *Ukraine* 75 Ef
Ochi, *Japan* 100 Ab
Ochil Hills, *Scotland* 23 Ed
Ochyemchiri, *Georgia* 75 Gg
Ocilla, *Georgia* 131 Ge
Ockelbo, *Sweden* 50 Fb
Ocmulgee R., *Georgia* 131 Gd
Ocna-Sibiului, *Romania* 67 Jd
Ocna Sugatag, *Transylva.* 67 Jb
Ocnele Mari, *Romania* 67 Kd
Ocoa, B. de, *Santo Domingo* 140 Cc
Ocona, *Peru* 145 Ce
Oconee R., *Georgia* 131 Gd
Oconto, *Wisconsin* 132 Ec
Ocos, *Guatemala* 140 Ee
Ocosta, *Washington* 136 Ab
Ocotal, *Nicaragua* 140 Fe
Ocracoke Inlet, *North Carolina* 131 Lc
Ócsa, *Hungary* 66 Eb
Ocsöd, *Hungary* 66 Fc
Octave, *Arizona* 135 Gd
Octeville, *France* 32 Da
Odádhahraun, *Iceland* 52 Eb
Odaka, *Japan* 97 Ec
Odate, *Japan* 97 Eb
Odawara, *Japan* 97 Dc
Odda, *Norway* 47 Cd
Oddernes, *Norway* 47 Ef
Oddesund N. & S., *Denmark* 45 Bb
Odebolt, *Iowa* 132 Bd
Odell, *Nebraska* 132 Ae
Odemira, *Portugal* 40 Bb
Odemis, *Turkey* 78 Ab
Odendaal Stroom, *Cape Prov.* 115 Ge
Odense, *Denmark* 45 Dc
Odenwald, *Baden, etc.* 58 Cb
Oder Geb., *Moravia* 57 Cd
Oder, R., *Prussia* 55 Kb
Oderzo, *Italy* 63 Gb
Odessa, *Ukraine* 75 Ef
Odienne, *Fr. W. Africa* 104 Ce
Odiham, *England* 14 Cd
Odivelas, *Portugal* 40 Ba
Ödmarden, *Sweden* 50 Fa
Odnes, *Norway* 46 Gd
Odolanów, *Poland* 57 Cb
Odoorn, *Holland* 29 Eb
Odorhei, *Transylvania* 69 Fb
Odur, *Madras States* 89 Bc
Odžaci, *Voyvodina* 66 Ed
Odzak, *Bosnia* 68 Da
Odzi and R., *S. Rhodesia* 113 Eb
Oeiras, *Brazil* 143 Fd
Oels 57 Cb
Oelwein, *Iowa* 132 Dd
Oensingen, *Switzerland* 42 Eb
Oesel (Saare Maa), *Estonia* 49 Bb
Oetling, *Argentina* 146 Cd
Of, *Turkey* 78 Da
Ofanto, R., *Italy* 64 Fc
Offaly, co., *Eire* 27 Ce
Offenbach, *Hesse* 58 Ca
Offenburg, *Baden* 58 Bc
Offingen, *Bavaria* 58 Ec
Offranville, *France* 30 Cb
Ogaki, *Japan* 100 Fd
Ogaki, *Ontario* 122 Da
Ogano, *Japan* 100 Gc
Ogasawara Jima, *Pacific Oc.* 149 Ec
Ogascanan L., *Quebec* 121 Aa
Ogbomosho, *Nigeria* 105 Bd
Ogbourne St. George, *England* 14 Cd
Ogden, *Nova Scotia* 120 Ed
Ogden, *Utah* 135 Ha
Ogdensburg, *New York* 123 Lc
Oggione, *Italy* 62 Db
Ogi, *Japan* 100 Fc
Ogilvie and Ra., *Yukon* 124 Bb
Oglat Sedra, *Morocco* 102 Cc
Oglio, R., *Italy* 62 Eb
Ogoja, *Nigeria* 105 Cd
Ogori, *Japan* 100 Ba
Ogowe, R., *Fr. Eq. Africa* 109 Bb
Ogre, *Latvia* 49 Cc
Ogulin, *Croatia* 69 Ac
Oguma, *Nigeria* 105 Cd
Oguta, *Nigeria* 105 Cd
Ohakune, *New Zealand* 158 Ec
Ohal, *Albania* 70 Aa
O'Higgins, prov., *Chile* 146 Ae
Ohio, state, *U.S.A.* 127 Jb
Ohio R., *U.S.A.* 129 Dc
Ohlau 57 Cc
Ohlsdorf, *Hamburg* 54 Fb
Ohra 56 Cb
Ohre R., *Bohemia* 60 Bc
Ohrid & L., *Serbia* 70 Bb
Ohringen, *Württemberg* 58 Db
Ohrnberg, *Württemberg* 58 Db
Ohura, *New Zealand* 158 Ec
Oi, *Japan* 100 Fd
Oil and R., *Kazak* 75 Jf
Oil City, *Pennsylvania* 129 Eb
Oildale, *California* 134 Dd
Oil Springs, *Ontario* 122 Gd
Oinói, *Greece* 71 Ee
Oirat Tura, *U.S.S.R.* 76 Jd
Oirschot, *Holland* 29 Dc
Oise, dep. and R., *France* 30 Eb
Oishi, *Japan* 100 Fd
Oissel, *France* 30 Db
Oita, *Japan* 97 Cd
Oíti, mt., *Greece* 71 De
Oítilon, *Greece* 71 Dg
Ojacasiro, *Spain* 38 Cb
Ojiya, *Japan* 100 Gc
Ojocaliente, *Mexico* 138 Dc
Ojo de Agua, *Argentina* 146 Cd
Ojoewa, *Suriname* 142 Cb
Oka R., *U.S.S.R.* 74 Gd
Okaba, *New Guinea* 156 Bc
Okaihau, *New Zealand* 158 Da
Okanagan R., *Washington* 136 Da
Okanagan Lake, *Brit. Columbia* 124 Ee
Okanda, *Ceylon* 89 Dd
Okanogan, *Washington* 136 Ca
Okayama, *Japan* 97 Cd
Okazaki, *Japan* 100 Fd
Okçular, *Turkey* 72 Eb
Okeechobee and L., *Florida* 131 Nh
Okeene, *Oklahoma* 133 Cb
Okefenokee Swamp, *Georgia* 131 Ge
Okegawa, *Japan* 100 Ge
Okehampton, *England* 17 Bb
Okhansk, *U.S.S.R.* 74 Jd
Okhotsk, and Sea of, *U.S.S.R.* 76 Pd
Okinawa Gunto, *Japan* 93 Ed
Okishima, *Japan* 97 Cc
Okkak, *Labrador* 119 Re
Oklahoma, state, *U.S.A.* 126 Fc
Oklahoma City, *Oklahoma* 133 Dc
Okmulgee, *Oklahoma* 133 Dc
Okolonia, *Mississippi* 130 Dc
Öksendal, *Norway* 46 Eb
Oksnöy, *Norway* 46 Cb
Okulovski, *U.S.S.R.* 74 Gb
Okuru, *New Zealand* 159 Be
Okushiri I. and Str., *Japan* 97 Db
Okusi Ambeno, *Timor I., East Indies* 99 Fe
Okwoga, *Nigeria* 105 Cd
Olafsfjördhur, *Iceland* 52 Da
Olanchito, *Honduras* 140 Fd
Öland, *Denmark* 45 Ca
Öland, I., *Sweden* 51 Ff
Olanga, *U.S.S.R.* 48 Jc
Olari, *Kenya* 110 Ec
Olary, *S. Australia* 154 Cb
Olathe, *Colorado* 135 Kb
Olathe, *Kansas* 133 Ea
Olavarria, *Argentina* 148 Db
Olba, *Spain* 38 Ed
Olbernhau, *Saxony* 55 Je
Oldcastle, *Eire* 26 Cd
Old Chitambo, *N. Rhodesia* 112 Bb
Old Crow, *Yukon* 125 Mc
Ölde, *Prussia* 54 Dd
Oldenburg, *Prussia* 54 Fa
Oldenburg and state, *Germany* 54 Db
Oldendorf, *Prussia* 54 Ec
Oldham, *England* 18 Bc
Oldham, *S. Dakota* 132 Ac
Old Meldrum, *Scotland* 23 Fb
Oldonyo Sambu, *Tanganyika Terr.* 110 Ee
Old Palapye (Palapshwe), *Bechuanaland* 113 Bd
Old Tati, *Bechuanaland* 113 Bc
Olean, *New York* 123 Jd
Oleggio, *Italy* 62 Cb
Oleiros, *Portugal* 37 Cc
Olekminsk, *U.S.S.R.* 76 Nc
Ölen, *Norway* 47 Be
Olenda, *Fr. Eq. Africa* 109 Bb
Olenitsa, *U.S.S.R.* 48 Lc
Oleron, Ile d', *France* 32 De
Olesa de Montserrat, *Spain* 39 Gc
Olette, *France* 34 Ee
Olevsk, *Ukraine* 75 De
Olga and B., *U.S.S.R.* 96 Ec
Olga L., *Quebec* 123 Ka
Olga Str., *Svalbard* 9 Mb
Olgiate, *Italy* 62 Cb
Olgod, *Denmark* 45 Bc
Olgos, *Tang. Terr.* 110 De
Olhão, *Portugal* 40 Cb
Oliana, *Spain* 39 Gb
Olib I., *Dalmatia* 63 Jc
Olifants R., *Cape Prov.* 114 Be
Olifants R., *Transvaal* 115 Jb
Olifants River Mts., *Cape Prov.* 114 Cf
Olimbía, *Greece* 71 Cf
Oliphant's Hoek, *Cape Prov.* 114 Ec
Oliva, *Spain* 41 Fb
Oliva, Cord. de, *Chile* 146 Bd
Oliva de Plasencia, *Spain* 37 Db
Oliveira, *Bahia, Brazil* 143 Fe
Oliveira, *Minas Geraes, Brazil* 147 Gc
Oliveira de Frades, *Portugal* 37 Bb
Olivenza, *Spain* 37 Cd
Olivone, *Switzerland* 43 Gd
Olkusz, *Poland* 57 Ec
Ollague, *Chile* 146 Bc
Ollague, mt., *Bolivia* 146 Bc
Ollerton, *England* 18 Cd
Olliergues, *France* 35 Fb
Ollita, Cord. de, *Chile* 146 Ae
Ölme, *Sweden* 50 Cc
Olmedo, *Sardinia* 64 Hf
Olmedo, *Spain* 38 Ac
Olmütz (Olomouc), *Moravia* 57 Cd
Olnes, *Alaska* 125 Kd
Olney, *England* 15 Db
Olney, *Illinois* 132 Ef
Olomouc (Olmütz), *Moravia* 57 Cd
Olona R., *Italy* 62 Db
Olon-bulak, *Sinkiang* 84 Ea
Olonets, *U.S.S.R.* 74 Ec
Oloron Ste. Marie, *France* 34 Bd
Olovo, *Bosnia* 68 Db
Olovyannaya, *U.S.S.R.* 96 Aa
Olsberg, *Prussia* 54 Dd
Olsnitz, *Saxony* 59 Ga
Olst, *Holland* 29 Eb
Olsztyn, *Poland* 57 Ec
Olte, Sa. de, *Argentina* 148 Cc
Olten, *Switzerland* 42 Eb
Oltenia, *Romania* 69 Ec
Olteniţa, *Romania* 69 Gc
Olton, *Texas* 133 Ac
Oltu, *Turkey* 78 Da
Oltul R., *Romania* 67 Kd
Olutanga I., *Philippines* 99 Fb
Olvega, *Spain* 38 Cc
Olvera, *Spain* 40 Ec
Olympia, *Brazil* 147 Fc
Olympia, *Washington* 136 Bb
Olympus, Mt., *Washing'n* 136 Bb
Olympic Mts., *Washing'n* 136 Ab
Olympus (Olimpus), mts., *Greece* 70 Dc
Olynthus, *Greece* 70 Ec
Omagh, *N. Ireland* 26 Cb
Omaguas, *Peru* 145 Cb
Omaha, *Nebraska* 126 Fb
Omalós Plain, *Crete* 71 Gj
Oman, *Ethiopia* 108 Dd
Oman, R., *Manchuria* 96 Bb
Oman, state and Gulf, *Arabia* 79 Ge
Oman Proper, *Oman* 79 Ge
Ombersley, *England* 14 Bb
Ombey, *Utah* 134 Ga
Ombo, *Norway* 47 Be
Ombwe, *Belgian Congo* 109 Eb
Omdraai Vlei, *Cape Prov.* 114 Ee
Omdurman, *A.-E. Sudan* 108 Bb
Omegna, *Italy* 62 Cb
Omei Mt., *China* 94 Bd
Omenee, *Ontario* 121 Ab
Omeo, *Victoria* 155 Ed
Omer, *Michigan* 122 Gc
Omerköy, *Turkey* 72 Fc
Ometepec, *Mexico* 139 Ed
Ominato, *Japan* 97 Eb
Omiš, *Dalmatia* 68 Bc
Omishima, *Japan* 100 Dd
Ōmiya, *Japan* 100 Gd
Ōmiya, *Japan* 100 Hc
Ommanney B., *N.-W.T.* 118 Jb
Ommen, *Holland* 29 Eb
Omö, *Denmark* 45 Ec
Omo & R., *Ethiopia* 108 Cd
Omoa, *Honduras* 140 Fd
Omokawa, *Japan* 100 Gc
Omoljica, *Voyvodina* 67 Fe
Omont, *France* 31 Gb
Omsk, *U.S.S.R.* 76 Hd
Omu, *Manchuria* 96 Dc
Omuerh R., *Manchuria* 96 Ca
Omura, *Japan* 100 Ab
Omuta, *Japan* 97 Cd
Omutinisk, *U.S.S.R.* 74 Jd
Ona, *Spain* 38 Bb
Onaga, *Kansas* 133 Da
Onalaska, *Wisconsin* 132 Dd
Onaping L. and R., *Ontario* 123 Hb
Onate, *Spain* 38 Ca
Onawa, *Iowa* 132 Be
Onaway, *Michigan* 122 Fc
Onda, *Spain* 39 Ee
Ondava R., *Slovakia* 60 Fd
Onterste Doorns, *Cape Prov.* 114 De
Ondozero, *U.S.S.R.* 48 Ke
Onega and R., *U.S.S.R.* 74 Fc
Onega L. (Onezhskoe), *U.S.S.R.* 74 Fc
Oneglia, *Italy* 62 Cd
Onehunga, *New Zealand* 158 Eb
Oneida and L., *New York* 123 Ld
O'Neil, *Nevada* 134 Fa
Oneonta, *Alabama* 130 Ed
Oneonta, *New York* 123 Ld
Onezhskaya G., *U.S.S.R.* 74 Fc
Onezhskoe (Onega L.) *U.S.S.R.* 74 Fc
Ongar, *England* 15 Ec
Ongerup, *W. Australia* 152 Be
Ongin, *China* 94 Cb
Ongole, *Madras* 91 Dd
Onitsha, *Nigeria* 105 Cd
Onja, *Korea* 97 Bb
Ono Is., *Pacific Ocean* 157 Ef
Onomichi, *Japan* 100 Dd
Ononiimachi, *Japan* 100 Hc
Onoto, *Venezuela* 144 Cb
Onotoa I., *Gilbert Is.* 157 Ed
Onrust, *Cape Prov.* 114 Cg
Onseepkans, *Cape Prov.* 114 Cd
Onslow, *W. Australia* 152 Ac
Onslow B., *N. Carolina* 131 Kc
Onsöy, *Norway* 47 Ge
Ontario, *Oregon* 136 Ed
Ontario, co., *Ontario* 121 Ab
Ontario L., *Can.-U.S.A.* 123 Kd
Ontario, prov., *Canada* 119 Mg
Ontake, mt., *Japan* 97 Dc
Onteniente, *Spain* 41 Fb
Ontiñena, *Spain* 39 Ec
Ontonagon, *Michigan* 122 Db
Ontong Java (Lord Howe Is.), *Pacific Oc.* 156 Jg
Ontur, *Spain* 41 Eb
Oodnadatta, *S. Aust.* 151 Fd
O'Okiep, *Cape Prov.* 114 Bd
Ooldea, *S. Australia* 150 Ee
Oolton, *California* 134 Ed
Oontoo, *Queensland* 153 Be
Oosterland, *Holland* 29 Db
Ootacamund, *Madras* 89 Bb
Opala, *Belgian Congo* 109 Db
Opanake, *Ceylon* 89 Dd
Opari, *A.-E. Sudan* 108 Be
Oparino, *U.S.S.R.* 74 Hd
Opatów, *Poland* 60 Fc
Opatówek, *Poland* 57 Db
Opava (Troppau), *Moravia* 57 Cd
Opdal, *Norway* 46 Fb

Opdol, *Norway* - - 46 Eb
Opelika, *Alabama* - 130 Fd
Opelousas, *Louisiana* - 130 Be
Open B., *New Britain* - 156 Eb
Opeongo L., *Ontario* - 121 Ab
Ophir, *Alaska* - - 125 He
Ophir, *Colorado* - - 135 Jc
Ophir Mt., *Malay States* 98 Bc
Ophir Mt., *Sumatra* - 98 Ac
Ophthalmia Ra., *W. Aust.* 152 Bc
O-pien, *China* - - 94 Bd
Opinaka R., *Quebec* - 119 Of
Opland, fylke, *Norway* 46 Ec
Opobo, *Nigeria* - - 105 Ce
Opochka, *U.S.S.R.* - 74 Dd
Opoczno, *Poland* - 57 Fb
Opodcpe, *Mexico* - 138 Ba
Opole (Oppeln), *Poland* - 57 Cc
Oporto (Porto), *Portugal* 37 Ba
Opotiki, *New Zealand* - 158 Fc
Opova, *Voyvodina* - 67 Fd
Oppeln (Opole), *Poland* - 57 Cc
Oppenheim, *Hesse* - 58 Cb
Optima, *Oklahoma* - 133 Bb
Opunake, *New Zealand* 158 Dc
Oputo, *Mexico* - - 138 Ca
Opuzen, *Dalmatia* - 68 Cd
Oqair, *Arabia* - - 79 Ed
Orab, *S.-W. Africa* - 114 Bb
Oradea, *Transylvania* - 67 Gb
Oradour-sur-Vayres, *France* - - - 34 Cb
Oræfajokull, *Iceland* - 52 Eb
Orai, *United Provs.* - 86 Cc
Oran, *Argentina* - - 146 Cc
Oran & dep., *Algeria* - 102 Db
Orang, *Assam* - - 88 Da
Orange, *Connecticut* - 128 Bc
Orange, *France* - - 35 Gc
Orange, *New Jersey* - 128 Ac
Orange, *New S. Wales* 155 Fc
Orange, *Texas* - - 133 Fe
Orange, *Virginia* - 129 Fc
Orange L., *Florida* - 131 Mg
Orange R., *Massachusetts* 128 Bb
Orange R., *S. Africa* - 114 Bd
Orangeburg, *S.Carolina* 131 Hd
Orange City, *Florida* - 131 Ng
Orange City, *Iowa* - 132 Bd
Orange Cliffs, *Utah* - 135 Hb
Orange Free State, prov., *S. Africa* - 101 Eh
Orangerie B., *New Guinea* 156 Dd
Orange River, *CapeProv.* 114 Ed
Orangeville, *Ontario* - 123 Hd
Orango I., *Port. Guinea* 104 Ad
Orani, *Sardinia* - - 64 Jf
Oranienburg, *Prussia* - 55 Jc
Oranje, *New Guinea* - 156 Bb
Oranje Geb., *Suriname* 142 Cb
Oranjefontein, *Transvaal* 113 Bd
Oranmore and B., *Eire* 27 Be
Orany - - - 60 Ha
Oraştie, *Romania* - 67 Jd
Oraviţa, *Romania* - 67 Gd
Oravska Magura, *Slovakia* 57 Ed
Oravsky Podzámok, *Slovakia* - - - 60 Ed
Orbassano, *Italy* - - 62 Bb
Orbe, *Switzerland* - 42 Cc
Orbec, *France* - - 30 Cb
Orbetello, *Italy* - - 64 Ba
Orbigo, R., *Spain* - 36 Eb
Orbisonia, *Pennsylvania* 129 Fb
Orbost, *Victoria* - - 155 Fe
Orchha, *Central India* - 86 Cc
Orciano, *Italy* - - 62 Ed
Orcières, *France* - - 35 Jc
Orco, R., *Italy* - - 62 Bb
Ord Mt., *Arizona* - 135 He
Ordenes, *Spain* - - 36 Ba
Ord R., *W. Australia* - 150 Db
Ordu, *Turkey* - - 78 Ca
Ordubad, *Nakhichevan* 75 Hh
Orduna, *Spain* - - 38 Cb
Ordway, *Colorado* - 135 Lb
Ordzhonikidze, *Ukraine* 75 Ff
Ordzhonikidze, *U.S.S.R.* 75 Gg
Ordzhonikidzegrad, *U.S.S.R.* - - 75 Ee
Öre, *Norway* - - 46 Db
Oreana, *Nevada* - - 134 Da
Örebro & Län, *Sweden* 50 Dc
Öreglak, *Hungary* - 66 Cc
Oregon, *Illinois* - - 132 Ee
Oregon, *Missouri* - 132 Be
Oregon, state, *U.S.A.* - 126 Ab
Oregon City, *Oregon* - 136 Bc
Öregrund and B., *Sweden* 50 Hb
Orehoved, *Denmark* - 45 Ed
Oreilles, *Wisconsin* - 132 Dc
Orekhov, *Ukraine* - 75 Ff
Orekhovo, *Bulgaria* - 69 Ed
Orekhovo-Zuevo, *U.S.S.R.* - - - 74 Fd
Orel, *U.S.S.R.* - - 75 Fe
Orellana, *Peru* - - 145 Bc
Orellana la Vieja, *Spain* 37 Ec
Orenburg (Chkalov), *U.S.S.R.* - - - 75 Je
Orense and prov., *Spain* 36 Cb
Oreoi & Str., *Greece* - 71 Ee
Orepuki, *New Zealand* 159 Ag
Orfaná, *Greece* - - 70 Dd
Orfani, *Greece* - - 70 Ec
Orford and Ness, *England* 15 Fb
Orford.Ness, *Queensland* 153 Bb
Orgaña, *Spain* - - 39 Gb
Organos, Sa. de los, *Cuba* 140 Ab
Orgaz, *Spain* - - 38 Be
Orgères, *France* - - 30 Dc
Orhaneli, *Turkey* - 72 Fc
Orhangazi, *Turkey* - 72 Gb
Orhei - - - 69 Hb
Orient, *Colorado* - - 135 Lb
Oriental, Cord., *Colombia* 144 Bb
Oriental, Cord., *Peru* - 145 Bc
Orihuela, *Spain* - - 41 Eb
Orih Vesi, *Finland* - 48 He
Orilla, *Ontario* - - 123 Jc
Orinoco, R., *Venezuela* 144 Db
Oriolo, *Italy* - - 65 Cb
Orissa, *India* - - 81 Eg
Oristano & Gulf, *Sardinia* - - - 64 Hg
Oriximiná, *Brazil* - 142 Cc
Orizaba, *Mexico* - - 139 Ed
Örje, *Norway* - - 47 He
Orjiva, *Spain* - - 41 Cd
Orkanger, *Norway* - 46 Fa
Orkdal, *Norway* - - 46 Fa
Orkney Is., *Scotland* - 24 Fd
Orland, *California* - 134 Bb
Orland, *Norway* - - 46 Fa
Orlando, *Florida* - - 131 Ng
Orlando, *Oklahoma* - 133 Db
Orléanais, old prov., *France* - - - 30 Dd
Orleans I., *Greenland* - 9 Hb
Orleans, I. of, *Quebec* - 123 Nb
Orléans and Forêt-d', *France* - - - 30 Dd
Orleansville, *Algeria* - 102 Ea
Orlovat, *Voyvodina* - 67 Fd
Orlovsk, *U.S.S.R.* - 75 Ee
Ormang, *Sinkiang* - 84 Fb
Ormenion, *Greece* - 72 Da
Ormesby, *England* - 18 Ca
Ormília, *Greece* - - 70 Ec
Ormond, *Florida* - 131 Hf
Ormondville, *New Zealand* - - 158 Fd
Ormoz, *Slovenia* - - 66 Bc
Ormskirk, *England* - 18 Ac
Ornavasso, *Italy* - - 62 Cb
Ornbau, *Bavaria* - - 58 Eb
Orne, dep. and R., *France* 30 Cc
Orno, *Sweden* - - 50 Hc
Örnsköldsvik, *Sweden* - 44 Dg
Orocue, *Colombia* - 144 Bc
Orofino, *Idaho* - - 136 Eb
Oro Grande, *California* 134 Ed
Oroluk I., *Caroline Is.* 157 Cc
Oron, *Switzerland* - 42 Cc
Orono, *Maine* - - 120 Ad
Oronsay I., *Scotland* - 22 Bd
Orosei & G., *Sardinia* - 64 Jf
Orosh, *Albania* - - 70 Bb
Orosháza, *Hungary* - 67 Fc
Orosi, Vol., *Costa Rica* 140 Fe
Oroville, *California* - 134 Cb
Oroya, *Peru* - - 145 Bd
Orpièrre, *France* - - 35 Hc
Orre, *Denmark* - - 45 Bc
Orroroo, *S. Australia* - 154 Bc
Orrskog, *Sweden* - - 50 Gb
Orsa, *Sweden* - - 50 Da
Orsara di Puglia, *Italy* 64 Fb
Orsaro, Mte., *Italy* - 62 Ec
Orsett, *England* - - 15 Ec
Orsha, *White Russia* - 75 De
Orsieres, *Switzerland* - 42 Dd
Orsk, *U.S.S.R.* - - 75 Ke
Orsogna, *Italy* - - 64 Ea
Orsova, *Romania* - 67 He
Orsta, *Norway* - - 46 Cb
Örsted, *Denmark* - 45 Dc
Orta, *Italy* - - 62 Cb
Orta Nova, *Italy* - 64 Fb
Orte, *Italy* - - 64 Ca
Ortegal, C., *Spain* - 36 Ca
Ortelsburg - - - 56 Ec
Orthez, *France* - - 34 Bd
Ortigosa, *Spain* - - 38 Cb
Ortigueira, *Spain* - - 36 Ca
Orting, *Washington* - 136 Bb
Ortiz, *Mexico* - - 138 Cb
Ortiz, *Venezuela* - - 144 Cb
Ortles Alps, *Italy* - 62 Ea
Ortona a Mare, *Italy* - 64 Ea
Ortonville, *Minnesota* - 132 Ac
Örtrask, *Sweden* - - 48 Cd
Orune, *Sardinia* - - 64 Jf
Orungo, *Uganda* - - 110 Cb
Oruro and dep., *Bolivia* 146 Bb
Orust, *Sweden* - - 50 Ad
Orvieto, *Italy* - - 63 Ge
Orvisburg, *Mississippi* 130 De
Orwell, *England* - - 15 Db
Orwell, *Vermont* - - 128 Bb
Os, *Norway* - - 47 Bd
Osa, *U.S.S.R.* - - 74 Kd
Osage, *Iowa* - - 132 Cd
Osage City, *Kansas* - 133 Ea
Osaka, *Japan* - - 97 Dd
Osaka-wan, *Japan* - 100 Ed
Osakis, *Minnesota* - 132 Bc
Osaonica, *Serbia* - - 68 Fc
Osara, *Trans-Jordan* - 80 Dc
Osawatomie, *Kansas* - 133 Ea
Osborne, *Kansas* - - 133 Ca
Osborne, *Ontario* - 121 Aa
Oscar Ra., *W. Australia* 152 Db
Osceola, *Arkansas* - 130 Cc
Osceola, *Iowa* - - 132 Ce
Osceola, *Missouri* - 130 Ba
Osceola, *Nevada* - - 134 Fb
Osceola, *Wisconsin* - 132 Cc
Oschatz, *Saxony* - - 55 Hd
Oschersleben, *Prussia* - 54 Fc
Oschiri, *Sardinia* - - 64 Jf
Oscoda, *Michigan* - 122 Gc
Oset, N., *U.S.S.R.* - 75 Gg
Oset, S., *Georgia* - - 75 Gg
Osh, *Kirghiz* - - 84 Cb
Oshawa, *Ontario* - - 121 Ac
Ōshima, *Japan* - - 97 Dd
Ōshima, *Japan* - - 100 Ee
Ōshima, *Japan* - - 100 Cb
Oshkosh, *Wisconsin* - 132 Ec
Oshoek, *Transvaal* - 115 Jc
Oshwe, *Belgian Congo* - 109 Cb
Osijek, *Slavonia* - - 66 Dd
Osimo, *Italy* - - 63 Hd
Osipenko, *Ukraine* - 75 Ff
Osipovichi, *White Russia* 75 De
Oskaloosa, *Iowa* - - 132 Ce
Oskarshamn, *Sweden* - 51 Fe
Oskarström, *Sweden* - 51 Cf
Oslo and Fjord, *Norway* 47 Ge
Oslob, *Philippines* - 99 Fb
Osman, *Texas* - - 133 Bf
Osmanabad, *Hyderabad* 90 Cb
Osmancik, *Turkey* - 78 Ca
Osmanlar, *Turkey* - 72 Ec
Osmanli, *Turkey* - - 72 Ea
Osnabrück, *Prussia* - 54 Dc
Osogovska Planina, *Serbia* 70 Da
Osone R., *Italy* - - 62 Eb
Osoppo, *Italy* - - 63 Ha
Osorno, *Spain* - - 38 Ab
Osorno and Mt., *Chile* - 148 Bc
Osowiec, *Poland* - - 56 Gc
Ospitale, *Italy* - - 63 Ga
Osprey Reef, *Queensland* 153 Cb
Oss, *Holland* - - 29 Dc
Ossa, Mt, *Bohemia* - 59 Hb
Ossa (Kíssavos), Mt., *Greece* - - - 70 Dd
Ossabaw I., *Georgia* - 131 He
Ossele, *Fr. Eq. Africa* - 109 Cb
Ossero & C. - - 63 Jc
Ossining, *New York* - 123 Me
Ossipee, *New Hampshire* 128 Cb
Os-Sjoen, *Norway* - 46 Hc
Ostaboining L., *Quebec* 121 Aa
Ostashkov, *U.S.S.R.* - 74 Ed
Östbirk, *Denmark* - 45 Cc
Ostellato, *Italy* - - 63 Gc
Osten, *Prussia* - - 54 Eb
Ostend, *Belgium* - - 29 Ac
Osterburg, *Prussia* - 55 Gc
Osterbymo, *Sweden* - 51 Ee
Osterdal, *Norway* - - 46 Gb
Oster Dal, *Sweden* - 44 Cg
Österdalälven, *Sweden* - 50 Ca
Ostergotland, län, *Sweden* 50 Ed
Osterhofen, *Bavaria* - 59 Hc
Österild, *Denmark* - 45 Ba
Osterkappeln, *Prussia* - 54 Dc
Osterö, *Færoe Is.* - 44 Oc
Osterode - - - 56 Ec
Osterode, *Prussia* - 54 Fd
Osteröy, *Norway* - - 47 Bd
Ostersund, *Sweden* - 44 Cg
Osterwieck, *Prussia* - 54 Fd
Ostfold, fylke, *Norway* 47 He
Osthammar, *Sweden* - 50 Hb
Ostia, *Italy* - - 64 Cb
Ostiano, *Italy* - - 62 Eb
Ostiglia, *Italy* - - 62 Fb
Ostnów, *Poland* - - 60 Dc
Oštrelj, *Bosnia* - - 68 Bb
Ostróg - - - 60 Jc
Ostrogozhsk, *U.S.S.R.* 75 Fe
Ostrołeka, *Poland* - 60 Fb
Ostrorog, *Poland* - - 57 Ba
Ostrov, *U.S.S.R.* - 74 Dd
Ostrova Novo Sibirskie Is., *U.S.S.R.* - - 76 Pb
Östvagöy, *Norway* - 48 Ab
Osumi Str., *Japan* - 97 Cd
Osuna, *Spain* - - 40 Eb
Oswaldkirk, *England* - 18 Cb
Oswego, *Kansas* - - 133 Eb
Oswego, *New York* - 123 Kd
Oswestry, *England* - 18 Ae
Oswiecim, *Poland* - 60 Ec
Osyka, *Mississippi* - 130 Ce
Oszmiana - - - 60 Ha
Ota, *Japan* - - - 100 Hc
Otago, prov., *New Zealand* - - - 159 Bf
Otago Pen., *New Zealand* 159 Cf
Otaki, *New Zealand* - 158 Ed
Otaru, *Japan* - - 97 Eb
Otavalo, *Ecuador* - - 145 Ba
Otawara, *Japan* - - 100 Hc
Otepaa, *Estonia* - - 49 Db
Othe, Forêt d', *France* 31 Fc
Othery, *England* - - 14 Bd
Othonoí (Fanós) I., *Greece* 70 Ad
Othris Mts., *Greece* - 71 Dd
Otira, *New Zealand* - 159 Ce
Otis, *New Brunswick* - 120 Bc
Otley, *England* - - 18 Cc
Otocac, *Croatia* - - 63 Kc
Otok, *Slavonia* - - 66 Dd
Otoka, *Bosnia* - - 68 Bb
Otorohanga, *New Zealand* 158 Ec
Otranto & C., *Italy* - 65 Eb
Otranto, Str. of, *Italy-Albania* - - 61 Ce
Otsego L., *New York* - 128 Ab
Otsu, *Japan* - - 97 Dc
Otsuki, *Japan* - - 100 Gd
Otta, *Norway* - - 46 Fc
Ottawa, *Illinois* - - 132 Ee
Ottawa, *Kansas* - - 133 Ea
Ottawa, *Ohio* - - 129 Bb
Ottawa, *Ontario* - - 121 Cb
Ottawa Is., *Hudson B., Canada* - - 119 Ne
Ottawa R., *Quebec-Ont.* 121 Aa
Otterburn, *England* - 21 Dc
Otteröy I., *Norway* - 46 Cb
Otter Peaks, mt., *Virginia* 129 Ed
Ottershaw, *England* - 15 Dd
Ottery St. Mary, *Eng.* 14 Ae
Otto, *Wyoming* - - 135 La
Ottosdal, *Transvaal* - 115 Fc
Ottoshoop, *Transvaal* - 115 Fb
Ottumwa, *Iowa* - - 132 Ce
Otuquis R., *Bolivia* - 146 Db
Oturkpo, *Nigeria* - - 105 Cd
Otway B., *Chile* - - 148 Be
Otway C., *Victoria* - 154 De
Otwock, *Poland* - - 60 Fb
Otztaler, *Italy* - - 62 Fa
Ouadane, *Fr. W. Africa* 104 Bb
Ouadda, *Fr. Eq. Africa* 105 Fd
Ouadda, *Fr. Eq. Africa* 105 Ee
Ouagadougou, *French W. Africa* - - 104 Dd
Ouahigouya, *Fr. W. Afr.* 104 Dd
Oualata, *Fr. W. Africa* 104 Cc
Ouanas R., *Finland* - 48 Fc
Ouanda Djalé, *Fr. Equat. Africa* - - 105 Fd
Ouango *Fr. Eq. Africa* 105 Fe
Ouaouizert, *Morocco* - 102 Ac
Ouargla, *Algeria* - - 103 Gc
Ouassoulou, *French W. Africa* - - 104 Cd
Oudenbosch, *Holland* - 29 Cc
Oudh, *United Provs.* - 86 Db
Oudtshoorn, *Cape Prov.* 114 Df
Oued Zem, *Morocco* - 102 Ac
Oued Zenati, *Algeria* - 103 Ha
Ouessant, I. d', *France* 32 Ab
Ouesso, *Fr. Eq. Africa* 109 Ca
Ouezzane, *Morocco* - 102 Bb
Oufu, *Manchuria* - - 96 Da
Ougarta, *Algeria* - - 102 Ce
Oughter, L., *Eire* - 26 Cc
Oughterard, *Eire* - - 25 Bc
Ouidah, *Fr. W. Africa* 105 Bd
Oujda, *Morocco* - - 102 Db
Oujeft, *Fr. W. Africa* - 104 Bb
Oulad-Nayls, Mts. des, *Algeria* - - - 103 Fb
Oulad Said, *Algeria* - 102 De
Ouled Djellal, *Algeria* - 103 Gb
Ouled Mahmoud, *Algeria* 102 Ee
Ouled Rahmoun, *Algeria* 103 Ha
Oullins, *France* - - 35 Gb
Oulmes, *Morocco* - - 102 Ac
Oulton, *England* - - 15 Fb
Oulu, *Finland* - - 48 Fd
Oulu Jarvi & R., *Finland* - - - 48 Gd
Oulx, *Italy* - - - 62 Ab
Oumé, *Fr. W. Africa* - 104 Ce
Oumenast, *Morocco* - 103 Nj
Oum er Rbia, R., *Morocco* 103 Nh
Oum Hadjer, *Fr. Equat. Africa* - - - 105 Ec
Oum Laaleg, *Morocco* 103 Ok
Oundle, *England* - - 15 Db
Ouray, *Colorado* - - 135 Kb
Ouray, *Utah* - - 135 Ja
Ouricury, *Brazil* - - 143 Fd
Ourinhos, *Brazil* - - 147 Ec
Ourique, *Portugal* - 40 Bb
Ourlal, *Algeria* - - 103 Gb
Ourlhana, *Algeria* - 103 Gc
Ouro Preto, *Brazil* - 147 Gc
Ouse R., *Norfolk, etc., England* - - - 15 Ea
Ouse R., *Yorks, Eng.* - 18 Cc
Ouse R., Little, *Eng.* - 15 Eb
Ousseukh, El, *Algeria* 102 Eb
Outakoski, *Finland* - 48 Gb
Outarde B., *Quebec* - 120 Ab
Outardes, R. aux, *Quebec* - - - 120 Ab
Outat el Hadj, *Morocco* 102 Cc
Outeiro, *Portugal* - 36 Dc
Outer I., *Quebec* - - 120 Fa
Outokumpu, *Finland* - 48 He
Ouvéa I., *Loyalty Is.* - 157 Df
Ouyeh, *Victoria* - - 154 Cd
Ouzouer, *France* - - 30 Ed
Ouzouer-le-Marche; *France* 30 Dd
Ovada, *Italy* - - 62 Cc
Ovalau I., *Fiji Is.* - 157 Pk
Ovalle, *Chile* - - 146 Ae
Ovar, *Portugal* - - 37 Bb
Ovce Polje, *Serbia* - 70 Cb
Overath, *Prussia* - - 54 Ce
Over Flakkee, *Holland* 29 Cc
Overijssel, prov., *Holland* 29 Eb
Överkalix, *Sweden* - 48 Dc
Overton, *England* - 14 Cd
Overton, *Nevada* - - 134 Fc
Overton, *Texas* - - 133 Ed
Övertornea, *Sweden* - 48 Ec
Oviedo and prov., *Spain* 36 Ea
Övre Fryk Sjö, *Sweden* - 50 Cb
Ovruch, *Ukraine* - - 75 De
Owaka, *New Zealand* - 159 Bg
Owashi, *Japan* - - 97 Dd
Owasso, *Oklahoma* - 133 Db
Owatonna, *Minnesota* - 132 Cc
Owego, *New York* - 123 Kd
Owen, *Wisconsin* - - 132 Dc
Owen Sd., *Ontario* - 123 Hc
Owenmore R., *Eire* - 25 Ba
Owens, *Arizona* - - 134 Gd
Owens L., *California* - 134 Ec
Owen's Pk., *California* 134 Dd
Owensboro, *Kentucky* - 130 Eb
Owen Sound, *Ontario* - 123 Hc
Owen Stanley Ra., *New Guinea* - - - 156 Dc
Owenton, *Kentucky* - 131 Fa
Owerri, *Nigeria* - - 105 Cd
Owosso, *Michigan* - 122 Fd
Owsa, *Hyderabad* - - 90 Cb
Owyhee Mts., *Idaho* - 136 Ed
Owyhee R., *Oregon, etc.* 136 Ed
Ox Mts, *Eire* - - 26 Bc
Oxberg, *Sweden* - - 50 Da
Oxborough, *England* - 15 Ea
Oxelösund, *Sweden* - 50 Gd
Oxford, *Idaho* - - 136 Hd
Oxford, *Kansas* - - 133 Db
Oxford, *Maryland* - 129 Fc
Oxford, *Mississippi* - 130 Dc
Oxford, *New York* - 123 Ld
Oxford, *North Carolina* 131 Jb
Oxford, *Nova Scotia* - 120 Dd
Oxford, *Ohio* - - 129 Bc
Oxford and co., *Eng.* - 14 Cc

Oxford Mills, Ontario - 121 Cb
Oxiá I., Greece - - 71 Ce
Oxilithos, Greece - - 71 Fe
Oxley, New S. Wales - 154 Dc
Oxnard, California - 134 Dd
Oxus, R., U.S.S.R., etc. 77 Kb
Oya, Sarawak - 98 Dc
Oyama, Japan - 100 Gc
Oyapock B. and R., Fr. Guiana-Brazil - - 142 Db
Oyem, Fr. Eq. Africa - 109 Ba
Oyeren L., Norway - 47 He
Oylo, Norway - - 46 Ec
Oyo, Nigeria - - 105 Bd
Öyslebo, Norway - 47 Df
Oyster B., Tasmania - 155 Kg
Oyster Bay, New York 128 Bc
Oysterville, Washington 136 Ab
Oystese, Norway - 47 Cd
Ozalj, Croatia - - 63 Kb
Ozark, Alabama - - 130 Fe
Ozark, Arkansas - - 130 Bc
Ozark, Missouri - - 130 Bb
Ozarks, L. of the, Missouri - - - 130 Ba
Ozd, Hungary - - 66 Fa
Ozieri, Sardinia - - 64 Hf
Ozinki, U.S.S.R. - - 75 He
Ozona, Texas - - 133 Be
Ozora, Hungary - - 66 Dc
Ozorkow, Poland - - 57 Eb
Ozuki, Japan - - 100 Ba
Paan, Burma - - 92 Cd
Paarl, Cape Prov. - 114 Cf
Paauwpan, Cape Prov. 115 Fe
Pab Ra., Baluchistan - 85 Aa
Pabba, Uganda - - 110 Cb
Pabjanice, Poland - 60 Ec
Pabna, Bengal - - 88 Bc
Pacaraima, Sa., Venez.-Brazil - - 144 Dc
Pacasmayo, Peru - - 145 Ac
Paceco, Sicily - - 65 Fg
Pachaimalai Hills, Madras 89 Cb
Pachbhadra, Rajputana 85 Db
Pachham I., W. India - 85 Bc
Pachino, Sicily - - 65 Jh
Pachmarhi, Central Provs. 86 Cd
Pachora, Bombay - - 90 Ba
Pachpahar, Rajputana 86 Eb
Pachuca, Mexico - - 139 Ec
Pacific, Missouri - - 130 Ca
Pacific Beach, California 134 Ee
Pacific Grove, California 134 Bc
Pacy, France - - 30 Dc
Padam, Kashmir - - 83 Gb
Padany, Sumatra - - 98 Ad
Padang I., Neth. Indies 98 Bc
Padangpanjang, Sumatra 98 Ad
Padang Sidimpoean, Sumatra - - - 98 Ac
Padang Tidji, Sumatra 98 Ab
Padang Tikar I., Netherlands Indies - 98 Cd
Padany, U.S.S.R. - 48 Ke
Padda, Nigeria - - 105 Cd
Paderborn, Prussia - 54 Dd
Padibe, Uganda - - 110 Cb
Padiham, England - - 18 Bc
Padilla, Bolivia - - 146 Cb
Padma R., Bengal - 88 Cc
Padra, Baroda - - 85 Dc
Padrauna, United Provs. 87 Eb
Padre, Sa. do, Brazil - 143 Gd
Padrela, Serra, Portugal 36 Cc
Padron, Spain - - 36 Bb
Padstow and B., England 17 Bb
Padua, Kashmir - - 83 Fb
Padua (Padova), Italy - 63 Fb
Paducah, Kentucky - 130 Db
Paducah, Texas - - 133 Bd
Padula, Italy - - 64 Fc
Padwa, Orissa - - 91 Fb
Paeroa, New Zealand - 158 Eb
Paestum, Italy - - 64 Ec
Pag I., Dalmatia - - 63 Jc
Paga, Bhutan - - 88 Ba
Pagan, Burma - - 92 Bb
Pagan, Marianas Is. - 157 Bb
Pagari, Idaho - - 136 Fd
Pagasaí, G. of, Greece - 70 Dd
Pagatan, Borneo - - 99 Dd
Pagi Is., Nether. Indies 98 Ad
Pagong L., Tibet - - 84 Dd
Pago Pago I., Samoa Is. 157 Fe
Pagosa Springs, Colorado 135 Kc
Pagouehi, Fr. W. Africa 104 Ce
Paguat, Celébes - - 99 Fc
Pagwachuan L. and R., Ontario - - - 122 Fa
Pahang, Malay States - 98 Bc
Paharpur, N.-W. F. P. 82 Db
Pahiatua, New Zealand 158 Ed
Pahlevi, Persia - - 79 Eb
Pahlevi Diz, Persia - 79 Fb
Pahranagat Val., Nevada 134 Fc
Pahroc Ra., Nevada - 134 Fb
Paianía, Greece - - 71 Ef
Paichuan, Manchuria - 96 Db
Paide, Estonia - - 49 Cb
Paignton, England - 17 Cc
Päijanne, Finland - 48 Ff
Paikakowmen, Manchuria 96 Bc
Pai Khoi Mts., U.S.S.R. 74 Lb
Paikoli, Manchuria - 96 Cb
Pailani, United Provs. - 86 Dc
Pailton, England - - 14 Cb
Paimbœuf, France - 32 Cc
Paimpol, France - - 32 Bb
Painan, Sumatra - - 98 Bd
Painesville, Ohio - - 129 Db
Painted Des., Arizona - 135 Hc
Paintsville, Kentucky - 131 Gb
Paisley, Ontario - - 123 Hc
Paisley, Oregon - - 136 Cd
Paisley, Scotland - - 23 De
Paita, Peru - - 145 Ac
Paithan, Hyderabad - 90 Bb
Pai Yar, U.S.S.R. - 74 Lb
Pajala, Sweden - - 48 Ec
Pajares, Spain - - 36 Ea
Pakala, Madras - - 90 De
Pakaraima Mts., British Guiana - 144 Db
Pakaur, Bihar - - 87 Gc
Pakchan, Burma - - 98 Aa
Pakhal and L., Hyderabad 91 Ec
Pak-hoi (Pei-hai), China 95 Ce
Pakhuis, Cape Prov. - 114 Cf
Pa-kow, Manchuria - 96 Bc
Paklan, Siam - - 98 Ab
Pak-lei, Siam - - 95 Bf
Paknam, Siam - - 95 Bg
Pakokku, Burma - - 92 Bb
Pakość, Poland - - 57 Ca
Pakpattan, Punjab - 82 Ec
Pakrac, Slavonia - - 66 Cd
Paks, Hungary - - 66 Dc
Pakse, Laos - - 95 Cf
Pakwach, Uganda - 110 Bb
Palacios, Spain - - 36 Db
Palafrugell, Spain - 39 Jc
Palagonia, Sicily - - 65 Hg
Palaiokhóra, Crete - 71 Gj
Pálairos (Zaverdha), Greece 71 Be
Palais, le, France - 32 Bc
Palaiseau, France - 30 Ec
Palakollu, Madras - 91 Ec
Palamás, Greece - - 70 Dd
Palamau, Bihar - - 87 Fd
Palamcottah, Madras - 89 Bc
Palamos, Spain - - 39 Jc
Palana, Rajputana - 82 Ee
Palanas, Philippines - 99 Fa
Palanga, Lithuania - 49 Ad
Palanka, Serbia - - 68 Fb
Palanpur, Rajputana - 85 Db
Palanque, Mexico - 139 Fd
Palapye Rd., Bechuanaland - - - 113 Bd
Palas, N.-W. F. P. - 82 Ea
Palas del Rey, Spain - 36 Cb
Palatka, Florida - - 131 Hf
Palau, Sardinia - - 64 Je
Palau Is., Pacific Oc. - 149 De
Palawan (Paragua) I., Philippines - - 99 Eb
Palawbun, Burma - - 88 Fa
Palazzo Adriano, Sicily 65 Gg
Palazzola, Italy - - 62 Db
Palazzolo Acreide, Sicily 65 Hg
Palazzo San Gervasio, Italy 65 Bb
Paldiski, Estonia - - 49 Bb
Palembang, Sumatra - 98 Bd
Paléna, Chile - - 148 Bc
Palena, Italy - - 64 Eb
Palencia and prov., Spain 38 Ab
Palenzuela, Spain - 38 Ab
Paleparto, Mte., Italy - 65 Cc
Palermo, Argentina - 146 Cc
Palermo & G. of., Sicily 65 Gf
Palestina, Chile - - 146 Bc
Palestine, Texas - - 133 Ee
Palestine, W. Asia - 77 Cc
Palestrina, Italy - - 64 Cb
Paletwa, Burma - - 92 Ab
Palghat, Madras - - 89 Bb
Palhoca, Brazil - - 147 Fd
Pali, Rajputana - - 85 Db
Pali, C., Albania - - 70 Ab
Palinges, France - - 35 Ga
Páliros, Greece - - 71 Dg
Palisade, Manchuria - 96 Cc
Palisade, Nevada - 134 Ea
Palitana, Western India 85 Cd
Paliyad, Western India 85 Cc
Palizada, Mexico - 139 Fd
Palizzi, Italy - - 65 Be
Palk B., Ceylon - - 89 Cc
Palk Str., India-Ceylon 89 Cc
Palkonda, Madras - 91 Fb
Palkonda Ra., Madras 90 De
Palkot, Bihar - - 87 Fd
Palla, Bechuanaland - 113 Bd
Palladam, Madras - 89 Bb
Pal Lahara, Eastern States 87 Fe
Pallanza, Italy - - 62 Cb
Palla Road, Bechuanaland 113 Bd
Pallaskenry, Eire - 27 Bf
Pallavaran, Madras - 91 Ee
Pallisa, Uganda - - 110 Cc
Palliser B. and C., New Zealand - - - 159 Ed
Pallivasal, Madras States 89 Bc
Palluau, France - - 32 Dd
Palma, Brazil - - 147 Gc
Palma, Mozambique - 112 Db
Palma, La, Spain - 40 Db
Palma & B., Balearic I. 39 He
Palma and R., Brazil - 143 Ee
Palma I., Canary Is. - 104 Aa
Palma del Rio, Spain - 40 Eb
Palma di Montechiaro, Sicily - - - 65 Gg
Palmanovo, Italy - 63 Hb
Palmares, Brazil - - 147 Ee
Palmas, Brazil - - 147 Ed
Palmas B., Mexico - 138 Cc
Palmas, C., Liberia - 104 Cf
Palmas, G. of, Sardinia 64 Hh
Palma Sola, Venezuela 144 Ca
Palm Beach, Florida - 131 Oh
Palmeira, Brazil - - 147 Ed
Palmer, Colorado - 135 Lb
Palmer, Massachusetts 128 Bb
Palmer Arch., Antarctica 160 –
Palmer Goldfield, Queensland - - 153 Bc
Palmerston, Ontario - 123 Hd
Palmerston, C., Queensland - - - 153 Cd
Palmerston I., Cook Is. 157 Ge
Palmerston North, New Zealand - - - 158 Ed
Palmerston South, New Zealand - - - 159 Cf
Palmerville, Queensland 153 Bc
Palmetto, Florida - 131 Mh
Palmi, Italy - - 65 Bd
Palmiet Fontein, C. Prov. 115 Ge
Palmira, Colombia - 144 Ac
Palms, Michigan - 122 Gd
Palms Is., Queensland - 153 Cc
Palmyra, Brazil - - 147 Gc
Palmyra, Missouri - 130 Ca
Palmyra, Syria - - 78 Cc
Palmyra I., Line Is. - 157 Gc
Palni, Madras - - 89 Bb
Palni Hills, Madras - 89 Bb
Palo, Italy - - 64 Cb
Palo, Sarawak - - 98 Dc
Palo Alto, California - 134 Bc
Paloe & B., Celébes - 99 Ed
Palombara Sabina, Italy 64 Ca
Palomera, Sa., Spain - 38 Dd
Palompan, Philippines 99 Fa
Palon, Burma - - 92 Bd
Palopo, Celébes - - 99 Fd
Palos, C., Spain - - 41 Fc
Palo Santo, Argentina - 146 Dd
Palosi, N.-W. F. P. - 82 Ea
Palouse, Idaho - - 136 Eb
Palouse Falls & R., Washington - - 136 Db
Palpa, Nepal - - 87 Eb
Pälsboda, Sweden - 50 Ec
Palu, Turkey - - 78 Cb
Palwal, Punjab - - 83 Gd
Pama, Fr. W. Africa - 105 Bc
Pamangkat, Borneo - 98 Cc
Pamekasan, Madoera I., Nether. Indies - - 99 De
Pamiers, France - - 34 Dd
Pamirs, Tadzhik - - 84 Cc
Pamlico Sd., N. Carolina 131 Kc
Pamoekan B., Borneo - 99 Ed
Pampa, Texas - - 133 Bc
Pampa del Castilla, Argentina - - 148 Cd
Pampanoea, Celébes - 99 Ed
Pampas, Peru - - 145 Cd
Pampas, terr., Argentina 146 Cf
Pampilhosa, Portugal - 37 Cb
Pamplona, Colombia - 144 Bb
Pamplona, Spain 38 Db
Pampoenpoort, Cape Prov. - - - 114 Ee
Pamyat Kirovo, U.S.S.R. 74 Jd
Pamzal, Kashmir - 83 Ha
Pana, Illinois - - 132 Ef
Panaca, Nevada - - 134 Fc
Panache L., Ontario - 123 Hb
Panama and Canal, Panama - - - 140 Hf
Panama, rep. & Gulf, Cent. America - - 140 Hf
Panama City, Florida - 130 Fe
Panaon I., Philippines 99 Fb
Panaro, R., Italy - 62 Ec
Panat, Siam - - 95 Bg
Panay I., Philippines 99 Fa
Panayiá, Crete - - 71 Jj
Panayia, Greece - - 70 Fc
Pancake Ra., Nevada - 134 Fb
Pančarevo, Serbia - 70 Db
Pancevo, Voyvodina - 67 Fe
Panchet Hill, Bihar - 87 Gd
Panch Mahals, Bombay 85 Dc
Panchun, Rajputana - 82 Ee
Pancota, Romania - 67 Gc
Pandan, Philippines - 99 Fa
Pandaria, Central Provs. 86 Dd
Pandassan, N. Borneo 99 Eb
Pan de Azucar, Chile - 146 Ad
Pandharpur, Bombay - 90 Bc
Pando, Uruguay - - 146 De
Pandora Pass, New Guinea - - - 156 Cc
Pandosa, California - 134 Ca
Pandu, Assam - - 88 Ca
Panevežys, Lithuania - 49 Cd
Panga, Belgian Congo - 109 Ea
Panga, Mt., Mozam.-S. Rhodesia - - 113 Eb
Panga, R., Manchuria 96 Ca
Pangaíon, Mt., Greece - 70 Ec
Pangal, Hyderabad - 90 Dc
Pangala Fr. Equat. Africa 109 Bb
Pangani & R., Tanganyika Terr. - - 111 Ff
Pangbourne, England - 14 Cd
Pangire, Tang. Terr. - 111 Dh
Pangkalan Brandan, Sumatra - - - 98 Ac
Pangkal Pinang, Bangka I., N. I. - 98 Cd
Pang-Khan, Burma - 92 Ca
Pangmi, Burma - - 92 Cb
Pangmuti, Mozambique 113 Fb
Pangnirtung, N.-W.T. 119 Qc
Pangong (Tsomonang) L., Kashmir-Tibet - 83 Hb
Pangrango, Mt., Java - 98 Ce
Pangtara, Burma - 92 Cb
Pangtsela, China - 94 Ad
Panguitch, Utah - - 135 Gc
Panguma, Sierra Leone 104 Be
Pangutarang Is., Philippines - - 99 Eb
Pangwe, Tang. Terr. - 111 Ff
Panhandle, Texas - 133 Bc
Pania Mutombo, Belgian Congo - - 109 Dc
Panipat, Punjab - - 83 Gd
Paniquia, Philippines - 99 Eb
Panir, Baluchistan - 82 Bd
Pánitsa, Greece - - 71 Dg
Panja, Mozambique - 112 Bd
Panjim (Nova Goa), Goa 90 Ad
Panjnad R., Punjab - 82 Dd
Panjshir, Afghanistan - 84 Bc
Pankop, Transvaal - 115 Hb
Pankow, Prussia - - 55 Jc
Panna, Central India - 86 Dc
Panokongba, Assam - 88 Eb
Panruti, Madras - - 89 Cb
Panshan, Manchuria - 96 Cc
Panshih, Manchuria - 96 Dc
Panta, N. Rhodesia - 112 Ab
Pantano, Arizona - - 135 Hf
Pantar I., Nether. Indies 99 Fe
Pantelleria I., Italy - 65 Fh
Panticeu, Transylvania 67 Jb
Pantun, Borneo - - 99 Ec
Pánuco, Mexico - - 138 Db
Pánuco R., Mexico - 139 Ec
Panyabungan, Sumatra 98 Ac
Panzi, Belgian Congo - 109 Cc
Panzos, Guatemala - 140 Fd
Pao-an, China - - 94 Da
Pão de Assucar, Brazil 143 Gd
Pão dos Ferros, Brazil 143 Gd
Pao-kang, China - - 94 Dc
Pao-king, China - - 94 Dd
Paola, Italy - - 65 Bc
Paola, Kansas - - 133 Ea
Paoli, Indiana - - 129 Ac
Pao-ngan, China - - 94 Cb
Pao-ning, China - - 94 Cc
Pao-teh, China - - 94 Db
Pao-ting, China - - 94 Db
Paotowchen, China - 94 Ca
Paotsing, Manchuria - 96 Eb
Paouignan, Fr. W. Africa 105 Bd
Pápa, Hungary - - 66 Cb
Papakura, New Zealand 158 Eb
Papaloapan, R., Mexico 139 Ed
Papanasam, Madras - 89 Cb
Papandajan, Java - 98 Ce
Papantala, Mexico - 139 Ec
Papar, N. Borneo - 99 Eb
Pápas (Araxos), C., Greece 71 Ce
Papa Stour, Zetland - 24 Gh
Papeete, Society Is. - 157 He
Papenburg, Prussia - 54 Cb
Papenwasser - - 55 Kb
Papile, Lithuania - 49 Bc
Papillion, Nebraska - 132 Ae
Papineau L., Quebec - 121 Cb
Papineauville, Quebec - 121 Cb
Pápóc, Hungary - - 66 Cb
Papoli, Italy - - 64 Da
Paposo, Chile - - 146 Ad
Papua (New Guinea) Pacific Oc. - - 156 Cc
Papua & Gulf of, New Guinea - - - 156 Cc
Papuk, Mt, Slavonia - 66 Cd
Papun, Burma - - 92 Cc
Para, state, Brazil - 142 Dc
Pará (Belem), Brazil - 143 Ec
Para, R., Brazil - - 143 Ec
Paracas, Pen. de, Peru 145 Bd
Paracatu and R., Brazil 147 Fb
Paracel Is. and Reefs, S. China Sea - - 95 Df
Parachilna, S. Australia 154 Bb
Parachinar, N.-W.F.P. 82 Db
Paraćin, Serbia - - 68 Gc
Paracurú, Brazil - - 143 Gc
Paradise, Kansas - 133 Ca
Paradise Valley, Nevada 134 Ea
Paradiso, Gran, mt, Italy 62 Bb
Parag, Persia - - 79 Hd
Paragould, Arkansas - 130 Cb
Paragua, La, and R., Venezuela - - 144 Db
Paraguana, Pen. de, Venezuela - - 144 Ca
Paraguari, Paraguay - 146 Dd
Paraguassu, Brazil - 147 Ec
Paraguay, rep., S. Amer. 141 De
Paraguay, R., Paraguay 146 Dd
Parah, Afghanistan - 79 Hc
Parahyba, R., Brazil - 147 Gc
Parahyba, state and R., Brazil - 143 Gd
Paraiso, Mexico - - 139 Fd
Parakou, Fr. W. Africa 105 Bd
Parakylia, S. Australia 154 Ab
Paramagudi, Madras - 89 Cc
Paramaribo, Suriname 142 Ca
Paramera de Avila, La, Spain - - - 37 Fb
Paramirim and R., Brazil - - - 143 Fe
Paramithiá, Greece - 70 Bd
Parana, Argentina - 146 Ce
Parana, state, Brazil - 147 Ec
Parana, R., Argentina 146 Dd
Paranagua, Brazil - 147 Fd
Paranapiacaba, Sa., Brazil - - - 147 Fc
Paranéstion, Greece - 70 Fb
Paranga, Uganda - - 110 Cb
Paranthan, Ceylon - 89 Dc
Parantij, Bombay - 85 Dc
Paraopéba, Brazil - 147 Fb
Parapanda, Sa., Spain 41 Cc
Parapato (Antonio Annes), Mozamb. - 112 Dc
Parapola (Belópoulo), Greece - - - 71 Eg
Parasan I., Philippines 99 Fa
Parashi, Tang. Terr. - 111 Fg
Parasnath Hill, Bihar - 87 Gd
Paratary L., Brazil - 142 Bc
Parattah, Tasmania - 155 Kg
Paray le Monial, France 35 Ga
Parbati R., Gwalior, etc. 86 Bc
Parbatipur, Bengal - 88 Bb
Parbhani, Hyderabad - 90 Cb
Parchim, Mecklenburg - 55 Gb
Parcq, Le, France - 30 Ea
Pardilla, Spain - - 38 Bc

PAR **Regional Atlas** PEN

Pardubice, *Bohemia* - 60 Cc
Pare Mts., *Tang. Terr.* 111 Ee
Parecis & Sa. das, *Brazil* 142 Ce
Paredes de Nava, *Spain* 38 Ab
Parenda, *Hyderabad* - 90 Bb
Parent, *Quebec* - - 123 La
Parentis-en-Born, *France* 34 Ac
Parenzo - - - 63 Hb
Pareora, *New Zealand* - 159 Cf
Pare Pare, *Celébes* - 99 Ed
Parey, *Prussia* - - 55 Ge
Párga, *Greece* - - 70 Bd
Pargi, *Hyderabad* - 90 Cc
Paria, Pen. and Golfo de, *Venezuela* - - 144 Da
Pariaguan, *Venezuela* - 144 Db
Pariaman, *Sumatra* - 98 Ad
Parida Grande, I., *Panama* - - - 140 Gf
Parigi, *Celébes* - 99 Fd
Parigi, *Java* - - 98 Ce
Parika, *British Guiana* 144 Eb
Parima, Sa., *Venez.-Brazil* 144 Dc
Parinari, *Peru* - - 145 Cb
Parinas, Pta., *Peru* - 145 Ab
Paring Mts., *Romania* - 67 Jd
Paringa, *S. Australia* - 154 Cc
Parintins, *Brazil* - - 142 Cc
Paris, *Arkansas* - - 130 Bc
Paris, *France* - - 30 Ec
Paris, *Idaho* - - 136 Hd
Paris, *Illinois* - - 132 Ff
Paris, *Kentucky* - - 131 Fa
Paris, *Missouri* - - 130 Ba
Paris, *Ontario* - - 123 Hd
Paris, *Tennessee* - - 130 Db
Paris, *Texas* - - 133 Ed
Parish, *Florida* - - 131 Mh
Parita B., *Panama* - 140 Gf
Pariz, *Persia* - - 79 Gd
Park Ra., *Colorado* - 135 Kb
Park City, *Utah* - - 135 Ha
Parker, *S. Dakota* - 132 Ad
Parker and Dam, *Arizona* - - - 134 Fd
Parkersburg, *W. Virginia* 129 Dc
Parkes, *New S. Wales* - 155 Fc
Park Falls, *Wisconsin* - 132 Dc
Parkfield, *California* - 134 Cd
Park Rapids, *Minnesota* 132 Bb
Parks, *Arizona* - - 135 Hd
Parkview, *New Mexico* 135 Kc
Parlakimedi, *Orissa* - 91 Gb
Parlakot, *Eastern States* 91 Eb
Parli, *Hyderabad* - 90 Cb
Parma, *Idaho* - - 136 Ed
Parma & R., *Italy* - 62 Ec
Parmele, *N. Carolina* - 131 Kc
Parna, *Brazil* - - 143 Fe
Parnahyba & R., *Brazil* 143 Fc
Parnassós, *Greece* - 71 De
Parnell, *Texas* - - 133 Bc
Párnis, Mt., *Greece* - 71 Ee
Pärnu, *Estonia* - - 49 Cb
Pärnu B. & R., *Estonia* 49 Cb
Paro, *Bhutan* - - 88 Ba
Paron, *Gwalior* - - 86 Bc
Paroo, R., *N.S.W.-Queensland* - - 154 Db
Paros I., *Greece* - - 61 Kf
Parowan and Ra., *Utah* 135 Gc
Parral, *Chile* - - 148 Bb
Parral, *Mexico* - - 138 Cb
Parramatta, *N. S. Wales* 155 Gc
Parras, *Mexico* - - 138 Db
Parre, *Italy* - - 62 Db
Parres (Arriondas), *Spain* 36 Ea
Parrett, R., *England* - 14 Bd
Parrsboro, *Nova Scotia* 120 Cd
Parry, C., *N.-W. Terr.* 118 Eb
Parry I., *Ontario* - 123 Hc
Parry Is., *N.-W. Terr.* 118 Ga
Parry Sound, *Ontario* - 123 Hc
Parsa, *Bihar* - - 87 Fc
Parseier Spitze, *Austria* 58 Ed
Parsons, *Kansas* - - 133 Eb
Parsons, *Mississippi* - 130 Dd
Parsonstown (Birr), *Eire* 27 Ce
Partabgarh, *Rajputana* 85 Eb
Partabgarh, *United Provs.* 86 Dc
Partabpur, *Eastern States* 87 Ed
Partabpur, *Eastern States* 91 Ea
Partanna, *Sicily* - - 65 Fg
Partenkirchen, *Bavaria* 58 Fd
Parthenay, *France* - 32 Ed
Parthenen, *Austria* - 58 Ee
Partinico, *Sicily* - 65 Gf
Partry Mts., *Eire* - 25 Bb
Parú, R., *Brazil* - - 142 Dc
Parur, *Madras States* - 89 Bb
Parva, *Transylvania* - 67 Kb
Parvatipuram, *Madras* 91 Fb
Parys, *O.F.S.* - - 115 Gc
Pas, The, *Manitoba* - 124 Jd
Pasadena, *California* - 134 Dd
Paşaköy, *Turkey* - 72 Db
Pasalimani I., *Turkey* - 72 Eb
Pasayigit, *Turkey* - 72 Db
Pascagoula and R., *Mississippi* - - 130 De
Paşcani, *Romania* - 69 Gb
Pas-de-Calais, dep., *France* 30 Ea
Paseo, *Washington* - 136 Db
Pasewalk, *Prussia* - 55 Kb
Pashkova, *U.S.S.R.* - 96 Eb
Pasi I., *Netherlands Indies* 99 Fe
Pasig, *Philippines* - 95 Fg
Pasing, *Bavaria* - - 58 Fc
Pasipas, *S. Rhodesia* - 113 Cc
Pasir, *Borneo* - - 99 Ed
Paska, *Ontario* - - 122 Ea
Paskuh, *Persia* - - 79 Hd
Pašman I., *Dalmatia* - 63 Kd
Paso de Indios, *Argentina* - - 148 Cc
Paso de los Libres, *Argentina* - - 146 Dd
Pasoeroean, *Java* - 99 De
Pasok, *Burma* - - 92 Bb
Paso Limay, *Argentina* 148 Bc
Paso Robles, *California* 134 Cd
Paspebiac, *Quebec* - 120 Cb
Pasrur, *Punjab* - - 83 Fb
Passaford, *S. Rhodesia* 113 Da
Passaic, *New Jersey* - 128 Ac
Passamaquoddy B., *New Brunswick* - 120 Bd
Passandaya B., *Madagascar* - - 112 Eb
Passau, *Bavaria* - - 59 Hc
Pass Christian, *Miss.* - 130 De
Passenheim - - 56 Ec
Passero, C., *Sicily* - 65 Jh
Passignamo, *Italy* - 63 Gd
Passo Borman, *Brazil* - 147 Ed
Passo Correse, *Italy* - 64 Ca
Passo Fundo, *Brazil* - 147 Ed
Passos, *Brazil* - - 147 Fc
Pastaza, R., *Peru* - 145 Bb
Pasto, *Colombia* - - 144 Ac
Pastrana, *Spain* - - 38 Bd
Pasvalys, *Lithuania* - 49 Cc
Pászto, *Hungary* - - 66 Eb
Pata I., *Philippines* - 99 Fb
Patan, *Baroda* - - 85 Cc
Patan, *Nepal* - - 87 Fb
Patan (Somnath), *Western India* - 85 Cd
Patancheru, *Hyderabad* 90 Dc
Pataudi, *Punjab States* 83 Gd
Patay, *France* - - 30 Dc
Pataz, *Peru* - - 145 Bc
Patchewollock, *Victoria* 154 Cd
Patchogue, *New York* 123 Me
Patea and R., *New Zealand* - - - 158 Ec
Pateley Bridge, *England* 18 Cb
Patentie, *Cape Prov.* - 115 Ff
Paterna, *Spain* - - 39 Ee
Paternion, *Austria* - 59 He
Paterno, *Sicily* - - 65 Hg
Paternoster Is., *Netherlands Indies* - 99 Ee
Paterson, *New Jersey* - 129 Gb
Paterson Ra., *W. Aust.* 152 Cc
Pathankot, *Punjab* - 83 Fb
Pathari, *Central India* - 86 Cd
Patheingyi, *Burma* - 92 Ca
Pathri, *Hyderabad* - 90 Cb
Pati, *Java* - - 98 De
Patiala, *Punjab States* - 83 Gc
Patiala, state, *Punjab States* - - - 83 Gd
Pa-tiao, *Laos* - - 95 Bf
Pativilca, *Peru* - - 145 Bd
Patjitan, *Java* - - 98 De
Patkai Hills, *Assam* - 88 Ea
Patna, *Bihar* - - 87 Fc
Patna, *Eastern States* - 87 Ee
Patnów, *Poland* - - 57 Db
Patokla, *Fr. W. Africa* 104 Ce
Paton, *United Provs.* - 83 Jc
Patos, *Brazil* - - 143 Gd
Patos, *Mexico* - - 138 Db
Patos, L., *Brazil* - - 147 Ee
Patos, L. de, *Mexico* - 138 Ca
Patquia, *Argentina* - 146 Be
Pátrai (Patros), *Greece* - 71 Ce
Patras & G. of, *Greece* - 71 Ce
Patrasayar, *Bengal* - 88 Ac
Patri, *Bombay* - - 85 Cc
Patricio Lynch I., *Chile* 148 Ad
Patrington, *England* - 19 Dc
Patrocinio, *Brazil* - 147 Fb
Pattanapuram, *Madras States* - - - 89 Bc
Patten, *Maine* - - 120 Ac
Patterson, *Louisiana* - 130 Cf
Patti, *Sicily* - - 65 Hf
Pattikonda, *Madras* - 90 Cd
Pattisons, *Texas* - - 133 Ef
Pattonsburg, *Missouri* 132 Be
Pattukkottai, *Madras* - 89 Cb
Patuakhali, *Bengal* - 88 Cc
Patuca R., *Honduras* - 140 Fe
Patutahi, *New Zealand* 158 Fc
Patuxent R., *Maryland* 129 Fc
Patzcuaro, *Mexico* - 138 Dd
Pau, *France* - - 34 Bd
Pau d' Arco, *Brazil* - 143 Ed
Pauk, *Burma* - - 92 Bb
Paulding, *Mississippi* - 130 De
Paulilatino, *Sardinia* - 64 Hf
Paulina Marsh, *Oregon* 136 Cd
Paulis, *Belgian Congo* - 109 Ea
Paulista, *Brazil* - - 143 Fd
Paulpietersburg, *Natal* 115 Jc
Paul Roux, *O.F.S.* - 115 Gd
Paul's Valley, *Oklahoma* 133 Dc
Paungbyin, *Burma* - 88 Eb
Paungde, *Burma* - 92 Bc
Pauni, *Central Provs.* - 86 Ce
Pauri, *United Provs.* - 83 Hc
Pausa, *Saxony* - - 59 Fa
Pavia, *Italy* - - 62 Db
Pavilosta, *Latvia* - 49 Ac
Pavlovsk, *U.S.S.R.* - 75 Ge
Pavlovsk, *Krasnodar, U.S.S.R.* - - - 75 Ff
Pavullo, *Italy* - - 62 Ec
Pawhuska, *Oklahoma* - 133 Db
Pawlett, England - 14 Bd
Pawnee, *Oklahoma* - 133 Db
Pawnee City, *Nebraska* 132 Ae
Pawtucket, *Rhode Is.* - 128 Cc
Paximádhia Is., *Crete* - 71 Hk
Paxoi I., *Greece* - - 71 Bd
Paxson, *Alaska* - - 125 Ke
Paxton, *Illinois* - - 132 Ee
Payaca Vol., *Guatemala* 140 Ee
Payenchow, *Manchuria* 96 Db
Payer Pk., *Greenland* - 9 Gc
Payerne, *Switzerland* - 42 Cc
Payette & R., *Idaho* - 136 Ec
Payne L., *Quebec* - 119 Pe
Paynesville, *Minnesota* 132 Bc
Paynesville, *W. Aust.* - 152 Bd
Payokumbu, *Sumatra* - 98 Bd
Payo Obispo, *Mexico* - 139 Gd
Paysandu and dep., *Uruguay* - - 146 De
Pays d'Albret, *France* - 34 Bc
Pays de Dombes, *France* 35 Ga
Payson, *Utah* - - 135 Ha
Paz, La, *Argentina* - 146 Be
Pazardzhik, *Bulgaria* - 69 Fd
Pazarköy, *Turkey* - 72 Ec
Pea R., *Alabama* - 130 Fe
Peabody, *Kansas* - 133 Da
Peace R., *Florida* - 131 Nh
Peace River, *Alberta* - 124 Fc
Peada, La, *Argentina* - 146 Ce
Peak, *South Carolina* - 131 Hc
Peak, The, *England* - 18 Cd
Peak Hill, *N. S. Wales* 155 Fc
Peak Hill, *W. Australia* 152 Bd
Peak Hill Goldfield, *W. Australia* - - 152 Bc
Peale I., *Pacific Oc.* - 157 Mh
Peale, Mt., *Utah* - - 135 Jb
Pearce, *Arizona* - - 135 Jf
Pearl, *Ontario* - - 122 Da
Pearl R., *Mississippi* - 130 Dd
Pearl Harbor, *Hawaiian Is.* 157 La
Pearsons Pk., *Nevada* - 134 Dc
Pearston, *Cape Prov.* - 115 Ff
Peary Land, *Greenland* 9 Fa
Pease R., *Texas* - - 133 Bc
Pebas, *Peru* - - 145 Cb
Pebble, *Idaho* - - 136 Hd
Pebble I., *Falkland Is.* 148 Ee
Peć, *Montenegro* - - 68 Fd
Pecanha, *Brazil* - - 147 Gb
Pecatonica R., *Wisconsin* 132 Ed
Pechenga (Petsamo), *U.S.S.R.* - - - 74 Eb
Pe-chih-li, Str. of, *Kwang-tung Terr.* - 97 Ac
Pechora R. and Sea, *U.S.S.R.* - - - 74 Jb
Pechorskaya Gulf, *U.S.S.R.* 74 Jb
Pecica, *Romania* - - 67 Gc
Peck, *Idaho* - - 136 Eb
Pecka, *Serbia* - - 68 Eb
Pecoaro, *Italy* - - 63 Fb
Pecora, *Sardinia* - 64 Hg
Pecos, *New Mexico* - 135 Ld
Pecos R., *New Mexico* 135 Le
Pecos R., *Texas* - - 133 Ad
Pecs, *Hungary* - - 66 Dc
Pécsvárad, *Hungary* - 66 Dc
Peddapuram, *Madras* - 91 Ec
Peddie, *Cape Prov.* - 115 Gf
Pedernales, *Spain* - 38 Ca
Pedernales, *Venezuela* - 144 Db
Pedernales R., *Texas* - 133 Ce
Pedhinón, *Greece* - 70 Dc
Pedralba, *Spain* - - 38 Ee
Pedras Salgadas, *Portugal* 36 Cc
Pedraza, *Venezuela* - 144 Bb
Pedregal, *Panama* - 140 Gf
Pedreiras, *Brazil* - 143 Ec
Pedro Affonso, *Brazil* - 143 Ed
Pedrogao, *Portugal* - 37 Bc
Pedro Juan Caballero, *Paraguay* - - 146 Dc
Pedroll, *Brazil* - - 143 Fc
Pedro Luro, *Argentina* 148 Db
Pedro Muñoz, *Spain* - 38 Ce
Pedrotallagalla, *Ceylon* 89 Dd
Peebinga, *S. Australia* 154 Cc
Peebles and co., *Scotland* 21 Cb
Pee Dee R., *South Carolina* - - 131 Jc
Peekskill, *New York* - 123 Le
Peel, *I. of Man* - - 19 Gf
Peel Inlet, *W. Australia* 152 Be
Peel R., *Yukon* - - 124 Ba
Peel Sd., *N.-W. Terr.* - 118 Kb
Peenemünde, *Prussia* - 55 Ja
Pegasus B., *New Zealand* 159 De
Peggau, *Austria* - - 59 Kd
Pegnitz, *Bavaria* - 58 Fb
Pegu, *Burma* - - 92 Cd
Pegu Yoma, *Burma* - 92 Bc
Pegwell B., *England* - 15 Fd
Pehcevo, *Serbia* - - 70 Db
Pehlivanköy, *Turkey* - 72 Da
Pehowa, *Punjab* - - 83 Gd
Pehuajo, *Argentina* - 148 Db
Péi, *China* - - 94 Ec
Peianchen, *Manchuria* 96 Db
Pei-ling, mts., *China* - 94 Bc
Peine, *Prussia* - - 54 Fc
Peio, *Italy* - - 62 Ea
Peiping (Peking), *China* 94 Ea
Peipsi, L. (Chudskoe), *U.S.S.R.-Estonia* - 74 Dd
Péi-shan (Paik-to-San) *Manchuria* - - 96 Dc
Peiskretscham - - 57 Dc
Pei-tang, *China* - - 94 Eb
Peitschendorf - - 56 Fc
Peitz, *Prussia* - - 55 Kd
Peixe, *Brazil* - - 143 Ee
Pekalongan, *Java* - 98 Ce
Pekan, *Malay States* - 98 Bc
Pekin, *Illinois* - - 132 Ee
Peking (Peiping), *China* 94 Ea
Pekuyonto, *Korea* - 97 Ac
Pélagos (Kirá Panayia) I., *Greece* - - 70 Ed
Pelaihari, *Borneo* - 99 Dd
Pelasyía, *Greece* - - 71 De
Pelee I., *Ontario* - - 122 Ge
Peleng I. and Str., *Netherlands Indies* - 99 Fd
Pelham, *Georgia* - - 131 Fe
Pelhrimov, *Bohemia* - 59 Kb
Pelican L., *Minnesota* - 132 Bb
Pelican Rapids, *Minnesota* 132 Bb
Peljesac I., *Dalmatia* - 68 Cd
Pella, *Cape Prov.* - 114 Cd
Pella, *Greece* - - 70 Cc
Pella, *Iowa* - - 132 Ce
Pellaro, *Italy* - - 65 Be
Pellegrini, *Argentina* - 148 Db
Pellérd, *Hungary* - 66 Dc
Pellestrina, *Italy* - 63 Gb
Pello, *Finland* - - 48 Fc
Pellworm I, *Prussia* - 54 Da
Pelly L., *N.-W. Terr.* - 124 Ja
Pelly R. and Ra., *Yukon* 124 Cb
Peloche, *Spain* - - 37 Ec
Peloncillo Ra, *Arizona* 135 Je
Peloponnese (Morea), div., *Greece* - - 71 Cf
Pelotas, *Brazil* - - 147 Ee
Pelsöcz, *Slovakia* - 67 Fa
Pelussin, *France* - - 35 Gb
Pelym, *U.S.S.R.* - - 74 Ld
Pemalang, *Java* - - 98 Ce
Pematang Siantar, *Sumatra* - - - 98 Ac
Pemba, *N. Rhodesia* - 112 Ac
Pemba B., *Mozambique* 112 Db
Pemba Chan., *E. Africa* 111 Ff
Pemba I., *Zanzibar* - 111 Ff
Pembas, *Sarawak* - 98 Dc
Pembina, *N. Dakota* - 132 Aa
Pemboeang, *Borneo* - 98 Dd
Pembridge, *England* - 14 Bb
Pembroke, *N. Zealand* 159 Bf
Pembroke, *Ontario* - 121 Bb
Pembroke and co., *Wales* - - - 20 Bd
Pembroke Dock, *Wales* 20 Ad
Pena, *U.S.S.R.* - - 75 Fe
Peña, Sa. de la, *Spain* - 38 Eb
Peña de Francia, Sa. de, *Spain* - - - 37 Db
Penafiel, *Portugal* - 37 Ba
Peñafiel, *Spain* - - 38 Ac
Peñaflor, *Spain* - - 40 Eb
Pena Iba, *Spain* - - 39 Ec
Peñalara, Pica de, *Spain* 38 Bd
Penalva, *Brazil* - - 143 Ec
Penang I., *Malay States* 98 Ab
Peñaranda, *Spain* - 38 Bc
Peñaranda de Bracamonte, *Spain* - - 37 Eb
Peñarroya, *Spain* - 37 Ed
Penarth, *Wales* - - 20 Ce
Peña Rubia, *Spain* - 36 Da
Peñas, C., *Spain* - - 36 Ea
Penas, G. de, *Chile* - 148 Bd
Peña Vieja, *Spain* - 36 Fa
Pendalofon, *Greece* - 70 Cc
Pendelikón, Mt., *Greece* 71 Ee
Pendembu, *Sierra Leone* 104 Be
Pender, *Nebraska* - 132 Ad
Pendik, *Turkey* - - 72 Gb
Pendlebury, *England* - 18 Bc
Pendleton, *Arkansas* - 130 Cd
Pendleton, *Oregon* - 136 Dc
Pend Oreille, L., *Idaho* 136 Ea
Pendulum I., *Greenland* 9 Hc
Penedo, *Brazil* - - 143 Ge
Penetanguishene, *Ontario* - - - 123 Hc
Peng, *China* - - 94 Cc
Penganga R., *Berar, C.P.* 90 Ca
Pengaron, *Borneo* - 99 Ed
Pengching, *Manchuria* 96 Cc
Penge, *Belgian Congo* - 109 Ea
Peng-shui, *China* - 94 Cd
Peng-tsz, *China* - - 94 Ed
Penguin, *Tasmania* - 155 Jg
Penhalonga, *S. Rhodesia* 113 Eb
Peniche, *Portugal* - 37 Ac
Penicuik, *Scotland* - 23 Ee
Penide I., *Nether. Indies* 99 Ee
Penig, *Saxony* - - 55 He
Peninsula and B., *Ontario* - - - 122 Ea
Penistone, *England* - 18 Cc
Penkridge, *England* - 14 Ba
Penmaen-mawr, *Wales* 20 Ca
Penna, Mte., *Italy* - 62 Dc
Pennabilli, *Italy* - - 63 Gd
Pennapolis, *Brazil* - 147 Ec
Penne, *Italy* - - 64 Da
Penner R., *Madras* - 90 Cd
Pennfield, *New Brunswick* - - 120 Bd
Pennine, Alpi, *Switz.* - 42 Ed
Pennine Chain, *England* 18 Ba
Pennington R., *Nigeria* 105 Be
Pennsylvania, state, *U.S.A.* - - - 127 Kb
Penny Str., *N.-W. Terr.* 118 Ja
Penn Yan, *New York* - 123 Kd
Penobscot B., *Maine* - 128 Da
Penokee Ra., *Wisconsin* 132 Db
Penola, *S. Australia* - 154 Cd
Penong, *S. Australia* - 151 Ee
Penonome, *Panama* - 140 Gf
Penrhyn I., *Pacific Oc.* 157 Hd
Penrhyndeudraeth, *Wales* 20 Bb
Penrith, *England* - 18 Ba
Penrith, *New S. Wales* 155 Gc
Penryn, *England* - 17 Ac
Pensacola & B., *Florida* 130 Ee
Pensford, *England* - 14 Bd
Pentecost I., *New Hebrides* - - - 157 De
Pentland, *Queensland* - 153 Cd
Pentland Firth, *Scotland* 24 Ed
Pentland Hills, *Scotland* 23 Ee
Pentwater, *Michigan* - 122 Ed
Penukonda, *Madras* - 90 Cd
Penybont, *Wales* - 20 Cc
Penza, *U.S.S.R.* - - 75 Ge
Penzance, *England* - 17 Ac
Penzberg, *Bavaria* - 58 Fd

Piribeyler, *Turkey* 72 Fc
Piritu, *Venezuela* 144 Ca
Pirmasens, *Saar Palatinate* 58 Bb
Pirna, *Saxony* 55 Je
Pirojpur, *Bengal* 88 Cc
Pirot, *Serbia* 69 Ed
Pir Panjal Ra. & Pass, *Kashmir* 83 Fb
Pirre, *Uganda* 110 Db
Pisa, *Italy* 62 Ed
Pisa R., *Poland* 56 Fc
Pisagua, *Chile* 146 Ab
Pisciotta, *Italy* 64 Fc
Pisco and R., *Peru* 145 Bd
Piseco, *New York* 128 Ab
Pisek, *Bohemia* 60 Cd
Pisek, *Moravia* 57 Cd
Pishin, *Baluchistan* 82 Bc
Pishin, *Persia* 79 Hd
Pisino 63 Hb
Pissis, mt., *Argentina* 146 Bd
Pisticci, *Italy* 65 Cb
Pistoia, *Italy* 62 Ed
Pistolet B., *Newfoundland* 120 Ha
Pisuerga R., *Spain* 38 Ab
Pita, *French W. Africa* 104 Bd
Pitar, *Western India* 85 Cc
Pitcairn I., *Pacific Oc.* 149 Oh
Pite R., *Sweden* 44 Df
Pitea, *Sweden* 44 Ef
Piteşti, *Romania* 69 Fc
Pithapuram, *Madras* 91 Fc
Pithiviers, *France* 30 Ec
Pithoria, *Central Provs.* 86 Cc
Pithoro, *Sind* 85 Bb
Piti, *Marianas Is.* 157 Ol
Pitigliano, *Italy* 63 Fe
Pitihra, *Central Provs.* 86 Cd
Pitkin, *Colorado* 135 Kb
Pitlochry, *Scotland* 23 Ec
Pitsani, *Bechuanaland* 115 Fb
Pitsea, *England* 15 Ec
Pi-tse-wo, *Kwang-tung Terr.* 97 Ac
Pi-tsiń, *China* 94 Bd
Pitt, Mt., *Oregon* 136 Bd
Pitt Pass., *Nether. Indies* 99 Gd
Pitt R., *California* 134 Ca
Pittenweem, *Scotland* 23 Fd
Pittsboro, *N. Carolina* 131 Jc
Pittsburg, *Kansas* 133 Eb
Pittsburg, *Texas* 133 Ed
Pittsburgh, *Pennsylva.* 129 Eb
Pittsfield, *Illinois* 132 Df
Pittsfield, *Massachusetts* 128 Bb
Pittsfield, *New York* 129 Ha
Pittston, *Pennsylvania* 129 Gb
Pittsworth, *Queensland* 153 De
Pitur Rani, mt., *Eastern States* 91 Eb
Piura and dep., *Peru* 145 Ac
Piute Pk., *California* 134 Dd
Piyai, *Greece* 70 Cd
Pizzo, *Italy* 65 Cd
Pizzoli, *Italy* 64 Da
Placentia & B., *Newfoundland* 120 Hc
Placer Guadalupe, *Mexico* 138 Cb
Placerville, *California* 134 Cb
Placerville, *Colorado* 135 Jb
Placerville, *Idaho* 136 Fd
Pladen, *Bohemia* 59 Ha
Plainby, *Queensland* 153 Dd
Plain Dealing, *Louisiana* 130 Bd
Plainfield, *Connecticut* 128 Bc
Plainfield, *New Jersey* 129 Gb
Plains, *Montana* 136 Fb
Plainview, *Minnesota* 132 Cc
Plainview, *Texas* 133 Bc
Plainville, *Connecticut* 128 Bc
Plainville, *Kansas* 133 Ca
Plainwell, *Michigan* 122 Fd
Plaka, C., *Crete* 71 Kj
Plan, *Italy* 63 Fa
Plana, *Bohemia* 59 Jb
Plana, *Hercegovina* 68 Dd
Plancoët, *France* 32 Cb
Planinski Chan., *Jugoslavia* 63 Jb
Planitz, *Saxony* 55 He
Plant City, *Florida* 131 Mh
Plaquemine, *Louisiana* 130 Ce
Plasencia, *Caceres, Spain* 37 Db
Plasencia, *Zaragoza, Spain* 38 Dc
Plaški, *Croatia* 63 Kb
Plassen, *Norway* 46 Jc
Plast, *U.S.S.R.* 74 Le
Plaster Rock, *New Bruns.* 120 Bc
Plaston, *Transvaal* 115 Jb
Plataiaí, *Greece* 71 Ee
Platamón, *Greece* 70 Dc
Plataniá, *Greece* 70 Fb
Plátanistos, *Greece* 71 Fe
Plátanos, *Akarnania and Aitolia, Greece* 71 Ce
Platanos *Akhaia and Ilia, Greece* 71 De
Plátanos, *Larissa, Greece* 71 Dd
Platanousa, *Greece* 70 Bd
Plathe 55 Lb
Plati, *Greece* 70 Dc
Platon Point, *Quebec* 121 Da
Plátsa, *Greece* 71 Dg
Platt Nat. Park, *Oklahoma* 133 Dc
Platte R., Nth., *Neb.-Wyo.* 126 Eb
Platte R., Sth., *Colorado* 135 Ma
Platte City, *Missouri* 130 Aa
Platteville, *Colorado* 135 La
Platteville, *Wisconsin* 132 Dd
Plattsburg, *Missouri* 130 Aa
Plattsburg, *New York* 123 Mc
Plattsmouth, *Nebraska* 132 Be
Plaue, *Prussia* 55 Hc
Plauen, *Saxony* 55 He
Plav, *Montenegro* 68 Ed
Plavinas, *Latvia* 49 Cc
Plavnica, *Montenegro* 68 Ed
Plāvnik, *Croatia* 63 Jc
Pławno, *Poland* 57 Ec
Playas, *New Mexico* 135 Jf
Plaza, Huincul, *Argentina* 148 Cb
Plean, *Scotland* 23 Ed
Pleasant B., *Maine* 120 Bd
Pleasant Grove, *Utah* 135 Ha
Pleasant Hill, *Louisiana* 130 Be
Pleasant Hill, *Missouri* 130 Aa
Pleasanton, *Kansas* 133 Ea
Pleasant Valley, *Nevada* 134 Ea
Pleasantville, *New Jersey* 129 Gc
Pleine Fougères, *France* 32 Db
Plenty, Bay of, *New Zealand* 158 Fb
Plerin, *France* 32 Cb
Plesetsk, *U.S.S.R.* 74 Gc
Plessé, *France* 32 Dc
Plessisville, *Quebec* 121 Ea
Pleszew, *Poland* 60 Dc
Pleternica, *Slavonia* 66 Cd
Pletipi L., *Quebec* 119 Pf
Plettenberg B., *Cape Prov.* 114 Eg
Plettenburg, *Prussia* 54 Cd
Pleumartin, *France* 30 Ce
Pleux, *France* 34 Eb
Pleven, *Bulgaria* 69 Fd
Pleyben, *France* 32 Ab
Pleystein, *Bavaria* 59 Gb
Plitvice, *Croatia* 63 Kc
Plješevica, mts., *Croatia* 68 Ab
Pljevlja, *Montenegro* 68 Ec
Płock, *Poland* 60 Eb
Plockenstein, *Austria* 59 Hc
Ploërmel, *France* 32 Cc
Ploeşti, *Romania* 69 Gc
Plogastel-St Germain, *France* 32 Ac
Plombièrres, *France* 31 Jd
Plomosa Mts., *Arizona* 134 Ge
Plöner See, *Prussia* 54 Fa
Plonge, Lac la, *Sask.* 124 Hc
Plonsk, *Poland* 60 Fb
Ploştina, *Romania* 67 Je
Plouaret, *France* 32 Bb
Plouay, *France* 32 Bc
Ploubalay, *France* 32 Cb
Ploudiry, *France* 32 Ab
Plouescat, *France* 32 Ab
Plouguenast, *France* 32 Cb
Plouguerneau, *France* 32 Ab
Plouharnel, *France* 32 Bc
Plouigneau, *France* 32 Bb
Plovdiv (Philippopolis), *Bulgaria* 69 Fd
Plumas, *California* 134 Cb
Plumtree, *S. Rhodesia* 113 Bc
Plunge, *Lithuania* 49 Ad
Pluvigner, *France* 32 Cc
Plymouth, *England* 17 Bc
Plymouth, *Indiana* 129 Ab
Plymouth, *Massachusetts* 128 Cc
Plymouth, *New Hamps.* 128 Cb
Plymouth, *N. Carolina* 131 Kc
Plymouth, *Pennsylvania* 129 Fb
Plymouth, *Vermont* 128 Bb
Plymouth, *Wisconsin* 132 Ed
Plzeň (Pilsen), *Bohemia* 60 Bd
Pnom Dang-rek, *Siam* 95 Bg
Pnom-Klia, *Cambodia* 95 Cg
Pnom Kmoch, *Cambodia* 95 Bg
Pnom-penh, *Cambodia* 95 Bg
Po, Mouths of the, *Italy* 63 Gc
Po R., *Italy* 62 Bb
Poarta, *Romania* 67 Hd
Pobe, *French W. Africa* 105 Bd
Pobla, La, *Spain* 39 Hb
Pobla de Segur, *Spain* 39 Fb
Pocahontas, *Arkansas* 130 Cb
Pocahontas, *W. Virginia* 129 Dd
Pocatello, *Idaho* 136 Gd
Pochep, *U.S.S.R.* 75 Ee
Pochinka, *U.S.S.R.* 75 Ge
Pochutla, *Mexico* 139 Ed
Počitelj, *Hercegovina* 68 Cc
Pocking, *Bavaria* 59 Hc
Pocomoke City, *Maryland* 129 Gc
Pocos de Caldas, *Brazil* 147 Fc
Podanur, *Madras* 89 Bb
Podareš, *Serbia* 70 Db
Podbiel, *Slovakia* 57 Ed
Podcetrtek, *Slovenia* 63 Ka
Podgorica, *Montenegro* 68 Ed
Podgorz, *Poland* 57 Da
Podili, *Madras* 90 Dd
Podlagovi, *Bosnia* 68 Dc
Podolinec, *Slovakia* 57 Fd
Podolsk, *U.S.S.R.* 74 Fd
Podor, *Fr. W. Africa* 104 Bc
Podujevo, *Serbia* 68 Gd
Podžeplje, *Bosnia* 68 Eb
Poel I., *Mecklenburg* 55 Ga
Poeroetjaoe, *Borneo* 99 Dd
Poerworedjo, *Java* 98 Ce
Poeting, C., *Borneo* 98 Dd
Pogamasing, *Ontario* 122 Gb
Poganico, *Italy* 63 Fe
Poggio, *Emilia, Italy* 63 Fc
Poggio, *Lombardia, Italy* 62 Fc
Poggio Mirteto, *Italy* 64 Ca
Pogorzela, *Poland* 57 Cb
Pogradec, *Albania* 70 Bc
Pohai, Gulf of, *China* 94 Eb
Pohonbatu, *Borneo* 99 Dd
Pohorela, *Slovakia* 57 Ee
Poide, *Estonia* 49 Bb
Poinsat, *France* 34 Ea
Point L., *N.-W. Terr.* 124 Ga
Point Arena, *California* 134 Ab
Point au Fer, *Louisiana* 130 Cf
Pointe à la Hache, *Louisiana* 130 Df
Pointe a Pitre, *Guadeloupe I.* 140 Kg
Pointe aux Trembles, *Quebec* 121 Ea
Pointe du Chene, *New Brunswick* 120 Cc
Pointe Noire, *Fr. Equat. Africa* 109 Bb
Point of Rocks, *Wyoming* 135 Ja
Poissons, *France* 31 Hc
Poissy, *France* 30 Dc
Poitiers, *France* 34 Ca
Poitou, old prov., *France* 34 Ba
Poix, *France* 30 Db
Pojan, *Albania* 70 Bc
Pokaran, *Rajputana* 82 De
Pokataroo, *N. S. Wales* 155 Fa
Pokegama, *Oregon* 136 Bd
Pokemouche, *New Brunswick* 120 Cc
Pokhara, *Nepal* 87 Fa
Pokotu, *Manchuria* 96 Cb
Pokran, *Sind* 85 Ab
Pokrovka, *U.S.S.R.* 96 Eb
Pokupsko, *Croatia* 66 Ad
Pokwani, *Cape Prov.* 115 Fc
Pola 63 Hc
Pola, *Philippines* 99 Fa
Pola de Gordon, La, *Spain* 36 Eb
Polana, mt., *Slovakia* 66 Ea
Poland, *Arizona* 135 Gd
Poland, *Cent. Europe* 53 Hb
Poleang, *Celébes* 99 Fd
Polesella, *Italy* 63 Fc
Polewali, *Celébes* 99 Ed
Polgar, *Hungary* 67 Gb
Polhov-Gradec, *Slovenia* 63 Ja
Poli, *Manchuria* 96 Eb
Poliçan, *Albania* 70 Bc
Policastro, Gulf of, *Italy* 64 Fd
Policka, *Moravia* 57 Bd
Polidhéndri, *Greece* 70 Dc
Poligny, *France* 31 He
Polikastron, *Greece* 70 Dc
Polikhrónon, *Greece* 70 Ec
Polillo, I., *Philippines* 95 Fg
Polipótamon, *Greece* 70 Cc
Polistena, *Italy* 65 Cd
Pölitz 55 Kb
Poliyíros, *Greece* 70 Ec
Polla, *Italy* 64 Fc
Pollachi, *Madras* 89 Bb
Pollensa & B., *Balearic Is.* 39 Je
Pollfoss, *Norway* 46 Dc
Pollica, *Italy* 64 Ec
Pollitt, *Texas* 133 Ee
Pollnow 55 Ma
Polloc, *Philippines* 99 Fb
Pollock, *Louisiana* 130 Be
Polmont, *Scotland* 23 Ee
Polna, *Bohemia* 59 Kb
Polnoyat, *U.S.S.R.* 74 Mc
Polo, *Illinois* 132 Ee
Polómka, *Slovakia* 57 Ee
Polotsk, *White Russia* 74 Dd
Polruan, *England* 17 Bc
Polson, *Montana* 136 Fb
Poltar, *Slovakia* 66 Ea
Poltava, *Ukraine* 75 Ef
Polur, *Madras* 90 De
Polva, *Estonia* 49 Db
Polyarnoe, *U.S.S.R.* 74 Eb
Polykhnitos, *Lesbos I., Greece* 72 Dc
Polynesia, *Pacific Oc.* 157 Ge
Polzin 55 Mb
Poma, *Argentina* 146 Bc
Poman, *Argentina* 146 Bd
Pomara, *Mexico* 138 Dd
Pomarico, *Italy* 65 Cb
Pombal, *Brazil* 143 Gd
Pombal, *Portugal* 37 Bc
Pomerania 55 Kb
Pomeranian B., *Prussia* 55 Ka
Pomeroy, *Ohio* 129 Cc
Pomeroy, *Washington* 136 Eb
Pomlana, *Assam* 88 Db
Pommerellia, *Poland* 56 Bc
Pomona, *California* 134 Ed
Pomona, *S.-W. Africa* 114 Ac
Pomona (Mainland), *Orkney Is.* 24 Ec
Pomorie, *Bulgaria* 69 Gd
Pomorze, *Poland* 56 Bc
Pompano, *Florida* 131 Nh
Pompeevka, *U.S.S.R.* 96 Eb
Pompeii, *Italy* 64 Ec
Pompey's Pillar, *W. Aust.* 152 Db
Ponape I., *Caroline Is.* 157 Cc
Ponca, *Nebraska* 132 Ad
Ponca City, *Oklahoma* 133 Db
Ponce, *Puerto Rico* 140 Jg
Ponce de Leon B., *Florida* 131 Nj
Pondaung Ra., *Burma* 92 Ba
Pond Creek, *Oklahoma* 133 Cb
Pond Inlet, *N.-W. Terr.* 119 Ob
Pondicherry (French), *Madras* 89 Cb
Pondoland, *Cape Prov.* 115 He
Ponferrada, *Spain* 36 Db
Pongau, dist., *Austria* 59 Hd
Pongoma, *U.S.S.R.* 48 Kd
Ponnaiyar R., *Madras* 89 Ca
Ponnani, *Madras* 89 Ab
Ponneri, *Madras* 91 De
Ponoi and R., *U.S.S.R.* 74 Gb
Ponomarevka, *U.S.S.R.* 75 Je
Pon-pi-sai, *Siam* 95 Bf
Pons, *France* 34 Bb
Pons, *Spain* 39 Gc
Pont, *Italy* 62 Bb
Ponta Grossa, *Brazil* 147 Ed
Pontailler, *France* 31 Hd
Pont-à-Mousson, *France* 31 Hc
Ponta Pora & terr., *Brazil* 146 Dc
Pontardawe, *Wales* 20 Cd
Pontarlier, *France* 31 Je
Pontassieve, *Italy* 63 Fd
Pont Audemer, *France* 30 Cb
Pontaumur, *France* 34 Eb
Pont Aven, *France* 32 Bc
Pontchartrain, L., *Louisiana* 130 Ce
Pont Château, *France* 32 Cc
Pont Croix, *France* 32 Ab
Pont-de-Bray, *France* 30 Cd
Pont-de-Montvert, Le, *France* 35 Fc
Pont-de-Roide, *France* 31 Jd
Pont-de-Salars, *France* 34 Ec
Pont de Suert, *Spain* 39 Fb
Pont-de-Veyle, *France* 35 Ga
Pont-du-Château, *France* 35 Fb
Ponte, *Switzerland* 43 Jc
Ponte all Isarco, *Italy* 63 Fa
Pontebba, *Italy* 63 Ha
Pontecorvo, *Italy* 64 Db
Pontedecimo, *Italy* 62 Cc
Ponte de Pungwe, *Mozambique* 113 Fb
Pontedera, *Italy* 62 Ed
Ponte de Sôr, *Portugal* 37 Bc
Pontefract, *England* 18 Cc
Ponteland, *England* 21 Ec
Ponte nell' Alpi, *Italy* 63 Ga
Ponte Nova, *Brazil* 147 Gc
Pontevedra & R., *Spain* 36 Bb
Pontevedra, prov., *Spain* 36 Bb
Ponthierville, *Belg. Congo* 109 Db
Pontiac, *Illinois* 132 Ee
Pontiac, *Michigan* 122 Gd
Pontianak, *Borneo* 98 Cc
Pontine Is., *Italy* 64 Cc
Pontinia, *Italy* 64 Db
Pontivy, *France* 32 Bb
Pont l'Abbe, *France* 32 Ac
Pont-l'Evêque, *France* 30 Cb
Pontoise, *France* 30 Db
Pontoon, *Eire* 25 Bb
Pontorson, *France* 32 Db
Pontotoc, *Mississippi* 130 Dc
Pontotoc, *Texas* 133 Ce
Pontremoli, *Italy* 62 Dc
Pontresina *Switzerland* 43 Jd
Pontrilas, *England* 14 Bc
Pont-St. Esprit, *France* 35 Gc
Pont-Ste Maxence, *France* 30 Eb
Ponts-de-Cé, Les, *France* 32 Ec
Pontypool, *England* 14 Ac
Pontypridd, *Wales* 20 Cd
Pony, *Montana* 136 Hc
Ponza I., *Italy* 64 Cc
Poole, *England* 14 Ce
Poona, *Bombay* 90 Ab
Poonarunna, *S. Aust.* 154 Ba
Poon Boon, *N. S. Wales* 154 Dd
Pooncarie, *N. S. Wales* 154 Dc
Poopalloe, L., *N. S. Wales* 154 Db
Poopo and L., *Bolivia* 146 Bb
Poorman, *Alaska* 125 Hd
Popa Mt., *Burma* 92 Bb
Po-pai, *China* 95 Ce
Popakai, *Suriname* 142 Cb
Popayan, *Colombia* 144 Ac
Poperinghe, *Belgium* 29 Ad
Pope's Creek, *Maryland* 129 Fc
Poplar Bluff, *Missouri* 130 Cb
Poplarville, *Mississippi* 130 De
Popo, *New Guinea* 156 Dc
Popocatepetl, *Mexico* 139 Ed
Popokabaka, *Belg. Congo* 109 Cc
Popovo polje, *Hercegovina* 68 Cd
Poprad, *Slovakia* 57 Fd
Poquis, mt., *Argentina* 146 Bc
Porahat, *Bihar* 87 Fd
Poraj, *Poland* 57 Ec
Porbandar, *W. India* 85 Bd
Porcuna, *Spain* 41 Bc
Porcupine, *Ontario* 123 Ha
Porcupine R., *Alaska-Yukon* 125 Lc
Pordenone, *Italy* 63 Gb
Pori, *Finland* 48 Df
Porjus, *Sweden* 48 Dc
Porkhov, *U.S.S.R.* 74 Dd
Porlamar, *Venezuela* 144 Da
Porlezza, *Italy* 62 Da
Porlock and B., *England* 17 Ca
Pornic, *France* 32 Cc
Póros, *Greece* 71 Ef
Poroszlo, *Hungary* 67 Fb
Porpac, *Hungary* 66 Bb
Porreras, *Balearic Is.* 39 Je
Porretta Terme, *Italy* 62 Ec
Porsanger Fd., *Norway* 44 Fe
Porsanger Halvoy, *Norway* 44 Fe
Porsgrund, *Norway* 47 Fe
Portachuela, *Bolivia* 146 Cb
Portacloy, *Eire* 25 Ba
Port Adams *Kwang-tung Terr.* 97 Ac
Port Adelaide, *S. Aust.* 154 Bc
Portadown, *N. Ireland* 26 Dc
Portaferry, *N. Ireland* 26 Ec
Portage, *Wisconsin* 132 Ed
Portage I., *New Bruns.* 120 Cc
Portage-du-Fort, *Quebec* 121 Bb
Portage la Prairie, *Manitoba* 124 Kd
Portage River, *New Brunswick* 120 Cc
Port Albert, *Victoria* 155 Ee
Portalegre, *Portugal* 37 Cc
Port Alfred *Cape Prov.* 115 Gf
Port Alice (Entebbe), *Uganda* 110 Cc
Port Allen, *Louisiana* 130 Ce
Port Angeles, *Wash.* 136 Ba

Roseburg, *Oregon* - 136 Bd
Rosedale, *Mississippi* - 130 Cd
Rosedale, *Queensland* - 153 Dd
Rosehearty, *Scotland* - 23 Fa
Roseires, *A.-E. Sudan* 108 Bc
Rosenallis, *Eire* - 27 Ce
Rosendal, *O.F.S.* - 115 Gd
Rosendale, *New York* - 128 Ac
Rosenhain - - 57 Cc
Rosenheim, *Bavaria* - 59 Fd
Rosen Tal, *Austria* - 59 Je
Rosetown, *Saskatchewan* 124 Hd
Rosetta (Rashid), *Egypt* 107 Hc
Roseville, *California* - 134 Cb
Roseworth, *Idaho* - 136 Fd
Rosheim, *France* - 31 Kc
Rosh Pinna, *Palestine* - 80 Db
Rosignano Marittima, *Italy* - - 62 Ed
Rosignol, *Brit. Guiana* 144 Eb
Rosiori de Vede, *Romania* 69 Fc
Roskilde, *Denmark* - 45 Ec
Roskilde Fjord, *Denmark* 45 Fc
Roslavl, *U.S.S.R.* - 75 Ee
Roslyn, *Washington* - 136 Cb
Rosmead Junc., *Cape Pr.* 115 Fe
Rösnæs, *Denmark* - 45 Dc
Rosö Fd., *Sweden* - 50 Gd
Rosolini, *Sicily* - 65 Hh
Rosporden, *France* - 32 Bc
Ross, *England* - 14 Bc
Ross, *French W. Africa* 104 Ac
Ross, *New Zealand* - 159 Ce
Ross, *Tasmania* - 155 Kg
Ross I., *Antarctica* - 160 —
Ross Sea and Quad., *Antarctica* - - 160 —
Rossach, *Bavaria* - 58 Ea
Ross and Cromarty, co., *Scotland* - - - 22 Ca
Rossano, *Italy* - - 65 Cc
Ross Carberry, *Eire* - 25 Bf
Rosscor, *N. Ireland* - 26 Cc
Rosseau L., *Ontario* - 123 Jc
Rossel (Arova) I., *Louisiade Arch.* - - 156 Lk
Rosshaupten, *Bavaria* - 58 Ed
Rossignol L., *Nova Scotia* 120 Cd
Rossinver, *Eire* - - 26 Bc
Rossland, *Brit. Columbia* 124 Fe
Rosslare Harbour, *Eire* 27 Dg
Rosslau, *Anhalt* - - 55 Hd
Rosslea, *N. Ireland* - 26 Cc
Rossnakill, *Eire* - - 26 Ca
Rossosh, *U.S.S.R.* - 75 Fe
Rossport, *Ontario* - 122 Ea
Rosstal, *Bavaria* - - 58 Eb
Rosswein, *Saxony* - 55 Jd
Rostanga, *Sweden* - 51 Cg
Rosthern, *Saskatchewan* 124 Hd
Rostock, *Mecklenburg* - 55 Ga
Rostov, *U.S.S.R.* - 75 Ff
Rostov, *Yaroslavl, U.S.S.R.* 74 Fd
Rostrenen, *France* - 32 Bb
Rostrevor, *N. Ireland* - 26 Dc
Ros Vatn, *Norway* - 44 Cf
Roswell, *Georgia* - - 131 Fc
Roswell, *New Mexico* - 135 Le
Rota, I., *Marianas Is.* - 157 Bb
Rotan, *Texas* - - 133 Bd
Rotenburg, *Hanover, Prussia* - - - 54 Eb
Rotenburg, *Hesse-Nassau, Prussia* - - - 54 Ee
Roten Turm, pass, *Romania* - - - 69 Fc
Roth, *Bavaria* - - 58 Fb
Rothaar Geb., *Prussia* 54 Dd
Rothbury, *England* - 21 Ec
Rothenburg, *Bavaria* - 58 Eb
Rother, R., *England* - 15 Ed
Rotherham, *England* - 18 Cd
Rothes, *Scotland* - - 23 Ea
Rothesay, *Scotland* - 22 Ce
Rothfliess - - - 56 Ec
Rothkreuz, *Switzerland* 43 Fb
Rothsay, *W. Australia* 152 Bd
Rothsurben - - 57 Cc
Rothwell, *England* - 15 Db
Roti, I., *Nether. Indies* - 99 Fe
Roto, *New S. Wales* - 155 Ec
Rotoke, *A.-E. Sudan* - 105 Fc
Rotonda, *Italy* - - 65 Cc
Rotondo, Mte., *Corsica* 33 Eg
Rotorua, *New Zealand* 158 Fc
Rottendorf, *Bavaria* - 58 Eb
Rottenmann, *Austria* - 59 Jd
Rotterdam, *Holland* - 29 Cc
Rottingdean, *England* - 15 De
Rottnest I., *W. Australia* 152 Ae
Rottweil, *Württemberg* 58 Cc
Rotuma, I., *Pacific Oc.* 157 Ee
Rotzo, *Italy* - - 63 Fb
Roubaix, *France* - 30 Fa
Rouen, *France* - - 30 Db
Rouge, *France* - - 32 Dc
Rouge R., *Quebec* - 121 Ca
Rougemont, *France* - 31 Jd
Rouille, *France* - - 34 Ca
Roulans, *France* - - 31 Jd
Roulers, *Belgium* - 29 Bd
Roumeli, *Crete* - - 71 Gj
Round Pond, *Newfound.* 120 Gb
Round Rock, *Texas* - 133 De
Roura, *Fr. Guiana* - 142 Db
Rous Pen., *Chile* - 148 Bf
Rousay, I., *Orkney Is.* 24 Ec
Rouse's Point, *New York* 123 Mc
Roussillon, *France* - 34 Ee
Routot, *France* - - 30 Cb
Rouvray, *France* - 31 Gd
Rouxville, *O.F.S.* - 115 Ge
Rouyn, *Quebec* - - 123 Ja
Rovaniemi, *Finland* - 48 Gc
Rovato, *Italy* - - 62 Db
Rovde and Fjord, *Norway* 46 Bb
Rovereto, *Italy* - - 62 Fb
Rovigno d' Istria - 63 Hb
Rovigo, *Algeria* - - 103 Fa
Rovigo, *Italy* - - 63 Fb
Rowan L., *Ontario* - 122 Ba
Rowena, *New S. Wales* 155 Fa
Rowley Shoals, *W. Aust.* 152 Bb
Równe - - - 60 Jc
Rox Sjo, *Sweden* - 50 Ed
Roxboro, *North Carolina* 131 Jb
Roxborough, *Queensland* 153 Ad
Roxburgh, *New Zealand* 159 Bf
Roxburgh, co., *Scotland* 21 Dc
Roxbury, *New York* - 128 Ab
Roxton Falls, *Quebec* - 121 Db
Royale, I., *Michigan* - 122 Db
Royan, *France* - - 32 Ee
Röykenvik, *Norway* - 47 Gd
Royston, *England* - 15 Db
Rožaj, *Montenegro* - 68 Fd
Rozel, *Channel Is.* - 17 Ef
Rozel, *Utah* - - 135 Ga
Rozoy, *France* - - 31 Gb
Rozsnyo, *Slovakia* - 67 Fa
Rozwadów, *Poland* - 60 Gc
Rtishchevo, *U.S.S.R.* - 75 Ge
Rua, *Belgian Congo* - 109 Da
Ruabon, *Wales* - - 20 Cb
Ruaha, *Tanganyika Terr.* 111 Eh
Ruahine Ra., *New Zealand* 158 Fd
Ruapehu, Mt., *New Zealand* - - - 158 Ec
Rubbiera, *Italy* - - 62 Ec
Rubungu, *Tang. Terr.* - 110 Bd
Rubungwa, *Tang. Terr.* 111 Cf
Ruby, *Alaska* - - 125 Hd
Ruby, *Colorado* - - 135 Kb
Ruby Ra. & L., *Nevada* 134 Fa
Ruby Hill, *Nevada* - 134 Eb
Ruby Valley, *Nevada* - 134 Fa
Rucava, *Latvia* - - 49 Ac
Ruchi, *U.S.S.R.* - - 74 Gb
Ruchugi (Uvinza), *Tanganyika Terr.* - - 111 Bf
Rudabánya, *Hungary* - 67 Fa
Rudauli, *United Provs.* 86 Db
Rudbar, *Afghanistan* - 79 Hc
Rudewa, *Tang. Terr.* - 111 Eg
Rudi, *Tanganyika Terr.* 111 Eg
Rudköbing, *Denmark* - 45 Dd
Rudnik, *Serbia* - - 68 Fd
Rudnik, Mt., *Serbia* - 68 Fb
Rudo, *Bosnia* - - 68 Ec
Rudok, *Tibet* - - 84 Dd
Rudoka Planina, *Serbia* 70 Bb
Rudolf, L., *Kenya, etc.* 110 Eb
Rudolstadt, *Thuringia* 54 Ge
Rue, *France* - - 30 Da
Rueda, *Spain* - - 38 Dc
Ruel, *Ontario* - - 123 Hb
Ruesta, *Spain* - - 38 Eb
Rufa'a, *A.-E. Sudan* - 108 Bc
Ruffec, *France* - - 34 Ca
Rufia, *Nigeria* - - 105 Bc
Rufiji, R., *Tang. Terr.* - 111 Eh
Rufino, *Argentina* - 148 Da
Rufisque, *Fr. W. Africa* 104 Ad
Rugby, *England* - - 14 Cb
Rugeley, *England* - 14 Ca
Rügen, I., *Prussia* - 55 Ja
Rügenwalde - - 55 Ma
Ruhama, *Palestine* - 80 Be
Rühimäki, *Finland* - 48 Ef
Ruhland, *Prussia* - 55 Jd
Ruhpolding, *Bavaria* - 59 Gd
Ruhr, R., *Prussia* - 54 Cd
Rui Khaf, *Persia* - 79 Gc
Ruislip, *England* - 15 Dc
Ruiwa, *Tanganyika Terr.* 111 Ch
Ruk, *Sind* - - - 82 Ce
Rukchen, *Kashmir* - 83 Gb
Rukhlovo, *U.S.S.R.* - 76 Nd
Rukowakuona Mts., *S. Rhodesia* - - 113 Da
Rukumkot, *Nepal* - 87 Ea
Rukwa, L., *Tang. Terr.* 111 Ch
Rum, *Hungary* - - 66 Bb
Rum, I., *Scotland* - 22 Bb
Ruma, *Slavonia* - - 66 Ed
Rumbek, *A.-E. Sudan* - 108 Ad
Rumburg, *Bohemia* - 59 Ja
Rumilly, *France* - - 35 Hb
Rumlang, *Switzerland* - 43 Fb
Rummelsburg - - 56 Bb
Rumoe, *Japan* - - 97 Eb
Rumsey, *California* - 134 Bb
Rumsey, *Montana* - 136 Gb
Rumuruti, *Kenya* - 110 Ec
Runanga, *New Zealand* 159 Ce
Runcorn, *England* - 18 Bd
Rundhögda, *Norway* - 46 Gb
Rungu, *Belgian Congo* 109 Ea
Rungwe & Mt., *Tanganyika Terr.* - - 111 Ch
Runn, L., *Sweden* - 50 Eb
Runton Ra., *W. Australia* 152 Cc
Ruovesi, *Finland* - 48 Ef
Rupa, *Assam* - - 88 Da
Rupar, *Punjab* - - 83 Gc
Rupbas, *Rajputana* - 83 Ge
Rupert, *Idaho* - - 136 Gd
Rupert House and R., *Quebec* - - - 119 Of
Rupnagar, *Rajputana* - 83 Fe
Ruppertown, *Tennessee* 130 Ec
Ruppichteroth, *Prussia* 54 Ce
Ruppin, Neu and Alt, *Prussia* - - - 55 He
Rupununi, R., *British Guiana* - - - 144 Ec
Rural Hall, *N. Carolina* 131 Hb
Rus, *Spain* - - - 41 Cb
Rusakovo, *U.S.S.R.* - 74 Ja
Rusapi, *S. Rhodesia* - 113 Eb
Rusco, *Italy* - - 63 Fc
Ruscova, *Transylvania* 67 Kb
Ruse, *Bulgaria* - - 69 Gd
Rush City, *Minnesota* - 132 Cc
Rushden, *England* - 15 Db
Rush Springs, *Oklahoma* 133 Cc
Rushville, *Illinois* - 132 De
Rushville, *Indiana* - 129 Bc
Rushville, *Missouri* - 132 Bf
Rushworth, *Victoria* - 154 Dd
Rusinga, I., *Kenya* - 110 Cd
Rusizi, R., *Belgian Congo* 109 Eb
Rusk, *Texas* - - 133 Ee
Russ and R. - - 56 Fa
Russas, *Brazil* - - 143 Gc
Russel Gulch, *Colorado* 135 Kb
Russell, *Alabama* - 130 De
Russell, *Arkansas* - 130 Cc
Russell, *Kansas* - - 133 Ca
Russell, *New Zealand* - 158 Ea
Russell I., *N.-W. Terr.* 118 Jb
Russell Is., *Solomon Is.* 156 Jg
Russell, Mt., *Alaska* - 125 Je
Russell, Mt., *W. Aust.* - 152 Dc
Russell Springs, *Kansas* 133 Ba
Russellville, *Alabama* - 130 Ec
Russellville, *Arkansas* - 130 Bc
Russellville, *Kentucky* - 130 Eb
Russian Mission, *Alaska* 125 Gf
Russian Turkistan, *U.S.S.R.* - - 76 Fe
Russki Zavorot, *U.S.S.R.* 74 Jb
Rustan, *Louisiana* - 130 Bd
Rustburg, *Virginia* - 129 Ed
Rustenburg, *Transvaal* 115 Gb
Rustringen, *Oldenburg* 54 Cb
Rutba, *Iraq* - - 78 Dc
Rute, *Spain* - - 40 Fb
Rutherfordton, *N. Carol.* 131 Gc
Rutherglen, *Scotland* - 23 De
Rüthi, *Switzerland* - 43 Hb
Ruthin, *Wales* - - 20 Ca
Ruthven, *Queensland* - 153 Bd
Rutland, *Cape Prov.* - 115 Fd
Rutland, *N. Dakota* - 132 Ab
Rutland, *Vermont* - 128 Bb
Rutland, co., *England* - 15 Da
Rutland I., *Andaman Is.* 91 Kk
Rutor, Testa dei, *Italy* 62 Bb
Rutshuru, *Belgian Congo* 109 Eb
Rutuku, *Belgian Congo* 109 Ec
Rutunguru, *Tang. Terr.* 110 Bd
Ruven, *Norway* - - 47 De
Ruvo di Puglia, *Italy* - 65 Ca
Ruvu, *Tanganyika Terr.* 111 Fg
Ruvuma, R., *Tang. Terr.-Mozamb.* - 111 Fj
Ruwa, *S. Rhodesia* - 113 Da
Ruwandiz, *Iraq* - - 78 Db
Ruwenzori Ra., *Uganda* 110 Bc
Ruwondo I., *Tang. Terr.* 110 Be
Ružaevka, *U.S.S.R.* - 75 Ge
Ruzomberok, *Slovakia* 60 Ed
Ryan, *Oklahoma* - - 133 Dc
Ryan, L., *Scotland* - 21 Bd
Ryazan, *U.S.S.R.* - 75 Fe
Ryazhsk, *U.S.S.R.* - 75 Ge
Rybachi, I., *U.S.S.R.* - 74 Eb
Rybinsk, *U.S.S.R.* - 74 Fd
Rybnik, *Poland* - - 57 Dc
Rybno, *Poland* - - 56 Dc
Rychtal, *Poland* - - 57 Cb
Ryde, *I. of Wight, Eng.* 14 Ce
Rydzyna, *Poland* - 57 Bb
Rye, *Denmark* - - 45 Cb
Rye, *England* - - 15 Ee
Ryfjallet, *Sweden* - 48 Ad
Ryfylke, *Norway* - 47 Ce
Ryhall, *England* - 15 Da
Rylane, *Eire* - - 25 Cf
Rynda, *U.S.S.R.* - 48 Mb
Rypin, *Poland* - - 60 Eb
Ryukyu Arch., *Japan* - 93 Ed
Ryumgaard, *Denmark* 45 Db
Rzeszow, *Poland* - 60 Fc
Rzhev, *U.S.S.R.* - 74 Ed
Saala, *Algeria* - - 102 De
Saaler B., *Prussia* - 55 Ha
Saalfeld - - - 56 Dc
Saalfeld, *Thuringia* - 55 Ge
Saane, R., *Switzerland* 42 Dc
Saanen, *Switzerland* - 42 Dd
Saarbrucken, *Saar Palatinate* - - - 58 Ab
Saare Maa (Oesel), *Estonia* - - - 49 Bb
Saari Selkä, *Finland* - 48 Gb
Saarlautern, *Saar Palatinate* - - - 58 Ab
Saar Palatinate, state, *Germany* - - - 58 Ab
Saavedra, *Argentina* - 148 Db
Saavedra, *Chile* - - 148 Bb
Saba, *Persia* - - 79 Ec
Saba, I., *Leeward Is.* - 140 Kg
Sabac, *Serbia* - - 68 Eb
Sabadell, *Spain* - - 39 Hc
Sabana, Arch. de, *Cuba* 140 Bb
Sabanalarga, *Colombia* 144 Ba
Sabancuy, *Mexico* - 139 Fd
Sabang, *Celébes* - - 99 Ec
Sabara, *Brazil* - - 147 Gc
Sabaragamuwa, *Ceylon* 89 Dd
Sabbla, Val., *Italy* - 62 Eb
Sabdarat; *Eritrea* - 108 Cb
Sabeta, *Mozambique* - 113 Fa
Sabetha, *Kansas* - 133 Da
Sabi, *S. Rhodesia* - 113 Dc
Sabi R., *Mozambique* - 112 Cd
Sabié, *Mozambique* - 115 Kb
Sabile, *Latvia* - - 49 Bc
Sabinanigo, *Spain* - 39 Eb
Sabinas, R., *Mexico* - 138 Db
Sabine, *Texas* - - 133 Ff
Sabine Is., *Greenland* - 9 Cb
Sabine L., *Louisiana* - 130 Bf
Sabine Pen., *N.-W. Terr.* 118 Ha
Sabine Pt., *Texas* - 133 Ef
Sabine R., *Texas* - 133 Ed
Sabini Mts., *Italy* - 64 Ca
Sabiwa, *S. Rhodesia* - 113 Cc
Sabkhet el Bardawil, *Egypt* - - - 107 Jc
Sablayan, *Philippines* - 99 Fa
Sablé, *France* - - 30 Bd
Sable, C., *Florida* - 131 Nj
Sable, C., *Nova Scotia* - 120 Ce
Sable I., *Nova Scotia* - 120 Ee
Sables d'Olonne, les, *France* - - - 32 Dd
Sabres, *France* - - 34 Bc
Sabria, *Tunisia* - - 103 Jc
Sabrina Land, *Antarctica* 160 —
Sabtan, I., *Philippines* 95 Fe
Sabugal, *Portugal* - 37 Cb
Sabula, *Iowa* - - 132 Dd
Saburo, *Fr. Equat. Africa* 109 Bb
Sabzawar, *Afghanistan* 79 Hc
Sabzawar, *Persia* - 79 Gb
Sabzko, *U.S.S.R.* - 48 Hg
Sacandaga Res., *New York* - - - 123 Ld
Sacaton, *Arizona* - 135 He
Sac City, *Iowa* - - 132 Bd
Sacco, R., *Italy* - - 64 Db
Sacco di Goro, *Italy* - 63 Gc
Sacedon, *Spain* - - 38 Cd
Sachihu, *Manchuria* - 96 Dc
Sachin, *Bombay* - - 90 Aa
Sacile, *Italy* - - 63 Gb
Sackets Harbor, *New York* - - 129 Ga
Sackville, *New Brunswick* 120 Cd
Saco, *Maine* - - 128 Cb
Sacoşul Mare, *Romania* 67 Gd
Sacramento, *Brazil* - 147 Fb
Sacramento and R., *California* - - 134 Cb
Sacramento Mts., *New Mexico* - - 135 Le
Sacro, Mte., *Italy* - 64 Gb
Sacueni, *Transylvania* - 67 Hb
Sacul, *Romania* - - 67 Hd
Sada, *Yemen* - - 78 Lg
Sadabad, *United Provs.* 83 He
Sadaich, *Persia* - - 79 Gd
Sadani, *Tanganyika Terr.* 111 Fg
Sadaseopet, *Hyderabad* 90 Cc
Sadazaki, *Japan* - - 97 Cd
Saddle Peak, *Andaman Is.* 91 Kj
Sadhaura, *Punjab* - 83 Gc
Sadi, *Belgian Congo* - 109 Dc
Sadirabad, *Azerbaijan* - 75 Hg
Sadiya, *Assam* - - 88 Ea
Sado, I., *Japan* - - 97 Dc
Sadovoe, *U.S.S.R.* - 75 Gf
Sadra, *Gujarat States* - 85 Dc
Sadras, *Madras* - - 91 Ee
Sadri, *Rajputana* - 85 Db
Sæby, *Denmark* - - 45 Da
Saelices, *Spain* - - 37 Db
Saerthu, *Manchuria* - 96 Cb
Safâga I., *Egypt* - - 107 Ke
Safed, *Palestine* - - 80 Cb
Safed Koh Ra., *Afghanistan-N.W.F.P.* - 82 Da
Saffa, *Palestine* - - 80 Cd
Safford, *Arizona* - - 135 Je
Saffron Walden, *England* 15 Eb
Saffurye, *Palestine* - 80 Cb
Safi, *Morocco* - - 103 Nh
Safidava, *Persia* - - 79 Gc
Safidon, *Punjab States* 83 Gd
Safra, Wady e', *Arabia* 78 Ce
Safranbolu, *Turkey* - 78 Ba
Saga - - - - 63 Ha
Saga, *Japan* - - 97 Cd
Sagaing, *Burma* - - 92 Bb
Sagaki, *Japan* - - 100 Ed
Sagalair R., *Madras* - 90 Dd
Sagami B., *Japan* - 97 Dc
Sagamore, *Massachusetts* 128 Cc
Sagan - - - 55 Ld
Saganaga L., *Ontario* - 122 Ca
Sagar, *Hyderabad* - 90 Cc
Sagar, *Mysore* - - 90 Bd
Sagar I., *Bengal* - - 88 Bd
Sagara, *Japan* - - 100 Gd
Sagauli, *Bihar* - - 87 Fb
Sage Plains, *Oregon* - 136 Cd
Sag Harbor, *New York* 123 Me
Sagho, Jeb., *Morocco* - 102 Bd
Saginaw, *Michigan* - 122 Fd
Saginaw, *Texas* - - 133 Dd
Saginaw B., *Michigan* - 122 Gd
Sagiz, *Kazak* - - 75 Kf
Saglek B., *Labrador* - 119 Re
Sagone and G., *Corsica* 33 Dg
Sagra, La, *Spain* - - 41 Dc
Sagres, *Portugal* - - 40 Bb
Sagsag, *New Britain* - 156 Dc
Sagthale, *Rajputana* - 85 Ec
Sagua la Grande, *Cuba* 140 Bb
Saguenay R., *Quebec* - 123 Na
Sagunto, *Spain* - - 39 Ee
Sagwara, *Rajputana* - 85 Dc
Sahagun, *Spain* - - 36 Eb
Saham, *Oman* - - 79 Ge
Sahara, desert, *N. Africa* 101 Bc
Saharanpur, *United Provs.* 83 Gd
Sahaswan, *United Provs.* 83 Hd
Sahel, R., *Algeria* - 103 Ga
Sahem, *Trans-Jordan* - 80 Db
Sahibganj, *Bihar* - 87 Gc
Sahin, *Turkey* - - 72 Da
Sahiwal, *Punjab* - - 82 Ec
Sahran, *Rajputana* - 85 Eb
Sahuajo, *Mexico* - 138 Dd
Sahuaripa, *Mexico* - 138 Cb
Sahwave Mts., *Nevada* 134 Db
Sahyadriparvat Ra., *Berar, etc.* - - 90 Ba
Sai R., *United Provs.* - 87 Ec
Saibai I., *New Guinea* - 156 Cc
Saïda, *Algeria* - - 102 Eb

Saidabad, *Afghanistan* 82 Ca
Saidabad, *Persia* - 79 Gd
Saidapet, *Madras* - 91 Ee
Saide, *French W. Africa* 104 Bc
Saidpur, *United Provs.* 87 Ec
Saifganj, *Bihar* - - 87 Gc
Saignelegier, *Switzerland* 42 Db
Saignes, *France* - - 34 Eb
Saigon, *Cochin-China* - 95 Cg
Saiki, *Japan* - - 97 Cd
Sailana, *Central India* - 85 Ec
Saimaa, *Finland* - - 48 Hf
St. Abbs Hd., *Scotland* 23 Fe
Ste. Adele, *Quebec* - 121 Cb
St. Affrique, *France* - 34 Ed
St. Agatha, *Maine* - 120 Ac
Ste. Agathe, *Quebec* - 121 Ca
St. Agnes, *England* - 17 Ac
St. Agnes, *Scilly Is.* - 17 Fh
St. Aignan, *France* - 30 Dd
St. Aignan (Misima), *Louisiade Arch.* - 156 Lk
St. Albans, *England* - 15 Dc
St. Albans, *Vermont* - 123 Mc
St. Alvère, *France* - 34 Cc
St. Amand, *Loir-et-Cher, France* - - - 30 Dd
St. Amand Nièvre, *France* 30 Fd
St. Amand, *Nord, France* 30 Fa
St. Amand-Mont Rond, *France* - - - 34 Ea
St. Amans, *France* - 34 Ec
St. Amant, *France* - 35 Fb
St. Ambroix, *France* - 35 Gc
St. Amour, *France* - 35 Ha
St. Andrä, *Austria* - 59 Je
St. André-les-Alpes, *France* 33 Bb
St. Andrew, C., *Madagascar* - - - 112 Dc
St. Andrews, *New Brunswick* - - 120 Bd
St. Andrews, *New Zealand* - - - 159 Cf
St. Andrews, *Quebec* - 121 Cb
St. Andrews, *Scotland* - 23 Fd
St. Andrews B., *Florida* 130 Fe
St. Ann and B., *Nova Scotia* - - 120 Ec
St. Anne, *Channel Is.* - 17 Ee
Ste. Anne, *Quebec* - 123 Ob
Ste. Anne, *Jac. Cartier, Quebec* - - 121 Db
Ste. Anne de Beaupre, *Quebec* - - 123 Nb
Ste. Anne de la Perade, *Quebec* - - 121 Da
Ste. Anne des Monts, *Quebec* - - - 120 Bb
St. Anns Bay, *Jamaica* 140 Bc
St. Anthony, *Idaho* - 136 Hc
St. Anthony, *Newfound.* 120 Ga
St. Anton, *Austria* - 58 Ed
St. Antonin, *France* - 34 Dc
St. Arnaud, *Algeria* - 103 Ga
St. Arnaud, *Victoria* - 154 Dd
St. Arvans, *England* - 14 Bc
St. Asaph, *Wales* - 20 Ca
St. Astier, *France* - 34 Cb
St. Auban, *France* - 33 Bb
St. Augustin, *Quebec* - 121 Cb
St. Augustin B., *Madagascar* - - - 112 Dd
St. Augustine, *Florida* 131 Hf
St. Austell, *England* - 17 Bc
St. Avold, *France* - 31 Jb
St. Barbe, I., *Netherlands Indies* - - 98 Cc
St. Barbe Is., *Newfound.* 120 Ha
St. Barbe du Tlélat, *Algeria* - - - 102 Db
St. Barthelemy, I., *Leeward Is.* - - - 140 Kg
St. Bečej, *Voyvodina* - 66 Ed
St. Bees Hd., *England* 18 Aa
St. Benin-d'Azy, *France* 31 Fe
St. Benoit, *France* - 34 Ca
St Bernard, *Louisiana* 130 Df
St. Bernard, Col du Gd., *Switz.-Italy* - 42 De
St. Blaize, C., *Cape Prov.* 114 Eg
St. Blazey, *England* - 17 Bc
St. Bonaventure, *Quebec* 121 Db
St. Boniface, *Manitoba* 124 Kd
St. Bonnet, *France* - 35 Jc
St. Bonnet-de-Joux, *France* - - - 35 Ga
St. Börge Fjell, *Norway* 44 Cf
St. Boswells, *Scotland* 21 Db
St. Briavels, *England* - 14 Bc
St. Bride's and B., *Wales* 20 Ad
St. Brieuc & B., *France* 32 Cb
St. Bris, *France* - - 31 Fd
St. Calais, *France* - 30 Cd
St. Camille, *Quebec* - 121 Eb
St. Canut, *Quebec* - 121 Cb
St. Catharines, *Ontario* 123 Jd
Ste. Catherine, *Quebec* - 121 Ea
St. Catherine I., *Georgia* 131 He
Ste. Cécile, *Quebec* - 123 Nc
St. Celestin, *Quebec* - 121 Da
St. Cernin, *France* - 34 Eb
St. Cesaire, *Quebec* - 121 Db
St. Chamond, *France* - 35 Gb
St. Chaptes, *France* - 35 Gd
St. Charles, *Algeria* - 103 Ha
St. Charles, *Michigan* - 122 Fd
St. Charles, *Minnesota* 132 Dd
St. Charles, *Missouri* - 130 Ca
St. Charles, C., *Labrador* 119 Sf
St. Christophe-en-Bazelle, *France* - - - 30 Dd
St. Christopher, I., *Leeward Is.* - - - 140 Kg
St. Clair, *Michigan* - 122 Gd
St. Clair, *Nevada* - 134 Db
St. Clair, *Pennsylvania* 129 Fb
St. Clair, L., *Mich.-Ont.* 122 Gd
St. Clair, L., *Tasmania* 155 Jg
St. Claud, *France* - 34 Cb
St. Claude, *France* - 35 Ha
St. Clears, *Wales* - 20 Bd
St. Clemens, *Michigan* 122 Gd
St. Cloud, *Minnesota* - 132 Bc
St. Columb, *England* - 17 Bc
Ste. Croix, *Quebec* - 121 Ea
Ste. Croix, *Switzerland* 42 Bc
St. Croix R., *Wisconsin* 132 Cc
St. Cyprien, *France* - 34 Cc
St. Cyr, *France* - 30 Dc
St. Cyr, *Quebec* - 121 Db
St. Cyrille, *Quebec* - 121 Db
St. Damiano, *Italy* - 62 Cc
St. David, *Arizona* - 135 Hf
St. David's & Hd., *Wales* 20 Ad
St. Denis, *France* - 30 Ec
St. Denis du Sig, *Algeria* 102 Db
St. Denis-les-Martel, *France* 34 Dc
St. Didier, *France* - 35 Gb
St. Die, *France* - - 31 Jc
St. Dizier, *France* - 31 Gc
St. Donat, *France* - 35 Gb
St. Elias, C., *Alaska* - 125 Lg
St. Elias, Mt., *Yukon* - 125 Mf
St. Elias Ra., *Yukon, etc.* 124 Bb
St. Eloy, *France* - - 35 Ea
Saintes, *France* - - 32 Ee
St. Esprit (Batas) Is., *Netherlands Indies* - 98 Cc
St. Étienne, *Basses Alpes, France* - - - 33 Aa
St. Etienne, *Basses Pyrénees, France* - - 34 Ad
St. Étienne, *Loire, France* 35 Gb
St. Étienne, *Quebec* - 123 Na
St. Étienne-de-Montluc, *France* - - - 32 Dc
St. Eustache, *Quebec* - 121 Cb
St. Eustatius, I., *Leeward Is.* - - - 140 Kg
St. Fabian, *Quebec* - 120 Ab
St. Felicien, *Quebec* - 123 Ma
St. Felix, *Quebec* - - 121 Da
Saintfield, *N. Ireland* - 26 Ec
St. Fillans, *Scotland* - 23 Dd
St. Finan's B., *Eire* - 25 Af
St. Firmin, *France* - 35 Jc
St. Florent, *France* - 30 Ed
St. Florent & G., *Corsica* 33 Eg
St. Florentin, *France* - 31 Fc
St. Florian, *Austria* - 59 Ke
St. Flour, *France* - 35 Fb
Ste. Foy-la-Grande, *France* - - - 34 Cc
St. Francis, *Kansas* - 133 Ba
St. Francis, *Maine* - 120 Ac
St. Francis C. & B., *Cape Prov.* - - 115 Fg
St. Francis L., *Ont.-Que.* - - - 121 Cb
St. Francis L., *Quebec* - 123 Nc
St. Francis R., *Arkansas* 130 Cc
St. Francis R., *Quebec* 121 Db
St. Francisville, *Louisiana* - - - 130 Ce
St. Francois, *Quebec* - 121 Da
St. Fulgent, *France* - 32 Dd
St. Gabriel, *Louisiana* - 130 Ce
St. Gabriel, *Quebec* - 121 Da
St. Gallen and canton, *Switzerland* - - 43 Hb
St. Gauburge, *France* - 30 Cc
St. Gaudens, *France* - 34 Cd
St. Gédéon, *Quebec* - 123 Na
Ste. Genevieve, *Missouri* 130 Cb
St. George, *New Bruns.* 120 Bd
St. George, *Queensland* 153 Ce
St. George, *S. Carolina* - 131 Hd
St. George, *Utah* - 134 Gc
St. George, *Windward Is.* - - - - 140 Kh
St. George Basin, *W. Australia* - - 152 Db
St. George, C., *Florida* - 130 Ff
St. George C. & B., *Newfoundland* - - 120 Fb
St. George Hd., *New S. Wales* - - 155 Gd
St. George I., *Bering Sea* 125 Eh
St. George I. & Sd., *Florida* - - - 131 Ff
St. Georges, *Belgium* - 29 Dd
St. Georges, *Eure-et-Loir, France* - - 30 Dc
St. Georges, *Haute-Loire, France* - - 35 Fb
St. Georges, *I. d'Oleron, France* - - - 32 De
St. Georges, *Vienne, France* - - - 30 Ce
St. Georges, *Fr. Guiana* 142 Db
St. George's Chan., *Bismarck Arch.* - - 156 Eb
St. George's Chan., *British Isles* - - - 13 De
St. Germain, *France* - 30 Dc
St. Germain des Fosses, *France* - - - 35 Fa
St. Germain-du-Bois, *France* - - - 31 He
St. German, *Puerto Rico* 140 Jg
Ste. Gertrude, *Quebec* - 121 Da
St. Gervais, *France* - 34 Ea
St. Géry, *France* - - 34 Dc
St. Gildas, Pte de, *France* - - - 32 Cc
St. Gildas-des-Bois, *France* - - - 32 Cc
St. Gilles, *France* - 35 Gd
St. Girons, *France* - 34 De
St. Goar, *Prussia* - 58 Ba
St. Gotthard, mt., *Switz.* 43 Gc
St. Gregory C. & Mt., *Newfoundland* - - 120 Fb
St. Guillaume, *Quebec* - 121 Db
St. Heddinge, *Denmark* 45 Fc
St. Helena, *California* 134 Bb
St. Helena B., *Cape Prov.* - - - 114 Bf
St. Helena I., *Atlantic Oc.* - - - 114 Nj
St. Helena I., *S. Carolina* 131 Hd
St. Helena Fontein, *Cape Prov.* - - 114 Bf
St. Helens, *England* - 18 Bd
St. Helens, *Oregon* - 136 Bc
St. Helens Mt., *Wash.* 136 Bb
St. Helier, *Channel Is.* - 17 Ef
St. Hilaire, *France* - 32 Db
St. Hilaire, *Minnesota* - 132 Aa
St. Hilaire, *New Bruns.* 120 Ac
St. Hilaire-au-Temple, *France* - - - 31 Gb
St. Hilaire-des-Loges, *France* - - - 32 Ed
St. Hippolyte, *Doubs, France* - - - 31 Jd
St. Hippolyte, *Gard, France* - - - 35 Fd
St. Hubert, *Belgium* - 29 Dd
St. Hyacinthe, *Quebec* - 121 Db
St. Ignace, *Michigan* - 122 Fc
St. Ignace I., *Ontario* - 122 Ea
St. Ignatius, *Montana* - 136 Gb
St. Imier, *Switzerland* - 42 Cb
St. Ingbert, *Saar Palatinate* - - - 58 Bb
St. Irénée, *Quebec* - 123 Nb
St. Ives, *Cornwall, England* - - - 17 Ac
St. Ives, *Hunts, England* 15 Db
St. Jacques, *Cochin-China* 95 Cg
St. Jacques, *New Brunswick* - - - 120 Ac
St. James, *Minnesota* - 132 Bc
St. James, C., *Br. Colum.* 124 Cd
St. Jean, *Quebec* - - 121 Db
St. Jean d'Angely, *France* 32 Ee
St. Jean-de-Losne, *France* 31 Hd
St. Jean-de-Luz, *France* 34 Ad
St. Jean de Matha, *Quebec* - - - 121 Da
St. Jean-de-Maurienne, *France* - - - 35 Jb
St. Jean de Monts, *France* 32 Cd
St. Jean-Pied-de-Port, *France* - - - 34 Ad
St. Jerome, *Quebec* - 121 Cb
St. Jo, *Texas* - - 133 Dd
St. Joachim, *Quebec* - 123 Nb
St. Johann, *Austria* - 59 Gd
St. John, *Kansas* - 133 Ca
St. John, *New Bruns.* - 120 Cd
St. John B., *Newfound.* 120 Ga
St. John (Chang-chwen) I., *China* - - - 95 De
St. John, L., *Quebec* - 123 Na
St. Johns, *Michigan* - 122 Fd
St. Johns, *Newfound.* - 120 Jc
St. Johns R., *Florida* - 131 Hf
St. Johnsbury, *Vermont* 128 Ba
St. John's Chapel, *England* - - - 21 Dd
St. Johns Highway, *Eng.* 15 Ea
St. John's Port, *Eire* - 26 Bc
St. Joseph, *Michigan* - 122 Ed
St. Joseph, *Missouri* - 132 Bf
St. Joseph, *Richelieu, Quebec* - - - 121 Da
St. Joseph, *Quebec* - 123 Nb
St. Joseph I., *Ontario* - 122 Gb
St. Joseph, L., *Ontario* 119 Lf
St. Joseph R., *Idaho* - 136 Eb
St. Joseph R., *Michigan* 122 Fe
St. Joseph's B., *Florida* 130 Ff
St. Jovite, *Quebec* - 121 Ca
St Juan, Mt., *Mexico* - 138 Bb
St. Julien, *Aube, France* 31 Fc
St. Julien, *Haute Savoie, France* - - - 35 Ja
St. Julien du Sault, *France* 30 Fc
Ste. Julienne, *Quebec* - 121 Db
St. Junien, *France* - 34 Cb
St. Just, *England* - 17 Ac
St. Just, *France* - - 35 Fb
Ste. Justine, *Quebec* - 123 Nb
St. Kilda, I., *Scotland* - 13 Bc
St. Laurent, *Isère, France* 35 Hb
St. Laurent, *Jura, France* 35 Ha
St. Laurent, *Vendée, France* 32 Ed
St. Laurent, *Fr. Guiana* 142 Da
St. Laurent-de-la-Salanque, *France* - - 35 Fe
St. Lawrence, *England* 15 Fb
St. Lawrence, *Queensland* - - - 153 Cd
St. Lawrence, G. of, *Quebec* - - - 120 Db
St. Lawrence I., *Alaska*, 125 De
St. Lawrence R., *Quebec* 119 Qg
St. Leonard, *France* - 34 Db
St. Leonard, *New Bruns.* 120 Bc
St. Leonards, *England* 15 Ee
St. Leonhard, *Austria* - 59 Je
Ste. Livrade, *France* - 34 Cc
St. Lô, *France* - - 32 Da
St. Louis, *France* - 35 Gd
St. Louis, *Fr. W. Africa* 104 Ac
St. Louis, *Michigan* - 122 Fd
St. Louis, *Missouri* - 130 Ca
St. Louis, L., *Quebec* - 121 Db
St. Louis R., *Minnesota* 132 Cb
St. Louis de Kent, *New Brunswick* - - 120 Cc
St. Loup, *France* - - 30 Be
St. Lucia, *Windward Is.* 140 Kh
St. Lucie, *Florida* - 131 Nh
St. Lucie Inlet, *Florida* 131 Nh
St. Luke's I., *Burma* - 98 Aa
St. Madeleine, *Quebec* - 121 Db
St. Magnus B., *Zetland* 24 Gh
St. Maixent, *France* - 34 Ba
St. Malo & Gulf of, *France* 32 Cb
St. Mamert, *France* - 35 Gd
St. Mamet, *France* - 34 Ec
St. Marc, *Haiti* - - 140 Cc
St. Marcellin, *France* - 35 Hb
Ste. Margaret B., *Newfoundland* - - 120 Ga
St. Margaret B., *Nova Scotia* - - 120 Dd
St. Margaret's Hope, *Orkney Is.* - - 24 Fd
Ste. Marie, C., *Madagas.* 112 De
Ste. Marie I., *Indian Oc.* 112 Fc
Ste. Marie-aux-Mines, *France* - - - 31 Kc
St. Maries, *Idaho* - 136 Eb
St. Marks, *Cape Prov.* - 115 Gf
St. Marks, *Florida* - 131 Fe
St. Martin, *Austria* - 66 Bb
St. Martin C., *Cape Prov.* 114 Bf
St. Martin, I., *Leeward Is.* 140 Kg
St. Martin-de-Londres, *France* - - - 35 Fd
St. Martine, *Quebec* - 121 Db
St. Martins, *New Bruns.* 120 Cd
St. Martin's, *Scilly Is.* - 17 Gg
St. Martin-Vesubie, *France* 33 Ca
St. Martinville, *Louisiana* 130 Ce
St. Mary, *Ontario* - 123 Hd
St. Mary, *Tasmania* - 155 Kg
St. Mary B., *Nova Scotia* 120 Bd
St. Mary, C., *Newfound.* 120 Hc
St. Mary Is., *Quebec* - 120 Fa
St. Mary R., *Michigan* - 122 Fb
St. Mary Bourne, *Eng.* 14 Cd
St. Mary Cray, *England* 15 Ed
St. Marys, *Georgia* - 131 He
St. Marys, *Kansas* - 133 Ea
St. Mary's, *Ohio* - - 129 Bb
St. Mary's, *Orkney Is.* - 24 Fd
St. Mary's, *Scilly Is.* - 17 Gg
St. Mary's, *W. Virginia* 129 Dc
St. Mary's & B., *Newfoundland* - - 120 Jc
St. Mary's L., *Scotland* - 21 Cc
St. Mary's Pk., *S. Aust.* 154 Bb
St. Mathieu, *France* - 34 Cb
St. Mathieu, Pte., *France* 32 Ab
St. Matthew I., *Alaska* 125 Df
St. Matthias Group, *Bismarak Arch.* - - 156 Eb
St. Maur, *France* - 30 Ec
St. Maurice, *Louisiana* 130 Be
St. Maurice, *Switzerland* 42 Cd
St. Maurice and R., *Quebec* - - - 121 Da
St. Mawes, *England* - 17 Bc
St. Maximin, *France* - 33 Ac
St. Méen, *France* - 32 Cb
St. Mellons, *England* - 14 Ac
Ste. Menehould, *France* 31 Gb
Ste. Mere Eglise, *France* 32 Da
St. Merouane, *Algeria* - 103 Ga
St. Michael, *Alaska* - 125 Fe
St. Michaelisdonn, *Prussia* - - - 54 Db
St. Michael's, *Maryland* 129 Fc
St. Michel, *France* - 35 Jb
St. Mihiel, *France* - 31 Hc
St. Moritz, *Switzerland* 43 Jc
St. Nazaire, *France* - 32 Cc
St. Neots, *England* - 15 Db
St. Nicholas, *Quebec* - 121 Ea
St. Nicolas, *Belgium* - 29 Cc
St. Nicolas, *France* - 31 Jc
St. Nicolas du Pelem, *France* - - - 32 Bb
St. Niklaus, *Switzerland* 42 Ed
St. Ola, *Ontario* - 121 Bb
St. Omer, *Oise, France* 30 Eb
St. Omer, *Pas-de-Calais, France* - - - 30 Ea
Saintonge, *France* - 34 Bb
St. Oskol, *U.S.S.R.* - 75 Fe
St. Osyth, *England* - 15 Fc
St. Ours, *Quebec* - 121 Db
St. Paul, *Algeria* - 103 Ha
St. Paul, *Arkansas* - 130 Bc
St. Paul, *Basses Alpes, France* - - - 35 Jc
St. Paul, *Landes, France* 34 Ad
St. Paul, *Minnesota* - 132 Cc
St. Paul B., *Newfound.* 120 Fb
St. Paul I., *Bering Sea* 125 Dh
St. Paul I., *Nova Scotia* 120 Ec
St. Paulin, *Quebec* - 121 Da
St. Paul-Trois-Châteaux, *France* - - - 35 Gc
Ste. Pazanne, *France* - 32 Dc
St. Pazova, *Slavonia* - 66 Fe
St. Peter, *Minnesota* - 132 Cc
St. Peter, *Montana* - 136 Gb
St. Peter, *Pr. Edward I.* 120 Dc
St. Peter, L., *Quebec* - 121 Da
St. Peter Port, *Channel Is.* 17 Ef
St. Peters, *Nova Scotia* 120 Ed
St. Petersburg, *Florida* 131 Mh
St. Pièrre, *Atlantic Oc.* - 120 Gc
St. Pièrre, *France* - 32 De
St. Pièrre, *Martinique, West Indies* - - 140 Kh
St. Pièrre, *Quebec* - 123 Nb
St. Pièrre, *Ste. Marie I.* 112 Fc
St. Pièrre Eglise, *France* 32 Da
St. Pièrre-le-Moutier, *France* - - - 30 Fe
St. Pièrreville, *France* - 35 Gc
St. Pois, *France* - - 32 Db
St. Pol, *France* - - 30 Ea
St. Pol-de-Leon, *France* 32 Ab
St. Polten, *Austria* - 59 Kc
St. Polycarp, *Quebec* - 121 Cb
St. Pons, *France* - - 34 Ed
St. Pourcain, *France* - 35 Fa

St. Priest-Taurion, *France* 34 Db
St. Prime, *Quebec* - 121 Db
St. Quentin, *France* - 30 Fb
St. Rambert, *Ain, France* 35 Hb
St. Rambert, *Drome, France* - - - 35 Gb
St. Raphael, *France* - 33 Bc
St. Raymond, *Quebec* - 121 Da
St. Regis, *Montana* - 136 Fb
St. Remi, *Quebec* - 121 Db
St. Rémi d'Amherst, *Quebec* - - - 121 Ca
St. Rémy, *Bouches-du-Rhône, France* - - 35 Gd
St. Rémy, *Puy-de-Dome, France* - - - 35 Fb
St. Remy-en-Bouzemont, *France* - - - 31 Gc
St. Rhemy, *Italy* - - 62 Bb
St. Roch, *Quebec* - 123 Nb
St. Rome-de-Tarn, *France* 34 Ec
St. Rosalie, *Quebec* - 121 Db
St. Sampson, *Channel Is.* 17 Ef
St. Saulge, *France* - 31 Fd
St. Sauveur, *Alpes Maritimes, France* - - 33 Ca
St. Sauveur, *Manche, France* - - - 32 Da
St.-Sauveur-en-Puisaye, *France* - - - 30 Fd
St. Sauveur Lendelin, *France* - - - 32 Da
St. Savin, *France* - 34 Ca
St. Savinien, *France* - 32 Ee
St. Sebastian B., *Cape Prov.* - - - 114 Dg
St. Sernin, *France* - 34 Ed
St. Servan, *France* - 32 Db
St. Sever, *France* - 34 Bd
St. Simeon, *Quebec* - 123 Nb
St. Simon, *Bagot, Quebec* 121 Db
St. Simon, *Quebec* - 120 Ab
St. Simons I., *Georgia* - 131 He
Ste. Sophie, *Quebec* - 121 Da
St. Stanislas, *Quebec* - 121 Da
St. Stephen, *New Bruns.* 120 Bd
St. Stephens, *Alabama* 130 De
St. Stephens, *England* - 15 Dc
St. Sulpice, *Switzerland* 42 Cc
St. Symphorien-de-Lay, *France* - - - 35 Gb
St. Thecle, *Quebec* - 123 Mb
St. Thegonnec, *France* - 32 Bb
Ste. Therèse, *Quebec* - 121 Db
Ste. Thérèse, L., *N.-W. Terr.* - - - 124 Eb
St. Thomas, *Nevada* - 134 Fc
St. Thomas, *Ontario* - 123 Hd
St. Thomas, *Virgin Is.* 140 Kg
St. Tite, *Quebec* - 121 Da
St. Tomas, Mt., *Philippines* - - 95 Ff
St. Trivier, *France* - 35 Ga
St. Trond, *Belgium* - 29 Dd
St. Tropez & G., *France* 33 Bc
St. Turá, *Slovakia* - 66 Ca
St. Valentin, *Austria* - 59 Jc
St. Valentino, *Italy* - 62 Ea
St. Valery, *France* - 30 Da
St. Valery-en-Caux, *France* - - - 30 Cb
St. Vallier, *France* - 33 Bb
St. Veit, *Austria* - 59 Je
St. Véran, *France* - 35 Jc
St. Vigilio, *Italy* - 63 Fa
St. Vincent, *Italy* - 62 Bb
St. Vincent, *Quebec* - 121 Db
St. Vincent, C., *Madagascar* - - 112 Dd
St. Vincent Gulf, *S. Aust.* 154 Bc
St. Vincent I., *Florida* 130 Ff
St. Vincent, I., *Windward Is.* - - - 140 Kh
St. Vincent-de-Tyrosse, *France* - - - 34 Ad
St. Vith, *Belgium* - 29 Ed
St. Vito, *Italy* - 63 Ga
St. Wolfgang, *Austria* - 59 Hd
St. Yrieix, *France* - 34 Db
Saipan, I., *Marianas Is.* 157 Bb
Saissac, *France* - 34 Ed
Saiyidwala, *Punjab* - 83 Ec
Saiyüan, *China* - 94 Da
Sajama, mt., *Bolivia* - 146 Bb
Sajiro, *Kenya* - 110 Fe
Sajo, R., *Hungary* - 67 Fb
Sajum, mt., *Tibet* - 84 Dd
Sakai, *Japan* - 100 Dd
Sakai, *Japan* - 97 Dd
Sakaka, *Arabia* - 78 Dd
Sakalilo, *Tangan. Terr.* 111 Ch
Sakania, *Belgian Congo* 109 Ed
Sakaria, R., *Turkey* - 78 Bb
Sakata, *Japan* - 97 Dc
Sakesar, *Punjab* - 82 Db
Sakha, *Arabia* - 78 De
Sakha, *Nepal* - 87 Ea
Sakhalin, *U.S.S.R.* - 93 Ga
Şakhra, *Trans-Jordan* - 80 Dc
Šakiai, *Lithuania* - 49 Bd
Sakishima Gunto, *Japan* 93 Ed
Sakmara, R., *U.S.S.R.* 74 Ke
Sakmarskoe, *U.S.S.R.* 75 Je
Sakobinda, *Belg. Congo* 109 Dd
Sakoi, *Burma* - 92 Cc
Sakoli, *Central Provs.* - 86 Ce
Sakon-lakon, *Siam* - 95 Bf
Sakonnet Pt. and R., *Rhode Island* - 128 Cc
Sakrivier, *Cape Prov.* - 114 De
Sakskõbing, *Denmark* - 45 Ed
Sakti, *Eastern States* - 87 Ed
Saktisgarh, *United Provs.* 87 Ec
Sakuma, *Japan* - 100 Fd
Sakurai, *Japan* - 100 Ed
Sakushu, *Korea* - 97 Bb
Sala, *Sweden* - 50 Fc
Salabangka Is., *Netherlands Indies* - 99 Fd
Sălaci, *Transylvania* - 67 Hb
Sala Consilina, *Italy* - 64 Fc
Saladillo, R., *Argentina* 146 Cd
Salado, R., *Argentina* - 148 Cb
Salado, R., *Argentina* - 146 Cd
Salado, R., *Mexico* - 139 Eb
Salaga, *Gold Coast* - 104 De
Salahiye, *Syria* - 78 Dc
Salaj, *Transylvania* - 67 Hb
Salajar I. and Str., *Netherlands Indies* - 99 Fe
Salala, *A.-E. Sudan* - 108 Ca
Salala, *Arabia* - 77 Gf
Salala, *Belgian Congo* - 109 Dc
Salama, *Guatemala* - 140 Ed
Salamanca, *Mexico* - 138 Dc
Salamanca, *New York* - 123 Jd
Salamanca and prov., *Spain* - - - 37 Eb
Salamanga, *Mozambique* 115 Kc
Salamaua, *New Guinea* 156 Dc
Salamina, *Colombia* - 144 Ab
Salamís, *Greece* - 71 Ef
Salamvrías (Piniós), R., *Greece* - - - 70 Dd
Sálard, *Transylvania* - 67 Hb
Salardu, *Spain* - 39 Fb
Salas, *Spain* - 36 Da
Salas de los Infantes, *Spain* - - - 38 Bb
Salatrucul, *Romania* - 67 Kd
Salaverry, *Peru* - 145 Bc
Salavina, *Argentina* - 146 Cd
Salawati, I., *Du. New Guinea* - - - 156 Ab
Salaya, *Western India* - 85 Bc
Salbris, *France* - 30 Ed
Salcha, *Alaska* - 125 Kd
Salcombe, *England* - 17 Cc
Salda, *U.S.S.R.* - 74 Ld
Saldana, *Spain* - 38 Ab
Saldanha B., *Cape Prov.* 114 Bf
Saldus, *Latvia* - 49 Bc
Sale, *England* - 18 Bd
Salé, *Morocco* - 102 Ab
Sale, *Victoria* - 155 Ee
Salebaboe, I., *Netherlands Indies* - - 99 Gc
Salegard, *U.S.S.R.* - 76 Gc
Saleh B., *Soembawa I., Nether. Indies* - - 99 Ee
Salem, *Illinois* - 132 Ef
Salem, *Indiana* - 129 Ac
Salem, *Madras* - 89 Cb
Salem, *Massachusetts* - 128 Cb
Salem, *Missouri* - 130 Cb
Salem, *New Jersey* - 129 Gc
Salem, *New York* - 128 Bb
Salem, *Ohio* - 129 Db
Salem, *Virginia* - 129 Dd
Salemi, *Sicily* - 65 Fg
Sälen, *Sweden* - 50 Ca
Salernes, *France* - 33 Bb
Salerno & Gulf of, *Italy* 64 Ec
Saletekri, *Central Provs.* 86 De
Salfit, *Palestine* - 80 Cc
Salford, *England* - 18 Bd
Salgotarjan, *Hungary* - 66 Ea
Sali, *Algeria* - 102 Ef
Sali, *Dalmatia* - 63 Kd
Salida, *Colorado* - 135 Lb
Salies, *Basses Pyrenées, France* - - - 34 Bd
Salies, *Haute Garonne, France* - - - 34 Dd
Salignac, *France* - 34 Dc
Salihler, *Turkey* - 72 Dc
Salin, *Burma* - 92 Bb
Salina, *Colorado* - 135 La
Salina, *Kansas* - 133 Da
Salina, *Oklahoma* - 133 Eb
Salina, *Utah* - 135 Hb
Salina I., *Italy* - 65 Hf
Salina Cruz, *Mexico* - 139 Ed
Salinas, *Matto Grosso, Brazil* - - - 146 Cb
Salinas, *Para, Brazil* - 143 Ec
Salinas, *Canary Is.* 104 Ba
Salinas, *Ecuador* - 145 Ab
Salinas, *Mexico* - 138 Dc
Salinas, *Spain* - 38 Cb
Salinas and R., *California* 134 Cc
Salinas C., *Balearic Is.* 39 Je
Salinas, Pta., *Angola* - 109 Bd
Salinas Grandes, *Argent.* 146 Be
Salindres, *France* - 35 Gc
Saline, *Italy* - 62 Ed
Saline R., *Kansas* - 133 Ca
Salines, les, *Tunisia* - 103 Ja
Salinitas, *Chile* - 146 Ac
Salins, *France* - 31 He
Salisbury, *England* 14 Cd
Salisbury, *Maryland* - 129 Gc
Salisbury, *Missouri* - 130 Ba
Salisbury, *New Bruns.* 120 Cc
Salisbury, *N. Carolina* - 131 Hc
Salisbury, *S. Australia* 154 Bc
Salisbury, *S. Rhodesia* 113 Da
Salisbury Chan., *Uganda* 110 Cd
Salisbury I., *N.-W. Terr.* 119 Od
Salisbury Plain, *England* 14 Cd
Saliste, *Romania* - 67 Jd
Sallent, *Spain* - 39 Gc
Salling, *Denmark* - 45 Bb
Sallins, *Eire* - 27 De
Sallisaw, *Oklahoma* - 133 Ec
Sallnas, *Mexico* - 138 Db
Sallyana, *Nepal* - 86 Da
Salmara, *Assam* - 88 Cb
Salmi, *U.S.S.R.* - 48 Jf
Salmijarvi, *Norway* - 48 Jb
Salmon and R., *Idaho* - 136 Fc
Salmon Mts., *California* 134 Ba
Salmon Falls R., *Idaho* 136 Fd
Salmon River Mts., *Idaho* 136 Fc
Salmoral, *Spain* - 37 Eb
Salo, *Finland* - 48 Ef
Salo, *Italy* - 62 Eb
Salon, *France* - 35 Hd
Salon, *United Provs.* - 86 Db
Salonica (Thessaloniki), *Greece* - - - 70 Ec
Salonta, *Transylvania* - 67 Gc
Salorno, *Italy* - 63 Fa
Salpau Selka, *Finland* 48 Ff
Salpi, Lago di, *Italy* - 64 Gb
Salsette I., *Bombay* - 90 Ab
Salsk, *U.S.S.R.* - 75 Gf
Salsomaggiore, *Italy* - 62 Dc
Salta and prov., *Argent.* 146 Bc
Saltash, *England* - 17 Bc
Saltburn, *England* - 19 Da
Saltcoats, *Scotland* - 21 Bb
Saltdal, *Norway* - 44 Cf
Saltee Is., *Eire* - 27 Dg
Saltholm, I., *Denmark* - 45 Fc
Saltillo, *Mexico* - 138 Db
Salt Lake City, *Utah* - 135 Ha
Salto, *Argentina* - 148 Da
Salto and dep., *Uruguay* 146 De
Salto Grande, *Brazil* - 147 Hb
Saltoluokta, *Sweden* - 48 Bc
Salton & L., *California* 134 Fe
Saltpond, *Gold Coast* - 104 De
Saltrou, *Haiti* - 140 Cc
Saltsjobaden, *Sweden* - 50 Hc
Salt Sulphur Springs, *W. Virginia* - - - 129 Dd
Saltville, *Virginia* - 129 Dd
Saluda, *Virginia* - 129 Fd
Saluda & R., *S. Carolina* 131 Gc
Salue, I., *Nether. Indies* 99 Fd
Salümbar, *Rajputana* - 85 Eb
Salur, *Madras* - 91 Fb
Saluzzo, *Italy* - 62 Bc
Saluzzola, *Italy* - 62 Cb
Salvacanete, *Spain* - 38 Dd
Salvador, rep., *Central America* - - - 140 Fe
Salvador, L., *Louisiana* 130 Cf
Salvaterra de Magos, *Portugal* - - - 37 Bc
Salvaterra do Extremo, *Portugal* - - - 37 Cc
Salvatierra, *Mexico* - 138 Dc
Salvatierra, *Alava, Spain* 38 Cb
Salvatierra, *Zaragoza, Spain* - - - 38 Eb
Salvatierra de Mino, *Spain* - - - 36 Bb
Salvatierra de Tormes, *Spain* - - 37 Eb
Salween and R., *Burma* 92 Cc
Salyany, *Azerbaijan* - 75 Hh
Salzbergen, *Prussia* - 54 Cc
Salzburg, *Austria* - 59 Hd
Salzburg, div., *Austria* 59 Gd
Salzkammergut, *Austria* 59 Hd
Salzmünde, *Prussia* - 55 Gd
Salzwedel, *Prussia* - 54 Fc
Samad, *Trans-Jordan* - 80 Dc
Samaden, *Switzerland* - 43 Jc
Samaguting, *Assam* - 88 Db
Samai, *Rajputana* - 85 Db
Samakh, *Palestine* - 80 Db
Samal I., *Philippines* - 99 Gb
Samalkot, *Madras* - 91 Fc
Samâlût, *Egypt* - 107 Hd
Samamit, *Rio de Oro* - 104 Bb
Samana, I., *Bahamas* - 140 Cb
Samannud, *Egypt* - 107 Hc
Samar, I., *Philippines* 99 Ga
Samarai, *New Guinea* - 156 Ed
Samaria, *Idaho* - 136 Gd
Samarína, *Greece* - 70 Cc
Samarinda, *Borneo* - 99 Ed
Samarkand, *Uzbek* - 84 Bc
Samarovo, *U.S.S.R.* - 76 Gc
Samarra, *Iraq* - 78 Dc
Samartin, *Dalmatia* - 68 Bc
Samastipur, *Bihar* - 87 Fc
Samawa, *Iraq* - 78 Ec
Sambalang, C., *Borneo* 99 Ec
Sambalpur, *Orissa* - 87 Fe
Sambas, *Borneo* - 98 Cc
Sambhal, *United Provs.* 83 Hd
Sambhar and L., *Rajputana* - - - 83 Fe
Sambiasè, *Italy* - 65 Cd
Sambo, *Angola* - 109 Cd
Sambor, *Cambodia* - 95 Cg
Sambor - - - 60 Gd
Samborombón, B., *Argentina* - - - 148 Eb
Sambro, C., *Nova Scotia* 120 Dd
Sambuca di Sicilia, *Sicily* 65 Fg
Samburu, *Kenya* - 111 Fe
Samdoemande, *New Guinea* - - - 156 Bc
Same, *Tanganyika Terr.* 111 Ef
Samer, *France* - 30 Da
Sametkyun, *Burma* - 92 Bb
Sami, *Baluchistan* - 79 Hd
Sami, *Greece* - 71 Be
Samira, *Arabia* - 78 Dd
Samiriya, *Palestine* - 80 Cc
Samit Pt., *Cambodia* - 95 Bg
Samka, *Burma* - 92 Cb
Samland - - - 56 Eb
Samnan, *Persia* - 79 Fb
Sam-nua, *Laos* - 95 Be
Samoa, *California* - 134 Aa
Samoan Is., *Pacific Oc.* 149 Jg
Samoded, *U.S.S.R.* - 74 Fc
Samokov, *Bulgaria* - 69 Ed
Samos, *Spain* - 36 Cb
Samos, *Voyvodina* - 67 Fd
Samos, I., *Ægean Sea* - 78 Ab
Samosköujfalu, *Hungary* 66 Ea
Samothrace (Samothraki), I., *Greece* - 72 Cb
Samothráki (Mathráki), I., *Greece* - - 70 Ad
Samothraki (Samothrace), I., *Greece* - - 72 Cb
Sampacho, *Argentina* - 146 Be
Samper de Calanda, *Spain* 39 Ec
Sampit and B., *Borneo* - 99 Dd
Sampwe, *Belgian Congo* 109 Ec
Samra, *Palestine* - 80 Db
Samsat, *Turkey* - 78 Cb
Sam-shui, *China* - 95 De
Samski, *U.S.S.R.* - 74 Lc
Samsö I. & Belt, *Denmark* 45 Dc
Samsun, *Turkey* - 78 Ca
Sam-tai, *Laos* - 95 Bf
Samthar, *Central India* 86 Cc
Samtredi, *Georgia* - 75 Gg
San, *French W. Africa* - 104 Dd
San'a, *Yemen* - 78 Lg
Sana, R., *Bosnia* - 68 Ba
Sanaga, R., *Fr. Eq. Afr.* 105 De
Sanak, I., *Alaska* - 125 Fj
San Ambrogio, *Italy* - 62 Eb
Sanana, I., *Nether. Indies* 99 Gd
Sanandaj, *Persia* - 79 Eb
San Andreas, *California* 134 Cb
Sânandrei, *Romania* - 67 Gd
San Andres Ra., *New Mexico* - - - 135 Ke
San Angelo, *Italy* - 62 Db
San Angelo, *Texas* - 133 Be
San Angelo in Vado, *Italy* 63 Gd
San Antioco and I., *Sardinia* - - - 64 Hg
San Antonio, *Argentina* 146 Bd
San Antonio, *Chile* - 146 Bc
San Antonio, *Chile* - 146 Ae
San Antonio, *Mexico* - 138 Bc
San Antonio, *New Mexico* 135 Ke
San Antonio, *Texas* - 133 Cf
San Antonio B., *Philippines* - - 99 Eb
San Antonio Pk., *New Mexico* - - - 135 Kc
San Antonio Ra., *Nevada* 134 Ec
San Antonio Abad, *Balearic Is.* - - 39 Kg
San Antonio de los Cobres, *Argentina* - - 146 Bc
San Antonio Oeste, *Argentina* - - 148 Dc
San Arcangelo di Romagna, *Italy* - - 63 Gc
San Ardo, *California* - 134 Cc
San Augustine, *Texas* - 133 Ee
San Bartolomé, *Mexico* 139 Fd
San Bartolomeo in Galdo, *Italy* - - - 64 Fb
San Baudilio de Llobregat, *Spain* - - 39 Gc
San Benedetto dell Tronto, *Italy* - - 63 He
San Benedetto Po, *Italy* 62 Fb
San Benedicto, I., *Mexico* 138 Bd
San Benito, *Mexico* - 139 Fe
San Benito Is., *Mexico* 138 Ab
San Bernardino, *Paraguay* - - - 146 Dd
San Bernardino and Ra., *California* - - 134 Ed
San Bernardino Pass, *Switzerland* - - 43 Hd
San Bernardino Str., *Philippines* - - 99 Fa
San Bernardo, *Chile* - 146 Ae
San Bernardo Is., *Colombia* - - - 144 Ab
San Blas, *Argentina* - 148 Dc
San Blas, *Nayarit, Mexico* 138 Cc
San Blas, *Sinaloa, Mexico* 138 Cb
San Blas, C., *Florida* - 130 Ff
San Blas, Pta. & Gulf, *Panama* - - - 140 Hf
San Borja, *Mexico* - 138 Bb
Sanborn, *Iowa* - 132 Bd
Sanborn, *Quebec* - 121 Eb
San Camilo, *Argentina* 146 Cc
San Candido, *Italy* - 63 Ga
San Carlos, *Cordoba, Argentina* - - - 146 Be
San Carlos, *Mendoza, Argentina* - - - 146 Be
San Carlos, *Salta, Argent.* 146 Bd
San Carlos, *Brazil* - 147 Fc
San Carlos, *Mexico* - 139 Ec
San Carlos, *Nicaragua* 140 Ge
San Carlos, *Uruguay* - 146 De
San Carlos, *Amazonas, Venezuela* - - 144 Cc
San Carlos, *Cojedes, Venezuela* - - 144 Cb
San Carlos, *Venezuela* - 144 Bb
San Carlos & L., *Arizona* 135 He
San Carlos B., *Florida* 131 Mh
San Carlos de Bariloche, *Argentina* - - 148 Bc
San Carlos de la Rapita, *Spain* - - - 39 Fd
San Casciano Val di Pesa, *Italy* - - - 62 Fd
San Cataldo, *Sicily* - 65 Gg
San Celoni, *Spain* - 39 Hc
San-cha, *China* - 94 Cc
Sanchez, *Santo Domingo* 140 Dc
Sanchor, *Rajputana* - 85 Cb
San-chow, *China* - 95 De
Sanchursk, *U.S.S.R.* - 74 Hd
San Clemente, *Spain* - 38 Ce
San Clemente I., *Calif.* 134 De
San Cosme, *Paraguay* - 146 Dd
San Cristobal, *Argentina* 146 Ce
San Cristobal, *Chiapas, Mexico* - - - 139 Fd
San Cristobal, *Vera Cruz, Mexico* - - - 139 Ed

Santa Cruz de la Palma, *Canary Is.* 104 Aa
Santa Cruz de la Sierra, *Bolivia* 146 Cb
Santa Cruz de la Zarza, *Spain* 38 Be
Santa Cruz del Retamar, *Spain* 38 Ad
Santa Cruz del Sur, *Cuba* 140 Bb
Santa Cruz de Moya, *Spain* 38 De
Santa Cruz de Mudela, *Spain* 41 Cb
Santa Cruz de Napo, *Philippines* 99 Fa
Santa Cruz de Tenerife, *Canary Is.* 104 Aa
Santa del Carmen, *Mexico* 138 Db
Santadi, *Sardinia* 64 Hg
Santa Elena, *Spain* 41 Cb
Santa Elena and B. de, *Ecuador* 145 Ab
Santa Eufemia, G. of, *Italy* 65 Bd
Santa Eugenia, Pta., *Mexico,* 138 Ab
Santa Eulalia, *Portugal* 37 Cc
Santa Eulalia del Rio, *Balearic Is.* 39 Kg
Santa Fé, *Galapagos Is.* 145 Eh
Santa Fe, *New Mexico* 135 Kd
Santa Fe, *Pinos, I., Cuba* 140 Ab
Santafe, *Spain* 41 Cc
Santa Fe and prov., *Argentina* 146 Ce
Santa Helena, *Maranhao, Brazil* 143 Ec
Santa Helena, *Parana, Brazil* 147 Ec
San-tai, *Sinkiang* 84 Fb
Santa Isabel, *Argentina* 148 Cb
Santa Isabel, *Fernando Po* 105 Ce
Santa Isabel, *Uruguay* 146 De
Santa Isabel I., *Solomon Is.* 157 Dd
Santa Leopoldina, *Brazil* 143 De
Santalnes, I., *Chile* 148 Be
Santal Parganas, *Bihar* 87 Gc
Santalpur, *Western India* 85 Cc
Santa Lucia, *Cuba* 140 Bb
Santa Lucia di Messina, *Sicily* 65 Jf
Santa Luzia, *Brazil* 147 Fb
Santa Margarita, I., *Mexico* 138 Bc
Santa Maria, *Argentina* 146 Bd
Santa Maria, *Balearic Is.* 39 He
Santa Maria, *Brazil* 147 Ed
Santa Maria, *California* 134 Cd
Santa Maria, *Galapagos Is.* 145 Eh
Santa Maria, *Honduras* 140 Fd
Santa Maria, *Philippines* 99 Fb
Santa Maria, L. and R., *Mexico* 138 Ca
Santa Maria, mt., *Argentina* 148 Cb
Santa Maria Capua Vetere, *Italy* 64 Db
Santa Maria de Huerta, *Spain* 38 Cc
Santa Maria di Leuca, *Italy* 65 Ec
Santa Maria la Real de Nieva, *Spain* 37 Fa
Santa Maria Nova, *Brazil* 143 Ed
Santa Marta, *Colombia* 144 Ba
Santa Marta, *Spain* 37 Dd
Santa Monica and B., *California* 134 De
Sântana, *Romania* 67 Gc
Sant' Ana do Paranahyba, *Brazil* 147 Eb
Santander, *Colombia* 144 Ac
Santander and prov., *Spain* 38 Ba
Santander, dep., *Colombia* 144 Bb
Sant' Angelo di Brolo, *Sicily* 65 Hf
San-tao-ho, *China* 94 Ca
Santa Olalla, *Spain* 38 Ad
Santa Paula, *California* 134 Dd
Santa Philomena, *Brazil* 143 Ed
Santa Quiteria, *Brazil* 143 Fc
Santarem, *Bahia, Brazil* 143 Ge
Santarem, *Para, Brazil* 142 Dc
Santarem, *Portugal* 37 Bc
Santa Rita, *New Mexico* 135 Je
Santa Rita, *Venezuela* 144 Ba
Santa Rita do Anta, *Brazil* 147 Eb
Santa Rosa, *Córdoba, Argentina* 146 Be
Santa Rosa, *Los Andes, Argentina* 146 Bc
Santa Rosa, *Bolivia* 146 Cb
Santa Rosa, *California* 134 Bb
Santa Rosa, *Honduras* 140 Fe
Santa Rosa, *New Mexico* 135 Ld
Santa Rosa, *Uruguay* 146 De
Santa Rosa I., *California* 134 Ce
Santa Rosa I., *Florida* 130 Ee
Santa Rosa Mts., *Nevada* 134 Ea
Santa Rosa de Toay, *Argentina* 148 Cb
Santa Rosalia, *Mexico* 138 Bb
Santa Sonoyta, *Mexico* 138 Ba
Santa Teresa di Riva, *Sicily* 65 Jg
Santa Victoria do Palmar, *Brazil* 147 Ee
Santee R., *S. Carolina* 131 Jd
Santeramo in Colle, *Italy* 65 Cb
Santesteban, *Spain* 38 Da
Santhia, *Italy* 62 Cb
Santiago, *Mexico* 138 Cc
Santiago, *Panama* 140 Gf
Santiago, *Santo Domingo* 140 Cc
Santiago, *Spain* 36 Bb
Santiago and prov., *Chile* 146 Ae
Santiago, Cerro, *Panama* 140 Gf
Santiago, Sa. de, *Bolivia* 146 Db
Santiago de Cuba, *Cuba* 140 Bc
Santiago del Esterro and prov., *Argentina* 146 Cd
Santiago do Boqueirao, *Brazil* 146 Dd
Santiago Papasquiaro, *Mexico* 138 Dc
Santiam R., *Oregon* 136 Bc
Santipur, *Bengal* 88 Bc
Santi Quaranta (Sarandë), *Albania* 70 Ad
Santisteban del Puerto, *Spain* 41 Cb
Santo, C. de, *Mozambique* 115 Kc
Santo Anastacio, *Brazil* 147 Ec
Santo Angelo, *Brazil* 147 Ed
Santo Antonio, *Angola* 109 Bc
Santo Antonio, *Brazil* 142 Be
Santo Antonio, *Matto Grosso, Brazil* 142 Bd
Santo Antonio, *Para, Brazil* 142 Dc
Santo Corazon, *Bolivia* 146 Db
Santo Domingo, *Cuba* 140 Ab
Santo Domingo, *Mexico* 138 Aa
Santo Domingo, rep., *West Indies* 140 Cc
Santo Domingo de Silos, *Spain* 38 Bc
Santolea, *Spain* 39 Ed
Santo Maria del Campo, *Spain* 38 Bb
Santona, *Spain* 38 Ba
Santorin, I., *Greece* 61 Kf
Santos, *Brazil* 147 Fc
Santos, Sa. de los, *Spain* 40 Ea
Santo Stefano di Camastra, *Sicily* 65 Hf
Santo Thome, *Argentina* 146 Dd
Santo Tirso, *Portugal* 36 Bc
Santo Tomas, *Mexico* 138 Aa
Santo Tomas, *Peru* 145 Cd
San Urbano, *Argentina* 146 Ce
San Vicente, *Salvador* 140 Fe
San Vicente, Sa. de, *Spain* 38 Ad
San Vicente de Alcantara, *Spain* 37 Cc
San Vicente de Beira, *Portugal* 37 Cb
San Vicente de la Sonsierra, *Spain* 38 Cb
San Vincente de la Barquera, *Spain* 38 Aa
San Vincenzo, *Italy* 62 Ed
San Vito, *Italy* 63 Gb
San Vito-Chietino, *Italy* 64 Ea
Sanya, *Tanganyika Terr.* 110 Ee
Sanzawa, *Tang. Terr.* 111 Df
São Antonio de Balsas, *Brazil* 143 Ed
São Antonio de Ica, *Brazil* 145 Db
São Benedicto, *Brazil* 142 Bc
São Borja, *Brazil* 146 Dd
São Christovão, *Brazil* 143 Ge
São Domingos, *Goyaz, Brazil* 143 Ee
São Domingos, *Para, Brazil* 143 Ec
São Felippe, *Amazonas, Brazil* 145 Cc
São Felippe, *Rio Negro, Brazil* 145 Da
São Felix, *Brazil* 142 Dd
São Francisco, *Ceara, Brazil* 143 Gc
São Francisco, *Minas Geraes, Brazil* 147 Gb
São Francisco, *Para, Brazil* 142 Cc
São Francisco and I. de, *Brazil* 147 Fd
São Francisco, R., *Brazil* 143 Gd
São Gabriel, *Amazonas, Brazil* 145 Da
São Gabriel, *Rio Grande do Sul, Brazil* 147 Ee
São Jeronymo, *Parana, Brazil* 147 Ec
São Jeronymo, *Rio Grande do Sul, Brazil* 147 Ee
São João, *Minas Geraes, Brazil* 147 Gb
São João, *Rio Grande do Sul, Brazil* 147 Ee
São João, *São Paulo, Brazil* 147 Fc
São João da Barra, *Brazil* 147 Gc
São João do Araguaya, *Brazil* 143 Ed
São João do Piauhy, *Brazil* 143 Fd
São Joaquin, *Para, Brazil* 142 Cc
São Joaquin, *Santa Catharina, Brazil* 147 Ed
São José, *Amazonas, Brazil* 142 Ac
São José, *Rio Grande do Sul, Brazil* 147 Ee
São José, *Santa Catharina, Brazil* 147 Fd
São José do Araguaya, *Brazil* 143 De
São José do Duro, *Brazil* 143 Ee
São José do Mipibú, *Brazil* 143 Gd
São José dos Martyrios, *Brazil* 143 Ed
São José dos Mattoes, *Brazil* 143 Fd
São José do Tocantins, *Brazil* 143 Ee
Sao-kan, *China* 94 Dc
São Leopoldo, *Brazil* 147 Ed
São Lourenço, *Brazil* 147 Ee
São Lourenço and R., *Brazil* 146 Db
São Luiz, I., *Brazil* 143 Fc
São Luiz de Maranhao, *Brazil* 143 Ec
São Luiz do Caceres, *Brazil* 146 Db
São Luiz Gonzaga, *Brazil* 146 Dd
São Manoel ou das Tres Barras, R., *Brazil* 142 Cd
São Marcello, *Brazil* 143 Ee
São Marco B., *Brazil* 143 Fc
São Matheus, *Espirito Santo, Brazil* 147 Hb
São Matheus, *Parana, Brazil* 147 Ed
São Miguel, *Brazil* 143 Ec
Saona, I., *Santo Domingo* 140 Dc
Saône, R., *France* 31 Hd
Saône-et-Loire, dep., *France* 35 Ga
Sao Paulo and state, *Brazil* 147 Fc
São Paulo de Olivencia, *Brazil* 145 Db
São Pedro do Sul, *Portugal* 37 Bb
São Raymundo Nonato, *Brazil* 143 Fd
São Salvador (Bahia), *Brazil* 143 Ge
São Sebastiao and I., *Brazil* 147 Fc
São Sebastian, C., *Mozambique* 112 Cd
São Simao, *Brazil* 147 Fc
São Thome, I., *Gulf of Guinea* 109 Aa
São Tiago de Caçem, *Portugal* 40 Ba
São Vicente, *Brazil* 143 Ed
São Vicente, *Brazil* 147 Fc
Saparoea, I., *Nether. Indies* 99 Gd
Sapaya, *Ecuador* 145 Ba
Sapele, *Nigeria* 105 Cd
Sapelo R., *Georgia* 131 He
Sape Str. and B., *Netherlands Indies* 99 Ee
Sapiéntza, *Greece* 71 Cg
Sapinero, *Colorado* 135 Kb
Sapoedi I. and Str., *Netherlands Indies* 99 De
Saposoa, *Peru* 145 Bc
Sappai, *Greece* 72 Ca
Sappiane 63 Jb
Sapporo, *Japan* 97 Eb
Sapucua, Sa. do, *Brazil* 142 Cc
Sapulpa, *Oklahoma* 133 Db
Saqqiz, *Persia* 79 Eb
Sar Planina, *Serbia* 70 Ba
Sarafand, *Palestine* 80 Bb
Sarafinia, *Fr. W. Africa* 104 Be
Saragossa, *Spain* 38 Dc
Saraikela, *Eastern States* 87 Gd
Sarajevo, *Bosnia* 68 Dc
Sarakinó, *Greece* 71 Fe
Saraklí, *Greece* 70 Dc
Saraktash, *U.S.S.R.* 75 Ke
Sarameti, mt., *Burma* 88 Eb
Saramon, *France* 34 Cd
Saran, *Bihar* 87 Fb
Saranac Inn, *New York* 128 Aa
Saranac Lake, *New York* 123 Lc
Saranda, *Bihar* 87 Fd
Saranda, *Tang. Terr.* 111 Df
Sarandë (Santi Quaranta), *Albania* 70 Ad
Sarandi del yi, *Uruguay* 146 De
Sarandi Grande, *Uruguay* 146 De
Sarang, *New Guinea* 156 Db
Sarangani B., *Philippines* 99 Fb
Sarangani Is., *Philippines* 99 Gb
Sarangarh, *Eastern States* 87 Ee
Sarangpur, *Central India* 86 Bd
Saranpau, *U.S.S.R.* 74 Lc
Saransk, *U.S.S.R.* 75 He
Saraorci, *Serbia* 68 Gb
Sarapul, *U.S.S.R.* 73 Jd
Sarasota and B., *Florida* 131 Mh
Saraspur Hills, *Assam* 88 Db
Sarat, *Queensland* 153 Ce
Saratoga, *Wyoming* 135 Ka
Saratoga L., *New York* 128 Bb
Saratoga Springs, *New York* 123 Md
Saratov. *U.S.S.R.* 75 He
Saratsi, *China* 94 Da
Sarawak, *N. Borneo* 99 Dc
Sarawak (Kuching), *Sarawak* 98 Cc
Sarawan, *Baluchistan* 82 Bd
Saray, *Turkey* 72 Ea
Sarbaz, *Persia* 79 Hd
Sarco, *Chile* 146 Ad
Sard, *Romania* 67 Jd
Sardarpur, *Gwalior* 85 Ec
Sardarshahr, *Rajputana* 83 Fd
Sardasht, *Persia* 78 Eb
Sardhana, *United Provs.* 83 Gd
Sardhínina, *Greece* 71 Ce
Sardinia, I., *Italy* 61 Bd
Sardis, *Mississippi* 130 Cc
Sarebas, *Sarawak* 98 Dc
Sareks Nat. Park, *Sweden* 44 Df
Sarektjakko, Mt., *Sweden* 44 Df
Sarentinio Alps, *Italy* 63 Fa
Sargans, *Switzerland* 43 Hb
Sargentes, *Spain* 38 Bb
Sargodha, *Punjab* 82 Eb
Sarhad, *Persia* 79 Fd
Sari, *Persia* 79 Fb
Sarikamis, *Turkey* 78 Da
Sari Kaya, *Greece* 70 Dc
Sarikol, *Tadzhik* 84 Cc
Sariköy, *Turkey* 72 Eb
Sarila, *Central India* 86 Cc
Sarilar, *Turkey* 72 Ea
Sarina, *Queensland* 153 Cd
Sariñena, *Spain* 39 Ec
Sar-i-Pul, *Afghanistan* 84 Bc
Sar-i-pul, *Persia* 79 Ec
Sariyer, *Turkey* 72 Fa
Sark, I., *Channel Is.* 17 Ef
Sarkad, *Hungary* 67 Gc
Sarköy, *Turkey* 72 Eb
Sarlat, *France* 34 Dc
Sarmasag, *Transylvania* 67 Hb
Sarmi, *New Guinea* 156 Bb
Sarmin-ola Mts., *Sinkiang* 84 Eb
Sarnada, *Portugal* 37 Bb
Sarnen, *Switzerland* 43 Fc
Sarnia, *Ontario* 122 Gd
Sarno, *Italy* 64 Ec
Sarny 60 Jc
Säro, *Sweden* 51 Ae
Saronic Gulf, *Greece* 71 Ef
Saronno, *Italy* 62 Db
Saros and Gulf, *Turkey* 72 Db
Sarospatak, *Hungary* 67 Ga
Sarpsborg, *Norway* 47 He
Sarpul, *Persia* 79 Fb
Sarpynya, *U.S.S.R.* 74 Lc
Sarrebourg, *France* 31 Jc
Sarreguemines, *France* 31 Kb
Sarria, *Spain* 36 Cb
Sarroch, *Sardinia* 64 Jg
Sarsawa, *United Provs.* 83 Gc
Sarsina, *Italy* 63 Gd
Sarstedt, *Prussia* 54 Ec
Sarthe, dep. & R., *France* 30 Cd
Sartilly, *France* 32 Db
Sartona, *Corsica* 33 Dh
Saru, *Japan* 97 Eb
Sarur, *Oman* 79 Ge
Sárvár, *Hungary* 66 Bb
Sarwar, *Ajmer-Merwara* 85 Ea
Sary Dangero Mts., *China* 94 Bc
Sarzana, *Italy* 62 Dc
Sarzeau, *France* 32 Cc
Sarzedas, *Portugal* 37 Cc
Sasaram, *Bihar* 87 Fc
Sasca Montana, *Romania* 67 Ge
Sásd, *Hungary* 66 Dc
Sasebo, *Japan* 97 Bd
Sasicu, L. 69 Hc
Saskatchewan, prov., *Canada* 118 Hf
Saskatchewan R., *Sask.* 124 Jd
Saskatchewan R., North, *Alta.-Sask.* 124 Gd
Saskatchewan R., South, *Alta-Sask.* 124 Gd
Saskatoon, *Sask.* 124 Hd
Sasovo, *U.S.S.R.* 75 Ge
Sassa, *Italy* 64 Da
Sassabaneh, *Ethiopia* 108 Dd
Sassandra, *Fr. W. Africa* 104 Cf
Sassari, *Sardinia* 64 Hf
Sassnitz, *Prussia* 55 Ja
Sass Town, *Liberia* 104 Cf
Sassuolo, *Italy* 62 Ec
Sastin, *Slovakia* 66 Ca
Sastre, *Argentina* 146 Ce
Satara, *Bombay* 90 Ac
Säter, *Sweden* 50 Eb
Sater Land, *Oldenburg* 54 Cb
Satevo, *Mexico* 138 Cb
Satka, *U.S.S.R.* 74 Kd
Satkhira, *Bengal* 88 Bc
Satmala Ra., *Hyderabad* 90 Db
Satna, *Central India* 86 Dc
Satoei, *Borneo* 99 Ed
Satoraljaújhely, *Hungary* 67 Ga
Satpura Ra., *Rajputana-Cent. Provs.* 85 Ed
Sa-tsan-tsa, *Sinkiang* 84 Fb
Satsi, *Bhutan* 88 Ca
Sattenapalle, *Madras* 91 Dc
Satti, *Kashmir* 83 Ga
Sattila R., *Georgia* 131 He
Sattimma, Mt., *Kenya* 110 Ed
Sattur, *Madras* 89 Bc
Satul, *Siam* 98 Bb
Satu Mare, *Transylvania* 67 Hb
Satyamangalam, *Madras* 89 Bb
Sauda, *Norway* 47 Ce
Saudhárkrókur, *Iceland* 52 Cb
Sauerlach, *Bavaria* 59 Fd
Sauerland, dist., *Prussia* 54 Cd
Saugeen Pen., *Ontario* 123 Hc
Saugerties, *New York* 123 Ld
Saugor, *Central Provs.* 86 Cd
Saugus, *California* 134 Dd
Sauherad, *Norway* 47 Fe
Saujon, *France* 32 Ee
Sauk, *Washington* 136 Ca
Sauk Center, *Minnesota* 132 Bc
Sauk Rapids, *Minnesota* 132 Bc
Saulce, *France* 35 Gc
Saulieu, *France* 31 Gd
Sault Ste. Marie, *Mich.* 122 Fb
Sault Ste. Marie, *Ontario* 122 Fb
Saulxures, *France* 31 Jd
Saulzais, *France* 34 Ea
Saumur, *France* 30 Bd
Saundersfoot, *Wales* 20 Bd
Sauqira B., *Arabia* 77 Hf
Saurimo, *Angola* 109 Dc
Sausa, *Celébes* 99 Fd
Sauvagnac, Puy de, *France* 34 Da

SER
Regional Atlas
SHO

Serabo, New Guinea - 156 Bb
Serafimovich, U.S.S.R. 75 Gf
Seraikeui, Turkey - 78 Ab
Seraing, Belgium - 29 Dd
Seram, Hyderabad - 90 Cc
Serampore, Bengal - 88 Bc
Serang, Java - 98 Ce
Serang, I., Neth. Indies 149 Cf
Serasan (High) I., Netherlands Indies - 98 Cc
Serasan Pass, Netherlands Indies - 98 Cc
Serbia, Jugoslavia - 68 Fc
Serdovsk, U.S.S.R. - 75 Ge
Sered, Slovakia - 66 Ca
Seregho, Italy - 62 Db
Seremban, Malay States 98 Bc
Serena, La, Spain - 37 Ed
Serengeti Plains, Tanganyika Terr. - 110 De
Serenje, N. Rhodesia - 112 Bb
Serenli, Ital. Somaliland 108 Gf
Sergach, U.S.S.R. - 74 Hd
Sergievsk, U.S.S.R. - 75 Je
Sergipe, state, Brazil - 143 Ge
Sergo, Ukraine - 75 Ff
Seriboe Dolok, Sumatra 98 Ac
Sérifos, I., Greece - 71 Ff
Seringapatam, Mysore - 89 Ba
Serir di Calanscio, Libya 106 Cd
Seros, Spain - 39 Fc
Serowe, Bechuanaland - 113 Bd
Serpa, Portugal - 40 Cb
Serpentara, I., Sardinia 64 Jg
Serpentine L., New Brunswick - 120 Bc
Serpents Mouth, Venezuela - 144 Db
Serpukhov, U.S.S.R. - 75 Fd
Serra, California - 134 Ee
Serra, Mte., Italy - 62 Ed
Serrai, Greece - 70 Eb
Serrania de Cuenca, Spain 38 Cd
Serra San Bruno, Italy 65 Cd
Serrat, C., Tunisia - 103 Ja
Serravalle, Italy - 62 Cc
Serres, France - 35 Hc
Serrezuela, Argentina - 146 Be
Serrieres, France - 35 Gb
Serrinha, Brazil - 143 Ge
Serro Azul, Brazil - 147 Fc
Sersou, Plat. du, Algeria 102 Eb
Sertã, Portugal - 37 Bc
Seruli, Bechuanaland - 113 Bc
Serutu, I., Neth. Indies 98 Cd
Seruwai, Sumatra - 98 Ac
Serverette, France - 35 Fc
Sérvia, Greece - 70 Cc
Serviceton, Victoria - 154 Cd
Servigliano, Italy - 63 Hd
Sesa, Spain - 39 Ec
Sesajap, Borneo - 99 Ec
Sesaloa, Bechuanaland - 113 Ac
Sese Is., Uganda - 110 Cd
Seseganaga, Ontario - 122 Ca
Seshachalam Hills, Madras - 90 Dd
Sesia, R., Italy - 62 Cb
Sessa Aurunca, Italy - 64 Db
Sessão, French W. Afr. 105 Bb
Sesto, Italy - 63 Ga
Sesto Fior, Italy - 63 Fd
Sestranj, Dalmatia - 63 Kc
Sestri Levante, Italy - 62 Dc
Sestri Pom, Italy - 62 Cc
Sestus, Turkey - 72 Db
Sesvete, Croatia - 66 Bd
Setana, Japan - 97 Db
Setberg, Iceland - 52 Bb
Sete, France - 35 Fd
Sete Lagoas, Brazil - 147 Gb
Setesdal, Norway - 47 De
Sétif, Algeria - 103 Ga
Setsu-san, Taiwan - 97 Hf
Settat, Morocco - 103 Oh
Sette Camma. Fr. Equat. Africa - 109 Ab
Settimo, Italy - 62 Bb
Settino, Italy - 62 Bb
Settle, England - 18 Bb
Setubal and B., Portugal 37 Bd
Seui, Sardinia - 64 Jg
Seul, Lac, Ontario - 119 Lf
Seurre, France - 31 Hd
Sevan (Gokcha), L., Armenia - 75 Hg
Sevastopol, Crimea - 75 Eg
Sevelen, Switzerland - 43 Hb
Seven Hds., Eire - 25 Cf
Seven Devils, Oklahoma 133 Ec
Seven Islands and B., Quebec - 120 Ba
Sevenoaks, England - 15 Ed
Seven Pagodas (Mahabalipur), Madras - 91 Ee
Severin, Romania - 67 Hd
Severn, Ontario - 121 Ab
Severn, R., England - 14 Bc
Severn, R., Ontario - 119 Mf
Severnaya Dvina, R., U.S.S.R. - 74 Gc
Severnaya Zemlya (North Land), U.S.S.R. - 76 Mb
Severn Stoke, England 14 Bb
Severy, Kansas - 133 Db
Seveso, Italy - 62 Db
Sevier L., Utah - 134 Gb
Sevier R., Utah - 135 Gb
Sevilla and prov., Spain 40 Eb
Seville, Spain - 40 Db
Seville (Sevilla), Spain 40 Eb
Sevnica, Slovenia - 63 Ka
Sevre, R., France - 32 Ed
Sevsk, U.S.S.R. - 75 Ee
Seward, Alaska - 125 Kf
Seward, Nebraska - 132 Ae
Seward Penin., Alaska 125 Fd
Seya, Kenya - 110 Ec
Seybaplaya, Mexico - 139 Fd
Seybouse, R., Algeria - 103 Ha
Seychelles, Is., Indian Ocean - 73 Hj
Seyches, France - 34 Cc
Seydhisfjördhur, Iceland 52 Gb
Seyitler, Turkey - 72 Fa
Seymour, Cape Prov. - 115 Gf
Seymour, Indiana - 129 Ac
Seymour, Texas - 133 Cd
Seymour, Victoria - 154 Ed
Seyne, France - 35 Jc
Seyne, la, France - 33 Ac
Sézanne, France - 31 Fc
Sezze, Italy - 64 Db
Sfakia (Khóra Sfakion), Crete - 71 Hj
Sfantu Gheorghe, Transylvania - 69 Fc
Sfax, Tunisia - 103 Kb
Sfinári, Crete - 71 Gj
Shaam, Oman - 79 Gd
Sha'ara, Arabia - 78 De
Shabani, S. Rhodesia - 113 Cc
Shabortai Gobi, Mongolia - 96 Ab
Shabunda, Belg. Congo 109 Eb
Shadadkot, Sind - 82 Be
Shadegan, Persia - 79 Ec
Shadforth, Mt., W. Aust. 152 Cb
Shadwân I., Egypt - 107 Ke
Shafa, Libya - 106 Dc
Shafah, Jeb., Arabia - 78 Cd
Shafter, Nevada - 134 Fa
Shaftesbury, England - 14 Bd
Shaga, Arabia - 78 Lg
Shagan, Kazak - 75 Kf
Shageluk, Alaska - 125 Ge
Shahabad, Bihar - 87 Ec
Shahabad, Hyderabad - 90 Cc
Shahabad, Punjab - 83 Gc
Shahabad, United Provs. 83 Je
Shahapur, Deccan States 90 Bd
Shahbandar, Sind - 85 Ab
Shahbeg, Sind - 85 Ab
Shah Dad, Persia - 79 Gc
Shahdadpur, Sind - 85 Bb
Shahdara, Delhi - 83 Gd
Shahdheri, Punjab - 82 Eb
Shahganj, United Provs. 87 Eb
Shahgarh, Rajputana - 82 Ce
Shahin, Persia - 79 Eb
Shahjahanpur, United Provs. - 83 Je
Shahjui, Afghanistan - 82 Bb
Shaho, Manchuria - 96 Cc
Shahpur, Punjab - 82 Eb
Shahpura, Central Provs. 86 Dd
Shahpura, Rajputana - 85 Eb
Shahpuri I., Burma - 92 Ab
Shah Rakht, Persia - 79 Hc
Shahr-i-Babak, Persia - 79 Gc
Shahrig, Baluchistan - 82 Bc
Shahr-i-Zabul, Persia - 79 Hc
Shahrud, Persia - 79 Gb
Shah-yar, Sinkiang - 84 Eb
Shaikh Shu'aib, Persia 79 Fd
Shaim, U.S.S.R. - 74 Lc
Shajapur, Gwalior - 86 Bd
Shajara, Arabia - 79 Ee
Shakan, Alaska - 125 Oh
Shakespeare I., Ontario 122 Da
Shakhrizyabs, Uzbek - 84 Bc
Shakhty, U.S.S.R. - 75 Gf
Shakhunya, U.S.S.R. - 74 Hd
Shakopee, Minnesota - 132 Cc
Shakotanzaki, Japan - 97 Db
Shalal, Egypt - 106 Mh
Shama, Gold Coast - 104 Df
Shambe, A.-E. Sudan - 108 Bd
Shamil, Persia - 79 Gd
Shammar, Jeb., Arabia 78 Dd
Shamokin, Pennsylvania 129 Fb
Shamva, S. Rhodesia - 113 Da
Shan, China - 94 Dc
Shanchengtze, Manchuria 96 Dc
Shandan, China - 94 Ca
Shanfana, Angola - 109 Cd
Shang, China - 94 Cc
Shangani, S. Rhodesia - 113 Cb
Shang-cheng, China - 94 Ec
Shang-hai, China - 94 Fc
Shang-hang, China - 95 Ee
Shang-sze, China - 95 Ce
Shan-hai-kwan, China - 94 Ea
Shanhotim, Manchuria 96 Dc
Shaniko, Oregon - 136 Cc
Shanklin, I. of Wight, England - 14 Ce
Shannon, New Zealand 158 Ed
Shannon I., Greenland - 9 Hb
Shannon R., Eire - 25 Bd
Shannon Harbour, Eire 27 Ce
Shansahiyat, Palestine 80 Be
Shan-si, prov., China - 94 Db
Shan States, Northern, Burma - 92 Ca
Shan-tan, China - 94 Bb
Shan-tung, prov., China 94 Eb
Shao-hing, China - 94 Fd
Shao-wu, China - 94 Ed
Shap, England - 18 Ba
Shapinsay I. and Sd., Orkney Is. - 24 Fc
Shaqiq, Arabia - 79 Fd
Shaqra, Arabia - 78 Dd
Sharakpur, Punjab - 83 Ec
Shara-kula, China - 94 Bb
Sharamuren, Manchuria 96 Bc
Shardi, Kashmir - 83 Fa
Shari and B., Japan - 97 Eb
Sharjah, Arabia - 79 Gd
Shark B., W. Australia 152 Ad
Shark Pt., Angola - 109 Bc
Sharon, Pennsylvania - 129 Db
Sharon Springs, Kansas 133 Ba
Sharon Springs, New York - 128 Ab
Sharqiya, Oman - 79 Ge
Sharr, Jeb. el, Arabia - 78 Cd
Sharya, U.S.S.R. - 74 Hd
Sha-si, China - 94 Dc
Shasta & Mts., California 134 Ba
Shasta Mt., California - 134 Ba
Shatra, Iraq - 79 Ec
Shatsk, U.S.S.R. - 75 Ge
Shatta, Palestine - 80 Cb
Shatt al-Arab, Iraq - 79 Ec
Shattuck, Oklahoma - 133 Cb
Shaukbin Hill, Burma - 92 Bc
Shawano, Wisconsin - 132 Ec
Shawinigan Falls, Quebec 121 Da
Shawnee, Oklahoma - 133 Dc
Shawneetown, Illinois - 130 Db
Sha-yang, China - 94 Ad
Shchgry, U.S.S.R. - 75 Fe
Shchors, Ukraine - 75 Ec
Sheboygan, Wisconsin - 132 Fd
Shechem (Nablus), Palestine - 80 Cc
Shediac, New Brunswick 120 Cc
Sheelin, L., Eire - 26 Cd
Sheepmoor, Transvaal - 115 Jc
Sheerness, England - 15 Ed
Shefaya, Palestine - 80 Bb
Sheffield, Alabama - 130 Ec
Sheffield, England - 18 Cd
Sheffield, New Zealand 159 Ce
Sheffield, Tasmania - 155 Jg
Shefford, England - 15 Db
Shegaon, Berar, C.P. - 86 Be
Sheikh Othman, Aden - 78 Mh
Sheinmaga, Burma - 92 Ba
Sheiten, China - 94 Ca
Shejara, Palestine - 80 Cb
Shekak, Ontario - 122 Fa
Shekhawati, Rajputana 83 Fe
Shê-ki-chên, China - 94 Dc
Sheklung, China - 95 De
Shek-shing, China - 95 Ce
Sheksna, R., U.S.S.R. - 74 Fd
Shelanda, N. Rhodesia 112 Ab
Shelbina, Missouri - 130 Ba
Shelburne, Nova Scotia 120 Ce
Shelburne, Ontario - 123 Hc
Shelburne B., Queensland - 153 Bb
Shelby, Alabama - 130 Ed
Shelby, Michigan - 122 Ed
Shelby, Montana - 136 Ha
Shelby, North Carolina 131 Hc
Shelbyville, Illinois - 132 Ef
Shelbyville, Indiana - 129 Bc
Shelbyville, Kentucky - 130 Fa
Shelbyville, Missouri - 132 Cf
Shelbyville, Tennessee - 130 Ec
Shelcan, Albania - 70 Bb
Sheldon, Iowa - 132 Bd
Shelekhova, G. of, U.S.S.R. - 76 Qc
Shelikof Str., Alaska - 125 Hh
Shella, Assam - 88 Cb
Shellborough, W. Aust. 152 Bb
Shell Lake, Wisconsin - 132 Cc
Shell Rock R., Iowa - 132 Cd
Shelpiny, U.S.S.R. - 48 Mb
Shelsley Walsh, England 14 Bb
Shelton, Alaska - 125 Fd
Shelton, Washington - 136 Bb
Shemakha, Azerbaijan - 75 Hg
Shen, China - 94 Eb
Shenandoah, Iowa - 132 Be
Shenandoah, Pennsylva. 129 Fb
Shenandoah Nat. Park, Virginia - 129 Ec
Shenandoah, South, R., Virginia, etc. - 129 Ec
Shen-chow, China - 94 Dd
Shencottah, Madras States - 89 Bc
Shendam, Nigeria - 105 Cd
Shendi, A.-E. Sudan - 108 Bb
Shenge, Angola - 109 Cd
Shëngjin (San Giovanni di Medua), Albania - 70 Ab
Shenkursk, U.S.S.R. - 74 Gc
Shen-mu, China - 94 Db
Shen-si, prov., China - 94 Cc
Sheopur, Gwalior - 86 Bc
Shepetovka, Ukraine - 75 De
Shepherdstown, W. Virginia - 129 Fc
Shepparton, Victoria - 154 Ed
Sheppey, Isle of, England 15 Ed
Shepton Mallet, England 14 Bd
Sherborne, England - 14 Be
Sherbro I. and R., Sierra Leone - 104 Be
Sherbrooke, N. Dakota 132 Ab
Sherbrooke, Nova Scotia 120 Dd
Sherbrooke, Quebec - 121 Db
Sherburn-in-Elmet, Eng. 18 Cc
Shergaon, Assam - 88 Da
Shergarh, Rajputana - 86 Bc
Sheridan, Arkansas - 130 Bc
Sheridan, Montana - 136 Gc
Sheridan, Oregon - 136 Bc
Sheridan, Wyoming - 126 Db
Sheridan, Mt., Wyoming 136 Hc
Sheriff Hutton, England 18 Cb
Sheringham, England - 19 Fe
Sherman, Texas - 133 Dd
Sherpur, Afghanistan - 82 Ca
Sherpur, Bengal - 88 Bb
Sherpur, Bengal - 88 Cb
Sherridon, Manitoba - 124 Jc
Sherwood, S. Rhodesia 113 Cb
Sherwood, Texas - 133 Be
Sherwood Forest, England 18 Cd
Shetland Is. (Zetland), Scotland - 24 Gh
Shevaroy Hills, Madras 89 Cb
Sheye, Ital. Somaliland 108 Gg
Sheyenne R., N. Dakota 132 Ab
Shibakawa, Japan - 100 Gc
Shibarghan, Afghanistan 84 Bc
Shibata, Japan - 97 Dc
Shibin el Kom, Egypt - 107 Hc
Shibotzu, I., Japan - 97 Fb
Shibushi, Japan - 97 Cd
Shi-chao, China - 94 Eb
Shi-chêng, China - 94 Ed
Shickshock Mts., Quebec 119 Qg
Shiel, L., Scotland - 22 Ce
Shieldaig, Scotland - 22 Ca
Shields, Kansas - 133 Ba
Shields, North and South, England - 21 Ec
Shifnal, England - 14 Ba
Shighnan, Tadzhik - 84 Cc
Shihan, Trans-Jordan - 80 De
Shih-nan, China - 94 Cc
Shih-tsien, China - 94 Cd
Shi-huo (Shikho), Sinkiang - 84 Eb
Shihwei, Manchuria - 96 Ca
Shikari, Mozambique - 113 Fb
Shikarpur, Mysore - 90 Bd
Shikarpur, Sind - 82 Ce
Shikart, Mozambique - 112 Bc
Shikho (Shi-huo), Sinkiang - 84 Eb
Shikohabad, United Provs. 83 He
Shikoku, I., Japan - 97 Cd
Shillelagh, Eire - 27 Df
Shillong, Assam - 88 Cb
Shiloh, Tennessee - 130 Dc
Shilole Ra., Brit. Somaliland - 108 Ed
Shiltigheim, France - 31 Kc
Shimabara, Japan - 97 Cd
Shimada, Japan - 100 Gd
Shimanovskoe, U.S.S.R. 96 Da
Shimba, Kenya - 111 Fe
Shi-men, China - 94 Dd
Shimisu, Japan - 97 Dc
Shimobara, Japan - 100 Dd
Shimoda, Japan - 97 Dd
Shimodate, Japan - 100 Hc
Shimoga, Mysore - 90 Be
Shimoni, Kenya - 111 Ff
Shimonoseki, Japan - 97 Cd
Shimosuwa, Japan - 100 Gc
Shin, L., Scotland - 24 De
Shinagawa, Japan - 100 Gd
Shinano, R., Japan - 97 Dc
Shinano Omachi, Japan 100 Fc
Shinas, Oman - 79 Ge
Shinchiku, Taiwan - 97 Hf
Shinghar, Baluchistan - 82 Cc
Shingu, Japan - 97 Dd
Shingwe, Bechuanaland 113 Bc
Shiniama, Belgian Congo 109 Ed
Shinjo, Japan - 97 Ec
Shinmataung, Burma - 92 Bb
Shinrone, Eire - 27 Cf
Shinshiro, Japan - 100 Fd
Shinshu, Korea - 97 Bc
Shinyanga, Tang. Terr. 111 Ce
Shionimizaki, Japan - 97 Dd
Ship I., Mississippi - 130 De
Shipdham, England - 15 Ea
Shipets, Japan - 97 Eb
Ship Harbour, Nova Scotia - 120 Dd
Shiplake, England - 15 Dd
Shipley, England - 18 Cc
Shippensburg, Pennsylva. 129 Fb
Shippigan and I., New Brunswick - 120 Cc
Shipston-on-Stour, Eng. 14 Cb
Shi-pu, China - 94 Fd
Shira, Nigeria - 105 Cc
Shirabad, Uzbek - 84 Bc
Shirahama, Japan - 100 Gd
Shirakawa, Japan - 97 Dc
Shiramba, Mozambique 113 Fa
Shirati & B., Tang. Terr. 110 Cd
Shiraz, Persia - 79 Fd
Shirbin, Egypt - 107 Hc
Shire, R., Nyasaland - 112 Cc
Shiringush, U.S.S.R. - 75 Ge
Shirkuh, Persia - 79 Fc
Shirley Mts., Wyoming 135 Ka
Shiroko, Japan - 100 Fd
Shiroro, Mozambique - 112 Cd
Shirwa, L., Mozambique 112 Cc
Shi-shan, China - 94 Ed
Shishmaref, Alaska - 125 Ed
Shishmaref Inlet, Alaska 125 Ec
Shi-tsui-tze, China - 94 Cb
Shiu-chow, China - 95 De
Shiuhing, China - 95 De
Shive, R., Manchuria - 96 Bb
Shivpuri, Gwalior - 86 Bc
Shizuoka, Japan - 97 Dc
Shklov, White Russia - 75 De
Shkoder (Scutari), Albania - 70 Aa
Shkotovo, U.S.S.R. - 96 Ec
Shlisselburg, U.S.S.R. - 48 Jg
Shoal Harbour, Newfoundland - 120 Hb
Shoals, Indiana - 129 Ac
Shoalwater B., Queensland - 153 Dd
Shobara, Japan - 100 Dd
Shodo, Japan - 97 Cd
Shoe Pt., Newfoundland 120 Jb
Shoeburyness, England 15 Ec
Shoina, U.S.S.R. - 74 Gb
Shojo, Japan - 100 Ed
Shoka, Taiwan - 97 Hf
Sholapur, Bombay - 90 Bc
Sholavandan, Madras - 89 Bc
Shomyo, Japan - 100 Ba
Shonga Dzong, Bhutan 88 Ca
Shorkot, Punjab - 82 Ec
Short, Missouri - 130 Cb
Shortland I., Solomon Is. 156 Jg
Shoshone, Nevada - 134 Ea
Shoshone L., Wyoming 136 Hc

General Index

Skagaströnd, *Iceland* - 52 Cb
Skagen, *Denmark* - 45 Da
Skager Sjö, *Sweden* - 50 Dc
Skagerrak, *Norway-Denmark* - - - 44 Ah
Skägganäs, *Sweden* - 51 Ff
Skagway (Skaguay), *Alaska* - - - 125 Ng
Skála, *Greece* - - - 71 Dg
Skala Oropoú, *Greece* - 71 Ee
Skälder B., *Sweden* - 51 Bf
Skallingen, *Denmark* - 45 Bc
Skalmarnesmuli, *Iceland* 52 Bb
Skalmierzyce, *Poland* - 57 Db
Skals and Aa, *Denmark* 45 Cb
Skamokawa, *Washington* 136 Bb
Skanderborg, *Denmark* 45 Cb
Skanee, *Michigan* - 122 Db
Skanevik and Fd., *Norway* - - - - 47 Be
Skånland, *Norway* - 48 Bb
Skänninge, *Sweden* - 50 Ed
Skantžoúra, I., *Greece* - 71 Fd
Skapiskis, *Lithuania* - 49 Cd
Skara, *Sweden* - - 50 Cd
Skaraborg, län, *Sweden* 50 Cd
Skarda I., *Dalmatia* - 63 Je
Skardorsfjella, *Norway* 46 Jb
Skardu, *Kashmir* - 84 Dc
Skarnes, *Norway* - 47 Hd
Skarsöy, *Norway* - 46 Ea
Skaw, The, *Denmark* - 45 Da
Skawina, *Poland* - 57 Ed
Skeena R., *Br. Columbia* 124 Dd
Skegness, *England* - 19 Ed
Skeidhararsandur, *Iceland* 52 Ec
Skellefte, R., *Sweden* - 44 Df
Skelleftea, *Sweden* - 44 Ef
Skelton, *England* - 21 Dd
Skelton, *Nevada* - 134 Fa
Skenderbent, mts., *Albania* - - - 70 Ab
Skender Vakuf, *Bosnia* 68 Cb
Skenfrith, *England* - 14 Bc
Skern and R., *Denmark* 45 Bc
Skerries, *Eire* - - 27 Dd
Skhídra, *Greece* - - 70 Dc
Skhíza, *Greece* - - 71 Cg
Ski, *Norway* - - 47 Ge
Skiathos, I., *Greece* - 70 Ed
Skibbereen, *Eire* - 25 Bf
Skiddaw, mt., *England* 18 Aa
Skien, *Norway* - - 47 Fe
Skierniewiec, *Poland* - 60 Fc
Skipsea, *England* - 19 Dc
Skipton, *England* - 18 Bc
Skir Dhu, *Nova Scotia* - 120 Ec
Skiropoúla, I., *Greece* - 71 Fe
Skíros and I., *Greece* - 71 Fe
Skive, *Denmark* - 45 Cb
Skjåk, *Norway* - 46 Ec
Skjalfandafljot, *Iceland* 52 Eb
Skjálfandi, *Iceland* - 52 Ea
Skjöld, *Norway* - 47 Be
Skjolden, *Norway* - 46 Dc
Skjönstå, *Norway* - 48 Ac
Skofja Loka, *Slovenia* - 63 Ja
Skog, *Sweden* - 50 Fa
Skoki, *Poland* - 57 Ca
Skole - - - 60 Gd
Sköllersta, *Sweden* - 50 Ec
Skopelos, *Lesbos I., Greece* - - - 72 Dc
Skópelos, I., *Greece* - 71 Ed
Skopin, *U.S.S.R.* - 75 Fe
Skoplje, *Serbia* - 70 Ca
Skorcz, *Poland* - 56 Cc
Skotoúsa, *Greece* - 70 Eb
Skotselv, *Norway* - 47 Fe
Skoulikariá, *Greece* - 71 Cd
Skoútari, *Greece* - 71 Dg
Skövde, *Sweden* - 50 Cd
Skrad, *Croatia* - 63 Jb
Skradin, *Dalmatia* - 68 Ac
Skrea, *Sweden* - 51 Bf
Skreia, *Norway* - 46 Hd
Skripoú, *Greece* - 71 Ee
Skruv, *Sweden* - 51 Ef
Skudeneshavn, *Norway* 47 Ae
Skukuza, *Transvaal* - 115 Jb
Skulerud, *Norway* - 47 He
Skuodas, *Lithuania* - 49 Ac
Skurup, *Sweden* - 51 Cg
Skvira, *Ukraine* - 75 Df
Skye, I., *Scotland* - 22 Bb
Slagelse, *Denmark* - 45 Ec
Slamet, Mt., *Java* - 98 Ce
Slammannon, *New S. Wales* - - - 154 Db
Slane, *Eire* - - 26 Dd
Slaney, R., *Eire* - 27 Dg
Slang Berg, *Cape Prov.* 114 De
Slanic, *Romania* - - 69 Fc
Slano, *Dalmatia* - - 68 Cd
Slany, *Bohemia* - - 59 Ha
Slate Is., *Ontario* - - 122 Ea
Slate Run, *Pennsylvania* 129 Fb
Slater, *Missouri* - - 130 Ba
Slatina, *Bosnia* - - 68 Cb
Slatina, *Romania* - 69 Fc
Slatina, *Slavonia* - - 66 Cd
Slatina, *Slovakia* - - 57 De
Slaughter, *Louisiana* - 130 Ce
Slave Coast, *N.-W. Africa* - - - 105 Bd
Slave R., *N.-W. Terr.* - 124 Gb
Slăveşti, *Romania* - 67 Je
Slavkov (Austerlitz), *Moravia* - - - 57 Bd
Slavonia, *Jugoslavia* - 66 Cd
Slavyansk, *Ukraine* - 75 Ff
Slavyansk, *U.S.S.R.* - 75 Ff
Slayton, *Minnesota* - 132 Bd
Slea Hd., *Eire* - - 25 Ae
Sleaford, *England* - 19 Dd
Sleat, Sd. of, *Scotland* - 22 Cb
Sleepers, The, *Hudson B., Canada* - - 119 Ne
Sleepy Eye, *Minnesota* 132 Bc
Sleetmute, *Alaska* - 125 Hf
Slide Mt., *New York* - 123 Ld
Slidell, *Louisiana* - 130 De
Slieve Aughty, *Eire* - 27 Be
Slieve Bernagh, *Eire* - 27 Bf
Slieve Bloom Mts., *Eire* 27 Ce
Slieve Car, mt., *Eire* - 25 Ba
Slieve Donard, *N. Ireland* 26 Dc
Slieve Mish, *Eire* - 25 Be
Slieve Miskish, *Eire* - 25 Bf
Slieve Snaght, *Eire* - 26 Ca
Sligachan, *Scotland* - 22 Bb
Sligo, co., *Eire* - - 26 Bc
Sligo and B., *Eire* - 26 Bc
Slite, *Sweden* - - 51 He
Sliven, *Bulgaria* - - 69 Gd
Slobozia Veche, *Romania* 69 Gc
Slochteren, *Holland* - 29 Ea
Sloinge, *Sweden* - 51 Bf
Słoka, *Latvia* - - 49 Bc
Slonim - - - 60 Hb
Slonta, *Libya* - - 106 Cb
Slough, *England* - - 15 Dc
Slovakia, *Czechoslovakia* 60 Ed
Slovenia, *Jugoslavia* - 63 Ja
Slovenjgradec, *Slovenia* 63 Ja
Slovodskoi, *U.S.S.R.* - 74 Jd
Slunj, *Croatia* - - 63 Kb
Slutsk, *White Russia* - 75 De
Slyne Hd., *Eire* - - 25 Ac
Smara, *Rio de Oro* - 104 Ba
Smederovo, *Serbia* - 68 Fb
Smela, *Ukraine* - - 75 Ef
Smerwick and Harb., *Eire* - - - 25 Ae
Smethport, *Pennsylvania* 129 Eb
Smetowo, *Poland* - 56 Cc
Smidovich, *U.S.S.R.* - 96 Eb
Smigadi, *Greece* - - 72 Ca
Smilde, *Holland* - - 29 Eb
Smiljevača, mt., *Bosnia* 68 Bb
Smiltene, *Latvia* - - 49 Dc
Smith, *Alberta* - - 124 Gc
Smith B., *Alaska* - 125 Ja
Smith B., *N.-W. Terr.* - 124 Ea
Smith I., *North Carolina* 131 Kd
Smith Sd., *N.-W. Terr.* 119 Oa
Smith Center, *Kansas* - 133 Ca
Smithers, *Brit. Columbia* 124 Dd
Smithfield, *N. Carolina* 131 Jc
Smithfield, *O.F.S.* - 115 Ge
Smithfield, *Utah* - - 135 Ga
Smithfield, *Virginia* - 129 Fd
Smithland, *Kentucky* - 130 Db
Smith River, *California* 134 Aa
Smiths Falls, *Ontario* - 121 Bb
Smithton, *Tasmania* - 155 Jg
Smithtown, *New York* - 128 Bc
Smithville, *Georgia* - 131 Fe
Smithville, *Texas* - 133 Df
Smockington, *England* 14 Ca
Smokovec, *Slovakia* - 57 Fd
Smoky R., *Alberta* - 124 Fc
Smoky Falls, *Ontario* - 122 Ga
Smoky Hill R., *Kansas* 133 Ca
Smöla, I., *Norway* - 46 Da
Smolensk, *Ukraine* - 74 Ee
Smólikas, mt., *Greece* - 70 Bc
Smolnik, *Slovakia* - 67 Fa
Smolyan, *Bulgaria* - 69 Fe
Smoothrock, *Ontario* - 123 Ha
Smoothstone L., *Sask.* 124 Hd
Smörstakkane, mt., *Norway* - - - 46 Cd
Smyrna, *Delaware* - 129 Gc
Smyrna, *Tennessee* - 130 Ec
Smyrna (Izmir), *Turkey* 78 Ab
Snaefell, *I. of Man* - 19 Hf
Snaefell, mt., *Iceland* - 52 Fb
Snaith, *England* - - 18 Cc
Snake R., *Minnesota* - 132 Cc
Snake R., *Ontario* - 121 Bb
Snake R., *Oregon, etc.* - 136 Ec
Snake R., *Yukon* - 124 Ca
Snake Creek, *Quebec* - 121 Aa
Snake River Plains, *Idaho* - - - 136 Gd
Snake River Ra., *Idaho* 136 Hd
Sneads, *Florida* - - 130 Fe
Sneek, *Holland* - - 29 Da
Sneem, *Eire* - - 25 Bf
Sneeuw Bergen, *Cape Prov.* - - - 115 Fe
Sniadowo, *Poland* - 56 Fc
Snizort, L., *Scotland* - 22 Ba
Snöfjellkolla, *Norway* - 46 Eb
Snohetta, mt., *Norway* 46 Fb
Snohomish, *Washington* 136 Cb
Snow Pk., *Wyoming* - 126 Db
Snow Crest Ra., *Montana* - - - 136 Gc
Snowdon, mt., *Wales* - 20 Ba
Snow Flake, *Arizona* - 135 Hd
Snow Hill, *Alabama* - 130 Ed
Snow Hill, *Maryland* - 129 Gc
Snowtown, *S. Australia* 154 Bc
Snowy Mts., *Victoria* - 155 Fd
Snowy Ra., *New Guinea* 156 Bb
Snyder, *Colorado* - 135 Ma
Snyder, *Texas* - - 133 Bd
Snyten, *Sweden* - 50 Fc
Soahazo, *Madagascar* - 112 Dc
Soai-rieng, *Cambodia* - 95 Cg
Soars, *Romania* - - 67 Kd
Soay, I., *Scotland* - 22 Bb
Soazza, *Switzerland* - 43 Hd
Sober, *Spain* - - 36 Cb
Sobotka, *Bohemia* - 59 Ka
Sobrado, *Brazil* - - 142 Dd
Sobral, *Brazil* - - 143 Fc
Sobral, *Portugal* - - 37 Ac
Sobraon, *Punjab* - - 83 Fc
Sobrarbe, *Spain* - - 39 Eb
Söby, *Denmark* - - 45 Dd
Sočanica, *Serbia* - - 68 Fc
Sochaczew, *Poland* - 57 Ea
Sochi, *U.S.S.R.* - - 75 Fg
Social Circle, *Georgia* - 131 Gd
Society B., *Kwangtung Terr.* - - - 97 Ac
Society Is., *Pacific Oc.* 157 He
Socompa, mt., *Chile* - 146 Bc
Soconi, *Tangan. Terr.* 111 Fg
Soconusco, Vol., *Mexico* 139 Fd
Socorro, *Colombia* - 144 Bb
Socorro, *New Mexico* - 135 Kd
Socorro, I., *Mexico* - 138 Bd
Socota, *Ethiopia* - - 108 Cc
Socotra I., *Indian Oc.* - 108 Fc
Soc-trang, *Cochin-China* 95 Ch
Soda, *A.-E. Sudan* - 108 Bc
Sodankylä, *Finland* - 48 Gc
Soda Springs, *Idaho* - 136 Hd
Sodaville, *Nevada* - 134 Db
Söderåkra, *Sweden* - 51 Ff
Söderfors, *Sweden* - 50 Gb
Söderhamn, *Sweden* - 50 Ga
Söderköping, *Sweden* - 50 Fd
Södermanland, län, *Sweden* - - - 50 Fc
Södertälje, *Sweden* - 50 Gc
Sodiri, *A.-E. Sudan* - 108 Ac
Soebi I., *Nether. Indies* 98 Cc
Soeda, *Japan* - - 100 Bb
Soekaboemi, *Borneo* - 98 Dd
Soekaboemi, *Java* - 98 Ce
Soekadana, *Borneo* - 98 Dd
Soekadana, *Sumatra* - 98 Ce
Soela Is., *Nether. Indies* 99 Fd
Soela Sd., *Estonia* - 49 Bb
Soemalata, *Celébes* - 99 Fc
Soemba I. and Str., *Netherlands Indies* - 99 Ee
Soembawa and I., *Netherlands Indies* - - 99 Ee
Soembing, Mt., *Java* - 98 Ce
Soenda Str., *Netherlands Indies* - - - 98 Be
Soengai Kakap, *Borneo* 98 Cd
Soengaipenoeh, *Sumatra* 98 Bd
Soepiori, I., *Du. New Guinea* - - - 156 Bb
Soerabaja, *Java* - - 98 De
Soerakarta, *Java* - - 98 De
Soeroelangoen, *Sumatra* 98 Bd
Soesoh, *Sumatra* - - 98 Ac
Soest, *Prussia* - - 54 Dd
Sofádhes, *Greece* - - 70 Cd
Sofala, *Mozambique* - 112 Bd
Sofala, *New S. Wales* - 155 Fc
Sofia, *Bulgaria* - - 69 Ed
Sofia and R., *Madagascar* - - - 112 Ec
Sofikón, *Greece* - - 71 Ef
Soga, *Tanganyika Terr.* 111 Fg
Sogamosa, *Colombia* - 144 Bb
Sogano, *Japan* - - 100 Hd
Sogndal, *Norway* - - 46 Dc
Sogndal, *Norway* - - 47 Cf
Sögne, *Norway* - - 47 Df
Sogne Fjord, *Norway* - 46 Bc
Sogne og Fjordane, fylke, *Norway* - - - 46 Bc
Sogud Gölü, *Turkey* - 78 Ab
Sögut, *Turkey* - - 78 Ba
Sohag, *Egypt* - - 107 He
Sohagpur, *Central India* 86 Dd
Sohagpur, *Central Provs.* 86 Cd
Soham, *England* - - 15 Eb
Sohar, *Oman* - - 79 Ge
Sohawal, *Central India* 86 Dc
Sohela, *Orissa* - - 87 Ee
Sohna, *Punjab* - - 83 Gd
Sohou Pass, *Idaho* - 136 Fb
Soignies, *Belgium* - 29 Bd
Soissons, *France* - - 30 Fb
Sojat, *Rajputana* - - 85 Db
Sojoło *Celébes* - - 99 Ec
Sokal - - - 60 Hc
Soke, *Turkey* - - 78 Ab
Sokele, *Belgian Congo* - 109 Dc
Sokendal, *Norway* - 46 Gb
Sokhós, *Greece* - - 70 Ec
Sokode, *Fr. W. Africa* 105 Bd
Sokol, *U.S.S.R.* - - 74 Fd
Sokolac, *Bosnia* - - 68 Dc
Sokółka, *Poland* - - 60 Gb
Sokolo, *Fr. W. Africa* - 104 Cd
Sokolów Podlaska, *Poland* - - - 60 Gb
Sokoto, *Nigeria* - - 105 Bc
Sôl, *Egypt* - - 107 Hd
Solai, *Kenya* - - 110 Ec
Solana, *New Mexico* - 135 Md
Solorio, Sa. del, *Spain* - 38 Cc
Solbergfoss, *Norway* - 47 He
Soldin - - - 55 Kc
Sole, Val. di, *Italy* - 62 Ea
Soledad, *Venezuela* - 144 Db
Soledade, *Brazil* - - 145 Dc
Sölen, mt. and Sjoen, *Norway* - - - 46 Hc
Solent, The, *England* - 14 Ce
Solenzara, *Corsica* - 33 Eh
Solesmes, *France* - 31 Fa
Solferino, *France* - 34 Ac
Soligalich, *U.S.S.R.* - 74 Gd
Solignano, *Italy* - - 62 Dc
Solihull, *England* - 14 Cb
Solikamsk, *U.S.S.R.* - 74 Kd
Solimoes, R., *Brazil* - 145 Db
Solin, *Dalmatia* - - 68 Bc
Solingen, *Prussia* - 54 Cd
Sollebrunn, *Sweden* - 51 Bd
Solleftea, *Sweden* - 44 Dg
Sollia, *Norway* - - 46 Gc
Sollies-Pont, *France* - 33 Ac
Sollinger Wald, *Prussia* 54 Ed
Sollum and G. of, *Egypt* 106 Ec
Sölnkletten, *Norway* - 46 Gc
Solofra, *Italy* - - 64 Ec
Sologne, *France* - - 30 Dd
Solok, *Sumatra* - - 98 Bd
Solola, *Guatemala* - 140 Ee
Solombo Is., *Nether. Indies* 99 De
Solomon, *Alaska* - - 125 Fd
Solomon, *Kansas* - 133 Da
Solomon Is., *Pacific Oc.* 157 Cd
Solomon R., *Kansas* - 133 Ca
Solomonsville, *Arizona* 135 Je
Solon, *Punjab* - - 83 Gc
Solor, *Norway* - - 47 Hd
Solor Is., *Netherlands Indies* - - - 99 Fe
Solothurn and canton, *Switzerland* - - 42 Db
Solovetskie, Is., *U.S.S.R.* 74 Fb
Solsona, *Spain* - - 39 Gc
Solt, *Hungary* - - 66 Ec
Soltau, *Prussia* - - 54 Ec
Soltsi, *U.S.S.R.* - - 74 Dd
Soluch, *Libya* - - 106 Cc
Solund, *Norway* - - 46 Ac
Sölvesborg, *Sweden* - 51 Df
Solvychegodsk, *U.S.S.R.* 74 Hc
Solway, *Minnesota* - 132 Bb
Solway Firth, *Scotland* 21 Cd
Som Sjö, *Sweden* - - 51 Ed
Soma, *Turkey* - - 72 Ec
Somabula, *S. Rhodesia* 113 Cb
Sombernon, *France* - 31 Gd
Sombo, *Mozambique* - 113 Gb
Sombor, *Voyvodina* - 66 Ed
Sombrerete, *Mexico* - 138 Dc
Sombrero Chan, *Nicobar Is.* - - - - 91 Jg
Sombrero, I., *Virgin Is.* 140 Kg
Sombrero Key, *Florida* 131 Nj
Somcuţa Mare, *Transylvania* - - - 67 Jb
Someren, *Holland* - 29 Dc
Somergem, *Belgium* - 29 Bc
Somerset, *Kentucky* - 131 Fb
Somerset, *Queensland* - 153 Bb
Somerset, co., *England* 14 Ad
Somerset I., *N.-W. Terr.* 119 Lb
Somerset E., *Cape Prov.* 115 Ff
Somerset W., *Cape Prov.* 114 Cg
Somersham, *England* - 15 Eb
Somerton, *England* - 14 Bd
Somerville, *Massachusetts* 128 Cb
Somerville, *Tennessee* - 130 Dc
Somes, *Transylvania* - 67 Jb
Someşul Mare, *Transylvania* - - 67 Kb
Somkele, *Natal* - - 115 Jd
Somma, *Italy* - - 64 Ec
Somme, dep. and R., *France* - - - 30 Eb
Sommen, *Sweden* - - 51 Ed
Sommerfeld - - 55 Ld
Sommieres, *France* - 35 Gd
Somnath (Patan), *Western India* - - - 85 Cd
Somogy, *Hungary* - 66 Cc
Somogyszob, *Hungary* - 66 Cc
Somoto, *Nicaragua* - 140 Fe
Sompeta, *Madras* - 91 Gb
Somra, *Burma* - - 88 Eb
Son, *Norway* - - 47 Ge
Son, *Spain* - - 36 Ab
Son R., *Bihar, etc.* - 87 Fc
Sonai R., *Assam* - - 88 Da
Sonakhan, *Central Provs.* 87 Ee
Sonamukhi, *Bengal* - 88 Ac
Sonargaon, *Bengal* - 88 Cc
Sonbarsa, *Bihar* - - 87 Gc
Sondalo, *Italy* - - 62 Ea
Sonderborg, *Denmark* - 45 Cd
Sondershausen, *Thuringia* 54 Fd
Söndervig, *Denmark* - 45 Ab
Sondrio, *Italy* - - 62 Da
Sone, *Mozambique* - 113 Fa
Sonepet, *Hyderabad* - 90 Cb
Song-bo (Black R.), *Tongking* - - - 95 Be
Songea, *Tangan. Terr.* - 111 Dj
Songelsk, *U.S.S.R.* - 48 Hb
Songeons, *France* - 30 Db
Song-ka, *Annam* - 95 Bf
Song-kan, *Annam* - 95 Cg
Song-koi (Red R.), *Tongking* - - - 95 Be
Songoya, *Fr. W. Africa* 104 Be
Songwe and R., *Tanganyika Terr.* - - 111 Ch
Sonhat, *Eastern States* - 87 Ed
Sonki, *A.-E. Sudan* - 108 Ba
Sonmiani (Miani), *Baluchistan* - - - 85 Ab
Sonneberg, *Thuringia* - 58 Fa
Sonnenburg - - 55 Kc
Sonning, *England* - 15 Dd
Sonnino, *Italy* - - 64 Db
Sonobe, *Japan* - - 100 Ed
Sonogno, *Switzerland* - 43 Gd
Sonoki, *Japan* - - 100 Ab
Sonoma, *California* - 134 Bb
Sonora, *California* - 134 Cb
Sonora, state and R., *Mexico* - - - 138 Bb
Sonoyta, *Mexico* - - 138 Ba
Sonpur, *Bihar* - - 87 Fc
Sonpur, *Eastern States* - 87 Ee
Sonson, *Colombia* - 144 Ab
Sonsonate, *Salvador* - 140 Ee
Sontai, *Tong-king* - 95 Ce
Sontiz, *Spain* - - 37 Ea
Sonyo, *Tangan. Terr.* - 110 De
Soochow, *China* - - 94 Fc
Soo Junction, *Michigan* 122 Fb
Soon Wald, *Prussia* - 58 Bb
Soperton, *Georgia* - 131 Gd
So-ping, *China* - - 94 Da
Sopris, *Colorado* - - 135 Lc
Sopron, *Hungary* - 66 Bb
Sopur, *Kashmir* - - 83 Fa
Sor Fd., *Norway* - - 47 Cd
Sora, *Italy* - - 64 Db
Söraby, *Sweden* - - 51 Db
Sorata, *Bolivia* - - 146 Be

STE Regional Atlas SUN

Steep Rock, Ontario - 122 Ba
Steffen, Argentina - 148 Bc
Steffisburg, Switzerland 42 Ec
Stege, Denmark - - 45 Fc
Stegi, Swaziland - - 115 Kc
Stehekin, Washington - 136 Ca
Steiger Wald, Bavaria - 58 Eb
Steinach, Austria - 59 Fd
Steinbeck, Prussia - 55 Jc
Steinfeld, S.-W. Africa 114 Bb
Steinjer, Norway - - 44 Bf
Steinkopf, Cape Prov. - 114 Bd
Steins Pass, New Mexico 135 Je
Stella, Cape Prov. - 115 Fc
Stella, Mte., Italy - 64 Fc
Stella, P., Italy - - 62 Da
Stella, R., Italy - - 63 Hb
Stellarton, Nova Scotia 120 Dd
Stellenbosch, Cape Prov. 114 Cf
Stelvio P., Italy - - 62 Ea
Stemshesten, mt., Norway - - - - 46 Db
Stendal, Prussia - - 55 Gc
Stenón, Greece - - 71 Df
Stenstorp, Sweden - 50 Cd
Stepanakert, Azerbaijan 75 Hh
Stephanieville, Fr. Equat. Africa - - 109 Bb
Stephen Ra., W. Aust - 152 Cb
Stephenson, Michigan - 122 Ec
Stephenville, Newfoundland - - - 120 Fb
Stephenville, Texas - 133 Cd
Sterea Ellás, div., Greece 71 Ce
Sterkstroom, Cape Prov. 115 Ge
Sterling, Colorado - 135 Ma
Sterling, Illinois - - 132 Ee
Sterling, Kansas - - 133 Ca
Sterling, Nebraska - 132 Ae
Sterling City, Texas - 133 Be
Sterlitamak, U.S.S.R. - 75 Je
Sternberk (Sternberg), Moravia - - 57 Cd
Sterren Mts., New Guinea - - - 156 Cc
Sterrett, Oklahoma - 133 Dd
Steszew, Poland - - 57 Ba
Stettin (Szczecin), Poland 55 Kb
Stettler, Alberta - - 124 Gd
Steubenville, Ohio - 129 Db
Stevenage, England - 15 Dc
Stevens, Alaska - - 125 Kc
Stevens Pk., Idaho - 136 Fb
Stevenson, Alabama - 130 Ec
Stevens Point, Wisconsin - - - 132 Dc
Stevensville, Montana - 136 Gb
Steventon, Scotland - 21 Bb
Stevns Klint, Denmark 45 Fc
Stewart, Br. Columbia 124 Dc
Stewart and R., Yukon 124 Bb
Stewart I., New Zealand 159 Ag
Stewartstown, N. Ireland 26 Db
Steyerberg, Prussia - 54 Dc
Steyning, England - 15 De
Steynsburg, Cape Prov. 115 Fe
Steynsrust, O.F.S. - 115 Gc
Steyr, Austria - - 59 Jc
Steyr, R., Austria - 59 Jd
Steytlerville, Cape Prov. 114 Ef
Stia, Italy - - - 63 Fd
Stickford, England - 19 Ed
Stigler, Oklahoma - 133 Ec
Stigliano, Italy - - 65 Cb
Stikine R. and Mts., Brit. Columbia - - 124 Cc
Stilís, Greece - - 71 De
Still Bay, Cape Prov. - 114 Dg
Stillinge, Denmark - 45 Ec
Stillwater, Oklahoma - 133 Db
Stillwater, Wisconsin - 132 Cc
Stillwater and Mts., Nevada - - 134 Db
Stillwater R., Montana 136 Jc
Stilwell, Oklahoma - 133 Ec
Stimigliano, Italy - 64 Ca
Stimlja, Serbia - - 68 Fd
Stip, Serbia - - 70 Db
Stira, Greece - - 71 Fe
Stirling, Ontario - - 121 Bb
Stirling and co., Scotland 23 Ed
Stirling Ra., W. Aust. - 152 Be
Stirling City, California 134 Cb
Stirone, R., Italy - - 62 Ec
Štites, Idaho - - 136 Eb
Stitnik, Slovakia - - 57 Fe
Stittville, Ontario - 121 Bb
Stjordal, Norway - - 46 Ga
Stockach, Baden - - 58 Dd
Stockaryd, Sweden - 51 De
Stockbridge, England - 14 Cd
Stockdale, Texas - - 133 Df
Stockerau, Austria - 59 Lc
Stockholm and län, Sweden - - - 50 Gc
Stockinbingal, New S. Wales - - - 155 Ec
Stockport, England - 18 Bd
Stockport, New York - 128 Bb
Stockton, Alabama - 130 Ee
Stockton, California - 134 Cc
Stockton, England - 14 Ba
Stockton, Kansas - 133 Ca
Stockton, Missouri - 130 Ab
Stockton, New S. Wales 155 Gc
Stockton-on-Tees, England - - - 18 Ca
Stoffberg, Transvaal - 115 Hb
Stoiceni, Romania - 67 Ke
Stoke Edith, England - 14 Bb
Stoke Ferry, England - 15 Ea
Stoke Fleming, England 17 Cc
Stokenchurch, England 15 Dc
Stoke-on-Trent, England 18 Bd
Stokesay, England - 14 Bb
Stokesley, England - 18 Cb
Stokkseyri, Iceland - 52 Cc
Stolac, Hersegovina - 68 Cc
Stolberg, Prussia - - 54 Be
Stolin - - - - 60 Jc
Stolnici, Romania - 67 Ke
Stolp - - - - 56 Bb
Stołpce - - - 60 Jb
Stolpmünde - - 56 Ab
Stolzenau, Prussia - 54 Dc
Stolzenfels, S.-W. Africa 114 Cd
Stómion, Greece - - 70 Dd
Ston, Dalmatia - - 68 Cd
Stone, Glos, England - 14 Bc
Stone, Staffs, England 18 Be
Stone Bridge, England - 14 Cb
Stoneby, Sweden - - 50 Bd
Stone Fort, Illinois - 130 Db
Stonegrave, England - 19 Db
Stonehaven, Scotland - 23 Fc
Stonehenge, England - 14 Cd
Stonehenge, Queensland 153 Bd
Stonehouse, England - 14 Bc
Stonehouse, Scotland - 21 Bb
Stone House, Nevada - 134 Ea
Stonington, Connecticut 128 Cc
Stony L., Ontario - 121 Ab
Stony Athi, Kenya - 110 Ed
Stony Cross, England - 14 Bb
Stony Man, mt., Virginia - - - 129 Ec
Stonypoint, New York 128 Ac
Stony Stratford, England - - - 15 Db
Stor Fjord, Norway - 46 Cb
Stor Fjord, Spitsbergen 9 Lb
Stor Sjoen, Norway - 46 Hc
Stora Le, Sweden - 50 Ac
Stora Lulevatten, Sweden - - - 44 Df
Stora Sjöfallets Nat. Park, Sweden - - 44 Df
Stord, Norway - - 47 Be
Stordal, Norway - - 46 Ha
Stordal, Norway - - 46 Db
Storekluken, Norway - 46 Ha
Stor-Elvdal, Norway - 46 Gc
Stören, Norway - - 46 Ga
Storhöpiggen, Norway - 46 Fc
Storkow, Prussia - - 55 Jc
Storm B., Tasmania - 155 Kh
Stormarn, Prussia - 54 Eb
Storm Berg, Cape Prov. 115 Ge
Stormberg Junc., Cape Prov. - - - 115 Ge
Storm Lake, Iowa - 132 Bd
Stornoway, Scotland - 24 Ba
Storo, Italy - - - 62 Eb
Storojineț - - - 69 Fa
Stórólfshvoll, Iceland - 52 Cc
Storsjön, Sweden - - 44 Cg
Storuma, Sweden - - 48 Bd
Storuman, Sweden - 44 Cf
Storvik, Sweden - - 50 Fb
Story City, Iowa - - 132 Cd
Stoughton, Massachusetts 128 Cb
Stoumont, Belgium - 29 Dd
Stour R., Dorset, England 14 Be
Stour, R., Essex, etc., England - - - 15 Fc
Stour, R., Kent, England 15 Fd
Stoúra (Stíra), Greece - 71 Fe
Stourbridge, England - 14 Bb
Stourport, England - 14 Bb
Stourton, England - 14 Bb
Stow, Scotland - - 21 Db
Stowmarket, England - 15 Eb
Stow-on-the-Wold, Eng. 14 Cc
Stra, Italy - - - 63 Gb
Strabane, N. Ireland - 26 Cb
Strachan, Quebec - 123 La
Stradbally, Kerry, Eire 25 Ae
Stradbally, Leix, Eire - 27 Ce
Stradbally, Waterford, Eire - - - 27 Cg
Stradbroke, England - 15 Fb
Stradbroke I., Queensland - - - 153 De
Stradella, Italy - - 62 Db
Stradone, Eire - - 26 Cd
Strahan, Tasmania - 155 Jg
Strakonice, Bohemia - 60 Bd
Stralsund, Prussia - 55 Ha
Strand, Cape Prov. - 114 Cg
Strand, Norway - - 46 Hc
Strandebarm, Norway - 47 Bd
Strandvik, Norway - 47 Bd
Strangford, N. Ireland 26 Ec
Strangford L., N. Ireland 26 Eb
Strängnäs, Sweden - 50 Gc
Strangways Springs, S. Australia - - 154 Aa
Stranorlar, Eire - - 26 Cb
Stranraer, Scotland - 21 Bd
Strasbourg, France - 31 Kc
Strasburg, Prussia - 55 Jb
Strassburg, Austria - 59 Je
Strasswalchen, Austria 59 Hd
Stratford, Eire - - 27 Df
Stratford, England - 15 Dc
Stratford, Michigan - 122 Fc
Stratford, New Zealand 158 Dc
Stratford, Ontario - 123 Hd
Stratford, Texas - - 133 Ab
Stratford, Victoria - 155 Ee
Stratford-on-Avon, Eng. 14 Cb
Strathalbyn, S. Aust. - 154 Bd
Strathaven, Scotland - 21 Bb
Strathblane, Scotland - 23 De
Strathcona Park, Brit. Columbia - - 124 De
Strath Halladale, Scotland - - - 24 Ee
Strathleven, Queensland 153 Bc
Strathmiglo, Scotland - 23 Ed
Strathmore, Queensland 153 Bc
Strathmore, Scotland - 23 Ed
Strathpeffer, Scotland - 23 Da
Strathroy, Ontario - 123 Hd
Strath Spey, Scotland - 23 Eb
Stratoníki, Greece - 70 Ec
Stratton, England - 17 Bb
Straubing, Bavaria - 59 Gc
Strausberg, Prussia - 55 Je
Straža, Slovenia - - 63 Jb
Streaky B., S. Australia 151 Ee
Streatham, England - 15 Dd
Streatley, England - 15 Dc
Streator, Illinois - - 132 Ee
Street, England - - 14 Bd
Strehaia, Romania - 67 Je
Strehlen - - - 57 Cc
Strelna, Alaska - - 125 Lf
Strencis, Latvia - - 49 Cc
Strengen, Norway - 47 Ee
Stretton, England - 15 Da
Strib, Denmark - - 45 Cc
Striberg, Sweden - - 50 Dc
Strickland, Ontario - 122 Ha
Strickland R., New Guinea - - - 156 Cc
Striegau - - - 57 Bc
Strimón, G. of, Greece - 70 Ec
Strofádhes Is., Greece - 71 Bf
Strokestown, Eire - 26 Bd
Stromboli I., Italy - 65 Bd
Strome Ferry, Scotland 22 Cb
Stromness, Orkney Is. - 24 Ed
Strömö, Færoe Is. - 44 Nc
Stromstad, Sweden - 50 Ad
Stromsund, Sweden - 44 Dg
Stroms Vattudal, Sweden 44 Cf
Strong City, Kansas - 133 Da
Strongilí, Greece - - 71 Bd
Strongoli, Italy - - 65 Dc
Stronsay, I., Scotland - 24 Fc
Strópones, Greece - - 71 Ee
Stroud, England - - 14 Bc
Strouds, Oklahoma - 133 Dc
Stroudsburg, Pennsylva. 129 Gb
Struanmore, Scotland - 22 Bb
Struer, Denmark - - 45 Bb
Struma, R., Bulgaria - 70 Eb
Struma (Strimon), R., Greece - - - 70 Eb
Strumica, Serbia - - 70 Db
Strydenburg, Cape Prov. 114 Ed
Stryj - - - - 60 Gd
Stryków, Poland - - 57 Eb
Strymi, Greece - - 72 Cb
Stryn, Norway - - 46 Cc
Strzelno, Poland - - 57 Da
Strzyzów, Poland - - 60 Fd
Stuart, Florida - - 131 Nh
Stuart, Iowa - - 132 Be
Stuart, Montana - - 136 Gb
Stuart, Virginia - - 129 Dd
Stuart, Mt., Washington 136 Cb
Stuart Ra., S. Australia 151 Ed
Stuart's Creek, S. Aust. 154 Aa
Stubbeköbing, Denmark 45 Fd
Stuben, Austria - - 58 Ed
Stubica, Montenegro - 68 Dd
Studley, England - - 14 Cb
Studnitz - - - 56 Bb
Stuen, Norway - - 46 Fb
Stugsund, Sweden - 50 Ga
Stung-treng, Cambodia 95 Cg
Stura, R., Italy - - 62 Bb
Sturgeon L., Ontario - 122 Ca
Sturgeon R., Ontario - 123 Hb
Sturgeon Bay, Wisconsin 132 Fc
Sturgeon Falls, Ontario 123 Jb
Sturgis, Michigan - 122 Fe
Sturminster, England - 14 Be
Stutterheim, Cape Prov. 115 Gf
Stuttgart, Arkansas - 130 Cc
Stuttgart, Würtemberg - 58 Cc
Stuurman, Cape Prov. - 114 De
Stuyvesant, New York 128 Bb
Stykkisholmur, Iceland 52 Bb
Styr, R. - - - 60 Hc
Styria, prov., Austria - 59 Jd
Su, China - - - 94 Ec
Suâdi, Egypt - - 107 Hd
Suakin, A.-E. Sudan - 108 Cb
Sual, Philippines - - 95 Ef
Suala Selka, Finland - 48 Eb
Suanhwa, China - - 94 Ea
Suan-wei, China - - 94 Bd
Suaqui, Mexico - - 138 Cb
Suarez, R., Colombia - 144 Bb
Suaji, Mozambique - 115 Kb
Subangala, Tang. Terr. 111 Bf
Subcetate, Romania - 67 Jd
Subeimanieh, Persia - 79 Fb
Suberieville, Madagascar 112 Ec
Subiaco, Italy - - 64 Cb
Subic, Philippines - 95 Fg
Sublette, Kansas - - 133 Bb
Subotica, Voyvodina - 66 Ec
Suceava, Romania - 69 Gb
Sucha, Poland - - 57 Ed
Suchan, U.S.S.R. - 96 Ec
Suchilapan, Mexico - 139 Fd
Suchow, China - - 94 Ec
Su-chow, China - - 94 Ab
Suchowola, Poland - 56 Hc
Süchteln, Prussia - 54 Bd
Suck, R., Eire - - 27 Be
Suckling, Mt., New Guinea - - - 156 Dc
Sucre, Bolivia - - 146 Bb
Sucre, state, Venezuela 144 Da
Sućuraj, Dalmatia - 68 Cc
Sud, Terr. du, Algeria - 102 Ed
Suda (Soúdha) B., Crete 71 Hd
Sudak, Crimea - - 75 Fg
Sudbury, England - 15 Eb
Sudbury, Ontario - 123 Hb
Sudbury, Victoria - 154 De
Suddie, British Guiana 144 Eb
Suderburg, Prussia - 54 Fc
Sudeten Mts., Germany-Czech. - - - 60 Bc
Sudetenland, Czechoslovakia - - - 60 Bc
Sudharam, Bengal - 88 Cc
Sudhavik, Iceland - 52 Ba
Sudi, Tanganyika Terr. 111 Fj
Sudoměřice, Bohemia - 59 Jb
Sudzha, U.S.S.R. - 75 Fe
Sueca, Spain - - 41 Fa
Süe-pau-ting, mt., China 94 Bc
Suez and Canal, Egypt - 107 Jc
Suez, G. of, Egypt - 107 Jd
Suf, Trans-Jordan - 80 Dc
Suffolk, Virginia - - 129 Fd
Suffolk, co., England - 15 Eb
Sugana, R., Italy - - 63 Fa
Sugar I., Michigan - 122 Fb
Sugar City, Colorado - 135 Lb
Sugar Land, Texas - 133 Ef
Sugar Loaf Key, Florida 131 Nj
Sugarloaf Res., Victoria 155 Ed
Suggsville, Alabama - 130 Ee
Suhara, Japan - - 100 Fd
Suhl, Prussia - - 54 Fe
Sui, China - - - 94 Ec
Sui-fu, China - - 94 Bd
Suihwa, Manchuria - 96 Db
Sui-ki, China - - 95 De
Suileng, Manchuria - 96 Db
Sui-ping, China - - 94 Dc
Suir, R., Eire - - 27 Cg
Sui-teh, China - - 94 Cb
Sui-ting, China - - 94 Cc
Suitung, Manchuria - 96 Cc
Suiyuan, Manchuria - 96 Eb
Suiyuan, prov., China - 94 Ca
Sujangarh, Rajputana - 83 Fe
Sujanpur, Punjab - 83 Fb
Sujanpur, Punjab - 83 Gc
Sukan Hills, Kenya - 110 Eb
Sukegawa, Japan - 100 Hc
Suket, Punjab States - 83 Gc
Sukhinichi, U.S.S.R. - 75 Ee
Sukhona, R., U.S.S.R. 74 Gc
Sukhumi, Georgia - 75 Gg
Sukkertoppen, Greenland - - - 9 Dd
Sukkur, Sind - - 82 Ce
Sukošan, Dalmatia - 63 Kc
Sula, Montana - - 136 Gc
Sula I. and Fd., Norway 46 Cb
Sulaiman Ra., Baluchistan - - - 82 Cd
Sulaimaniya, Iraq - 78 Eb
Sulaimiya, Arabia - 79 Ee
Suldals Vatn, Norway - 47 Ce
Sulemanke, Punjab States 83 Ec
Sulet, I., Dalmatia - 68 Bc
Suliki, Sumatra - - 98 Bd
Sulima, Sierra Leone - 104 Be
Sulimov, U.S.S.R. - 75 Gg
Sulina, Romania - - 69 Hc
Sulingen, Prussia - 54 Dc
Sulitelma, mt., Norway-Sweden - - - 44 Df
Sullana, Peru - - 145 Ab
Sullivan, Illinois - - 132 Ef
Sullivan, Indiana - 129 Ac
Sullivan, Missouri - 130 Ca
Sulmona, Italy - - 64 Da
Sulphur, Oklahoma - 133 Dc
Sulphur Springs, Texas 133 Ed
Sultanabad, Hyderabad 90 Db
Sultan Bulak, Persia - 79 Eb
Sultan Hamud, Kenya 110 Ee
Sultaniyeh, Persia - 79 Eb
Sultanpur, Punjab States 83 Fc
Sultanpur, United Provs. 86 Db
Sulu Arch. and Sea, Philippines - - 99 Fb
Sulzbach, Bavaria - 59 Fb
Sulzbach, Saar Palatinate 58 Bb
Sulze, Mecklenburg - 55 Ha
Sulzer, Alaska - - 125 Oj
Sumatra, I., Nether. Indies 98 Ac
Sumbangala, Tang. Terr. 111 Bg
Sumbawanga, Tang. Trr. 111 Bg
Sumbu, N. Rhodesia - 109 Fc
Sumburgh Hd., Zetland 24 Gj
Sumdum, Alaska - 125 Oh
Sümeg, Hungary - - 66 Cc
Sumeriya, Es., Palestine 80 Cb
Sumesar Ra., Nepal - 87 Fb
Sumiswald, Switzerland 42 Eb
Summan, Arabia - - 79 Ed
Summer L., Oregon - 136 Cd
Summerside, Prince Edward I. - - 120 Dc
Summersville, W. Virginia - - - 129 Dc
Summerville, Georgia - 130 Fc
Summerville, S. Carolina 131 Jd
Summit, California - 134 Ed
Summit, Mississippi - 130 Ce
Summit, Nevada - - 134 Eb
Summit, S. Dakota - 132 Ac
Sumner, Iowa - - 132 Cd
Sumner, Washington - 136 Bb
Sumony, Hungary - 66 Cd
Sumperk, Moravia - 60 Dd
Sumpter, Oregon - - 136 Dc
Sumter, South Carolina 131 Hd
Sumterville, Florida - 131 Ng
Sumy, Ukraine - - 75 Ee
Sumya, Trans-Jordan - 80 Dc
Sun R., Montana - 136 Gb
Sunagawa, Japan - 97 Eb
Sunam, Punjab States - 83 Fc
Sunamganj, Assam - 88 Cb
Sunart, L., Scotland - 22 Cc
Sunbury, Pennsylvania 129 Fb
Suncho Corral, Argentina 146 Cd
Sün-chow, China - - 95 Ce
Suncook, New Hampshire 128 Cb
Sund, Norway - - 47 Bd
Sundarbans, Bengal - 88 Bd

Talbot, C., *W. Australia* 152 Da
Talbotton, *Georgia* - 131 Fd
Talca and prov., *Chile* - 148 Bb
Talcahuano, *Chile* - 148 Bb
Talcher, *Eastern States* - 87 Fe
Taldan, *U.S.S.R.* - 96 Ca
Taldora, *Queensland* - 153 Bc
Taleh Sap, *Siam* - 98 Bb
Talgarth, *Wales* - 20 Cd
Talghemt, *Morocco* - 102 Bc
Taliaboe, I., *Neth. Indies* 99 Fd
Ta-lien-wan, *Kwang-tung Terr.* - 97 Ac
Ta-li-fu, *China* - 94 Bd
Ta-ling-ho, R., *Manchuria* 96 Cc
Talisayan, *Philippines* - 99 Fb
Taliwang, *Soembawa I., Netherlands Indies* - 99 Ee
Talka, *Transylvania* - 67 Gc
Talkeetna & Mts., *Alaska* 125 Ke
Talki Mts., *Sinkiang* - 84 Eb
Talla, *Italy* - 63 Fd
Tallac, *California* - 134 Cb
Talladega, *Alabama* - 130 Fd
Tallahassee, *Florida* - 131 Fe
Tallahatchie R., *Miss.* - 130 Dc
Tallangatta, *Victoria* - 155 Ed
Tallapoosa, *Georgia* - 130 Fd
Tallapoosa R., *Alabama* 130 Fd
Tallard, *France* - 35 Jc
Tallassee, *Alabama* - 130 Ed
Tallinn, *Estonia* - 49 Cb
Tallow, *Eire* - 27 Cg
Tallulah Falls, *Georgia* - 131 Gc
Talmaciu, *Romania* - 67 Kd
Talmine, *Algeria* - 102 De
Talmont, *France* - 32 Dd
Talnoe, *Ukraine* - 75 Ef
Taloda, *Bombay* - 85 Ed
Talodi, *A.-E. Sudan* - 108 Bc
Taloe, *Sumatra* - 98 Ac
Taloek, *Sumatra* - 98 Bd
Taloga, *Oklahoma* - 133 Cb
Talpoş, *Transylvania* - 67 Gc
Talsarnau, *Wales* - 20 Bb
Talsi, *Latvia* - 49 Bc
Talsint, *Morocco* - 102 Cc
Talsona, *Alaska* - 125 Ke
Ta Luang, *Siam* - 95 Bf
Talvik, *Norway* - 48 Eb
Talybont, *Wales* - 20 Cd
Talzaza, *Morocco* - 102 Cd
Tamacha, *Cape Prov.* - 115 Gf
Tamale, *Gold Coast* - 104 De
Tamames, *Spain* - 37 Db
Tamana, I., *Gilbert Is.* - 157 Ed
Tamanar, *Morocco* - 103 Nj
Tamanthi, *Burma* - 88 Eb
Tamar, *Bihar* - 87 Fd
Tamar, R., *England* - 17 Bb
Tamar R., *Tasmania* - 155 Jg
Tamaris, *France* - 33 Ac
Tamarite de Litera, *Spain* 39 Fc
Tamási, *Hungary* - 66 Dc
Tamatave, *Madagascar* - 112 Ec
Tamaulipas, state, *Mexico* 139 Ec
Tamaya, *Chile* - 146 Ae
Tamazanchale, *Mexico* - 139 Ec
Tamba, *Belg. Congo* - 109 Bc
Tambacounda, *Fr. W. Afr.* 104 Bd
Tambara, *Mozambique* - 113 Fa
Tambelan & I., *Neth. Indies* 98 Cc
Tambilaban, *Sumatra* - 98 Bd
Tambo, *Queensland* - 153 Cd
Tambo de Mora, *Peru* - 145 Bd
Tambohorano, *Madagascar* 112 Dc
Tambora, Mt., *Soembawa I., Nether. Indies* - 99 Ee
Tamboril, *Brazil* - 143 Fc
Tambov, *U.S.S.R.* - 75 Ge
Tambre, R., *Spain* - 36 Bb
Tambura, *A.-E. Sudan* - 108 Ad
Tame, *Colombia* - 144 Bb
Tamel Aiken, *Argentina* 148 Bd
Tamera, *Tunisia* - 103 Ja
Tamerza, *Tunisia* - 103 Hb
Tamesi, R., *Mexico* - 139 Ec
Tamgak Mts., *Fr. W. Afr.* 105 Cb
Tamiahua & L. de, *Mexico* 139 Ec
Ta-ming, *China* - 94 Eb
Tamins, *Switzerland* - 43 Hc
Tâmîya, *Egypt* - 107 Hd
Tamlelt, Plaine de, *Morocco* 102 Cc
Tamluk, *Bengal* - 88 Ac
Tampa, *Florida* - 131 Mh
Tampa B., *Florida* - 131 Mh
Tampere, *Finland* - 48 Ef
Tampico, *Mexico* - 139 Ec
Tamra, *Palestine* - 80 Cb
Tamrihand, *Orissa* - 91 Fb
Tamsula, *Estonia* - 49 Cb
Tamuin, *Mexico* - 139 Ec
Tamworth, *England* - 14 Ca
Tamworth, *New S. Wales* 155 Gb
Tamworth, *Ontario* - 121 Bb
Tana Fd., *Norway* - 44 Ge
Tana, I., *New Hebrides* - 157 De
Tana, L., *Ethiopia* - 108 Cc
Tana, R., *Kenya* - 110 Fe
Tana, R., *Norway-Finl'd* 48 Gb
Tanabe, *Japan* - 97 Dd
Tanabu, *Japan* - 97 Eb
Tanaga I., *Aleutian Is.* - 125 Um
Tanagura, *Japan* - 100 Hc
Tanah Bala, *Neth. Indies* 98 Ad
Tanahgrogot, *Borneo* - 99 Ed
Tanah Jampea, *Netherlands Indies* - 99 Ee
Tanah Masa, *Neth. Indies* 98 Ad
Tanah Merah, *Malay States* 98 Bb
Tanahpoetih, *Sumatra* - 98 Bc
Tana Keke, I., *Netherlands Indies* - 99 Ee
Tanakpur, *United Provs.* 83 Jd
Tanana, *Alaska* - 125 Jd
Tanana R., *Alaska* - 125 Ld
Tanana Crossing, *Alaska* 125 Le
Ta-nan-hu, *China* - 94 Ec
Tanant, *Morocco* - 103 Oj
Tancanhuitz, *Mexico* - 139 Ec
Tan-chow, *China* - 95 Cf
Tancitaro, Pico de, *Mexico* 138 Dd
Tanda, *United Provs.* - 87 Eb
Tan Daği, *Turkey* - 72 Fb
Tanda Urmar, *Punjab* - 83 Fc
Tandawanna, *Queensland* 153 Ce
Tandi, *Punjab* - 83 Gb
Tandil & Sa. de, *Argent.* 148 Eb
Tandjoeng, *Borneo* - 99 Ed
Tandjoeng Balai, *Sumatra* 98 Ac
Tandjoeng Pandan, *Billiton I., Nether. Indies* - 98 Cd
Tandjoengpinang, *Bintan I., Nether. Indies* - 98 Bc
Tandjoeng Pura, *Sumatra* 98 Ac
Tandjoengrebed, *Borneo* 99 Ec
Tandjoengselor, *Borneo* - 99 Ec
Tando Adam, *Sind* - 85 Bb
Tando Bago, *Sind* - 85 Bb
Tando Muhammad Khan, *Sind* - 85 Bb
Tandou L., *New S. Wales* 154 Cc
Tandur, *Hyderabad* - 90 Db
Tandur, *Hyderabad* - 90 Cc
Tanduri, *Baluchistan* - 82 Cd
Taneatua, *New Zealand* - 158 Fc
Tanegashima, *Japan* - 97 Cd
Tanemai, *Japan* - 97 Fb
Tang, *China* - 94 Dc
Tanga, *Tanganyika Terr.* 111 Ff
Tanga Is., *Pacific Oc.* - 156 Fe
Tangail, *Bengal* - 88 Cb
Tanganyika, L., *Cent. Afr.* 111 Af
Tanganyika Terr., *E. Afr.* 101 Ff
Tangar, *China* - 94 Bb
Tangarong, *Borneo* - 99 Ed
Tangen, *Norway* - 46 Hd
Tangermünde, *Prussia* - 55 Gc
Tang-ho, *Laos* - 95 Be
Tangi, *Bengal* - 88 Cc
Tangier (International Zone), *N.-W. Africa* - 102 Ab
Tangla, *Assam* - 88 Ca
Tangla Ra., *Tibet* - 81 Gd
Tangorin, *Queensland* - 153 Bd
Tangyuan, *Manchuria* - 96 Db
Tanimber Is., *Neth. Indies* 149 Df
Ta-ning, *China* - 94 Cc
Tanit B., *Fr. W. Africa* - 104 Ac
Tanje, L., *Mozambique* - 113 Ga
Tanjong Peninjut, *Malay States* - 98 Bc
Tank, *N.-W.F.P.* - 82 Db
Tankse, *Kashmir* - 83 Ha
Tanlay, *France* - 31 Gd
Tannay, *France* - 31 Fd
Tanne, *Brunswick* - 54 Fd
Tannen Geb., *Austria* - 59 Hd
Tannenburg, - 56 Ec
Tannu-Ola, mts., *Mongolia* 93 Ba
Tannu-Tuva, rep., *Asia* - 93 Ba
Tanouchert, *Fr. W. Africa* 104 Bb
Tanout, *Fr. W. Africa* - 105 Cb
Tanque, *Arizona* - 135 Je
Tansui, *Taiwan* - 97 He
Tanta, *Egypt* - 107 Hc
Tantabin, *Burma* - 92 Ba
Tântăreni, *Romania* - 67 Je
Tantpur, *United Provs.* - 83 Ge
Tantura, *Palestine* - 80 Bb
Tanuf, *Oman* - 79 Ge
Tanum, *Sweden* - 50 Ad
Tanunda, *S. Australia* - 154 Bc
Tanyo, *Korea* - 97 Bc
Tao & R., *China* - 94 Bc
Taodeni, *Fr. W. Africa* - 104 Db
Taofuhs, *China* - 94 Bc
Tao-kow, *China* - 94 Db
Tao-lai-chao, *Manchuria* 96 Dc
Taolin, *China* - 94 Da
Taonan, *Manchuria* - 96 Cb
Taongi Is., *Marshall Is.* - 157 Eb
Tao-ping, *China* - 95 Ee
Taormina, *Sicily* - 65 Jg
Taos, *New Mexico* - 135 Lc
Taounot, *Morocco* - 102 Bb
Taourirt, *Algeria* - 102 Df
Taourirt, *Morocco* - 103 Oj
Taouz, *Morocco* - 102 Bd
Tapa, *Estonia* - 49 Cb
Tapachula, *Mexico* - 139 Fe
Tapah, *Malay States* - 98 Bc
Tapajoz, R., *Brazil* - 142 Cc
Tapaktoean, *Sumatra* - 98 Ac
Tapalque, *Argentina* - 148 Db
Tapan, *Sumatra* - 98 Bd
Tapanahuni, R., *Suriname* 142 Cb
Tapanui, *New Zealand* - 159 Bf
Taparapeco, Sa., *Venez.* 144 Cc
Ta-pa-shan, *China* - 94 Cc
Tapat, I., *Nether. Indies* - 99 Gd
Tapauá, *Brazil* - 142 Bd
Tapaw, *Burma* - 92 Ff
Tapera do Retiro, *Brazil* 142 Bd
Tapingshao, *Manchuria* - 96 Cc
Tápiószele, *Hungary* - 66 Eb
Tapolca, *Hungary* - 66 Cc
Tappahannock, *Virginia* 129 Fd
Tapti R., *Bombay, etc.* - 85 Dd
Taptugara, *U.S.S.R.* - 96 Ca
Ta-pu, *China* - 95 Ee
Tapuku, *Manchuria* - 96 Ca
Tapul Is., *Philippines* - 99 Fb
Taqali, *A.-E. Sudan* - 108 Bc
Taquanalsinho, *Brazil* - 142 Cd
Taquara, *Brazil* - 147 Ed
Taquaretinga, *Brazil* - 143 Gd
Tar R., *N. Carolina* - 131 Jb
Tara, *Eire* - 27 Dd
Tara, *U.S.S.R.* - 76 Hd
Tara, R., *Montenegro* - 68 Ed
Taraclia, - 69 Hc
Taradale, *New Zealand* - 158 Fc
Tarago, *New S. Wales* - 155 Fd
Tarahumare, Sierra, *Mexico* - 138 Cb
Tarakan, I., *Nether. Indies* 99 Ec
Tarakki, *Afghanistan* - 82 Bb
Tarakli, *Turkey* - 78 Ba
Taraku, I., *Japan* - 97 Fb
Tarana, *New S. Wales* - 155 Fc
Taranaki, prov., *New Zeal.* 158 Ec
Taranaki Bight, N. and S., *New Zealand* - 158 Dc
Tarancón, *Spain* - 38 Ce
Taransay, I., *Scotland* - 22 Aa
Taranto & Gulf of, *Italy* 65 Db
Tarapaca, prov., *Chile* - 146 Bb
Tarapoto, *Peru* - 145 Bc
Taraqua, *Brazil* - 145 Db
Tarare, *France* - 35 Gb
Tararua Ra., *New Zealand* 159 Ed
Tarascon, *Ariège, France* 34 De
Tarascon, *Bouches-du-Rhône, France* - 35 Gd
Tarash, *Kenya* - 110 Db
Tarata, *Peru* - 145 Ce
Tarauaca, R., *Brazil* - 145 Dc
Tarawa, *New Britain* - 156 Dc
Tarawa, I., *Gilbert Is.* - 157 Ec
Tarawera, *New Zealand* - 158 Fc
Tarazona, *Salamanca, Spain* 36 Ec
Tarazona, *Zaragoza, Spain* 38 Dc
Tarbagatai Mts., *Kazak* - 76 Je
Tarbat Ness, *Scotland* - 23 Ea
Tarbert, *Eire* - 25 Bd
Tarbert, *Harris, Scot.* - 22 Ba
Tarbert & L., *Argyll, Scotland* - 22 Ce
Tarbert, L., *Jura, Scotland* 22 Be
Tarbert L., E. and W., *Harris, Scotland* - 22 Ba
Tarbes, *France* - 34 Cd
Tarboro, *N. Carolina* - 131 Kc
Tarcento, *Italy* - 63 Ha
Tarcoola, *S. Australia* - 151 Ee
Tarcutta, *New S. Wales* 155 Fd
Tardajos, *Spain* - 38 Bb
Tardienta, *Spain* - 39 Ec
Taree, *New S. Wales* - 155 Gb
Taref Mts., *Egypt* - 107 Fc
Tärendö, *Sweden* - 48 Dc
Tarentais, *France* - 35 Jb
Tarentum, *Pennsylvania* - 129 Db
Târgovişte, *Romania* - 69 Fc
Targu Frumos, *Romania* 69 Gb
Targuist, *Span. Morocco* - 102 Bb
Targu-Jiu, *Romania* - 67 Jd
Târgul Săcuilor, *Transylvania* - 69 Gb
Târgu Mures, *Transylva.* 67 Kc
Târgu-Ocna, *Romania* - 69 Gb
Tarhit, *Algeria* - 102 Cd
Tarhuna & Jeb., *Libya* - 106 Ok
Tarifa, *Spain* - 40 Ec
Tarija and dep., *Bolivia* 146 Cc
Tarikere, *Mysore* - 90 Be
Tarim R., *Sinkiang* - 84 Eb
Tarkastad, *Cape Prov.* - 115 Gf
Tarkwa, *Gold Coast* - 104 De
Tarlac, *Philippines* - 95 Ff
Tarm, *Denmark* - 45 Bc
Tarma, *Peru* - 145 Bd
Tarn, R. & dep., *France* 34 Ed
Tärna, *Sweden* - 50 Fc
Tarnava Mare, *Romania* 67 Kc
Tarnava Mica, *Transylva.* 67 Kc
Tarn-et-Garonne, dep., *France* - 34 Dc
Tarnopol(Ternopol), *Ukraine* 60 Hd
Tarnów, *Poland* - 60 Fc
Tarnowskie Góry, *Poland* 57 Dc
Tarn Taran, *Punjab* - 83 Fc
Taro, R., *Italy* - 62 Dc
Taroetoeng, *Sumatra* - 98 Ac
Taroka, *Kenya* - 110 Ed
Taroom, *Queensland* - 153 Ce
Taroubdit, *Morocco* - 102 Bc
Taroudant, *Morocco* - 103 Nj
Tarpa, *Hungary* - 67 Ha
Tarpon Springs, *Florida* 131 Mg
Tarporley, *England* - 18 Bd
Tarquinia, *Italy* - 64 Ba
Tarragona & prov., *Spain* 39 Gc
Tarrasa, *Spain* - 39 Gc
Tarrega, *Spain* - 39 Gc
Tarrytown, *New York* - 128 Bc
Tarshi Pass, *Manchuria* - 96 Cb
Tarshiha, *Palestine* - 80 Ca
Tarsus, *Turkey* - 78 Bb
Tartagal, *Argentina* - 146 Cc
Tartaro, R., *Italy* - 62 Eb
Tartas, *France* - 34 Bd
Tartna Point, *N. S. Wales* 154 Dc
Tartola, *Finland* - 48 Fc
Tartu, *Estonia* - 49 Db
Tarum, *Persia* - 79 Gd
Tarutino, - 69 Hb
Tarves, *Scotland* - 23 Fb
Tăşad, *Transylvania* - 67 Hc
Taschereau, *Quebec* - 123 Ja
Tascosa, *Texas* - 133 Ac
Ta-shang (Gt. Sandbank), *China* - 94 Fc
Tashang tsi Dzong, *Bhutan* 88 Ca
Ta-shi-kiao, *Manchuria* - 96 Cc
Tashiro, *Japan* - 100 Gc
Ta-shi-shan, *China* - 94 Bc
Tashkent, *Uzbek* - 84 Bb
Tashkurghan, *Afghanistan* 84 Bc
Tashkurghan, *Sinkiang* - 84 Dc
Tashmalik, *Sinkiang* - 84 Dc
Tåsjö, *Sweden* - 48 Ad
Tasköprü, *Turkey* - 78 Ba
Tasman B. and Mts., *New Zealand* - 159 Dd
Tasman Mt., *New Zealand* 159 Ce
Tasman Pen., *Tasmania* 155 Kh
Tasman Sea, *Australasia* 149 Fj
Tasmania I. & state, *Aust.* 151 Hg
Tasnad, *Transylvania* - 67 Hb
Tasov, *U.S.S.R.* - 96 Fb
Tasserat, *Fr. W. Africa* 104 Bb
Tasurchai Mts., *China* - 94 Bc
Tata, *Hungary* - 66 Db
Tatakoto, I., *Tuamotu Ar.* 157 Ke
Tatar, *U.S.S.R.* - 74 Jd
Tatar Bunar, - 69 Hc
Tatarlar, *Turkey* - 72 Da
Tatarsk Str., *U.S.S.R.* - 93 Gb
Tatau, *Sarawak* - 99 Dc
Tate, *Georgia* - 131 Fc
Tathlina, *N.-W. Terr.* - 124 Fb
Ta-ting, *China* - 94 Cd
Ta-ting, *China* - 94 Da
Tatitlek, *Alaska* - 125 Kf
Tatlock, *Ontario* - 121 Bb
Tatnam C., *Manitoba* - 124 Lc
Tatong, *Victoria* - 155 Ed
Tatra, mts., *Czech.-Poland* 60 Ed
Tatta, *Morocco* - 103 Ok
Tatta, *Sind* - 85 Ab
Tattershall, *England* - 19 Dd
Tatuhy, *Brazil* - 147 Fc
Ta-tung, *China* - 94 Bb
Ta-tung, *Sinkiang* - 84 Fb
Ta-tung-kow, *Manchuria* 96 Cd
Tau Passage, *Siam* - 98 Bb
Tauapeçaçú, *Brazil* - 142 Bc
Tauarga, *Libya* - 106 Pk
Taueil, *Fr. W. Africa* - 104 Ac
Taufikia, *A.-E. Sudan* - 108 Bd
Taufkirchen, *Bavaria* - 59 Gc
Tauha, *Brazil* - 143 Fd
Taujénai, *Lithuania* - 49 Cd
Taumarunui, *New Zeal'd* 158 Ec
Taungdwingyi, *Burma* - 92 Bb
Taung-gyi, *Burma* - 92 Cb
Taung-myo Ra., *Burma* 92 Cd
Taungnyo, *Burma* - 92 Bc
Taungs, *Cape Prov.* - 115 Fc
Taungtha, *Burma* - 92 Bb
Taungup, *Burma* - 92 Bc
Taunsa, *Punjab* - 82 Dc
Taunton, *England* - 14 Ad
Taunton, *Massachusetts* - 128 Cc
Taunus, mts., *Prussia* - 58 Ca
Taupo, L., *New Zealand* 158 Fc
Taurage, *Lithuania* - 49 Bd
Tauranga and Harb., *New Zealand* - 158 Fb
Taurate, *Brazil* - 147 Fc
Taureau Res., *Quebec* - 121 Da
Taurus, Mts., *Turkey* - 78 Bb
Tauste, *Spain* - 38 Dc
Tauti, *Romania* - 67 Gc
Tauves, *France* - 34 Eb
Tavannes, *Switzerland* - 42 Db
Tavares, *Florida* - 131 Ng
Taverne, *Switzerland* - 43 Gd
Taveta, *Kenya* - 110 Ee
Tavira, *Portugal* - 40 Cb
Tavistock, *England* - 17 Bb
Tavolara, I., *Sardinia* - 64 Jf
Tavoy, *Burma* - 81 Hh
Tavsanli, *Turkey* - 78 Ab
Taw, R., *England* - 17 Ba
Tawa, *Burma* - 92 Cd
Tawa, *Tang. Terr.* - 111 Fh
Tawang, *Assam* - 88 Ca
Tawao, *N. Borneo* - 99 Ec
Tawas City, *Michigan* - 122 Gc
Tawe, R., *Wales* - 20 Cd
Taweisha, *A.-E. Sudan* - 108 Ac
Tawila I., *Egypt* - 107 Je
Tawi Tawi I. and Group, *Philippines* - 99 Fb
Tawmaw, *Burma* - 88 Fb
Tawng Peng, *Burma* - 92 Ca
Tawutsingtze, *Manchuria* 96 Db
Taxco, *Mexico* - 139 Ed
Tay, Firth of, *Scotland* - 23 Ed
Tay, L., *Scotland* - 23 Dc
Tay, R., *Scotland* - 23 Ed
Tayabas, *Philippines* - 95 Fg
Tayan, *Borneo* - 98 Dc
Tayeh, *China* - 94 Dc
Tayfur, *Turkey* - 72 Db
Taylor, *Arizona* - 135 Hd
Taylor, *Texas* - 133 De
Taylor Hd., *Nova Scotia* 120 Dd
Taylor Mt, *New Mexico* 135 Kd
Taylors Falls, *Minnesota* 132 Cc
Taylorsville, *Alabama* - 130 Ec
Taylorsville, *N. Carolina* 131 Hc
Taylorville, *Illinois* - 132 Ef
Tayport, *Scotland* - 23 Fd
Taytay, *Philippines* - 99 Ea
Taza, *Morocco* - 102 Bb
Tazewell, *Virginia* - 129 Dd
Tazoult, *Morocco* - 103 Oj
Tazzarine, *Morocco* - 102 Bd
Tazzouguert, *Morocco* - 102 Cc
Tbilisi, *Georgia* - 75 Gg
Tchaguen, *Fr. Eq. Africa* 105 Ec
Tchang, *Fr. Eq. Africa* - 105 Dd
Tchula, *Mississippi* - 130 Cd
Tczew, *Poland* - 60 Ea
Teaca, *Transylvania* - 67 Kc
Team Valley, *England* - 21 Ed
Te Anau, L., *N. Zealand* 159 Af
Teano, *Italy* - 64 Eb
Teapa, *Mexico* - 139 Fd
Te Aroha, *New Zealand* - 158 Eb
Te Awamutu, *New Zealand* 158 Eb
Teb, *A.-E. Sudan* - 108 Cb
Teba, *Spain* - 40 Fc
Tebang Mt., *Sarawak* - 99 Dc
Tebay, *England* - 18 Bb
Tébessa & Mts. de, *Algeria* 103 Hb
Tebingtinggi, *Palembang, Sumatra* - 98 Bd
Tebingtinggi, *Sumatra* - 98 Ac
Tebingtinggi, I., *Netherlands Indies* - 98 Bc
Tebourba, *Tunisia* - 103 Ja
Teboursouk, *Tunisia* - 103 Ja
Tecamachalco, *Mexico* - 139 Ed
Te-chow, *China* - 94 Eb
Tecka, *Argentina* - 148 Bc

Tifton, *Georgia* - - 131 Ge
Tiganca - - - 69 Hb
Tigara, *Alaska* - - 125 Eb
Tigda, *U.S.S.R.* - - 96 Da
Tiger Berg, *Cape Prov.* - 115 Ff
Tiger I., *Annam* - - 95 Cf
Tiger Is., *Nether. Indies* 99 Fe
Tiger's Tooth, mt., *Annam* 95 Cf
Tighanimine, *Algeria* - 103 Hb
Tighina Gainari - - 69 Hb
Tighnabruaich, *Scotland* 22 Ce
Tigiria, *Eastern States* - 87 Fe
Tignish, *Pr. Edward I.* - 120 Dc
Tigris, R., *Iraq* - - 79 Ec
Tigyaing, *Burma* - - 92 Ca
Tih, Des. & Jeb el, *Egypt* 107 Kd
Tihuta, *Transylvania* - 67 Kb
Tijesno, *Dalmatia* - - 63 Kd
Tikamgarh (Tehri), *Central India* - - 86 Cc
Tikhoretsk, *U.S.S.R.* - 75 Ff
Tikhtozersk, *U.S.S.R.* - 48 Hd
Tikhvin, *U.S.S.R.* - - 74 Ed
Tikkenlik, *Sinkiang* - 84 Fb
Tikopia, I., *Pacific Oc.* - 157 De
Tikrit, *Iraq* - - - 78 Dc
Tikse, *Kashmir* - - 83 Ga
Tiksi, *U.S.S.R.* - - 76 Nb
Tikura, *Idaho* - - 136 Gd
Tilamoela, *Celébès* - - 99 Fc
Tilburg, *Holland* - - 29 Cc
Tilbury, *England* - - 15 Ed
Tilcara, *Argentina* - - 146 Bc
Tilgremt, *Algeria* - - 103 Fc
Tflissos, *Crete* - - 71 Jj
Tillabery, *Fr. W. Africa* 105 Bc
Tillamook & B., *Oregon* - 136 Ac
Tillamook Hd., *Oregon* - 136 Ac
Tillberga, *Sweden* - - 50 Fc
Tillingham, *England* - 15 Ec
Tillsonburg, *Ontario* - 123 Hd
Tilmas Ferkla, *Algeria* - 102 Fe
Tilpa, *New S. Wales* - 154 Db
Tilsit - - - - 56 Fa
Tilton, *New Hampshire* - 128 Cb
Tim, *U.S.S.R.* - - 75 Fe
Tima, *Egypt* - - - 107 He
Timagami L., *Ontario* - 123 Jb
Timahoe, *Eire* - - 27 Cf
Timanski Mts., *U.S.S.R.* 74 Hb
Timar, *Montenegro* - - 68 Ed
Timaru, *New Zealand* - 159 Cf
Timbakion, *Crete* - - 71 Hj
Timbalier B., *Louisiana* - 130 Cf
Timbédra, *Fr. W. Africa* 104 Cc
Timbo, *Fr. W. Africa* - 104 Bd
Timboon, *Victoria* - - 154 De
Timboroa, *Kenya* - - 110 Dc
Timbue, I., *Mozambique* 113 Gb
Timbu Mata, *E. Indies* - 99 Ec
Timelloughit, *Morocco* - 103 Oj
Timerein, *A.-E. Sudan* - 108 Cb
Timesgadioume, *Morocco* 103 Nj
Timfristós, mt., *Greece* - 71 Ce
Timhadit, *Morocco* - - 102 Bc
Timidert, *Morocco* - - 103 Oj
Timimoun & Sebkra de, *Algeria* - - - 102 Ee
Timis, *Romania* - - 67 Gd
Timiskaming and co., *Quebec* - - - 121 Aa
Timiskaming L., *Quebec-Ontario* - - - 123 Jb
Timişoara, *Romania* - 67 Gd
Timişul, R., *Romania* - 67 Hd
Timkerdat, *Rio de Oro* - 104 Bb
Tlmmins, *Ontario* - - 123 Ha
Timmoudi, *Algeria* - - 102 De
Timor I., *E. Indies* - - 99 Ge
Timor Sea, *Australasia* - 149 Cg
Timoshevsk, *U.S.S.R.* - 75 Ff
Timote, *Argentina* - - 148 Db
Timpahute Ra., *Nevada* 134 Fc
Timpas, *Colorado* - - 135 Mc
Timperley Ra., *W. Aust.* 152 Cd
Timpson, *Texas* - - 133 Ee
Timuria, *Nepal* - - 87 Fa
Tinahely, *Eire* - - 27 Df
Tin Assaguid, *Fr. W. Afr.* 105 Bb
Tinca, *Transylvania* - 67 Gc
Tindivanam, *Madras* - 89 Ca
Tindouf, *Algeria* - - 104 Ca
Tineo, *Spain* - - - 36 Da
Ting, *China* - - - 94 Db
Tinga Maria, *Peru* - - 145 Bc
Ting-an, *China* - - 95 Df
Tinga-tingana, *S. Aust.* - 154 Ca
Ting-chow, *China* - - 94 Ed
Ting-hai, *China* - - 94 Fc
Tinghir, *Morocco* - - 102 Bd
Tinglev, *Denmark* - - 45 Cd
Ting-nan, *China* - - 95 De
Tingsryd, *Sweden* - - 51 Ef
Tingstäde, *Sweden* - - 51 He
Tinguere, *Fr. Eq. Africa* 105 Dd
Tingvoll & Fjord, *Norway* 46 Eb
Ting-yüen, *China* - - 95 De
Ting-yuen, *China* - - 94 Ec
Tinhare, I., *Brazil* - 143 Ce
Tinian, I., *Marianas Is.* - 157 Bb
Tinn, *Norway* - - 47 Ed
Tinn Sjo, *Norway* - - 47 Ee
Tinnevelly, *Madras* - 89 Bc
Tinnoset, *Norway* - - 47 Fe
Tinoasa, *Transylvania* - 67 Kc
Tinogasta, *Argentina* - 146 Bd
Tinombo, *Celébes* - - 99 Fc
Tinos, I., *Greece* - - 61 Kf
Tin-pak, *China* - - 95 De
Tinsukia, *Assam* - - 88 Ea
Tintagel, *England* - - 17 Bb
Tinteniac, *France* - - 32 Db
Tintern, *England* - - 14 Bc
Tintern Abbey, *Eire* - 27 Dg
Tintic, *Utah* - - 135 Gb
Tintina, *Argentina* - - 146 Cd
Tintinara, *S. Australia* - 154 Cd
Tinto, *Nigeria* - - 105 Cd
Tinto Hill, *Scotland* - 21 Cb
Tinto, I., *Korea* - - 97 Bd
Tinto, R., *Spain* - - 40 Db
Tinwald, *New Zealand* - 159 Ce
Tin Zaouatene, *Fr. W. Africa* - - - 105 Bb
Tioro, *Fr. Eq. Africa* - 105 Ea
Tiout, *Algeria* - - 102 Dc
Tipasa, *Algeria* - - 102 Fa
Tiporo, *Celébes* - - 99 Ed
Tippera, *Bengal* - - 88 Cc
Tipperary and co., *Eire* - 27 Bg
Tipton, *England* - - 14 Ba
Tipton, *Indiana* - - 129 Ab
Tipton, *Iowa* - - 132 De
Tipton, *Missouri* - - 130 Ba
Tipton, *New Mexico* - 135 Ld
Tipton, *Oregon* - - 136 Dc
Tipton, *Wyoming* - - 135 Ja
Tipton, Mt., *Arizona* - 134 Fd
Tiptree, *England* - - 15 Ec
Tiracumba, Sa. de, *Brazil* 143 Ec
Tiran, I., *Arabia* - - 78 Bd
Tirana (Tirane), *Albania* 70 Ab
Tirangole, *A.-E. Sudan* - 108 Be
Tirano, *Italy* - - - 62 Ea
Tiraspol, *Moldavia* - - 75 Df
Tiraz Mts., *S.-W. Africa* 114 Bb
Tire, *Turkey* - - - 78 Ab
Tireboli, *Turkey* - - 78 Ca
Tiree, I., *Scotland* - - 22 Bc
Tires, *Italy* - - - 63 Fa
Tiri, *Kashmir* - - 83 Hb
Tirilye, *Turkey* - - 72 Fb
Tirlemont, *Belgium* - 29 Cd
Tirma, *U.S.S.R.* - - 96 Ea
Tírnavos, *Greece* - - 70 Dd
Tirol, div., *Austria* - 58 Fd
Tirós, *Greece* - - 71 Df
Tirso, R., *Sardinia* - 64 Hg
Tiruchendur, *Madras* - 89 Cc
Tiruchengodu, *Madras* - 89 Bb
Tirukkoyilur, *Madras* - 89 Ca
Tirumangalam, *Madras* - 89 Bc
Tirupati, *Madras* - - 90 De
Tiruvallur, *Madras* - 90 De
Tiruvannamalai, *Madras* 89 Ca
Tisa, R., *Voyvodina* - 66 Fd
Tisbury, *England* - - 14 Bd
Tishomingo, *Oklahoma* - 133 Dc
Tista R., *Bengal* - - 88 Ba
Tisted & B., *Denmark* - 45 Bb
Tistutin, *Span. Morocco* - 102 Cb
Tisza (Tisa), R., *Hungary* 66 Fb
Tiszafoldvár, *Hungary* - 66 Fc
Tiszafured, *Hungary* - 67 Fb
Tiszalok, *Hungary* - - 67 Ga
Tit, *Algeria* - - - 102 Ef
Titabar, *Assam* - - 88 Ea
Titaf, *Algeria* - - 102 Df
Titalyah, *Bengal* - - 88 Ba
Ti-tao, *China* - - 94 Bb
Titicaca, L., *Bolivia-Peru* 145 De
Titonka, *Iowa* - - 132 Bd
Titule, *Belg. Congo* - 109 Ea
Titusville, *Florida* - - 131 Ng
Titusville, *Pennsylvania* - 129 Eb
Tivane, *Mozambique* - 113 Dd
Tivaouane, *Fr. W. Africa* 104 Ac
Tiveden, *Sweden* - - 50 Dd
Tiverton, *England* - - 14 Ae
Tivoli, *Italy* - - - 64 Cb
Tiwi, *Oman* - - - 79 Ge
Tixcocob, *Mexico* - - 139 Gc
Tixla, *Mexico* - - 139 Ed
Tizi, *Algeria* - - - 102 Eb
Tizimin, *Mexico* - - 139 Gc
Tizi Ouzou, *Algeria* - 103 Ga
Tiznit, *Morocco* - - 103 Nk
Tjareme, mt., *Java* - 98 Ce
Tjiamis, *Java* - - 98 Ce
Tjibuli Hill, *S. Rhodesia* 113 Cb
Tjilatjap, *Java* - - 98 Ce
Tjöme, *Norway* - - 47 Ge
Tjörn, *Sweden* - - 51 Ae
Tkearcheli, *Georgia* - 75 Gg
Tlacotalpan, *Mexico* - 139 Ed
Tlaltenango, *Mexico* - 138 Dc
Tlapa, *Mexico* - - 139 Ed
Tlaring, *Bechuanaland* - 115 Ec
Tlaxcala, *Mexico* - - 139 Ed
Tlaxiaco, *Mexico* - - 139 Ed
Tlemcen & Monts de, *Algeria* - - - 102 Db
Tleta de Sidi Embarek, El, *Morocco* - - 103 Nh
Tłumacz - - - - 60 Hd
Tmimi, *Libya* - - 106 Db
Toa, *Belgian Congo* - 109 Ec
Toand Ra., *Nevada* - 134 Fa
Toay, *Argentina* - - 148 Db
Toba L., *Sumatra.* - - 98 Ac
Toba and Kakar Ra., *Baluchistan* - - 82 Bc
Tobacco R., *Montana* - 136 Fa
Tobago, I., *Windward Is.* 140 Kh
Tobalai, I., *Nether. Indies* 99 Gd
Tobantirenda, *Argentina* 146 Cc
Tobarra, *Spain* - - 41 Eb
Tobelo, *Halmahera, N.I.* 99 Gc
Tobercurry, *Eire* - - 26 Bc
Tobermore, *N. Ireland* - 26 Db
Tobermory, *Scotland* - 22 Bc
Tobo, *Japan* - - 100 Ab
Toboli, *Celébes* - - 99 Fd
Tobolsk, *U.S.S.R.* - 76 Gd
Tobruk, *Libya* - - 106 Db
Tocantins, R., *Brazil* - 143 Ec
Tocaya, *Brazil* - - 142 Ac
Toccoa, *Georgia* - - 131 Gc
Tochigi, *Japan* - - 97 Dc
Toco, *Chile* - - - 146 Bc
Toco, *Florida* - - 131 Hf
Tocopilla, *Chile* - - 146 Ac
Tocqueville, *Algeria* - 103 Gb
Tocra, *Libya* - - 106 Cb
Tocumwal, *New S. Wales* 155 Ed
Tocuyo, *Venezuela* - - 144 Bb
Tôd, *Egypt* - - - 107 Jf
Todal, *Norway* - - 46 Eb
Todd Ra., *W. Australia* 152 Dd
Todenyang, *Kenya* - - 110 Da
Todgarh, *Ajmer-Merwara* 85 Eb
Todi, *Italy* - - - 63 Ge
Todjo, *Celébes* - - 99 Fd
Todmorden, *England* - 18 Bc
Todos os Santos, B. de, *Brazil* - - - 143 Ge
Todos Santos, *Mexico* - 138 Bc
Todos Santos, B., *Mexico* 138 Aa
Todtnau, *Baden* - - 58 Cd
Toeban, *Java* - - 98 De
Toekang Besi Is., *Netherlands Indies* - - 99 Fd
Toeslaan, *Cape Prov.* - 114 Dd
Tofo, *Chile* - - - 146 Ad
Tofty, *Alaska* - - 125 Jd
Tofua, I., *Tonga Is.* - 157 Fe
Toge, *Japan* - - - 100 Ed
Toggenburg, *Switzerland* 43 Hb
Togi, *Japan* - - - 100 Fc
Togian Is., *Nether. Indies* 99 Fd
Togo & terr., *Fr. W. Afr.* 105 Bd
Tohakopa, *New Zealand* 159 Bg
Tohana, *Punjab* - - 83 Fd
Tohatchi, *New Mexico* - 135 Jd
Tohil, *Fr. Eq. Africa* - 105 Eb
Tohmajärvi, *Finland* - 48 Je
Toijala, *Finland* - - 48 Ef
Toima, *U.S.S.R.* - - 74 Hc
Toinya, *A.-E. Sudan* - 108 Ad
Toiyabe Ra., *Nevada* - 134 Eb
Tokachi, *Japan* - - 97 Eb
Tokaj, *Hungary* - - 67 Ga
Tokala, Mt., *Celébes* - 99 Fd
Tokamachi, *Japan* - - 100 Gc
Tokanui, *New Zealand* - 159 Bg
Tokar, *A.-E. Sudan* - 108 Cb
Tokara Gunto, *Japan* - 93 Fd
Tokat, *Turkey* - - 78 Ca
Tokeen, *Alaska* - - 125 Oh
Tokelau Is., *Pacific Oc.* - 157 Fd
Tokmak, *Kirghiz* - - 84 Cb
Tokomaru, *New Zealand* 158 Gc
Tokoto, *China* - - 94 Da
Toksun, *Sinkiang* - - 84 Fb
Tokusa, *Japan* - - 100 Ba
Tokushima, *Japan* - - 97 Cd
Tokuyama, *Japan* - - 100 Ba
Tokyo and B., *Japan* - 97 Dc
Toledo, *Chile* - - 146 Ad
Toledo, *Iowa* - - - 132 Ce
Toledo, *Ohio* - - - 129 Bb
Toledo, *Oregon* - - 136 Bc
Toledo and prov., *Spain* 38 Ae
Toledo, Mtes. de, *Spain* - 38 Ae
Tolentino, *Italy* - - 63 Hd
Tolfa, *Italy* - - - 64 Ba
Tolga, *Algeria* - - 103 Gb
Tolga, *Norway* - - 46 Gb
Tolima, dep. and vol., *Colombia* - - - 144 Ac
Tolleshunt D'Arcy, *Eng.* 15 Ec
Tollo, *Italy* - - - 64 Ea
Töllöse, *Denmark* - - 45 Ec
Tolmeta, *Libya* - - 106 Cb
Tolmezzo, *Italy* - - 63 Ha
Tolmino - - - - 63 Ha
Tolna, *Hungary* - - 66 Dc
Tolo, *Belg. Congo* - - 109 Cb
Tolo (Tomaiki), Gulf, *Celébes* - - - 99 Fd
Tolong & B., *Philippines* 99 Fb
Tolós, *Greece* - - - 71 Df
Tolosa, *Spain* - - 38 Ca
Tolovana, *Alaska* - - 125 Kd
Toltec, *New Mexico* - 135 Kc
Toluca, *Illinois* - - 132 Ee
Toluca, *Mexico* - - 139 Ed
Toluca, Nevada de, *Mexico* 139 Ed
Tolunnoerh (Dolunnor), *China* - - - 96 Bc
Tölz, *Bavaria* - - 59 Fd
Tomah, *Wisconsin* - - 132 Dc
Tomahawk, *Wisconsin* - 132 Ec
Tomakomai, *Japan* - - 97 Eb
Tomar, *Portugal* - - 37 Bc
Tomari, *Honshu, Japan* - 97 Eb
Tomari, *Kunashiri, Japan* 97 Fb
Tómaros, mt., *Greece* - 70 Bd
Tomaszów, *Łódź, Poland* 60 Ec
Tomaszów, *Lublin, Poland* 60 Gc
Tomat, *A.-E. Sudan* - 108 Cc
Tombador, Sa. do, *Brazil* 142 Ce
Tombari, *Mozambique* - 112 Bd
Tombe, *A.-E. Sudan* - 108 Bd
Tombigbee R., *Mississippi* 130 Dd
Tombouctou, *Fr. W. Afr.* 104 Dc
Tombstone, *Arizona* - 135 Jf
Tombuco, *Celébes* - - 99 Fd
Tomburke, *Transvaal* - 113 Bd
Tome, *Chile* - - - 148 Bb
Tome, *New Mexico* - 135 Kd
Tomelilla, *Sweden* - - 51 Cg
Tomelloso, *Spain* - - 41 Da
Tomiko, *Ontario* - - 123 Jb
Tomini (Gorontalo), Gulf of, *Celébes* - - - 99 Fd
Tomintoul, *Scotland* - 23 Eb
Tommerup, *Denmark* - 45 Dc
Tomobe, *Japan* - - 100 Hc
Tomori, Gulf, *Celébes* - 99 Fd
Tomsk, *U.S.S.R.* - - 76 Jd
Tom's River, *New Jersey* 129 Hb
Tonala, *Mexico* - - 139 Fd
Tonawanda, *New York* - 129 Ea
Tonbetu, *Japan* - - 97 Ea
Tonbridge, *England* - 15 Ed
Tondano, *Celebes* - - 99 Gc
Tondela, *Portugal* - - 37 Bb
Tonder, *Denmark* - - 45 Bd
Tondern, *Ontario* - - 122 Fa
Tondi, *Madras* - - 89 Cc
Tone, R., *England* - - 14 Ad
Tonga, *A.-E. Sudan* - 108 Bd
Tonga Is., *Pacific Oc.* - 157 Fe
Tongaat, *Natal* - - 115 Jd
Tongala, *Victoria* - - 154 Ed
Tongareva I., *Pacific Oc.* 149 Lf
Tongataba, I., *Tonga Is.* 157 Ff
Tonghong, *Assam* - - 88 Eb
Tong-king, *Fr. Indo-China* 95 Be
Tong-king, Gulf of, *Fr. Indo-China* - - 95 Cf
Tongoy, *Chile* - - 146 Ae
Tongres, *Belgium* - - 29 Dd
Tongsa, *Bhutan* - - 88 Ca
Tongue, *Scotland* - - 24 De
Tonichi, *Mexico* - - 138 Cb
Tonj, *A. E. Sudan* - 108 Ad
Tonk, *Rajputana* - - 85 Ea
Tonkour, *Fr. W. Africa* 105 Cc
Tonle Sap (Great L.), *Siam-Cambodia* - - 95 Bg
Tonneins, *France* - - 35 Cc
Tonnerre, *France* - - 31 Fd
Tönning, *Prussia* - - 54 Da
Tonopah, *Nevada* - - 134 Eb
Tonsberg, *Norway* - - 47 Ge
Tonstad, *Norway* - - 47 Cf
Tonto, *Arizona* - - 135 Hd
Tonuoka, *Japan* - - 100 Ee
Tonya, *Uganda* - - 110 Bc
Toodyay, *W. Australia* - 152 Be
Tooele, *Utah* - - - 135 Ga
Tooligie, *S. Australia* - 154 Ac
Toompine, *Queensland* - 153 Be
Toomyvara, *Eire* - - 27 Bf
Toowoomba, *Queensland* 153 De
Top L., *U.S.S.R.* - 48 Kd
Topaz, *Idaho* - - - 136 Hd
Topeka, *Kansas* - - 133 Ea
Topla, *Central Provs.* - 86 Dd
Toplanë, *Albania* - - 70 Aa
Toplica, R., *Serbia* - 68 Gc
Toplice, *Slovenia* - - 63 Jb
Toplok, *Sinkiang* - - 84 Eb
Topock, *Arizona* - - 134 Fd
Topola, *Voyvodina* - - 66 Ed
Topolčane, *Serbia* - - 70 Cb
Topolčany, *Slovakia* - 66 Da
Topólia, *Greece* - - 71 Ee
Topolobampo, *Mexico* - 138 Cb
Topozero, *U.S.S.R.* - 74 Eb
Toppenish, *Washington* - 136 Cb
Topsham, *England* - - 14 Ae
Toquema Ra., *Nevada* - 134 Eb
Toquerville, *Utah* - - 134 Gc
Tor, *Egypt* - - - 107 Jd
Torbay, *Nova Scotia* - 120 Ed
Torchiara, *Italy* - - 64 Fc
Torcopuri, *Bolivia* - - 146 Bc
Tordera, *Spain* - - 39 Hc
Tordesillas, *Spain* - - 36 Ec
Tore, R., *Italy* - - 62 Ca
Torello, *Spain* - - 39 Hb
Toreno, *Spain* - - 36 Db
Torgau, *Prussia* - - 55 Hd
Torgilsbu, *Greenland* - 9 Ee
Torhamn, *Sweden* - - 51 Ef
Tori, *Bihar* - - - 87 Fd
Tori Fathpur, *Cent. India* 86 Cc
Toriñana, C., *Spain* - 36 Aa
Torino (Turin), *Italy* - 62 Bb
Torino di Sangro, *Italy* - 64 Ea
Torit, *A.-E. Sudan* - 108 Be
Torla, *Spain* - - - 39 Eb
Torma, *Estonia* - - 49 Db
Tormac, *Romania* - - 67 Gd
Tormentine C., *New Bruns.* 120 Cc
Tormes, R., *Spain* - - 37 Eb
Torne Elv, *Sweden-Finland* 48 Ec
Torne Träsk, *Sweden* - 44 Ee
Tornio, *Finland* - - 48 Fd
Tornquist, *Argentina* - 148 Db
Toro, *Spain* - - - 36 Ec
Toro, El, *Spain* - - 38 Ed
Toro, dist., *Uganda* - 110 Bc
Torodi, *Fr. W. Africa* - 105 Bc
Toroiaga, mt., *Transylvania* 67 Kb
Törökszentmiklós, *Hungary* 67 Fb
Toróni (Kassándra), G. of, *Greece* - - - - 70 Ed
Torontal, *Romania* - - 67 Gd
Toronto, *Kansas* - - 133 Db
Toronto, *New S. Wales* - 155 Gc
Toronto, *Ohio* - - 129 Db
Toronto, *Ontario* - - 123 Jd
Toronto, *S. Dakota* - 132 Ac
Torontola, *Italy* - - 63 Fd
Tororo, *Uganda* - - 110 Dc
Torozos, Mtes. de, *Spain* 38 Ac
Torpe, *Norway* - - 46 Ed
Torquay, *England* - - 17 Cc
Torrance, *New Mexico* - 135 Ld
Torre, *It. Somaliland* - 108 Gf
Torre Annunziata, *Italy* 64 Ec
Torre Astura, *Italy* - 64 Cb
Torreblanca, *Spain* - 39 Fd
Torre del Greco, *Italy* - 64 Ec
Torre de Moncorvo, *Portugal* - - - 37 Ca
Torre de Passeri, *Italy* - 64 Da
Torredonjimeno, *Spain* - 41 Bc
Torregaveta, *Italy* - - 64 Dc
Torre la Carcel, *Spain* - 38 Dd
Torrelaguna, *Spain* - 38 Bd
Torrelavega, *Spain* - 38 Aa
Torremaggiore, *Italy* - 64 Fb
Torrens, L., *S. Australia* 154 Bb
Torrente, *Spain* - - 38 Ee
Torrente de Cinca, *Spain* 39 Fc
Torreon, *Mexico* - - 138 Db
Torreorgaz, *Spain* - - 37 Dc
Torre Orsaja, *Italy* - 64 Fc
Torreperogil, *Spain* - 41 Cb
Torres, *Brazil* - - 147 Fd
Torres, *Mexico* - - 138 Bb
Torres Is., *New Hebrides* 157 De
Torres de Alcala, *Span. Morocco* - - - 102 Bb
Torres de Cotillas, La, *Spain* 41 Eb

Tu-chow, *China*	-	94	Ed	Tung-po, *China*	-	94	Dc	Tuskegee, *Alabama*	-	130	Fd	Ubian, I., *Philippines*	-	99	Fb	Ulmeni, *Transylvania*	-	67	Jb

Tu-chow, *China* - 94 Ed
Tuchuan, *Manchuria* - 96 Cb
Tuckerton, *New Jersey* - 129 Gc
Tucson & Ra., *Arizona* - 135 He
Tucuman & prov., *Argent.* 146 Bd
Tucumcari, *New Mexico* - 135 Md
Tucunare, *Brazil* - 142 Cd
Tucupita, *Venezuela* - 144 Db
Tudela, *Navarra, Spain* - 38 Db
Tudela, *Valladolid, Spain* 38 Ac
Tuen, *Queensland* - 153 Ce
Tugarakshan, *Kazak* - 75 Jf
Tugba, *Fr. W. Africa* - 104 Cc
Tugela and R., *Natal* - 115 Jd
Tugidak I., *Alaska* - 125 Hh
Tuguegarao, *Philippines* - 95 Ff
Tuimaza, *U.S.S.R.* - 74 Je
Tukums, *Latvia* - 49 Bc
Tukushima, *Japan* - 100 Fd
Tukuyu, *Tang. Terr.* - 111 Ch
Tula, *Mexico* - 139 Ec
Tula, *U.S.S.R.* - 75 Fe
Tula I., *Ital. Somaliland* 108 Gg
Tulagai Sor, *Kazak* - 75 Jf
Tulagi, I., *Solomon Is.* 157 Cd
Tulancingo, *Mexico* - 139 Ec
Tulare, *California* - 134 Dc
Tularosa, *New Mexico* - 135 Me
Tulasi, mt., *Eastern States* 91 Eb
Tulbagh, *Cape Prov.* - 114 Cf
Tulbagh, mt., *Cape Prov.* 114 De
Tulcan, *Ecuador* - 145 Ba
Tulcea, *Romania* - 69 Hc
Tulchin, *Ukraine* - 75 Df
Tulear, *Madagascar* - 112 Dd
Tuli and R., *S. Rhodesia* 113 Cc
Tulia, *Texas* - 133 Bc
Tulivary, *U.S.S.R.* - 48 Je
Tuljapur, *Hyderabad* - 90 Cb
Tul Karm, *Palestine* - 80 Cc
Tulla, *Eire* - 27 Bf
Tullahoma, *Tennessee* - 130 Ec
Tullamore, *Eire* - 27 Ce
Tullamore, *New S. Wales* 155 Fd
Tulle, *France* - 34 Db
Tullet Pt., *N.-W. Terr.* - 118 Da
Tullow, *Eire* - 27 Df
Tullu, *Austria* - 59 Kc
Tully Cross, *Eire* - 25 Db
Tulsa, *Oklahoma* - 133 Eb
Tulsk, *U.S.S.R.* - 75 Fe
Tulua, *Colombia* - 144 Ac
Tumac Humac, Sa., *Brazil* 142 Db
Tumaco, *Colombia* - 144 Ac
Tumbarumba, *N. S. W.* 155 Fd
Tumbes and dep., *Peru* - 145 Ab
Tumbes, Desierto de, *Peru* 145 Ab
Tumby Bay, *S. Australia* 154 Ac
Tumkur, *Mysore* - 90 Ce
Tumlong, *Sikkim* - 88 Ba
Tummel, R., *Scotland* - 23 Dc
Tump, *Baluchistan* - 79 Hd
Tumsar, *Central Provs.* - 86 Ce
Tumshuk, *Sinkiang* - 84 Db
Tumu, *Gold Coast* - 104 Dd
Tumupasa, *Bolivia* - 145 Dd
Tumut, *New S. Wales* - 155 Fd
Tuna, *Philippines* - 99 Fb
Tuna, *Western India* - 85 Cc
Tunas, *Cuba* - 140 Bb
Tunbridge Wells, *England* 15 Ed
Tundra, *U.S.S.R.* - 76 Kb
Tunduru, *Tang. Terr.* - 111 Ej
Tundzha R., *Bulgaria-Turkey* - 69 Gd
Tung, *China* - 94 Eb
Tungabhadra R., *Hyderabad* 90 Cd
Tungara, *N. Borneo* - 99 Eb
Tung-chang, *China* - 94 Eb
Tung-chow, *China* - 94 Cc
Tung-chwan, *Sze-chwan, China* - 94 Bc
Tung-chwan, *Yun-nan, China* - 94 Bd
Tung-hai I., *China* - 95 De
Tunghi, *Mozambique* - 112 Db
Tu-nghia, *Annam* - 95 Cf
Tungho, *Manchuria* - 96 Db
Tung-hwa, *China* - 95 De
Tung-hwa, *Manchuria* - 96 Dc
Tung-jen, *China* - 94 Cd
Tung-kiang, *China* - 94 Cc
Tung-kiang R., *China* - 94 Bd
Tungkiang, *Manchuria* - 96 Eb
Tung-kwan, *Kwang-tung, China* - 95 De
Tung-kwan, *Shen-si, China* 94 Dc
Tunglaio, *Manchuria* - 96 Cc
Tungning, *Manchuria* - 96 Ec
Tungpei, *Manchuria* - 96 Db
Tungpin, *Manchuria* - 96 Db
Tung-ping, *China* - 94 Eb

Tung-po, *China* - 94 Dc
Tung-shan, *China* - 95 Ee
Tung-siang, *China* - 94 Cc
Tung-tai, *China* - 94 Fc
Tung-ting-hu, *China* - 94 Dd
Tungtzuchen, *Manchuria* 96 Dc
Tunguski Mts., *U.S.S.R.* 76 Lc
Tunguska, R., Lr. and Upper, *U.S.S.R.* - 76 Kc
Tung-wei, *China* - 94 Cb
Tungyang, *China* - 94 Ed
Tunhwa, *Manchuria* - 96 Dc
Tuni, *Madras* - 91 Fc
Tunia, *Kenya* - 110 Fd
Tunica, *Mississippi* - 130 Cc
Tunis, *Tunisia* - 103 Ja
Tunis, G. de, *Tunisia* - 103 Ka
Tunisia, *N. Africa* - 101 Cb
Tunja, *Colombia* - 144 Bb
Tunkhannock, *Pennsylvania* 129 Fb
Tunö, I., *Denmark* - 45 Dc
Tunstall, *Staffs, England* 18 Bd
Tunstall, *Suffolk, England* 15 Fb
Tunuyan & R., *Argentina* 146 Be
Tuolumne, *California* - 134 Cc
Tuparoa, *New Zealand* - 158' Gb
Tupelo, *Mississippi* - 130 Dc
Tupilco, *Mexico* - 139 Fd
Tupinambaranas, I., *Brazil* 142 Cc
Tupiza, *Bolivia* - 146 Bc
Tupper Lake, *New York* 128 Aa
Tuquarussu, *Brazil* - 143 Ee
Tuque, La, *Quebec* - 123 Mb
Tuquerres, *Colombia* - 144 Ac
Tura, *Assam* - 88 Cb
Tura, *Tanganyika Terr.* - 111 Cf
Turaba, *Arabia* - 78 Lf
Turaiyur, *Madras* - 89 Cb
Turakom, *Laos* - 95 Bf
Turana Mts., *U.S.S.R.* - 96 Ea
Turany, *Slovakia* - 57 Dd
Turbat-i-Heideri, *Persia* 79 Gb
Turbat-i-Sheikh Jam, *Persia* 79 Hb
Turbenthal, *Switzerland* 43 Ca
Turbo, *Colombia* - 144 Ab
Turbo, *Kenya* - 110 Dc
Turcin, mt., *Serbia* - 70 Ba
Turda, *A.-E. Sudan* - 108 Ac
Turda, *Transylvania* - 67 Jc
Turfan, *Sinkiang* - 84 Fb
Turgutlu, *Turkey* - 78 Ab
Turi, *Estonia* - 49 Cb
Turia, R., *Spain* - 39 Ee
Turin (Torino), *Italy* - 62 Bb
Türje, *Hungary* - 66 Cc
Turjoe, *A.-E. Sudan* - 105 Fc
Turka - - 60 Gf
Turkestan Mts., *Uzbek, etc.* 84 Bc
Túrkeve, *Hungary* - 67 Fb
Turkey, *Europe-Asia* - 77 Db
Turkey Creek, *W. Aust.* 152 Db
Turkheim, *Bavaria* - 58 Ec
Turkmen, *U.S.S.R.* - 76 Ge
Turks Is., *Bahamas* - 140 Cb
Turku, *Finland* - 48 Ef
Turkwel, R., *Kenya* - 110 Db
Turnberry, *Scotland* - 21 Bc
Turneffe Is., *Br. Honduras* 140 Fd
Turners Falls, *Massachus.* 128 Bb
Turnhout, *Belgium* - 29 Cc
Türnitz, *Austria* - 59 Kd
Turnov, *Bohemia* - 59 Ka
Turnu-Magurele, *Romania* 69 Gd
Turnu Rosiu, *Romania* - 67 Kd
Turnu Severin, *Romania* 67 Hc
Turö, *Denmark* - 45 Dc
Turon, *Kansas* - 133 Cb
Turquino, Pico de, *Cuba* 140 Bc
Turrialba, *Costa Rica* - 140 Gf
Turriff, *Scotland* - 23 Fa
Turshiz, *Persia* - 79 Gb
Tursi, *Italy* - 65 Cb
Turtle I., *W. Australia* 152 Bb
Turtle Is., *Nether. Indies* 99 Ge
Turtle L., *Quebec* - 121 Aa
Turtle Rapids, *Washington* 136 Da
Turtucaia - - 69 Gd
Turun, *Persia* - 79 Gb
Turut, *Persia* - 79 Gb
Turvo, *Brazil* - 147 Gc
Turya, *U.S.S.R.* - 74 Jc
Tury Assu & B., *Brazil* - 143 Ec
Turzovka, *Slovakia* - 57 Dd
Tuscaloosa, *Alabama* - 130 Ed
Tuscarora, *Nevada* - 134 Ea
Tuscola, *Illinois* - 132 Ec
Tuscor, *Montana* - 136 Fb
Tuscumbia, *Alabama* - 130 Ec
Tuscumbia, *Missouri* - 130 Ba
Tu-shan, *China* - 94 Cd
Tu-shan, *Manchuria* - 96 Bc
Tushka, *Egypt* - 106 Lh

Tuskegee, *Alabama* - 130 Fd
Tusket, *Nova Scotia* - 120 Ce
Tüskevár, *Hungary* - 66 Cb
Tuslu Geul, *Persia* - 79 Fc
Tustna, I., *Norway* - 46 Da
Tutaev, *U.S.S.R.* - 74 Fd
Tuticorin, *Madras* - 89 Cc
Tuttlingen, *Württemberg* 58 Cd
Tutuila I., *Samoa Is.* - 157 Fe
Tuwaiq, Jeb., *Arabia* - 79 Ed
Tuxford, *England* - 19 Dd
Tuxpan, *Mexico* - 139 Ec
Tuxtepec, *Mexico* - 139 Ed
Tuxtla, *Mexico* - 139 Fd
Tuxtla (Gutierrez), *Mexico* 139 Fd
Tuy, *Spain* - 36 Bb
Tuyen-Kwang, *Tong-king* 95 Be
Tu-yun, *China* - 94 Cd
Tuz Gölü, *Turkey* - 78 Bb
Tuzla, *Bosnia* - 68 Db
Tværaa, *Færoe Is.* - 44 Od
Tvedestrand, *Norway* - 47 Ef
Tveitekvitingen, *Norway* - 47 Bd
Twante, *Burma* - 92 Cd
Tweed, *Ontario* - 121 Bb
Tweed, R., *Scotland* - 21 Db
Tweeddale, *Cape Prov.* - 115 Fe
Tweedsmuir Hills, *Scot.* 21 Cb
Tweedsmuir Park, *Brit. Columbia* - 124 Dd
Tweeling, *O.F.S.* - 115 Hc
Twenty-five de Mayo, *Argentina* - 148 Db
Twenty-five de Mayo, *La Pampa, Argentina.* - 148 Cb
Twenty-four Parganas, *Bengal* - 88 Bc
Twickenham, *England* - 15 Dd
Twillingate, *Newfoundland* 120 Hb
Twin Bridges, *Montana* - 136 Gc
Twin Buttes, *Arizona* - 135 Hf
Twin Falls, *Idaho* - 136 Fd
Two Harbors, *Minnesota* 132 Cb
Two Mountains, L. of, *Quebec* - 121 Mb
Two Rivers, *Wisconsin* - 132 Fc
Two Rivers, R., *Minnesota* 132 Aa
Tworog - - 57 Dc
Two Waters, *Cape Prov.* 115 Ff
Twycross, *England* - 14 Ca
Twyford, *Berks, England* 15 Dd
Twyford, *Hampshire, Eng.* 14 Cd
Tybee, *Georgia* - 131 He
Tybo, *Nevada* - 134 Eb
Tyborön, *Denmark* - 45 Bb
Tydal, *Norway* - 46 Ha
Tyee, *Alaska* - 125 Nh
Tykocin, *Poland* - 56 Gc
Tylden, *Cape Prov.* - 115 Gf
Tyldesley, *England* - 18 Bc
Tyler, *Texas* - 133 Ed
Tymbark, *Poland* - 57 Fd
Tyne, R., *England* - 21 Ed
Tynemouth, *England* - 21 Ec
Tyngeri Des., *China* - 94 Bb
Tyre, *Lebanon* - 78 Cc
Tyri Fd., *Norway* - 47 Gd
Tyrone, *Pennsylvania* - 129 Eb
Tyrone, co., *N. Ireland* - 26 Cb
Tyrrell L. & R., *Victoria* 154 Dd
Tyrrhenian Sea, *Italy* - 61 Cd
Tysfjord, *Norway* - 48 Bb
Tysnesöy, *Norway* - 47 Be
Tyssedal, *Norway* - 47 Cd
Tyumen, *U.S.S.R.* - 76 Gd
Tyvoll, *Norway* - 46 Hb
Tzaneen, *Transvaal* - 115 Ja
Tzariser Mts., *S.-W. Afr.* 114 Bb
Tzenin, El, *Span. Morocco* 102 Bb
Tzia (Kéa, Kéos), I., *Greece* 71 Ff
Tzuhsinho, *Manchuria* - 96 Cb
Tzu-kiang, *China* - 94 Dd
Uallel, Mt., *Ethiopia* - 108 Cd
Uanda, *Queensland* - 153 Cc
Uanetzi, *Mozambique* - 115 Jb
Ua Pou, I., *Marquesas Is.* 157 Kd
Uarandab, *Ethiopia* - 108 Dd
Uaroo, *W. Australia* - 152 Bc
Uasin Gishu Plat., *Kenya* 110 Dc
Uassary, Sa., *Br. Guiana* 144 Cc
Uatuma, R., *Brazil* - 142 Cc
Uaupes, R., *Brazil* - 145 Db
Uba, *Brazil* - 147 Gc
Ubangi, R., *Belgian Congo* 109 Ca
Ubangi-Shari, col., *Fr. Equat. Africa* - 105 Ed
Ubatuba, *Brazil* - 147 Gc
Ubeda, *Spain* - 41 Cc
Uberaba, *Brazil* - 147 Fb
Uberlandia, *Brazil* - 147 Fb
Uberlingen, *Baden* - 58 Dd

Ubian, I., *Philippines* - 99 Fb
Ubigau, *Prussia* - 55 Jd
Ubo, *China* - 94 Bb
Ubombo, *Natal* - 115 Kc
Ubrique, *Spain* - 40 Ec
Ubun, *Siam* - 95 Bf
Ucayali, *Peru* - 145 Cc
Ucero, *Spain* - 38 Bc
Uch, *Punjab States* - 82 Dd
Uchinoumi, *Japan* - 100 Dd
Uchiza, *Peru* - 145 Bc
Uch-musduk, *Sinkiang* - 84 Db
Uckfield, *England* - 15 Ee
Uckro, *Prussia* - 55 Jd
Ucles, *Spain* - 38 Ce
Udain, *Yemen* - 78 Lh
Udaipur, *Tripura, Eastern States* - 88 Cc
Udaipur, *Eastern States* - 87 Ed
Udaipur, *Rajputana* - 83 Fe
Udaipur & state, *Rajputana* 85 Db
Udaiyarpalaiyam, *Madras* 89 Cb
Udamalpet, *Madras* - 89 Bb
Udayagiri, *Madras* - 90 Dd
Udayagiri Hill, *Orissa* - 91 Ha
Udbina, *Croatia* - 68 Ab
Uddeholm, *Sweden* - 50 Cb
Uddevalla, *Sweden* - 50 Ad
Uddingston, *Scotland* - 23 De
Uddjaur, *Sweden* - 44 Df
Udekwa, *Tang. Terr.* - 111 Eg
Udgir, *Hyderabad* - 90 Cb
Udi, *Nigeria* - 105 Cd
Udine, *Italy* - 63 Ha
Udipi, *Madras* - 90 Be
Udmurt, *U.S.S.R.* - 74 Jd
Udong, *Cambodia* - 95 Bg
Ueda, *Japan* - 100 Gc
Uele, R., *Belg. Congo* - 109 Da
Uezzen, *Libya* - 103 Kd
Ufa, *U.S.S.R.* - 74 Ke
Uganda, protectorate, *E. Africa* - 101 Fe
Ugashik, *Alaska* - 125 Gh
Ugento, *Italy* - 65 Ec
Ugie, *Cape Prov.* - 115 He
Ugines, *France* - 35 Jb
Uglich, *U.S.S.R.* - 74 Fd
Ugljevik, *Bosnia* - 68 Db
Ugoi (Ujiji), *Tang. Terr.* 111 Af
Uh, R., *Carpatho-Ukraine* 60 Gd
Uig and B., *Scotland* - 24 Aa
Uige, *Angola* - 109 Cc
Uinta Mts., *Utah* - 135 Ma
Uiski, *U.S.S.R.* - 74 Le
Uist, North, *Scotland* - 22 Aa
Uist, South, *Scotland* - 22 Ab
Ui-tal, *Sinkiang* - 84 Db
Uitenhage, *Cape Prov.* - 115 Ff
Uithuizen, *Holland* - 29 Ea
Ujae Is., *Marshall Is.* - 157 Dc
Ujelang I., *Marshall Is.* - 157 Db
Ujhani, *United Provs.* - 83 He
Uji, *Japan* - 100 Ed
Ujiji (Ugoi), *Tang. Terr.* 111 Af
Ujina, *Japan* - 100 Ca
Ujjain, *Gwalior* - 85 Ec
Ujpest, *Hungary* - 66 Eb
Ujscie, *Poland* - 56 Ac
Ukamas, *S.-W. Africa* - 114 Cc
Ukara I., *Tang. Terr.* - 110 Cd
Ukerewe I., *Tang. Terr.* 110 Ce
Ukermark, *Prussia* - 55 Jb
Ukhta, *U.S.S.R.* - 74 Eb
Ukiah, *California* - 134 Bb
Ukk, *Hungary* - 66 Cb
Ukraine, rep., *U.S.S.R.* 75 Gg
Ukrina, R., *Bosnia* - 68 Cb
Ukta, *E. Prussia* - 56 Fc
Ukushima, *Japan* - 97 Bd
Ula Dag (Olympus), *Turkey* - 72 Gb
Ulan, *U.S.S.R.* - 75 Gf
Ulan Bator Hoto, *Mongolia* 93 Cb
Ulan Ude, *U.S.S.R.* - 76 Ld
Ulborg, *Denmark* - 45 Bb
Uled Saidan (Fugha), *Libya* - 106 Ae
Ulefoss, *Norway* - 47 Fe
Ulete, *Tanganyika Terr.* - 111 Dh
Uliassutai, *Mongolia* - 93 Bb
Ulithi Is., *Caroline Is.* - 157 Ab
Uljan, *Dalmatia* - 63 Kc
Uljma, *Voyvodina* - 67 Gd
Ulladulla, *New S. Wales* 155 Gd
Ullapool, *Scotland* - 22 Ca
Ullared, *Sweden* - 51 Be
Ulldecona, *Spain* - 39 Fd
Ullswater, *England* - 18 Ba
Ulm, *Montana* - 136 Ha
Ulm, *Württemberg* - 58 Dc
Ulmarra, *New S. Wales* - 155 Ha

Ulmeni, *Transylvania* - 67 Jb
Ulmin, *U.S.S.R.* - 96 Da
Ulog, *Hercegovina* - 68 Dc
Ulricehamn, *Sweden* - 51 Ce
Ulsberg, *Norway* - 46 Fb
Ulstein, *Norway* - 46 Db
Ulster, prov., *Eire* - 26 Cb
Ultimo, Val di, *Italy* - 62 Fa
Ulua & R., *Honduras* - 140 Fd
Uluguru Mts., *Tang. Terr.* 111 Eg
Ulukisla, *Turkey* - 78 Bb
Ulundi, *Natal* - 115 Jd
Ulustu-bulak, *Sinkiang* - 84 Fa
Ulva, I., *Scotland* - 22 Bd
Ulven, *Norway* - 47 Hd
Ulverston, *England* - 18 Ab
Ulverstone, *Tasmania* - 155 Jg
Ulvik, *Norway* - 46 Cd
Ulyanovsk, *U.S.S.R.* - 75 He
Ulysses, *Kansas* - 133 Bb
Ulzen, *Prussia* - 54 Fc
Umago - - 63 Hb
Uman, *Ukraine* - 75 Ef
Umanak, *Greenland* - 9 Dc
Umanaks Fd., *Greenland* - 9 Dc
Umanarsuk, *Greenland* - 9 Dd
Umarkot, *Sind* - 85 Bb
Umatilla, *Washington* - 136 Dc
Umb, L., *U.S.S.R.* - 48 Lc
Umbeluzi, *Mozambique* - 115 Kc
Umbertide, *Italy* - 63 Gd
Umboi (Rooke) I., *Bismarck Arch.* - 156 Dc
Umbozero, *U.S.S.R.* - 74 Eb
Umbria, *Italy* - 63 Ge
Umčari, *Serbia* - 68 Fb
Umeå, *Sweden* - 44 Eg
Umfolozi, *Natal* - 115 Jd
Umgazi, *Cape Prov.* - 115 He
Umgusa, *S. Rhodesia* - 113 Bb
Um Hagar, *Eritrea* - 108 Cc
Umm Ajjua, *Palestine* - 80 Ae
Umm Badr, *A.-E. Sudan* 108 Ac
Umm el 'Amad, *Trans-Jordan* - 80 Dd
Umm el Qulban, *Arabia* 78 Dd
Umm el Walid, *Trs.-Jordan* 80 Dd
Umm Jose, *Trans-Jordan* 80 Dd
Umm Keddada, *A.-E.Sudan* 108Ac
Umm Khalid, *Palestine* - 80 Bc
Umm Lej, *Arabia* - 78 Cd
Umm Qala, *Trans-Jordan* 80 De
Umm Qasr, *Iraq* - 79 Ed
Umm Qeis, *Trans-Jordan* 80 Dd
Umm Ruwaba, *A.-E. Sudan* 108Bc
Umnak I. and Pass., *Aleutian Is.* - 125 Ek
Umpqua, *Oregon* - 136 Bd
Umrer, *Cent. Provs.* - 86 Ce
Umri, *Gwalior* - 86 Bc
Umsinduzi, *Natal* - 115 Jd
Umsinga, *Natal* - 115 Jd
Umtali, *S. Rhodesia* - 113 Eb
Umtata, *Cape Prov.* - 115 He
Umtwalumi, *Natal* - 115 Je
Umurbey, *Turkey* - 72 Db
Umvuma, *S. Rhodesia* - 113 Db
Umzimkulu, *Cape Prov.* - 115 He
Umzinto, *Natal* - 115 Je
Una, *Brasil* - 147 Hb
Una, *Punjab* - 83 Gc
Una, R., *Bosnia* - 69 Bc
Unadilla, *New York* - 128 Ab
Unaka Mts., *Tennessee* - 131 Fc
Unalakleet, *Alaska* - 125 Ge
Unalaska & I., *Aleutian Is.* 125 Ek
Unangua, *Mozambique* - 112 Cb
Unao, *United Provs.* - 83 Je
Uñatuya, *Argentina* - 146 Cd
Uncastillo, *Spain* - 38 Db
Uncia, *Bolivia* - 146 Bb
Uncompahgre Plateau, *Colorado* - 135 Md
Und Sjö, *Sweden* - 50 Dd
Underberg, *Natal* - 115 Hd
Underbool, *Victoria* - 154 Cd
Unga, *Alaska* - 125 Gj
Ungarie, *New S. Wales* - 155 Ec
Ungava B., *Quebec* - 119 Cc
Uniao, *Piauhy, Brazil* - 143 Fc
Uniao, *Terr. do Acre, Brazil* - 145 Cc
União da Victoria, *Brasil* 147 Ed
Uniao Marara, *Brazil* - 142 Bc
Uniara, *Rajputana* - 85 Eb
Unie I. - - 63 Jc
Unîket, *China* - 96 Bb
Unimak I. and Pass., *Aleutian Is.* - 125 Fj
Union, *La Rioja, Argentina* 146 Bd
Union, *San Luis, Argentina* 148 Cb
Union, *Georgia* - 131 Gd

Union, *Indiana* 129 Ac
Union, *Mexico* 138 Dd
Union, *Missouri* 130 Ca
Union, *Nebraska* 132 Ae
Union, *Oregon* 136 Dc
Union, *S. Carolina* 131 Hc
Union, la, *Spain* 41 Fc
Union Pk., *Wyoming* 126 Cb
Union City, *Pennsylvania* 129 Db
Union City, *Tennessee* 130 Db
Uniondale, *Cape Prov.* 114 Ef
Union of Soviet Socialist Republics, *Asia* 73 Gb
Union Pass, *Arizona* 134 Fd
Union Springs, *Alabama* 130 Fd
Uniontown, *Alabama* 130 Ed
Uniontown, *Kentucky* 130 Eb
Uniontown, *Pennsylvania* 129 Ec
Unionville, *Nevada* 134 Da
Unionville, *Missouri* 132 Ce
Unisław, *Poland* 56 Cc
United Provinces, *India* 81 De
United States, *N. America* 117 Fe
Uniti, R., *Italy* 63 Gc
Uniut, *Manchuria* 96 Bc
Universales, Mtes., *Spain* 38 Dd
Unkel, *Prussia* 54 Ce
Unkovsky B., *Korea* 97 Bc
Uno, *Japan* 100 Dd
Unruhstadt 55 Lc
Unst, I., *Zetland* 24 Hg
Unter 63 Ha
Unterlüss, *Prussia* 54 Fc
Unterwalden, canton, *Switzerland* 42 Fc
Unturan, Sa. de, *Venezuela* 144 Cc
Uorra Ilu, *Ethiopia* 108 Cc
Uotsu, *Japan* 100 Fc
Upar Ghat, *Eastern States* 87 Ed
Upata, *Venezuela* 144 Db
Upavon, *England* 14 Cd
Upernivik, *Greenland* 9 Dc
Upesa, *Tanganyika Terr.* 111 Bf
Uphall, *England* 15 Eb
Upham, *New Mexico* 135 Ke
Upington, *Cape Prov.* 114 Dd
Upminster, *England* 15 Ec
Upolu I., *Samoa Is.* 157 Fe
Upper Chindwin, *Burma* 88 Eb
Upper Egypt, *Egypt* 107 Je
Upper Klamath L., *Oregon* 136 Cd
Upper Musquodoboit, *Nova Scotia* 120 Dd
Upper Ohio, *Nova Scotia* 120 Ce
Upper Palatinate (Ober Pfalz), *Bavaria* 59 Fb
Upper Sandusky, *Ohio* 129 Cb
Upphärad, *Sweden* 50 Bd
Uppingham, *England* 15 Da
Uppsala and län, *Sweden* 50 Gc
Upsala, *Ontario* 122 Ca
Upstart C. & B., *Queensl'd* 153 Cc
Upton, *England* 14 Bb
Uracoa, *Venezuela* 144 Db
Uraga, *Japan* 100 Gd
Urakawa, *Japan* 97 Eb
Ural, R., *U.S.S.R.* 76 Fe
Ural Mts., *U.S.S.R.* 76 Fd
Uralla, *New S. Wales* 155 Gb
Uralsk, *Kazak* 75 Je
Urambo, *Tangan. Terr.* 111 Bf
Urandangi, *Queensland* 153 Ad
Urandy, *Brazil* 143 Fe
Urapunga, *N. Terr., Aust.* 151 Ea
Uraricoera, R., *Brazil* 142 Bb
Urasa, *Japan* 100 Gc
Urawa, *Japan* 97 Dc
Urbakh, *U.S.S.R.* 75 He
Urbana, *Illinois* 132 Ee
Urbana, *Ohio* 129 Cb
Urbana, *Queensland* 153 Bd
Urbana, La, *Venezuela* 144 Cb
Urbania, *Italy* 63 Gd
Urbino, *Italy* 63 Gd
Urcos, *Peru* 145 Cd
Urda, *Kazak* 75 Hf
Urda, *Spain* 38 Be
Urdaneta, Mt., *Philippines* 99 Gb
Ures, *Mexico* 138 Bb
Urfa, *Turkey* 78 Cb
Uri, canton, *Switzerland* 43 Gc
Uribe, *Colombia* 144 Bc
Uribia, *Colombia* 144 Ba
Urindima, *Belg. Congo* 109 Da
Urkarakh, *U.S.S.R.* 75 Hg
Urlingford, *Eire* 27 Cf
Urnes, *Norway* 46 Dc
Uroševac, *Serbia* 68 Gd
Urosozoro, *U.S.S.R.* 48 Le
Urroz, *Spain* 38 Db
Urshult, *Sweden* 51 Df
Ursine, *Nevada* 134 Fc
Urskog, *Norway* 47 He
Urson, R., *Manchuria* 96 Bb
Uruapan, *Mexico* 138 Dd
Urubamba and R., *Peru* 145 Cd
Urucará, *Brazil* 142 Cc
Urucú, *Brazil* 147 Gb
Uruguay, rep., *S. America* 141 Df
Uruguay, R., *Uruguay, etc.* 146 De
Uruguayana, *Brazil* 146 Dd
Urumchi, *Sinkiang* 84 Fb
Urundi, *Belg. Congo* 109 Eb
Urusan, *Korea* 97 Bc
Urusha, *U.S.S.R.* 96 Ca
Urussanga, *Brazil* 147 Ed
Urussuhy, *Brazil* 143 Fd
Uryupinsk, *U.S.S.R.* 75 Ge
Urzhum, *U.S.S.R.* 74 Hd
Urziceni, *Romania* 69 Gc
Urzulei, *Sardinia* 64 Jf
Usa, *Tanganyika Terr.* 110 Ee
Usa, R., *U.S.S.R.* 74 Lb
Usagara, *Tang. Terr.* 110 Ce
Usak, *Turkey* 78 Ab
Usami, *Japan* 100 Gd
Usborne, *Falkland Is.* 148 Ee
Ušće, *Serbia* 68 Fc
Usdum, Jeb., *Palestine* 80 Ce
Usedom, *Prussia* 55 Jb
Usedom, I., *Prussia* 55 Ja
Useri, *Kenya* 110 Ee
Ushakovo, *U.S.S.R.* 96 Da
Ushetu, *Tangan. Terr.* 111 Cf
Ushnuiyeh, *Persia* 78 Db
Ushuaia, *Argentina* 148 Ce
Usinskaya, *U.S.S.R.* 74 Kb
Usk and R., *England* 14 Bc
Uska, *United Provs.* 87 Eb
Uskedalen, *Norway* 47 Be
Uskoplje, *Hercegovina* 68 Dd
Uskudar (Scutari), *Turkey* 72 Ga
Üsküp, *Turkey* 72 Ea
Usman, *U.S.S.R.* 75 Fe
Usmayo, *Tangan. Terr.* 110 Ce
Usoke, *Tangan. Terr.* 111 Cf
Uspenka, *U.S.S.R.* 96 Eb
Usquil, *Peru* 145 Bc
Usseglio, *Italy* 62 Bb
Ussel, *France* 34 Eb
Ussuri, *U.S.S.R.* 96 Eb
Ussuri R., *Manchuria* 96 Eb
Uster, *Switzerland* 43 Gb
Usti, *Bohemia* 60 Bc
Usti, *Moravia* 57 Bd
Ustikolina, *Bosnia* 68 Dc
Ustipraća, *Bosnia* 68 Dc
Ust Izhma, *U.S.S.R.* 74 Jb
Ust Kamchatsk, *U.S.S.R.* 76 Rd
Ust Kozhva, *U.S.S.R.* 74 Kb
Ust Kulom, *U.S.S.R.* 74 Jc
Ust Niman, *U.S.S.R.* 96 Ea
Ustron, *Poland* 57 Dd
Ust Shchugor, *U.S.S.R.* 74 Kc
Ust Tsilma, *U.S.S.R.* 74 Jb
Ust Ukhta, *U.S.S.R.* 74 Jc
Ust Unya, *U.S.S.R.* 74 Kc
Ust Usa, *U.S.S.R.* 74 Kb
Ust Vimskoe, *U.S.S.R.* 74 Jc
Ust Vorkuta, *U.S.S.R.* 74 Lb
Ust Yeniseiski Port, *U.S.S.R.* 76 Jb
Ustyuzhna, *U.S.S.R.* 74 Fd
Usuki, *Japan* 100 Bb
Usumbura, *Belg. Congo* 109 Eb
Uszod, *Hungary* 66 Dc
Uta, *New Guinea* 156 Bb
Utah, state, *U.S.A.* 126 Cc
Utah L., *Utah* 135 Ga
Utelle, *France* 33 Cb
Utena, *Lithuania* 49 Cd
Utengule, *Tangan. Terr.* 111 Ch
Utengule, *Tangan. Terr.* 111 Dh
Utete, *Tanganyika Terr.* 111 Fh
Uthal, *Baluchistan* 85 Ab
Utiarity, *Brazil* 142 Ce
Utica, *Mississippi* 130 Cd
Utica, *New York* 123 Ld
Utiel, *Spain* 38 De
Utima, *Kenya* 110 Dd
Utimba, *Tang. Terr.* 110 Ce
Utirik Is., *Marshall Is.* 157 Eb
Utlak Soak, *Greenland* 9 Bb
Utö, *Sweden* 50 Hd
Utraula, *United Provs.* 87 Eb
Utrecht, *Natal* 115 Jc
Utrecht & prov., *Holland* 29 Db
Utrera, *Spain* 40 Eb
Utsjoki, *Finland* 48 Gb
Utsunomiya, *Japan* 97 Ec
Uttangarai, *Madras* 89 Ca
Uttendorf, *Austria* 59 Gc
Uttoxeter, *England* 18 Ce
Utupua, I., *Santa Cruz Is.* 157 De
Uuksu, *U.S.S.R.* 48 Jf
Uusikaarlepyy, *Finland* 48 Ee
Uusikaupunki, *Finland* 48 Df
Uva, *Wyoming* 135 La
Uva Prov., *Ceylon* 89 Dd
Uvac and R., *Serbia* 68 Ec
Uvada, *Utah* 134 Gc
Uvalde, *Texas* 133 Cf
Uvinza (Ruchugi), *Tanganyika Terr.* 111 Bf
Uvira, *Belg. Congo* 109 Eb
Uwajima, *Japan* 100 Cb
Uxbridge, *England* 15 Dc
Uxbridge, *Massachusetts* 128 Cb
Uxbridge, *Ontario* 121 Ab
Uxmal, *Mexico* 139 Gc
Uyuni & Salar de, *Bolivia* 146 Bc
Uzbek, *U.S.S.R.* 76 Ge
Uzdin, *Voyvodina* 67 Fd
Uzerche, *France* 34 Db
Uzes, *France* 35 Gc
Uzes le Duc, *Algeria* 102 Eb
Uzhorod, *Carpatho-Ukraine* 60 Gd
Užice, *Serbia* 68 Ec
Užok, *Carpatho-Ukraine* 60 Gd
Uzpaliai, *Lithuania* 49 Cd
Uzunköprü, *Turkey* 72 Da
Vaago, *Færoe Is.* 44 Nc
Vaal, R., *Transvaal* 115 Gc
Vaala, *Finland* 48 Gd
Vaalfontein, *Cape Prov.* 114 Ce
Vaalwater, *Transvaal* 115 Gb
Vaal-Wilge Confluence Dam, *O.F.S.* 115 Gc
Vaasa, *Finland* 48 De
Vac, *Hungary* 66 Eb
Vaca Keys, *Florida* 131 Nj
Vacaville, *California* 134 Cb
Vache, I. la, *Haiti* 140 Cc
Vad, *Transylvania* 67 Hc
Vadas, *Transylvania* 67 Gc
Vaddigudem, *Madras* 91 Ec
Vadheim, *Norway* 46 Bc
Vadi (Wari), *Deccan States* 90 Ad
Vadna, *Hungary* 67 Fa
Vado, *Italy* 62 Cc
Vadsbro, *Sweden* 50 Fd
Vadsö, *Norway* 48 Ha
Vadstena, *Sweden* 50 Dd
Vaduz, *Liechtenstein* 43 Jb
Vag R., *Slovakia* 66 Ca
Vaga, R., *U.S.S.R.* 74 Gc
Vågåmo, *Norway* 46 Ec
Vaganovo, *U.S.S.R.* 96 Da
Vageva, *Estonia* 49 Db
Vaggeryd, *Sweden* 51 De
Vagos, *Portugal* 37 Bb
Vagsellye, *Slovakia* 66 Ca
Vågsöy, *Norway* 46 Ac
Váh, R., *Slovakia* 60 Dd
Vaiden, *Mississippi* 130 Dd
Vaigach, I., *U.S.S R.* 74 Kb
Vaigai R., *Madras* 89 Cc
Vaijapur, *Hyderabad* 90 Bb
Vaikam, *Madras States* 89 Bc
Vaike Maarja, *Estonia* 49 Db
Vailly, *France* 31 Fb
Vairowal, *Punjab* 83 Fc
Vaison, *France* 35 Hc
Vaitolahi, *U.S.S.R.* 48 Ka
Vaitupu, I., *Ellice Is.* 157 Ed
Vajka, *Slovakia* 66 Ca
Vajszló, *Hungary* 66 Dd
Valais, canton, *Switzerland* 42 Dd
Valamazski, *U.S.S.R.* 74 Jd
Valamo, *U.S.S.R.* 48 Jf
Valandovo, *Serbia* 70 Db
Valáxa, I., *Greece* 71 Fe
Valbonnais, *France* 35 Hc
Val Brillant, *Quebec* 120 Ab
Valcani, *Romania* 67 Fd
Valcartier, *Quebec* 121 Ea
Vâlcea, *Romania* 67 Jd
Valcheta, *Argentina* 148 Cc
Valcourt, *Quebec* 121 Db
Valcov 69 Hc
Valdagno, *Italy* 63 Fb
Valdai, *U.S.S.R.* 74 Ed
Valdai Hills, *U.S.S.R.* 74 Ed
Val d'Ajol, *France* 31 Jd
Valdecaballeros, *Spain* 37 Ec
Valdemarpils, *Latvia* 49 Bc
Valdemars B., *Sweden* 51 Fd
Valdemeca, Sa. de, *Spain* 38 Dd
Valdepeñas, *Spain* 41 Cb
Valderies, *France* 34 Ed
Valdestillas, *Spain* 38 Ac
Valdez, *Alaska* 125 Lf
Valdez, Pen., *Argentina* 148 Dc
Valdieri, *Italy* 62 Bc
Valdivia and prov., *Chile* 148 Bb
Valdosta, *Georgia* 131 Ge
Valdoviño, *Spain* 36 Ba
Valdres, *Norway* 46 Ec
Vale, *Oregon* 136 Ec
Valea-Dosului, *Romania* 67 Jc
Valea Florilor, *Transylva.* 67 Jc
Valea lui Mihai, *Transylva.* 67 Hb
Vålebru, *Norway* 46 Gc
Valeggio, *Italy* 62 Eb
Valença, *Brazil* 143 Fd
Valença, *Portugal* 36 Bb
Valence, *Drôme, France* 35 Gc
Valence, *Gers, France* 34 Cd
Valencia, *Venezuela* 144 Ca
Valencia & prov., *Spain* 39 Ee
Valencia I. and Harb., *Eire* 25 Af
Valencia de Alcantara, *Spain* 37 Cc
Valencia de Don Juan, *Spain* 36 Eb
Valencia del Ventosa, *Spain* 37 Dd
Valenciennes, *France* 31 Fa
Valensole, *France* 33 Ab
Valentano, *Italy* 64 Ba
Valentin, mt., *Chile* 148 Bd
Valenza, *Italy* 62 Cb
Vale of Sorek, *Palestine* 80 Bd
Våler, *Norway* 46 Hd
Valestrand, *Norway* 47 Be
Valga, *Estonia* 49 Dc
Valgrana, *Italy* 62 Bc
Valgrund, *Finland* 48 De
Valguernera, *Sicily* 65 Hg
Valiente, C., *Panama* 140 Gf
Valikardhë, *Albania* 70 Bb
Valjala, *Estonia* 49 Bb
Valjevo, *Serbia* 68 Eb
Valkjärvi, *U.S.S.R.* 48 Hf
Valladolid, *Mexico* 139 Gc
Valladolid, *Philippines* 99 Fa
Valladolid & prov., *Spain* 38 Ac
Valle, *Norway* 47 De
Valle, El, *Colombia* 144 Ab
Vallecas, *Spain* 38 Bd
Vallecitos, *New Mexico* 135 Kc
Vallecorsa, *Italy* 64 Db
Valle de Cauca, dep., *Colombia* 144 Ac
Valle de La Pascua, *Venezuela* 144 Cb
Valle de Santiago, *Mexico* 138 Dc
Valledolmo, *Sicily* 65 Gg
Valledupar, *Colombia* 144 Ba
Valle Fertil, *Argentina* 146 Be
Vallejo, *California* 134 Bb
Vallenar, *Chile* 146 Ad
Vallet, *France* 32 Dc
Valletta, *Malta* 65 Kk
Valley City, *N. Dakota* 126 Fa
Valley Falls, *Kansas* 133 Ea
Valleyfield, *Quebec* 121 Cb
Valley Junction, *Iowa* 132 Ce
Valley Mills, *Texas* 133 De
Valley Springs, *California* 134 Cb
Vallikodu, *Madras States* 89 Bc
Valloire, *France* 35 Jb
Vallon, *France* 35 Gc
Vallorbe, *Switzerland* 42 Bc
Vallöy, *Norway* 47 Ge
Valls, *Spain* 39 Gc
Valluru, *Madras* 91 Ec
Valmaseda, *Spain* 38 Ba
Valmiera, *Latvia* 49 Cc
Valmojado, *Spain* 38 Ad
Valmontone, *Italy* 64 Cb
Valmy, *France* 31 Gb
Valognes, *France* 32 Da
Valona (Vlonë), *Albania* 70 Ac
Valona, B. of, *Albania* 70 Ac
Valonga, *Portugal* 37 Ba
Valora, *Ontario* 122 Ca
Valparaiso, *Indiana* 129 Ab
Valparaiso, *Mexico* 138 Dc
Valparaiso & prov., *Chile* 146 Ae
Valpovo, *Slavonia* 66 Dd
Valsequillo, *Spain* 37 Ed
Valtellina, *Italy* 62 Da
Valuevka, *U.S.S.R.* 75 Gf
Valuiki, *U.S.S.R.* 75 Fe
Val Venosta, *Italy* 62 Ea
Valverde de Jucar, *Spain* 38 Ce
Valverde del Camino, *Spain* 40 Db
Valverde de Llerena, *Spain* 40 Ea
Vamdrup, *Denmark* 45 Cc
Vámos, *Crete* 71 Hj
Van and Golu, *Turkey* 78 Db
Van Alstyne, *Texas* 133 Dd
Vana-Vandra, *Estonia* 49 Cb
Van Buren, *Arkansas* 130 Ac
Van Buren, *Maine* 120 Bc
Van Buren, *Missouri* 130 Cb
Vance, *Colorado* 135 Jc
Vanceboro, *Maine* 120 Bd
Vancouver, *Brit. Columbia* 124 Ee
Vancouver, *Washington* 136 Bc
Vancouver, C., *Alaska* 125 Ef
Vancouver, C., *W. Aust.* 152 Be
Vancouver I., *Br. Columbia* 124 De
Vancouver, Mt., *Yukon* 124 Bb
Vandalia, *Illinois* 132 Ef
Vandalia, *Missouri* 130 Ca
Vandellos, *Spain* 39 Fd
Van Diemen, C., *Queensl'd* 153 Ac
Van Diemen, C. & G., *N. Terr., Australia* 150 Da
Vandoies, *Italy* 63 Fa
Vanduzi, *Mozambique* 113 Eb
Vāne, *Latvia* 49 Bc
Vanegas, *Mexico* 138 Dc
Väner L., *Sweden* 50 Cc
Vänersborg, *Sweden* 50 Bd
Vang, *Norway* 46 Ec
Vanga, *Kenya* 111 Ff
Vangaindrano, *Madagascar* 112 Ed
Vangi, *Liberia* 104 Ce
Vangunu I., *Solomon Is.* 156 Jg
Vanikoro, I., *Santa Cruz Is.* 157De
Vanimo, *New Guinea* 156 Cb
Vaniyambadi, *Madras* 90 De
Vankaner, *Western India* 85 Cc
Vankerckhovenville, *Belgian Congo* 109 Ea
Vanleek Hill, *Ontario* 121 Cb
Vannas, *Sweden* 44 Dg
Vanndale, *Arkansas* 130 Cc
Vannes, *France* 32 Cc
Van-phong B. of, *Annam* 95 Cg
Van Reenen, *Natal* 115 Hd
Van Rees Mts., *New Guinea* 156Bb
Vanrhynsdorp, *Cape Prov.* 114 Ce
Vansittart B., *W. Aust.* 152 Da
Vansittart I., *N.-W. Terr.* 119 Nc
Vanua Levu, I., *Fiji Is.* 157 Fe
Van Wert, *Ohio* 129 Bb
Van Wyks Vlei, *Cape Prov.* 114 De
Vanylven, *Norway* 46 Bb
Vanylvsgapet, *Norway* 46 Bb
Var, R., *France* 33 Cb
Vara, *Sweden* 50 Bd
Vara, R., *Italy* 62 Dc
Varades, *France* 32 Dc
Varaita, R., *Italy* 62 Bc
Varaklani, *Latvia* 49 Dc
Varalto, *Italy* 62 Gb
Varangar Halvoy, *Norway* 44 Ge
Varanger Fd., *Norway* 44 Ge
Varaždin, *Croatia* 66 Bc
Varaždinske Toplice, *Croatia* 66 Bc
Varazze, *Italy* 62 Cc
Varberg, *Sweden* 51 Be
Vardar R., *Serbia* 70 Cb
Vardarska, *Serbia* 70 Ca
Varde, *Denmark* 45 Bc
Vardhousia Mts., *Greece* 71 De
Vardiste, *Bosnia* 68 Ec
Vardo, *Norway* 44 Ge
Varel, *Oldenburg* 54 Db
Varella, C., *Annam* 95 Cg
Varena, *Lithuania* 49 Cd
Varennes, *France* 31 Hd
Varennes, *Quebec* 121 Db
Varennes-sur-Allier, *France* 35 Fa
Vares, *Bosnia* 68 Db
Varese, *Italy* 62 Cb
Varful Pietrosul, *Transylvania* 67 Kb
Vargebre, *Norway* 46 Dd
Variás, *Romania* 67 Fc
Väring, *Sweden* 50 Cd
Varkaus, *Finland* 48 Ge
Varmland, lan, *Sweden* 50 Bc
Varna, *Bulgaria* 69 Hd
Varnamo, *Sweden* 51 De
Väro, *Sweden* 51 Be
Väroslöd, *Hungary* 66 Cb
Varpalota, *Hungary* 66 Db
Vars, *France* 34 Cb
Vars, *Ontario* 121 Cb
Varsinsk, *U.S.S.R.* 48 Mc
Varsuga & R., *U.S.S.R.* 48 Lc
Vartholomión, *Greece* 71 Cf
Vartöfta, *Sweden* 51 Cd
Varzi, *Italy* 62 Dc
Varzo, *Italy* 62 Ca
Vas, *Hungary* 66 Bb
Vásárosnameny, *Hungary* 67 Ha
Vascau, *Transylvania* 67 Hc
Vascongadas, *Spain* 38 Cb
Vashka, R., *U.S.S.R.* 74 Hc
Vasht, *Persia* 79 Hd
Vasilikón, *Euboea, Greece* 71 Ee
Vasilikón, *Ioannina, Greece* 70 Bc
Vasilikós, *Greece* 71 Ee

Vasilkov, *Ukraine* 75 De
Vaškovo, *Montenegro* 68 Ec
Vaskút, *Hungary* 66 Dc
Vaslui, *Romania* 69 Gb
Vassar, *Michigan* 122 Gd
Vastanfors, *Sweden* 50 Ec
Västerås, *Sweden* 50 Fc
Västerdalälven, *Sweden* 50 Ca
Våsterfjall, *Sweden* 48 Bc
Västervik, *Sweden* 51 Fe
Västland, *Sweden* 50 Gb
Västmanland, län, *Sweden* 50 Ec
Vasto, *Italy* 64 Ea
Vasvár, *Hungary* 66 Bb
Vatersay, I., *Scotland* 22 Ac
Vathi (Avlídhos), *Greece* 71 Ee
Vatican, City of the, *Italy* 64 Cb
Vaticano, C., *Italy* 65 Bd
Vátika B., *Greece* 71 Eg
Vatna Jokull, *Iceland* 52 Eb
Vatne, *Norway* 46 Cb
Vatneyri, *Iceland* 52 Bb
Vatomardry, *Madagascar* 112 Ec
Vatra Dornei, *Romania* 69 Fb
Vätter L., *Sweden* 51 Dd
Vatu Lele, I., *Fiji Is.* 157 Ok
Vaucluse, dep., *France* 35 Hc
Vaucouleurs, *France* 31 Hc
Vaud, canton, *Switzerland* 42 Cc
Vaudreuil, *Quebec* 121 Cb
Vaufranche, la, *France* 34 Ea
Vaughn, *Kansas* 133 Ca
Vaupes, *Colombia* 144 Bc
Vauvert, *France* 35 Gd
Vauvillers, *France* 31 Jd
Vavau, I., *Tonga Is.* 157 Fe
Vavoua, *Fr. W. Africa* 104 Ce
Vavuniya, *Ceylon* 89 Dc
Vaxholm, *Sweden* 50 Hc
Växjö, *Sweden* 51 Df
Vayalpad, *Madras* 90 De
Váyia, *Greece* 71 Ee
Vaysal, *Turkey* 72 Da
Veche, *Romania* 67 Ge
Vechelde, *Brunswick* 54 Fc
Vechta and R., *Oldenburg* 54 Dc
Vecilla, la, *Spain* 36 Eb
Veckerhagen, *Prussia* 54 Ed
Vecpiebalga, *Latvia* 49 Cc
Vedbæk, *Denmark* 45 Fc
Vedia, *Argentina* 148 Da
Veendam, *Holland* 29 Ea
Vega, *Norway* 44 Bf
Vega, La, *Granada, Spain* 41 Cc
Vega, La, *Orense, Spain* 36 Db
Vegadeo, *Spain* 36 Ca
Vegarshei, *Norway* 47 Ef
Veggli, *Norway* 47 Fd
Vegorrítis, L., *Greece* 70 Cc
Vegreville, *Alberta* 124 Gd
Veike Lasce, *Slovenia* 63 Jb
Veiveriai, *Lithuania* 49 Bd
Veivirzenai, *Lithuania* 49 Ad
Vejen, *Denmark* 45 Cc
Vejer de la Frontera, *Spain* 40 Dc
Vejle & Fjord, *Denmark* 45 Cc
Veksö, *Denmark* 45 Fc
Vela, *Argentina* 148 Eb
Vela, La, *Venezuela* 144 Ca
Velachha, *Baroda* 85 Dd
Vela Luku, *Dalmatia* 68 Bd
Velanai I., *Ceylon* 89 Cc
Velasco, *Texas* 133 Ef
Velburg, *Bavaria* 59 Fb
Velcan Mokra, *Albania* 70 Bc
Velebit Mts., *Jugoslavia* 63 Kc
Velenje, *Slovenia* 63 Ka
Velentzikon, *Greece* 70 Cd
Veles, *Serbia* 70 Cb
Velestínon, *Greece* 70 Dd
Velez Malaga, *Spain* 41 Bd
Velez Rubio, *Spain* 41 Dc
Velika Kapela, *Croatia* 63 Kb
Velika Kikinda, *Voyvodina* 67 Fd
Velika Plana, *Serbia* 68 Fb
Velikie Luki, *U.S.S.R.* 74 Ed
Veliki Ustyug, *U.S.S.R.* 74 Gc
Veliko Gradište, *Serbia* 68 Gb
Velikonda Ra., *Madras* 90 Dd
Velilla de Cinca, *Spain* 39 Ec
Velilla de Ebro, *Spain* 39 Ec
Veli Meše, *Turkey* 72 Ea
Velimje, *Montenegro* 68 Dd
Velingara, *Fr. W. Africa* 104 Bd
Velizh, *U.S.S.R.* 74 Ed
Veljun, *Croatia* 63 Kb
Velká, *Slovakia* 57 Fd
Vellach, *Austria* 59 Je
Vella Lavella, I., *Solomon Is.* 157 Cd
Velletri, *Italy* 64 Cb
Vellore, *Madras* 90 De
Velo, *Italy* 62 Fb
Velsk, *U.S.S.R.* 74 Gc
Velvendós, *Greece* 70 Dc
Vem, *Denmark* 45 Bb
Vemalwada, *Hyderabad* 90 Db
Veme, *Norway* 47 Gd
Vempalle, *Madras* 90 Dd
Venado, *Mexico* 138 Dc
Venado Tuerto, *Argentina* 146 Ce
Venafro, *Italy* 64 Db
Vena Park, *Queensland* 153 Bc
Vence, *France* 33 Cb
Vendas Novas, *Portugal* 37 Bd
Vendee, dep., *France* 32 Dd
Vendes, *France* 34 Eb
Vendeuvre, *France* 31 Gc
Vendom I., *Greenland* 9 Fd
Vendôme, *France* 30 Dd
Vendrell, *Spain* 39 Gc
Venétiko, *Greece* 71 Cg
Venezia (Venice), *Italy* 63 Gb
Venezuela, rep., *S. Amer.* 141 Cb
Venezuela, G. de, *Venez.* 144 Ba
Vengurla, *Bombay* 90 Ad
Venice, *California* 134 Dd
Venice, *Florida* 131 Mh
Venice (Venezia), *Italy* 63 Gb
Venice, G. of, *Italy* 63 Gb
Venjan, *Sweden* 50 Cb
Venkatagiri, *Madras* 90 Dd
Venkatapuram, *Madras* 91 Eb
Venlo, *Holland* 29 Ec
Vennachar, L., *Scotland* 23 Dd
Venosa, *Italy* 64 Fc
Ventana, Sa., *Argentina* 148 Db
Ventersburg, *O.F.S.* 115 Gd
Ventersdorp, *Transvaal* 115 Gc
Venterstad, *Cape Prov.* 115 Fe
Ventimiglia, *Italy* 62 Bd
Ventnor, *I. of Wight, Eng.* 14 Ce
Ventotene, I., *Italy* 64 Dc
Ventspils, *Latvia* 49 Ac
Ventuari, R., *Venezuela* 144 Cb
Ventura, *California* 134 Dd
Venus B., *Victoria* 154 Ee
Vepriai, *Lithuania* 49 Cd
Vera, *Argentina* 146 Cd
Vera, La, *Spain* 37 Ec
Vera Cruz, *Mexico* 139 Ed
Veragua, Cord de, *Panama* 140 Gf
Veramin, *Persia* 79 Fb
Veraval, *Western India* 85 Cd
Verbicaro, *Italy* 64 Fd
Vercelli, *Italy* 62 Cb
Vercheres, *Quebec* 121 Db
Verclanuova, *Italy* 62 Eb
Verde, *California* 134 Cd
Verde, C., *Fr. W. Africa* 104 Ad
Verde R., *Arizona* 135 He
Verde, R., *Mexico* 139 Ed
Verden, *Prussia* 54 Ec
Verdiaris R., *Oklahoma* 133 Eb
Verdun, *France* 31 Hb
Verdun, *Quebec* 121 Db
Verdun-sur-le-Doub, *France* 31 He
Vereeniging, *Transvaal* 115 Gc
Vereshchagino, *U.S.S.R.* 74 Jd
Vergara, *Spain* 38 Ca
Vergara, *Uruguay* 147 Ee
Vergara (Amayantir), *Philippines* 99 Fb
Vergato, *Italy* 62 Fc
Vergemont, *Queensland* 153 Bd
Vergennes, *Vermont* 128 Ba
Verin, *Spain* 36 Cc
Verkeerdevlei, *O.F.S.* 115 Gd
Verkhne Ufaleiski, *U.S.S.R.* 74 Kd
Verkhneuralsk, *U.S.S.R.* 74 Ke
Verkhoture, *U.S.S.R.* 74 Ld
Verkhoyansk, *U.S.S.R.* 76 Oc
Verkhoyansk Mts., *U.S.S.R.* 76 Nc
Verlegen Huken, *Spitsbergen* 9 La
Verma, *Norway* 46 Eb
Vermaas, *Transvaal* 115 Gc
Vermenton, *France* 31 Fd
Vermilion, *S. Dakota* 132 Ad
Vermilion B., *Louisiana* 130 Bf
Vermilion R., *Quebec* 123 Mb
Vermilion Bay, *Ontario* 122 Ba
Vermillion, *S. Dakota* 126 Fb
Vermillion L., *Minnesota* 132 Cb
Vermont, state, *U.S.A.* 127 Lb
Vernal, *Utah* 135 Ja
Vernayaz, *Switzerland* 42 Dd
Verner, *Ontario* 123 Hb
Verneuil, *France* 30 Cc
Verneukpan, *Cape Prov.* 114 De
Vernio, *Italy* 62 Fc
Vernon, *Brit. Columbia* 124 Fd
Vernon, *France* 30 Db
Vernon, *Texas* 133 Cc
Vernoux, *France* 35 Gc
Verny, *France* 31 Jb
Vero Beach, *Florida* 131 Nh
Véroia, *Greece* 70 Dc
Verona, *Italy* 62 Fb
Verona, *Montana* 136 Ha
Verona, *Ontario* 121 Bb
Verpelet, *Hungary* 66 Fb
Verpilliere, *France* 35 Hb
Verplanck, *New York* 128 Bc
Verrès, *Italy* 62 Bb
Verrieres, les, *Switz.* 42 Bc
Versailles, *France* 30 Dc
Versailles, *Kentucky* 131 Fa
Versailles, *Missouri* 130 Ba
Versam, *Switzerland* 43 Hc
Versmold, *Prussia* 54 Dc
Verte B., *Newfoundland* 120 Ha
Verte, I., *Quebec* 123 Ob
Verteneglio 63 Hb
Vértes Mts., *Hungary* 66 Db
Vertou, *France* 32 Dc
Verulam, *Natal* 115 Jd
Vérvaina, *Greece* 71 Df
Verviers, *Belgium* 29 Dd
Vervins, *France* 31 Fb
Vešala, *Serbia* 70 Ba
Veseli, *Moravia* 57 Ce
Veshensk, *U.S.S.R.* 75 Gf
Vesoul, *France* 31 Jd
Vespolate, *Italy* 62 Cb
Vest Fd., *Norway* 44 Cf
Vesta, *Costa Rica* 140 Gf
Vesta, *Minnesota* 132 Bc
Vest-Agder, fylke, *Norway* 47 Df
Vesterålen, *Norway* 44 Ce
Vesterö, *Denmark* 45 Da
Vestfold, fylke, *Norway* 47 Fe
Vestmannaeyjar, *Iceland* 52 Cc
Vestnes, *Norway* 46 Cb
Vestone, *Italy* 62 Eb
Vesturhorn, *Iceland* 52 Fb
Vesuvius, Mte., *Italy* 64 Ec
Veszprém, *Hungary* 66 Cb
Vesztö, *Hungary* 67 Gc
Vetluga & R., *U.S.S.R.* 74 Hd
Vetralla, *Italy* 64 Ba
Veules, *France* 30 Cb
Veum, *Norway* 47 De
Vevay, *Indiana* 129 Bc
Vevey, *Switzerland* 42 Cd
Vezelay, *France* 31 Fd
Vézer, R., *France* 34 Db
Vezseny, *Hungary* 66 Fb
Viacha, *Bolivia* 146 Bb
Viana do Castelo, *Portugal* 36 Bc
Viadona, *Italy* 62 Ec
Viana del Bollo, *Spain* 36 Cb
Viana do Alentejo, *Portugal* 40 Ca
Vianna, *Brazil* 143 Ec
Viareggio, *Italy* 62 Ed
Vibonati, *Italy* 64 Fc
Viborg, *Denmark* 45 Cb
Vibo Valentia, *Italy* 65 Cd
Viby, *Denmark* 45 Db
Vicenta, *Mozambique* 112 Cc
Vicente, *Uruguay* 147 Ee
Vicenza, *Italy* 63 Fb
Vich, *Spain* 39 Hc
Vichada, *Colombia* 144 Bc
Vichado, R., *Colombia* 144 Cc
Vichuquen, *Chile* 146 Ae
Vichy, *France* 35 Fa
Vicksburg, *Mississippi* 130 Cd
Vico, *Corsica* 33 Dg
Vicopisano, *Italy* 62 Ed
Vicor, Sa. de, *Spain* 38 Dc
Vicosoprano, *Switzerland* 43 Jd
Victor, *Idaho* 136 Hd
Victor, *Montana* 136 Fb
Victor Emanuel Ra., *New Guinea* 156 Cb
Victor Harbour, *S. Aust.* 154 Bd
Victoria, *Argentina* 146 Ce
Victoria, *Brazil* 147 Gc
Victoria, *Alagoas, Brazil* 143 Gd
Victoria, *Vancouver I.* 124 Ee
Victoria, *Chile* 148 Bb
Victoria, *China* 95 De
Victoria, *Fr. W. Africa* 104 Bd
Victoria, *Nigeria* 105 Ce
Victoria, co., *Ontario* 121 Ab
Victoria, state, *Australia* 151 Gf
Victoria Falls, *Zambesi R.* 113 Aa
Victoria Fd., *Greenland* 9 Ea
Victoria I., *N.-W. Terr.* 118 Gb
Victoria I., *Pacific Oc.* 149 Kf
Victoria, L., *E. Africa* 110 Cd
Victoria, L., *Victoria* 155 Fe
Victoria Land, *N.-W. T.* 118 Hc
Victoria Mt., *Burma* 92 Ab
Victoria, Mt., *New Guinea* 156 Dc
Victoria Pk., *Philippines* 99 Eb
Victoria Quad., *Antarctica* 160 —
Victoria Ra., *W. Aust.* 152 Ad
Victoria R., *N. Terr., Australia* 150 Eb
Victoria East, *Cape Prov.* 115 Gf
Victoria Nile, R., *Uganda* 110 Bb
Victoria Point, *Burma* 98 Aa
Victoria River Downs, *N. Terr., Australia* 150 Db
Victoriaville, *Quebec* 121 Ea
Victoria West, *Cape Prov.* 114 Ee
Victorica, *Argentina* 148 Cb
Victory Mills, *New York* 128 Bb
Vidago, *Portugal* 36 Cc
Vidalia, *Mississippi* 130 Ce
Vidauban, *France* 33 Bc
Videle, *Romania* 69 Fc
Videmangué, *Fr. Eq. Afr.* 105 De
Vidin, *Bulgaria* 69 Ec
Vidlitsa, *U.S.S.R.* 48 Kf
Vidostern, *Sweden* 51 Ce
Viechio, *Italy* 63 Fd
Viechtach, *Bavaria* 59 Gb
Viedma, *Argentina* 148 Dc
Viedma, L., *Argentina* 148 Bd
Viekšniai, *Lithuania* 49 Bc
Viella, *Spain* 39 Fb
Vielsalm, *Belgium* 29 Dd
Vienna, *Georgia* 131 Gd
Vienna, *Missouri* 130 Ba
Vienna (Wien), *Austria* 59 Lc
Vienne, *Isère, France* 35 Gb
Vienne, *Loir-et-Cher, France* 30 Dd
Vienne, dep. & R., *France* 34 Ca
Vien-tiane, *Laos* 95 Bf
Vieques, I. de, *Puerto Rico* 140 Jg
Vierfontein, *O.F.S.* 115 Gc
Viersen, *Prussia* 54 Bd
Vierwaldstatter See, *Switz.* 43 Fb
Vierzon-Ville, *France* 30 Dd
Viesca, L., *Mexico* 138 Db
Viesite, *Latvia* 49 Cc
Vieste, *Italy* 64 Gb
Vietri, *Tong-king* 95 Ce
Vietzig 56 Bb
Vieuna, *Chile* 146 Ae
Vig, *Denmark* 45 Ec
Vigan, *Philippines* 95 Ff
Vigan, le, *France* 35 Fd
Vigeois, *France* 34 Db
Vigevano, *Italy* 62 Cb
Viggiano, *Italy* 65 Bb
Vigia, *Brazil* 143 Ec
Vigia, La, *Venezuela* 144 Bb
Vigia Chicho, *Mexico* 139 Gd
Viglio, Mte., *Italy* 64 Db
Vigo and R., *Spain* 36 Bb
Vigone, *Italy* 62 Bc
Vigrestad, *Norway* 47 Bf
Vigsö B., *Denmark* 45 Ba
Vigy, *France* 31 Jb
Vihanti, *Finland* 48 Fd
Vihiers, *France* 32 Ec
Viipuri (Vyborg), *U.S.S.R.* 48 Hf
Vijapur, *Baroda* 85 Dc
Vijayadurg, *Bombay* 90 Ac
Vijosë, R., *Albania* 70 Ac
Vik, *Iceland* 52 Dc
Vik, *Norway* 46 Cc
Vik Sjö, *Sweden* 50 Dd
Vikersvik, *Sweden* 50 Dc
Vikesund, *Norway* 47 Ge
Vikna, *Norway* 44 Bf
Vikoc, *Bosnia* 68 Dc
Vila, *New Hebrides* 157 De
Vila Bocage, *Mozambique* 113 Fa
Vilac, *Montenegro* 68 Ed
Vilada, *Spain* 39 Gb
Vila do Bispo, *Portugal* 40 Bb
Vila do Conde, *Portugal* 36 Bc
Vila Flor, *Portugal* 37 Cc
Vila Fontes, *Mozambique* 112 Cc
Vila Franca de Xira, *Portugal* 37 Ad
Vilaine, R., *France* 32 Dc
Vilaka, *Latvia* 49 Dc
Vila Luzo, *Angola* 109 Cd
Vila Machado, *Mozambique* 112 Bc
Vilanculos, *Mozambique* 112 Bd
Vila Paiva d'Andrade, *Mozambique* 113 Fb
Vila Pereira, *Mozambique* 113 Ga
Vila Pery, *Mozambique* 113 Eb
Vila Real de Santo Antonio, *Portugal* 40 Cb
Vilarelho, Sa. de, *Portugal* 36 Cc
Vila Silva Porto, *Angola* 109 Cd
Vila Teixeira da Silva, *Angola* 109 Cd
Vila-Velha de Rodão, *Portugal* 37 Cc
Vila Vicosa, *Portugal* 37 Cd
Vildtland, *Greenland* 9 Fa
Vilhelmina, *Sweden* 48 Ad
Vilhena, *Brazil* 142 Be
Viljandi, *Estonia* 49 Cb
Vilkaviškis, *Lithuania* 49 Bd
Vilkija, *Lithuania* 49 Bd
Villa Ahumada, *Mexico* 138 Ca
Villa Angela, *Argentina* 146 Cd
Villaba, *Spain* 38 Db
Villa Bella, *Bolivia* 142 Ae
Villa Bittencourt (Narino), *Brazil* 145 Db
Villablanca, *Spain* 40 Cb
Villablino, *Spain* 36 Db
Villacañas, *Spain* 38 Be
Villacarlos, *Balearic Is.* 39 Mj
Villacarriedo, *Spain* 38 Ba
Villacarrillo, *Spain* 41 Cb
Villach, *Austria* 59 He
Villacidro, *Sardinia* 64 Hg
Villa Cisneros, *Rio de Oro* 104 Ab
Villa Constitucion, *Argentina* 146 Ce
Villa Coronada, *Mexico* 138 Db
Villa Curuguaty, *Paraguay* 146 Dc
Villa de Don Fadrique, *Spain* 38 Be
Villa de Rosario, *Argentina* 146 Ce
Villa de Rosario, *Paraguay* 146 Dc
Villadiego, *Spain* 38 Bb
Villa d'Nevoso 63 Jb
Villa Dolores, *Argentina* 146 Be
Villa d'Ossola, *Italy* 62 Ca
Villafamés, *Spain* 39 Ed
Villa Federal, *Argentina* 146 De
Villa Feijo, *Brazil* 145 Cc
Villafeliche, *Spain* 38 Dc
Villafranca, *Italy* 62 Eb
Villafranca, *Spain* 38 Db
Villafranca del Bierza, *Spain* 36 Db
Villafranca del Campo, *Spain* 38 Dd
Villafranca del Cid, *Spain* 39 Ed
Villafranca de los Barros, *Spain* 37 Dd
Villafranca de los Caballeros, *Spain* 38 Be
Villafranca del Panades, *Spain* 39 Gc
Villagarcia, *Spain* 41 Ea
Villagarcia de Arosa, *Spain* 36 Bb
Villagio, *Libya* 106 Cf
Villagonzalo, *Spain* 37 Dd
Villa Grove, *Colorado* 135 Kb
Villaguay, *Argentina* 146 De
Villa Guillermina, *Argentina* 146 Cd
Villa Hermosa, *Mexico* 139 Fd
Villahermosa, *Spain* 39 Ed
Villa Hidalgo, *Mexico* 138 Db
Villa Huidobro, *Argentina* 146 Be
Villaines-la-Juhel, *France* 30 Bc
Villa Iris, *Argentina* 148 Db
Villa João Belo, *Mozambique* 112 Be
Villa Jordão, *Brazil* 145 Cc
Villajoyosa, *Spain* 41 Fb
Villalba, *Spain* 39 Fc
Villalba, *Lugo, Spain* 36 Ca
Villaldama, *Mexico* 138 Db
Villalon de Campos, *Spain* 36 Eb
Villalonga, *Argentina* 148 Db
Villalpando, *Spain* 36 Ec
Villa Luiza, *Mozambique* 112 Be
Villamalea, *Spain* 38 De
Villamanrique, *Spain* 41 Db
Villamar, *Sardinia* 64 Hg
Villa Maria, *Argentina* 146 Ce
Villamartin, *Spain* 40 Ec
Villamayor de Santiago, *Spain* 38 Ce
Villa Mercedes, *Argentina* 146 Be
Villa Monte, *Bolivia* 146 Cc
Villa Murtinho, *Brazil* 142 Ae
Villa Nora, *Transvaal* 113 Bd
Villa Nova, *Amazonas, Brazil* 142 Cd
Villa Nova, *Sergipe, Brazil* 143 Ge
Villanova, *Italy* 62 Bc
Villanova Monteleone, *Sardinia* 64 Hf
Villa Novo, *Brazil* 142 Dc
Villanueva, *Mexico* 138 Dc
Villanueva, *Spain* 38 Dc
Villanueva de Cordoba, *Spain* 37 Fd
Villanueva de Gallego, *Spain* 38 Ec
Villanueva de Gomez, *Spain* 37 Fb
Villanueva de la Jara, *Spain* 38 Ce
Villanueva de la Serena, *Spain* 37 Ed
Villanueva de la Vera, *Spain* 37 Eb

Walachia (Muntenia), Romania - 69 Fc
Walcha, New S. Wales - 155 Gb
Walchen, Austria - 59 Gd
Walcheren, I., Holland - 29 Bc
Walcourt, Belgium - 29 Cd
Waldburg Ra., W. Aust. 152 Bc
Walden, Colorado - 135 Ka
Waldenburg (Walbrzych) 55 Me
Waldenburg, Switzerland 42 Eb
Waldenburg, Württemberg 58 Db
Waldens Ridge, Tennessee 131 Fc
Waldheim, Saxony - 55 Jd
Waldia, Ethiopia - 108 Cc
Waldkeppel, Prussia - 54 Ed
Waldkirchen, Bavaria - 59 Hc
Waldmünchen, Bavaria 59 Gb
Waldo, Arkansas - 130 Bd
Waldo, Florida - 131 Gf
Waldo L., Oregon - 136 Bd
Waldport, Oregon - 136 Ac
Waldron, Arkansas - 130 Ac
Waldsassen, Bavaria - 59 Gb
Waldsee, Württemberg - 58 Dd
Waldshut, Baden - 58 Cd
Walen See, Switzerland - 43 Hb
Wales, Alaska - 125 Ed
Wales, Great Britain - 13 Ee
Walese, Belgian Congo - 109 Ea
Walford, England - 14 Bb
Walgett, New S. Wales - 155 Fb
Walhalla, S. Carolina - 131 Gc
Walhalla, Victoria - 155 Ee
Walikale, Belg. Congo - 109 Eb
Walkaway, W Australia 152 Ad
Walker, Minnesota - 132 Bb
Walker, Quebec - 121 Da
Walker B., Cape Prov. - 114 Cg
Walker L., Nevada - 134 Db
Walkerburn, Scotland - 21 Cb
Walker River Ra., Nevada 134 Db
Walkers Ra., Oregon - 136 Cd
Walkerton, Ontario - 123 Hc
Walkerville, Ontario - 122 Gd
Wall, Mt., W. Australia 152 Bc
Wallace, Idaho - 136 Eb
Wallaceburg, Ontario - 122 Gd
Wallal, W. Australia - 152 Cb
Wallangarra, Queensland 153 De
Wallaroo, S. Australia - 154 Ac
Wallasey, England - 18 Ad
Wallaston, N. Terr., Aust. 150 Eb
Walla Walla, N. S. W. - 155 Ed
Walla-Walla, Washington 136 Db
Walldurn, Baden - 58 Db
Wallekraal, Cape Prov. - 114 Be
Wallenstadt, Switzerland 43 Hb
Wallingford, England - 14 Cc
Wallingford, Vermont - 128 Bb
Wallis Is., Pacific Oc. - 157 Fe
Wallisville, Texas - 133 Ef
Wallowa R. and Mts., Oregon - 136 Ec
Walls, Zetland - 24 Gh
Wallsee, Austria - 59 Jc
Wallsend, England - 21 Ed
Wallsend, New S. Wales 155 Gc
Wallula, Washington - 136 Db
Walmer, Cape Prov. - 115 Fg
Walney, I., England - 18 Ab
Walnut Cove, N. Carolina 131 Hb
Walnut Grove, Mississippi 130 Dd
Walpole, New Hampshire 128 Bb
Walrus I., Bering Sea - 125 Eh
Walsall, England - 14 Ca
Walsenburg, Colorado - 135 Lc
Walsh, Queensland - 153 Bc
Walsingham, N.-W. Terr. 119 Rc
Walsrode, Prussia - 54 Ec
Waltair, Madras - 91 Fc
Walterboro, S. Carolina - 131 Hd
Walters, Oklahoma - 133 Cc
Waltersdorf - 55 Ld
Waltham, England - 19 De
Waltham, Massachusetts 128 Cb
Waltham, Quebec - 121 Bb
Waltham Abbey, England 15 Ec
Waltham Cross, England 15 Dc
Waltham, Gt. & Lit., Eng. 15 Ec
Walton, Somerset, England 14 Bd
Walton, Suffolk, England 15 Fc
Walton, New York - 129 Ga
Walton, Nova Scotia - 120 Dd
Walton-on-the-Naze, England - 15 Fc
Wal Wal, Ethiopia - 108 Ed
Wamala, L., Uganda - 110 Cc
Wamba, Belgian Congo - 109 Ea
Wamba, Kenya - 110 Ec
Wambeka, New Guinea - 156 Bc
Wamego, Kansas - 133 Da
Wamlana, Boeroe I., N.I. 99 Gd
Wampsville, New York - 123 Kd
Wamsisi, Boeroe I., N.I. 99 Gd
Wana, N.-W. F. P. - 82 Cb
Wanaaring, New S. Wales 154 Da
Wanaka, L., New Zealand 159 Bf
Wanapitei, L., Ontario - 123 Hb
Wanbi, S. Australia - 154 Cc
Wanchese, N. Carolina - 131 Lc
Wanchuan, China - 94 Da
Wandamen B., New Guinea 156 Ab
Wandiwash, Madras - 90 De
Wandoan, Queensland - 153 Ce
Wandsbek, Hamburg - 54 Fb
Wang, China - 94 Cb
Wanganella, New S. Wales 154 Dd
Wanganui and R., New Zealand - 158 Ec
Wangara, S. Australia - 154 Ac
Wangaratta, Victoria - 155 Ed
Wangching, Manchuria - 96 Dc
Wangen, Switzerland - 42 Eb
Wangen, Württemberg - 58 Dd
Wangerooge, I., Prussia 54 Cb
Wangford, England - 15 Fb
Wangga Meti, Soemba I., Netherlands Indies - 99 Fe
Wangi Wangi, Netherlands Indies - 99 Fd
Wang-je-fu, China - 94 Bb
Wangkwei, Manchuria - 96 Db
Wan-hsien, China - 94 Cc
Wanke, Ital. Somaliland 108 Gf
Wankie, S. Rhodesia - 113 Bb
Wankung, Manchuria - 96 Bb
Wanlockhead, Scotland - 21 Cc
Wansen - 57 Cc
Wansford, England - 15 Da
Wantage, England - 14 Cc
Wantu, Burma - 92 Aa
Wanyin, Burma - 92 Cb
Wanzleben, Prussia - 55 Gc
Wapakoneta, Ohio - 129 Bb
Wapello, Iowa - 132 De
Wapheton, N. Dakota - 126 Fa
Wapi, Idaho - 136 Gd
Wapiti R., Alberta - 124 Fd
Wapou, Fr. W. Africa - 104 Cf
Wappingers Falls, New York - 128 Bc
Warabes, Kenya - 110 Fe
Warabi, Japan - 100 Gd
Warangal, Hyderabad - 90 Dc
Warangwa, A.-E. Sudan 108 Bd
Waratah, Tasmania - 155 Jg
Waratah B., Victoria - 155 Ee
Warboys, England - 15 Db
Warburg, Prussia - 54 Ed
Warburton, Victoria - 155 Ee
Warburton R., S. Aust. 154 Aa
Ward, Colorado - 135 La
Warden, O.F.S. - 115 Hc
Wardha and R., Central Provs. - 86 Ce
Ward Hunt Str., New Guinea - 156 Dc
Wardner, Idaho - 136 Eb
Ware, England - 15 Dc
Wareham, England - 14 Be
Wareham, Massachusetts 128 Cc
Waremme, Belgium - 29 Dd
Waren, Mecklenburg - 55 Hb
Warenda, Queensland - 153 Bd
Warendorf, Prussia - 54 Cd
Waresley, England - 15 Db
Warialda, New S. Wales 155 Ga
Warji, China - 94 Ac
Warkworth, England - 21 Ec
Warmbad, S.-W. Africa 114 Cd
Warmbad, Transvaal - 115 Hb
Warmbrunn - 55 Le
Warmington, England - 15 Da
Warminster, England - 14 Bd
Warmspring, Oregon - 136 Cc
Warm Springs, Virginia 129 Ec
Warmwaters Berg, Cape Prov. - 114 Df
Warnemünde, Mecklenburg 55 Ga
Warner L., Oregon - 136 Dd
Warnier, Algeria - 102 Ea
Warnsdorf, Bohemia - 59 Ja
Waromge B., New Guinea 156 Ab
Warora, Central Provs. - 86 Ce
Warr, Uganda - 110 Bb
Warracknabeal, Victoria 154 Cd
Warragul, Victoria - 155 Ee
Warramboo, S. Australia 154 Ac
Warrego Ra., Queensland 153 Cd
Warrego R., Queensland 153 Ce
Warren, Arkansas - 130 Bd
Warren, Colorado - 135 La
Warren, Massachusetts - 128 Bb
Warren, Minnesota - 132 Aa
Warren, New S. Wales - 155 Fb
Warren, Ohio - 129 Db
Warren, Ontario - 123 Hb
Warren, Pennsylvania - 129 Eb
Warren, Wisconsin - 132 Dd
Warrenpoint, N. Ireland 26 Dc
Warrensburg, Missouri - 130 Ba
Warrenton, Cape Prov. - 115 Fd
Warrenton, Georgia - 131 Gd
Warrenton, Missouri - 130 Ca
Warrenton, N. Carolina 131 Jb
Warrenton, Virginia - 129 Ec
Warri, Nigeria - 105 Cd
Warrina, S. Australia - 154 Aa
Warrington, England - 18 Bd
Warrington, Florida - 130 Ee
Warrnambool, Victoria - 154 Ce
Warroad, Minnesota - 132 Ba
Warsaw, Illinois - 132 De
Warsaw, Indiana - 129 Ab
Warsaw, Kentucky - 131 Fa
Warsaw, Missouri - 130 Ba
Warsaw, New York - 123 Jd
Warsaw, N. Carolina - 131 Kc
Warsaw (Warszawa), Poland 60 Fb
Warsheik, Ital. Somalilaud 108 Hf
Warstein, Prussia - 54 Dd
Warszawa (Warsaw), Poland 60 Fb
Warta, Poland - 57 Db
Warta, R., Poland - 60 Db
Wartburg, Tennessee - 131 Fb
Wartenburg - 56 Ec
Wartha - 57 Bc
Warthe, R. - 55 Lc
Warthe Bruch - 55 Kc
Warwick, New York - 128 Ac
Warwick, Quebec - 121 Eb
Warwick, Queensland - 153 De
Warwick, Rhode Island - 128 Cc
Warwick & co., England 14 Cb
Wasatch Mts., Utah - 135 Hb
Waschbank, Natal - 115 Jd
Wasco, Oregon - 136 Cc
Wase, Nigeria - 105 Cd
Waseca, Minnesota - 132 Cc
Wash, The, England - 19 Ee
Washakie Needle, Wyoming 126 Db
Washburn, Texas - 133 Bc
Washburn, Wisconsin - 132 Db
Washburn, Mt., Wyoming 136 Hc
Washington, Arkansas - 130 Bd
Washington, Dist. of Columbia - 129 Fc
Washington, Georgia - 131 Gd
Washington, Indiana - 129 Ac
Washington, Iowa - 132 De
Washington, Kansas - 133 Da
Washington, Missouri - 130 Ca
Washington, N. Carolina 131 Kc
Washington, Ohio - 129 Cc
Washington, Pennsylvania 129 Db
Washington, Utah - 135 Gc
Washington, state, U.S.A. 126 Aa
Washington I., Line Is. - 157 Gc
Washington Land, Greenland - 9 Ca
Washir, Afghanistan - 79 Hc
Washita R., Arkansas - 130 Bd
Washita R., Oklahoma - 133 Cc
Washoe, Nevada - 134 Db
Wasile, Halmahera, N.I. 99 Gc
Wasilkow, Poland - 56 Hc
Wasilla, Alaska - 125 Kf
Wassen, Switzerland - 43 Cc
Wasser, S. W. Africa - 114 Cc
Wasseralfingen, Wurttemb'g 58 Dc
Wasserbillig, Luxembourg 29 Ee
Wasserburg, Bavaria - 59 Gc
Wasserkuppe, mt., Prussia 58 Da
Wassertrüdingen, Bavaria 58 Eb
Wassigny, France - 31 Fa
Wasson, Colorado - 135 Kc
Waswanipi L. and R., Quebec - 123 Ka
Watampone, Celébes - 99 Fd
Watamu, Kenya - 110 Fe
Wataroa, New Zealand - 159 Ce
Watchet, England - 14 Ad
Watchfield, England - 14 Bd
Waterbeach, England - 15 Eb
Waterbury, Connecticut - 128 Bc
Waterbury, Vermont - 128 Ba
Wateree R., S. Carolina 131 Hc
Waterford, Cape Prov. - 115 Ff
Waterford, Connecticut - 128 Bc
Waterford, New Brunswick 120 Cd
Waterford, New York - 128 Bb
Waterford, S. Rhodesia - 113 Ab
Waterford and co., Eire 27 Cg
Waterford Harb., Eire - 27 Cg
Waterklip, Cape Prov. - 114 Be
Waterloo, Alabama - 130 Ec
Waterloo, Belgium - 29 Cd
Waterloo, Illinois - 130 Ca
Waterloo, Iowa - 132 Cd
Waterloo, Ontario - 123 Hd
Waterloo, Quebec - 121 Db
Waterpoort, Transvaal - 113 Cd
Waterton Lakes National Park, Alberta - 124 Ge
Watertown, New York - 123 Lc
Watertown, S. Dakota - 126 Fa
Watertown, Wisconsin - 132 Ed
Waterval Boyen, Transvaal 115 Jb
Watervale, Colorado - 135 Mc
Water Valley, Mississippi 130 Dc
Waterville, Maine - 128 Da
Waterville, Minnesota - 132 Cc
Waterville, New York - 128 Ab
Waterville, Quebec - 121 Eb
Waterville, Washington - 136 Db
Watervliet, New York - 129 Ga
Waterways, Alberta - 124 Gc
Watford, England - 15 Dc
Watkins, New York - 129 Fa
Watkins Mts., Greenland 9 Fd
Watlings (San Salvador) I., Bahamas - 140 Cb
Watlington, England - 15 Dc
Watonga, Oklahoma - 133 Cc
Watrous, New Mexico - 135 Ld
Watrous, Saskatchewan - 124 Hd
Watsa, Belg. Congo - 109 Ea
Watseka, Illinois - 132 Fe
Watson, Utah - 135 Jb
Watson Pk., Arizona - 135 Gd
Watsonville, California - 134 Bc
Watt, New Brunswick - 120 Bd
Watton, England - 15 Ea
Wattsville, Alabama - 130 Ed
Wattwil, Switzerland - 43 Hb
Wau, A.-E. Sudan - 108 Ad
Wauchope, New S. Wales 155 Gb
Wauchula, Florida - 131 Nh
Waukaringa, S. Australia 154 Bb
Waukegan, Illinois - 132 Fd
Waukesha, Wisconsin - 132 Ed
Waukomis, Oklahoma - 133 Db
Waukon, Iowa - 132 Dd
Waupaca, Wisconsin - 132 Ec
Waupun, Wisconsin - 132 Ed
Waurika, Oklahoma - 133 Dc
Wausau, Wisconsin - 132 Ec
Wauseon, Ohio - 129 Bb
Wautoma, Wisconsin - 132 Ec
Wauwatosa, Wisconsin - 132 Fd
Wave Hill, N. Terr., Aust. 150 Eb
Waveney, R., England - 15 Fb
Waverly, Iowa - 132 Cd
Waverly, New York - 123 Kd
Waverly, Ohio - 129 Cc
Waverly, Tennessee - 130 Eb
Wavre, Belgium - 29 Cd
Wawa, Nigeria - 105 Bc
Wawa, Ontario - 122 Fa
Wawa Central, Nicaragua 140 Ge
Waxahachie, Texas - 133 Dd
Waxhaw, N. Carolina - 131 Hc
Waya, I., Fiji Is. - 157 Oj
Waycross, Georgia - 131 Ge
Wayland, Ontario - 122 Ga
Wayne, Nebraska - 132 Ad
Wayne, W. Virginia - 129 Dc
Waynesboro, Georgia - 131 Gd
Waynesboro, Mississippi 130 De
Waynesboro, Pennsylvania 129 Fc
Waynesburg, Pennsylvania 129 Dc
Waynesville, Missouri - 130 Bb
Waynesville, N. Carolina 131 Gc
Waynoka, Oklahoma - 133 Cb
Wayuaki, Timor I., N.I. 99 Ge
Wazirabad, Punjab - 83 Fb
Waziristan, N. and S., N.-W. F.P. - 82 Cb
We I., Sumatra - 98 Ab
Weald, The, England - 15 Ed
Wear, R., England - 21 Ed
Wearhead, England - 21 Dd
Weatherford, Oklahoma - 133 Cc
Weatherford, Texas - 133 Dd
Weaver, R., England - 18 Bd
Weaverville, California - 134 Ba
Webb, Mississippi - 130 Cd
Webb City, Missouri - 130 Ab
Webbe Shibeli, Ital. Somaliland - 108 Gf
Webbwood, Ontario - 122 Gb
Webster, Massachusetts - 128 Cb
Webster City, Iowa - 132 Cd
Webster Springs, W. Virginia - 129 Dc
Weda and B., Halmahera, Netherlands Indies - 99 Gc
Weda Is., Nether. Indies 99 Gd
Weddell I., Falkland Is. 148 De
Weddell Sea and Quad., Antarctica - 160 —
Wedderburn, Victoria - 154 Dd
Wedel, Prussia - 54 Eb
Wedgeport, Nova Scotia 120 Be
Wedmore, England - 14 Bd
Wednesbury, England - 14 Ca
Wedza, S. Rhodesia - 113 Cc
Weed, California - 134 Ba
Weedon, England - 14 Cb
Weedon, Quebec - 121 Eb
Weeks, Louisiana - 130 Cf
Weenen, Natal - 115 Jd
Weener, Prussia - 54 Cb
Weeping Water, Nebraska 132 Ae
Weeringerwerf, Holland 29 Cb
Weert, Holland - 29 Dc
Weesen, Switzerland - 43 Hb
Weesp, Holland - 29 Cb
Weetzen, Prussia - 54 Ec
Wee Waa, New S. Wales 155 Fb
Weggis, Switzerland - 43 Fb
Wegrow, Poland - 60 Fb
Wehlau - 56 Fb
Wehrden, Prussia - 54 Ed
Wei, China - 94 Eb
Wei-chang, Manchuria - 96 Bc
Weida, Thuringia - 55 Ge
Weide R., Prussia - 57 Cb
Weidenau, Prussia - 54 De
Wei-hai-wei, China - 94 Fb
Wei-ho, China - 94 Eb
Wei-hwei, China - 94 Db
Weikersdorf, Austria - 59 Kc
Weikersheim, Wurttemberg 58 Db
Weilheim, Bavaria - 58 Fd
Weimar, Texas - 133 Df
Weimar, Thuringia - 54 Ge
Weinan, China - 94 Cc
Weiner, Arkansas - 130 Cc
Weinfelden, Switzerland 43 Ha
Weingarten, Wurttemberg 58 Dd
Weinheim, Baden - 58 Cb
Wei-ning, China - 94 Bd
Weiningen, Switzerland - 43 Fb
Weiser, Oregon - 136 Ec
Weishaho, Manchuria - 96 Dc
Wei-si, China - 94 Ad
Weissenbach, Austria - 58 Ed
Weissenburg, Bavaria - 58 Fb
Weissenfels, Prussia - 55 Hd
Weissenhorn, Bavaria - 58 Ec
Weisskugel, mte., Italy - 62 Ea
Weissrand Mts., S.-W. Africa - 114 Cb
Weisstannen, Switzerland 43 Hb
Weisswasser, Prussia - 55 Kd
Weitin, Mecklenburg - 55 Jb
Weiz, Austria - 59 Kd
Wejh, Arabia - 78 Cd
Wejherowo, Poland - 56 Cb
Welch, W. Virginia - 129 Dd
Welden, Bavaria - 59 Gb
Weldon, England - 15 Db
Weldon, N. Carolina - 131 Kb
Welford, Queensland - 153 Be
Welgegund, Cape Prov. - 115 Fe
Welland, Ontario - 123 Jd
Welland, R., England - 15 Da
Wellesbourne, England - 14 Cb
Wellesley Is., Queensland 153 Ac
Wellin, Belgium - 29 Dd
Wellingborough, England 15 Db
Wellington, Cape Prov. - 114 Cf
Wellingtou, Salop, Eng. 14 Ba
Wellington, Somerset, England - 14 Ae
Wellington, Kansas - 133 Db
Wellington, New S. Wales 155 Fc
Wellington, New Zealand 159 Ed
Wellington, Ohio - 129 Cb
Wellington, Ontario - 121 Bc
Wellington, S. Australia 154 Bd
Wellington, Texas - 133 Bc
Wellington, prov., New Zealand - 158 Ec
Wellington Channel, N.-W. Terr. - 119 La
Wellington I., Chile - 148 Ad
Wellington, L., Victoria 155 Ee
Wells, Norfolk, England 19 Ee
Wells, Somerset, Eng. - 14 Bd
Wells, Minnesota - 132 Cd
Wells, Nevada - 134 Fa
Wells, L., W. Australia 152 Cd
Wellsboro, Pennsylvania 129 Fb
Wellsburg, W. Virginia 129 Db
Wells River, Vermont - 128 Ba
Wellston, Ohio - 129 Cc
Wellsville, Missouri - 130 Ca
Wellsville, New York - 123 Kd

WEL General Index WIN

Wellsville, *Ohio* 129 Db
Welney, *England* 15 Ea
Wels, *Austria* 59 Jc
Welsford, *New Brunswick* 120 Bd
Welshpool, *Wales* 20 Cb
Welwyn, *England* 15 Dc
Wem, *England* 18 Be
Wemyss Bay, *Scotland* 22 De
Wenatchee, *Washington* 136 Cb
Wên-chow, *China* 94 Ed
Wen-chow B., *China* 94 Fd
Wendell, *California* 134 Ca
Wendelstein, *Bavaria* 58 Fb
Wendesi, *New Guinea* 156 Ab
Wendisch-Buchholz, *Prussia* 55 Jc
Wendling, *England* 15 Ea
Wendover, *England* 15 Dc
Wendover, *Ontario* 121 Cb
Wendover, *Utah* 134 Ga
Wen-hsien, *China* 94 Bc
Wen-shan, *China* 94 Ed
Wen-teng, *China* 94 Fb
Wentworth, *New S. Wales* 154 Cc
Wepener, *O.F.S.* 115 Gd
Wer, *Rajputana* 83 Ge
Werben, *Prussia* 55 Gc
Werdau, *Prussia* 55 He
Werder, *Prussia* 55 Hc
Werdohl, *Prussia* 54 Cd
Werlte, *Prussia* 54 Cc
Wermelskirchen, *Prussia* 54 Cd
Werne, *Prussia* 54 Cd
Werneuchen, *Prussia* 55 Jc
Wernigerode, *Prussia* 54 Fd
Werribee, *Victoria* 154 De
Werris Creek, *N. S. W.* 155 Gb
Werzebaun 55 Lc
Werzig, *Prussia* 55 Kc
Wesel, *Prussia* 54 Bd
Wesenberg, *Mecklenburg* 55 Hb
Weser, R., *Germany* 54 Db
Weseritz, *Bohemia* 59 Hb
Wesermunde, *Prussia* 54 Db
Weshi, *Burma* 92 Ff
Wessel Is., *N. Terr., Aust.* 151 Fa
Wesson, *Mississippi* 130 Ce
West B., *Louisiana* 130 Df
Westacre Junction, *S. Rhodesia* 113 Cc
West Allis, *Wisconsin* 132 Ed
West Banas R., *W. India* 85 Cc
West Bay, *Texas* 133 Ef
West Bay City, *Michigan* 122 Fd
West Bend, *Wisconsin* 132 Ed
West Branch, *Michigan* 122 Fc
West Bromwich, *England* 14 Ca
Westbrook, *Alabama* 130 Ed
Westbrook, *Maine* 128 Cb
Westbury, *England* 14 Bd
Westbury, *Quebec* 121 Eb
Westbury, *Tasmania* 155 Jg
West Calder, *Scotland* 23 Ee
West Chester, *Pennsylvania* 129 Gb
Westcliffe, *Colorado* 135 Lb
Westerburg, *Prussia* 54 De
Westerham, *England* 15 Ed
Wester-Kappeln, *Prussia* 54 Cc
Westerly, *Rhode Island* 128 Cc
Western Australia, state, *Australia* 150 Cd
Western India, States of, *India* 81 Cf
Western Prov., *Ceylon* 89 Cd
Westerstede, *Oldenburg* 54 Cd
Westerville, *Ohio* 129 Cb
Westerwald, *Prussia* 54 Ce
Westfield, *Massachusetts* 128 Bb
Westfield, *New Brunswick* 120 Bd
Westfield, *New York* 123 Jd
West Fork, *Iowa* 132 Bd
West Frankfort, *Illinois* 130 Db
West Gallatin R., *Montana* 136 Hc
Westgate, *England* 15 Fd
West Ham, *England* 15 Ec
West Hartlepool, *England* 18 Ca
Westhaven, *Connecticut* 128 Bc
West Indies, *Caribbean Sea* 137 Fc
West Kilbride, *Scotland* 21 Bb
Westlake, *Louisiana* 130 Be
Westland, prov., *New Zealand* 159 Be
West Leichhardt, *Queensland* 153 Ad
Westleigh, *O.F.S.* 115 Gc
Westleton, *England* 15 Fb
Westley, *California* 134 Cc
West Liberty, *Iowa* 132 De
West Liberty, *Kentucky* 131 Gb
West Linn, *Oregon* 136 Bc
West Linton, *Scotland* 21 Cb
West Lothian, co., *Scotland* 23 Ee
West Meath, co., *Eire* 27 Ce
Westminster, *Maryland* 129 Fc
Westmoreland, *Kansas* 133 Da
Westmorland, co., *England* 18 Bb
Westmount, *Quebec* 121 Db
West Nicholson, *S. Rhod.* 113 Cc
Weston, *Idaho* 136 Gd
Weston, *N. Borneo* 99 Eb
Weston, *Oregon* 136 Dc
Weston, *W. Virginia* 129 Dc
Weston-super-Mare, *England* 14 Ad
West Palm Beach, *Florida* 131 Nh
West Pawlett, *Vermont* 128 Bb
Westphalia, prov., *Prussia* 54 Cd
West Pittston, *Pennsylvania* 129 Fb
Westplains, *Missouri* 130 Cb
West Point, *Arkansas* 130 Cc
West Point, *Georgia* 131 Fd
West Point, *Mississippi* 130 Dd
Westpoint, *Nebraska* 132 Ae
West Point, *Virginia* 129 Fd
Westport, *California* 134 Ab
Westport, *Eire* 25 Bb
Westport, *New York* 128 Ba
Westport, *New Zealand* 159 Cd
Westport, *Ontario* 121 Bb
Westray, I. and Firth, *Orkney Is.* 24 Fc
Westrich, dist., *Saar Palatinate* 58 Bb
West Riding, *Yorks, Eng.* 18 Cc
West St John, *New Brunswick* 120 Bd
West Shefford, *England* 14 Cd
West Spitsbergen, *Spitsbergen* 9 Lb
West Union, *Iowa* 132 Cd
West Union, *W. Virginia* 129 Dc
Westville, *Nova Scotia* 120 Dd
Westville, *Oklahoma* 133 Ec
West Virginia, state, *U.S.A.* 127 Jc
Westwood, *California* 134 Ca
Wetar I., *Nether. Indies* 99 Ge
Wetaskiwin, *Alberta* 124 Gd
Wetherby, *England* 18 Cc
Wetlands, *Queensland* 153 Bd
Wetterau, *Hesse* 58 Ca
Wetumpka, *Alabama* 130 Ed
Wetwun, *Burma* 92 Ca
Wetzlar, *Prussia* 54 De
Wewak, *New Guinea* 156 Cb
Wewoka, *Oklahoma* 133 Dc
Wexford and co., *Eire* 27 Dg
Wexford Harb., *Eire* 27 Dg
Wey, R., *England* 15 Dd
Weybridge, *England* 15 Dd
Weyburn, *Saskatchewan* 124 Je
Weymont, *Quebec* 123 Mb
Weymouth, *England* 14 Be
Weymouth, *Massachusetts* 128 Cb
Weymouth, *Nova Scotia* 120 Cd
Weymouth, C., *Queensland* 153 Bb
Whakataki, *New Zealand* 159 Fd
Whakatane, *New Zealand* 158 Fb
Whale Sd., *Greenland* 9 Bb
Whalsey, I., *Zetland* 24 Hh
Whangarei, *New Zealand* 158 Ea
Wharanui, *New Zealand* 159 Ed
Wharfe, R., *England* 18 Cc
Wharton, *Texas* 133 Ef
What Cheer, *Iowa* 132 Ce
Wheatland, *California* 134 Cb
Wheatland, *Wyoming* 135 La
Wheatley, *England* 14 Cc
Wheaton, *Minnesota* 132 Ac
Wheeler, *Texas* 133 Bc
Wheeler Pk., *Nevada* 134 Fb
Wheeling, *W. Virginia* 129 Db
Whidbey, I., *Washington* 136 Ba
Whipsnade, *England* 15 Dc
Whistler, *Alabama* 130 De
Whitacre, *England* 14 Ca
Whitbourne, *Newfoundland* 120 Jc
Whitburn, *England* 21 Ed
Whitby, *England* 19 Db
Whitby, *Ontario* 123 Jd
Whitchurch, *Hampshire, England* 14 Cd
Whitchurch, *Hereford. England* 14 Bc
Whitchurch, *Salop, Eng.* 18 Be
Whitchurch, *Wales* 20 Cd
White B., *Newfoundland* 120 Ga
White Mts., *California* 134 Dc
White Mts., *New Hamps.* 128 Ca
White Mts. (Lévka Ori), *Crete* 71 Gj
White R., *Arkansas* 130 Bb
White, R., *Indiana* 129 Ac
White R., *Ontario* 122 Gb
White R., *S. Dakota* 126 Eb
White R., *Utah-Col.* 135 Jb
White Sea, *U.S.S.R.* 74 Fb
White Abbey, *N. Ireland* 26 Eb
White Bear R., *Newfoundland* 120 Gc
White Bear Lake, *Minnesota* 132 Cc
White Bluffs, *Washington* 136 Db
White City, *Kansas* 133 Da
White Cliffs, *N. S. Wales* 154 Db
Whitedeer, *Texas* 133 Bc
White Earth, *Minnesota* 132 Bb
White Face R., *Minnesota* 132 Gb
Whitefield, *New Hampshire* 128 Ca
Whitefish, *Montana* 136 Fa
Whitefish B., *Mich.-Ont.* 122 Fb
Whitefish L., *Quebec* 121 Cb
Whitehall, *Eire* 27 Df
Whitehall, *Illinois* 132 Df
Whitehall, *Michigan* 122 Ed
Whitehall, *Montana* 136 Hc
Whitehall, *New York* 123 Md
Whitehall, *Wisconsin* 132 Dc
Whitehaven, *England* 18 Aa
Whitehorse, *Yukon* 124 Bb
White Horse Hills, *Eng.* 14 Cc
White Lake, *Ontario* 121 Bb
White Mark, *Flinders I., Tasmania* 155 Kg
White Mesa, *Arizona* 135 Hc
White Mountain, *Alaska* 125 Fd
White Nile (Bahr el Abiad), *A.-E. Sudan* 108 Bc
White Otter L., *Ontario* 122 Ca
White Pass, *Brit. Columbia* 124 Cc
White Pine, *Montana* 136 Fb
White Pine Mts., *Nevada* 134 Fb
White Plains, *Georgia* 131 Gd
White Plains, *New York* 128 Bc
White River, *Ontario* 122 Fa
White River Plat., *Colorado* 135 Kb
White Rock, *Nevada* 134 Ea
White Russia, *U.S.S.R.* 75 De
White Salmon R., *Wash.* 136 Cb
Whitesboro, *Texas* 133 Dd
Whitesburg, *Kentucky* 131 Gb
White Springs, *Florida* 131 Ge
White Sulphur Springs, *Montana* 136 Ha
Whiteville, *N. Carolina* 131 Jc
Whiteville, *Tennessee* 130 Dc
White Volta, R., *Gold Coast* 104 De
Whitewater, *Colorado* 135 Jb
White Water, *New Mexico* 135 Je
Whitfield, *Victoria* 155 Ed
Whithorn, *Sotland* 21 Bd
Whiting, *Indiana* 129 Ab
Whiting, *New Jersey* 129 Gc
Whitland, *Wales* 20 Bd
Whitley Bay, *England* 21 Ec
Whitney, *England* 14 Ab
Whitney, *Ontario* 121 Ab
Whitney, *Texas* 133 De
Whitney, Mt., *California* 134 Dc
Whitstable, *England* 15 Ed
Whitsunday I. and Pass, *Queensland* 153 Cd
Whittier, *California* 134 Ee
Whittingham, *England* 21 Dc
Whittle, C., *Quebec* 120 Fa
Whittlesea, *Cape Prov.* 115 Gf
Whittlesey, *England* 15 Da
Whitway, *England* 14 Cd
Whitwell, *England* 18 Cd
Whitwick, *England* 14 Ca
Wholdaia L., *N.-W. Terr.* 124 Hb
Whupperthal, *Cape Prov.* 114 Cf
Whyalla, *S. Australia* 154 Ac
Whyte, *Minnesota* 132 Db
Wiarton, *Ontario* 123 Hc
Wiawso, *Gold Coast* 104 De
Wichita, *Kansas* 133 Db
Wichita Falls, *Texas* 133 Cd
Wichita Mts., *Oklahoma* 133 Cc
Wichita R., *Texas* 133 Cd
Wichman, *Nevada* 134 Db
Wick, *England* 14 Bd
Wick, *Scotland* 24 Ee
Wickenburg, *Arizona* 135 Ge
Wickepin, *W. Australia* 152 Be
Wickes, *Arkansas* 130 Ac
Wickes, *Montana* 136 Hb
Wickford, *England* 15 Ec
Wickham Market, *England* 15 Fb
Wickliffe, *Kentucky* 130 Db
Wicklow and co., *Eire* 27 Df
Wicklow Mts., *Eire* 27 Df
Wickwar, *England* 14 Bc
Widdifield, *Ontario* 121 Aa
Wide B., *Queensland* 153 De
Wide Bay, *New Britain* 156 Eb
Widener, *Arkansas* 130 Cc
Widgemooltha, *W. Aust.* 152 Ce
Widminnen 56 Fc
Widnes, *England* 18 Bd
Wiecbork, *Poland* 56 Bc
Wiedenbrück, *Prussia* 54 Dd
Wiehen Geb., *Prussia* 54 Dc
Wieliczka, *Poland* 57 Fd
Wielka Wies, *Poland* 56 Cb
Wieluń, *Poland* 60 Ec
Wien (Vienna), *Austria* 59 Lc
Wiener Wald, *Austria* 59 Kc
Wiener Neustadt, *Austria* 59 Ld
Wienhausen, *Prussia* 54 Fc
Wierden, *Holland* 29 Eb
Wieren, *Prussia* 54 Fc
Wieringen, *Holland* 29 Db
Wierschutzin 56 Bb
Wierzbnik, *Poland* 60 Fc
Wies, *Austria* 59 Ke
Wiesau 55 Ld
Wiesbaden, *Prussia* 58 Ca
Wiesen, *Switzerland* 43 Jc
Wiesenburg, *Prussia* 55 Hc
Wiesensteig, *Württemberg* 58 Dc
Wiesloch, *Baden* 58 Cb
Wiesmath, *Austria* 66 Bb
Wietings Moor, *Prussia* 54 Dc
Wietstock 55 Kb
Wietze, *Prussia* 54 Ec
Wigan, *England* 18 Bc
Wiggins, *Colorado* 135 La
Wight, Isle of, *England* 14 Ce
Wigmore, *England* 14 Bb
Wigston Magna, *England* 14 Ca
Wigton, *England* 21 Cd
Wigtown & co., *Scotland* 21 Bd
Wigtown B., *Scotland* 21 Bd
Wigwam, *Colorado* 135 Lb
Wijk, *Holland* 29 Dc
Wijnkoops B., *Java* 98 Ce
Wil, *Switzerland* 43 Hb
Wilbarston, *England* 15 Db
Wilber, *Nebraska* 132 Ae
Wilberforce, *Ontario* 121 Ab
Wilbur, *Washington* 136 Db
Wilburton, *Oklahoma* 133 Ec
Wilby, *England* 15 Db
Wilcannia, *New S. Wales* 154 Db
Wilczyn, *Poland* 57 Da
Wildalpen, *Austria* 59 Jd
Wildon, *Austria* 59 Ke
Wild Rice R., *Minnesota* 132 Ab
Wild Spitze, *Austria* 58 Ee
Wildwood, *Florida* 131 Gf
Wildwood, *New Jersey* 129 Gc
Wildwood, *Oregon* 136 Bd
Wilejka 60 Ja
Wilhelma, *Palestine* 80 Bc
Wilhelmina, Mt., *New Guinea* 156 Bb
Wilhelmina Geb., *Suriname* 142 Cb
Wilhelmsburg, *Austria* 59 Kc
Wilhelm II. Land, *Antarctica* 160 —
Wilhelmshaven, *Oldenburg* 54 Cb
Wilkes I., *Pacific Oc.* 157 Mh
Wilkes Land, *Antarctica* 160 —
Wilkes Barre, *Pennsylva.* 129 Gb
Wilkesboro, *N. Carolina* 131 Hb
Willacoochee, *Georgia* 131 Ge
Willamette, *Oregon* 136 Bc
Willapa Harbor, *Wash.* 136 Ab
Willard, *New Mexico* 135 Ld
Willard, *Utah* 135 Ha
Willaumez Penin., *New Britain* 156 Ec
Willcox, *Arizona* 135 He
Willemstad, *Holland* 29 Cc
Willenberg 56 Ec
Willenhall, *England* 14 Ba
Willerby, *England* 19 Dc
Willersley, *England* 14 Bb
Willesden, *England* 15 Dc
Willet, *Ontario* 122 Da
William, C., *Celébes* 99 Ed
William Creek, *S. Aust.* 154 Aa
Williams, *Arizona* 135 Gd
Williams, *W. Australia* 152 Be
Williamsburg, *Kentucky* 131 Fb
Williamsburg, *Virginia* 129 Fd
Williamsport, *Indiana* 129 Ab
Williamsport, *Newfoundland* 120 Ga
Williamsport, *Pennsylva.* 129 Fb
Williamston, *N. Carolina* 131 Kc
Williamstown, *New York* 128 Ab
Williamsville, *Missouri* 130 Cb
Willimantic, *Connecticut* 128 Bc
Willingham, *England* 15 Eb
Willington, *England* 21 Ed
Willis Is., *Pacific Oc.* 149 Fg
Willisca, *Iowa* 132 Be
Williston, *Cape Prov.* 114 De
Williston, *N. Dakota* 126 Ea
Williton, *England* 14 Ad
Willits, *California* 134 Bb
Willmar, *Minnesota* 132 Bc
Willochra & R., *S. Aust.* 154 Bb
Willoughbys, *S. Rhodesia* 113 Cb
Willow, *Alaska* 125 Jf
Willow R., *Minnesota* 132 Cb
Willow Creek, *Montana* 136 Hc
Willowmore, *Cape Prov.* 114 Ef
Willows, *California* 134 Bb
Willow Springs, *Missouri* 130 Bb
Willowvale, *Cape Prov.* 115 Hf
Willunga, *S. Australia* 154 Bd
Wilmette, *Illinois* 132 Fd
Wilmington, *California* 134 De
Wilmington, *Delaware* 129 Gc
Wilmington, *N. Carolina* 131 Jc
Wilmington, *S. Australia* 154 Bc
Wilmot, *S. Dakota* 132 Ac
Wilmslow, *England* 18 Bd
Wilno, *Ontario* 121 Bb
Wilno (Vilna), *Lithuania* 49 Cd
Wilson, *Kansas* 133 Ca
Wilson, *N. Carolina* 131 Jc
Wilson, Mt., *Arizona* 134 Fd
Wilson Pk., *New Mexico* 135 Jc
Wilson's Prom., *Victoria* 155 Ee
Wilsonville, *Alabama* 130 Ed
Wilthen, *Saxony* 55 Kd
Wilton, *England* 14 Cd
Wilton Junction, *Iowa* 132 De
Wiltshire (Wilts), co., *England* 14 Cd
Wiltz, *Luxembourg* 29 De
Wiluna, *W. Australia* 152 Cd
Wimbledon, *England* 15 Dd
Wimborne, *England* 14 Ce
Wimmis, *Switzerland* 42 Ec
Winamac, *Indiana* 129 Ab
Winburg, *O.F.S.* 115 Gd
Wincanton, *England* 14 Bd
Winchburgh, *Scotland* 23 Ee
Winchcomb, *England* 14 Cc
Winchelsea, *England* 15 Ee
Winchendon, *Massachusetts* 128 Cb
Winchester, *England* 14 Cd
Winchester, *Illinois* 132 Df
Winchester, *Indiana* 129 Bb
Winchester, *Kentucky* 131 Fb
Winchester, *New Hamps.* 128 Bb
Winchester, *Ohio* 129 Cc
Winchester, *Tennessee* 130 Ec
Winchester, *Virginia* 129 Ec
Winchester B., *Oregon* 136 Ad
Windala, *W. Australia* 152 Ac
Wind Cave Nat. Park, *S. Dakota* 126 Eb
Windell Windell Pool, *W. Australia* 152 Bc
Winder, *Georgia* 131 Gd
Windermere and Lake, *England* 18 Bb
Windermere L., *Ontario* 122 Fb
Wind Eschenbach, *Bavaria* 59 Gb
Windham, *Alaska* 125 Oh
Windhoek, *S.-W. Africa* 101 Dh
Windich Spring, *W. Aust.* 152 Cd
Windischgarstein, *Austria* 59 Jd
Windom, *Minnesota* 132 Bd
Windorah, *Queensland* 153 Be
Wind River Mts., *Wyoming* 126 Cb
Windsor, *Colorado* 135 La
Windsor, *Connecticut* 128 Bc
Windsor, *England* 15 Dd
Windsor, *Missouri* 130 Ba
Windsor, *New S. Wales* 155 Gc
Windsor, *New York* 128 Ab
Windsor, *N. Carolina* 131 Kb
Windsor, *Nova Scotia* 120 Cd
Windsor, *Ontario* 122 Gd
Windsor Pt., *New Zealand* 159 Ag
Windsor Mills, *Quebec* 121 Eb
Windsorton, *Cape Prov.* 115 Fd
Windward Is., *West Indies* 140 Kh
Windward Pass., *W. Indies* 140 Cc
Winfield, *Kansas* 133 Db
Winfield, *W. Virginia* 129 Dc
Wingen, *New S. Wales* 155 Gb
Wingham, *New S. Wales* 155 Gb
Wingham, *Ontario* 123 Hd
Winisk R., *Ontario* 119 Mf
Winkelsdorf, *Moravia* 57 Cc
Winkleman, *Arizona* 135 He
Winklern, *Austria* 59 Ge
Winlock, *Washington* 136 Bb
Winneba, *Gold Coast* 104 De
Winnebago, *Minnesota* 132 Bd
Winnebago L., *Wisconsin* 132 Ec
Winnemucca and L., *Nevada* 134 Da